ENCYCLOPEDIA OF WESTERN LAWMEN & OUTLAWS

Jay Robert Nash

First Paragon House Trade edition, 1992

Published in the United States by

Paragon House
90 Fifth Avenue
New York, N.Y. 10011

Condensed from the ENCYCLOPEDIA OF WORLD CRIME

Published by arrangement with CrimeBooks, Inc.

Library of Congress Cataloging-in-Publication Data

Nash, Jay Robert
     Encyclopedia of western lawmen & outlaws / Jay Robert Nash. — 1st
Paragon House trade ed.
          p.   cm.
     Includes bibliographical references and index.
     ISBN 1-55778-507-4 : $49.95
     1. West (U.S.) — Biography — Encyclopedias. 2. Peace officers — West
(U.S.) — Biography — Encyclopedias. 3. Outlaws — West (U.S.) — Biography — Encyclopedias. I. Title. II. Title:
Encyclopedia of western lawmen & outlaws
F591.N38 1992
978'.00992 — dc20

                                               91-46116
                                               CIP

BOOKS BY JAY ROBERT NASH

FICTION

On All Fronts
A Crime Story
The Dark Fountain
The Mafia Diaries

NONFICTION

Dillinger: Dead or Alive?
Citizen Hoover
Bloodletters and Badmen
Hustlers and Con Men
Darkest Hours
Among the Missing
Murder, America
Almanac of World Crime
Look for the Woman
People to See
The True Crime Quiz Book
The Innovators
Zanies
The Crime Movie Quiz Book
Open Files
The Toughest Movie Quiz Book Ever
The Dillinger Dossier
Murder Among the Mighty
Jay Robert Nash's Crime Chronology

REFERENCE

The Motion Picture Guide (12 vols.)
The Encyclopedia of World Crime (6 vols.)

THEATER

The Way Back
Last Rites for the Boys (*1947*)

POETRY

Lost Natives & Expatriates

JAN 1993

FOREWORD

Contrary to popular conception, there was little glamour in the Old West, and the wonderful adventure it offered in the books and films that chronicled its past was largely mythical. It was a place of unspeakable hardships and dangers. Early death threatened the pioneers at all turns, from hostile Indians to vicious weather, disease, and roaming white renegades who slaughtered the innocent indiscriminately to obtain and hold the West's most precious commodity—land. It was the land that caused the range wars, where cattle barons attempted to wipe out the small ranchers, the immigrant farmers, or the sheepherders whose flocks vied with cattle for the grazing lands.

It was the land that became precious once the railroads sliced through its far horizons in search of the cattle to be shipped east to beef-hungry millions. Along the steel paths of the railroads mushroomed the cattle towns of the West —Ellsworth, Hays, Wichita and Dodge City in Kansas, and with these early-day settlements came the cowboy, adept with horse and gun, the tools he would later employ in robbing banks and trains and killing for hire.

The towns themselves, from Leadville to Deadwood, from Silver City to Tombstone, were little more at the beginning than a huddle of clapboard shacks and rutted mud streets. Hygiene was practically nonexistent, and settlers died prematurely of diseases long since vanquished by modern medicine. Saloons and bordellos were usually in greater number than churches and schools in these towns, if any of the latter existed at all. The women of the town were mostly prostitutes who casually spread veneral diseases of all sorts.

Those women married to businessmen of the manipulating merchant class kept to small rooms in dark hotels and rooming houses in town; those wedded to small ranchers and farmers dwelled in rough-built farmhouses squatting in the desolate landscape, cooking and cleaning their lives away. The women who became celebrated in the West were invariably prostitutes who prospered and became gamblers, or ribald characters such as Calamity Jane. The so-called "bandit queens," Belle Starr and Cattle Kate Watson, were really inconsequential persons within the ranks of the outlaws and were thought of as such by their male counterparts.

Belle Starr, despite the Hollywood treatment she later received, was nothing more than a petty horse thief, an ugly harridan who used her gunfighter husbands to shoot down individuals she disliked. Cattle Kate Watson merely stocked the cattle stolen by her lover Jim Averill, for which she was later hanged. Calamity Jane (Martha Jane Canary), the most historically overblown female of the Old West, was never anything more than a common prostitute and a drunk. Her supposedly torrid love affair with gunman James Butler "Wild Bill" Hickok was the stuff of dime novel fiction. Calamity's claim following Hickok's death—that she was married to the famed gunfighter—was merely her wild hope of clinging to the odd fame of the Old West, but one she insisted upon with such fervor that she was eventually buried next to Hickok, who hardly knew her in real life.

It was a man's world indeed, one in which a man generally prospered if he carried and used a gun well, or could afford to hire gunmen to protect his interests. The gunmen who hired out to the cattle barons or the merchant princes did not magically spring from the windswept western earth. They were homegrown, as it were, from the cattle ranches, these gunfighters and bandits beginning as cowboys or farm hands who visited the lawless railheads when driving herds of cattle from the south and southwest.

These unschooled youths, most of them illiterate, had become experts with the six-gun and the rifle while battling Indians, rustlers, and the wild animals of the plains. They rode horses with ease and thought nothing of traveling hundreds of miles in the saddle. The cowboy knew little of civilization, except when visiting its rough precincts in the cattle towns, thus he had no use for its laws or those charged with enforcing them. He easily became a bandit or a gunfighter without having to make a moral decision based upon an appreciation of ethics and morality he had never acquired. He became a "bad man" only in the eyes of those who understood his actions as crimes. Murder and robbery to the unschooled outlaw were survival actions, ways of life.

Like his twentieth-century counterpart, the western bad man was boldest when working with gangs. It was the old western gangs, many held together with blood ties, that launched the first daring raids against banks and railroads. Most of these outlaw bands were made up of brothers such as the Burrow gang, the Renos, the James-Younger band, and the Daltons. When the gangs were exterminated, splintered, or disbanded, the individual bandit became a furtive desperado who took unrealistic chances and increased his risk of capture. Rather than face the possibility of jail—an abhorrent thought to any western criminal—many an outlaw, when cornered with no hope of escape, committed suicide. Such was the case of Harvey Logan (Kid Curry), Harry Tracy, Grant Wheeler, and possibly the notorious Sundance Kid and Butch Cassidy.

Suicide as a self-inflicted act was less prominent among western gunfighters, who made their living as killers-for-hire, enforcing the edicts of the land-greedy cattle barons. They killed mostly from ambush and seldom, unless drunk in a saloon, fought it out with opponents in head-to-head combat. Most of these gunmen, who had learned their special knowledge of weapons and marksmanship as youthful cowboys, were little more than hired assassins, such as Jim "Killer" Miller. In general, the Old West was never noble or altruistic, although it had a smattering of principled men of the law to lend that illusion to latter day historians. There were few high noon duels in which gunman and lawman faced one another bravely and fought to the death, the rare exception being the gunfight between the Earp and the Clanton-McLowery factions in Tombstone in 1881. For the most part the western gunman was a sneaky, back-shooting killer who fired from ambush, lurking in the shadows of dark alleys or behind walls, rocks, and trees while waiting to send an anonymous bullet into his victim.

There existed, however, a special breed of gunfighter who thrived on gunfighting alone, having no ambition other than to best an opponent with a faster draw and a deadlier aim. These men were rare in the West, egotistical to the point of lunacy, and certainly many could have been certified as insane. These gunmen included the mercurial Billy the Kid, the unpredictable Clay Allison, the hot-tempered Ben Thompson, and the vainglorious John Wesley Hardin, who proudly claimed to have killed forty men in gun duels be-

fore he himself was shot in the back while rolling dice in a saloon.

The western lawmen who faced these maniacs were also special individuals, as courageous as the outlaws were devious. They too had learned gunmanship at an early age, most being the sons of pioneers. It is interesting to note that in the backgrounds of most of the famous lawmen, such as Wyatt Earp, a strong family unit was present with parents who preached early to their sons the moral necessity of obeying and upholding the law. Even more interesting is the fact that these men, for the most part, had both mother and father throughout their childhoods, whereas a good deal of the outlaws, bandits and gunmen that plagued the Old West grew up with only one parent, invariably a stern father with little time to spend with sons, the mother having died early. Many of the worst outlaws were orphaned as youths and had no parental guidance at all.

The father of Frank and Jesse James deserted his family to join the California Gold Rush, which led to his early death; he left his two sons to be raised by a mother who dominated their lives and was fiercely loyal to them, excusing their crimes to come and defending them against all who criticized their outlaw ways. It was the same case with the Daltons and their mother. (This same attitude was ruthlessly displayed in the twentieth century by Ma Barker, mother of the notorious Barker Brothers.)

Outlaw sons seemed also to have an almost pathological devotion to their mothers. When Pinkerton detectives accidentally blew off the arm of Jesse James's mother, the outlaw traveled to Chicago and lay in wait to kill the firm's founder, Alan Pinkerton. Before their last bank robbery—the disastrous 1892 raid in Coffeyville, Kansas—Bob, Grat, and Emmett Dalton rode to their homestead and, fearing to go nearer lest waiting lawmen capture them, watched their mother during the night inside the lighted Dalton farmhouse in silent farewell to the person who meant most in their nefarious lives.

The Wild West was not a term of hindsight. It was called that during its own time and for good reason. Life and humanity meant little to its anxious inhabitants, and during the heyday of the lawless bandits and gunmen, between 1850 and 1900, only a few resolute men with tin stars stood up to the lawbreaker, risking and losing their lives at an alarming rate to win the West for unborn generations. The willing courage of these few good men is the true legacy of the Old West, to be found now only in the myriad boot hills that marked their way.

Jay Robert Nash
1991

ACKNOWLEDGMENTS

Grateful acknowledgment is given to the thousands of persons who, over the years, have assisted the author in obtaining valuable source information, research materials of all kinds, photos, illustrations, trial reports, and tracts. Without the splendid and wonderful cooperation of these persons and organizations, this work would not have come into existence. Organizations deserving special recognition in this area include correctional facilities, criminal investigation agencies, government offices, historical societies, libraries, newspaper and other media, and police departments worldwide.

Some of the most helpful include:

CORRECTIONAL FACILITIES: Alabama Dept. of Corrections (Montgomery, Ala.); Arizona Dept. of Corrections (Phoenix, Ariz., Jo Stephens); Baystate Correctional Center (Norfolk, Mass., Deodato Arruda); Bureau of Prisons (Washington, D.C., Helen Butler, Tina Cloyd); California Dept. of Corrections (Sacramento, Calif., Lisa Korb); Connecticut Dept. of Correction (Hartford, Conn.); Delaware Dept. of Correction (Smyrna, Del., Kathryn Pippin); District of Columbia Dept. of Corrections (Washington, D.C., Pat Wheeler); Federal Bureau of Prisons - North Central Region (Kansas City, Mo.); Florida Dept. of Corrections (Tallahassee, Fla.); Georgia Dept. of Corrections (Atlanta, Ga.); Illinois Dept. of Corrections (Springfield, Ill.); Indiana Dept. of Corrections (Indianapolis, Ind.); Kansas Dept. of Corrections (Topeka, Kan., Thomas J. Sloan); Kentucky Corrections Cabinet Dept. of Adult Correctional Institutions; Lackawanna County Prison (Scranton, Pa.); Maryland Dept. of Public Safety and Correctional Services; Massachusetts Dept. of Probations and Records (Boston, Mass.); Minnesota Dept. of Corrections (St. Paul, Minn.); Missouri Dept. of Corrections and Human Resources; Nevada Dept. of Prisons (Carson City, Nev.); New York State Dept. of Corrections (Albany, N.Y., Kelly Priess); New Jersey Dept. of Corrections (Trenton, N.J.); North Carolina Dept. of Corrections (Raleigh, N.C., David Guth); Ohio Department of Rehabilitation and Correction (Columbus, Ohio); Oklahoma Dept. of Corrections (Oklahoma City, Okla., Michelle Matthews); Olmstead County (Minn.), Dept. of Corrections; Pennsylvania Dept. of Corrections (Harrisburg, Pa., Kenneth G. Robinson); South Carolina Dept. of Corrections (Columbia, S.C., Judy Bode); Tennessee Dept. of Correction (Nashville, Tenn., William C. Haynes, Jr.); Texas Dept. of Corrections (Huntsville, Texas); U.S. Medical Center for Federal Prisoners (Springfield, Ill.); Leavenworth (Kan.) Penitentiary; Marion (Ill.) Penitentiary; Utah Dept. of Corrections (Salt Lake City, Utah).

COURT OFFICIALS: Nell E. Anderson (Clerk of the District Court, Teller County, Cripple Creek, Colo.); Tom Bigbee (Record Planning Commission, Canton, Ala.); C. Edward Bourassa (Register of Probate, Hillsborough County Probate Court, Nashua, N.H.); Richard P. Brinker (Clerk, Probate Division of Circuit Court of Miami, Fla.); Arlene D. Connors (Deputy Register in Probate, Milwaukee County, Milwaukee, Wis.); John J. Corcoran (Acting County Clerk, Los Angeles, Calif.); Susan Cottrell (Deputy, San Diego, Calif.); Virginia Crane (Deputy Court Clerk, Neptune, N.J.); John T. Curry (Circuit Clerk, Probate Division, Macon County, Ill.); Director of Licensing, Public Service Level, Minneapolis, Minn.; B.J. Dunavant (Clerk of the Probate Court, Shelby County, Memphis, Tenn.); Bremer Ehrler (Clerk, Jefferson County Court, Probate Division, Louisville, Ky.); C. Fatni (Record Clerk, Surrogate's Court, Kings County, N.Y.); Mildred Fulton (County Clerk, Cherokee County, Rusk, Texas); Mildred Gonder (Deputy Clerk, Probate Court, New Albany, Ind.); Harriet L. Gosnell (Trust Officer, People's Bank of Bloomington, Ill.); Jackie Griffin (Chief Deputy, Ellis County, Texas); Carole J. Hals

(Deputy Clerk, County Court, Probate Division, Stark, Minn.); James B. Kelley, Jr. (Register, Probate Court, Taunton, Mass.); Julia Kowrak (Register of Wills, City Hall, Philadelphia, Pa.); Leland Larrison (Clerk, Probate Court, Terre Haute, Ind.); Madelina S. Marting (Deputy Clerk, Putnam County, N.J.); Sarah Montjoy (Deputy Clerk, Jefferson County Court, Probate Division, Louisville, Ky.); Olmsted County Court, Probate Division (Minn.); Carl M. Olsen (Deputy Clerk, San Francisco, Calif.); Mrs. Lana J. Olson (Register of Probate, Luce County, Newberry, Mich.); Lorna Pierce (Secretary to Judge Donald Gunn, Probate Court of St. Louis, Mo.); Port Arthur, Texas, Probate Court; Providence, R.I., Probate Court ; William J. Regan (Judge of the Surrogates Court, Buffalo, N.Y.); Elisabeth F. Sachse (Deputy Clerk of Court, Baton Rouge, La.); St. Joseph County Health Department (South Bend, Ind.); San Mateo County Sheriff's Office (Hall of Justice, Redwood City, Calif.); Joan R. Saunder (Deputy Register of Wills, Clerk of the Probate Division, Washington, D.C.); Jean Smith (Deputy Clerk of Court, Watonwan County, St. James, Minn.); Nancy M. Spaulding (Chief Clerk, Schoharie, N.Y.); Storey County (Nev.) Probate Clerk; Surrogates Court of Essex, N.J.; Irene Thuringer (Deputy Clerk, Probate Dept., Pima County, Tucson, Ariz.); John M. Walker (Chief of Public Services, Los Angeles, Calif.); David M. Warren (Assistant Chief Deputy, Probate Courts Department, Harris County, Houston, Texas); R.D. Zumwalt (County Clerk, San Diego, Calif.).

CRIMINAL INVESTIGATION AGENCIES: Atlanta, Ga., U.S. Attorney's Office; Boston, Mass., U.S. Attorney's Office; Boston, Mass., District Attorney's Office; Brooklyn (N.Y.) District Attorney's Office; Bryan, Texas, District Attorney's Office (Bill Turner); Chicago, Ill., U.S. Attorney's Office; Columbus, Ohio, U.S. Attorney's Office; Cook County State's Attorney's Office (Chicago, Ill., Merle Aguilar); Cook County State's Attorney-Criminal Records Dept. (Chicago, Ill.); Danville, Ill. U.S. Attorney's Office (Rick Cox); Denver, Colo., District Attorney's Office (Dave Heckenbach, Assistant D.A.); Ft. Smith, Ark., District Attorney's Office (Steven Snyder, Assistant D.A.); Franklin County Prosecutor's Office (Columbus, Ohio, Thomas Tornabene); Geneva, Ill., State's Attorney's Office; Hamilton County (Ohio) Prosecutor's Office; Lee County State's Attorney's Office (Ft. Myers, Fla.); Livingston County, Ill., District Attorney's Office; Los Angeles City Attorney's Office (Mike Qualls); Los Angeles, Calif., District Attorney's Office (Grace Denton); Manhattan District Attorney's Office (New York, N.Y.); Montgomery County District Attorney's Office (Cheltenham, Pa.); New Bedford, Mass., District Attorney's Office; New Orleans, La., U.S. Attorney's Office; Reno, Nev., District Attorney's Office; San Jose, Calif., District Attorney's Office; Shiawassee City, Mich., District Attorney's Office; Suffolk County (N.Y.) Assistant District Attorney's Office (Jermyn Ray); Westchester County District Attorney's Office (N.Y.); Will County State's Attorney's Office (Joliet, Ill.).

GOVERNMENT OFFICES: Camden County (N.C.) Clerk's Office; Crown Point, Ind., Mayor's Office; Dept. of Treasury, Public Affairs Office (Washington, D.C., Robert R. Snow); FBI, Special Productions Branch (Washington, D.C., Melanie McElhinney); Federal Bureau of Investigations (Washington, D.C.); Hamilton County Clerk's Office (Cincinnati, Ohio); Municipal References & Resource Center of New York City (New York, N.Y., Devra Zetlan); Shiawassee County (Mich.) Clerk's Office; Tallahassee, Fla., City Clerk's Office (Becky Pippin); U.S. Information Agency (Washington, D.C., Scott Righetti).

HISTORICAL SOCIETIES: Anoka (Minn.) County Historical Society; Arizona State Historical Society (Tucson, Ariz.); Blair County Historical Society (Altoona, Pa., Sylva L. Emerson, Curator); California Historical Society (Los Angeles, Calif., Peter Evans); Chicago Historical Society; Colorado State Historical Society (Denver, Colo.); Connecticut Historical Society (Hartford, Conn.); Detroit Historical Society; Historical Society of Pennsylvania (Philadelphia, Pa.); Historical Society of Pennsylvania (Pittsburgh, Pa.); Illinois Historical Society (Chicago, Ill.); Illinois State Historical Society (Springfield, Ill.); Kansas State Historical Society (Topeka, Kan.); Kentucky Historical Society (Frankfort, Ky.); Massachusetts Historical Society (Boston, Mass.); Minnesota Historical Society (St. Paul, Minn.); Missouri State Historical Society (Columbia, Mo.); New Jersey Historical Society (Newark, N.J.); New York Historical Society (New York, N.Y., Mariam Touba); Oregon Historical Society (Portland, Ore.); Virginia Historical Society (Richmond, Va.); Wyoming State Historical Society (Cheyenne, Wyo.).

LIBRARIES: Alachua County Library District (Gainesville, Fla., Phillis Filer); Boston Public Library; Bridgeport Public Library (Bridgeport, Conn., Louise Minervino); Broward County Library (Ft. Lauderdale, Fla., Juanita Alpuche, Allison M. Ellis); California State Library (Sacramento, Calif.); Chicago Public Library (Chicago, Ill.); Columbia University Law Library (New York, N.Y.); Deerfield Public Library (Deerfield, Ill., Jack Hicks); Denver Public Library (Denver, Colo., James H. Davis, Picture Librarian); Detroit Public Library; Drug Enforcement Administration Library (Washington, D.C., Edith A. Crutchfield); Harvard Law School Library (Cambridge, Mass.); Illinois State Library (Springfield, Ill.); Indiana State Library (Indianapolis, Ind.); John Crerar Library (Chicago, Ill.); Library of Congress (Washington, D.C., Dan Burney); Metropolitan Library System (Oklahoma City, Okla.); Monroe County Law Library (Monroe, Mich., Judge Sullivan); New Orleans Public Library (New Orleans, La.); New York City Public Library (New York, N.Y.); New York State Law Library (Albany, N.Y.); Newberry Library (Chicago, Ill.); North Carolina State Library (Raleigh, N.C.); Northwestern University Law Library (Chicago, Ill.); Scotland Yard Library (London, England); Special Collections Library, Northwestern University (Evanston, Ill., Russell Maylone); University of California Library (Berkeley, Calif., William F. Roberts, Reference Librarian); University of Chicago Library (Chicago, Ill.); University of Missouri Law Library (Columbia, Mo.); University of Missouri Library (Columbia, Mo.); University of Oklahoma (Norman, Okla., Jack D. Haley, Assistant Curator, Western History Collections); University of Wisconsin Criminal Justice Reference and Information Center (Madison, Wis., Sue L. Center, Dir.); Wisconsin Dept. of Justice, Law Library (Madison, Wis., Michael F. Bemis); Yale University Law Library (New Haven, Conn., Robert E. Brooks, Reference; Jo Anne Giammattei, Acquisitions).

MISSING PERSONS BUREAUS: Chicago Police Dept. (Chicago, Ill., Lts. Bill Bodner, John Doyle, Bill Frost); New York Police Department (New York, N.Y., Detective John Griffin).

NEWSPAPERS/MEDIA: *Adam Smith's Money World* (New York, N.Y., Anne Hansen); Albuquerque (N.M.) *Journal;* Arizona *Daily Star* (Tucson, Ariz.); Arizona *Republic* (Phoenix, Ariz.); Arkansas *Democrat* (Booneville, Ark.); Atlanta (Ga.) *Constitution* (Diane Hunter); Baltimore (Md.) *Sun*; Bangor (Maine) *Daily News;* Boston (Mass.) *Herald* (Betsy Warrior); Boston (Mass.) *Globe* (William Boles); Capital News Service (Los Angeles, Calif., Jerry Goldberg); Charleston (W. Va.) *Gazette* (Ron Miller); *Chicago Sun-Times* (Chicago, Ill.); *Chicago Tribune* (Chicago, Ill.); Cincinnati (Ohio) *Enquirer; Clarion-Ledger* (Jackson, Miss.); Cleveland (Ohio) *Plain Dealer* (Eileen M. Lentz); *Daily Northwestern* (Oshkosh, Wis.); *Daily Oklahoman* (Oklahoma City, Okla.); Dallas (Texas) *Morning News;* Dayton (Ohio) *Daily News;* Detroit (Mich.) *Free Press;* Detroit (Mich.) *News;* Gallatin (Tenn.)

Examiner (John Cannon); Greenville (S.C.) *News;* Houston (Texas) *Post;* Houston (Texas) *Chronicle* (Sherry Adams); Indianapolis (Ind.) *Star* (Nadine Moore); Japan *Times* (Tokyo, Japan, Shigeo Shimada); Las Vegas (Nev.) *Sun* (Jenny Scarantino); Los Angeles (Calif.) *Times* (Renee Nembhard); Louisville (Ky.) *Courier-Journal* (Patrick Chapman); Miami (Fla.) *Herald* (Liz Donovan, Nora Paul); *Morning Call* (Allentown, Pa., Lynn M. Dubbs); New York (N.Y.) *Daily News* (Faigi Rosenthal); New York (N.Y.) *Times* (Tom Wicker); *Newsday* (Garden City, N.Y., Elizabeth Whisnant); Omaha (Neb.) *World Herald;* Philadelphia (Pa.) *Inquirer;* Pittsburgh (Pa.) *Post Gazette;* Portland (Ore.) *Oregonian* (Sandra Macomber); *Press Telegram* (Long Beach, Calif., George Choma); Providence (R.I.) *Journal;* Reno (Nev.) *Gazette-Journal* (Carole Keith, Nan Spina); *Rocky Mountain News* (Denver, Colo.); St. Louis (Mo.) *Post-Dispatch* (Mike Marler); Salt Lake *Tribune* (Salt Lake City, Utah); San Antonio (Texas) *Express-News* (Judy Zipp); San Diego (Calif.) *Union;* San Francisco (Calif.) *Chronicle* (Nikki Bengal); San Francisco (Calif.) *Examiner;* Seattle (Wash.) *Times;* Seattle (Wash.) *Post-Intelligencer;* Selma (Ala.) *Times Journal* (Nicki Davis Maud); *Spokesman-Review* (Spokane, Wash.); Tampa *Tribune* (Tampa Bay, Fla.); *The State* (Columbia, S.C., Dargan Richards); *Times News* (Cumberland, Md., Linda Shuck); Topeka (Kan.) *Capital-Journal;* Trenton (N.J.) *Times;* Tucson (Ariz.) *Daily Citizen;* Tulsa (Okla.) *Daily World;* Wichita (Kan.) *Eagle Beacon;* Winnipeg *Free Press* (Winnipeg, Manitoba, Canada); WTEN-TV (Albany, N.Y., David A. Lamb).

POLICE DEPARTMENTS: Aurora (Ill.) Police Dept.; Baltimore (Md.) Police Dept. (Dennis S. Hill, Dir. Public Info. Div.); Boston (Mass.) Police Dept. (Allison Woodhouse, Research & Analysis); Brooklyn Organized Crime Strike Force (Brooklyn, N.Y.); Chicago (Ill.) Police Dept. (Dennis Bingham, Public Information; Tina Vicini, Dir. News Affair Div.); Chicago (Ill.) Police Dept. Academy (Sgt. Anthony Consieldi); Dallas (Texas) Police Dept. (Capt. J.E. Ferguson); Deerfield (Ill.) Police Dept. (Richard Brandt, Chief of Police; Thomas A. Creighton, Youth Dir.); Indianapolis (Ind.) Police Dept. (Maj. Robert L. Snow); Los Angeles (Calif.) Police Dept. (Stephen F. Hatfield, Public Information Dir.); Metropolitan Police Dept. (St. Louis, Mo.); Miami (Fla.) Police Dept. (Maj. Dean De Jong); Minneapolis (Minn.) Police Dept. (Ted Faul, Deputy Chief of Services; J.E. Bender, Officer); New Scotland Yard (London, England, Annette Eastgate, Robin Goodfellow, Steve Wilmot); Oshkosh (Wis.) Police Dept.; Pennsylvania State Police Troop H; Philadelphia (Pa.) Police Dept. (Mary Ann Edmunds); Portland (Ore.) Police Dept. (Candy Hill Turay); San Diego (Calif.) Police Dept. (Pliny Castanien); Washington, D.C., Police Dept.

NON-GOVERNMENT AGENCIES: Alcatraz Ferry (San Francisco, Calif.); Chicago Crime Commission (Chicago, Ill.).

OTHER CONTRIBUTORS: American Red Cross (Washington, D.C., Margaret O'Connor); Amnesty Int'l (New York, N.Y., Janice Christianson); Chinese Consulate's Office (New York, N.Y.); Joseph Dillman, Registered Pharmacist (Libertyville, Ill.); Japanese Consulate's Office (Chicago, Ill.); Korean Consulate's Office (Chicago, Ill.); Yuri Morozov, Translator; Northwestern University Language Dept. (Evanston, Ill., Rolf Erickson); Anthony J. Pellicano, Private Detective (Los Angeles, Calif.); Pinkerton's, Inc. (New York, N.Y., G.F. O'Neill); Salvation Army (Chicago, Ill., Col. Lloyd Robb); Seaman's Institute of New York City (New York, N.Y., Barbara Clauson).

HOW TO USE THIS ENCYCLOPEDIA

ALPHABETICAL ORDER

Each entry name in the *Encyclopedia of Western Lawmen & Outlaws* is listed alphabetically. Biographical entries are alphabetized by the subject's last name. Everything preceding the comma is treated as a unit when alphabetizing. Hyphens, periods following initials, and spaces do not influence its alphabetization. Names with prefixes such as **de**, **von**, or **le** are listed under the most common form of the name. Names beginning in **Mc** or **M'** are treated as if spelled **Mac**. Identical names are alphabetized chronologically. When the names of two or more people head an entry, it is usually alphabetized according to the most prominent person's last name.

ENTRY HEADINGS

Entry names appear in boldface. Parenthetical remarks immediately following an entry name indicate an alternate spelling, that person's original or maiden name, or the entry's alias if preceded by **AKA:**. These names also appear in boldface.

Following the name are **date(s)** relevant to that entry. The letter **b.** preceding the date signifies that only the person's date of birth is known, while the letter **d.** signifies that only the person's date of death is known. The letter **c.** (circa) signifies that the date which immediately follows is approximate. In some cases **prom.** (prominent) is used to denote the year(s) in which that entry was noteworthy.

A number of entries may include more than one person if the criminals or professionals worked together. When the relevant dates of a **multiple name entry** coincide, one date will follow the last person named in the entry heading.

The **country** designation in each entry heading refers to the country in which the crime was committed or the country in which a lawman was known professionally. The **category** defining the entry follows.

REFERENCES

Cross references immediately following an entry refer the reader to entries containing additional information relevant to the case, person, place, or event being consulted. Direct references are also used frequently throughout to lead the readers from a well known name (alias, victim, event) to the name under which that entry appears (**Happy Jack**, See: **Morco, John**).

KEY TO ABBREVIATIONS

abduc.	= abduction		Colo.	= Colorado
Ala.	= Alabama		Conn.	= Connecticut
Arg.	= Argentina		crim. law.	= criminal lawyer
Ariz.	= Arizona		Del.	= Delaware
Ark.	= Arkansas		det.	= detective
Aus.	= Australia		Ecu.	= Ecuador
Bol.	= Bolivia		execut.	= executioner
Braz.	= Brazil		Fla.	= Florida
Brit.	= Britain		forg.	= forgery
Calif.	= California		Ga.	= Georgia
Can.	= Canada		Ill.	= Illinois
			Ind.	= Indiana
			jur.	= jurist
			Kan.	= Kansas
			Ky.	= Kentucky
			La.	= Louisiana
			lynch.	= lynching
			Mass.	= Massachusetts
			Md.	= Maryland
			Mex.	= Mexico
			Mich.	= Michigan
			Minn.	= Minnesota
			Miss.	= Mississippi
			Mo.	= Missouri
			Mont.	= Montana
			mur.	= murder
			N.C.	= North Carolina
			N.D.	= North Dakota
			N.H.	= New Hampshire
			N.J.	= New Jersey
			N.M.	= New Mexico
			N.Y.	= New York
			Neb.	= Nebraska
			Nev.	= Nevada
			Okla.	= Oklahoma
			Ore.	= Oregon
			Pa.	= Pennsylvania
			prom.	= prominent
			pros.	= prostitution
			R.I.	= Rhode Island
			rob.	= robbery
			S.C.	= South Carolina
			S.D.	= South Dakota
			Tenn.	= Tennessee
			U.S.	= United States of America
			Urug.	= Uruguay
			Va.	= Virginia
			Venez.	= Venezuela
			vigil.	= vigilantism
			Vt.	= Vermont
			W.Va.	= West Virginia
			Wash.	= Washington
			Wis.	= Wisconsin
			Wyo.	= Wyoming

A

Alexander, William, prom. 1889, U.S., outlaw. William Alexander was a Mexican-American who was convicted of murdering his business partner, David C. Steadman, on Oct. 21, 1889. He was one of only a few felons to be spared from the gallows at Fort Smith (Ark.), during the long reign of the "Hanging Judge," Isaac Parker. Alexander was shrewd enough to engage attorney J. Warren Reed, who proved to be a worthy adversary to Parker in the 1890s. In West Virginia and southeastern Ohio, Reed was called the "lawyer who always wins his cases." His tactic was simple. If a murderer was found Guilty and sentenced to die, Reed appealed the conviction to the president regardless of the circumstances. In many cases, the condemned man was given executive clemency or a pardon.

Such was the case with William Alexander, whose guilt was established through purely circumstantial evidence and the statements given in court by one J.G. Ralls, a Muskogee attorney who conferred with the defendant a few days after the murder. Reed was convinced that Parker's decision to admit Ralls' statements constituted a breach of justice. An appeal was filed with the Supreme Court, and the conviction was overturned on the grounds that Ralls' testimony was "incompetent." Alexander was remanded for a second trial, but the jury failed to reach a verdict. On Christmas Eve, 1892, the prosecuting attorney agreed to *nolle prosequi* the case, which permitted Alexander to walk free. See: **Parker, Isaac.**

Allee, Alfred Y., 1855-96, U.S., lawman. Allee, born in DeWitt County, Texas, was appointed deputy sheriff of Karnes County, Texas, in 1882 and in that year he reportedly shot a robbery suspect but was later charged with murder. Some claimed that Allee was merely settling an old score. He was acquitted. Allee was made deputy sheriff of Frio County, Texas, and a short time later he began arguing with another deputy named Rhodes about who was faster on the draw. Both men drew their weapons and Allee, firing two six-guns, pumped eight bullets into Rhodes, four finding the victim's heart. Amazingly, Allee was again acquitted of murder, some friendly witnesses insisting that Rhodes drew first.

Much was said of Allee's ability to shoot down prisoners already cowed and victims unprepared for his lightning temper and fast draw, but the lawman proved his mettle in September 1888, when he was assigned to track down the wild, vicious train- and bank-robber Brack Cornett. The outlaw had evaded a posse of Texas Rangers and was heading for Arizona when he was intercepted by Allee, who had trailed him across the prairie. In a pitched gun battle, both men raced their horses toward each other. Using two guns, they blazed away at each other as they rode forward. Allee's aim was good and Cornett was shot dead from the saddle.

Allee's temper was short and his hatred for blacks pronounced. Once, when boarding a train, it was alleged, a black porter shoved him back down the stairs when he ordered the porter out of his way. Allee fell backward, grabbed a rail outside the sleeping car to balance himself, and then jerked himself back up the stairs; a pistol in his hand barked once and sent a bullet into the porter's heart. He was quickly acquitted in a trial where statements were made regarding blacks who "don't know their place." The explosive peace officer escaped death many times, but his own violent past caught up with him in Laredo, Texas, on Aug. 19, 1896, when he was stabbed in a barroom brawl, dying almost instantly. See: **Cornett, Brack.**

Western lawman Alfred Allee seldom took prisoners.

Allen, Charles (AKA: **Big Time Charlie**), prom. 1910s, U.S., outlaw. Allen had, by his own boasting, great adventures in the Alaskan gold strikes and in Mexico, riding and scouting for Pancho Villa in his wars against dictators Diaz and Huerta. He appeared in the Denver area about 1916 and soon became rich by managing hundreds of whores as a master pimp. His method was to addict young girls to heroin and opium and then place them in the lowly cribs and bordellos he owned, paying them slave wages which were mostly in the form of dope. Within a period of four years, it was estimated that Allen accumulated more than $1 million from his prostitution empire, at least half of this paid to local authorities who allowed him to operate without interference. Prostitution was one thing, according to the liberal-minded officials of Denver, but hard drugs could not be tolerated, and when Allen made moves to begin wholesale distribution of drugs throughout the community, police cracked down on him. His home was raided in 1919 and significant quantities of heroin and opium were seized. He was sent to Leavenworth to serve five years for illegal drug trafficking, which smashed his prostitution racket.

Allen, Joseph, d.1909, U.S., lynch. Allen joined with Jesse West in saloon operations and later a booming cattle business throughout Oklahoma, developing a bitter feud with cattle baron A.A. Bobbitt. When Allen and West could not best Bobbitt, they hired a professional killer, Jim Miller, to murder the cattle baron. Bobbitt's riddled body was found on Feb. 26, 1909, and Allen, West, Miller, and another confederate, Berry B. Burrell, who had "spotted" Bobbitt for Miller, were arrested. While awaiting trial in Ada, Okla., Allen imported a prominent criminal attorney, Moman Pruiett, who seldom lost a defense case. (His record later showed that Pruiett won 303 acquittals out of 343 murder cases where he acted as the defense attorney.) The consensus of opinion in Ada had it that the old Texas killer-for-hire and his employers would get off. A mob of more than forty men broke the prisoners from the local jail on Apr. 19, 1909, dragged the four accused men to a nearby livery stable and, after a few words which condemned the conspirators, promptly lynched all four men. Miller, who insisted that he by hanged with his hat on, was undoubtedly the most dangerous killer in Texas, Oklahoma, and New Mexico. He bragged with his last words that he had murdered fifty-one men. The vigilantes who executed this murderous band were never brought to justice. See: **Miller, James B.**

Allen, Malachi, d.1889, U.S., gunman. After quarreling over the ownership of a saddle, Malachi Allen shot and killed Shadrach Peters and Cy Love in the Chickasaw Nation on July 15, 1888. Allen engaged in a vicious gunfight with Deputy Marshal McAlester and the posse which had been organized to bring the desperado back to Fort Smith (Ark.). In the heat of the battle, Allen sustained a serious wound in his shooting arm. He was taken back to Fort Smith where the arm was amputated shortly before the hangman affixed the noose to his neck on Apr. 19, 1889.

Allison, Robert A. (Clay), 1840-87, U.S., gunman. That Clay Allison was unbalanced from an early age there was no doubt. He had a mean streak running to his marrow and a seething anger that seemed never to abate. His clubfoot and a condition that was occasionally diag-

nosed as "epileptic" may have contributed to his mercurial temper. Allison worked on his parents' farm near Waynesboro, Tenn., until he was twenty-one. Immediately upon the outbreak of the Civil War, he enlisted in the Confederate Army and went off willingly to fight for the South. His clubfoot did not seem to hamper his ability to perform active duty. He saw action in several battles but was sent home in March 1862 to recuperate from wounds that seemed more mental than physical, a Confederate doctor stating that Allison was suffering from a condition that was "partly epileptic and partly maniacal." He had reportedly threatened to shoot his superiors follow-

Quick-draw gunman Clay Allison, killer of a half dozen men.

ing one battle because they refused to pursue and execute retreating Union troops.

A short time later, Allison got the chance to vent his anger on one Union soldier, a corporal of the Third Illinois Cavalry who rode onto the Allison farm and announced to Allison's mother that he intended to take everything valuable on the premises. Clay went to a closet, got out a gun, and promptly shot the Union soldier dead. Following the end of the war, Allison, his two brothers, Monroe and John, his sister Mary, and her husband, Lewis Coleman, migrated to Texas. While Allison was waiting to take a ferry across the Red River, he became incensed when ferryman Zachary Colbert tried to double-charge them. Allison beat up Colbert and left him unconscious while the family took the ferry across the Red, paying nothing.

Once in Texas, Allison signed on with several cattle barons as a cowboy, helping to blaze the Goodnight-Loving Trail through Texas, New Mexico, and Colorado in 1866. He became an expert, tough cowhand, working first for Oliver Loving and Charles Goodnight, then for cattle barons M.L. Dalton and Isaac Lacy. He drove a huge herd of cattle to New Mexico in 1870 and demanded as pay 300 head of cattle. With this small herd Allison began his own ranch near Cimarron, N.M., which was soon lucrative. It was on October 7 of that year that Allison's true savagery emerged. Allison brooded about a locally convicted murderer, Charles Kennedy, while drinking heavily in the saloon at Elizabethtown. He stirred up sentiment against Kennedy and then led a lynch mob across the street to the jail. Allison and others battered down the door, knocked the deputies senseless, and dragged Kennedy screaming from his cell. He was taken to a local slaughterhouse where Allison and others not only lynched Kennedy but mutilated his corpse with the huge knives employed for butchering cattle. Allison then cut the body down and, using an ax, decapitated the corpse and jammed the head on a pole, riding with this gory trophy all the way to Henry Lambert's saloon in Cimarron where Allison put the head on display.

Those who befriended Allison stayed fiercely loyal to the gunman. His enemies, on the other hand, not only hated him but vowed to kill him whenever the opportunity arose. One of these was gunslinger Chunk Colbert who had secretly planned to kill Allison ever since Clay beat up his uncle Zachary some nine years earlier at the Red River crossing. Colbert rode into Cimarron and challenged Allison to a horse race. Both men rode their horses wildly and the race wound up in a dead heat. They decided to rest up at the Clifton House, an inn near Allison's ranch. Both men sat down to eat large dinners. (One madcap Western historian went so far as to state that the two men eyeballed each other intently while they stirred their coffee with the barrels of their six-guns.) They talked amiably, but Allison noticed Colbert reach for his cup of coffee with one hand and his pistol with another. Before Colbert could lift the six-gun beyond the rim of the table, Allison tipped his chair backward, falling toward the floor which caused Colbert to hurry his shot which, in turn, plowed into the table top. As he fell backward, however, the cool-under-fire Allison aimed a single shot that smashed into Colbert's head, going in above the right eye and killing the gunman.

After Colbert was buried behind the Clifton House, someone asked Allison why he would sit down to dinner with a man he knew intended to kill him. Quipped the sardonic gunman, "Because I didn't want to send a man to hell on an empty stomach." Charles Cooper, a friend of Colbert's who had been present at the shoot out, did not take part in the gunfight, but he stated to friends that he would settle matters with Allison later. On Jan. 19, 1874, Cooper was seen riding toward Cimarron and then was never seen again. It was widely believed that Allison killed Cooper and buried the body on the prairie. Two years later, the gunman would be charged with murdering Cooper but the prosecution could produce no body nor any evidence that Allison committed the crime; the gunman was released.

As time passed, Clay Allison earned the reputation of a mad gunfighter who feared no one and could be counted on to do the unexpected. It was reported that Allison, totally drunk, stepped from a saloon in Canadian, Texas, wearing nothing but his ten-gallon hat, his boots, and his six-guns, to march up and down the main street challenging any and all to face him. There were no takers. Another report had the gunman and a drinking companion, Mason T. Bowman, stripping to their underwear and dancing wildly about a saloon and then shooting up the floor at each's others feet to quicken the pace without bloodying a single toe.

On Oct. 30, 1875, Allison took part in another lynching, helping to hang one Cruz Vega, under arrest for murder in Colfax County, N.M. As Vega was dragged to a telegraph pole by Allison and others, he shouted out that he was not the killer, but that the murder he stood accused of had been committed by Manuel Cardenas. It mattered not to Allison and his friends. Cruz was strung up and while he slowly strangled to death the compassionate Allison shot him in the back "to put the poor Mex out of his misery." The gunman then had the body taken down; he tied the end of the lynch rope to his saddle and rode through the streets, dragging the body outside of town, over rocks and heavy brush, until the face was unrecognizable. He left Vega's body to rot in the desert.

Cruz's employer, rancher and feared gunman Francisco Pancho Griego, showed up in Cimarron on Nov. 1, 1875, asking for Allison. With him were Luis Vega, the 18-year-old son of the lynch mob victim, and Griego's partner, Florencio Donahue. Allison boldly confronted the trio outside the St. James Hotel and suggested they step inside the bar to talk things over. The men had a few drinks and seemed to talk amiably. Then Griego motioned to a corner of the bar and he and Allison walked to the spot. As Allison turned he saw that Griego had removed his large sombrero and had begun to fan himself, an uncommon gesture on one of the coldest nights of the year. Allison had also prepared for treachery with a trick of his own; having palmed a small pistol, he fired this weapon as soon as Griego's sombrero stopped at his gunbelt. The lights in the saloon suddenly went out (thanks to a friend of Allison's), and when the lamp was next lit the body of Francisco Pancho Griego was seen sprawled on the floor, a bullet in his heart. Allison had disappeared.

Colfax County citizens began a campaign to get rid of the lethal Allison, urging the editor of the Cimarron *News and Press* to write some scathing articles about the New Mexico badman. One of the those behind the publicity campaign was none other than Allison's own brother-in-law, Lewis Coleman. The gunman's response to this civic campaign to run him out of the territory was to ride into Cimarron and wreck the entire offices of the *News and Press*, putting it out of business. Though Allison's neighbors were nervous about his presence, total strangers living in towns Allison visited on his trail drives were positively traumatized when he and his cowboys rode into town. Such was the situation when Clay and John Allison appeared in Las Animas, Colo., on the night of Dec. 21, 1876. They had just sold a herd of cattle and were looking to entertain themselves, at the expense of the local citizenry, of course.

Spotting festivities in progress at the Olympic Dance Hall, the Allison brothers stomped inside and began dancing with the wives of local merchants, both of them almost drunk and impolitely stepping upon the toes of their partners. Town constable and deputy sheriff Charles Faber quietly walked up to the Allisons and asked them to check their six-guns but they ignored him. Faber stepped outside and quickly deputized two men, getting a shotgun and returning to the dance hall. Just as he entered, someone shouted, "Look out!" John Allison, who was still attempting to dance with a cringing local lady, spun around, appearing to draw his gun. Faber let loose with a blast from one of the shotgun barrels. Clay Allison, who was at the bar and had his back to the scene, wheeled around with his pistols in his hands (he usually wore one gun but on occasion wore two). As John Allison received a load of buckshot in his chest and arm, Clay fired four deliberate shots at Faber, hitting him only once, but this shot ripped through the deputy's chest, killing him. As Faber fell, his shotgun went off once more, the second barrel of buckshot slamming into John Allison's leg, sending the brother toppling to the floor. (As was the case with most Western shootouts, all this gunfire took only a few seconds to occur.)

Allison then chased the two deputies outside, firing at them as they ran for their lives down the street, escaping uninjured in the darkness. Returning to the hall, Allison went to his brother and then called for a doctor. He reached over to Faber's fallen body and yanked the bloody corpse next to the semi-conscious John Allison, telling his brother, "Look here, this man is dead, John, not to worry, vengeance is ours! Not to worry."

John Allison eventually recovered from his wounds and Clay Allison managed to escape punishment by proving self-defense. This shootout spread the reputation of Allison far and wide through the hell holes and cow towns. Legends about the fierce gunman began to appear in the penny dreadfuls and police gazettes of the East where Allison was portrayed as the most dangerous gunman of the Old West, a man who outdrew and backed down the most esteemed of lawmen, including the venerable Wyatt Earp and deadly Wild Bill Hickok. Of course, these stories were apocryphal and only occurred in the fertile brains of writers who never crossed the Mississippi.

To the citizens of Colfax County, however, Allison was infamous enough. He found that few in the area wished to befriend him, or, worse, do business with him. Losing money on cattle he could not sell, Allison moved to greener territory, buying a ranch in Hemphill County, Texas. There he married and his wife gave birth to two girls, Patsy, born a cripple, and Clay, who was born after Allison's strange, premature death. The gunman seemed to temper a bit and began to avoid confrontations with other gunfighters. His

fortunes rising once more, Allison bought another ranch in Lincoln County, N.M., and here he developed considerable herds. On one trail drive to Wyoming, Allison stopped off in Cheyenne, so the tale goes, where he went to a local dentist with a howling toothache. The dentist, learning the identity of his patient, nervously worked on the wrong tooth. Allison pushed his hand away and went to another dentist, who filled the right cavity. So incensed was Allison at the first dentist's ineptitude that he raced back to the first man, strapped him into his own chair, and yanked out the dentist's front tooth. He intended to pull every one of his teeth but a rescuing crowd heard the dentist's screams and pulled Allison away before he could do more damage. There is little support for this story, in fact, and none for the tale which graphically described how Allison, forced to share a room with another gunman one night, shot his roommate for snoring too loudly.

Allison's end was ignominious and grimly ironic. On July 1, 1887, Allison was returning from Pecos, Texas, where he purchased supplies for his ranch. Apparently he had been drinking, for about forty miles from Pecos, the gunfighter toppled from the buckboard he was driving and fell beneath the wheel of the heavily laden wagon. The horses jerked forward and the wheel crushed Allison's head, almost decapitating him, which caused some to later recall how Allison had severed the head of the killer Kennedy seventeen years earlier. It was said, following Allison's death, that he was heading toward a rendezvous where he planned to murder his neighbor, John McCullough, with whom he had had a recent argument, but this was mere fiction. The contemporary tale-tellers of Allison's era could not accept a mundane end for one of the worst killers of the West. Fate, they would have it, intervened to prevent the gunman from claiming one more victim.

Historians later estimated that the six-foot, blue-eyed gunman had shot and killed *at least* fifteen men during his notorious career. Shortly before his death, Allison told a newsman, "I never killed a man who didn't need it." He then added that in all his gunfights he was merely "protecting the property holders of the country from thieves, outlaws, and murderers." He could have numbered himself among these miscreants, for Allison was no simple rancher with a hair trigger. Throughout his days on the range he practiced wholesale rustling of cattle and horses. On one occasion, he even attempted to steal a herd of army mules but the stubborn beasts would have none of him. He fell from his horse amidst the herd, and they began kicking him. He actually drew his gun, frothing with rage and intent upon shooting several of the mules, but he received another kick and the gun accidentally went off, sending a bullet into Allison's good foot. This caused Allison to place added pressure to the clubfoot, increasing a lifelong pain and developing a permanent limp. Allison used a cane after that until the very day of his death. See: **Earp, Wyatt**; **Hickok, James Butler**.

Almer, Jack (AKA: **Jack Averill; Red Jack**), d.1883, U.S., outlaw. Almer was chief of the Red Jack gang that preyed on Arizona stagecoaches during the early 1880s, particularly active along the San Pedro River. The gang held up the Globe stage on Aug. 10, 1883, near Riverside. When the Wells Fargo guard insisted that the stage was not carrying any gold, and showed signs of resisting the robbers, a female passenger jumped from the stage, lifting her skirts high and bellowing in a decidedly bass voice that he was a liar. It was Almer, disguised as a female passenger, dark veil and all. In that impossible impersonation Almer had witnessed the gold being placed under a seat on the stage and thus signaled his men to move in when the stagecoach passed a spot where the gang was waiting. The guard went for his gun and Almer reached inside his skirt and pulled his own six-gun, shooting the Wells Fargo man dead. The gang took $2,800 in gold and bills and fled. Sheriff Bob Paul organized a strong posse and hunted the Red Jack gang down one by one. Paul and his men unearthed Almer hiding near Wilcox, Ariz., on Oct. 4, 1883, and shot him to pieces when he tried to battle his way to freedom.

Alvord, Burton, 1866-c.1910, U.S., lawman-outlaw. Moving west with his father, a justice of the peace, Alvord settled in Tombstone, Ariz., where, as a teenager, he found a job as a stable hand at the O.K. Corral. Shortly after he began work there, Alvord witnessed one of the most spectacular gunfights of the Old West, the showdown shoot-out between the Earp-Holliday clan and the Clanton-McLowery outlaws, a bullet-spitting incident that he would recall for the remainder of his days. Though he was only fifteen at the time of this legendary gun battle on Oct. 26, 1881, Alvord watched carefully as the Earps bested the outlaws by their cool composure and deliberate aim, a hallmark that was to be Alvord's adopted character when acting as a lawman or an outlaw.

At age twenty in 1886, Alvord was selected as a deputy by John Slaughter, the newly-elected sheriff of Cochise County. Slaughter had already seen the mettle of this young man a year earlier when Alvord had been challenged by a local Tombstone tough ubiquitously named "Six-shooter Jimmy." Both men had gone for their guns and Alvord had killed his opponent with one deliberately-aimed shot. From 1886 to 1890 Alvord served as Slaughter's back-up man in

many a shoot-out with outlaws, rustlers, and gunmen of all kinds. Alvord accompanied Slaughter and another deputy, Cesario Lucero, in May 1888, in a pursuit after three Mexican train robbers, tracking these men down to their camp near the Whetstone Mountains one night. The lawmen found the thieves sleeping in their blankets around a smoldering campfire and ordered them to surrender. The three bandits dove for their guns and a pitched battle took place in which one of the train robbers was shot. When he fell, the other two men meekly surrendered to the three lawmen.

A month later, in the same area, on May 7, 1888, Alvord helped Slaughter capture three more Mexican bandits. Again, the lawmen crept up on their prey at night and caught the robbers asleep. A gun battle ensued and one of the bandits was killed, another wounded, the unharmed bandit surrendered quickly. The wounded Mexican, however, managed to escape. The following year, in February of 1889, Alvord began to slip from his role as the ramrod tough deputy. He began drinking heavily and frequently mixed with the outlaw element that drifted into Tombstone. On one oc-

Western lawman turned outlaw, Burt Alvord.

casion, Alvord got drunk with two surly cowboys named Fortino and Fuller, the threesome then in a private house near Slaughter's residence. Fuller exploded over a remark made by Fortino and seized Alvord's six-gun, shooting Fortino to death with it. The deputy was too drunk to stop Fuller at the time. When Slaughter arrived and learned of his deputy's involvement and how Alvord's own weapon was used in a killing, the sheriff exploded, verbally chastising Alvord in front of dozens of witnesses. The deputy was put on notice; either he mended his ways or he would be an unemployed lawman.

Alvord soured on Slaughter and Tombstone following this incident and he moved to Fairbank, Ariz., in the early 1890s where he became the town constable. His drinking and cavorting with known criminals soon caused town fathers to ask for his resignation and Alvord move on to Wilcox, Ariz., where he was made the town constable. He continued to drink heavily and most of the young outlaws labelled him a hopeless alcoholic from whom they had nothing to fear. One such gunman was Billy King, a rough-and-tumble cowboy who harassed Wilcox one day in 1898.

Alvord appeared and ordered King to put up his gun and stop racing his horse up and down the main street. King gave the constable a winning smile and suggested that the two "settle matters over drinks" in the nearby saloon. Alvord and King went to the saloon and belted down a few drinks, but the cowboy grew sullen and threatening so Alvord asked him to step outside. As soon as King went through the back door of the saloon, Alvord drew his pistol and fired every bullet in his gun into King's face, killing him instantly. Burt Alvord was not a man to waste time.

By the turn of the century Alvord had given up on keeping the peace. He would rather break it and join with the outlaws he had befriended over the years. He had physically changed into a dour-faced man with a bald head and a black beard; his dark eyes were full of anger and menace. For some years he led a band of ruthless train robbers. He was arrested first in 1900 and then in 1903 when he and his sidekick, Billy Stiles, were imprisoned. Both men managed to escape after Stiles was made a trustee at the Tombstone Jail and stole the keys to the lockup, allowing him to set Alvord free. Alvord, then much wanted, reasoned that the best way to effect a permanent escape was to play dead. He and Stiles located two corpses (they either killed two Mexicans or unearthed them from recent graves) and sent these bodies to Tombstone in sealed coffins, spreading the word that the pine boxes contained the wanted outlaws, Burt Alvord and Billy Stiles. The ruse failed, however, when suspicious lawmen broke open the coffins and found the ripening bodies of the Mexicans.

Arizona rangers set off in grim pursuit of Alvord and Stiles, locating the pair at their secret camp near Nigger Head Gap, Mex. The rangers ignored international law and crossed the border into Mexico to confront the two bad men. Both Alvord and Stiles went for their guns and both were wounded in the battle, Alvord shot twice in the leg, Stiles in the arm. Alvord was immobilized and could not reach his horse while Stiles managed to get into the saddle and ride wildly out of the trap, escaping. The rangers took Alvord into custody and he was sent to the Arizona prison at Yuma, serving two years for robbery. He was released in 1906 and decided that he would leave the American west forever, seeking his fortune in Central America. He was later reported to be in Venezuala and Honduras and, as late as 1910, the year he was presumed to have died, seen working as a canal employee in Panama. See: **Earp, Wyatt; Holliday, John H.; Slaughter, John Horton; Stiles, William Larkin.**

American Horse, d.1902, U.S., fraud. American Horse, the son of Chief Sitting Bear, was the leader of the True-Oglala division of the Sioux. He claimed to have personally killed Captain William J. Fetterman at the notorious Fetterman Massacre, fought near Fort Phil Kearny, Wyo., on Dec. 21, 1866. In 1889 American Horse cooperated with the U.S. government and helped negotiate the fraudulent sale and transfer of valuable Sioux lands. His actions greatly displeased fellow tribesmen, and in the Ghost Dance uprising of 1890, American Horse's house was destroyed and his livestock run off.

Anderson, David L. (AKA: **Billy Wilson; Buffalo Billy**), 1862-1918, U.S., outlaw. Born in Ohio, Anderson moved to Texas at an early age with his family and there became a cowboy. When he was eighteen he resettled in White Oaks, N.M., where he ran a small livery stable. There he was known as Billy Wilson. Anderson sold his stable in 1880 to a sharper who reportedly paid him off in counterfeit bills. When Anderson began to pass these bills they were identified as bogus currency and he was arrested and indicted. Skipping bail, Anderson fled and joined the band of Billy the Kid. On the night of Nov. 29-30, 1881, a sheriff's posse trapped the Kid and Wilson, shooting the horses out from under both men, but the resourceful outlaws managed to escape on foot in the dark.

The Kid and Anderson then joined with Dave Rudabaugh and, obtaining fresh mounts, boldly rode into White Oaks where they spotted Deputy James Redman who had been part of the posse that had attacked them the night before. All three men opened fire on Redman who had the presence of mind to run for cover, escaping injury. At the sound of this gunfire, dozens of well-armed citizens appeared on the street and began firing at the three outlaws who promptly galloped out of town. The following night a posse tracked the three men to the ranch house of Jim Greathouse where they opened negotiations with the outlaws in arranging their surrender. Billy the Kid agreed to exchange Greathouse, then ostensibly a hostage, for posse leader Jim Carlyle. It was Carlyle's reasoning that, once inside the ranch house, he would persuade the Kid, Anderson, and Rudabaugh to surrender. The posse waited for some time and then witnessed Carlyle's body crashing through a window, three bullets having been pumped into the deputy. While the posse members stood in shock, the outlaws made their getaway. The frustrated possemen vented their wrath on the ranch house, burning it to the ground.

A later story had it that Anderson had tried to reason with the Kid when Carlyle stepped inside the Greathouse building, saying that he had no important charge against him and that he would rather surrender. The Kid talked him out of that and a short time later cold-bloodedly turned and shot Carlyle three times and then smashed his body through the window. Pat Garrett, who would later become famous for shooting down Billy the Kid, then assumed command of the posses in the area, searching for the gang. Garrett set a trap for the gang near Fort Sumner, N.M., and, with a number of deputies, waited for the outlaws to appear. On Dec. 19, 1880, the Kid, Anderson, Rudabaugh, Charlie Bowdre, Tom O'Folliard, and Tom Pickett appeared on the road leading to the old hospital. Garrett, Lon Chambers, and several other deputies leaped from cover, with Garrett ordering the outlaws to halt. But the possemen did not wait for the outlaws to respond to Garrett's command. They opened fire on Pickett and O'Folliard, who were riding in front, and shot them from their saddles. Rudabaugh's horse collapsed, killed in the hail of bullets but Rudabaugh managed to jump onto the horse ridden by Anderson and escaped with the Kid and Bowdre.

Trapped later by Garrett and a large posse at Stinking Springs, Anderson surrendered his six-gun to the lawman, and it was later alleged that this very weapon was used by Garrett to kill Billy the Kid. Anderson was tried for murder and robbery and was convicted in 1881, sent to the prison at Santa Fe, N.M. He managed to escape and flee to Texas where he lived under his real name, Anderson. For years, Anderson lived quietly in Sanderson, Tex., a town begun in 1880 by a relative. He married and raised a family, operating the Old Cottage Bar. He became so popular that Anderson was elected sheriff in 1905 and he proved himself to be an upstanding lawman, keeping the peace with a resolute, steady hand. By that time, Anderson's outlaw career as Billy Wilson was known to authorities and, because of his years of faithful service to the law, men like Pat Garrett had successfully moved to have old charges against him dropped.

The violent past, however, caught up with Anderson on June 14, 1918, when he was asked to go to the train station in Sanderson to quell a disturbance. At the depot he found a drunken cowboy named Ed Valentine whom he knew. Anderson felt he could reason with the rowdy who had been drunkenly brandishing his pistol. But when Anderson arrived the young cowboy ran to a shed and refused to come out. Sheriff Anderson stepped in front of the opened door and called into the darkness for Valentine to come out. A single shot came out of the gloom and pierced Anderson's chest. He fell mortally wounded, dying within an hour. So incensed were local residents by this senseless killing that Valentine was quickly seized and lynched. See: **Billy the Kid; Garrett, Patrick Floyd.**

Anderson, Hugh, d.1873, U.S., gunman. Texas cowboy Anderson was part of a trail herd that moved from Saledo, Tex., to Newton, Kan., in 1871. While on the trail he and several other cowhands were asked to hunt down a killer named Juan Bideno, and this gunman was tracked to Bluff City, Kan., where he was killed by Texas gunslinger John Wesley Hardin. Upon arriving in Newton, Anderson learned that his good friend and gambler William Bailey had been shot to death by a rough-and-tumble railroad foreman, Mike McCluskie, who had left town following the killing. Anderson and his friends let it be known that they intended to seek revenge on McCluskie when, if ever, he returned to Newton. McCluskie returned to Newton on Aug. 20, 1871, and Anderson immediately went after him as the burly railroad foreman sat playing faro in Perry Tuttle's Dance Hall.

Without waiting for McCluskie to make his move, Anderson raced up to him, swore, and pumped several shots into the foreman before he could draw his gun. This set off one of the wildest gun battles ever witnessed in the West, later called the Newton General Massacre. Anderson had made good his boast; he had killed McCluskie but had been severely wounded and, before he could be arrested, the quick-triggered cowboy was spirited out of town by friends who tended his wounds. Two years later, in June 1873, McCluskie's brother, Arthur McCluskie, who had been looking for Anderson, arrived in Medicine Lodge, Kan. Anderson was tending bar at Harding's Trading Post. A man named Richards who had helped McCluskie locate Anderson, went into Harding's bar and told Anderson that Arthur McCluskie was outside waiting to settle the score over the killing of his brother, giving Anderson a choice of knives or guns. Anderson chose guns, asking Harding to be his second in a duel that was very formal for the Old West. He then closed the bar, telling grumbling patrons that he had "a chore to do" and would be back in a few minutes. He never returned.

Once outside, Hugh Anderson stood back to back with Arthur McCluskie, walked twenty paces and, at the command, turned around and fired reapeatedly, as did his opponent. A crowd in the hundreds had gathered around the blood fight and were making loud wagers as the first shots went wild. Then McCluskie's second bullet found its mark, smashing into Anderson's arm and breaking it. The cowboy-bartender sank to his knees in pain, attempting to stop the flow of blood from an artery. He then aimed at McCluskie with his good hand and his bullet smashed into McCluskie's mouth. McCluskie spat out gobs of blood and broken teeth and fired again, advancing on Anderson. With deliberate aim, Anderson fired twice more, his bullets striking McCluskie in the leg and the stomach. Now McCluskie crashed to the ground and appeared to be dying.

He worked himself to a kneeling position and fired another shot at Anderson, striking him in the abdomen. Anderson pitched backward, gasping for air.

Both men appeared to be dying but McCluskie showed some signs of life, pulling out a knife and then crawling painfully to his foe where he sank the knife to the hilt in Anderson's side. At the same moment, Anderson, his own knife in his hand, swiped McCluskie's neck, cutting his throat. Both men then collapsed and died within seconds of each other. The gamblers collected their wagers and the bodies were dragged off for a quick burial. Harding, who had seconded Anderson, showed remarkable restraint in this duel. When both men were shot to the ground and before they pulled their knives, many in the crowd began to step forward to stop the battle but Harding, holding a shotgun, warned them not to interfere, allowing the combatants to kill each other, according to the rules they had agreed upon. See: **Hardin, John Wesley; Newton General Massacre.**

Anderson, Reese, prom. 1880s, U.S., vigil. Anderson was a cowboy who worked for the Granville Stuart ranch in Montana. When the nearby area, known as the Lower Judith Basin, welled up with scores of bandits and robbers in 1884, Anderson volunteered to lead two dozen of Stuart's cowhands in a vigilante sweep of the area. Anderson and his men rode into the hideout area between the Musselshell and Judith rivers and surprised the outlaws, capturing and hanging twenty-three horse thieves caught red-handed with stolen herds.

Anderson, Scott L., prom. 1870s, U.S., gunman. Scotty Anderson was a fearless guard for the Northwestern Stage amd Transportation Company, guarding the firm's considerable gold shipments in the Dakotas. One particular run, the Deadwood-Pierre, S.D., was plagued by a bold band of bandits headed by an ex-company guard, Boston Joe. Several guards had been killed and more than $50,000 in gold shipments stolen. Anderson, a tough, unflinching hard case who carried two shotguns along with three pistols, was hired as chief guard to protect this run. On his first assignment, Anderson and four guards, heavily armed and protecting more than $100,000 in gold, took the Deadwood-Pierre stage which was stopped by Boston Joe and his gang near Deadman's Creek. The bandits and guards opened up on each other, blazing away as the stage made a run for it. Boston Joe and his men dashed after it, firing as they attempted to catch the stage. Anderson, though wounded several times, managed to kill Boston Joe. The other guards shot three of the remaining outlaws dead in their saddles before two of the guards were killed and the driver wounded. Anderson brought the stage in safely to Pierre to report the end of the outlaw band.

Anderson, William (AKA: Bloody Bill), 1837-64, U.S., outlaw. Born in Jefferson County, Mo., on Feb. 2, 1837, Anderson enlisted in the guerilla band of William Clarke Quantrill, a Confederate group, in 1863, having operated with his own guerilla band since the beginning of the Civil War. Often as not, this most fierce of Quantrill's raiders, operated with his own band of men, about sixty-five strong. Anderson was feared throughout the border states of Missouri-Kansas as an out-and-out killer—aptly nicknamed Bloody Bill—who preferred to murder anyone with Union sympathies. While Quantrill would earn his notoriety at the sacking and burning of Lawrence, Kan., Anderson's complete annihilation of Centralia, Kan., in 1864 would make the vicious outlaw's name synonymous with murder.

This fierce killer who, like his men wore his hair long and unkempt, postured as a Confederate soldier, but he and his men, in reality, were most often nothing more than

Civil War Confederate guerrilla William "Bloody Bill" Anderson committed mass murder at Centralia, Kan., in 1864.

raiding plunderers of small, defenseless towns. Contemporary accounts reported that Anderson's three sisters had all died when the building where they were being guarded by Union troops caught on fire. Anderson claimed that his sisters had been brutally raped and then locked in the building which was then purposely torched, and this was the reason why he showed no mercy to Union troops and sympathizers. Most historians, however, agreed that Anderson was simply a bloodlusting lunatic who enjoyed inflicting pain and death. Jim Cummins, who later rode with Jesse James and had been a member of Quantrill's legions during the war, later stated that Anderson was "the most desperate man I ever met." Union forces operating in Missouri and Kansas were grimly aware of the fact that Anderson never took prisoners but always shot captives out-of-hand. This was never more in evidence than during Bloody Bill's raid on Centralia.

While attempting to join up with regular Confederate Army troops under the command of General Sterling Price, Anderson and about seventy men swooped down on Centralia on Sept. 27, 1864. As soon as the local merchants recognized the savage looking Anderson and his ragged troops with their long, tangled hair and filthy long dusters, they realized they were at the mercy of the worst guerilla raider of the war. The shopkeepers and their families fled their homes and stores into the open county. Several women were dragged back and raped by Anderson's men while others set fire to the entire town and executed those they thought were Union supporters. Whiskey barrels were located in one store and Anderson and his men gulped down great quantities of this raw alcohol, using their shoes as cups.

Anderson, checking the train schedules at the depot, realized that a train was scheduled to pass through Centralia at noon that day and he ordered a huge barricade built across the tracks. At noon a passenger train was forced by the barricade to stop at Centralia. Its passengers were herded onto the depot platform, including twenty-six Union soldiers under the command of a Lieutenant Peters, men who had been furloughed and were en route to St. Joseph, Mo. Peters, recognizing Anderson from a train window and realizing that the guerilla leader was known to murder any Union officers, threw a blanket over himself, jumped from the train, and attempted to hide beneath the platform of the burning depot.

The guerilla chieftan spotted the cowardly officer and yelled to his men, "Pull that bastard out of there!" Peters was dragged from beneath the platform and, as Anderson approached him, guns in hands, broke free and tried to run for his life. Anderson took careful aim and fired six bullets into him, killing Peters. He then ordered the remaining twenty-six Union troopers lined up in an open field. All knew of Anderson's no quarter policy and that he had given his men strict orders to kill all Union prisoners. Most fell on their knees to pray or beg sobbingly for mercy. Anderson paraded up and down in front of them, bristling with guns. (He was a walking and riding arsenal, usually with four Navy Colt pistols in his waistband, four rifles on his horse, a sabre, a hatchet, and a bag of pistols wrapped around the horn of his saddle.)

Anderson ignored the pleas from the troopers that their lives be spared. He stopped, stuck a cigar in his mouth and lighted this, then asked softly, "Boys, do you have a sergeant in your ranks?" None of the men answered, all fearing that anyone admitting to the rank of sergeant would be tortured. Anderson repeated his question calmly several times, indicating that if the Union troops cooperated, their lives would be spared. Finally, Sergeant Thomas M. Goodman stepped forward, admitting his rank. "Fine," smiled Anderson around his cigar. "We'll use you to exchange for one of my men that the damned Yankees have caught." Goodman was ushered out of line. The guerilla chieftan than withdrew two of his Colts and went down the line, firing until the chambers of both guns were empty. He took two more pistols and emptied these and then two more, until all twenty-six Union soldiers had been murdered in cold blood.

Goodman would later escape to tell the tale of Anderson's brutal slaughter but by that time the guerillas had already ridden off to attack Union troops elsewhere. While in Texas some weeks later, Anderson married a young girl and brought her back to Ray County, Mo., settling briefly in a small farmhouse before riding off once more to lead his men in more murderous raids. Anderson's bloody crimes were halted, however, on Oct. 27, 1864, when, at the head of his guerilla column, riding near Orrick, Mo., he was ambushed by Union troops under the command of Captain S.P. Cox. Anderson was struck by dozens of bullets and was dead in his saddle. His men fought wildly to retrieve his body but were driven off. Anderson's corpse was taken to Richmond, Mo., where it was propped up in a chair and a pistol placed in its dead hand and then photographed. A few minutes later, Union soldiers, full of hatred for this butcher, cut off Anderson's head and impaled it on a telegraph pole and placed at the entrance of the town to assure one and all that the terrible guerilla leader was indeed dead. His carcass was then tied to a rope and dragged up and down the streets, before the remains were dumped into an unmarked grave at the outskirts of town.

It was later claimed that Anderson was not killed at the Orrick ambush and that another man, a look-alike, was killed and that Anderson changed his name and escaped to Oklahoma where he ran a saloon for several years in Erin Springs. Another report has it that the mass killer went to Texas after the war and settled in Salt Creek, Brown County, where he lived peacefully under an alias for sixty years. Some credibility was attached to this last story in that a man bearing a slight resemblance to Anderson died in Salt Creek on Nov. 2, 1927. On the table next to his deathbed was found an ancient photograph of three young women who were later identified as Anderson's long-dead sisters. See: **Quantrill, William Clarke.**

Anderson, William, prom. 1870s, U.S., gunman. Anderson was a drunken gunman who lived in Delano, the vice district of Wichita, during the 1870s. He was forever getting into trouble with the law and, in the spring of 1873, he was involved in a violent argument in a Wichita livery stable. He pulled a gun, as did others, and a brief shootout occurred where one of Anderson's shots smashed into the forehead of a passerby, killing him. The death was ruled accidental and Anderson was released. A short time later, on Oct. 27, 1873, Anderson was lounging inside of Rowdy Joe Lowe's Delano bar when an enraged cowhand, Edward T. "Red" Beard, burst into the bar. He had been jilted by one of the saloon girls, Annie Franklin, and he sought revenge, pulling his gun and shooting the girl in the stomach. Lowe let loose with his shotgun and blasted Beard who fired back as he staggered outside. In the exchange of bullets, Anderson was caught in the crossfire, taking a load of buckshot in the head which caused him to become permanently blind. Anderson spent the rest of his days sitting outside cowtown saloons, hat in hand, begging coins. See: **Beard, Edward T.; Lowe, Joseph**.

Anderson, William H., d.1878, U.S., lawman. Anderson, born in Illinois, moved as a youth to Texas and served in the Confederate Army during the Civil War, later deserting to serve with an Illinois regiment. He moved back to Texas following the war and was appointed a U.S. deputy marshal, a post he served with distinction, having a reputation as an expert marksman. He invariably captured any felon he sought out. In 1878 he was ordered to track down outlaw Bill Collins, last surviving member of the Joel Collins outlaw band. Doggedly trailing the Collins brother through several states, Anderson finally cornered his man in Manitoba, Can. Outside the small hamlet of Pembina, both Anderson and Collins shot it out, killing each other. Anderson's body was returned to Texas for burial and his family was given the considerable reward that had been placed on Collins' head.

Andrew, Robert, prom. 1870s, U.S., lawman. An Oklahoma lawman and detective, Andrew was responsible for discovering the Doolin gang hideout. This resulted in the Ingalls, Okla., raid on Sept. 1, 1893, and the capture of many members of that band. See: **Doolin, William**.

Antrim, Henry (Kid Antrim; William Antrim), See: Billy the Kid.

Apache Kid (Zenogalache, AKA: **The Crazy One**), b.1867-c.1910, U.S., outlaw. Next to Geronimo, the most fierce and feared Apache of the old Southwest was the Apache Kid, the son of Toga-de-chuz, a chief who was murdered by a rival for the Kid's mother. The boy, who was never known by any other name than the Apache Kid to whites, but whose Apache name was Zenogalache, waited many years before taking his revenge, eventually murdering his father's killer near the Aravaipo River. At an early age the orphaned Kid was taken in at the San Carlos Indian Agency, N.M. Here the famous cavalry scout, Al Sieber, educated the boy and taught him the use of

The Apache Kid, terror of the Southwest.

firearms and the codes of the military, later getting the Apache Kid an appointment as the first sergeant of the Apache Government Scouts which were under the command of the U.S. Cavalry. The Scouts served as agency policemen who made arrests among their own people.

Following the murder of the old Indian who had killed the Kid's father, Sieber ordered the Apache Kid into San Carlos. He appeared with ten of his heavily armed men. When Sieber told other Indian policemen to take the group to the guardhouse, the Kid ordered his men to fire on Sieber and he was wounded in the leg before the band rode pell-mell from the agency. There was a price on the Kid's head ever after. In addition to the military, several scouts and gunmen joined in the hunt for the Kid, and this included the famous Tom Horn, later hanged for murder. The Kid and his band, increased to about thirty, rode for the Mexican border and en route stole a herd of horses from the Atchley Ranch near Table Mountain, killed a trapper in his cabin, one Bill Diehl, and tortured and murdered rancher Mike Grace as the desperadoes moved southward.

For two years the Kid and his men eluded capture but were finally taken and sentenced to death following a quick trial. The Kid insisted that he was innocent of the Diehl and Grace killings, that others in his band had done the deeds. His plea reached President Grover Cleveland's ears and the chief executive granted him a pardon. But as soon as he was released, the Kid led another band on bloody raids through the territory, stopping freight wagons, murdering the drivers and taking the goods. Sheriff Glenn Reynolds of Gila County, Ariz., led a huge posse after the Kid and managed to capture him. This time the Kid was sent to prison for seven years. However, en route to the

Yuma Prison, on Nov. 1, 1889, the guards and their six prisoners camped near Riverside in the Pinal Mountains. The Kid and his men broke free and murdered his guards, Reynolds, and Bill Holmes. Another guard, Eugene Middleton, badly wounded, survived the Kid's wrath and limped into Globe, Ariz., to tell authorities how the Kid escaped after murdering the guards while they slept.

After six of the Kid's band were captured and two were hanged (the other four committed suicide by strangling each other with their loin cloths while in their cell the morning before the execution), the Kid went on a murder rampage, killing several settlers. He attacked a prairie schooner in which a woman, her young son, and an infant were traveling to meet the woman's husband. The Kid stopped the covered wagon, shot the woman and boy to death but oddly spared the infant. This crime incensed the military and civilian population and hundreds set out to hunt down the killer Indian. One scout named Dupont abruptly came across the Kid on a trail in the Catalinas. Both men had single shot rifles and paused, staring at each other. Neither wanted to waste one shot and be at the mercy of the other so they dismounted, sat on rocks through the long day, glaring at each other while the sun beat down upon them. At dusk, the Kid stood up and grunted, "Me leaving." With that the killer mounted his horse and rode off while Dupont heaved a heavy sigh of relief.

For several years the Kid and a small band of renegade Apache followers raided ranches and freight lines throughout New Mexico, Arizona, and northern Mexico, hiding out in the Mexican Sierra Madre mountains. A price of $5,000 was placed on the Apache Kid's head but no one ever claimed the reward. Edward A. Clark, who had been the partner of Bill Diehl, continued to live on his horse ranch which the Kid raided several times, the last attack occuring in 1894 when the Kid and his men surrounded the ranch house and lay siege to Clark, his new partner, John Scanlon, and a visiting Englishman named Mercer. When night fell, Clark slipped out of the house and worked his way to the corral where he saw two Indians leading away his favorite horse. He fired two shots and in the morning found the body of a squaw, the Kid's wife. He also found a trail of blood leading from the spot where the woman's corpse sprawled. Clark followed the trail of blood but it petered out in the rocks of the high hills. "It was the Kid all right," Clark later claimed. "He crawled away to die somewhere, I know."

Supporting Clark's theory was a sudden silence from the Apache Kid. No more ranches were raided or settlers and freightman killed. The outlaw's trail ceased to exist. One account by Mrs. Tom Charles insists that a posse led by Charles Anderson trapped the Kid near Kingston on Sept. 10, 1905, and shot him dead. Some later reports had it that the Apache Kid simply retired to his mountain hideout in Mexico and lived well into the twentieth century, dying of consumption sometime around 1910. This claim has never been substantiated. See: **Horn, Tom.**

Archer Brothers, prom. 1880s, U.S., outlaws. The Archer Brothers of Indiana were the scourge of Orange and Marion counties for several decades, bandits who regularly robbed stagecoaches, trains, and travelers, escaping back to their homes where relatives and friends protected them against arrest. The Archer clan operated in much the same fashion as had the Reno Brothers of Indiana two decades earlier, robbing when low on funds, then resuming the ostensibly respectable roles of farmers and shopkeepers. The nominal leader of the holdup gang was Thomas Archer and his brothers included Morton, John, and Samuel. All four brothers were finally caught by possemen in March 1886. Vigilantes hanged Tom, Mort, and John without trial. Sam Archer, the youngest of the gang, was held for trial and, following a speedy conviction for robbery and murder, was officially hanged on July 10, 1886. See: **Reno Brothers.**

Arcine, James (or **Arcene**), and **Parchmeal, William**, d.1885, U.S., outlaws. To avoid the gallows, James Arcine told Judge Isaac Parker at Fort Smith (Ark.), that he was only ten years old when he shot and killed Henry Feigel, a Swedish laborer. If true, Arcine is the only person in the U.S. to be executed for a crime committed when he was so young. Arcine and a friend, William Parchmeal, were Cherokee Indians living near the U.S. Army base at Fort Smith. On Nov. 25, 1872, Henry Feigel set out from Talequah, capital of the Cherokee Nation, en route to Fort Gibson.

Two miles out of town Feigel was overtaken by Arcine, who fired at him and then completed the job with a large stone. Parchmeal later claimed he stood helplessly by, fearing Arcine would kill him if he intervened. Arcine removed Feigel's half-soled boots and later would boast that he had stolen them from a dead man. Feigel's body was found in a thicket the next day.

Although Arcine and Parchmeal were strongly suspected, no arrests were made and the affair was dropped for the next thirteen years. In 1884 the case attracted the attention of Deputy U.S. Marshal Andrews, who uncovered new evidence that established their guilt. Following his arrest, Arcine told authorities that he was thirty-three years old, which meant he was actually age twenty when the crime was committed. Parchmeal confessed and led Andrews to the exact spot where the killing had occurred. His attempt to secure leniency from the court failed, for Parchmeal's confession only served to place the noose squarely around his and Arcine's necks. An appeal was made directly to President Chester Arthur, who refused them clemency. June 26, 1885, was set as the date of execution. The two convicted murderers prayed and sang in the Cherokee language up to the minute they were led to the gallows.

Arizona Rangers, 1901-10, U.S., lawmen. The Arizona Rangers were formed just after the turn of the century to assist local lawmen in the state who were overwhelmed by the number of criminals infesting the state. Arizona was then making the transition from Old West traditions to modern statehood, employing new police techniques that had yet to take hold. Desperadoes were still being chased on horseback at this time and the days of the posse, the vigilante, and the rangers were on the wane. The rangers were, nevertheless, a potent factor in fighting crime. Headed by the celebrated Captain Burton C. Mossman, the Arizona Rangers formed the nucleus of what later became the modern-day state police, as did the Texas Rangers. Though the organization saw only a decade of life, the Arizona Rangers became a legendary organization which tracked down numerous public enemies on horseback such as the vicious gunman Augustin Chacon and lawman-turned-outlaw Burt Alvord. See: **Alvord, Burton; Chacon, Augustin; Mossman, Burton C.**

Armstrong, John Barclay, 1850-1913, U.S., lawman. Born in McMennville, Tenn., in January 1850, Armstrong, son of a dentist, left home at an early age and drifted about the southwest until reaching Austin, Texas, in 1870 where he married and began life as a rancher, raising a large family of seven children. Armstrong was an early advocate of law and order and to that end, joined the Travis Rifles in 1871, this group being a paramilitary organization put together to combat rampant lawlessness in Texas. In 1875, Armstrong enlisted with the Texas Rangers and became one of its most famous members, first serving under L.H. McNelly where he quickly reached the rank of sergeant because of his excellent service. So dedicated was Armstrong and so fearless in battling outlaws when accompanying his superior that he was dubbed "McNelly's Bulldog."

On Oct. 1, 1876, Armstrong and a company of rangers cornered a band of rustlers and outlaws near Espinoza

Lake. Several outlaws escaped but four of them elected to shoot it out and all were killed by Armstrong and his men. Another two rustlers were later shot by a small contingent of Armstrong's command. Armstrong and another ranger, Leroy Deggs, were assigned to arrest John Mayfield, a rancher who had been charged with murder and on whose head a considerable reward had been placed. On Dec. 7, 1876, Armstrong and Deggs rode to Mayfield's ranch in Wilson County, Tex. They found their man in a corral and Amrstrong told Mayfield that he was under arrrest. He laughed and reached for his gun. The lawmen pulled their pistols and shot the rancher dead. A dozen ranchhands came running and threatened to kill the two rangers if they attempted to take the body with them. Armstrong and Deggs thoughtfully withdrew without the corpse which was later buried secretly to prevent Amstrong from collecting the reward.

The next man Armstrong went after was the most wanted outlaw of his day, as well as the fastest and most feared gunslinger of the era, John Wesley Hardin. A $4,000 reward had been posted for Hardin's arrest for murder. The ranger spent months tracking the elusive Hardin, learning that the outlaw was somewhere in the Gulf State area. The trail led him to Florida where, on Aug. 23, 1877, Armstrong learned that Hardin would be on a train stopping at Pensacola. Though he had no actual authority in the area, Armstrong appointed a few local men as deputies and boarded the train when it arrived.

A large, burly man with an intent gaze and an unswerving nature, Armstrong intended to take Hardin dead or alive and told his nervous deputies to walk behind him as he marched through the coaches, looking for his prey. Armstrong spotted Hardin sitting in a coach seat with a member of his gang, Jim Mann. Three other heavily armed Hardin associates sat in nearby seats. Armstrong motioned for his deputies to sit apart from him and he took a seat directly across from Hardin and Mann while the train idled in the station. (At the time Armstrong was limping and using a cane, having accidentally shot himself in the leg while cleaning a pistol, and this image of being crippled thoroughly disarmed Hardin's normally accute suspicions.) Slowly, Armstrong drew forth his long-barreled .45-caliber pistol, put this in his lap, then stood up and aimed it at Hardin and Mann. "I am a ranger and you are both under arrest," Armstrong calmly announced. "Surrender your weapons."

Hardin jerked his head back, exclaiming, "Texas, by God!" He reached for his pistol but in his awkward effort to stand up from the cramped train seat, Hardin hooked the long barrel in his suspenders. While he was struggling to untangle himself, his partner, 19-year-old Mann, drew his pistol and fired across the aisle at Armstrong, blowing the ranger's stetson from his head, missing his scalp by half an inch. Armstrong stood up wobbly-legged, balancing his bad leg with his cane in one hand and with the other carefully, cooly aimed his six-gun, firing one shot which plowed into Mann's chest. The young outlaw dove head first out the open train window, got to his feet, took a few steps down the station platform and then crashed downward, dead.

Hardin by then was on his feet, still struggling to release the hammer of his weapon from his suspenders. In frustration he kicked Armstrong in the chest and sent the law-man reeling backward down the aisle. The ranger got to his feet and jumped forward, bringing his gun butt down on Hardin's head several times, pistol-whipping him into uncon-sciousness. During this en-tire incident, which lasted only a few minutes, Har-din's three other outlaw companions sat frozen in their seats. With Hardin down and unconscious, Armstrong turned to them and quietly asked for their guns. They turned them

Texas Ranger Armstrong, who cap-tured John Wesley Hardin.

over meekly, and Armstrong took the entire gang into custody, later delivering them to Texas authorities. This time the ranger did collect the reward and used the $4000 to purchase more than 50,000 acres of cattle land in Willacy County, Tex., calling his spread the XIT ranch, one of the largest at that time.

Armstrong did not retire from the rangers, however, but continued to battle outlaws such as King Fisher, cleaning out that rustler baron's operations in South Texas and rising to the rank of captain. This most respected of rangers retired in 1882 to attend to his lucrative cattle ranch. He accepted the post of U.S. marshal for his area for a brief period, then returned to his ranch. He maintained a large crew of cowhands and rigidly bossed their work, much as he had when operating as a Texas Ranger. One cowboy, a truculent sort, refused to take Armstrong's harsh order on Nov. 18, 1908, and shot his boss out of his saddle. (The cowboy was later sent to prison for attempted murder.) Armstrong survived this attack as he had so many others and died peacefully in his bed on his ranch, May 1, 1913. See: **Hardin, John Wesley.**

Arrington, George W., 1844-1923, U.S., lawman. One of the greatest Texas Rangers on record, Arrington was born in Greensboro, Ala., on Dec. 23, 1844, and fought for the Confederacy in Mosby's Raiders. Following the Civil War, Arrington joined other Confederate soldiers and went to Mexico, offering his services to the doomed Em-peror Maximilian and then moved on to seek adventure in Central America before returning to the U.S. in 1867. He eventually moved to Texas and joined the Texas Rangers in the early 1870s, fast rising through the ranks until he was appointed a captain. Arrington's territory was the Panhandle of Texas, then one of the worst nightmares for any lawmen. The area was overrun with hostile Indians and hundreds of hardcase outlaws who would rather shoot it out than talk truce. Whenever Arrington and his com-pany of twenty men went out in sweeps to capture outlaws, fugitives by the scores were either captured or killed. In one month a-lone, July 1878, Arrington and his company rounded up forty men, half of these having separate murder charges against them.

Capt. George W. Arrington.

As a captain of the rangers, Arrington proved himself fearless. Often as not, if his men were on duty elsewhere, he would go after several desperadoes alone and invariably bring in two or three rustlers. He was as tough as any outlaw on the plains, and his strict discipline was applied to his own men. Whenever he caught one of his own rangers tipsy he would order him locked up as a common drunk. Arrington was living proof that the Rangers, like the Mounties, always got their man. He would track fugitives to both ends of the continent. He trailed one wealthy cattle rustler all the way to New England, returning him to Texas secretly. Arrington knew that the wealthy fugitive would have lawyers waiting in each state through which they would travel so the intrepid lawman purposely changed trains at regular intervals and stayed in hotels using aliases for himself and his captive.

Arrington left the Rangers in the early 1880s and became sheriff of Wheeler County, a post he kept for eight years before retiring to his Rocking Chair Ranch in 1890. The old lawman came out of retirement briefly to become sheriff for the same county in 1894 and during this time he was confronted by six tough drunken cowboys in a local saloon who dared him to throw them into jail. Arrington had a small jail and no deputy so he did the next best thing. The lawman handcuffed the six men to the bar rail and held them in custody for twenty-four uncomfortable hours, until all promised to leave town without creating further disturbances. Arrington died on his ranch, Mar. 31, 1923.

Aten, Ira, 1863-1953, U.S., lawman. Born in Illinois on Sept. 3, 1863, Aten moved with his family when a child to Round Rock, Texas, where his father had a small farm and traveled the Bible Belt as a Methodist minister. As a youth, Aten and his brothers Edwin (b.1871) and Franklin (b.1860) were exposed to the rough-and-tumble westerners inhabiting and visiting their community, from wild cowboys to dedicated gunslingers and bandits. In 1878, when Ira was only fifteen, he and his brothers saw Sam Bass, the infamous outlaw, brought into Round Rock, mortally wounded after a gun battle with a posse following a robbery. His father, the Reverend Mr. Aten, was called to Bass' deathbed where he gave him spiritual aid in his last

Texas Ranger Ira Aten, one of the most dedicated and tough lawmen in the Southwest.

moments and heard the outlaws's last words. ("Let me go—the world is bobbing around," slipped from Sam Bass' mouth before he died.) From that moment on, Ira Aten vowed that he would never follow the path of the gunman but would become a champion for law and order, promising his father that he would join the Texas Rangers as soon as he was of age. Aten went on to become one of the most respected rangers in the Lone Star State.

Known to lawmen then as an expert marksman, Aten joined Company D, Frontier Battalion of the Texas Rangers, serving under Captain L.P. Sieker in March 1883. He had just turned twenty and was immediately assigned to cover the most dangerous territory in Texas, the border along the Rio Grande which was awash with rustlers running stolen cattle from Texas into Mexico. At the Rio Grande River in March 1884, Aten accompanied Sieker and five other rangers in a sweep of the area. About eighty miles south of Laredo, the rangers came upon a gang of rustlers who immediately tried to escape across the border. Sieker, Aten, and Ben Reilly rode ahead of the other rangers and cut the outlaws off from reaching the Mexican border. In a running gunfight, Sieker was hit by a bullet in the heart, toppling dead from his horse. Reilly received a blast in the thigh and was also shot from the saddle. This left Aten to attack the two outlaws alone. Pumping his Winchester, the Ranger shot one bandit in the shoulder, the other in the hand and, joined by the remaining Rangers, brought the wounded outlaws to the Webb County Jail but were themselves arrested and thrown into jail and the outlaws released. This was the doing of Sheriff Dario Gozalez, a corrupt lawman who was on the payroll of the region's rustlers. Aten and the other Rangers spent three weeks locked up in the Webb County Jail before being released.

In 1887 Aten, who had been promoted quickly to the rank of corporal and then sergeant in the Rangers, was assigned to track down the much-wanted outlaw, Judd Roberts, who had escaped from the San Antonio Jail. In April 1887, Aten learned that Roberts would be visiting a ranch in Williamson County and he lay in wait for the outlaw. As Roberts arrived, Aten jumped from behind his cover and ordered him to surrender. The outlaw drew his gun and fired off several wild shots which missed the resolute Aten. The Ranger took careful aim, fired one shot and blasted the six-gun out of Roberts' hand. The outlaw, however, spurred his horse around and escaped. Aten cornered Roberts two months later in June when he rightly guessed that Roberts would attack rancher John Hughes of Liberty Hill, Burnet County, Texas; Hughes had earlier made an enemy of the outlaw. When Roberts arrived at the ranch in the dead of night, creeping up to a window, gun in hand, ostensibly to murder Hughes, Aten stepped from the darkness and told Roberts he was under arrest. The outlaw fired a shot which whizzed past Aten and the lawman returned fire, again wounding the outlaw in his shooting hand. Roberts ran to his horse and again escaped.

Hughes, realizing that the vengeful Roberts would return, offered his services to Aten in tracking down the outlaw and the two men set off on a month-long chase after Roberts, one that took them through the Texas Panhandle. There, on a small ranch where Roberts was known to have a sweetheart, Aten and Hughes trapped the killer. Roberts ran from the ranch house, his girl friend running after him. Instead of surrendering, Roberts again chose the gun and fired blindly at Aten and Hughes. Both returned fire and Roberts fell to earth with six bullets in him; his sweetheart cradled him in her arms until he died minutes later. It was at this time that Aten persuaded Hughes to join the Texas Rangers. He did, becoming one of its valued members for twenty-eight years.

Aten was a sergeant of the Rangers when he led Hughes, Bass Outlaw and Sheriff Will Terry after the cattle-rustling Alvin and Will Odle, two brothers known for their lethal gunfights. On Dec. 25, 1889, the lawmen cornered the brothers near Vance, Texas, as they were running stolen cattle by moonlight. In the resulting gunfight both Odle boys were killed. Aten then retired from the Rangers and was promptly appointed sheriff of Fort Bend County which was plagued by a Democrat-Republican political fight later known as the Jaybird-Woodpecker War, one which involved Texans attempting to eradicate the last of the carpetbag politicians left over from the Civil War. Aten and his deputies soon put a stop to the wholesale shootings that took several lives, and the lawman is credited with halting this deadly Texas feud.

The next year, 1891, Aten bought a small ranch near Dimmitt, Texas, and was soon opposing two conniving brothers, Andrew and Hugh McClelland. The McClellands had migrated from Tennessee and intended to win election to high office and then set a land-grabbing scheme in motion. Aten's small but important ranch was part of the scheme. During a heated election for county judge, Andrew McClelland, a laywer by trade, addressed a large crowd in Dimmitt. Aten, who had campaigned against McClelland, was in the crowd and the lawyer singled out the ex-Ranger, calling him a liar and a crook. After the election, which resulted in McClelland's defeat, Aten went to Dimmitt and told McClelland to arm himself so that he could avenge his honor. The lawyer went to a hardware store while Aten waited in the street. In minutes McClelland leaped into the street with two new .45-caliber pistols in his hands, both spitting bullets in Aten's direction. Aten fired one shot which shattered McClelland's arm. The lawyer collapsed but managed to get off another shot which harmlessly chewed up some dust between Aten's feet. He was carried off by friends as Aten holstered his weapon.

No sooner had the ex-lawman put away his pistol than a bullet sang past Aten's face, one fired by the other McClelland brother, Hugh. Aten drew his weapon once more as Hugh McClelland ducked behind a wooden shack. Aten fired through the thin boards twice, wounding the other brother who was also carried away to the doctor's office. Aten then turned himself in to local authorities. The McClelland brothers survived and Aten was released as having fired in self-defense. Aten, who retired officially as a captain of the Texas Rangers, was elected sheriff of

Castro County in 1893 and served well for almost a year, rounding up rustlers and bandits with regularity. He became known for his humane treatment of prisoners as well as his ability to take fugitives alive, this mostly due to his ability to shoot weapons out of the hands of his prey.

In 1895 Aten quit his sheriff's post and permanently retired to the position of superintendent of 600,000 acres of XIT ranchland, a job he held until 1904. He then moved his wife and five children to the Imperial Valley in California to raise oranges, dying in Burlingame on Aug. 6, 1953, at age ninety-one. Both Aten's brothers Edwin and Franklin also became members of the Texas Rangers. In Edwin's case it was a no-choice decision. Edwin shot and killed a card cheat who drew a pistol and tried to murder him. His brother Ira arrested him and gave him only one option. Either he would go to jail and stand trial or become a Texas Ranger. He chose the latter and went on to become an excellent lawmen, responsible for the arrest of dozens of rustlers along the Rio Grande when serving with Captain Frank Jones of Company D, at Alpine, Texas. As fearless as his brother Ira, Edwin Aten crossed many times into Mexico in pursuit of the dreaded Jesus Maria Olguin and his gunfighter sons. Edwin Aten was with the redoubtable Captain Jones when they and other Rangers pursued Olguin into Mexico in June 1893 which ended in a wild gunfight that claimed the life of Jones. Franklin Lincoln Aten, the oldest of the Aten brothers, never served as a lawman, content to remain a beekeeper all his days. Like his brothers he lived a long life; he was more than 100 when he died. See: **Bass, Samuel; Hughes, John; Jaybird-Woodpecker War; Jones, Frank; Outlaw, Bass.**

Austin, Harris, d.1890, U.S., outlaw. After accusing Thomas Elliott of stealing his whiskey at Tishomingo, in the Chickasaw Nation, Harris Austin fired two bullets at close range into the man's body on May 25, 1883. Austin discharged a third shot into Elliott's temple, which left a powder burn on the victim's face. Austin escaped into the surrounding hills, and remained at large until Deputy Marshal Carr and a posse tracked him down in April 1889. He was taken to Fort Smith (Ark.) where he was hanged on Jan. 16, 1890.

Averill, James (Jim), and **Watson, Ella**, d.1889, U.S., gunmen. The bloody Johnson County War in Wyoming was largely precipitated by the gruesome fates of gunman-rancher Jim Averill and his buxom paramour, Ella Watson, better known as Cattle Kate. Averill's background is sketchy, though it was claimed by contemporary historians that he was either a graduate of Yale or Cornell. He arrived at Sweetwater, Wyo., in late 1887, just when the powerful Wyoming Stock Growers' Association was planning to wipe out the newly arrived hordes of immigrant settlers who had streamed into the area to cultivate the rich land for farms. The ranges were soon fenced off with barbed wire, and the classic battle for land was waged between settlers and small ranchers lined up against the cattle barons.

Shortly after arriving, Averill bought a small ranch and established a combination store-saloon-post office. The approximately eighty residents of Sweetwater soon elected him justice of the peace and Averill's reign over this little frontier dynasty led him to believe that he could defy the ruthless cattle barons headed by Albert Bothwell. He began complaining to authorities about the encroachments of the cattlemen and was bitterly opposed to the Maverick Act which the Association had forced into existence. The wealthy cattlemen, who owned Wyoming's governor and most of its state senators, ordered the new law which allowed all unbranded calves to become the property of the Association. Thus, the thousands of stray cattle, no matter who rightfully owned them, went into the pens of the cattle barons. Men like Bothwell also coveted the entire Wyoming range and those who refused to sell their claims to the cattlemen were either run out of the territory or murdered by gunmen like Frank Canton, a glorified stockman's detective who was nothing more than killer for hire.

Jim Averill, gunman and cattle rustler who was hanged with his sweetheart Ella Watson, 1889.

While the range battles expanded, Averill was besieged by his saloon customers to provide some female companionship for their amusement. He remembered a voluptuous woman named Ella Watson whom Averill had met in Rawlins. Watson was the daughter of a wealthy farmer in Smith County, Kan., and by the time she was eighteen she had already been married and separated from her husband. (Whether or not she was ever divorced is still unanswered, but she later claimed that her marriage was ruined because of her spouse's "infidelity.") Ella Watson was known to many men other than Averill, having earned her living as a prostitute in Denver, Cheyenne, and Rawlins. Averill penned her a purple-prosed letter, asking her to join him, ostensibly as his lover. She replied that she

was on her way. It was later suggested that Watson was lured to Sweetwater by Averill on the promise of marriage and that when she arrived, penniless and with nowhere else to go, he made her his concubine and then the communal sexual property of the small ranchers who supported his store and saloon. Watson soon established a claim for a spread adjoining that of Averill's and she ordered stock pens built on her land since she took as pay for her sexual favors in the form of cattle. Thus this statuesque, tough woman earned the sobriquet of Cattle Kate.

Kate was a tall, big-boned woman whose stamina with her cowboy lovers was legendary. She rode horses as would a man, never side-saddle, and was quite frank in her spoken ambitions to amass a cattle fortune, believing that Averill, whom she truly loved, would marry her and they would together establish a powerful cattle empire on their own. Watson remains somewhat of an enigma to this day, described as feminine and demure by her relatives and friends and as a hellion by the press and her enemies. The Cheyenne *Mail Leader*, for instance, reported that she was "of a robust physique, a dark devil in the saddle, handy with a six-shooter and a Winchester, and an expert with a branding iron." This unflattering profile was written following Kate's brutal demise as a way of supporting the cattlemen's claim that Kate rebranded and penned the cattle Averill stole from the cattle barons in preparation for resale. Watson's father described her in a contradictory statement, "She was a little girl, between one hundred and sixty to one hundred and eighty pounds."

Averill's attitude toward Watson was one of economics. He considered Kate a good investment, and the maverick cattle he and his men, including foreman Frank Buchanan, rounded up on the range, were brought to Kate's pens and there branded with Averill's own brand before being shipped to eastern markets. The cattlemen in the area were incensed with Averill's free-and-easy ways with their livestock, but they took little direct action. Averill was usually surrounded by several gunmen and Buchanan, an expert with rifle and shotgun, seemed always to be at his side. He was himself an expert gunman and had shot several men in the past. One of these, a man named Johnson, quarreled with Averill and the rancher shot him dead. Before turning himself in for this shooting, Averill wrote the local judge a flowery letter in which he claimed self defense, a missive that caused his later release. It was Averill's talent with pen and paper that eventually brought about his demise. In the spring of 1889 he began to write to several local newspapers, venting his spleen on the cattlemen and branding them thieves and killers, after the Association made claim to his own spread. He also expressed indignant anger over the stockmen's claim that his partner Kate was running a "hog ranch." Kate was a highly respected cattle rancher, Averill insisted.

The cattlemen suffered greatly during the 1888 blizzards which depleted their herds but the cattle in Kate's pens seemed to increase and she and Averill were growing rich. Averill began buying expensive clothes, gold cufflinks, and watch chains and he even sent off for imported cigars while he took Kate on shopping trips to Denver where she bought new dresses by the dozen. Kate thought to make her burden less by returning from Denver with another girl who was to satisfy her crude customers. Instead the poor girl almost died at the hands of a drunken Jim Averill who attacked her, then tied her to a wagon and left her to the savage elements. She was found the next morning half frozen to death. Sobering, Averill apologized (some said only after Kate leveled a shotgun at him) and gave the girl a generous amount of money.

Meanwhile, Averill and his men kept rounding up range strays, branding them, and shipping them off to market. At the same time, Averill kept up his barrage against the Association by writing letters to local papers. The Cheyenne *Weekly Mail* published his most bitter attack on the stockmen on Apr. 7, 1889, a letter that caused gunman Frank Canton to insist that Averill and his prostitute partner

"Cattle Kate" Watson on horseback, alongside the pens holding the herds of stolen cattle for which she and Jim Averill were hanged by vigilantes.

be eradicated. Adding fuel to this idea was an incident occuring in early June of that year. A cattleman rode to Watson's pens and identified some of his own cattle, asking Kate where she obtained them. Averill gave his usual laconic reply, "I bought them." The cattleman accused her

of buying stolen cattle and Watson raced into her cabin and returned with a Winchester. The cattleman promised he would return and lay claim to his calves, then rode quickly away while Kate resolutely aimed her rifle in his direction.

A short time later a herd of cows belonging to Bothwell was raided by Averill, Buchanan, and others and the calves cut out and driven to Kate's pens (or so the story was later related by Association supporters). To keep the mothers from trailing behind the calves, Averill and his men slew the cattle and this bloody trail was followed almost to Watson's pens by cowboys working for Bothwell. When informed of this raid, Bothwell exploded, declaring that he would take the law into his own hands. First, Bothwell sent a spy to the Averill-Watson ranches and this man reported that he watched the pair get drunk at Kate's house. Thinking the couple would be suffering from hangovers and be easily caught off-guard, Bothwell, on July 20, 1889, ordered twenty of his best gun hands to follow him to the Sweetwater claims. The cattlemen first stopped at Watson's ranch. One report had it that both Watson and Averill were found in drunken stupors, "sitting next to a crude fireplace, the room clouded with tobacco smoke, a whiskey bottle and glasses on the table and firearms within easy reach." The facts are otherwise.

The cattlemen found Watson alone, returning from the outhouse in a skimpy nightgown. She tried to run into the ranch house but gunmen stopped her and dragged her before Bothwell who motioned to a wagon the posse had brought along. "You're going to Rawlins," he said, indicating that Watson and Averill would be brought before the law in that town and charged with rustling. Cattle Kate's reply was typically female, "I can't go to Rawlins. I don't have a new dress." Bothwell ordered her into the wagon and the big woman was lifted up and tossed onto the rough planks of the wagon which was then whipped on to Averill's place. There gunmen surrounded Averill's store-saloon and ordered him to step outside. He stepped outside, blinking at the bright sunlight. Bothwell lied in telling Averill that a warrant for his arrest had been posted and he was being taken to Rawlins. Unarmed, Averill, in his shirtsleeves, was grabbed and thrown into the wagon. Averill and Cattle Kate sat together wholly unconcerned about their fate, joking and laughing, making fun of the men who rode silently next to the wagon.

The taunting by Averill and Watson only seemed to strengthen the resolve of the possemen who rode to a small canyon through which snaked the Sweetwater River. Ropes were placed around the necks of the two captives and they were led over rocks to the water's edge. One of the possemen told Kate that they intended to drown her and Averill in the river. She looked at the shallow stream and laughed; it was still a joke to her. "Hell, there ain't enough water in there to give you hogbacks a bath!" she snorted. While the possemen hesitated, Averill's foreman, Frank Buchanan, who had followed the posse's trail, stood on a cliff looking down on the party. He began firing at the possemen but the return fire was so withering that he was forced to flee.

This attack bolstered the possemen and they quickly led Averill and Watson to a split cottonwood tree, threw the ropes over the limbs and then ordered them to jump from rocks on which they were perched. An idiotic grin clung to Averill's face; he believed the vigilantes were continuing their joke. Watson, however, suddenly realized that this grim exercise was real. They were about to be hanged. She punched out wildly at the men around her and tried to remove the tightly drawn noose from around her neck. Two men held her arms while a cattleman stepped forward and casually kicked Averill's legs out from under him, sending him into space. Watson screamed and was then pushed off the rock where she stood. So eager were the cattlemen to lynch the pair that they had forgotten to tie the hands of their victims and both Averill and Watson clawed at the nooses that slowly strangled them. According to a report appearing in the Casper *Mail*, "the kicking and writhing of those people was awful to witness."

It took quite a while for the couple to die. Finally, their bodies went limp as their eyes bulged hideously and bloody foam dripped from their mouths. The cattlemen left them dangling from the cottonwood tree and slowly rode away. Some of the members of this posse later regretted the double lynching, saying that they only meant "to frighten" Averill and Watson but the charade went too far. Others claimed that had Buchanan not fired on them the couple would have been taken to authorities and charged with cattle rustling. But these were merely tales designed to absolve the guilty, others claimed and that the whole incident was nothing more than premeditated murder, that Averill and Watson were respectable ranchers and had stolen no cattle at all. They were murdered because they would not give up their land to the covetous cattlemen.

Two days later the bodies of Averill and Watson were cut down and opinion quickly turned against the Association and its lynch-bent members, the Casper *Mail* demanding retribution and angrily asking in an editorial, "Is human life held at no value whatever?" Kate's father, Thomas Watson, arrived in Rawlins to claim his daughter's body, telling reporters that the cattlemen were liars, that his child was incapable of cattle rustling. "She never branded a hoof or threw a rope," he insisted. A dark stranger wearing two guns rode into Rawlins and buried Averill. He was identified as Averill's brother, and he busied himself for some time in rounding up witnesses against the possemen. Six of those who had been part of the lynch mob were subse-

quently arrested, but the process was a farce from the beginning. Rawlins authorities were in the pockets of the Association, and these six defendants were permitted to sign each other's bail bond. None were convicted. The deaths of Jim Averill and Cattle Kate did serve, however, to inspire homesteaders and small ranchers to stand up to the Association and a full-scale bloody range war erupted in Johnson County. Inside that death-filled turmoil, Frank Buchanan disappeared, presumed murdered by Frank Canton on behalf of the cattlemen. One of the more intriguing stories concerning the legends that gathered about Averill and Watson is that the couple produced a son, Thomas Averill, or so one Thomas Averill later claimed. He stated that he was five when the possemen arrived at his mother's cabin and that they shot him in the throat and left him for dead. He was raised by Indians and went on to work in many Wild West shows where he was known as Buffalo Vernon. When the Johnson County War ground down, Cattle Kate's small cabin was sold at auction for a mere $14.19, purchased by one of the possemen who had put the nooses around the necks of Jim Averill and Cattle Kate Watson. See: **Canton, Frank; Johnson County War.**

B

Baca, Elfego, 1865-1945, U.S., lawman. Born in Socorro, N.M., Elfego Baca moved to Kansas with his family while in his teens. His father got into an argument with two cowboys in 1882 and shot both of them dead which caused him to receive a long prison sentence. The family moved back to Socorro where Baca worked in a store. He nevertheless harbored visions of becoming a lawman and a man who, like his father, was not afraid to use a gun. To that end he purchased a mail-order lawman's badge and two six-guns which he wore proudly. In October of 1884, a cowboy named McCarty got drunk in Frisco, N.M., where Baca was working. McCarty began to "hurrah" the town, picking Mexicans as his targets, causing many of these hapless people to "dance" to the music of his bullets. Baca rushed to the scene and, pinning on his badge, the self-styled lawman arrested McCarty after drawing his two guns. He marched the tipsy cowboy to the town square where he informed citizens that he would take McCarty to Socorro where he would be tried for disturbing the peace.

At that moment, more cowboys led by their foreman, a

Elfego Baca in old age.

man named Perham, arrived in the plaza and demanded that McCarty be released. Perham and McCarty, citizens informed Baca, both worked for the largest rancher in the area, Tom Slaughter, a man unused to having his cowboys arrested without his approval. Baca shrugged and then told Perham that he would count to three and if they did not leave the plaza he would start shooting. Without waiting for a response, Baca rapidly counted to three and then opened fire on the cowboys, wounding one in the knee. Another one of

Baca's shots struck the horse Perham was riding, causing the animal to crash to earth, mortally injuring Perham. Citizens led by J.H. Cook then approached Baca and convinced him to turn his prisoner over to a local justice of the peace. McCarty was fined $50 for disturbing the peace and Baca's sense of justice was served. He stated that he intended to leave for Socorro the next day, but when he began to leave town he suddenly faced more than eighty well-armed cowboys under the command of Tom Slaughter.

It was never determined who fired the first shot, but suddenly Baca was blazing away with both six-guns at the entire Slaughter band. He turned and darted down an alleyway to a small Mexican hut which was made of poles and mud, ordering the small family inside to escape. Just as they did so, Slaughter's men surrounded the hut and began to fire at it, riddling the walls and door. Baca crouched low and fired through the eighteen-inch opening beneath the door, his bullets smacking into Jim Herne as he rushed the hut with rifle in hand. Herne died in the dusty street outside the hut, his body dragged away by a dozen cowboys pouring a deadly barrage into the hut. Slaughter's men lay siege to the small building, hour after hour pouring tremendous fusillades into the walls of the hut so that the hail of bullets literally tore away the walls and cut the wooden door to shreds. Baca occasionally returned fire and his aim proved to be deadly accurate. One cowboy after another fell wounded by Baca's pinpoint firing. The Slaughter people finally strung ropes between buildings and placed blankets over these so they could walk about freely without Baca picking them off.

Slaughter's men, using shotguns and buffalo guns, poured several volleys into the roof of the hut at sundown, causing the roof to collapse. It took Baca two hours to dig himself out from under the debris. He continued to fire back at his antagonists. At midnight some of Slaughter's men worked their way close enough to the hut to hurl a lighted stick of dynamite which blew away half of the hut, but Baca remained uninjured, having crouched in an undamaged corner of the building. Again he rose to fire at the cowboys, managing to wound two or three more. At dawn, Baca was seen to calmly cook his breakfast in the ruins of the hut which brought cheers and applause from the many Mexican spectators viewing the battle from afar. Still, the Slaughter cowboys were determined to ferret out the upstart Baca. Some of their more inventive numbers ripped out some heavy cookstoves from nearby buildings and used these as metal shields, moving them across the open ground around the half-demolished hut, but Baca picked off those behind them, creasing the skull of one cowboy and winging another in the arm. The cowboys gave up the idea of trying to rush the 19-year-old "deputy sheriff."

Before the Slaughter group unleashed another barrage, Cook, a deputy sheriff named Ross and Francisquito Naranjo approached the hut under a flag of truce and persuaded Baca to surrender, promising that he would be delivered safely to the authorities in Socorro. He agreed, but only if he could keep his guns. Amazingly, this was agreed to by the Slaughter band, who apparently had been instilled with a great deal of respect for the sharpshooting

Baca. More than thirty cowboys escorted Baca to Socorro but the cowboys rode in front of a buckboard in which Baca sat with Cook and Ross. Throughout the journey to Socorro, Baca kept his guns trained on his captors lest they go back on the promise he had been made.

In Socorro, the evidence was heard. Four men had been killed by Baca and at least ten other cowboys had been wounded by the self-styled lawman. Yet his heroic defense of the hut so impressed the court, along with its belief that Baca was acting in self-defense, that he was acquitted in two hotly-argued murder trials. Following his release, this survivor of New Mexico's most famous gunfight sought many public offices and was generally elected by landslides. He served as deputy sheriff, county sheriff, mayor of Socorro, school superintendent, and district attorney. He narrowly missed being elected to the governorship. Baca, although he rarely drew his gun as a lawman, was, because of the legendary Frisco fight, the most feared gunman in the territory. At age fifty he was again called upon to draw his six-guns.

In 1915, Baca was approached by an old enemy, Celestino Otero, who accosted the aging lawman as he stepped from the Paso del Norte Hotel in El Paso. Otero and some of his henchmen jumped out of a car and Otero pulled a revolver. He fired at Baca but the shot went wild. Baca drew both six-guns and fired a bullet from each, both striking Otero in the chest and killing him immediately. Baca was again tried for murder and acquitted. In 1919, Baca was again elected sheriff of Socorro County. Upon taking office, he went through all the wanted circulars of his own and neighboring counties and then wrote letters to these wanted felons, demanding that they immediately turn themselves in or he would strap on his six-guns and bring them back head down over a saddle. Such was Baca's fierce reputation that a half dozen of the most deadly outlaws in the area came meekly to Socorro to surrender to the famous sheriff. He died at age eighty in Albuquerque, N.M., in 1945.

Baird, P.C., d.1928, U.S., lawman. P.C. Baird served with the Texas Rangers and rose to the rank of sergeant in Company D, Frontier Battalion. Baird and two other Rangers encountered several fence-cutters near the Greer ranch near Green Lake on July 29, 1884, the offenders being known outlaws. When the Rangers ordered these men, about five in number, to surrender, the outlaws fired on them. In the return fire, Baird shot and killed John Bailey, also known as John Mason. A Ranger was wounded in the gunfight but all the outlaws were captured. Baird was elected sheriff of Mason County in 1888 and in the following year, a gunfight broke out in Mason inside Garner's Saloon. Baird and a deputy raced down the street to investigate, and at that moment, two brothers, Jesse and John Simmons, stepped from the saloon with shotguns blazing at the lawmen. Baird and his deputy stood calmly in the middle of the street and took aim at the brothers who were advancing on them, both in an obvious state of drunkenness. Baird fired a single shot which hit John Simmons, killing him, and his deputy dispatched Jesse Simmons. Baird served as sheriff of Mason County through 1898 and then retired. He died on Mar. 9, 1928, in San Antonio, Texas.

Baker, Cullen Montgomery, 1835-69, U.S., outlaw. Baker was born in Weakley County, Tenn., on June 22, 1835, the son of a poor farmer who took his family to Cass County (later Davis County), Texas, in 1839. The boy grew up dirt poor and, because of his homespun trousers and bare feet, was the butt of jokes by other boys. Slender, sallow-faced Baker finally fought back, beating the biggest boy in the area. Baker was a lonely, withdrawn boy who read books of knights and ancient heroes and dreamed of becoming a valiant westerner who would command respect. He obtained an old pistol at age twelve and began practicing a quick draw from his waistband. He then acquired a rusty but workable rifle and practiced shooting each day with both weapons, becoming an expert marksman by the time he was fifteen—the age when he took his first long drink of whiskey. When in his teenage cups, the drunken boy would challenge adults who annoyed him to "go for your guns." But Baker's reputation of being a crack shot caused all to back away from him. This encouraged a growing braggart personality that boasted of great deeds never accomplished. On one occasion, just for the sadistic joy it gave him, Baker pulled his pistol on an old man and terrorized him in a local town, driving the old man from the city limits and laughing hysterically.

At the age of nineteen, Baker ordered all the youths in the area to stage a mock cowboys-and-Indians battle—a wild fight in which he was struck in the head with a tomahawk and knocked unconscious. The blow seemed to bring Baker to his senses as he lay in bed for several weeks recovering. He told his parents that he had been a fool, that someone would eventually come along and best him at his own vicious games and he would wind up dead. He vowed to reform. Some weeks later, in January 1854, still wearing a head bandage, Baker married 17-year-old Jane Petty and he settled down to quiet farming. But he soon tired of this routine and took up his old ways of violence. He forced other teenagers to carry him on their shoulders through the towns while he drove them on by pecking at their heads with knives or slamming the butt of his pistol against the sides of their heads. One youngster named Stallcup, an orphan, received the brunt of Baker's bullying. Baker chased him about with a whip on an August day in 1854, lashing the terrified child. His guardian brought suit against Baker and a farmer named Bailey, who had witnessed the whipping, testified in court against Baker who was heavily fined, warned to mind his manners, and sent on his way.

Baker showed up at Bailey's house an hour after the trial, his pistol tucked into his waistband. He called Bailey outside and the farmer stepped onto his porch, a pistol in his hand, limp at his side. "So you'd talk against me, huh, Bailey," Baker said with a sneer. "Well, you got a gun. Use it while you got the chance!" The farmer hesitated for a moment, then yanked the pistol upward and fired a quick shot that whizzed past Baker's head. Baker drew his weapon and fired two shots, one hitting Bailey in the chest, the other in the head, propelling him backward through his front door so that he fell dead in front of his horrified family. Baker rode quickly away and was absent from Cass County, hiding out with relatives in Perry County, Ark., for almost two years. He took his ugly nature with him to Arkansas where he stabbed to death a man named Wartham in an argument about horses. Baker returned to Cass County in 1856 but fled when he learned that he was still wanted to face murder charges in the killing of Bailey. After another two years in Arkansas, Baker once more returned to Texas, but only to retrieve his wife and daughter, resettling them in Arkansas. His wife died on July 2, 1860, and Baker took their child to Sulphur County, Texas, and the home of Hubbard Petty, his daughter's grandfather, leaving the child in the old man's care. He never saw his daughter again.

Authorities in Perry County, Ark., pressed charges against Baker for the Wartham killing and he fled back to Cass County, Texas, where officials dropped murder charges against him for the killing of Bailey. Baker told one and all he was through with killing, that he was a reformed man, but it was an old story. A local belle, Martha Foster, fell in love with Baker and they were married on July 1, 1862. A short time later, Baker was conscripted into the Confederate Army and sent to Little Rock, Ark., to serve with his company. He was a poor soldier, often absent without leave, returning to Texas to ostensibly visit his wife and family but in reality to escape the discipline of army life. Finally, Baker refused to return to his company, settling near Spanish Bluffs, Ark., on a small farm, stating that he was growing corn for the Confederacy, a much more important role than soldiering since the South needed food. The area was occupied by northern troops under the command of Captain F.S. Dodge in Spring 1864. These Union soldiers were all blacks, which incensed the southerners in the area, particularly Baker, who hated Negroes. Three black soldiers and a sergeant entered the local saloon at Spanish Bluffs where they saw a single customer at the bar. It was Baker, wearing a broad Confederate hat. The sergeant demanded identification papers from Baker and he turned with a gun in his hand, shooting the sergeant and then the other three soldiers.

Now Baker was wanted by both sides, by the Confederate Army as a deserter and by the Union forces as a killer. He fled to Little Rock, which had also been occupied by northern troops, and there took the oath of allegiance and joined the Union Army using a false name and claiming that he had been a Confederate officer. Ironically, he was placed in charge of a company of black troops. He deserted the Union Army and returned to Texas, staying with his uncle, Tom Young. By late 1864, Texas was overrun with deserters from both armies, and these freebooters roamed the countryside as bandits. Baker fell in with one group and soon became their leader, robbing farmers trying to flee the area as they crossed the Saline River. He looted farms and ranches throughout the territory.

One story, perhaps apocryphal, has Baker and his band of thieves rustling a great herd of cattle, including livestock taken from a widow named Drew, near Jefferson. Baker stopped at Mrs. Drew's farm where she told him that robbers had just taken her herd. She offered Baker a substantial reward if he could find the rustlers and deal with them, returning her cattle. He promised to do what he could, pretending to be shocked at the wholesale robbery. A short time later, Baker caught up with his band, ordering them to separate the Drew cattle from the rest, and these were driven back to the Drew ranch where Baker received a cash reward which was more than what he and his men would have realized had they sold off the stolen cattle elsewhere.

When the war ended, Baker, to avoid arrest for his many robberies, moved to the Sulphur River area in southwestern Arkansas where he became the manager of the Line Ferry, settling down for a while with his wife Martha, who took ill and died on Mar. 1, 1866. Baker seemed to have truly loved his second wife; he was grief-stricken for weeks, even making a lifelike effigy of her which he adorned with her clothes and placed upon his front porch for all the neighbors to see. He was finally persuaded to remove this mannequin in the interest of good taste. Baker later proposed to Bell Foster, his dead wife's 16-year-old sister, but she rejected him in favor of local schoolteacher, Thomas Orr. Baker later picked a fight with Orr and cracked the teacher's head with a tree limb. He later went to Orr's small school and ridiculed Orr before his students, cursing him and threatening to shoot his head "off from your shoulders!" So bitter was Baker at being rejected by Bell Foster that he continued to plague the teacher, who had a crippled arm, with threats, writing Orr letters in which he promised to beat or shoot the teacher if he ever found out that Orr missed any classes.

By early 1867, Baker had returned to Cass County, Texas, where he continued to make a nuisance of himself, exercising his bullyboy tactics at every opportunity. On June 1, 1867, Baker arrived at the Rowden store and, finding it locked, broke inside and took whatever goods he wanted. Before he rode away, Mrs. Rowden arrived and asked him what he was doing. Baker told her he would pay for the goods later. When Rowden returned and heard from his wife how Baker had helped himself to his provisions, the shopkeeper rode to Baker's small ranch and demanded payment. He carried a shotgun at his side. "Sure, I'll pay you in a few days," Baker told him. On June 5, 1867, Baker appeared at Rowden's store and called the storekeeper outside. Mrs. Rowden and her children begged Rowden not to go outside, knowing the fierce reputation of Cullen Baker. Rowden nevertheless grabbed his shotgun and stepped onto the porch of his store.

"What do you mean by speaking so disrespectfully to me?" Baker shouted to Rowden.

"I'm sure I never meant to do such a thing," Rowden replied.

Before another word could be uttered, Baker whipped out his six-gun and fired four shots into the store owner. He was hit in the chest by all four bullets and fell forward, dead. Baker returned home to hear some days later that citizens in the area were organizing a huge posse to arrest him for the Rowden killing. He sent a message to town stating that he would kill anyone who attempted to bring him to trial over a "fair fight," pointing out that Rowden had been armed with a shotgun. Texas was still occupied by Union troops at the time and the Union commander at Jefferson, Texas, sent a patrol to Pett's Ferry, where Baker was staying, to arrest the gunman. A sergeant and a private found Baker at the ferry and asked him his name.

"It's Johnson," Baker lied, "but what in hell makes you so particular?"

"We thought you might be Cullen Baker," the sergeant told him, fingering his pistol, "the man we are searching for. From your weapons and the way you're dressed, I am inclined to believe you are Baker." The sergeant, a fearless type, pulled his pistol but before he could level it at Baker, the gunman whipped out his own six-gun and blazed off four shots, all of which struck the sergeant, blowing him off the saddle, dead. The private lashed his horse about and raced back to the detachment to report the killing.

Baker fled, going down river and hiding in Bowie County, but troops scouring the area for him, encircled his hiding place the next day. Baker, realizing that he had no chance against a company of soldiers, began to shout: "Charge them, boys! Charge them!" The soldiers, believing that they were facing a large band of outlaws led by Baker, fled in panic. Some days later, a small group of soldiers encountered Baker riding a mule and a gunfight erupted. Baker shot one of the soldiers dead before the rest of the troopers took flight. On Oct. 10, 1867, Baker stopped a Union supply wagon escorted by a four-man patrol. The driver reached for his pistol but Baker shot him dead and drove off the other soldiers with withering gunfire. He then stole the supply wagon. Baker was now a much-wanted man with a $1,000 reward posted for his capture, dead or alive.

More than 600 soldiers were assigned to track the outlaw down and these troopers fanned out in small contingents throughout the territory. One, led by Captain Kirkham, found Baker in Boston, Texas. Baker, seeing he was surrounded by at least two dozen heavily-armed troopers, boldly marched up to Captain Kirkham and said: "I'm Cullen Baker. You looking for me?"

Kirkham went for his pistol but Baker's lightning draw produced his pistol first which barked and sent a single bullet into Kirkham's head, killing him instantly. Before Kirkham's men could react, Baker jumped on his horse and raced out of town. In November 1868, Baker organized another outlaw band which raided farms and ranches along the Red River and ranged as far as Sevier and Little River counties in Arkansas. Baker and his men, in one raid, shot and killed two government agents named Andrews and Willis. When Baker received news that more than a thousand troopers were searching for him, he stole an officer's uniform and impersonated a Union captain, requesting and receiving supplies from local farmers, saying that his troops needed fresh supplies in their search for the notorious outlaw, Cullen Baker.

With the troopers and lawmen of two states looking for him, Baker took to writing letters to local newspapers in which he attempted to justify his actions, portraying himself a victim of the Civil War, a defender of the white man's rights against black carpetbaggers, and that he would willingly submit himself to the justice of "unbiased men" if any could be found who were not influenced by the lies spread throughout Texas and Arkansas about him. Baker then rode back to the Foster home, still seething about Bell Foster, who had since married Thomas Orr. He and his men surrounded the Foster home and Baker demanded that his ex-father-in-law turn Orr over to him. Foster did so, on the promise that the crippled school teacher would not be harmed. It was Baker's sadistic intention to show Bell that he could do what he pleased with her ineffectual husband. He forced the teacher to ride behind one of his men with a rope affixed about his neck, the end of which Baker held in his hand as he rode ahead. He stopped a few miles away and tied the rope around the limb of dogwood tree, then ordered the man behind whom Orr was riding to spur his horse onward, leaving the teacher dangling.

Baker and his men rode on, but the bandit chief had second thoughts about losing his best rope. He turned to one of his men and shouted: "Cut down that wretch and drag him away! And bring me that rope!" Orr was cut down and left for dead as the band rode away. But Orr miraculously survived his own hanging and vowed to track down his tormentor. On Jan. 6, 1869, Orr, with three others, followed Baker and an accomplice to a hideout in southeastern Arkansas, coming upon the two men just as they were squatting next to a fire, having lunch. Orr and the others did not call out to the outlaws to surrender, knowing what their answer would be. The teacher and his companions rode down on Baker and his henchman with their six-guns blazing, shooting both men dead on the spot. Orr found that his old adversary was a walking arsenal. Strapped to his side was a double-barrelled shotgun. Baker was also wearing four six-guns, three derringers, and six knives. Also found on Baker's corpse was a carefully kept packet of newspaper clippings which described him as "the Arkansas brigand," and the most feared gunman in the Lone Star State who had spread "a reign of terror in Texas." Many historians have portrayed Baker as a soft-spoken southern gentlemen who was compelled to take up the gun, although he kept his scruples intact and was a gentleman when treating with women and children. He was anything but this, a vicious gunman, an immoral, ruthless killer, a man who despised culture and education. His death at the hands of a meek-mannered school teacher was poetic justice indeed.

Baldwin, Thurman (AKA: **Skeeter; Balding; Jack Pipkin**), b.1867, U.S., outlaw. Thurman Baldwin worked in Oklahoma as a cowboy and joined the Bill Cook gang in the early 1890s and participated in the gang's many robberies. He was at large for some months after the Cooks were rounded up in 1894-95, but was captured in late 1895 outside of Wichita Falls by Texas Rangers Bob McClure, W.J.L. Sullivan, and W.J. McCauley, along with two other lesser lights of the

Thurman "Skeeter" Baldwin

Cook gang, Jess Snyder and Will Farris. Baldwin, who admitted to having committed some robberies with the Cooks, was tried for robbery before Judge Isaac Parker who sentenced him to thirty years, as severe a sentence as possible for his crimes. Parker, who was known as "The Hanging Judge," stated that it was not his intention to sentence Baldwin so severely for his crimes of robbery but that he did so because he believed such "severe sentences deter others" from committing similar offenses. Baldwin, a tall, rangy man of few words but one who possessed a considerable sense of humor, replied: "This is a helluva court for a man to plead guilty in." He served ten years and, following his release, is presumed to have led an exemplary life since no criminal record exists beyond that time nor any other trace of the last of the Bill Cook gang.

Barkley, Clinton (AKA: **Bill Bowen**), prom. 1870s, U.S., outlaw. Clinton Barkley was a Texas gunman who was wanted for murder in 1873, and sought the help of his brother-in-law, Merritt Horrell, of the five battling Horrell Brothers. Horrell promised Barkley that if he came to Lampasas, Texas, Horrell home territory, he would be defended against any lawmen by Horrell guns. As soon as Barkley arrived in Lampasas, a local murder warrant was issued for his arrest and, on Mar. 19, 1873, Captain Thomas Williams, accompanied by three officers, entered Jerry Scott's Matador Saloon in Lampasas, knowing Barkley and the Horrells were inside. The minute Williams and his men stepped through the swinging doors, Barkley, Martin, Tom, and Sam Horrell, along with saloon owner Scott, opened fire with their six-guns. Williams and two of his men dropped to the floor dead while the third deputy returned fire as he backed out of the saloon, his shots wounding Martin and Tom Horrell.

Martin Horrell, who had been taken to a relative's home in Lampasas after being shot, was arrested, along with saloon owner Scott, both jailed in Georgetown to await trial for murder. A few days later, the Horrells roared into Georgetown and stood guard in front of the jail while Barkley calmly got off his horse with a sledgehammer and assaulted the jail door. Enraged citizens began pot-shooting at the outlaws, slightly wounding Barkley in the shoulder, but he kept swinging the sledgehammer at the door and the Horrells returned fire, wounding lawyer, A.S. Fisher, which caused the rest of the citizens to put up their guns. Barkley broke down the jail door and the Horrells rushed inside, rescuing Martin Horrell and Scott.

Barkley continued to serve the Horrells throughout the bloody Horrell-Higgins war. He was a member of the Horrell faction that raided a Higgins camp in June 1877, rustling some cattle and shooting down two of Higgins' cowhands. On June 14, 1877, Tom, Martin, and Sam Horrell, accompanied by Barkley, his brother Tom, and two other Horrell men, ran into a Higgins group headed by John Pinckney Calhoun Higgins, his top aide, Bill Wren, his brother-in-law, Frank Mitchell, and half a dozen other Higgins men. Both sides went for their guns and a wild shootout ensued. Wren was wounded by Barkley and the Horrells shot and killed Mitchell. Citizens managed to persuade the gunmen to call a truce which ended the battle. More than a dozen Higgins men sought revenge the following month, July 1877, by boldly attacking the Horrell ranch. For two days, the ranch house was peppered incessantly by the Higgins faction, managing to severely wound two Horrell men before Pink Higgins called off the attack. Barkley was badly unnerved by this last battle and decided to quit the gunslinger business. He packed up his belongings and quietly rode away and out of western history. See: **Horrell-Higgins Feud.**

Barnes, Seaborn (Seaborne or Seab or Sebe, AKA: Nubbins Colt), 1853-78, U.S., outlaw. Born in Tarrant County in north Texas, Barnes was an illiterate hardcase who went to work as a cowboy in his early teens. His father, a lawman, died while Barnes was a small child and his widowed mother moved with her five children to Handley, Texas, a few miles from Fort Worth. There Barnes and his family lived off the charity of relatives and the boy grew up embittered over being a have-not. He went to work early, lacking any kind of education, cooking for local ranchers. He also worked briefly as a potter in Denton County. When he was only seventeen, Barnes was jailed for a year in Fort Worth over a shooting. He did not hold his liquor well and was involved in many barroom fights. He was arrested several times for assault and was jailed in 1874 in Calahan County, but he escaped wearing his leg irons. Hobbling across the street from the jail, Barnes forced the local blacksmith to hack off the shackles before he fled on a stolen horse. He joined Sam Bass, already a notorious Nebraska bandit who arrived in the Fort Worth-Dallas area in 1878. Barnes became Bass' most loyal lieutenant, following the bandit chief in several desperate holdups in the spring of 1878. Others in the band included Thomas Spotswood, Arkansas Johnson, Frank Jackson, Henry Underwood, Sam Pipes, and Albert Herndon.

Barnes participated in all the train robberies Bass engineered, helping to rob the Texas Central at Allen Station on Feb. 22, 1878, stopping a train on the same line at Hutchins, Texas, on Mar. 18, looting the mail car of a Texas and Pacific train near Eagle Ford on Apr. 4 and stopping a train of the same line at Mesquite on Apr. 10. It was during this last robbery that the Bass gang met strong opposition. As they approached the mail car a tremendous fusillade was unleashed by citizens in the passenger cars, along with guards who were escorting some captives to prison and armed railway detectives. Several of the gang were wounded, Barnes being the worst hit. Three bullets struck his right leg and one punctured the left. Barnes barely managed to mount his horse and gallop off with the rest of the gang.

Following the spate of train robberies, which netted the gang little more than $1,000, the Texas Rangers and local lawmen by the score began searching for the outlaws. A posse led by Texas Ranger captain June Peak and Sheriff W.F. Eagan, cornered the Bass gang near Salt Creek in Wise County on June 13, 1878. A terrific gun battle ensued in which Arkansas Johnson was killed and others were wounded. Bass, Barnes, and others managed to escape on foot after the posse captured their horses. They slipped by the posse during the night, reached a nearby farm where they stole some horses, and then escaped. The gang, now down to Bass, Barnes, Frank Jackson, and Jim Murphy, planned to rob the bank at Round Rock, Texas, on Sept. 20, 1878. Murphy had secretly agreed to inform on the gang some time earlier to extricate his family from felony charges. He informed the local contingent of the Texas Rangers of the impending raid on Round Rock and when the gang rode into town a day earlier than the planned bank robbery to survey the town, the Rangers were waiting for them, trapping them in a local store as they were buying tobacco.

Barnes was approached in Koppel's Store by Deputy Sheriffs Morris Moore and Ellis Grimes. Grimes noticed a bulge beneath Barnes' coat. He put his hand on Barnes' shoulder, telling him that there was a local ordinance against carrying firearms. "Are you armed, young man?" Grimes asked Barnes from behind his back. Barnes turned, reached beneath his coat and pulled forth his pistol, which he fired. Grimes fell backward, dead. Deputy Moore returned fire but he was hit several times by shots from Bass and Jackson. Murphy was not present, having told Bass that he would look around town to see "if the Rangers were about." The trio fled the store but a hail of bullets slammed into them from the guns of a half dozen Rangers and lawmen running toward the outlaws. Barnes tried to untether his horse but Ranger Dick Ware, who had not expected the outlaws until the next day and had been in the barbershop, raced to the street with lather on his face. He drew his weapon and fired only once, but his bullet struck Seaborn Barnes square in the forehead and killed him instantly.

Jackson and Bass galloped from the scene. Bass was by

then mortally wounded and died a short time later. Jackson made a permanent escape. Murphy, the traitor, identified Barnes by the four bullet wounds in his legs.

Barnes was buried next to his bandit chieftan, and on his tombstone read the words: "He was right bower (sea anchor) to Sam Bass." See: **Bass, Samuel; Jackson, Frank.**

Barnett, Wesley, d.1889, and **Thompson, Dan**, prom. 1889, U.S., gunmen. A $500 reward was placed on the heads of gunmen Wesley Barnett and his accomplice Dan Thompson, who were charged with the murder of Deputy U.S. Marshal John Phillips in the Indian territory surrounding Fort Smith (Ark.). Barnett was a wild, hell-raising rabble-rouser who rode into the capital of the Creek Indian Territory and fired twenty-six bullets into the cupola of a building.

Deputy U.S. marshals tracked Barnett to his Okmulgee campsight near the Arkansas River in January 1889. Three possemen, William Sevier, John Barnell, and Wallace McNack, stopped at the residence of John Porters to spend the night. At about 10:00 p.m., Barnett, along with an Indian named Wiley Bear, turned their guns on the lawmen. In the flurry of gunfire that followed, Barnett was shot and killed, but Wiley Bear managed to make his escape. Barnett's accomplice, Dan Thompson, who was a full-blooded Creek Indian, had been arrested earlier and jailed at Fort Smith.

Barter, Richard (AKA: **Rattlesnake Dick; Dick Woods**), 1834-59, U.S., outlaw. Richard Barter was born in Quebec, Can., (some reports state England), the son of a British officer. He migrated to California during the Gold Rush days and, not finding gold, decided to steal his fortune, beginning with rustling horses. Barter was not successful, being captured and imprisoned for two years. Upon his release he formed another gang made up of Cy and George Skinner and some others. In 1856, Barter learned from a drunken mining engineer that large gold shipments were being sent down Trinity Mountain from the mines of Yreka. Barter sent George Skinner and three others to intercept the gold shipment which was packed on mules. Skinner accomplished the task easily, stopping the gold shipment outside of Nevada City, holding guns on the muleskinners who meekly turned over more than $80,000 in gold bullion. Skinner and his men did not have to fire a shot. They made off with the shipment to keep a rendez-vous with Barter and Cy Skinner. But Rattlesnake Dick did not keep the appointment; he and Skinner had been jailed

for stealing mules.

Barter immediately sought out George Skinner to obtain his share of the gold shipment robbery, an enormous amount for those days. But George Skinner was already dead. Skinner had found it next to impossible to take the heavy gold shipment down the mountain passes without fresh mules, so he buried most of the stolen gold and headed for Folsom to meet Barter. He and his con-federates were intercepted by Wells Fargo detectives who shot and killed him in a wild gun battle. His confederates fled. Barter and Cy Skinner spent weeks trying to find the gold and then gave up. (This treasure is still being unsuc-cessfully sought.) Barter went back to robbing stagecoaches but his luck soon ran out. Sheriff J. Boggs trapped Barter and Skinner in a mountain pass near Auburn, Calif., on the night of July 11, 1859. Boggs fired one bullet which entered the heart of Rattlesnake Dick, killing him instantly. Skinner was wounded, taken into custody, and later given a long prison sentence.

Bascom Affair, 1861, U.S., mur. A misunderstanding between an inexperienced army lieutenant and the Apache chief Cochise triggered a long and devastating series of Indian wars that exacted a heavy toll on human life for about a dozen years.

In October 1860, an Arizona rancher named Johnny Ward, who lived near the Sonoita Creek, reported to the U.S. Army the abduction of his adopted son and the theft of some cattle. Ward blamed the Apache Indians for the crime, and demanded that the army do something about it. Second Lieutenant George N. Bascom and sixty of his men were ordered to investigate the matter. Cochise and several of his braves were invited to the army camp at Apache Pass for what the Indian leader believed to be a friendly discussion. Once inside the tent, Bascom ordered Cochise arrested, but the chief managed to escape by cutting a hole in the canvass. The six braves who had accompanied Cochise to the campsite were captured, however.

There was no real evidence to link the Apaches to the kidnapping and cattle rustling, but tensions between whites and Indians were already at a straining point. Having failed in his efforts to win the release of his men, Cochise ab-ducted six whites and offered them in exchange, but Bascom refused. Between Feb. 4-11, 1861, the rampaging Apaches tortured and killed sixteen whites. Bascom retaliated by hanging the six Apaches on the eleventh. The failure to arrive at a peaceful accord with Cochise triggered a war that lasted until 1872, when Major General O.O. Howard reached a settlement with the chief. The abducted boy, Felix Tellez, turned up about ten years later. Contrary to what the white settlers believed, Tellez, who used the name "Mickey Free," was taken by a Western Apache tribe, not Cochise. See: **Cochise.**

Bass, Samuel (Sam), 1851-78, U.S., outlaw. The lore and legend of Sam Bass became a permanent part of Texas history almost before this daring outlaw met his early end by the tool of his trade, the six-gun. In his short criminal career—a span of about four years—Bass managed to rob stagecoaches, trains, and banks with lightning speed, committing holdups with such alacrity that the lawmen of several states began hunting him as one of the most infamous desperadoes of the Old West. He seemed to be everywhere, from the Black Hills to the Texas Panhandle. Unlike most Texas outlaws, Bass was not a homegrown bad man. He was born in Mitchell, Ind., near Woodville, on July 21, 1851. His parents died when Sam was a small child, one of ten children in the Bass family. The children were sent to relatives to be raised and it was Sam's bad luck to be put in the care of a tight-lipped, skinflinted uncle, David Sheeks. The uncle denied his small nephew any sort of education, compelling the boy to work his farm as soon as he was strong enough to fetch and carry. Throughout his youth Bass knew nothing but work, first slaving for his uncle and later working as a millhand and teamster. At the age of eighteen in 1869, Bass built a raft and floated down the Mississippi to St. Louis. From there he drifted to Rosedale, Miss., where he worked for a year.

Sam Bass at age sixteen. He died from a gunshot wound on July 21, 1878, his twenty-seventh birthday.

There was nothing revealed in Bass' background or steady personality that indicated a bent for crime. In 1870, Bass, working as a teamster, drove some supplies to Denton, Texas. He stayed on in Denton to work for the local sheriff, W.F. "Dad" Eagan, who ran a supply company. It was Eagan who would later spend months trying to capture Bass when he turned outlaw. In the beginning, Bass proved to be a thrifty, hardworking employee who followed his uncle's tightwad practices, refusing to ever pay more than $5 for a suit, and when making deliveries, Eagan had to remind young Sam to make sure that he fed the horses regularly rather than keeping them on short rations to save money. With his hard-earned savings, Bass bought a sorrel

mare, a fast horse he entered in several races. The mare won on several occasions and Bass collected enough from bets to quit Eagan.

With money in his pocket, Bass began to drink in the local saloons, befriending such rowdies as Henry Underwood. One hot day in 1875, Bass and Underwood bought melons which they attempted to slice apart. Bass dropped his melon, causing a group of young blacks standing nearby to hoot and jeer at the pair. Bass and Underwood began to stone the blacks, which caused Denton's Sheriff Gerren to place them under arrest. Both men jumped on their horses and raced out of town. Gerren swore out warrants against them. For this prosaic offense, Sam Bass became an outlaw. Underwood, born in 1846, also in Indiana, had fought with Jennison's Jayhawkers against Quantrill's guerrillas and was both mean-streaked and criminally inclined, influencing the naive Bass against a law-abiding life. Following their escape from Sheriff Gerren, Bass and Underwood split up, Underwood riding to southwest Texas where he had a small ranch and an upstanding wife. Bass rode to San Antonio. There Bass met Joel (Joe) Collins, a hell-raiser who came from a fine San Antonio family. Both invested their money in a small herd of cattle which they drove north, making a considerable profit from its sale in Sidney, Neb. A cowboy and gunman, Jack Davis, befriended Bass and Collins in a local saloon and suggested that they could make a fortune in a boomtown called Deadwood, in South Dakota. The pair invested their money in a freight company there but later sold out to invest in a mine which did not pay off.

Bass and Collins decided to take what they wanted. They recruited a number of freight handlers who had worked for them, most of them fast-draw gunmen, which included Tom Nixon, Bill Heffridge, Jack Davis, and James Berry. The bandits robbed seven Deadwood stages in the Black Hills area between 1876 and 1877 but they quit this line of robbery after stopping one stage filled with heavily armed guards who let loose a deadly barrage in their direction. Bass and Collins returned fire before riding off, leaving the stage driver dead in his seat. These robberies had not proved lucrative, the band taking in only small amounts of money. Jack Davis, a California bandit, suggested that the gang attack a Union Pacific train, saying that these trains carried huge gold shipments from the West, consigned to Wells Fargo and routed to eastern banks. Collins perfected a plan to rob the Union Pacific train at Ogallala, Neb. The group, which included Bass, Collins, Nixon, Davis, Heffridge, and Berry, arrived in Ogallala, but Collins thought too many people were present and decided that the band would attack at Big Springs, Neb. Here, on Sept. 19, 1877, the band boarded the train at 10 p.m. at a water station, taking more than $60,000 in newly minted twenty-dollar gold pieces from the mail car, being shipped from the Denver Mint. They took an additional $1,300 from the startled passengers, and $450 from the mail car safe. (It should be noted that Bass and his men *did* rob the passengers of this train, contrary to denials from so-called western experts, whereas the gang led by Bass later in Texas did not have time to rob passengers on the trains they robbed.)

The gang split up following the robbery, going in pairs in separate directions, knowing that the enormity of the theft would soon bring posses down on them. Joel Collins and Bill Heffridge followed the Kansas Pacific Railroad line

Sam Bass, standing left; J.E. Gardner, right; seated, unknown and Joel Collins (with gun).

and were overtaken on Sept. 26, 1877, by a huge posse led by Sheriff Bardsley near Buffalo Station. Both outlaws decided to make a fight of it and were killed. About $25,000 in twenty-dollar gold pieces was found in Collins' saddlebags. In the middle of October, Berry was trapped and wounded in a gunfight with officers who surrounded his Mexico, Mo., home. He told lawmen the details of the Big Springs robbery and gave them the names of his fellow bandits, saying that he believed Tom Nixon had boarded a train headed for Chicago and from there intended to return to his native Canada. Authorities in Texas refused to believe this story and arrested Henry Underwood, whom they believed to be one of the Big Springs bandits, using the alias of Tom Nixon. Underwood was innocent of the crime, as authorities later learned. Nixon, who had been a blacksmith by trade, utterly disappeared with about

$10,000 in gold pieces.

Following the breakup of the first gang, Bass, now emulating his boyhood heroes, the Reno Brothers of Indiana, first to rob trains in the U.S., gathered about him a new group of bandits with the intent of robbing Texas trains. These new recruits included Seaborn Barnes, a tough western gunman, Frank Jackson, Tom Spotswood, Henry Underwood, Arkansas Tom Johnson, all hardcases, and, at the end, Jim Murphy, a novice thief from a clan of thieves whose disloyalty to Bass was to equal in legend the betrayal of Jesse James by the notorious Ford Brothers. With Barnes, Spotswood, Jackson, and Underwood, Bass went back to robbing stages, stopping a coach outside of Mary's Creek, near Fort Worth, in October 1877, but the take of $43 was so miserable that the bandits quit stagecoach robbery altogether. They would concentrate on Texas trains, Bass vowed.

The gang stopped the Houston & Texas Central express at Allen Station on Feb. 22, 1878, taking $1,280. The raid was committed by Bass, Spotswood, Barnes, Jackson, and Underwood, who stopped another flyer of the same line at Hutchins on Mar. 18. The same group struck the Texas and Pacific line on Apr. 4, at Eagle Ford, robbing the safe in the mail car. On Apr. 10, 1878, the bandits attacked a Texas and Pacific express while it was stopped at Mesquite, but here they ran into serious trouble for the first time. The train was loaded with convicts en route to prison and their heavily armed guards opened fire on the outlaws from windows as soon as they appeared. Passengers and train employees also grabbed guns and let loose a withering barrage that wounded several gang members. Seaborn Barnes was struck once in the left thigh and three times in the right leg. Grabbing what little loot they could, the bandits leaped on their horses and escaped without losing a man. Barnes recovered from his wounds within a few weeks. (These rather hurriedly planned train robberies netted the gang about $1,500 each; Bass did not have the special kind of information Jack Davis had brought to him about west-to-east gold shipments in the Big Springs robbery and lacked the effective tactics employed by Joel Collins, whom many still believe to be the real brains of the first Sam Bass gang.)

The four train robberies committed by the Bass gang so alarmed authorities in the Dallas-Fort Worth area that an army of lawmen assembled in the region—sheriffs, deputies, bounty hunters, and local militia, hundreds of heavily armed men all looking for the most notorious outlaw in Texas, Sam Bass. He was an elusive quarry, however, moving from one remote hideout to another in Denton County. Since the Texas Rangers were short-handed in the area, a company of thirty men was organized under the command of one-time deputy sheriff, city marshal June Peak, who at the time was recorder for the city of Dallas. Peak was a determined, hard-riding lawman; he promised that he would bring in the Bass gang dead or alive. Meanwhile, Bass and his men hid out in the dense, vast Elm and Hickory Bottoms, an enormous swamp area where, as one newsman of the day described it, "the foliage is dense—the vines hang in masses and it is not good daylight until 12 noon." Bass and Underwood knew these bottoms well, having gone hunting and fishing here years earlier.

Ranger Peak, now a captain in the force, with thirty men, accompanied by a large posse, under the command of Sheriff W.F. Eagan, Bass' old employer, were combing the back areas of Wise County on June 12-13, 1878, when they encountered the Bass gang camped at Salt Creek. The outlaws were cooking breakfast in the pre-dawn hours when the lawmen rode down on them, firing as they came. Arkansas Tom Johnson pulled two six-guns and picked off three riders far ahead of the posse as they splashed across the creek but other Rangers behind these wounded men riddled Johnson, who collapsed in a heap, dead. Bass and the others returned fire but quickly realized that they were hopelessly outnumbered, and they scrambled up a small gorge to retrieve their horses. They discovered that the Rangers and Eagan's men had cut them off, having captured their mounts. The outlaws slipped into a long gulley and fled on foot. Later they stole some horses from a nearby ranch and made good their escape. This escape so enraged state law enforcement officials that rewards were increased for each gang member, particularly Bass.

Sam Bass shortly before the fatal Round Rock raid.

The gang was reported to be in five different counties in a single day, which caused Rangers and lawmen to ride about in a confused search. But on May 21, 1878, a break in the manhunt appeared in the form of James W. Murphy, who, along with his father, Henderson Murphy, had been charged with harboring the Bass gang and faced certain imprisonment. Jim Murphy approached Captain Peak with a proposition. He would deliver the Bass gang if charges against him and his father were dropped. Authorities agreed to the deal. Murphy then joined the gang as a full-fledged member, waiting for an opportunity to betray Bass and his men. Several traps were set but the wily outlaws always managed to slip from the grasp of the lawmen. Murphy was present when the gang held a meeting and decided to rob the bank at Round Rock, Texas, on July 20, 1878. He managed to write a letter to Major John B. Jones of the Rangers, telling him that the bandits would raid Round Rock on July 20, and "for God's sake" to get there first with his men.

Jones sent a large contingent to Round Rock, telling them to expect Bass and his men on July 20. Unexpectedly, Bass and the others decided to go into the town a day before the planned robbery "to look things over." Both Davis and Murphy had looked over the small town twice earlier. Jackson said he thought there were too many cowboys at Round Rock and that they might be lawmen waiting to spring a trap. Murphy told him that some large cattle herds had just been driven into the area and that explained the presence of so many gun-carrying men. On July 19, 1878, all four bandits rode into town to make sure everything was safe for the robbery planned for the next day. The town was divided into Old Round Rock and Newtown, where new buildings had mushroomed because of the cattle boom, and this is where the bank, fat with cash, was located. As the gang passed through Old Round Rock, Murphy, looking for a chance to separate himself from the doomed gang, said to Bass: "I think I'll look around here to see that things are safe, maybe buy some grub for the horses." Bass nodded in his direction. The others rode into Newtown and tied their horses up in an alley next to Koppel's store which was next to the bank. Bass, Barnes, and Jackson walked into the store to buy some tobacco and other supplies.

The Rangers, include Major Jones, were spread about the town, not expecting the outlaw band until the next day. Murphy, in Old Round Rock, desperately searched for lawmen to inform them that the gang had arrived earlier than expected. Meanwhile, Sheriff Hoke Grimes and his deputy, Morris Moore, spotted the three men going into Koppel's store and followed them inside. All three men were wearing long coats with suspicious bulges beneath them. Grimes, not thinking that the visitors were members of the Bass gang, believed they were wearing concealed weapons and this was against a local ordinance. He stepped up behind Seaborn Barnes and, putting a friendly hand on the outlaw's shoulder, asked if he was armed. Barnes tore open his coat and whipped out his six-shooter, turning and firing, blasting two bullets into the startled sheriff, who died on his feet. Before he fell, Bass and Jackson shot Grimes four more times and sent two bullets into Moore's lungs. The deputy got off one shot before collapsing, the bullet ripping through Bass' hand. The three men dashed to the street and turned the corner to the alley, going for their horses.

At the first sound of gunfire, Rangers flew to the street. Major Jones saw the three gunmen turn the corner and shouted for his men to attack them. A dozen rangers and other lawmen converged on the alley, firing as they ran, with the outlaws firing back. Ranger Dick Ware had been having a shave in the barbershop and at the first shots in the store, he jumped from the barber's chair still wearing the striped bib around his neck, his face coated with lather. He ran with two guns in his hands and when he turned the corner into the alley, he saw the bandits trying to mount their skittish horses. Barnes had one foot in the saddle when he saw Ware, twisting about to take aim with his pistol. But Ware came to a dead stop and fired deliberately, hitting the outlaw square in the forehead and killing him. Seaborn Barnes fell into the alleyway, dead. Bass was struggling with his horse, the animal moving about wildly, frightened by the gunfire. A Ranger knelt at the mouth of the alley and fired. Bass groaned as the shot tore into his back and burst through his chest. Another shot from a second Ranger shattered his arm. Frank Jackson, unhurt, returned fire, driving the Rangers back somewhat into the street as he went to the bandit chief and helped his leader into the saddle. Holding the reins of Bass' horse, Jackson spurred his horse out of the back of the alley and down another street.

Murphy, who had taken refuge in a doorway in Old Round Rock, crouched low to see Jackson and Bass gallop past him down the street. He later stated: "I was sitting in a door at Old Round Rock as they came by, and Frank was holding Bass on his horse. Bass looked pale and sickly, and his hand was bleeding and he seemed to be working cartridges into his pistol. Jackson looked at me, as much as to say, 'Jim, save yourself if you can.' I then saw Major Jones go by and hallooed to him, but he did not hear me." Murphy went to Newtown and identified the body of Seaborn Barnes by pointing out the four bullet wounds the outlaw had received during the shootout at the abortive Mesquite robbery. At first the crowd of irate citizens thought to lynch Murphy as one of the outlaws but Major Jones returned, his horse spent in pursuit of the fleeing Bass and Jackson, and ordered the crowd to let Murphy go. All charges against Murphy were later dropped and he was given a large reward, but Murphy's name became synonymous with traitor. Even members of the valiant Texas Rangers condemned Murphy for his betrayal of Bass. Captain Jesse Lee Hall described Murphy as "a veritable Judas in every sense of the word."

Frank Jackson, with a superficial wound in his shoulder, managed to steer Bass' horse for several miles. Near Bushy Creek, Bass asked to stop. His saddle was coated with blood from his terrible back and chest wound and he told Jackson he could not go on. Jackson helped him from his horse and put him beneath a shady tree. "Go on, Frank," Bass told his last lieutenant. "I'm finished but you get going before the law gets here." Jackson argued with him, telling him that he would bind up his chief's wounds and they would make their escape. Bass said he was too badly wounded and then ordered Jackson to flee, telling him to take all the gold in his saddle bags. Jackson complied and rode away. He returned briefly to Denton, Texas, and then rode on and out of history, completely vanishing.

Bass was found by Jones and other Rangers that night. As the Rangers approached him, Bass held up his uninjured arm and said weakly: "Don't shoot. I am the man you are looking for. I am Sam Bass." The Rangers noticed that the outlaw had torn his shirt to pieces in order to bandage his awful chest wound which still seeped blood. Bass was carried back to Round Rock where a Dr. Cochran tended to his wounds but gave no hope that the bandit chieftain would survive. Major Jones sat by the outlaw's deathbed, questioning him about past robberies but he got little or no information from Sam Bass. At one point Bass told Jones: "It's agin my profession to blow (inform) on my pals! If a man knows anything, he ought to die with it in him." On the morning of July 21, 1878, Bass' twenty-seventh birthday, the outlaw still thought he might recuperate and asked Dr. Cochran about his chances. The physician minced no words, telling Bass that "the end is very near." Bass nodded and replied: "Let me go." A few moments later he said: "The world is bobbing around." These were the last words of Sam Bass. He was buried in a grave next to Seaborn Barnes in the little Round Rock cemetery.

Following the death of Sam Bass, the man who betrayed him, Jim Murphy, lived a nightmare existence. The 200-pound Murphy, who wore a red mustache and chin beard and whose small blue eyes seemed watery and darted everywhere at once, lived in mortal fear that Frank Jackson or some other friend of Sam Bass would seek him out and kill him. He claimed to have received word that Jackson was looking for him. Murphy spent most of his time holed up in a small room in Round Rock, writing lengthy letters to Major Jones, begging him to protect him against possible killers, phantom outlaws that so plagued Murphy that he asked to sleep in the small jail, being locked inside a cell at night with two six-guns next to his sleeping form. Finally, on June 7, 1879, Murphy could no longer bear the strain. He swallowed poison and died. See: **Barnes, Seaborn; Hall, Jesse Lee; Reno Brothers**.

Bassett, Charles, prom. 1870s-90s, U.S., lawman. Charles Bassett, a steady, level-headed officer who seldom displayed any kind of alarm no matter the crisis, became the first sheriff of Ford County and Dodge City, Kan., on June 5, 1873, and later served for many years as the town marshal. It was Bassett who appointed Wyatt Earp a deputy marshal. He was present at many confrontations between lawmen and outlaws, as well as shootouts between local residents. Bassett was not really a gunman but an officer who generally backed up such men as Ed and Bat Masterson and the Earp Brothers. Bassett helped Earp track down James "Spike" Kennedy, killer of beautiful Dodge City showgirl Dora Hand in 1878. It was Bassett who disarmed Cock-Eyed Frank Loving after his famous lethal duel in Dodge City with Levi Richardson on Apr. 5, 1879. On that occasion, the smoke still curling from the barrel of Loving's gun, Bassett arrived at the scene and calmly walked up to Loving without drawing his own gun. He reached out and took Loving's six-gun which was pointed at his chest, and then arrested him. Through the 1880s and 1890s Bassett served consistently as a lawman until his retirement shortly before the turn of the century. See: **Earp Brothers; Kennedy, James; Masterson, Edward J.; Masterson, William Barclay; Richardson, Levi.**

Baugh, Andrew T., d.1885, U.S., outlaw. A former Confederate officer, Andrew T. Baugh turned to cattle rustling in Georgia in the 1870s, and the early 1880s, he moved to Texas where he and a small band of rustlers continued to steal cattle. Baugh was captured in Texas by a posse of cowboys who interrupted Baugh and his men as they were driving a stolen herd of cows toward Mexico. He was hanged in 1885.

Bean, Roy, c.1823-1903, U.S., jur. Nothing was orthodox about Roy Bean, and little in his life qualified him to sit in judgment of others, yet this uneducated, colorful, and contrary man set himself up as the only "law West of the Pecos" in Langtry, Texas, and ruled this dust-blown hamlet with harshness and humor for twenty years. Bean's background was hazy at best, but it is known that he was born about 1823 in a crude cabin along the Ohio River in Mason County, Ky. His parents, Francis and Anna Bean, were uneducated hill people who barely scraped a living from the wildness and young Roy, having little, soon developed a taste for the finer things of life. His brothers, Sam and Josh, left home first, Sam going to Mexico where he later fought in the Mexican-American War and, still later, settling in Dona Ana County, N.M., becoming its first sheriff. Josh went further, traveling to California where he became the first mayor of San Diego. He was murdered

in 1852. Roy Bean left the hardscrabble life in Kentucky while in his teens, seeking his fortune in Mexico with his brother Sam.

Both arrived in Chihuahua in 1848 and there got into an argument with a drunken Mexican cowboy who reportedly drew a knife on young Roy, who pulled a pistol and, with one shot, drilled a bullet into his antagonist's forehead. To

Judge Roy Bean, the only "Law West of the Pecos."

the Americans in Chihuahua the killing was self-defense, but local authorities labeled Bean's shooting murder and Roy fled to California where he worked for his brother Josh briefly, ran a saloon, joined the California Rangers and, when his brother was slain in 1852, fled once more, this time going to Mesilla, N. M. Roy later told the tale that he had fought a duel on horseback in San Diego and left that town after killing his opponent. He also said, some years later, that he stole a beautiful Spanish girl from her Mexican lover near the Mission of San Gabriel outside Los Angeles. The boyfriend and his friends supposedly lynched Roy Bean for his transgressions and left him to dangle but he was cut down by the sweetheart and escaped with rope burns around his neck.

During the Civil War, Bean organized a guerilla band which he dubbed The Free Rovers, a group of scavengers that ostensibly robbed from wealthy landowners and converted the loot into supplies for the Confederacy. Bean's group, however, was considered to be nothing more than a band of rustlers and robbers who stole in the name of the southern cause. Following the war, Bean moved to San Antonio, Texas, where, for eighteen years, he enmeshed himself in a myriad of money-producing schemes that produced little or no money. He worked as a butcher, a dairy operator, a saloon-keeper, and a freighter. Bean was in and out of court so often, pressing claims and mostly losing, that he became a regular fixture in the San Antonio courthouse. In the course of his many suits, the unschooled, almost illiterate Bean learned much about the law, knowledge he would later put to effective use. During this long dry spell, Bean wed a child-bride, Virginia Chavez. After bearing two sons and two daughters for the hard-drinking, easy living Bean, Virginia left her failed husband.

Bean, however, saw the advance of the railroads as his opportunity and he followed the railhead as it worked across West Texas, first at Vinagaroon where he was appointed a justice of the peace by the drunken road-gang workers he befriended and who were impressed with Bean's law-spouting speeches. When Vinagaroon died, Bean moved on with the Southern Pacific, getting off at a desolate spot called Langtry. Here Bean established his little empire that was to win him fame across the state of Texas and earn him a lasting, if curious, lore as one of the strangest judges of the West. Bean later claimed that he named the tiny town of Langtry, a half-dozen broken down shacks that butted up against the rail line, after the popular British actress. Bean saw a picture of the "Jersey Lily" in a magazine and exclaimed: "By gobs, what a purty critter!" He kept the magazine clipping until the day he died, nailing it to the wall of his saloon where it faded and yellowed year after year.

Armed with a copy of the Revised Statutes of Texas, 1879 edition, Bean got himself appointed justice of the peace in Langtry on Aug. 2, 1882, occupying a twenty-by-fourteen-foot shack adorned with signs that read: "Judge Roy Bean, Notary Public," "Justice of the Peace," "Law West of the Pecos," and "Ice Beer." The place was entitled with another prominent sign, reading: "The Jersey Lilly," named after Bean's heart-throb, Lily Langtry. The sign was misspelled by a illiterate sign-painter who worked off one of Bean's notorious fines by painting the signs while drunk.

Bean's actions as a judge became more and more eccentric. He once found a body with forty dollars in gold and a pistol in one of the dead man's pockets. He fined the corpse forty dollars for carrying a concealed weapon and pocketed the money. Bean would officiate at any occasion, for a price, of course. He charged $2 for inquests, and there were many of these in Langtry where everyone carried weapons and fired first and talked later, if anyone was left alive to talk. For weddings and divorces, Bean charged $5 for each ceremony. He had no right, of course, to grant divorces and when challenged on one of these actions, he snorted: "I guess I got a right to unmarry 'em if it don't take." His wedding ceremonies were somber affairs and Bean usually rushed through the traditional rites. When he finished he would invariably stare long and hard at the

groom and state: "And may God have mercy on your soul," a comment usually reserved for those who had been condemned to death.

The judge was as concerned about selling his liquor as he was about dispensing justice. Before any important court hearing, Bean would suggest that everyone buy "a good snort" to liven up the proceedings. Though he was supposedly loved by children and animals, Bean was a harsh man with a dark humor who favored white citizens and considered all others worthless. On one occasion a railroad worker who had shot a Chinese laborer was brought before him. Bean leafed through his one law book briefly and then looked up and said: "There ain't a damned law here that says it's illegal to shoot a Chinaman! Defendant is discharged." Of course, Bean bent over backwards for anyone who worked for the railroad since the Southern Pacific made a regular stop at his small town. The railroad was the only source of supplies and business, especially when trains stopped long enough to allow passengers to visit The Jersey Lilly, and buy a few drinks. The inside of the place was part saloon and part courtroom with a small back room

Judge Bean, sitting on porch wearing sombrero, trying a horse thief at Langtry, Texas, 1900.

where Bean slept. If any customer got drunk in the courtroom area instead of the saloon, Bean promptly fined the offender.

Lily Langtry remained Bean's lifelong obsession. No one could bring up her name in his ramshackle saloon without buying a drink and toasting her picture which was behind the bar. When the actress toured America in 1888, Bean traveled to a San Antonio theater to see her, wearing his best suit and a battered top hat, paying a staggering price for a front-row customer. He sat bug-eyed throughout the performance but did not have the courage to visit the actress backstage later. When Bean returned to tell his tale of seeing the actress, he called for a week-long celebration. The judge's reign was interrupted twice, in 1886 and in 1896 when elections he claimed were rigged put others in his place. Bean, however, continued to win the post of justice of the peace and by the turn of the century his legendary character and judicial decisions had reached eastward, drawing hundreds of visitors to the dusty town of Langtry just to get a glimpse of Bean sitting on the porch of his establishment, meting out justice to drunks, wife-beaters, and rowdies.

Even Lily Langtry finally came to visit the famous judge in 1903 but her most ardent fan was by then dead. Bean had gone into San Antonio on Mar. 15, 1903, where he witnessed a cockfight in the Mexican quarter. So aroused by the blood sport was he that he went on an extended bender and was taken back to his shack in Langtry in an almost comatose state. He lingered in his back room for some hours, unable to recognize his own son, Sam, who had ridden a horse to death to get to his father's deathbed. He died on Mar. 16, 1903. Toward the end of the year, Lily Langtry alighted from a passenger train and toured Bean's miserable shack, which still bore her picture over the bar. The natives gave her the judge's pet bear which had been chained for years to Bean's bed, but the animal ran off once it was released. Then Lily was given the judge's revolver which she took home with her to England where she placed it on a mantle to remind her of the "strange little man in America" who loved her and who never met her.

Bean was buried in Del Rio, Texas, with little pomp. His children were present and his daughter, fifty years later, objected to the critical stories about her father, stating in his defense: "The only thing about Papa that anybody could object to was that he was a Republican and favored a high tariff...He was a wonderfully kind, good and gentle father...And he was a honest, fair and impartial judge." Judge Roy Bean was also one of the most unusual jurists ever seen in the annals of the West.

Beard, Edward T., c.1828-73, U.S., gunman. Raised with wealth and education, Edward Beard married and produced three children in Beardstown (named after his father), Ill. Without any explanation, Beard suddenly left his family and went West in 1861, becoming a notorious rowdy and gunman in California, Oregon, and Arizona. When he heard of the cattle boom in Kansas, Beard moved to Wichita and opened a notorious dance hall in nearby Delano, a hangout for soldiers stationed nearby. On June 3, 1873, a drunken soldier argued with a prostitute named Emma Stanley over her price for the night, and fired a bullet into her leg. Beard leaped over the bar and ran toward the group of soldiers, blindly firing his six-gun. He shot one soldier in the throat and another in the leg, neither being the culprit who escaped out a back door and deserted the army that night. Two nights later, thirty troopers sought revenge by invading Beard's dance hall and shooting up the place, wounding a gambler named Charles Leshhart, shooting Emma Stanley in the other leg, and wounding another dance hall girl. Before retreating, the soldiers torched the dance hall and then watched from the street, cheering as it burned to the ground.

After rebuilding his dance hall, Beard was immediately at odds with the dreaded gunman Rowdy Joe Lowe, who had built a saloon next to Beard's (winning in a race to see who could build a dance hall first). On Oct. 27, 1873, Beard, drinking heavily, accused one of his prostitutes, Jo DeMerritt, of stealing from him. DeMerritt threw a bottle at him and fled next door to Lowe's saloon. The drunken Beard followed her, staggered into Lowe's, and in the smoke-filled place mistook another prostitute, Annie Franklin, as being DeMerritt. He fired a shot which struck the woman in the stomach. Lowe then grabbed a shotgun and exchanged shots with Beard. Lowe's shot missed but Beard's bullet grazed Lowe's neck. A stray bullet struck and wounded bystander Bill Anderson who was standing at the bar.

Beard fled and Lowe, as drunk as his quarry, went after him. Both men, mounted on horses and racing out of town, had a running gunfight. Lowe caught up with Beard near the river bridge and emptied his shotgun into him, then rode back to town where he turned himself in to the sheriff. Beard was found critically wounded in the arm and thigh, loaded with buckshot. He clung to life for two weeks, but through loss of blood died on Nov. 11, 1873.

Bear River Tom, See: Smith, Thomas J.

Beaubien, Carlos (Charles Hipolyte Trotier), 1800-64, U.S., jur. Born in French-speaking Canada, Carlos Beaubien went to St. Louis as a boy. There he joined French fur trader Auguste Chouteau, who taught him the business. In 1823 Beaubien traveled west while working for fur trader Antoine Robidoux, who took the young man on an expedition to New Mexico. Beaubien was impressed with the surroundings and decided to become a Mexican citizen. He settled in Taos and in 1827 married Paula Lobato. After the Americans occupied New Mexico in 1846, General Stephen W. Kearny (who formed his own civilian government) appointed Carlos Beaubien to serve as one of the first judges of the newly created superior court.

Beaubien presided over the trial charging a group of Taos Indians with the murder of Beaubien's son Narciso and Governor Charles Bent during the aborted 1847 Tao uprising. Beaubien sentenced the men to death.

Beck, H.O. (AKA: Ole; Edward Welch), d.1912, U.S., outlaw. Beck was an old-time western train and stagecoach robber who had been serving time with Ben Kilpatrick, the "Tall Texan" of Wild Bunch fame. Both men were released from federal prison in early 1912 and immediately planned a train robbery of the Southern Pacific's *Sunset Express* in a remote desert spot. They boarded the train at Dryden, Texas, a small water stop, on Mar. 13, 1912, and attempted to rob the Wells Fargo car of its cargo of $65,000, but the guard, David Trousdale, attacked both men, killing Beck and Kilpatrick and delivering their bodies to officials at the next stop as if he were casually dropping off some mailbags. See: **Kilpatrick, Benjamin**.

Beckwith, John H., d.1879, and **Beckwith, Robert W.**, 1858-78, U.S., lawmen. Beckwith and his brother Bob were born in New Mexico and were ranchers who were deputies battling the McSween "Regulators" which included Billy the Kid. John and Robert Beckwith were with a group of deputies who stopped rancher John Tunstall on Feb. 18, 1878, killing him, and setting off the infamous Lincoln County (N.M.) war. John Beckwith was involved with a number of shoot-outs, one, on Aug. 16, 1878, in the home of his hardcase father, Henry, who killed his son-in-law, William Johnson, during a wild argument in the ranch house, a fight where John tried to intervene and was almost shot to death by his own father. On Aug. 26, 1879, Beckwith encountered rustler John Jones stealing some of the Beckwith herd, and both men went for their guns. Beckwith was shot dead from the saddle.

Robert Beckwith operated a cattle ranch with his older brother John in Lincoln County and was deputized in the Lincoln County War, as a member of the Murphy-Dolan faction. Robert accompanied six others of the "Seven Rivers Crowd" on Apr. 30, 1878, when, near Lincoln, N.M., they encountered Regulator chief Frank McNab and two of his men, Ab Sanders and Frank Coe, who were watering their horses in a stream. McNab and Sanders had already dismounted and they were shot down immediately by Beckwith and the other men, but Coe, still mounted, spurred his horse on while firing at his pursuers. The horse was killed and Coe was arrested. When the Beckwith faction returned to the stream they saw that McNab was still alive, trying to crawl to safety. They shot him to pieces. Sanders, who was left for dead, later recovered.

On July 15-19, 1878, during the siege of Alexander McSween's store, Robert Beckwith, shortly before his twentieth birthday, stepped into clear view and announced to those inside the store that he was a deputy sheriff. He boldly marched to the door of the store, throwing it open and announcing that anyone who gave himself up would go unharmed. The response was a hail of gunfire, one shot smashing Beckwith's wrist, a second plowing into his left eye and killing him. McSween and the others came charging out of the house and McSween was shot to death by Beckwith's companions, falling over young Beckwith's body. See: **Billy the Kid; Lincoln County War**.

Beckwourth, James (James Pierson, AKA: Jim or James Beckwith), c.1806-c.66, U.S., outlaw. Son of Jennings Beckwith, an Irish nobleman, and a mulatto slave, James Beckwourth was born in Virginia but was a freed slave by 1822 when he moved west to Missouri. He joined several expeditions through the Rocky Mountains and the Sierras, becoming a famed Indian fighter and scout over the next fifteen years, guiding countless wagon trains to California. Beckwourth was employed by the Rocky Mountain Fur Company, and worked there until 1828 when he was adopted by a tribe of Crow Indians. Caleb Greenwood, Beckwourth's erstwhile partner and fellow fur trapper, convinced Chief Big Bowl that Beckwourth was the chief's son who was captured by the Cheyenne when he was a child and sold to the white people. For whatever reason—historians suggest that it was a clever ruse designed to get beaver pelts for his employer Kenneth McKenzie—Beckwourth went along with the deception and was welcomed into the tribe. He lived as an Indian for the next six years, and according to his later accounts, participated in many important raids and battles. In 1837 he turned up in Florida, where he enlisted as a paid volunteer in a Missouri regiment fighting in the Seminole War. From there he traveled to present-day Pueblo, Colo., where he settled with a group of squatters in 1842.

Two years later, Beckwourth left for California. There he discovered that considerable profit lay in selling horses to immigrants. To obtain sizeable herds, he and other celebrated mountain men, Pegleg Smith and Old Bill Williams, assembled a huge gang of horse thieves—some reports say more than 150 men—and began raiding ranches throughout California.

This gang of horse thieves, the most feared in the history of California, looted horses from almost every ranch in middle and southern California in 1840, stripping the horse herds of the San Bernadino and San Gabriel valleys. The gang was pursued by Jose Antonio Carillo, the Spanish governor, and a small army which trapped the rustlers at

Resting Springs. A full scale battle ensued where dozens on both sides were killed and wounded, but Beckwourth managed to fight his way through to freedom, escaping with most of his men and more than 1,000 horses.

The shootout proved too hazardous even for the adventure-seeking Beckwourth and he later gave up horse stealing to take up ranching, storekeeping, and eventually scouting for the army. He served as a guide to Colonel John M. Chivington in 1864 and was part of the Sand Creek Massacre. Beckwourth's death is unclear. While some sources report he was poisoned to death in 1866 by Crow Indians as he sat at one of their campfires eating a meal especially prepared for him, other sources claim he may have died in 1867 near Denver, Colo.

In 1854, Beckwourth was interviewed by Thomas D. Bonner, a New England writer who in 1856 published a book titled *The Life and Adventures of James P. Beckwourth; Mountaineer, Scout, Pioneer, and Chief of the Crow Nation.* Bonner, who allegedly changed the spelling of Beckwith's name to Beckwourth, captured the colorful tales of the adventurous mountain man.

Behan, John, d.1917, U.S., lawman. The Missouri-born Behan arrived in Prescott, Ariz., in the 1860s and, after serving time in the territorial legislature, he became tax collector and sheriff of Yavapai County in 1879. Behan later became deputy to Charles Shibbell, sheriff of Pima County and, notably, Tombstone, an end-of-the-trail hellhole which was dominated by gun-happy cowboys who were more gunmen than cattlemen, including the notorious McLowery and Clanton families of dedicated rustlers. Shibbell, in order to bring some law and order to the town, asked Wyatt Earp and his brothers to become his deputies. The coming of the Earps aggravated Behan and his own followers, who later elected Behan sheriff. It was Behan, a devout Democrat as were the cowboy factions, who became one of Wyatt Earp's most bitter enemies. Earp and his brothers were Republicans and sided with the town elders, the storekeepers, and the saloonkeepers.

Behan was later accused of siding with the gunslinging Clantons and McLowerys, encouraging their outlaw exploits and their eventual confrontation with the Earps in the legendary gunfight at the O.K. Corral in 1881. It was Behan who tried to stop the Earps and Doc Holliday from going down to the Corral when he heard they were about to confront the outlaw Clanton-McLowery faction. He was getting a shave at the time (some reports had him lurking in an alleyway with a shotgun, preparing to backshoot the Earps but deciding against this at the last moment). He allegedly leaped out of the barber chair and raced to the street, lather still on his face, and argued with the Earps briefly, telling them they had no authority to disarm the cowboys at the Corral. Wyatt Earp gave him a menacing look, hand on his holstered gun and told him to step aside. Behan stepped aside and the Earps walked into legend.

Following the gunfight Behan and his faction slowly took control of Tombstone but, by that time, the Earps had moved on. Behan was never anything more than a titular lawman who desired public office and the authority of that office. As sheriff of Tombstone he did manage to keep the peace the Earps had secured but seldom used his guns to quell the rowdy and reckless. He was forced into a gunfight with Dick Tolby some time later, and fired all the shots in his six-gun, hitting Tolby who died later and was buried in the crowded Tombstone cemetery, Boot Hill. Behan still later served as a state clerk and, goaded by friends to uphold a reputation he had slimly earned, joined Theodore Roosevelt's Rough Riders during the Spanish-American War, serving in Cuba, the Philippines, and in China. This record allowed him to secure the position of U.S. treasury agent in El Paso, Texas. Behan died in Tucson in 1917. See: **Earp, Wyatt**.

Beidler, John X., 1831-90, U.S., vigil. German-born John X. Beidler first came to prominence as a vigilante in Kansas where he single-handedly broke up a gang of cowboys "hurrahing" a town by firing a small howitzer loaded with printer's type into their midst, causing them to pick lead slugs out of their bodies for weeks. Later, when Beidler moved to Montana, he fearlessly led vigilantes without wearing the traditional mask, challenging the friends of those he hanged to seek him out. None did.

Vigilante and lynching expert John X. Beidler.

A squat, fierce little man with a walrus mustache, Beidler always went armed with a rifle; some said he slept with the weapon. He was so aggressive in his lynching of desperadoes and horse thieves that many believed he performed the executions more out of perverse pleasure than as justice-seeking acts of retribution against criminals. It was Beidler who invariably provided his "long rope" for the lynching of captured outlaws. When Helena, Mont., finally established a police force, Beidler and his friends retired, the dogged vigilante becoming a customs inspector for Montana and

Idaho, a position he held until his death on Jan. 22, 1890. See: **Slade, Joseph Alfred.**

Bell, Hamilton, prom. 1880s-90s, U.S., lawman. Bell followed Bat Masterson as sheriff of Ford County, Kan. He was a rigid, stand-up lawman who seldom drew his guns and was known, after thirty years of law enforcement, as a sheriff who never shot a man nor beat one over the head with a pistol. Still, it was reported that Hamilton Bell took more men into custody, using warrants, than any other lawman of the Old West. He retired about 1911 and, at the age of ninety, was operating a pet shop in Dodge City, selling canaries, his favorite bird. See: **Masterson, William Barclay.**

Bell, James W. (AKA: **Lone Bell**), d.1881, U.S., lawman. James W. Bell had been a Texas Ranger in the mid-1870s, serving under Captain Dan Roberts in San Saba County, Texas. He later served as a deputy to Pat Garrett who had captured Billy the Kid. He was one of the two guards killed by Billy when the Kid escaped from the jail in Lincoln, N.M., on Apr. 28, 1881, even though he befriended the young outlaw and had been kind and considerate to his prisoner. The other deputy, Robert Olinger, was also murdered by Billy the Kid as he escaped the jail. See: **Billy the Kid; Garrett, Patrick Floyd.**

Bell, Tom (Dr. **Thomas J. Hodges**), 1825-56, U.S., outlaw. Tom Bell, a brilliant Alabama-born surgeon who had served in the U.S. Army during the Mexican-American War, turned bandit in 1855 and terrorized the California counties of Yuba, Nev., and Placer about two years after the death of the notorious outlaw, Joaquin Murieta. Bell had been raised in Rome, Tenn., and had received a good education. He went on to medical school, then served with the Tennessee Volunteers under Colonel Cheatham in the Mexican-American War. He went West to follow the gold strikes, but he wound up broke and then turned to banditry, looting a San Francisco cabin. He was caught and sent to Angel Island, then a state prison in the middle of San Francisco Bay, where he served a year. Here he met the men who later made up his outlaw band: Bill Gristy, also known as Bill White; Ned Connor, a fierce-looking bandit with long red whiskers, and Jim Smith, an escape artist whose entire body was covered with tattoos.

When released, Bell and these men were joined by Bob Carr who called himself "English Bob," Montague Lyon, also known as "Monte Jack," and Juan Fernandez, a killer and thief wanted in Mexico. Unlike the fierce Murieta, noted for his cruelty to his victims, Bell was often considerate of those he preyed upon and showed them pity when depriving them of their valuables. He and his men robbed stagecoaches but often stopped wagon drivers such as Dutch John who was robbed by Bell and his men near Volcano, Calif. He turned over $30.25; Bell took the cash but returned the coin, telling John to "buy a drink and forget this incident."

A flat nose made Bell easy to remember and this was the first thing his victims described to lawmen seeking him, that and the fact that he was also very handsome, with blue eyes, sandy hair, blond mustache and goatee, a tall man standing well over six feet. Bell was early identified, even by his own men who had the habit of boasting that they were "Tom Bell's men." The band stopped John McMillan, a wagon driver for a mining company, and took more than $3,000 in gold dust from his shipment. He was tied to a tree and blindfolded, but Bell made sure that the bonds were loose and McMillan could free himself within a short time. When the victim removed his blindfold he found that Bell had left him food and a hunting knife so that he could survive in the wilderness.

Lawmen searching for Bell were confounded by his knowledge of which travelers would be carrying gold and money. Then, by interviewing these victims, officers realized that almost all of the victims had been guests at the Western Exchange Hotel or Hog Ranch, located on the main road between Sacramento and Nevada City. The hotel owner, Elizabeth Hood, of course, was being paid by Bell to supply him with information on wealthy travelers and gold shipments. Other innkeepers at the Mountaineer House on Auburn Road and the California House near Marysville, also provided Bell with similar information for a price or a share of the loot stolen. On Mar. 12, 1856, Bell and his band stopped a mule train laden with $21,000 in gold, taking the gold bags, and tying the five drivers to trees, again leaving pocket change with the mining men. When this pack train was stopped, Wells Fargo guard S.T. Barstow had half-pulled his gun when Bell shouted to him: "Stop that! We don't want to kill you but we must have your money." Again, the robber had proved his inclination to avoid bloodshed. This was soon changed with a bloody stagecoach robbery some months later.

Bell and his men were soon rich, but they were hunted by scores of posses and vigilantes throughout northern California. Bell decided that he would make one more "strike" and then go east and resume his career in medicine. He learned that a huge gold shipment of more than $100,000 would be shipped on Aug. 12, 1856, from Camptonville to Marysville. The gold's owner, a man named Rideout, rode ahead on horseback, the stage rumbling behind him, guarded by driver John Greer and messenger Bill Dobson; both cradled shotguns. Bell, ever cautious, planted one of his men on the stage in the disguise of a miner. This man got off the stage at the California House and there signaled to another gang member that the gold was indeed aboard the stage.

Rideout continued leading the stage once it was back on the wilderness road and was soon surrounded by Bell and two other men, Gristy and Carr. Riding up on the stage from behind were Monte Jack, Connor, and Fernandez. The outlaws ordered Greer to bring the stage to a halt but the seasoned driver only whipped them to faster speeds. Infuriated, three of the bandits opened fire on the stage-coach, raking it, and killing a female passenger, Mrs. Tilghman, the wife of a barber in Marysville. A bullet struck her directly in the forehead. Two male passengers cried out when they, too, were wounded. Greer was wounded in the arm but kept hold of the reins while Dobson let loose with his shotgun, then his pistols, blasting Fernandez from his horse and wounding first Bell's horse, then Bell in the arm. The outlaws tried to stop the stage once more at another spot up the road, but Greer whipped his horses past them at such speed that the stationary outlaws could do nothing. When the stagecoach arrived in Marysville, a posse was quickly formed and, headed by Police Captain William King, and Sacramento detectives Robert Harrison and Daniel Gay, went immediately in pursuit of the Bell gang. The posse returned empty-handed.

Bell by this time thought himself immune to capture and he taunted Captain King with letters in which he stated: "Catch me if you can!" Rewards were posted and one citizen recognized a member of the Bell gang, William Carter, who was captured and quickly revealed the hideouts of his fellow outlaws. Detective Harrison and others rounded up the gang members, one by one, each informing on the others. Bill Gristy was identified in Knights Ferry and he was taken prisoner by the local sheriff. He quickly revealed Bell's hideout at Firebaugh's Ferry near the San Joaquin River. On Oct. 4, 1856, a posse led by Judge Belt and Robert Price, overcame the outlaw on the trail and decided not to turn him over to officials but to hang him vigilante style. Bell accepted his fate laconically but asked if he could write two letters, one to his mother, the other to a Mrs. Hood who had harbored him at the Western Exchange Hotel. To his mother the outlaw wrote touchingly:

Dear Mother:

I am about to make my exit to another country. I take this opportunity to write you a few lines. Probably you may never hear from me again. If not, I hope we may meet where parting is no prodigal career in this country, I have always recollected your fond admonitions, and if I had lived up to them, I would not have been in my present position; but, dear Mother, though my fate has been a cruel one, yet I have no one to blame but myself. Give my respects to all my old and youthful friends. Tell them to beware of bad associations, and never to enter into any gambling saloons, for that has been my ruin. If my old grandmother is living, remember me to her. With these remarks, I bid you farewell forever.

Your only boy,
Tom

Possemen came forward with a bottle of whiskey, offering the condemned man a drink. He accepted gratefully, lifting the bottle to his executioners, thanking them for their thoughtfulness. "I have no bitterness toward any one of you," he said. He showed not a bit of nervousness as his hands were tied behind his head and a rope was placed over the limb of a sycamore tree, the other end looped around his neck. He was given a few minutes to pray and this Bell did, lowering his head and quietly saying words only he could hear. He lifted his head and nodded to the possemen as a signal that he was ready. His horse was whipped forward and Tom Bell, California's most dangerous outlaw, swung into space.

Bent, Charles, 1799-1847, U.S., mur. vict. Charles Bent was the eldest of two brothers who established a thriving mercantile firm in the Southwest. Born in Virginia, he organized the firm of Bent, St. Vrain, and Company in 1830 in New Mexico. In time, it was to become the largest U.S. business firm in the Southwest. Then, in 1833, Charles and his brother William built what came to be known as Bent's Fort on the north bank of the Arkansas River near Purgatoire, in what is now Colorado. The fort became a hub of the Indian trade in the region. The Bent brothers and their partner, Ceran St. Vrain, sold blankets and buffalo robes, drove New Mexican sheep to Missouri, and engaged in the lucrative fur trade within the walls of the fortress.

In the 1830s, Bent moved part of his business to Taos, N.M., where he ingratiated himself with Governor Manuel Armijo. Using his influence, Bent persuaded the governor to award land grants to several of Bent's cronies. When the U.S. gained control of the region following the conclusion of the Mexican War, Bent, as one of only a handful of politically connected whites in the territory, was appointed governor by Stephen Kearny.

Bent was a strong-willed figure who was not afraid to speak his mind. His candor earned him numerous enemies including the powerful Martinez family that was influential in Taos. Bent further antagonized the Taos Indians by trading with their sworn enemies. During the Taos rebellion in January 1847 against U.S. government rule, Charles Bent was murdered.

Bickerstaff, Benjamin F., d.1869, U.S., outlaw. A native of Sulphur Springs, Hopkins County, Texas, Benjamin Bickerstaff served in the Civil War as a guerrilla, and, following the war, he turned outlaw. While traveling in Louisiana in 1867, Bickerstaff murdered a freed slave who spoke defiantly to him. He then went back to Sulphur Springs and raised an outlaw band of about twenty men, raiding Union supply depots and killing many federal troops who were part of the Army of Occupation after the war. Bickerstaff was looked upon as a local hero, but he was nothing more than a bandit who used public animosity toward Union troops as an excuse for his criminal operations.

So effective were Bickerstaff's men in sacking federal warehouses and ambushing Union patrols, that three full companies were moved into Hopkins County and "forts" were established throughout the area around Sulphur Springs in an attempt to capture the band. A $1,000 reward was placed on Bickerstaff's head, dead or alive, but no local residents would think to turn the bandit into authorities, let alone shoot him down. This attitude changed a few years later when Bickerstaff and his men turned on Texans, shooting and robbing citizens at will. When Bickerstaff and his men roared into the town of Alvarado, Johnson County, on the night of Apr. 5, 1869, the gang "hurrahed" the town by firing weapons into the air and some into the store windows. Irate citizens spilled into the street heavily armed, warned in advance of the arrival of the gang, and gunned down several members, including Bickerstaff who was shot dead from his horse by a load of buckshot from a shotgun fired almost point blank into his face.

Bideno, Juan, d.1871, U.S., outlaw. Mexican-born Juan Bideno worked as a cowboy but was known as a fast-gun and hired out for killings, one report has it. In June

1871, Bideno signed on to a cattle drive from Texas to the railhead at Abilene, Kan. The trail boss was 22-year-old Billy Cohron, who noticed Bideno's slack work and called him on it several times, leading to hard words between the pair. As the herd crossed the Cottonwood River in Kansas on July 5, 1871, Cohron and Bideno again fell to arguing and then went for their guns. Bideno shot the youthful trail boss dead and fled, riding south toward Texas.

A self-appointed posse of cowboys tracked the killer to Bluff Creek, Kan. The four men following Bideno were John Cohron, the victim's brother, Hugh Anderson, Jim Rodgers, and a young Texan who would later be known as the fastest gun in the West, John Wesley Hardin. Several different stories of Hardin's gunfight with Bideno exist. According to one, Bideno was just mounting his horse when Hardin and the others rode into town and Hardin challenged the killer. Both men then rode at a full gallop down the street toward each other blazing away with their six-guns. Hardin proved to be the far superior and quicker shot, as he sent a bullet straight into Bideno's heart, killing him instantly.

Another story reported how Cohron, Anderson, and Rodgers surrounded the cafe where Bideno was eating and Hardin went inside alone. As Hardin approached Bideno's table he told him that he had been deputized to arrest him and that if he surrendered to him he would not be hurt. The Mexican gunman dropped his knife and fork, leaned back in his chair so that his holsters were free and went for his guns. Hardin, walking solemnly across the room, pulled his six-gun with lightning speed and drilled a bullet into Bideno's brain, instantly killing the outlaw. See: **Hardin, John Wesley.**

Billee, John, and **Willis, Thomas**, d.1890, U.S., outlaws. After robbing and murdering W.P. Williams and burying his body in a ravine in Oklahoma's Kiamichi Mountains on Apr. 12, 1888, John Billee and Thomas Willis were apprehended by three deputies, Will Ayers, James Wilkerson, and Perry DuVall. While en route back to Fort Smith, Oklahoma Territory, for trial, the three lawmen and the two prisoners bedded down in a deserted cabin near Muskogee, Okla. During the night, Billee managed to free one hand from the handcuffs which bound him to one of the deputies and reached for the deputy's gun. He shot Ayers, DuVall, and Wilkerson, wounding them, but Wilkerson managed to wound the outlaw before Billee made good his escape. All three wounded deputies, embarrassed at being jumped, were publicly denounced when they delivered their prisoners to Fort Smith. Billee and Willis were convicted of murder and sentenced to death. After several legal delays, they were both hanged at Fort Smith on Jan. 16, 1890.

Billy the Kid (William H. Bonney, AKA: Henry Antrim; Kid Antrim; William Antrim; Henry McCarty), 1859-81, U.S., outlaw. Next to Jesse Woodson James, no other outlaw of the American Old West still captures the imagination and near-obsession of the public than Billy the Kid, a lethal phenomenon who killed, according to legend if not record, twenty-one men before his twenty-first birthday. This famed bad man was reportedly born in New York City on Nov. 23, 1859, the son of William and Kathleen (or Catherine) McCarty Bonney, and named William H. Bonney. Another story has it that he was born on Sept. 17, 1859, as Patrick Henry McCarty to Catherine and Patrick McCarty. And still another account has it that he was born in Indiana to Joseph McCarty of Cass County. The first report seems to be the most reliable, especially since the Kid used the name of William H. Bonney, signing his letters as such. Yet a reliable account has Mrs. Bonney or McCarty living in Indianapolis, Ind., with William Antrim and moving west with him and her two sons, Henry and Joseph in 1870, settling first in Wichita, Kan., where Mrs. Bonney ran a laundry and dabbled in small real estate holdings. One report has it that the family lived for a while in the newly establish town of Coffeyville, Kan., and it was here that Billy first got into trouble, arrested for pilfering butter and other items from a local store.

Mrs. McCarty-Bonney decided to move to the Southwest with Antrim, marrying him in Sante Fe, N.M., on Mar. 1, 1873. The Antrims, along with the two boys, Henry (Billy) and Joseph, moved to Silver City where Antrim became a miner and Mrs. Antrim ran a small boarding house. Always a sickly, frail woman, Mrs. Antrim died on Sept. 16, 1874, after a short illness. Billy was then about fifteen and did not get along with his stepfather, William Antrim, who thought the boy was a troublemaker as he had been in some minor scrapes in Silver City where he went to school and did odd jobs. He and another youth, George "Sombrero Jack" Shaffer, stole some clothes from a Chinese laundry, mostly as a prank, and were arrested. Billy, rather than face the wrath of his stern stepfather, left town, drifting about Arizona, performing odd jobs on ranches and in small towns.

It was during this loosely recorded period of wandering that the Kid supposedly shot his first man. One account claimed he killed an unknown gunman in Coffeyville even before he and his family left that town and, a few years later, shot and killed three Apache braves near the Chiracachua Reservation, killed a blacksmith in Fort Bowie, three

cardsharps in Mexico, two more Indians in the Guadalupe Mountains, and so on. It is known that he was first called the Kid in 1877 when he got into an argument with Irish blacksmith Frank P. Cahill at Camp Grant, Ariz., on Aug. 17, 1877. The blacksmith who was in a saloon owned by George Adkins, called Billy a pimp, slapped the Kid's face, and threw him to the floor. The Kid realized he was no match for the burly Cahill and he immediately drew his six-gun as the blacksmith came toward him, firing a single shot that mortally wounded Cahill who died the following day. Billy was locked up in the post guardhouse but he escaped and began running.

This was the first recorded killing by Billy the Kid, official or not. Not until the outbreak of the Lincoln County War in New Mexico did the Kid's guns claim known victims. The first and second of these were Frank Baker and Billy Morton. These two men, with others, stopped the gentleman English rancher J.H. Tunstall while he was driving his buckboard along a lonely road and shot him to death. Billy, who worked for Tunstall and had been almost adopted by him, vowed that he would kill every man responsible for Tunstall's death. He had wandered into Lincoln County in late 1875 and was hired as a ranch hand by the Murphy-Dolan forces. L.G. Murphy and J.J. Dolan owned giant ranches in Lincoln County and were in mortal combat with other ranchers for water rights and grazing land, chiefly Alexander McSween and John Tunstall who were supported by the greatest cattle baron of that day, John Chisum.

Billy spent most of his time rustling Chisum's cattle from the sprawling Jinglebob Ranch and turning these over to Murphy who sold them to Mexican and Indian buyers. By accident, the Kid met John Tunstall, a cultured, kingly man who became the father figure Billy never had. The Kid went to work for him, idolizing Tunstall and his gentlemanly ways, trying to emulate his mentor's style and sense of nobility. Tunstall thought the Kid showed promise and was later quoted as having said of Billy: "That's the finest lad I ever met. He's a revelation to me every day and would do anything on earth to please me. I'm going to make a man of that boy yet."

Tunstall's plan for Billy never materialized. On Feb. 18, 1878, he was stopped on the road by a group of gunmen who had been deputized by Sheriff William Brady, a Murphy-Dolan backer. This band included many of Billy's former friends before he had switched sides in the Lincoln County War, including Billy Morton, Jesse Evans, Jim McDaniel, and Frank Baker. These so-called deputies informed Tunstall that they were going to take part of his herd, cattle which they claimed belonged to Murphy. Tunstall objected, pointing out that all his cattle were branded and if they checked the brands, they would see for

Billy the Kid

Catherine Bonney Antrim

William Antrim

John Tunstall

Alexander McSween

Susan McSween

Richard Brewer

Tom O'Folliard

themselves that Murphy could not lay claim to them. Evans and the others drew their guns and ordered Tunstall to surrender. He got out of his buckboard and handed over his gun, saying: "I don't want bloodshed." As he was handing Evans his gun, Evans fired a bullet into the helpless man who pitched downward to the road. Billy Morton then cruelly fired a bullet into Tunstall's head, killing him.

When the Kid heard the news of Tunstall's death he said: "He was the only man who ever treated me kindly, like I was free born and white." He then gritted his teeth and said in a rage: "I'll get every s.o.b. who helped kill John if it's the last thing I ever do." This remark was passed along to the members of the Murphy-Dolan clan and many of its members became apprehensive, knowing that Billy the Kid was a single-minded man who would ride miles out of his way to confront an enemy, and that his marksmanship was unfailing, starting with a fast draw no one had beat to date. The Kid at this time was not an impressive looking fellow. He stood about five-feet-ten-inches tall, had a receding chin, an overbite that made him appear to have exaggerated buck teeth, and narrow, squinting eyes of icy blue that were piercing to look into, eyes that seemed to dart about nervously whenever danger was near. He was a clever killer, an expert bushwacker who would not hesitate to shoot from ambush, fire a bullet into an enemy's back, or sneak up on an adversary in the middle of the night with a knife and dispatch his man without a second of sorrow.

The first to feel the bite of Billy's bullets were Billy Morton and Frank Baker. When the Kid heard that Richard M. "Dick" Brewer had been sworn in as a special constable to arrest Tunstall's killers, he joined the group of "regulators," being sworn in as a deputy. After several days of searching, on Mar. 6, 1878, Brewer's posse found a group of riders about six miles from the Rio Pecos. The band rode off, breaking up in small groups, with Brewer's men in hot pursuit. The Kid raced after Morton and Baker, firing his six-gun and Winchester as he rode. He ran both men down after their horses collapsed and took them prisoner, but he vowed to kill both men. The prisoners were taken to the Chisum ranch and, on Mar. 9, 1878, the Kid was a member of the regulators removing the prisoners to Lincoln. The party stopped at Roswell, about five miles from Chisum's ranch so Morton could mail a letter. Morton told the postmaster there, M.A. Upson, to notify his relatives if any harm came to him. Upson asked him if he thought the posse taking him and Baker to Lincoln would injure them. Morton said that the posse had promised John Chisum to deliver the prisoners safely to authorities in Lincoln and he trusted their word.

At that point, William McCloskey, one of the regulators, stepped forward, having heard the conversation between Morton and Upson, saying to Morton: "Billy, if harm comes to you two, they will have to kill me first." The posse rode off, the Kid and Charlie Bowdre in the lead, some distance in front of the posse and its prisoners, looking out for Murphy-Dolan men who might try to release Morton and Baker. Then rode Morton and Baker with McCloskey and John Middleton right behind them. Following were Dick Brewer, Henry Brown, Frank McNab, Sam Smith, Jim French, J.G. Skurlock, and Fred Wayt. The posse and its prisoners never reached Lincoln.

On Mar. 11, 1878, McNab appeared in Roswell and reported that Morton and Baker had tried to escape, pulling McCloskey's guns from their scabbards and killing him, and then being shot to death by the posse. This was later proven to be a lie. The posse, with the exception of McCloskey, had apparently agreed to kill the prisoners. It was unclear whether or not the Kid and Bowdre knew of this plan, which may have been developed as the posse rode along, the men in the rear making the decision. McNab, a short time after the posse had left Roswell, near a spot called the Black Water Holes (also called Steel Springs), rode up to McCloskey and put a six-gun to his head, saying: "You are the s.o.b. who's got to die before harm can come to these fellows, are you?" He fired, blowing out McCloskey's brains, his corpse falling from the horse. Morton and Baker, realizing they were marked for execution, then spurred their horses on, and the Kid, turning to see them flee, pursued them, overtaking them and firing two bullets which killed them both.

The posse split up, McNab returning to Chisum's ranch where he worked, the others going off to separate destinations. The bodies of McCloskey—who was thought to be in league with the prisoners—Morton, and Baker were left where they fell and were later buried by Mexican sheepherders. The Kid went to Lincoln, working for McSween. Later, he heard that Andrew L. "Buckshot" Roberts, a dedicated Murphy-Dolan man, was hunting him and the other killers of Morton and Baker. Brewer got together his regulators, including the Kid, and sought out Roberts, finding him in early April 1878 at Blazer's Saw Mill, about forty miles south of Lincoln. As the regulators rode into the area, Roberts, on horseback, saw them, and bravely charged them alone on horseback, firing his Winchester as he rode. Roberts was a western hardcase of incredible courage. He had been a soldier and had been in many gunfights. He was a crack shot with his Winchester and equally accurate with his six guns. As Roberts raced forward, he sent a rifle bullet whizzing past the Kid's head. Billy jumped from his horse and fired a shot that struck Roberts in the abdomen, but the tough old gunfighter managed to dismount, grab his guns, and take refuge in an outhouse. The regulators peppered the outhouse with dozens of shots and it appeared to them that Roberts had been killed. Brewer stood up and began to advance on the tiny building when Roberts thrust his Winchester through a hole and fired, his bullet crashing through Brewer's head, killing him. Roberts' Winchester barked again and this time Charley Bowdre was seriously wounded in the side, but his heavy cartridge belt had deflected the bullet and saved his life. Again the regulators riddled the outhouse, this time hitting Roberts several times, mortally wounding him. He died clutching his Winchester.

The Kid, now that Brewer was dead, vowed to continue his purge of the Murphy-Dolan faction. To this end he sought out Sheriff William Brady and his deputies George Hindman and J.B. Matthews. The Kid and Matthews had already confronted each other on the streets of Lincoln and Matthews had avoided a gunfight by slipping into a building and hiding. On Apr. 1, 1878, the Kid and five of his friends rode unseen into Lincoln and hid behind an adobe wall. They cut holes in the wall through which they could see the entire main street, with a view of the courthouse and through which they could fire their weapons. A short time later Sheriff Brady, Hindman, and Matthews appeared on the street, all carrying rifles and six-guns. As soon as they came under the Kid's guns he and his companions opened fire from their ambush. Brady fell dead with several bullets in him. Hindman fell next to him, mortally wounded. Matthews raced to a row of buildings and took refuge. The Kid ran to the fallen lawmen, intent on taking Brady's weapons, but when he picked up Brady's rifle, Matthews fired a shot that blew it out of his hand, the bullet grazing Billy's side. He retreated to the adobe wall and then the Kid's party saddled up and rode out of Lincoln. The Kid's brutal ambush of Brady and Hindman was one of the most ruthless, cowardly murders ever committed in the territory and it lost Billy the support of many who, up to that time, had backed him.

With the deaths of Brady and Hindman, the count of those killed by Billy the Kid, depending on whose count one accepted, had reached seventeen. He would kill five more men before he himself was slain by a man he had known for years, a friend at one time, a lawman only at the time he fired his fatal shot into the Kid. Following Brady's murder, George "Dad" Peppin became the new sheriff of Lincoln and he put together a large force to capture the Kid who made himself available to Peppin and his men by visiting McSween in his large Lincoln mansion with fourteen men. They barricaded the place and were soon surrounded by Peppin and about forty of the toughest gunfighters in the territory. Marion Turner, a Roswell merchant who had once been aligned with Chisum but had gone over to the Murphy-Dolan faction, had control of Peppin's posse and ordered it to open fire on the McSween mansion. This occurred on July 15, 1878. The gun battle raged for five

days before a truce was called.

Turner then called out to the bullet-ridden mansion that he had warrants for the Kid and his men, charging them with the murder of Sheriff Brady and Deputy Hindman. There was a moment's silence, then Billy shouted back: "We too, have warrants for you and all your gang which we will serve on you hot from the muzzles of our guns!" The fight again ensued. The Turner-Peppin forces aided by a company of U.S. infantry commanded by Lieutenant Colonel Nathan Augustus Monroe Dudley, made a shambles of the mansion, but the occupants fired back at their attackers with vigor and many were wounded on both sides. Colonel Dudley threatened to fire his two field cannons at the house, reducing it to rubble unless the Kid's forces surrendered, but the guns remained silent. The battle was witnessed by several newsmen who later wrote fabulous, untrue reports. One had it that Mrs. McSween "encouraged her wild garrison by playing inspiring airs on her piano, and singing rousing battle songs until the besieging party, getting the range of the piano from the sound, shot it to pieces with their heavy rifles." This, of course, was nonsense. Mrs. McSween and three other females left the house before the battle commenced.

One of the Mexicans inside the McSween house, exhausted with the battle, called out that those inside the mansion would surrender, but the Kid leaped across the room and knocked him senseless with his gunbutt. Outside, the call had been heard and Robert Beckwith approached the kitchen door of the house, with John Jones next to him. He called out for McSween as he stood in the open doorway. Billy sent a bullet into his skull, killing Beckwith instantly. Jones was also shot as the Kid shouted to his comrades: "Come on!" With that, Billy, two guns blazing in his hands, jumped over Beckwith's body, followed by his friends, as they made their mass escape, hundreds of bullets smashing into the building around them. The Kid miraculously fought his way through the lines of besiegers, wounding several, and made it to the nearby river, plunging in and getting to the other side where he was covered by high reeds. His friends, including Tom O'Folliard, followed and most were wounded. McSween refused to desert his home. He stepped into the yard and was shot to death, nine bullets entering his body.

The Lincoln County War was the disgrace of New Mexico and President Rutherford B. Hayes replaced Governor Axtell with Lew Wallace. As the new territorial governor, Wallace resolved to bring the bloody war to an end. He announced that a general amnesty was in effect for all those involved in the war, except for those who had been charged with murder. This meant Billy the Kid. But the Kid had cleverly seen his chance to escape murder warrants some time earlier. He had witnessed the killing of Huston Chapman, a lawyer for the McSween faction, who was shot down in cold blood on the streets of Lincoln by William Matthews, William Campbell, and James Dolan, but he had not gone for his guns. He went instead to Governor Wallace, offering to turn state's evidence against the three killers in exchange for a full pardon.

Wallace met with the Kid on Mar. 17, 1789. Billy walked into the home of John Wilson, holding a Winchester and a six-gun, asking if Wallace was there. Governor Wallace stood up and was shocked to see a slender boy with only a faint stubble of beard, finding it hard to believe that the Kid was the most feared gunman in the West. Wallace said that if he surrendered and testified against Matthews and the others in the Chapman killing he would receive a full pardon. Billy said he did not like the idea of surrendering; it would appear that he was a coward. He would be arrested then, Wallace volunteered, a fake arrest but one that would convince everyone that the Kid had put up a fight. The arrest was made and the Kid testified against the killers, so much enjoying the widespread publicity he received that he talked non-stop about all the outlaws in the territory, providing details on their rustling and thieving activities, thus breaking the code of silence binding all criminals. But he was Billy the Kid and he reveled in his black fame; he did as he pleased.

Part of the bargain the Kid made with Governor Wallace was to stand trial for the murder of Brady and Hindman. Wallace had promised that Billy would be set free but the Kid grew uneasy waiting for his day in court and suddenly decided to leave his loosely guarded confines in the back of a store, simply ambling to the street where he mounted someone else's horse and rode away, going to see his friends at Fort Sumner. Here he ran into Texas gunman Joe Grant who had told anyone who would listen that he intended to make his reputation by gunning down Billy the Kid. The Kid had also heard the story and, when meeting Grant, told him how much he admired Grant's expensive six-gun, asking if he could inspect it. Grant foolishly handed over the gun and Billy reportedly turned the cylinder to three empty chambers. A short time later, after the Kid had returned the gun, Grant and Billy squared off and fired at each other. Grant's gun only clicked as he fired an empty chamber but Billy's shot killed the ambitious Grant on the spot, or, at least, that is the story still told.

Billy and his gang were surrounded in a ranch house some time later by a posse and the Kid asked for a truce to negotiate. Gunman Jimmy Carlyle stepped from cover to talk and the Kid shot him down. When Carlyle was killed, the rest of the posse fled in terror, and the Kid and his men rode away without interference. It seemed as if New Mexico was to be forever plagued by the gunplay of Billy the Kid. That changed in 1880 when Pat Garrett was made sheriff of Lincoln County. He had known the Kid well; they had both ridden for the Maxwell ranch and had played cards and gotten drunk together on their days off. There was a deep and genuine friendship between them, but that too changed when Garrett put on his badge. He had been ordered to capture the Kid at all costs by Governor Wallace, who had placed a $500 reward on the Kid's head for not keeping his promise to stand trial for the Brady killing.

Garrett lost no time forming a posse and setting a trap for the Kid and his band on Dec. 18, 1880. With more than a dozen men laying in wait with him, Garrett, who had received a tip that the Kid and his men would be approaching Fort Sumner, saw Tom O'Folliard riding point for the gang and opened fire. O'Folliard was hit and his horse bolted but the mortally wounded O'Folliard turned about and limped back to Garrett. Blood gushed from O'Folliard's chest and the gunman said to Garrett: "Don't shoot again, Garrett, I'm killed." Garrett told him to dismount but O'Folliard said he could not, that he was dying and needed help to get off his horse. The Kid and his friends fled. O'Folliard died about an hour later.

The Kid and his men were now on the run and Garrett pursued them relentlessly, finally cornering the band in a deserted farmhouse near Stinking Springs on Dec. 21, 1881. Inside of the house were Billy, Charlie Bowdre, Dave Rudabaugh, Tom Pickett and Billy Wilson, the Kid's closest friends and most ardent followers. The lanky Garrett stepped out from cover in the moonlight and called for the gang to surrender. The Kid's response was typical; he fired off several shots, attempting to kill his one-time friend. Garrett and his men, about twenty strong, opened up a withering fire on the farmhouse. When Bowdre crossed in front of an open window he was hit in the chest and let out a piercing scream. "I'm killed, Billy, they killed me," he said as he crouched in the one-room farmhouse.

Billy stood Bowdre up and shoved him to the door, ruthlessly telling his friend: "They have murdered you, Charlie, but you can get revenge! Go out there and kill some of the s.o.b.'s before you go!" With that, the Kid swung the door open and shoved his friend Bowdre out into a hail of bullets. Bowdre lifted his six-gun but did not have the strength to fire. He was hit several more times and fell face forward, saying: "I wish...I wish...I wish..." Then he died and his body rotted there as Garrett and his men kept up the siege for two days. The Kid and his men, starving and panting for water, surrendered and were taken to Santa Fe. Here the Kid sent a letter to Governor Wallace, reminding him of his promise to pardon him. Wallace refused to answer, telling newsmen that the Kid reneged on *his* promise to stand trial for the murder of Sheriff Brady. There would be no pardon.

Pat Garrett (on white horse) brings in Billy the Kid.

Deputy Bob Ollinger.

The Kid escaped from the Lincoln County Courthouse.

Governor Lew Wallace.

Pat Garrett, left, with friends.

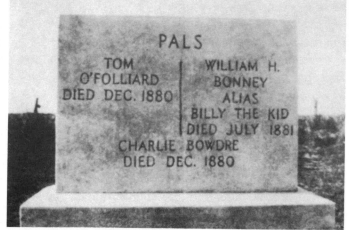

The grave of Billy the Kid and pals.

With great fanfare, the Kid was taken to Mesilla, N.M., where he was tried before Judge Warren Bristol for killing Andrew "Buckshot" Roberts. He was convicted and Judge Bristol, a stern, unrelenting jurist, sentenced the Kid to death, telling the stoic Billy that he would hang "until you are dead, dead, dead!" The Kid reportedly yelled back: "And you can go to hell, hell, hell!" While awaiting execution, the Kid gave expansive interviews to eager newsmen, posing as a persecuted victim in the one-sided Lincoln County War, telling reporters: "I expect to be lynched. It's wrong that I should be the only one to suffer the extreme penalties of the law." He went on to complain that he was being singled out for punishment where there were many others more deserving of the hangman's rope. He was removed to Lincoln to await execution by two of Garrett's top deputies, J.W. Bell and Robert Ollinger. On the trip, Ollinger, who had been a Murphy-Dolan henchman during the Lincoln County War, made no secret of his hatred for the Kid. Once the Kid was locked up in the old courthouse in Lincoln, Ollinger kept prodding Billy with the butt of his shotgun whenever the Kid had to go to the washroom, saying: "I can save you from the hangman, Kid. Just make a run for it...I'd love to put a load of buckshot in your back...give it to you the way you gave it to Sheriff Brady!"

Billy said nothing, only took the punishment, biding his time. Bell, on several occasions, told Olliger to stop persecuting the Kid. His kindness toward Billy caused the Kid to become friendly with the deputy but this was only an act. He was determined to escape and he would kill anyone who got in his way, including the gentle deputy. On Apr. 28, 1881, Billy asked Bell to help him to the latrine which was down the stairs and in back of the courthouse. As he was hobbling in leg chains toward the stairs en route to the outhouse, the Kid knocked Bell down with his shoulder and hopped quickly into Garrett's gun room which was only a few feet away, grabbing a pistol. Bell came running into the room and saw the gun in the Kid's hands, pleading with him to put it down. "Sorry, Bell," said the Kid and shot the deputy dead. He then hobbled over to the outside second-story balcony with a loaded shotgun and waited for Bob Ollinger whom he knew would come running at the sound of the shot that killed Bell.

Ollinger, who had been drinking in a nearby saloon, soon appeared, running toward the court house. "Hello, Bob," a friendly voice called out, and Ollinger looked up to see Billy on the balcony, a shotgun aimed straight at his head. Juggling the weapon and the heavy manacles about his wrists, the Kid pulled back both hammers of the shotgun as Ollinger stood petrified in the middle of the street. Billy let loose both barrels at the hated Ollinger and the lawman was blown twenty feet into the ruts of the road, his head almost blown away. The Kid hobbled down the stairs and

stopped a handyman, ordering him to get an ax. Then the handyman was ordered to chop off the manacles from the Kid's ankles and wrists, which he did. Billy gathered several pistols, a Winchester, and the shotgun, went to the street and mounted a horse tethered to a hitching post outside the courtroom. He rode up to the spot where Ollinger's body lay and dropped the shotgun next to it. To startled witnesses gaping at him, Billy the Kid, ever the limelighter, swept off his wide hat and waved it, shouting: "Adios, amigos!" Then he galloped out of town as the news of his spectacular escape was flashed across the country.

Such daring caused local residents to believe that Billy the Kid, who escaped the noose two weeks before his scheduled execution, would never be brought to justice. Garrett vowed he would get the Kid and spent three months tracking him all over New Mexico. Finally, on the night of July 14, 1881, he rode onto the old Maxwell ranch where he and the Kid had worked and spent many happy hours together. The Kid was visiting a young Mexican woman at the ranch and stepped out of a bedroom, into the moonlight, when he heard the hoofbeats of horses outside. Garrett, meanwhile, had entered the large ranch house, gone down a corridor and entered the darkened bedroom. The Kid stood outside in the shadows, calling in a loud whisper in Spanish: "Quien es?...Quien es?...Quien es?" (Who is it?) When no one answered, the Kid stepped back through the outside door to the bedroom, he turned to see his old friend Garrett holding a gun on him. The Kid was armed, according to Garrett's later report: "He came there (into the bedroom) armed with a pistol and a knife expressly to kill me if he could. I had no alternative but to kill him or suffer death at his hands." Two shots rang out and Billy the Kid, living legend, fell to the bedroom floor dead. Garrett's first shot struck the outlaw in the heart and killed him instantly, the second shot going wild.

Possemen who had accompanied Garrett to the ranch and who nervously waited in the shadows outside were shocked to see Garrett suddenly dash outside, yelling triumphantly: "I killed the Kid! I killed the Kid!" He stood outside the ranch house for some time, trembling and saying nothing. Then he went back into the bedroom where Deluvina Maxwell, the pretty woman the Kid had come to see, held the lifeless body of the killer boy in her arms. She looked up at Garrett, accusing the lawman of shooting her lover in the back, adding with a sneer: "You didn't have the nerve to kill him face to face."

As with most of the Kid's story, his death remained a subject of heated controversy for decades and still causes endless debate. Did Garrett, one time friend of the outlaw, murder the youthful gunman when his back was turned? Was Billy armed? It did not matter in 1881. Garrett was praised, for the most part, as a hero, even though murder charges were brought against him. He was acquitted by a coroner's jury who ruled the shooting of Billy the Kid "justifiable homicide." The $500 reward was not paid to Garrett for some time. In fact, a special act by the territorial legislature had to be passed before Garrett collected the reward. Billy the Kid, who died four months before his twenty-second birthday, was first buried at the Maxwell ranch in clothes that were too large for his slender body. Deluvina Maxwell placed a cross over his grave with a marker stating "Duerme bien, Querido." (Sleep well, beloved.)

Souvenir hunters, however, soon arrived and the grave was despoiled many times until the body was removed to the common grave at Fort Sumner where Billy the Kid was buried with his two best friends, Tom O'Folliard and Charlie Bowdre, who had died for their outlaw chief. The stone over this grave bore the names of its three occupants and the word "Pals." Garrett went on to fame but little reward. He had a small ranch and employee problems. On Feb. 28, 1908, he was shot to death by an angry tenant rancher who felt Garrett had cheated him out of wages. Of the two, Billy the Kid's name became the most remembered and attached to it is a strange lore that has somehow overshadowed the true nature of this ruthless killer, one that will not admit to his cold-blooded murders, his total disregard for humanity, his utter lack of mercy. In this twisted legend of the Old West, the Kid's victims are not human beings but notches on a gun, twenty-one of them. See: **Bell, J.W.; Garrett, Patrick Floyd; Lincoln County War.**

Bisbee, Ariz., 1917, U.S., abduc. IWW (Industrial Workers of the World, known as the Wobblies) workers struck the enormous copper mining company, Phelps-Dodge Copper, in Bisbee, Ariz., in 1917. Management refused to negotiate and secretly organized a 1,000-man posse under the command of Sheriff Harry Wheeler. More than 2,000 workers were seized in a midnight raid and herded into waiting cattle cars, which were locked and then shipped across the state line into New Mexico. This proved to be the largest *en masse* abduction in U.S. history, one which effectively broke the back of the IWW in Arizona. Phelps-Dodge was so influential that no legal suits against the firm for this abduction were permitted by local courts.

Bitter Creek, See: **Newcomb, George.**

Black, Isaac (Ike), d.1895, U.S., outlaw. Ike Black was a native of Kansas who drifted to Oklahoma when in his teens and there became a cowboy and, later, a cattle rustler. He became a member of the notorious Doolin Gang in the early 1890s and later joined Zip Wyatt (Dick Yeager) in committing several holdups. On Aug. 1, 1895, Black, Wyatt, and others rode into a posse trap near Skelerton Creek, outside of Sheridan, Okla. The posse, headed by U.S. Marshal W.D. Fossett and Sheriff Bill Banks, opened fire when the outlaws refused to surrender and shot Black from his saddle. He was dead by the time the lawmen reached him. Wyatt was wounded but managed to escape; he was later captured. One of the members of the posse, the son of lawman Fossett, had gone to grade school with Black and he spent considerable time worrying about whether or not his bullets were the ones who killed his boyhood friend. Black's corpse was taken to Canton, Okla., where it was put on display; the morbidly curious paid a dime each to see the dead outlaw stretched out on a wooden plank. See: **Wyatt, Nathaniel Ellsworth.**

Black Bart (Charles E. Boles, AKA: **Charles E. Bolton; T.Z. Spalding**), 1832-c.1917, U.S., outlaw. One of the most unusual stagecoach robbers in American history was an old man known in the annals of the West as Black Bart. He used many aliases, including Charles E. Bolton and Charles E. Boles, the latter, most probably his true name. Bart, in addition to being an expert lone bandit who robbed more than two dozen stages in California in 1877-78, exercised a sardonic brand of humor in the form of doggerel scratched on foolscap and left in the empty strongboxes he looted. He was frivolous and capricious, a jokester whose laughing nature endeared him even to his victims.

Bart first struck on a mountain pass called Funk Hill, four miles outside of Copperopolis, Calif., on July 26, 1875. The driver of the Wells Fargo stage, John Shine (later a U.S. marshal and a California state senator), brought up his team short, startled at the strange apparition before him. Bart wore a long, white duster over his clothes, and over his head was a flour sack with holes that had been cut for the eyes. A deep voice commanded: "Throw down the box!" The driver reached beneath his seat and withdrew the Wells Fargo strongbox containing several thousand dollars. He tossed down the wooden box, reinforced with iron bands, which was padlocked. Bart grabbed the box and slipped into a nearby woods. Shine drove off some distance and then stopped the stage, walking back down the road to see a half dozen guns leveled at him from outlaws positioned behind boulders. He stood rock still and then realized the outlaws were not moving. Shine approached one, and then another boulder, to discover dummies with sticks for guns pointed at him. (Bart accomplished his robberies by pretending to have a large gang positioned behind several large boulders, and when he first stopped the stage, he would call out to his imaginary gang: "If he dares to shoot, give him a solid volley, boys!")

The lone bandit continued to stop Wells Fargo stages with alacrity, always along mountain roads where the driver was compelled to slow down at dangerous curves. (It was later estimated that Bart robbed as much as $18,000 from Wells Fargo stages over the course of four years, striking twenty-nine times.) He left no clues whatsoever, although

The infamous stagecoach robber Black Bart.

he did leave a spare gun after one robbery, and he was always extremely courteous to passengers, especially women travelers, refusing to take their jewelry and cash, telling them: "I don't want your money, only Wells Fargo boxes." He made a favorable impression on drivers and passengers alike as a courteous, gentlemanly robber who apparently wanted to avoid a gunfight at all costs. On Aug. 3, 1877, the lone bandit, again appearing in his duster and flour sack, stopped the Arena stagecoach, en route to Duncan's Mill on the Russian River. He took the strongbox and its contents of $300 in cash and a check for a similar amount.

Some days later a posse found the empty box, and inside of it was a note reading:

> I've labored long and hard for bread,
> For honor and for riches
> But on my corns too long you've tred,
> You fine-haired sons-of-bitches.

The stage robber had signed the note with a name that would go down in Western history: "Black Bart, PO-8." The letters and number mystified lawmen as much as the name Black Bart. Tracking posses found no trace of the elusive bandit, and superstition had it that the stage indeed had been robbed by a ghost. For a year the robber was not to be seen. Then, on July 26, 1878, Bart held up another Wells Fargo stage, one traveling between Quincy and Oroville, Calif. Again, he wore the same weird outfit, the long flowing duster and the flour sack, and again, his voice, described as "hollow and deep," ordered the driver to "throw down the box!" This time Bart made off with

$379. He also helped himself to a passenger's $200 diamond ring and a gold watch worth $25.

Once more, pursuing lawmen found the empty strongbox with another note which stated:

> Here I lay me down to sleep
> To wait the coming morrow,
> Perhaps success, perhaps defeat
> And everlasting sorrow.
> Yet come what will, I'll try it once,
> My conditions can't be worse,
> And if there's money in that box,
> 'Tis money in my purse.

Again there were no clues to follow. The bandit seemed to have vanished into thin air. Bart himself was responsible for a trail that led nowhere. Wells Fargo drivers noticed that when he stopped a stage, he wore large socks over his boots so that he would leave no heel marks in the dirt to be followed. Moreover, he never used a horse but slipped into the wilderness on foot and thus left no trail of horse tracks. Bart, it was later discovered, was an excellent hiker and outdoorsman who traveled great distances on foot, camping out for weeks to get to and from his robbery sites which he scouted carefully. He used a shotgun most times in his robberies, but not once in all of his many robberies did he ever fire it. As it turned out, he could not have fired the weapon since he never loaded it, or at least that is what he told arresting officers later.

Bart was not a rampant pillager of Wells Fargo. He only robbed stages periodically, sometimes with as much as nine months' time between robberies, and he later stated that he "took only what was needed when it was needed." Most stagecoach drivers were submissive to Bart, seldom defying him with a cross word and obediently tossing down the strongbox when ordered to do so. This was not the case with hardcase George W. Hackett who, on July 13, 1882, was driving a Wells Fargo stage some nine miles outside of Strawberry, Calif. Bart suddenly darted from a boulder and stood in front of the stage, stopping it and leveling a shotgun at Hackett. He politely said: "Please throw down your strongbox." Hackett was not pleased to do so; he reached for a rifle and fired a shot at the bandit. Bart dashed into the woods and vanished, but he received a scalp wound that would leave a permanent scar on the top right side of his forehead.

Robberies became increasingly difficult for Bart, and his last, on Nov. 3, 1883, almost spelled his doom. He stopped another Wells Fargo stage on that day, almost in the exact spot where he robbed the first stagecoach in 1875. A lone rider following the stage, Jimmy Rolleri, fired a shot at Bart as he was dragging the strongbox into the underbrush, and wounded him in the hand. Bart used his handkerchief to wrap around the wound; this was later found with a San Francisco laundry mark on it. The men assigned to track down Black Bart were two shrewd, tough detectives, James B. Hume and Henry Nicholson Morse, one-time sheriff of Alameda County. Harry Morse realized that there were ninety-one laundries in San Francisco, but he set out to visit each one of them and, at Ferguson & Bigg's California Laundry, his search was rewarded with an identity, that of Charles E. Bolton, a mining engineer. Morse and Hume, accompanied by local police, arrested Bolton-Bart in his hotel. He would not admit to being the bandit, and denied that his name was either Charles E. Bolton, the name under which he had been living in San Francisco for years, or his supposedly given name, Charles E. Boles. When booked, he gave his name as T. Z. Spalding.

Found in Bart's hotel room was a Bible which had been given to him by his wife in 1865. It bore the name of Charles E. Boles. He was born and raised in upper New York State and had been a farmer, until he married and moved to Illinois just before the Civil War. He served as a sergeant in 116th Illinois Volunteer Infantry. When his family members died, he moved to California to seek his fortune. He had tried a number of jobs and even tried panning for gold before he turned to stagecoach robbing. With his loot, he had invested in several small businesses which brought him a modest income, but he could not resist the urge to go back to robbing stages when money became short. After days of denying he was the famous Black Bart, the bandit finally admitted that he had committed several robberies of which he stood accused, but only those occurring before 1879—mistakenly believing that the statute of limitations would protect him against prosecution. Bart was convicted and given a six-year prison sentence in San Quentin Prison, arriving there on Nov. 21, 1883.

Bart served about four years and was released on Jan. 21, 1888. By then he had aged considerably, with one ear gone deaf, his eyesight failing, his shoulders stooped, and his hair whitened. His spirit was crushed, and he sought only to escape the newsmen surrounding him when he stepped from the prison gates. He disappeared and was later thought to have returned to his bandit ways, especially since another Wells Fargo stage was robbed on Nov. 14, 1888. The lone bandit left another bit of doggerel that read:

> So here I've stood while wind and rain
> Have set the trees a'sobbin'
> And risked my life for that damned stage
> That wasn't worth the robbin'.

Detective Hume examined the note and compared it with the genuine Black Bart bits of poetry of the past. He declared the new verse a hoax and the work of another man, declaring that he was certain Black Bart had permanently retired. This gave rise to the later notion that Wells Fargo had actually pensioned off the robber on his promise that he would stop no more of its stages, paying him a handsome annuity until his death, which was reported in New York newspapers as being sometime in 1917, although this was never officially confirmed. The last time Detective Jim Hume heard of Black Bart's whereabouts was sometime in 1900, when he received a report that the old man had died in the high California mountains while hunting game. This rather pedestrian end was unacceptable to those who bore the legend of Black Bart into the next century. Writers and reporters had the outlaw living in a hundred different places and robbing stages until Wells Fargo decided to close its last stage routes. Today the legend and reality of Black Bart are almost impossible to separate, which is undoubtedly the way the bandit would have wanted it.

Blackburn, Duncan (AKA: **Tom Blackburn**), prom. 1870s, U.S., outlaw. Duncan Blackburn was a stagecoach robber who operated around Deadwood, Dakota Territory. He often rode with another outlaw, Jim Wall. Blackburn's activities ceased in 1877 when Boone May, a fierce stagecoach guard, became famous for killing four bandits who had been plaguing the very stage line Blackburn and others had preyed upon. Little is known about this outlaw except a host of rumors. One has it that he had an affair with Calamity Jane who bore him a son and, after serving a long prison term, Blackburn returned to his native Baltimore with this boy, settling down and becoming a prominent businessman.

Black Face Charlie: See: Bryant, Charles.

Blackwell, Okla., Shoot-out, 1896, U.S. A well-intentioned posse sometimes fell short of the mark, evidenced by the deadly shoot-out at Bert Benjamin's ranch outside of Blackwell, Okla., on Dec. 4, 1896. In the early dawn hours a heavily armed six-man posse surrounded a wooden shack where a gang of bank robbers were believed to be holed up. As the sun appeared on the horizon, Deputy Sheriff Alfred Lund called to the occupants of the cabin: "Throw up your hands!" The men inside answered with a burst of gunfire. As the first shots were fired three of the possemen turned tail and ran. Lund stood up to the robbers, killing one of them, who was later identified as a petty thief named Buck McGregg. He wounded a second bandit, Ben Cravens, a rustler and murderer, who was taken into custody but later escaped. The third casualty turned out to be a cow belonging to Bert Benjamin, which caused the residents of Blackwell considerable amusement.

Lund examined the dead man and foolishly concluded that he had bagged himself a real prize: "Dynamite" Dick Clifton, who was wanted for bank robbery and had a $3,500 reward on his head. The dead man (McGregg) was missing three fingers—just like Clifton. McGregg was only a small-time thief, and his death was hardly cause for celebration. The local gazette took solace in the fact that the surrounding notoriety had caused "a marked advance in the local real estate market." See: **Clifton, Daniel; Cravens, Ben.**

Blake, John (AKA: **Tulsa Jack**), d.1895, U.S., outlaw. A Kansas cowboy during the late 1880s, John Blake moved south to the Oklahoma Territory where he met Bill Doolin and joined his gang, becoming one of Doolin's most loyal and stouthearted followers. He participated in many bank robberies and train robberies committed by the Doolin gang at Perry, Okla., and other places. At the wild gun battle between the Doolin band and lawmen at Ingalls, Okla., on Sept. 1, 1893, Blake shot his way through barricades from a hotel to the stable where the gang's horses were kept, freeing the animals and leading them back to gang members who, along with Blake, mounted them and made good their escape, leaving only gang member Roy Daugherty (Arkansas Tom) who was trapped in a second-story hotel room.

The Doolin gang continued its robbing spree and, on May 20, 1894, the gang robbed the bank in Southwest City, Mo., where Bill Dalton, the only member of the Dalton gang to ride with the Doolins, shot J.C. Seaborn, former state auditor and one of the leading citizens of the state. Seaborn, along with dozens of other citizens, joined the local lawmen in harassing the gang as it attempted to make its escape. Blake was one of these and it was later claimed that his deadly marksmanship was responsible for wounding several vigilantes firing at the gang while it thundered down the main street of town. Blake, the most

Tulsa Jack Blake, shown in death.

daring of the gang, was the last man out of town, covering the retreat. Though hundreds of shots were fired at him, he miraculously escaped injury.

This was not the case following the gang's robbery of a Rock Island train near Dover, Okla. The Doolin band rode to their hideout on the Cimarron River and encamped. In the early morning of May 5, 1895, a large posse led by the redoubtable lawman Chris Madsen came upon the Doolins as they were asleep in their camp. Tulsa Jack Blake was on guard at the time and, spotting Deputy William Banks sneaking up on the sleeping forms of his fellow bandits, pulled his six-gun and fired at the lawman. The bandits leaped to their feet and a roaring gun battle ensued. Blake continued to exchange shots with deputy Banks and one of Banks' shots struck his cartridge belt, exploding a shell that tore into Blake's stomach, causing a mortal wound. Tulsa Jack died as Bill Doolin and the others leapt into their saddles and splashed across the Cimarron to make their thunderous escape. See: **Clifton, Daniel; Dalton Brothers; Daugherty, Roy; Doolin, William; Newcomb, George; Pierce, Charles; Raidler, William; Weightman, George; West, Richard.**

Blevins Family, prom. 1880s, U.S., outlaws. The Blevins family, five brothers, assorted cousins and nephews, were deeply involved in the Arizona range war of the 1880s called the Graham-Tewksbury Feud. All were ranchers located in Pleasant Valley, but most of the clan members doubled as hired gunmen, and some of them were dedicated killers like Andy Blevins, who was also known as Andy Cooper. Andy Blevins was a rustler and killer who hired out to the Graham cattlemen who were battling the sheep herders headed by the Tewksburys. On Sept. 2, 1887, Andy Blevins led some of his brothers and other cattlemen on a night ambush of the Tewksbury sheep camp, shooting clan leaders John Tewksbury and Bill Jacobs in cold blood as the sheepmen went to check on their horses. Mrs. Tewksbury raced from the house to go to her fallen husband, but Andy Blevins fired several shots driving her off. The sheepmen then came under siege from the Blevins faction and later slipped away under cover of darkness. Andy Blevins was so infuriated about the other sheepmen eluding him that he let some hogs eat the bodies of Tewksbury and Jacobs.

Sheriff Perry Owens, one of the deadliest shots in the West, then gathered a posse and rode out to the Blevins ranch near Holbrook on Sept. 4, 1887. He advanced on the ranch house with a rifle in his hand, apparently intending to serve warrants on Andy Blevins for the murder of Tewksbury and Jacobs. At that moment, Andy Blevins fired at

Owens from behind the front door of the ranch house but his shot was wild. Owns fired a rifle shot that smashed into Blevins' chest and sent him reeling backward into the arms of his mother. Then John Blevins, the oldest brother, stepped to the door and fired at Owens; the lawmen's responding fire brought him down, too. Mose Roberts, a brother-in-law of the Blevins, then raced outside, firing at Owens, but Owens killed him with a single, mortal shot. Next, 16-year-old Sam Houston Blevins charged toward Owens with a blazing sixgun, but the sheriff fired one shot, killing the boy. Only John Blevins survived this gunfight.

Another brother, Charles Blevins, was shot to death in front of Perkins Store in Holbrook on Sept. 27, 1887, when he opened fire on Sheriff William Mulveron who returned fire and killed him. Hampton Blevins had already been killed on Aug. 10, 1887, in another shootout at the Middleton ranch. Except for John Blevins, the Blevins family members were decimated in the bloody Graham-Tewksbury Feud. John Blevins later became a lawman and helped chase the Apache Kid in 1889 after the Kid had murdered Sheriff Glenn Reynolds. See: **Apache Kid, The; Graham-Tewksbury Feud.**

Outlaw Blue Duck, with wife Belle Starr.

Blue Duck, prom. 1880s, U.S., outlaw. Blue Duck was a half-breed lover of Belle Starr's who was under a sentence of death for having murdered a farmer in the Indian Nations in 1886. Scheduled to die on July 23, 1886, at Fort Smith, Blue Duck was saved through the actions of his common-law wife, Belle Starr, who hired a lawyer. The lawyer managed to get Blue Duck several reprieves and later a commutation to life imprisonment at the federal penitentiary in Menard, Ill. Blue Duck was later paroled, but by then Belle Starr, a horsethief, had been shot and killed. See: **Starr, Belle.**

Blumner, Charles (AKA: **Carlos**), prom. 1853-57, U.S., lawman. Charles Blumner signed his business correspondence "Carlos" in an apparent attempt to build good relations with the Hispanic population, where he was appointed to serve as marshal of the New Mexico Territory on Dec. 10, 1853. Blumner had occupied the treasurer's office—a position he would again take over after resigning his post four years later.

Blumner, much like his predecessors, was required by law to open each session of the federal court. It was estimated that a complete circuit through the New Mexico Territory required eight weeks of travel over 1,000 miles of terrain. Blumner's good work in enforcing the customs cases in West Texas and New Mexico, and his tireless efforts on behalf of the local population earned him great praise. When he stepped down in 1857, he was awarded with a silver pipe for his many contributions to federal law enforcement in the region.

Bogles, Gus, d.1888, U.S., outlaw. Gus Bogles was one of the most ornery, unrepentant prisoners ever to occupy a jail cell at Fort Smith (Ark.). During his incarceration he would howl like a crazed animal, for no other reason than to annoy his fellow prisoners. Bogles was arrested in Denison, Texas, for the June 27, 1887, murder of J.D. Morgan, a railroad official who worked at the McAlester station. He confessed to having wrapped a strap around Morgan's neck and pistol whipping him to death after being put off a train for not having a ticket. Morgan's body was found the next day near the station house; he had been stripped of his coat, hat, shoes, and trousers.

During his trial, before Judge Isaac Parker at Fort Smith, Bogles swore that he had never set eyes on Morgan in his life, and claimed that the marshals had coerced a false confession out of him by torture. Parker scolded Bogles for what was obviously a lie. "In your efforts to escape the consequences, you have added to your crime that of perjury," Parker said. "This, of course, is not to be wondered at...it is expecting too much of wicked and depraved human nature for us to look for truth from one who has stained his hands with innocent human blood." Bogles was convicted, and hanged at Fort Smith on July 6, 1888.

Bojorques, Narciso, and **Chevez, Cleovara**, and **Garcia, Antonio**, and **Ponce, Noratto**, and **Soto, Juan**, and **Vasquez, Tiburcio**, prom. 1860-75, U.S., outlaws. Bojorques and his companions were the ringleaders of a gang of Mexican desperados who terrorized the southern portion of California in the 1860s and 1870s. The murderous Bojorques rode north to Alameda in 1863 where he shot down a husband and wife named Golding, and their young child, before setting fire to their ranch house. In 1865 Sheriff Harry Morse engaged Narciso Bojorques in a shootout near San Jose where the bandit was badly wounded. He escaped, but was cornered in Copperopolis, and killed by a western outlaw named One-Eyed Jack.

Boles, Charles E., See: **Black Bart.**

Bolton, Charles E., See: **Black Bart.**

Bonney, William, See: **Billy the Kid.**

Border Boss, See: **Hughes, John Reynolds.**

Bowdre, Charles, See: **Billy the Kid.**

Boyce, Reuben H. (AKA: **Rube**), d.1927, U.S., gunman. According to stories told by retired Texas Rangers, Reuben Boyce headed a group of cutthroat rustlers and thieves nicknamed the "Pegleg stage robbers." Boyce was arrested by Ranger Dan Roberts, who jailed him in Austin, Texas. However the Kimble County outlaw managed to escape with the help of a gun smuggled into his cell with his laundry. Boyce was arrested a second time by Ranger Charles Nevill and five other lawmen on a charge

of murdering his brother-in-law. He was turned over to the sheriff of Kimble County, but again the clever Boyce managed to escape his jailers.

Recaptured at Socorro, N.M., Boyce was returned to Austin where he was at last put on trial for his misdeeds. The court believed him when he said he was not a member of the Pegleg Gang. However, a list of fugitives published in Brown County in 1900 included the name of Reuben Boyce. The description of the man with the gimpy leg seemed to match Boyce, who in later years liked to boast that he was a member in good standing of the Texas Rangers. This assertion was vigorously denied by veteran Rangers who maintained that Boyce was always on the wrong side of the law.

Brann, William Cowper, 1855-98, U.S., gunman. William Cowper Brann was a frontier journalist whose invective and vituperation appearing in the newspapers and magazines he published caused him to be repeatedly attacked and finally killed in a Texas gunfight. Born Jan. 5, 1855, in Cole County, Ill., Brann became a newspaperman early in life and moved with his family in 1886 to Texas where he worked for the Galveston *Tribune*. He later worked on the Houston *Post* with such literary luminaries as O. Henry and M.E. Foster. Brann specialized in stinging, biting editorials which earned him myriad enemies. He started a magazine in Austin, Texas, in 1892 which he called *The Iconoclast*. He sold the magazine and later started it again in Waco, Texas, where his enemies beat him up many times and even wrecked his press. Yet, this outspoken journalist, whose motto was to attack "injustice, intolerance, and stupidity," saw *The Iconoclast* rise in circulation until it had more than 100,000 national subscribers. Brann dipped his pen once too often in acid and T.E. Davis, one of his most bitter enemies, read an editorial that caused him to seek out Brann on the streets of Waco on Apr. 1, 1898. The editor, who also wore a gun and had been in many close brushes, met Davis on the street. Davis, a lightning draw, pulled his pistol and shot Brann in the side. Brann, whirling, yanked his six-gun from its holster and fired off four shots, all of which struck Davis and killed him instantly. Brann died a short time later.

Brazzleton, William, d.1878, U.S., outlaw. The Arizona Territory was a lawless, untamed wilderness in the late 1870s, populated by stagecoach robbers, highwaymen, and tinhorn gamblers. Successive U.S. marshals proved inept at curbing the steady and overwhelming stream of desperados that entered the territory from Mexico and points east. One of the vicious outlaws who came to the attention of the local authorities during this time was William Brazzleton. By the time he was fifteen, he had already killed his first man. In 1876, he entered the territory from California as the proprietor of a traveling show. Brazzleton mastered the art of clever disguises through his stage work. In 1878, he committed a series of stagecoach robberies in the territory, but was killed in August of that year after being betrayed by one of his comrades. The *Arizona Citizen* reported that he looked dangerous even in death.

Breakenridge, William Milton (Billy), 1846-1931, U.S., lawman. Born in Watertown, Wis., William Milton Breakenridge sold newspapers as a boy and ran away from home to join the Union army during the Civil War. Following the war, Breakenridge sought fame and fortune by moving west where he held a variety of jobs in Denver and then became a page boy in the Colorado legislature. He next enlisted in the Third Colorado Cavalry under Colonel Chivington and participated in the Sand Creek Massacre. After leaving the cavalry, Breakenridge became a train brakeman, then a storekeeper in Sidney, Neb. After wandering about the West, Breakenridge became a deputy sheriff in Phoenix, Ariz., in 1878. He later moved to Tombstone, Ariz., where he hauled lumber, then became a deputy sheriff, working for his close friend, Sheriff John Behan. On May 25, 1881, Breakenridge entered a saloon in Galeyville, Ariz., and was immediately confronted by two of the toughest gunmen and rustlers in the area, William "Curly Bill" Brocius and Jim Wallace, a hardcase gunman who had participated in the Lincoln County war. Wallace, after spotting the star on Breakenridge's vest, drew his gun and challenged him to a duel. The lawman laughed off Wallace's insults and asked everyone to join him in a drink. Brocius, admiring Breakenridge's courage, talked Wallace out of gunfighting, but when the lawman began to leave, Brocius, by then drunk, tried to pick a fight with Breakenridge.

Ignoring Curly Bill's antagonizing remarks, Breakenridge walked to his horse, but Brocius followed him and mounted his horse. Curly Bill began to shout insults at the lawman and finally, Breakenridge had had enough. He pulled his gun and fired a shot that struck Curly Bill in the neck, the bullet emerging out of his right cheek, knocking out a tooth. Brocius recovered from this ugly wound but was so unnerved by the incident that he reportedly took off his guns forever and left Arizona, a claim much contested by Wyatt Earp. In 1882, Breakenridge, John C. Gillespie, and two other lawmen named Allen and Young tracked down two

outlaws, Billy Grounds (real name Boucher) and Zwing Hunt, who had committed a robbery in Charleston, a small town near Tombstone.

Breakenridge and his men located the outlaws at the Stockton ranch about ten miles from Tombstone. They rode up quietly, hid their horses, then surrounded the small cabin. Then, inexplicably, Gillespie marched toward the front door of the cabin, demanding that Grounds and Hunt surrender. The outlaws threw open the front door and fired, killing Gillespie on the spot. Next a ranch hand named Lewis came dashing from the cabin, screaming that he was innocent, but the outlaws shot him in the back. Then Allen and Young were both wounded from the withering gunfire by the outlaws. Breakenridge, alone, aimed a shotgun directly at the open door and, as soon as he saw movement inside, he let loose a blast that caught Grounds in the face, sending him to the floor. He died of this wound a short

Legendary lawman Billy Breakenridge, who penned a famous book on the Old West.

time later. Hunt raced out the back door but Breakenridge and the injured Allen fired at him and a bullet struck his back, knocking him down. Hunt got up and began running once more but the lawmen later found him sprawled unconscious. He was taken to jail but later escaped and disappeared. Some reports had it that Hunt was killed by Indians or went to Texas where he changed his name and lived to a ripe old age.

In 1883, Breakenridge quit his deputy sheriff's position and turned to ranching, but when this failed he went back to law enforcement, becoming a U.S. marshal. He was involved in many dramatic shoot-outs and was also involved in the notorious Wham case in 1889. Major Joseph Wham, U.S. Army paymaster, and a large contingent of soldiers were ambushed near Fort Thomas by thirteen outlaws who wounded eight troopers and drove off the rest of the soldiers before scooping up a payroll of $29,000. Breakenridge and other officers rounded up many suspects who were later charged with the sensational robbery, most of these being Mormons with strong political connections. The accused men were defended by Marcus Aurelius Smith, one of the most effective and successful lawyers and politicians in the territory, and when Major Wham and his men failed to identify any of the defendants in court, they were all acquitted. Breakenridge later claimed that political pressure allowed the robbers to go free.

Breakenridge was elected surveyor of Maricopa County in 1888, and he later became a special investigator for the Southern Pacific Railroad, performing guard duty and conducting detective work, retiring in 1918 at age seventy-two. Ten years after retiring, in 1928, Breakenridge published his famous book of the Old West, *Helldorado,* which made him rich and even more famous than when he hunted outlaws along dusty Arizona trails. He died at age eighty-five of a heart attack on Jan. 31, 1931, in Tucson. See: **Behan, John; Brocius, Curly Bill; Earp, Wyatt.**

Brewer, Richard M., 1852-78, U.S., lawman-gunman. Born in St. Alban's Vt., Richard M. Brewer moved with his family in 1860 to Wisconsin, and at age eighteen he left home and headed west. He moved to Lincoln County, N.M., and became a rancher, breeding horses. Brewer befriended his neighbor, John Tunstall, and later became Tunstall's foreman, keeping his horses with Tunstall's. In September 1877, several of Brewer's prized horses and a pair of mules were rustled by Jesse Evans, Frank Baker, Tom Hill, and others. Brewer, who had received a deputy sheriff's commission, raised a fifteen-man posse to track down the thieves. Evans, Baker, and the others were found hiding in a dugout and were ordered to surrender. When they refused, Brewer told them that they would all be killed if they continued to fight. The outlaws surrendered and were taken to Lincoln, N.M., where they were placed in a deep hole in the ground, the town having a jail too small to hold them for trial. Some days later, thirty-two men working for rival ranchers L.G. Murphy and James J. Dolan, rode into Lincoln and freed the outlaws.

The Murphy-Dolan faction and the McSween-Tunstall combine then squared off in what later became the infamous Lincoln County War. After Tunstall was murdered, Brewer organized a band of "regulators," deputizing Billy the Kid, Frank McNab, Charlie Bowdre, John Middleton, Henry Brown, Josiah "Doc" Scurlock, and others, and sought out Tunstall's killers. Brewer and his men captured and later murdered two of the killers, Billy Morton and Frank Baker in March 1878. On Apr. 4, 1878, Brewer and his men encountered an ally of the Murphy-Dolan faction, Andrew L. "Buckshot" Roberts, at Blazer's Mill, N.M. Bowdre pulled his gun and ordered Roberts to surrender. The tough Roberts sneered and roared: "Not much, Mary Ann!" Bowdre then shot Roberts in the stomach but the tough westerner began firing his Winchester, retreating into an outhouse, wounding Middleton and George Coe in the process.

Brewer raced forward to a pile of logs in front of the outhouse and began firing into the small structure. Inside, Roberts had found a Sharps .50-caliber buffalo gun and he carefully propped this heavy gun on a log, aiming through a knothole. Brewer let loose another barrage, then ducked. When he poked his head above the wood pile, Roberts fired a roaring blast from the buffalo gun which tore off the top of Brewer's head. Roberts yelled in triumph: "I killed the s.o.b.! I killed him!" With that, Billy the Kid and the others riddled the outhouse with dozens of bullets and then retreated, taking their wounded with them and leaving the dead Brewer. After the gunsmoke cleared, the owner of the place, Dr. Emil Blazer, cautiously opened the outhouse door to see that Roberts was dead, shot full of holes. He buried Brewer and Roberts side by side on his property. See: **Billy the Kid; Lincoln County War; McNab, Frank; Middleton, John; Scurlock, Josiah.**

Briant, Elijah S. (AKA: **Lige**), 1854-1932, U.S., lawman-jur. Elijah S. Briant was a druggist who also served as the sheriff of Sonora, Texas. Briant, a mild-mannered, tall, lean man with light brown hair and a penetrating stare, was described by one of his contemporaries as "absolutely fearless" when facing outlaws who invaded his town. This was evident on the night of Apr. 2, 1901, when a youth ran into his drugstore and told him that "suspicious strangers" were in the town's bakery, and they looked as if they intended to rob the store. Briant collected two deputies and the town constable and marched into the bakery where two rough-looking gunmen faced him. Briant asked the men to identify themselves and both went for their guns. In a wild shootout, both outlaws were riddled and the lawmen escaped injury. During this fight, Briant cooly drew his weapon and fired three bullets into each man, as the men also emptied their weapons into the gunmen who fired wildly at the lawmen. Killed, with seven bullets in his body was Will Carver, infamous member of Butch Cassidy's Wild Bunch. Wounded, with fourteen bullets in him, was George Kilpatrick, brother of the notorious Ben Kilpatrick, the Tall Texan, and one of Butch Cassidy's closest lieutenants.

Briant's nerveless gunfight with Carver and Kilpatrick earned him a large slice in western folklore. He later became a county judge and then retired to San Angelo where he died on Dec. 22, 1932, at age seventy-eight. See: **Carver, William; Cassidy, Butch; Kilpatrick, Benjamin; Wild Bunch, The.**

Bridges, Jack L., b.1838, U.S., lawman. A peace officer in Kansas City for fifteen years, Jack L. Bridges was made a deputy U.S. marshal in 1869, working in Hays City, Kan., and later in Wichita. The most serious gunfight in which Bridges was involved occurred in Wichita on Feb. 28, 1871, when he attempted to arrest infamous horse thief, J.E. Ledford. Bridges, accompanied by twenty-five soldiers, went to arrest Ledford who owned the Harris House Hotel. At the hotel, Bridges was told that Ledford was not on the premises. Bridges harbored deep resentment against Ledford who had pistol-whipped him some months earlier in an argument, and he had vowed to "get even" with the horse thief. Ledford, knowing this, realized that his life was in the balance when Bridges sought him out on the horse thieving charge. When Bridges could not locate Ledford at his hotel, he then scouted the area and saw a man run into an outhouse behind the Harris House. Bridges, military scout Lew Stewart, and an officer approached the outhouse with guns in hand. Ledford then came running from the outhouse, his pistol blazing. He shot Bridges who, along with the others, emptied their guns into the fleeing horse thief. Leford was hit four times and died a few hours later. Bridges was severely wounded and he moved back to his birthplace in Maine to recuperate from the wounds. Once healed, he headed west to Colorado and finally returned to Kansas, being appointed city marshal of Dodge City where he had numerous confrontations with hardcase cowboys and gunmen, not the least of whom was Luke Short. When William Tilghman replaced Bridges as marshal of Dodge City, the ex-lawman left town and faded into oblivion.

Brocius, Curly Bill (or **Brosius**, AKA: **William Graham**), prom. 1880s, U.S., outlaw. Background on this western gunman is sketchy at best. He was six feet tall with black curly hair and blue eyes, supposedly a light-hearted cowboy who was head wrangler at the McLowery ranch. He was also portrayed as a vicious, drunken gunman who would draw his six-guns at the slightest provocation. Many murders were credited to him, including that of the Haslett Brothers in 1881 in their store at Huachita after the Hasletts reportedly shot and killed two members of the Clanton-McLowery clan. A known rustler and gunman with a fast draw, Curly Bill Brocius led members of the Clanton-McLowery rustling gang into Arizona towns to "buffalo" the citizens, taking over the saloons and racing up and down the streets on their pintos, firing weapons into the air. On Oct. 28, 1880, Brocius and other cowboys entered Tombstone and were "hurrahing" the town. Drunk, the cowboys blindly fired their six-guns. This caused Fred White, Tombstone's first marshal, to deputize Virgil Earp, Wyatt

Earp's brother, before both men went hunting for Brocius. They found him in an alley and when White tried to disarm Brocius, the gunman's pistol went off, mortally wounding White.

Almost immediately after the weapon went off, Wyatt Earp appeared and marched up to Brocius, pulled his foot-long Special from its holster and crashed it down on Brocius' head, knocking him unconscious, and then dragged him to jail. Brocius was later acquitted of White's death since White himself, with his dying breath, stated that he had been accidentally shot. Brocius' next confrontation with the law occured on May 25, 1881, when he met and began an argument with tough lawman William Breakenridge. The lawman, goaded by a drunken Brocius, finally shot his antagonist in the mouth—a terrible wound from which Brocius recovered, but one that convinced him to hang up his guns, or so it was later claimed, and leave Arizona, later settling in Texas under the name of William Graham which may or may not have been his real name. According to Wyatt Earp, Brocius was involved with the Clanton-McLowery rustling gang throughout its confrontation with the Earp Brothers, and that he tracked down and killed the outlaw some time after the gunfight at the O.K. Corral. See: **Breckenridge, William Milton; Clanton-McLowery Gang; Earp, Wyatt.**

Brock, Leonard Calvert (AKA: **Will Waldrip; Joe Jackson; Henry Davis; W.L. Brock**), 1860-90, U.S., outlaw. Leonard Calvert Brock was a member of the Burrow Brothers gang of train robbers. Born on July 13, 1860, Brock and his brother, W.L. Brock, joined the Burrow gang in 1888 and aided the notorious brothers in train robberies in Texas and Alabama. He was identified as one of the bandits accompanying the Burrow Brothers when they robbed a Mobile and Ohio train on Sept. 25, 1889. A substantial reward was posted for Brock, who was arrested on a train in Columbus, Miss., in July 1890. He was quickly convicted and given a long prison term, committing suicide on Nov. 10, 1890, by jumping from the fourth tier of the cell block of his prison. See: **Burrow, Reuben Houston.**

Brooks, James Abijah, 1855-1944, U.S., jur.-lawman. Born in Bourbon County, Ky., on Nov. 20, 1855, James Brooks moved to Collin County, Texas, in 1876 and spent some time ranching before moving to San Antonio, Texas, in 1880. Brooks joined the Texas Rangers in 1889 and served with distinction, solving widespread cattle thefts from the King Ranch in 1902 by rounding up a number of rustlers. Brooks resigned from the Rangers in 1906 and served in the state legislature. Brooks County was named after this upstanding lawman, who later became a county judge in the county named after him.

Brooks, William L. (AKA: **Buffalo Bill** or **Billy; Bully**), 1836-74, U.S., lawman-gunman-outlaw. Elected first city marshal of Newton, Kan., in 1872, William L. Brooks, a noted Buffalo hunter, also had a reputation as a fierce gunman. On June 9, 1872, Brooks stopped several cowboys from harrassing Newton residents and was wounded in the neck for his efforts, later arresting his attackers, James Hunt and Joe Miller. He moved to Ellsworth where he served briefly as a city policeman, and then he moved to Dodge City where he quarreled frequently with other cowboys and gunslingers, getting into several shootouts, the first being on Dec. 23, 1872. He argued with a Santa Fe Railroad yardmaster named Brown and both went for their

William L. "Buffalo Bill" Brooks, who was elected first city marshal of Newton, Kan.

guns. Brooks was wounded, but Brown was killed by a single shot from Brooks' six-gun. Five days later, on Dec. 28, 1872, Brooks took revenge on saloon keeper Matthew Sullivan, who had thrown him out of his establishment the night before. Brooks crept up on Sullivan, who was standing next to an open window in his saloon, poked his six-gun through the window, and fired an almost point-blank bullet into the saloon keeper, killing him instantly. Brooks was never charged with the killing.

On Mar. 4, 1873, Brooks took issue with comments made by another Buffalo hunter, Kirk Jordan. Before he could pull his six-gun, Brooks saw Jordan leveling his buffalo gun at him and dove behind two water barrels in the street. The blast from Jordan's gun exploded the barrels and almost killed Brooks who apologized to Jordan immediately and then went on his way. Brooks turned outlaw the following year and was rounded up by a posse which captured several horse thieves near Caldwell, Kan. On the night of July 28, 1874, a lynch mob broke into the Caldwell Jail and dragged out Brooks, L.B. Hasbrouck, and Charley Smith, all horse thieves. They immediately hanged the three men. Brooks struggled violently after the rope failed to break his neck. He slowly strangled to death.

Brown, Angus (AKA: **Arapaho, Red**), prom. 1892, U.S., lawman. Angus Brown was the sheriff of Buffalo, Wyo., during the notorious Johnson County war. He took the side of the homesteaders against the cattlemen. Brown moved to Wyoming from Tennessee in the 1880s and was extremely well read, said to have one of the few libraries in the territory. He was later killed by two cowboys representing the cattle barons.

Brown, Henry Newton, 1857-84, U.S., lawman-gunman-outlaw. Henry Newton Brown was orphaned at an early age and raised by relatives in Rolla, Mo., until he was seventeen when he headed west to be a cowboy. He worked on Colorado ranches and then drifted southward to Texas where he killed a cowboy in a gunfight outside a Panhandle town. Brown then moved to Lincoln County, N.M., where he became involved in the Lincoln County war, fighting on the side of the McSween-Tunstall faction. He befriended Billy the Kid and helped the Kid shoot down Sheriff William Brady on Apr. 1, 1878, in Lincoln, N.M., as he, the Kid, and others hid behind an adobe wall and fired from ambush. Brown was also with Billy the Kid and others at Blazer's Mill on Apr. 4, 1878, when Andrew L. "Buckshot" Roberts shot and killed Richard Brewer, leader of the so-called "regulators" to which Brown, the Kid, and others belonged. Roberts was also killed at this shootout, Brown helping to riddle the outhouse in which Roberts had taken cover. Brown was present at the Lincoln, N.M., siege of the McSween house in which Billy the Kid and others were trapped.

Gunman and outlaw Henry Newton Brown.

Brown and two others were in a little storehouse nearby and sniped at the Murphy-Dolan men surrounding the McSween house. He escaped with the Kid and others.

In the fall of 1878, Brown accompanied Billy the Kid and others to the Texas Panhandle and there the band busied itself with rustling horses. When the Kid returned to New Mexico, Brown decided to stay in Texas and most probably saved his life for a few years. He tracked horse thieves and later got an appointment as a deputy sheriff in Oldham County, Texas, but he was fired for picking fights with drunks. Next Brown worked for ranches in Oklahoma and then moved on to Caldwell, Kan., where he was first appointed deputy marshal and then city marshal. Caldwell was a tough town at the time, and Brown asked his friend Ben Wheeler (real name Ben Robertson) to work as his deputy. The two men cleaned up the town quickly. In April 1883, Brown, Wheeler, and other lawmen chased the notorious Ross gang to their hideout in Hunnewell and captured its members after shooting one of the sons of the leader. On May 14, 1883, Brown ordered a drunken Indian named Spotted Horse to leave Caldwell, but the Indian went for his gun and Brown pumped four bullets into him, killing the Indian.

A gambler named Newt Boyce threatened to kill both Wheeler and Brown for locking him up after he cut two men in a Caldwell saloon. On the night of Dec. 15, 1883, Brown went after Boyce who met him in the street. The gambler reached inside his coat pocket, ostensibly for a der-

Four men to hang: left to right, John Wesley, Henry Newton Brown, Bill Smith, Ben Robertson, captured after they robbed the bank in Medicine Lodge, Kan., in 1884; following the taking of this photo, the four were served meals and wrote letters to their families before their executions.

ringer, but Brown fired a single shot from his Winchester and mortally wounded Boyce. Brown and Wheeler decided that their wages as peacemakers needed to be supplemented. Under the ruse of traveling to Oklahoma to look for a murderer, both men left Caldwell and joined up with two outlaws, William Smith and John Wesley. These four men then rode to Medicine Lodge, Kan., and there held up the Medicine Valley Bank. President E.W. Payne reached for his gun and Brown shot him to death. Chief Cashier

George Geppert was also shot to death by the other outlaws, even though he had raised his hands. The cashier staggered to the vault and managed to close it before he fell dead to the floor.

Brown and the others fled the town with nine citizens hotly pursuing them. One of the vigilantes was Barney O'Connor, a rancher who had once employed Brown and recognized him as he rode pell-mell out of Medicine Lodge. The outlaws rode mistakenly into a box canyon and surrendered after a two-hour gun battle. The outlaws were kept prisoner in a small house and given two meals before their picture was taken. Then the prisoners were told to write letters to their loved ones and Brown wrote a letter to his wife, which stated: "It was all for you. I did not think this would happen." Brown anticipated a lynch mob would arrive that night to string up the outlaws. He managed to get out of his handcuffs and when the mob broke into the makeshift jail at 9 p.m., Brown dashed through the open door, squirmed through the mob, and ran down an alley. A farmer fired both barrels of a shotgun as Brown raced past him and tore the gunman in half. Though Brown was already dead, several citizens fired bullets into his body, so angry were they that he had cheated them of a hanging. Wheeler also tried to escape the mob and was wounded but he was dragged with Wesley and Smith to a nearby tree and hanged. See: **Billy the Kid**; **Brewer, Richard**; **Lincoln County War**.

Brown, Sam (AKA: **Fighting Sam; Long-Haired Sam**), d.1861, U.S., gunman. Mississippi born and raised, Sam Brown moved to the Nevada mining camps in the late 1850s where he reportedly killed fifteen men before he met his own violent end. Brown lived in the high timber of Sun Mountain and was a southern sympathizer just after the outbreak of the Civil War, attempting to control the mines and the unions. A large, big-boned man with long hair and a fierce look about him, Brown was habitually starting fights and encouraging gunplay, although he was not reportedly fast on the draw. As he rode down Sun Mountain he was heard to shout repeatedly: "I must have a man for supper!" This bully came to his fate on July 7, 1861, when he threatened to kill Henry van Sickles, an innkeeper at Gold Canyon, unless he was given the best room in Sickles' inn, one that was already occupied. Sickles went for his gun and the slow-drawing Brown was shot dead from his horse. A quickly convening coroner's jury concluded that Long-Haired Sam had "come to his death from a just dispensation of an all-wise Providence."

Brown, William, d.1881, U.S., outlaw. Gunman William Brown intended to ambush a man whose name was Moore near White Bead Hill in the Chickasaw Nation on Aug. 19, 1880. Brown had harbored a lingering grievance against Moore over the outcome of a certain horse race. Later, in a case of mistaken identity, he shot down the wrong man, who was identified as Ralph Tate. William Brown was apprehended in Texas, and was returned to Fort Smith (Ark.) where he was convicted, and hanged on Sept. 9, 1881.

Bryant, Charles (AKA: **Black Face Charlie**), d.1891, U.S., outlaw. Born in Wise County, Texas, Charles Bryant had been a cowboy since his teens and lived most of his life in the saddle. While still a youth, Bryant got into a gunfight and a pistol was fired at pointblank range next to his face, the grains of black powder from the shot permanently disfiguring him and resulting in his odd nickname. Bryant joined the Dalton gang in 1890 and was with the Daltons when they robbed the Santa Fe's Texas Express train near Wharton, Okla., on May 9, 1891. He was also in the Dalton band that robbed the Santa Fe train near Red Rock in the Cherokee Strip, Okla., area some weeks later, and it was reportedly Bryant who suggested to the Daltons that the passengers on this train be robbed. The Daltons refused, sneering at such a low-life notion, and telling Bryant that they did not prey upon people, only on railroads and banks. Black Faced Charlie, it was claimed, also shot a telegraph operator during this holdup.

There was a maniacal, almost suicidal, streak in Bryant, who loved gunplay of any kind. The Daltons were forever warning him to "go easy with your trigger finger," and they considered Bryant the most unreliable of their dedicated band of outlaws, believing him to be a "little crazy." After a shootout with a posse sometime in 1891, Bryant strutted about a campfire while the exhausted Dalton gang members collapsed on their bedrolls. The gunfight, in which the gang just barely managed to escape, had filled him with exhilaration and, in this manic state, Bryant yelled to his indifferent fellow thieves: "Me, I want to get killed in one hell-firing minute of smoking action!" He got his wish.

Bryant got sick while in the outlaw camp near Buffalo Springs, Okla., and gang members arranged for him to see a doctor in Hennessey, Okla. While recuperating in a hotel room in that town, Deputy U.S. Marshal Edward Short learned of Bryant's whereabouts and kicked open the door to Bryant's room, holding two six-guns. He had no trouble arresting the weakened Bryant, who had by then a $1,000 reward posted for his capture. Short then got aboard a train with Bryant on Aug. 3, 1891, intending to deliver his prisoner to the federal court district in Wichita, Kan., riding in the express car. During the trip that day, Short had to relieve himself and told the express messenger to guard the prisoner, handing him a pistol. He checked Bryant's handcuffs and then left the car. The messenger, seeing that Bryant was ill and asleep in a chair, put the pistol in a pigeonhole in his desk and went about sorting mail and other chores. Bryant was only feigning sleep. As the train neared Waukomis Station, he went to the desk when the messenger's back was turned, and grabbed the pistol just as Short reentered the car.

With his hands still manacled together, Bryant managed to snap off a shot at Short, the bullet hitting the marshal in the chest. Short lifted his rifle and pumped several bullets at Bryant, one of these ploughing into the outlaw's chest and emerging at the back, severing Bryant's spinal column. As he fell to the express car floor, the outlaw emptied the pistol in Short's direction. As he was dying, Black Faced Charlie yelled: "I can't die with my boots on! Please pull them off." Short and the messenger picked up Bryant's body and placed it on a cot. Then Short laid down on another cot and died from his wounds. When the train stopped at Waukomis, both bodies were laid out on the station platform to await the undertaker. Black Faced Charlie, curious train passengers noted, wore no boots. See: **Dalton Brothers.**

Buck Gang, prom. 1895, U.S., outlaw. The Buck Gang, led by Rufus Buck, was made up of five illiterate Indians who terrorized the Old Indian Territory of Arkansas-Oklahoma. The Cherokee Nation was suddenly gripped by a reign of terror when Buck, an Uche Indian, accompanied by four young Creek Indians—Lucky Davis, Lewis Davis, Naomi July, and Sam Sampson—began raiding farmhouses and ranches, raping and killing as they rode wildly through a two-week crime spree, beginning on July 28, 1895. On that day, the five men gathered in tiny Okmulgee, Okla., collecting weapons for their rampage (some later said a traditional warpath was declared by Rufus Buck). They were spotted by a black U.S. deputy marshal, John Garrett, who stopped them, and asked them why they were so heavily armed. All five men wheeled about blazing away with their six-guns and rifles, killing the lawman. Mounting their ponies, the Indians rode out of town.

The gang struck randomly for thirteen days after that, riding to lonely ranches between Fort Smith and Muskogee, robbing stores, raping women. The first woman taken by the gang was a widow named Wilson whom they came upon as she was riding to town in her wagon. All five men raped the woman, then took her shoes away, and shot at her feet so that she fled, half dead from fear. Next, near Berryhill Creek, the gang robbed a man named Stanley, taking his watch, horse, and $50 in cash. The Buck Gang struck the ranch of Gus Chambers, looting it of horses and riddling the Chambers house with bullets after the rancher put up a fight. Days later, they raided the farm of Henry Hassan, and while they held the rancher under guard, several gang members forced Rosetta Hassan to have sex with them, despite her pleas to remain with her children. When she resisted, Lucky Davis pushed her toward the bedroom, saying: "You must go with me or I will throw the damned brats of yours into the creek!" Later, the sadistic gang forced Hassan and one of his hired hands to fight each other and then made them dance while they shot at their feet. On the road the next day, the gang held up a drummer named Callahan. When a boy who worked for the elderly Callahan protested the rough treatment of Callahan, he was shot in the back and seriously wounded by Rufus Buck and others.

On Aug., 9, 1895, the gang robbed two stores, Norberg's and Orcutt's, near the town of McDermott. A huge posse of federal marshals and a company of Creek Indian police, the Creek Lighthorse, under the command of Captain Edmund Harry, was assembled and ordered to bring in the Buck Gang "dead or alive." Steve Burke, toughest of the U.S. marshals in the district, led the posse, which tracked the gang to a cave hideout near Okmulgee on Aug. 10, 1895. A wild gun battle took place, but all five outlaws were captured and taken by Marshal S. Morton Rutherford to McDermott. Here, hatred for the rapist-killers was so intense that Rutherford had to sneak his captives out of town to keep them from being lynched. The Buck Gang members, all manacled together by chain, were then taken to Muskogee and put on a train to Fort Smith, where they were quickly tried on Sept. 20, 1895, before Judge Isaac Parker. Hassan and his 30-year-old wife, as well as others, testified against the renegades, describing their perverted crimes. The jury quickly found all the gang members Guilty of rape and, on Sept. 25, 1895, Judge Parker passed sentence.

Parker asked the defendants if they had anything to say, and Lucky Davis jumped up and shouted: "Yes, suh! I wants my case to go to the Supreme Court."

"I don't blame you," replied Judge Parker sardonically. Then he stated: "I want to say in this case that the jury, under the law and the evidence, could come to no other conclusion than that which they arrived at. Their verdict is an entirely just one, and one that must be approved by all lovers of virtue. The offense of which you have been convicted is one that shocks all men who are not brutal. It is known to the law as a crime offensive to decency, and

as a brutal attack upon the honor and chastity of the weaker sex. It is a violation of the quick sense of honor and the pride of virtue which nature, to render the sex amiable, has implanted in the female heart, and it has been by the lawmakers of the United States deemed equal in enormity and wickedness to murder, because the punishment fixed by the same is that which follows the commission of the crime of murder...

"Your crime leaves no ground for the extension of sympathy...You can expect no more sympathy than lovers of virtue and haters of vice can extend to men guilty of one of the most brutal, wicked, repulsive and dastardly crimes known in the annals of crime. Your duty now is to make an honest effort to receive from a just God that mercy and forgiveness you so much need. We are taught that His mercy will wipe out even this horrible crime; but He is just and His justice decrees punishment unless you are able to make atonement for the revolting crime against His law and against human law that you have committed. This horrible crime now rests upon your souls..."

Parker then sentenced all five men to hang on Oct. 31, 1895. Buck and the others "exhibited no sign" of emotion. They merely listened to their death sentences and then silently filed back to their cells. Later, Buck insisted that he could provide an alibi, that he was not present at any of the crimes committed by the gang. Judge Parker permitted a stay of execution while lawyers prepared appeals. The U.S. Supreme Court refused to hear the case and Parker's decision was affirmed without opinion. Parker rescheduled the hanging for July 1, 1896. The five men, on that day, were escorted to a large scaffold where they were to be hanged simultaneously. They stood on the large trapdoor in front of a great crowd while ropes were fixed around their necks.

None except Lucky Davis had anything to say. Davis asked for a priest and the chaplain prayed with him for a few moments. Then Davis spotted his sister in the crowd and shouted: "Goodbye, Martha!" Rufus Buck's father, a large, heavyset man, came into the courtyard and tried to walk up the stairs to the gallows. He was drunk and had to be escorted to a chair nearby and subdued by guards while he watched his son hang. Only Lucky Davis showed any signs of emotion; his face twitched and his eyes darted about furtively. At 1:28 p.m., the large trapdoor swung down and all five men fell with jerks to the ends of their ropes. Lewis Davis, Naomi July, and Sam Sampson died almost at once, their necks broken. Lucky Davis and Rufus Buck slowly strangled to death, their bodies jerking and drawing upward several times while they struggled for life.

Following the execution, a guard went into Buck's cell and found a photograph of Buck's mother on the wall. On the back of the photo, Buck had written the following poem:

I dreamt I was in Heaven
Among the Angels fair;
I'd never seen none so handsome,
That twine in golden hair.
They looked so neat and sang so sweet
And played the Golden Harp.
I was about to pick an angel out
And take her to my heart:
But the moment I began to plea,
I thought of you my love.
There was none I'd ever seen so beautiful
On earth or Heaven above,
Goodbye my dear wife and Mother.
Also my sister.
Remember me, Rock of Ages.

Judge Parker, who had sentenced so many men to the gallows that he later earned the dark sobriquet, "The Hanging Judge," had delivered his most blistering sentence

Members of the Buck Gang, all hanged for rape, 1896; left to right, Naomi July, Sam Sampson, Rufus Buck, Lucky Davis, Lewis Davis.

to the members of the Buck Gang for the crime of rape, not murder. Parker considered this crime against females the most "intolerable" offense of all the many felonies he had to review in his "court of the damned." See: **Parker, Isaac.**

Buckskin, Frank, See: **Leslie, Nashville Franklin.**

Buffalo Bill, See: **Cody, William Frederick.**

Bullion, Laura (AKA: **Della Rose; Clara Hays**), b.1873, U.S., outlaw. Kentucky-born Laura Bullion moved to Texas with her family at an early age and quit school while in her teens, becoming a prostitute who later befriended and lived with many outlaws, including the brothers Tom and Sam Ketchum, and, following their capture, consorting with Wild Bunch train robbers Will Carver and Benjamin Kilpatrick. It was Ben Kilpatrick with whom Bullion became most closely associated, riding with him on raids with the Wild Bunch and accompanying him when Kilpatrick split from the gang, going his own way. Bullion was slender, five-foot-three-inches, with hazel eyes and black hair that she kept cropped close to her head, unlike the long-haired style of her day. She was not an attractive woman but much sought after by outlaws in that she was willing to share their hardships and take chances with them in their wild robberies. She was with Ben Kilpatrick when both were arrested in St. Louis on Nov. 15, 1901. Lawmen found a large amount of cash and unsigned notes in the room she shared with Kilpatrick—loot, it was later proved, from a recent train robbery committed by the Wild Bunch at Wagner, Mont. Bullion was given a five-year prison sentence in Kentucky and Kilpatrick received a fifteen-year sentence in the federal penitentiary at Atlanta. Following her release, Bullion disappeared. See: **Kilpatrick, Benjamin; Wild Bunch.**

Bunch, Eugene (AKA: Capt. **J.F. Gerard**), d.1892, U.S., outlaw. Born in Mississippi, Eugene Bunch was a well-educated teacher and editor who turned to train robbery to make his fortune and wound up being shot to death by lawmen in a Louisiana swamp. Bunch, a mild-mannered man of six feet with blue eyes, earned his living as a teacher in Louisiana. He later moved to Gainesville, Texas, where he edited the local newspaper. He and a few other bandits robbed trains in Texas, Mississippi, and Louisiana in 1888, at the time the more celebrated Burrow gang was robbing trains almost every month. Introducing himself as Captain J.F. Gerard to train passengers, Bunch politely tipped his hat to ladies while refusing to take their purses, and he was just as gentlemanly when taking the wallets of male train passengers. When standing inside express cars he spoke quietly to the messengers, telling them in a soft, mellifluous voice that if they did not open the safes in their custody they would have their "brains blown out." Bunch reportedly stole more than $30,000 from six trains he robbed in 1888-92. In November 1888, Bunch robbed a New Orleans and Northwestern train of $10,000, and his biggest haul was in 1892 when he stopped a train near New Orleans and took $20,000. Shortly after this robbery, Pinkerton detectives tracked Bunch to a swamp near Franklin, La., and, on Aug. 21, 1892, shot and killed Bunch and his cohorts. See: **Burrow, Reuben Houston.**

Buntline, Ned (**Edward Zane Carroll Judson**), 1823-86, U.S., writer. After serving in the Navy, Ned Buntline became a newsman in Cincinnati, Ohio, and later established a sensational magazine, *Ned Buntline's Own*, in Nashville, Tenn., in 1845. Buntline was arrested and charged with murder in 1846, and a lynch mob strung him up, but he was cut down alive and bore the rope burns around his neck for the rest of his life. He was subsequently found Not

Ned Buntline

Guilty. Buntline traveled to the West in 1869 and gathered material for the hundreds (some reports had it at more than 1,000) of trashy short novels based on western gunmen and adventurers. He lionized William F. Cody, a legendary cavalry scout, in many of his stories, and he introduced Cody to eastern audiences in his theatrical extravaganza, *The Scouts of the Plains*. Buntline, who dubbed Cody "Buffalo Bill," was responsible for having Cody establish his great Wild West show in later years. Buntline's tales, which preceded the dime novels of the 1880s and 1890s, also glorified such lawmen-gunmen as James Butler "Wild Bill" Hickok and Wyatt Earp. Buntline designed a foot-long six-gun for Earp which the lawman used with great effect, this weapon being forever known as the Buntline special. See: **Cody, William Frederick; Earp, Wyatt; Hickok, James Butler.**

Burrow (or **Burrows**), **Reuben Houston** (**Rube**, AKA: **Charles Davis**), 1854-89, U.S., outlaw. Born in Lamar County, Ala., on Dec. 11, 1854, Reuben H. Burrow owned a farm in Arkansas and tilled the soil. In 1872, he moved to Stephenville, Texas, where he maintained a ranch for fourteen years. He married a Wise County girl in 1876 and the union produced two children. He was considered to be an upstanding citizen, a cracker-barrel philosopher, and a member in good standing of the local Masonic Lodge. Burrow's first wife died in 1880 and he was left to take care of two small children. He remarried in 1884 and bought a small farm near Alexander, Texas, but his fortunes

diminished when his crops failed. In 1886, Burrow, who had earned a reputation as a crack marksman in local shooting meets, decided to take up train robbing. He collected a band of hardcases, including his brother Jim Burrow, W.L. and Leonard Brock, and Nep Thornton.

With his brother Jim and Thornton at this side, Rube Burrow rode north to Bellevue in Clay County where, on Dec. 1, 1886, he and the others held up the Fort Worth and Denver train. While Thornton jumped into the engine's cab to hold the engineer and fireman at bay with two six-guns, Rube and Jim Burrow went through the passenger cars, robbing the startled travelers. The outlaws decided not to rob the mail car, believing this to be heavily guarded, but when they entered the last passenger car, the Burrow brothers discovered a squad of black soldiers sleeping in their seats. They disarmed these troopers and took the weapons, along with considerable ammunition. This robbery netted Burrow and his men only a few hundred dollars. The bandit chief resolved to rob the mail car of the next train they held up. With the Brock brothers and Thornton, the Burrow brothers stopped a Texas and Pacific train near Gordon, in Palo Pinto County, Texas, on Jan. 23, 1887. This time the outlaws forced the engineer and fire-

Southern train robbers, Rueben and Jim Burrow.

man to go to the mail car and order the messenger inside to open the door. When the messenger refused, Burrow fired several shots, saying that he had just killed the engineer and fireman, although he fired these shots into the air, and that he would start shooting the passengers if the messenger did not open the door. The door was opened and the bandits made off with more than $2,000.

Burrow, his brother Jim, the Brock brothers, and Thornton stopped another Texas and Pacific train near Benbrook in Tarrant County in June 1887, and the gang removed more than $3,000 from the mail car. In September 1887, an exact duplication of this robbery occurred with the same band stopping the same train with the same crew in the same spot and getting almost the same amount of cash. On

Dec. 9, 1887, Burrow and his gang stopped a train of the St. Louis, Arkansas and Texas R.R. near Genoa Station, Ark., breaking into the mail car and forcing at gunpoint the messenger for the Southern Express Company to open the safe. They grabbed $3,500 in cash and fled just as the local sheriff arrived at the scene with a large posse, responding to an urgent call from a stationmaster up the line who sent out the alarm when he noted that the train was long overdue. The band continued to stop trains with such regularity that railroad detectives and lawmen came to believe that Burrow was being supplied information on cash shipments by someone working for the railroads, although this was never proven.

The Burrow gang next stopped a Fort Worth and Denver train in January 1888 and took more than $3,000 from the safe and passengers. A few weeks later the band held up a Texas and Pacific train, taking away $2,000. This time one of the outlaws made a serious mistake, leaving behind a new black raincoat. This was traced to Leonard Brock, who was arrested in his Texas home and confessed. He was given twenty years in prison but committed suicide on Nov. 10, 1890, by leaping to his death from a fourth-floor prison tier. The Burrow gang had, by early 1888, become the most infamous train robbers since Jesse James, and were sought by hundreds of lawmen throughout the South and Southwest. Scores of Pinkerton detectives searched for them at the request of their clients, the railroads. The Pinkertons barely missed capturing Jim Burrow at his ancestral Alabama home in Lamar County in January 1888, firing at him as he fled out the back door of the rickety farmhouse.

Posters describing the outlaws and showing them in drawings, were distributed to all conductors on trains. On Jan. 23, 1888, Jim and Rube Burrow were recognized by a conductor when they got aboard a Louisville and Nashville train. He wired ahead to Montgomery, Ala., and when the train came into the station, police poured into the cars, only to find that the brothers had already left their car. They were on a Montgomery street when newspaperman Neil Bray recognized them from wanted posters and called police. As he was doing so, Jim Burrow ordered him to stop. Bray kept yelling for police, who were coming down the block from the train station. When Bray continued to call for the police, Jim Burrow shot him and he and Rube escaped down an alley.

Another conductor spotted the brothers on a train as it was pulling into Nashville, Tenn., some weeks later and again police were called. This time lawmen trapped the outlaws in a passenger car, but Rube Burrow managed to shoot his way to freedom. Jim Burrow was taken into custody and bragged about the gang's exploits. William Pinkerton visited the outlaw in his cell in the Texarkana Jail and the pacing outlaw snarled to the detective: "My name

is Jim Burrow, and the other man on the train is my brother Rube, and if you give us two pistols apiece we are not afraid of any two men living!" James Buchanan Burrow never got hold of another pistol. He died in his prison cell of consumption on Oct. 5, 1888. Rube Burrow was now alone and the subject of one of the most widespread manhunts in American history. Every detail known of his life and habits related in wanted posters. Americans knew that this fair-haired, six-foot-tall outlaw wore a mustache and sometimes a goatee, that he had a "lounging gait and carried his hands in his pockets in a leisurely way," that he did not smoke or chew tobacco or gamble, and that he drank only on rare occasions. He was an adept player of the game of "seven-up," and also a fascinating storyteller, "relating stories of snake, dog, and catfights."

It was also known that Reuben Houston Burrow was a cold-blooded killer. On Dec. 15, 1888, Burrow and two other men robbed an Illinois Central Train at Duck Hill, Miss. A passenger, Chester Hughes, protested the taking of his wallet and Rube Burrow shot him dead in his seat. In June 1889, an Alabama postmaster refused to give a package addressed to Burrow to one of the gang leader's relatives. The relative had been sent to retrieve the package, but the postmaster stated that unless Burrow himself arrived to sign for the package he would not release it. Burrow then rode into town, called the postmaster into the street and shot him dead in front of his horrified wife. He then tipped his hat and rode leisurely out of town. The package contained a false beard which Burrow intended to use in his next robbery.

Burrow, like Jesse James in Clay County, Mo., was protected in his home area of Lamar County, Ala., by scores of relatives and friends. He returned constantly to his broken-down farm where he knew he would be safe since his friends would notifiy him whenever lawmen entered the wilderness area. Moreover, he had constructed a secret room in the cabin, three feet by nine, where he slept. This room was not found until years after Rube Burrow's death. Here the outlaw had dug out firing slits in the thick log walls and made pine slab ports which he could open from the inside and through which he could fire weapons, if need be.

On Sept. 29, 1889, Burrow and a new recruit, Joe Jackson, stopped a Mobile and Ohio train near Buckatunna, Ala., fleeing with $11,000. Many train robberies were then occurring in Alabama, Louisiana, Arkansas, Oklahoma, and Texas, and most of these were attributed to the infamous Rube Burrow, but some of these train holdups were committed by another wild desperado, Eugene Bunch, later killed in Louisiana. Many men were mistaken for Burrow, including one of his own cousins, who was shot and killed in Marshall County, Ala., on Nov. 17, 1889, by A.D. Scott, who attempted to collect the considerable reward on Rube Burrow's head. The man he killed, however, stated with his dying breath: "My name is Rube Smith." Rewards for Burrow totaled $7,500, a fortune for that era and the Pinkerton Detective Agency in Chicago was flooded with "tips" from thousands of people in the South and Southwest, reporting the whereabouts of the elusive bandit. "It appears," moaned William Pinkerton, "that Rube Burrow had a thousand twins." After Joe Jackson was captured and sent to prison, Rube Burrow continued robbing trains alone. Fifty miles north of Mobile, Ala., in mid-1890, Burrow held up a Louisville and Nashville train, taking more than $4,000 from the Southern Express Company's safe in the mail car. It was his last train robbery.

On Oct. 7, 1890, Rube Burrow entered the small town of Linden, Ala., going into a store operated by C. Carter. He asked to look at some rifles on display and as he was examining the weapons, Carter, who fancied himself a detective, went into the back room and checked some Pinkerton wanted posters, identifying his customer from one of them as the infamous Reuben Houston Burrow. He came out of the back room holding a rifle on the outlaw and marched him into a storeroom where Burrow was locked up. Then Carter went to the train depot to wire the Pinkertons in Chicago that he had captured the notorious outlaw. While Carter was waiting for a reply at the train station, Burrow escaped from the storeroom and armed himself.

Instead of fleeing, the desperado was so humiliated at being captured by a mere clerk that he went looking for Carter, vowing to kill him. He spotted the shopkeeper at the depot and opened fire, striking Carter's arm. Carter drew his own six-gun and began blasting away, one shot hitting Burrow and tearing open the outlaw's stomach. Burrow, clutching his stomach and almost bent in half, backed down the street, firing as he went, while Carter, his arm wound bleeding profusely, staggered after him, also firing. Both men emptied their guns and then collapsed. Burrow died in the street. Carter recovered and was given the reward money, but not until Pinkerton agents arrived in Marengo, the county seat, and thoroughly examined and photographed the body of the big outlaw as it lay in its coffin. Then the body was put aboard a Southern Express car and taken to Burrow's relatives in Lamar County.

Thousands lined the route of this train in hopes of getting a look at the remains of the famous outlaw. When the train stopped in Birmingham, more than 1,000 persons climbed in and out of the express car to glance at the body in its open coffin. When the train reached the depot at Sulligent Station in Lamar County, Burrow's mother and father were on the platform. Detectives threw open the door of the express car and then the body, bruised and battered, was literally thrown from the car so that it spilled from the open coffin at the feet of the elderly Burrows, a horrible act by lawmen who obviously could not control their hatred even after their nemesis was dead. Moreover, the body bore horrible scars and bruises that Burrow had not received in his battle with Carter. It was easily concluded that the lawmen aboard the train had mutilated the corpse before delivering it so viciously at Sulligent Station. See: **Brock, Leonard Calvert; Bunch, Eugene; James, Jesse.**

Burton, Isaac, prom. 1835, U.S., lawman. On Oct. 17, 1835, Daniel Parker put forth a resolution which created a corps of Texas Rangers "whose business shall be to range and guard the frontiers between the Brazos and Trinity Rivers." The measure was passed into law on Nov. 24, 1835, and Isaac Burton was chosen as one of the first five captains to head up this newly created agency, which entered the struggle for territorial sovereignty from Mexico. One of his first assignments was to comb the coastal regions in search of hostile Mexican ships seeking access to Texas. In the early morning hours of June 3, Burton and his men captured five Mexicans who came ashore from their vessel, the *Watchman*, in search of provisions. A squad of sixteen Rangers boarded the ship and seized the vessel at gunpoint. Two other ships, the *Comanche* and the *Fanny Butler*, were likewise taken, and directed to sail to the port of Velasco where the supplies in the hold were deposited with the army of Texas. For this, Burton's gallant band was dubbed the "horse marines."

Burts, Matthew (Matt), prom. 1899, U.S., lawman-outlaw. Matthew Burts was a deputy sheriff in Pearce, Ariz., in charge of prisoners, but he was really in collusion with the gang led by the sometime-lawman, sometime-outlaw Burt Alvord. He reportedly participated in several train robberies with Alvord and others and allowed one of Alvord's men, Billy Stiles, to escape prison. For this and other crimes, Burts himself was given a long term in Yuma Prison.

Outlaw Matt Burts.

Following his release, Burts went to California, where he had a small ranch. He was allegedly killed in a gunfight as

late as November 1925, but other western historians claim
that he was killed about 1908 in a Wyoming gunfight.

C

Caballero, Guadalupe (AKA: **The Owl**), prom. 1890s, U.S., outlaw. A strange little bandit, the cross-eyed Guadalupe Caballero stood only five feet tall and was a member of Vicente Silva's notorious cattle-rustling gang in Las Vegas, N.M. This runty bandit spent most of his time in a section of Las Vegas known as Old Town, squatting on the streets, pretending to be asleep but alert to lawmen or traitors who might betray Silva's operations. He was often sent by Silva to the nearby mountains to drive stolen herds to Silva's nearby ranch when they were ready for sale. Caballero was convicted of being an accessory in the murder of Pete Maes in 1894 and sent to prison for ten years.

Cadete, d.1872, U.S., mur. vict. Cadete was the tribal chieftain of a faction of Mescalero Apaches whose land extended from the Rio Grande River eastward and beyond the Pecos River. He was murdered in 1872 by a band of white men in retaliation for the testimony he gave against their cohorts, who were accused of selling whiskey to the Indians.

Calabaza, Ariz., prom. 1870s-1880s, U.S., fugitive haven. This area, frequented by the worst criminal element in Arizona, was just across the Mexican border, near Nogales, and served as a "sheriff-proof" hideout for wanted felons, much the same as the notorious Hole-in-the-Wall or Oklahoma's Indian Territory. No lawman in his right mind would enter this area in search of wanted men as dozens, often hundreds, of gunmen were always present. The camp was destroyed when two huge outlaw factions battled each other and caused the clapboard camp to burn down in the process. The surviving residents limped across the border to resettle in Nogales. See: **Hole-in-the-Wall; Indian Territory**.

Calamity Jane (**Martha Jane Canary** or **Cannary**), 1852-1903, U.S., pros. Much has been written about Calamity Jane, a western character who was often a mistress to lawmen and gunmen, and, periodically, a common prostitute in such western towns as Deadwood, S.D., where she met the famous lawman and gunfighter, James Butler Hickok, better known as Wild Bill. Very little of the vast amount of literature produced about this frontier character is factually reliable. Calamity Jane, as she is known in legend, was created from an illiterate, alcoholic, common prostitute. She apparently had a brief affair with Hickok but there was never a lasting relationship between these two. Calamity Jane was more man than woman, tall and muscular and wearing men's clothing. Following Hickok's death, Calamity Jane was celebrated by dime novel writers as "the White Devil of the Yellowstone" and all kinds of wild adventures were attributed to her, almost all of them pure inventions, particularly her scouting for the U.S. cavalry and fighting Indians. Calamity Jane supposedly captured Jack McCall after he shot Hickok to death, cornering the backshooter with a cleaver in a butcher shop a short time after the killing but this, of course, is pure fiction, as Calamity Jane herself admitted some years later. She appeared in a few Wild West shows but was invariably fired for being drunk. Calamity Jane briefly married but this union was ruined by her alcoholism. As late as 1900, Calamity Jane was found working in a brothel. She died in Terry, S.D., on Aug. 1, 1903, not far from Deadwood, calling out Wild Bill's name and insisting that she be buried next to the western hero, a wish that was granted. Thus, ironically, Hickok, who thought Calamity Jane a nuisance in life, lies next to her in eternity. See: **Hickok, James Butler.**

Camp Grant Massacre, 1871, U.S., mur. As the Arizona frontier began to shrink, the migrant Apache Indian tribes, who had called this land home for generations, began to feel increasingly threatened. Negotiations with the U.S. government failed to placate the warlike Apaches who attacked settlements at will, usually resulting in retaliatory strikes against the Indians. In 1871, the Arivaipa faction of the San Carlos group of the Western Apache tribe sought asylum within five miles of Camp Grant, a U.S. military installation near the San Pedro River in southern Arizona. The Indians, whose intentions were peaceful, wanted nothing more than to live off the land.

First Lieutenant Royal Emerson Whitman, who commanded the cavalry, was not sure he had the proper authority to grant the Indians asylum and sought the advice of General George Stoneman. An officious bureaucrat, Stoneman refused to issue a formal reply unless the message was properly summarized on the outside of the envelope. Whitman went ahead on his own and helped the Apaches, and for a time things went well. Some 500 of them lived on the grounds of the fort, which presented more than the usual problems after an Apache brave attacked a train in the Pinal Mountains, murdered one of the passengers, and carted away a woman. Although the incident occurred a distance of fifty miles from Camp Grant, the citizens of that area traced the blame to the local Apaches. In March 1871 there were further outbreaks of violence, which the editorial writers at the Tucson *Citizen* laid at the doorstep of Eskiminzin and his tribe who lived at Camp Grant.

In the early morning of Apr. 30, 1871, the Tucson Committee of Public Safety, composed of six white men, forty-eight Mexicans, and some Papago Indians (the sworn enemy of the Apaches) descended on the sleeping encampment and wantonly slaughtered 100 men, women, and children. Twenty-seven Apache children were sold into slavery, or simply "given" to the Papago. The residents of Tucson called for the removal of Whitman, who was called an Indian lover. The army ordered a general court-martial, but the charges were eventually dropped. When news of the Camp Grant Massacre filtered east, there was a public outcry for the perpetrators to be put on trial. The trial of the Committee members was held in December 1871, but after five days of deliberation a verdict of Not Guilty was handed down against all the defendants. U.S. president Ulysses Grant called the unprovoked attack "purely murder."

Canary, Martha Jane, See: **Calamity Jane**.

Canton, Frank M. (**Joe Horner**), 1849-1927, U.S., lawman-gunman. Born Joe Horner near Richmond, Va., Frank M. Canton moved as a child to Texas with his family. Here, while in his teens, he became a cowboy, herding cattle from North Texas to the Kansas railheads in the late 1860s. In 1871, Canton dropped from sight, becoming a bank robber and rustler. He was next heard from when he got into a quarrel with black cavalry troopers from Fort Richardson. Canton was in a Jacksboro, Texas, saloon on Oct. 10, 1874, when one of the black soldiers made a remark about white women. Canton demanded an apology and a gunfight erupted with Canton killing one black cavalryman and wounding another. He was jailed in 1877 for robbing the bank at Comanche, Texas, but he managed to escape and returned to cattle herding. After driving a herd to Ogallala, Neb., he officially changed his name to Frank Canton and vowed to uphold law and order. To that end he hired on as the top enforcer of the Wyoming Stock Growers' Association, a group of powerful cattlemen intent upon driving out the immigrant farmers who had settled in Johnson County. Canton ran his own ranch near Buffalo,

Wyo., and was later elected sheriff of Johnson County.

In 1885, Canton married and the union produced two daughters, one of them dying in childhood. He then resigned as sheriff to accept a well-paying job with his former employers, the Wyoming Stock Growers' Association. At the same time, Canton was made a deputy U.S. marshal and he enforced the law as the cattlemen wanted it enforced. One of the leaders of the opposition, the settlers, was Nathan Champion who had been branded a

Lawman and gunman Frank M. Canton, enforcer for the Wyoming Stock Growers' Association during the Johnson County War.

rustler by the cattlemen, and, thus labeled, he was ordered to be arrested. This was essentially an order to murder Champion and Canton proceed to carry out this order without questioning his employers. He rode to Champion's cabin on the Powder River on Nov. 1, 1891, accompanied by Joe Elliott, Fred Coastes, and Tom Smith, who was a friend of Champion's. Once outside the cabin, the four men drew their guns and then burst inside. Champion, sick in bed, jumped up with his six-gun barking. Smith and Coates were slightly wounded as they exchanged gunfire with Champion and then Canton ordered his men to flee, all four gunmen running from the cabin, mounting their horses and riding pell mell out of the area as Champion blazed away at them with a rifle that his one-time friend Tom Smith had given to him some time earlier.

Canton then joined Frank Wolcott's Regulators, a group of more than fifty gunmen hired by the cattlemen to wipe out the settlers in Johnson County, especially the settlement at Buffalo. Wolcott, Canton, and Tom Smith led this small army toward Buffalo, Wyo., on Apr. 9, 1892, when they heard that Champion and a fellow gunman, Nick Ray, were holed up at the nearby K.C. ranch. As they approached the ranch, Canton spotted Jack Flagg driving a wagon near the ranch; this man was on the murder list of the Regulators and the gunmen fired at him. He managed to escape but left his wagon which the Regulators torched and then sent crashing into the log cabin ranch building where Champion and Ray were defending themselves. The place blazed up and Champion, his clothes smoking, dove through the front door with two six-guns firing, but fifty guns zeroed in on him and he was riddled with bullets, dying instantly.

This killing was too much for Canton to bear. In the

months to come his nerves began to come apart. He had nightmares and would bolt upright from a dead sleep as he and his men slept about campfires and shout: "Do you hear them? They're coming! Get to your guns, boys!" The slightest sound, the wind, horses galloping in the distance, would cause Canton to tremble and become incoherent. He began seeing the ghosts of the dead, including James Averill and Ella "Cattle Kate" Watson, two rustlers who had defied the cattle barons and who were lynched by vigilantes, at Canton's insistence. The gunman quit the cattlemen's group and moved south to serve as a deputy U.S. marshal under Judge Isaac Parker who was headquartered in Fort Smith. Here Canton made a name for himself as a lawman who would stand up to any gunman. In Pawnee, Okla., in 1893, Canton tracked down and arrested a fugitive wanted on a murder charge, trapping him in a livery stable owned by gunman Len McCool. When McCool entered the stable and saw his friend, the fugitive, tied up and being made ready for the trip back to Judge Parker's courtroom, he slapped Canton and began to draw his gun. Canton jumped backward and produced a derringer, shooting McCool in the face, the bullet entering just under the left eye. Canton left McCool for dead and traveled back to Fort Smith. McCool, however lived, but got into a fistfight some time later and a blow to the wound inflicted by Canton brought about his death.

In the winter of 1895, Canton joined a posse that tracked down outlaws Bill and John Shelley, who had escaped from the Pawnee jail and had barricaded themselves in a cabin on the Arkansas River in Pawnee County. The posse peppered the cabin with more than 800 bullets in a five-hour gun battle but failed to dislodge the fugitives. Then Canton found a wagon filled with hay and, as he had done in the case of Nate Champion years earlier, sent this crashing into the ranch house. The resulting fire drove the outlaw brothers outside and they were quickly arrested and taken to Fort Smith. Outlaw Bill Dunn, a friend of the Shelley brothers, who was being hunted by Canton, rode into Pawnee, Okla., on Nov. 6, 1896, cornering Canton as the lawman was about to enter the courthouse. "Damn you, Canton," cried Dunn, "I've got it in for you!" He made a motion toward his gun but the lightning-fast Canton flung a six-gun from his wasitband and fired a single shot which struck Dunn square in the forehead. The outlaw fell backward, pulling out his gun as he fell but he died before he could fire a shot.

The restless Canton left his family in 1897 and accepted an appointment as U.S. deputy marshal in Alaska where he underwent many harrowing adventures. Canton reportedly tamed the entire lawless town of Dawson and befriended the writer Rex Beach and was used by Beach as role model for many of the frontier heroes he portrayed in his novels.

Canton was snowbound in 1888 and barely survived a winter which caused him to go snowblind. He returned to Oklahoma and once more became a lawman. In 1907 Canton became adjutant general of the Oklahoma National Guard and held this post until his death in 1927. See: **Averill, James; Champion, Nathan D.; Johnson County War.**

Captain Jack (AKA: **Keintpos**), 1837-73, U.S., mur. A Modoc Indian, Captain Jack was the leader in the Modoc War in Oregon which raged between 1872-73. Captain Jack, as he was called by whites, had left the reservation near Klamath, Ore., in 1865 when Indian agents refused to acknowledge his authority, appointing others as chiefs. After an absence of four years, Captain Jack led his band back to the reservation only to find that he and his followers had been branded pariahs, and they once more left the reservation. A contingent of forty soldiers, under the command of

Modoc Chief Captain Jack.

T.B. Odeneal, superintendent of the reservation at Klamath, tracked Captain Jack and his Modocs to Lost River and there attempted to disarm them on Nov. 29, 1872. A fight ensued and several troopers and Indians were shot.

A full-scale war broke out with pitched battles being fought through 1873, the most notable of which was on Jan. 17, 1873, when fifty Modocs under Captain Jack repelled more than 300 soldiers in the Lost River area. President Ulysses S. Grant ordered a truce with the Indians and a peace settlement to be arranged. To that end, General Edward R.S. Canby, Methodist preacher Eleasar Thomas, and Albert B. Meacham, one-time superintendent of the Modoc Reservation at Klamath, met with Captain Jack on Apr. 11, 1873. As Canby approached the Modoc leader under a flag of truce, Captain Jack raised his rifle and shot Canby to death. Other Modocs opened fire on Meacham and Thomas, killing Thomas. Meacham managed to run back to his horse and escape. The cold-blooded murder of General Canby, a Civil War hero and the only general ever killed by Indians, caused the U.S. Army to launch full-scale attacks against the Modocs, soundly defeating the Indians at Dry Lake a short time later. On May 22, 1873, the Modocs surrendered, offering to lead the soldiers to the hideout of Captain Jack, which they did.

Captain Jack was tried for the murders of General Canby

and Thomas and, with five others, was found Guilty and sentenced to death. Two of these Indians were reprieved and sent to Alcatraz for life. Captain Jack, Schonchin John, Black Jim, and Bogus Charley were hanged on Oct. 3, 1873. The Modoc tribe was transplanted to Oklahoma and held in custody until 1909 when survivors were permitted to return to Klamath. The Modoc War cost the U.S. government more than $500,000 and added another stain to the already tarnished Grant administration.

Carney, Thomas, prom. 1860s-70s, U.S., gambler. Thomas Carney was a successful entrepreneur who had briefly served as governor of Kansas from 1863-65. He fancied himself somewhat of a cardsharp, and when he turned up in Dodge City in 1877 there were few people, least of all the press, who truly believed he was on a mission to buy wholesale buffalo hides. The Dodge City *Times* reported on Carney's presence in the town, cautioning the populace that the former governor intended to "entice our unsophisticated denizens into the national game of draw poker. The Governor's reputation and dignified bearing soon enabled him to decoy three of our business men into a social game."

The three "business men" referred to in the story were Colonel Charles Norton, Charles Ronan, and Robert Gilmore—all professional gamblers. The game quickly progressed to high stakes. In those days, poker was played with a fifty-three card deck that included a joker that was played as an ace. Governor Carney mistook the joker to be an ace of spades—a fatal mistake in this game. "A breathless silence pervaded the room as Governor Carney spread his four kings on the table with his left hand and affectionately encircled the glittering heap of gold, silver, greenbacks, and precious stones with his right arm, preparatory to taking in the spoils," the paper recounted.

To Carney's utter horror, his worthy adversary spread four aces on the table, beating the governor's "imperial trump," which he counted on to carry him to victory. "I forgot about the cuter (joker)," Carney whispered. When next seen, the governor was on board an east-bound train, relieved of all his possessions. "Gov. Carney is not buying bones and hides in this city anymore," the *Times* reported.

Carson, Thomas, prom. 1871, U.S., lawman. A nephew of famous frontiersman Kit Carson, Thomas Carson was appointed a peace officer in Abilene, Kan., in June 1871. He quickly established a reputation as a man dangerous when provoked. After being reprimanded by his su-

periors, Carson left Abilene to accept employment in Newton, a boomtown best remembered as the site of the bloody "Newton General Massacre." Later that year, the Abilene city fathers rehired him.

Lawman-gunman Tom Carson.

Carson was again discharged after shooting bartender John Man in the hip on Nov. 22, 1871, without apparent provocation. In January 1872, Carson fired on Brocky Jack Norton, a former peace officer. The two men quarreled bitterly, and Carson settled matters the way he knew best: with pistols blazing. Norton survived the attack, but Carson was held over for trial. Deciding that freedom was preferable to a likely prison sentence, Tom Carson made his escape before going to trial.

Carver, William (AKA: **Will; News Carver**), d.1901, U.S., outlaw. William Carver was born in Texas and was a cowboy until joining up with the Ketchum gang in the

William "News" Carver of the Wild Bunch.

early 1890s, robbing trains and banks in both Texas and New Mexico. When the Ketchums were captured and hanged, Carver rode to Hole-in-the-Wall and joined the Wild Bunch, robbing trains and banks with Butch Cassidy, the Sundance Kid, Ben Kilpatrick, Harvey Logan, and others. When this gang broke up, Carver went on robbing banks and trains long after the heyday of the western bandit was over. He was finally trapped in 1901 in Sonora, Texas, following a robbery. Cornered by Sheriff Lige Briant and a large posse, Carver refused to surrender, preferring to shoot it out. He was shot to pieces and some reports later had it that Carver put a bullet into his own head rather than be taken prisoner. See: **Cassidy, Butch; Kilpatrick, Benjamin; Logan, Harvey; Sundance Kid, The.**

Cassidy, Butch (Robert LeRoy Parker, AKA: George Cassidy; William T. Phillips; Ingerfield; Lowe Maxwell), 1866-c.1908, U.S., outlaw. Butch Cassidy and his Wild Bunch members were the last of the old time western bank and train robbers, a motley group of outlaws with distinctive personalities and a flair for the flamboyant. Cassidy was no mean-minded desperado but a fun-loving, easy-going bandit who preferred to use his brains rather than his six-gun. He was backed up in most of his gun play by the lightning fast-draw artist, the Sundance Kid. His gang members included Will Carver, addicted to reading press notices about the gang; Ben Kilpatrick, the towering bandit known as the Tall Texan; and the most deadly of the group, Harvey Logan, who was also known as Kid Curry, a dead-eyed killer who vowed he would never be taken alive by the law and kept his word. Born Robert Leroy Parker in Beaver, Utah, on Apr. 13, 1866, Cassidy was one of ten children and had no formal education. Cassidy became a cowboy while still in his teens when he met outlaw Mike Cassidy, adopting Cassidy's name after he joined him in rustling cattle in Utah and Colorado.

Cassidy taught Butch how to shoot so that he was able to hit a playing card dead center at fifty paces and his draw was much faster than historians later described. Mike Cassidy led a small band of robbers and rustlers but, after having shot a Wyoming rancher, he disappeared. Butch Cassidy took over the gang. The gang's hide-out was at Robber's Roost, located in the southwest corner of Utah, a rough, mountainous area which was difficult to find, even by the outlaws who re-turned again and again to the rocky haven. In early 1887, Cassidy met Bill and Tom McCarty, hard-riding outlaws who headed up their own gang which in-

Robert LeRoy Parker, better known as celebrated outlaw, Butch Cassidy, leader of the famed Wild Bunch.

cluded Matt Warner (real name Willard Christianson), Tom "Peep" O'Day, Silver Tip (Bill Wall), Gunplay Max-well, and Indian Ed Newcomb.

When the McCarty boys suggested Cassidy join them in a train robbery, the apprentice outlaw happily agreed. On Nov. 3, 1887, Cassidy and the McCartys stopped the Denver and Rio Grande express near Grand Junction, Colo. The stubborn express guard refused to open the safe in the mail car and Bill McCarty put a six-gun to his head. "Should we kill him?" he asked.

"Let's vote," Cassidy said.

The gang members voted not to kill the guard and the train moved off leaving the bandits with not a dime in loot. Cassidy became disheartened with robbery and went back to rustling and occasional work as a cowboy or a miner in the local Colorado and Utah mines. It was almost a year and a half before Cassidy agreed to once more accompany the McCartys on another raid. This time the gang picked out the First National Bank of Denver, robbing it of $20,000 on Mar. 30, 1889. Tom McCarty approached the bank president that day and, expressing his sense of macabre humor, stated: "Excuse me, sir, but I just overheard a plot to rob this bank."

The bank president trembled so that he appeared to be undergoing an apoplectic fit, then managed to say: "Lord! How did you learn of this plot?"

"I planned it," McCarty said, pulling his six-gun. "Put up your hands."

Four men, Cassidy, Tom and Bill McCarty, and Matt Warner rode out of Denver with $5,000 each from the robbery, a fortune for those days. Warner immediately opened a saloon. Cassidy and the McCartys, however, decided to raid another bank and, on June 24, 1889, robbed the bank of Telluride, Colo., taking $10,500. Like the bank robbery in Denver, the gang never fired a shot. They merely trained guns on the bank employee, emptied the tellers' cages and looted the opened vault, then rode quietly out of town. Lawmen, however, formed huge posses and conducted wide and long searches for the bandits. This caused Cassidy and the others to go into hiding. Cassidy decided to follow the straight and narrow path and he took several jobs with ranches as a cowboy. He even worked as a butcher in Rock Springs, Wyo. which is where he earned his sobriquet "Butch." But such legitimate pursuits never worked out for Cassidy. A drunk picked a fight with him while he was serving customers and Cassidy knocked the man cold which caused his arrest. He was convicted of disturbing the peace and served a short term in the local jail. When released, Cassidy vowed he would never again work for a living.

Cassidy and Al Hainer, another cowboy, then began an extortion racket, selling Colorado ranchers protection, telling them that they would make sure that cattle was not rustled nor any of their property damaged by fire or other man-made hazards. Cassidy and Hainer were the man-made hazards, of course, and any rancher who did not pay his monthly protection fee had his cattle rustled by Cassidy and Hainer. Complaining cattlemen caused Wyoming lawmen John Chapman and Bob Calverly to hunt Cassidy and Hainer down to their cabin hideout near Auburn, Wyo. The lawmen crept up on Hainer as he was tending to the horses, wrestled him to the ground and tied him to a tree. Calverly then entered the cabin, his six-gun drawn. As soon as Cassidy spotted him he leaped for his two six-guns and gun belt, which were on a chair. Calverly fired four shots, one of which creased Cassidy's scalp and knocked him unconscious. Both men were quickly tried for extortion, sentenced to two years, and sent to the penitentiary at Rawlins, Wyo., on July 15, 1894. The man who had sworn out the arrests for Cassidy and Hainer, rancher Otto Franc, of the Big Horn Basin, was mysteriously murdered in 1903. Cassidy was released on Jan. 19, 1896, and immediately headed for a place called Hole-in-the-Wall, the last great hideout of the western outlaws. He had learned of this place behind the walls of the penitentiary and he resolved to put together the last super-bandit gang.

Hole-in-the-Wall was located in Colorado, more of a fortress than Cassidy's old Utah haven, Robber's Roost. At Hole-in-the-Wall, Cassidy was welcomed by the notorious Logan brothers, Harvey and Lonnie. Harvey Logan was the worst killer of the Wild Bunch, a brooding, small-bodied man with piercing black eyes, who had taken the name of Kid Curry, after another Hole-in-the-Wall bandit, Big Nose George Curry. Cassidy also met such gunmen and outlaws as Bob Meeks and William Ellsworth "Elzy" (or "Elza") Lay. Cassidy talked long and hard to these men about the mistakes he and others had made which resulted in imprisonment or death. He talked about how his friend Bill McCarty and another McCarty brother, Fred, had been shot to pieces in Delta, Colo., on Sept. 27, 1893, when they attempted to rob the bank there and how Matt Warner had been captured and sent to prison for a long prison term. (Warner would later reform and lecture against crime, dying in 1937.) Cassidy warned his fellow bandits that it was no good to merely ride into a town and rob the bank unless the town was scouted and it was learned whether or not a local vigilante group existed, or how strong the local sheriff's force was, how many deputies were in that town, and chiefly, how much money was really in the bank. Usually, he pointed out, such information could be easily learned by merely visiting the bank in advance and asking a few questions of its employees.

On Aug. 13, 1896, Cassidy led Bob Meeks and Elzy Lay to the Montpelier Bank, which they successfully robbed of $7,165. Butch had scouted this bank some weeks ahead of the robbery, learning that money would be transferred to this bank a few days before he raided it. Next, Cassidy, with Elzy Lay and Joe Walker, rode to the large mining camp at Castle Gate, Utah, on Apr. 21, 1897, a camp where Butch had once worked as a miner. He knew when payrolls were received and paid and he and his fellow bandits arrived just in time to scoop up $8,000. Before the outlaws fled, Cassidy had Walker cut the telegraph wire so that the local lawmen could not be warned. Cassidy then rode to a New Mexico ranch with Lay where the two of them

took jobs as cowboys. This was part of Butch's plans. He no longer drew attention to himself by freely spending the money he had robbed. He would put up a good "front" by pretending to work while posses were searching for shiftless thieves.

Cassidy and Lay left the ranch in early June, rode back to Hole-in-the-Wall and gathered more men, Harvey Logan, Walt Putney, Tom "Peep" O'Day, and Indian Billy Roberts. These men then rode to Belle Fourche, S.D., on June 27, 1897, and robbed the bank there, taking about $5,000. On May 13, 1898, Joe Walker was killed with another man by a posse seeking cattle rustlers near Thompson, Utah. When the two bodies were brought in, the entire town of Thompson turned out to cheer, thinking that the other man was the dreaded Butch Cassidy, but the corpse was that of Johnny Herring, a lesser-known outlaw who bore some resemblance to Butch. Cassidy was far from dead. In fact he had, by then, carefully planned a train robbery at Wilcox, Wyo., on June 2, 1899.

The gang consisted of Cassidy, George "Flatnose" Curry, Elzy Lay, Harvey Logan, Lonny Logan, Ben Kilpatrick, the Sundance Kid (Harry Longbaugh or Longabaugh), and Ben Beeson. The bandits stopped the Union Pacific's Overland Flyer on a small trestle which was barricaded. When the train came to a halt, Cassidy ordered the engineer, W.R. Jones, to uncouple the express car. He refused and Harvey Logan pistol-whipped the engineer. He still refused and Lay took the controls in the engine's cab and forced the train forward. Just as it crossed the trestle the small bridge

Butch Cassidy, cowboy turned outlaw.

blew up. Cassidy and his men had forgotten a small charge of dynamite they had placed there. Once the train was some distance from the smashed trestle, the gang stood outside the express car and called out to the guard inside, a man who identified himself as Woodcock. He was ordered to open the express car door and come out.

"Come in and get me!" the defiant guard shouted to the bandits. A charge of dynamite was placed next to the door and the fuse lighted. The bandits dove into a nearby ditch and the resulting explosion tore the express car in half, sending Woodcock hurling outward. He was injured but alive. Harvey Logan ran up to the stubborn guard, pulling his six-gun and putting this next to the man's head. "This damned fellow is going to hell!" Logan shouted.

Cassidy ran up to him and brushed his gun aside, saying: "Now, Harvey, a man with that kind of nerve deserves not to be shot." Meanwhile the rest of the bandits ran about wildly, picking up more than $30,000 in bank notes and securities which had been blown every which way. This spectacular raid caused the Union Pacific to bring in the Pinkerton Detective Agency which sent scores of agents after the outlaws. Lawmen also, in dozens of posses led by such famous manhunters as Charles Siringo and N.K. Boswell, were on the trail of the gang. Cassidy decided that the best way for the outlaws to escape was for the Wild Bunch to split up. He, the Sundance Kid, who had become Cassidy's most loyal companion, and Ben Kilpatrick rode toward Hole-in-the-Wall while Logan, Curry, and Lay took a more circuitous route and were cornered by a large posse near Teapot Creek, Wyo.

The outlaws took refuge behind boulders while several possemen, including Sheriff Joe Hazen, charged their position. Hazen was shot off his horse, dead, by the sharp-shooting Harvey Logan. The outlaws then mounted their horses and, blazing away with their six-guns, shot their way through the ranks of the disorganized posse. Logan and Curry rode on alone while Lay joined notorious bandits, Thomas "Black Jack" Ketchum and G.W. Franks, and held up a Colorado Southern train on July 11, 1899, at Twin Mountains, N.M., stealing $30,000. The next day, the three bandits were surrounded at Turkey Creek Canyon, N.M., by a determined posse. A gunfight ensued and Lay was wounded twice and Ketchum once. The outlaws shot and killed Sheriff Edward Farr, Tom Smith, and W.H. Love before escaping. Ketchum was later captured and hanged for train robbery in a gruesome execution. Lay was trapped by lawmen in August 1899 and subdued after a desperate fight; he was sent to the New Mexico Territorial Prison on Oct. 10, 1899, given a life term. He would be paroled in 1906 and reform, living until 1934.

Despite losing some of his best riders, Cassidy put together another band of outlaws for another train raid. These bandits included Harvey Logan, who had managed to ride through several posses and return to Hole-in-the-Wall following the wild Wilcox robbery, the Sundance Kid, Ben Beeson, Ben Kilpatrick, and Laura Bullion, the Tall Texan's girlfriend. They stopped the Union Pacific's Train Number 3 at Tipton, Wyo., on Aug. 29, 1900. Ironically,

the express guard, Woodcock, was in the mail car and he again refused to open the door to the bandits. Butch shook his head in disgust and then said to the engineer: "You tell that iron-headed Woodcock that if he doesn't open the door *this* time, we're going to blow up him and the whole damned car sky high!" When the engineer pleaded with Woodcock, the plucky guard finally relented and threw open

The dynamited remains of the express car in Cassidy's robbery of the Union Pacific's Overland Flyer in 1899 near Wilcox, Wyo.

the door. The bandits blew open the safe and took more than $50,000, the largest haul taken by the gang up to that time.

Joe Lefors, one of the most feared lawmen of the era, was assigned by the Union Pacific to track down Cassidy and his gang at all costs. He wore out fifty men and twice as many horses chasing the Wild Bunch across Wyoming but lost them when they slipped into their mountainous hideout, Hole-in-the-Wall. The gang rode out again to strike the bank at Winnemucca, Nev., taking $30,000 on Sept. 19, 1900. Next the gang rode far afield, all the way to Wagner, Mont., where Cassidy, Logan, Kilpatrick, the Sundance Kid, and Deaf Charley Hanks stopped the Great Northern Flyer on July 3, 1901. (The Sundance Kid had robbed a train near this spot almost ten years earlier.) Two of the men boarded the train, and as the train got up steam, Logan climbed into the engineer's cab by crawling over the coal tender, dropping down with two six-guns in his hands and ordering the engineer to stop the train. The Sundance Kid and Ben Kilpatrick raced through the passenger cars, firing their six-guns into the ceiling and shouting to the startled passengers: "Keep your heads inside the car!"

When the train came to a small trestle, it ground to a stop where Cassidy and Hanks were waiting. Cassidy planted a charge of dynamite beneath the Adams Express car and blew off its side. More than $40,000 was taken from the safe but most of it was in unsigned bank notes. This never bothered the Wild Bunch. Bill Carver or someone else with good penmanship merely signed the notes and these were quickly cashed or passed. During this holdup, Laura Bullion was present, tending to the horses. She was Ben Kilpatrick's girl, although she had been a mistress to many an outlaw before him. Following the Wagner robbery, the Wild Bunch split up for the last time. Ben Kilpatrick and Laura Bullion rode east and were later arrested in Memphis with part of the loot taken from the Wagner robbery. Both were given long prison terms. When Kilpatrick was released in 1912, he attempted another train robbery and was killed by an aggressive express car guard. Harvey Logan was later trapped by a posse and, rather than be taken captive, sent a bullet into his brain.

The fate of Butch Cassidy and the Sundance Kid after that has been much in debate. It is known that Cassidy and Sundance rode to Fort Worth, Texas, to relax in Fannie Porter's luxurious brothel. The Sundance Kid then took up with a bored teacher and housewife, Etta Place, a beautiful statuesque brunette who longed for adventure and left with Cassidy and Sundance when they decided that the West was too "hot" for them, all three going first to New York to stay in the finest hotels, eat in the best restaurants, and have their photos taken while wearing evening attire. The trio then traveled to Bolivia where they hid out by taking jobs as miners for the American-owned Concordia Tin Mine. While living in employee quarters (Sundance and Etta living as man and wife), the three went off on several raids. They reportedly took a vacation to Argentina and robbed a bank in Mercedes, San Luis Province, in 1906. Once more in Bolivia, Etta decided to leave the outlaws and returned to the U.S., where she changed her name and drifted into oblivion. Butch and Sundance, however, continued their errant ways. In Spring 1908 they robbed a Bolivian payroll in Aramayo and were trapped in the small village of San Vincente by a regiment of troops who had been looking for the "gringo" bandits. After a fierce gun battle in which Cassidy and Sundance killed a number of troopers, the bandits were finally killed, shot full of holes. A variation of this report has Cassidy wounded, looking upon his dead friend, and, rather than falling into the hands of the Bolivian soldiers, he put his six-gun to his temple and pulled the trigger.

Another story has it that only Sundance was killed in the murderous crossfire and that he gave his money belt and a letter to his best friend Cassidy, telling him to give these items to Etta Place, whom he had married. Cassidy reportedly watched the mortally wounded Sundance die and then, under the cover of darkness, escaped, returning to the U.S. There are many unsupported stories claiming that Cassidy returned to his birthplace of Circleville, Utah, and changed his name, living out his life there and dying in 1929. Another story has it that he moved to Johnnie, Nev., and lived there until 1937, running, of all things, a western curiosity shop. Still another tale insists that the celebrated outlaw survived until 1943 or 1944, dying in either California or Washington. See: **Carver, William; Curry, George; Ketchum, Thomas; Kilpatrick, Benjamin; Lay, William Ellsworth; Logan, Harvey; McCarty Brothers; Sundance Kid, The; Wild Bunch, The.**

Catron, Thomas Benton, 1840-1921, U.S., fraud. The name of Thomas Benton Catron is forever associated with the Santa Fe Ring, a notorious band of grafters who swindled the government of New Mexico, often resorting to acts of violence to further their aims. Catron was born in Lexington, Mo., and fought for the Confederacy during the Civil War. In 1866 he moved to Santa Fe to begin a law practice with his friend Stephen B. Elkins. In 1872, he was appointed U.S. Attorney for New Mexico, a position which greased the way for his entry into territorial Republican politics. Before he was through with public life, Catron would serve as mayor of Santa Fe, president of the New Mexico Bar Association, and the first state senator when the territory was admitted into the Union in 1912.

An unscrupulous politician who would stop at nothing to achieve his goals, Catron's Santa Fe Ring controlled the political patronage and the ultimate destiny of the region. Businessman Lawrence G. Murphy, backed by his influential friends in the Santa Fe Ring, waged constant warfare with cattleman John Chisum between 1878-81. Chisum, who owned vast herds of cattle, set up a rival mercantile enterprise that threatened Murphy's stranglehold on the economy. The war dragged on until 1878, when the Murphy-Dolan faction laid siege to the McSween property. The five-day battle more or less ended the hostilities, though peace was not fully realized until Chisum's death in 1884. Catron's name was smeared once again as a result of the Maxwell Land Grant frauds of 1875-79, but through it all Catron maintained a firm grip on his power. See: **Lincoln County War.**

Cattle Kate, See: **Averill, James.**

Chacon, Augustin (AKA: **Paludo; Peledo; The Hairy One**), d.1901, Mex.-U.S., outlaw. Part Indian and part Mexican, Augustin Chacon was one of the most feared outlaws to raid the Arizona Territory in the late 1890s. He was a tall, hairy man with a fierce disposition and a decided inclination toward murder. Chacon was born and raised in Sonora, Mex., and served as a youth with the Mexican army. He attended school for a few years, which passed for a higher education in that illiterate era. By 1895, Chacon had deserted the army and had put together a ruthless band of outlaws in Sonora, raiding into Arizona. In Morenci, Ariz., Chacon and his men robbed a storeowner and when he resisted, Chacon drew a machete and hacked the man to pieces. He and his men robbed a gambling house in Jerome, Ariz., then killed two prospectors and, near Phoenix, the band shot two sheepherders to death for no apparent reason other than for the sadistic joy of killing.

The outlaws struck next at Agua Fria, stopping and robbing a stage there. In Clifton, Ariz., a posse cornered Chacon and his men while they were freely spending their loot in the Longfellow House. A wild gunfight ensued in which Chacon shot and killed one of his old friends, Pablo Salcido, one of the deputies who had gone to the beseiged building under a flag of truce. Chacon, however, was wounded when he attempted to escape the trap and he was placed in the local jail, later removed to the stronger jail at Solomanville. He bribed a guard there and made an escape. Dozens of lawmen and vigilantes hunted Chacon who, after committing several robberies, was again captured. He was tried at Solomanville, found Guilty, and sentenced to be hanged on July 18, 1897.

Again, however, the wily Chacon escaped. He fled back to the sanctuary of Mexico. The bandit was finally caught by the indomitable Arizona Ranger captain Burton Mossman, a lawman who was one of the deadliest gunmen in the West. Mossman lost two rangers to the guns of Chacon and he vowed to track the killer down. He did, shooting it out with the bandit and wounding him several times. So powerful was Chacon that, though wounded, he leaped upon Mossman when the lawman came close and Mossman had to club him into unconsciousness with his six gun. Chacon finally kept his long overdue date with the gallows, being hanged on Nov. 21, 1902, in Solomanville. See: **Mossman, Burton.**

Chadwell, William, See: **James, Jesse Woodson.**

Chambers, Lon, prom. 1880s, U.S., lawman. Lon Chambers carried his badge and enforced the law in the Texas Panhandle throughout the late 1870s. About the time that Billy the Kid was terrorizing the Southwest, Chambers left his job to join Pat Garrett's posse, bent on taking Billy dead or alive. At Fort Sumner, N.M., on Dec. 19, 1881, Garrett and Chambers got their chance. They set an ambush for The Kid.

That night, Chambers was assigned to serve as a lookout outside the post hospital where the posse had gathered to await The Kid's arrival. When Billy the Kid's gang rode into town, the posse was ready. Garrett called, "Halt!" but Tom O'Folliard and Thomas Pickett, riding in the lead, did not heed this warning. O'Folliard reached for his gun, but Chambers was faster on the draw. O'Folliard slumped, wounded and bleeding, in his saddle and tried to ride away, but the severity of his gunshot wound forced him to surrender. He died within the hour, but Billy the Kid escaped.

A year later, Chambers quit law enforcement for good and formed his own holdup gang. They pulled their biggest job at Coolidge, Kan., on Sept. 29, 1883. Three masked men boarded a westbound train that had made a brief stop at Coolidge, one of them believed to be Chambers. They ordered engineer John Hilton to take the train out of the station, and when he was slow to comply one of the gunmen shot him through the heart. The express messenger returned the fire, which drove the robbers from the train. Chambers was eventually arrested, but was released for lack of evidence. See: **Billy the Kid.**

Champion, Nathan D. (AKA: Nate), 1852-92, U.S., gunman. Born near Round Rock, Texas, Nathan Champion and his twin brother Dudley became cowboys at an early age and both helped to drive herds north to Wyoming where they settled down and began small ranches. At the outbreak of the Johnson County War, Nate and Dudley Champion sided with the homesteaders and small ranchers against the wealthy cattle barons. Nate Champion was the gunman of the family, a deadly shot and quick on the draw. He did more than his share of rustling which earned him the title of "King of the Rustlers," a sobriquet bestowed upon him by his one-time friend Frank Canton who worked as a Regulator for the cattlemen. Champion not only attacked the cattlemen verbally, but, like Jim Averill before him, he wrote letters to local newspapers denouncing the greedy, ruthless cattle barons. For this, Champion was marked for death.

On Nov. 1, 1891, Frank Canton, Fred Coates, Joe Elliot, and Tom Smith rode to the line shack owned by W.H. Hall on the Powder River where Champion and Ross Gilbertson were living. Canton and his men had but one assignment from their cattle baron employers: Kill Champion. They crept up on the shack, kicked open the door, and dashed inside, guns drawn. Shouted Canton, according to one report: "Give up, we've got you this time!" (This seemed to be an unlikely command for gunfighters sent to kill Champion, not capture him.) Champion, who was on the only bunk in the shack, bolted upright, grabbing his six-gun from its holster, saying: "What's the matter, boys?" Champion and Canton fired at the same time, both shots going wild, but Champion received powder burns on the face. More shots from the invading gunmen smashed into the wall next to the bunk. Champion's next two shots were more accurate, striking one gunman in the arm, another in the side. Canton and his men, getting the worst of it, fled the shack.

The gunmen left their overcoats, a few weapons and some horses when they ran to safety. Champion dashed outside and traded shots with Joe Elliott, who was later arrested on Champion's complaint, and charged with attempted murder, but when it came time for his trial, the case collapsed since the only witness, Gilbertson, had fled Johnson County under the threat of murder. The Canton raid caused Champion to move operations to the KC Ranch, which he leased with Nick Ray. This ranch was near the famous outlaw hideout, Hole-in-the-Wall. On the night of Apr. 8, 1892, two trappers, Ben Jones and Bill Walker, visited Champion and Ray. The four pioneers spent the evening drinking and singing along with the music creaked out by Walker on his fiddle. The next morning, Jones went outside to fill a pail of water from the nearby well. He was jumped by several Regulators and dragged away; more than fifty Regulators had surrounded the ranch house before dawn, intent upon murdering Champion and Ray. When Walker stepped outside to look for Jones a half hour later, he, too, was dragged away and held prisoner.

Ray then stepped from the cabin door and dozens of shots brought him down. Champion came outside, guns blazing, shooting at Regulators positioned in the nearby stable and along the creek bed, but their firepower drove him back into the cabin. He dashed out once more to grab Ray and drag him back inside. Then began a siege where the Regulators peppered the small ranch house. Inside, both Ray and Champion were wounded but they managed to keep fighting back. During lulls of the siege, Champion recorded the attack in a small diary. Ray bled to death by 9 a.m. but Champion continued the battle, refusing to surrender, knowing he would be shot down.

At 3 p.m., Champion, peering out of a window, saw one of his friends, Jack Flagg, riding in a wagon. Flagg fired on the Regulators, but when the fifty guns of this group were turned on him, he fled, abandoning his wagon. Frank Canton ordered the wagon filled with flammable materials, set afire, and rolled down a hill toward the cabin which blazed up when the wagon crashed into it. The fire finally drove Champion outside. He held two six-guns and both blasted away at his enemies as he tried to get to a ravine some fifty yards from the cabin. The Regulators caught him in a crossfire and he was shot to pieces. He fell on his back

and the Regulators, so fearful of this gunman, continued to fire bullets into Champion's dead body. Twenty-eight wounds were later found in his corpse. Champion's diary was crumpled in his dead hand and this was given to Sam Clover, a newspaperman who had accompanied the Regulators on their raid and had even helped set fire to the wagon. Clover later published excerpts of Champion's diary in his paper, the Chicago *Herald*. Before leaving, Canton pinned a note to the shirt of his old enemy, Champion, one that read: "Cattle thieves, beware." Champion's riddled body was left to be buried by his friends. This wanton murder was never called to justice and Champion's killers, most of them known, were never charged with the brutal killing. Nate Champion's twin brother Dudley was killed in 1893 by range detective Mike Shonsey, who had had several encounters with the Champion brothers in the past. See: **Averill, James; Canton, Frank; Johnson County War.**

Cherokee Bill, See: Goldsby, Crawford.

Childers, John, Jr., 1849-73, U.S., outlaw. Born near Cowskin Creek in the Cherokee Nation, John Childers was the half-breed son of John Childers, Sr., and his Indian wife, Katy Vann. The young man spent much of his early life engaged in evil pursuits, and traveled with a dangerous band of outlaws that roamed the plains in the 1860s. On the morning of Oct. 14, 1870, Childers met up with an old man named Reyburn Wedding near Caney Creek in the Cherokee Nation. Wedding had with him a prized black horse that Childers wanted to buy. He asked the old man if he would accept a trade for the animal, but Wedding declined. The horse, he said, was not for sale. Childers refused to give up and continued to badger the peddler, who would not give in. Childers grew angry and pulled a knife from his sheath, slashing the old man across the neck. Wedding died instantly.

After dumping his remains in the creek, Childers rode off with the prized horse. He was arrested by Deputy Marshal Vennoy at his home in Klo Kotchka in the Creek Nation, and was taken to Van Buren, Ark., for arraignment on Dec. 2, 1870. While waiting for the opening of the court session, Childers and six other men tunneled their way to freedom and fled into the woods. Childers joined up with a renegade gang of marauders that terrorized the inhabitants of the Cherokee and Creek nations and remained at large for many months. The gunman might never have been caught if not for his indiscreet confession to a Fort Smith (Ark.) prostitute. For $10 the woman related what she had learned to Marshal Vennoy, who laid a trap for Childers in his old haunt. The lawman quickly snapped on the handcuffs and led Childers away. During the time of his escape, the U.S. Court for the Western District of Arkansas had been switched from Van Buren to Fort Smith. It was here, on May 15, 1871, that Childers was indicted for murder. The date of execution was set for Aug. 15, 1873, but on the appointed moment of death, a remarkable thing happened. Childers was led to the gallows by Marshal John Sarber and Deputy James Messler. In a rare conciliatory gesture, the lawmen offered his life in exchange for information about the other gang members. Childers, however, was no squealer. "Didn't you say you were going to hang me?" he asked.

"Yes," Sarber replied.

"Then, why in hell don't you!" snapped Childers.

Messler released the bolt, dropping Childers through the trap. At that precise moment, a powerful bolt of lightning crashed down on the frame of the gibbet. The rain poured down on the hushed crowd, who truly believed that they had witnessed a supernatural event. An examination of Childers' body confirmed that he was quite dead, and that spiritual intervention had not saved him as some towns-people had claimed. Childers thus became the first man to hang at the new territorial court at Fort Smith.

Chinese Riots, prom. 1870s-80s, U.S., mob violence. The tremendous influx of Chinese immigrants to the West Coast during the 1870-80s stirred up feelings of racial hatred among whites who targeted the Chinese for selective harassment, often erupting into violence and murder. The fact that the Chinese were legally restricted from testifying against their white persecutors in open court no doubt encouraged gangs of rowdys to further terrorize the worker population.

In 1871, eighteen Chinese were killed in Los Angeles in retaliation for the shooting of a white man. Six years later the scene shifted to San Francisco, where large numbers of Chinese peasants were forced to vacate their homes. Many simply returned to China on the first available boat. Further contributing to the open hostility shown the Asians was the incorporation of the so-called "Chinese Question" into the realm of national politics. The government was under pressure from many quarters to impose strict immigration laws to stem the tide of Chinese who were coming to the West Coast to take advantage of employment opportunities in the booming railroad construction field. During the national campaign of October 1880, which pitted Republican James Garfield against Democrat Winfield Hancock, a Chinese person was brutally murdered in

Denver. Whites then rampaged through Chinatown, burning and gutting the dwellings.

Five years later, on Sept. 2, 1885, twenty-eight Chinese coal miners and general laborers were killed in Rock Springs, Wyo., by a mob of 150 whites who were upset about their refusal to join a strike against the Union Pacific Coal Department. Those who survived were allowed to return to work. In 1887, the U.S. government paid $147,748.74 in restitution to China as a result of this clash. The ink was barely dry on the agreement when a masked gang of men lynched five Chinese in Pierce, Idaho. The victims were suspected of having murdered a white merchant. There were additional anti-Chinese riots in King County, Wash., in September 1885, and in Seattle the following February. The violence against the Chinese abated only after the government passed into law a series of restrictive measures to curb immigration into the U.S.

Christian, Will (AKA: Black Jack; Ed Williams; 202), d.1897, U.S., outlaw. Will Christian and his gang of Oklahoma robbers were active in New Mexico and in Arizona's Sulphur Springs Valley throughout the 1890s, when the American frontier was fast disappearing. Will and his brother, Bob, led the "High Fives," a gang that robbed stagecoaches, banks, and trains. Christian was originally nicknamed "202" because of his considerable girth, but his ability with a gun soon earned him the name "Black Jack."

Will "Black Jack" Christian

Both brothers were arrested in Guthrie, Okla., in the summer of 1895 after fatally shooting a peace officer. They broke out of jail a short time later and fled to Arizona, where they remained active for the next two years. In Nogales on Aug. 6, the High Fives attempted to rob the International Bank. The attempt failed when newspaperman Frank King opened fire on Bob Hays and Jess Williams as they tried to leave town with the sack of loot, causing Williams to drop the money.

Later that month, a deputized posse from Tucson led by Sheriff Bob Leatherwood intercepted the gang near Skeleton Canyon. Deputy Frank Robson was killed in the shootout, but Christian and his men escaped across the border into Mexico. After hearing that Christian and his henchman had returned to Arizona in 1897, a second posse was organized. They ambushed the desperadoes in Black

Jack Canyon. In the gun battle that followed, Christian was shot in the side and killed. Christian's body was thrown on top of a lumber wagon and taken to town for display.

Christianson, Willard Erastus (AKA: Matt Warner; Mormon Kid), 1864-1938, U.S., outlaw. Born of hardworking immigrant parents from Sweden and Germany who came to Utah to practice the Mormon faith, Willard Christianson nearly killed a man when he was only fourteen. Without knowing his victim's fate, Christianson ran away from his parents home in Levan to become a range cowboy. He began calling himself the "Mormon Kid" and joined a band of rustlers operating in the Robber's Roost area. During these years on the run, Christianson met up with Butch Cassidy and committed several crimes with his gang.

Christianson married Rose Morgan, and together they ran a cattle ranch with Tom McCarty in Washington's Big Bend country. In 1892, Christianson and the two McCarty Brothers, Tom and Bill, held up a bank in Roslyn, Wash. The "Invincible Three" as they came to be known, escaped two lengths ahead of the furious townsmen. Shortly afterward, Christianson was captured and imprisoned in the Ellensburg, Wash., jail. While awaiting trial, Christianson and another inmate, George McCarty, attempted to escape by sawing through the wall of the jail. They were recaptured following a brief gunfight, but were freed by the courts two days later.

Christianson returned to Diamond Mountain, Utah, and lived there for the next four years. On an expedition to the Uinta Mountains in 1896, Christianson and his party were ambushed by a gang of gunslingers led by Dave Milton, and Ike and Dick Staunton. Although Christianson's horse was shot from under him, he began firing and killed Milton and Dick Staunton. Ike Staunton was shot in the knee.

When the shooting was over, Christianson sent for the sheriff. He was arrested, tried, and convicted on a charge of manslaughter in the deaths of Milton and Staunton, and sent to the Utah State Prison. After Christianson's release from prison in 1900, he was law-abiding most of the time. He moved to Carbon County where he was elected justice of the peace. He also served as a night watchman, and was involved in bootlegging. Christianson died of natural causes in 1938. See: **Cassidy, Butch; Wild Bunch, The.**

Christie, Ned, 1852-92, U.S., outlaw. Ned Christie, a full Cherokee, evaded lawmen for nearly seven years. Christie worked as a blacksmith near Tahlequah, Okla., where he also sold guns, stole horses, and ran whiskey. In

1885 Christie drove away a lawman who attempted to take him into custody. For the next seven years, a state of siege existed between Christie and the government.

Subsequent assaults against his various strongholds failed to roust the determined Cherokee. However, early one morning in 1889 while Christie and his family slept, deputy marshals L.P. Isbel, Dave Rusk, and Heck Thomas set fire

Outlaw Ned Christie, dead, 1892.

to his house in Tahlequah. Alerted by a watchdog, Christie opened fire on the lawmen. During a break in the shooting, his wife and son fled from the burning house but lawmen spotted and shot at them. Christie's son was hit in the lung and hips, but Christie managed to escape despite having his right eye put out and the bridge of his nose broken. He retreated to the mountains to build a two-story fortification that the lawmen found virtually impossible to penetrate. Various attempts to burn Christie's Fort Mountain failed. Law enforcement officials even tried to blast it open with sticks of dynamite, but failed.

On Nov. 2, Deputy U.S. Marshal Paden Tolbert and sixteen lawmen lugged a small cannon up the mountain in an all-out effort to dislodge Christie from his fortress. To

Ten members of the seventeen-man posse that flushed outlaw Ned Christie from his heavily fortified stronghold.

Tolbert's dismay, the cannon shells merely bounced off the thick log walls. When the posse regrouped after dark, Tolbert fashioned a barricade from a burned lumber wagon that had been used in an earlier attack on the fort. A few minutes after midnight, the rolling wall was pushed close to the cabin. Inside, Christie and his companion Arch Wolf emptied a fusillade of shot into the barricade with no effect. Lawman Charley Copeland placed six dynamite sticks against the south wall and stood back. The intensity of the blast finally pierced a hole in the structure.

With his fortress penetrated, Christie made a break for the woods but found himself confronted by Deputy Wess Bowman, who shot him in the head. Sam Maples, whose father had been killed by Christie in Tahlequah in 1885, emptied his revolver into Christie's lifeless body.

Claiborne, William (AKA: **Billy the Kid**), 1860-82, U.S., gunman-outlaw. A cowboy who worked for the Clanton-McLowery gang, William Claiborne is often confused with the more famous Billy the Kid, because they shared the same sobriquet. Claiborne was a teenage drifter who stood only five-feet-four-inches in height. He had black hair and dark eyes. When he appeared in Tombstone, Ariz., in about 1877, he at first went to work in the mines. He later signed on as a cowhand for John Slaughter, who had been a friend of Claiborne's family. He then went on Ike Clanton's payroll, more as a rustler and gunman than a ranch worker. In October 1881, Claiborne first came to the attention of local lawmen after he shot and killed a tough saloon brawler, James Hickey (or Hicks), in Charleston, N.M., a small mining town a few miles outside of Tombstone. When Hickey refused to drink with the diminutive Claiborne, the Kid, with a lightning draw, drilled a single shot into the brawler's heart. Claiborne was arrested by the local marshal, Virgil Earp, of the famous Earp Brothers, but Claiborne managed to escape. He was later acquitted of the killing, winning a "self defense" verdict.

When the Earp Brothers faced the Clanton-McLowery gang at the O.K. Corral on Oct. 26, 1881, in Tombstone, Claiborne was present, backing the outlaw faction. When the guns went off, Claiborne, instead of going for his gun, dove to the ground and watched as Billy Clanton, and Frank and Tom McLowery were shot to death in the terrific gun battle. He saw the outlaw ringleader, Ike Clanton, his boss, run from the scene and Claiborne followed, a single bullet from Wyatt Earp's six-gun nipping at his heels. Claiborne had only a few months left to live but he spent most of that time carousing through Tombstone's saloons and berating the Earps and their friends. One Earp associate, Buckskin Frank Leslie, was in the Oriental Saloon on the night of Nov. 14, 1882, when Claiborne entered and began insulting him, condemning him for killing one of his friends, John Ringo (a gunfighter reportedly killed by Leslie's friend, Wyatt Earp).

Buckskin Frank was a noted gunfighter and he told Claiborne to shut up or go elsewhere to drink. The youth faced Leslie for a moment, then decided that back-shooting the gunman was a better course. He went outside and retrieved his rifle from the scabbard on his horse. Then he crouched behind a fruit stand, close to the saloon, waiting for Leslie to step outside, intending to shoot Leslie in the back. Buckskin Frank was an old hand at such confrontations and, suspecting a sneak attack, which was the usual ploy of the Clanton-McLowery crowd, he stepped from the Oriental via a side exit. Leslie approached Claiborne from behind and when the Kid heard him approaching in the dimly lighted street, he turned, gasped, then fired a quick shot at Leslie. The experienced gunman drew his six-gun and fired a single bullet which entered Claiborne's left side and exited from the back. Leslie marched resolutely forward and Claiborne, who was now cradled in the arms of a bystander, cried out: "Don't shoot again! I am killed!" Claiborne was taken to a private home where a doctor could only dress his wounds and watch him die. He died some six hours later, cursing the name of Buckskin Frank Leslie.

Clanton-McLowery Gang, prom. 1870s-80s, U.S., outlaws. The toughest cattle rustling gang of outlaws in the Southwest was without a doubt the Clanton-McLowery band which was led by Newman H. Clanton, known as Old Man Clanton, the patriarch of the Clanton family. N.H. Clanton was a crusty, tough pioneer who settled near Fort Thomas, Ariz., in 1850. He later moved to Texas, then California, then back to Fort Thomas where he settled with his large family, building the Clanton House hotel. He later sold this hotel and moved to a sprawling ranch near the San Pedro River, close to Lewis Springs and a few miles outside of the small town of Charleston, which was near Tombstone. His sons Joseph Isaac "Ike" Clanton, Finneas "Finn" Clanton, and William "Billy" Clanton, became hardworking cowboys as soon as they were old enough to ride, working for their father. N.H. Clanton led his sons into rustling until the Clanton ranch was an enormous stockpen of stolen cattle, all rustled from Mexico.

The motherless Clanton boys (their mother having died shortly after giving birth to William, the youngest child) were led by the oldest, Ike Clanton, a crafty gunfighter who had no nerve for standup gun battles but preferred the ambush and the sneak attack. Finn Clanton was an easy-going cowboy who merely went along with his brothers but he avoided gunfights. Billy Clanton, who was well over six feet when sixteen, was the wildest of the boys, a hell-raiser and a deadly shot. He was fearless and foolish, seeking confrontations with gunmen where he could best them and build a reputation as a fast gun. The McLowery Brothers, Frank and Tom, who had a small ranch adjoining the Clanton spread, worked with the Clantons in their rustling raids into Mexico and invariably backed the Clantons in their confrontations with lawmen. The McLowerys (sometimes spelled McLaury) were born in Iowa and drifted into Arizona in the late 1870s where they began two small ranches. While Tom worked these ranches, Frank hired out to the Clantons to raise money. Both brothers were soon deeply involved in cattle rustling led by Ike Clanton.

Ike Clanton, leader of Tombstone's Clanton-McLowery gang.

Tombstone, the thriving city in the area, was under the control of the Clanton family by 1878, the town sheriff, John Behan, being in their employ, receiving kickbacks from the sale of the stolen cattle the Clantons had rustled. Behan was a smug little man, vainglorious and full of self-importance, but he was in reality, nothing more than a Clanton stooge who exercised his authority only when it benefited the Clanton-McLowery faction. Regardless of the attempts by certain western writers to whitewash the rustlers for whatever reasons, the Clanton-McLowery group was nothing more than a murderous band of outlaws. These men did as they pleased in Tombstone and the honest citizens there were under their criminal grip. With the coming of the Earp Brothers to Tombstone in 1879, the lawlessness of the area came to an end.

Wyatt Earp had come to Tombstone at the request of his brother Virgil Earp, who was then city marshal, to act as a deputy in helping to clean up the town. To support themselves beyond the meager pay they received as lawmen, the Earps, including Morgan Earp, who accompanied Wyatt to Tombstone, along with John "Doc" Holliday, Wyatt's friend, were given interests in certain gambling operations, a standard gratuity of the day, one which was extended to James Butler "Wild Bill" Hickok and other great lawmen of the Old West. It was claimed that Wyatt Earp and Ike Clanton befriended each other when Earp first arrived in Tombstone but that the two later fell out when Clanton refused to help Earp locate bandits who had been robbing the local stage line. This, of course, was impossible for Clanton, since it was he and his brothers, along with the McLowerys, who had been robbing the stages.

A feud between the two factions developed so that by 1881, a bloody confrontation was inevitable. For several days in October 1881, Ike Clanton and the McLowery brothers spent an unusual amount of time in Tombstone, confronting the Earps and Doc Holliday. On Oct. 25, Ike Clanton got into a fight with Virgil Earp and was pistol-whipped. On Oct. 26, 1881, Frank McLowery stepped from a store to see Wyatt Earp tethering McLowery's horse to a hitching post. McLowery ordered Earp to take his hands off his horse and the marshal told McLowery to keep his animal off the sidewalk. McLowery then rode to the O.K. Corral where he was joined by his brother Tom, Ike and Billy Clanton, and Billy Claiborne.

The outlaws then sent word to the Earps to meet them in a showdown at the corral. A short time later, Wyatt, Morgan, and Virgil Earp, accompanied by Doc Holliday, came down the street, armed with six-guns and shotguns. When they reached the corral, the Earps demanded that the rustlers throw down their guns and submit to arrest for various robberies. The outlaws fired on the lawmen who fired back, and in the space of a few minutes, Frank and Tom McLowery and Billy Clanton were shot dead. Ike Clanton, the braggart leader of the outlaws, fled at the first sound of gunfire with Billy Claiborne hot on his heels. Virgil and Morgan Earp were wounded but recovered while Wyatt Earp and Doc Holliday remained unscathed.

Claiborne was killed a few months later by Buckskin Frank Leslie in Tombstone, but Ike Clanton still headed a powerful group of gunmen, including Curly Bill Brocius, John Ringo, Frank Stilwell, Pete Spence, Florentino Cruz, and others. For months after the celebrated O.K. Corral battle, Ike Clanton schemed revenge on the Earps, arranging to have Virgil Earp ambushed in December 1881, which left him an invalid, and also employing killers to murder Morgan Earp in 1882. Wyatt Earp and others hunted down the killers and killed them one by one. Ike Clanton fled to Mexico but the cowardly gunfighter returned to Arizona after the Earps and Holliday had moved away from Tombstone.

Clanton started another small ranch on Bonita Creek near Fort Grant, but when he once more took up rustling in 1887, local lawmen J.V. Brighton and George Powell confronted him at his ranch. Clanton, in an act of rare courage, went for his gun and both deputies shot him to death. N.H. Clanton was by then dead; he had been killed before his sons lined up against the Earps in the battle of the O.K. Corral. In July 1881, N.H. Clanton and several of his rustlers, ambushed a group of Mexican cowboys driving a herd through Guadalupe Canyon, killing nineteen

Mexican vaqueros, a slaughter that was later known as the Guadalupe Canyon Massacre. Old Man Clanton paid for this butchery a few weeks later when he and four of his men were killed in the same canyon by Mexican cowboys seeking revenge for the earlier ambush. Finn Clanton survived in this terrible family of outlaws, dying peacefully in bed at the turn of the century. See: **Brocius, Curly Bill; Claiborne, William; Earp, Wyatt; Holliday, John Henry; Leslie, Nashville Frank; O.K. Corral; Ringo, John.**

Clark, Jim Cummings, 1841-95, U.S., outlaw. Missouri-born gunfighter Jim Clark committed his first criminal act at age seventeen when he stole his stepfather's mule and set out to find fortune and adventure in San Antonio, Texas. Clark sold the mule there and stole $1,400 from a rancher before returning to Missouri. When the Civil War broke out, the young outlaw signed up with William Quantrill's renegade cavalry that pillaged and burned dozens of Union strongholds in Kansas and Missouri.

In the 1870s Clark drifted into Leadville, Colo., where he boxed in the ring for hundred-dollar fees. When Clark tired of boxing, he moved to Telluride and secured an appointment as city marshal. Persistent rumors that Clark consorted with outlaws resulted in his eventual dismissal. He remained in town, however, threatening to kill city council members for fifteen cents a head or two for twenty-five cents.

On Aug. 6, 1895, Clark was shot outside the Colombo Saloon while in the company of a man known only as Mexican Sam. An errant bullet pierced Clark's heart, and he died within the hour.

Clark, Richard Brinsley Sheridan, 1838-93, U.S., gambler. Born in New York State and named after the great eighteenth-century Irish dramatist, "Dick" Clark is best remembered as the owner of the infamous Alhambra saloon and gambling resort in Tombstone, Ariz. Clark disdained formal education, and from the time he was old enough to learn the value of four aces in the hand, he wanted nothing more than to be a professional gambler. He spent much of his youth in Saginaw, Mich., where he learned how to cut, shuffle, and deal a hand of cards to an opponent. Along the way, he learned something of human nature, an important key to success on the green cloth.

Before his twenty-first birthday, Clark made his way west to begin his card-playing career. When the Civil War began, Clark enlisted in the Union army, where he could wile away the hours playing games of chance with soldiers for their pay. When the war ended, he decided to re-enlist. With the coming of the western cattle trade to Abilene in 1867, Clark soon realized there were ample new fields to conquer.

The young gambler became known throughout the cow towns as a gambler with a keen eye and nerves of steel. The Topeka *Daily Commonwealth* remarked that Clark "has the reputation of being one of the best-hearted men and cleverest poker players in the country. His face, while engaged in play, is one of the most impassive and stony I ever saw." Clark followed the buffalo hunters and drifted as far south as Fort Mobeetie, Texas, where he found it necessary on occasion, to use a gun to defend his life and property. Clark disdained violence—unless it was a life and death matter. He was an elegant dresser, with a gentlemanly air about him, but few bothered to tangle with Dick Clark, for he always packed a six-shooter.

In 1880, Clark opened his Alhambra resort in Tombstone. Clark enjoyed engaging his clientele in high stakes poker games. In one such encounter with Senator Horace Tabor, his winnings was a carload of silver ore standing on the railroad tracks outside of town. "It was the closest I ever came to owning a mine," Clark liked to boast.

The Alhambra became nationally famous, and many card players of note would seek out Clark for all-night card games at the saloon. The gambler led a rather solitary, remorseful life, however. He contracted tuberculosis and developed an addiction to morphine that often took him away from a high stakes game at the most inopportune times. In 1888 Clark attempted to turn his life around by taking 17-year-old Louisa D'Argentcourt as his wife. They bought a home in Tombstone and settled down to raise their adopted child. Later he bought a cattle ranch in the San Pedro Valley and attempted to work his way into the good graces of the big-time cattlemen who had money to burn at their annual conventions. For several years he traveled the cattle circuit plying his gambling games on an eager clientele. But his R.C. Ranch proved to be a financial drain, and in 1890, three years before his death, he sold the remaining cows for a meager $420.

Beset by his terminal illness and drug addiction, Clark sought the expert help of some Chicago doctors who pronounced his case hopeless. After seeing the attractions of the World's Fair, Dick Clark returned to Arizona in October 1893. He made it as far as Albuquerque where he died in a local hotel. Clark was buried with great honors in Boothill Cemetery—alongside rustlers, thieves, and gunmen. A national day of mourning was declared for this beloved local figure.

Clayton, William H.H., prom. 1874-93, U.S., lawman. William Clayton served as the U.S. Attorney for the Western District at Fort Smith (Ark.) from July 1874 until he was replaced by James Read, a political appointee of President Grover Cleveland, in 1893. Except for a four-year period from 1885-90, when Cleveland replaced him with M.H. Sandel, Clayton was involved in nearly every major case docketed in Judge Isaac Parker's courtroom. Attorney Clayton prosecuted over 10,000 cases, convicting eighty men of murder, forty of whom went to the gallows.

Clayton served on the side of the Union in the Civil War, and was admitted to the Arkansas bar in 1871. Two years later he was named judge of the First Judicial Circuit Court. He resigned in 1874 to accept President Ulysses Grant's appointment to serve as the U.S. Attorney. See: **Parker, Isaac.**

Clements, Emmanuel, Jr. (AKA: Mannie), d.1908, U.S., gunman-lawman. Following in his father's footsteps, Emmanuel Clements, Jr., became a feared western gunman. No matter which side of the law Clements was on, he was dangerous when provoked.

In 1894, Mannie Clements arrived in El Paso, Texas, where he became deputy constable and then deputy sheriff. Mannie had fled from Murphysville, where he had been hired to kill local bad man Pink Taylor. Clements had fired at Taylor through an open window, but missed and hit the wrong man. In the 1890s, Clements teamed up with his cousin, John Wesley Hardin, and his brother-in-law, "Killin'" Jim Miller. The three of them operated together on the wrong side of the law for many years.

Emmanuel Clements, Jr., a hot-headed gunman and lawman.

Clements was indicted for armed robbery in 1908, but was acquitted because the jury did not dare return a Guilty verdict. Though he had been cleared, Clements's law enforcement career was ruined. He began drinking heavily, and turned to smuggling to earn a living. It is believed that his fatal shooting at the El Paso Coney Island Saloon on Dec. 29, 1908, was the result of an argument with the bartender, Joe Brown. Brown was also involved in the illegal importation of Chinese workers into the U.S. See: **Clements, Emmanuel, Sr.; Hardin, John Wesley.**

Clements, Emmanuel, Sr. (AKA: Mannen), d.1887, U.S., outlaw. Emmanuel Clements, known as Mannen, was one of four brothers brought up on a cattle ranch near Smiley, Texas. Mannen was the most notorious of the brothers, and was accused occasionally of cattle rustling. His cousin was the legendary gunman John Wesley Hardin, who came to live on the Clements ranch for a time and worked as a cowhand. Hardin took the brothers' herd on a trail drive and fought against the Sutton clan, who were feuding with the Taylors, blood relatives of the Clements family. In October

Emmanuel Clements, Sr.

1872, Mannen repaid Hardin's many kindnesses by springing him from his jail cell. Hardin sawed through the bars of the cell and Mannen used his lariat to pull the escapee to freedom.

The Clements clan became very wealthy as they continued to drive cattle to the Kansas railheads throughout the 1870s. But in 1877, Mannen found himself sharing a cell with Hardin, Johnny Ringo, and Bill Taylor. A decade later, Mannen ran for sheriff of Runnels County. The distinction between lawmen and outlaws frequently blurred in the Old West.

While campaigning for elective office, Clements was shot and killed at the Senate Saloon in Ballinger, Texas, on Mar. 29, 1887, by Marshal Joe Townsend. See: **Hardin, John Wesley.**

Clever, Charles P., prom. 1858-62, U.S., lawman. Prussian-born Charles Clever served as deputy marshal under Charles Blumner, but was tainted by a scandal after speculating in jurors certificates (receipts given to jurors by federal marshals, who would exchange them for currency when the U.S. government paid the marshal). In his official capacity, Clever purchased the certificates from jurors at a substantial discount, resulting in his dismissal. Clever discredited himself in other ways. He provided grist for political opponents by maintaining a Mexican mistress. Yet he remained a powerful force in New Mexico's political and business circles for many years.

Clever arrived in New Mexico Territory in 1850. After

taking out citizenship papers, he formed a partnership with Sigmund Seligman, a wealthy German Jew who paved the way for Clever to become director of the *Santa Fe Weekly Gazette*. After serving his apprenticeship under Blumner, Charles Clever was appointed marshal on Mar. 30, 1858, largely through the efforts of territorial delegate Miguel A. Otero who prevailed upon President James Buchanan. Clever was appointed over the objections of Governor William Carr Lane who recommended an easterner named Samuel Ellison for the job.

Two months after taking office Clever appointed Sheriff Jesus Maria Sena y Baca as his deputy. It was a wise political move aimed at winning Clever Hispanic support—and one that was soundly praised in the pages of the marshal's very own paper—the *Weekly Gazette*.

Marshal Charles P. Clever.

As a lawman, Charles Clever often found himself relying on the abilities of the local militia unit, which in those days were often incapable of maintaining order in remote territories. Hubert Howe Bancroft described the army garrison as "lazy, careless, indifferent, and stupid." Yet, Clever counted on their support when Juan Ortega and his Mesilla Guard savagely murdered eight Apache Indians in 1858. The local residents refused to organize a posse, because they sympathized with the Mexican. Clever was forced to turn to the army for help. They obliged by swearing out a warrant and providing a military guard to accompany the marshal. Clever succeeded in arresting Ortega and thirty-five members of his renegade band, and bringing them to trial in Socorro.

Charles Clever was the last of New Mexico's pre-Civil War marshals. His term expired in 1861, but Clever remained in office until Aug. 16, 1862, when Albert W. Archibald, a Nova Scotian gold seeker, was named to replace Clever. Archibald was disqualified after failing to post the proper bond and never served.

Clifton, Daniel (AKA: **Dynamite Dick**), d.1896, U.S., outlaw. Dan Clifton was an Oklahoma cattle rustler who turned to bank robbery. In the 1890s, he joined Bill Doolin's "Oklahombres," who terrorized the Southwest for nearly a decade. Clifton supplied the firepower for the Doolin mob, who were relentlessly pursued by local posses.

In Southwest City, Mo., on May 20, 1895, the Doolin gang held up the bank. With guns blazing, Clifton, Doolin, and Bill Dalton fought their way out of town. The three gunfighters shot and killed former Missouri state auditor J.C. Seaborn and escaped after sustaining only minor injuries themselves.

Doolin and Clifton were arrested in Guthrie the next year, but they bribed a prison guard and made a clean escape. Dan Clifton did not live long enough to enjoy his freedom. With a posse on his trail, Clifton holed up at Sid Williams' farm sixteen miles outside of Newkirk, Okla. He was trapped there on Dec. 4, 1896, by deputy marshals George Lawson and W.H. Bussey. When Clifton tried to escape on horseback, a bullet from Lawson's rifle shattered his arm, knocking him off the horse, to the ground.

Dan "Dynamite Dick" Clifton, a member of Bill Doolin's outlaw band killed by an Oklahoma posse.

The wounded outlaw hid in a cabin deep in the woods, but his pursuers caught up with him later that night. Clifton burst out of the cabin, shooting wildly at the deputies as he ran, but they shot him in the back. Clifton died minutes later. See: **Doolin, William M.**

Cochise, c.1824-74, U.S., rob. Cochise led the Chiricahua Apaches into battle against white settlers and the U.S. Army during the 1860s. In 1861 he was captured by the army for kidnapping a Mexican-American child named Felix Tellez, a crime he denied. He escaped from the territorial prison, taking with him several hostages. Within two months, 150 non-Indians including soldiers, miners, and settlers were brutally murdered. Many homesteaders simply abandoned their property rather than square off against the marauding Apaches. Cochise evaded capture and plundered and pillaged the Arizona territory and Mexican borderlands for ten years, until 1872 when a peaceful settlement was reached, whereby a large reservation of land was set aside for the Apache tribe. See: **Bascom Affair**.

Cockeyed Frank, See: **Loving, Frank.**

Cody, William Frederick (AKA: **Buffalo Bill**), 1846-1917, U.S., gunman. No man typified the myth and folklore of the Old West better than William Cody, whose genius for self-promotion translated into a rich harvest, both for himself and the financial backers who organized "Buffalo Bill's Wild West" a traveling circus and side show that charmed audiences around the world for nearly thirty-five years. Blending myth and fact together into one pleasing package, Cody succeeded in romanticizing the West in such a way that it was to become grist for countless dime store novels, stage plays, Hollywood movies, and television programs.

Cody was born and reared in Scott County, Iowa. In 1854 his father Isaac, a politician, moved the family to the Salt Creek Valley near Fort Leavenworth, Kan. While speaking before a gathering over the issue of Kansas being admitted as a free or slave state, the elder Cody was violently stabbed. Although Cody's father survived, family members later attributed his death in 1857 to this injury. Following his father's untimely death, young Bill Cody was forced to seek work as a messenger with Majors & Waddell, an overland express company later known as Russell, Majors & Waddell. Cody later became a Pony Express rider for the same company, working under a division headed by the notorious gunfighter Joseph A. Slade. When the Civil War broke out, Cody attached himself to several independent militias and effectively served them as a "jay-hawker"—someone who steals horses. Near the war's conclusion, in 1864, Cody officially enlisted as a private in the Seventh Kansas Volunteer Cavalry, which saw action against reknowned Confederate generals Nathan Bedford Forrest and Sterling Price.

After the war, Cody married and attempted to settle down as an innkeeper at Salt Creek Valley. This business venture proved unsuccessful and did not suit the tastes of the restless Cody, who, in 1867, signed an agreement with the Union Pacific's Eastern Division to supply buffalo meat to the construction workers on the line. His legendary ability as a buffalo hunter during this period earned him his famous nickname.

"Buffalo Bill" Cody came to the attention of Lieutenant General Philip H. Sheridan, who hired him as chief of scouts for the Fifth U.S. Cavalry. He held down this post for four years (1868-72), during which time he engaged in sixteen Indian fights. Cody fought a hand-to-hand battle with Cheyenne Chief Yellow Hand immediately following Custer's massacre, killing and scalping the chief, holding up the chief's scalp and shouting: "First coup for Custer!" For this and other actions during the Indian wars, Cody was awarded the Congressional Medal of Honor. An expert marksman, Cody distinguished himself against the Cheyenne at Summit Springs on July 11, 1869. That year he met up with the famous western writer Edward Zane Carroll Judson, who wrote many popular dime novels under the pen name of "Ned Buntline." Intrigued by Cody's exploits as a "great white hunter," Buntline made him the hero in dozens of mass-produced short stories. In 1872 the author talked Cody into going on stage as an actor. Cody did so and performed convincingly in many one-act plays for the next eleven theatrical seasons.

Following a successful July 4, 1883, pageant at North Platte, Neb., Cody was inspired to organize the "Buffalo Bill's Wild West," a show which brought to a circus tent or stage "true scenes" from the West as it was being lived. Cody took the show to England in 1887 for Queen Victoria's Jubilee celebration. The show included a re-enactment of Custer's Last Stand, a riding and roping exhibition, and a display of marksmanship by Annie Oakley, who was known to all as "Little Sure Shot." The Wild West show received such critical acclaim that it went on tour, appearing before enthusiastic audiences at the 1893 World's Columbian Exposition in Chicago.

The show continued for many years. Cody orchestrated the main events and supervised every aspect of production. Thanks to Buffalo Bill Cody, the history of the Old West was elevated to mythic proportions. The public was fascinated and desired to learn more about a time and place that had all but vanished from the scene. See: **Slade, Joseph Alfred.**

Coe, Frank, d.1931, U.S., gunman. As a young man, Frank Coe worked as a farmer and ranch hand in Lincoln County, N.M., just before that county's infamous war. Coe and his cousin, George, pooled their money together and invested in the first thresher in Lincoln County. When the Lincoln County War started, the Coe cousins joined the Chisum-McSween-Tunstall coalition and engaged in a series of pitched gun battles against the faction fighting for the politically influential James Dolan and James Riley, owners of the powerful mercantile store, The House. On Apr. 4, 1878, George Coe and John Middleton were shot and wounded when they sat down to lunch at Blazer's Mill, N.M., by Buckshot Roberts. Dick Brewer, leader of the McSween Regulators, and Frank Coe shot it out with Roberts. Both Roberts and Brewer were killed in the battle.

There were many more such skirmishes in the following months. On Apr. 30, Cow, Frank McNab, and Ab Sanders were ambushed by Murphy-Dolan supporters near McNab's ranch. McNab was killed, Sanders seriously wounded, and Coe, his horse shot from under him, was captured. When the Lincoln County War had finally ended, the Coe cousins moved to San Juan County, then left New Mexico before Frank Coe returned to Lincoln County in 1884. Coe lived there with his wife and six children until he died in 1931. See: **Billy the Kid; Coe, George Washington; Lincoln County War.**

Coe, George Washington, 1856-1941, U.S., gunman. George Coe's father was a Civil War veteran, who had moved his family from Brighton, Iowa, to Missouri. After his eighteenth birthday in 1874, Coe moved to Fort Stanton, N.M., to work on his cousin Frank's ranch. Four years later, he leased his own piece of property in Lincoln County, just when the Lincoln County War flared up. Many local ranchers were drawn into the power struggle between the Murphy-Dolan faction on one side, and John Chisum, Alexander McSween, and John Tunstall on the other. Although only a bystander to these events, George Coe was arrested by William Brady, the puppet sheriff controlled by Murphy-Dolan, and subjected to various physical tortures.

Coe was released, but he swore vengeance. With his cousin, Frank, Coe fought on the side of Chisum, Tunstall, and McSween. He was badly injured on Apr. 4, 1878, at Blazer's Mill, N.M. Buckshot Roberts, a member of the rival faction had just ridden into town, and Coe and his partners tried to persuade the armed gunman to surrender peacefully, but he answered them with a spray of gunfire. George Coe's hand was shattered by a stray bullet from Roberts' rifle. Buckshot Roberts was shot and killed.

George Coe led a number of armed raids against the Lincoln cow camps, and fought with reckless abandon alongside Billy the Kid and others. His activities in the Lincoln County War made Coe a wanted man. When the hostilities ceased, he petitioned Governor Lew Wallace for amnesty. In 1884, after brief stays in Nebraska and Colorado, Coe settled permanently in Lincoln County, where he operated the Golden Glow Ranch. He became a respected member of the community and lived in peace until his death. See: **Billy the Kid; Coe, Frank; Lincoln County War.**

Coe, Philip Haddox, d.1871, U.S., gunman. Philip Coe was an itinerant gambler who associated with the Second Texas Mounted Rifles near the Rio Grande Valley in 1862. Coe was instantly popular, and the men elected him a lieutenant, which violated military protocol. The regimental officers ordered him to enlist properly, or stop posing as an officer. When he refused, the army simply drafted him, but Coe fled to Mexico to sit out the Civil War. When the South surrendered in 1865, Coe drifted into Abilene, Kan., a fierce cow town known for its lawlessness. There he opened the Bull's Head Saloon with fellow gamblers Ben Thompson and Tom Bowles. The saloon stood on the outskirts of town, and was the first friendly place the trail hands encountered when they rode in. Coe advertised with a hanging sign that depicted the bull's anatomy in graphic detail.

Coe had sold his interests in the saloon by the time the citizens of Abilene prevailed upon their sheriff, Wild Bill Hickok, to cover the offensive portion of the sign. Coe and Hickok became bitter enemies. The situation was further complicated when Coe became involved with Hickok's former mistress.

Coe and fifty drunken cowboys from Texas ambled into Abilene on Oct. 5, 1871. They accosted townsmen in the street, and became generally disruptive. In one of many saloons, Coe and his friends ran into Marshal Hickok, who bought them a round of drinks. Later that night, when a shot was fired in the streets, Hickok ran out and told Coe he was endangering the lives of Abilene's citizens. Coe said he fired at a dog, wherein Hickok reached for his six-shooter. Coe fired first, but his shot passed harmlessly through the marshal's coat. Hickok took aim and drilled Coe through the stomach.

At that moment, Deputy Mike Williams rushed to Hickok's assistance. An angry crowd had gathered in the street, but the marshal, who suffered from poor eyesight, did not recognize Williams. He spun around and fired two shots into the young man's head by accident. Coe's life had ended, but so did Hickok's career in law enforcement. The next year he joined Buffalo Bill's Wild West Show. See: **Hickok, James Butler.**

Colbert, Chunk, d.1874, U.S., gunman. Chunk Colbert enjoyed a modest reputation as a gunslinger, having killed at least seven men in Texas, New Mexico, and Colorado during the 1870s. In the early 1870s he shot Charles Morris dead in Cimarron, N.M., after becoming convinced that the man had been trifling with Colbert's wife.

Clay Allison proved to be a better gunman than Colbert, however. On Jan. 7, 1874, the two men went to Clifton House, an inn in Colfax County, N.M., to eat after failing to resolve their differences in a horse race. The quarter-mile trot between the two men ended in a dead heat. After finishing his meal, Allison relaxed over a cup of coffee. Colbert, meanwhile, resolved to kill his adversary. But as Colbert fingered his holstered gun nervously, the astute Allison pulled out his own revolver and blasted him through the forehead. Colbert was buried behind the inn.

See: **Allison, Clay.**

Cole, James, prom. 1886-87, U.S., lawman. James Cole, a marshal and peace officer assigned to the Indian Territories during the 1880s, often dispensed frontier justice from the point of his gun. He and Deputy Marshal Frank Dalton were once sent to the Cherokee reservation to capture suspected horse thief Dave Smith. They tracked him to his camp near the Arkansas River, where he was joined by his brother-in-law Lee Dixon, fellow horse thief William Towerly, and Dixon's wife.

The gang spotted Cole first, and opened fire. Dalton was shot through the chest, fell to the ground, and was finished off by Towerly, who emptied his Winchester into the deputy. Cole was shot in his side by Smith, but he refused to retreat. Cole killed Dixon's wife and Smith, and wounded Dixon. Towerly managed to escape, but only temporarily. He was soon killed in a shootout. Cole brought Dixon back to Fort Smith, where he died of his wounds.

Coleman, William Tell, 1824-93, U.S., lawman. William Coleman was the law unto himself during the heyday of the San Francisco Vigilance Committee—that collection of vain glorious civic boosters, do-gooders, and businessmen who pooled their resources to stamp out wrongdoing and put to death the criminal element. Coleman was a native Kentuckian who made his way to Sacramento, Calif., in 1849, where he founded the mercantile firm of William T. Coleman & Company almost one year later.

In 1851, Coleman replaced Sam Brannan as leader of the vigilante movement, but the group remained dormant until 1856 when newspaper editor James King was shot to death. Coleman was instrumental in stirring up a local frenzy, which led to a public hanging of the perpetrators. Coleman personally sanctioned much of the violence that was to follow, although he is thought by some to have been a stabilizing influence on the group. When the anti-Chinese hysteria swept through San Francisco in July 1877, Coleman organized another vigilante band, the Committee of Public Safety, which he armed with pick handles.

Though in many ways Coleman was a pillar of the business community for many years, his activities on behalf of the vigilante groups was clearly outside the law. Author Robert Louis Stevenson glowingly referred to Coleman as the "Lion of the Vigilantes," a self-aggrandizing description that was later borrowed by James A.B. Scherer, who wrote a biography of Coleman in 1939. See: **San Francisco**

Colfax County War, 1875-85, U.S., feud. The complex history of this range war between homesteaders, cattlemen, and unscrupulous land speculators dates back to 1841, when the Mexican governor Manuel Armijo awarded a land grant to Carlos Beaubien, a prominent Taos merchant, and his associate Guadelupe Miranda who was the collector of customs for New Mexico. After Beaubien died in 1864, his son-in-law Lucien Bonaparte Maxwell bought the outstanding claims as well as the lands owned by Miranda. Maxwell soon found himself occupying a position of enormous power. His holdings included some 97,000 acres of land in northeastern New Mexico and southern Colorado.

When gold was discovered in 1867, thousands of prospectors poured into Maxwell's land with little regard for his existing claim. Realizing his dilemma, the Mexican made it known in 1869, that the grant was for sale. Two groups of investors immediately stepped forward: a Denver group headed by Jerome B. Chaffee, a well-to-do mine owner, and the New Mexico Republican district attorney Stephen Elkins. Chaffee and Elkins were granted an option to buy, and in 1870 the purchase was concluded for the sum of $1.35 million. The Maxwell Land Grant and Railroad Company was organized for the sole purpose of returning a handsome profit on the investment. To achieve these ends, the company skirted the law by having the grant surveyed as a 2-million-acre plot rather than the actual 97,000-acre limit established in 1869. Two years later Secretary of the Interior Columbus Delano ruled that the grant covered only 97,000 acres as specified in the original 1869 ruling. Chaffee and Elkins found themselves in an untenable position. Facing financial ruin, they attempted to press their claim in Congress, but first it was necessary to organize a grassroots political movement to grease the way. Out of sheer necessity, the Santa Fe Ring, composed of wealthy Republican businessmen and politicians who shared a common interest in exploiting the rich natural resources of New Mexico and Colorado, was organized.

Despite the formidable organization behind them, Elkins and Chaffee faced bankruptcy proceedings in 1875. The claim was sold in order to cover tax liability, but through some rather shifty financial and legal maneuvering, it ended up in the hands of Elkins' former law partner, Thomas B. Catron. Compounding the thorny legal problems facing Elkins, was the presence of squatters on company lands. Gold miners occupied a campsite near Elizabethtown. The Texas ranchers, who coveted the rich grazing lands, allowed their herds to roam freely on Maxwell territory. It was inevitable that a clash of wills would occur over these hotly disputed lands.

The first phase of the Colfax County War started in September 1875, when a Methodist minister, the Reverend T.J. Tolby, was ambushed near Cimarron, allegedly by two Mexicans, Cruz Vegan and Manuel Cardenas, who were forced to "confess." The gunmen were allegedly hired by Robert Longwill, probate judge of Colfax County, and three of his cronies. Reverend Tolby had threatened to blow the whistle on Judge Joseph Palen, an associate of the company engaged in shady financial dealings. When the local authorities indicated that they were not interested in tracking down the killers, Tolby's friends took matters into their own hands. Vega was lynched by an angry mob of settlers led by the Reverend Oscar P. McMains, and Cardenas was ambushed while on his way to court. After Pancho Griego, an intimate of Longwill was murdered by the Texas gunman Clay Allison, the frightened judge placed himself in the protective custody of Marshal John Pratt in Santa Fe.

When the violence threatened to erupt into anarchy, Governor Samuel B. Axtell proclaimed the county in a state of riot. The Colfax County courts were abolished in January 1876 and attached to Taos County for expediency. Governor Axtell ordered special agent Ben Stevens into Cimarron to arrest Clay Allison, and provided him with a detachment of U.S. Army regulars to help out. Allison surrendered without incident. When a grand jury refused to return indictments against him in June 1876, Allison walked out of court a free man.

Stymied by the courts, the squatters lodged a formal complaint in Washington, accusing Thomas Catron and his henchmen with masterminding the murder of Reverend Tolby and for falsifying a set of charges brought against the wife of William R. Morley, a political enemy of Elkins. Morley told the attorney general that Thomas Catron had slandered him in Cimarron society. Catron accused the *Cimarron News and Press*, a paper owned by Morley, of fomenting hysteria and whipping up the vigilantes. The political cabal that controlled New Mexico politics and the federal judiciary was ultimately exposed. Marshal Pratt, who later left office, was discredited, as well as others.

The Colfax County War dragged on for nearly a decade. In 1879 U.S. land commissioner James A. Williamson handed down a ruling to the effect that a surveyor's recommendation would determine the size of a claim rather than the Colonization Law. Elkins ordered a new survey drawn, and the Maxwell Land Grant Company received patents for 1,714,764 acres. The patents were upheld by the U.S. Supreme Court in 1887. The company continued to thrive well into the 1960s when its holdings were divided up and sold to private investors. See: **Allison, Clay; Pratt, John;**
Catron, Thomas Benton.

Collins, Ben, d.1906, U.S., lawman. Ben Collins represented law and order in the Indian Territory of Oklahoma during the 1890s. He was appointed deputy U.S. marshal in 1898, which brought him into contact with some of the most infamous characters in the vast ungoverned lands. In 1905, in Emet, Okla., Collins was ordered to arrest Port Pruitt, one of the town's leading citizens. Pruitt brandished a gun, but Collins dropped him with a single shot. As it turned out, the shot permanently crippled Pruitt, who swore revenge. Later that year, he paid an assassin $500 to kill Collins. The killer took his $200 advance and skipped the country.

On Aug. 1, 1906, Marshal Collins was ambushed near his home in Emet by "Killin'" Jim Miller, who shot him in the stomach while Collins' wife looked on. See: **Miller, James.**

Collins, William, d.1878, U.S., outlaw. A brother of the more celebrated Joel Collins, William Collins, began robbing trains after his brother Joel was killed by lawmen in 1877. Following a train robbery in Mesquite, Texas, Collins fled north on horseback, a posse tracking him through Colorado, Wyoming, the Black Hills, and then into Canada. U.S. marshal Bill Anderson alone finally cornered Collins in Pembina, Manitoba, Can. On Nov. 8, 1878, both Collins and Anderson faced each other, drawing their six-guns, advancing on each other, and emptying their revolvers at the same time. Both died from their wounds. Anderson's body was shipped back to Texas and his widow was given the $10,000 reward posted for Collins. The outlaw's body was buried in Pembina.

Connelly, Charles T., d.1892, U.S., lawman. Charles T. Connelly was the city marshal at Coffeyville, Kan., at the time when the Dalton gang raided two banks on Oct. 5, 1892. When the outlaws attacked the banks, Connelly was in an upstairs room. He ran to the street

Charles T. Connelly

and tried to borrow a rifle from George Cubine, who was using the weapon to fire on the Daltons. Cubine told him to find a rifle of his own. Connelly finally managed to grab a rifle and he raced into the street, firing at Grat Dalton, who turned his horse about and raced down the street straight at Connelly, killing him with a single shot at a distance of twenty feet. See: **Dalton Brothers.**

Cook, David J., 1842-1907, U.S., lawman. Though not as well known as Wild Bill Hickok, Wyatt Earp, and other legends of the Old West, David Cook attained prominence in his own right, for arresting more than 3,000 outlaws. In 1882, he published his memoirs, *Hands Up! or Twenty Years of Detective Work In the Mountains and on the Plains.* Cook's career began in 1859, when he moved to Colorado.

He joined the Colorado Cavalry, and spent the Civil War years hunting down Confederate spies and smugglers. In 1866, Cook was appointed city marshal of Denver, and later worked as a federal marshal and private eye. Marshal Cook tracked down the dreaded Musgrove-Franklin Gang. In 1868, he put Lee Musgrove behind bars, and then lured Franklin to Denver to try to spring his partner from jail. Cook cornered Franklin in his room at the Overland Hotel. When the gunman reached for his pistol, Cook drilled him through the heart. Throughout his lengthy career, Cook seems to have lived by his one simple credo: "Never hit a man over the head with a pistol, because afterward you may want to use your weapon and find it disabled."

Cook, Thalis T., prom. 1895, U.S., lawman. Thalis Cook was a God-fearing gunfighter who belonged to Company D of the Texas Rangers. His work on behalf of the church belied his reputation as a dangerous gunman. He was involved in the 1895 shootout at Marathon, Texas. Cook and his partner, Jim Putnam, were sent in to arrest Fin Gilliland for murder. Gilliland pulled his .45-caliber pistol and took aim at Cook as the men passed on horseback.

The shot hit Cook in the knee, which caused him permanent disability. Ran-

Lawman Thalis T. Cook.

ger Putnam shot Gilliland's horse from under him, forcing the fugitive to take cover behind the carcass. In the exchange of shots, Gilliland was hit between the eyes. Neither Cook nor his partner was sure who fired the shot.

Cook, William Tuttle (AKA: **John Williams; John Mayfield**), b.1873., U.S., outlaw. William Cook was born near Fort Gibson in the Cherokee Nation and was left homeless at age fourteen when his mother died in 1887. Cook served as a scout for U.S. marshals from Fort Smith, Ark., guiding them through the Indian Territory. Judge Isaac Parker in Fort Smith sentenced Cook to forty days in

Bill Cook who led a notorious band of outlaws in the early 1890s.

jail in 1893 for the illegal sale of liquor in the Indian Territory. Cook vowed that when he was released, he would put together an outlaw gang and take his revenge. In June 1894, Cook organized one of the most vicious outlaw bands in the territory. Members included Crawford Goldsby, known as Cherokee Bill; Thurman "Skeeter" Baldwin; Jess Snyder; William Farris; Curtis Dayson; Elmer "Chicken" Lucas; Jim French; George Sanders; Sam Mc-Williams, also known as the Verdigris Kid; Lon Gordon, and Henry Munson. The gang raided banks and trains at will, until dozens of lawmen tracked down these outlaws one by one. Gordon and Munson were trapped after the Cook gang robbed the Chandler, Okla., bank, on July 31, 1894. Both Gordon and Munson shot it out with an entire troop of the Creek Light Horse at Sapulpa, Okla., on Aug. 2, 1894. Munson and Gordon were both killed in this battle.

The gang then robbed the Kansas City and Missouri Express at Coretta, Okla., on Oct. 20, 1894. At this time

Cook ordered his men to go through the coaches while the train was at a standstill, cursing the passengers and firing his six-gun into the air. Unlike Crawford Goldsby, the real killer of the band, Cook was no gunman and avoided gunplay at all costs. Following the Coretta train robbery, the Cook gang robbed a number of stores and company offices, stealing large payrolls. When the gang robbed the Schufeldt and Son store in Lenapah, Goldsby, for no apparent reason, shot and killed a prominent citizen, Ernest Melton, who was standing in the store looking out a window at the time.

The gang members rode off in different directions, but determined sheriffs and U.S. marshals tracked them down. Dayson and Lucas had been captured after the Chandler, Okla., bank robbery. Both were sent to prison to serve long terms. Then Baldwin, Snyder, and Farris were captured and they, too, were given long prison terms. French, Sanders, and the Verdigris Kid were shot to death by lawmen when they resisted arrest. Goldsby was captured and later hanged for the Melton murder. Cook himself was finally apprehended in a bloodless capture by Sheriff Thomas D. Love of Borden County, Texas, and Sheriff C.C. Perry of Chaves County, N.M., near Fort Sumner, N.M., on Jan. 11, 1895. He was tried for bank robbery before Judge Isaac Parker on Feb. 12, 1895, and found Guilty. Cook was sent to the federal prison at Albany, N.Y., to serve forty-five years. He died some time later in prison. See: **Baldwin, Thurman; Goldsby, Crawford.**

Cooley, Scott, 1845-c.1876, U.S., outlaw. Scott Cooley, a former member of the Texas Rangers, spurred the Mason County War of 1875 through an act of vengeance against Deputy Sheriff John Worley. Cooley held Worley responsible for the death of his friend and benefactor Tim Williamson.

Lawman-turned-outlaw Scott Cooley.

In September 1875, Deputy Sheriff Worley arrested Williamson on suspicion of cattle rustling. While he was in jail, an angry mob shot Williamson to death. That incident marked the start of the Mason County War, which pitted the German cattlemen of Texas against the native-born Texans. Williamson had been killed by the Germans, and when Cooley got word of it, he went to Worley's home. He found the deputy working on his well with an assistant, who had been lowered over the side. Cooley shot Worley dead, and the well worker, who had clung to a rope,

tumbled to the bottom.

Cooley cut off his victim's ears, showed them to the anti-Williamson faction, and then killed Peter Border, the second man on his death list. The war dragged on for another year, with many deaths on both sides, until the Texas Rangers restored order. Cooley escaped from a posse at the Llano River in 1875, and was never heard from again, though some say he died in 1876.

Copeland, James, 1815-57, U.S., outlaw. James Copeland and his gang of ruthless "land pirates" gained a popular following in Mississippi in the 1840s. Despite their reputation for depravity, the Copeland gang had dealings with the upper crust, land-owning Wage family of Augusta. The Wages used their political ties to protect Copeland from the law. In return, Copeland performed various "services," for the family, including murder.

"Land pirate" James Copeland.

On July 15, 1848, Copeland shot and killed James Harvey in revenge for the murder of Gale H. Wages. Gale's father paid Copeland $1,000 to carry out the murder. Copeland was quickly identified as the killer, arrested, tried, and convicted. Although it was common knowledge in Augusta that Wages had hired Copeland to kill Harvey, Copeland steadfastly refused to implicate Wages. As a testament to the family's power, Copeland stayed alive for nine years. He was hanged on Oct. 30, 1857.

Cornett, Brack, d.1888, U.S., outlaw. A member of the Bill Whitley band, Brack Cornett was born and raised in Goliad County, Texas. Along with Whitley and others, Cornett robbed banks and trains in southwest Texas in the late 1880s. In 1888, Whitley, Cornett, and others robbed the bank at Cisco, Texas, taking $25,000 and, a few days later, they stopped an I&GN train near McNeill in Travis County, stealing $20,000 from the express car. Cornett's gang stopped another Southern Pacific train at Harwood, but a sheriff's posse was on board waiting for them and the gang was driven off. The band was successful in robbing another train near Flatonia. At Floresville in Wilson County, Texas, the band was finally trapped by U.S. marshals on Sept. 25, 1888. The gang members elected to shoot it out and Whitley was killed, another member was captured, and Cornett escaped in a wild ride across the plains. Sheriff Alfred Allee tracked the bandit across Arizona and, at Frio, shot it out with him, killing Cornett.

Cortez, Gregorio, 1875-1916, U.S., outlaw. The Mexican-born Gregorio Cortez migrated to Texas in 1887 where, in his teens, he worked as a ranch hand, or a *vaquero*. He and his brother Romaldo rented a few acres of land in Karnes County where they had lived for eleven years, raising some corn crops. Cortez had never had any trouble with the law and was considered a quiet, law-abiding ranch worker. He was married and had four children. On June 10, 1901, Sheriff W.T. "Brack" Morris, a 41-year-old lawman who had seen many years service with the Texas Rangers, and who had been sheriff of Karnes County for four years, received a message from the sheriff of Atacosa County that a Mexican had recently stolen a horse and he had been trailed to Karnes County. Morris was asked to look for the horse thief. Having only a brief description, Morris went to the Cortez farm, on June 12, having heard that Cortez had recently traded, not sold, a horse.

Morris met with Romaldo and Gregorio Cortez and asked Gregorio if he had recently traded a horse. He denied having done so. Cortez' historical defenders later insisted that Cortez would have answered "yes" to that question if Morris had asked him if he had traded a *mare,* which is about the thinnest kind of hairsplitting. When Morris heard this—already having the statement from another Mexican that Cortez had, indeed, traded a horse recently—he got off his horse, stepped through the rails of a fence and told Gregorio and Romaldo Cortez that he was arresting them for horse stealing. Morris' remarks were translated into Spanish by Boone Choate, who had accompanied Morris to the ranch, a useless chore in that Gregorio Cortez spoke English but made no effort to speak the language and let Choate labor through his translations. Gregorio Cortez, who was wearing a six-gun, was about twelve feet from Morris and he spoke quickly in Spanish to the sheriff, words later interpreted by Choate to mean: "No white man can arrest me."

Cortez pulled his gun as the unarmed Romaldo "ran at Morris" as if to seize him. Morris drew his weapon and first shot Romaldo, wounding him. He turned to Cortez and both men fired, Morris' bullets going wild. Cortez fired four bullets into Morris who reeled down the fence. When he fell, Cortez ran to him and pumped another bullet into the sheriff. The unarmed Choate jumped from a buggy and ran into a wooded area where he found a deputy, John

Trimmell, who was armed. Both men thought it prudent to go to Kennedy and form a posse. This they did.

Meanwhile, Gregorio packed his wounded brother in a buckboard, along with his family, and fled, leaving Sheriff Morris to bleed to death. Gregorio took his wounded brother to Kennedy where he was left with relatives and then he struck out on foot, wearing low cut, pointed shoes, leaving his two horses behind, correctly reasoning that the posse that would be looking for him would head south toward the Rio Grande, figuring that he would head for Mexico. Cortez walked eighty miles in forty hours, finally staying with Martin Robledo near Ottine.

Robert M. Glover, sheriff of Gonzales County, went to the jail in Kennedy where the Cortez family had been locked up and talked to three women, Cortez' mother, wife, and sister-in-law. One of the women, it was never learned which, told Glover that Cortez was headed for the Robledo ranch. The sheriff and a large posse thundered after the killer. Glover and his men arrived at the Robledo ranch at night and gunfire immediately ensued. Which side fired first was never determined, but Cortez, wearing no shoes after his long walk, marched boldly toward Glover who was on horseback, trading shots with him until his bullets slammed into Sheriff Glover and knocked him dead from the saddle. Also killed was Henry Schnabel, a member of the posse and owner of the land worked by the Robledo family. He was killed by either Cortez or, as some later claimed, by bullets fired from the posse.

While the posse rounded up the Robledo family, Cortez fled, hiding in the bush. After the lawmen left the Robledo house, he returned, put on his shoes and then went to another friend, Ceferino Flores who gave him a fast mount and a six-gun. Cortez then set out for Mexico with hundreds of lawmen, militia, and vigilantes swarming all over southern Texas in search of him. He rode two horses nearly to death, hiding in small towns and pretending to be a common laborer, harbored by sympathetic Mexicans who looked upon him as a hero. The outlaw had covered an enormous amount of ground, walking almost 100 miles and riding more than 400. He was only a few miles from the Rio Grande and Mexico. By then a $1,000 reward had been posted for Cortez' capture by the governor of Texas. Jesus Gonzalez spotted Cortez near the border and informed a nearby hunting party where they could find the outlaw, who was arrested without a struggle on June 22, 1901.

Cortez was jailed in San Antonio and, at that time, a campaign headed by the Miguel Hidalgo Workers' Party in San Antonio was begun to raise a huge defense fund for Cortez. Cortez was tried at Gonzalez on July 24, 1901, for the murders of sheriffs Morris and Glover and sentenced to fifty years. His lawyers filed one appeal after another, insisting that Sheriff Morris had denied Cortez his rights when arresting him for horse stealing since he had no warrant for this arrest. The legal battle for Cortez raged for several years and a number of trials were reversed and tried again while Cortez spent twelve years in prison, nine of them in Huntsville Penitentiary. He was pardoned by Texas governor Oscar Branch Colquitt and released on July 14, 1913.

Cortez later went to Mexico and fought with the despised despot General Victoriano Huerta against the revolutionaries under Pancho Villa and Emiliano Zapata. Wounded, Cortez returned to Texas to recuperate. In 1916, at Anson, while celebrating his fourth marriage (his other wives were still alive and not divorced), Cortez drank heavily, then complained of severe pains. Before the horrified eyes of his guests and new bride, he turned black and died on the spot. The life of Gregorio Cortez was lionized by writers and Hollywood wherein he was portrayed as a legendary hero, a hunted member of a persecuted minority. Although there is truth in this claim, there is also the reality of the two murders Cortez committed while resisting arrest.

Cortina, Juan (Juan Nepomuceno Cortinas), 1824-92, U.S., outlaw.

A hero to the Mexican peasant class, and

Mexican outlaw Juan Cortina.

a common rustler to U.S. landowners, Juan Cortina was a figure of enduring controversy throughout much of his life. Cortina was born on the Texas side of the Rio Grande River, and was heir to a large ranch that spanned both sides of the border. He became a leader in the Mexican-American community by virtue of his wealth and power, yet he was forced to defend his holdings against U.S. encroachers who were taking sections of his land as part of a broader-based policy of discrimination. During these years, he killed many land grabbers, and a warrant was issued for his arrest.

On Sept. 13, 1859, he shoved aside the marshal of Brownsville, Texas, as he was beating one of Cortina's former ranch hands. The ranch hand escaped, which further angered the marshal, who stewed over this insult. In response, Cortina organized 1,000 cutthroats into an armed band that captured the city of Brownsville. According to U.S. reports, the guerilla leader executed many people during the siege, and held the town ransom for $100,000.

Under pressure from less militant family members, Cortina withdrew his army from the town center, permitting a Brownsville resident to summon the Texas Rangers. The Rangers engaged Cortina in combat at the nearby Palo Alto, but were quickly routed by the superior firepower of the renegade soldiers. Cortina moved on, capturing the towns of Edinburg, and Rio Grande City, where he exacted a ransom payment of $100,000 in gold. By Christmas Day, 1859, the Rangers had driven Cortina across the border into Mexico, but found it impossible to circumvent his periodic forays into U.S. territory. A full 900,000 head of cattle were taken by the marauders over the next several years, an act that Mexicans viewed as retribution for what they had lost to the Yankees over several previous generations.

In later years Cortina served as a general in the army of Mexican president Benito Juarez, and then as military governor of the state of Tamaulipas. In 1875, Juan Cortina was imprisoned by the new regime, headed by Porfirio Diaz. He remained behind bars until 1890, and lived out the last two years of his life near the U.S.-Mexican border.

Courtright, Timothy Isaiah (AKA: Longhaired Jim), 1848-87, U.S., gunman-lawman.

Born in Iowa, Courtright served under General John "Black Jack" Logan

during the Civil War, and continued a personal friendship with Logan for much of his life. When the war ended, Courtright moved to Texas where Logan hired him as an army scout. In 1876, he was appointed city marshal of Fort Worth, Texas, a position he held for the next three years. He then moved to Lake Valley, N.M., a mining camp where he guarded silver ore mined for the American

Gunman Jim Courtright.

Mining Company. Here he was reunited with Logan who retained him as ranch foreman.

Courtright's job was little more than that of hired gun. Trespassers and cattle rustlers had been roaming Logan's property at will, and it was Courtright's duty to secure the land. In 1883, near Silver City, N.M., Courtright shot and killed two squatters, a crime that forced him to flee from the territory under threat of imprisonment. He returned to Fort Worth and opened a private detective agency, but when federal agents served extradition papers on him, he fled to western Canada. He completed his self-imposed exile in the Pacific Northwest before heading back to New Mexico to clear his name.

Returning to New Mexico around 1887, Courtright reopened his T.I.C. Commercial Agency, which provided "protection" to gambling dens and saloons in return for a portion of their profits. On Feb. 8, Luke Short, part owner of the White Elephant Saloon, refused to pay the extortion money. Short, in the company of Bat Masterson, confronted Courtright outside a Fort Worth shooting gallery that night. A quarrel ensued, and Short drew his gun and shot Courtright to death. Short was later freed on the grounds that Courtright had fired first. See: **Short, Luke**.

Crane, Jim, d.1881, U.S., outlaw. Cattle rustler and stagecoach robber Jim Crane rode with the Clanton-McLowery gang in southern Arizona until shortly before his death in 1881. Crane's most famous gunfight occurred near Contention, Ariz., when he attempted to rob a Wells Fargo shipment of bullion valued at $26,000. Twelve miles from Tombstone, Ariz., Crane, Bill Leonard, Luther King, and Harry "the Kid" Head overtook the stagecoach after Wells Fargo special agent Bob Paul had changed places with driver Budd Philpot. In a narrow ravine, the gang of robbers stepped out of the shadows and ordered Paul to stop the coach. Before he could respond, Crane fatally shot Philpot. A passenger riding in the stage, Peter Roerig, was also killed, but agent Paul relieving Philpot on the box, regained control of the frightened horse team and managed to pull away without losing his precious cargo. Wells Fargo offered a $2,000 reward for each of the four, and lawman Wyatt Earp offered Ike Clanton, an Arizona outlaw, $3,600 to lure the stage robbers into a trap.

A posse headed by Sheriff John Behan and Wyatt Earp later arrested King, who told them the names of his accomplices. Wanted by the law, Bill Leonard and "Kid" Head attempted to rob the Haslett Brothers general store in Eureka, N.M. Their holdup was thwarted by Bill and Ike Haslett who opened fire on the gunmen. Head was killed instantly, but Leonard lived long enough to implicate Crane as the murderer of Philpot. Unaware of this sellout, Crane recruited several others to help him massacre the Haslett Brothers outside of Eureka. The Hasletts killed two members of the gang and wounded three more before falling in a hail of gunfire. Crane fled across the border into Mexico where he was shot and killed.

Cravens, Ben, 1868-1950, U.S., outlaw. Ben Cravens was the last of a generation of Oklahoma gunfighters to roam the plains. Born in Lineville, Iowa, Cravens was the son of a respected farmer. He had a yen for adventure, and he ran away to the Indian Territory, where in a few short years, he became a train robber, horse thief, and whisky runner. It seemed as if there wasn't a jail secure enough to hold Cravens who had escaped from custody in three different states—Kansas, Oklahoma, and Iowa.

Outlaw Ben Cravens, a gunfighter who outlived most of his cohorts.

After marrying a Missouri woman, Cravens attempted to go straight. He even settled down to a life of farming before his past caught up with him. In 1896, after attempting to rob a train in Blackwell, Kan., Cravens was arrested, convicted, and sentenced to serve fifteen years in the state penitentiary. He escaped a year later after whittling the facsimile of a gun from a piece of wood. He wrapped the stick into a wad of silver tinfoil he had saved from cigarette packages, and made his escape from the prison coal mine.

Near Red Rock, Okla., on Mar. 19, 1901, Cravens murdered a postmaster at a combination store and postal agency. As he made his escape, he turned his gun on Bert Welty, a former convict who had helped him plan the heist. Welty survived the shotgun blast, and later identified Cravens as his assailant. By this time, however, Cravens was already serving a jail sentence under an alias.

Crawford, Ed, d.1873, U.S., lawman. Ed Crawford was discharged from the Ellsworth, Kan., police department along with the rest of the officers on the day Sheriff C.B. Whitney was killed in a card game by a group of carousing Texans. Crawford was soon reappointed to the force, and while lounging in front of a local store on Aug. 20, 1873, saw the same Texans appear, led by Cad Pierce and Neil Cain.

"Hello Hogue!" Pierce called to city marshal Ed Hogue. "I understand you have a white affidavit for me. Is that so?" The marshal tried to calm Pierce down, but there were angry words and then shots. Crawford, who was sitting with Hogue, wounded Pierce in the arm and then beat him to death with the butt of a rifle. Crawford was suspended from the police force for his action, and the Texans warned him to leave town, which he did, only to return early in November. Crawford burst in on Pierce's brother-in-law, Putnam, who was with a prostitute. The drunken ex-lawman fired at Putnam, who drew his six-shooter and killed Crawford. Putnam's friends from Texas burst into the room and fired thirteen slugs into the dead man.

Crawford, Foster, d.1896, U.S., outlaw. A one-time Oklahoma cowboy, Foster Crawford was reportedly a member of the Al Jennings gang before going to Texas where he teamed up with Elmer Lewis, better known as the

Bank robbers Foster Crawford and Elmer "Kid" Lewis, lynched, 1896.

Slaughter Kid, Kid Lewis, or The Mysterious Kid. Crawford, who had an abiding passion for French poetry and often quoted such poets as Francois Villon, decided with Lewis to rob the bank in Wichita Falls, Texas. He and Lewis rode into the town on Feb. 25, 1896, and walked into the City National Bank with guns drawn, demanding all the cash on hand. The cashier of this bank, Frank Dorsey, resisted opening the vault, and was killed. A clerk was also wounded by the outlaws before they fled the bank with about $2,000.

A company of Texas Rangers, led by Captain W.J. McDonald, was soon in pursuit and captured the outlaws some hours later. The two were jailed in Wichita Falls. After the Rangers left town, on Feb. 27, 1896, a mob broke into the jail and dragged Crawford and Lewis out to a telephone pole and lynched both of them. One of the witnesses to this lynching was Tex Rickard, who had worked with Crawford as a cowhand on ranches near Henrietta in Clay County, Texas. Crawford had invited Rickard to join him and Lewis in the bank raid but Rickard had refused, telling Crawford: "If you boys go and do a damned fool thing like that the Rangers will ride you down. You're asking me to join you in boot hill and I say no to that!" Rickard later went on to become the first great impresario of boxing, managing the career of Jack Dempsey and promoting the first million-dollar fight. Rickard died a

multimillionaire. See: **Lewis, Elmer**.

Credit Mobilier, prom. 1870s, U.S., fraud. In 1864 Thomas C. Durant, vice president of the Union Pacific Railroad Company, secured controlling interest in the Pennsylvania Fiscal Agency and renamed it the Credit Mobilier of America. The company, brazenly named after a joint-stock firm that defrauded many French investors during the 1850s, was authorized to build the nation's first transcontinental railroad, the Union Pacific, at an enormous cost. Durant and his Union Pacific colleagues who owned stock saw handsome profits from government bonds and land grants—reportedly as high as $23 million—mostly authorized by congressmen who owned stock in the company. Construction costs were wildly exaggerated, sometimes as much as double the amount. The Union Pacific paid Credit Mobilier, which, in turn, returned the money back to the railroad for stocks and bonds to fulfill a legal requirement that the company stock be purchased for cash at par value. Credit Mobilier was then free to sell the stock for whatever the market could bear.

To prevent legislation against the Credit Mobilier's methods, Congressman Oakes Ames of Massachusetts gave shares to his fellow congressmen, often at no charge. None of the congressmen/stockholders complained about the enormous returns they were receiving on their investments until the New York *Sun* published names of congressmen allegedly bribed by Oakes Ames, the front man and major stockholder in the Credit Mobilier, in the fall of 1872.

Congress formally censured Ames for distributing the shares and also censured Congressman James Brooks of New York, probably more for being a Democrat than for illicit behavior. Both men died shortly afterward. A special Senate investigating committee voted to remove New Hampshire Senator James W. Patterson from office, but, with only five days remaining in his term, Patterson was allowed to stay. Congressional inquiries also implicated James A. Garfield, later U.S. president, Vice President Schuyler Colfax, William D. Kelley of Pennsylvania, John Bingham of Ohio, and John A. Logan. Durant was removed from the directorate of the Union Pacific on May 25, 1869.

Crow Killer, See: **Johnson, John**.

Crumpton, Bood, 1872-91, U.S., outlaw. As he stood

on the scaffold about to meet death, 19-year-old murderer Bood Crumpton had some timely advice to offer those who came to witness his hanging. "To all you who are present, especially you young men—the next time you are about to take a drink of whiskey, look closely into the bottom of the glass and see if you cannot observe in there a hangman's noose. There is where I first saw the one which breaks my neck."

Crumpton's life was extinguished as a result of a drunken quarrel with his companion Sam Morgan, whom he shot in the back and dumped near the Pawnee Indian Agency.

Cruz, Florentino, d.1882, U.S., gunman. Florentino Cruz, a Mexican-American renowned for his gunplay, killed Wyatt Earp's brother, Morgan, on Mar. 18, 1882, in Tombstone, Ariz. Earp was playing a game of billiards at Campbell and Hatch's establishment when Cruz, Pete Spence, Frank Stilwell, and "Indian" Charley appeared. Wyatt was sitting near the billiard tables watching the game when Cruz suddenly fired a shot into Morgan Earp's back. A second shot narrowly missed Wyatt's head.

The two surviving Earp brothers, along with Doc Holliday, Jack Johnson, and Sherman McMasters took off after Morgan's killers. They gunned down Stilwell in Tucson, and returned to Tombstone on Mar. 22 to look for Cruz. Wyatt Earp was told by informant Theodore Judah that he could find Cruz working on a woodpile near the Pete Spence camp. When Judah returned to the woodpile, he found Cruz's bullet-riddled body. See: **Earp, Wyatt**.

Cummings, Samuel M. (AKA: **Doc**), d.1882, U.S., gunman-lawman. Samuel Cummings' association with Texas gunslinger Dallas Stoudenmire ultimately cost him his life. Prior to his association with Stoudenmire, Cummings had owned a hotel in San Marcial, N.M., and raised sheep in West Texas. Beginning in 1870 when Cummings' sister married Stoudenmire, the two men became partners.

Stoudenmire, who was unpopular with the local gunslingers, served as marshal of El Paso in 1881. On the night of Apr. 17, Cummings was riding with his brother-in-law through town when a hired assassin named Bill Johnson shot at the two men. When Johnson missed, Stoudenmire and Cummings killed him with their six-guns.

Marshal Stoudenmire believed the attack was instigated by the Manning brothers of El Paso. Tensions between the two factions continued for the next several months until Cummings ran into Jim Manning at the Coliseum Variety Theatre on Feb. 14, 1882. Cummings had been drinking heavily, and challenged Manning to a fight. Although Cummings drew first, Manning and the bartender David Kling outdrew him. Cummings staggered out of the saloon and died. See: **Stoudenmire, Dallas**.

Curry, George (AKA: **Flat Nose; Big Nose**), 1871-1900, U.S., outlaw. Born on Prince Edward Island, Can., George Curry moved as a young boy to a farm in Chadron, Neb. At the age of fifteen, Curry moved west and became a stock thief. After a horse kicked him in the nose he became known as "Flat Nose." Curry rode with the Wild Bunch for several years during the late 1890s. In October 1897, Curry, the Sundance Kid, and Harvey

George "Big Nose" Curry

Logan rode into southern Montana where they planned to hold up a train. Their plan was thwarted by "Six-Shooter" Bill Smith and an ambitious bounty hunter. Curry and the Kid were arrested and taken to the Deadwood jail, but managed to escape. They returned to Nevada and spent the next few months breaking horses for local ranchers.

In 1899 Curry held up a train at Wilcox Siding. A posse led by sheriffs Jesse Tyler and William Preece trailed Curry all the way to Castle Gate, Utah, where, on Apr. 17, 1900, they trapped him on a ranch. Curry ran for six miles, before he was hit in the head with a bullet from a long-range rifle. Before Curry's body was dumped into a common grave at Thompson, Utah, souvenir hunters ripped away portions of his skin. See: **Cassidy, Butch; Logan, Harvey; Sundance Kid, the; Wild Bunch, The**.

Cutler, Abraham, prom. 1862-67, U.S., lawman. The first of New Mexico's war-time marshals, Abraham Cutler of Kansas was appointed by President Abraham Lincoln on the recommendation of Senator James H. Lane. A staunch upholder of the Union, and a strident foe of slavery, Cutler took office on Aug. 16, 1862. It was Marshal Cutler's responsibility to enforce martial law and the First and Second Confiscation Acts, which permitted the government to seize the property of Confederate sympathizers intended for hostile use. Cutler interpreted the language of the law in the broadest of terms. He indiscriminately crossed over into El Paso County, Texas, which was under the control of a Union army occupation force. He defended his actions within the context of primal jurisdiction. He believed that the Customs District of Paso del Norte, comprising New Mexico *and* El Paso County gave him the right to uphold the law in both regions. The Santa Fe *New Mexican* which opposed Cutler's high-handed methods, accused of him of confiscating $500,000 worth of Texas property.

Cutler had little regard for abiding by the letter of the law. According to the First Confiscation Act, he was legally bound to share the "spoils" of a seizure with the person who had tipped him off. Cutler allegedly fabricated an "informant's" letter, and then began his seizures knowing full well that he could charge exorbitant fees to libel the person's property and purchase condemned lands under fictitious names. In July 1864, for example, Cutler purchased an interest in Sylvester Mowry's confiscated mine in southern Arizona. Later, he bought 320 acres of valuable real estate for the trifling sum of $30. The greedy marshal signed the deed in the name of Carrie F. Cutler, his wife. Mowry later filed a lawsuit against Cutler asking for $1.129 million in damages, but the case was dropped after Cutler proved that there were not sufficient grounds to justify continued legal action.

When Marshal Cutler left office in 1866, he was charged with embezzlement by an Albuquerque grand jury. Cutler was ordered to return the proceeds from the sale of all confiscated property. Since the list of such properties was unspecified, the court had to rely on Cutler's word alone as many official documents pertaining to the case had mysteriously disappeared from the clerk's office in Albuquerque. (The papers had been stolen and were held for ransom but were eventually recovered by clerk Benjamin Stevens.) The former marshal submitted a bogus report in which he billed the government for $571.29. In May 1867, he produced a report which was closer to the truth. The following October Cutler pleaded not guilty to the charges before the court and was acquitted by the jury. An additional lawsuit was later filed by one of Cutler's victims, but before the claim could be settled, the discredited lawman had fled the territory.

D

Dake, Crawley P., prom. 1878-82, U.S., lawman. Crawley Dake, who commanded a company of Michigan volunteers during the Civil War, took over from Wiley W. Standefer as the Arizona marshal on June 12, 1878. Dake was a well-known figure in Michigan before the Civil War. He held a variety of government offices, before losing his senatorial bid. Prior to his appointment as Arizona's marshal, he had served briefly as the chief deputy marshal of Detroit. His appointment to fill the vacated marshalcy in Arizona was enabled by his considerable influence among members of the Michigan delegation in Washington. It was largely through the intervention of senators Zachariah Chandler and T.W. Terry of Michigan that Dake received his appointment. Governor John P. Hoyt, however, had strongly objected.

Dake took over the Arizona marshalcy under less than ideal circumstances. The territorial residents were still incensed by the callous treatment shown Jack Swilling, who had perished in the Yuma jail that summer. There were loud demands for Dake to remove the controversial Standefer holdover—deputy Joseph W. Evans. Dake refused to be compromised. He announced that Evans would remain, while at the same time he named seven other new men to the post including Virgil Earp, brother of the famous Tombstone lawman Wyatt Earp. Marshal Dake soon found himself hampered by the same financial problems that had plagued the office since its inception. The lack of funding and bureaucratic red tape that accompanied each robbery (marshals were required to solicit "special instructions" from Washington following each crime) prevented him from going after criminals with all the available resources. In September 1878, he posted a $500 reward for the capture of a group of stagecoach robbers. It was a surreptitious action done without the approval of his superiors. "If I am to protect the people, I must have funds to do it," he wrote to Washington. Dake rounded up the bandits, but the cooperation he had sought from Washington was slow in coming.

Dake fostered a new spirit of cooperation between the various governmental agencies and the Mexican officials in his war against Mexican bandit gangs and holdup men. Dake and Governor Hoyt were praised for their efforts to extradite felons from Mexico, and for having the courage to send the *posse comitatus* across the international boundary lines in pursuit of holdup men. In 1880, a gang of horse thieves and border ruffians known as the "Cowboys," began terrorizing the inhabitants of southern Pima County. A shooting war soon erupted between the American bandits and Mexican officials. The Tucson *Daily Arizona Journal* questioned why a group of 100 bandits could reap so much

havoc, and yet evoke so little response from the marshal. In May 1881, Acting Governor John J. Gosper informed the Secretary of the Interior Samuel J. Kirkwood that more funds were needed to actively pursue the Cowboys. Attorney General Wayne MacVeagh replied in June 1881, that

Marshal Crawley P. Dake.

Dake should arrest the bandits who were led by the Clanton brothers and the McLowerys, but no mention was made of the money needed to support such an operation. Later, government officials informed Dake that he must first reduce his official debt below the $20,000 penalty bond before an appropriation could be made. On Aug. 1, 1881, a representative of Governor Pesqueira of Sonora was murdered by the Cowboys while en route to Tombstone. The death of the Mexican government official compelled the militia to cross the border and retaliate against the American bandit leaders, including Newman H. Clanton and Jim Crane. Meanwhile, the Cowboys tangled with Virgil, Morgan, and Wyatt Earp, and Doc Holliday in a deadly confrontation at Tombstone on Oct. 26, 1881—the Gunfight at O.K. Corral. Two McLowerys and Billy Clanton lay dead in the field, but the celebrated gun battle finally spurred the government into action. On Nov. 17, 1881, acting Attorney General Samuel F. Phillips ordered Marshal Dake to take immediate steps against the Cowboys. Phillips somberly added: "Your deputy Mr. (Virgil) Earp is more disposed to quarrel than to cooperate with local authority." Dake failed to take the hint and remove Earp who had engaged in a deadly gun battle without the necessary federal warrants. Wyatt Earp's feud with the Clantons was motivated more by personal ambition, rather than a hatred of the gunfighters. Earp was stymied in his attempt to win the office of sheriff from John E. Behan, and had used the Clantons as a publicity springboard in his private election campaign. Marshal Dake did little, if anything, which prompted Phillips to issue a second directive, this time it came from the president himself.

Feeling powerless to act, Dake communicated with the governor concerning his views on suppressing the Cowboy uprising. Gosper suggested that Dake field a *posse comitatus* led by a man of sterling character whose fees would be paid by private contribution. Dake then presented the recommendation to Acting Attorney General Phillips, adding that there were "no braver men in Arizona" than the Earps, whom he believed would drive the last of the Cowboys from the border. When Virgil Earp was shot by one of the Cowboys on Dec. 28, Wyatt telegraphed Dake seeking appointment as a deputy marshal. Dake complied. The surviving members of the Cowboys gang were in no mood for a fight, and attempted instead to have the Earps and Doc Holliday tried for murder. There was little the courts would do to placate the vengeful outlaws, which resulted in a renewal of the shooting war. Morgan Earp fell before the blazing guns of the outlaws on Mar. 18, 1882. The bloody vendetta eventually ran its course, but only after the Earps had gunned down William "Curley Bill" Brocius, Johnny Ringo, and others. The gunplay of the Earp brothers did much to discredit the integrity of the federal marshals in Arizona at that time. Before the shooting was over, however, President Chester A. Arthur was forced to issue a proclamation against the Cowboys and declared that part of Arizona in a state of rebellion. Governor Frederick A. Tritle persuaded Marshal Dake to deputize liveryman John H. Jackson who headed up the Tombstone vigilante committee. Jackson and his posse took the place of the departed Earps, and restored the peace to Cochise County.

Dake escaped public censure for his inability to contain the escalating violence between the Earps and the Clantons. Political opponents castigated him for making poor choices in his selection of deputies, but the public seemed willing to forgive him. However, in August 1885, three years after leaving office, Crawley Dake was implicated in a serious scandal involving misappropriation of funds. A government examiner, Leigh Chalmers, reported that Dake admitted to having "feloniously converted" some $50,000 in government funds to his private account and had used this to pay for private expenses. This money had apparently been placed in the account of Deputy Marshal Wyatt Earp in Tombstone, who used it in his relentless war against the Cowboys. Dake had spent $300 of this money in a drunken orgy with several posse men at a local sporting house. Former Marshal Dake was eventually exonerated of wrongdoing, but the scandal underlined a deeper problem plaguing Cochise County in those days: the greed of the ruling cabal of politicians who exploited the natural resources of the region for profit. Crawley Dake was a cog in that Republican group headed by Governor John C. Fremont, a protégé of the Michigan senator who engineered Dake's appointment, Zachariah Chandler. See: **Behan, John E.; Clanton-McLowery Gang; Earp, Wyatt; Earp Brothers; Holliday, John Henry; O.K. Corral.**

Dallam, Richard, prom. 1846-48, U.S., lawman.

Following the surrender of the Mexican forces to U.S. troops at the conclusion of the Mexican War, General Stephen Watts Kearny formed a provisional U.S. government and named several prominent local citizens to fill key posts. Among these was Richard Dallam, who had made a small fortune for himself in the mining and merchandising business of Santa Fe. Dallam had no outstanding qualifications for the office of marshal other than his favorable dealings with Kearny.

Marshal Dallam chose the capital city of Santa Fe, headquarters of the First Judicial District, to serve as his base of operations. In January 1847, the Taos Rebellion broke out in the counties north of Santa Fe. It was an armed insurrection pitting the resentful Hispanic population against the U.S. civilian government. Governor Charles Bent, a crony of General Kearny and an influential New Mexican merchant, was killed in the affray along with the sheriff of Taos. Marshal Dallam was unprepared to suppress the revolt, but he signed on with a militia unit as a sergeant. When hostilities ceased, Dallam returned to northern New Mexico to resume his duties as marshal. In March 1847, he opened the session of the Third District Court in Taos, which was convened in order to try rebel leader Antonio Maria Trujillo.

The growing resentment against the provisional government on the part of the native population compelled the U.S. Congress to direct the War Department to abolish the marshalcy and district attorney's office on Jan. 11, 1847. Dallam remained in office until June 22, to see the trial of the remaining rebels through to its conclusion. In February 1848, General Sterling Price eliminated the office of marshal by decree, and in October the governor was replaced by a military officer. See: **Bent, Charles.**

Dalton, J. Frank, 1847?-1951, U.S., outlaw. As early as 1935, J. Frank Dalton of Gladewater, Texas, publicly claimed that he was the one and only Jesse Woodson James and that he had not been killed by Bob Ford in 1882, rather that a stranger was killed instead. Researchers at the time traced Dalton back to about 1886 when a man by that name was wanted for horse stealing in Limestone County, Texas. Dalton was also identified as a fake in 1935 by several old-time circus riders who insisted that he had traveled with their show shortly before 1900, playing an "old-time frontiersman." In the late 1930s, Dalton gave another interview to a disbelieving newsman in Corpus Christi, again claiming that he was the real Jesse James. He claimed that he had fought with the guerilla leader William Quantrill during the Civil War and that he had helped to set up a double who was shot to death in St. Joseph, Mo., by the

Ford brothers in a scheme in which he could escape while another man's body was passed off as that of James. He offered little evidence then, or later, in 1949, when J. Frank Dalton made national headlines, thanks to promoter, Rudy Turilli.

At that time, Turilli "discovered" Dalton in Lawton, Okla., where the old man, claiming to be 100 years of age, again insisted that he was Jesse James. Turilli located a few doddering old westerners who supported the old man's claims, supposedly identifying Dalton as James, but these men hardly knew the real Jesse James. Bandit Al Jennings visited the old man at Meremac Caverns near Stanton, Mo., a small resort which was managed by Turilli, and where Turilli had brought Dalton to appear as a side-show attraction for tourists. Jennings took one look at the old man and unhesitatingly exclaimed: "It's Jesse, by God!" The

Al Jennings, left, with J. Frank Dalton, who claimed to be Jesse James.

identification, however, was unimpressive to experts since it was well known that Al Jennings belonged to a generation of bandits who operated long after the killing of Jesse James in 1882. Jennings had never met Jesse James, which was a documented fact.

The most telling interview with J. Frank Dalton was conducted by Homer Croy, an expert on Jesse James. He asked Dalton to hold up his left middle finger, and the old man complied. Croy then announced that Dalton was the most unique human being he had ever met, pointing out that Jesse James had blown off the tip of his finger while cleaning a pistol when riding with Quantrill; Dalton appeared to have grown a new finger. This fact and many other glaring discrepancies soon convinced most experts that J. Frank Dalton was nothing more than a colorful, colossal fraud. The old man died on Aug. 16, 1951, and was buried

in Granbury, Texas. See: **James, Jesse Woodson**.

Dalton Brothers, prom. 1890s, U.S., outlaws. The Dalton brothers and their dedicated riders comprised the last great bandit gang of the Old West, one as daring and outlandish as the James and Younger boys. For the most part they upheld the oddly chivalric codes of the West, refusing to rob women on trains and stagecoaches, shooting it out with lawmen rather than surrendering as a matter of their homespun honor, and insisting on "dying game." For all these reasons and more, the Daltons came to ruin and death in Coffeyville, Kan., in 1892. The Dalton boys, or more precisely, the four sons who became outlaws, were distant blood relatives of the notorious Younger brothers, and even more distantly related, it was claimed, to the James boys. Like the infamous James-Younger brothers, the Daltons were born in Missouri, which was aptly named in the nineteenth century the "Mother of Bandits."

Lewis Dalton was born in Kentucky and fought in the Mexican War of 1848. He moved to Missouri where he married Adeleine Younger, whose father was a cousin to the Younger brothers. This union produced fifteen children in all, most of whom grew up to be law-abiding citizens. Four sons, all born in Cass County, Mo., did not. These were Emmett (1871-1937); Grattan, called Grat, (1865-92); Robert, called Bob, (1868-92); and William Marion, called Bill, (1866-95). The boys were raised behind a saloon Lewis Dalton ran, but Dalton decided that this atmosphere was a bad influence on his sons. They moved, first to Kansas where the family struggled to maintain a small farm, and later to the Indian Territory, living near Coffeyville, Kan., which would be the scene of a bloody shootout in 1892 that would take the lives of two of his sons.

The family moved again to Oklahoma where the first of the sons, Frank Dalton, took up the gun, not as an outlaw, but on the side of the law, becoming a U.S. marshal in 1884 for Judge Isaac Parker in Fort Smith in 1884. Dalton was a courageous officer who was killed on Nov. 27, 1887, while attempting to arrest three peddlers illegally running whiskey to the Indians. Seeking vengeance, the three youngest boys, Grat, Bob, and Emmett, applied for silver stars. Grat was appointed to fill Frank Dalton's position as U.S. Marshal by Marshal John Carroll. Bob joined Grat as a posseman and was later appointed deputy marshal, and Emmett, the youngest, worked on a ranch but later became a posseman under the direction of his older brothers. The Daltons were effective lawmen, fast with their guns and fearless when running down wanted felons. They also became a law unto themselves, rustling herds of horses and selling these to willing buyers near Baxter Springs, Kan.

Above left, Frank Dalton, a brave lawman and the only Dalton brother who remained honest.
Above right, Bill Dalton, who rode with the Doolin Gang and was later killed by lawmen while reportedly playing with his children.
Middle right, Bill Dalton shown in death.

Gang leader Bob Dalton and sweetheart Eugenia Moore, 1889.

Left, Grat Dalton and, right, Emmett Dalton, who lived until 1937.

The Condon Bank in Coffeyville, Kan., scene of the Daltons' doom.

Judge Parker was enraged at this outlawry and revoked the Daltons' appointments, issuing warrants for their arrest. But the boys had by that time fled to Oklahoma to visit their mother who was living with their brothers, Charles and Henry, who had developed successful farms near Kingfisher. Their father, Lewis Dalton, had died in 1889 in Oklahoma. The Dalton brothers held a family meeting. Bob and Grat wanted the boys to travel to California to join another brother, Littleton, who had moved to the West Coast years earlier to farm. Bob Dalton, who was to become the aggressive leader of the Dalton Gang, suggested all the brothers go to California and "pick the trains and banks clean." Charles and Henry said no, that a bandit's life was not for them. They would stay in Oklahoma and take care of their mother. Bob and Grat would go to California. Emmett wanted to travel with Bob and Grat, but his older brothers told him he was too young and that he was to stay at home with Mrs. Dalton. Emmett pleaded his case, reminding his brothers that he had helped Bob rob a faro game in 1890. "That don't make you no train robber," snorted Grat. Emmett stayed in Oklahoma while Bob and Grat rode west to California.

Littleton Dalton wanted no part of robbery and told his brothers Bob and Grat that he intended to continue farming. Bill Dalton, however, joined his younger brothers and the three Daltons stopped the Southern Pacific's Train Number 17 on Feb. 6, 1891, near Alila, Calif. Wearing masks, Bob and Grat leaped into the engine's cab and forced engineer George Radcliff to bring the train to a halt. Bill Dalton, using a rifle, then began firing above the heads of the passengers to keep them crouching in their seats, while Grat and Bob forced Radcliff to accompany them to the express car. When Radcliff tried to slip away in the darkness, one of the brothers wheeled about and sent a bullet into his stomach, killing him.

More trouble awaited the brothers inside the express car. Guard Charles C. Haswell refused to unlock the express car door. Several loads of buckshot from shotguns were fired into the door, and Haswell grabbed his own shotgun and fired several times from a small hole in the door. He claimed later that he hit one of the bandits who, failing to get the door to the express car open, fled in disgust and anger. The first train robbery attempted by the Daltons had ended in utter failure. Bill and Grat were later captured while Bob Dalton managed to escape, riding back to Oklahoma. Bill Dalton was freed after a quick trial, but Grat was sentenced to twenty years. He managed to escape and he, too, rode back to the familiar landscape of Oklahoma. There Emmett joined his older brothers, now dedicated to a life of crime which Bob tried to excuse by blaming the Southern Pacific for placing rewards of $6,000 each on their heads. "They put the running irons on our

hides," Bob was fond of saying. This was an old excuse, one used by the James and Younger brothers before them, but the Daltons saw themselves as heroic outcasts who had been driven to banditry by the forces of evil establishments.

At this time, the Daltons rounded up some of the toughest, meanest gunmen and thieves in the Oklahoma Territory, forming a fearsome gang that would soon make outlaw history. Members included Dick Broadwell, Charley Pierce, Bill McEhanie, Bill Doolin, George "Bitter Creek" Newcomb, and "Black Face Charley" Bryant. The gang first struck the Santa Fe's Texas Express near Wharton, Okla., in early 1891. This time when the bandits ordered the guard to open the door to the express guard, there was no resistance. The outlaws easily forced the safe inside and took more than $14,000. The robbery was without gunfire, which disturbed Black Face Charley Bryant who told the Daltons that he was looking forward to some gunplay. Bryant once stated that "I want to get killed in one hell-firing minute of smoking action." He would later get his wish. As the bandits were about to ride away from the train, Bryant halted and said, "We should go into those passenger cars and get everything those people have." Bob Dalton, with his brothers backing him up, snorted: "Those are working folks like us and we don't steal from them." With that he ordered the gang to ride away. Black Face Charley closed his mouth and rode with them in silence.

Bryant took his share of the robbery to Hennessey, Okla., where he promptly got drunk and then staggered into the street, firing his six-gun wildly into second-story windows. Marshal Ed Short arrested him and, after learning that he had apprehended the infamous Black Face Charley, put Bryant aboard a train headed for Wichita, where he would stand trial before a federal judge on charges of bank and train robbery. While Short left Bryant manacled to a steel post in the baggage car to take a smoke, the outlaw managed to free himself and grab a gun just as the lawman re-entered the car. Both men leveled their six-guns at each other and fired, emptying their guns into one another. They both fell dead.

The fate of Black Face Charley did not bother the Daltons, especially Bob Dalton, the most daring and inventive of the gang. Dalton told members of his gang that Bryant had been a fool and that if they kept their heads and followed his methodical plan of train and bank robbing, all of them would be able to "retire in about twelve months." With that thought in mind, the gang next raided a Missouri-Kansas & Texas Express outside of Lellietta, Okla., stopping the train and quickly looting the express car on the night of Sept. 15, 1891, taking between $3,000 and $14,000, according to varying reports. None of the train passengers were molested or robbed, according to Dalton custom, and the robbery took less than fifteen minutes, with no gunfire exchanged between the Daltons and the express car guard. The gang was becoming proficient.

Aiding the bandits was Eugenia Moore, Bob Dalton's sweetheart. Unknown to other members of the gang, including Bob's own brothers, Moore acted as an undercover intelligence agent. She would inquire of various railroads which trains were the best protected, on the pretense that she intended to ship money and valuables but was fearful of robbery since so many trains were being held up. She was assured by railroad officials that her valuables would be safe on trains carrying considerable cash, payrolls, and bank shipments, since these trains would be guarded by armed express agents in the mail cars. Thusly, Eugenia Moore obtained the schedules of trains carrying considerable cash and passed this information on to her lover, Bob Dalton, who then planned and executed the robberies with lightning efficiency. To his brothers and other followers Bob Dalton seemingly possessed an uncanny ability to select just the right trains to rob.

Moore learned that a Santa Fe train would be carrying a large amount of cash. This train was stopped on July 1, 1892, near Red Rock in the Cherokee Strip at about 9 p.m. when seven bandits, their faces covered by kerchiefs, fired their six-guns and intimidated the crew and passengers. They quickly forced the door of the express car and held the guard at bay while they took $11,000 from the small safe. Within twenty minutes, the bandits had remounted their horses and ridden off into the hills, whooping and hollering triumph as they went. Flushed with this success, the Daltons struck again only two weeks later, seven or eight of its members walking into the depot at Adair, Okla., in the Cherokee Strip at 9 p.m. on Sept. 15, 1892. The gang held up the station master, looting the safe in his office. When the Missouri-Kansas & Texas train pulled into the station, the bandits were waiting for it. One outlaw jumped into the cab of the engine, holding the engineer at gunpoint, while the rest of the gang went to the express car, backing a wagon up to it.

The express guard refused to open the door to the mail car, but after the bandits fired several shots through the door and threatened to use dynamite to blow up the entire car if need be, the guard opened the door. Some of the Daltons jumped inside and quickly took $17,000 from the safe. As they threw the money bags onto the back of the wagon, the bandits were startled by the sudden fusillade unleashed from some of the passenger cars which carried a large force of Indian police and railroad detectives. The bandits drove the wagon away as they returned shots, a withering crossfire that wounded Dr. B. Youngblood and killed Dr. W.L. Goff, who were sitting on the porch of a nearby drugstore when the gun battle erupted and had no time to take cover. Also wounded was Chief Charley

LaFlore of the Territorial Police and L.L. Kinney, a railroad detective. Deputy Marshal Sid Johnson was also wounded by one of the bandits he thought he recognized as Grat Dalton. Ironically, Johnson had served with Grat and Bob Dalton when they had all been marshals in Fort Smith. Although hundreds of shots had been fired, miraculously none of the bandits were wounded, and they escaped intact with the stolen money.

The robbery at Adair caused the Daltons to be identified as the most feared gang of outlaws in the West. Their bold raids and their ability to escape capture time and again made them legends within two years of the time the gang began operating. The gang managed to evade the hundreds of lawmen searching for them. They had benefited well through their experiences as U.S. marshals, knowing the tracking techniques of their pursuers. They also had dozens of hideouts where they were safe from detection, especially the caves in which they once played in as boys along the Canadian River, and other hard-to-find areas throughout the Indian Nation. But this on-the-run life had, the Daltons knew, only won them the image of infamous outlaws.

To Emmett Dalton, such notoriety meant the doom of his plans to marry his childhood sweetheart, Julia Johnson. Before the Red Rock raid, Emmett Dalton had ridden to the Johnson ranch and, while his brothers stood guard, visited Julia for what he believed would be the last time. He told her that he wanted to marry her but that he had thrown in his lot with his brothers Bob and Grat and there was no turning back now. He was headed, not toward the altar, but for Boot Hill. Emmett would later write: "What had I to offer Julia, a man with a price on his head and no clear way to extricate myself from the compounding results of crime? I rode away. An outlaw has no business having a girl, no business thinking of marriage."

All that Bob Dalton was thinking about was achieving something that even the notorious James-Younger gang had failed to do—rob two banks at the same time. Jesse and Frank James, with the Younger brothers and others, had ridden into Northfield, Minn., in 1876, intending to rob two banks, but the raid proved to be disastrous when the local citizens fought them off and decimated the gang. This time, Bob Dalton vowed, it would be different. He would lead the Dalton Gang into his old hometown of Coffeyville, Kan., and there boldly rob the Condon and First National Banks. Before this raid, Bob Dalton must have had deep reservations about his surviving his own wild scheme. Only a few weeks before the bloody Coffeyville raid, he learned that his girl, Eugenia Moore, had suddenly died of cancer after only a short illness. He stared at her picture for some hours before throwing it into the campfire around which the Daltons warmed themselves. The following day the three Dalton brothers rode to Kingfisher to see their mother for what might be the last time. They sat on their horses, watching the ranch house from the cover of trees, afraid to go near the house since they rightly believed that it was being watched by possemen who were hunting the Daltons throughout the southwest.

The brothers watched their mother move past the windows of their boyhood home as they sat silent that night on horseback, all thinking back to an earlier time. Wrote Emmett later: "For a moment we saw her in the distant window, her flitting form setting the house in order for the night. None of us dared look at each other. With one accord we spurred our horses. And at the sound I saw her turn her face to the window, listening intently, as if she heard the passing hoofbeats. Such was Bob and Grat's last outspoken salute to the grand old lady who bore them." The gang that headed north toward Coffeyville and into western legend the next day included Bob, Grat, and Emmett Dalton, Dick Broadwell, Bill Powers, and Bill Doolin, the last three all experienced hardcase outlaws from Oklahoma. In the early morning of Oct. 5, 1892, when the gang was only twenty miles outside of Coffeyville, Bill Doolin's horse began to limp and he dismounted. He told Bob Dalton that he would return to a ranch they had passed a few miles back and get another horse and catch up with the gang. Dalton nodded and Bill Doolin began walking his horse back down the road. This accident was to save Doolin's life. By the time he located a horse and raced after the Daltons, he was already too late. He heard the muttering gunfire in Coffeyville and realized the raid was a failure. He turned his horse about and headed for Oklahoma.

Emmett Dalton was a reluctant member of the gang that rode into Coffeyville. He had originally argued with Bob Dalton against the raid. He pointed out that they had relatives buried in Coffeyville and that many of the townspeople were their friends. Bob Dalton had ignored this plea and went ahead with the raid. Rather than let his brothers ride into danger alone, Emmett, ever loyal, decided to go with them. As the outlaws neared Coffeyville, they slipped false beards on their faces, but when they rode down Maple Street at 9:30 a.m. the Daltons were recognized by Aleck McKenna who had known the brothers when they were boys. McKenna watched as the gang rode to an alley between Maple and Walnut streets, one that would later be called Death Alley, and tethered their horses. Then Grat Dalton, Powers, and Broadwell walked across the street to the C.M. Condon Bank, while Bob and Emmett Dalton went into the First National Bank.

McKenna went to the window of the Condon Bank and, peering inside, saw Grat Dalton draw his six-gun and aim it at the cashier, Charles Ball. McKenna turned on his heels and raced down the middle of the street, shouting:

"It's the Daltons! It's the Daltons! They're robbing the bank!" Several passersby thought McKenna had gone out of his mind, some laughed. But Cyrus Lee, who had also known the Daltons when they were youngsters, recognized Bob Dalton inside the First National Bank and took up the cry of alarm. Dozens of Coffeyville citizens raced to the hardware store and armed themselves, then ran back outside and trained their guns on the fronts of the two banks.

Inside the First National Bank, Bob and Emmett Dalton heard the cries of their names but kept about their business. Bob held two guns on Thomas G. Ayres, cashier, and W.H. Shepherd, the teller, along with three customers, J.H. Brewster, C.L. Hollingsworth, and A.W. Knott, who was a deputy sheriff. Emmett was behind the teller's cage, shoving more than $21,000 into a grain sack. Grat Dalton, Powell, and Broadwell were having less success inside the Condon Bank. Before him stood Vice President Charles T. Carpenter, bookkeeper T.C. Babb, and Charles Ball, the cashier, who was arguing with Dalton, telling him he could not open the safe.

"Open the safe and be quick about it," Grat Dalton ordered Ball.

The cashier shook his head, repeating the same line he had earlier delivered: "It's a time lock and it won't open until 9:45 a.m." Ball, of course, knew that the safe, containing $18,000, was closed but unlocked. He was stalling for time.

The oldest of the Dalton brothers leveled his gun only a few inches from Ball's head, snarling: "Open it or I'll kill you!"

Again the courageous cashier repeated his lie about the time lock. He then began to push several bags of money from behind the teller's cage, most of it in small bills and silver, about $4,000 worth, an attempt by Ball to keep the bandits from the substantial cash inside the safe.

Grat looked at the clock on the wall and saw that it was 9:42 a.m. "We'll wait," he said—a wait of three minutes which would cost four of the five bandits their lives.

Bob and Emmett Dalton grabbed the grain sacks with the large bills inside the First National Bank and began heading for the door when they saw the street filling with gun-carrying citizens. Bullets began crashing through the bank windows and thudding into the walls and teller's cage. Bob Dalton stood in the open doorway for a moment, then slammed it shut. "The back way," he told Emmett. He motioned with his six-gun for Shepherd, Ayres, and Knott to go before them out the back door and into the street. Lucius M. Baldwin, a clerk who had grabbed a rifle at the first alarm, was approaching the group from the First National. Bob Dalton handed the grain sack full of money to Emmett, saying to him: "Look after the money sack. I'll

Bob Dalton in death.

Bill Powers in death.

Bob and Grat Dalton, dead, held by Coffeyville lawmen.

Grat Dalton in death.

Dick Broadwell in death.

The lesson of the Coffeyville raid: four dead outlaws, left to right, Bill Powers, Bob and Grat Dalton, Dick Broadwell.

do the fighting. I have to get that man." He then raised his rifle just as Baldwin was aiming his own gun. Dalton fired first, a dead shot that plowed into Baldwin's head. The clerk toppled to the dusty street, dying of the fatal wound.

By now the outlaws abandoned their hostages. Bob and Emmett Dalton were trotting toward the alley where their horses were tied. From across the street, Grat Dalton, Broadwell, and Powell were running toward the same spot. Dozens of guns barked after them, kicking up dust from the street, banging into buildings. Bootmakers George Cubine and Charles Brown, who had fixed the shoes of the boys when they were young, had taken up positions in a chemist's shop; both held rifles in their hands. Cubine took aim to fire at Bob Dalton as he ran past the shop, but the outlaw whirled about and fired a single bullet that killed him. When he fell, Brown caught the rifle dropped by Cubine; before he could fire it, another shot from the deadly accurate Bob Dalton killed him also. Almost at that second, Thomas Ayres, the cashier from the First National Bank who had raced to Isham's Hardware Store when Bob and Emmett released him, ran to the street with a rifle, aiming at Bob Dalton. Before he could shoot, Dalton fired one shot from the hip and again his aim was true, the bullet striking Ayres in the cheek, killing him.

By the time the five bandits reached the alley and their horses, they quickly realized that they had run into a death trap. Dozens of citizens converged on the alley from both ends, letting loose a withering fire. "Get out, get out," Grat Dalton shouted to the others, but there was nowhere to go. As they struggled to lead their horses out of the alley and mount them, they were greeted by walls of deadly gunfire. Several bullets struck Powers, the first to be shot down, but he leaped up again, firing two six-guns at his tormentors. Broadwell was shot in the arm, then in the back, and fell; he, too, got up once more, firing. Bob Dalton was then shot, then Emmett. At that moment, Marshal Charles T. Connelly, who had once been the schoolteacher of both Bob and Grat, came marching down the alley, firing his six-gun at Grat Dalton. The outlaw advanced on the lawman, firing his own weapon. Dalton's bullets cut down Connelly, but as the marshal fell he sent a bullet into Grat Dalton's chest. Bob Dalton moaned in anguish as he saw Grat sink slowly against a wall and die.

Bill Powers, wounded several times, managed to get into the saddle, but just as his horse galloped out of the alley, Powers was riddled, blown from his mount. He lay dead in the street as the vigilantes stepped over his body, advancing on the other bandits. With an amazing burst of energy, Dick Broadwell leaped into the saddle of his horse. Bleeding from several wounds, Broadwell spurred his mount at a gallop down the other end of the alley, smashing through a group of citizens who pumped bullet after bullet into him. Broadwell went a short distance before falling dead from the saddle. Now only two of the outlaws were left alive and on their feet—Bob and Emmett Dalton. Livery stable owner John J. Kloehr, and the town barber, Carey Seaman, raced down the alley with shotguns in their hands. At a distance of five feet, Kloehr fired a barrel into Bob Dalton's chest, sending him to the ground with a mortal wound.

Emmett Dalton fired several rounds which drove Kloehr and Seaman to temporary cover. He threw the money sack over his saddle, crawled up on his mount and was about to make his getaway when he heard his brother Bob groan. He reached down to pull Bob Dalton up behind him on the horse, but the outlaw leader said with his last breath: "Don't mind me, boy. I'm done for. Don't surrender! Die game!" As the brothers clasped each other's hands, Kloehr jumped out from behind a doorway and fired another barrel from his shotgun, sending the load into Emmett Dalton. The last outlaw fell to the ground. For an eerie moment, all was silent. Only the heavy gunsmoke drifted from the mouth of the alley. The citizens walked slowly forward and finally one of them shouted: "They're all down!" The vigilantes were surprised to find Emmett Dalton still alive, although he had been shot twenty times. He was taken to a local doctor and given medical attention and survived. A rush of angry citizens crowded about the slain outlaws. Many cut locks of hair from the heads of Bob and Grat Dalton. Then the bodies of Broadwell, Powers, and both Dalton boys were placed on boards and propped up so that Coffeyville lawmen and citizens could pose with the corpses for photographs that later became famous in the West. Such was the inglorious end of the last great western outlaw band. Bill Dalton and Bill Doolin would, within a few years, join Bob and Grat Dalton in early death as a result of their bandit ways. Only Emmett Dalton was to outlive his criminal brothers and friends and the wild era that spawned them. Bill Dalton would later ride with the Doolin Gang and be shot to death by lawmen.

Emmett Dalton was tried for the murders of Cubine and Baldwin, even though many had witnessed Bob Dalton committing these murders. Emmett Dalton was sent to prison for life, but he proved to be a model prisoner and was released in 1907. Waiting for him was Julia Johnson. They were married and lived happily together for thirty years. Emmett Dalton would prove to be a model citizen and an implacable foe of crime, championing law and order in his writings and lectures. He would live until 1937, but six years before that time, the last of the Dalton brothers returned to Coffeyville to visit the common grave that held the bodies of Broadwell, Powers, and his brothers Bob and Grat. He stood before this solemn plot of ground and then, as he pointed to the spot, said for the benefit of many standing next to him: "I challenge the world to produce the history of any outlaw who ever got anything out of it but that, or else be huddled in a prison cell...The biggest fool on earth is the one who thinks he can beat the law, that crime can be made to pay. It never paid and it never will and that was the one big lesson of the Coffeyville raid." See: **Bryant, Charles; Doolin, William M.**

Daly, James, d.1864, U.S., gunman-outlaw. Daly was a member of the gang led by "Three-Fingered Jack" McDowell, operating outside of Aurora, Nev. Daly and McDowell ran a saloon in Aurora and were credited with many gunfights. A man named Lloyd picked a fight with Daly, shooting him in the leg. Daly slowly drew his gun and shouted as he fired: "I'll dance to your music all night." As Lloyd fired several wild shots at Daly, the gunman fired a single shot that brought Lloyd down. Vigilantes later arrested Daly, McDowell, and two others and hanged them for various crimes in February 1864 near Aurora. See: **McDowell, Jack.**

Daniels, Benjamin F., prom. 1900s, U.S., lawman. Daniels began as a buffalo hunter in the 1870s while a teenager and was a deputy sheriff in Arizona in the early 1880s. In 1887, Daniels was bartending at Fort McKavett, in Menard County, Texas, when John Vaden, a gunman, goaded Daniels into a duel. Both men drew their six-guns and fired at almost the same instant. Daniels' aim was true, and he killed Vaden on the spot. He was never indicted for the shooting.

Lawman Ben Daniels, who served with Theodore Roosevelt's Rough Riders.

In 1884, Daniels tracked down William Delaney, a lethal desperado who was one of the killers responsible for the Bisbee, Ariz., Massacre. Daniels later worked as a deputy in Oklahoma under Bill Tilghman and served with Teddy Roosevelt's Rough Riders in the Spanish-American War, fighting at San Juan Hill and earning Roosevelt's praise. Roosevelt later appointed Daniels a U.S. marshal. He served in Arizona and New Mexico with distinction during the 1900s and retired with honors. See: **Bisbee, Ariz., Massacre; Delaney, William E.**

Daugherty, Roy (AKA: **Arkansas Tom Jones**), 1870-1924, U.S., outlaw. Roy Daugherty drifted from Missouri to Oklahoma under an assumed name when he was only fourteen. He called himself "Arkansas Tom Jones" because he claimed to have hailed from there. In the 1890s, he joined Bill Doolin's gang in holding up a number of banks in Oklahoma. On Sept. 1, 1893, Daugherty was trapped by lawmen in a hotel in Ingalls, Okla. Doolin and the others had left town, leaving Daugherty to fight off the posse from his second-floor room. When he refused to surrender, Deputy Jim Masterson

Roy Daugherty, alias Arkansas Tom Jones, who tried to become a Hollywood actor after robbing banks with the Bill Doolin Gang.

emptied the hotel and threatened to bomb it with dynamite.

Daugherty was captured, tried, and convicted of manslaughter. Sentenced to a fifty-year prison term, he was paroled in 1910, thanks to the efforts of his brothers, both ministers. For a short time he ran a restaurant in Drumright, Okla., and then drifted to Hollywood, where he hoped to make money acting in westerns. But Daugherty soon returned to bank robbery. With the law on his heels, Daugherty took refuge in the home of Red Snow in Joplin, Mo. Detectives trapped him there on Aug. 16, 1924, and killed him in a gunfight. See: **Doolin, William M.**

Day, Alfred, prom. 1870s, U.S., gunman-outlaw. Alfred Day was a follower of Jim Taylor during the bloody Sutton-Taylor feud in south Texas in the 1870s. He drove cattle north to the railheads in Kansas for the Taylor family and doubled as a gunman when needed. He reportedly shot Bill Sutton in the Bank Saloon at Cuero, Texas, and he was listed as a fugitive in 1876 in Gonzales County. Day survived the Sutton-Taylor feud and lived into the next century, writing a book about his experiences in the 1930s. See: **Sutton-Taylor Feud.**

Deady, Matthew Paul, 1824-93, U.S., jurist. Admitted to the Ohio bar in 1847, Matthew Deady resettled in the Oregon Territory two years later while employed as a blacksmith for the U.S. Mounted Rifle Regiment. Deady entered politics in 1850, when he was elected to the territorial house of representatives. He served as an associate justice on the territorial supreme court for six years (1853-59) and later codified all general state laws (in 1864, and again in 1872). Deady was named a U.S. district judge for Oregon in 1859. It was a position he held until his death.

Deger, Larry, prom. 1870s, U.S., lawman. Corpulent, pugnacious Larry Deger served as marshal of Dodge City, Kan., during the late 1870s. In the spring of 1877, Deger, an enormous man who weighed 300 pounds, tangled with Bat Masterson, an event which proved to be his own undoing. The bad feelings between the two started when Deger attempted to arrest a saloon lounger named Bobby Gill on a charge of disturbing the peace. Gill, it seems, did not walk to the jail fast enough to suit Marshal Deger, who kicked him several times to urge him on. Masterson, who happened to be standing nearby, grabbed Deger by the throat, allowing Gill to escape.

Deger's friends answered his call for help and were able to restrain Masterson, who received a thorough pistol whipping before he was dragged off to jail. "Every inch of the way was closely contested," reported the Dodge City *Times*, "but the city dungeon was reached at last, and in he went. If he had got hold of his gun before going in, there would have been a general killing." Ed Masterson, who had recently been appointed assistant marshal, arrested the troublesome Bobby Gill, and threw him in a jail cell alongside his brother Bat. The next day in court, Gill was released after paying a five-dollar fine and was given a free railroad ticket out of town. Bat was ordered to pay $25 plus court costs, which he did, but his anger with Marshal Deger had not yet peaked. Masterson found an unexpected ally in Dodge City—Mayor James "Dog" Kelley, who owned a saloon on Front Street. Kelley was in direct competition with Deger, who also owned a saloon on Front Street.

Deger had used his powers of office to harass and intimidate Kelley. One day Deger ambled into Kelley's bar and ordered the arrest of his bartender on a spurious charge. Kelley stormed to the jail and demanded the release of his bartender. When Deger refused, the mayor suspended him from office. Kelley then ordered Assistant Marshal Ed Masterson to arrest the marshal. Deger whipped out a pistol and warned him not to take a step further. After some delicate negotiation, Deger agreed to be locked up until the affair could be straightened out.

Deger filed a complaint against the mayor for interfering with a lawman in the discharge of his duty. The confusing series of events was finally untangled by the city council which reinstated Deger and directed the police court to dismiss the charge against Kelley. The mayor resented Deger, but lacked the political wherewithall to removed him from office, at least until he secured enough political support to tilt the scales. Kelley quietly gathered his forces for the next election by bringing in some ambitious newcomers, including Bat Masterson, the under sheriff of Ford County, Lloyd Shinn, editor of the Dodge City *Times*, and Mike Sutton, county attorney. They began calling themselves "The Gang," and in 1877 they slated Masterson for county sheriff against Deger. The sympathetic *Times* played up all of Masterson's virtues. "Bat is known as a young man of nerve and coolness in cases of danger. He is qualified to fill the office and if elected will never shrink from danger." A "People's Mass Convention" held at the Lady Gay Saloon endorsed Masterson wholeheartedly.

In the general election the dapper, young gunfighter was swept to victory by a narrow margin—three votes. Mayor Kelley then decided to move against Deger. By consent of the city council the incumbent marshal was dismissed, and replaced by Ed Masterson. For the time being, Dodge City was in firm control of "The Gang," headed by the Mastersons. See: **Masterson, Edward J.; Masterson, William Barclay (Bat).**

Delaney, William E. (AKA: **Bill Johnson; Mormon Bill**), 1856-84, U.S., outlaw. Born in Scranton, Pa., on July 11, 1856, William E. Delaney later tended bar in Harrisburg and left that town in 1880 after being involved in a murder, moving to Arizona. He worked briefly as a miner and was later reported to have killed a man in Graham County. In 1883, Delaney killed three men in saloon shootout in Clifton, Ariz., according to one account. On Dec. 3, 1883, Delaney rode into Bisbee, Ariz., with John Heath, Daniel Kelly, and others, holding up a store and killing four persons, including a woman, and wounding a dozen more. Delaney had been one of the gang members stationed outside the store and he was clearly seen to shoot down two men and may have killed the woman.

The gang members split up with Delaney riding to Sonora, Mexico, later moving to Minos Prietas where lawman Ben Daniels tracked him down and arrested him on Jan. 5, 1884. He was returned to Tombstone, Ariz., where he and three others were convicted of the Bisbee Massacre and sentenced to hang. Delaney boasted that he did not fear the hangman, saying: "No man will stand it better than I." He insisted that he and Heath were innocent of the Bisbee killings, right up to the moment that he mounted the gallows in Tombstone on Mar. 3, 1884. See: **Bisbee, Ariz., Massacre; Daniels, Benjamin F.; Heath, John.**

Delony, Lewis S., b.1857, U.S., lawman. The son of a Texas Ranger who fought in the Mexican and the Civil Wars, Lewis Delony left home at the age of fourteen to seek his fortunes on the road. In Clinton, he became a store clerk, an assistant postmaster, and a deputy sheriff before accepting a temporary appointment as a Texas Ranger in 1877. For the rest of his life, Delony served as a part-time law enforcement official while running several businesses in Texas.

His most notable gunfight occurred in Eagle Pass, Texas, in the spring of 1882. While riding with Spencer Adams, a young boy alerted the two rangers to the murder of a deputy sheriff in town. Adams and Delony rode into town and found the outlaw dancing in the local saloon over the bodies of the fallen lawman and a Mexican woman. Delony arrested the killer, but as he prepared to lead him away, another man lunged at him with a knife. Delony whirled around and shot the assailant in the chest. The two Texas Rangers were forced to retreat from town by a hostile crowd before arresting the sheriff's slayer. However, Delony was able to return to arrest his prisoner.

de Rana, Patas (AKA: El Coyote), prom. 1890s, U.S., gunman-outlaw. Patas de Rana was a member of the Forty Thieves Gang headed by the ruthless Vincente Silva who controlled Las Vegas, N.M., in the early 1890s. He was said to have been one of Silva's most trusted lieutenants until the outlaw chieftan shot his wife and the gang turned against him, electing de Rana to shoot Silva. It was also reported that Antonio Valdez, another top Silva gunman, did the actual shooting of Silva, but both shared the $10,000 reward for this feared outlaw leader. The gang later broke up and de Rana was imprisoned for a number of years before disappearing. See: **Silva, Vincente.**

Devol, George, 1829-1902, U.S., gambler. George Devol was a cardsharp, a cheat, and skilled player of three-card monte during the forty years he spent sailing the great paddle wheel ships that traversed the Mississippi River during the mid-nineteenth century. His partner, Canada Bill Jones, played the role of the gullible dupe, while Devol raked in $2 million by his own estimate. Recalling Canada

Bill years later, Devol described his confederate as a "character one might travel the length and breadth of the land and never find his match, or run across his equal. Imagine a medium-sized, chicken-headed, tow-haired sort of man with mild blue eyes, and a mouth nearly from ear to ear, who walked with a shuffling, half-apologetic sort of gait, and who, when his countenance was in repose, resembled an idiot. His clothes were always several sizes too large and his face was as smooth as a woman's and never had a particle of hair on it." Canada Bill Jones is credited with coining a famous line that has become a standard part of American vernacular. One night Bill was playing a rigged gang of faro in a small town along the banks of the Mississippi. His losses were substantial, which prompted one overly-considerate observer to inquire as to why he would play in a game that was so obviously slanted in the dealer's favor. "Yes," he replied in a slow sure manner, "But it's the only game in town."

Devol was born in Ohio but ran away from home when he was only ten. He found work as a riverboat cabin boy, earning four dollars a month. He learned his future trade during the Mexican War, when he was tutored by a veteran card sharp who plied his trade on the Rio Grande. Instead of enlisting in the army as he originally intended, Devol remained a safe distance from the fight, preferring instead to pick the pockets of the soldiers in rigged games of chance. When he completed his apprenticeship, Devol returned to New Orleans with $2,700 jingling in his pockets.

In his published memoirs entitled *Forty Years a Gambler on the Mississippi*, Devol described himself as "a cabin boy in 1839; could steal cards and cheat the boys at eleven; stack a deck at fourteen...fought more rough and tumble fights than any man in America and was the most daring gambler in the world." Three-card monte, and rigged games of poker were his particular specialties. Victims who recognized that they were being cheated would not hesitate to pull a gun or knife. During these tense moments when his life hung in the balance, the gambler would extricate himself from the dilemma by "butting" heads with the swindled victim. Devol's cranium was the envy of the Mississippi con men. He used it many times to cold-cock adversaries, and became known as the man with the "most awesome cranium."

From time to time Devol would butt heads with circus performers for prize money. He knocked unconscious the famous Billy Carroll of Robinson's Circus, who promoted himself as "the man with the thick skull," or "the great butter"—a title Carroll was forced to relinquish. "Gentlemen, I have found my papa at last," he said. In 1887, Devol published his memoirs and drifted into semi-retirement. By his own estimate he had won perhaps $2 million, but like most men of his profession, it was money that was easily spent. "It is said of me that I have won more money than any sporting man in this country," he wrote in 1886. "I will say that I hadn't sense enough to keep it; but if I had never seen a Faro bank, I would be a wealthy man today." Indeed, faro was his only weakness. After stepping off the riverboat which was Devol's second home, he would dispose of his earnings as easily as any gullible western farmer. After his death, the Cincinnati *Enquirer* stated that Devol had won and lost more money than any other gambling blackleg in history.

Diamond, Dick, See: **St. Leon, Ernest.**

Dickason, Isaac Q., prom. 1871, U.S., lawman. The appointment of Isaac Q. Dickason to the Arizona marshalcy on Apr. 15, 1871, was greeted with cautious skepticism by the press, following revelations that former marshal Edward Phelps had perished in the Mexican interior after absconding with $12,000 in federal money. The Prescott *Arizona Mirror* took satisfaction in noting that Dickason was not an "imported pilferer," and was "intelligent, hard working, and a successful farmer." In 1870, Dickason sold his Leonara Valley farm and later joined the throngs of people lured to northern Arizona on the wild rumor that a trove of diamonds had been discovered.

Dickason had only occupied his office a short time when reports of malfeasance began circulating in the territory. In September 1871, a complaint of dereliction of duty was filed by the acting attorney general, Benjamin H. Bristow. A series of letters passed between Dickason and the attorney general's office, in which the discredited lawman tried to defend himself from the charges. Meanwhile Dickason and District Attorney Rowell had been making preparations for the trial over the Camp Grant Massacre in which 100 Apache Indian men, women, and children were killed outside the fort in April 1871. Although controversy existed as to the justification of the massacre, Dickason gained the respect of local citizens for his part in affirming Arizonans' right to defend themselves against Indians and gained the citizens' support. Dickason further shifted some of the criticism away from himself by becoming the first federal law officer to pay the expenses of the U.S. courts in Arizona in January 1872. "Better keep Dickason in office," the Tucson *Citizen* advised.

Political opponents renewed their attack against Dickason in the spring of 1873. He was accused of neglect of duty after taking a short hiatus to prospect for diamonds. It was the second time he had been lured away from his post to chase down the precious stones, the existence of which was wholly unsubstantiated. Later that summer U.S. District Attorney James E. McCaffry, alleged that Dickason had gambled public money on these foolish ventures, and was away from his office for much of the time. In October, Isaac Dickason simply disappeared. He left no forwarding address and was not tracked down for another five years. Published reports out of Deadwood, S.D., told of Dickason's sudden demise in that city. He had died while working as a barkeep in a saloon. This latest scandal involving the Arizona Marshal's office so shocked and outraged the government, that the post was left vacant from July 1873 to January 1874 when George Tyng was appointed. See: **Camp Grant Massacre; Phelps, Edward; Tyng, George.**

Diggs, James, d.1878, U.S., outlaw. James Diggs might have gotten away with murder if not for the determination of Deputy Marshal James Wilkinson, who refused to let the case be forgotten, even after the Western District Court of Arkansas decided there was no evidence to convict the accused.

Diggs was accompanying J.C. Gould, a cattle-driver, in the northern section of the Indian Territory near the Kansas line on Aug. 4, 1873. When nightfall set in Gould, Diggs, and a third man—Hiram Mann—decided to set up camp in an abandoned cabin. The following morning Diggs told several of the area residents that during the night two men had ridden into the camp and murdered his companions as they slept.

A posse was organized to search the countryside for the killers, but first they decided to search the campsite for clues. They discovered Hiram Mann breathing, but unconscious. No evidence, however was found to corroborate Diggs' original story. In addition, the lawmen found $27 in Diggs' coat—the exact amount of Gould's paycheck.

Diggs was brought to Fort Smith where he was charged with murder. However, the government was unable to come up with a witness to the crime other that Mann, who was incapacitated with a gun shot wound. The case collapsed and Diggs was released. When Judge Isaac Parker was appointed to the bench in 1875, he drew Deputy Marshal Wilkinson into the case. Nearly five years had passed but Wilkinson located Diggs and arrested him. In his search for witnesses, he tracked down Mann who was living in Michigan. Mann and the other witnesses Wilkinson had located were brought to Fort Smith where they related their stories. When all the facts were in, Diggs was convicted of murder and hanged on Dec. 20, 1878.

Dodge City Gang, prom. 1879, U.S., outlaw. In the summer of 1879, a gang of desperados known as the Dodge City Gang made their first appearance in San Miguel County, forty miles east of Santa Fe in the New Mexico Territory. The first Santa Fe railroad train steamed into the territory that summer, and with it came a whole host of gamblers, ruffians, and unsavory characters. They became known as the "Dodge City Gang," since so many of them had earned reputations for violent behavior in the western cow towns of Kansas.

Remarkably, several members of the gang managed to secure law enforcement positions within the Las Vegas (also known as New Town), N.M., city government. Hyman G. Neill, known as "Hoodoo Brown," was appointed justice of the peace in Las Vegas. Neill filled several key law enforcement vacancies with some of the most infamous gunslingers of the day. For chief of police he selected Joe Carson, and for deputy, David "Mysterious Dave" Mather, a descendent of Cotton Mather who was not anything like his pious Puritan forefather. Neill saw to it that other cronies were taken care of, including a well-known train robber, Dave Rudabaugh, who was appointed a policeman.

Las Vegas was firmly in control of a criminal cartel bent on thumbing their noses at the law. Between August and October 1879, the Dodge City Gang, led by Hoodoo Brown, held up two stagecoaches and two Santa Fe trains. Marshal John Sherman attempted to deal with the problem by selecting men he considered to be trustworthy and reliable for the deputyship of Las Vegas. In August James H. Dunagan, a veteran of the Union army, applied for the post. He noted his former law enforcement experience—he had served as deputy sheriff of San Miguel County, the bailiwick of Hoodoo Brown. However, before Sherman could act on his application, Dunagan disqualified himself by participating in a stagecoach robbery.

For inexplicable reasons, Sherman chose Mysterious Dave Mather, perhaps believing that his shady past, coupled with his prior experience in Kansas as a lawman made him a good candidate in dealing with men of his own kind. In the fall of 1879, Sherman and his deputies scoured the countryside looking for train robbers. Sherman's unorthodox methods finally paid off, when deputies and postal agents arrested a dozen suspects including the disgraced policeman David Rudabaugh. See: **Mather, David H.; Sherman, John E, Jr..; Rudabaugh, David.**

Dolan, James J., 1848-98, U.S., gunman. James Dolan immigrated to the U.S. from Ireland and served on the Union side during the Civil War, later serving in the West and being mustered out at Fort Stanton. He went to work as a clerk for L.G. Murphy in Lincoln, N.M. He became a junior partner to Murphy, who was a cattle baron at war with John Tunstall, Alexander McSween, and others, including Billy the Kid. Dolan was proficient with a six-gun, an expertise that he proved on May 1, 1877, when he shot and killed 20-year-old Heraldo Jaramillo, an employee who pulled a gun on him. Dolan insisted at his trial that Jaramillo tried to murder him on behalf of the Tunstall faction, and he was acquitted. After Murphy died, Dolan became the chief opponent of the Tunstall-McSween faction, using his vast funds to hire an army that eventually shot down all his adversaries. Dolan was later

Gunman James Dolan, victor in the Lincoln County War.

elected to the Territorial Council and died on his large ranch, the Flying H, on the site of John Tunstall's old ranch, on Feb. 26, 1898. See: **Billy the Kid; Lincoln County War.**

Donahue, Cornelius (AKA: **Lame Johnny**), 1850-78, U.S., lawman-outlaw. "Lame Johnny," Cornelius Donahue, attended college in Philadelphia, but yearned to experience firsthand the thrills and dangers of the western frontier. He moved to Texas to become a cowboy, but his physical impairment kept him away from the big jobs. In desperation he became a horse thief.

Donahue left Texas in the mid-1870s when things got too hot for him. In Deadwood, a rough frontier town in the Dakota Territory, Donahue was hired as a deputy sheriff. He quickly demonstrated his skills with a six shooter. Later on he found a job in the mines, but someone recognized him in 1878 as a Texas horse thief. Donahue fled, and began holding up stagecoaches and stealing horses from the Pine Ridge Indian Reservation. A livestock detective named Frank Smith arrested Johnny on Indian land, and attempted to return him to Deadwood on a stage coach. On the way back to town, a masked rider pulled the coach over and waved Donahue out. It was first thought that one of his pals had come to free him, until they found the body of Lame Johnny swinging from a tree the next day. The identity of the gunman was never established, but the miners who remembered him renamed a creek in the Black Hills the "Lame Johnny."

Doolin, William M., 1858-96, U.S., outlaw. Bill Doolin, the son of an Arkansas farmer, rode into the Indian Territory (later Oklahoma) in 1881, working as a cowboy at the H-X Bar ranch, where the Dalton Brothers occasionally worked. Doolin was a taciturn, tough cowboy who was quick with his gun, and he left the ranch after being involved in a shooting in Coffeyville, Kan., in 1891. Two lawmen had tried to break up a beer party, and when they began pouring the brew on the floor, several cowboys, including Doolin, pulled their six-guns and fatally shot the two deputies. Doolin fled, joining the Daltons. Doolin participated in several train and bank robberies with the gang, but he escaped being killed with most of the Daltons on Oct. 5, 1892, when the gang raided two banks in Coffeyville.

Doolin missed the Coffeyville raid when his horse ostensibly pulled up lame and he told Bob Dalton that he would go to a nearby ranch to find another mount and join the gang later. By the time Doolin arrived at the Coffeyville city limits, the Daltons had died in a hail of bullets fired by irate citizens. Another story has it that Doolin quit the gang just before the Coffeyville debacle after arguing with Bob Dalton over how the spoils from the raid would be divided.

In 1893, Doolin married a preacher's daughter and then organized one of the most notorious outlaw bands in Oklahoma history—Doolin's "Oklahombres." The gang included Bill Dalton, one of the remaining outlaw brothers; Dan Clifton, known as Dynamite Dick; George "Bitter Creek" Newcomb; George "Red Buck" Weightman; Tulsa Jack Blake; Charley Pierce; Bob Grounds; Little Dick West; Roy Daugherty, also known as Arkansas Tom Jones; Alf Sohn; Little Bill

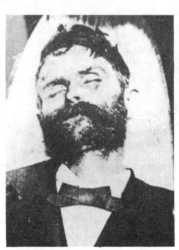
Oklahoma outlaw Bill Doolin, dead.

Raidler; and Ole Yantis. For three years this gang raided banks, trains, and stagecoaches, headquartering in the wide-open town of Ingalls, Okla.

On May 30, 1893, Doolin and three of his gang robbed a train near Cimarron, Kan. As they were fleeing, a large posse led by the noted lawman Chris Madsen cut off the band and a wild gunfight ensued in which Doolin was shot in the right foot. The outlaws escaped under the cover of darkness. After a number of robberies, a small army of lawmen slipped unnoticed into the outlaw town of Ingalls on Sept. 1, 1893. Inside the Ransom and Murray saloon,

Doolin, Dalton, Clifton, Weightman, Newcomb, and Blake were drinking heavily. Roy Daugherty went to his room on the second floor of the City Hotel. As the gang members sat down to a poker game, Newcomb stepped into the street to check the horses. Dick Speed, one of the deputies who had taken cover across from the saloon, impulsively fired a shot at Newcomb and the battle of Ingalls commenced. Newcomb gave the alarm and then escaped by riding out of town in a hail of bullets. Meanwhile, the outlaws inside the saloon and Daugherty from his room fired their weapons from windows at the posse members.

As Deputy Speed raced down the street, one of the gang members shot him dead. Errant bullets killed Del Simmons, a boy watching the fight, and struck another citizen in the chest. The guns fell silent for some minutes and one of the deputies called out to Doolin, asking him and his men to surrender. "You go to hell!" Doolin shouted back and the fighting again erupted. Doolin and his men then dashed to the livery stable, mounted their horses, and fired wildly at the lawmen who shot at them as they rode in the same direction as Newcomb. Bill Dalton was trapped behind a fence and lost his horse. Deputy Lafe Shadley ran forward to kill Dalton with a shotgun but Dalton whirled about and shot Shadley dead. Then Doolin reappeared, racing down the street on his horse, riding to the spot where Dalton stood. He pulled Dalton up on the back of his horse and the two raced out of town.

The gang continued their raids, the largest haul being about $40,000, taken from an East Texas bank, but their days were numbered as more and more lawmen took to their trail. The greatest lawmen of the day, Chris Madsen, Bill Tilghman, and Heck Thomas, formed posses and chased the Doolins through five states, never giving gang members a moment's peace. Doolin was considered a fair-minded man and he reportedly saved Tilghman's life one night by stopping the gang's arch killer, Red Buck Weightman, from shooting Tilghman from ambush. Tilghman's posse was close on the heels of the Doolins one morning. Doolin and his men had just eaten a large breakfast at a farmhouse. As the gang leader stepped outside, he saw Tilghman and his men riding down a distant hill toward the farm. The hospitable farmer thought that the Doolins were part of a posse. Doolin told him that "the other boys coming along now" would be hungry and would want breakfast, too, and that they would pay for all the meals. Tilghman and his men arrived, ate a hearty meal, and were then told by the farmer that "the other boys" had told them Tilghman would pay for the meals. The lawman reluctantly dug into his pocket and paid the farmer for the food his own men and the outlaws had eaten.

In Southwest City, Mo., on May 20, 1895, the Doolin gang raided a local bank, but J.C. Seaborn, the state auditor, seized a gun and tried to stop the bandits. He was dead and Doolin seriously wounded in the head when the outlaws rode from the town. A few weeks later, near Dover, Okla., the gang was camped near the Cimarron River when lawmen suddenly swooped down on them. Tulsa Jack Blake, on guard, warned the gang and traded shots with the posse. Blake was shot and died of his wounds as Doolin and the others escaped. By this time, there was little left of the Doolin gang. Most of its members had ridden off to their own bloody fates. Doolin's own end was also drawing near. He was in Eureka Springs, Okla., when Bill Tilghman tracked him to a bathhouse where the two men fought with fists until the powerful Tilghman knocked Doolin cold and arrested him. Tilghman brought his notorious prisoner to Gutherie, Okla., to stand trial for train and bank robbery. Thousands lined the streets of the town to catch a glimpse of the outlaw. Doolin was cheered as he was taken to jail. He vowed he would never go to prison, and some weeks later he engineered a mass jail break in which he and thirty-seven other prisoners escaped.

Riding to Mexico, Doolin hid out at the ranch of writer Eugene Manlove Rhodes, but he pined for his family and was determined to have his wife and child with him. He rode back to his family, who were then living in Lawson, Okla. On the night of Aug. 25, 1896, Doolin was approaching his father-in-law's farmhouse, where his wife and child were staying. Lawmen led by Heck Thomas, however, had learned of Doolin's presence in the area and were waiting in ambush. Doolin appeared on foot, leading his horse, carrying a rifle, whistling as he walked in the bright moonlit night. Suddenly Thomas shouted from behind some bushes, calling to the outlaw to surrender. Doolin raised his rifle which was shot out of his hand by several shots fired by posse. Doolin then drew his six-gun and fired twice before a blast from a shotgun fired by Deputy Bill Dunn and rifle bullets fired by Thomas cut him to pieces. The outlaw's body was later displayed, naked from the waist up, to show the many holes made by shotgun pellets. See: **Blake, John; Clifton, Daniel; Dalton Brothers; Daugherty, Roy; Madsen, Christian; Newcomb, George; Pierce, Charles; Raidler, William; Thomas, Henry Andrew; Tilghman, William Matthew, Jr.; Waightman, George; West, Richard.**

Dow, Leslie (Les), d.1896, U.S., lawman. Lawman Les Dow was born in Texas, but became deputy sheriff of Chaves County in New Mexico after giving up his hotel and saloon business. He later became a cattle inspector and range detective for the Texas and New Mexico Sanitary Association. His career in law enforcement also included a stop in Eddy County, N.M., where he served as sheriff and deputy U.S. marshal.

Dow was involved in a number of gunfights on the New Mexico and Arizona frontier, including the famous 1896 shootout in the San Simon Valley with Black Jack Christian and his gang. Dow and his posse of seven lawmen fired on the gang as they prepared to break camp. Christian and two other outlaws escaped. In April 1896, Dow was shot down in Carlsbad, N.M., while scanning a pile of letters in the postal station. The gunman was an old adversary named Dave Kemp, who fled from the building before Dow could get off a shot.

Downing, William, prom. 1890s, U.S., lawman-outlaw. William Downing served as a deputy under Burt Alvord and reportedly organized the posse that searched for Alvord after he turned outlaw and robbed a train near Cochise, Ariz., on Sept. 9, 1899. Out of deference to his old boss, it was said, Downing allowed Alvord to escape. Downing later went into the lumber business and then started down the outlaw path himself. One report has it that Downing, an enigmatic person, killed more than thirty men. Another claim was that Downing was the mysterious Frank Jackson, the only gang member who escaped during the disastrous Round Rock robbery

Outlaw Bill Downing.

of 1878 when Sam Bass was killed. Even Downing's death is a mystery. He was reported killed in 1900 in Wilcox, Ariz., by Deputy Billy Speed. Another report has it that Downing was killed in 1908 when officers arrived to arrest him on a wife-beating charge. According to another account, Downing lived into the 1920s. See: **Alvord, Burton; Bass, Samuel.**

Duffield, Milton B., prom. 1863-66, U.S., lawman. By an act of Congress, the Arizona Territory in 1863 was separated from the jurisdiction of the New Mexico marshal, at that time Abraham Cutler. On Mar. 10, of that year, President Abraham Lincoln selected Milton B. Duffield, a fanatical unionist and sworn enemy of the Confederacy, to serve as the region's first marshal. Duffield was a protégé of Kansas senator Samuel Pomeroy and was involved in the scheme to relocate former slaves into a Central American colony. When it came time to select the Arizona territorial marshal, Pomeroy convinced Lincoln to name Duffield, a bigamist, who openly maintained an octoroon wife in Tucson. (His other wife lived elsewhere.)

Duffield arrived in the territory in 1864. He maintained an office in his private home, and since the territorial government had not provided him with a jail facility, he used the military guardhouse. When this area became overcrowded, Duffield was known to chain a prisoner to the wall of a house. The new marshal focused much of his attention on rebel sympa-thizers. One afternoon in Tucson he encountered a former Confederate officer named Kennedy. Follow-ing an angry exchange of words, Duffield threw him to the ground and re-peatedly kicked him in the head. "I allowed him to get up," Duffield later wrote, "(and) he ran like a dog leaving his chivalry behind, and for the pur-pose of extracting any re-

Milton B. Duffield, first marshal of the Arizona Territory.

mainder that might be left, I sent a Derringer Pill after him making an issue through his right ham." Duffield wrote to Secretary of State William Seward about the matter. "If I am molested again I will go to work in earnest and place the balls a little higher up."

Duffield was not well liked, and in turn did little to mask his displeasure with the government troops, the amount of his salary, the inhabitants of the territory, and the politicians whom he accused of "persecuting" him. "Arizona seems a kind of 'Rogues Paradise,'" he wrote to the New York *Tribune* a year after submitting his resignation in 1866, "for a class of government contractors and quiet, pleasure seeking officers; and to give the appearance of action, occasionally are read accounts of successes obtained by the troops...I do not hesitate, over my own signature to declare them false." Duffield resigned on Apr. 1, 1866, in protest of his wholly inadequate salary. His decision to leave greatly pleased his opponents and certain newspapers including the *Arizona Miner* which believed the marshal was insane.

Dumont, Eleanore (AKA: **Simone Jules; Madame Moustache**), 1829-79, U.S., gambler. Eleanore Dumont could rightfully be called California's first lady card sharp.

She found work at San Francisco's Bella Union in the early 1850s, and was such an immediate sensation that rival saloons found it necessary to hire women just to keep up with the competition. In 1854, Dumont, who began calling herself "Madame Simone Jules," left San Francisco to take up residence in Nevada City, Calif. With her unmistakable French accent, the locals in this one-horse town quickly identified her as the famous lady gambler from the Barbary Coast. Her purpose was not to entice a man, but to open a gambling den on Main Street. Her resort became a favorite rendezvous for thirsty gold miners, and the rough-housing Nevada City clientele. The game they most com-monly played was called *vingt-et-un*.

For the next two years business was good. But the local economy was tied to the gold fields and when the mines ceased to produce, the town suffered. Such was the case in 1856 when Dumont found it necessary to move on. She would spend the next twenty-three years of her life tra-versing the backwater towns of Nevada, South Dakota, Idaho, Montana, and Oregon. As she approached thirty, however, her youthful good looks began to fade, and more alarming to a bevy of former suitors, was the appearance of facial hair under her nose. The men began to call her "Madame Mustache," an unkind, yet accurate sobriquet. In the 1870s, Dumont's travels took her into Fort Benton, Mont., where she operated a saloon and brothel. An itinerant steamboat man named Louis Rosche, filed this description of the bagnio. "The click of dice, the rattle of the roulette ball, and the slap of cards greeted my ears as, with my heart beating fast with excitement, I entered the door of the weather-beaten two-story frame building and stepped into the gambling hall. The none too clean looking bar ran along one wall. Faintly from one of the upstairs rooms I could hear the gibberish of a drunken man and the high, shrill laughter of a woman who was quite sober."

Rosche demanded to see the famous proprietor of the establishment—Madame Moustache. "I'm here for a fling at the cards tonight with your lady boss," Rosche told one of the scantily attired demimondes. "Now you take this and buy yourself a drink. Come around after I clean out the Madame, and maybe we can do a little celebrating." The wizened prostitute warned the man that "he should not hold his breath." Eleanore Dumont soon appeared at the table. She sat down and began shuffling the deck of cards and asked him what his pleasure was. Rosche indicated that he had no preference. "Ma'am, there's more than $200 there. Let's get going now, and I don't want to quit until you've got all my money, or until I've got a considerable amount of yours."

Dumont informed him that she preferred *vingt-et-un*. The cards were divvied up and the game began. It took only an hour for Rosche to lose his entire bankroll. When the game ended, the gambler stood up and prepared to leave the saloon, but Dumont suddenly ordered him to sit down and have a drink on the house. The bartender brought a glass of milk, for it was customary for the "trimmed" loser to partake of this drink. Rosche later surmised this custom was the result of Madame Mustache's reasoning that "any man silly enough to lose his last cent to a woman deserved a milk diet or...that the milk would keep him going until his next meal."

In September 1879, the final chapter of the lady gambler's life was played out in the mining town of Bodie, Calif. Professional gamblers descended on her saloon and broke the bank, leaving her destitute. Dumont offered no excuses, nor did she solicit anyone for help. She coolly exited her bar and headed a safe distance out of town where she took her life with her own hand.

Dunlap, Jack (Dunlop, AKA: **Three-Fingered Jack**), prom. 1890s, U.S., outlaw. Jack Dunlap was an Arizona bank and train robber active in the 1890s. Following his release from custody in 1895, he joined "Black Jack" Christian's gang, and later the Burt Alvord-Billy Stiles mob, which held up trains.

In Fairbank, Ariz., on Feb. 15, 1900, Dunlap and his co-

Western outlaw "Three-Fingered" Jack Dunlap.

horts—among them Louis Owens and Owens' brother George, Bravo Juan Yoas, and Bob Brown—tried to stick up an approaching train. They fired on the express messenger, Jeff Milton, but managed only to clip him in the arm. Milton recovered his wits and fired some buckshot into Dunlap's side. Badly wounded, the outlaw was rescued by his companions and removed to safety.

Dunn, Bill, d.1896, U.S., gunman. Bill Dunn and his four brothers Bee, Dal, Calvin, and George most often operated as bounty hunters. But the Dunn brothers were better known as the proprietors of a road ranch outside Ingalls, Okla., where passing travelers were waylaid after being put up for the night. On May 2, 1895, two desper-

ados known as Charley Pierce and Bitter Creek Newcomb arrived at the Dunn ranch to spend the night. As they stabled their horses, Bill and one of his brothers ambushed them outside the barn to collect the $5,000 bounty on Newcomb in Guthrie. A year later, on Aug. 25, 1896, the outlaw leader Bill Doolin was killed much the same way. Dunn was part of the posse surrounding Doolin's farm in Lawson, Okla., and waited for the fugitive to appear at the door. When he showed himself, his surrender was demanded.

Doolin refused and was shotgunned to death. Later that year, the people of the county grew angry over Dunn's tactics. On Nov. 6, Dunn answered his critics by blaming Deputy Sheriff Frank Canton for the brutal way in which Newcomb and Pierce had been killed. In the streets of Pawnee, Canton confronted Dunn. Dunn drew first, but Deputy Canton fired a .45-caliber slug into Dunn's forehead, killing him instantly. See: **Canton, Frank; Doolin, William**.

Dutch Henry (Henry Borne), d.1930, U.S., outlaw. Henry Borne, a German immigrant called Dutch Henry, became known for horse thievery. After arriving in the U.S., he joined the Seventh Cavalry, but quit in the late 1860s. Shortly afterward, Borne was arrested at Fort Smith, Ark., for absconding with twenty government mules. He was sentenced to prison, but escaped just three months later and became a full-time horse thief, an avocation he pursued until the automobile replaced the horse. Dutch Henry sometimes had over 300 men on his payroll who were prepared to steal any herd, no matter how large.

It was said that the crafty Dutchman once sold a sheriff his own recently stolen horse, and "Dutch Henry" came to mean a stolen horse. In 1878, Bat Masterson arrested Henry, but he escaped punishment. The state of Arkansas finally succeeded in putting Dutch Henry away after they connected him with the Fort Smith robbery years earlier. He spent the next twenty years behind bars, and emerged from prison to discover that there was no longer a market for horse thieves. Hollywood borrowed his legendary name for many scripts featuring western badmen.

Dynamite Dick, See: **Clifton, Daniel**.

E

Earhart, Bill, d.1896, U.S., gunman. Bill Earhart, an itinerant cowboy, was born in Jack County, Texas, and moved to New Mexico in 1883 with two friends, Jim and Clay Cooper. In 1888 Earhart became embroiled in a dispute with cattleman John Good, an influential rival of the Cooper brothers whose ranch Earhart worked on. The altercation sparked a bitter range war in 1888 between the Coopers and the Goods. In August John Good's son was allegedly killed by five men, including Earhart, near Las Cruces, N.M. There was a lengthy shootout but the only fatalities were two horses. Peace was eventually restored to the region, and Earhart drifted back into Texas, where he was killed in a saloon brawl in Pecos in Fall 1896.

Earp, Wyatt Berry Stapp, 1848-1929, U.S., lawman. No other American lawman of the Old West inspired more legends than the soft-spoken, nerveless Wyatt Earp. Unlike most of his peers, Earp survived countless gun battles and physical encounters with outlaws because of his extraordinary patience and resolute manner. He was not a fast-draw artist. While gunslingers pulled their weapons and wildly shot away at him, Earp would coolly draw his own weapon and, while bullets whizzed and thudded about him, take careful aim and fire. His aim was generally true, as was his purpose as a lawman in a half-dozen western towns where the rule of the day was robbery and murder.

The Earp family, of Scottish origin, dated back to pre-Revolutionary Virginia. Earp's parents, Nicholas and Virginia Earp, settled in Hartford, Ky., and here produced seven children: James, 1841; Virgil, 1843; Martha, 1845; Wyatt, 1848; Morgan, 1851; Warren, 1855; and Adelia, 1861. Wyatt, named after his father's commander during the Mexican-American War, Colonel Wyatt Berry Stapp, also had a half-brother, Newton, born in 1840 to his father and his first wife. The Earps moved to Iowa and here established a large farm. The Earp boys learned early to respect the law. Their father, according to Wyatt's later recollection, had a "regard for the land (that) was equaled by his respect for the law and his detestation for the lawless elements so prevalent in the West. I heard him say many times that while the law might not be entirely just, it generally expressed the will of the decent folks who were trying to build up the county, and that until someone could offer a better safeguard for a man's rights, enforcement of the law was the duty of every man who asked for its protection in any way."

The older sons, Newton, James, and Virgil Earp, served in the Union army during the Civil War. James was so severely wounded that he returned home, permanently disabled, but this did not prevent him from later serving as a lawman in several western towns. Wyatt attempted to enlist at age fifteen but his father caught him and returned him to the family farm. The family then moved to California and, en route, to protect against marauding Indians, Nicholas Earp gave Wyatt his first weapon, "a cumbersome weapon," Earp recalled later, a combination rifle and shotgun. He later acquired a six-gun and practiced shooting every day, becoming a deadly marksman. He left California, going East in the mid-1860s where he worked as a buffalo hunter for the railroads and the U.S. Cavalry, a railroad worker, and sometimes a scout for wagon trains, as his father had been.

According to his own recollection, Earp met James Butler "Wild Bill" Hickok in Kansas City in 1871, along with the legendary gunmen, scouts, and western legends of their own day. These included Jack Gallagher, Jack Martin, Billy Dixon, Billy Ogg, and Jim Hanrahan. "The names may not mean much to another century," Earp recalled in the 1920s, "but in my younger days, each was a noted man." It was Hickok who convinced Earp to become a buffalo hunter, pointing out that he had made thousands of dollars at hunting these beasts to provide food for U.S. troops. "Bill Hickok was regarded as the deadliest pistol shot alive," Earp would later recall, "as well as a man of great courage. The truth of certain stories of Bill's achievements may have been open to debate but he had earned the respect paid to him."

Earp was a rare exception among his fellow frontiersmen. He did not drink, never cursed, and enjoyed only one vice—gambling, chiefly poker. Earp, during the early 1870s, operated mule and wagon trains and this job took him to Ellsworth, Kan., in August 1873. It was here that the Earp legend began. Ellsworth was the railhead where huge herds of cattle, driven from Texas, were shipped east to the slaughterhouses of Chicago. The town was wild with drunken cowboys spending their pay, shooting up the town, and creating havoc. Two of these were Billy and Ben Thompson, lethal gunmen who would rather resort to gunplay than talk out an argument. On Aug. 15, 1873, both Thompsons were drunk and had started several arguments with two gamblers, John Sterling and Jack Morco, the latter also a local policeman. The Thompsons exchanged shots with Sterling and Morco, who had charged into a saloon, guns blazing at the Thompsons. Ben Thompson fired several shots and drove them off, but Billy Thompson, a homicidal maniac and a hopeless alcoholic, inexplicably turned his gun on Sheriff Chauncey B. Whitney, a friend of the Thompsons who had been drinking with them at the bar. Billy let loose both barrels from his shotgun, killing

An early photo of Wyatt Earp, 1879.

Morgan Earp, 1881.

"Big Nose" Kate Fisher

Left, Wyatt Earp in 1881, and, right, in old age.

Wyatt Earp's close friend, John H. "Doc" Holliday.

Left, James Earp, and, right, Virgil Earp, 1881.

Wyatt Earp, 1880, and his second wife, Celia Blaylock.

Whitney on the spot. Ben Thompson turned about in shock and shouted at his brother: "My God, Billy! You've shot your best friend." Ben Thompson then ushered his drunken brother outside, put him on a horse, and sent him out of town.

Across the street, Wyatt Earp watched these events without interfering. He saw Ellsworth mayor James Miller enter the saloon and demand that Thompson surrender his guns. Thompson refused and Miller stepped outside, going to Marshal J.W. Norton and his deputies Ed Crawford and Charlie Brown, who stood petrified at the Pacific Depot down the street, refusing to go after Thompson. Miller, swearing in frustration at his immobile police force, passed Earp who reportedly said to him: "It's none of my business but if it was me I'd get me a gun and arrest Ben Thompson or kill him." Miller then went to Norton, tore the badge from his shirt, and walked back to Earp, saying: "I'll make it your business. Here's your badge. Go into Beebe's (hardware store) and get some guns and arrest Ben Thompson." Earp nodded, went to the store and strapped on two used .45-caliber six-guns and then went after Thompson, who had stepped into the street. Thompson, who knew Earp, asked what he wanted. Earp told him to throw down his shotgun.

"What are you going to do with me?" Thompson asked him.

"Kill you or take you to jail," Earp replied.

Thompson threw down his shotgun and Earp marched him to jail. He was later fined $25 for disturbing the peace and released. A murder warrant was sworn out for his brother Billy. This, at least, was the story told by many who supported the Earp legend. The great lawman's detractors, however, insisted that Earp never faced down Thompson. There is documentary evidence, however, that proves Earp was present in Ellsworth on Aug. 15, 1873, and Mayor Miller's documents indicate that he not only deputized Earp to disarm and arrest Thompson but that he later offered him the job of town marshal at $125 a month. Earp declined, handing Miller back his badge, and told him that he intended to go into the cattle business with his brothers. He left Ellsworth to meet his brothers in Wichita, but waiting for him was another call to keep law and order. The tall, strong, slender Earp rode into Wichita in 1874 and here he would face an army of gunmen, all looking to establish a reputation by killing lawmen.

Mayor Jim Hope encountered Earp on the streets of Wichita and made him a deputy marshal, serving under the town marshal. Hope had heard of Earp's arrest of the lethal Ben Thompson in Ellsworth and wanted this fearless man on the local police force. Legend and fact mixed freely concerning Earp's exploits in Wichita. There were stories recounting how Earp cowed the gunslinging Manning

brothers, Gyp, Joe, and Jim, and how he squared off against the towering brute, George Peshaur, knocking him unconscious after a ten-minute slug match (Earp was a better-than-average boxer). Ben Thompson arrived in Wichita, but whenever he saw deputy marshal Earp, he crossed the street and sulked in shadows. When cattle baron Abel Head "Shanghai" Pierce arrived in Wichita at the head of a huge herd, his wild, reckless cowboys threatened to wreck the town. Pierce led his men up and down the main streets as they fired their pistols in the air, creating mayhem—a practice then called "hurrahing the town." Earp stopped this by walking calmly up to Pierce and yanking the cattleman from his horse, clubbing him alongside the head, and dragging him to a cell while his stupefied men stood paralyzed in shock.

Most of Earp's duties consisted of tax collecting, a chore he found distasteful, and rounding up drunken cowboys, many of whom were gunmen who looked for combat with lawmen, eager to carve more notches on their guns. One such cowboy, W.W. Compton, was wanted for horse stealing. Earp identified Compton as he emerged from a saloon one night and collared him. Compton shouted that his name was "Jones," but Earp ignored this plea. He dragged the wanted man to a lamp post and looked him over. "You're Compton all right and you're under arrest," Earp told him. Compton squirmed from the lawman's grasp and dashed away, crossing the street and cutting through a back yard, Earp in pursuit. The lawman ordered Compton to halt and when he continued running, Earp fired a single shot that struck the horse thief in the buttocks. Compton pitched forward over a clothesline, bringing down womens' undergarments which had been drying there. Earp picked up the cursing Compton and dragged him to jail while he was still adorned with fluttering nighties.

William Smith, the other deputy marshal in Wichita, decided to run for the office of marshal, that position then held by Michael Meager, who was Earp's friend and favored him. One night in 1876, Smith made insulting remarks about his boss Meager while drinking in a Wichita saloon. Earp ordered him to keep quiet, "or step outside." Smith, drunk, made the mistake of going into the street where Earp beat him senseless in a rather one-way brawl. Smith filed a complaint against his fellow deputy Earp. The town council, to save face, ordered Earp removed from the police force and fined him $30. Earp, disgusted at being punished for defending the honor of his employer, left Wichita, his brother Morgan at his side, and rode to Dodge City, then called the Queen of the Cow Towns, the wildest, most dangerous town in Kansas.

Located near Fort Dodge, the railroads made Dodge City the railhead for all cattle shipping. The vast herds of the southwest were driven to this town, and with them came a mushrooming community, where cash was plentiful and saloons and bawdy houses flourished. Gamblers, prostitutes, gunmen, and thieves of all stripes flowed into Dodge which was soon dubbed "the Gomorrah of the Plains." Mayor George M. Hoover had heard of Earp's no-nonsense reputation and sent for him. When Earp arrived he was quickly made a deputy marshal. His job was to police the lawless red light district, and to arrest drunks and gunmen. He invariably kept his six-gun holstered and used his fists to corral unruly citizens, but he did draw his weapon when outnumbered on several occasions, not to fire it but to use the butt as a club. He received $250 each month in salary and $2.50 per arrest. Earp earned every dollar.

Earp's prowess with a gun was proven on enough occasions to cause the Dodge City *Times* to warn gunslingers not to draw their guns on Earp "unless you got the drop and meant to burn powder without any preliminary talk." Earp, as chief deputy, established what came to be known as the Deadline, prohibiting the carrying of guns north of the railroad tracks, the "civilized" part of Dodge with its better shops, a school, and a church. Any gunman stepping into this area wearing his six-gun was quickly arrested by Earp and his deputies, Morgan Earp, William Barclay "Bat" Masterson, and Jim Masterson. By the fall of 1876, Earp wearied of his knuckle-breaking chores. He turned in his badge and, accompanied by Morgan Earp, the lawman set out for the Black Hills outside of Deadwood, S.D., where gold had been found. He returned to Dodge City on May 7, 1877, after James H. "Dog" Kelley, Dodge City's new mayor, wired him, asking him to help with the Texas cowboys who were shooting up the town. Kelly made Earp assistant city marshal.

Only days after pinning another star on his chest, a group of drunken cowboys rode up to the marshal and pulled their guns, taunting him. At that moment, John Henry Holliday, a young dentist from Georgia who had rented an office on the second floor of the Dodge House, leaned out a window with a shotgun, which he trained on the cowboys as he shouted down to them: "The marshal has his gun put away! Put yours away!" The cowboys nervously looked up to see the shotgun aimed at them and then holstered their weapons, all except the ringleader. Earp reached up and pulled this man from his saddle, knocking the gun out of his hand, and hitting him so hard he knocked him senseless. Before dragging the man off to jail, Earp looked up at Holliday and waved. The lawman and the deadly dentist were close friends ever after. Holliday would go on backing Earp's play, risking his life time and again for Wyatt Earp, especially on that fateful day when he walked with Wyatt, Morgan, and Virgil Earp down to O.K. Corral in Tombstone in 1881 to face the roaring guns of the Clanton-McLowery gang.

Bat Masterson was then sheriff of Ford County, a position he was elected to after his good friend Wyatt Earp encouraged him to run for the office. On many occasions, Masterson and Earp would confront a half-dozen drunken cowboys and subdue them with their pistol butts rather than shoot them. Only flying bullets compelled Earp to draw his weapon. So incensed were certain cattle barons at Earp's manhandling of their cowboys that they posted a $1,000 reward to anyone who would kill Wyatt Earp. A few misguided gunmen tried to collect, one of these being George R. Hoyt.

One night while Earp stood outside the Comique Theater in front of the plaza, listening to the packed crowd inside applaud comedian Eddie Foy, Hoyt rode wildly through the streets, six-gun in hand. He spied Earp and wheeled his horse about, racing across the plaza and, while his horse reared and bucked, fired shot after shot at the marshal. He emptied his gun at Earp, his wild shots missing. Earp coolly withdrew his weapon and fired three times. His first two shots missed the gunman, who was being tossed about by his skittish horse, but the third shot ploughed into Hoyt's forehead. The gunman toppled from his horse, mortally wounded. Hoyt died of his wound a month later.

Earp had to deal with all kinds of killers. James W. "Spike" Kennedy was a hot-headed Texas gunman whose family had showered wealth and favor upon him. Kennedy fell in love with the lovely Dora Hand, who was also known in Dodge City as Fannie Keenan. Dora had been raised in a proper Boston family, had studied voice, and reportedly begun a promising opera career before some unknown tragedy caused her to move West. She had sung in a dozen western hellholes, like Hays and Abilene, and in Dodge City she sang for the raucous, drunken cowboys in saloons and bawdy houses. Mayor James H. Kelley, called Dog, because he once handled General Custer's hounds, made Dora a star by featuring her at his saloon-theater, the Alhambra. Here Kennedy met her and attempted a clumsy seduction. Kelley grabbed the young Texan and threw him out of his place. Kennedy swore revenge and, early one October morning before dawn, rode into Dodge City and fired two bullets through the front door of Kelley's two-room frame shack. The mayor was not there at the time, but Dora Hand was asleep in the back room and one of the bullets slammed through a wall and killed her.

Kennedy then rode wildly out of town, hooting, and firing his weapon. Earp found the dead woman a short time later and then organized one of the most spectacular posses on record, one that included Bat Masterson, Charles Bassett, and William Tilghman, all famous lawmen of their day. For more than a hundred miles, the four lawmen, Earp in the lead, raced across the prairie after Kennedy. The lawmen brought along extra horses and rode them in relays, whereas

Kennedy simply rode his poor mount to death. It collapsed near Meade City. The Texan was kind enough to send a bullet into the stricken animal, but this loud report echoed across the plains and brought the lawmen in hot pursuit. They raced up to Kennedy who took cover behind the body of his dead horse, and fired at them. Masterson, an expert shot, fired a single shot from his rifle. This struck Kennedy's arm, shattering it so that he could not fire his six-gun. Earp and the others closed in as Kennedy shouted: "You s.o.b.'s, I'll get even with you for this!"

As the lawmen rode back to Dodge City, Earp turned in the saddle and told Kennedy: "Your shot killed Dora Hand, not Kelley."

The tough cowboy began to weep and then sobbed: "I wish you had killed me."

In Dodge City, Kennedy was taken to a doctor who removed four inches of bone from his shot-up arm. He was then tried for the murder of Dora Hand but freed for "lack of evidence." Kennedy rode back to Texas where his wealthy parents took him in. He was not heard from again. There were other wild men to tame and Earp stayed in Dodge until 1879, keeping the peace. His pay was meager and the gratitude of citizens was even thinner. In 1879, Earp received a letter from the owners of the Oriental Saloon in Tombstone, Ariz., asking him to come to that town with his brothers to protect the lavish emporium from the gunmen and thugs employed by rival saloon owners. Earp was offered a partnership in the Oriental, which would guarantee him a fortune, more than $1,000 a month. Scarred and worn out with keeping the peace in a half-dozen towns, Earp and his brothers Morgan, Virgil, and James, agreed to the deal and left for Tombstone in 1879. The ever-loyal Doc Holliday also packed up his guns, his cards, and his Bowie knife, and rode along with the Earps.

Tombstone was then the last of the wide-open hellholes. The town teamed with rustlers, thieves, gunmen, gamblers, and whores—the worst flotsam of the West. The community had been founded by wandering prospector Edward Schieffelin. He told a friend that he would find gold or silver in the shadows of the Dragoon Mountains in southeastern Arizona. The friend replied: "All you'll ever find is your tombstone." Schieffelin did strike a bountiful vein of silver, which caused a stampede to the area. Miners quickly dug through silver veins yielding more than $30 million, and the strike then evaporated. What was left was a ramshackle community peopled by the worst dregs of society, a town Schieffelin had whimsically named Tombstone, after the fate his friend had predicted for him.

When Wyatt Earp, his brothers, and Holliday arrived in Tombstone, Pima County sheriff Charles Shibbell made Earp a deputy. As a deputy county sheriff, Earp worked with town marshal Fred White but he found Cochise County sheriff John H. Behan siding with the local gunmen. Behan, Earp quickly learned, supported and received money from the most notorious cattle thieves and rustlers in the West, the burgeoning Clanton-McLowery gang, which was headed by Newman H. Clanton, or Old Man Clanton, as he was called. Behan and his crooked deputies looked the other way while the Clantons looted cattle and horses and held up stagecoaches, parceling out some of their spoils to the corrupt sheriff. Clanton's sons, Joseph Isaac (known as Ike), Peter, Finneas "Finn" Clanton, and Billy Clanton, were hard riding cowboys who learned at an early age the art of rustling from their criminally bent father. Frank and Tom McLowery (or McLaury) worked a small ranch next to the Clanton spread and also worked the Clanton herds, which were mostly stolen and which the McLowerys had helped to thieve from Mexican ranches south of the border.

In addition to the quick guns of the Clantons and McLowerys, lawmen had to contend with an army of fast-draw artists such as Curly Bill Brocius (William B. Graham), Johnny Ringo (Ringgold), Pony Deal, Pete Spence, Frank Patterson, Billy Claiborne, and Frank Stilwell. All of these men, especially Brocius and Ringo, were dour-faced, alcoholic killers, and would shoot a man for staring at them. Stilwell was a sneaky murderer who ran livery stables in the towns of Charleston and Bisbee. He had shot a Mexican cook to death some years earlier simply because the man served him tea instead of coffee. He reportedly killed an elderly miner and took his claim, which Spence used to obtain the livery stables.

It was Brocius who first ran headlong into Wyatt Earp. On an October night in 1880, Billy Clanton, Frank and Tom McLowery, Pony Deal, and Brocius rode up and down Allen Street firing their weapons recklessly and harassing anyone foolish enough to walk the rickety slatboard side-walks. Sheriff White stopped the cowboys at Sixth and Allen streets, and Brocius began to draw his holstered weapon. White reached out and grappled with the gunman, grabbing Brocius' gun, which went off. The bullet struck White in groin and he fell to the dusty street. Just then Earp appeared, ran to Brocius and, pulling his six-gun, brought it down with such force on Brocius' head that he knocked the gunslinger unconscious.

White was rushed to a doctor's office and there magnanimously told witnesses that he had been shot by his own carelessness. He then died. Earp, meanwhile, had confronted the other gunmen, telling them that he would kill any one of them that reached for a weapon. He ordered them out of town and they meekly complied as Earp dragged the unconscious Brocius to jail. Brocius, thanks to White's dying statement, was later released. He would later be shot in the mouth on May 25, 1881, by lawman William Breakenridge, and then hang up his guns,

Outlaws Newman H. Clanton and his son, Isaac Clanton.

The O.K. Corral, Tombstone, Ariz., mid-1880s.

Outlaws Frank and Tom McLowery, Clanton allies.

The Earps and Clantons battle in the O.K. Corral.

The robbery of the Tombstone stage by Clanton outlaws, 1881.

Pete Spence, killed by Wyatt Earp.

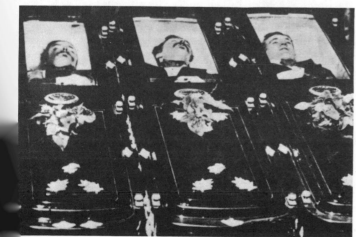

Tom and Frank McLowery and Billy Clanton, in their coffins, 1881.

Sheriff John Behan.

John Clum, Earp ally.

moving to Texas to live out his life in obscurity. Earp, however, later claimed that he tracked down Brocius and killed him.

Meanwhile, Doc Holliday, who busied himself in gambling and gunfights, confronted Sheriff Behan one day in the Oriental when Behan accused Holliday of manipulating a faro game. The deadly dentist challenged Behan, who quickly retreated when Holliday taunted him in front of a jeering crowd. From then on, Behan hated both Earp and Holliday, who later stated that Behan "would spend money to have me killed." But the men who wanted the Earps and Holliday dead were the Clantons. Earp had warned the leader of the gang, Ike Clanton, that he would no longer tolerate the gang's lawless ways in Tombstone. He also ordered Clanton to run his stolen herds of cattle back into Mexico. Then, in March 1881, the Kinnear & Co. stagecoach leaving Tombstone was robbed and driver Bud Philpot was killed by the holdup men. So, too, was passenger Peter Roerig, who was riding atop the stage when the holdup gang began firing at it. The stagecoach, driven by guard Bob Paul, who had answered the bandits with gunfire, managed to elude the thieves and reach Benson.

Earp put together a posse of his brothers Morgan and Virgil Earp, "Buckskin Frank" Leslie, Bat Masterson, and others and began tracking the bandits. The lawmen managed to corner a small-time thief, Luther King, who confessed that he had held the horses of the bandits in their abortive attempt to stop the stagecoach. He named the thieves as Harry Head, Jim Crane, and Bill Leonard, all friends of the Clantons. Earp turned King over to Behan, who was part of the posse and the sheriff returned to Tombstone with the prisoner while Earp and his posse sought the other bandits. They failed to track down the killers and rode into Tombstone to discover that King had escaped from Behan's jail. He simply walked out an unlocked back door, according to most reports, while the crooked Behan looked the other way. When Earp accused Behan of letting King escape, the sheriff then claimed that Doc Holliday, Earp's friend, had tried to rob the stage.

Holliday laughed this charge off, pointing out that Behan hated him for earlier embarrassing the sheriff in front of half of the town. The gun-toting dentist then pointed out that he would have gotten the bullion on the stage by simply shooting the horses, if he had been present which, he insisted, he had not. Earp then concocted a plan to catch the real criminals. He went to Ike Clanton and asked him to bring Head, Crane, and Leonard to a rendezvous. If Clanton cooperated, Earp said, Clanton would receive the sizeable reward then offered for the killer of Philpot and Roerig. He, Earp, would be credited with the arrest and would surely be swept into the office of Pima County Sheriff in the next election. At least, that is the story the insidious

Ike Clanton later told to embarrass Wyatt Earp.

Further confusion was created by Big Nose Kate Fisher, also known as Elder. Drunk some time later, she slobbered to Behan a story about how her estranged lover Doc Holliday had indeed held up the stage and shot Philpot and Roerig. Behan swore out an arrest for Holliday the next day, but Earp and friends put up a $5,000 bail. When Big Nose Kate sobered up the next day, she admitted lying about Holliday. He was released and Big Nose Kate left Tombstone and the arms of Doc Holliday forever.

The Bisbee stage was then held up on Sept. 8, 1881, and lawmen interviewed the passengers, who said that one of the masked holdup men had grabbed the $2,500 in gold bullion and then said to the other bandits: "Have we got all the sugar?" Earp, Billy Breakenridge, and others were shocked to hear this statement which they knew was a favorite phrase of Frank Stilwell, who was Sheriff Johnny Behan's chief deputy. Boot marks at the scene of the robbery were matched to Stilwell's boots. He and Pete Spence, Stilwell's livery stable partner, were arrested in Bisbee and returned to stand trial in Tombstone. Both men, of course, were close associates of Ike Clanton, who was incensed that his friends were jailed. He began a smear campaign against Wyatt Earp, saying to anyone who would listen: "Wyatt Earp is telling lies about me in town."

Then one of Clanton's riders, Billy Claiborne, who liked to be called "Billy the Kid," a drunk, braggart, and killer-from-ambush, was arrested and charged with a murder and placed in the Charleston jail. Ike Clanton and others led a raid that freed Claiborne and at the time the gang leader boasted that if the Earps ever dared to jail one of his men in Tombstone, the same thing would happen, a brag that made its way back to Wyatt Earp. All of Tombstone knew that the simmering feud between the Clantons and Earps would break into open warfare. This was looked upon as a family against family confrontation by those who favored the Clantons which removed the myriad illegal acts of the Clantons from the consideration they deserved. The Earp faction was headed by law-and-order citizens such as Mayor John Clum, who had appointed Virgil Earp city marshal in June 1881. Clum and his vigilance committee wholly backed the Earps and were considered the "good citizens" of Tombstone. They were hopelessly outnumbered by the outlaws and gunmen.

The feud boiled over on Oct. 25, 1881, just after midnight. Several gunmen, including Ike Clanton and Doc Holliday, had gathered for a predawn snack in the lunchroom of the Alhambra. Holliday was absolutely fearless, some said mentally unbalanced. He had a long record of bloody gunfights in Denver, Dodge City, and other cattle towns where his fast gun was legendary. "He had a mean disposition and an ungovernable temper," according to his

The deadly gunfighter Ben Thompson, who was disarmed by Wyatt Earp in Ellsworth, Kan., shown circa 1875.

William Smith, with whom Earp had a bloody fistfight in Wichita, Kan., shown at right in 1875.

The legendary lawman, William Barclay "Bat" Masterson and Dodge City, Kan., circa 1879.

Drunken killer Billy Thompson and Tombstone, Ariz., at the time of the Earp-Clanton feud, 1881.

friend Bat Masterson, "and under the influence of liquor was a most dangerous man...among men who did not fear him (he) was very much disliked." The small-framed Holliday, armed with a six-gun despite the ordinance against carrying firearms (a law few in Tombstone obeyed), approached Clanton and said: "Ike, you threaten the Earps again and you'll have to face me, you and your rotten gang." Clanton sneered and swore at Holliday. "You s.o.b. of a cowboy!" Holliday roared back. "Go get your gun and go to work."

"The Earps are going to get plenty of fight from us," Clanton said to Holliday.

Just then Morgan Earp entered the room, heard the remark, and told Clanton: "Go heel yourself! You can have all the fight you want right now."

Clanton spread back the bottom of his coat to show that he was not armed. In a quavering voice he said: "Don't shoot me in the back, will you, Morg?" He then turned and walked out of the lunchroom but he returned a half hour later, still unarmed, going to the gambling hall of the Alhambra and boldly sitting down to a poker game with, of all people, Morgan Earp. But also sitting at the table was the venal Johnny Behan, Clanton's sponsor, along with Tom McLowery, Clanton ally. The game broke up some hours later, and Clanton was about the leave the Alhambra. Doc Holliday appeared and again berated Clanton. Jim Flynn, a city policeman, appeared and broke up the argument. It was about 7 a.m., Oct. 26, 1881.

Two hours later Ike Clanton saw city marshal Virgil Earp in the middle of the street and walked up to him, a sneer on his face. The loud-mouthed Clanton said: "If you were one of them threatening me last night, you can have your fight." The gang leader then turned about and sauntered away. Virgil Earp thought he was still half drunk. About noon Morgan and Virgil Earp, patrolling the streets, saw Ike Clanton and approached him, seeing that he carried a gun in his belt hidden beneath his coat. They ordered him to turn in his gun and he refused. Virgil Earp pulled his six-gun and, with a lightning move, banged it against Clanton's head. Clanton, half conscious, was then dragged by the Earps into court where Judge Wallace fined the gunman $25 for carrying a concealed weapon.

Just as the cowed Clanton was about to be released, Tom McLowery ran into the court room, screaming oaths at the Earps. Wyatt Earp was on hand and he slammed his six-gun against McLowery's head. He then dragged the unconscious McLowery to the street and threw him into the mud. Clanton then helped McLowery to his feet and, both swearing at the three Earp brothers, they went down the street, vowing revenge. A half hour went by before a town drunk appeared before the three Earps and told them: "There are some men want to see you fellows down at the O.K. Corral."

Wyatt Earp stepped forward and asked: "Who are these men?"

"The McLowery brothers, the Clantons, and Bill Claiborne."

The somber lawman turned to his brothers Virgil and Morgan and said: "Let's go." The three tall Earps fingered their six-guns. They began their historic walk to the O.K. Corral wearing long black coats, black, broad-rimmed hats, shiny boots, and starched white shirts with string ties. Before they had gone half a block, Doc Holliday suddenly appeared. He was carrying a shotgun. Wyatt Earp nodded in his direction and the loyal gunman joined the Earps, all four men striding confidently down Fremont Street. The residents of Tombstone watched them go by, resolute and knowing what waited for them at the narrow, small corral which squatted between two adobe buildings down the street.

Someone on the sidewalk standing close to Doc Holliday as he passed by, said to the determined dentist: "Let them have it."

"All right," was Holliday's only reply.

Johnny Behan, who was sitting in a barber shop getting a shave, saw the Earps marching down the street. He jumped out of the chair and ran into the street, the barber's sheet still tucked about his neck, lather on his face. Behan was close to the O.K. Corral at Fourth and Fremont streets and he was soon joined by Frank McLowery. The two conferred and then McLowery walked quickly back to the O.K. Corral where he joined his brother Tom, Ike and Billy Clanton, and Billy Claiborne. Behan turned and went up the street where he approached Virgil Earp, having a brief conversation with him. Behan later claimed that he told Earp that it was his duty to disarm the men at the O.K. Corral, not to bring a gunfight to them, a lie. Behan actually tried to arrest the Earps but Wyatt brushed him aside, saying: "We won't be arrested today by you, Behan."

They continued on their way, with Behan standing in the middle of the street looking after them. A few minutes later the four men turned about and faced the entrance of the little corral where the five rustlers stood waiting. Virgil Earp was the ranking lawman and he spoke for the Earps: "You men are under arrest. Throw up your hands!"

Frank McLowery and Billy Clanton reached for the six-guns on their hips. Virgil Earp shouted: "Hold it, I don't mean that. I've come to disarm you!" Behan later insisted that Tom McLowery claimed he was not armed and that Billy Clanton shouted to the lawmen and Holliday: "Don't shoot me. I don't want to fight." According to best reports, these were typical Behan fabrications. All of the outlaws were armed, not only with six-guns but with rifles, either in their hands or in scabbards on their nearby horses and within reach.

The two groups stood motionless for some moments. Then, almost at the same second, Billy Clanton and Wyatt Earp drew their guns. Then Frank McLowery drew his six-gun and both he and Billy Clanton fired at Wyatt at the same time, their shots going wild. Wyatt fired once, his bullet striking Frank McLowery in the stomach. At that second, the boastful coward, Ike Clanton, leaped forward, running to Wyatt Earp and whining as he grabbed the lawman's sleeve: "Don't shoot me! Don't kill me! I'm not fighting!"

"The fighting has now commenced," Earp shouted at him. "Go to fighting or get away!"

Ike Clanton left his brother Billy and his friends by dashing across the street and disappearing down an alley while the gunfight went on. "Throw up your hands!" said Virgil Earp but the outlaws were now firing rapidly at the Earps. Frank McLowery, the first to receive a mortal wound, staggered through the smoke of the banging six-guns and moved slowly across the street, gun still in hand. He pitched forward and fell on the wooden sidewalk but he managed to get off another shot which whizzed past Wyatt Earp. Billy Claiborne fired several shots at Virgil Earp and then fled in the direction Ike Clanton had taken, running into the street, firing as he ran, racing into the nearby photographic studio owned by C.S. Fly, where he hid from the lawmen.

Tom McLowery, six-gun blazing, stepped toward the entrance of the corral. He fired a shot at Morgan Earp and two at Doc Holliday which ripped through Holliday's coat. Holliday aimed his shotgun and fired both barrels into McLowery, blasting him to death. As he fell, the second McLowery brother to die, he squeezed off a round that ploughed into Morgan Earp's shoulder. Billy Clanton, age nineteen, had received a wound in his right hand from a shot fired either by Morgan or Virgil Earp, but the tough little gunman shifted his six-gun to the left hand and fired several bullets, one of which struck Virgil Earp in the leg and sent him to the ground. He then followed Billie Claiborne's escape route, running down the street toward Fly's photographic gallery. As he ran, he fired at the Earps, one of his bullets creasing Holliday's back. The Earps fired back at him and he was hit another three times. He fell in front of the gallery.

Everyone was now down. Only Wyatt Earp stood alone, unharmed, as the smoke from gun battle drifted down the street, offering a clear view of the carnage. Earp turned and followed Billy Clanton, standing over him. The mortally wounded gunman looked up at Earp, cursing him and saying: "God, God, won't someone give me some more cartridges for a last shot?" He then sank back and died. The historic gunfight at the O.K. Corral was over and within days became western legend. It had lasted no more than two or three minutes and from thirty to fifty shots had been fired by both factions. Two lawmen, Virgil and Morgan Earp, were seriously wounded, and Doc Holliday was slightly injured. Three dead outlaws lay in the street: Tom and Frank McLowery and Billy Clanton. Stories and whole books would be written about this most famous of Western gun battles and more than a half-dozen motion pictures would record the event. Few such incidents in the history of the Old West were marked with such passionate lore. And, because of this standup, high noon fight, the memory of Wyatt Earp would be forever linked to the image of raw courage and dedication to duty.

Wyatt Earp walked back to his stricken brothers and he and the slightly wounded Holliday lifted Morgan and Virgil Earp to their feet and helped them back up the street to a doctor's office. While Virgil and Morgan were recuperating, Virgil Earp was discharged as city marshal and Wyatt Earp and Doc Holliday were arrested on charges of murder, on warrants sworn out by the cowardly Ike Clanton and his sneaky sidekick, Sheriff Behan. Justice of the peace Wells Spicer heard the case and quickly dismissed the charges against Earp and Holliday. This was not the end of the Clantons, however.

Ike Clanton organized other outlaws who would shoot down the Earps from ambush in the coming months. Virgil Earp, who had recovered from his wounds, was entering the Oriental Saloon on the night of Nov. 28, 1881. Several shots were fired at him from the shadows and a bullet entered his back. He was crippled for the rest of his life. Morgan Earp was next. On the night of Mar. 17, 1882, four Clanton henchmen, Pete Spence, Frank Stilwell, Hank Swilling, and Florentino "Indian Charlie" Cruz, slipped behind a stack of kegs in Hatch's Saloon and when Morgan Earp entered and began to play pool, the four gunmen opened up and shot Earp in the back, killing him.

Wyatt Earp, joined by Holliday, put the body of Morgan Earp on a westbound train. They, along with the crippled Virgil Earp and James Earp, who had been permanently crippled in the Civil War and did not serve as a lawman, traveled west toward California. But Wyatt and Holliday got off the train at Tucson, Ariz. There they were met by Warren Earp, who had rounded up Texas Jack Vermillion, Turkey Creek Jack Johnson, and Sherman McMasters, three specially appointed lawmen. This posse then went in search of the killers who had shot down Morgan and Virgil Earp. Wyatt had received word that Clanton gunmen would be waiting at Tucson to ambush the surviving Earp family members in the train yards.

Wyatt and the other posse members searched the yards and, according to Wyatt's later statements, they saw four figures crouching behind some flatcars. Wyatt approached them and one of them, Pete Spence, bolted, running on top of a flatcar and then turning to fire on Earp. Wyatt fired a single bullet from his six-gun which smashed into Spence's heart, killing him. When he turned, now cradling a shotgun, Earp saw Frank Stilwell step from the shadows. He had reserved his anger for Stilwell who was the one who had led the ambush of Morgan Earp. Outlaw and lawmen stood only a foot or so apart and, in Earp's own words, "Stilwell caught the barrel of my Wells Fargo gun with both hands. I forced the gun down until the muzzle of the right barrel was just underneath Stilwell's heart. He found his voice: 'Morg!' he said, and then a second time, 'Morg!' I've often wondered what made him say that...I let him have it. The muzzle of one barrel was just underneath the heart. He got the second before he hit the ground."

With his brother Warren, Doc Holliday, Vermillion, Johnson, and McMasters at his side, Wyatt Earp tracked down each and every one of Clanton's hired killers. According to his own later statements, Earp found Florentino "Indian Charlie" Cruz outside of Tombstone. Wyatt told the gunman to count to three and both men then drew. Cruz fell with a bullet in his heart. Wyatt raced after Curly Bill Brocius, both men riding their mounts to death on a harrowing plains chase which ended at Iron Springs. Here Brocius advanced on Earp as the intrepid lawman stoically marched toward his prey, both firing as they moved. Brocius fell, shot to death, as Earp pumped one bullet after another into him. In the shadows of the Whetstone Mountains, Earp tracked down and killed Johnny Ringo.

The Clanton family had been reduced to N.H. "Old Man" Clanton, Ike, and Finn. N.H. Clanton was shot to death in July 1881 while he was on a rustling raid. Finn, a non-violent member of the clan, lived out a calm life, dying at the turn of the century. Ike Clanton, while Earp and his men sought out the killers of Morgan Earp, fled to Mexico and hid under an assumed name. When Earp gave up the search for him, he returned to the Tombstone area, but he took up his old rustling ways and was shot to death in 1887 by lawmen.

Doc Holliday, Earp's good and loyal friend, lived only a few more years after the historic O.K. Corral gunfight. Wracked with consumption, he was taken to a sanitorium near Glenwood Springs, Colo., by Wyatt Earp and here the deadly dentist died, his Bowie knife still tied about his neck, his six-gun at his side, and his shotgun on the bed with him. Wyatt Earp outlived them all. His life was nomadic for several decades. The great lawman had married for the first time in 1870, but his wife died a few months following the wedding. Earp's second wife, Celia "Mattie" Blaylock, who had accompanied him to Tombstone, separated from the lawman after his Tombstone days and tragically wound up living in the seedy gold and silver towns as a prostitute,

committing suicide in Pinal, Ariz., on July 3, 1888.

Earp finally moved to his family home at Colston, Calif., marrying again, to Josie Earp in 1882 while in San Francisco. He returned to Tombstone briefly and then wandered about the West through the gold camps of Idaho and Colorado, but his reputation was too much with him. He traveled to Alaska during the gold rush at the turn of the century. Earlier he was a referee of notable boxing matches. (His most notable fight was the championship battle between Bob Fitzsimmons and Tom Sharkey in 1896.) Earp raised thoroughbred horses in San Diego in the 1890s. He and his wife prospected throughout Nevada and briefly owned and operated a Tonopah saloon. They finally settled in Los Angeles. Only a few months before his death in 1929, Earp told his story to Stuart Lake.

He died at the age of eighty on Jan. 13, 1929, in the arms of his wife, Josie. Wyatt Earp's last words to his biographer were: "The greatest consolation I have in growing old is the hope that after I'm gone they'll grant me the peaceful obscurity I haven't been able to get in life." Some claimed he had stretched the truth, but if he had, it mattered little. The facts of his astounding, spectacular life needed no embellishment. He remains, in fact and fiction, the greatest U.S. lawman of the Old West, and the considerable efforts on the part of certain revisionist historians have failed to change that image. Wyatt Earp lived and the great deeds of his day happened in a West where the legend of the hero cannot perish. See: **Bassett, Charles; Brocius, Curly Bill; Claiborne, William; Clanton-McLowery Gang; Holliday, John Henry; Masterson, William Barclay; Ringo, John.**

Earp Brothers, prom. 1870s-1880s, U.S., lawmen. Born and raised in the Midwest by a hard-working farming father, the Earp brothers, Morgan, Virgil, Warren, and Wyatt, all became law enforcement officers. Morgan, the most easy going of the brothers, served as a marshal in Butte, Mont., and was later sheriff of Ford County, Kan. before joining his brothers Virgil and Wyatt in Tombstone, Ariz., in 1880. He and Virgil and Wyatt Earp, and John H. "Doc" Holliday faced the Clanton-McLowery clan in the 1881 battle of the O.K. Corral. Morgan Earp was killed on Mar. 18, 1882 while playing billiards with Bob Hatch in Campbell and Hatch's Billiard Parlor in Tombstone. Several armed men, members of the Clanton-McLowery gang, shot Morgan Earp through an open back door of the billiard parlor and then fled. Bullets penetrated his spinal column and stomach. Wyatt Earp was watching the game at the time and rushed to the alleyway but found the killers had fled.

Morgan Earp was taken to a couch in an adjoining card

room and there, while his brothers Wyatt, Virgil, Warren, and James stood by with the Earp wives, he died in less than an hour. Three doctors tried desperately to save Earp but his wounds were fatal. When several men tried to remove him to a doctor's office, Morgan cried out: "Stop, I can't stand it! This is the last game of pool I'll ever play." He whispered a few words into Wyatt's ear and then died. Wyatt Earp and others avenged the murder of Morgan Earp by tracking down and killing the murderers of Morgan Earp.

Virgil Earp served in the Union Army during the Civil War, along with his older brothers James and Newton. After the war, Virgil drove a stagecoach out of Council Bluffs, Iowa, and was, with his brothers Morgan, James, and Wyatt, later involved in a wild two-hour street brawl with five other men in Lamar, Mo., where Wyatt was a peace officer. He later served on the Dodge City police force and moved to Arizona in 1876, prospecting and farming. He briefly served as a deputy and helped to track down two outlaws, killing one in a gun battle. He arrived in Tombstone to serve as marshal in June 1881.

The following October, Virgil, along with his brothers Morgan and Wyatt, and Doc Holliday, shot it out with the Clanton-McLowery outlaws at the O.K. Corral. Following this battle, Clanton gunmen, on the night of Dec. 28, 1881, shot Virgil Earp from ambush as he left Tombstone's Oriental Saloon. The gunmen fired shotguns from the shadows, wounding Virgil, who was rushed to a doctor's office where buckshot had peppered his left side and arm, along with his back. His wife Allie appeared and Virgil told her: "Never mind, I've still got one arm left to hug you with."

Wyatt Earp arrived and, just before Virgil was given gas in preparation of an operation, he said to his brother: "Wyatt, when they get me under, don't let them take my arm off. If I have to be buried I want both arms on me." He survived and kept his arm but was a cripple for life. Virgil Earp was taken to the family homestead in Colton, Calif., where he recovered from his wounds. He later prospected with his wife and, still later, was elected city marshal of Colton. He then returned to prospecting with his wife Allie and died of pneumonia in Goldfield, Nev., in 1905.

Warren Earp, the youngest of the Earps who served as lawmen, joined his brothers Morgan, Virgil, and Wyatt in Tombstone in 1880. He was made a deputy by his brother Virgil, then marshal, but he was absent from Tombstone when his brothers Virgil, Morgan, and Wyatt shot it out with the Clanton-McLowery outlaws. Warren Earp later joined Wyatt in tracking down the killers of Morgan Earp. Warren Earp later prospected and served as a stage driver in Globe, Ariz. He moved to Wilcox, Ariz., and there, in 1900, got into a drunken fight with a cowboy named Johnny Boyet. Boyet shot and killed Warren, who was unarmed at the time. Boyet was acquitted on grounds of self-defense, the jury believing that even an Earp without a gun was more dangerous than an opponent with a blazing six-gun in his hand. See: **Clanton-McLowery Gang; Earp, Wyatt Berry Stapp; Holliday, John Henry; O.K. Corral.**

Elliott, Joe (AKA: **Little Joe**), prom. 1870-80, U.S.-Turk., outlaw. Joe Eliott was a counterfeit artist to whom no currency was foreign. He operated in the U.S. and in Turkey, creating and passing forged documents. After escaping from a Turkish prison, where he had been housed after being found Guilty of counterfeiting, Eliott returned to the U.S. and fell in love with actress Kate Castleton. He pursued the theater queen for months, bombarding her with flowers, expensive dinners, and jewelry he had stolen. The couple eventually married, but it was not long before someone told the former Miss Castleton how her new husband made his living. When she confronted Eliott, he admitted guilt and promised to go straight. After a year of relative calm, Eliott was arrested in New York on charges of attempting to forge a $64,000 check. Castleton stuck with her husband while he served his prison sentence, but one year later the couple were divorced.

Eliott talked his wife into a second marriage, but it was short-lived as the convict could not abandon his criminal lifestyle. The couple were divorced a second time and Eliott went on to commit a number of robberies and pull off a number of counterfeiting scams in Europe.

Elliott, William (AKA: **Colorado Bill**), d.1879, U.S., gunman. William Elliott was a much feared gunman who was wanted for murder in four states. On Feb. 23, 1879, he claimed his fifth victim: David J. "Cooke" Brown, who was passing through the Choctaw Nation. Elliott was apprehended for this crime and was sentenced to death on May 28, 1879, at Fort Smith by Judge Isaac Parker. In commenting on the charges brought against Elliott, the local newspaper *Elevator* dryly noted that: "He will hardly be wanted by any other state after they get through with him here." The prophecy was correct for the desperado was hanged on Aug. 29, 1879.

Escobar, Rafael, prom. 1850s, U.S., outlaw. Rafael Escobar was a bandit who plagued southern California in the early 1850s, robbing stagecoaches and stores almost at will. He reportedly shot and killed a number of people who resisted his robberies. He was tracked down and taken to Jackson, Calif., but he was hanged by the local vigilance committee before reaching trial.

Espinosa Brothers, prom. 1860s, U.S., outlaws. In 1861, three Mexican citizens, Julian, Felipe, and Victorio Espinosa entered the U.S. reputedly to avenge the deaths of six relatives who had perished during the Mexican-American War, by killing 100 "gringos." The Espinosas travelled to Colorado, where, in the next two years they killed twenty-six U.S. citizens. Most of the Espinosas' victims were also robbed, often immediately after being paid—a fact which casts some doubt on their professed motive of revenge.

When the trio's leader, Felipe Espinosa, offered to stop the killings in return for a land grant of 5,000 acres, Colorado officials responded by posting a reward of $2,500 for Felipe—dead or alive. When the killing continued, local vigilante groups were organized, and tried to catch the Espinosas, but often ended up hanging the wrong person. Finally, Victorio Espinosa was caught in the Fairplay-California gulch and lynched. Felipe remained at large and continued killing.

In desperation, the U.S. Army hired Tom Tobin, a renowned U.S. scout, to bring in the two remaining Espinosas. Eschewing a fifteen-man backup, Tobin, riding alone, caught up with the two renegades at Indian Creek and killed them before they could fire a shot. Tobin cut off their heads and returned to Fort Garland to claim his reward money. Because of a cash shortage Tobin received only $1,500 and a quantity of buckskins. The heads of the Espinosas became a ghoulish but popular local attraction. As late as 1955, Kit Carson III was exhibiting them in sideshows. When local experts denounced the heads as fakes, Carson, grandson of Tom Tobin, said that he had always insisted the real skulls were buried behind Fort Garland.

Estabo, Tranquellano, prom. 1890s, U.S., gunman. Within a few months in 1895 this notorious Mexican outlaw was involved in three gunfights. Near Phoenix, N.M., Tranquellano Estabo and some friends got into a fight with Walter Paddleford and some other men. Three of the Mexicans were killed in the shootout, but Estabo escaped unhurt. A few months later, after mortally wounding a man during a card game in a Phoenix saloon, Estabo went into

the street and began shooting his pistols. When ordered to stop by Sheriff Dee Harkey and his assistant Cicero Stewart, Estabo replied with gunfire. When Estabo jumped on his horse and tried to escape, Harkey gave chase. Three miles out of town. Estabo was forced to surrender. The frightened gunman was returned to town where he was nearly killed by Stewart. Estabo's life was spared and he was put in jail to await trial.

Evans, Christopher (AKA: Bill Powers), 1847-1917, U.S., outlaw. Born in Vermont, Christopher Evans moved as a child to Canada and served in the Union Army during the Civil War. Following the war, Evans served as a scout for the U.S. Cavalry and reportedly worked as a guide to Major Marcus Reno of the 7th Cavalry. Evans later claimed that he was at the Battle of the Little Big Horn and survived with the remnants of Reno's command. He later moved to California with his brother Tom, and after

California bandit Chris Evans.

years prospecting and working as a miner, bought a quarter section of "railroad land" in Tulare County. Nearby was a mine owned and operated by George and John Sontag. When the Sontags turned to train and bank robbery, Evans joined them.

The Sontags and Evans robbed throughout California, and one report had it that they robbed a train at Kasota Junction, Minn., in 1892. The trio robbed a train in California earlier, according to one account, and Grat Dalton was wrongly convicted of this raid. In January 1892, a posse tracked down Evans and the Sontags in a San Joaquin Valley barn. Following a fierce battle, George Sontag was captured but Evans and John Sontag escaped.

Lawmen continued to pursue Evans and Sontag and finally cornered them on Sept. 13, 1893, at Sampson's Flat, Calif. In an eight-hour battle, two deputies and John Sontag were killed. Evans was wounded many times by detective Frank Burke. He was dragged unconscious to jail. On Dec. 13, 1893, Evans was convicted of murder and robbery, but he escaped jail with the help of Ed Morrel, a fellow prisoner. He and Morrel were recaptured after being wounded near Slick Rock, Calif., and Evans was sent to prison for life, entering Folsom Prison in February 1894.

Released in May 1911 at age sixty-four, Evans moved to Oregon to homestead and died on Feb. 9, 1917. See: **Sontag Brothers**.

Evans, Jesse, b.1853, U.S., outlaw. Jesse Evans arrived in Lampasas County, Texas, when he was a young man. He worked for a short time as a cowboy before drifting into New Mexico in 1872 to work on John Chisum's ranch. A few years later he became an outlaw, primarily engaged in cattle rustling and armed robbery. He rode the range with Billy the Kid, Frank Baker, and Tom Hill. When the Lincoln County War broke out Evans sided with the Murphy-Dolan faction. The first violence in the protracted range war occurred when rancher John Tunstall was murdered on Feb. 18, 1878. As part of a posse formed by Sheriff William Brady, Evans, Hill, and other Murphy-Dolan supporters confronted Tunstall on his ranch. Finding him helpless and on foot, they shot and killed him.

With a price on his head, Evans fled to Southwest Texas where he resumed his cattle rustling activities. On July 3, 1880 near Presidio, Evans shot and killed Texas Ranger George Bingham near Cibola Creek. Ranger Tom Carson shot John Gross through the head, and the remaining members of the gang were forced to surrender. Jesse Evans was sentenced to ten years in prison but managed to escape from a work detail in May 1882 and was never heard from again. See: **Lincoln County War**.

F

Fellows, Dick (George Bret Lytle; Richard Perkins, AKA: **Richard Kirtland**), prom. 1870s-80s, U.S., outlaw. Stagecoach robber Dick Fellows had to ride horseback to carry out his crimes, but the California badman was no equestrian, as he proved in his miserable attempt to rob a Wells Fargo Stage bound for Caliente, Calif. Fellows had been released from San Quentin in 1874 after serving nearly four years for robbery and assault when Governor Newton Booth was duped into believing that he had become a Christian in jail. Fellows hired a horse from a livery man before setting

California bandit Dick Fellows.

out to rob the stage on Dec, 4, 1875. Since holdups were common, the Wells Fargo Company assigned four guards disguised as passengers to ride on the stage to guard three boxes of gold. Fellows had not counted on a balky horse when he set out. Just out of town the animal reared and threw the robber to the ground. Fellows was knocked unconscious. The horse went back to the stable of its own accord, leaving its rider on the ground. When he returned to town a short time later, Fellows decided that he would rob the northbound stage instead.

Fellows stopped the Bakersfield stage at gunpoint and ordered the driver to give him the strongbox. Then, to everyone's surprise, he began whistling "The Arkansas Traveler." "A most creditable performance," wrote the San Francisco *Chronicle* later. The second horse proved more cooperative, but he had forgotten to bring his tools. Once he was safely away from the stagecoach, he was hindered by the darkness and could not find a suitable stone to open the box, so he picked it up and walked back to his horse. The animal suddenly ran away, leaving Fellows. He set off on foot, carrying the heavy box over his shoulder. In the darkness he stumbled down an eighteen-foot embankment, landed in Tunnel Number Five of the Southern Pacific Railroad, and broke his left leg. Fellows dragged himself to the tent of a Chinese laborer where he took an axe. He then opened the box and took out $1,800, made a pair of crutches for himself, and made his way to the Fountain Ranch. There he stole a horse and rode to an abandoned hut where he was eventually arrested by company detectives. The *Chronicle* commented on the affair, reporting, "When it is considered that the stage was robbed by a man with a

broken leg and with a little single-barreled pistol, it becomes ludicrous."

On June 8, 1876, Fellows was sentenced to eight years in prison. By the next morning, Fellows had escaped through a hole tunneled in the floor and made his way to the Kern River where he took a horse. But Fellows was captured, and this time, he was sent straight to San Quentin where he was given a job in the prison library. He was freed in May 1881, and sought legitimate employment with the Santa Cruz *Daily Echo*. He offered his services as a Spanish teacher, but soon reverted to armed robbery. On July 19, he held up the San Luis Obispo-Soledad stage, but his take was only $10. Close to the Russian River, Fellows robbed the Mills-Point Arena coach, but the box contained only a letter in Chinese. Between July 1881 and January 1882, Fellows robbed three stage coaches around San Luis Obispo. With Wells Fargo agents pursuing him, Fellows was captured in a cabin outside Los Gatos. They jailed him in San Jose on Feb. 4, 1882, and some 700 spectators came to gaze upon the wily bandit. Then Fellows was taken to San Francisco and sentenced to life at Folsom State Prison. Fellows had barely arrived when he made his third escape from prison. Several blocks away, Fellows grabbed the reins of a horse and tried to ride away, but the horse threw him to the ground and he was taken into custody again.

Finch, William, c.1852-83, U.S., outlaw. While being returned to Fort Sill from Decatur, Texas, William Finch shot and killed two military guards. Finch was a convicted horse thief who had stolen a horse from an Indian named Quinette. Finch was recaptured in Texas and was extradited to Fort Smith where he was hanged on June 29, 1883.

Fisher, John King (AKA: **King Fisher**), 1854-84, U.S., lawman-gunman. John King Fisher was born in Collin County, Texas. His mother died when he was five and his father, a cattleman who established several ranches throughout Texas, left the boy on his own. At the age of fifteen, Fisher stole a horse and, following his arrest, he escaped, hiding out on one of his father's ranches. At sixteen, he broke into a house in Goliad, Texas, was caught and was sentenced to the state penitentiary for a year, though he served only four months. Upon his release, Fisher became an honest cowboy and learned how to break wild horses, and drive cattle. Old hands taught him how to use a six-gun and he became a crack shot and a quick draw. He later bought a ranch which he called the Pendencia near Eagle Pass, Texas. It was here that he placed a sign at a crossroad which read: "This is King Fisher's road. Take the other one!"

During the 1870s, Fisher took up rustling and he also became a shrewd gambler. He was quick to anger and quicker to draw his gun. He claimed in 1878 that he had killed seven men, mostly in gambling arguments, and he was not including "several Mexicans." He was a colorful dresser who favored

Texas gunman turned peace officer, John King Fisher.

fringed shirts, red sashes, and bells on his spurs. Anyone ridiculing his apparel, inevitably faced his guns. The most persistent legend about Fisher was the story of his killing four Mexican *vaqueros* in a cattle pen on his own ranch. These men arrived at Fisher's place to buy cattle, but it appeared to him as though they were about to steal his herd.

When they refused to leave his ranch, Fisher suddenly brought down a branding iron on the skull of one, crushing it. He outdrew a second Mexican and killed him with a single shot through the head. Then he spun around and shot the other two men as they, too, were drawing their weapons, killing both *vaqueros*. These four deaths were never verified, except in tall tales about King Fisher which abounded throughout Texas during his lifetime and after. He was arrested several times for rustling and murder in 1875 but the charges were later dropped.

In 1876, Fisher married and subsequently sired four daughters. His new domestic life did not temper his outlaw impulses. He went on rustling and was arrested many times for murder, although the charges were invariably dropped for lack of evidence. In most of these instances, Fisher simply threatened witnesses with death if they dared to testify against him. Fisher was not the best of drinking companions. While in a bar in Zavala County, Texas, on Dec. 25, 1876, a cowboy named William Donovan refused to buy Fisher a drink, and the gunman fired three bullets into Donovan, killing him. In 1877, Fisher was arrested by Texas Ranger Lee Hall, who charged him with murder. Fisher however, was expertly defended in court by Major T.T. Teel and was found Not Guilty.

Fisher began to reform in the late 1870s, so much so, that instead of shooting another gunman in an argument he thought better of it and tried to reholster his six-gun. He was drunk at the time and his gun went off accidentally and

Fisher shot himself in the leg. He was tried for another murder but was cleared of this charge. By 1881, Fisher became a champion of law and order and he was sworn in as a deputy sheriff in Uvalde County. For a short time he served as acting sheriff. In 1883, while acting sheriff of Uvalde County, Fisher rode out to the ranch owned by Tom and Jim Hannehan. The brothers were suspected of having robbed a stagecoach. When Fisher confronted them, both brothers went for their guns. The lightning-fast Fisher shot Tom Hannehan dead and wounded his brother who surrendered and turned over the money stolen from the stage.

Early in 1884, Fisher announced that he was a candidate for sheriff in the upcoming election. He went to Austin, Texas, on official business and there met an old friend, the fierce gunfighter Ben Thompson who gave Fisher an autographed photo of himself. After visiting several Austin bars together, Thompson decided to accompany Fisher to San Antonio which was along the route Fisher was taking when returning to Uvalde. Once in San Antonio, both men caroused through the saloons and talked boisterously of their gunslinging pasts. Thompson began to abuse a black porter in one saloon and Fisher warned him to stop this. Both men were theater-goers and they attended a play at the Turner Hall Opera House on the night of Mar. 11, 1884.

When the pair left the Opera House at 10:30 p.m., they decided to attend the Vaudeville Variety Theater, an inappropriate selection in that Thompson had been in this gambling hall two weeks earlier and had killed its proprietor, Jack Harris. Thompson and Fisher had several drinks at the bar there, then went upstairs to the theater to watch the show. They sat in a large box, drinking heavily, and were shortly joined by Joe Foster and Billy Simms, former partners of the deceased Jack Harris. Bouncer Jacob Coy then joined the group in the box. Thompson made sev-

Gunman Ben Thompson, killed with Fisher in a San Antonio theater.

eral critical remarks about Harris and when Foster objected, Thompson jerked his six-gun from its holster, jammed the barrel into Foster's mouth, and playfully cocked the weapon.

Coy leaped forward and grabbed Thompson's weapon. Fisher stood and took several steps backward in the box, saying he was leaving "before trouble started." Thompson then joined him but before the two men could leave the box, Coy, Foster, and Simms pulled their weapons and blasted the two men. They were aided by three armed men lurking in the shadows of the next box, gambler Canada Bill (no relation to famous Canada Bill Jones), Harry Tremaine, a performer at the theater and close friend of the slain Jack Harris, and a bartender named McLaughlin. These men had aimed shotguns and rifles into the box and had stationed themselves as part of the planned ambush of Ben Thompson. Fisher and Thompson were riddled with bullets, Fisher struck thirteen times in the head and chest and killed on the spot. Thompson was struck with nine bullets and also collapsed dead in the box. As he fell, the still deadly Ben Thompson managed to get off several shots. Coy received a minor wound and Foster was struck in the leg, the bullet striking an artery. Foster's leg had to be amputated and he died a few days later from shock and loss of blood. Despite his attempt to reform and work on the side of the law, John King Fisher's past embraced him at the end and brought about his bloody, premature death at the age of thirty. See: **Thompson, Ben**.

Flatt, George W., d.1880, U.S., lawman. In 1879, George Flatt was a lawman in Caldwell, Kan., with the reputation for having killed men before. He also operated an elegant saloon with William Horseman.

On July 7, 1879, in Caldwell, Flatt was involved in a shootout after two men, George Wood and Jake Adams, began firing pistols while drinking at the Occidental Saloon. Constable W.C. Kelly and Deputy John Wilson, accompanied by Flatt and W.H. Kiser, entered the saloon. During the ensuing shootout Flatt killed the two outlaws, while Kiser was grazed in the temple and Wilson was wounded in the wrist.

On Oct. 29, 1879, Flatt, by now the marshal, and his deputy, Red Bill Jones, sought to arrest John Dean for being drunk and disorderly. As Flatt approached Dean, the latter turned and fired. When the shots missed their mark, Dean escaped on horseback. On June 19, 1880, Flatt himself became drunk and raucous and began to have trouble with Frank Hunt. Flatt was persuaded to leave for home, but insisted instead on stopping at Louis Segerman's restaurant. As he approached the restaurant, he was fatally shot at the base of the skull, his spinal cord severed. While his killers were never brought to justice, Frank Hunt and William Horseman were widely suspected.

Flores, Juan, 1835-57, U.S., outlaw. Juan Flores was a cattle rustler and horse thief who became famous after he was sentenced to San Quentin in 1856. He escaped with other prisoners from the seemingly impregnable prison by stealing a provision ship tied to the wharf. A grand plan to sail to Australia dissipated quickly, and the gang landed on the shore south of the prison. Flores, with a newly recruited gang of fifty marauders, terrorized the area, looting small towns, robbing stagecoaches, and pillaging mining camps from a hideout in the hills above San Juan Capistrano. The gang kidnapped travelers and held them for ransom. One of their victims was a German settler who was shot to death in a public square after refusing to pay.

In January 1857, Sheriff James R. Barton organized a posse to apprehend the gang of thugs. However, Flores was formidable, and only three lawmen returned. Sheriff Barton was slain by gang member Andres Fontes. A larger Mexican-American posse led by Don Andres Pico was organized, which disrupted the gang and killed several members. But Flores and Fontes escaped. On Feb. 1, 1857, Flores was apprehended by a third posse led by Doc Gentry. He escaped from a ranch house, but was caught two days later and brought to Los Angeles. On Feb. 14, Flores was sentenced to be hanged, and the sentence was carried out immediately. Fontes escaped to Mexico, where he died in a gunfight shortly thereafter.

Foraker, Creighton M., b.1861, U.S., lawman. Creighton Foraker, a political dark horse in the Republican Party, replaced Edward L. Hall as marshal of New Mexico in 1897. Born into a distinguished Hillsboro, Ohio, family in 1861, Foraker headed west to Colorado where he worked as a mining prospector with his brother Charles. Later, they resettled in Grant County, N.M. He earned respect in October 1887 by slaying a mountain lion that had been killing livestock at various goat ranches in the area. The Silver City *Enterprise* described Foraker as a "model pioneer who fought mountain lions like a dime novel hero."

Creighton M. Foraker, who served as marshal of New Mexico for fifteen years.

Foraker was the first marshal to serve under the newly enacted salary system, enacted by the U.S. Congress in the spring term of 1896. No longer would the marshal be encumbered by the outmoded "fee" system which had existed since the early frontier days. Marshal Foraker upgraded the skill levels of his deputies, and required each of them to speak Spanish and to carry out their duties in a professional manner. They were given fixed incomes and elevated to a position of respectability. Foraker also did away with the ancient practice of hiring local sheriffs to assist in investigations. In the past, political partisanship and conflicting loyalties had interfered with their job performance. During his fifteen years in office, Foraker introduced the automobile to New Mexico law enforcement.

An outbreak of banditry in the territory between 1896-1906 tested the levels of cooperation between the federal and local law enforcement agencies. Two trains were robbed in 1896; three a year later; two in 1899; one each in 1901, 1903, and 1905. The most serious threat to law and

Marshal Creighton Foraker (center) shown with five members of his staff in 1908.

order was William "Black Jack" Christian, the leader of a gang of Oklahoma train robbers who had killed Deputy Frank Robinson near Skeleton Canyon, Ariz. In April 1897 Foraker's men eventually tracked down the vicious deputy killer near Black Jack Canyon, where Christian was shot and killed.

Another "Black Jack" of note, outlaw and train robber Thomas E. Ketchum, was captured, tried, and convicted of train robbery by Foraker's deputies. Ketchum was hanged in 1901; the only man to be executed under the stringent territorial laws enacted against train robbing. Faced with these challenges, Foraker made a good showing. He was re-appointed four times and according to one source, was "possibly personally known to more people in the territory than anyone." Foraker, who did much to restore integrity to the marshal's service in that region of the country, was forced to step down in 1912 due to the changing political climate in Washington. Supporters of President William Howard Taft demanded the appointment of former Las Vegas court clerk, Secundino Romero, to ensure that the New Mexico delegation to the national nominating convention would be firmly on the side of the incumbent president. Thus, ended the career of one of the

frontier's finest lawman. See: **Ketchum, Thomas E.; Christian, Will.**

Ford, John S. (AKA: **Rip**), prom. 1858-60, U.S., lawman. John S. Ford, one of the bravest, most capable men to the wear the star of the Texas Rangers, was named supreme commander of all state forces by Governor Hardin R. Runnels on Jan. 28, 1858. There were Indian uprisings from the Red River to the Rio Grande, and the governor was anxious to quell the threat by appointing a man of stature and forthright character. "I impress upon you the necessity of action and energy," the governor wrote. "Follow any and all trails of hostile or suspected hostile Indians you may discover, and if possible, overtake and chastise them if unfriendly." Ford proved he was up to the task. The Comanche uprising was easily suppressed, and for his troubles Ford was given the task of putting down another revolt, the one engineered by the Mexican guerilla leader Juan Nepomuceno Cortina.

On Sept. 29, 1859, Cortina and his renegade band seized control of Brownsville, Texas, and demanded payment of a $100,000 ransom. When reports came through that Cortina had burned Corpus Christi and was laying waste to Texas, Governor Runnels appointed Ford major in command of all state forces on the Rio Grande. A force of fifty-three well-armed Rangers under the leadership of Ford approached Cortina's camp on Dec. 14. The opposing forces were already under siege from the combined forces of Major S.P. Heintzelman and Captain W.G. Tobin when Ford arrived. Pooling their resources, they drove Cortina out of Brownsville and followed the rebel leader eighteen miles up the river to Rio Grande City, a small town located between a hill and the waterway. Heintzelman and Ford laid a trap for Cortina by sending a de-

Texas Ranger John S. "Rip" Ford, who was appointed to command all state forces on the Rio Grande.

tachment of Rangers on a circuitous route through the hills in order to cut off his escape route. There was a pitched gun battle between Cortina, the Rangers, and the detachment of army regulars. It is doubtful that the soldiers participated in much of the action, due to the fact that sixteen Rangers sustained injury. The Mexicans listed sixty dead.

The Rangers reclaimed Rio Grande City, and by Christmas Day Cortina had crossed the border into Mexico. There was trouble brewing among the Rangers, however. Since Ford had taken on a largely volunteer force, it was customary for the men to elect their own officers, even though Runnels had clearly made his choice for major. Captain W.G. Tobin, a vain and ambitious man, talked himself up among the men and cut a few deals in return for their votes. Ford, naturally enough, was unaware of this and ended up losing the election by a scant six votes. He politely thanked the men for their support, commended them for a good fight, and returned to Brownsville.

Immediately after he had left the camp, disorder broke out. Tobin's men ran amuck in the community, and there were reports from one rancher that the Rangers had stolen some livestock and had set fire to his pens. These reports crossed the desks of commissioners Robert H. Taylor and Angel Navarro before Ford even reached Brownsville.

Ford was presented with a directive authorizing him to take command of a newly re-organized regiment as its captain. Major Tobin was summarily mustered out of the service. With a full complement of men, Ford undertook a trip to La Bolsa Bend, thirty-five miles from Brownsville. It was there that Cortina had indicated he would take a stand. On Feb. 4, 1860, Ford engaged the enemy in a brief skirmish that claimed the life of a Texas Ranger named Woodruff. The Mexicans fired on the Rangers' steamboat the *Ranchero*, sending a bullet through the flag on the masthead. At this critical point, Ford made the decision to cross over the border into Mexico to go after his elusive quarry.

Using the steamer as a landing vehicle, a force of thirty-five men and another ten belonging to the discredited Major Tobin moved upstream until they approached the stockade where Cortina was holed up. Ford later recalled the fierce gun battle that followed: "They rushed upon the Mexicans, six-shooters in hand, drove them, rolled them up on the center, and routed them. The fleeing Mexicans were pursued by Texans." Cortina commanded an army of 200 to 400 heavily armed men, including cavalry. Yet they proved hopelessly ineffective before the small band of on-rushing Texas Rangers.

With his troops scattered and put to flight, Cortina turned on the Rangers with his guns blazing. The Texas Rangers returned the fire, but the bullets harmlessly struck his saddle and belt, and even clipped a lock of his hair. With the darkness fast approaching, Cortina was able to make his escape on horseback. Ford continued to patrol the border and made a number of independent raids into Mexico, but Cortina had long since retreated to the safety of the Burgos Mountains. To avoid an international incident, the U.S. Secretary of War sent an emissary to Texas to confer with Ford on Apr. 7 about the necessity of ceasing his forays into the interior of Mexico. The emissary was the new commander of the Department of Texas—Colonel Robert E. Lee. See: **Cortina, Juan**.

Ford, Robert, 1861-92, U.S. outlaw. Robert Ford's name became synonymous with the word traitor at the very moment he squeezed the trigger of the six-gun that shot and killed America's most celebrated western bandit, Jesse James. Bob Ford and his older brother Charles were farm boys who lived in Ray County, Mo. By 1879, they had been recruited into the notorious gang headed by James, and were reportedly involved in several train and bank robberies

Robert Ford, posing with the gun he used to kill Jesse James, 1882.

led by James. Ford was a hanger-on and did odd jobs for the gang, as well as accompany James and the others on raids, invariably as the one who held the horses. He enjoyed consorting with outlaws and often made his home and that of other Ford family members available to gang members who were being sought by lawmen.

In January 1882, Wood Hite and Dick Liddell, members of the James gang on the run from the law, took refuge in the home of Martha Bolton, Bob Ford's widowed sister. At breakfast, Hite and Liddell fell to arguing while Ford sat quietly sipping his coffee. Suddenly the outlaws swore at each other and drew their guns. Hite fired four rapid shots at Liddell, one of his bullets striking Liddell's right thigh. As he was falling to the floor, Liddell shot a bullet into Hite's arm. As the two men blasted at each other, Bob Ford drew his own gun and, being Liddell's close friend, fired a single bullet at Hite, striking him in the head. Hite collapsed to the floor and died a few minutes later. Ford wrapped Hite's body in a blanket and carried it outside, slipping it over the back of a mule. He then led the animal into the woods and, about a mile from his sister's house, buried Hite's corpse in a shallow, unmarked grave.

Charles Ford, terrified that Frank James was hunting him for the killing of his brother Jesse, committed suicide in 1884.

Word of this shooting caused authorities to arrest Ford, but he was not prosecuted when he informed detectives that he had access to the much-wanted Jesse James. Missouri governor Thomas T. Crittenden met secretly with Ford and told him that if he killed the notorious outlaw, he would receive a full pardon for the Hite murder as well as the killing of James, and also receive a large reward. Ford agreed to perform the deed. Bob Ford then went to his brother Charlie and told him to have Jesse swear him in as a full-fledged member of the gang. James, though he had told several people that he did not trust the Ford brothers, especially Bob, accepted the Fords as gang members. The brothers visited the James home in St. Joseph, Mo., on the morning of Apr. 3, 1882.

Bob and Charlie went to the barn to tend the horses and then entered the house. Jesse had just sent his two children outside to play. Mrs. Zeralda James was in the kitchen, and James entered the parlor where the Ford boys were sitting. Jesse outlined his plans for another robbery. He complained of the heat and took off his coat. Then he removed his two

Outlaw Jesse James, shot by "the dirty little coward" in 1882.

guns and wrapped the holsters about the arm of a chair. He noticed a picture hanging crooked on the wall and stood on a chair to adjust it. As he did so, Charlie nodded at Bob, and the brothers pulled their six-guns. Jesse heard the

Ford's tent saloon, second structure from left, in Creede, Colo., where Ford was killed in 1892.

hammers cock on their pistols and started to turn. As he did, Bob Ford fired a bullet into the back of his head. Jesse James toppled to the floor, dead.

Mrs. James ran into the room and Bob Ford, backing toward the front door with his brother Charlie, told her: "The gun went off accidentally."

Kneeling to cradle the bloody head of her husband, Zee James, sobbing, replied: "Yes, I guess it did."

Bob and Charlie Ford then ran from the James home, Bob shouting down the street: "I killed him! I shot Jesse James!" A few minutes later the brothers arrived at the telegraph office and sent a wire to Governor Crittenden claiming the reward. The wire read: "I have killed Jesse James. St. Joseph. Bob Ford."

Ford was charged with murdering Wood Hite *and* Jesse James, but Governor Crittenden pardoned him while he stood trial for the murder. Ford and his brother were given large rewards and returned to the home of their parents in Richmond, Mo. Residents, however, found the traitorous killing of Jesse James so distasteful that they made life unbearable for the Fords. Charlie Ford fled Richmond when he heard that Jesse's brother, Frank James, was searching for the brothers to kill them in revenge for Jesse's death. So terrified was Charlie Ford that he kept running from town to town for two years, changing his name several times. He finally committed suicide in 1884.

Capitalizing on his betrayal of Jesse James, Bob Ford took to the stage, appearing in an act entitled *Outlaws of Missouri*. Night after night, Ford stood before the footlights chanting out that last fateful morning of Jesse James. He carefully avoided describing how he shot down America's legendary bandit *in the back*. Still, he was greeted with catcalls, jeers, hoots, and challenges shouted from the audience: "Traitor! Step outside and get what's coming to you! Frank James is looking for you, Judas!" Even his fellow troupers found Ford repulsive, all except a young chorus girl, Nellie Waterson, who fell in love with the good-looking young killer. They were married and left Missouri.

Ford took a job with P.T. Barnum's freak show and traveled through the East to again tell disgusted audiences how he shot down the man who trusted him. To the Easterner, indoctrinated with the legend of Jesse James through dime novels, countless pamphlets, stories, and newspaper columns which incorrectly portrayed James as a heroic figure, Bob Ford was a loathsome creature who had committed a foul murder. He had killed a man he feared so much that he had shot him in the back rather than risk facing him in a fair gunfight. He was again greeted by angry audiences who chanted the words of a song then popular: "The dirty little coward who shot Mr. Howard (the alias James was using when killed), and laid poor Jesse in his grave!" Ford's response to the negative audience reaction was to drink heavily and squander his considerable earnings in gambling.

Dick Liddell, Ford's old outlaw friend, later joined Ford in establishing a saloon in Las Vegas, N.M., but the operation failed, chiefly because of lack of customers. Those who did enter the place kept picking fights with Ford and Liddell, calling them traitors and murderers. The Las Vegas saloon soon closed and Ford moved on to Creede, Colo., where a silver boom had begun. N.C. Creede, an old prospector, had discovered two rich silver veins, and armies of prospectors moved into the area when hearing the news, the boom town mushrooming overnight and being named Creede. When Ford arrived, there were few buildings, and he simply put up a large tent saloon and quickly prospered, charging hefty prices for his beer and whiskey. He dressed as a dandy in brocaded vests, long tailcoats, and a diamond stickpin. He made so much money he soon bought his wife Nellie a diamond brooch and other expensive jewels.

In 1892, Ford took a business trip to Pueblo, N.M., and there had to share a room with another man in a crowded hotel. The other guest was Ed O. Kelly, a man with a shady past. Ford and Kelly nodded and then had a drink together before bedding down for the night. When Ford awoke, he discovered a diamond ring missing and he angrily accused Kelly of stealing it. The two men parted with angry words, with Kelly still denying he took the ring. Kelly later heard that Ford was telling everyone in Creede that he had stolen his diamond ring. After brooding about this, Kelly went to Creede on June 8, 1892, and stormed into Ford's tent saloon. He demanded that Ford retract his statements about the diamond ring theft, but Ford refused, and, with the help of a bartender, threw Kelly out of his saloon.

Kelly obtained a shotgun and returned to the saloon, almost running toward the bar where Ford stood talking to some customers. As Ford turned to face Kelly, the shotgun roared, both barrels of buckshot tearing into Ford. One pellet drove Ford's collar button through his throat, killing him. Kelly was arrested and tried for murder. He was convicted and given a twenty-year sentence in the Colorado Penitentiary. Nellie Ford returned her husband's body to Richmond, Mo., where it was buried in the Ford family plot. See: **James, Jesse Woodson; Kelly, Edward O.**

Fountain, Albert Jennings, 1838-96, U.S., gunman. Born in 1838 in New York City, Albert Jennings Fountain traveled the world before ending up in California in the 1850s. In 1859 he began the first of many careers as a reporter for the Sacramento *Union* covering Latin America. He fought in the Civil War as a soldier in the First California Infantry Volunteers, later moving to New Mexico, where he married 14-year-old Mariana Perez, with whom he eventually had twelve children. Fountain organized a militia to fight Indians and was wounded in 1865. The family moved to El Paso where he first became a deputy collector of customs, then county surveyor, and attorney. Fountain also fought in the Mexican War as colonel to Benito Juarez. In 1868, Fountain was elected to the Texas Senate, and was named Senate President. Later he was made a brigadier general of the Texas State Police.

On Dec. 7, 1870, Fountain and Judge Gaylord Judd Clarke were accosted in El Paso by a lawyer, B.F. Williams. Fountain, unarmed, was hit three times by Williams but was able to stagger home. Returning with a shotgun, Fountain wounded Williams, who was fatally shot by police captain A.H. French. Although he had not provoked the assault, Fountain's public career faltered. Five years later he moved his family back to New Mexico, where he served as an assistant U.S. attorney and a state representative. He returned to his Indian wars, using his Mexican friends as allies. In March 1883, Fountain and his son Albert were returning by train from El Paso with three fugitives. One of the three, Doroteo Saenz attempted to escape as the train slowed in Canutillo, Texas. The alert Fountain followed the fugitive, and killed him before he could escape.

Fountain began a bitter struggle with Albert B. Fall in the late 1880s. The feud escalated until Jan. 31, 1896, when Fountain and his 9-year-old son Henry were killed in White Sands, N.M., while returning home to Mesilla. Fountain, by that time a territorial judge, had been involved in a grand jury investigation involving alleged cattle rustling. Three men, James Gililland, Oliver Lee, and William McNew were charged with the murders, but were later acquitted. Many prominent individuals including Albert Fall were suspected, but nobody was ever convicted of the brutal double murder. Jim "Deacon" Miller, a hired gunman, was credited with the Fountain murders. See: **Miller, James B.**

Fowler, Joel, 1849-84, U.S., outlaw. Indiana-born Joel Fowler arrived in Fort Worth, Texas, about 1875. He was a tall, striking man, who always carried himself well in social situations. Fowler's calm demeanor and command of the English language greatly contrasted his true criminal nature. After allegedly murdering a Texan during a domestic quarrel, Fowler fled to Las Vegas, N.M., during the time that village was besieged by the Dodge City Gang. During the few short months he lived in Las Vegas, Joel Fowler ran a saloon dance hall and then later bought into a ranch at Carrizozo. Reportedly, Fowler got into an altercation with another man and shot his adversary to death. He was forced to return to Texas, where he opened a ranch near San Antonio. For a time the business prospered and the future seemed promising, but Fowler was an unrestrained man with little in the way of self-discipline. He began drinking heavily and murdered Jim Cale in the Grand Central Hotel of Socorro, N.M., on Oct. 10, 1883. Fowler was arrested, tried, and sentenced to hang. While languishing in the Socorro jail, a vigilante mob broke in and pulled him out of the cell and lynched him on Jan. 21, 1884.

Frazer, George A. (AKA: **Bud**), 1864-96, U.S., lawman. Texas sheriff Bud Frazer had more trouble with his deputy, Jim Miller, than with criminals. Born in 1864, the son of a judge, Frazer became a Texas Ranger in 1880. In 1890, he was elected Reeves County sheriff. He fired Deputy Miller for stealing a pair of mules from a Mexican prisoner whom Miller had shot to death, allegedly for resisting arrest. Miller was charged, and though subsequently released, he fostered ill will which would surround the two men for the following six years. Miller opposed Frazer for the office of sheriff in 1892 and was defeated, but managed to be

Western lawman Bud Frazer.

appointed city marshall of Pecos.

On Apr. 12, 1894, Frazer shot Miller in the right arm in front of a Pecos hotel. Miller returned the fire, but succeeded only in wounding an innocent bystander. Frazer then shot Miller repeatedly in the chest and left him for dead. Miller, however, survived. In November 1894, Frazer lost his bid for reelection and left Texas to operate a stable in New Mexico. Returning to Pecos on Dec. 26, 1894 to complete his move, Frazer encountered Miller for the second time, and shot him in the arm and leg. This time, Frazer was arrested for attempted murder and jailed. He was acquitted in May 1896. He completed the move to New Mexico, but, on Sept. 14, 1896, returned to Toyah, Texas, to visit his mother and sister, where he once again encountered Miller. This time, Miller shot first, killing Frazer with a shotgun blast to the face. See: **Miller, James B.**

French, Jim, prom. 1878, U.S., gunman. Jim French, a New Mexico cowboy, was one of the primary participants in the Lincoln County War of 1878. On Mar. 9, 1878, French was a member of a posse of regulators who apprehended accused murderers Frank Baker and Billy Morton. The prisoners escaped briefly, but were soon killed by the posse. Less than a month later, on Apr. 1, French turned to the other side of the law and joined four outlaws including Billy the Kid in killing Sheriff William Brady and Deputy George Hindman. French was wounded by John Long as the ambushers fled.

In mid-July 1878, French was involved in the final shoot-out of the regional war, defending the store of Alexander McSween. On July 19, the store was set afire and almost totally burned. French was able to escape, and after surveying the fate of his comrades, decided to retire from the turbulence of New Mexico, and live a more obscure existence.

Fulsom, Edward, d.1882, U.S., outlaw. Edward Fulsom was a hardened criminal and horse thief, who fled to the Indian territory to escape justice in February 1881. Fulsom got into trouble again in a tough saloon near the Arkansas-Indian Territory line. In a barroom brawl Fulsom beat William Massingill to death with his pistol butt. Fulsom was arrested, convicted, and hanged at Fort Smith on June 30, 1882. Being slight of build, the drop did not snap Fulsom's neck and the outlaw's pulse continued for sixty-three minutes until the doctors pronounced him dead.

G

Gabriel, Peter, prom. 1880s, U.S., lawman. A long-time lawman in Arizona, Gabriel had chased bandits through Pima County, Ariz., from 1883 when he was the sheriff of the county. He fired one of his deputies, Joe Phy, for disorderly and drunken conduct and later arrested him in Casa Grande for assault. The two men feuded throughout an election for sheriff in 1888 which Gabriel won. On May 3, 1888, in Florence, Ariz., Phy called Gabriel to the street from a saloon where both men had been drinking. The two men went for their six-shooters and, in a wild gun battle in which eleven shots were exchanged, Gabriel shot Phy several times. Gabriel was wounded in the groin and in the chest near the heart. The Sheriff walked away from the fallen Phy and staggered into the O.K. Stable where he collapsed. Phy died four hours later but Gabriel survived to stand trial and be exonerated for the shooting on grounds of self-defense.

Gallagher, Jack (AKA: **Three-Fingered Jack**), d.1864, U.S., outlaw. Gallagher was a member of the feared Henry Plummer gang of Montana, a gunslinger who killed an estimated six men before he was hanged in Virginia City, Mont., on Jan. 13, 1864 (some accounts state Jan. 14). Plummer had already been killed by vigilantes and Gallagher and other Plummer gang members had sworn vengeance. This notorious band of train and stagecoach bandits, the vigilantes knew, would show no mercy. The vigilantes decided to act first. They rounded up Jack Gallagher, George "Clubfoot" Lane, Frank Parish, Boone Helm, and Hayes Lyons. "Three-Fingered Jack" was the fiercest of the lot. He had been Plummer's top aide and was quick on the draw. The vigilantes found him asleep in the gambling room of the Arbor Restaurant.

While Gallagher yelled oaths at the vigilantes, he was dragged outside and to the place of execution, in front of an unfinished log building at Van Buren and Wallace streets. He wore a fancy cavalryman's coat trimmed with beaver and he continued to swear at his executioners as he was lined up with the other members of the Plummer gang. All five were placed upon boxes, and ropes tied to a crossbeam were then placed about their necks.

Boone Helm thought it all a great, grim joke. He made several remarks about Gallagher's resplendent cavalry coat and then shouted to Gallagher: "Jack, give me that coat! You never gave me anything!"

Gallagher snorted: "Damned sight of use you'd have for it." He then spied someone he knew standing in the window of the Virginia Hotel across the street and shouted:

"Hey, old fellow, I'm going to Heaven! I'll be there in time to open the gate for you!"

Somehow, Gallagher managed to free one hand from the ropes binding both arms behind his back and produced a small knife which he used in a vain attempt to slit his own throat. A vigilante wrestled the knife from Gallagher's hand. His arms were again tied. He asked for a drink of whiskey before he was hanged. This was brought and poured down his throat so that he was coughing when asked to make his last statement. Choking, Gallagher said: "I hope forked lightning will strike every one of you bastards dead!" Then, defiantly, he leaped off the box on which he had been placed, hanging himself and depriving the vigilantes of performing the execution. Following Gallagher to eternity were Helm, Lane, Parrish, and Lyons.

Boone Helm, the joker among the condemned outlaws, clowned and bluffed his courage out to the last. He looked up to see Gallagher in his death throes and shouted: "Kick away, old fellow, I'll be in hell with you in a minute!" Then he said to the vigilantes about to kick the box from beneath his feet: "Every man for his principles. Hurrah for Jeff Davis (Jefferson Davis, the President of the southern Confederacy)! Let her rip!" A vigilante knocked the box out from beneath him and Helm dangled in death from the rope.

Several thousand spectators witnessed this mass vigilante execution and one of them approached the chief hangman, John X. Beidler, a leading vigilante.

"When you put that rope around Gallagher's neck," asked the spectator of Beidler, "didn't you feel for him?"

"Yes," Beidler dryly replied, "I felt for his left ear."

Garcia, Manuel (AKA: **Three-Fingered Jack**), d.1853, U.S., outlaw. One of the most fierce bandits in California history, Manuel "Three-Fingered Jack" Garcia is almost as legendary in the annals of western outlaws as is his bandit chieftain, Joaquin Murieta. For years before he began following Murieta, Garcia had been robbing stagecoaches and travelers along the wild California roads, and lawmen had been searching for him. When he joined Murieta, this brigand proved to be the most bloodthirsty of Murieta's terror band.

On one occasion, after Murieta's band had roared into a mountain mining area and rounded up all the Chinese miners, Garcia reportedly hanged dozens of these hapless laborers by their queues and then, wielding a razor-sharp hunting knife, casually marched along the line of dangling victims and slit each throat with a single slash. He was later quoted as boasting of this mass slaughter, reveling to his chieftain: "Ah, Murieta, this has been a great day! How my knife lapped up their blood!" This, of course, was part and parcel of the kind of lurid dime novel narratives employed when describing the awful deeds of the mythical Murieta in the 1850s.

Murieta's band had so terrorized the residents of northern California that the governor appointed a former Texan, Harry Love, to head a special force of twenty California rangers whose specific purpose it was, no matter the cost or time it took, to hunt down Murieta and his men and bring them to justice. Captain Love and his men, who were as fierce and lethal as their prey, doggedly tracked down a band of Mexican outlaws identified as the Murieta gang, coming upon these men west of Tulare Lake near Panoche Pass on July 23, 1853.

The Mexicans were squatting about a fire and eating dinner when Love's rangers appeared, surrounding them and approaching cautiously, guns at the ready. The rangers began to ask harsh and pointed questions which the Mexicans naturally resented and said so. A handsome young Mexican stood up and walked a few paces toward the rangers, announcing that he was the leader of the band, and if the rangers wanted to ask questions they must direct them to him. The young man's actions seemed to be a signal to the other Mexicans who suddenly reached for their six-guns.

A wild gunfight erupted which saw the Mexican leader fall mortally wounded. A fierce-looking Mexican who tried to come to his rescue was shot several times and he dashed for the band's horses tethered nearby, but a withering cross fire from the rangers cut him off. He stumbled off into the thick woods, running along a trail, the rangers in pursuit. The Mexican, two guns in his hand, fired his weapons as he ran until his six-guns were empty. He then whirled, threw a hunting knife at the ranger closest to him, and fell dead of his wounds. This man was identified as Manuel "Three-Fingered Jack" Garcia. The youthful leader of the band was identified as the celebrated Joaquin Murieta.

Determined that their feats be recognized and rewards given, the rangers cut off Murieta's head and placed this in a jar of alcohol so it could be preserved and returned to Mariposa as proof of the rangers' triumph. Garcia's head was too badly shot up to preserve, but his right hand, which had been mutilated years earlier in an accident, a well-known fact, was cut off and preserved so that identification was certain. The corpses of the dead Mexican bandits were left to rot in the thick forest. Several other Mexicans had escaped in the wild melee, but two of the band were captured alive and put on horses, their hands tied behind their backs. The rangers headed for Mariposa.

Both Mexicans refused to admit that the dead leader of

their band had been the famed Murieta. They remained silent and spoke only briefly to each other in Spanish, saying they held no hope of surviving the mobs waiting for them in Mariposa. When the rangers crossed a deep river, one of the Mexicans leaped from his horse and dove into the waters and quickly drowned. The other was delivered to the jail in Mariposa, but before he could be brought to trial a mob broke into the small frame building, dragged him out, and lynched him. The head of Murieta and the hand of the savage Garcia were put on display and drew great crowds of curious settlers who had heard of Murieta and Garcia only through wild rumor and tales that approached fable, both of these bandits being part of California folklore long before their reported demise. See: **Murieta, Joaquin.**

Garrett, Patrick Floyd (Pat), 1850-1908, U.S., lawman. Raised in Louisiana, Patrick Garrett was one of six children. His parents died shortly after the Civil War and at eighteen, in 1869, Garrett went west to seek his for-

New Mexico lawmen, standing (left to right): W.S. Mabry, Frank James, C.B. Vivian, Ike P. Ryland; sitting (left to right): Jim East, Jim McMasters, and Pat Garrett, 1884.

tune. He worked as a cattle driver in the Texas Panhandle and later became a buffalo hunter. While working in Texas, Garrett killed his first man. Near Fort Griffin, Texas, in November 1876, Garrett got into an argument with Joseph Briscoe, a burly Irish skinner. Garrett made a derogatory remark about Briscoe washing his clothes in a stream and both men got into a wild fistfight. Briscoe was a short, squat man and Garrett was six-foot-four-inches tall. He easily bested the mule skinner but Briscoe grabbed an ax and raced toward Garrett who, in turn, lifted his rifle and fired into Briscoe's chest. The mule skinner died a few minutes later with Garrett standing over him, tears running down his ruddy cheeks.

The plains-hardened Garrett, who had become an expert with a gun, arrived in Sumner, N.M., driving cattle. Here he got a job tending bar and later opened a small cafe. He married in 1879, but his teenage bride died of illness and Garrett married again. While tending bar and running his restaurant, Garrett also spent a considerable amount of time gambling, and at the tables he met most of the young cowboys who later became gunslingers involved in the infamous and bloody Lincoln County War. One of these was Billy the Kid. The two became so close that they were known as Big Casino and Little Casino, nicknamed after their sizes and because they were constantly playing casino poker.

When the Lincoln County war erupted between warring cattle barons, Billy the Kid and his friends shot and killed several gunmen who had murdered John Tunstall, the Kid's former employer and mentor. In 1880, Garrett was elected county sheriff with specific instructions to halt the bloody war and, most importantly, bring Billy the Kid, his former friend, to justice. So Garrett and his deputies set out after the Kid's gang and, in early December 1880, Garrett and others encountered Tom O'Folliard on the trail in Lincoln County, N.M. O'Folliard was riding to join the Kid at the time, and once he spotted the posse, he fired his Winchester several times in a running gunfight with the pursuing lawmen before outdistancing them.

Garrett, in December 1880, had just delivered some prisoners to Puerto de Luna, N.M., when he encountered a boisterous Mariano Leiva in a store. Leiva saw Garrett, by then a noted lawmen, and began stomping about the store, snarling: "No gringo can arrest *me!*" He then went to the street and shouted for all to hear, particularly the patient, tight-lipped Garrett: "By God, even that damned Pat Garrett can't take me!"

Garrett stepped onto the porch of the store, faced his antagonist, and pushed him into the street. Leiva went for his gun, firing a single bullet that went wild. Garrett drew his six-gun and snapped off two shots, one missing Leiva, the other ploughing into Leiva's left shoulder, smashing the blade. The would-be gunman was thrown over a saddle and led to jail. He was later fined $80 for attempting to murder Garrett.

In an effort to capture Billy the Kid and his gang, Garrett and a number of lawmen moved into the post hospital at Fort Sumner. One of the Kid's riders, Charlie Bowdre, had a wife who lived at the post, and Garrett was expecting that Bowdre and the others would soon ride into Fort Sumner to visit the woman. He was correct. On the evening of Dec. 19, 1880, Billy the Kid, accompanied by Charlie

Bowdre, Tom O'Folliard, Billy Wilson, Tom Pickett, and Dave Rudabaugh, rode into the post. Garrett, Lon Chambers, and others stepped onto the porch of the hospital and

Billy the Kid, shot by Pat Garrett in 1881.

saw O'Folliard and Picket riding ahead of the Kid and the rest of the riders.

"Halt!" shouted Garrett and at that moment O'Folliard drew his six-gun and began blazing away at the lawmen. Garrett and Chambers fired back simultaneously and a bullet stuck O'Folliard in the chest. He and Picket, along with the Kid and the others behind him, turned their horses about and galloped away. Pickett was wounded and Ruda-baugh's horse later died from a wound. But the gang escaped, riding pell-mell from the post, except for O'Fol-liard, who suddenly wheeled his horse about and trotted back to face the lawmen. O'Folliard shouted: "Don't shoot, Garrett! I'm killed!"

Barney Mason, one of the deputies, aimed his six-gun at the wounded O'Folliard, saying: "Take your medicine, boy."

Garrett stopped him from shooting and ordered O'Fol-liard: "Throw up your hands! Surrender!"

"I can't raise my arms," O'Folliard said weakly as he rode slowly forward. He then fell from his horse into the arms of the lawmen, who took him to the hospital where he was put on a couch and doctors told him he had a fatal wound.

Lawman Pat Garrett, on white horse, bringing in Billy the Kid.

A bizarre scene then ensued with Garrett and his deputies sitting at a nearby table, playing poker, while talking to the dying O'Folliard, asking him to name the members of the gang.

"Tom," Garrett told him, "your time is short." He then asked for the names of the gang members.

Replied O'Folliard: "The sooner the better. I will be out of pain." He then moaned out the names of his fellow outlaws: The Kid, Wilson, Rudabaugh, Pickett, and Bowdre. O'Folliard also gave Garrett the locations of the Kid's hideouts. About half an hour later he died. O'Folliard would later be buried in a common grave with Bowdre and Billy the Kid.

Four days later, on Dec. 23, 1880, with the knowledge of the identities of the gang and their hideout, Garrett led a large posse to a rock house at Stinking Springs, N.M. The lawmen surrounded the crumbling rock house and Garrett gave orders that when the Kid stepped from this structure in the morning, he was to be shot immediately. By this time, Garrett knew that Billy the Kid was lethal and that asking him to surrender was a futile gesture. The next morning Charlie Bowdre, who was about the same size as the Kid, stepped from the rock house. From a distance, he

appeared to be the Kid and Garrett raised his rifle, a signal which caused the posse to open a withering fire. Bowdre was hit twice in the chest and sent reeling back through the door of the rock house. Someone inside the house slam-med the door shut and gunfire erupted from its windows.

Then Billy Wilson could be heard to call out to Garrett that Bowdre was dying and that he wanted to step outside. Garrett shouted back that Bowdre should step from the rock house with his hands up. Suddenly, Bowdre was shoved outside by the vicious Billy the Kid, who screamed to his friend: "Kill some of the sons-of-bitches before you die, Charlie!" Bowdre, clutching his chest and bleeding heavily, could only stagger forward blindly. He fell into Garrett's arms. The lawman put the dying outlaw on his own bedroll where Bowdre murmured: "I wish—I wish—I wish..." He then died.

The Kid and his men then tried to pull some of their horses tied up outside to the doorway into the house, but Garrett shot and killed one horse and the outlaws aban-doned this attempt. Gunfire was exchanged periodically between the outlaws and the posse until Garrett shouted: "How are you doing, Kid?"

The Kid replied: "Pretty well, but we have no wood to get breakfast."

Shouted Garrett to his former friend: "Come out and get some. Be a little sociable."

There was no reply. Garrett stared at Bowdre's corpse and told other lawmen that he felt bad about the youth's death. Then he told his men to make several fires and begin cooking bacon and other food. This was done and the thick odor of the food being made wafted to the rock house. A white handkerchief on a stick was then waved from a window and Rudabaugh stepped outside to ask for food. Garrett, after some discussion, told Rudabaugh that if he and the others surrendered, they would be well fed and go unharmed. The Kid and the others slowly stepped from the rock house and surrendered. The Kid was taken to Lincoln and locked up, but he later shot his way to freedom, killing two of Garrett's best deputies while Garrett was away on official business. Garrett now set out to get the Kid, accompanied by Tip McKinney and Frank Poe. They rode into Fort Sumner on July 14, 1881, following a tip that the Kid was hiding with friends at the post.

Several accounts had it that when entering the crowded old fort, Garrett and the Kid actually passed each other, but neither recognized the other. That night, Garrett approached Pete Maxwell, a friend of the Kid's, asking if the Kid was in the vicinity. He entered Maxwell's house and went into the bedroom, sitting on the bed and question-ing Maxwell. The room was unlighted and the door opened. The Kid stood there, framed in the light from the hallway. He had just left his sweetheart and had come to

Maxwell to ask for the key to the meat locker so he could prepare a steak.

The Kid was in his stocking feet and wore no hat. He had a butcher knife in his hand in preparation of cutting the steak. A six-gun was jammed into his waistband. Maxwell, cowering on the bed, whispered to Garrett in the darkness: "That's him."

Billy stood squinting into the dark room, unable to see its occupants but knowing someone was there after hearing Maxwell speak to Garrett in hushed tones. Said the Kid: "Quien esta? Quien esta?" ("Who's there? Who's there?") He pulled out his six-gun and stepped into the room. Garrett fired a single shot which slammed into the Kid's chest. Then Garrett dove to the floor, expecting the Kid's six-gun to spit. The lawmen fired another shot as he leaped, but the bullet went wild. Maxwell ran from the room and Garrett followed him. The Kid lay on the floor, silent forever. His body was removed a short time later and he was buried the next day in the common grave holding Charlie Bowdre and Tom O'Folliard.

The killing of Billy the Kid brought Garrett fame and criticism. He was lauded for ridding Lincoln County of its most ferocious murderer, a youth who claimed to have killed twenty-one men. But the manner in which Garrett shot his quarry caused him severe criticism, especially from the supporters of Billy the Kid and those who never knew the vicious killer and had romanticized his bloody actions. In truth, he was a cheap, illiterate, back-stabbing slayer who shot from ambush and killed seemingly without cause. To those who idolized his legend, the Kid was the victim of a traitorous friend. Garrett claimed the reward for the Kid and even had to hire a lawyer to obtain this cash. The Republican Party refused to renominate him for sheriff and Garrett went into ranching, establishing operations near Fort Stanton in 1884.

Later, working for a special branch of the Texas Rangers, Garrett chased outlaws along the Texas-New Mexico border. He later supervised operations for other ranchers, established another ranch near Roswell that failed, and then tried to launch an irrigation scheme in the Pecos Valley that did not work. In 1890 Garrett ran for the office of sheriff in Chaves County, but was rejected by voters, a defeat that left him embittered. He moved to Uvalde, Texas, and set up a horse ranch. There he befriended a political power-house named John Nance "Cactus Jack" Garner, later vice president in the Franklin D. Roosevelt administrations (1933-41). Garrett was elected a county commissioner in 1894, with Garner's help.

In 1896, Garrett was called back to the six-gun when Judge Albert J. Fountain and his young son disappeared and were presumed to be mysteriously murdered in White Sands, N.M. Garrett became sheriff of Dona Ana County with the specific assignment of tracking down the killer of the Fountains. These murders reportedly stemmed from a dispute over a huge cattle empire and were apparently carried out by Jim "Deacon" Miller. Although Garrett suspected Miller, an independent gunman for hire and killer of dozens of persons, he could prove nothing. The Fountain case remained unsolved.

While still sheriff of Dona Ana County, Garrett and four other deputies rode out to a ranch near Wildy Well on July 13, 1898, to arrest Oliver Lee and James Gilliland, who stood accused of murder. The Lee ranch, which was about thirty miles south of Alamogordo, was well-guarded and, as the lawmen approached, a ranch hand gave the alarm. The posse members, advancing on the house, were blasted by heavy gunfire from Lee and Gilliland after Garrett had ordered the pair to surrender. Garrett received a slight wound in the side and his deputy, Kent Kearney, was mortally wounded. So intense was the gunfire from the well-barricaded Lee and Gilliland that the lawmen were forced to retreat in disgrace. Both men later surrendered, but Lee and Gilliand were acquitted after a widely publicized trial.

This disgrace, coupled with his failure to find the killer of the Fountains, caused Garrett to lose his job as sheriff of Dona Ana County. He later opened a livery stable in Las Cruces, N.M., then moved to El Paso, Texas, where he was made a customs inspector through special appointment of President Theodore Roosevelt, again with the help of John Nance Garner. He refused another appointment in 1905 and began ranching again near Las Cruces. Pressed for cash, Garrett began leasing some of his best acreage. Some of this land was leased by Wayne Brazil (or Brazel) for cattle. When Brazil put herds of goats onto the land, Garrett said that he had violated their agreement and threatened to shoot Brazil unless he removed the goats. This led to a bitter feud.

Pat Garrett, in 1898, shown during his term as sheriff of Dona Ana County.

On Feb. 29, 1908, Garrett met with Jim "Deacon" Miller and Carl Adamson, who claimed that they themselves would lease the land Brazil had been leasing. This was an apparent ruse. Miller, the suspected killer of the Fountains twelve years earlier, had apparently been brought in to murder the stubborn Garrett. Garrett, Adamson, and Brazil then rode together to inspect the land in question. Miller rode a circuitous route and lay in ambush about four miles outside of Las Cruces. When Garrett stopped his buggy to relieve himself, a bullet suddenly smashed through the back of his head and exited above the right eye. He spun around and another bullet tore into his stomach. The lawmen fell to the earth, dead. Brazil later reported that he and Garrett had quarreled and both had drawn their six-guns and Brazil had killed the lawman. Miller, however, was the real killer. Neither Brazil nor Miller were ever tried for the murder. See: **Billy the Kid; Fountain, Albert Jennings; Lincoln County War; Miller, James B.**

Gathings, James, and **Nicholson, Sol,** prom. 1870, U.S., mur. Martial law was declared in Hill County, Texas, following the outbreak of racial violence that erupted when two white men, James Gathings and Sol Nicholson, were arrested for the murder of two blacks in December 1870. A detachment of Texas Rangers, led by Lieutenant W.T. Pritchett, appeared at the Gathings home and demanded that the accused men surrender. The Rangers did not have a proper warrant. "You cannot search my house with your damned Negro police!" the indignant Colonel J.J. Gathings snapped. Pritchett pushed passed the man and proceeded to ransack the entire house. They could not locate Nicholson or James Gathings on the premises. While this was going on, an angry group of twelve to fifteen men who called themselves law officers gathered in front of the house and arrested Pritchett and his men. A judge later fixed Pritchett's bail at $500. "By God, if the bond is not made strong and substantial, I will rearrest him and hold him until the day of the trial!" threatened Colonel Gathings with clenched fist. Pritchett, who was released, forfeited his bond on the grounds that he was only being held so that the murderers could make their escape.

Adjutant General James Davidson, a Yankee carpet-bagger of the worst kind, arrived in Hill County where he immediately declared martial law and ordered the arrest of Colonel Gathings and seven other men. Brought before the military men, Gathings was told that he could avoid a court martial by paying $100 a day for every day that martial law was in force. It was extortion pure and simple, and it had little to do with justice for the murdered men. Gathings explained that he lacked the financial resources to pay the demand, whereby Davidson said that $3,000 in currency would satisfy the debt. He warned Gathings that unless the money was promptly paid, he would be tried and sent to prison before an appeal could be filed. Gathings was given

fifteen minutes to make up his mind. Finally, he agreed, raising $2,765, which Davidson accepted. The martial law decree was rescinded and Davidson quietly returned to Austin. An editor for the Waco newspaper editorialized: "Here we behold the melancholy and humiliating spectacle of an officer engaged in plundering a citizen of his property by aid of a military power...It is a robbery which is not sustained nor covered by Radical legislation."

Gillett, James Buchanan, 1856-1937, U.S., lawman. In 1875, after two years as a cowboy, 19-year-old James Gillett enlisted in the Texas Rangers. He spent the next six and a half years fighting Indians and hunting fugitives and was involved in two gunfights. In January 1877, Gillett and five colleagues sought to apprehend Dick Dublin, who had worked with Gillett in his pre-Ranger days. They found Dublin at a ranch in Menard County, Texas, but the fugitive

Lawman James B. Gillett.

disappeared into a ravine when he saw the lawmen approaching. Gillett followed, and fatally shot Dublin when the fugitive refused to surrender. A year later, in February 1878, Gillett, in a party led by Lieutenant N.O. Reynolds, was escorting five prisoners to Austin for trial. Again, while in Menard County, the lawman spotted fugitive Starke Reynolds. Reynolds tried to flee, but Gillett apprehended him after a mile and a half chase. On Dec. 26, 1881, Gillett retired from the Rangers to become a railroad guard, and later became the city marshall in El Paso, Texas. In 1885, he retired to a 30,000-acre cattle ranch near Marfa, Texas, where he lived until his death in 1937. See: **Gilliland, Fine.**

Gilliland, Fine, d.1891, U.S., gunman. Fine Gilliland worked as a cowboy for the Dubois and Wentworth ranch near Hovey in Brewster County. He was also known to be deadly with a six-shooter and was involved in many gunfights. Gilliland was sent to the Leoncita water holes to round up strays when he encountered another cowboy, Henry Harrison Powe, who had lost an arm while serving in the Confederate army during the Civil War.

The two men, who both worked for the same ranch, had

been feuding for some time and fell to arguing about how a steer should be branded. Gilliland, who was armed, told Powe to "get some iron." Powe borrowed a six-shooter from Manning Clements who was standing nearby and then both Gilliland and Powe faced each other and drew. Gilliland was faster and shot Powe through the head. He then turned about and branded the steer in question.

Gilliland was marked as a murderer, despite his protests that he shot Powe in self-defense. Before he could be arrested, Gilliland mounted a fast horse and headed for the Glass Mountains. Texas Ranger Captain Jim Gillett headed a posse, including noted lawmen Thalis Cook and Jim Putnam, which overtook Gilliland. When the lawmen ordered him to surrender, Gilliland charged. The outlaw shot Putnam in the knee, but the posse's bullets cut him to pieces. His body was returned to Brewster County for burial. His fellow cowboys were so incensed that they retrieved the steer over which Gilliland and Powe had argued and branded it with large letters to read: "Murder" and the date of Gilliland's death. This steer wandered throughout the county for some years as a western curiosity.

Gladden, George, prom. 1870s, U.S., gunman. A friend of gunmen Johnny Ringo and Scott Cooley, Gladden recruited both these men and others for a Texas feud that was known as the Hoodoo War, which occurred in Mason County, Texas, in 1875. In September, Gladden and one of the Beard Brothers were involved in a fierce gunfight with dozens of gunmen from Mason County. Beard was killed and Gladden was wounded nine times. Dan Hoerster, who had a wild fistfight with Gladden earlier and represented the Mason County cattlemen, was found murdered and the killing was attributed to Gladden and Ringo. Both outlaws were captured on Nov. 7, 1876, after Ringo and Gladden had killed another range enemy, Pete Bader. They were jailed, but Ringo escaped and rode to Arizona where he would later confront the Earp Brothers as a member of the Clanton-McLowery outlaw band. Gladden, however, was sentenced to ninety-nine years. He was pardoned some time later and vanished.

Goldsby, Crawford (AKA: **Cherokee Bill**), 1876-96, U.S., outlaw. Born at Fort Concho, Texas, on Feb. 8, 1876, Crawford Goldsby was of mixed blood, being part white, Hispanic, and black, and was rejected by all races. The boy was not only a social pariah but was homeless at age seven when his parents separated. An old black woman, Amanda Foster, undertook to raise Goldsby at

Fort Gibson, but she could do little with the wild boy. At age twelve, Goldsby was quite large, often confronting grown men. One such man was a brother-in-law who told him to feed some hogs. The boy grabbed a gun and fatally shot the man. He was not prosecuted because of his age.

As a teenager, the tall, heavyset Goldsby took to petty thievery. He got into fights regularly and, when he could not settle an argument with his fists, he went for his six-

Oklahoma bandit-killer Crawford "Cherokee Bill" Goldsby.

gun, having become an expert shot by the age of fifteen. Goldsby attended a dance at Fort Gibson in 1894 and here he fell to arguing with a burly black man, Jake Lewis, over a woman. The two began a slugfest where Goldsby got the worst of it. Knocked down, the youth drew his six-shooter and fired a shot that wounded Lewis. Goldsby fled. Lawmen pursued him on a charge of assault with intent to kill.

At age eighteen, Goldsby fell in with the worst outlaws of the Indian nation in the Oklahoma Territory, William and James Cook. Goldsby, who was dubbed "Cherokee Bill" by Bill Cook, was with the Cook brothers when a posse cornered the three men near Tahlequah, Okla., in June

1894. Lawmen had a warrant for the arrest of Jim Cook on a charge of larceny, but when they moved forward to arrest Cook, all three youths went for their guns. The outlaws drove back the posse and then mounted their horses, riding wildly away from their camp near Fourteen Mile Creek. Goldsby, seeing one of the lawmen gaining on him, turned in the saddle and fired a single shot killing Deputy Sequoyah Houston, who fell dead from his horse.

Goldsby rode to the home of his sister, Maud Brown, and remained here, hiding from the law. Her husband, George Brown, a vicious drunkard, took a whip to Maud one day for not responding fast enough to his orders. While he was beating the woman, Goldsby walked up behind him and shot him to death. He then rejoined the

Artist rendering of the execution of Cherokee Bill on the Fort Smith gallows.

Cook brothers and others and this infamous band began robbing trains, banks, and stores throughout Oklahoma. In the summer of 1894, Goldsby appeared alone at the train depot in Nowata. He held up the station agent, Richard Richards, who went for a gun. Goldsby shot him to death, then leisurely stepped to the station platform and waited for the next train. When it pulled in, Goldsby banged on the door of the express car with the butt of his six-gun, ordering those inside to "open up and give me the money." The door flew open and conductor Sam Collins ordered Goldsby to depart. Goldsby shot Collins in the face, killing him. When a brakeman came running down the platform, Goldsby shot and wounded the man. He then mounted his horse and galloped off.

In 1894, Goldsby and others entered the Shufeldt & Son general store at Lenapah, Okla., and held up the owners. Ernest Melton, a curious resident, stuck his head in the door and the lightning-fast Goldsby pumped a single bullet into his head, killing him. For this killing, committed before a number of witnesses, Judge Isaac Parker of Fort Smith, Ark., announced a reward of $1,300 for Goldsby, dead or alive. This was the murder for which Goldsby would pay with his life. Capturing the wily Goldsby, however, was another thing. Deputy Marshal W.C. Smith then learned

that Goldsby was infatuated with a Cherokee girl, Maggie Glass, a cousin of Isaac "Ike" Rogers, who had been a deputy for Smith on several occasions when posses were needed. Smith arranged to lure Goldsby to Rogers' remote farmhouse to meet his cousin Maggie.

Goldsby appeared on the night of Jan. 29, 1895, and when he fell asleep, Rogers and a neighbor, Clinton Scales, jumped the powerful Goldsby, pinning him to the couch on which he slept, and then bound him and dragged him to a buggy. The outlaw was delivered to Fort Smith to await trial for murder. On Feb. 26, 1895, Goldsby was tried for the murder of Melton by jury before Judge Parker. He was found Guilty. His mother and sister wept in court at the news, but Goldsby, confident that he would never see the hangman, turned to them and snapped: "What's the matter with you two? I ain't dead yet."

Judge Parker sentenced the smirking killer to death on Apr. 13, 1895, but Goldsby seemed unconcerned about his fate. He returned to a holding cell in the jail where he promptly sat down to play cards with Bill Cook, by then a prisoner, and others. Goldsby joked about the sentence, bragging that no one would ever put a noose around his neck. His date of execution had been set for June 25, 1895, but his lawyer, J. Warren Reed, managed to file several appeals pushing the death date further and further back.

Sherman Vann, a Negro trusty at the jail, smuggled a six-gun to Goldsby for an undisclosed price and the outlaw hid this in a hole in the wall of his cell. He knocked out a brick, broke it so that only its front half remained, and put the gun behind this. On July 26, 1895, while his lawyer was still delaying his execution through a barrage of appeals, Goldsby pointed his six-gun at armed guard Lawrence Keating, a father of four, and shouted through the bars of his cell: "Throw up your hands and give me that pistol damned quick!"

Keating reached for his gun, but not to hand it to the outlaw. He began to level it at Goldsby, when the outlaw fired a bullet into his stomach. Keating wheeled about and staggered down the corridor as Goldsby sent another bullet into his back. The guard fell dead in the main office. Goldsby was tried for this murder, convicted, and sentenced to death. Again his lawyers filed numerous appeals and the death sentence, originally fixed for Dec. 2, 1895, was put off. The U.S. Supreme Court upheld the verdict in the Keating murder, and the Goldsby's execution date was set for Mar. 17, 1896. No avenue of escape was left for Goldsby except a direct appeal to the president. This was rejected.

On Mar. 17, St. Patrick's Day, Goldsby, still arrogant, was led from his cell. He tried to convince his mother, sister, and Amanda Foster, the old Negro woman who had raised him, that he was unconcerned about his gruesome fate. Goldsby sang ditties and whistled as he walked outside to the courtyard of the Fort Smith jail. Goldsby took one look at the scaffold and said: "This is about as good a day to die as any." The murderous outlaw stood on the gallows with a rope around his neck when he was asked if he had any final words. Defiant to the last, Goldsby snarled: "No! I came here to die, not make a speech." A minute later his large body shot through the trap. His mother took the body to Fort Gibson and buried it. See: **Cook, William Tuttle.**

Good, John, prom. 1877-88, U.S., gunman. John Good, a large, intimidating cattle rancher in the Texas hill country, became involved in a gunfight in Blanco City on June 10, 1877. A man named Robinson accused him of being a horse thief, but Robinson's revolver got tangled in his clothing as he attempted to shoot Good. The rancher killed Robinson with four shots. Good had also been present when Ed Crawford killed Cad Pierce in Newton, Texas, and after the shootout with Robinson, Good sold his ranch and opened a hotel in Coleman, Texas. He quickly wore out his welcome and continued to move, first in 1880, to a ranch in Colorado City, and later to another ranch near La Luz, N.M. He began a relationship with Bronco Sue Yonker, a tryst which led to his second gunfight. Yonker had killed a man in 1884.

In 1885, Good's wife and children arrived in La Luz and Yonker began a relationship with a man named Charley Dawson. On Dec. 8, 1885, Good killed Dawson after a quarrel over the affections of Yonker. This time he remained in the area, building a large adobe ranch house, and accumulating a great deal of money. But his temper resurfaced in 1888 when he had a bitter argument with George McDonald. After McDonald was killed, his friends retaliated by killing Good's son, Walter. The body of Walter Good was found in the White Sands Desert. Good set out with a five-man posse to avenge his son's death and found McDonald's friends near Las Cruces. After a fierce battle, Good and his party were forced to retreat, after which he sold his ranch and moved to Arizona. He was last known to be working in Oklahoma for hourly wages.

Goodwin, Francis H., prom. 1870s, U.S., lawman. Described by former marshal Milton Duffield as the "most confirmed rebel in Arizona," Francis Goodwin of Georgia faced stiff opposition when he was named to succeed George Tyng as marshal in February 1875. Goodwin settled in Arizona after the Civil War. He was serving as the clerk of Pima County when Tyng became the marshal in 1870,

and was named to fill Tyng's unexpired sheriff term in Yuma County by Governor Anson Peacely-Killen Safford.

Goodwin served as Arizona marshal from February 1875 until July 1876. His term of office was uneventful except for the increased lawlessness that pervaded the territory. Goodwin was negligent in answering his correspondence, and on at least one occasion he was remiss in providing for the subsistence of federal prisoners. Goodwin moved against the law breakers only when necessity dictated. He did little to track down the killers who massacred the John Baker family in Gila Valley in 1871, on the grounds that it did not involve federal statutes. When residents of that same area complained about the presence of a band of armed Mexican revolutionaries, Goodwin replied that he lacked the proper authority to deal with "unorganized"

Arizona marshal Francis H. Goodwin, whose term was highlighted by his departure from office.

bands. The U.S. cavalry finally intervened, and the revolutionaries were put to flight.

Goodwin stepped down in July 1876, to everyone's considerable relief. During his tenure of office, the onus of responsibility for enforcing all laws fell on Governor Safford, who presented a series of recommendations to the assembly to protect his territory. He asked that highway robbery be elevated to the status of a capital crime. He also requested a twenty-man patrol to safeguard the lives of the people living near the Gila Road, and for the authority to pay rewards for information leading to the apprehension of known criminals. The legislature only agreed to the latter request.

Gordon, Lon, d.1894, U.S., outlaw. Lon Gordon was a member of the ferocious Bill Cook gang, which looted and terrorized its way through the Indian territory in Oklahoma during the early 1890s. After the Cook gang struck the Chandler Bank in Oklahoma, the Creek Light Horse Police Force, made up of Indians from the Cherokee Strip, tracked the Cook gang across the territory and finally cornered Gordon and Henry Munson near Supulpa. The outlaws chose to shoot it out with the Indian police and both were killed in the battle on Aug. 2, 1894.

Gosling, Harold L., 1853-85, U.S., lawman. Harold Gosling was appointed a U.S. marshal for the Western District of Texas in 1884. Prior to this time, the Shelbyville, Tenn., native attended the Annapolis Naval Academy, studied law in Washington, and had owned a newspaper in Medina County, Texas, where he also set up a legal practice. At the time of Gosling's appointment to the marshal's service, there was a rash of stagecoach robberies in the San Antonio-Comfort road area, between Fredericksburg and Comfort and near Boerne. In early 1885, two highwaymen and postal robbers, James Pitts and Charles Yeager, who had terrorized Lampasas and Burnet counties, were tried and convicted in federal court. Marshal Gosling was assigned to convey the two from Austin to San Antonio, pending their incarceration.

Gosling permitted his prisoners to be accompanied by two female relatives, who were no doubt responsible for the tragic events that unfolded. At the Wetmore train station, the two men suddenly produced guns from the food baskets brought on board the train by the women. Marshal Gosling was shot down before he had a chance to react. A second law enforcement officer shot and wounded the female accomplice and killed one of the fleeing suspects. The second prisoner was apprehended a month later and returned to prison.

Graham, Dayton, prom. 1901, U.S., lawman. In 1901, Dayton Graham, a law officer from Bisbee, Ariz., became a sergeant in the Arizona Rangers. Within a few months, he was involved in a shoot-out with fugitive outlaw Bill Smith in the town of Douglas. Graham, accompanied by Tom Vaughn, a Douglas sheriff, was answering a complaint by a local merchant. Smith shot Graham in the chest and arm and wounded Vaughn in the neck. Graham appeared to be mortally wounded and his family gathered at his bedside, but he miraculously recovered and vowed to avenge his shooting. He began searching southern Arizona, and one day in 1902 found Smith at a card table in a saloon. This time Graham fired first, and Smith died from two shots to the stomach and one to the head. See: **Arizona Rangers.**

Graham, William, See: **Brocius, Curly Bill.**

Graham Brothers, prom. 1870s, U.S., outlaws. The Graham brothers, Albert (also known as Charles Graves and Ace Carr), Charles, and Dollay, joined the Jesse Evans outlaw band which robbed its way through Texas and New Mexico. All of them were born and raised in Llano County, Texas, and they became rustlers at an early age, later joining Evans in robbing stores in Davis. Rangers cornered the gang and Dollay Graham was shot and killed. Albert and Charles Graham escaped to pillage west Texas.

Graham-Tewksbury Feud, 1887-88, U.S., feud. The Graham-Tewksbury Feud was waged over range rights and the cattlemen's claims that sheep ruined the grazing lands for cattle-raising. It took place in the Pleasant Valley, Ariz., area near Globe, and began in 1887 when the Tewksbury clan started raising sheep on their ranch and the adjoining range. Cattleman John Graham and his men attacked the Tewksbury family and, in return, John D. Tewksbury and his three sons, Edwin, James and John, Jr., led raids against the Grahams. Several other families joined both factions. The Blevins family, led by Andy Blevins, were fierce allies of the Grahams and fought many gun battles with the Tewksburys, resulting in several deaths. Although the feud supposedly ended in 1888, hatred flared up between the quarelling parties for the next few years. The feud officially ended on Aug. 2, 1892, when John Graham, head of the Graham family, was shot and killed by Ed Tewksbury and ally John Rhodes. See: **Blevin Family; Tewksbury, Edwin; Tewksbury, Jim.**

Grannon, Riley (or **Grannan**), 1868-1908, U.S., gambler. Riley Grannon, a western entrepreneur, foresaw the future of Nevada. In 1907, he purchased land in Rawhide intending to create a great gambling center. He specialized in handicapping horse races, and had won as much as $275,000 in a single afternoon. Grannon sought to modernize gambling casinos, replacing dusty saloons filled with card cheats and vigilante violence with an atmosphere reflecting the tastes of a more sophisticated populace. He was correct, but his timing was forty years premature. In April 1908, Grannon died penniless, having squandered a fortune in pursuit of his dream. In death he was heralded as a great public benefactor for his many charitable deeds on behalf of many down-and-out gamblers and prostitutes.

Griego, Francisco (AKA: **Pancho**), d.1875, U.S., gunman. Pancho Griego, a Colfax County, N.M., businessman and cowboy, was known for his mercurial temperament. On May 30, 1875, he encountered soldiers from the Sixth U.S. Cavalry at a hotel saloon in Cimarron, N.M. During an argument at a card table, Griego shot two soldiers to death, and killed another with a knife. Later that year, a gang led by Clay Allison lynched Cruz Vega, Griego's business associate. On Nov. 1, Griego found Allison in the same Cimarron hotel. The two men had a drink and as Griego was leaving, Allison shot him to death. See: **Allison, Robert A.**

Gristy, Bill (AKA: **Bill White**), prom. 1856, U.S., outlaw. Bill Gristy, a California bandit and arsonist, joined Thomas Hodges in launching a crime wave in 1856. The pair had escaped from prison together after Gristy had been sentenced for murder. Forming a gang under Hodges' alias, Tom Bell, they robbed a wagon driver in early 1856. After a brief gunfight, Gristy made off with $300. On Aug. 11, near Marysville, Calif., the gang tried to rob a stagecoach, but were repelled by the driver, a messenger, a security man, and several passengers. A gang member and a passenger were killed, and several passengers were wounded. A posse was organized to apprehend the bandits. The following month, detectives Anderson and Harrison from Sacramento found Gristy and four others hiding near the Mountaineer House. The robbers tried to shoot their way to freedom. One of them named Walker was fatally wounded by Detective Harrison, while another bandit, Pete Ansara, was shot in the leg. Two others surrendered peacefully, but Gristy escaped. Detective Anderson apprehended him after a brief chase on horseback. Gristy was returned to prison, but was promised leniency for informing on Hodges. See: **Bell, Tom.**

H

Hall, Jesse Lee (AKA: **Red**), 1849-1911, U.S., lawman. In 1871 Jesse Lee Hall retired from his job as a schoolteacher and became the city marshal of Sherman, Texas, rising within two years to deputy sheriff in nearby Denison. Hall was wounded during a gun battle in 1873, after agreeing to take part in a duel with an outlaw he was attempting to arrest. Two passersby fatally wounded the fugitive, saving Hall's life. In 1876, Hall left the local force to become a lieutenant with the Texas Rangers. He was immediately assigned to quell the notorious Sutton-Taylor Feud, and earned a reputation for fearlessness after he walked unarmed into a room filled with the feuding outlaws and arrested seven of them for murder.

Lawman Jesse Lee Hall.

Hall was promoted to captain, and within two years had arrested more than 400 criminals. As captain of the Rangers, he patrolled the Mexican border and was present when the infamous Sam Bass was cornered and shot to death at Round Rock, Texas. In 1880, Hall married, retired from the Rangers, and became a cattle rancher. He befriended a young man named William Porter while Porter was recovering from a childhood illness. Later, Porter chronicled many of his ranch experiences under the pen name of O. Henry.

In 1885, Hall became an Indian agent in Anadarko, Indian Territory. Two years later, he was suspected of accepting bribes and was fired, a charge he was exonerated of in 1889. Afterward, he held several law enforcement positions, including deputy sheriff of San Antonio. During the Spanish-American War, he organized several regiments of men to fight in the tropics because they were immune to yellow fever. In 1899, he joined the army and served in the Philippines. He returned to the U.S. and guarded gold mines in Mexico, and speculated in oil before he died in San Antonio on Mar. 17, 1911.

Hampton, Silas, 1868-87, U.S., outlaw. On Dec. 9, 1886, Silas Hampton, an 18-year-old Cherokee, robbed and murdered farmer Abner N. Lloyd, near the town of Tishomingo (Okla.) With the $7.50 he rifled from the dead man's pocket, Hampton purchased a bright red handker-

chief and several baubles which he proudly displayed to the townspeople. His carelessness led to his arrest. As Hampton was led away he pleaded with the marshals, "Don't take me to Fort Smith; kill me right now!" The marshals were not amused. Hampton was taken to the fort where he was tried before Judge Isaac Parker, found Guilty, and hanged on Oct. 7, 1887.

Hanks, Orlando Camillo (AKA: **Charley Jones; Deaf Charley**), 1863-1902, U.S., outlaw. O.C. Hanks was one of the most notorious train robbers in the West during the late nineteenth century, often aligning himself with Butch Cassidy's Hole-in-the-Wall Gang. Despite his loss of hearing, Hanks was particularly adroit at covering an entire railroad car full of passengers, as associates stole their possessions. He was imprisoned at the Deer Lodge Penitentiary in 1892, receiving a ten-year sentence for robbing a Northern Pacific train at Big Timber, Mont. He rejoined Cassidy after his release on Apr. 30, 1901, accumulating a great deal of money from the successful robberies. He drifted to Texas to spend some of the funds, but attracted the attention of local lawman Pink Taylor, who shot him to death on Oct. 22, 1902. See: **Cassidy, Butch; Hole-in-the-Wall; Wild Bunch, The.**

Happy Jack, See: **Morco, John.**

Hardin, John Wesley (AKA: **J.H. Swain**), 1853-95, U.S., outlaw-gunman. The most feared gunman in Texas, killer of at least twenty-one men, was John Wesley Hardin. He was a quick-draw artist, perhaps the fastest gun alive until he was shot in the back and died ignominiously, without a friend to mourn his passing. Before that shoddy fate embraced Hardin, he wrote his autobiography, a thrilling dime-novel affair which made up in imagination what it lacked in honesty. He claimed to have killed forty men—certainly the record for any gunman in the history of the Wild West.

Born in Bonham, Texas, on May 26, 1853, Hardin had the benefit of upstanding, hard-working parents. His background was anything but criminal, rooted in religion, nurtured by a God-fearing father who made a living as a hard-working Methodist circuit preacher. Hardin's forefathers had illustrious positions in the history of Texas. One had fought at San Jacinto and another had signed the Texas Declaration of Independence in the fight against Santa Ana. Hardin's grandfather served with distinction in the Congress of the Texas Republic. Hardin County, Texas, was named after another of Hardin's relatives, Judge William B. Hardin. Somehow, Hardin's father believed that his son would follow in his footsteps and named him after the esteemed Methodist leader, John Wesley. None of this affected the conduct of John Wesley Hardin.

Outlaw John Wesley Hardin.

The Hardin family resettled in southeastern Texas when Hardin was an infant. He grew up in these wilds, learning early the use of firearms as a hunter and was a marksman by the age of ten. He practiced by shooting at effigies of Abraham Lincoln, the most hated man in the South during the Civil War. He also demonstrated a killer instinct at an early age. When only eleven, Hardin got into a vicious knife fight with another boy. He stabbed the boy in the back and chest but the youth survived.

At age fifteen, in November 1868, Hardin visited his uncle who had a plantation near Moscow, Tex. He got into a wrestling match with one of his uncle's ex-slaves, a burly man named Mage and bested him. Mage told Hardin that he would kill him and when the boy was riding home, Mage stepped into the road with a large stick. When he stepped toward Hardin, the youth pulled an old Colt from his waistband and fired three shots into Mage's chest. The former slave died of his wounds two days later. Hardin fled, and went into hiding at a friend's farm in Sumpter, Texas.

He later wrote in his memoirs that he was being persecuted by Union soldiers who still occupied the territory for defending himself against a black man who "came at me with a big stick." He had run from the law of the Union military "not from justice but from the injustice and misrule of the people who had subjugated the South." Hardin heard that three Union soldiers were approaching the ranch where he was hiding and rode out to meet them, carrying a shotgun and a six-gun. He lay in wait in a creek bed and when the soldiers rode by jumped up and emptied the shotgun into two of them at close range, blowing them off their horses. The remaining soldier wheeled his horse about and began firing at the youth but Hardin drew his .44 and fired several shots, killing the third soldier. Ex-

Confederate soldiers then arrived and buried the bodies of the three dead Union men while Hardin fled.

Hardin later claimed that when he was on the run in early 1869, he and his cousin, Simp Dixon, shot and killed two more Union soldiers who were chasing them. On Dec. 25, 1869, Hardin was playing cards in Towash, Texas. He won many hands and a town tough, Jim Bradley, a big loser, suddenly jerked forth a knife and threatened: "You win another hand and I cut out your liver, kid." Hardin was unarmed at the time and politely excused himself. He went to his room and strapped on two six-guns.

By then he had developed what was perhaps the fastest draw in the West, an unusual cross-draw. Hardin had sewn two holsters into a vest so that the butts of his two six-guns pointed inward across his chest. Hardin's draw was one sweeping movement where he crossed his arms, yanked forth the two six-guns and moved them in a lightning fast arch. This required one motion, a movement he practiced for hours a day, figuring that it was much faster than the traditional draw, where one reached to the side, drew a six-gun out of a hip holster and then leveled it to fire, a three-motion movement.

That night, Hardin stepped into the main street of Towash wearing his two guns. Down the street stood Jim Bradley, who also wore a gun and had been looking for Hardin. The tall youth with black hair and dark smoldering eyes resolutely walked toward Bradley who cursed him and then fired a shot in Hardin's direction, the bullet missing its mark. Hardin's hands flashed across his chest and his two six-guns were suddenly in his hands, both exploding at the same moment. The two bullets found their marks, one striking Bradley in the head, the second smashing into the gunman's chest. He crumpled to the street dead. This gunfight was witnessed by a dozen or more people who quickly spread the word that John Wesley Hardin was the fastest gun in the West, a reputation the boy upheld at every opportunity.

In January 1870, Hardin and a friend rode into Horn Hill, Texas, to see a local circus that had come to town. Several roustabouts from the circus got drunk that night and one of these big-shouldered men, half-drunk, spotted Hardin wearing his two guns. When he ridiculed Hardin, the youth told him to shut up. The circus man then slammed his huge fist into Hardin's face. Both men went for their guns but Hardin shot the man dead before he ever drew his six-gun. A few days later, Hardin arrived in Kosse, Texas, where he went into a cheap bar and met a saloon girl. While escorting her home, a man jumped Hardin from a dark alleyway, struggling to take his money. Hardin leaped backward and threw his money to the ground. The thief stooped to reach for the money and Hardin fired a single bullet into his head, killing him. He ran for his horse and raced out of town, a procedure that would become monotonous for the gunfighter.

Lawmen finally caught up with Hardin, arresting him for a killing he insisted he did not commit. Hardin and several other prisoners were being moved to Waco, Texas, to stand trial. Only two guards rode with the prisoners who were shackled at the hands. On the second night of the trip, the group camped near Marshall, Texas. One of the guards rode off to a nearby ranch to obtain food for the horses. While he was gone, Hardin, using a six-gun smuggled to him in the Marshall Jail, shot and killed the other guard and fled on horseback. He later forced a blacksmith to cut away the shackles. Hardin claimed that three Union troopers then chased him across the Texas prairies for days, until his horse gave out and he ran on foot. The troopers tried to ride him down but, according to his own account, he turned and shot all three dead from their horses before they could get off a single shot.

Hardin next went to work as a cowboy for William C. Cohron, a trail boss, and while herding cattle in February 1871, in the company of his cousin, Emmanuel "Mannen" Clements, Hardin stopped at a Mexican camp in Gonzales County, Texas. Here he and Clements played cards with three Mexican *vaqueros* but a quarrel broke out and Hardin shot and wounded two of the Mexicans before riding off. Two months later, while rounding up strays in the Indian Territory, Hardin found an Indian trying to steal a cow and he shot and killed him with a single bullet. Then he and others hurriedly buried the Indian, fearing that if the body was found, his tribesmen would hunt down Hardin and the others. Cattle rustlers were a problem and one of the worst of these was Juan Bideno. He gave up rustling briefly to join Cohron's trail herd as a cowboy but he was suspected of working in league with a band of rustlers who were waiting to steal Cohron's herd. Cohron accused Bideno of avoiding work and the Mexican threatened him. When the herd crossed the Cottonwood River in Kansas on July 5, 1871, Cohron accused Bideno of shirking his duties. Bideno went for his gun, shot Cohron dead, and then fled. Hardin, who was a close friend of Cohron's, heard the news when he was in Abilene, Kan., and, the next day, July 6, he organized a small posse to hunt down Bideno. Before leaving town that day, Hardin ran afoul of Charles Cougar, a tough gunman who threatened to kill him. Hardin pulled his gun and killed Cougar with a single shot, the bullet striking the gunslinger in the middle of the forehead from a distance of forty feet.

The next day, Hardin, with Hugh Anderson and Jim Rodgers at his side, rode into tiny Bluff City, Kan. They carried a warrant for the arrest of Juan Bideno, one issued to them by lawman John Cohron, who was a brother of the slain Billy Cohron. Hardin had learned that Bideno was in Bluff City and he located the rustler in a small cafe where he was eating dinner. While his friends surrounded the cafe, Hardin boldly entered the cafe and saw Bideno sitting at a table, a plateful of food before him. Hardin told Bideno that he carried a warrant for his arrest on the charge of murdering Cohron. He then ordered the Mexican to surrender.

Bideno smiled, dropped his knife and fork, and then leaned slowly back in his chair so that his holsters were clear. As he began to drop his hands to his holsters, Hardin whipped out his two six-guns in what was now a famous cross-draw and fired two bullets into Bideno's head, killing him. Another version of this shooting had Hardin challenging Bideno to a duel. Both men then reportedly mounted their horses and charged each other from opposite ends of the street, Bideno firing wildly as he rode madly toward Hardin. Hardin fired only one bullet, which took off the top of the Mexican's head.

In September 1871, two black Union soldiers, Green Parramore and John Lackey, were hunting Hardin for a previous killing. They stopped in Smiley, Texas, hearing that Hardin was in the vicinity. As they were eating crackers and cheese in the general store, a tall, dark-haired youth wearing two guns on his vest walked inside.

"I hear you two are looking for John Wesley Hardin. Do you know what he looks like?" the youth asked the soldiers.

"No, sure don't," said Parramore. "We have never seen him but we are looking for him and when we find him we'll arrest him."

"Well," said John Wesley Hardin, "you see him now!" With that, his hands a blur as they flashed across his chest, Hardin drew both guns and emptied them into both soldiers. Parramore fell, dead, but Lackey, wounded badly in the chest and mouth, ran from the store and survived.

It was in the year 1871, according to Hardin, that he backed down one of the great lawmen of the West, James Butler "Wild Bill" Hickok. According to Hardin's memoirs, he rode into Abilene, got drunk one night, and then stepped into the street. To liven up the town, Hardin began firing his gun into the air as he moved, wobbly-legged and half tipsy, down the street. He suddenly heard footsteps behind him and turned to see the six-foot-two-inch, long-haired Wild Bill glaring at him. Hickok, town marshal, told him in a low voice: "You can't hurrah (frighten or bully) me, I won't have it!"

"I haven't come to hurrah you," Hardin said, "but I'm going to stay in Abilene."

"I'll have your guns first," Hickok told him.

Hardin then offered his two six-guns to the famous marshal but as Hickok reached for them, his own hands extended far from his holsters, Hardin performed the famous "border roll" or "gun-spin." As Hardin later told it:

"While he was reaching for them, I reversed them and whirled them over on him with the muzzles in his face, springing back at the same time. I told him to put his pistols up and he did."

Hickok historians take issue with Hardin's claim to this day, refusing to believe that the wily Wild Bill would ever fall for the "border roll," but it is a fact that Hardin did stay in Abilene and did not have another encounter with Hickok, a man Hardin openly admired. Hardin frequented the Bull's Head Saloon and Gambling House which was owned and run by Ben Thompson, one of the most feared gunmen in the West who hated Hickok for cowing him on several occasions.

Even Thompson was timid about confronting his nemesis, Wild Bill. He approached Hardin one night and told him that he would pay the gunman a considerable sum if he shot Hickok dead. Hardin was offended by this killer-for-hire offer, he later claimed, and told Thompson: "If Bill needs killing, why don't you do it yourself?" Thompson was disinclined to do so and dropped the matter. Hardin left Abilene abruptly a short time later after gunning down a saloon thug who announced that he hated all Texans and tried to crush his head with a pipe. Knowing Hickok would be looking for him, Hardin leaped on his horse and rode from the town.

In June 1872, Hardin arrived in Hemphill, Texas, with a herd of cattle for sale. A local policeman named Spites interrupted Hardin when he was quarreling about the sale of the cattle and warned him not to start any trouble. The officer had no idea who Hardin was but quickly learned that he was dealing with a lethal cowboy when, in a few seconds, a derringer appeared in Hardin's hand. Hardin fired a shot which wounded the lawman in the shoulder. At the same time someone shouted: "Watch out, that's Wes Hardin you got there!" Spites, clutching his shoulder and with a terrified look on his face, turned on his heel and ran down the street. Hardin hurriedly grabbed some cash for the sale of his cattle and then rode quickly out of town.

The gunman rode to Trinity City, Texas, in July 1872 to visit relatives. He and a cousin then got into a bowling contest which Hardin purposely lost. Phil Sublett, a local gunman who had been watching the match, then suggested he play Hardin for $5 a set. Hardin quickly beat Sublett six straight games and the gunmen realized that he had been suckered into the match. He began screaming that he had been swindled but Hardin drew his gun and forced Sublett to continue playing until he was out of money.

Then, while still holding the six-gun on his defeated foe, Hardin marched Sublett to a nearby saloon and bought him several drinks. Sublett then angrily left the bar, but returned a few minutes later with a shotgun, shooting both barrels in Hardin's direction. One load of buckshot caught

the gunfighter in the side. Wounded, Hardin still managed to draw his six-guns and stagger into the street, chasing a fleeing Sublett. He shot his attacker in the back before he collapsed. Hardin's relatives picked him up and spirited him out of town to a hiding place, a deserted ranch house in Angelina County, Texas. In August 1872, while Hardin was recovering from his painful wounds, two policemen crept up on the ranch, going to a window to see the gunfighter lying on a bed. They fired rifles at him through the window and wounded him in the thigh, but then Hardin rolled off the bed, grabbed a shotgun, and managed to get to the door where he began blasting at them. The officers, both wounded, hobbled off and did not return.

Somehow, in the busy year of 1872, Hardin managed to meet and marry Jane Bowen. Their union produced two girls and a boy, but these children seldom saw their father,

Hardin in his early twenties.

who was either on a cattle drive somewhere or was busy earning the reputation of the fastest gun in the West. Hardin did make an attempt at rehabilitation. Influenced by his young wife, Hardin rode into Gonzales, Texas, and surrendered his guns to Sheriff Richard Reagan, stating that he would face all charges against him and "wipe the slate clean."

As Hardin was being put into a cell in the local jail, a jittery guard, terrified of the now infamous gunfighter, nervously fingered his six-gun and accidentally sent a bullet into Hardin's leg. This was removed while Hardin languished in jail and authorities busied themselves with collecting all the charges against him. Hardin had second thoughts about his voluntary surrender, especially when he heard that he would be tried for several murders and he was expected to be found guilty and then hanged. Using a saw smuggled to him by a relative, Hardin cut through the bars of his cell's window and escaped. He went to DeWitt County where his relatives, the numerous members of the Taylor clan, were battling with the Sutton family.

The Sutton-Taylor feud had been raging since 1868 when Buck Taylor had been shot from ambush by William Sutton. The Taylors presented a formidable array of gunmen, more than 100 under the leadership of Pitkin, Creed, Josiah, William, and Rufus Taylor. Against them were more than 200 gunmen led by the Suttons. These included the ranch hands and gunslingers employed by cattle baron Joe Tumilson and the notorious brawler Abel Head "Shanghai" Pierce, who had, with his wild cowboys, terrorized the towns of Abilene, Dodge City, Wichita, and countless other cowtowns that served as railheads to which Pierce drove his massive Texas herds. Jack Helm, who was an official in the state police force, also backed the Suttons, who paid him handsomely to take their side in any dispute.

Hardin worked for the Clements family, headed by Mannen Clements, his cousin. They were allies and relatives of the Taylors. The Clements were headquartered in the little town of Cuero, Texas, and here Hardin entered a local saloon and encountered J.B. Morgan, one of Jack Helm's deputies and a stalwart Sutton man. Morgan shouted at Hardin that he was ugly, stupid, and a gunman who had earned his reputation by killing helpless drunks. Both men drew their guns at the same time. Hardin reported that, "I pulled my pistol and fired, the ball striking him just above the left eye. He fell dead. I went to the stable, got my horse, and left town unmolested."

The Sutton-Taylor war raged on. In 1873, Jack Helm arrested two Taylor men and allowed his deputies to murder them. A few days later Pitkin Taylor was shot to death while he sat on the front porch of his ranch house. His son, Hardin's best friend, Jim Taylor, vowed that he would "wash my hands in old Bill Sutton's blood!" Hardin and Taylor were in Albuquerque, Texas, in July 1873, at a blacksmith's shop having their horses re-shod, when Jack Helm and six of his deputies rode past and spotted them. Helm and his men dismounted, hands on guns, and headed for the blacksmith's shack.

At the time, Helm no longer held any official position as a lawman, having been dismissed from the state police force for his ruthless treatment of prisoners. Helm was in the lead. He pulled forth a large knife as he walked, then ran toward Taylor, aiming this weapon at Taylor's chest. Hardin was holding a shotgun at the time and he leveled it at Helm, pulling both triggers and blasting Helm in the chest. Taylor then shot the writhing Helm in the head, killing him. Both Hardin and Taylor then turned their guns on the other deputies and drove them off with a barrage of flying lead.

After Jim Taylor fulfilled his vow by killing William Sutton in Indianola in 1874, the Sutton-Taylor feud ended and Hardin went to Comanche, Texas, to join his family. On May 26, 1874, the town of Comanche held horse races in honor of its native son, John Wesley Hardin, who was celebrating his twenty-first birthday. The local sheriff, John Karnes, was one of the few Texas sheriffs who held no warrants for Hardin's arrest. Karnes liked Hardin and often played cards with the gunfighter in one of Comanche's six roaring saloons. On that day, however, Comanche County Deputy Sheriff Charles Webb rode into town, intent upon arresting or gunning down Hardin. He made no show of doing so. In fact, he pretended he did not even know Hardin. Hardin, on the other hand, had been warned that Webb intended to arrest him. When Webb approached one of the saloons, Hardin was suddenly on the wooden sidewalk in front of him. The gunfighter spread his coat backward to reveal the jutting gunbutts in his vest holsters. "Have you any papers for my arrest?" Hardin asked Webb coolly.

"I don't know you," Webb lied. He had studied photographs of Hardin for weeks before going to Comanche.

"My name is John Wesley Hardin," the gunfighter said.

"Now I know you," Webb replied, "but I have no papers for your arrest."

Hardin nodded and then invited Webb to have a drink in the saloon. Webb agreed and Hardin turned his back, starting toward the saloon's swinging doors. At that moment one of Hardin's friends, Bud Dixon, shouted to Hardin: "Look out!"

In one movement of incredible speed, Hardin whirled about, cross-drawing his six-guns as he turned, and fired as he faced Webb, whose gun had just cleared the holster. Webb's bullet was fired after Hardin's guns roared. It struck Hardin in the side, but the gunfighter sent a bullet into the sheriff's head. As he fell, certainly dead or dying, a reflex movement caused Webb to get off another shot. Jim Taylor and Dixon, who were standing nearby, then shot Webb as he lay dying in the dust of the street. Webb was the fortieth man to be killed by John Wesley Hardin, according to the gunfighter's own careful count.

The Webb killing caused an uproar throughout Texas. Although Webb's actions had proved him to be shifty and double-dealing (understandably so since he was dealing with the worst killer in Texas history), the thousands of citizens of the state who held Webb in high regard demanded that Hardin be brought to justice. Hardin knew this shooting would be his downfall. He kissed his wife and children good-bye, and then, leading a string of fresh, fast horses behind him, fled eastward, planning to outrun any posse by regularly changing mounts. The posses pounded after him and, in their pursuit of Hardin, they caught up with many of his friends and relatives, those who had shielded and harbored him for years. A mob grabbed Hardin's older brother Joe, a completely innocent person, and lynched him. Lynch mobs hanged the Dixon brothers, Bud (also known as Bill) and Tom. Alex Barrickman and Ham Anderson, close friends of Hardin's, were then hunted down and shot to death. The state of Texas announced a dead-or-alive reward for Hardin and posted $4,000 for that purpose.

Powerful organizations sent scores of men to track down the gunfighter, including the Pinkerton Detective Agency and the Texas Rangers. Dozens of fast-draw gunfighters also searched for Hardin, hoping to shoot him down and gain a reputation as well as a reward for doing so. Posses numbering from ten to fifty heavily-armed men combed Texas for Hardin, and other lawmen kept vigil at his ranch in Comanche, expecting the gunfighter to return home. But John Wesley Hardin disappeared, as if swallowed by the vast Texas landscape itself. He was rumored to be robbing banks and trains in Florida, Georgia, Louisiana, and Alabama.

It was the Texas Rangers who finally tracked down the elusive gunfighter. For three years the Rangers searched for Hardin and finally learned that he would be boarding a train in Pensacola, Fla., on Aug. 23, 1877, with four gunmen, bound for his hideout in Alabama. Lt. John B. Armstrong of the Texas Rangers led a contingent of men to Pensacola and then boarded the train on which Hardin would be traveling. Armstrong limped to a seat with the aid of a cane; he was recovering from a recent injury. He sat down and looked across the aisle to see Hardin sitting alone in a seat, his head in the palm of his hand and his elbow resting on the window sill. Rangers piled on board the train car at either end. Then Armstrong got up and pulled his Peacemaker from its holster, pointing the seven-and-one-half-inch barrel at Hardin's head.

The gunfighter turned slightly, saw the weapon and shouted: "Texas, by God!" He reached for his own weapons but his guns got tangled in his suspenders. Armstrong brought the Peacemaker down hard on the gunfighter's head, knocking him unconscious. Jim Mann, nineteen, one of Hardin's men, jumped from another seat and fired a shot that tore Armstrong's hat from his head. Armstrong fired a shot that hit Mann in the chest. For a few moments, the youth did a wild dance in the train car aisle, cursing the lawman, then dove through a window, landed on the station platform and staggered a few steps and fell dead at the feet of another ranger, James Duncan.

Put aboard a Texas-bound train, Hardin insisted that the rangers had made a mistake, that he was J.H. Swain, a businessman. He had been in Pensacola buying timber, he said. The gunfighter kept up this pretense until the wide Texas landscape came into view. He then admitted that he was the man they were looking for, John Wesley Hardin. He was taken to the sturdy jail in Austin, Texas, and held there to await trial for the murder of Sheriff Webb. He was in notorious company. Hardin's fellow prisoners at that time included the infamous Johnny Ringo who would later join the Clanton-McLowery rustling gang of Tombstone, Ariz., and go down before the guns of Wyatt Earp. Also on hand was Mannen Clements and Bill Taylor.

Hardin was placed on trial at Gonzales, Texas, and he chose to defend himself in court. Hardin surprised everyone with his eloquence and inspired oratory. "Gentlemen," the gunfighter told his jury, "I swear before God that I never shot a man except in self-defense. Sheriff Webb came to Comanche for the purpose of arresting me, and I knew it. I met him and I defied him to arrest me, but I did not threaten him...I knew it was in his mind to kill me, not arrest me. Everybody knows he was a dangerous man with a pistol." Hardin then looked about the courtroom, noting the scores of strange faces staring back at him. "I know I don't have any friends here but I don't blame them for being afraid to come out for me. My father was a good man and my brother, who was lynched, never harmed a man in his life."

Moving slowly about the courtroom, the tall, good-looking Hardin, dressed in a neat black suit, a starched white shirt and black string tie, appeared to be a preacher and his bearing was that of a man with authority and immense self-respect. It was later remarked that Hardin was, at that moment, mimicking the posture and presence of his own preacher-father whom he had studied as a child when the elder Hardin held his revival meetings. Certainly Hardin was out to save a soul that day—his own. The young man peered intently at the jury, saying: "People will call me a killer, but I swear to you gentlemen that I have shot only in defense of myself. And when Sheriff Webb drew his pistol, I had to draw mine. Anybody else would have done the same thing. Sheriff Webb had shot a lot of men. That's all, gentlemen." He walked slowly back to the defendant's table and sat down.

The jury retired and then shuffled back into the courtroom within an hour and a half. It found Hardin Guilty of second-degree murder. The gunfighter's eloquence had saved his own life. He was sentenced to twenty-five years at hard labor. Guards escorted the gunman from the court and took him to the train depot en route to Rusk Prison in Huntsville, Texas. He served sixteen years of his prison term and spent most of his time behind bars studying law. When he emerged he told the press that he was completely reformed. He omitted the fact that during his first ten years of confinement he had created havoc by attempting many escapes and leading prison revolts. He had been whipped and starved and had spent months in solitary confinement before he stopped rebelling against the prison system. He became a model prisoner and settled down to the study of law in the last six years of his imprisonment.

Hardin was forty-one when he was released from prison. He had no place to go. His wife Jane had died about two years before he was set free and his children had grown up and gone off to make lives of their own. The gunfighter moved to El Paso where he studied law and stayed out of trouble. Hardin proved to be a model citizen and was hailed in the El Paso *Times* as a living example of modern penal rehabilitation. Callie Lewis, an 18-year-old woman, met the gunfighter at a social gathering. She was impressed with the legend of John Wesley Hardin, and the two were wed, but on Hardin's wedding night, he reverted to his old ways and went to a saloon, got drunk, and picked a fight he did not win. He returned home, battered and bruised. Callie Lewis took one look at this bleeding hulk and packed her bags, leaving Hardin on their wedding night.

After taking to drink, Hardin caroused through the worst dives of El Paso and was often found in a drunken stupor in the gutter. He then took up with a married, overweight prostitute, Mrs. Martin McRose, whose husband was wanted for rustling. McRose, Tom Finnessey, Vic Queen, and others in the rustling band had been hiding in Mexico. When this gang crossed into the U.S., they were met by a large group of lawmen led by Ranger Jeff Milton and U.S. marshals George Scarborough and Frank McMahon. The outlaws were shot down to the last man, including McRose. When Hardin heard this, he drunkenly bragged in several El Paso saloons that he had paid the lawmen to kill McRose and the others so he could have McRose's wife to himself. Ranger Jeff Milton, one of the finest lawmen on the frontier, heard of Hardin's boasting and confronted him in a saloon, incensed at the thought that he could be paid to kill the husband of someone's paramour.

Milton accused Hardin of lying and then demanded the aging gunfighter apologize to him. Hardin told Milton that he was not carrying guns and that Milton knew it or he would not dare speak to him in such a way.

"You're lying," Milton said, "you're always armed. And you can go for your gun right now or tell all these men here

and out loud that you lied."

Hardin shrugged, turned to his drunken friends, and said without hesitating: "Gentlemen, when I said that about Captain Milton, I lied."

Days later, Mrs. McRose was thrown into the El Paso jail for drunk and disorderly conduct. Hardin berated the policemen in the case, John Selman, and his father, John Selman, Sr. He met the elder Selman on the street and cursed him, promising loudly that he would later kill both

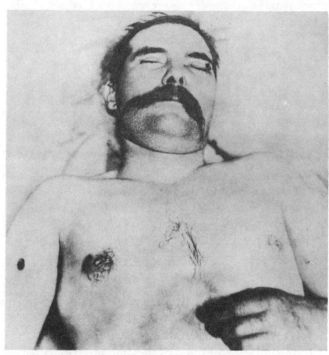

John Wesley Hardin, killer of forty men, dead of gunshot wounds, 1895.

him and his son. He then spread the word through the saloons that the Selmans, especially the elder Selman, were marked for his guns. Apparently Hardin and the elder Selman had hated each other for years over a past but unstated grievance. "Old John had better go fixed at all times," Hardin kept repeating to his associates.

When the elder Selman heard this, he resolved to rid himself and El Paso of the lethal Hardin. He heard that Hardin was in the Acme Saloon on July 19, 1895, and he headed for this place. The gunfighter had been drinking all night, bragging about how he would "fix those damned Selmans." At 11 p.m., he was still at the bar, playing dice with a local businessman, H.S. Brown. He rolled the dice, watched the cubes bounce and stop on the bar, and then uttered his last words, saying to Brown: "Four sixes to beat!" He looked up a moment later to see in the mirror behind the bar the figure of old John Selman standing behind him. Before he could turn, Selman fired a bullet into the back of Hardin's head. The bullet took off the back of his head and emerged above the left eye. He toppled to the floor dead but Selman was taking no chances.

He pumped two more bullets into the prone body, one slug going into the left arm, the other into the chest.

Selman insisted that Hardin had uttered a threat and had gone for his deadly guns in his vest holsters but none of the witnesses supported this claim. Selman was charged with murder and defended by Albert Fall, who was later the central figure in the Teapot Dome Scandal. Fall managed to persuade a jury that Hardin intended to kill Selman and that the old man had acted in self defense. He also maintained that the gunfighter had reached for his guns, causing Selman to defend himself. Selman was acquitted but no one, including the jury members at Selman's trial, believed that John Wesley Hardin had reached for his guns, or it would have been Hardin on trial for murder. See: **Armstrong, John Barclay; Bideno, Juan; Clements, Emmanuel, Jr.; Clements, Emmanuel, Sr.; Hickok, James Butler; Pierce, Abel Head; Ringo, John; Selman, John, Sr.; Sutton-Taylor Feud; Thompson, Ben.**

Hargraves, Dick, 1824-82, U.S., gambler. Born in England, Dick Hargraves immigrated to New Orleans as a 16-year-old, and after a short time as a bartender, became a renowned Mississippi riverboat gambler. Hargraves won a much as $30,000 from a single poker game and accumulated a fortune of $2 million. During his gambling career, he killed ten men who thought their losses to Hargraves were the result of his cheating.

Hargraves wore the finest clothes imported from England and France, and with his gambling ability, he attracted the attention of many women. He fought a duel with a banker over the affections of the man's wife, and was forced to shoot and kill the dead man's brother as well. Upon returning home, he was stabbed by the banker's wife, who then committed suicide. Hargraves recovered from the attack and retired to a more sedentary life, marrying a girl he had saved in a fire. He traveled to Cuba, and later became a Union officer in the Civil War. After the war, wealthy but suffering from tuberculosis, Hargraves moved to Denver where he lived until his death in 1882.

Harkey, Dee, 1866-1948, U.S., lawman. Dee Harkey was born in Texas in 1866 and became a lawman shortly after his sixteenth birthday. Orphaned at the age of three and raised by his older brother, Harkey witnessed a number of Indian raids as a child, and lost three brothers to gunfights before he was twenty-one. He eschewed an education, working on farms and on the range before becoming the teen-aged deputy of San Saba County, Texas, serving

under his older brother Joe who was the elected sheriff. Two years later, in 1884, Harkcy and another deputy arrested a man named Quinn in Richland Springs on the charge of stealing a mule. While the prisoner changed clothes at a hotel, Harkey and his partner were attacked by Quinn's wife and daughter. Harkey was slightly wounded in the abdomen by the girl.

In 1886, Harkey retired, married, and became a rancher in Bee County, Texas. Shortly afterward, he quarreled with neighbor George Young and during the argument, stabbed Young to death. Two years later, Harkey moved to Carlsbad, N.M., where he became a butcher, but continued to have trouble with his neighbors. He was involved in two shooting incidents with a customer named George High, impressing the citizenry enough with his skill with a gun to be named a deputy U.S. marshal. He served in that capacity until he retired from law enforcement for a second time in 1911. In 1895, in Phoenix, N.M., Harkey and Sheriff Cicero Stewart apprehended Tranquellano Estabo, a local gunman who was shooting up the town. In 1908, near Sacramento Sinks, Harkey led a posse of four lawmen in pursuit of Jim Nite, a member of the Dalton Gang who had escaped from a Texas jail. Nite and his accomplice, Dan Johnson, were found at daybreak and apprehended after a brief exchange of gunfire. Harkey later worked various jobs including town marshal and livestock inspector for a cattle raiser's association.

Harpe, William Micajah (AKA: **Big**), and **Harpe, Wiley** (AKA: **Little**), prom. 1790s, U.S., outlaws. The Harpe Brothers were long remembered by the U.S. settlers who traveled west along the Wilderness Trail in the 1790s. William Micajah "Big" Harpe and his brother Wiley "Little" Harpe were born into a Tory family in North Carolina. When the British surrendered in 1781, the brothers fled west to escape persecution. In the lawless frontier, the Harpes quickly gained a reputation as a pair of cold-blooded killers. They often disemboweled their victims and threw the remains into the Barren River, weighted down with stones. A $300 reward was posted in the Tennessee territory, but the brothers moved on to Ohio, where they holed up in a remote fortress known as Cave-In-the-Rock. River pirates described the Harpes as "men turned into wild wolves."

The brothers murdered numerous settlers, one because he snored too loudly. In 1799, a posse trapped the Harpe brothers in the woods. Wiley escaped, but Micajah was shot off his horse. The posse members began to hack off his head while he still lived. Micajah then cursed them and told them to get on with it. Later, they boiled his head and nailed the skull to a tree to deter potential desperadoes. Legend has it that Wiley was eaten by a pack of wolves sometime after 1800.

Harris, Jack, d.1884, U.S., gambler-gunman. Jack Harris, born and raised in Texas, led an adventuresome life. At an early age he worked for the U.S. Army as a scout and Indian fighter. During the Civil War, Harris served in the Confederate cavalry. Following the war, he fought in

Central American revolutions, losing a finger in Nicaragua. Returning to the U.S., Harris was one of the last great Buffalo hunters, providing meat and skins for the railroads moving west in the late 1870s. He then moved to San Antonio where he served briefly as a policeman, later becoming a gambler and winning several small fortunes. He and another gambler, Ernest Hart, formed a partnership and opened the Green Front Saloon, which had a full theater, the Vaudeville House, on the second floor. Harris' wealth grew, and he was well-liked in San Antonio. One of Harris' few enemies was Texas gunfighter Ben Thompson. The two men, who had earlier been friends, fell out in a poker game in 1880. Thompson nurtured a grudge ever after, believing Harris had cheated.

Texas gambler and gunman Jack Harris.

On July 11, 1882, Thompson rode into San Antonio drunk. He continued to drink and then stormed into the Green Front Saloon, demanding that Harris get a gun and meet him in the street. Harris, who entered the saloon after Thompson had left, got a gun and waited inside the saloon for his nemesis. Thompson appeared a short time later and saw Harris waiting with a shotgun behind some venetian blinds. Before Harris could fire, Thompson squeezed off a fatal round that smashed through the blinds and into Harris' right lung. The gambler fell to the floor and Thompson fired another round at him and left. Harris got to his feet, staggered upstairs to his apartment, and died there that night. Thompson, who was the city marshal of Austin, Texas, at the time, resigned and turned himself over to the San Antonio sheriff. He pleaded self-defense in a quick trial and was acquitted. See: **Thompson, Ben**.

Hart, Pearl (Pearl Taylor, AKA: Mrs. L.P. Keele), 1871-1925?, U.S., outlaw. Pearl Hart was the last Western bandit to rob a stagecoach and the only woman ever recorded as having committed that crime. Unlike Belle Starr or Cattle Kate Watson, Hart was not bred into Wild West crime. Born and raised in Lindsay, Ontario, Can., to a middle-class and respectable family, Pearl Taylor was one

Pearl Hart, last of the stagecoach robbers.

of several children. She was sent to a finishing school at an early age and, in 1888, at age seventeen, was seduced by a gambler, Frederick Hart. Pearl eloped with him but marriage to Hart proved to be one hardship after another. Hart was a small-time gambler and occasional bartender. Somehow he managed to scrape enough money together to take Pearl to Chicago to see the Columbian Exposition of 1893. There Hart became a barker for sideshows and Pearl worked odd jobs. She was thrilled at the Wild West shows and became enamored of the Old West, believing in all its legends and heroes.

Pearl left her ne'er-do-well husband abruptly and moved to Colorado where she gave birth to a son. She returned to her home in Lindsay briefly to leave the child in the care of her mother. She then went Phoenix, Ariz., where she quickly discovered that the Old West was no more and mostly likely never existed. To survive, she cooked in a lunch room and took in laundry. Her husband suddenly showed up in late 1895 and begged Pearl to return to him, promising that he would get a job. The couple was reunited, and Hart worked as a bartender and hotel manager.

For three years there was domestic peace and a second child, a girl, was born.

In 1898, Hart told Pearl that he was tired of supporting her and the child. During a fight, he knocked her unconscious and left, joining the army and going off to fight the Spanish in Cuba with Teddy Roosevelt's Rough Riders. Pearl took her second child to her home in Canada and then drifted back to the western mining camps. She worked in these hellholes as a cook until taking up with a carefree miner, Joe Boot. In 1899, Pearl received a letter from her brother telling her that her mother was ill and needed money for medical attention. Desperate, she talked to Boot about her dilemma. Boot suddenly had the idea to rob the Globe, Ariz., stage.

Boot said he knew all about the stagecoach that ran between Florence and Globe, Ariz.—that it always carried salesmen who had hundreds of dollars and that, since no one had robbed a stagecoach in years, it carried no shotgun rider, only an unarmed driver. This stage run was one of the last in the Arizona Territory, an antiquated form of transportation in 1899. By then the railroad reached into almost every town of the West. Pearl agreed to rob the stage with Boot, and the two rode to a watering hole where they knew the stagecoach would stop to rest the horses. Pearl was armed with an old .44 Colt. Boot carried a .45-caliber six-gun.

When the Globe stagecoach appeared, Pearl and Boot jumped in front of it, holding their guns on the driver. They ordered him to halt. Pearl was dressed as a man, wearing a man's gray flannel shirt, jeans, and boots. She had cut her hair short and had tucked the longer strands beneath a wide white sombrero. At first the driver thought she was a boy. Boot trained his weapon on the driver while Pearl ordered the passengers to step from the stage and line up.

After she took the driver's six-gun, Pearl held her gun on the passengers while collecting their money, about $450. Then, acting out the part of the Western badman, she peeled off three $1 bills from the stolen money and gave a bill to each of the three passengers, saying: "For grub and lodging." The passengers were then ordered to get back into the coach. Boot ordered the driver to whip the horses onward, and the stagecoach resumed its journey while Pearl and Boot mounted their horses and rode into the hills. The daring bandits had given little thought to their escape. They promptly got lost and, after wandering about in the wilds for several days, fell asleep next to a large campfire. Possemen roused them from their slumbers and put them under arrest.

Pearl Hart played her part as lady bandit to the hilt, telling the smiling lawmen that they would never have taken her alive if she had gotten to her gun. They agreed and then took her and Boot to jail. Pearl became an overnight celebrity as the last bandit to rob a stage. The fact that she was a woman made her even more of a curiosity, drawing crowds of admirers to the Globe jail to collect her autograph. She strutted behind the bars of her cell, playing the part of the outlaw. Some time later, with another prisoner, Ed Hogan, Pearl escaped. News of the manhunt for her spread through the newspapers of the East, further enhancing her fast-growing legend. When she was recaptured some days later, Pearl again played the part of the desperado.

Before her trial on charges of highway robbery, Pearl Hart made a flamboyant suicide attempt, one that was obviously intended to glean headlines, not insure death. While one of her guards stood in front of her cell, she suddenly cried out that she did not care to live any longer and threw a white powder into her mouth, then collapsed. A doctor was rushed to her cell and, after examining her, shook Pearl and shouted: "Stop pretending Pearl and get up!" As her eyes blinked open, the physician said: "No one ever killed themselves by swallowing talcum powder, Pearl."

Her trial took place in Florence, but Pearl insisted that no court had the right to place her on trial, loudly stating: "I shall not consent to be tried under a law in which my sex had no voice in making." Thus, Pearl Hart became one of the first champions for women's rights, giving interviews and urging her fellow females to revolt against the laws of the land until they were given the right to vote. Public sentiment was in favor of Pearl, who was tried separately from Boot. After listening to her lawyer plead that this was her first offense and that she had struggled all her life to obey the law, the jury retired and returned in fifteen minutes to acquit her.

Judge Doan was furious and ordered another jury impaneled immediately to try Pearl on stealing the six-gun from the driver of the stage. Judge Doan warned the members of this second jury that they should not allow their natural sympathies for a woman to cloud their reason. The all-male jury listened to the case and found Pearl Guilty in ten minutes. Judge Doan then sentenced the lady bandit to five years imprisonment at the Territorial Prison at Yuma "to cure her of robbing stagecoaches." Joe Boot, in a separate trial, was convicted of highway robbery and sent to the same prison for thirty years. Reporters rode the train with Pearl to Yuma, filing colorful accounts which detailed her every move and utterance, including the fact that she smoked cigars during the trip and livened up the trip with her "salty conversation."

The warden at Yuma Prison had to prepare a special cell for Pearl, separating her from the all-male population. Within a few weeks, Pearl began to spread the gospel, giving fellow prisoners long lectures on their sinful ways and how crime does not pay. She continued this evangelistic campaign for a year and a half until scores of Arizona citizens, hearing of her newly found religious beliefs, petitioned for her release. She was set free after serving eighteen months, on Dec. 19, 1902, along with another female prisoner, Rosa Duran. Governor A.W. Brodie released these two women on the grounds that the state prison had no accommodations for women, but he was really bowing to overwhelming public pressure to release Pearl Hart.

Pearl left for Kansas City where she joined her sister who had written a play about her and Pearl starred in this dime novel production which was titled *The Arizona Bandit*. The play closed after a short run and Pearl disappeared. She was arrested under the name of Mrs. L.P. Keele, in Kansas City two years later for buying stolen canned goods and given a brief jail term. Again Pearl disappeared and was not seen again until 1924 when she returned to Arizona and inspected the courthouse where she had been tried, smiling and telling an attendant that "nothing has changed." When the attendant asked who she was, she turned at the doorway and dramatically stated: "Pearl Hart, the lady bandit." She was thought to have died in 1925 in Kansas City while operating a cigar stand but other reports have it that she moved to the far West, perhaps San Francisco, where she lived until the mid-1950s.

Hassells, Samuel (AKA: **Bob Hays**), d.1869, U.S., outlaw. Born in Laporte, Iowa, Samuel Hassells went west at an early age and joined several gangs, committing many robberies. While living in Gonzales County, Texas, he reportedly was captured and drew a five-year prison sentence. He escaped four months before finishing this term in Huntsville, Texas. Hassells was identified as a member of a gang that robbed the post office in Separ, N.M., in October 1869. On Nov. 28, 1869, a large posse cornered the gang at the Diamond A ranch, about sixty miles south of Separ. A wild gun battle ensued and Hassells was killed.

Hays, Bob, d.1896, U.S., outlaw. Bob Hays was one member of Black Jack Christian's outlaw gang which attempted to rob the International Bank of Nogales, Ariz., on Aug. 6, 1896. Hays and fellow bank robber Jess Williams were inside the bank when newspaperman Frank King accosted gang members stationed outside. When King began firing, Hays and Williams were forced to abandon their efforts and flee. Despite the failed attempt, the gang was pursued by an eight-man posse and was cornered at a hideout in San Simon Valley. In an exchange of gunfire,

Hays was shot to death by lawman Fred Higgins.

Hays, John Coffey (**Jack**), 1817-83, U.S., lawman. Born in Wilson County, Tenn., John Coffey Hays, who was later known as Jack Hays to his men in the Texas Rangers and the outlaws he doggedly hunted down, moved to San Antonio, Tex., in 1837, working as a frontier surveyor. He also developed a reputation as a gunman who would fight to uphold the law. When the Texas Rangers were formed in 1840, Hays was elected a major in this sterling organization. He led many posses in tracking down outlaws and thieves and more than once arrested deadly gunmen by simply

John Coffey Hays, a Texas Ranger who became the first sheriff of San Francisco.

walking up to them and knocking them senseless with the butt of his sixgun, a tactic successfully employed by Wyatt Earp. Hays is credited with introducing the Colt revolver to the Rangers.

Hays served the Texas Rangers for ten years and then moved to California where he became fabulously rich. He purchased a huge tract of land across the Bay from San Francisco, and this he later established as the city of Oakland. Hays became the first sheriff of San Francisco County (1850-53), and through him many police reforms were instituted. Hays, though a lawman all his life, had the distinction of never being wounded in a gunfight.

Head, Harry (AKA: **Harry the Kid**), d.1881, U.S., outlaw. Harry Head was a cattle rustler and a member of Ike Clanton's gang. He was personally involved in a number of daring stagecoach robberies in southern Arizona, including the famous holdup near Contention on Mar. 15, 1881. The stagecoach had left Tombstone with eight passengers and $26,000 of Wells Fargo bullion in the safe. The loot was guarded by Bob Paul, a veteran of many encounters with western desperados.

As the stage passed through Contention, Ariz., Budd Philpot, the stagecoach driver, and Paul found themselves under attack from Harry Head, Bill Leonard, and Jim Crane. Paul tried to defend the passengers and cargo as best he could. But when bullets struck a passenger, Peter Roerig, and the driver, Paul was forced to lay down his gun and try to secure the reins of the stagecoach before it flipped over.

The Wells Fargo Co., posted a $2,000 reward for the arrest and capture of Head, Leonard, and Crane. A fourth man, Luther King, was seized a day after the robbery by Morgan Earp. Not to be outdone by his brother, Wyatt Earp allegedly offered the Clanton boys $3,600 if they would lure the three fugitives into a trap. The three men remained at large until June 1881, when they ran low on cash and were forced to hold up a store in Eureka, N. Mex. Owners Bill and Ike Haslett pulled out their guns from under the counter, and in a fast and furious exchange of shots, Head and Leonard were killed. Crane would later extract his vengeance against the Haslett brothers before being killed.

Heath, John (or **Heith**), 1851-84, U.S., outlaw. John Heath was Texas born and raised, and at an early age became involved in criminal activities, including rustling and

The end of outlaw John Heath, lynched by a Tombstone mob in 1884.

robbery. He reformed briefly and became a deputy sheriff in Cochise County, Texas, but resigned because of poor pay

and went back to thieving. Heath later opened a dance hall and saloon in Clifton, Ariz., which became a hangout for many desperadoes and gunmen. Befriending William Delaney and Daniel Kelly, both notorious gunmen who had been credited with killing several men, Heath joined these men and others in a robbery of a Bisbee, Ariz., store on Dec. 8, 1883. In the course of this robbery, four people including a woman were killed before the robbers fled. This notorious raid was later known as the Bisbee Massacre, and the outlaws were tracked down one by one by determined lawmen.

Heath was arrested in his Clifton saloon on suspicion and taken to Bisbee, where he was convicted of second-degree murder in a quick trial on Feb. 21, 1884, after witnesses identified him as one of the killers in the store robbery. He was sentenced to life in prison but he served only one day of this term. Housed in the Tombstone jail, Heath was dragged from his cell by an incensed group of miners the day after his conviction and taken to a telegraph pole where a rope was looped over a crossbeam and the other end around his neck. Heath claimed to be innocent of the crime for which he was convicted, but when he realized the determination of the miners to see justice done, he became philosophical in his last moments, saying: "I have faced death too many times to be disturbed when it actually comes." As the miners began to yank him skyward, Heath cried out: "Don't mutilate my body or shoot me full of holes!" He died seconds later as he dangled from the telegraph pole. See: **Bisbee, Ariz., Massacre; Daniels, Benjamin F.; Delaney, William E.**

Helm, Boone, 1823-64, U.S., outlaw. At an early age, Boone Helm was considered a fierce criminal. While in his teens he stabbed to death a man named Littleburg in his native Log Branch, Mo., before fleeing west. In the 1850s, Helm roamed through California, prospecting for gold but, often enough, robbing miners. In 1858, he reportedly shot a miner in California before leaving for Oregon where he became a mountain man. One account has Helm starving in the mountains and slaying a pioneer family, then eating their remains. Helm then moved to Utah and hired his gun to the highest bidder, taking part in the Mountain Meadows Massacre. Helm was later described as "a low, coarse, cruel, animal ruffian," and he became one of the most feared outlaws of his day.

Helm joined Henry Plummer's outlaw gang, robbing and killing through Idaho and Montana. He shot and killed a man in Florence, Idaho, and was jailed, but he bribed the jailer and was allowed to escape. He used many aliases while hiding out in the Montana mining camps, aware of several warrants issued for his arrest. He rejoined the Plummer gang but vigilantes put an end to these outlaws on Jan. 13 (or Jan. 14, according to another account), and was hanged, along with Jack "Three-Fingered Jack" Gallagher, Hayes Lyons, George "Clubfoot" Lane, and Frank Parish in Virginia City, Mont.

These five men were placed on boxes with ropes around their necks, the ropes tied to a crossbeam of an unfinished log building at Van Buren and Wallace streets. Helm treated his miserable fate as if it were a gruesome joke. He was slightly drunk at the time and laughingly asked Gallagher for his handsome coat, telling his fellow outlaw: "Jack, give me that coat. You never gave me anything!" Gallagher was hanged first and Helm shouted up to his dangling body: "Kick away, old fellow, I'll be in hell with you in a minute!" He then announced his loyalty to the Confederacy by shouting to the vigilantes: "Every man for his principles! Hurrah for Jeff Davis! Let her rip!" A vigilante kicked the box out from beneath Helm and he was dead minutes later. See: **Gallagher, Jack; Plummer, Henry.**

Helm, Jack, d.1873, U.S., lawman. Jack Helm, a Texas cowboy, served in the confederate army during the Civil War, once killing a black man for merely whistling a Yankee song. Returning to Texas, he became involved in the bloody Sutton-Taylor feud, and became the unofficial leader of 200 Sutton regulators. In San Patricio County in July 1869, Helm and C.S. Bell murdered Taylor men John Choate and his nephew Crockett Choate. On Aug. 23, Helm and Bell killed Jack Hays Taylor and wounded his brother Doboy during an ambush at the Taylor ranch. That month, Helm was appointed captain of the Texas State Police. In 1873, Helm was ordered to arrest Taylor relatives, William and Henry Kelly. Helm and his posse, consisting of Sutton supporters, apprehended the pair in DeWitt County and murdered them in a spate of vigilante justice. Following a public outcry, Texas governor E.J. Davis fired Helm from the state police, but he continued as sheriff of DeWitt County. The infamous outlaw and Taylor relative, John Wesley Hardin, encountered Helm several times, once killing his deputy, and another time shooting two Sutton supporters after an intended truce meeting. In July 1873, while in Albuquerque, Texas, Helm spotted Hardin and Jim Taylor in a blacksmith's shop. As he approached, Hardin turned and killed him with a shotgun blast. See: **Hardin, John Wesley.**

Hickok, James Butler (AKA: **Wild Bill**), 1837-76,

U.S., lawman. Born on May 27, 1837, in Homer, Ill. (later Troy Grove), Hickok was the fourth of six children. His father, William Alonzo Hickok, was a farmer and operator of a general store which was also used as part of the underground railroad where runaway slaves were hidden and smuggled to "safe" farms. As a boy, Hickok helped guide slaves to freedom. Big for his age, Hickok had a wild brawl with Charlie Hudson, a fellow teamster, in 1855. The teenage Hickok so badly beat Hudson that he thought he had killed him. He fled with his brother Lorenzo, going to St. Louis and then to Kansas, which was then torn between pro-slavery and anti-slavery forces. Hickok joined the ranks of Jim Lane, leader of the anti-slavery men, known as Redlegs. Learning that their mother, Polly Butler Hickok, was ill, Lorenzo returned home, but Hickok stayed on, becoming the town constable of Monticello in Johnson County.

There was little or no work for Hickok, except to lock up an occasional drunk. He busied himself by homesteading and then took a job as a stagecoach driver, following the Santa Fe Trail. In 1860, he became a freighter for Russell, Majors & Waddell. One day at Raton Pass, a ravenous bear jumped Hickok and badly mauled him before Hickok killed the beast with two guns and a knife. He recuperated from severe wounds in Kansas City. The freight line then assigned Hickok to handle their Rock Creek Station in Nebraska. It was during this period that Hickok befriended the hunter and cavalry scout William Frederick Cody, the celebrated Buffalo Bill. They became fast friends and Hickok often visited the Cody home in Leavenworth, Kan.

At Rock Creek, Hickok worked as a stock tender. Also at the station was its manager, Horace Wellman, his common-law wife, and Doc Brink, a stable hand. Living nearby was rancher David McCanles, who had financial difficulties with the Russell freight line. Moreover, Hickok took to visiting McCanles' mistress, Sarah Shull. McCanles insulted Hickok on several occasions, calling him "Duck Bill" because of the shape of his nose and mouth, and a hermaphrodite.

On July 12, 1861, McCanles, enraged at Hickok's seeing his mistress once again, went to the Rock Creek Station, standing outside the cabin and calling for Hickok to come outside. Hickok refused and McCanles went to a side door. It is unclear whether or not he pulled his six-gun. "Come out and fight fair!" McCanles shouted. Hickok did not step outside. Then McCanles shouted that he would go inside the cabin and drag Hickok outside. "There'll be one less s.o.b. if you try that," Hickok shouted back. McCanles then entered the side door of the cabin and Hickok shot him through the heart. McCanles' 12-year-old son, Monroe, ran into the cabin to hold his dying father.

Meanwhile, McCanles' cousin, James Woods, and James

Gordon, a ranch hand who worked for McCanles, came toward the cabin. Hickok shot Woods twice and sent a bullet into Gordon. Both men fled but Wellman appeared with a hoe and ran after Woods, knocking him down and hacking him to death. Doc Brink raced after Gordon and killed him with a shotgun blast. These killings were later much in debate and it was claimed that McCanles was unarmed when he threatened Hickok. One report had it that Hickok shot McCanles from ambush, standing behind a curtain and firing through it.

Following this incident, Hickok, in October 1861, hired out as Union freighter, working in Sedalia, Mo. He later worked as a spy for Union general Samuel R. Curtis. He was also credited in 1862 as having fought as a sharpshooter at the battle of Pea Ridge, Ark. It was during the Civil War that Hickok earned his sobriquet, Wild Bill. One report has it that he was given this name to distinguish him from his younger brother, Lorenzo, who was called Tame Bill. Hickok became Wild Bill. Another story has it that Hickok stopped a lynch mob from hanging a youth and a woman shouted: "Good for you, Wild Bill!" The name stuck and would follow Hickok to the grave and beyond into legend.

By the summer of 1865, Hickok and other scouts had been mustered out of the Union Army. Hickok was then in Springfield, Mo. He was well known in the streets, always armed with two revolvers. With him was his friend Davis Tutt, who also wore two six-guns. Both men reportedly courted the same woman, one Susanna Moore, and this led to a break in their friendship. Hickok and Tutt next met in the Lyon House, a Springfield saloon and gambling hall, on the night of July 20, 1865. Hickok beat Tutt at cards and Tutt threw down his cards, snarling that Hickok owed him $40 for a horse trade. Hickok paid him. Then Tutt recalled another old debt, one for $30. Hickok said no, it was only $25 he owed Tutt and he said he would settle that matter later. Tutt grabbed Hickok's valued Waltham watch from the gaming table, telling him he would wear it the next day on market square. Hickok told Tutt that if he tried that, he would pay with his life.

The gunfight was set for 6 a.m., and half the town was up to witness the duel between Hickok and Tutt. Both men appeared on opposite sides of the square and slowly advanced toward each other. When they were separated by about seventy-five yards, Hickok yelled: "Don't come any closer, Dave!" Tutt kept moving toward Hickok. He pulled his six-gun and fired a shot that went wild. Hickok then drew his gun with his right hand and steadied it with his left, slowly squeezing off a round that smashed into Tutt's heart, killing him instantly. Hickok promptly turned himself into Union authorities and was charged with murder, a charge later reduced to manslaughter. He was tried on

Aug. 5-6, 1865, and was found Not Guilty.

The verdict upset many people in Springfield, especially those who had been friendly to Tutt. Yet Hickok remained in Springfield, where he later campaigned for the post of town marshal. Out of five candidates, Hickok ran second. Wild Bill then left for the West and for the next four years served as a scout for the U.S. Cavalry. He was a scout for General George Armstrong Custer and the famed Seventh Cavalry. He left the service in 1869, taking various jobs in Colorado Territory. There, in July 1869, Hickok got drunk and was involved in a shooting scrape. He shot no one but received three minor wounds.

Hickok then went to Hays City, Kan., where, in the summer of 1869, he was elected sheriff. On Aug. 22, 1869, a local tough, Bill Mulvey (or Melvin, or Mulrey) started to shoot up the town. Hickok confronted the drunken ex-cavalryman, ordering him to surrender his guns and submit to arrest. Mulvey, who was with a number of equally drunken friends, shouted that he would never be arrested. He fumbled for his six-gun and Hickok shot him once. Mulvey was taken to a doctor's office where he died the next morning. Hays City was a wild town in those days, a freight and cattle center, and it attracted some of the worst gunmen of the day. One of these was a brutish teamster named Samuel Strawhim who arrived with a half dozen teamsters on Sept. 27, 1869. He and his friends stormed into John Bitters' Beer Saloon that night and began to wreck the place.

A few minutes later Hickok, accompanied by Deputy Peter Lanihan, arrived at the saloon and ordered Strawhim to surrender his guns. Strawhim laughed and drew his guns. Wild Bill drew both his 1851 Navy Colts, blasting Strawhim to death. A coroner's jury later stated that the Strawhim shooting was justifiable homicide. Aside from cattlemen, teamsters, and gamblers, Hickok also contended with numerous drunken cavalrymen from nearby Fort Hays. On July 17, 1870, Hickok was in a saloon when seven intoxicated troopers jumped him and held him down. One of them held a six-gun to Wild Bill's ear and pulled the trigger but the gun misfired. Wild Bill managed to regain his feet and he pulled his pistols, shooting Private Jerry Lanihan through the wrist and knee and another trooper, John Kile, who was hit in the stomach. The rest of the troopers backed off as Hickok retreated from the saloon. Lanihan survived but Kile died the next day.

Hickok's reputation as a fearless lawman was now firmly established and the authorities of Abilene, Kan., one of the roughest cattle towns on the frontier, sent for him. He became marshal of Abilene on Apr. 15, 1871. Abilene was then experiencing a boom in Texas cattle but the cowboys who drove the great herds to the railhead in Abilene were fast draw artists, not the least of whom was John Wesley

Left to right, "Wild Bill" in 1867, gunman Samuel Strawhim, killed by Hickok in 1869, and gunman David McCanles, killed in 1861 by Hickok.

Left, "Wild Bill" turns on hostile crowd after shooting Dave Tutt, 1865, and, right, feeding his horse in a Deadwood saloon, 1875.

Left, an artist's sketches of Hickock-McCanles fight at Red Creek, and, right, "Wild Bill" sitting down to his last poker hand in Deadwood.

Hardin. Hickok confronted Hardin one night while the Texan was shooting up the town. He ordered Hardin to turn over his two six-guns but, according to Hardin, the gunman pulled his guns out of two holsters sewn to his vest, drawing cross-armed, handing the guns' butts first to Hickok. When the marshal reached for the guns, Hardin twirled the guns about in a "border roll" and got the drop on the lawman before leaving town. This story, of course, was all Hardin's and is unsupported elsewhere.

Another story has it that Ben Thompson, then one of the most feared gunmen on the frontier, had had several run-ins with Hickok and that the lawman had pistol-whipped Thompson, disgracing him in front of his friends and employees in a saloon Thompson was then running in Abilene. Thompson, who invariably would face any man with his guns, could not work up his courage to meet Wild Bill in a showdown. Hickok may have been the slower gun but his accuracy was deadly. He was probably the greatest marksman in the West with his Navy Colts, firing with unerring aim whenever he was forced into a gunfight. Thompson reportedly asked young John Wesley Hardin to kill Hickok, offering to pay Hardin several thousand dollars to do the job. To Hardin's credit, he told Thompson that Hickok was an honorable man and if Thompson wanted the lawman dead he had better shoot him himself, if he could. Thompson dropped the matter.

One story that was not apocryphal is Hickok's meeting with the deadly gunman and gambler, Phil Coe, who had confronted the marshal on several previous occasions. On Oct. 5, 1871, Coe led about fifty Texans into town. Hickok warned Coe and the others to behave themselves, but at 9:00 that night a shot was fired outside the Alamo Saloon and Hickok went to investigate. When he arrived, he saw a dozen Texans, including Coe, with guns in their hands. Coe admitted that he had fired the shot, claiming that he fired at a wild dog. Hickok drew his guns, saying as he did so that Coe had to surrender his six-guns. Coe fired twice at Hickok at a distance of about fifteen feet. Both shots whizzed through Wild Bill's coat. Hickok fired once, his bullet smashing into Coe's stomach. The gunman crumpled to the ground. Hickok said: "I have fired too low."

At that moment, Mike Williams, a friend of Hickok's, thought to help the marshal. He broke through the crowd and crossed in front of Hickok who thought he was a member of the Texas group trying to shoot him. Wild Bill fired off two shots, killing Williams on the spot. Coe was carried away and he lingered in agony for three days before dying. Hickok was depressed at having accidentally shot Williams. He paid for the man's funeral and was said never to have fired another shot at any man.

For several years, Hickok participated in several Wild West shows sponsored by his good friend Buffalo Bill Cody, although he was a reluctant showman, according to most reports, drinking heavily and grousing about having to "play act" to earn a living. By 1876, Hickok was in Deadwood, Dakota Territory, where he spent much of his time drinking and gambling. He knew Calamity Jane in those days but only as a friend. He was never this tomboy's lover, as Calamity Jane later claimed. Hickok had earned many enemies up to that time, after his several years as a lawman. One of those who hated him was a small, cross-eyed little man, Jack McCall, a common laborer who was also known as Bill Sutherland. On Aug. 1, 1876, McCall had lost $110, all the money he possessed, to Hickok in a card game. Even though Hickok had loaned McCall money to have breakfast, McCall swore revenge.

The following day, Hickok was sitting in Saloon Number 10, playing poker with William Rodney Massie, a one-time riverboat captain, Charlie Rich, and Carl Mann, who was part owner of the saloon. Wild Bill was apparently uneasy since his chair faced two open doors to the saloon. On several occasions, Hickok asked Rich, whose chair was against a wall, to exchange seats with him. Rich laughed and refused each time, saying that he did not want to get shot in the back. At about 4 p.m., McCall entered Saloon Number 10. He ordered a drink at the bar. He slowly walked up behind Hickok and then pulled an old six-gun, firing once into Wild Bill's back. The great gunman toppled sideways in his chair, falling to the floor dead. He clutched his poker hand, aces and eights, which was forever after known as "The Dead Man's Hand." The other poker players at first did not realize what had happened until they saw McCall standing with the smoking gun in his hand. Bartender Anson Tipple jumped over the bar and tried to grab McCall who unsuccessfully tried to fire his weapon at Tipple. McCall dashed out the side door of the saloon while several persons ran about the streets of Deadwood, shouting: "Wild Bill has been shot! Wild Bill is dead!" The bullet that killed Hickok passed through his body and lodged in Massie's wrist. The gambler never had it removed and it was still embedded in Massie's wrist when he died in 1910.

McCall was later found hiding in a nearby barber shop. He was arrested and charged with murder. Some claimed that McCall had been given $200 by Hickok's enemies to kill Wild Bill, although this claim was never corroborated. Meanwhile, Wild Bill was buried the next day with great ceremony. A huge throng was present for the services. McCall was tried on Aug. 3, 1876, the day of Wild Bill's funeral. He was tried before Judge W.L. Kuykendall. He was prosecuted by Colonel George May and he was defended by Judge Miller. McCall insisted that he was blinded with rage since Hickok had killed his brother years earlier in Kansas. This, of course, was a lie, but the jury

Left to right, "Wild Bill" Hickok, the deadly gunslinging lawman in 1863, 1871, and 1874.

Left to right, "Wild Bill" with "Texas Jack" Omohundro and William F. "Buffalo Bill" Cody.

"Wild Bill" in buckskins, 1869.

believed McCall and he was acquitted.

McCall, fearing that Wild Bill's friends would seek him out and kill him, fled first to Cheyenne and then to Laramie City. Here he was again arrested for killing Hickok. It was ruled that the Deadwood trial was illegal and McCall was again tried on Dec. 4-6, 1876, in Yankton, Dakota Territory. He was found Guilty of murdering Wild Bill and, on Jan. 3, 1877, he was sentenced to death. He appealed this sentence but President U.S. Grant refused to intervene. McCall went to the gallows on Mar. 1, 1877. He stood quaking on the scaffold, trembling and begging for someone to save him. The rope was placed around his neck and just before he fell through the trap to his death, McCall cried out: "Oh, God!" The body went into an unmarked grave. Hickok's body was later removed to Mount Moriah, where an elegant marker was later built. It is visited yearly by thousands of travelers who still seek the legend of Wild Bill. See: **Calamity Jane; Hardin, John Wesley; Thompson, Ben.**

Hickory, Sam (AKA: **Downing**), prom. 1891, U.S., outlaw. Deputy U.S. Marshal Joseph Wilson was a Texan assigned to the Muskogee District. Wilson was given the task of serving a warrant on Sam Hickory, a liquor runner who lived on Fourteen Mile Creek near Tahlequah (Okla.). Hickory was picked up by Wilson on Sept. 21, 1891, in one of the fields surrounding his home. The prisoner walked back to the farmhouse with Wilson to retrieve a riding saddle for the journey back to the Fort Smith prison. He slipped away from Wilson for an instant and grabbed his revolver.

The lawman drew his gun and fired a shot at Hickory, which landed harmlessly in the door of the house. Hickory returned the fire, dropping Wilson from his horse. The body of the dead marshal was taken to a ravine about a mile away and left there. Three days later Wilson's body was recovered. His throat had been slit and there was a bullet wound in his knee. At his trial, Hickory claimed the shooting was in self defense. Wilson had shot at him, so he ran inside the house to fetch a gun in order to defend himself. The evidence against Hickory suggested he was lying, and accordingly, the jury returned a verdict of Guilty.

Defense Attorney J. Warren Reed appealed on the grounds that Judge Isaac Parker had issued improper instructions to the jury. The motion was upheld in the U.S. Supreme Court, and the conviction was overturned. Hickory was brought to trial a second time, and again he was convicted. Undaunted, Reed objected for a second time to Parker's instructions to the jury. The case went before the Supreme Court a second time, and a favorable decision was again handed down to the defendant. By the

time Hickory appeared in court for his third trial, the charges had been reduced to manslaughter. The jury convicted him, and Parker ordered him to jail for five years.

Higgins, Fred R., prom. 1890s, U.S., lawman. In the 1890s, Fred Higgins was a deputy U.S. marshal in the Arizona Territory. In the San Simon Valley in 1896, Higgins and seven other lawmen formed a posse to pursue Black Jack Christian, Bob Hays, and two other bandits. The lawmen found the fugitives' lair and set up an ambush. When the outlaws appeared, a furious gunfight broke out. Hays fired three shots at Higgins, who was sprayed with splinters of rock, but not hit. Higgins returned the fire and killed Hays with two shots. The other criminals escaped. The following year, on Apr. 28, Higgins and three others, while still in pursuit of the remaining three bandits, tracked them to a cave near Clifton, Ariz. Again while attempting an ambush, they mortally wounded Black Jack Christian, but the other two bandits escaped. A few years later, Higgins moved to New Mexico and became the sheriff of Chaves County.

Higgins, John Calhoun Pinckney (AKA: **Pink**), 1848-1914, U.S., gunman. Pink Higgins, born in Georgia

John Pinckney Higgins (first row, far right) and his men.

in 1848, moved to Texas in 1857 and settled with his family on a ranch in Lampasas County. As a young man, he became a fervent member of the Ku Klux Klan, and owned a saloon and butcher shop. Higgins was wounded twice during Indian battles, and in the 1870s became a central figure in a feud with the notorious Horrell clan. The two families had been friendly, even combining their cattle on common range land, but in 1873, the Horrell brothers killed one of Higgins' relatives and two other law officers. Higgins retaliated by killing two Horrell cowboys, Zeke Terrell in 1874 and Ike Lantier a year later. The feud escalated on Jan. 22, 1877, when Higgins killed the unarmed Merritt Horrell in a Lampasas saloon. Two months later, Higgins was among a group which ambushed Sam and Mart Horrell, but both men survived. The hostility continued on June 14, 1877, when Higgins and three others fought seven Horrells for several hours on the streets of Lampasas, leaving Frank Mitchell, Higgins' brother-in-law, dead. Citizens finally convinced the two factions to ride out of town in opposite directions, but the following month the feud continued after Higgins, with a full complement of men, invaded the Horrell ranch. They contained the Horrells in the ranch buildings, but after a two-day siege, the Higgins forces ran out of ammunition and were forced to retreat. The Texas Rangers, making dire threats to both families, forced the two factions to sign a peace treaty.

Higgins stayed out of trouble until 1884, when he shot a man to death at the border town of Ciudad Acuna, Mex., after the man had reneged on the sale of 125 horses. Higgins escaped by swimming back across the Rio Grande after nightfall. In the early 1900s, Higgins became embroiled in a feud with a Texan named Bill Standifer. On Oct. 4, 1903, in Kent County, Texas, they drew rifles on each other. Standifer's shot struck Higgins' horse, but the return was on the mark, and Standifer was dead from a bullet wound to the heart. Higgins died of a heart attack at age sixty-six in 1914.

Hill, Tom (AKA: **Tom Chelson**), d.1878, U.S., outlaw. Tom Hill became acquainted with crime in the early 1870s as a cattle rustler in New Mexico with a gang led by Jesse Evans. After an October 1877 raid on the ranches of Dick Brewer and John Tunstall in Lincoln County, Hill, Evans, Frank Baker, and a man named Davis were apprehended by a fifteen-man posse after a two-day chase. All four surrendered after a furious exchange of gunfire and were taken to the jail in Lincoln, N.M. Two weeks later, thirty-two members of the Evans gang raided the jail and freed the four prisoners. In January 1878, the gang tried to rustle a herd of horses in Grant County, but Hill and Evans were wounded in the struggle.

A month later, on Feb. 18, 1878, as sides were being taken in the impending Lincoln County War, a posse which included Hill confronted John Tunstall on his ranch. Finding Tunstall alone and on foot, Hill shot Tunstall to death. On Mar. 13, 1878, Hill and Evans tried to rob the camp of a sheepherder at Alamo Springs, N.M. They surprised a camp guard, but after looting a wagon, and preparing to steal the livestock, they were involved in a gun battle as they tried to leave. The thieves wounded the guard, but he crawled to camp and shot the two armed bandits at point-blank range, killing Hill and wounding Evans' wrist.

Hindman, George W., d.1878, U.S., lawman-gunman. In 1875, George Hindman moved a herd of cattle to New Mexico from his native Texas, and decided to stay and work on a ranch in Lincoln. But Bill Humphreys, part owner of the herd, became angry with Hindman's desertion, and after an argument, both men drew their guns. Hindman's shot grazed Humphreys' head, knocking him unconscious, while Hindman was wounded by a shard of metal when a bullet hit his gun. Hindman escaped and became a ranch hand for Robert Casey. Hindman encountered a more stalwart foe when he wrestled a grizzly bear who refused to die after being shot. The bear mauled Hindman, permanently crippling his arm and hand. In 1877, Hindman was appointed deputy sheriff to William Brady, and the following February was part of a posse which instigated the Lincoln County War with the fatal shooting of John Tunstall. On Apr. 1, 1878, Hindman was accompanying Sheriff Brady to the Lincoln courthouse when they were ambushed by an outlaw gang which included Billy the Kid, Henry Brown, Jim French, John Middleton, and Fred Wait. Brady died instantly, and Hindman shortly thereafter.

Hite, Robert Woodson (AKA: **Wood**), 1848-81, U.S., outlaw. Wood Hite was a Kentucky cousin of Jesse James. After serving in the Confederate Army during the Civil War, Hite joined his illustrious relative's gang in 1870. After the gang's disastrous 1876 holdup attempt in Northfield, Minn., and a few train robberies in Kentucky, he returned to his father's home disenchanted. In 1881, Hite shot a black man to death after a brief argument. However, he bribed a jail guard with a $100 bill and escaped to the Missouri home of Bob Ford. While there, he began feuding with Dick Liddell, another fugitive, over the affections of Martha Bolton, Ford's widowed sister. The feud culminated one day in January 1882 when the two exchanged gunshots one morning. Hite was wounded in the right arm and Liddell was hit in the leg. While Hite writhed on the floor,

Ford murdered him in cold blood. See: **Ford, Robert; James, Jesse Woodson.**

Hodges, Dr. Thomas, See: **Bell, Tom.**

Holder, Lewis, d.1894, U.S., outlaw. After hearing the news from Judge Isaac Parker that he was going to die on the gallows, Lewis Holder let forth a piteous scream and then collapsed to the floor, paralyzed with fear. There was an immediate concern that Holder had died from fright, but the defendant was still very much alive. Holder, who had been convicted of murdering his partner George Bickford in the San Bois Mountains (Okla.) on Dec. 28, 1891, vowed that he would return to Fort Smith in spirit form and would haunt Judge Parker and the jurymen if he were indeed hanged.

No one paid much attention to the desperate warnings of a condemned man. Holder was executed as scheduled on Nov. 2, 1894. About one month later, jailer George Lawson was startled by a moaning sound coming from the direction of the jail yard gallows. Upon further examination, a thoroughly inebriated man was found lying prone on the wooden gallows.

Holdout Jackson, prom. 1890s, U.S., gambler. Professional cardsharp Holdout Jackson rode into a mining camp in the Yukon one day, looking for some action. The miners were on to him and prudently declined his invitation to wager. The only man willing to go up against Jackson was Stuttering Smith, whose reputation for honesty was none too good. Smith, as his name suggests, had a difficult time getting his words out. To help correct his stammer, Smith would hold pebbles in his mouth; when this did not work he substituted pellets.

Holdout Jackson had come to a party with a fat bankroll, which Stuttering Smith eyed greedily. The two gamblers played each other to a virtual standoff. Jackson held his ground against the more capable Smith by using the famous "Kepplinger Sleeve Holdout," a mechanical device favored by professional card cheats for producing a winning hand. Jackson was soon ahead by $500. Smith soon figured out that a Kepplinger device was concealed inside of Jackson's coat vest and by bending forward ever so slightly, Jackson triggered the pulley which produced the winning hand.

Smith called Jackson's wager, and with a fresh deck a new game began. When Jackson bent forward, Smith spit out a No. 7 pellet, which struck Jackson in the head. Jackson paused and then bent forward again and was hit by another of Smith's pellets. The card cheat thought a bee had stung him. Smith offered that it could very well be the bothersome little pests since spring was coming. His trick discovered, Jackson folded. "You take the pot mister! All of a sudden my hand went bust!" Holdout Jackson raced out of town, having been trimmed of his fortune.

Hole-in-the-Wall, prom. 1890s-1900s, U.S., outlaw hideout. The Hole-in-the-Wall was a seemingly impenetrable hideout used by Butch Cassidy and members of the Wild Bunch during the heyday of this last of the Old West's super bandit gangs. This hideout, which no one has been able to pinpoint to this day, was somewhere in the deep mountain ravines and gorges near the meeting place of the Colorado, Utah, and Wyoming state lines. It was reportedly discovered by George "Big Nose" Curry, one of the elder statesmen of the Wild Bunch, and it was home for more than twenty years to the likes of Butch Cassidy, the Sundance Kid (Harry Longbaugh), Kid Curry (Harvey Logan), O.C. Hanks, Ben Kilpatrick, William "News" Carver, Harry Tracy, Elza Lay, and dozens of other desperadoes. When these outlaws were all either imprisoned or killed, use of Hole-in-the-Wall ceased. The exact location of this legendary hideout is still a mystery.

Holliday, John Henry (AKA: **Doc**), 1852-87, U.S., gunman. John Holliday was, on occasions, either a self-appointed lawman or an outlaw and gunman for hire. Born in Griffin, Ga., Holliday was raised as a polite scion of a rich southern family. He studied dentistry while in his twenties and practiced the profession whenever in need of funds. About 1872, this slender man with florid manners contracted tuberculosis and traveled west to seek a dry climate.

From 1873 to the late 1870s, Holliday demonstrated an apparently innate skill with firearms.

The deadly gunfighter John Henry "Doc" Holliday, who was both lawman and outlaw.

His aim was deadly. Unlike most of the western gunslingers of his day, Holliday was never impatient to pull his six-guns. He drew his weapons with dedicated calm, and while his opponent was firing wildly at him, this beady-eyed killer, would carefully level his Colt and nervelessly fire, invariably inflicting a mortal wound upon his enemy.

Holliday's reputation in the West as a deadly gunslinger was earned in the boom towns of Dallas, Cheyenne, Denver, Pueblo, Leadville, Dodge City, Tucson, and Tombstone. It was during the early 1870s that Holliday befriended a man to whom he gave his undying loyalty, Wyatt Earp, the legendary lawman whose cool-headedness and gritty dedication Holliday sought to emulate. The deadly dentist undoubtedly studied Earp's mannerisms when Earp faced dozens of bad men in the saloons and gambling halls of Ellsworth, Wichita, Dodge City, and especially, in Tombstone, Ariz., where both men, along with Earp's two stoic brothers, Virgil and Morgan, shot it out with the fierce Clanton-McLowery band in the historic gunfight at O.K. Corral.

Holliday's fearful reputation as a gunman was established more by rumor than reality. The actual record of his gunfights reveal a limited number of smoking pistol show-downs. The earliest verifiable gunfight in which Holliday participated was in Dallas, Texas, on Jan. l, 1875. He was gambling in a saloon owned by a man named Austin. An argument over a card hand caused Holliday and Austin to fire single bullets at each other. Neither was injured and both parties decided to settle their differences without further gunplay.

Saloons, dance halls, and bordellos formed the social world of Doc Holliday. An inveterate gambler, Holliday often served as the "in-house" cardsharp. Suckers were invited to try their luck with Holliday and he invariably won, sharing his winnings with the saloon owner who financed his play. Though a small man, Doc was wiry and strong, and he often doubled in a saloon as the resident gunman and bouncer so he not only fleeced patrons with alacrity and dexterity, but he quickly cowed their indignation at being euchred.

By 1879, Holliday was earning goodly sums as a part owner of a saloon in Las Vegas, N.M. His partner and financial backer was one-time lawman for Dodge City, John Joshua Webb. On July 19, 1879, Webb and Holliday were seated at a card table in the saloon when Mike Gordon, a bully boy and former army scout, began an argument at the bar, ordering one of the saloon women, who had been his mistress and who had lately rejected him, to quit her job and leave town with him. The woman rejected Gordon's offer and he stormed from the saloon, standing in the street and shouting obscenities at Holliday. Gordon then drew his gun and began firing bullets into the front of the building and this drew Holliday forth. Doc stepped outside and a bullet from Gordon's pistol whizzed past him. He drew his gun slowly, then fired a single shot which sent Gordon crashing into the dirt. The wound was fatal and Gordon died the following day, cursing Holliday with his last breath.

In June 1880, Holliday entered a Las Vegas saloon and quickly got into an argument with bartender Charley White, a man Doc had run out of Dodge City some months earlier. Both men pulled guns, and as usual, Holliday's aim was better. White collapsed behind the bar, Doc assuming he was dead. Holliday left him there and was surprised to learn the next day that White had survived, having received only a slight wound.

Much has been written about the strange friendship Holliday developed with Wyatt Earp. Earp presented the image of the incorruptible lawman but he was seen regularly with Holliday in the Kansas cow towns where he kept the peace. Holliday, on the other hand, was considered by most upstanding citizens as a decided lowlife. Stories abound with pithy details that describe how Earp saved Holliday from a lynch mob but the location is sketchy, or how the lawman actually financed Holliday's gambling operations, taking a sly share of the profits. That Holliday looked up to Earp there is no doubt; he openly admired Earp's nervy and decisive behavior with bad men. As their legends began to grow from cow town to cow town, Holliday was more than content to be known as Earp's "back-up" man, an unofficial peace officer who made it his responsibility to see that Earp was not shot in the back. Earp, in turn, paid oblique homage to little Doc, spreading the gunman's reputation with surly strangers who came to town so they would quickly realize that to face Earp with guns was also to face Holliday.

Doc Holliday was a man who truly had but one friend, Wyatt Earp. The gunman wanted it that way, seeking the company of only those who played cards with him or drank with him at the bar. He was closed-mouthed and mean-minded, quick to see an insult where none was intended and even quicker to prompt gunplay, which, as he knew, would seldom come to reality because of his terrible reputation, earned or not. Countless times, he would force an issue with a bar patron or a green cowboy so that he could have the pleasure of seeing his victim cringe and beg off. Night after night, Holliday would go through this tireless routine of challenge, taking grim pleasure in seeing the other man back away, a weak smile on his face that edged up the huge handlebar mustache adorning a heavy upper lip. In this regard, Holliday was typical of most western gunmen, thriving each night on such petty triumphs and feeding a dime novel vanity that insisted he go to bed victorious.

Only one woman was known to have won Holliday's guarded affections, an ungainly prostitute, Big-Nosed Kate

Fisher (real name Katherine Elder) who left Davenport, Iowa, as a young girl and traveled west to seek her fortune, landing in a Kansas bordello where Holliday allegedly met her. She was a large woman who stood inches above Doc and was loud, crass, and drunk most of the time. Yet, Holliday, for many years, was inexplicably drawn to her, showing her the kind of attention usually reserved for respectable ladies. One unsupported story had it that Holliday and Big-Nosed Kate were actually married in St. Louis in the late 1870s.

Big-Nosed Kate followed the little gambler around from town to town, and she was present in Tombstone in 1881 when Holliday backed the Earp brothers in their famous fight with the Clanton-McLowery group at O.K. Corral. Fisher and Holliday were a twosome in Tombstone until Spring 1881. The Wells Fargo Stage was held up by a band of outlaws and the driver, Bud Philpot, was shot and killed by the bandits, who were driven off by shotgun guard Bob Paul.

Holliday was accused of leading the bandits by his then-sworn enemies, the Clanton brothers whom Big-Nosed Kate had befriended after Doc had thrown her out of his rooms following a drunken argument. Fisher, seething with anger at Holliday, and undoubtedly nursing a severe hangover, made out a deposition that stated Holliday had bragged to her about holding up a stage. Holliday was politely asked by the local sheriff, John Behan, to answer the deposition. The gunman walked to the jail and flatly denied the charge, pointing out that the bandits failed to get the money in the stage's strongbox. "If I had pulled that job," Holliday told Behan, "I'd have gotten the eighty thousand!" With that, Holliday strolled out of the jail and back to the Oriental Saloon to resume his card game. He was never indicted, especially since his good friend Wyatt Earp was presently U.S. deputy marshal and exonerated Doc from all responsibility concerning the robbery, later bringing in his own suspects.

Holliday, however, was incensed by the accusation and he told Kate Fisher that she was never to speak to him again. When he heard that Mike Joyce, a Tombstone bar owner who had taken Fisher in, was also repeating her story about the stage robbery, Holliday rushed into Joyce's saloon. Both men drew weapons and Doc shot the pistol out of Joyce's hand, sending a bullet through the palm, a feat that enhanced Holliday's reputation as an expert marksman, which he was not; it was a lucky shot, Holliday quietly admitted later.

The gunman's real anger was aimed at the Clanton-McLowery clan for both stealing Kate Fisher and accusing him of the stage holdup. He sought out Ike Clanton on Oct. 26, 1881, and cursed him loudly in one of Tombstone's saloons. Clanton, by nature a cowardly creature who created arguments without the nerve to settle them with guns, pleaded to be spared and was later pistol-whipped in the street by Wyatt Earp. This caused the Clanton and McLowery brothers to send out a challenge to the Earps the next day to meet them in a showdown at the O.K. Corral.

With the Earps, walking toward the corral that day, was Holliday, Wyatt's ever-loyal friend. During that famous gun battle, Holliday produced a shotgun (some said from beneath his long coat) and shot Tom McLowery to death with it after having been slightly wounded in the side by Frank McLowery. Seeing Ike Clanton fleeing from scene, Holliday pulled out his pistol and fired after the catalyst of the battle, but Doc's shots failed to find their mark.

The feud raged on for another year, with Morgan Earp being murdered in Tombstone on Mar. 18, 1882. Holliday joined Wyatt Earp and others in a posse that went after one of Morgan Earp's killers, Frank Stilwell. They found the gunman in the Tucson train station on Oct. 20 and Stilwell, drawing his pistol, was killed by thirty bullets, some from the gun held in Holliday's hand. Another member of the murder band who had shot Morgan Earp from ambush, Florentino Cruz, was tracked down by Earp, Holliday, and others and killed outside of Tombstone on Mar. 22.

Tombstone was the last of the roaring cow towns where Holliday held court. When Wyatt Earp packed away his family and guns and headed for California, Holliday decided to stay behind in the West he knew, one of saloons, dirt streets, and gunplay. He was part of a dwindling society of gunmen who were compelled to ride into the backwater towns as law and order came to the West.

By the time Holliday arrived in Leadville in 1884 his health was failing; he had been forced to retreat several times to crude sanitoriums in the high mountains to fill his wheezing lungs with thin air. The tuberculosis afflicting him caused him to go into painful coughing fits that sometimes went on for days. Moreover, Holliday's luck ran out at the card tables. Broke, he began to borrow money and seldom repaid it. Bill Allen, a Leadville bartender, became irate at Holliday when the gunman was late in paying back five dollars.

Allen was not impressed with Holliday's reputation. As far as the bartender was concerned, Doc Holliday was a has-been. He nagged Doc about the $5 debt and bragged to his friends that if Holliday did not repay the loan soon he would "lick the tar out of him." When he next encountered Holliday, Allen demanded his money and insulted Holliday, but the gunman merely waved him away and walked into a saloon. Allen rushed after him, charging him at the bar, fists raised. Holliday stared for a moment, then drew his gun. Allen was a big man who outweighed Doc by seventy pounds and the gunman had no intention of fighting him. Holliday fired one shot into Allen's upraised arm which sent the bartender running outside where he was taken to a doctor. He survived and wrote off the debt, but Holliday was arrested and charged with attempted murder. He was tried but acquitted. This was Doc Holliday's last recorded gunfight.

In late 1887, Holliday was an emaciated wreck and went to his favorite health spa in Glenwood Springs, Colo., to "take another cure." But he found no cure and certainly no peace of mind. His nights were haunted by terrible dreams of blood and death and he kept next to his bed a fully loaded shotgun, a Bowie knife, and his nickel-plated six-gun, ready to battle the phantoms of his sleep. In his waking hours he gulped down great quantities of whiskey. On the morning of his death, Nov. 8, 1887, Doc Holliday asked a nurse to pour him one more drink and begged that his boots be put on his bare feet. By the time the boots were found in a closet, Holliday had coughed himself to death. See: **Earp, Wyatt Berry Stapp; O.K. Corral**.

Hollister, Cassius M. (AKA: **Cash**), 1845-84, U.S., lawman. Cash Hollister moved to Caldwell, Kan., from his native Cleveland as a thirty-one year old in 1877. Two years later, he was elected mayor after the sudden death of the incumbent. He exhibited a tempestuous temperament, frequently got involved in fights, and was fined for assaulting a man named Frank Hunt. In 1880, Hollister chose not to run for reelection, but three years later was appointed a deputy U.S. marshal. On Apr. 11, 1883, he became embroiled in a shootout near Hunnewell, Kan., while trying to arrest a family of horse thieves. One brother was killed and another wounded before the remaining Ross family members surrendered. On Nov. 21, 1883, Hollister and Ben Wheeler tried to arrest Chet Van Meter, who was accused of beating his family and threatening others. Van Meter fired at the lawmen as they approached, but was killed by five shots in the chest. A year later, on Nov. 20, 1884, Hollister attempted his final arrest. Bob Cross, the son of a minister, was accused of adultery after he abandoned his wife for the daughter of a local farmer. Hollister and three other lawmen went to the Cross farm in Hunnewell, Kan. Cross' wife and sister denied he was there, but as the posse searched the house, two shots fatally wounded Hollister.

Hoover, Tuck, d.1894, U.S., gunman. Tuck Hoover, was a rancher near Alleyton, in South Texas. In 1878, while with Dallas Stoudenmire and others, Hoover encountered another group of men led by two brothers named Sparks.

The two groups had a violent argument over the ownership of a herd of cattle, and in the ensuing gun battle the Hoover faction killed Benton Duke and his son and wounded one of the Sparks brothers. Around 1894, Hoover began arguing with a man named Burtshell, the owner of an Alleyton saloon. During the following gun battle, Hoover shot Burtshell to death. Hoover was arrested, but was released on bond only to lose his final gunfight in Alleyton to a young rowdy named Jim Coleman.

Horn, Tom (AKA: **James Hicks**), 1860-1903, U.S., lawman-outlaw. Tom Horn was a legendary western scout, Pinkerton detective, and range detective. When his luck ran out, he hired his gun to the highest bidder for murder and for this, he went to the gallows. Born in Memphis, Mo., on Nov. 21, 1860, Horn was raised on a farm. As a youth he liked the outdoors, but hated school and was often truant. His father, a strict disciplinarian, took the boy aside when he was fourteen and gave him such a severe whipping that Horn ran away from home, going west. He worked on the railroad, drove wagons for a freight company, and later became a stagecoach driver.

Horn was a scout for the army at age sixteen and was involved in many campaigns for more than a decade. In 1885, Horn replaced the celebrated Al Sieber as chief of scouts in the Southwest and he was involved in the historic Geronimo campaign in 1886. It was the intrepid Horn who, as chief of scouts, tracked Geronimo and his band to his hideout in the Sierra Gordo outside of Sonora, Mex. He rode into the Indian camp alone and negotiated Geronimo's surrender. Geronimo, with Horn guiding him and his tribe, crossed the border, officially surrendering, and ending the last great Indian war in America.

After quitting his post as chief of scouts, Horn wandered through the gold fields and then became a ranch hand. He proved himself to be a great cowboy, entering the rodeo at Globe, Ariz., in 1888 and winning the world's championship in steer roping. Horn joined the Pinkerton Detective Agency in 1890 and used his gun with lethal effectiveness. He worked out of the agency's Denver offices, chasing bank robbers and train thieves throughout Colorado and Wyoming. He was fearless (some said mad) and would face any outlaw or gunman. On one occasion, Horn rode into the outlaw hideout known as Hole-in-the-Wall and single-handedly captured the notorious Peg-Leg Watson (alias McCoy) who had recently robbed a mail train with others. Horn tracked Watson to a high mountain cabin and called out to him, telling the outlaw that he was coming for him.

Watson stepped from the cabin with two six-guns in his hands. He watched, open-mouthed, as Horn walked resolutely toward him across an open field, his Winchester carried limply at his side. Watson never fired a shot and Horn took him to jail without a struggle, bragging that Watson "didn't give me too much trouble." This feat was heralded across the West and Horn became a living legend. Still, working for the Pinkertons bothered Horn. He had reportedly killed seventeen men as an agent. Hunting down men very much like himself upset the lawman, however, and he quit, saying: "I have no stomach for it anymore." Yet Horn had

Tom Horn, calvary scout.

enough stomach to hire out as a gunman in 1892 to the Wyoming Cattle Growers' Association.

It was Horn's job to recruit gunmen for the association and he put together a formidable army which later attacked and slaughtered homesteaders in the bloody Johnson County War, although there is no indication that Horn participated in this one-sided battle. In 1894, Horn was working as a horse breaker for the Swan Land and Cattle Company. His real duties were to track down and kill rustlers and hector settlers homesteading on the range. He demanded and got $600 for each rustler he shot and killed. Horn proved to be a methodical manhunter and ruthless killer.

He would spend several days tracking a rustler, learning the man's habits and observing him as the rustler made camp each night. Finally, using a high-powered, long-distance Buffalo gun, Horn would lay a careful ambush and kill his man with a single, well-aimed bullet. Horn was no longer the stand-up gunman who faced his adversaries in a fair fight. He killed from hiding and he killed often. Rustlers, more than a dozen, were found shot to death on the range. Beneath each man's head was a large rock. This was Horn's trademark. "Killing men is my business," he announced one night in a saloon when questioned about his activities. Tom Horn's legend changed to that of a fearsome murderer, one who killed with the law behind him and one who apparently enjoyed taking lives. The residents of Cheyenne came to know and fear him as a blood-stained slayer.

When the Spanish-American War broke out in 1898, Horn left the West and joined the cavalry. He served with distinction in Cuba but saw little action, being in charge of Teddy Roosevelt's pack trains. Following the war, Horn returned to Wyoming and went to work for wealthy cattle baron, John Coble. He was once again a hunter of rustlers

and his tactics had changed little since he began this bloody business a decade earlier. Typical of Horn's ambush techniques was the manner in which he killed rustler Matt Rash. He tracked Rash to his cabin near Cold Springs Mountain in Routt County, Colo., pretending to be a prospector named James Hicks. Rash invited him to dinner and Horn joined him on the evening of July 8, 1900. Following the meal, Horn excused himself and went outside. He hid behind a tree, and as his host stepped outside, Horn pumped three bullets into him. Horn then rode to Denver to set up an alibi. Rash lived long enough to try to write the name of his killer with his own blood, but wrote the alias Horn had given him and Horn was therefore not immediately identified.

A black cowboy, Isom Dart, who, with a gang of five other black cowboys, had been rustling cows, was found at his Routt County hideout by Horn on Oct. 3, 1900. Horn hid behind a large rock and, after Dart and his companions had their breakfast and left their cabin to inspect the cattle pens that held their rustled cattle, Horn fired two shots from a .30-.30 rifle. Both bullets struck Dart's head, shattering his skull and killing him instantly. His five companions raced back to the cabin and cowered there while Horn mounted his horse and rode away.

Horn's last killing was his undoing. He had perfected the art of long-distance murder, using powerful weapons that could bring down a target at a

Horn at the time he turned killer in the 1890s.

distance of hundreds of yards. On the morning of July 18, 1901, on the Powder River Road near Cheyenne, Wyo., Horn lay in wait for rancher Kels P. Nickell, who had been marked for death by competing ranchers. He had only seen Nickell once from a distance, so Horn did not recognize Willie Nickell, the rancher's tall 14-year-old son, who appeared that morning, driving his father's wagon out of the ranch yard. Willie wore his father's coat and hat and when he got down from the wagon to open a gate, Horn fired a shot that struck the boy. Willie Nickell staggered to his feet and tried to get back to the wagon but Horn fired another shot, striking him in the back of the head and killing him.

Though this killing was immediately attributed to Horn because of its method, no real proof could link him to the murder. Joe Lefors, one of the great lawmen of the West, resolved to uncover the truth and bring Horn to justice. He rode to Denver and there got Horn drunk in a small saloon. While using a crude listening device, Lefors' deputies hid in a back room while Horn talked about the Nickell killing, describing it in such detail that his words amounted to a confession. Lefors arrested Horn for the killing and returned him to Cheyenne where he was later tried and condemned to death. The wealthy cattleman, Coble, along with Glendolene Kimmel, a schoolteacher whose father was also a cattle baron and who was Horn's sweetheart, attempted to obtain a commutation for Horn, but public resentment against the hired killer was so intense that none was forthcoming.

Tom Horn awaiting execution; he was hanged with the rope he is shown making.

Horn, realizing that he would soon face the hangman, broke out of the Cheyenne Jail with another prisoner, Jim McCloud. They leaped on Deputy Sheriff Richard Proctor, struggling for his gun in a hallway of the jail. Proctor squeezed off four shots, wounding McCloud, before he was overpowered. McCloud ran outside and leaped on the only available horse, riding wildly out of town. Horn fled on foot, followed by O.M. Eldrich, a citizen. Eldrich fired several shots at Horn, one of these grazing his head. As he struggled to work the jammed gun he had taken from Proctor, Eldrich and other residents charged up to Horn and knocked him to the ground. They began beating him with sticks and clubs until Proctor arrived and stopped them. Horn was restrained and returned to his cell, and McCloud was also recaptured and taken back to the Cheyenne Jail.

Horn resigned himself to his death, spending his last months writing his memoirs and weaving a rope that was later used to hang him. The hired killer mounted the gallows in Cheyenne on Nov. 20, 1903. His sweetheart, Kimmel, and his employer John Coble stood by as witnesses. Tom Horn looked down at them and then turned to the executioner, telling him to "hurry it up. I got nothing more to say." He was promptly hanged.

Horner, Joe, See: **Canton, Frank.**

Horrell-Higgins Feud, prom. 1870s, U.S., feud. The six Horrell brothers, Ben, John, Mart, Merritt, Sam, and Tom, returned from the Civil War to rustle cattle and cause mayhem in Texas and New Mexico in the 1870s. John Horrell became the first casualty when he was shot to death in Las Cruces, N.M., but the other five built a ranch near Lampasas, Texas, and with neighbor John Calhoun Pinckney Higgins participated in a joint cattle drive in 1872. But Higgins feuded with Tom Horrell, and began a five-year battle which became known as the Horrell-Higgins Feud.

On Mar. 19, 1873, members of the Texas State Police led by Captain Tom Williams tried to arrest Horrell ranch hand Clint Barkley at the Matador Saloon in Lampasas. During a shoot-out, Williams was killed and Mart and Tom Horrell were wounded. Mart was later arrested. A few days later, the remaining Horrells battered their way into a Georgetown, Texas, jail and freed their brother. They all traveled to Lincoln County, N.M. On Dec. 1, 1873, Ben Horrell got drunk and became embroiled in a gunfight in Lincoln. Ben was killed, as were his companions Jack Gylam and Dave Warner, as well as lawman Juan Martinez. Ben suffered a final indignity by losing a gold ring to a thief who chopped off his finger. The four remaining brothers avenged his death on Dec. 20 when they invaded a Mexican wedding party and killed four guests and wounded two. The Horrells returned to Lampasas and the feud with Higgins continued.

On Jan. 22, 1877, again in the Matador Saloon, Merritt Horrell was shot to death by Higgins after being accused of tampering with a herd. Two months later, on Mar. 26, Tom and Mart Horrell were ambushed by members of the Higgins gang as they were on their way to court in Lampasas. Tom was wounded, but both escaped. In June, the Horrells counter-attacked, killing a Higgins ranch hand and wounding another in an ambush at dawn. On June 14, the feud escalated into a three-hour public gunfight on the streets of Lampasas. Higgins lost Frank Mitchell, his brother-in-law, and Bill Wren before the townspeople convinced the two factions to take the feud elsewhere. The following month, Higgins and fourteen gunmen invaded the Horrell ranch and kept their rivals under siege. Two Horrell ranch hands were wounded during the two-day siege, which ended when the Higgins party ran short of ammunition. The Horrells retaliated again on July 25, 1877, when they ambushed Carson Graham, a Higgins employee. Mart, Sam, and Tom Horrell were all arrested by a Texas Ranger party led by Major John B. Jones. Exasperated, Jones brought both factions together and a peace treaty was signed. However, in 1878, after being suspected of robbing and murdering a Bosque County merchant, Mart and Tom Horrell were lynched in their jail cell as they awaited trial. Samuel Horrell, the last brother, left Texas in 1880 to live a peaceful life in New Mexico with his two daughters. See: **Higgins, John Calhoun Pinckney.**

Houston, Temple L., 1860-1905, U.S., crim. law. Temple Houston practiced law with a singular style during the late nineteenth century in the West. The son of Sam Houston, he was known as much for his appearance as for his oratory, with his shoulder-length hair, white sombrero, and rattlesnake ties. Houston often practiced outrageous methods of defense. Defending a gunman at trial, he drew and fired a gun loaded with blanks at a jury. As the jury scattered and mingled with spectators, Houston declared them no longer sequestered and after a second trial, won freedom

Criminal lawyer Temple Houston.

for his client. Houston once killed an opposing lawyer after a trial and successfully won his own acquittal by pleading self-defense. Adept with a pistol, Houston often led posses in search of fugitives, and once bested Bat Masterson in a shooting contest. This unique criminal lawyer died of a stroke at age forty-five while visiting Woodward, Okla.

Houston, Tom, d.1893, U.S., lawman. Tom Houston was a law officer in the Oklahoma Territory during the early 1890s. On Nov. 29, 1892, in Orlando, Okla., Houston, accompanied by Chris Madsen and Heck Thomas, tried to apprehend bank robber Ol Yantis. They cornered him at his sister's farm, and after a brief exchange, Houston killed him. On Sept. 1, 1893, Houston and a large posse traveled to Ingalls, Okla., in search of the Doolin Gang. After a ferocious gun battle, the gang escaped, with the exception of Arkansas Tom Jones. Before he was arrested, Jones killed three lawmen, Dick Speed, Lafe Shadley, and Houston.

Hoyt, George, See: **Earp, Wyatt Berry Stapp.**

Hughes, John Reynolds (AKA: **Border Boss**), 1857-1946, U.S., lawman. John Hughes was born in Illinois, but moved to Texas at age fourteen. A year later he was shot in the right arm during a battle with Choctaw Indians. Hughes ranched until 1886, when he sold out, unable to fight the cattle rustlers. He had recently killed four rustlers and wounded another two after trailing them for a week through northwestern Texas. In July 1887, Hughes and Texas Ranger Ira Aten trailed Judd Roberts, an escaped murderer, to the Texas Panhandle. Six shots killed Roberts as he tried to escape the lawmen.

Texas Ranger John R. Hughes.

Hughes became a Texas Ranger the following month, and by 1889, attained the rank of corporal and had made a reputation for his border patrol along the Rio Grande. Later that year, Hughes was doing undercover work in a Shafter, Texas, silver mine after some of the ore was reported missing. Hughes discovered that a crooked foreman placed the silver on burro trains bound for the Mexican border. Setting a trap at the mine entrance with rangers Lon Oden and Ernest St. Leon, Hughes fought an hour-long gun battle. The Rangers finally killed three of the thieves and apprehended and arrested the foreman. On Christmas Day, near Vance, Texas, Hughes and a ranger posse killed Will and Alvin Odle, two brothers who were violently resisting arrest for cattle rustling.

In 1893, while arresting Desidario Duran in the San Antonio Colony, the rangers killed Florencio Carrasco, who was trying to free his friend. In March 1896, Hughes and his rangers arrested notorious bandit Miguel de la Torre when they surprised him on a street in Bajitas, Texas, and tied him on an extra horse. Later that year, on Sept. 28, Hughes and his men trailed three cattle rustlers to Nogalitos Pass. The fugitives fired at the posse, and during the ensuing gunfight the lawmen killed two of them, brothers Art and Jubel Friar, while Ease Bixler, the third man, escaped. Hughes retired from the Rangers in 1915, and committed suicide in 1946 at age eighty-nine.

Human Wildcat, The, See: **Soto, Juan.**

Hunt, J. Frank, d.1880, U.S., lawman. In 1880, J.

Frank Hunt was the deputy marshal of Caldwell, Kan., a frontier boomtown. On June 19, 1880, George Flatt, a drunken former lawman was shot to death as he neared a Caldwell restaurant. A man identified as Hunt was seen fleeing the murder scene. Flatt's death was avenged on Oct. 11, 1880, when an unidentified gunman fatally wounded Hunt as he sat near a window at the Red Light saloon and dance hall.

I

Indian Territory, 1834-96, U.S., crime district. The Indian Territory, also called The Cherokee Strip for the Indians that occupied it, was a strip of land in what is now Oklahoma, an area which remained without statehood for sixty-two years. With the town of Ingalls at its hub, this region was also referred to as Bad Man's Territory because it was a known sanctuary for many notorious outlaws who mistakenly believed that no U.S. law enforcement officer had jurisdiction there. As a territory, the Indian Territory fell under the jurisdiction of the Western District of Arkansas at Fort Smith, where Federal Judge Isaac Parker presided. Parker, known as the "Hanging Judge," supervised a small army of U.S marshals who made regular sweeps each month through the rough terrain of the Indian Territory in search of wanted desperadoes.

Prior to the Civil War, the Territory was indeed utterly lawless. Because no court existed in the Territory no extradition could be legally made from it to an existing state

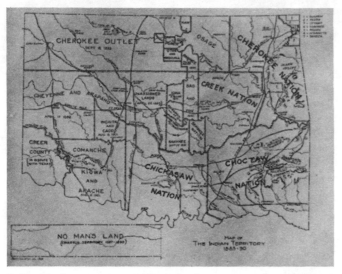

Indian Territory encompassed land that is now presentday Oklahoma. It was home to the "Five Civilized Tribes" and the Plains Indians.

where a fugitive was wanted on felony charges. From about 1870 to 1896, when it became part of the Oklahoma Territory, even the U.S. marshals were cautious when riding through the Indian Territory and seldom rode into Ingalls to confront the outlaws who gathered there. On Sept. 1, 1893, however, this did actually happen; Bill Doolin's gang was trapped by a small army of lawmen, resulting in a wild gun battle in which several men died.

The Indian Territory was, for the most part, inhabited by prostitutes, cattle and horse thieves, whiskey peddlers, escaped convicts, and many outlaw gangs. The more notorious outlaws who rode in and out of the Indian Territory included the Dalton Brothers, the Doolin Gang, Belle Starr, Jim Reed, Ned Christie, the Buck Gang,

Crawford Goldsby (better known as Cherokee Bill), Jim French, the Cook Gang, and the last of the old-time outlaws, Henry Starr and Al Spencer. By the time Oklahoma became a state in 1907, the Indian Territory and the hordes of outlaws that had once called it home had long disappeared. See: **Buck Gang; Christie, Ned; Cook, William Tuttle; Dalton Brothers; Doolin, William M.; French, Jim; Goldsby, Crawford; Parker, Judge Isaac; Spencer, Al; Starr, Belle; Starr, Henry.**

Ishtanubbee, Gibson, and **Seely, Isham**, d.1876, outlaws. On May 10, 1873, a pair of itinerant drifters, Isham Seely and Gibson Ishtanubbee, knocked on the door of "Squirrel" Funny, a white farmer who lived with his black housekeeper and cook in a small cabin near Stonewall (Miss.) in the Chickasaw Nation. The two men asked if they might be allowed to spend the night before continuing their travels the next morning. The farmer agreed to their request and showed them where they could bunk down for the evening. Just before dawn the following morning, Istanubbee grabbed an ax from the yard and drove it into Funny's skull as he slept; Seely beat the housekeeper to death with a pistol, and the two looted the house. The gunmen buried a dress belonging to the woman in a hollowed-out log. They sold a pair of boots that had belonged to the farmer before attempting to flee from the Chickasaw Nation. Seely and Ishtanubbee did not get far before they were arrested and taken to Fort Smith for trial. They were tried and convicted by Judge Isaac Parker who sentenced them to death on the gallows, Apr. 21, 1876. Before Seely was dropped to eternity he let loose with a fearful war whoop: "Chicak-a-mah!"

Ivers, Alice (AKA: **Poker Alice**), 1851-1930, U.S., gambler. Born in Sudbury, Devonshire, England, on Feb. 17, 1851, Alice Ivers immigrated with her family to the U.S., settling in Virginia first, then moving to Fort Mead, Colo., where her father was a school teacher. She married a mining engineer, who introduced her to the fast world of the gamblers and their known haunts. Ivers greatly admired the card sharps and high-hatted gamblers that traveled the cow towns and soon she learned their card-playing wiles. While in her teens, Ivers went to Deadwood, S.D., where she became a dealer, specializing in poker and soon earning the sobriquet "Poker Alice." After her husband died, she devoted the rest of her life to gambling; traveling through

Arizona, Oklahoma, Kansas, South Dakota, Texas, and New Mexico, or wherever the stakes were high and the whiskey smooth. She smoked thick, black cigars, and during the 1870s and 1880s, became a well-known and successful gambler in all the famous cow towns, from Deadwood to Tombstone, Ariz. In her heyday, she would spend $6,000 in the fancy New York-run shopping stores buying the finest garments, but later, in old age, Ivers took to wearing army-surplus clothes.

Poker Alice would not tolerate a cheat and was never challenged by other gamblers. She was known to carry several guns, one in her purse and one in a pocket of her dress. On occasion, she would practice her marksmanship by shooting knobs off the frames of pictures hanging in bars to warn gambler gunmen that she was capable of defending herself. Wild Bill Hickok reportedly asked Poker Alice to sit in with him and others during a game of poker in Saloon No. 10 in Deadwood on the day he was shot by Jack McCall; she declined, saying that she had already agreed to play with another group down the street in Mann's Saloon.

Poker Alice Ivers, lady gambler.

When hearing that Wild Bill had been shot in the back, Ivers rushed to Saloon No. 10 and saw Hickok sprawled dead on the floor and McCall fleeing out the back door. "Poor Wild Bill," she said of Hickok, peering down at his corpse, "he was sitting where I would have been if I had played with him." She later claimed that she had refused to play with Wild Bill on that fateful day because she "had a queer feeling that all would not be right that day."

Alice Ivers later married Frank Tubbs, a gambler who did not possess half her playing talents and one who took to drink early in their marriage. Poker Alice was forever getting her husband out of trouble. Tubbs was knifed one night by a disgruntled player, and Poker Alice stormed into the bar and shot the man in the stomach, wounding him from a distance of thirty feet. She and Tubbs moved on to Silver City, Nev., where she broke the bank in the biggest saloon, winning an estimated $150,000. She and Tubbs then bought a huge Colorado ranch which Poker Alice later lost. Following her husband's death, Poker Alice moved to Rapid City, S.D., where she ran a small poker club. She died there, a grand old lady of western lore, on Feb. 27,

1930. See: **Hickok, James Butler.**

J

Jackson, Charles W., prom. 1840, U.S., gunman. A shooting war between two rival factions began in Shelby County, Texas, on a warm autumn day in 1840, when Charles Jackson shot Joseph Goodbread through the chest. Jackson had taken exception to Goodbread's duplicity in a business deal that had gone awry. His decision to terminate the life of Goodbread sparked a four-year war between the self-proclaimed "Moderators" and "Regulators" that eventually spread to five adjacent counties in Texas. By the time it was over, at least fifty people had been killed in the feud and acres of land had been laid to waste.

District court judge John Hansford, was assigned the disagreeable task of trying the politically connected Jackson for murder. When he arrived in the town of Pulaski to open the session, he was greeted by 150 armed men. Twenty of them, including the sheriff and the defendant Jackson—who was also armed—followed Hansford into the courthouse. Hansford ordered the sheriff to pay a fine for allowing a defendant in a murder case to carry a weapon into court. Judge Hansford did not comprehend the natural order of things in Shelby County—Jackson had committed the murder on the sheriff's *behalf*. A jury was selected, but as the day wore on, Hansford became more uneasy.

The following morning the judge departed town, leaving a note of explanation with the sheriff. "Being unwilling to risk my person in the courthouse any longer where I see myself surrounded by bravos and hired assassins, and no longer left free to preside as an impartial judge at this special term of court called for the trial of Charles W. Jackson, I order you to adjourn the court at 8:00 by proclamation without delay." Jackson was given a mock trial by his friends, found Not Guilty on the grounds of self-defense, and was released. The bullet-riddled remains of Judge Hansford were found a few days later several miles outside of Pulaski. See: **Regulator War.**

Jackson, Frank (AKA: **Blockey**), b.1856, U.S., outlaw. Born in Texas in 1856, Frank Jackson was trained to be a tinsmith after being orphaned as a youth. His interest in his trade quickly waned, and by the time he turned twenty he was working as a cowboy in Denton, Texas, on the Murphy ranch, notorious for harboring the outlaw Sam Bass. Jackson started his life as an outlaw by murdering Henry Goodall, a black man accused of stealing horses. The two fought over a stolen horse, and settled when Goodall gave Jackson a mount. They rode off together, but as they stopped to water the horses, Jackson shot Goodall and cut his throat.

Jackson next joined Bass for a two-year career of robbing trains and banks. On Apr. 10, 1878, the gang lost a number of members during a retreat from an aborted train robbery in Mesquite, Texas. Two months later, on June 13, the gang narrowly escaped an ambush near Salt Creek, Texas, losing only Arkansas Johnson. By July the gang had dwindled to four. In Round Rock, Texas, on July 19, 1878, the gang was surprised by lawmen who had been tipped off by Jim Murphy, a remaining gang member. In a store next to the bank, the gang killed Deputy Ellis Grimes and wounded his assistant, Morris Moore. As they left the store, outlaw Seaborn Barnes was shot to death and Bass was critically wounded. Bass escaped with Jackson's help, but was found bleeding to death the following day. He died without revealing Jackson's destination, and the final member of the Bass gang was never found. If, in his final moments, Bass revealed the location of the loot he acquired over a lifetime of crime, Jackson may have retired as a prosperous man. See: **Bass, Sam.**

James, Calvin, d.1886, U.S., outlaw. Calvin James commanded a gang of three liquor runners who operated with impunity in the Chickasaw Nation. James and his confederates, Henry Robey, Albert Kemp, and Tony Love, were passing through Texas on Aug. 1, 1885. The four rumrunners were drunk and ready for action after purchasing four gallons of whiskey apiece. Without warning James suddenly turned on Love and shot him in the head to gain control of the man's whiskey. Kemp and Robey were riding on ahead and did not witness the shooting.

James attempted to cover the crime by hiding the body in the brush off the road. The dead man's horse was then turned loose. Calvin James threatened the other two members of the gang with death if they were to ever breathe a word of the crime to anyone. The authorities eventually arrested all three for murder, but in order to save their lives, Robey and Kemp testified against James in return for leniency. Calvin James was found Guilty and was hanged at Fort Smith on July 23, 1886.

James, Jesse Woodson (AKA: **Dingus; Thomas Howard**), 1847-82, U.S., outlaw. Born on his father's farm near Kearney, Clay County, Mo., on Sept. 5, 1847, Jesse Woodson James would become America's most famous bandit, rivaling in lore and legend that of England's Robin Hood. Millions of words would be written about this handsome, dashing, and utterly ruthless bank and train robber. To many of his peers, he appeared a folklore hero who took vengeance in their name upon an industrial society that was grinding the old agrarian lifestyle to ashes. To others, he and his band represented the last vestiges of the Old South and its lost cause of secession.

A good deal of truth was in the tale that Jesse James the bandit was created by oppressive troops of the Union Army, and worse, operatives working for the then widely disliked Pinkerton Detective Agency. Detectives of this agency killed innocent members of the James family and thus unified the rural communities of Missouri in protecting and nurturing this greatest of outlaws. Beyond the myriad propaganda and countless myths about this western legend, lived a farm boy who became a professional thief and a cold-blooded killer. He was at large for sixteen years. He committed dozens of daring robberies and killed at least a half dozen or more men. He died at the age of thirty-four.

Jesse James was raised with little formal education. His father, Robert James, was a Baptist preacher and his mother, Zerelda Cole Mimms, was a hard-working, strong-willed farm woman. Jesse's older brother, Frank (Alexander Franklin James, 1843-1915), a taciturn, withdrawn, and Bible-reading youth, later followed his younger, more aggressive brother into banditry. It was because of the notorious and celebrated exploits of the James Brothers, the Younger Brothers who rode with them, and the Dalton Brothers who came later, the state of Missouri, their home state, became known as "The Mother of Bandits." The James and Younger boys were products of what was then known as the Middle Border, the wild and still unsettled states of Missouri and Kansas.

The parents of the James boys were hardy pioneers. Robert James married Zerelda Cole Mimms when she was seventeen. The couple moved from Kentucky to western Missouri where James became the pastor of a small Baptist Church outside of Kearney, Mo. He and his wife, with the help of neighbors, built a log cabin in the wilderness and began to carve out a farm. On Jan. 10, 1843, the couple's first child, Alexander Franklin James, was born. Jesse was born four and a half years later. Robert James, though a cleric, was consumed by the gold fever, and in 1850, when Jesse was only three, left his family and went to California to seek his fortune, telling his wife that he would send for her as soon as he struck it rich. He slaved in the gold fields and found nothing but an early death from pneumonia.

A short time later, Zerelda James married a man named Simms, but their marriage dissolved within a few months. She was a woman of strong opinions who fiercely guarded her sons from criticism, one of the contributing factors in the breakup of her second marriage. In 1855, she married a third time, to Dr. Reuben Samuels. The physician was well-to-do, docile, and allowed his wife to make important family decisions. When it came to the boys, Mrs. Samuels made all the decisions. A third child, Archie Samuels, was born. He was retarded and was kept close to home, his older brothers doting upon him.

The James brothers stayed on the farm begun by their father, and through Dr. Samuels' acquisition of adjoining property, the James holdings grew. The family bought some slaves to work the land, and Frank and Jesse also farmed through their teenage years. When the Civil War broke out, the James brothers sided with the Confederacy. First Frank, then Jesse, rode off to fight with Confederate guerrillas under the command of William Clarke Quantrill. They later fought with William "Bloody Bill" Anderson and were part of the guerilla band that attacked and sacked Lawrence, Kan. In 1863, Union soldiers swooped down on the James farm, looting the place, setting fires to crops, and driving the slaves off the property. When the teenage Jesse attempted to stop the soldiers, he was beaten almost to death.

When he recovered, 17-year-old Jesse rode off to join his brother Frank and Cole Younger, who were fighting Union troops and raiding Union towns with Quantrill. Jesse was by then an expert horseman and crack shot with pistols and rifles. He was part of Anderson's contingent when it raided and burned Centralia, Kan., in 1864, helping to shoot down seventy-five Union prisoners in what later became known as the Centralia Massacre. A large Union force pursued Anderson's detachment, but the Confederates turned about and ferociously attacked the Union troops, routing them and slaying dozens. Jesse James was seen riding pell-mell into the Union ranks, the reins of his horse held by his teeth, firing two pistols. He shot down six northern soldiers and was credited with killing three of them.

That night, Jesse James sat at a campfire, taking no part in the discussion about the day's battle. He spent his time cleaning his pistol. Suddenly, the gun's hair trigger went back and a bullet took off the tip of James' left middle finger. He stared momentarily at the bloody finger, then said as he wrapped a kerchief about it: "Well, if that ain't the dingus-dangest thing!" His fellow guerrillas laughed with him and nicknamed him "Dingus" James. The James boys grew to such prominence that the Samuels were singled out for persecution by Union troops, who raided the farm and compelled the Samuels family to move to Nebraska. Following the end of the war, the James brothers returned to a ruined and vacant farm. As guerrillas that were not part of regular Confederate armed forces, they were still considered outlaws and rewards were posted for them dead or alive.

In early 1865, when a general amnesty was offered guerrillas, Jesse James led a small band toward Lexington, Mo., intending to surrender. The group included his brother, Frank James, and Cole Younger. A company of Union troops ignored the amnesty, and waiting in ambush, opened fire on the Confederate guerrillas. Jesse, in the lead, was shot off his horse, a bullet puncturing his lung. As the guerrillas fled, Jesse crawled to nearby underbrush. Two Union soldiers pursued him, but he shot and killed one of their horses and they thought better of trying to capture Jesse, who escaped. He was found by a friendly farmer the next day in a creek bed, trying to tend to his severe gunshot wound. The farmer bandaged Jesse's wound and then helped him travel to Nebraska, where his mother and stepfather nursed him back to health.

Jesse, believing he would not recover, begged his mother to take him back to Missouri, saying: "I don't want to die in a northern state." She and her husband put him in a wagon and rode slowly to Harlem, Mo., taking Jesse to a boarding house owned by Mrs. Samuels' brother, John Mimms. There, Jesse met young Zerelda Mimms, his cousin, who had been named after his mother. She nursed him back to health and the two fell in love. Zee, as she was called, was too young to marry, but the two promised to wed in the future. Nine years later they took their vows. When Jesse was almost well, his mother and stepfather took him back to the family farm near Kearney. He worked sporadically with Frank in the fields, although he had relapses with his wounded lung and was often bedridden. Both he and Frank, when in the fields, wore guns on their hips, and kept saddled horses nearby in the event Union troops acting as occupying forces in Missouri after the war swooped down to arrest or even shoot them, such was the bitterness that survived the war.

The war had changed much in the national character of the U.S. and it had also changed the perspective of the farm boys who fought in it. The James boys had tasted battle and blood, adventure, and danger. They had survived the worst carnage ever seen in the country, and either out of boredom or an ambition that went beyond the dull chores of their farm, they, like many others in that turbulent era, buckled gun belts, mounted horses, and rode into small towns to rob banks. The rationale the raiders later said was "we were driven to it." They blamed Yankee bankers and railroad magnates for impossible farm mortgages and threatening foreclosure in underhanded land-grabbing schemes. And to some small degree it was true.

The first bank robbery attributed to the James Brothers occurred on Feb. 13, 1866. Ten men rode into Liberty, Mo. While eight waited outside with the horses, two went into the Clay County Savings Bank. One of these men was later identified as Frank James. The other was Cole Younger, the oldest and most daring of the Younger Brothers (this included three out of thirteen children who later took up robbery, Coleman, James, and Robert).

One of the robbers, allegedly Frank James, approached father and son cashiers Greenup and William Bird, and said: "If you make any noise, you will be shot." He then demanded all the money behind the teller's cage and in the vault be stuffed into a wheat sack. Both men held pistols aimed at the Birds. The robbers emerged from the bank without incident a few minutes later. Inside the wheat sack was more than $60,000 ($15,000 in gold and $45,000 in non-negotiable securities).

The men outside joined the two coming from the bank and the ten rode slowly out of town. Then George "Jolly" Wymore, en route to classes at William Jewell College, paused in the town square and stared at one of the riders as if he knew him. The rider slowed his horse, rode a few feet away from Wymore, then wheeled in his saddle, drawing his pistol and firing three shots into the startled Wymore, who collapsed and died on the spot. Apparently, the rider realized that Wymore had recognized him. As Wymore fell, the entire gang drew weapons and began firing wildly into the air as they spurred their horses down the street and out of town. A posse was quickly formed, but it lost the bandits, who had crossed the Missouri River on a ferry and disappeared in a raging snowstorm.

The Liberty raid was the first daylight bank robbery in the U.S. by an organized band of robbers. (The first U.S. bank robbery was committed by lone postal employee Edward W. Green, who held up a bank in Malden, Mass., on Dec. 15, 1863.) Whether or not Jesse James was present at the Liberty bank robbery was debated by several western historians. Some claimed he was at home nursing his old lung wound. Others insist that Jesse was outside the bank with the other riders, waiting for his brother Frank and Cole Younger to emerge. However, Jesse James was certainly a member of the same gang that robbed the Alexander Mitchell Bank in Lexington, Mo., on Oct. 30, 1866.

A tall young man who stood a little under six feet entered the bank while another young man stood outside the front entrance. The first young man went to a teller's cage and held out a $50 bill to cashier J.L. Thomas. "Can you change this for me?" he asked. "No," the suspicious Thomas said, remembering the Liberty bank had just been robbed and that a man first asked to change a large bill.

The young man then drew a gun and leveled it at Thomas. Three other men entered the bank and also drew guns, training these on the bank employees. The tall young man said: "You've got one $100,000 in this bank. Unless you turn it over to me, you'll be killed."

"That's not true," Thomas said, denying the bank had that much money.

The original James-Samuel cabin in Clay County, Mo.   Jesse, left, and Frank James in their twenties.

Zerelda James Samuels   Jesse James as a teenager.   Frank James at twenty.

Jesse when he rode with Bill Anderson.   Frank James during the Civil War.   Frank James, 1867.

"Let's have the key to the vault," the tall young man demanded.

"I don't have it," Thomas told him.

The bandits went through Thomas' pockets and found nothing. They then stuffed $2,011 into a wheat sack and left cursing. Actually, the vault held considerably more cash. The tall young man was identified as Jesse James and this was the first time the bandit was linked to robbery.

On Mar. 2, 1867, the James-Younger gang rode into Savanna, Mo., and went into the local bank. They aimed guns at bank president, Judge John McClain, who refused to turn over the vault keys. One bandit stepped forward and shot McClain in the chest. The bandits ran from the bank and rode quickly from the town. McClain survived. On May 22, 1867, it was a different story. The James-Younger gang decided to adopt guerrilla tactics when raiding the Hughes and Wasson Bank of Richmond, Mo. They rode into town shooting their weapons and whooping like drunken cowboys. Pedestrians ran in all directions while six men—Jesse and Frank James, Cole, Jim, and Bob Younger, and James White—broke down the locked front door of the bank. The bandits stuffed $4,000 into a wheat sack and then raced to the street.

Citizens grabbed their guns and began firing on the bandits as they mounted their horses and attempted to flee. Mayor John B. Shaw tried to rally residents as he ran to the bank with a pistol in his hand. The bandits fired many shots at him and Shaw fell to the street dead, seven bullets in him. Impetuously, the bandits decided to attack the jail instead of fleeing, having heard that several ex-guerrillas were being held there. They tried to batter down the jail's front door. Frank Griffin, the 15-year-old son of the jailer, ran behind a tree with a rifle and began shooting at the bandits. They rode past him and riddled his body, killing him. His father, B.G. Griffin, then raced forward, but a bandit caught him and fired a bullet into his head, leaving him dead beside his son.

The gang then rode quickly out of town, but a large posse caught up with them at sundown. A pitched battle ensued and the bandits escaped under the cover of darkness. Several were tracked down. The first was Payne Jones. A young girl guided a posse to the Jones farm and Jones came running out of his farmhouse with two guns blazing. He shot down the girl and killed a posse member. Jones was captured but later killed in a gun battle. Next, Richard Burns was tracked to his farmhouse near Richmond. Vigilantes took him to a large tree, and with torches flickering, quickly tried and convicted him of the Richmond robbery and murders. He was then hanged. Andy Maguire and Tom Little, identified as Richmond raiders; were apprehended and lynched.

The James brothers were also identified and several vigilante groups assembled. Before the vigilantes rode to the James farm, "alibi cards" were sent to the vigilante leaders. The cards bore signed statements from Frank and Jesse James saying they had no part in the Richmond bank raid, and incredibly, their word was accepted. If the James brothers said they were innocent, then that was the end of the matter, such was their reputation in western Missouri. Nowhere in Clay or Ray counties would a Missourian betray these men. Anyone who continued to insist that they had robbed the bank risked being shot and killed while traveling lonely roads. Merchants who labeled the boys thieves and murderers risked boycotts and being put out of business. This fierce loyalty to the ex-guerrillas lasted until the day Jesse Woodson James was executed by two traitorous men.

The James-Younger gang continued robbing banks despite the threat of Union soldiers, lawmen, and vigilantes. There were always farmers, men who had fought in the Civil War on the southern side, who were willing to ride with them on a raid or two to get enough money to pay off a mortgage or support a family. The James and Younger brothers were the professionals and kept most of the loot. After Richmond they were careful to select banks some distance from their homes and made only a few raids each year, then returning to their farms to resume peaceful, law-abiding ways. In these early years they robbed with leisure, but later they became desperate, infamous and much-wanted. So they sought the "big strike," a robbery that would yield enough to allow them to permanently retire in California or Mexico or even South America.

Jesse and Frank James and Cole and Jim Younger, along with four other men, rode far afield on Mar. 21, 1868, arriving in Russellville, Ky. Actually, Frank James had been in the area for some days, scouting the Southern Bank of Kentucky. He had used the alias Frank Colburn, pretending to be a cattle buyer from Louisville. He entered the bank and approached the managers, Nimrod Long and George Norton. He asked Long to cash a $100 bill, but Long became suspicious. Frank James pointed to a tall, blue-eyed man standing in the door of the bank. "I've got to pay off one of my hired hands," he said.

Long looked over the bill carefully and then said: "This bill is counterfeit, Mr. Colburn."

Frank James laughed, took the bill back and tucked it into his vest pocket, saying: "I reckon it is." He then drew his pistol and aimed it at Long. "But this isn't, Mr. Long. Open the vault."

The young man in the doorway was also holding a pistol and aiming it at him. Long turned and then dashed for the rear door of the bank, but Jesse fired a single shot that grazed the banker's scalp and sent him unconscious to the floor. Then Jesse ran to him and hit Long on the head repeatedly with his gun butt. Long, a burly man, rolled over and grabbed the bandit's hands. Frank James stood next to the struggling men, shouting for Jesse to "finish him!" He aimed his pistol at the banker but could not fire for fear of hitting his brother.

Suddenly, Long found enough strength to throw off Jesse and jump up. He ran to the door and outside into an alley. Jesse and Frank fired at him, but the two bullets merely struck the door frame. Once outside, Long raced down the alley, yelling: "They're robbing my bank! They're robbing my bank!" Citizens misunderstood Long's message and thought his bank was on fire. Several raced about the streets grabbing water buckets. Meanwhile, Frank and Jesse James dragged two sacks full of gold from the bank, about $14,000, and put the heavy sacks on the saddles of the gang's horses. An old man, half blind, wandered into the middle of the street. Cole Younger rode up to him, saying: "Old man, we're having a little serenade here, and there's danger of you getting hurt. Just get behind my horse here and you'll be out of the way." Younger moved his horse gently next to the old man so that he edged him out of the road. The bandits then formed a single line and raced out of the town hollering and firing their weapons as if in a cavalry charge. A fifty-man posse gave pursuit but lost the experienced riders in the wilderness.

The Pinkerton Detective Agency was hired by an association of bankers and began its long crusade to capture the James-Younger band. Their detectives interviewed George Hite, a neighbor of the James Brothers, but he insisted he knew nothing of the Russellville raid and that the James Brothers were innocent. He was lying. His own sons often rode with Jesse and Frank James and it was George Hite, upon Jesse's assassination, who explained how the gang met in barns and in kitchens of farmhouses to plan their robberies. They would scout a town and determine whether or not the local bank held a substantial amount of cash. They might send someone from the gang to make deposits, who, as a depositor, would ask questions about security and whether or not the bank was solvent and thus learn from the bankers the amount of money usually kept on hand.

In these days, the gang operated democratically, its members selecting a target bank and then voting whether to rob it. Jesse James was not then the leader of the gang, although he was considered by its members as the most daring and the one most likely to kill anyone who interfered in a robbery. Not until the gang's disastrous raid on Northfield, Minn., in 1876 did Jesse become the overall leader, and by then his authority rested upon his widespread reputation which he enjoyed and used to advance his own image among his fellow outlaws. He was also by then a deadly killer, who even threatened to shoot his own brother Frank for disagreeing with him.

Frank James was almost as much an enigma as his younger brother Jesse. Well-read, Frank liked to quote the Bible and Shakespeare, but his fellow bandits thought him sanctimonious, hypocritical, and overly cautious to the point of annoyance. He vexed the impetuous Younger brothers, especially the good-natured Cole Younger. But Frank James was no mere toady to Jesse. He was resolute and a deadly marksman, as feared a gunman as his younger brother. It was Cole Younger, however, who was the most experienced horseman and gunman, and it was Cole who lent balance and authority to the gang. Jesse and Frank James showed their murderous natures on Dec. 7, 1869, when they rode into Gallatin, Mo., going into the Davies County Savings Bank.

Frank James offered a $100 bill to cashier John W. Sheets, asking him to change it. Sheets began walking to his desk. Sheets had been a Union officer during the Civil War and the brothers apparently held a deep hatred for him. It was later claimed that it had been Sheets who had commanded the Union troops who had fired on Jesse and wounded him when he had attempted to surrender in 1865. Jesse James, without warning, suddenly shot and killed Sheets as he stood next to his desk. Jesse fired twice, hitting Sheets in the head and chest. Frank James then ran behind the counter and gathered up about $500, which he threw into a wheat sack. William McDowell, a clerk, ran toward the front entrance of the bank and Frank shot him in the arm. The wounded clerk staggered to the street and shouted an alarm. The bandit brothers raced to their horses. Frank mounted, but Jesse's foot caught in the stirrup of his expensive horse and the animal bolted, dragging the outlaw almost forty feet down the middle of the street. Frank turned back, stopped Jesse's horse, allowing the younger James to jump on Frank's horse. They rode from town with bullets smacking at their single horse's hooves. They later stole another horse and finished their escape.

The horse the bandits left behind was identified as having belonged to Jesse James, but he reported that his horse had been stolen just before the Gallatin robbery. Jesse had earlier established another identity for himself after robbing the Gallatin bank. As he and Frank left town, they stopped a Methodist minister named Helm, and Jesse told the pastor that he was "Bill Anderson's brother. I just killed S.P. Cox who works back there in the bank at Gallatin. He killed my brother in the war and I got him at last!" Jesse had purposely lied about himself and his victim, wrongly identifying Sheets, to cover his murder. But this ruse did not work. A large posse headed for the James farm on Dec. 15, 1869, and when they arrived, Jesse and Frank James, mounted two fast horses and raced from the barn. The posse pursued them, with Deputy Sheriff John Thomason in the lead. Thomason dismounted and trained his rifle on the two fleeing James boys, but his horse bolted and spoiled his shot. Thomason's horse then caught up with the James brothers and Jesse shot the animal dead. The boys escaped.

Somehow, the James boys managed to convince local authorities that they were not the bandits responsible for the bloody Gallatin holdup, even though most citizens were certain they were. For almost two years, the James gang remained inactive. Then, on June 3, 1871, Jesse and Frank James, Cole, Jim and Bob Younger, Jim Cummins, Charlie Pitts (alias Samuel Wells), and Ed Miller took a leisurely ride to the sleepy little hamlet of Corydon, Iowa. Jesse and Frank James and Cole Younger entered the Ocobock Brothers Bank and found only one clerk behind the counter. The other bandits waited outside the bank and noticed the streets were empty. Frank asked the clerk where everyone had gone and the clerk explained that Henry Clay Dean, a celebrated Methodist preacher, was giving a lecture at the local church, and the entire town had turned out to hear him.

"All the better," Jesse said, drawing his pistol and aiming it at the clerk. Within a few minutes the bandits had cleaned out the bank, taking with them more than $45,000 in gold and bills. The bandits rode slowly out of town, but when they came to the church where the townspeople had gathered, Jesse smiled and told his men to wait. He got off his horse and went into the church, standing in the middle of the aisle at the back of the church, where he loudly announced: "Folks, you should know that some riders were just down to the bank and tied up the cashier. All the drawers are cleaned out. You folks best get down there in a hurry!" He then began to laugh loudly and, while the congregation stared in awe at the tall young man with piercing blue eyes, he turned and walked back to his horse. He and his men rode out of town slowly, all laughing uproariously. Finally, one man in the church shouted: "For God's sake! It's the James gang! They've just robbed the bank!" After finding the cashier bound and gagged, the citizens of Corydon hastily formed a posse and rode after the bandits, but the gang outdistanced them and they lost all trace of the thieves by the time they reached Clay County, Mo.

On Apr. 29, 1872, the gang executed its next raid, this time riding to Columbia, Ky. Jesse and Frank James entered the bank. Outside waiting with the horses were Clell Miller and Cole Younger. Jesse demanded the key to the safe but cashier R.A.C. Martin balked and Jesse shot him three times, killing him. Frank James casually stepped over Martin's body and cleaned out the cash drawers, taking only $600. The gang rode quickly out of town. A huge posse seeking vengeance for the Martin slaying rode after the bandits, but the James gang, old hands at evasion by then, doubled back on their own trail twice, circled Columbia, and then rode on to Missouri, completely confusing the pursuing lawmen.

On May 23, 1872, Jesse James, Cole and Bob Younger, Clell Miller, and Bill Chadwell (alias Bill Stiles) rode into Ste. Genevieve, Mo., entering the local bank where cashier O.D. Harris recognized the bandits. He quickly complied with their demands and filled a grain sack with more than $4,000 in gold and bills, and the gang left town at a gallop. No posse pursued the robbers. By then, it seemed inevitable that every town in Missouri would receive a visit from the James-Younger gang and most local lawmen became apathetic in their efforts to catch the thieves, knowing that the bandits were protected by almost everyone in Clay and Ray counties. A short distance outside of Ste. Genevieve, Jesse dismounted to readjust the gold sack hanging from his saddle and, at that moment, his skittish horse ran off into a field.

A farmer appeared on the road and Jesse asked him to go after the animal. He refused but quickly changed his mind when the other members of the gang aimed six-guns at him. The farmer chased the horse across the field and returned him to Jesse. He grinned at the outlaw chief with a toothless smile and then asked with a thick accent: "I catch der horse. Vot do I get for dot, yah?"

Jesse mounted the animal and replied: "Your life, Dutchy. Vot you tink, yah?" He rode off laughing. By then Jesse James was very much aware of his growing reputation and he enjoyed his notoriety. He even played up to his self-image of the unbeatable bad man, a daring bandit with a sense of humor and intelligence to outwit any country bumpkin posse. He demonstrated his belief in his fame on Sept. 26, 1872, when he, Frank James, and Cole Younger rode to the fairgrounds outside of Kansas City, Mo. At the main gate, Jesse dismounted and went to the cashier. He smiled at Ben Wallace, the cashier, and then said in a pleasant voice: "What if I was to say that I was Jesse James and I told you to hand out that tin box of money? What would you say?"

"I'd say I'd see you in hell first," snapped Wallace.

"Well, that's just who I am and you'd better hand it out pretty damned quick or..." He aimed a pistol at Wallace. The cashier handed over the money in the tin box, $978. Stuffing this in the traditional sack, Jesse mounted his horse. The feisty Wallace ran from the cashier's box and grabbed the stirrup on Jesse's horse, holding on to it. "It's the James gang!" he shouted, but few in the crowd heard him. Jesse turned the horse away from Wallace, drawing his pistol and firing a shot that went wild and struck a girl in the leg. The three men then galloped into some nearby woods and vanished. En route home, Jesse cursed the bad luck. Frank

The First National Bank at Northfield.

Some of Northfield's citizens who fought the James gang.

Jesse James in 1876.

Cole Younger

Clell Miller, dead.

Jim Younger

Bill Chadwell, dead.

Frank James in 1876.

REWARD!
- DEAD OR ALIVE -

$5,000.00 will be paid for the capture of the men who robbed the bank at

NORTHFIELD, MINN.

They are believed to be Jesse James and his Band, or the Youngers.

All officers are warned to use precaution in making arrest. These are the most desperate men in America.

Take no chances! Shoot to kill!!

J. H. McDonald.

Reward poster for the James boys.

Bob Younger

Charlie Pitts, dead.

James said nothing. He had scouted the fair and had reported that as much as $10,000 was kept on hand with the cashier. He had been right, but shortly before the bandits arrived to rob the cashier, thousands of dollars had been taken from the strongbox and sent to a local bank for safekeeping.

The paltry sum taken at Kansas City caused the bandits to believe that certain types of robberies were not worth the effort. Even banks were unreliable in having large sums of cash on hand. Trains, however, always carried large amounts of gold, silver, and currency. They knew well that the first train robbery had been committed by the ill-fated Reno Brothers of Indiana, but they felt themselves superior to the Hoosier bandits and believed they would have no trouble in successfully looting trains. So the gang rode to Adair, Iowa, in mid-July 1873. Frank James had taken several trains west, as far as Omaha, Neb., riding the Chicago, Rock Island, and Pacific Express (while reading *Pilgrim's Progress*). He reported to the rest of the gang that when the Express reached Adair on July 21, 1873, it would be carrying more than $100,000 in gold, destined for eastern banks.

Gang members arrived outside Adair on that day and removed a section of track. These included Jesse and Frank James, Cole and Jim Younger, Clell Miller, Bob Moore, and Commanche Tony. As the Express came around a bend, its engineer, John Rafferty, saw the break and reversed the engine. It was too late. The engine raced into the open track and crashed onto its side, crushing Rafferty to death. Jesse and his men rode from a nearby wood and went to the baggage car, pointing guns at the clerks who opened the safe to give them not $100,000 but only $2,000 in federal reserve notes. The gold that was supposed to have been on board had been rescheduled that morning and had gone through Adair four hours earlier on a fast Express. The bandits rode back to Missouri discouraged. They decided to go back to farming, and for six months the James-Younger gang was inactive.

Before attacking their next train, the James-Younger gang committed a vintage holdup. On Jan. 15, 1874, the bandits rode south to Arkansas and, outside of Malvern, held up the Concord Stagecoach, one of their few such robberies. Cole Younger, who was the experienced hand and practical hub of the gang, proved during this robbery that he, too, had his moments of caprice. After the gang stopped the stage, driver and passengers were ordered to step down and line up before the gang as guns were trained on them. More than $4,000 in gold, bills, and jewels were taken from the well-to-do passengers. When Cole Younger took a gold watch from a man who protested in a strong southern accent, the bandit paused. "Are you a southerner?" he asked, a rather ridiculous question since there were few northerners traveling in Arkansas at that time.

"Yes, suh," replied the gentleman traveler.

"Were you in the Confederate Army?"

"I had that distinction, suh."

"State your rank, regiment, and commanding officer," Younger demanded.

When the passenger gave Younger this information, he was startled to see Younger hand him back his watch. "We are all Confederate soldiers," Younger said with some pride, enjoying his magnanimity. "We don't rob southerners, especially Confederate soldiers." He pointed his finger at the rest of the passengers and said in a solemn voice: "But Yankees and detectives are not exempt."

In fifteen days, the gang had ridden back to Missouri, and on Jan. 31, 1874, entered the small flag station at Gadshill, Mo., a depot along the line of the Iron Mountain Railroad. The bandits, which included Jesse and Frank James, Cole, Jim, and Bob Younger, Jim Cummins, Clell and Ed Miller, Sam Hildebrand, Arthur McCory, and Jim Reed, flagged down the Little Rock Express. As the train came to a stop, the bandits jumped into the baggage car and quickly opened the safe, shooting off its locks. They took from it more than $22,000 in gold and bills. Some of the bandits went through the cars, robbing the passengers. Jesse James then mounted his horse and rode up to the engineer's cabin where Cole Younger held the engineer under his gun. "Give her a toot, Cole!" Jesse shouted to him. Cole Younger grabbed the whistle cord and yanked on it. As the whistle shrieked, Younger laughed like a small boy with a new toy.

Before the gang departed, Jesse threw a stick to the engineer. Around it was wrapped a piece of paper. James told the engineer: "Give this to the newspapers. We like to do things in style." The scrap of paper contained Jesse's own press release of the robbery which he had written only a few hours before the train had been stopped. It read:

THE MOST DARING TRAIN ROBBERY ON RECORD!

The southbound train of the Iron Mountain Railroad was stopped here this evening by five [there were ten bandits] heavily armed men and robbed of _____ dollars. The robbers arrived at the station a few minutes before the arrival of the train and arrested the agent and put him under guard and then threw the train on the switch. The robbers were all large men, all being slightly under six feet. After robbing the train they started in a southerly direction. They were all mounted on handsome horses.

PS: They are a hell of an excitement in this part of the country.

After the Gadshill raid the robberies stopped, and it seemed as if the James-Younger gang had been swallowed by the earth. There was no trace of any of the bandits for almost a year. With the spoils from the robbery, Jesse decided to finally wed Zeralda Mimms, his cousin. They had met often in wooded retreats and lonely cabins in the wilderness. Now Zee Mimms insisted that they either marry or never see each other again. Jesse and Zee went to Kansas City and were married. They then traveled to Galveston, Texas, where a reporter for the St. Louis *Dispatch* interviewed Jesse before he and Zee boarded a steamer headed for Vera Cruz where they planned to honeymoon. Jesse candidly told the reporter: "On the 23rd of April, 1874, I was married to Miss Zee Mimms, of Kansas City, and at the house of a friend there.

"About fifty of our mutual friends were present on the occasion and quite a noted Methodist minister (Reverend William James, Jesse's uncle) performed the ceremonies. We had been engaged for nine years and through good and evil report, and not withstanding the lies that had been told upon me and the crimes laid at my door, her devotion to me has never wavered for a moment. You can say that both of us married for love, and that there cannot be any sort of doubt about our marriage being a happy one." Jesse and Zee James, however, did not take ship for Vera Cruz but traveled back to Missouri and settled on a small farm near Kearney, living in a log cabin. Jesse James was by then dedicated to a way of crime and had no thought to retire or reform. His wife's attitude about his criminal ways was never learned, but Wood Hite, a family friend, later stated that "she looked the other way...out of love." Hite went on to say that Jesse James was a devoted husband and loved his wife very much. The couple produced two children, Jesse, Jr., and Mary James. The outlaw spent a great deal of time with his children, playing with them whenever he was home. The couple continued to travel, living in Texas, then Tennessee, and even in the heart of Kansas City.

Frank James would also marry two years later, eloping with 17-year-old Annie Ralston, a union that would produce a son, Robert, in 1878. While Jesse was settling down to a farming life, the Pinkerton Detective Agency increased its efforts to arrest and try the James boys for their past crimes. Detectives roamed in pairs and in groups through western Missouri, seeking the James brothers and their allies, the Youngers. The detective agency had been waging a private war with the James-Younger clan for sometime. On Mar. 16, 1874, Jim and John Younger were riding through the woods near Osceola, Mo. Two Pinkerton detectives, Louis J. Lull and E.B. Daniels, who had been trailing them, suddenly found themselves faced by the two Youngers. The detectives claimed they were cattle buyers but Jim Younger correctly guessed them to be Pinkertons. The detectives and the Youngers both went for their guns at the same time and Lull and Daniels were killed. So was John Younger. A month later Jesse James, Clell Miller, and James Latche, killed another Pinkerton agent, John W. Whicher. From that day on, the Pinkertons hounded the James-Young gang.

The Pinkertons watched the Samuels farm on and off, believing that Jesse and Frank would pay their mother a visit. Detectives learned, on Jan. 26, 1875, that the boys would arrive at the Samuels farm after sundown. They stationed men near the farmhouse and then shouted for Jesse and Frank to come outside. A light in the window went out and then a bomb of some sort was thrown through the window by one of the Pinkerton men. It exploded with a deafening roar. The bomb blew off Mrs. Samuel's arm and a fragment of the bomb tore through the side of Archie Peyton Samuel, the 8-year-old half-brother of Jesse and Frank. The child died within an hour in great pain and agony.

No other act than this "inexcusable and cowardly deed," as the press termed it, could have earned more sympathy for the James boys. The newspapers vilified the Pinkertons, who were universally hated, and labeled them child killers and inhuman monsters who attacked defenseless women. Even though Allan Pinkerton repeatedly denied that any of his men had thrown a bomb into the Samuels' home, his agency fell into disgrace. Jesse was so incensed at the killing of his little half-brother and the mutilation of his mother that he spent long hours planning the execution of Allan Pinkerton. According to Wood Hite, he actually took a train to Chicago and spent hours waiting for Pinkerton to show up at his headquarters there, planning to shoot the detective on sight. He did see Pinkerton but did not shoot him on a crowded Chicago street. He later told Hite: "I had a dozen chances to kill him when he didn't know it. I wanted to give him a fair chance but the opportunity never came."

For some time after this, Jesse and Frank James fell out. Frank had apparently tried to convince his younger brother to retire, that bank and train robbing were getting too dangerous. Jesse, on the other hand, called Frank a coward, especially since he refused to try to track down Allan Pinkerton and take vengeance on him for the death of his half-brother. Frank refused to associate with Jesse or the rest of the gang for some time. He remained on a farm, reading and writing letters to Missouri newspapers, attempting to vindicate himself and stating that he was not responsible for the robberies attributed to him. He went on to say that he and his brother Jesse "were not good friends (at the time of Kansas City fairgrounds robbery) and have not been for several years."

By early 1875, the brothers were reunited and led the Youngers to Texas where, on May 12, they robbed the San Antonio stage of $3,000. Cole Younger reportedly had to be persuaded to join the band. He was busy romancing Belle Starr, the daughter of Collins County rancher John Shirley. Cole Younger then had the notion to quit banditry. He told Jesse and Frank James that he was thinking of settling in Dallas, where he had a job offer as a census taker. Jesse talked him out of this idea and Younger followed the James boys back to Missouri where an important train robbery was planned.

Through a bribed railroad clerk, the gang learned that the United Express Company would be shipping more than $100,000 on the Missouri Pacific Railroad. On July 7, 1875, Jesse and Frank James, Cole, Jim and Bob Younger, Clell Miller, Charlie Pitts, and Bill Chadwell were waiting for the train as it slowed to cross an old railroad bridge east of Otterville, Mo. The gang trained pistols on the engineer who brought the engine to a halt. The bandits then approached the Adams Express car and entered it, ordering guard John Bushnell to open the safe. "It can't be done," Bushnell nervously told Jesse. "I don't have the keys to it. It's locked all the way through and the keys are at the other end of the run."

"Get an ax," Jesse told Bob Younger who took a fire ax from the wall of the baggage car and began chopping away at the safe. It was useless. All Younger succeeded in doing was making a few dents in the heavy iron safe. Then Cole Younger demanded the ax. A tall, powerful man, Younger repeatedly swung his 200 pounds against the safe for ten minutes, finally making a small hole in the top of the safe. Jesse reached through the hole and pulled up a leather pouch from which the bandits took more than $75,000. They stuffed the money into a grain sack and then tossed it to Frank James and the others waiting outside. Jesse, Cole, and Bob Younger then climbed on their horses, but before riding off, Jesse told Bushnell: "If you see any of the Pinkertons, tell 'em to come and get us."

This strike, the gang's largest to date, convinced Jesse and the others that with the proper information they could commit robberies that would bring them quick fortunes and enough money to retire. Bill Chadwell, a native of Minnesota, was sent to scout the large First National Bank in Northfield, Minn., reputedly one of the wealthiest banks in the Midwest. Though far afield from their regular haunts, the Northfield bank promised as much as $200,000 in cash and gold, perhaps more. The gang members were further lured to rob this bank because its two principal stockholders were Ben Butler and W.A. Ames, who had been Union officials in the Civil War and were still much hated for the oppressive measures they employed when occupying southern cities. Butler, the general in charge of

conquered New Orleans, had issued an order which allowed his soldiers to treat women there as common streetwalkers. Ames was considered the worst carpetbagger to ever plague the South. Both men had enriched themselves through the spoils of war and the misfortune of the devastated southerners.

In August 1876, the James-Younger band began its ride north, moving slowly and with great confidence. They had never experienced any serious setbacks and their members had remained unharmed in ten years of robbery. The bandits were all mounted on the finest horses available and looked prosperous. All wore new suits, shiny black boots, and long linen dusters like those worn by cattle buyers. They carried new carbines and heavy Colt pistols on their hips. Jesse wore two more Colts in shoulder holsters.

The eight men rode into Northfield, Minn., on Sept. 7, 1876. To the bandits, Northfield looked like any other town they had raided, with a main street and small stores nestled next to the bank. Yet Northfield was unlike any town the gang had ever visited. Its residents were industrious pioneers who placed great value on thrift and an even greater value on the law. Minnesota was not Missouri, where roving bands of outlaws were commonplace. The state was relatively free of such bandits and the natives of Northfield were fiercely protective of their town and the savings in their bank. And, as they proved with lethal dedication, they would battle anyone who tried to take what they had earned by the sweat of their brows.

At 2 p.m., Jesse, Charlie Pitts, and Bob Younger entered the First National Bank while Cole Younger and Clell Miller waited outside the bank, holding the horses. At the end of the street Frank James, Bill Chadwell, and Jim Younger sat on their horses, guarding the exit of the town, ready to protect the gang when it fled Northfield. Trouble began almost immediately. J.A. Allen, a hardware store owner, spotted the men outside the bank and walked over to investigate. Clell Miller grabbed his arm and said: "Keep your goddamned mouth shut!" Allen broke free of Miller's grip and began to run down the street, shouting: "Get your guns, boys! They're robbing the bank!" Henry Wheeler, a university student home on vacation, saw Allen and took up the alarm. He, too, began to shout: "Robbery! Robbery! Robbery! They're all at the bank!" Cole Younger and Miller quickly mounted their horses and they were joined by Frank James, Jim Younger and Chadwell. The five outlaws began racing up and down the street, shouting to the startled residents: "Get in! Get in!" This technique had worked many times in Missouri where gun-shy natives raced for cover. But the citizens of Northfield did just the opposite. Dozens of men, young and old, grabbed pistols, rifles, and shotguns and ran to the street or took positions in windows, behind doors, and at the corners of buildings.

Inside the bank, Jesse James held his pistol on acting bank cashier Joseph Lee Heywood, telling him: "Don't holler! There's forty men outside the bank." Heywood nodded as Jesse added in a menacing voice: "Open the goddamned safe before I blow your head off!" "I can't do that," Heywood said, "there's a time lock on it." Pitts ran forward with a knife and cut the cashier's throat slightly. He and Bob Younger both stuck their pistols into Heywood's stomach. The cashier kept insisting that the safe was on a time lock. None of the bandits bothered to check the safe. Heywood was lying. The safe was unlocked and had no time lock. Then a clerk, A.E. Bunker, ran into a back room. Pitts fired a shot at him but missed. Bob Younger went through the cash drawers and found only a small amount of money. Firing could be heard in the street and Pitts went to the front entrance of the bank. He turned to Jesse and shouted: "The game's up! Pull out or they'll be killing our men!"

Bob Younger and Jesse James followed Pitts out the front door, but one of them—it was never determined which—turned and shot Heywood in the head. He fell dead to the bank floor. The scene that greeted Jesse as he stepped into the street was as bloody as any battle he had experienced in the Civil War. Clell Miller was riding crazily about, his face blasted to pulp and gushing blood. Elias Stacy, a resident, had rushed him moments earlier and let loose a shotgun blast that caught Miller full in the face. He was unrecognizable. His flesh hung in shreds from his jaw and his shirt front was soaked with blood. He moaned and screamed wildly, firing his six-gun indiscriminately. One of Miller's wild shots struck and killed Nicholas Gustavson, a terrified immigrant who was trying to reach the cover of a building.

A bullet smacked into Cole Younger's shoulder. Then A.B. Manning fired a shot that struck Bill Chadwell square in the heart. The outlaw stood straight up in his saddle for a moment then toppled to earth, dead. Wheeler, the university student, had gotten a gun and repeatedly shot the already wounded Clell Miller until he also fell from his horse dead. Bob Younger raced forward on his horse, firing at Manning, and Wheeler fired a shot at him, wounding him in the hand. Younger switched his weapon to the other hand and fired back at Wheeler.

By that time the citizens had blocked both ends of the street and dozens of men were firing at the outlaws who rode up and down the street through a murderous cross fire, looking desperately for an escape route. A bullet struck Charlie Pitts, then Jim Younger, then Cole Younger. The gang was being shot to pieces. "It's no use, men!" Jesse shouted to the others. "Let's go! Let's go!" Bob Younger, who had been shot from his horse, managed to climb up

behind his brother Cole and what was left of the gang rode wildly down the street through heavy fire. Scores of citizens who did not have weapons threw rocks at them.

Some miles outside Northfield, the gang rested for a few minutes. Jesse looked at Bob Younger's wounds and then told his cousin Cole Younger that Bob was too seriously wounded to continue. He suggested that either Bob be left behind or "we put him out of his misery." Reaching for his six-gun, Cole Younger, who had taken Jesse's orders for years, glared at Jesse and told him that he would not leave his brother behind. "Maybe it's best we split up," he said. Jesse and Frank, the only bandits in the gang not wounded, nodded and then rode off in one direction.

The Younger brothers and Pitts headed in another direction. The Youngers were slowed by their wounds and left a clear trail for pursuing lawmen to follow. Fourteen days later they were trapped in a swamp outside of Madelia, Minn. More than fifty men surrounded them and a full-scale battle ensued. An hour later, Sheriff Glispen shouted to the outlaws who were behind a large fallen tree: "Do you men surrender?" As the lawmen waited for an answer, they reloaded their weapons and prepared for further battle. Then the silence was pierced by a voice from behind the large tree. "I surrender!" Bob Younger, bleeding from five wounds, stood up unsteadily and waved the possemen forward. "They're all down, except me." The lawmen came forward cautiously, guns at the ready. They found Cole Younger wounded seven times and Jim Younger wounded five times. Both were still alive. Charlie Pitts lay flat on the ground, his six-guns and rifle empty of bullets. There were five bullet wounds in his chest. He was dead.

The Younger Brothers were taken into custody, and as they rode in an open cart through the small Minnesota towns, en route to medical attention, citizens came out by the thousands to see them, curious about these strange men from Missouri who had traveled hundreds of miles to risk their lives. All three brothers were tried and sentenced to life imprisonment. As they entered the state penitentiary at Stillwater, Minn., Cole Younger was asked why he and his brothers had turned to crime. "We were victims of circumstances," he explained, not half believing his own oft-repeated words. "We were drove to it, sir."

The Northfield raid made national headlines and Jesse and Frank James became the most sought-after outlaws in the U.S. But they were nowhere to be found. Hundreds of possemen scoured Minnesota, Wisconsin, and Iowa for them as the brothers moved slowly south. They traveled on foot, stole horses, and then abandoned them. They slept in abandoned farm buildings during the day and moved only at night. They ate raw vegetables and hid from sight, believing that all were their enemies. It took them three weeks to reach Missouri and by then they looked like scarecrows, their clothes in rags. Both Jesse and Frank realized that they were too notorious now to remain in Missouri. The murders they had committed in Northfield had branded them cold-blooded killers. Even many of their former supporters in Missouri found it hard to excuse their actions. Hiding in a covered wagon, Jesse and Frank were driven to Tennessee. Both purchased small farms outside of Nashville and lived there in obscurity for three years with no thought of returning to the outlaw trail.

Jesse, however, ran low on money and organized a new gang in Fall 1879; it included his brother Frank, Bill Ryan, Dick Liddell, Ed Miller, Tucker Basham, and Wood Hite. On Oct. 7, 1879, the gang held up the Alton Express near Glendale, Mo., and took more than $35,000 from the baggage car safe. The outlaws were inactive for almost a year and a half before they robbed a stage in Muscle Shoals, Ala., of only $1,400. On July 10, 1881, Jesse led the same men to Riverton, Iowa, where they held up the Sexton Bank, looting it of $5,000. Five days later, they stopped the Chicago, Rock Island, and Pacific train at Winston, Mo. When Frank McMillan tried to interfere with the robbery, Jesse shot him dead. The train engineer, William Westfall (or Westphal), refused to do as Jesse ordered and the bandit chief shot him dead in the engine cabin. The outlaws got only $600 from this bloody robbery which caused Missouri governor Thomas T. Crittenden to offer a $10,000 reward for the capture and conviction of Frank and Jesse James.

This amount of money was staggering for the day. In earlier times, this kind of reward would not have tempted any member of the James gang. The Younger brothers, cousins to the James boys, were blood kin and absolutely loyal. Other earlier members were fellow veterans of the guerrilla battles of the Civil War and were tied to the James and Younger brothers through old associations and loyalties. But the new members Jesse had recruited for the band had little or no allegiance to them. This included Robert and Charles Ford, two young men who had learned of the reward and planned to murder Jesse.

Bob Ford, the younger of the Ford Brothers was not a regular member of the gang. He spent time around gang members, clamoring to ride with the bandits, but was mostly used to run errands, a fact which caused him to become resentful and embittered. Charlie Ford rode with Jesse and Frank James, however, on Aug. 7, 1881, in a strange robbery that occurred near Blue Cut, outside Glendale, Mo., near the site where the gang had stopped a train two years earlier. The gang, consisting of Jesse and Frank James, Charles Ford, Wood and Clarence Hite, and Dick Liddell, stopped the train by piling large timbers across the track.

Engineer Jack Foote brought the train to a halt and the bandits used a pickax to chop their way into the locked express car. They hammered open the safe but were disappointed at the small amount of money in the safe. The outlaws then walked through the train, robbing the passengers. Jesse, wearing a thick, black beard, and the only bandit without a mask, made no effort to disguise himself. In fact, he reveled in his notoriety. He had taken to collecting the dime novels that Eastern presses had churned out about his exploits. "I'm Jesse James," he said to several stunned passengers and then he boldly introduced other members of the gang. The bandits rode off grumbling about the meager loot, less than $1,500. This was Jesse James' last robbery.

Following this robbery, Frank rode back to his farm near Nashville. Jesse, accompanied by the Ford Brothers, rode to Missouri to visit his mother. The three men slept in the Samuels barn. Jesse kept his pistols at the ready, believing that the Pinkertons might arrive at any moment. When he fell asleep, the Ford Brothers began discussing how to kill the man they followed. They had been planning to murder Jesse for months but were cautious and fearful of this deadliest of outlaws. Robert Ford was already in contact with Governor Crittenden, promising him that he would kill Jesse James in the near future. After having breakfast at his mother's home for the last time, Jesse, still accompanied by the Ford Brothers, rode to St. Joseph, Mo., where he was living under the name of Thomas Howard with his wife and two children. The family occupied a small but comfortable house atop a hill and in this quiet community, Jesse went on planning robberies. He sent the Ford boys out to scout several banks he was thinking of robbing.

The second James gang began to disintegrate quickly. Ed Miller was found dead, his body shot to pieces and dumped on a rural Missouri road. Jim Cummins later claimed that Jesse had murdered Miller after learning that Miller planned to turn himself in and inform on the rest of the gang. Wood Hite was then killed by Dick Liddell and Bob Ford over a split of the loot from the second Glendale train robbery at Blue Cut. Liddell, thinking that the Ford brothers intended to murder him, surrendered and confessed all he knew. His statements led to the arrest of Clarence Hite, who was tried and convicted of robbery and sent to prison for twenty-five years.

Only four active members of the James gang were now at large: Jesse, Frank, and the Ford brothers. Still, Jesse was undaunted and planned another robbery, summoning the Fords to his St. Joseph home on the morning of Apr. 3, 1881. Zee James made breakfast for the three men and the two small James children were sent out to play in the back yard. Following the meal, Jesse and the Fords went into the small parlor to further plan the robbery of the Platte County bank. When Jesse glanced at a newspaper

Jesse James, 1881.

PROCLAMATION
$5,000⁰⁰
REWARD
FOR EACH of SEVEN ROBBERS of THE TRAIN at
WINSTON, MO., JULY 15, 1881, and THE MURDER of
CONDUCTER WESTFALL
$ 5,000,00
ADDITIONAL for ARREST or CAPTURE
DEAD OR ALIVE
OF JESSE OR FRANK JAMES
THIS NOTICE TAKES the PLACE of ALL PREVIOUS
REWARD NOTICES.
CONTACT SHERIFF, DAVIESS COUNTY, MISSOURI
IMMEDIATELY
T. T. CRITTENDEN, GOVERNOR
STATE OF MISSOURI
JULY 26, 1881

Reward poster, 1881.

Bob Ford holding the gun he used to kill Jesse James.

Jesse's home in St. Joseph, Mo., where he was killed.

Charlie Ford, a suicide.

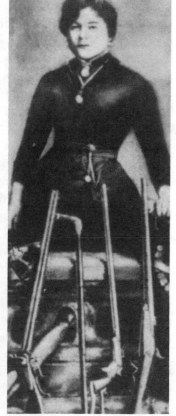

Jesse James, dead, 1882.

Jesse's children, Mary and Jesse James, Jr.

Jesse's wife, Zee James.

containing Dick Liddell's confession, Charlie Ford, according to his later statements, was suddenly gripped by fear that Jesse would learn of the Fords' secret meeting with Governor Crittenden. Bob Ford also became nervous, and later stated at James' inquest: "I knew then that I had placed my head in the lion's mouth. How could I safely remove it?"

James put the newspaper aside, stood up, walked to the window and looked outside to see his children playing. He then turned and spotted a picture that was hanging crooked on the wall. According to the Fords, he then removed two gun belts, one about his hips, another around his shoulders. Each belt contained two big Colts, four guns in all. James looped the gun belts around a chair. Why he took the belts off was never known. The Fords may have told this story to make their target all the more dangerous. Some claimed that Jesse wore no guns in the house at any time, at least not *four* weapons, especially in the company of men he trusted. Given his belief in his invulnerability, it is most likely that James was never armed that morning.

The outlaw chief stood upon a small stool to reach the picture on the wall. As he adjusted the picture, Jesse exposed his back to the Fords. Robert pulled his pistol and aimed it squarely at the bandit's back. His hand shook so that the had to steady it with the other. At a distance of about four feet, he fired several times. James turned slightly to give his assassin a fierce look and then fell lifeless to the floor. Zee James rushed in from the kitchen, and kneeling at her husband's side, cradled his head in her arms, sobbing. Robert Ford sputtered that his gun went off by accident.

The Fords raced from the house. As Bob Ford ran down the hill toward the telegraph station he yelled loudly to anyone who would listen: "I killed him! I killed Jesse James! I killed him! I killed him! I killed Jesse James!" Only a few minutes later, he wired Governor Crittenden that the most wanted man in the U.S. was dead, that he, Bob Ford, had killed the infamous Jesse James. He immediately demanded his reward. The Ford Brothers were later charged with murder, but Crittenden, keeping his word, had the charges dropped and the reward money sent to the Fords.

The news of the bandit's murder was bannered in almost every newspaper in the U.S., from New York to California, from Maine to Texas. "Jesse by Jehovah!" read the front page headline in the St. Joseph *Gazette*. "Goodbye, Jesse!" read the Kansas City *Journal*. The newspapers and the dime novelists who had churned out endless copy on the outlaw for sixteen years lamented his passing, if only for commercial reasons. Almost immediately, the legend and lore of Jesse James began to be embellished so that within a few months, he was known as a hero. The ruthless killer and thief, the real Jesse James, was somehow forgotten and in his place sprang up a sterling, enviable Robin Hood.

The heavily bearded body of the outlaw was officially identified by his wife and by Mrs. Zee Samuels, his mother. The old woman appeared the next day at an inquest where the Ford brothers and Dick Liddell testified. When Mrs. Samuels took the stand, she wept and said: "I live in Clay County and I am the mother of Jesse James...My poor boy...I have seen the body since my arrival and I have recognized it as that of my son Jesse...The lady by my side is my daughter-in-law and the children hers...He was a kind husband and son." Then she fixed her eyes on the Fords and Dick Liddell. She held up the stump of her arm and shook an empty sleeve in their direction, shouting: "Traitors!" The Fords and Liddell were hurried out of the courtroom by officers. Their lives were thought to be in great jeopardy; Frank James could appear at any moment, leading a large band of men, with the single thought of killing the Fords.

Mrs. Samuels took Zee Mimms and her children back with her to the Clay County farm and with them the body of her son, which had been placed in a $500 coffin, an expensive casket for that day. The outlaw was buried on the Samuels farm and a white marble headstone was placed over the grave. It read:

> Jesse W. James
> Died April 3, 1882
> Aged 34 years, 6 months, 28 days
> Murdered by a traitor and a coward
> Whose name is not worthy to
> appear here.

On Oct. 5, 1882, five months after his brother's murder, Alexander Franklin James, last of the outlaw band, surrendered to Governor Crittenden. The 39-year-old bandit marched into the governor's office and took off his gun belt, placing it before Crittenden and saying: "Governor Crittenden, I want to hand over to you that which no living man except myself has been permitted to touch since 1861." The governor promised James protection and a fair trial. James was a celebrated prisoner and reporters flocked to interview him. One asked: "Why did you surrender? No one knew where you were hiding."

"What of that," James replied. "I was tired of an outlaw's life. I have been hunted for twenty-one years. I have literally lived in the saddle. I have never known a day of perfect peace. It was one long, anxious, inexorable, eternal vigil. When I slept it was literally in the midst of an arsenal. If I heard dogs bark more fiercely than usual, or the hooves of horses in a greater volume than usual, I stood to my arms. Have you an idea of what a man must endure who

Left, crowds running to the James house following the outlaw's murder.

Right, Frank James in 1882.

THE DAILY GRAPHIC

AN ILLUSTRATED EVENING NEWSPAPER

39 & 41 PARK PLACE

VOL. XXVIII. | NEW YORK, TUESDAY, APRIL 11, 1882. | NO. 2814

HIC JACET
JESSE JAMES

Cartoon showing how Jesse James was glorified for children.

Jim Cummins

Jesse James, Jr., 1900.

leads such a life? No, you cannot. No one can unless he lives it for himself."

Universal sympathy for Frank James and the James family was exhibited. The cowardly way the Ford brothers had killed Jesse almost assured Frank James an acquittal. After a number of long trials, that is exactly what he received. He returned to the Samuel farm and took up peaceful pursuits, working as a horse trainer and a racetrack starter. After the turn of the century, he appeared in a small Wild West show with his friend Cole Younger, who, by then, had been released from prison. Frank James died in a small bedroom of the Samuels farmhouse on Feb. 18, 1915.

Cole and Jim Younger were not released from the penitentiary at Stillwater, Minn., until July 10, 1901. Bob Younger had died in prison of pneumonia on Sept. 16, 1889. Jim Younger fell in love with a young woman in St. Paul, but she rejected him when he asked her to marry him. Younger went to his hotel room and shot himself to death. Cole Younger returned to Lee's Summit, Mo., where he lived a quiet life. He became a farmer and later appeared at local fairs, sometimes with Frank James. As the two bandits aged, they gave lectures to Sunday school classes and at ladies tea parties, thundering their condemnation of the outlaw life. The tall and muscular Cole Younger was the last of the outlaw band to die, suffering a heart attack on Mar. 21, 1916.

The Ford brothers, following Jesse's death, enjoyed some brief notoriety but were mostly shunned as "vile cowards." Charlie Ford was consumed by fear that Frank James or some of Jesse's other relatives would hunt him down and kill him. He was plagued by nightmares and became an insomniac. He finally committed suicide. Bob Ford moved west, traveling from town to town, opening up several saloons with the reward money he had received. He was finally shot to death in Creede, Colo., a decade after he became the most infamous "traitor" in the U.S. by shooting Jesse James in the back. Ford's shooting of Jesse James was challenged by J. Frank Dalton, who appeared in the late 1940s to claim that he was Jesse James and that the man shot in 1882 in St. Joseph, Mo., was an imposter. But it was generally agreed that Dalton was the impersonator and that the man buried in James' grave was indeed Jesse.

From the moment Jesse Woodson James was put into his grave, his life became a great fiction and he was lionized as a hearty pioneer, a brave son of the Middle Border, an embodiment of the spirit of adventuresome America. Fabulous tales were told of his kindliness and generosity. One abiding canard involved a widow woman who had given the James boys breakfast as they fled from a bank robbery. She informed her guests that she was about to lose her farm, that she did not have the money to pay the mortgage.

Jesse reportedly gave her the money and then hid as the land owner appeared and collected this sum from the woman, signing back the deed to the farm to her. Jesse then rode after the landlord and held him up, recouping his loan to the widow woman. Jesse was kind to children and chivalrous to women. Journalists of the day took pains to point out that he never robbed a woman in a bank, in a stagecoach, or on a train. They omitted the many murders he was known to have committed.

Most of these tales had no foundation, but generations of small boys were thrilled by these stories and Jesse James became their tarnished idol, much to the chagrin of lawmen and parents. A decade later, the Dalton Brothers tried to emulate the James boys and were destroyed at Coffeyville, Kan. In the next century, the likes of John Dillinger and Charles Arthur "Pretty Boy" Floyd, who both admired Jesse James in their youth, not only followed his career closely, but copied his bank robbing techniques. The bandit's myth deepened so that it became part of the core of the American character or psyche, one of dash and quick action, one of fearless adventure. A song created by an amateur composer came into existence almost overnight following the bandit's death and did much to perpetuate the legend of this strange and mysterious man whom few called friend and whom no one really knew. This melodramatic ballad captured the myth if not the reality of Jesse Woodson James:

Jesse James was a lad who killed many a man.
He robbed the Glendale train.
He stole from the rich and he gave to the poor,
He'd a hand and a heart and a brain.

(Chorus)
Jesse had a wife to mourn for his life,
Two children, they were brave,
But that dirty little coward that shot Mister Howard
Has laid poor Jesse in his grave.

It was Robert Ford, that dirty little coward,
I wonder how does he feel,
For he ate of Jesse's bread and he slept in Jesse's bed,
Then he laid Jesse James in his grave.

Jesse was a man, a friend to the poor.
He'd never seen a man suffer pain,
And with his brother Frank, he robbed the Gallatin bank
And stopped the Glendale train.

It was on a Wednesday night, the moon was shining bright.

He stopped the Glendale train.
And the people all did say for many miles away,
It was robbed by Frank and Jesse James.

It was on a Saturday night, Jesse was at home,
Talking to his family brave.
Robert Ford came along like a thief in the night,
And laid Jesse James in his grave.

The people held their breath
When they heard of Jesse's death
And wondered how he ever came to die.
It was one of the gang called little Robert Ford,
Who shot Jesse James on the sly.

Jesse went to his rest with his hand on his breast,
The devil will be upon his knee.
He was born one day in the County of Shea
And he came from a solitary race.

This song was made by Billy Garshade,
As soon as the news did arrive,
He said there was no man with the law in his hand
Could take Jesse James when alive.

See: **Anderson, William; Dalton Brothers; Dalton, J. Frank; Ford, Robert; Quantrill, William Clarke; Reno Brothers; Starr Belle; Younger Brothers.**

Jaybird-Woodpecker War, 1889, U.S., range war. The Jaybird-Woodpecker War occurred in Fort Bend County, Texas, and involved two large cattle ranches and dozens of cowboys. Several gun battles between these two factions resulted in a half dozen deaths. Ira Aten is credited with bringing this feud to an end. See: **Aten, Ira.**

Jenkins, James Gilbert, 1834-64, U.S., outlaw. James Jenkins was a professional criminal having a long history of highway robberies and murders. It was reported that he had killed eight white men and ten Indians throughout Missouri, Texas, Iowa, and California. While living in Napa City, Calif., Jenkins became acquainted with Patrick O'Brien in order to establish a sexual liaison with O'Brien's wife. Mrs. O'Brien, a lusty, attractive woman with a strong will, goaded Jenkins into murdering her husband, or so he later said, although Jenkins' willingness to murder needed no encouragement.

Jenkins got drunk, marched into O'Brien's home, and

shot him, but he was caught almost immediately and quickly confessed. Mrs. O'Brien denied having anything to do with the murder and was released. Jenkins was convicted and sentenced to death. Before he was hanged, Jenkins lamented his sloppy habits and the fact that he had gotten drunk, believing that if he had been meticulous in his killing of O'Brien, he never would have been caught. His last words on the scaffold were: "That whiskey that I drank the morning before I shot O'Brien was what caused me to do it when I did, and in so careless a manner."

Killer and robber James Gilbert Jenkins.

Jennings, Alphonso J. (Al), 1863-1961, U.S., outlaw. One of the more comic characters of the Old West, Al Jennings, was raised with his brothers Edward, Frank, and John at Kiowa Creek, Okla., near the town of Woodward. The Jennings boys, sons of Judge J.D.F. Jennings, were a fun-loving lot who dreamed of becoming bandits. In the mid-1890s, while working as cowboys they met some outlaws who later became members of the Bill Doolin gang. Al and Frank Jennings decided to become outlaws. They started off by obtaining fake U.S. marshal's badges and using them to collect "tolls" from gullible trail herders moving their cattle through the Oklahoma Territory.

Train robber Al Jennings.

Ed and John Jennings had followed their father's lead and became lawyers. The Jennings boys practiced in their father's court but they proved to be unorthodox and hotheaded. On Oct. 8, 1895, both brothers acted as defense for some young cowboys accused of stealing some barrels of beer. Acting for the prosecution was the flamboyant Temple Houston, son of Texas' greatest hero Sam Houston. Temple Houston, who was later the role model for Yancy Cravat in Edna Ferber's *Cimarron,* was an excellent lawyer;

he was also deadly with a gun and took insults from no man. When the Jennings brothers began to shout at him in court, Houston accused both of them of being "grossly ignorant of the law."

Ed Jennings slammed his hand down hard on a table and then shouted at Houston: "You're a damned liar!" Both he and his brother drew their guns just as Temple Houston's six-gun cleared its holster. Before a shooting battle erupted, the opponents were restrained. That night, Judge Jennings reproached his sons, telling them that their uncontrollable tempers had embarrassed him. He warned them to curb their emotions if they intended to practice law. Some hours later Ed and John Jennings entered the Cabinet Saloon in Woodward and went to the bar. They saw Temple Houston playing cards in a nearby room and took their guns from their holsters, carrying them at their sides. They entered the gambling room and Houston stood up. "Ed, I want to see you a minute," Temple Houston said to Jennings, motioning for Ed Jennings to accompany him out a back door.

Jennings was apparently drunk. He shouted at Houston: "See me here and now, you s.o.b.!" Both men pointed their guns, as did John Jennings. Houston fired six shots at both Jennings brothers. John was hit in the arm. Ed was struck in the head by a stray bullet from his brother's gun. When two more of Houston's bullets struck Ed Jennings he fell dead onto the barroom floor. John Jennings staggered out of the bar with half his arm in shreds. Though John Jennings had accidentally fired the shot that killed his brother, Houston was charged with murder. He was acquitted on grounds of self-defense.

Al Jennings told his father when they buried Ed that he intended to kill Houston but Judge Jennings shook his head, saying: "Do you want to heap another tragedy on this one?" Jennings, rebuked by his father, saddled his horse and, with his brother Frank, rode into southern Oklahoma where he was joined by several members of the Doolin gang. They planned to rob trains. On the night of Aug. 16, 1897, Al and Frank Jennings, with Little Dick West and Morris and Pat O'Malley, stopped a southbound Santa Fe train at Edmond but found it impossible to shoot or blast the safe open.

A few nights later Al Jennings tried to flag down another train by standing directly in the center of the tracks, holding a lantern and frantically waving a red flag. The engineer, however, kept his hand on the throttle and the train roared forward. Jennings, screaming for the engineer to halt, finally leaped out of the way at the last moment. The train raced on into the night as Jennings and the rest of the outlaws stood cursing in the darkness. A few days later Jennings and his brother Frank rode alongside a fast-moving Santa Fe train, near Bond Switch, firing their six-guns in the air as a signal to the engineer to stop. The engineer merely waved a friendly hello and kept going. The Jennings brothers, their horses exhausted, fell behind and then came to a panting stop as they watched their prey chug from sight.

These miserable failures were capped by a disastrous raid on a southbound Rock Island passenger train at 11 a.m. on Oct. 1, 1897. Al and Frank Jennings, Little Dick West and the O'Malley brothers found the train stopped at a water station eight miles south of Minco. They boarded the baggage car but again could not open the safe. "I've been waiting for that," Al Jennings said and he produced several sticks of dynamite. He tied these together, stuck a long fuse into one stick, lit it, and placed it alongside the safe. The baggage car clerk and the outlaws leaped from the train car and ran some distance from it, waiting.

Al Jennings in Hollywood, 1940.

"How much dynamite did you use, Al?" Frank Jennings asked his brother.

"You got to use a lot of dynamite to dent a big safe like that," Al Jennings answered knowingly.

A few seconds later, the entire car blew up, sending a shower of wooden and iron splinters in all directions. There was no safe, let alone money, to be found. The frustrated gang members then went through the passenger coaches and robbed everyone down to their last dollar. They also took diamond stickpins, women's jewelry, even a new pair of boots from a traveling salesman. The gang fled into the Indian nation where, on Oct. 29, 1897, they robbed the till of the Crozier and Nutter Store in the town of Cushing in Payne County. The robbery netted the thieves a mere $15. This was the last straw for Little Dick West and the O'Malleys. They rode in one direction, the Jennings brothers in another direction.

Little Dick West disappeared and would not be found until Apr. 7, 1898, when he was tracked down by Sheriff Frank Rinehart and other lawmen at the Harmon Arnett ranch southwest of Guthrie where he was working. At first Little Dick gave an alias, claiming he was merely a hired hand. Sheriff Rinehart told him to "cut the act" and arrested him under his real name. West broke away, pulled a six-gun and began firing at the lawmen who then shot him dead. The O'Malley brothers were captured earlier. This left only the inept Al and Frank Jennings at large. Marshal

James F. "Bud" Ledbetter of Muskogee, Okla., one of the toughest lawmen in the West, then received a tip that the Jennings brothers would be hiding in a covered wagon moving through the Indian Nation. He tracked down the wagon and ordered Al and Frank Jennings to come out from some heavy blankets under which they had been hiding.

The boys meekly surrendered and Ledbetter captured them without firing a shot. He threw them a rope and ordered them to tie each other up. Thus hog-tied, Ledbetter threw them over the backs of horses and led them ignominiously to town. This was the end of the Al Jennings gang, an outlaw band that never really got started and one that earned its members less than $200 each. Frank Jennings and the O'Malleys were given five-year terms in Leavenworth. Their leader and mastermind of the most absurd train robbery attempts on record, Al Jennings, was sent to the federal prison at Columbus, Ohio, to serve a life term. Here Jennings met the writer William Sydney Porter, who wrote under the pseudonym of O. Henry. Jennings filled Porter's ears with mythical stories about himself which the writer later used in some of his best stories.

Al Jennings was freed within five years. His brother Frank had been set free earlier and returned to the family homestead in Oklahoma. Al, however, refused to settle down and headed for California. He settled in Hollywood where he became a fixture, an "adviser" on motion pictures about the West. He told wild tales of his outlaw years, almost all of his claims being complete fabrications. Sheriff Jim Herron of Oklahoma later stated: "Old Al Jennings was around California for years, stuffing dudes with nonsense and telling them wild yarns about himself in the early days." Jennings convinced many a film producer that he was an expert on western banditry and he earned a considerable living as a consultant. He even wrote two books about his imagined life and his story was made into a motion picture. Although none of his claims were true, Jennings came to believe he was not only one of the most celebrated bad men of the West but he also had been a peer and friend of Jesse James.

When the ancient imposter, J. Frank Dalton, appeared in 1948 to claim that he was Jesse James, it was Al Jennings who rushed to his side. Jennings took one look at the old man and shouted with glee: "It's him! It's Jesse!" It made no difference to Al Jennings that he had never met the notorious Jesse James. Jennings babbled on about his fabulous exploits until his death in 1961, believing himself to be one of the great outlaws of the Old West. See: **Dalton, J. Frank; Doolin, William M.; Houston, Temple L.; West, Richard.**

Jennings, Napoleon Augustus, 1856-1919, U.S., lawman. Born and raised in Philadelphia, Napoleon Jennings ventured to Texas as an 18-year-old and lived a life filled with adventure for the next ten years, before returning to the East. He worked initially as a farmhand, later becoming a Cavalry clerk and a surveyor's aid. In 1876, Jennings became a Texas Ranger under the direction of L.H. McNelly and John B. Armstrong. He was immediately thrust into the Sutton-Taylor feud, fought along the Mexican border, and was with Jesse Lee Hall when the rangers ended the disturbance.

On Oct. 1, 1876, Jennings was involved in the raid of an outlaw camp near Carrizo, Texas, which resulted in the death of two of the ten fugitives. One bandit named McAlister was arrested after being wounded by Jennings. Four days later, Jennings and two other Rangers were involved in a case of mistaken identities when a group of men firing upon Jennings' party turned out to be a reinforcement contingent of Rangers. Jennings retired from the Rangers after two years, moving further west to work as a cowboy, stage driver, and gold prospector. In 1884, his thirst for adventure sated, Jennings returned East to write for newspapers and magazines until his death in 1919.

Johnny Behind the Deuce, See: O'Rourke, John.

Johnson, Jack (AKA: **Turkey Creek**), prom. 1870s, U.S., lawman-gunman. Jack "Turkey Creek" Johnson roamed the high plains to the Arizona Territory from the mid 1870s until the early 1880s. Originally a gold miner in Deadwood, Dakota Territory, he moved to Arizona after killing his two partners in a gunfight. Following a quarrel in the Deadwood saloon in late 1876, the three retired to a local cemetery where Johnson killed the two men. He paid for their burials, although dynamite had to be used to make a hole in the frozen ground.

In Arizona, he became a temporary deputy marshall to Wyatt Earp, and aided in the apprehension of stage robbers. On Mar. 20, 1882, two days after the murder of Morgan Earp, Johnson joined a posse which included Wyatt and Warren Earp, Doc Holliday, and Sherman McMasters, in pursuit of Frank Stilwell, the presumed murderer. The posse cornered Stilwell near Tucson and shot him to death. Two days later, while in pursuit of other murder suspects, Johnson and others encountered Florentino Cruz in a wood camp near Tombstone. Cruz was thought to have confessed to a murder before he was killed in the hail of a bullets.

Johnson and Sherman McMasters later drifted into Utah and northern Texas.

Johnson, John (AKA: **Liver-Eating Johnson; Crow-Killer**), prom. 1880s, U.S., lawman. Moving from Missouri to Montana in 1870, John Johnson became a mountain man who trapped deer, bear, and buffalo and was considered the greatest hunter of his day. He maintained a cabin near Rock Creek, near Red Lodge, Mont., which William "Buffalo Bill" Cody used as a camp for his buffalo hunting expeditions. Johnson reportedly maintained a private war with the Crow Indians, who murdered his Indian wife and child. He killed dozens of tribe members over ten years. One Easterner who hired Johnson to take him into the hills to hunt bear witnessed Johnson creep up on an Crow camp and attack it single-handedly, wounding several Indians and killing two. He then casually butchered the two corpses and ate their livers, thus earning the sobriquet "Liver-Eating Johnson."

John "Liver-Eating" Johnson in old age.

A large man who stood more than six feet tall and weighed 200 pounds, Johnson was a keen-eyed hunter and agile runner. He was also an expert knife-thrower, and he served for some years as an Indian scout for the U.S. Cavalry under General Nelson Miles. In 1880, he was appointed sheriff of Coulson, Mont., a rough-and-tumble town of mountain men and miners. He carried a rifle around town, never a six-gun. He always settled disputes with his fists and he later proudly stated that he never had to shoot a man to keep the peace. Offered princely sums to appear in Cody's Wild West shows, Johnson refused to travel to the East, stating that "civilization will kill you faster than God's great outdoors." Johnson maintained law and order for several years in Coulson before moving into the high mountains and disappearing.

Johnson, Richard, prom. 1860s-70s, U.S., outlaw. Richard Johnson, called Dick, was a Texas cowboy who sided with the Lee faction in the bloody Lee-Peacock Feud that raged through Grayson County, Texas, during the 1860s. Johnson was a half brother of the Dixon Brothers, Simp, Bob, and Charles, who all fought with Bob Lee against the forces of Lewis Peacock. Bob Lee, leader of the Lee faction, was killed in June 1869 and Johnson moved to west Texas to raise cattle. When Charles Dixon was killed by the Peacocks in 1871, Johnson returned to Grayson County to hunt down and kill Lewis Peacock, leader of the Peacock clan. Accompanied by Joe Parker, Johnson went to Peacock's ranch and climbed into a tree in the middle of the night, perching there with a rifle. At dawn on July 1, 1871, Lewis Peacock emerged from his ranch house and stood on the front porch. Johnson fired a bullet into

Western gunman Richard Johnson.

Lewis Peacock's heart, killing him on the spot. He then fled and was never apprehended for this murder. The Lee-Peacock Feud came to an abrupt end. See: **Lee-Peacock Feud; Peacock, Lewis**.

Johnson, William H., d.1878, U.S., lawman-gunman. Following the Civil War, Confederate Captain William Johnson moved west to New Mexico, married the daughter of prominent rancher and fellow southerner Henry Beckwith, and became co-owner of a cattle ranch. In 1876 he was drawn into the Lincoln County War, he and his partner Wallace Olinger joining the Murphy-Dolan faction. During the feud he was made a deputy to Sheriff William Brady. On Apr. 22, 1877, at Seven Rivers, Johnson defended his father-in-law's ranch from a raid led by John Chisum, who was convinced that Beckwith was stealing his herd.

A year later, on Apr. 30, 1878, Johnson joined a posse seeking to apprehend outlaws Frank Coe, Frank McNab, and Ab Sanders. The posse caught up with the band when they stopped to water their horses near Lincoln, N.M. The posse shot McNab and Sanders to death and arrested Coe. Johnson returned to ranching, but his relationship with his father-in-law became uncomfortable. On Aug. 16, 1878, after arguing at Beckwith's ranch, the old man fatally shot Johnson in the neck and chest with a double-barreled shotgun. Johnson's partner, Olinger, returned the fire, hitting Beckwith in the face, but the old man survived.

Johnson County War, 1892, U.S., feud. In 1892, the owners of the largest ranches in Johnson County, 250 miles northwest of Cheyenne, Wyo., declared war on the smaller ranchers and local homesteaders in the guise of driving out cattle rustlers. Many of these "homesteaders" were actually professional cowboys, formerly employed by the large cattle companies. When their term of employment ended, these disgruntled cowboys built their own herds at the expense of the stock companies by simply applying their own brand to the hide of the pilfered animals. The big ranchers sought relief in the courts, but evidence was hard to come by and the juries tended to sympathize with the small entrepreneur and against the conglomerate. Frustrated by the system, the larger firms hired "range detectives" to kill a few alleged rustlers, hoping to scare off smaller ranchers who were vying for the land.

The barons then attempted to influence the state legislature and the press. They ordered the lynching of a prostitute named Ella "Cattle Kate" Watson, who was equally adept with both a branding iron and a six-shooter, and her paramour Jim Averill. Averill used Watson's corral as the drop off point for the Johnson County rustling ring. It was also believed she accepted stolen beef for her sexual services. In the evening of July 20, 1889, twenty stockmen rode to Watson's ranch and took Kate and Averill captive. The gunmen proceeded to a nearby canyon, where the two were hanged. The lynching of Cattle Kate and Averill precipitated the Johnson County War.

Within the Wyoming Stock Growers' Association a secret "hit" list naming the alleged rustlers was prepared by the injured parties and sent to the association secretary for approval. Many of the men on the list were dangerous felons wanted in several states for cattle rustling and other criminal acts. Forty-six vigilantes (or Regulators as they were sometimes called) led by Major Frank Wolcott and Frank M. Canton, himself wanted for murder, were sent to the ranges to carry out the "invasion" following the close of the annual spring meeting of the Stock Grower's Association. Interestingly, two newspaper reporters acting as "observers" were on board the Union Pacific train when it steamed out of Cheyenne on Apr. 5, 1892. The nineteen cattle growers, accompanied by twenty-two hired gunmen from the area, occupied three passenger cars. The horses, weaponry, and provisions were lodged in the baggage cars.

The party arrived in Casper, where it was necessary to continue the rest of the journey on horseback. The Regulators succeeded in killing suspected rustlers Nate Champion and Nick Ray, but other small ranchers organized a resistance army of 200 men who chased the invaders back to Buffalo, Wyo., where they were arrested by the sheriff and his men at a local ranch. Champion emerged as a local martyr after managing to stave off fifty Regulators for

nearly twelve hours, before he was finally burned out of his shack and shot dead. The news of the "war" soon reached Cheyenne and acting Governor Amos Barber, who, with the help of senators Francis E. Warren and Joseph M. Carey, ordered a detachment of U.S. Cavalry troops into the region to end the hostilities. The cavalry refused to surrender the

Members of the Sixth Cavalry returning from duty in the Johnson County War.

Regulators to Red Angus, the sheriff of Cheyenne who was known to be sympathetic to the homesteaders. Placed in protective custody, the Regulators were escorted back to Cheyenne where they were to be put on trial in January 1893. They were to have been defended by Willis Van Devanter (who was later named an associate justice on the U.S. Supreme Court), but in a move that caught many people off guard, the prosecution requested that the court dismiss all charges against the men. The prosecuting attorneys were unable to produce the two trappers who had witnessed the shooting of Champion and Ray. The witnesses had been spirited out of town by friends of the Regulators. The financially beleaguered Johnson County owed the state $18,000 in trial expenses and the treasury was empty. Johnson County leaders refused to pay this sum, and it was not until 1899, when the state agreed to an appropriation, that the matter was quietly resolved.

Although none of the Regulators were prosecuted, the devastating effects of this ill-fated "war" hurt the local economy for years to come, and contributed to an ideological and political split that resulted in the election of a Democratic governor and five Populists to the legislature. The Republican machine that had represented the powerful stock growers for so many years was derailed as a result of the Johnson County War, but the Democratic governor and Populist legislators who took their place deadlocked on the issues, resulting in a political vacuum that left Wyoming without a senator for the next two years. See: **Averill, Jim; Wolcott, Frank; Canton, Frank.**

Jones, Frank, 1856-93, U.S., lawman. Frank Jones became a Texas Ranger at seventeen and quickly proved himself as a lawman. A year later, Jones killed two Mexican horse thieves and arrested another when they ambushed him. In 1880, Jones shot an outlaw and arrested two others, while searching for Scott Cooley, who sparked the 1875 Mason County War. Jones also killed a couple of rustlers in separate barroom incidents, including the notorious Tex Murietta.

Texas Ranger Frank Jones.

In October 1891, Jones and a seven-man posse chased four train robbers in Crockett County, Texas. During a shootout at Howard's Well the posse wounded three of the bandits, while the fourth, John Flint, committed suicide as he was about to be nabbed after an eight mile chase. Jones' last gunfight occurred on June 29, 1893, when he attempted to arrest a Mexican cattle thief, Jesus Maria Olguin and his son, Severio. He and his Ranger posse trailed them across the border to the settlement of Tres Jacales, Mex., where they fired at the two men, wounding them. As the lawmen attempted to enter a building where the two men were hiding, Jones was shot to death by the bandits inside. The Olguins were never prosecuted because the incident occurred on the Mexican side of the Rio Grande.

Jones, Jefferson, d.1890, U.S., outlaw. Sixty-year-old Henry Wilson was passing through the Winding Stair Mountains in the Choctaw Nation on Mar. 12, 1889, when Jefferson Jones killed Wilson and robbed him for a mere $12. The badly decomposed body was discovered a week later. Jones was arrested and taken to Fort Smith where Judge Isaac Parker sentenced him to die on the gallows, Jan. 16, 1890.

Jones, John, d.1879, U.S., outlaw. Born in Iowa, John Jones moved to New Mexico in 1866, and became embroiled in the Lincoln County War a decade later. The Jones family drifted to several different ranch sites, selling a ranch at one time to the infamous Horrell brothers, who were fleeing justice in Texas. In 1878, Jones became a cattle rustler with the Murphy-Dolan Gang. During a gunfight, he killed Bob Riley and avoided prosecution in the unruly Lincoln County.

On July 15, 1878, at the climactic battle of the bloody war, Jones and forty others attacked the store owned by Alexander McSween, the leader of the opposing group. After setting the store on fire, Jones and his men systematically slaughtered McSween, Harvey Morris, Vincent Romero, and Francisco Zamora as they fled the burning building. Tom O'Folliard and Hijino Salazar were also shot, but survived. On Aug. 26, 1879, at Seven Rivers, N.M., Jones shot John Beckwith to death following an argument over the ownership of cattle. Jones was pursued by lawmen Bob Olinger and Milo Pierce, who caught up with him a month later in Lincoln County. Jones angrily demanded a settlement to the rumors that he had killed Beckwith, cocking his rifle and firing a shot toward Olinger. The lawman responded with three shots which fatally wounded John Jones. See: **Lincoln County War.**

Jones, John B., 1834-81, U.S., lawman. Born in South Carolina on Dec. 22, 1834, John B. Jones was four when his family resettled in Travis County, Texas. Jones attended Baylor College and Zion College in Winnsboro, S.C. After serving in the Confederate Army in the Civil War, Jones was elected to the Texas legislature in 1868. He was later commissioned a major in the Frontier Battalion of the Texas Rangers and he became one of the leading law enforcement administrators in Texas, com-

John B. Jones, Texas Ranger.

manding six companies of Rangers and sending them across thousands of miles to battle outlaws and Indians. He often accompanied his men in various sweeps when dozens of desperate fugitives were captured. Jones was involved with a number of gun battles with outlaw bands and he was responsible for bringing the bloody Horrell-Higgins Feud to an end. Jones died in Austin, Texas, on June 19, 1881. See: **Horrell-Higgins Feud.**

Jones, John G., prom. 1851-53, U.S., lawman. In 1848 after several years of vigorous campaigning on the part of the U.S. citizens residing in the New Mexico territory, the Treaty of Guadelupe Hidalgo was ratified by the U.S. Congress, and the land was formally annexed into the union.

John G. Jones was appointed the first territorial marshal under civilian rule. Jones was familiar with the politics of the region, having lived most of his life in the Southwest and was considered somewhat of an expert on Indian policy when he assumed his duties on Mar. 12, 1851. Jones also doubled as sheriff of Santa Fe County. In order to placate the resentful Hispanic-Indian population, Jones shrewdly selected Lafayette Head, a merchant from Abiquiu, Rio Arriba County, to serve as deputy sheriff. Head was married to one of the prominent Spanish families in the region and was a special agent for the Jicarilla Apaches and the Utes.

Marshal Jones received little financial support from the depleted coffers of the territorial government. There was simply no money to feed the fourteen prisoners housed in the small, woefully inadequate Taos jail. In March 1852, Jones reported to the governor that the "poor wretches" would either starve to death, or be released. The governor issued a humane pardon, with the condition that the inmates must leave the territory for good. After two years in office, Marshall Jones was succeeded by Charles S. Rumley on Apr. 5, 1853. See: **Rumley, Charles S.**

Jones Brothers, d.1900, U.S., outlaw. John and Jim Jones were raised in Dallas County, Mo., and both young men, originally farmers, became outlaws in 1892. They moved to Texas where they reportedly killed the sheriff of Hamilton County. The Jones Brothers then fled to Colorado, where they held up stagecoaches and small banks. The Jones brothers robbed a Union Pacific train near Hugo, Colo., on Aug. 11, 1900, taking a small amount of money from the baggage car. A large posse pursued the Jones Brothers for hundreds of miles and finally cornered them in a small ranch house. The lawmen

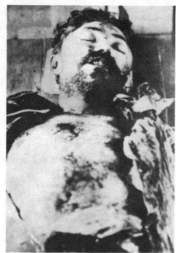

Outlaw John Jones, dead, 1900.

and outlaws exchanged fire for several days until officers set fire to the building. Jim Jones, rather than surrender, shot himself inside the burning building. His brother, John, leaped through the front door, two six-guns blazing. He was riddled by rifle fire and fell dead.

Judson, Edward Zane Carroll, See: **Buntline, Ned.**

K

Kalijah, Seaborn, d.1887, U.S., outlaw. Seaborn Kalijah was taken into custody on Jan. 17, 1887, for selling whiskey to Creek Indians in defiance of local laws. Deputy Marshal Phillips entrusted the prisoner to three of his possemen, Henry Smith, Mark Kuykendall, and William Kelly, while he attended to another matter in Eufaula, Okla. It was the responsibility of these three to safely convey the prisoner to Fort Smith for trial. Kalijah, a merciless killer, managed to break free from his shackles in the middle of the night. He grabbed an ax and chopped up Smith and Kuykendall as they slept by the fire. The third man, Kelly, was shot to death and his body mutilated. When Phillips returned the next day he found the bloody remains at the campsite. He followed Kalijah's trail back to the family home where he was promptly arrested. Seaborn Kalijah was removed to Fort Smith where he was hanged for murder on Oct. 7, 1887.

Keating's Saloon, Battle of, 1881, U.S., gunfight. Keating's Saloon was the worst pesthole in El Paso, Texas, and was the site of one of the wildest and bloodiest shootouts in western history. The Manning Brothers, notorious rustlers, had stolen a huge herd of cattle in Mexico and had driven the cattle into Texas to sell at handsome prices. Texas Ranger Ed Fitch and two Mexican officers named Sanchez and Juarique investigated the cattle raid. The two Mexicans, searching for the stolen herd, were shot and killed from ambush near the Manning ranch. This provoked a huge Mexican posse of more than seventy-five men to cross into Texas seeking revenge.

The Mexicans demanded an inquest for the deaths of Sanchez and Juarique. This was held on Apr. 15, 1881, with constable Gus Krempkau acting as interpreter. Krempkau, at noon that day, left the courtroom in El Paso and went to Keating's Saloon, where he obtained a rifle, even though no firearms were allowed in court. As Krempkau went through the swinging doors of the saloon, he was faced by cowboy George Campbell, a friend of the Mannings. Drunk, Campbell shouted to Krempkau that town marshal Dallas Stoudenmire should have arrested the armed Mexicans who had ridden into town that day and not have harassed the Manning brothers.

Dallas Stoudenmire, one of the most feared lawmen of the era, a fast-drawing peace officer who took no insults from anyone, was at that moment eating a bowl of stew in the Globe Restaurant only 200 yards away from Keating's Saloon. Meanwhile, Krempkau, not one to seek trouble, ignored Campbell's remarks. He walked to his horse and slipped the rifle into a holster. Campbell continued berating him, shouting: "Any American who befriends Mexicans should be hanged!"

"George," Krempkau said to the cowboy, "I hope you don't mean me."

"If the shoe fits, wear it," snarled Campbell.

At that moment, John Hale, a drunken bully and friend of Campbell's, staggered from Keating's Saloon and, hearing the exchange between Krempkau and Campbell, rushed to Krempkau and jammed a six-gun into Krempkau's chest. "Turn loose, Campbell," Hale shouted to his friend. "I've got him covered!" Though Krempkau made no move, Hale then shot the lawmen in the lungs. Hale looked down at the coughing Krempkau and then realized what he had done. He ran behind a post in front of the saloon just as Marshal Stoudenmire appeared with two six-guns in his hands. He had rushed from the Globe Restaurant when he heard the shot.

Stoudenmire saw his deputy crawling up the stairs of the saloon and he spied Hale trying to hide behind a post. He fired two shots on the run. The first wounded a man emerging from the saloon, the second struck Hale in the center of his forehead, killing him instantly. Then Stoudenmire turned to Campbell, who had caused the shooting of Krempkau. Campbell stood in the street, waving a six-gun at a crowd collecting nearby, telling the spectators to go away. "Gentlemen," he said, "this is not my fight!"

Krempkau called him a liar, and with his last ounce of strength pulled his six-gun and fired all six shots from a prone position, striking Campbell in the wrist and toe. Krempkau then fell against the steps of the saloon, dead. Campbell, whose six-gun had been shot out of his hand, picked up the weapon with his uninjured hand and sent a slug into the already dead Krempkau.

Stoudenmire than pumped three bullets into Campbell, who crashed to the street, shouting: "You s.o.b., you have murdered me!"

Patrick Shea, another town drunk, staggered across the street and picked up Cambpell's weapon. He leaned close to the dying Campbell and said: "You're a goner, George. Do you want your gun?"

Marshal Stoudenmire moved to the prone Campbell and waved his six-gun in Shea's face. "Put down that gun and move on, you little rat!" Shea dropped the gun and staggered off the street.

Three men were dead in a senseless argument and near comic opera gun battle. The killers of the two Mexican officers were never caught.

Keaton, Pierce, 1868-1931, U.S., outlaw. A Texas cowboy, Keaton fell in with bad company, notably Bud Newman and Bill and Jeff Taylor, who had been robbing banks and trains in Texas. Keaton participated in several robberies, and on June 9, 1898, he, the Taylor brothers, and Newman stopped a train outside of Coleman, Texas. Lawmen who were on the train, as well as armed crew members, put up a fierce fight; Newman was wounded in the arm and Keaton in the leg. Keaton

Outlaw Pierce Keaton.

fired a wild shot when he was struck by a bullet; this wounded fireman Lee Johnson, who died a few hours later. The outlaws fled on horseback, but a posse tracked them down four hours later, capturing all but Jeff Taylor. Bud Newman and Bill Taylor were given lengthy prison terms. Keaton was convicted of killing Johnson and sent to prison for life. Pierce Keaton was paroled in 1915, and he later settled in Bisbee, Ariz., where he died in 1931. See: **Newman, Bud**.

Kelly, Dan (AKA: **Yorky**), 1859-84, U.S., outlaw. Leaving his family and friends behind, young Dan Kelly left his home in Cork County, Ire., in 1881 for a chance at a new life in the U.S. What he found instead, was the hangman's noose—western justice for those who refused to abide by the laws of the land, and those sworn to uphold it. Kelly was living near Clifton, Ariz., in December 1883 when a gang of outlaws raided the town of Bisbee and killed several people. Dan Kelly was one of the men suspected of holding up a store with two other hardcases, Red Sample and Tex Howard. He left town and headed north, where his movements were almost impossible to trace due to a blinding snowstorm that had hit the area. Kelly boarded a train at Bowie Station on Dec. 11, but was put off near Deming after claiming that he was an itinerant hobo. Kelly was eventually arrested and taken back to Tombstone, Ariz., to stand trial for the Bisbee robbery. Kelly claimed he was innocent but was sentenced to hang on the gallows on Mar. 8, 1884. He was not fearful of that moment and remained talkative and full of good spirit. "I will walk up rightly," Kelly said of his approaching date with the gallows. On Mar. 8, he signaled the executioner to proceed and shouted, "Let her loose." In an instant he was

dead. Kelly's remains were transported to Boothill cemetery.

Kelly, Edward O. (AKA: **Red**), d.1904, U.S., outlaw. Living for some time on reward money he and his brother had collected after shooting Jesse James, Bob Ford made the choice when he ran out of money of going on the stage and becoming an actor. After meeting actress Nellie Waterson, he went with her to a Colorado mining camp called South Creede, where they opened a rowdy resort in a tent opposite the Foretone Hotel. Deputy Sheriff Edward Kelly, who had served as marshal of Batchelor, Colo., took issue with the way Ford ran the resort, and the two men became enemies.

Fighting at Creede Exchange on Feb. 17, 1892, neither was seriously in-

Edward O. Kelly, killer of Bob Ford.

jured but Kelly got the worst of the deal. On June 8 of that same year, Kelly approached Ford's saloon and without warning instantly killed Ford with a shotgun blast. Arrested immediately, Kelly was turned over to Sheriff Gardner, and charged with murder. Convicted, he was sentenced to life imprisonment and served eight years before gaining his freedom in 1900. Following his release Kelly moved to Oklahoma City, Okla., where on June 13, 1904, officer Joseph Burnett attempted to arrest him and was attacked and overpowered by Kelly. Burnett drew his revolver and killed the one-time deputy sheriff. See: **Ford, Robert**.

Kemp, David, d.c.1930s, U.S., lawman-gunman. In Hamilton, Texas, David Kemp was sentenced to hang while still a youth, but escaped to lead a life on both sides of the law. Breaking both ankles in a leap from the second story of the courthouse where he had been sentenced to death, he was recaptured. His sentence was commuted to life before receiving a full gubernatorial pardon. He had killed a man named Smith in 1885 in Hamilton after interfering in an argument between Smith and a man named Bogan. Kemp moved to New Mexico, established a butcher shop in Eddy, now Carlsbad, and co-owned a casino in nearby Phoenix, Ariz., before becoming the sheriff of Eddy County in 1889. He was a crooked lawman, catering to the interests of gamblers, and soon got involved in a feud with Dee Harkey, the newly appointed deputy U.S. marshal. Harkey caught Kemp rustling cattle and forced him to leave the county. But after spending a short time in Arizona, Kemp returned when Les Dow was appointed as his replacement. The two had been bitter enemies, and in April 1896, at the post office in Carlsbad, Kemp met Dow as he left the building and shot him to death. The former sheriff was acquitted on a plea of self-defense after forcing the only eyewitness to the murder to leave town. Kemp returned to cattle rustling and moved back to Texas, where he came to a violent end in the 1930s when he was shot to death by his sister.

Kennedy, James (AKA: **Spike**), prom. 1878, U.S., outlaw. In October 1878, James Kennedy, the heir to a Texas fortune, was in love with Dora Hand, the most popular woman in Dodge City, Kan. Unfortunately, Dora was also involved with James H. "Dog" Kelley, the mayor, and oversaw his prostitution operations. When Kelley noticed Kennedy becoming overly affectionate to Dora at his Alhambra Club, he ordered Kennedy evicted. Kennedy vowed revenge, and soon after sneaked up to the mayor's bedroom window and blindly fired a couple of shots into the darkened room. The mayor was still out on the town, but the shots killed Dora Hand instantly. A posse led by Sheriff Bat Masterson and including deputies Wyatt Earp, Charlie Bassett, Neal Brown, and Bill Tilghman apprehended Kennedy after a wild chase which ended when Masterson shot the fugitive in the arm. Kennedy asked only if he had been successful in killing his intended target. When told he had killed the woman he loved, he said he had no will to live. However, at his murder trial, helped by his father's wealth, Kennedy was found Not Guilty for lack of evidence.

Ketchum, Thomas E. (AKA: **Black Jack**), 1866-1901, U.S., outlaw. Born in San Saba County, Texas, Thomas Ketchum was raised in New Mexico and, with his brother Samuel, became a cowboy at an early age. He had little education and was emotionally unstable. A crack shot with a short temper, Ketchum became a notorious outlaw in the late 1890s, after putting together a tough band of outlaws gathered from the celebrated Hole-in-the-Wall area in Wyoming. He was known as Black Jack Ketchum, although his brother Sam was also called Black Jack at times. Although Ketchum was a feared gunman, he was

an uninspired robber who was easily tracked by lawmen when they realized that Ketchum would rob the same train or stagecoach over and over again and in the same location.

The outlaw's love life was a source of constant vexation to him. Ketchum, at one time, was seeing a young woman named Cora who was two-timing him. On one occasion, after he had seen her home and kissed her good night, another man entered her embrace only minutes after Ketchum rode off into the moonlight. She later wrote a letter to Ketchum rejecting him, a cruel missive which Ketchum read in front of a number of other cowboys at a ranch where he worked.
"No more than you were out of sight," the woman had written, "than we went to Stanton and got married."

Ketchum reacted to this letter by taking his six-gun from its holster and beating his own head with the butt until blood ran from the scalp. In between the vicious blows he administered to himself, Ketchum shouted at himself for being so foolish as to trust

Outlaw and train robber "Black Jack" Ketchum.

his emotions with another. "You will, will you?" he yelled. Then he struck himself again and again, yelling: "Take that! And that!" After punishing himself in this manner, Ketchum then went to the nearby Pecos River and waded into the water to the tops of his boots. His fellow cowboys stood gaping at him as Ketchum continued beating himself with his lariat. He did not quit this brutal self-punishment until he fell down exhausted.

This experience so unhinged Ketchum that he immediately launched into a vindictive criminal career. He went out of his way to punish anyone who even mildly disagreed with him. He organized a gang of desperadoes in 1898, hardcase outlaws that included his brother Sam Ketchum, G.W. Franks, and William Ellsworth "Elza" Lay (alias Bill McGinnis), who had been one of Butch Cassidy's most trusted riders in the old Wild Bunch. The gang robbed a number of small banks and stagecoaches in 1898. Lawmen tracking this gang soon realized that Ketchum and his men would return time and again to the same spot to stop the same stagecoach. Ketchum's predictable habits almost ended in his capture on several occasions, and he escaped hard-riding posses by only several minutes. It was as if he was daring the lawmen to apprehend him.

There was some confusion on the part of lawmen searching for the gang since Sam Ketchum, sometimes led a separate gang of men which included Will Carver and Elza Lay, one-time members of the Wild Bunch. Sam Ketchum and Carver had been longtime friends, the two having opened a saloon and gambling house in San Angelo in 1894. The place was notorious for shootings and rigged gambling tables and was soon closed by authorities. Sam went back to working at ranches as a cowboy, but he tired of this and readily joined his brother Tom in a career of crime, one that would lead to his own premature death.

On July 2, 1899, Tom Ketchum arrived in Cape Verde, Ariz., and immediately got drunk in a saloon. He then sat down to a poker game with several miners. When two burly miners made fun of his drunken conduct, Ketchum suddenly sobered. He jumped up and swept back his long black coat so that his two guns showed and then ordered the miners to go for their guns. He was a fearsome sight, with dark, piercing eyes, heavy, dark eyebrows and a thick, black handlebar mustache. The miners reached for their guns and Ketchum shot them both, mortally wounding them. He then fled the town.

In 1899, Ketchum, his brother Sam, Lay, and Franks stopped three Santa Fe Railroad trains at the Twin Mountain curve near Folsom, N.M. The gang took only a few hundred dollars with each robbery, but Black Jack Ketchum was identified and several posses began searching for him in earnest. After robbing the Sante Fe for the third time, the Ketchum gang split up, with Tom Ketchum going his own way and Sam Ketchum, Franks, and Lay riding to a hideout in Turkey Canyon, N.M. A large posse tracked them to this area on July 12, 1899, and surrounded the campsite, waiting for the outlaws to go to sleep around their smoldering campfire. Just before dawn the next day, the lawmen ordered the outlaws to surrender. The bandits replied with intense gunfire and scurried behind some rocks.

The battle lasted for hours. Sam Ketchum's marksmanship was as deadly accurate as his brother's. He shot and killed Sheriff Edward Farr of Colorado and a deputy, W.H. Love. Another lawman named Tom Smith was also killed by one of the outlaws. Ketchum was wounded in the shoulder and Lay was struck by two bullets, but the three wily outlaws managed to get to their horses and escape. The wounded Ketchum, however, limped off to a ranch owned by Henry Lambert near Ute Park. Here he took refuge in a barn but the bullet in his arm caused gangrene to set in. Lambert and a ranch hand realized that only amputation would save Sam's life. They cut off his arm in a crudely performed operation. A few days later, lawmen tracked Ketchum to the Lambert ranch and arrested him, taking him to Santa Fe Prison. Here officers questioned Sam Ketchum incessantly, seeking to know the whereabouts of his brother, Tom. Sam, in typical outlaw tradition, refused to say anything. He finally blurted: "Black Jack, my

brother, is dead and buried." Sam Ketchum's condition worsened and, because of the amputation, he went into shock and died on July 24, 1899.

Black Jack Ketchum was now alone but, undaunted, he stopped a Colorado & Southern train near Folsom, Ariz., on Aug. 16, 1899. As Ketchum was scooping up a few hundred dollars in cash from the baggage car safe, the guard reached for a gun and Ketchum shot him in the jaw.

The hanging of Thomas "Black Jack" Ketchum, Apr. 25, 1901.

He then leaped from the car and began to run toward his horse when conductor Frank Harrington jumped down from a passenger car, firing at him with a shotgun. Ketchum turned and faced Harrington and both men advanced upon each other, blazing away. Ketchum shot Harrington but not before the conductor unloaded a blast of buckshot into Ketchum. The outlaw dropped his six-gun, crawled beneath the train, crossed over the tracks, and crawled into the brush. He escaped under the cover of darkness. A train crew found him the next day a short distance down the line. He was propped against a tree, painfully picking the buckshot out of his chest.

Taken to Santa Fe, Ketchum was tried and convicted of train robbery and was sentenced to death. (Train robbery was by then a capital offense in certain western states, although Ketchum seems to be the only outlaw who was ever executed for this crime.) He was imprisoned in the jail at Clayton, N.M., and watched from his cell window as workmen erected the gallows from which he was to hang.

As the carpenters finished their task, Ketchum shouted out to them from the window of his cell: "You did a fine job, boys, but why not tear down the stockade so the fellows can see a man hang who never killed anyone?"

On the day of his execution, Apr. 25, 1901, Ketchum refused to talk to a priest who came to visit him in his cell. "I'm gonna die as I've lived," he told the clergyman, "and you ain't gonna change me in a few minutes." The warden arrived and asked Black Jack if he had any last requests. The celebrated outlaw smiled and then said: "Have someone play a fiddle when I swing off." Many newspaper men were present to record the outlaw's last moments and he played to them with great bravado. When he was led into the courtyard, he saw the scaffold and suddenly increased his gait, almost sprinting up the steps of the gallows. Standing beneath the noose of the hangman's rope, Ketchum said loudly to the many witnesses standing at the foot of the gallows: "I'll be in hell before you start breakfast, boys!" The noose was affixed around Ketchum's neck and a black hood was placed over his head and face. The crowd fell silent.

A moment before the trap door was flung wide, Black Jack Ketchum's last words roared out from beneath the darkly sinister shroud: "Let her rip!" The executioner pulled the lever and the trap door shot backward and Ketchum plummeted to his death. His last words were gruesomely prophetic. The hangman had improperly fixed the rope around the outlaw's neck and the weights on his legs so that the outlaw went through the trap at terrific speed and was decapitated. The gore from the headless torso soaked the front ranks of the visitors at the foot of the scaffold. It was one of the most grisly executions on record. See: **Carver, William; Cassidy, Butch; Lay, William Ellsworth; Wild Bunch.**

Kettle, Jack, d.1889, U.S., outlaw. Jack Kettle led a large band of thieves and outlaws in Wyoming in the late 1880s. The band roamed through Fremont and Johnson counties, robbing stores, settlers, and stagecoaches. Several deaths were attributed to Kettle and his ruthless gang. The gang became so powerful that it built a sprawling log "castle" or fort in the Big Horn Mountains with a second fort at the mouth of a canyon leading to the main headquarters. Vigilantes finally resolved to wipe out the band and more than 150 people stormed the Big Horn bastion in 1889. They seized eleven of the band, including Kettle, and lynched them. One newspaper report of the day related that "the bodies were buried before they were cold."

Kid Curry, See: Logan, Harvey.

Kilpatrick, Benjamin (AKA: **The Tall Texan; Benjamin Arnold**), 1876-1912, U.S., outlaw. Born and raised in Texas, Ben Kilpatrick came from a large family. He and his brother George began working as cowboys at an early age and joined Butch Cassidy's Wild Bunch in the late 1890s. Kilpatrick was slow to use his gun and had an

Wild Bunch members William Carver, left, and Ben "The Tall Texan" Kilpatrick, right, who rode with the infamous outlaws Butch Cassidy and the Sundance Kid.

amiable nature. He stood six feet, two inches and was known as The Tall Texan. Kilpatrick was one of Cassidy's top lieutenants and was present during almost all of the major train and bank robberies committed by Cassidy and his Wild Bunch gang, proving himself to be nerveless and dependable. Kilpatrick was reportedly with Cassidy, Harvey "Kid Curry" Logan, William Ellsworth "Elza" Lay, and George "Flat Nose" Curry when the gang stopped and robbed the Union Pacific's Overland flyer on Apr. 25, 1898. They gang blew up the express car with dynamite and made off with more than $30,000.

The Tall Texan was present when Cassidy, Logan, Bill Carver, and O.C. Hanks robbed the Union Pacific's Train No. 3 at Table Rock, near Tipton, Wyo., on Sept. 29, 1900. The gang took a little more than $5,000 from the express car. Cassidy, Harry Longbaugh (better known as the Sundance Kid), Logan, Hanks, and Kilpatrick robbed the First National Bank of Winnemuca, Nev., on Sept. 19, 1900, taking $32,000. On July 3, 1901, Kilpatrick helped Cassidy, Logan, Hanks, and the Sundance Kid rob the Great Northern train at Wagner, Mont., taking $40,000 from the express car, again using dynamite to blow wide the bolted doors of the car.

Following the Wagner robbery, Cassidy's Wild Bunch was pursued by dozens of posses as the last great outlaw band of the West. So intense was the manhunt for this gang that its members decided to split up and leave the Wyoming-Colorado-Utah area. Cassidy and the Sundance Kid reportedly traveled to New York and then to South America to continue robbing banks and payrolls in Bolivia where they were killed in a shootout with a small army of federal troops (some later reports have it that Cassidy survived and returned to the U.S. to live into old age).

Kilpatrick, with Laura Bullion, alias Della Rose, one of the female camp followers of the gang, traveled east but as trailed by detectives to St. Louis and captured there on Nov. 8, 1901. More than $7,000 from the Wagner robbery was found in Kilpatrick's suitcase. He was then using the alias of Benjamin Arnold. Kilpatrick confessed his part in the Wagner robbery but would offer no information about his fellow bandits. On Dec. 12, 1901, he was sentenced to fifteen years in the federal penitentiary at Atlanta. Laura Bullion was given a five-year sentence in a women's prison in Tennessee.

While serving time in Atlanta, Kilpatrick struck a fast friendship with his cell mate, Ole Beck, also known as Howard Benson. Beck was a small-time thief and he thrilled to Kilpatrick's exciting tales of his western outlaw days. Both men resolved that when they were released they would again follow the outlaw trail made famous by The Tall Texan and his Wild Bunch friends. Kilpatrick was released on June 11, 1911. Beck was released a short time later and both men rode to Texas. On this trip, Kilpatrick soon came to realize that the Old West he had known and roamed was no more. Automobiles were everywhere and he and Beck found it difficult to ride their horses down the streets of any sizeable city without getting run over. Telephone poles dotted the western landscape and police drove about in large black wagons.

When the pair reached Ozona, Texas, they were spotted on the street by newspaper editor Marvin Hunter who had known Kilpatrick decades earlier. He invited them into the office of his newspaper, the Ozona *Kicker*. The two outlaws sat sipping coffee and telling Hunter that they had seen for themselves how the country had changed, how banks were protected by alarm systems and that the outlaws of Kilpatrick's days could not survive in the modern era. They were going straight, they said, telling Hunter that they had

gotten jobs on a nearby sheep ranch. No, the days of robbing and running were over for them. Nothing could have been further from the truth.

Kilpatrick and Beck had been monitoring the run of the Southern Pacific's *Sunset Flyer* between Sanderson and Dryden, Texas. On the night of Mar. 13, 1912, both men were waiting at Sanderson Draw when the train stopped for water. This was a regular water stop which had been noted by Kilpatrick. He and Beck got onto the passenger car just

Kilpatrick and Ole Beck, dead, Mar. 13, 1912; their killer, express guard David Trousdale, stands at left, holding up Kilpatrick's corpse.

in front of the express car and then knocked on the door of the express car. A young baggage car guard, David A. Trousdale, opened the door a crack. Beck said to him: "I'm a Southern Pacific detective. We've just got wind of a robbery attempt on you. Let us inside."

Trousdale opened the door and Beck entered, followed by Kilpatrick. Beck carried an old six-gun, holding this at his side, pretending to check the car's security. Kilpatrick held a Winchester rifle, an old 40-82 make. The Tall Texan moved close to Trousdale and said: "Where do you keep the currency consignment?" This question alerted Trousdale to the fact that the two men were not who they claimed to be. "You fellows are railroad detectives and *you* don't know where we keep the cash?"

He reached for a rifle in a wall rack but Kilpatrick jammed his ancient weapon into Trousdale's stomach. "Don't try it, young fellow," Kilpatrick warned him. There was a loud noise like a door banging coming from the next car and Kilpatrick turned his head to see if anyone else was entering the car. At that moment Trousdale grabbed a large mallet which was nearby and was used for smashing ice for the water cooler. He brought this down on Kilpatrick's head with terrific force, crushing the outlaw's skull and killing him on the spot. Beck wheeled about but Trousdale grabbed Kilpatrick's rifle and fired almost point blank at Beck as the outlaw ran toward him. Beck fell dead from a bullet in his heart.

A few minutes later the train continued its journey uninterrupted. When it reach Dryden, Trousdale dumped the two bodies onto the station platform and a local photographer took a photo of the two dead outlaws being held up by train and station workman. This ignominious end for the once-proud Ben Kilpatrick signaled the end of the old-time western outlaws. Trousdale, the young baggage car guard who had dispatched two bandits in a matter of a minute, was given a large reward by Southern Pacific and a long vacation, along with the gratitude of the railroad's executives for saving a cash shipment of a few thousand dollars.

Said Trousdale of the whole affair: "They thought they were such smooth workers at the game. But it made me sore the way they acted. So I decided to take some of the conceit out of them...I am more worried about what to do with the vacation and the reward the company has given me than I am about killing those two." See: **Bullion, Laura; Carver, William; Cassidy, Butch; Curry, George; Hanks, Orlando Camillo; Logan, Harvey; Wild Bunch, The.**

Kimble County, Texas, prom. 1877, U.S., outlaws. In the early winter months of 1877, an epidemic of lawlessness spread through Kimble County, Texas, which prompted local officials to seek the help of the Texas Rangers in arresting the gang of cutthroats who had succeeded in virtually abolishing all civil authority. "This is the worst section of the country there is for men to work in and a better hiding place for rascals than any other part of Texas," reported Lieutenant Pat Dolan of the Rangers, after a thug named Goodman stabbed and wounded one of his men while being transported to jail.

Horse thieves and rustlers were making life difficult for the ranchers and cattle growers living near the junction of the Llanos. Ranger H.B. Waddill added an alarming postscript to the intolerable conditions that abounded: "A man that isn't a thorough expert at stealing has no show of holding his own...these men make forays into other counties and burn cattle beyond recognition...Everyone that is not known is looked upon as an enemy." The law-abiding citizens began stocking up on guns and ammunition, in anticipation of a shooting war with the desperados. Judge W.A. Blackburn of the Seventeenth Judicial District was not at all sure if he would be able to open the spring session of court. He notified Major John B. Jones of the Texas Rangers that on any given day, forty to a one hundred gunmen could be raised to prevent law enforcement officers from serving legal papers. The session was scheduled to begin on Apr. 30, but Judge Blackburn requested that the Rangers provide an escort from his home in Lampasas. Major Jones replied that he would be dispatching three companies to the region by Apr. 15 to clean up Kimble County.

Jones assembled his forces near the headwaters of South Llano on Apr. 18 and began moving on the town of Junction the next day. Five detachments of Rangers descended on Kimble County the following day. They were welcomed enthusiastically by the local people who were taken completely by surprise. In some instances the residents of Kimble County offered to take up arms in order to assist in the cleanup. The Rangers combed the woods for outlaws, and sometimes came upon these men by surprise as they slept in their cabins. In the next few days, forty-one criminal suspects were arrested—thirty-seven in Kimble County alone. They were charged with a variety of crimes including forgery, assault, prison escape, theft, and suspicion. The courts went to work on the defendants, and within a short period of time twenty-five indictments were returned, including ones charging the sheriff and county judge with malfeasance. Not one life had been lost in the sweep, and Major Jones had earned much praise and respect for his work. See: **Jones, John B.**

King, Frank, b.1863, U.S., lawman. Frank King was a dedicated lawman who served as a deputy sheriff in Phoenix, Ariz., during the 1880s, and in Texas, New Mexico, and California in the following decade. While serving a brief term as a guard at the Yuma Prison in 1889, a massive prison break was attempted in which five prisoners were shot to death, most of them by sharpshooter King the only man in the main tower at the time. King was one of the lawmen who fought a gun battle with the Black Jack Ketchum gang when it attempted to rob a bank in Nogales, Ariz., on Aug. 6, 1896, beating off the outlaws. King lived into the 1920s and was considered one of the toughest lawmen of his era.

King, Sandy, prom. 1881, U.S., outlaw. Sandy King was a tall cowboy with an addiction for red kerchiefs, which he wore around his neck. He was a rustler and thief when not working at ranches and often rode with William "Curly Bill" Brocius, raiding herds in New Mexico and Arizona. King was a hard-drinking gunman who appeared in Shakespeare, N.M., in late 1880. He got into several barroom brawls and was considered the town bully. When Russian Bill, one of King's friends, was caught red-handed stealing a horse, he was brought to Shakespeare and tried by a vigilance committee on Jan. 1, 1881. Russian Bill admitted stealing the horse and was promptly sentenced to be hanged. Someone on the vigilance committee proposed that Sandy King be hanged at the same time on the charge of being "a damned nuisance." The committee agreed and King, who was in a makeshift courtroom at the time, was seized. It was pointed out that recently he had gotten drunk, entered the local general store and had gotten into an argument with the clerk, shooting the clerk's finger off when he did not move fast enough to suit King.

In his own defense, King pointed out to the vigilantes that others had committed worse acts and had not been punished. He cited the recent case of Bean-Belly Smith who had, some weeks earlier, entered the dining room of the hotel and shot a man to death over the last egg in the house. The vigilantes ignored this argument and took King and Russian Bill to the lobby of the hotel and threw ropes about the high rafters. Bill begged for his life but King merely requested a glass of water because "my throat is dry after talking so much to save my life." After King gulped down the water, both men were hanged from the rafters and left dangling for several hours "so the people about town could ride in and see how justice had overtaken two bad characters." See: **Brocius, Curly Bill**.

Kuhns, Marvin (AKA: **J.W. Wilson**), b.1865, U.S., outlaw. Marvin Kuhns was a thief and bank robber operating from 1890 to the turn of the century. After one robbery, Kuhns, who had been wounded five times by police bullets, was imprisoned in the Fort Wayne, Ind., jail on Dec. 12, 1890. Born in Noble County, Ind., Kuhns and his brother Walter robbed several small-town banks in Indiana and Illinois before being captured in a hotel in Green Hill, Ind., by Marshal Elmer Laird and others in 1901. Kuhns was known to sleep with two revolvers so the posse entered his room in their stocking feet. Laird put a gun to Kuhns' head, then shook him and ordered him not to reach for his revolvers. Ignoring the command, Kuhns still reached and Laird shot him in the head. The bandit survived, however, and was sent to prison. He was later paroled but was shot and killed by a farmer in Illinois while rustling some livestock.

L

Labreu, Jason, prom. 1880s, U.S., gunman. Jason Labreu was a Creole cowboy who kept his sinister past well hidden from Leona Devere, the daughter of a western Arkansas farmer whom he was courting. One night, Labreu, who was wanted for murder in Texas and New Orleans, took the young girl on a walk through a lush meadow in order to pick some flowers. Devere never returned to her parents home. Her body was found in a brook; she had been brutally raped and drowned.

Deputy Marshal H.D. Fannin was assigned to the case. He found Labreu working as a hired hand in the Chickasaw Nation at a ranch belonging to Jack Crow. The lawman appealed to Crow to hire him on, so that he could get into Labreu's good graces. For many weeks Fannin worked in the fields side by side with the killer, trying to get him to carelessly confess to the Devere murder. Finally, Labreu let his guard down and exclaimed: "I've killed a dozen men myself, but I was never bothered in my sleep until I killed that girl." Fannin said that he had shot a woman once, but she did not die. "I drowned the one I killed," Labreu interjected.

Deputy Fannin waited for the right moment to arrest Labreu. The gunman always kept his Winchester near his side, in case he was threatened. Finally, Labreu made a mistake. He left the weapon just long enough for the lawman to grab hold of it, and aim it at Labreu's face. With the help of Jack Crow, Labreu was placed in shackles for the trip to Fort Smith (Ark.). They were only a few miles away from the stockade when Labreu made a desperate bid for freedom. Deputy Fannin dismounted from his horse in order to wait for a train to pass. As Fannin tightened a cinch on his horse, Labreu kicked the animal in such a way that the bucking action snapped the lead rope. Fannin's horse galloped off, and with it, Labreu.

However, the deputy coolly drew out his six-shooter and took aim at the escaping cowboy. He fired a shot that struck Labreu in the back. The gunman fell to the ground dead. For Deputy Fannin it was an unfortunate mishap, because he had forfeited his fees and mileage expenses after shooting the prisoner. Furthermore, it was the legal responsibility of the lawman to pay for the burial expenses of a prisoner if no one came forward to claim the body. Fannin had to pay $60 to bury the troublesome Jason Labreu.

Lacy, Robert, d.1877, U.S., outlaw. Robert Lacy was a notorious western gambler and gunman who allegedly shot several men throughout New Mexico. Afterwards, he moved north to Rawlins, Wyo., where he continued gambling and frequently cheated several residents of the town.

Infuriated by Lacy's consistent swindles, several of his victims formed a vigilante group and stormed into the saloon where Lacy was playing poker. He was dragged outside with another cardsharp and both scoundrels were promptly hanged.

Robert Lacy, right, and another cardsharp, lynched at Rawlins, Wyo., 1877.

Lamb, James, and **O'Dell, Albert**, d.1887, U.S., outlaws. Edward Pollard and George Brassfield leased a farm near the town of Lebanon in the Chickasaw Indian Nation. In the fall of 1885, the two farmers hired James Lamb and Albert O'Dell to assist them in the harvest. Lamb, a handsome young rake, took a fancy to Mrs. Pollard. Within days they had begun an illicit affair. At the same time George Brassfield's wife conducted an amorous flirtation with O'Dell. The goings on at the Lebanon ranch quickly became a scandal of major proportions.

Brassfield finally decided to leave his wife, but Pollard hung on gamely, hoping that this was nothing more than a passing fancy. It was not, and on the night of Dec. 26, Lamb and O'Dell hid in the bushes waiting for Pollard to return from a business trip to Lebanon. When he appeared on the road, they ambushed and killed him, concealing the body in a nearby location. Afterward, a preacher was summoned to marry Lamb and Mrs. Pollard. The woman explained that her husband had run off and would not be coming back. Two months later the decayed remains were found, and the case was assigned to Deputy Marshal Mershon.

The facts of the case slowly came to light. Mershon arrested the two men in the company of Mrs. Pollard near Buck Horn Creek. They were brought back to the jail at Fort Smith (Ark.) to await trial. Mrs. Pollard posted bail, and returned to the family home in Missouri where she gave birth to Lamb's child. Interestingly, Mrs. Brassfield also bore her lover's children—twins—but they died a few hours after leaving the womb. Lamb and O'Dell employed separate attorneys at their trial. Each blamed the other for the murder of farmer Pollard. The women were enlisted as prosecution witnesses, and their testimony helped convict

Lamb and O'Dell who were both hanged on Jan. 14, 1887.

Larn, John M., 1849-78, U.S., lawman-outlaw. John M. Larn was born in Mobile, Ala., in 1849. In his early teens, he ran away to Colorado and worked as a ranch hand until he killed his boss in an argument over a horse. Larn then fled to New Mexico, where he killed a sheriff he thought was hunting him. Larn made his way to Fort Griffin, Texas, and took a job as a trail boss for Bill Hays, a local rancher. On the way to California, Larn became embroiled in a dispute with a pair of Mexicans and as usual, settled the argument by shooting the men to death. He had their bodies thrown into the Pecos River.

Larn eventually settled down in Fort Griffin and married Hays' daughter. By 1876, he was known as an established citizen of Shackelford County, and rode with the local vigilante committee. In April 1876, Larn was elected county sheriff. During his tenure, Larn frequently deputized his old friend, gunfighter John Selman, who also helped in a cattle rustling scheme Larn devised. Larn had signed a contract to deliver three steers a day to the military garrison and was rustling them from his neighbors' herds. As their herds dwindled and Larn's did not, his neighbors discovered the rustling scheme and forced Larn to resign as sheriff on Mar. 7, 1877. In June 1878, Larn wounded a local rancher named Treadwell, who may have been the man who uncovered the rustling. On June 22, 1878, Larn was arrested by his successor, Sheriff William Cruger. In the jail in Albany, Cruger had the local blacksmith shackle Larn to the cell floor to keep his supporters from freeing him. When the Fort Griffin vigilantes arrived at the jail at midnight on June 23, to lynch Larn and could not release him from his shackles, they formed a firing squad and killed him in his cell.

Las Cuevas, Mex., War, prom. 1875, U.S. In the fall of 1875, there were widespread rumors of an impending war with Mexico. For some time, Mexican cattle rustlers had been crossing the Rio Grande to steal livestock from white ranchers, and then driving the herds south to Monterey. The unwillingness of the Mexican government to assist in the manhunt for these thieves angered the settlers on the U.S. side of the Rio Grande, and contributed to a growing pro-war sentiment. Captain Leander H. McNelly, a former Confederate army officer commanded a special detachment of Texas Rangers assigned to apprehend the rustlers.

McNelly spent from June to October in search of the roving band of Mexicans, but he met with little success despite an intricate spy system set up to clock their movements in the vicinity of Brownsville and Rio Grande City. In October, McNelly returned to his home in Washington County to recuperate from a lingering illness. Later that

A monument to Gen. Juan Flores was erected by the peasants shortly after his death in the Las Cuevas Mexican War.

month he received reports that the bandits had stolen another 200 head of cattle from Cameron County. McNelly notified his intentions to his superiors: "I am in communication with my spies on the other side, and I feel satisfied that within a short time will be able to send you a good report. I have met with Commander Kells of the U.S.A. boat *Rio Bravo*, and if he does as much as he says he will, you may expect some stirring news soon."

McNelly received permission from Attorney General George Clark to engage U.S. forces, if necessary, in the pursuit of the criminals. There is little doubt that the captain interpreted this in the broadest of terms. Kells and McNelly were anxious for war and may have hatched a conspiracy to unwittingly lure the Mexicans into battle. So hungry for war was McNelly, that it was suggested his own men fire upon the *Rio Bravo* to provoke a fight. The leader of the Las Cuevas renegades was Juan Flores, who had driven hundreds of Texas cattle across the river.

On Nov. 19, 1875, after receiving a tip from a Mexican informant that the rustlers were preparing to cross a big herd of cattle near Las Cuevas, Captain McNelly gathered his forces and told them they would be crossing the river in canoes. However, the U.S. troops were unable to cooperate in such a foolhardy scheme. The Mexican forces were three times the size, and such action could lead to an international incident that might spark a full blown war. McNelly however, was not deterred. He gathered his men and presented the facts to them. "Boys," he said, "you have followed me as far as I can ask you to unless you are willing to go farther. Some of us may get back, or maybe all of us will get back, but if any of you do not want to go over with me, step aside. You understand there is to be no surrender—we ask no quarter nor give any."

The Rangers were in agreement: they would accompany McNelly on this crusade. They crossed the river at 4:00 a.m., and proceeded to the heavily fortified Las Cuevas ranch. "Kill all you see except old men, women, and children," McNelly ordered. There were only thirty Rangers, and at least ten times as many Mexicans. Against these odds, McNelly hoped his situation would lure U.S. troops into the fold if he succeeded in capturing the ranch. The signal to attack was given. Lieutenant Robinson let out a fearful whoop and headed for the target. The other Rangers followed, descending on the sleeping ranch. "Many of the men were on their woodpiles cutting wood while their wives were cooking breakfast on little fires out of doors," stated Ranger Bill Callicott. "We shot the men down on the woodpiles until we killed all we saw in the ranch. Then the pilot told the Captain that we had made a mistake in the ranch. This was the Las Curchas—the Cuevas Ranch was a half-mile up the trail."

McNelly accepted the news calmly and ordered his men to Las Cuevas, where they encountered 250 Mexican soldiers. With the element of surprise no longer in their favor, McNelly ordered a retreat back to the river. Having failed in his initial attempt, the captain regrouped his forces

The home of Mexican rebel leader Juan Flores.

and ordered them to take cover in the brush. Flores and his men appeared on horseback a short time later to give chase to the fleeing Americans. Recalled Callicott: "When the Mexicans did not see any of us on the bank, they thought we were swimming the river, and so here they came, twenty-five horsemen led by General Juan Flores, owner of Las Cuevas. The captain said 'Charge them boys!' and we ran up the cowtrail to the top of the bank and formed a line. 'Open up on them as fast as you can!' McNelly ordered."

Flores was shot off his horse. He fell to the ground, riddled with Ranger bullets. Having observed the gunfight from the U.S. side of the river, Captain Randlett of the

army contingency crossed forty soldiers into Mexico. He justified his actions on an earlier order which stipulated that troops were only authorized to assist in the fighting if there was a genuine threat of massacre. This scenario was wildly exaggerated, but in his official report, Randlett stated he believed McNelly's command was "in danger of annihilation." Once across the river, McNelly tried to persuade the soldiers to accompany him to the Las Cuevas ranch for an assault on the rustlers. Randlett remained at the riverbank where his men repulsed attacks by the Mexicans.

As the day wore on the size of the troops increased. At a critical juncture in the confrontation a messenger from the Chief Justice of the state of Tamaulipas suddenly appeared with a message. The Mexicans would agree to return the stolen cattle and apprehend the thieves if the troops would retreat to the other side of the river. The compliment of soldiers complied, leaving McNelly and his band to stand alone against a large, imposing Mexican army. The stand-off continued. The next day McNelly sent a dispatch to General William Steele, asking for further instructions. The news was communicated to Washington, and the federal authorities entreated McNelly to surrender to the Mexicans, lest his actions provoke a war.

The brazen McNelly advised the Mexicans that he would attack with his force of thirty men unless the cattle and the thieves were handed over. On the afternoon of the twenty-first, the Mexicans complied with the demands and returned seventy-six head of cattle to Ringgold. The Las Cuevas raid, which claimed the life of General Flores and at least four other men, was a success. The strange little "war" was not fought over boundary rights, freedom, or military oppression, but to secure the border from Mexican bandits, and to assure a safe passage for Texas longhorns on the way to market. See: **McNelly, Leander H.**

Latham, James V., 1859-1936, U.S., lawman. James V. Latham, born in Vienna, Mo., on July 7, 1859, moved to Texas in 1880 and became a Texas Ranger, serving with that distinguished group of lawmen for almost twenty years. Latham also served as a deputy sheriff in El Paso, Texas, and later in New Mexico. He died on Nov. 17, 1936.

Lay, William Ellsworth (AKA: **Elza; Elzy; William McGinnis**), 1862-1934, U.S., outlaw. William Ellsworth Lay, known alternately by the nickname "Elzy" and the alias William McGinnis, is suppose to have masterminded the most successful bank and train robberies of Butch Cassidy's Wild Bunch. Although the film which popularized

Cassidy's turn-of-the-century escapades casts the Sundance Kid in the role, Lay was actually Cassidy's most frequent partner. Lay, born in Ohio in 1862, traveled west as a teenager, and collaborated with Cassidy in many two-man robberies.

The pair met while doing ranch work in Wyoming and worked together for a couple of years. In April 1897, Lay

Outlaw "Elza" Lay, Wild Bunch member.

helped Cassidy and the Wild Bunch rob the Castle Gate, Utah, mining camp of $8,000. Lay's last hold-up with the Wild Bunch was the robbery of the Union Pacific train at Wilcox, Wyo., on June 2, 1899. A train robbery at Twin Mountains, N.M., with the Black Jack Ketchum Gang on July 11, 1899, marked the end of Lay's brief career as an outlaw. He was injured in the Twin Mountains holdup, and though he managed to escape, a posse apprehended him the following month. Lay served seven years at the New Mexico Territorial Prison. On Jan. 10, 1906, he received a pardon as a reward for his part in quelling a prison riot, and returned to Baggs, Wyo., where he ran a saloon. In 1909, Lay married his second wife, Mary Calvert, with whom he raised two daughters. When Lay's oil drilling endeavors failed, he moved to California with his family. After a few years as a professional gambler in Mexico, Lay returned to California where he worked as the head water master for the Imperial Valley Irrigation System. Lay died in Los Angeles in 1934. Concerning the rumor that Butch Cassidy visited Lay at Baggs, Wyo., in 1929-30, Lay admitted nothing. If Cassidy survived the 1909 shoot-out with Bolivian soldiers and returned to the U.S., Lay died without sharing the knowledge. See: **Cassidy, Butch; Wild Bunch, The.**

Leach, William, d.1876, U.S., gunman. John Wadkins was a traveling minstrel performer who was attempting to negotiate his way through uncharted lands in the Cherokee Nation when he met William Leach, who was familiar with the territory. Wadkins hired Leach to safely convey him to Fayetteville, Ark., where the minstrel was scheduled to give a performance the second week of March, 1875.

Leach disguised his murderous intentions and agreed to escort Wadkins to his destination. The minstrel show performer never arrived. A month later, a hunter found the charred bones of Wadkins in an abandoned campsite on the frontier. Deputy marshals identified several fragments of clothing and a knife and screwdriver that had belonged to the dead man. When Leach tried to sell Wadkins' boots in town, he was arrested and brought to Fort Smith on murder charges. William Leach was found Guilty of the crime and was sentenced to death by Judge Isaac Parker. He was hanged along with four other men on Apr. 21, 1876.

Ledbetter, James F. (AKA: **Bud**), prom. 1880s-90s, U.S., lawman. Bud Ledbetter was born in Arkansas, where he began his career as a lawman. He moved to Oklahoma and became a deputy U.S. marshal under Morton Rutherford, who was in charge of the Eastern Indian Territory District. Ledbetter later served under U.S. Marshal E.D. Nix of that district. Ledbetter, who was a fierce fighter and quick with his six-gun, is credited with single-handedly rounding up four members of the Al Jennings

Lawman Bud Ledbetter.

gang after the gang bungled several train robberies. Ledbetter later became police chief of Muskogee, Okla., while serving as the sheriff of the county. See: **Jennings, Alphonso J.**

Lee, James, d.1885, U.S., outlaw. In the mid-1880s, Cooke County, Texas, and the Chickasaw Nation were plagued by a gang of horse and livestock thieves led by James Lee and his brothers Tom and Pink. Both the white settlers and natives were up in arms about this lawlessness, which Detective Jack Duncan vowed he would bring to an end. On May 1, 1885, a five-man posse made up of Bill Kirksey, U.S. Marshal James Guy, Frances Mathes, and Andy and James Roff was sent to arrest Jim Lee at the Cold Branch ranch. The posse cautiously approached a log cabin, noting the sinister presence of gun portholes cut into the walls of the building. The lawmen called to Ed Stein, who directed them to the rear of the cabin. The possemen were ambushed and caught in a trap from which they seemed powerless to escape. A hail of lead spit forth from the cabin, killing four of the lawmen. The gang members managed to escape, and hid at Stein's store at Delaware Bend on the Texas side. Rewards totalling $7,000 were posted for Jim and Pink Lee. Stein and Lee were arrested and brought back to Fort Smith where they were acquitted.

On Dec. 7, the two remaining Lee brothers were trapped in a hay field near Dexter by a posse led by Heck Thomas and Jim Taylor. The Lees were caught off-guard on the John Washington ranch where they were attending to a broken fence. Surrounded by the posse, the two fugitives were ordered to surrender, but they answered with their Winchesters and were dropped in their tracks. "Died Fighting!" the newspaper proclaimed the next day. "The Lee brothers, the most notorious desperadoes in Texas finally go down with their boots on." The papers attributed at least forty other murders to the Lee Gang, which cannot be verified with certainty since there is so little surviving information about this particular gang.

Lee, Oliver Milton, 1866-1941, U.S., outlaw. Oliver Milton Lee spent time on both sides of the law. At the age of eighteen, Lee and his family moved to a ranch in the Tularosa Valley of New Mexico. A few years later, a feud developed between Lee and a neighboring rancher, John Good. The murder of Lee's boyhood friend, George McDonald, started a range war. The murder was allegedly committed by Good's son, Walter Good or one of Good's henchmen. In August 1888, a gang including Lee captured Walter Good and shot him to death, leaving his body in the desert. Good's father found the body, and shortly after engaged Lee and his gang in a gunfight.

Lee served time for his part in Good's shooting, and on his release worked diligently to develop his ranch. He also served as deputy sheriff and deputy U.S. marshal. In February 1893, Lee trailed a herd of stolen cattle almost to El Paso, Texas, where he shot and killed rustlers Charley Rhodius and Matt Coffelt.

Lee turned back to the outlaw life in the late 1890s and became a fugitive after reportedly murdering A.J.Fountain and his 8-year-old son. A posse including Pat Garrett tracked Lee and James Gilliland, also suspected of the murders, and on July 13, 1898, surprised the two fugitives just south of Alamogordo, N.M. Lee and Gilliland outshot and outwitted the posse, who finally withdrew. The two later surrendered, stood trial, and were acquitted. Lee returned to tending his Dog Canyon Ranch. After selling out in 1914 to several businessmen, he was elected twice to the New Mexico legislature. Lee died in 1941.

Lee, Robert, b.1861, U.S., outlaw. Bob Lee was a cousin of the notorious Harvey and Lonie Logan, and it was Lee who led the Logan Brothers to the celebrated Hole-in-the-Wall hideout, where they met Wild Bunch members Butch Cassidy, the Sundance Kid, Ben Kilpatrick, William Carver, and others. Lee was a gambler and gunman, a tall, handsome man who participated in some of the train robberies committed by the Wild Bunch. He was arrested at Cripple Creek, Colo., on Feb. 28, 1900, on suspicion of robbing the Union Pacific train at Wilcox, Wyo., the previous year. Lee was later sent to prison to serve a short sentence and he disappeared upon his release.

Outlaw Bob Lee.

Lee-Peacock Feud, 1860s, U.S. Lewis Peacock, a wealthy landowner in Grayson County, Texas, organized the Reconstruction Union League following the Civil War. This was a carpetbagging, uniform-wearing organization that was reportedly designed to help former slaves obtain jobs and buy property. But Peacock, his enemies claimed, had established this organization merely as a land-grabbing scheme. Hatred for blacks ran high and many of the gunfights that erupted in this feud were racially motivated. Bob Lee, another important cattleman and rancher in Grayson County, led the opposition to Peacock's group. Many former Confederate soldiers joined Lee in his battles with the Peacock clan, including the Dixon family, notably Simp, Bob, and Charles Dixon, and Richard Johnson, a sharp-shooting gunman. Lee was killed in 1869 and Peacock was shot to death in 1871, ending this seven-year feud. See: **Johnson, Richard; Peacock, Lewis.**

Robert E. Lee of the Lee-Peacock Feud.

Lefors, Joseph, b.1865, U.S., lawman. Joe Lefors was

one of the toughest, most relentless lawmen in the history of the West. He was born in Paris, Texas, where his mother died when he was twelve. He and his father then moved to the Panhandle to ranch but were attacked and captured by Comanche Indians. A company of Texas Rangers rescued Lefors and his father. Lefors never forgot the experience, vowing to later become a lawman and emulate the Rangers.

Lawman Joe Lefors, left, about to pursue the Wild Bunch.

At first Lefors worked as a cowboy and later as a cattleman. He drove herds from Texas and Wyoming to the railheads in Kansas in the 1880s and later worked for the Montana Livestock Association as a range detective. He was also hired as a railroad detective and led a fifty-man posse in a 1,000-mile pursuit of the Wild Bunch after its members robbed a Union Pacific train in 1900, but he failed to catch the elusive Butch Cassidy and the Sundance Kid. Lefors served as a deputy U.S. marshal in 1898 in Wyoming, and still later, in the same capacity, Lefors tracked down Tom Horn, lawman-turned-outlaw, and got Horn to indirectly confess to the killing of a young boy—a crime for which Horn was later hanged. See: **Cassidy, Butch; Horn, Tom; Wild Bunch.**

Leonard, Bill, d.1881, U.S., outlaw. Originally a jeweler in New Mexico, Bill Leonard traveled to Arizona in the late 1870s where he became involved with cattle thieves, including N.H. "Old Man" Clanton. On Mar. 15, 1881, Leonard, Harry Head, Jim Crane, and Luther King laid in wait for the Tombstone stage, which carried $26,000 in bullion. When the stage slowed down on a hill, Leonard, Head, and Crane stepped in front of it and ordered it to stop. Wells Fargo agent Bob Paul, who was driving the stage, shot Leonard in the groin. In the ensuing gunfire, the usual driver of the stage, Budd Philpot, was shot and killed, as well as a passenger inside the coach. Because of Paul's courageous action, no other passengers were injured and the robbers fled without the bullion. In June 1881, King was captured and revealed the identities of the other robbers. Leonard stayed at large until later that month when he was shot while attempting a robbery in Eureka, N.M. Bill Leonard died just a few hours later, after admitting his part in the stagecoach robbery and naming Jim Crane as the killer of the driver. See: **Earp, Wyatt**

Berry Stapp.

LeRoy, Kitty, 1850-78, U.S., gambler. Kitty LeRoy, born in Texas, was among the best women gamblers in the West. LeRoy began her career as a performer at the age of ten, and by the age of twenty was the toast of Dallas. She eventually gave up her theatrical career to become a faro dealer. Her skill at dealing and shooting became legendary. LeRoy allegedly never went to the faro table without several bowie knives and revolvers on her person, and she was noted for stopping arguments with a deftly placed near miss.

LeRoy married four times, selecting the first husband because he was the only man in town with the nerve to let her shoot apples off his head as she galloped by on horseback. Her next husband was a rich German. Leroy's third marriage appeared to be the result of her guilty conscience. She shot a man she considered too ardent in his attentions, and then married him several hours before he died of his wounds. In 1876, LeRoy moved to Deadwood in the Dakota Territory with her fourth husband and opened the Mint Gambling Saloon. In 1878, LeRoy's husband shot and killed her and himself in a jealous fit over her alleged affairs with outlaws Sam Bass and Wild Bill Hickok.

Leslie, Nashville Franklin (AKA: Buckskin Frank) 1842-c.1925, U.S., gunman. "Buckskin" Frank Leslie served as an Indian scout in Texas, Oklahoma, and the Dakotas in the 1870s. In 1880, he arrived in Tombstone, Ariz., and opened the Cosmopolitan Hotel. Leslie began seeing a married woman and, on June 22, 1880, when her jealous husband came after him, Leslie shot and killed the man. A week later, May Killeen, the man's widow, became Mrs. Frank Leslie.

Two years later, Leslie got into an argument with

"Buckskin" Frank Leslie

Billy Claiborne, a survivor of the gunfight at the O.K. Corral. Claiborne had already shot three men who laughed when he demanded to be called "Billy the Kid." When Claiborne asked the same of Leslie, Leslie declined and, shortly thereafter, killed Claiborne in a shoot-out. In the mid-1880s, Leslie twice aided the army during Apache uprisings and also served for a short time as a mounted customs inspector along the Rio Grande.

After seven years of marriage, Leslie's wife divorced him, citing as one reason his habit of practicing his shooting by standing her against a wall and tracing her outline with bullets. Leslie then became involved with Mollie Williams, a prostitute. On July 10, 1889, Leslie came home drunk and killed Mollie during an argument. He was found Guilty and sentenced to twenty-five years in prison.

Leslie was pardoned after serving only eight years in the territorial prison at Yuma. After his release, he became a field assistant in Mexico to Professor Dumell, a geologist searching for coal deposits. Leslie also spent some time in the Alaska gold fields. He ran a pool hall in Oakland, Calif., between 1913 and 1922 when he disappeared. Some sources report that he committed suicide.

Lewis, Alexander, prom. 1888-92, and **Johnson, Jim**, prom. 1888, and **Queen, Kelp**, and **Barber, John**, d.1888, U.S., outlaws. Benjamin C. Tarver, a cattleman from Rose, Texas, was on his way home from Chicago the evening of June 15, 1888, when a gang of outlaws held up the Missouri-Kansas-Texas passenger train he was riding. Tarver was shot and killed, and the four gunmen made their escape. Two of the gang members, Kelp Queen and John Barber were later killed in shootouts with deputy U.S. marshals. A third man, Jim Johnson, was arrested in Texas on an unrelated charge and was sentenced to the penitentiary for a term of twenty-five years.

A fourth member of the gang, Alexander Lewis, was apprehended in December 1890 after a youth who had once lived in his home confessed that he had overheard the gang members formulating their plan to rob the train. His testimony was supported by a mass of evidence assembled by railroad detective J.J. Kinney, who brought the felon to justice at Fort Smith (Ark.). Lewis was tried and convicted, but on appeal from Defense Attorney J. Warren Reed, Judge Isaac Parker's sentence was overturned by the U.S. Supreme Court on the grounds that he had directed "secret challenges" to be made away from the jurors.

Reed was equally brilliant in the second Lewis murder trial. He assailed the integrity of the government witnesses under cross-examination, and his unvarnished courtroom theatrics helped win his client a verdict of Not Guilty. At no time, he maintained, could anyone place Lewis at the murder scene. It was an argument the jury found difficult to refute; Lewis was acquitted.

Lewis, Elmer (AKA: **Slaughter Kid; Mysterious Kid**), 1877-96, U.S., outlaw. At nineteen, Elmer Lewis was working on a ranch in Henrietta County, Texas. He met Foster Crawford and decided to rob banks. He and Crawford held up the City National Bank in Wichita Falls, Texas, on Feb. 25, 1896, taking about $2,000 after killing the bank cashier, Frank Dor-

sey, and wounding a clerk. Lewis and Crawford fled. The two outlaws then raided the town of Electra, Texas, robbing two stores and the post office. Marshal W.D. McDonald finally caught up with the outlaws and returned them to Wichita Falls. Both men were jailed pending trial, but a mob broke into the jail, dragged Lewis and Crawford outside, and

Outlaw Elmer Lewis, dead.

hanged them from a telephone pole. See: **Crawford, Foster**.

Lincoln County War, 1878-81, U.S., feud. The Lincoln County War, which some have taken to be a blood feud between Billy the Kid and the murderers of John Tunstall, was actually a conflict between rival banking, mercantile, and ranching interests in Lincoln County, N.M. In the early 1870s, famed cattleman John Chisum brought his herds to the Pecos Valley, a remote and lawless section

L.G. Murphy and J.J. Dolan.

of the New Mexico Territory. Until Chisum's arrival, the area had been controlled by Lawrence G. Murphy, owner of a huge general store called The House. The store's prominence made Murphy and his successors, James J. Dolan and James H. Riley, political powers as well. In contrast to Chisum, Murphy owned no cattle, but managed to maintain tight control over the small ranchers and all the judges, politicians, and lawmen in the county. The House of Murphy enjoyed a virtual monopoly on the selling of beef to army posts and Indian reservations. Dolan and Riley collaborated with a group of corrupt Republican office holders known as the Santa Fe Ring to fix prices on the beef. The Ring sought to control local commerce in all of New Mexico, though its actual existence and sphere of influence is still a matter of conjecture.

Chisum objected to the cattle cartel and formed an alliance with lawyer Alexander McSween, who arrived in Lincoln County in 1875, and rancher John Tunstall, an Englishman who later brought Billy the Kid into the conflict. McSween initially went to work for Murphy, but quickly grew disillusioned with his methods and defected to the Chisum camp. Tunstall and McSween went into business together, and soon opened a store similar to The House but offering better terms to farmers and small ranchers. Murphy finally had enough and decided to sell his holdings to Riley and Dolan, who were unable to counter the threat to the business posed by the Tunstall-McSween faction. With their political clout slowly ebbing away, Dolan began applying legal and economic sanctions against Tunstall.

Antagonisms between the two rival mercantile groups increased, forcing the small ranchers, farmers, and businessmen to choose sides. Chisum, for all of his political independence and integrity, succeeded in driving many of the small ranchers into the Dolan camp by swallowing up large segments of public land in the Pecos Valley. McSween and Tunstall attracted a number of Dolan's unhappy creditors and members of the Spanish-speaking community who were anxious to escape the economic tyranny inflicted on them by The House of Murphy. Compounding Dolan's problems were rumors to the effect that he was stealing cattle to satisfy his government contracts. Nevertheless, Dolan still had the local law enforcement officers on his side, and he continued to use these men to apply continued pressure on Tunstall in the form of legal writs and physical harassment.

In February 1878, Sheriff William Brady, a puppet of Dolan and Riley, sent out a posse to serve a writ of attachment on some cattle at the Tunstall ranch. The possemen included a number of Dolan supporters who had crossed paths with the law on numerous occasions. Deputy Jacob B. "Billy" Matthews, a silent partner in the Dolan firm, led the force of riders which included gunmen Jesse Evans, Frank Baker, Tom Hill, William "Buck" Morton, Andrew L. "Buckshot" Roberts, George Hindman, Manuel Segovia, Johnny Hurley. They found the Tunstall ranch to be heavily defended by Dick Brewer, John Middleton, deputy U.S. Marshal Robert Widenmann, Billy the Kid, and several

other men. Matthews announced his intention to examine a head of cattle in connection with a pending case against Alexander McSween. Brewer indicated that there was no problem with that provided Matthews did not take any of the cattle away. The matter might have been resolved peacefully at this point, but the hot-headed Widenmann stepped forward to curtly inform Matthews that he intended to arrest Evans, a known outlaw, and two of his cohorts. Matthews refused, explaining that Dolan would not sanction such a thing. For the moment Widenmann did nothing.

Brewer then offered Matthews and his men lunch inside. During the meal, Evans turned to Widenmann and asked: "Do you want to arrest me?" Widenmann replied, "You will find it out quickly enough when I want to arrest you." Angry words passed between the supporters of the two factions. Frank Baker whispered to Roberts, that all this talk was getting them nowhere. "What the hell's (the) use of talking? Let's pitch in a fight, and kill all the damned s.o.b.s!" Matthews decided that he should seek further instructions from Dolan regarding the cattle. For his part, however, Widenmann felt that he should speak with Tunstall, who was not present at the ranch when the posse arrived.

On Feb. 18 the two rival factions crossed paths a second time on the road between Roswell and Lincoln. Widenmann, Brewer, Middleton, and Billy the Kid were riding with Tunstall when suddenly they were attacked from behind by Brady's men, who were seeking to arrest Tunstall. Tunstall found himself cut off from the other four men. Shots rang out, and within a minute or two the wealthy businessman, who disdained violence as a solution to the present difficulties, lay dead. Widenmann recognized his old foe Jesse Evans, as one of the gunmen. Neither he nor Billy the Kid bothered to give chase after realizing that they were hopelessly outnumbered. In his report to Dolan, "Buck" Morton stated that Tunstall had resisted arrest and had opened fire on them. This was the standard alibi given by the Dolan faction throughout the course of the Lincoln County War.

Billy the Kid pledged to avenge Tunstall's death. He was among a group of "Regulators" who apprehended two members of the Morton posse responsible for the shooting. Before they could be returned to Lincoln, Billy shot them both as well as a member of his own posse, who apparently tried to protect them. Before Billy the Kid could track down and kill Evans and the others, he was arrested by Sheriff Brady, who had refused to arrest Tunstall's murderers although warrants for their arrest had been issued. McSween concluded that the present legal authorities in Lincoln County would offer no protection for those aligned with Chisum. Following his release, Billy the Kid returned to Lincoln where he became McSween's head gunfighter.

On Apr. 1, 1879, Billy and his cohorts killed Sheriff Brady in an ambush outside the Tunstall store and wounded George Hindman. Twenty-five mounted soldiers from Fort Stanton arrived in town to track down Billy the Kid, but he had vanished into the countryside.

The gunplay in Lincoln County continued. On Apr. 4, "Buckshot" Roberts was killed by McSween partisans at Blazer's Mill after he had pumped a fatal shot into Brewer's head. Dick Brewer, a temperate young rancher from Rio Ruidoso who possessed no real vices, had served as Tunstall's slavishly devoted foreman. His death was a major setback for the McSween faction. By default, Billy the Kid became the leader of the rapidly thinning ranks of McSween supporters.

The climax of the Lincoln County War occurred during a five-day siege at the McSween store between July 14-19, 1878. Troops dispatched from Fort Stanton did little to ease the tensions, and may in fact, have sided with the Dolan gang. Alexander McSween was killed on July 19, after the Murphy-Dolan men set fire to the store. Blinded

Alexander McSween and John Tunstall.

and choking from smoke, he ran from the smoldering building with three other men in a desperate bid for freedom. Billy the Kid had out maneuvered his opponents again, and succeeded in escaping under the cover of darkness. Not so lucky were McSween and three Mexicans who were shot. Just who fired the fatal shots is hard to say, though western historians attribute the shooting to John Jones, Joe Nash, and Andy Boyle, who were present in the yard when McSween emerged from the burning building.

With McSween's death, The House and the Santa Fe Ring emerged the victors of the Lincoln County War, though sporadic outbreaks of violence continued into 1884. Pat Garrett was named sheriff of Lincoln County, and in 1881 the New Mexico governor felt confident the county was finally in a "state of quiet." Chisum remained powerful up until the time of his death in 1884, but he never really managed to overtake his opposition. Billy the Kid, angered at John Chisum's refusal to compensate him for supporting Tunstall and McSween, embarked on a crime spree unparalleled in the history of the Old West. See: **Billy the Kid; Widenmann, Robert.**

Lindsey, Seldon T., b.1854, U.S., lawman. Born in Louisiana, Seldon T. Lindsey moved with his family to McClennan County, Texas, just after the Civil War. At the age of sixteen, Lindsey began working as a cowboy, and for the next few years trailed cattle to the railheads in Kansas. As a young man, Lindsey also spent time buffalo hunting, and allegedly met "Buffalo" Bill Cody. In 1873, Lindsey's family decided to leave McClennan County because of trouble with a local gang. As Lindsey and his father were leaving town, a member of the gang followed them. When he pulled a gun, Seldon Lindsey shot him out of the saddle. Lindsey was charged with murder but was acquitted.

Lindsey married in 1881, and over thirty-two years, fathered eleven children. In 1890, he was appointed a deputy U.S. marshal. Also that year, he returned to Louisiana in search of a man named Barber who had killed his business partner. With the help of another gunman, Lindsey found and killed Barber. Lindsey was involved in several other manhunts and gun battles in the following years.

Little Bill, See: Raidler, William.

Little Dick, See: West, Richard.

Little Reddie from Texas, See: McKemie, Robert.

Liver-Eating Johnson, See: Johnson, John.

Logan, Harvey (AKA: **Kid Curry**), 1865-1904, U.S., outlaw. Born in Tama, Iowa, Harvey Logan and his three younger brothers grew up with little supervision after their mother died while they were small children. At nineteen, Logan and his younger brothers Lonie and Johnny, accompanied by an older cousin, Bob Lee, rode west, going to Wyoming where they began rustling cattle. The boys moved their large stolen herds to a ranch near Landusky,

Wyo., in 1888. The Logan boys hired their guns out to the Red Sash gang during the bloody Johnson County war but when leader Nathan D. Champion was killed in 1892, the Logans returned to rustling and ranching.

Harvey Logan was the leader of the Logan clan, a mean-spirited, tight-lipped young man who possessed a murderous

Harvey "Kid Curry" Logan

nature. He was vicious and enjoyed terrorizing his rancher neighbors and the town of Landusky. Logan seduced one of the step-daughters of Pike Landusky, the town's founder. The girl later gave birth to an illegitimate child Logan refused to accept as his own. He mocked the girl and quickly incurred the seething wrath of Landusky, a burly 55-year-old miner who had been involved in several brawls and shoot-outs over the years.

On Dec. 24, 1894, the Logans rode into Landusky to celebrate Christmas. Harvey and Lonie Logan and fellow rustler, Jim Thornhill, got drunk and began harassing the towns-people. They sauntered in-to the saloon and general store operated by Lan-dusky. The husky miner was at the bar where he had been drinking heavily and cursing Harvey Logan as a no-account. When Logan entered the saloon, he walked past Landusky, slapping the miner's face as he went to the bar. Landusky ran after him and the two began to battle, a fistfight that lasted for several minutes until the younger Logan knocked Landusky down.

Logan leaped upon him and even though Landusky had cried out that he had had enough, Logan kept bashing the miner's head on the floor. Landusky reached for his six-gun, pulling this from his coat. Logan jumped backward and, while Landusky was still on his knees, shot him to death. Lonie Logan and Thornhill, guns drawn, covered Harvey Logan's retreat from the saloon. Logan jumped into a buckboard owned by Landusky and the others mounted their horses. The three then rode out of town, laughing uproariously as Logan whipped the team at a furious pace.

Rancher Jim Winters, who had been plagued by the rustling Logan brothers, informed lawmen about their activities. When Harvey Logan heard about this, he and his brothers Lonie and Johnny rode to the Winters ranch in January 1896. Winters was waiting for them behind a barricaded house, having been told that the outlaws were hunting for him. When the Logan brothers arrived, Winters opened a deadly barrage of rifle fire that toppled Johnny Logan from his saddle, killing him. Harvey and Lonie Logan returned fire and then fled.

In mid-January 1896, with the law on his trail, Harvey Logan rode to the notorious Hole-in-the-Wall, a rocky hideout for western bad men near Diamond Mountain, Colo. It was later said of Logan that by the time he rode to the rocky outlaw haven he had already killed eight men in street duels, but little real evidence exists to support this claim. Bob Lee and Jim Thornhill rode to this outlaw retreat with Logan, as Lee had been there many times. At Hole-in-the-Wall Logan was taken under the wing of George "Flat Nose" Curry, an elderly bank and train robber. Logan so much admired the crafty old Curry that he took his name, preferring to be called Kid Curry. A short time later, after Butch Cassidy was released from prison, he rode to Hole-in-the-Wall to form what was later known as the Wild Bunch. Harvey Logan became one of Cassidy's lieutenants, along with Benjamin Kilpatrick and the Sun-dance Kid, whose real name was Harry Longabaugh.

Logan was with Cassidy in many bank and train robberies through 1896-97, but he proved to be difficult. Cassidy, an unusual outlaw who preferred to use his six-gun only as a last resort, found himself continually at odds with Logan, who was obsessed with killing train guards and crew members whenever the gang stopped a train. Cassidy invariably stopped him and more than once it appeared that the two men would end up in a gunfight. At these mo-ments, the Sundance Kid, Cassidy's closest friend, a taciturn man with a lightning draw, would side with Butch, and Logan, who feared the two guns Sundance wore, would back down.

By 1897, Logan had formed his own splinter gang and was committing bank and train robberies without Cassidy and the chief members of the Wild Bunch. He, the Sun-dance Kid, Tom O'Day, and Walt Putney robbed the bank at Belle Fourche, S.D., on June 27, 1897, then rode to a hideout on Musselshell River near Lavina, Mont. The four men were tracked to this campsite by lawmen on Sept. 24, 1897, and a wild shoot-out took place after Sheriff John Dunn of Carbon County called on the outlaws to surrender. Logan, who was just tethering his horse, drew his gun and began shooting at Dunn, deputies W.D. Smith, Dick Hicks, and a local constable named Calhoun. The other two outlaws also began to fire on the small posse. As Logan mounted his horse a bullet struck Logan's hand, knocking his six-gun from his grasp and tearing through the neck of his mount. He nevertheless galloped away. A few miles distant the horse fell dead and Logan, along with the Sundance Kid, O'Day, and Putney, were captured and taken to the jail in Deadwood. On Oct. 31, 1897, the four men escaped the jail after bribing a guard.

Logan rejoined Cassidy and the Wild Bunch and was with them on Apr. 25, 1899, when the gang stopped the Union Pacific's Overland Flyer near Wilcox, Wyo. Engineer W.R. Jones refused to uncouple the express car and Logan pistol-whipped him into unconsciousness. He was about to shoot the fallen engineer but was stopped by Cassidy. When the express guard refused to open the door, the gang blew the side of the car off with dynamite. The guard, a man named Woodcock, was thrown out by the blast but survived. Logan ran up to him and placed a six-gun to his head, shouting: "This s.o.b. has caused us a lot of trouble and he must die for it!" Cassidy brushed aside Logan's gun with a smile and said: "Leave him be, Kid. A man with his nerve deserves not to be shot."

The gang then blew up the safe which they had dragged from the express car; this sent more than $30,000 in currency and negotiable securities skyward, causing the outlaws to chase wildly after the windswept money. Following the robbery, the gang split up, Logan and two others fleeing northward. They were tracked to the Red Fork of the Powder River on June 5, 1899, by a large posse led by Sheriff Joseph Hazen of Converse County. Lawmen closed in on the outlaws just as they were sitting down to eat their supper. After Hazen called to Logan and the others to surrender, Logan dropped his plate of beans and jumped up shooting a rifle. One of his bullets struck Hazen in the chest, killing him on the spot. The outlaws scrambled on foot for the roaring Powder River with posse members firing at them. Logan and the others managed to escape by diving into the river; rushing waters carried them downstream.

Logan and a few others rode south, and in early 1900 the outlaw busied himself with rustling cattle in Arizona. He was tracked down near San Simon, Ariz., on Apr. 5, 1900, by George Scarborough, an experienced lawman, and a deputy named Birchfield. Cornered in a box canyon, Logan proved his deadly marksmanship by sending a rifle bullet into Scarborough's leg and then riding past his pursuers whooping with excitement. Scarborough's wound was so severe that his leg was later amputated. Logan rode north, hiding out in the Book Mountains, near the small town of Thompson, Utah. Here, on May 26, 1900, he and some other outlaws were surprised by lawmen led by Sheriff Jesse Tyler who was accompanied by deputies P. Day and Sam F. Jenkins.

The lawmen thought they had found an Indian campsite.

They were startled to walk within a few yards of a smoldering fire to find Logan and two others facing them. "Hello, boys," Tyler said. Logan saw the badge on Tyler's chest and went for his six-guns. As he did, Tyler and Jenkins ran for their horses to retrieve their rifles. Logan pumped a bullet into the back of each man, killing them on the spot. Deputy Day, who was mounted, rode his horse from the scene to inform another posse combing the nearby hills for Logan. By the time the other lawmen returned to the campsite, Logan and his men had fled.

In June 1900, Logan was reported to have encountered two brothers named Norman who came upon his campsite and quarreled with him when he refused to offer them food. He shot both brothers dead when they appeared to go for their guns. Logan had killed almost a dozen men by this time and was, after the more celebrated Butch Cassidy and the Sundance Kid, the most wanted man in the West. He moved about continuously, traveling from one western state to the next. On Mar. 27, 1901, he appeared in Painted Rock, Texas. Within minutes he had picked a fight with Oliver Thornton, a resident. Both men drew their six-guns and Logan shot Thornton to death with one well-aimed bullet to the heart.

Logan then rode back to Hole-in-the-Wall to join Cassidy and others in robbing the Great Northern Flyer on July 3, 1901. The gang members rode the train as passengers. As the train neared Wagner, Mont., Logan got up from his seat and went to the front of the train. He climbed over the tender and dropped into the engineer's cab, training two six-guns on the engineer and fireman, ordering them to stop the train. As the train was halted, Cassidy and others went to the express car and planted a package of dynamite under it, setting this off and blowing away the side of the car. The outlaws took more than $40,000 from the safe and rode off. Cassidy and the Sundance Kid went to Fort Worth, Texas, to hide out in a brothel owned by Fannie Porter. From there they would flee east with Etta Place, going to New York and then to South America where they reportedly died in a wild gunfight with federal troops in Bolivia. Harvey "Kid Curry" Logan and the other members of the gang split up.

Logan had decided at this time to take his revenge on rancher Jim Winters who had shot and killed his brother Johnny five years earlier. Logan rode to the Winters ranch on July 26, 1901. Catching the rancher off-guard, Logan emptied his six-gun into Winters, killing him. Logan then rode east with many posses on his trail. He hid in Knoxville, Tenn. There, on Dec. 13, 1901, Logan went into a pool hall and began to play a game of pool with a local tough who pulled a gun after losing several games. Logan pulled his own six-gun and smashed it down on his adversary's head, knocking him to the ground. At that moment several policemen were called and Logan shot and wounded three of them before fleeing out the back door.

Logan fell thirty feet into a culvert and as he was climbing out of this drainage area, one of the wounded policeman managed to shoot the outlaw in the shoulder. Logan staggered off into the darkness. Bandaging his wound with his shirt, Logan fled on foot. A large posse, led by bloodhounds, found him twenty miles outside of Knoxville and brought him back to jail. His identity was unknown, but when Pinkerton detective Lowell Spence, who had been trailing Logan for years, was given a description of the gunman, he went to the Knoxville jail and identified him. As Spence walked from the jail, Logan said to one of his guards: "Some day I'm going to kill that man. He's very troublesome."

Prolonged legal delays ensued. Many states wanted to try Logan for robbery and murder, but his lawyers successfully fought off extradition. He was found Guilty of shooting the Knoxville policemen and given a long jail term, but Harvey Logan vowed he would never serve out his full term. On June 27, 1903, Logan used a homemade garrotte to loop around the neck of a guard who had his back to his cell, forcing the guard to give him the keys to the cell. He locked up the guard and took his gun, then escaped the jail. Lowell Spence of the Pinkerton Detective Agency was soon on his trail. Logan, like a homing pigeon, had gone back to his old haunts in the West. He had gone to Hole-in-the-Wall but none of the outlaws from the Wild Bunch were left; the bandits of Kid Curry's day had either been killed, were in prison, or, like Butch Cassidy and the Sundance Kid, had left the country. Even his brother Lonie, whom he led to the outlaw trail, had been killed in a wild shoot-out in Missouri in 1900.

Logan managed to round up two rustlers, and the three men stopped a small train near Parachute, Colo., on June 7, 1904. When they forced open the safe in the express car they discovered only a few dollars. Logan cursed his bad luck. He then fled with a large posse led by Lowell Spence on his trail. The following day, June 8, Logan and his men were trapped in a box canyon by Spence's twenty-man posse. A shootout broke out with the deadly Logan firing his rifle as he ran from boulder to boulder. When he was sprinting to the cover of a large rock, a lawman took careful aim and shot Logan in the shoulder. He tumbled behind the rock. One of Logan's men was heard by lawmen to shout to him: "Are you hit?"

There was a long silence and then Logan answered: "Yes, and I'm going to end it here." The lawmen heard a shot and rushed the boulder. Behind it lay Harvey Logan, the notorious Kid Curry, most feared killer of the West. He had committed suicide by sending a bullet into his left temple. See: **Carver, William; Cassidy, Butch; Curry, George; Hanks, Orlando Camillo; Kilpatrick, Benjamin; Lay, William Ellsworth; Logan, Lonie; Sundance Kid, The; Wild Bunch.**

Logan, Lonie, 1871-1900, U.S., outlaw. Lonie Logan was born in Dodson, Mo., in 1871. Orphaned and raised by an aunt, he and his brothers Harvey and Johnny decided to ride west when Lonie was just thirteen. Along with a cousin, Bob Lee, they reached Wyoming, where they began rustling livestock. After four years, the Logans and Lee drove a herd of stolen cattle into Montana and started a ranch of their own.

Lonie was involved in various criminal activities, and hired out to Nate Champion's Red Sash Gang during the Johnson County War. He and Harvey also became members of Butch Cassidy's Wild Bunch. When the Pinkertons began closing in on Cassidy in the late 1890s, Lonie left and opened a saloon in Harlem, Mont. Word reached him that Charles Siringo and other detectives were closing in on him, so Logan sold the saloon and became a fugitive. In February 1900, a posse led by Pinkerton detective Bill Sayles traced Logan to his aunt's home in Missouri. When Logan tried to escape, he was shot and killed. See: **Logan, Harvey.**

Long, John (AKA: Long John), prom. 1870s, U.S., lawman-gunman. The first prominent mention of John Long, nicknamed Long John, in the Old West, occurred when he got into a fight in Fort Griffin, Texas, around 1876. In the exchange of gunfire, Long killed Vergil Hewey and a black soldier assigned to the Tenth Cavalry at the fort. Long was then appointed deputy sheriff in Lincoln County, N.M.

Long became involved in the Lincoln County War, an extended, bloody struggle between opposing financial interests. On Apr. 1, 1878, Long, Sheriff William Brady, George Hindman, Billy Matthews, and George Peppin were ambushed by a group led by Billy the Kid. Brady and Hindman were killed, but Long and the others survived. A few weeks later, Long, as a member of the Seven Rivers Gang, repaid the attack by ambushing Frank McNab, Frank Coe, and Ab Sanders. On July 13 of the same year, Long, looking for Billy the Kid in order to serve him with a warrant, found him near San Patricio, N.M., with Alexander McSween and nine other gunmen. Long's horse was killed in the gunfire, but Long himself managed to escape. In the four-day battle outside McSween's store that finally ended the Lincoln County War, Long set fire to the kitchen, which drove McSween and his gang out of the building where some, including McSween, were killed and others wounded. See: **Billy the Kid.**

Long, Steve (AKA: **Big Steve**), d.1868, U.S., gunman. A professional gunman, Steve Long teamed up with Ace and Con Moyer to establish a saloon in Laramie City, Wyo. The Moyer brothers had founded the town and appointed themselves justice of the peace and marshal, respectively, making gunman Steve Long their deputy marshal. They ruled with an iron hand and their saloon was correctly called The Bucket of Blood. Numerous murders were committed by the Moyer brothers and Long in the back room of the saloon, where crooked card games were the rule.

"Big Steve" Long, left, and the Moyer Brothers, lynched, 1868.

It was here that Long meted out the "justice" decreed by the Moyer brothers. Ranchers were ordered to sign over the deeds to their lands; miners were forced to give up their claims. Those who refused were shot to death by Long on the pretense that the victim reached for a weapon.

Long was also moonlighting as a thief, and on Oct. 18, 1868, he tried to ambush and rob prospector Rollie "Hard Luck" Harrison. In the ensuing firefight, Harrison shot Long, who retreated. Back in Laramie City, Long's fiancee treated the wound, but when she discovered how he received it, she turned him over to a vigilante group, organized by local rancher N.K. Boswell, when they stormed into The Bucket of Blood on Oct. 28. They seized Long and the Moyer brothers and dragged them to a partially finished cabin, where they were hanged from the rafters. Before Long was hanged, he asked the vigilantes to remove his boots. "My mother always said that I would die with my shoes on," he said. He was hanged in dangling bare feet.

Longabaugh, Harry, See: **Sundance Kid, The.**

Longley, William Preston (AKA: **Wild Bill; Rattling Bill; Tom Jones; Jim Patteson; Jim Webb; Bill Black; Bill Henry; Bill Jackson**), 1851-78, U.S., gunman. William Longley, born at Mill Creek, Texas, on Oct. 6, 1851, learned how to use a gun before he was a teenager. He was never unarmed and he proved to be one of the fastest draw artists in Texas, deadly accurate and fearless in gunfights. He reputedly had killed thirty men in various gunfights in small western towns, chiefly in Texas. Longley reportedly never stole. He worked as a rancher and sometimes a freight driver.

Texas gunman Bill Longley.

His reputation as a fast-draw spread and he was sought out by those wanting to establish themselves as feared gunmen. These challengers invariably lost when calling Longley into the street.

Longley himself picked many a fight with anyone he suspected of being a Yankee sympathizer or a carpetbagger. He also hated blacks and whipped them whenever they crossed his path. This fierce racist, who stood six feet tall and "carried himself like a prince," according to one report, feuded with Wilson Anderson for years. When Longley heard that Anderson had shot one of his cousins from ambush, he rode to Evergreen, Texas, and shot Anderson to death in a duel. He was nevertheless charged with murder and fled with a posse on his trail. Not until two years later was Longley captured and taken to Giddings, Texas, where he was tried and convicted for the murder of Wilson Anderson.

He was sentenced to hang and while he awaited the executioner, Longley wrote the governor, asking for clemency. He carped in his letter that John Wesley Hardin, the most infamous gunmen Texas ever produced, received only twenty-five years in prison for his *forty* killings—ten more than were credited to Longley. Why then, Longley wanted to know, was he being sent to the hangman? The governor did not respond, and on Oct. 11, 1878, Longley was taken to a scaffold and a rope was placed about his neck. Longley wore his best Sunday suit and stood erect and proud on the gallows. He held up his hand, saying: "I deserved this fate. It is a debt I have owed for a wild and reckless life. So long, everybody!" He then nodded to the executioner and was sent downward through the trap to his death. See: **Hardin, John Wesley.**

Loving, Frank (AKA: **Cock-Eyed Frank**), 1854-82, U.S., gunman. During the 1870s, professional gambler Frank Loving got into a feud over a woman with Levi Richardson, a local rowdy in Dodge City, Kan. In the famed Long Branch Saloon, Richardson drew his pistol on Loving. Richardson reportedly got off five shots, but failed to wound Loving seriously. Loving's first three shots hit a wall, but the next three hit Richardson, mortally wounding him. Loving enjoyed tremendous celebrity as a result of this fight, and claimed that his unconventional slow draw was an intentional technique.

Loving spent some time in Las Vegas, N.M., and then moved on to Trinidad, Colo., where in 1882 he encountered former lawman Jack Allen. They argued and began duelling. They fired sixteen shots without a single hit. When they met the next day, Allen fired first and killed Loving.

Lowe, Joseph (AKA: **Rowdy Joe; Red Joe; Monte Joe**), 1845-99, U.S., gunman. Illinois-born Joseph "Rowdy Joe" Lowe and his wife Kathryn, also known as "Rowdy Kate," left the Midwest after the Civil War and roamed through the cow towns, establishing saloons, whorehouses, and gambling dens. About 1870, Lowe set up a combination saloon-gambling den-whorehouse in Delano, Kan., the worst section of Wichita. This rough-and-tumble place was the scene of several shootings, some of which included Lowe, who was fast on the draw and a good shot. Anyone complaining about Lowe's rigged card games received a severe beating. He became so infamous that no one would gamble in his place.

In 1871, the Lowes moved to Newton, Kan., where they established another saloon. Here, on Feb. 19, 1872, after Lowe and his wife had argued, a gunman, A.M. Sweet, got Rowdy Kate drunk, then took her to a brothel run by Fanny Grey for a quick assignation. Lowe, armed with two six-guns, showed up at the brothel the next morning and kicked open the door to the room where Sweet and his wife were in bed. Sweet drew a six-gun but Lowe fired two shots which struck Sweet in the chest. He died three hours later. The shooting caused Joe and his tramp wife to depart Newton and return to Wichita where they set up another saloon, but Rowdy Joe again began battering his customers when they got drunk. He pistol-whipped Joseph Walters so viciously on the night of July 19, 1872, that Walters almost died.

E.T. "Red" Beard, a brawling saloon owner like Lowe, owned a dive next to Lowe's in Delano. He was a roughhouse killer and he went into a rage on the night of Oct. 27, 1873, when a whore, Josephine DeMerritt, began to argue with him. DeMerritt ran out of Beard's place and into Lowe's. Beard was so drunk that when he entered Lowe's saloon looking for DeMerritt he mistook Annie Franklin for her and shot Franklin in the stomach. The woman staggered to the bar where Rowdy Joe had drawn a shotgun. Lowe fired both barrels at Beard but missed. Beard, suddenly sober, fired several shots from his six-gun and then dashed outside with Lowe running after him. One of Beard's bullets struck a cowboy named Bill Anderson, blinding him.

Gambler and gunman Joseph "Rowdy Joe" Lowe.

Outside, Lowe caught up with Beard. Even though Rowdy Joe had been struck by one of Beard's bullets in the neck and was bleeding profusely, he carefully aimed his shotgun at Beard and sent a full blast of buckshot into Beard's right arm, side, and leg. Beard was carried to a doctor's office. It appeared that he would survive but his wounds became infected and three weeks later he was dead. Lowe traveled south in late 1873, drifting into Dennison, Texas. Here he opened a bar named the Crystal Palace. He was soon in trouble and the local sheriff arrested him for brawling. As Rowdy Joe held his hands over his head he kicked the six-gun out of the sheriff's hand and it went off, killing Billy Campbell, a saloon customer.

Lowe was reported to have joined Sam Bass, Joel Collins, and other outlaws, participating in several robberies before he set up another saloon in Dodge City, Kan. In his travels, Rowdy Joe met his match in the form of several famous lawmen, including Wyatt Earp, who reportedly ran him out of Wichita in 1875, and James Butler "Wild Bill" Hickok, who ran him out of Deadwood after delivering a well-placed kick in Rowdy Joe's posterior. Lowe moved on, from one town to the next. By 1899, Lowe had moved to a small ranch outside of Denver. He swore that he had given up his wild ways, but on Feb. 11, 1899, Rowdy Joe went to the Walrus Saloon in Denver and promptly got drunk. When he learned that a man at the bar, E.A. Kimmel, was an ex-policeman, Lowe began to insult the Denver police department. Kimmel, who knew Lowe was a feared gunman, pulled a six-gun and before Rowdy Joe could draw, fired five bullets into Lowe, killing him on the spot. When Lowe was rolled over on the barroom floor, it was discovered that he was unarmed.

Lyons, Haze, 1840-64, U.S., outlaw. As a young cowboy, Haze Lyons traveled from California to Montana and joined Sheriff Henry Plummer's gang, the Innocents. Lyons engaged in numerous robberies, and at Plummer's request, tried to kill Plummer's deputy, Bill Dillingham. Lyons and his accomplices failed and were caught. Lyons was convicted by a miners' court and sentenced to death. Just as he was to be hanged, someone read aloud a letter Lyons had written to his mother. The sentimental poem apparently softened the miners' hearts toward Lyons, and they released him with an admonition to go home to his mother. Instead Lyons returned to Plummer's gang, and on Jan. 14, 1864, he was taken prisoner by vigilantes and hanged.

M

McCall, John (AKA: **Broken Nose Jack; Bill Sutherland**), c.1850-77, U.S., gunman. After moving west from his home in Louisville, Ky., John McCall joined a group of buffalo hunters. In 1876, he appeared in Deadwood, S.D., using the name Bill Sutherland. Deadwood was town of one saloon after another. Gambling halls and other places of ill repute were the norm in this legendary rough-and-tumble town, a little more than thirty miles northwest of Rapid City. After only a few weeks in Deadwood, McCall shot and killed Wild Bill Hickok with a bullet to the back of Hickok's head. At his trial, McCall said he shot Hickok over a poker debt, but it was thought that McCall had been hired to murder Hickok. McCall also falsely claimed to be the brother of Samuel Strawhim, whom Hickok killed in 1869. The jury believed McCall's side of the story and acquitted him.

McCall left Deadwood for Cheyenne where, while drunk, he began boasting about his successful lie. A deputy U.S. marshal overheard McCall and arrested him. This time he stood trial for first-degree murder in Yankton, Dakota Territory. McCall was found Guilty, and on Mar. 1, 1877, was hanged. See: **Calamity Jane; Hickok, James Butler.**

McCall, Thomas P., 1831-1902, U.S., lawman. Born in Belfast, Ire., on June 7, 1831, Thomas P. McCall immigrated to the U.S. in 1844, living in New York where he became a carpenter and shipbuilder. In 1848, McCall moved to Texas, where he was a rider for the pony express and a stagecoach driver, driving a stage from San Antonio, Texas, to Santa Fe, N.M. McCall was appointed sheriff of Medina County, Texas, in 1858.

Lawman Thomas P. McCall.

Governor Sam Houston reappointed McCall to this post in 1860. For the next three decades, McCall served the law throughout Texas, a tough and uncompromising peace officer who seldom used his six-guns to keep law and order. When McCall did reach for his guns, his marksmanship proved deadly accurate. As sheriff of Bexar County, McCall was credited with shooting three outlaws and rounding up numerous rustlers during his ten years in office.

McCanles, David C., See: **Hickok, James Butler.**

McCarty, Henry, See: **Billy the Kid.**

McCarty, Patrick, d.1887, U.S., outlaw. During the winter months, it was customary for Thomas Mahoney and his brother to close up their farm near Fort Scott, Kan., to work with a railroad grading crew that was laying track for the Atlantic and Pacific line in the Cherokee Nation. The pay was good, and if all went well the Mahoney brothers could clear $200 for their troubles before returning to Fort Scott for the spring planting season. On the night of Feb. 17, 1886, the Mahoneys set up camp seven miles outside of Coffeyville. They were accompanied by Patrick McCarty who had joined them several days earlier. McCarty, mindful of the amount of cash the brothers carried and the expensive tools loaded on their rig, decided that he should lay claim to it.

When the brothers drifted off to sleep, McCarty shot one of them, and bludgeoned the other with the sharp end of an ax. Afterward, he burned the bodies beyond recognition and made off with the cash and provisions. McCarty's crime was unraveled, however, and he was arrested in Springfield, Mo., and taken to Fort Smith (Ark.) to stand trial. Judge Isaac Parker sentenced him to die on the gallows on Jan. 14, 1887, but the defense attorneys secured a last minute stay of execution to file an appeal with President Grover Cleveland. Parker vigorously protested the action and filed a brief with the president, who decided not to intervene in the matter. With all the legal appeals exhausted, McCarty was hanged at Fort Smith on Apr. 8, 1887.

McCarty, Tom, c.1855-c.1900, U.S., outlaw. Tom McCarty was raised on a Mormon ranch in Utah and at an early age began a life of banditry. He is credited with introducing Butch Cassidy into a life of outlawry.

At eighteen McCarty married Teenie Christianson, sister of outlaw Willard Erastus Christianson (AKA: Matt Warner), also Mormons. Around 1892, he, along with his brother-in-law Christianson and his brother, Bill McCarty, held up a bank in Roslyn, Wash. When an angry crowd approached him, Tom opened fire, wounding two men. All three of the bandits escaped. The following year, the Mc-Carty brothers and a nephew, Fred McCarty, robbed the Farmers and Merchants Bank of Delta, Colo. During the robbery, Tom McCarty shot and killed cashier A.T. Blachey, who yelled for help before he died. Citizens heard the gunfire and rushed the bank. Merchant Ray Simpson shot and killed both Bill and nephew Fred McCarty.

Tom McCarty escaped a furious posse and fled to Montana, where he turned to sheepherding. McCarty was shot

Outlaw brothers Bill and Tom McCarty.

and killed around 1900 in the Bitteroot county of Montana when a quarrel led to a gunfight. See: **Cassidy, Butch.**

McCluskie, Arthur, d.1873, U.S., gunman. Arthur McCluskie earned his reputation as a western gunman for avenging his brother's death. In 1871, Texan Hugh Anderson killed Mike McCluskie. In June 1873, Arthur McCluskie found Anderson in Medicine Lodge, Kan., and challenged him to a duel with either pistols or knives. Anderson chose pistols and the two men prepared to face each other in the street.

While a crowd of seventy watched, McCluskie and Anderson turned and fired on each other. Both first shots by each gunfighter missed. McCluskie's second bullet tore through Anderson's arm, breaking it. While Anderson's second shot slammed into McCluskie's mouth. As McCluskie charged Anderson, the smaller man fired round after round into McCluskie. McCluskie dropped to the ground but raised himself back up and shot again, hitting Anderson in the stomach. McCluskie dragged himself to where Anderson lay in the street. Anderson drew his knife and slashed McCluskie in the neck. McCluskie then stabbed Anderson in the side, ending the struggle with the deaths of both men. See: **Anderson, Hugh; McCluskie, Mike.**

McCluskie, Mike (AKA: **Arthur Delaney**), d.1871, U.S., lawman-gunman. As Mike McCluskie often went by the name Arthur Delaney, his background is somewhat unclear. It is known that he was the foreman of a crew of workmen employed by the Atchison, Topeka & Santa Fe Railroad. A strapping Irishman with a quick temper and an ability to control those under him, he moonlighted as a police officer in Newton, Kan.

On Aug. 11, 1871, McCluskie was in Newton with his railroad crew when a special election was called. A hard-drinking gambler named Bill Wilson was recruited to serve as a special election deputy. A poor choice on the part of the townsmen, Wilson (alias William Bailey) became drunk and offensive to election officials. McCluskie intervened and gave him a verbal reprimand. Later that evening the two men encountered each other in the Red Front Saloon. Still in his cups after a full day of drinking, Wilson ordered McCluskie to buy a round of drinks for the boys. It was an affront to McCluskie's pride, and when Wilson rudely shoved him McCluskie dealt him a solid blow to the jaw which sent Wilson reeling backward through the swinging doors and into the street.

McCluskie followed him outside, but Wilson had drawn his gun. The Irishman reacted quickly and fired two shots in quick succession which killed the drunken Wilson. The next morning, McCluskie caught the first train out of town in hopes of avoiding retaliation by the dead man's friends. On Aug. 19, he slipped back into Newton and proceeded directly to Perry Tuttle's dance hall. Here he was greeted with an angry epitaph coming from the Texas cowboy Hugh Anderson, who then shot at him. The first bullet only grazed McCluskie's neck. The second one, however, caught him in the leg, dropping him to the floor. McCluskie fired errantly at Anderson, who fired back, hitting his mark. McCluskie was carried away to a boarding house where, before dying the next day, he claimed his real name was Arthur Delaney and that his mother still resided in St. Louis. Two years later, in June 1873, Arthur McCluskie avenged his brother's death at Medicine Lodge, Kan., where he and Anderson killed each other in a gun and knife fight. See: **Newton Massacre; McCluskie, Arthur; Riley, Jim.**

McConnell, Andrew, b.c.1835, U.S., gunman. Andrew McConnell came from Massachusetts to homestead outside Abilene, Kan. On Oct. 23, 1870, McConnell got into an argument with his neighbor, John Shea, who was driving cattle across McConnell's land. Shea drew his pistol and misfired twice. Next McConnell fired his rifle, putting a bullet directly through Shea's heart. McConnell then went for a doctor and turned himself in, but Shea was already dead. McConnell was arrested, but released when Moses Miles testified on his behalf.

Soon thereafter, neighbors began to question Miles' testimony and another warrant was issued for McConnell's arrest. Tom Smith, the marshal of Abilene, rode out to McConnell's property with Deputy J.H. McDonald to serve the warrant. Smith and McDonald were met by McConnell and Miles. While Smith was reading the warrant, McConnell shot him in the chest. Smith returned the fire, slightly injuring McConnell. The two wounded men then began to wrestle. Miles and McDonald also exchanged fire, and although Miles was injured, McDonald fled. Miles beat Smith to the ground, and then nearly chopped off Smith's head with an ax. Three days later, Miles and McConnell were arrested, found Guilty, and sent to prison. Miles was sentenced to sixteen years and McConnell to twelve years in prison.

McCord, Myron, prom. 1901-06, U.S., lawman. The Arizona Territory had grown considerably by the time Myron McCord, a New Yorker, assumed office on June 6, 1901. The lawless frontier was now inhabited by 123,000 and increasing yearly. Political considerations, and not law enforcement skills, continued to remain the criteria for which the territorial marshal was chosen. Myron McCord had resided in the Arizona Territory since 1893 and had served on the Board of Control, which oversaw the affairs of the prison, the insane asylum, and the reform school. Early in his public service career, McCord had served as a congressman while living in Wisconsin. He also became acquainted with future president William McKinley, and through his connections with the Ohio politician, McCord secured an appointment to the marshalcy of Arizona.

Myron McCord, who served as the marshal of Arizona, was replaced twice by Benjamin F. Daniels.

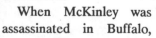

When McKinley was assassinated in Buffalo, N.Y., in September 1901, McCord assumed that his job status would be protected by the incoming president, Theodore Roosevelt. This, however, was not the case. The new president named Benjamin F. Daniels, a fellow Rough Rider of Roosevelt's, assistant city marshal of Dodge City, Kan., and big game hunter to fill the post of Arizona marshal in 1902. Daniels, who had earned a reputation as a gunfighter and an unsavory character early in life, served a prison term for stealing a horse when he was eighteen. When these facts came to light, Roosevelt asked for Daniels resignation, and McCord was reappointed marshal on Mar. 18, 1902.

Marshal McCord quickly became involved in the Burton Alvord case. Alvord, a former lawman turned outlaw, was arrested by McCord in December 1902 on federal charges of mail robbery. In July 1903, Marshal McCord transported Alvord and five members of his gang from Yuma Prison to testify before a grand jury in Tombstone. The prisoners had to be separated to prevent collusion in their testimony, a situation that greatly troubled McCord who feared that they might escape from the poorly maintained Tombstone jail. Alvord and his partner Billy Stiles escaped from their flimsy cells and succeeded in reaching Mexico, where they were later recaptured by the Arizona Rangers following a desperate gun battle. (The Rangers were a special police force created by the Arizona Legislature in 1901 to assist the marshal in tracking down criminals.)

In a strange twist of fate, the discredited Ben Daniels replaced McCord as marshal in April 1906 by order of the president who had always harbored warm feelings for his former comrade in arms. The Kansas City *Journal* was quick to pick up on Roosevelt's strategy. Since assuming office, he had placed eighteen former Rough Riders in key government and law enforcement posts in Arizona, New Mexico, and Oklahoma. Burton Mossman, captain of the Arizona Rangers bitterly complained that "the devastating blight of the Rough Riders was spreading all over the Southwest." See: **Alvord, Burton**; **Daniels, Benjamin F.**; **Mossman, Burton**.

McDowell, Jack (AKA: **Three-Fingered Jack**), d.1864, U.S., gunman. A western hardcase, Jack McDowell ran a saloon in Aurora, Nev., a place where beatings, mayhem, and murder were the norm. "Three-Fingered Jack" McDowell and several other rough and tumble gunmen bullied the town and cheated the card players who were foolish enough to frequent McDowell's saloon. If any players were provoked by the underhandedness of the establishment, then McDowell and his confederates merely took matters into their own hands and forced the unfortunate gambler to take his losses like a man.

After a man named Sears was murdered in McDowell's saloon, a law-abiding Aurora citizen threatened to tell the local authorities the identities of the killers, those being McDowell, Jim Daley, Jim Buckley, and another gunslinger. The ruffians took quick action and cut the throat of the would-be informer and then threw the body of the hapless man into the muddy street to rot. So incensed at this bestial conduct, the horror-stricken citizens of Aurora formed a vigilante group and attacked McDowell's saloon on Feb. 5, 1864. McDowell, Daley, Buckley, and the un-

Jack McDowell and friends being hanged, 1864.

named gunman were easily overpowered and disarmed, then locked up. They were hanged a short time later on a quickly constructed gallows.

McGee, Orpheus, d.1876, U.S., outlaw. On Apr. 20, 1874, a vengeful Orpheus McGee lured Robert Alexander out of his home by gobbling like a turkey. Annoyed by the cackling bird, Alexander grabbed his rifle and appeared on the front porch of his home. McGee took dead aim on Alexander, whom he blamed for the unsolved murder of a close friend. Alexander was dead before he could get a shot off. McGee was quickly arrested and brought to Fort Smith (Ark.) where he was tried before Judge Isaac Parker. Orpheus McGee was found Guilty of murder and was one of five men hanged at Fort Smith on Apr. 21, 1876.

McGrath, Price, prom. 1850s-60s, U.S., gambler. Price McGrath, born in Kentucky, was originally a tailor who arrived in New Orleans after winning fortunes in Kentucky and on Mississippi riverboats. He established a posh casino in New Orleans and made a fortune by the end of the 1860s, since many of his games were rigged.

McIntire, James, 1846-1902, U.S., lawman-outlaw. James McIntire, born in Ohio, moved to Texas at an early age and became a cowboy when he was in his teens. In

Fort Griffin, Texas, McIntire served briefly as a deputy sheriff and was noted for his ability to catch horse thieves. McIntire served as a Texas Ranger for a short period and was later city marshal in Las Vegas, N.M., at the time Pat Garrett arrested Billy the Kid. After serving in several more law enforcement posts, McIntire got involved in a range war and was charged with murdering two men in 1883 near Silver City, N.M. A $1,000 reward was posted for McIntire and his friend, Jim Courtright. Both men fled but were later cleared of the murder charges.

Lawman James McIntire.

McIntire later moved to El Paso, Texas, where he died. See: **Courtright, Timothy Isaiah.**

McKemie, Robert (McKimie, AKA: **Little Reddie from Texas**), prom. 1870s, U.S., outlaw. A rider with the Sam Bass gang when it operated in the Dakotas, Robert McKemie reportedly shot John Slaughter in the head during the stagecoach robbery of the Deadwood-Pierre stage at Gold Run Creek in April 1877. When Bass gave up stagecoach robberies for train holdups, McKemie went his own way, preferring to remain a stagecoach robber. He joined Dunc Blackburn, Bill Bivins, Jim Wall and Boston Joe in holding up several stagecoaches, but at South Pass City a posse caught the gang red-handed and shot

Western gunman Robert McKemie.

several members, killing Boston Joe. McKemie returned to his native Ohio and there formed a new gang, committing holdups in Highland, Pike, and Ross counties. McKemie was later captured and sent to prison. See: **Bass, Sam.**

McKinney, Thomas L. (AKA: **Tip**), prom. 1882, U.S., lawman. Thomas L. "Tip" McKinney was born into a prestigious Texas family and finally settled down in Roswell, N.M., where he was appointed deputy sheriff by

Pat Garrett. On May 8, 1881, McKinney was tracking Bob Edwards and three other rustlers who had stolen twenty-one horses from an Arizona ranch. McKinney caught up with them near Rattlesnake Springs, N.M. As McKinney drew abreast of Edwards' horse, Edwards opened fire with a Winchester. McKinney quickly returned fire with his six-gun, killing Edwards. Two months later, McKinney was with Garrett when Billy the Kid was killed.

McLaughlin, Archie, d.1878, and **Brown, Jim**, prom. 1878, and **Caswell, Alex**, and **Mansfield, Billy**, and **Smith, Jack**, d.1878, U.S., outlaws. Archie McLaughlin led a gang of bandits who robbed the Wells Fargo stagecoaches outside of Deadwood, S.D., more than thirty miles northwest of Rapid City. McLaughlin's gang included Jim Brown, Alex Caswell, Billy Mansfield, and Jack Smith. Belle Siddons, alias Lurline Monte Verde, McLaughlin's lover, accidentally let it be known that a robbery was planned for July 2, 1878, at Whoop-up Canyon, between Deadwood and Rapid City. The cargo was a large treasure taken from the Homestead Mine. The passengers, however, were heavily armed Wells Fargo detectives.

McLaughlin's expected surprise attack turned into a rout. The detectives shot Caswell dead with a bullet to the head and seriously wounded Brown in his thigh. The remaining three gang members escaped with Brown. McLaughlin, slightly wounded, had Mansfield contact Siddons and bring her to their hideout to help the dying outlaw. Siddons, who had once been a doctor's assistant, arrived and saved Brown's life. Brown was captured soon after his recovery and confessed to his involvement in the attempted holdup and also informed on his three surviving companions. All three fled to Canada, but later returned to the U.S. and were apprehended in Cheyenne, Wyo. On Nov. 3, 1878, a stagecoach transporting McLaughlin, Mansfield, and Smith was overtaken by masked vigilantes, and all three were lynched north of Fort Laramie. See: **Siddons, Belle.**

McLowery Brothers, See: Clanton-McLowery Gang.

McMahon, Francis Marion, 1870-1940, U.S., lawman. Francis Marion McMahon was born in Missouri and raised in McCulloch County, Texas. He joined the Texas Rangers in 1893 and proved to be one of the toughest and most fearless rangers of this legendary law enforce-ment group. McMahon arrested the notorious and deadly bandit, Bass Outlaw, on Apr. 4, 1894, in El Paso, Texas, after Outlaw was shot during an exchange of gunfire with Constable John Selman. McMahon was appointed deputy U.S. Marshal in El Paso in May 1894. By 1896 McMahon gave up his public position to work for the Southern Pacific Railroad as a detective. McMahon later worked as an immigration official and then chief postal inspector in San Diego, Calif., before dying on Mar. 6, 1940. See: **Outlaw, Bass.**

Lawman Frank M. McMahon.

McMasters, Sherman, prom. 1882, U.S., lawman. Sherman McMasters sided with the Earp brothers in their long feud with the Clantons. Wyatt Earp appointed McMasters deputy sheriff so he could help pursue stage robbers. McMasters was present when Morgan Earp was fatally shot, and ran down Morgan's killers with the Earp brothers. They fatally shot one of the killers, Frank Stilwell, when they spotted him near the train depot after they sent Virgil Earp, wounded in an earlier gunfight, to safety in California. Two days later, on Mar. 22, 1882, a posse including McMasters, Wyatt and Warren Earp, Doc Holliday, and Turkey Creek Jack Jackson caught up with and killed Florentino Cruz, another suspect in Morgan's murder. See: **Earp, Wyatt Berry Stapp.**

McNab, Frank, d.1878, U.S., gunman. Frank McNab worked as cattle king John Chisum's foreman on Chisum's Seven Springs Ranch in New Mexico. When the Lincoln County War broke out between Chisum and the owners of The House, a powerful mercantile exchange, McNab aligned himself with Chisum and his partners, Alexander McSween and John Tunstall. When the opposition shot and killed Tunstall in March 1878, McNab, Billy the Kid, and several other Regulators (the name given to the Chisum gunmen) rode in search of his killers. They found two of them, Frank Baker and William Morton. Baker, Morton, and one of the Regulators, William McCloskey, were shot and killed before they ever reached Lincoln. Reports of Frank Baker's and William Morton's death conflict. One version named McNab as their killer and suggested McCloskey was accidentally shot. In another account, Billy the Kid shot Baker, Morton, and McCloskey because he was opposed to killing the prisoners.

When Dick Brewer was killed at Blazer's Mill, McNab took over the Regulators. Soon after, in April 1878, McNab and Regulators Frank Coe and Ab Sanders were ambushed by two dozen men. They abducted and wounded Sanders but later released Coe. Frank McNab was shot to death. See: **Billy the Kid; Lincoln County War.**

McNelly, Leander H., 1844-77, U.S., lawman. When the Texas Rangers were organized in 1874, Leander H. McNelly, a former captain in the Confederate army, was placed in command of the Special Battalion assigned to unusual missions such as dealing with rustling rings or inter-

Texas Ranger, Captain Leander H. McNelly.

national smugglers. McNelly and his rangers were given the job of settling the Sutton-Taylor feud in DeWitt County and of dealing with the U.S. outlaws terrorizing the Nueces Strip near the Mexican border. The feud dated back to 1867-68, when one of Creed Taylor's men was killed by William Sutton during a scrape with Union troops sent in to preserve order during the Reconstruction period. McNelly and his men succeeded in curtailing the violence until the spring of 1875, when he was transferred to the Mexican border to end the lawlessness plaguing the region.

McNelly had a number of encounters with the army of Juan Cortina, a Mexican bandit who had troubled Texas for more than fifteen years. On one occasion, McNelly and his men caught up with Cortina's group and killed twelve of the rustlers as they were herding cattle stolen from the King Ranch toward the border. The two groups clashed several times, and McNelly and his men once chased the rustlers back across the border. Revered by his men almost to the point of fanaticism, McNelly would have led them deep into the interior of Mexico if not for the U.S. Army, which stopped him. "Give my compliments to the secretary of war, and tell him United States troops can go to hell!" he told army officers. Even so, McNelly's raid against Cortina effectively ended large-scale rustling in that part of Texas.

Despite failing health, McNelly continued to perform his duties. When tuberculosis prevented the lawman from riding on horseback, McNelly directed his men from a wagon. He was finally forced to resign in February 1877 and died on Sept. 4 of that year. See: **Cortina, Juan.**

Madsen, Christian, 1851-1944, U.S., lawman. After stints in several European armies, Christian Madsen arrived in New York in 1876 and joined the U.S. Cavalry. In fifteen years of service, he fought in the Indian campaigns and witnessed Buffalo Bill Cody's scalping of Cheyenne warrior Yellow Hand. In 1891, Madsen accepted a post as deputy U.S. marshal, first in El Reno, and later in Guthrie, Okla. Alone or with the help of others, Madsen caught members of the Dalton Gang, killers Kid Lewis and Foster Crawford, and train robber Henry Silva. Madsen's success made him, along with Heck Thomas and Bill Tilghman, one of the legendary Three Guardsmen.

Lawman Chris Madsen, one of the legendary Three Guardsmen.

In 1898, Madsen joined up with Teddy Roosevelt's Rough Riders. In 1911, he assumed the post of U.S. marshal for Oklahoma. From 1918 to 1922, Madsen was a special investigator for Oklahoma governor J.B.A. Robertson. Madsen died on Jan. 9, 1944.

Maledon, George, 1834-1911, U.S., executioner. George Maledon, who implemented the sentences of "Hanging Judge" Isaac C. Parker of Fort Smith (Ark.), was born in Detroit to German immigrant parents. He moved to Fort Smith and joined the police department. Following the Civil War, in which he served on the Union side, Maledon became deputy U.S. marshal in Fort Smith. For additional income, Maledon always offered to act as hangman, and with Judge Parker's arrival in 1875, his future was assured.

George Maledon, hangman.

Maledon took particular pride in his hangman's work, and rarely if ever, smiled. He prepared carefully for each execution, oiling and stretching the ropes to assure a drop that would quickly and neatly kill the condemned. "Get out your oil can, Maledon," was the standing joke in the courtroom after Parker had handed down the sentence of death. For the condemned prisoner, Maledon graciously provided new suits and coffins, and arranged for the transportation of the unclaimed body to a cemetery.

He considered multiple executions a particular challenge and had a twelve-man gallows erected. When the multiple gallows were used for the notorious "Dance of Death," in which six men were hanged, the public apparently thought Maledon and Parker had gone too far. In 1882, the government ordered that the executions be closed to the public, after such events had taken on all the aspects of a carnival freak show. A stockade was constructed around the gallows, and Maledon was given the additional responsibility of issuing passes to those persons who were allowed inside.

For twenty-one years, Maledon hanged almost all of the eighty-eight men Parker condemned. When Parker died, Maledon continued his hangman's work for a few years, and then went on the road, displaying the tools of his trade in a sort of sideshow. When asked if he suffered from a guilty conscience the jailer replied: "No, I simply did my duty. I never hanged a man who came back to have the job done over." Maledon died on May 6, 1911. See: **Parker, Isaac.**

Manley, Amos, and **Manley, Abler**, d.1881, U.S., outlaws. The slaying of Ellis McVay, a farmer who lived with his wife, two children, and hired hand William Burnett on the boundary of the Creek and Choctaw Indian nations, was one of the most heinous crimes in the history of the region. Amos Manley and his brother Abler were passing through the area on a miserably cold night, Dec. 3, 1880, when they spotted the glowing light of McVay's cabin. The two men prevailed on McVay for lodging for the night, saying that they would be on their way the next morning. There were jobs opening up in the Choctaw Nation, and the Manley brothers were eager to make some money. The cabin was narrow, but McVay consented and allowed the Manleys to sleep on a pallet in the corner of the room.

At 3:00 a.m., the Manleys reached for their guns and crept toward the sleeping McVay. Amos fired his weapon first, striking the farmer in the head. Abler finished off McVay with two shots to the abdomen. Burnett reached for his gun and tried to defend Mrs. McVay and the two children. In the confused struggle that followed, the murderous Manley brothers chopped off Burnett's right hand and dealt him a severe gash to the neck. Meanwhile, the woman slipped out the back door and fled barefoot with her children into the countryside. The killers left Burnett for dead, and took off. But they were caught the next day and remanded for trial to Fort Smith (Ark.). The severed hand was offered as evidence in court, and the testimony of the surviving victims helped convict the pair. The Manleys were hanged on Sept. 9, 1881.

Manning, James, c.1845-1915, U.S., gunman. The Manning brothers, Doc, Jim, John, Frank, Joe, and Gyp, born on a plantation in Alabama, fought for the Confederacy in the Civil War. When the South was defeated, they moved to the Texas Gulf Coast. The four brothers built a sloop and sailed to Mexico, where they fought for Maximillian. Upon their return to the U.S., they scattered to various parts of Texas. Around 1875, William Manning was killed in an ambush while the brothers were trailing a cattle herd to Texas. The three remaining brothers chased the man responsible for the shooting and killed him.

Sometime after 1881, Jim, Frank and John ran a ranch together near Canutillo which developed a reputation as a hangout for rustlers and outlaws. By February 1882, Jim Manning owned the Coliseum Variety Theater in El Paso, Texas. He was approached by Doc Cummings, brother-in-law to Dallas Stoudenmire, a lawman and bitter enemy of the Mannings. Manning ignored Cummings' taunts for a time, but finally strapped on his pistols and drew on Cummings, killing him in the exchange that followed. Later that year, Jim Manning came upon Stoudenmire and Doc

Cummings wrestling on the ground. Stoudenmire had been shot twice, and Manning once. Jim Manning shot and killed Stoudenmire.

Manning then ran a saloon in Seattle, but a fire destroyed it. He moved his family to Anacosta, Wash., and opened another saloon. Toward the end of his life, he returned to the Southwest and invested in silver and copper mines around Parker, Ariz. He died of cancer in Los Angeles in 1915. See: **Stoudenmire, Dallas.**

Marlowe, Boone, 1865-89, U.S., gunman. Boone Marlowe's family lived at various times in California, Texas, Missouri, Oklahoma, New Mexico, Mexico, and Colorado. The elder Marlowe was a doctor and farmer. The family, which included four other sons, Charley, Alf, Epp, and George, left their home in Wilbarger County, Texas, in 1886 when Boone killed James Holdson. Boone was riding up to the house of a married sister when Holdson, either drunk or thinking about an old grudge, drew and fired on him. Boone returned the fire, killing Holdson. In Colorado, where the family settled next, all five brothers were arrested for stealing. When the charges were dropped, they moved back to Texas, this time to Vernon. There, in 1888, a posse tried to arrest Boone for murder. Boone shot his way free, but all four of his brothers were arrested for complicity. While being transferred to a more secure jail, the four Marlowes and their captors were ambushed. One lawman and Alf and Epp Marlowe were killed. George and Charley, though wounded and each shackled to a dead brother, picked up the guards' weapons and continued to fight. Both George and Charley survived the incident. A group of bounty hunters found Boone, poisoned him, and brought his body back to Fort Sill, Okla., on Jan. 28, 1889, where they collected a $1,700 reward.

Mason County War (AKA: **Hoodoo War**), 1870s, U.S., feud. The Mason County War in Texas, which began in 1875 with the shooting of Tim Williamson, became a bloody confrontation that lasted more than a year, claiming at least a dozen lives. Williamson, who had been arrested for stealing livestock, was abducted and shot to death by a mob of his enemies. A close friend of Williamson, Scott Cooley, decided that deputy sheriff John Worley, who was escorting Williamson to jail at the time of the ambush, had been in collusion with the ambushers. Cooley avenged Williamson's murder by shooting Worley and cutting off his ears. Cooley and some friends then killed Daniel Hoerster, whom they also suspected of having been part of the group

who killed Williamson. Some of Cooley's enemies caught and hanged two of his confederates, Elijah and Pete Backus. In return, Cooley's forces killed Pete Bader and Luther Wiggins. The murders continued for more than a year until the Texas Rangers put an end to the bloodshed. Cooley disappeared, and only a few minor gunmen were ever charged. One of them, Johnny Ringo, was imprisoned for murder, but managed to escape and left Texas.

Mason County gunman Scott Cooley.

Massey, Robert, d.1883, U.S., outlaw. Robert Massey and his business associate Edmond Clark had driven a herd of cattle from Dodge City, Kan., to the Dakota Territory in the summer of 1881. After completing the sale of the cattle, they headed back to their homes in Texas. On Dec. 1 they had just set up camp on the South Canadian River, a distance of 200 miles from Fort Smith (Ark.), when Massey reached for his revolver and shot Clark in the back of the head.

Massey took off with the money received from the livestock sale and continued on to his home in Grayson County, Texas. The following April he was arrested with the murder weapon still in his possession. Robert Massey was returned to Fort Smith where he was hanged on Apr. 13, 1883, following a short trial.

Masterson, Bat, See: **Masterson, William Barclay**

Masterson, Edward J., 1852-78, U.S., gunman. Ed Masterson, older brother of Bat Masterson, believed in talking his way out of difficulties. He was the eldest of seven children born in Canada to Thomas and Catherine Masterson. After the Civil War, the family moved to a farm near Wichita, Kan. Ed and Bat soon left home, working first as grading contractors and then as buffalo hunters. In June 1877, Ed Masterson was appointed deputy marshal of Dodge City. His policy as a lawman was to keep his gun holstered as much as possible.

Masterson was wounded in the chest while trying to arrest Texas cowboy Bob Shaw. Masterson held the marshal's job for only a matter of months. On Apr. 9, 1878, he was shot after disarming a disorderly cowboy in the Lady Gay Dance Hall. Masterson took a gun from Jack Wagner and gave it to Wagner's boss, A.M. Walker, who returned the gun to the drunken Wagner. Both Wagner and Walker then rushed Masterson. While Wagner and Masterson struggled, Walker prevented Masterson's deputy marshal, Nat Haywood, from coming to his aid. Wagner shot Masterson in the stomach, firing at such close range that the charge set the marshal's clothes on fire. Masterson managed

Lawman Edward J. Masterson, killed in 1878.

to fire four shots, one of which hit Wagner, mortally wounding him. The other three hit Walker, wounding but not killing him. Masterson died within the hour of his wounds. His funeral was one of the biggest ever seen in Dodge City. See: **Masterson, William Barclay**.

Masterson, James P., 1855-95, U.S., lawman-gunman. James P. Masterson, younger brother of Bat and Edward Masterson, was born in Iroquois County, Ill., in 1855, raised in New York state, and moved with his family in 1871 to Wichita, Kan. Jim left the family farm and spent a few years hunting buffalo before joining his brothers in Dodge City. There, in 1878, shortly after his brother Ed's death, Jim was appointed to the police force. He was also a Ford County deputy sheriff. In 1879, he was promoted to city marshal.

Lawman James Masterson.

In April 1881, Jim, then a part-owner in the Lady Gay Saloon and Dance Hall, got into a fight with bartender Al Updegraff. Shots were fired but no one was hurt. Two days later, Jim's brother Bat, summoned from Tombstone, Ariz., by telegram, arrived in Dodge City. As soon as Bat stepped off the train, he

spotted Updegraff and began firing. Jim Masterson soon joined the fight and Updegraff was killed. Both Masterson brothers were forced to leave town.

In 1889, Jim Masterson was involved in the struggle between Cimarron and Ingalls, Okla., two villages vying to be the county seat of newly formed Gray County. On one occasion, Masterson and three other gunfighters were trapped inside the city hall of Cimarron while trying to steal the county records. They were caught there until an agreement was reached to release them to the county sheriff, an Ingalls sympathizer who released them the following day. Masterson took part in the Oklahoma Land Rush of 1889 and became one of the first settlers of Guthrie, Okla. He served as a deputy sheriff of Guthrie, and in 1893, he was appointed deputy U.S. marshal. In September 1893, Masterson participated in the arrest of the infamous Doolin Gang. Two years later, still in Guthrie, Masterson died of the "galloping consumption." See: **Masterson, William Barclay**.

Masterson, William Barclay (AKA: **Bat**), 1853-1921, U.S., lawman. William Barclay Masterson, who was known throughout the West as "Bat," was born on Nov. 26, 1853, in Quebec, Can., the second of seven children born to Thomas and Catherine Masterson. He was raised on farms in Canada, New York, and Illinois until moving with his family to Wichita, Kan., in 1867. Bat and his older brother Ed left home and went to work for the Atchison, Topeka, and Santa Fe Railroad as a section hand. He later became a buffalo hunter and then an Indian scout for General Nelson Miles at $75 a month.

After three months, Masteron left the army and his whereabouts were uncertain. He surfaced in Mobeetie, Texas, where, on Jan. 24, 1876, he was drinking in a local saloon with a bar girl, Molly Brennan. A trooper named King, who had been seeing Brennan, roared into the bar, blazing away with his six-gun at Masterson and Brennan. Bullets struck both of them but Masterson managered to fire a round from his own gun which struck King, killing him. Molly Brennan died of her wound a short time later.

Returning to Kansas, Masterson opened a saloon in Dodge City in 1877. He ran afoul of the law a short time later by helping a prisoner escape. Masterson was beaten up by the town marshal and vowed that he would never again be on the wrong side of the law. Masterson managed to get himself appointed a deputy sheriff of Ford County. His brother Ed at the same time was a policeman in Dodge City. Masterson proved himself an effective peace officer and was elected sheriff of Ford County in 1877. He excelled in maintaining law and order, preferring to talk troublemakers into leaving town.

Sheriff Masterson used his six-gun only on rare occasions when his glib tongue or fists would not solve an issue. He manhandled such tough customers as Ben Thompson and his equally lethal brother Billy Thompson by simply telling these lightning-fast gunfighters that if they did not obey the laws of Ford County, he and his deputies would be forced to shoot them on sight. Masterson's reputation as a gunfighter was by then widely established but mostly on Masterson's own statements. He was not a gunfighter by any means, and, oddly, he had only a few real gunfights in his past. However, his friendships with gunmen such as John "Doc" Holliday, and the Earp brothers, who served as lawmen throughout Kansas, caused the bad men visiting Dodge City to believe that if they shot and killed Masterson, they would have to deal with his friends, a prospect no gunfighter, drunken or sober, wished to entertain.

One of Masterson's more famous manhunts involved James W. "Spike" Kennedy, son of a wealthy cattleowner.

William Barclay "Bat" Masterson as the top lawman of Dodge City.

In 1878, Kennedy, a hellion and gunfighter who was used to having his own way, fell in love with a dance hall girl, Dora Hand, who rebuffed him. Kennedy created such a disturbance that he was ordered to leave Dodge City. He rode back into town and fired several bullets through the windows of the home of Mayor James H. "Dog" Kelley, the man who had banished Kennedy. One wild shot struck Hand by accident; she had been sleeping in a back room. Kennedy then rode quickly out of town. Hand died within minutes and a small posse was quickly assembled, one consisting of Wyatt Earp, Bat Masterson, Charlie Bassett, and Bill Tilghman, probably the most formidable group of lawmen ever assembled on the frontier.

The four lawmen rode after Kennedy on a relentless pursuit, stopping only for water and a few meals, riding the extra mounts they had brought along in relays. Kennedy, who realized he was being followed, rode an excellent stallion, but rode the poor horse to death. After a frantic chase of more than a hundred miles across the prairie, Kennedy's horse collapsed near Mead City. He fired a bullet into the animal to put it out of its agony. That single shot echoed across the wide open range and was heard by the pursuing lawmen who galloped to where Kennedy was stranded. The gunman opened fire, but Masterson slipped

his rifle from the holster on his saddle and fired a single bullet that slammed into Kennedy's arm, disabling him. When he was told that he had killed Dora Hand, not Mayor Kelley, the object of his wrath, Kennedy broke down and sobbed: "I wish you had killed me." He was released after being found Not Guilty for "lack of evidence."

Masterson's brother Ed was killed by gunman Jack Wagner in 1878, and his younger brother James Masterson later became a lawman in Dodge City, working with Wyatt Earp. It was because of James Masterson that Bat almost lost his life in his most serious gunfight. James Masterson had entered into an uneasy partnership with A.J. Peacock, both of them being owners of the Lady Gay Dance Hall and Saloon. The two men began arguing over James Masterson wanting Peacock to fire a truculent bully, Al Updegraff, who was a bartender at the Lady Gay. When Peacock refused to fire Updegraff, James Masterson sent for his brother Bat, who was then in Tombstone, Ariz.

Taking the train from Tombstone, Bat Masterson arrived in Dodge City on Apr. 16, 1881. A few minutes after he left the train he spotted Peacock and Updegraff walking down a street. He angrily shouted to them: "I have come over a thousand miles to settle this! I know you are heeled—now fight!" All three drew their sixguns and began blazing away at each other. James Masterson and Charlie Ronan joined the battle, also shooting from cover.

Bat Masterson had taken refuge behind some logs, and Peacock and Updegraff were hiding around the corner of the

"Bat" Masterson in old age when he was a sports columnist.

local jail. Bullets flew wildly in all directions, wounding passerby James Anderson in the back. The firing went on for some minutes with bullets passing through Bat Masterson's clothes and hat. At one point, while he was firing from a prone position, a bullet struck the ground only inches from his face, sending a clump of dirt into his open mouth. Masterson's return shot caught Updegraff in the chest, entering his right lung. He fell to the ground.

Mayor A.B. Webster and Sheriff Fred Singer suddenly appeared on the street carrying shotguns. The firing stopped at Webster's order. Updegraff and Anderson were rushed to a doctor's office and both men later recovered. Bat Masterson, whose reputation and prior service as a lawman in the area worked on his behalf, was only charged with disturbing the peace and fined but a small amount of money. Some in Dodge City wanted him charged with attempted murder, but they were hooted down in a quick hearing. Masterson agreed to leave town immediately and he did, on the next train heading for Colorado.

Masterson drifted about for several years, moving to Fort Worth, Texas, where he supported himself through gambling. In addition, Masterson promoted racetrack events and purchased a few race horses that earned considerable prize money. Masterson had a talent for telling stories and related his experiences in newspaper articles that became widely popular. In 1891, he married Emma Walters. So successful were Masterson's newspaper columns, especially those on sports, that he was hired as the chief sports writer for the New York *Morning Telegraph* in 1901. He moved to New York where he became a permanent fixture in the popular night spots, regaling customers with his tales of the old Wild West. President Theodore Roosevelt appointed Masterson a special U.S. Marshal in 1905, but Masterson resigned the position a short time later, explaining that his newspaper duties demanded too much of his time.

On Oct. 25, 1921, Masterson, who was suffering from a cold, arrived at the offices of the *Morning Telegraph* and went to his desk to catch up on some belated sports articles. He sat down and began writing in pen and ink. He wrote: "There are those who argue that everything breaks even in this old dump of a world of ours. I suppose these ginks who argue that way hold that because the rich man gets ice in the summer and the poor man gets it in the winter things are breaking even for both. Maybe so, but I'll swear that I can't see it that way..." These were Bat Masterson's last words, spoken or written. He was found a few minutes later, his head on his desk, the pen still clutched in a hand that once held six-guns. He was dead of a heart attack. See: **Bassett, Charles; Earp, Wyatt Berry Stapp; Kennedy, James; Masterson, Edward J.; Masterson, James P.; Thompson, Ben; Tilghman, William Matthew, Jr.**

Mather, Dave H. (Mathers, AKA: Mysterious Dave), b. 1845, U.S., outlaw-lawman. Around 1873, Dave Mather became involved in cattle rustling in Sharp County, Ark. By 1874, Mather had made his first appearance in Dodge City, where he was to return frequently as both lawman and lawbreaker. By 1878, Mather had found his way to Mobeetie, Texas, and into the company of Wyatt Earp, where, one suspicious account related, the two ran a con game selling "gold" bricks to gullible cowboys.

In 1879, Mather and several other men were arrested with outlaw Dutch Henry Borne. Mather was released, but was soon picked up for complicity in a train robbery near Las Vegas. Once acquitted, Mather got himself appointed

constable in Las Vegas, but left town after being accused of "promiscuous shooting." Mather served for a short time as assistant marshal in El Paso, Texas. After an altercation in a brothel in which Mather was slightly wounded, he returned to Dodge City where he was hired as assistant city marshal. When he lost the position in an election in 1884, a feud began between him and his successor, Tom Nixon. On the evening of July 18, 1884, Nixon finally drew a gun and fired at Mather, but only sprayed him with a few splinters. Three days later, Mather approached Nixon from

Western gunman Dave Mather.

behind and fired four bullets into his back, killing him instantly.

Although Mather was acquitted of Nixon's murder, he killed another man the following year and was run out of town by Marshal Bill Tilghman. After serving as city marshal in a couple small towns in Kansas and Nebraska, Mather disappeared.

Matthews, Jacob B., 1847-1904, U.S., gunman. After the Civil War, Jacob B. Matthews, who had served in the Fifth Tennessee Cavalry, drifted west. By 1867, Matthews was a miner in Elizabeth, N.M. In 1873, Matthews moved on to Lincoln, where he served as circuit court clerk and began working for L.G. Murphy and James J. Dolan, later forming a partnership with Dolan and John H. Riley just in time for the bloody Lincoln County War. The war was a struggle between two factions vying for economic control of the Lincoln County area, with Dolan and Riley as the incumbent power holders and John Chisum, Alexander McSween, and John Tunstall challenging their empire. Matthews was appointed deputy to Sheriff William Brady and was at the head of the posse that killed John Tunstall under questionable circumstances. After Tunstall's death, the fighting between the two factions intensified. On Apr. 1, 1878, Billy the Kid, who had pledged to avenge Tunstall's death, ambushed Brady, Matthews, Deputy George Hindman, George Peppin, and John Long on the main street of Lincoln. Brady and Hindman were mortally wounded in the gunfire. Matthews, though hit, drove off the attackers. Matthews also took part in a four-day pitched battle at McSween's house which began on July 15, in which McSween was shot and killed, effectively ending the Lincoln County War. In February 1879, James Dolan, Matthews, Jesse Evans, and William Campbell met lawyer Huston Chapman on the street near the Lincoln post office. Campbell, who was drunk, fired on Chapman. The others in Campbell's group also drew and fired, killing Chapman.

Eventually, Matthews moved to Roswell, N.M., where in 1898 he was appointed postmaster by President William McKinley. Theodore Roosevelt reappointed Matthews in 1902. Matthews died on June 3, 1904. See: **Billy the Kid.**

Meade, William Kidder, prom. 1880s-90s, U.S., lawman. William Meade served two terms as the Arizona marshal, both times during the administration of a Democratic president. Meade was born in Virginia in 1851, but he spent most of his adult life in Arizona investing in mining property. He was active in local government, and as a delegate to the 1884 Democratic nominating convention, he was instrumental in attaching a plank to the party platform calling for the appointment of local residents to key offices in the territory. In 1885 he traveled to Washington to lobby for an appointment to the governorship, but had to settle for the marshalcy instead.

Meade, who succeeded Marshal Zan Tidball, labeled himself a Democratic reformer and, according to published reports, took office "with a flourish of trumpets." At the outset of his first term, Meade made good on his promises. He selected deputies who were sensitive to the needs of members of the Church of Jesus Christ of Latter-Day Saints, who had been treated rather roughly and with prejudice, during the previous administrations. Meade set an unusual precedent by allowing the Mormons to appear in court voluntarily, rather than submit to the humiliating ordeal of having a process server give them a summons. Therefore, it was ironic that the Mormons should figure so prominently in the one incident that marred Meade's first term of office.

On May 11, 1889, thirteen American outlaws ambushed and robbed an army paymaster, Joseph Wham, who was stationed at Fort Thomas in Graham County. Meade took personal charge of the investigation and sent two of his deputies, C.T. Dunavan, and William "Billy" Breakenridge on the trail of the felons. Breakenridge became convinced that the robbers had sought refuge in a Mormon settlement near the Gila River. Consequently, several Mormons, including Gilbert and Wilfred Webb, David Rogers, Thomas N. Lamb, and Warren and Lyman Follett, were arrested and put in jail. Mormon leaders charged Meade and his men with willful persecution, noting that the lawmen had ignored the suspicious movements of another group of men, who had fled the county under strange circumstances. The Mormons traced the deputy marshal's motive to greed—for each arrest made, there was a $500 reward promised.

Marshal William K. Meade.

The Mormon church demanded the ouster of Meade, and with the change to a Republican administration in Washington, rumors circulated that the marshal's days were numbered. Meade and his deputies worked tirelessly on the case. The editor of the Tucson *Daily Citizen* noted that the Wham case had "probably furnished more work for the deputy marshals...than any previous case in the history of the territory." The trial of the Wham defendants began on Nov. 11, 1889, and continued until mid-December. On the witness stand, Joseph Wham proved to be unreliable. He admitted that he had not seen the robbers too clearly and it was difficult to make a positive identification. A verdict of Not Guilty was returned against the Mormons, which only served to make Marshal Meade a political scapegoat. The Missouri *Republican*, which harbored no sympathy for Meade, accused him of making no effort to apprehend the suspects until a sizeable reward was posted. Under these circumstances, Meade had little recourse but to step down, which he did on Mar. 4, 1890. The failure of his successor Robert H. Paul to placate the bruised feelings of the Mormons in the wake of the Wham case, and the hint of financial impropriety in his handling of government money disappointed many Arizonians who expected more than they had received.

With the restoration of Grover Cleveland to the White House in 1892, Meade was re-appointed Arizona marshal. He was in office a mere seven months when a gang began robbing stagecoaches in Graham County. On Jan. 6, 1894, this same outlaw band robbed a Southern Pacific train at Teviston Post Office near Bowie. To track the culprits down, Marshal Meade hired Alexander Ezekiels, a noted bounty hunter. Two weeks later Meade jubilantly reported the arrest of Wilfred Webb, deputy postmaster at Pima, and a relative of one of the suspects in the Wham case. Three other outlaws associated with Webb were quickly rounded up and placed on trial in December 1894. The three men each received ten years in prison for robbery of the mails. The special prosecutor in the case was William E. Barnes, who had made an enemy of Meade in the Wham case. It was personal vindication for Meade and a significant victory for the government in its first test of federal justice in the raw Arizona territory.

Meade resigned from his post on June 15, 1897, having carved out an enviable legacy for himself. He had strengthened the powers of his office, and restored a degree of respect to the federal institution in the wake of the poorly handled Wham robbery case. In this sense, he had lived up to his reform banner which he took into office in 1885. See: **Paul, Robert H.**

Meagher, Mike, 1843-81, U.S., lawman. From their home in County Cavar, Ire., Mike Meagher, his brother John, and his father immigrated to the U.S., settling first in Illinois. After fighting in the Civil War, the brothers made their way into Kansas as stage drivers. In 1871, Mike was appointed marshal of Wichita, then a wild cattle town, and made John his deputy.

Meagher rarely drew his gun to settle a dispute. After three years as marshal, Mike left Wichita for Indian Territory where he worked as a carpenter and drove a freight wagon. In 1874 he became a deputy U.S. marshal and was also appointed first lieutenant of a militia company organized to scout Indians. In 1875, Meagher again was elected marshal of Wichita.

On New Year's Day 1877, a drunken stage driver, Sylvester Powell, angry that Meagher had arrested him earlier, crept up on the marshal, who was using the outhouse behind Hope's Saloon. Powell fired several shots at Meagher through the outhouse door, wounding him slightly. Meagher later shot Powell to death.

He then moved to Caldwell, Kan., where he opened a saloon, and in 1880 was elected mayor. Meagher served occasionally as a deputy for the local marshal. In December 1881, a drunken Texas cowboy, Jim Talbot, shot and killed Meagher.

Meldrum, Bob, b.1865, U.S., lawman-gunman. It was widely believed that Bob Meldrum had worked with Pinkerton detective Tom Horn in the 1890s for ranchers and mine operators who wanted troublemakers eliminated. In 1900, Meldrum was working as a harness maker in Dixon, Wyo., when he saw a reward notice on a co-worker, Noah Wilkinson. Meldrum allegedly shot Wilkinson in the back of the head and collected the reward.

Meldrum next moved to Colorado, where he worked as a strike breaker for mine operators. The murder of a number of strikers were attributed to Meldrum. In 1908, the Snake River Cattlemen's Association in Wyoming hired Meldrum to rid the area of rustlers. When Meldrum shot and killed John "Chick" Bowen, the ranchers raised his $18,000 bail. Meldrum jumped bail and eluded authorities for six years before he surrendered to stand trial. He was sentenced to five to seven years for manslaughter, but served only three months before being paroled into the custody of a rancher. After his imprisonment, Meldrum worked in the saddler's trade.

Menczer, Augustus (AKA: **Gus; The Kid**), 1856-82, U.S., outlaw. With his partner Bill Burbridge of Tarrant County, Texas, Gus Menczer opened a saloon at Raton, N.M., which became popularly known as the "Bank Exchange." In 1882, the two friends had a falling out which resulted in a showdown. Menczer and Burbridge agreed to resolve their differences in a shootout inside the Raton saloon. "Kid" Menczer shot Burbridge and then was pursued into the streets by an angry mob that supported Burbridge. Menczer led them on a wild chase through town, in which two of the townsmen were killed. The Kid was finally subdued after he ran out of ammunition. On June 28, 1882, he was hanged in front of the Raton Bank.

Middleton, John, d.1885, U.S., gunman. Sometime in the 1870s, John Middleton wandered into New Mexico from Kansas. Just before the infamous Lincoln County War broke out, rancher John Tunstall hired Middleton and Billy the Kid as part of his posse of "Regulators," who later killed Frank Baker and Billy Morton in retribution for Tunstall's murder. Middleton also took part in an ambush a short time later in which Sheriff William Brady and Deputy George Hindman were killed and Billy Matthews was wounded. Just a few weeks after the Regulators killed Brady and Hindman, they encountered a member of the opposition at Blazer's Mill. Gunfire broke out, in which Middleton was seriously injured. The Regulators withdrew from the fight to get help for Middleton and another injured man, Frank Coe.

After the encounter at Blazer's Mill, Middleton seemed to lose his taste for gunfights. He recuperated at Fort Sumner and then moved to Sun City, Kan., where he opened a grocery store. In 1885, he allegedly became involved with Belle Starr in Oklahoma while Belle's husband, Sam, was away. In the spring of 1885, Middleton was ambushed and shot to death. See: **Billy the Kid.**

Middleton, Thomas (AKA: **Doc**), 1851-1913, U.S., gunman. A tall, handsome man, who was said to be a ladies man, Thomas Middleton and his brother Joe arrived in Texas in 1875, where they worked as cowboys in San Saba and Llano counties. Tensions between rival cattle companies were high in that part of Texas, and men were getting killed on a daily basis. "Doc" Middleton, a desperate gunman in his own right,

shot and killed two soldiers in Sidney, Texas, one night after returning from a cattle drive along the North Platte River. But it was for the crime of horse theft—and not murder—that he was arrested in 1879. Middleton was sentenced to five years in the Nebraska state prison, actually serving time from Sept. 24, 1879, to June 18, 1883.

Two years later, Middleton and the "Pony Boys" were loose on the plains, stealing horses and trying

Tom Middleton

to keep one step ahead of the law. In later years, Middleton ran a saloon in Ardmore, S.D., and promoted a horse race that was run between Gillette, Wyo., and Chicago, Ill. His final scrape with the law occurred on Nov. 1, 1913, when he was arrested in Nebraska for running a blind pig saloon. While in jail, he contracted a serious illness and died. This colorful figure of the western plains was aptly described as "an outlaw of the worst kind, a horse thief, a handsome cuss."

Miller, Clelland, d.1876, U.S., gunman. Born near the Missouri homestead of Jesse James, Clelland Miller idolized the famed western badman and was determined to join him as soon as the James gang would have him. Always in need of men, Jesse and Frank James allowed Miller to join them. He soon proved to be handy with a gun, as evidenced by an incident that occurred at the Clay County, Mo., home of Daniel H. Askew on Apr. 12, 1875.

Suspecting that Askew was harboring a Pinkerton agent, the James brothers surrounded the house and waited for the owner to emerge. At 8:00 p.m., Askew went to his well to draw water. Three shots rang out. Mrs. Askew ran forth to assist her dying husband, whom she believed was gunned down by the James brothers and Clell Miller. There was no positive proof, however, to link Miller to the crime.

On Sept. 7, 1876, the townsmen in Northfield succeeded in shooting members of the James Gang—a feat no lawman had been able to achieve. Miller was one of eight robbers who entered Northfield intent on robbing the First National Bank. Miller and Cole Younger remained outside the bank on the look out for the sheriff. When J.S. Allen, the proprietor of a hardware store, was ordered away from the entrance of the bank by Miller, he became suspicious and alerted the townspeople. "Get your guns boys!" he yelled. "They're robbing the bank!" The shooting actually began inside the building and then moved outside. As Miller tried to mount his steed, Elias Stacy shot him in the face with a volley of buckshot, but Miller was not seriously wounded. He composed himself in the saddle and prepared to ride away when Henry Wheeler, a medical student, took careful aim. His bullet pierced Miller in the chest, killing him instantly. Clell Miller's short, but violent ride with the James Gang was over before it barely began. See: **James, Jesse Woodson; Younger Brothers.**

Miller, James B. (AKA: **Killin' Jim; Killer Miller; Jim the Killer; Deacon**), 1866-1909, U.S., outlaw. Born in Van Buren, Ark., on Oct. 24, 1866, James B. Miller moved

with his parents to Franklin, Texas, when he was one year old. Both his parents died when he was young, and when his older sister married, Miller was sent to live with his grandparents in Coryell County. In 1874, when Miller was only eight, both his grand-

Professional assassin James B. Miller.

mother and grandfather were found murdered, and he was arrested for the killings. He was not prosecuted, however, because of his age. He was placed in the custody of his sister, but Miller did not get along with his brother-in-law, John Coop. On July 30,

1884, when Miller was seventeen, he attended church with a Miss Georgia Large. During the meeting he left for about forty minutes. During that time, Coop was murdered by someone unleashing a shotgun blast into him while he was asleep on a porch hammock. Miller was convicted of the murder and sent to prison for life.

After Miller's lawyers appealed on a technicality, the youthful killer was again tried and was acquitted for lack of evidence. He was released and rode to San Saba County where he hired out his gun to the highest bidder. Miller told those who hired him that he would murder anyone for $1,000, and he was soon in the employ of cattlemen and businessmen who wanted rivals or truculent partners out of the way. Miller killed with alacrity, but was seldom charged with murder since no motive could be established and eyewitnesses did not exist. Miller was careful to shoot his victims always from ambush and mostly at night. He invariably used a shotgun so that the spread of pellets would find their mark and his work would be done with a single blast from his favorite weapon.

By the early 1890s, Miller had selected West Texas as his area of operations. He associated himself with Mannen and Joe Clements and his outlaw family and accepted many murder assignments from Clements. Miller also had some dealings with the notorious gunfighter, John Wesley Hardin, who was, a short time later, killed by John Selman, Sr. After arranging the murder of a cattleman, Con Gibson, Miller was confronted by Sheriff Bud Frazer in Pecos, Texas, on Apr. 12, 1894. Frazer did not give Miller time to reach for his shotgun but opened fire on the killer while Miller was fixing a wagon. The first bullet from Frazer's gun bounced harmlessly off Miller's chest as did four more shots. Miller, wounded in the right arm, drew his gun and tried to fire with his left hand as he advanced on the startled Frazer. The sheriff fired another shot and this one struck Miller in his side, felling him.

Miller's friends rushed him to a doctor's office. The long, black frock coat Miller always wore, no matter the heat, was removed and so was Miller's shirt. It was then that the solid steel plate Miller wore hidden beneath his clothes, strapped to his chest, was seen. Four dents from Frazer's bullets had been made in it, but it had saved the killer's life. When Miller recovered, he immediately stalked Frazer and shot and killed the sheriff while he was playing cards. Miller was later confronted by Frazer's sister who held a gun on him. Miller drew his own gun and aimed it at the grief-stricken girl, snarling: "If you try to use that gun, I'll give you what your brother got! I'll shoot you right in the face!" The girl put the gun down and went home.

The ruthless gunman went on killing for profit. On Feb. 29, 1908, Miller and Carl Adamson met with the famous Pat Garrett, retired lawman and killer of Billy the Kid. Garrett owned some rich land near Las Cruces, N.M., which another cattlemen coveted. He hired Miller to murder Garrett in order to steal the land. Miller and Adamson pretended to be interested in leasing some of Garrett's land, and when the old lawmen rode out to a remote spot to show them the land available, Miller shot and killed Garrett from ambush. He was never prosecuted for the crime for the usual reason—lack of evidence.

Miller had grown rich in the murder business. He owned a large house in Forth Worth, Texas, and he had several large bank accounts. He wore fine suits and ate in the best restaurants. Miller owned a string of thoroughbred horses and did not need to continue killing for a living. He nevertheless accepted another murder assignment, and it was clear by then that Miller enjoyed killing people. Angus A. Bobbitt, a cattle baron living near Ada, Okla., was his next victim. Jesse West, Berry B. Burrell, and Joe Allen hired Miller to kill Bobbitt, planning to acquire the Bobbitt holdings once its owner was safely buried.

Bobbitt had been a sheriff and was still handy with his six-gun. Miller took no chances with this victim, shooting him from ambush with his shotgun, but he was seen by Oscar Peeler, a 19-year-old cowboy as he rode away from the slain Bobbitt. At first Peeler refused to say anything

"Jim the Killer" Miller, at left, hangs from the rafter of a livery stable in Ada, Okla., 1909, along with three of his fellow murderers.

about Miller, but when he learned that he was about to be charged with Bobbitt's murder, Peeler told lawmen in Ada everything he knew, saying that he had been paid $50 to escort Miller to Bobbitt's ranch and that Miller had admitted to him that he had traveled from Fort Worth to murder the Oklahoma rancher.

Lawmen in Fort Worth were contacted, and Miller was extradited to Oklahoma where he stood trial. He, West, Burrell, and Allen were all convicted and sentenced to death, but Miller only laughed. The finest criminal lawyers in the West were on his payroll, and he soon bragged that he would be released after his attorneys filed their appeals. A crowd of vigilantes did not wait for these legal procedures to take place. They knew that Miller, who had bragged of killing as many as thirty men (twelve could be proven), might again cheat justice through his highly paid lawyers. On the night of Apr. 19, 1909, a lynch mob broke into the jail and dragged Miller and the others out to a livery stable. Though the other men begged for their lives, Jim "The Killer" Miller showed no signs of fear. He only asked that his diamond ring be given to his wife and that he be permitted to wear his black stetson while he was being hanged.

The vigilantes granted these wishes. Then Miller, standing on a box, displayed his last act of bravado, shouting: "Let 'er rip!" He then voluntarily stepped off the box to be jerked by the rope around his neck which was tied to a rafter in the stable. He dangled as the other three were strung up. The bodies were left hanging for some hours in order to allow a local photographer to take enough photos of the lynchings. These photos sold for many years in Ada to tourists. The only surviving photo shows Miller hanging with the others, his black hat on his tilted head.

Mills, James, d.1889, and **Robin, Tom**, d.1887, U.S., outlaws. James Mills and Tom Robin shot and killed John Windham in the Seminole Nation on Dec. 15, 1887. After Windham had fallen to the ground, the gunmen pumped two more bullets into him. A vigilante group attempted to arrest the pair, but in the fracas, Mills managed to escape. Robin, who had sustained a serious wound in his scrape with the vigilantes, was taken to Fort Smith (Ark.), where he died of his wounds. Mills was captured the following January. He refused to supply the marshals with a motive for the shooting and went to the gallows quietly on Apr. 19, 1889.

Milton, Jeff Davis, 1861-1947, U.S., lawman. Jeff Davis Milton was born on the family plantation in Marianna, Fla., the youngest of ten children of the Civil War governor of Florida. In 1877, at the age of sixteen, Milton moved to Navasota, Texas, then west to a cattle ranching job at Fort Phantom Hill, and from there to Huntsville, where he supervised convicts on a prison farm. In 1880, Milton joined the Texas Rangers and served with them for three years before quitting to work in a general store.

Milton soon moved to Murphyville, Texas, where he signed on as a deputy marshal and later opened a saloon. In 1884, he moved to New Mexico, where he first worked on a ranch near San Marcial, then homesteaded in the San Mateos, and later became deputy sheriff of Socorro County. In 1885, Milton joined "Russell's Army" and campaigned in

Arizona against Apache marauders. In 1887, Milton became a mounted inspector patrolling the long Arizona-Mexico border. Between 1890 and his retirement in 1930, Milton ran a small horse ranch, worked as a fireman, and then a conductor, on the Southern Pacific Railroad, and served as police chief of El Paso. He also worked for Wells Fargo as an express messenger, prospected in the Sierra Madres, and explored oil leases in Texas and Baja California.

Lawman Jeff Milton.

Milton's last job was with the Immigration Service, where he was assigned to stop the smuggling of Chinese aliens through Arizona and California. He later accompanied a shipload of aliens being deported to revolutionary Russia. Milton married in 1919 and spent the last years of his life with his wife on a small ranch near Tombstone, Ariz. He died on May 7, 1947.

Miner, William (AKA: **Old Bill**), 1847-1913, U.S., outlaw. Educated in the public schools of Jackson, Ky., William "Old Bill" Miner made his way west to San Diego, Calif., in 1863 to become a messenger for the U.S. Army during the Apache Indian war. Although his job was dangerous and required stealth and nerve, Miner realized there was a profit potential. He went into business for himself delivering the mail of San Diego citizens to points east at an exorbitant charge of $25 per letter.

Miner squandered his money and soon found himself in a financial hole. He turned to crime, specifically stagecoach robbing, to finance his extravagant habits. In 1869, he held up the Sonora stagecoach, taking $200 from the driver. As Miller attempted to flee, his horse collapsed and a posse chasing him had no trouble bringing him to justice. Miner was sentenced to fifteen years in prison but was out in ten for good behavior. Released in 1879, Miner teamed up with Bill LeRoy in Colorado and together they robbed a number of stagecoaches and trains. They were cornered by a posse one night but Miner shot his way out of the trap, dropping three deputies in their tracks. LeRoy was was arrested and hanged.

In 1879, Miner collected his savings and sailed to Europe, where, according to his own account, he worked as a slave trader in Turkey. From there he pushed on to Rio de Janeiro and hired himself out as a gunrunner. Arriving in the U.S. in November 1880, Miner held up the Sonora stage a second time, netting himself $3,000. With a fresh bank-roll, Miner traveled to Chicago where he joined a bank robber named Stanton T. Jones. Together they rode into Colorado where they robbed the Del Norte stage of $3,000, but the two men barely escaped. Returning once more to California, Miner held up the Sonora stage for a third time on Nov. 7, 1881. He was captured three days later, convicted, and sentenced to San Quentin for twenty-five years.

Old Bill was paroled on June 17, 1901. He tried to go straight, deciding that it was perhaps the prudent thing to do for a man of his years (he was then fifty-four). But after two years he gave it up and returned to crime. On Sept. 23, 1903, he robbed a passenger train near Corbett, Ore., but made off with only a few hundred dollars. Miner headed north into British Columbia in 1904, where he robbed the Canadian Pacific express at Mission Junction of $10,000. Old Bill had at last hit the jackpot. He lived in the finest hotels while passing himself off as a wealthy, retired cattleman. The money lasted until 1906, when he robbed the Canadian Pacific. On May 8 of that year, he stopped the Transcontinental Express near Furrer, B.C. The Northwest Mounted Police nabbed him a month later, and he eventually received a life sentence at the New Westminster Penitentiary at Victoria.

On Aug. 9, 1907, after a year of digging, Miner escaped through a thirty-foot tunnel under his cell. The Mounties contacted the Pinkerton Detective Agency to assist them in the chase. Reward money totalling $12,500 was offered for his capture. Undaunted, Miner committed two more robberies of note. In July 1909, he robbed a Portland, Ore., bank of $12,000. Two years later on Feb. 18, 1911, he held up the Southern Railroad Express in Sulphur Springs, Ga., and made off with $3,500. Company officials hired the Pinkertons to track down this "elder statesman" of crime, who was barely able to hold his six-gun straight during the Southern Express holdup. Henry W. Minster, assistant superintendent of the Pinkerton office in Philadelphia, was in Atlanta preparing to open a branch office at the time of the holdup. He rushed to Gainesville, Ga., to interview the train conductor and engineers on board the express at the time of the holdup. Deciding that Miner's surest way of escape was through the Blue Ridge Mountains, he alerted local law enforcement officials. Two days later, the Lumpkin County sheriff received word that an old man was camped out in the woods. Miner was quickly arrested and shuttled off to prison, where he died in 1913 at age sixty-six. Turning to a deputy at the time of his last arrest, he said with a tinge of sadness, "I'm really getting too old for this sort of thing."

Mitchell, William (AKA: **Baldy Russell**), 1853-1928, U.S., gunman. Texas gunman William Mitchell got involved in a feud with the Truitt family, members of which raided Mitchell's ranch in 1874. Mitchell and Mit Graves, a handyman working for the Mitchell family, then raided the Truitt ranch and killed two members of the family. Mitchell fled, and while hiding, his father was hanged by vigilantes for the Truitt killings. A year later Mitchell reappeared and killed James Truitt, the last member of the rival clan. Mitchell then turned outlaw and using the alias of Baldy Russell, robbed stagecoaches and banks with several southwestern gangs. He was not apprehended until 1912 when he was sentenced to life imprisonment for the Truitt killings. Within months, Mitchell escaped and lived in hiding until he died in 1928.

Moore, William, prom. 1870s-80s, U.S., outlaw. William Moore compensated for his one bad eye by using the other to take dead aim on all those who displeased him in some small way. Moore gunned down one of his own family members, a black cowboy, and two of his New Mexico neighbors before fleeing to Alaska, where at last report, he became a trapper under an assumed name.

Morco, John (AKA: **Happy Jack**), d.1873, U.S., gunman. John "Happy Jack" Morco killed four unarmed men in California who tried to stop him from beating his wife. Morco fled to Ellsworth, Kan., then in its heyday as a railhead, where he was hired onto the police force. On Aug. 15, 1873, Morco, who drank excessively, was involved in a saloon brawl, in which Sheriff C.B. Whitney was killed. Morco was fired and left town after stealing a pair of expensive six-guns. When Morco returned to Ellsworth, policeman Charlie Brown confronted him. Morco refused to surrender his pistol and drew on Brown, who responded by shooting Morco through the head and heart, killing him.

Morse, Harry N., 1835-1912, U.S., lawman. Harry N. Morse, a New Yorker by birth, came to California in the 1849 Gold Rush. In 1863, Morse was elected sheriff of Alameda County, and developed a reputation as a clever and persistent man hunter. In October 1865, Morse and another lawman tracked killer Norrato Ponce to a hideout, but Ponce, though wounded, managed to escape the relentless lawman. The next month, when Morse tracked Ponce into Contra Costa County, Ponce tried to escape again, but

Morse shot and killed the murderer.

In 1871, Morse and several other lawmen trailed Juan Soto, a criminal known as the Human Wildcat into the Sausalito Valley. After a confrontation with a dozen Mexicans, Morse shot Soto to death. Morse retired in 1878 and started a detective agency in San Francisco. He was responsible for the arrest of the notorious stagecoach robber Black Bart. Morse moved to Oakland to raise a family and diversified his business interests into real estate, publishing, and mining. See: **Soto, Juan.**

Lawman Harry N. Morse.

Moss, George, d.1888, and **Smith, Sandy**, and **Jones, Factor**, and **Butler, Dick**, d.c.1887, U.S., outlaws. Frontier justice finally caught up with four hardcases who conspired to steal cattle on the range and murder anyone who tried to stand in their way. George Moss, and his three henchmen, Sandy Smith, Factor Jones, and Dick Butler, proceeded to the Red River Bottoms in the Choctaw Nation where they stole a steer belonging to a local farmer named George Taff. Shots were fired, which brought an alarmed Taff to the scene of the shooting. Moss was a man who was true to his word. He took aim on farmer Taff and shot him. During the melee, Moss' horse escaped. It was an unlucky break for the cattle rustlers, because the discovery of the horse led the marshals back to the body of Taff. Since Jones and Butler were citizens of the Choctaw Nation, and thereby governed by laws of the Indian jurisdiction, they could not be prosecuted at Fort Smith (Ark.).

Outraged by the cold-blooded nature of the crime, the local gentry organized a vigilante party and seized the two men, who were then riddled with bullets on the same spot where their neighbor Taff was killed. Sandy Smith died in prison before the case went to trial, leaving only George Moss to legally answer for his crime. He was duly convicted and hanged on Apr. 27, 1888.

Mossman, Burton C., 1867-1956, U.S., lawman. Born in Aurora, Ill., in 1867, Burton C. Mossman moved west with his family, eventually ending up in the New Mexico Territory by the time he was twenty-one. Mossman began working as a ranch foreman, and by the age of thirty, was managing the two-million acre Hash Knife ranch. One of his primary duties was to clear the property of rustlers.

Lawman Burton Mossman.

Mossman was appointed a deputy sheriff of Navajo County, Ariz., but continued managing the Hash Knife and ran a stagecoach line. Mossman even built an opera house in Winslow and later profitably sold it. In 1901, he became first captain of the newly organized Arizona Rangers. During his short term as captain, Mossman captured Augustin Chacon, one of the era's most active and dangerous rustlers.

When Mossman resigned his post in 1902, rustling was under control. Mossman married in 1905, became one of the Southwest's prominent ranchers, and retired in 1944. He died at Roswell, N.M. See: **Arizona Rangers.**

Murieta, Joaquin, (Murrieta; Joaquin Carrillo), 1830-c.1853, U.S., outlaw. Murieta was a Mexican outlaw who emerged as a folk hero in the 1850s to thousands of immigrant Sonorans, who resented U.S. exclusionary laws that barred them from striking claims in the Sacramento gold fields. Murieta attempted to avenge the injustice the "Yanquis" had heaped upon himself and his people by embarking on a murderous rampage.

Born in the province of Sonora in 1830, Joaquin Murieta was the son of a prosperous land owner who was well-respected in his community. In Spring 1850, Murieta eloped to California with his young bride, Rosita Feliz. The couple arrived in Stanislaus County to join other prospectors in the hunt for gold, but Murieta had underestimated the anti-Mexican feeling among the miners. Six "Yanqui" rough-necks came to their residence one night to tell Murieta that his kind was not welcome in Stanislaus County, then bound and gagged him and raped his wife. Driven from his claim, Murieta moved his wife and belongings to Calaveras County in April 1850. A short time later Murieta's half-brother arrived from Mexico. He loaned Joaquin a horse he had purchased, which had been stolen from a resident of the county. Murieta did not know this, and upon meeting the rightful owner he found himself in a terrible predicament. A mob quickly formed, and it appeared briefly as if Murieta

Left, one of the best likenesses of the California bandit, Joaquin Murieta.

Right, a cover for one of the many lurid dime-novel books on the legendary bandit Murieta.

Below, Murieta depicted as a blood-thirsty savage, riding his wild black stallion.

A fictionalized Murieta shown attacking a helpless female.

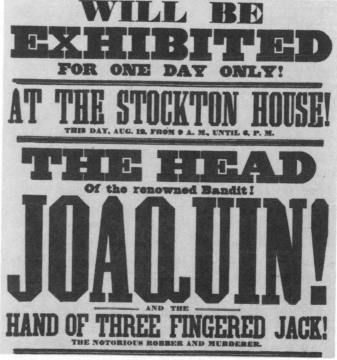

Advertisement for a grisly exhibit, the head of bandit Murieta.

was going to be lynched. Joaquin explained what had happened and insisted that his half-brother would give a good account of himself. The mob agreed to hear the half-brother's story and followed Joaquin back to the hovel where the Murietas lived, but they were not satisfied with the brother's excuses. The Americans lynched the brother and horsewhipped Joaquin. When it was over, Murieta vowed revenge against all Americans.

Not long after that the mangled body of a miner was found near a campsite. It was one of the men who had taken part in the lynching. Several weeks later a physician Murieta suspected of being part of the mob was shot at as he walked down a road late at night. Panic-stricken, the doctor and many others fled the county. The remaining "vigilantes" were all gunned down by Murieta and the Mexican brigands he had recruited for the job. At the age of twenty, Joaquin Murieta became one of California's most feared outlaws, heading a band of cutthroats that included the legendary Manuel Garcia, known as "Three-fingered Jack"; Reyes Feliz, a brother of Joaquin's wife; Pedro Gonzales; and Joaquin Valencia, who had once served under Padre Jurata, a famous Mexican guerilla chieftain.

The Murieta band was opposed to the Greaser Act of 1850 and the Foreign Miners Act, which were passed by the Sacramento legislature to keep Mexicans out of the gold fields. During the next three years the outlaw leader and his men rampaged through the San Joaquin and Sacramento Valleys, robbing miners, holding up stagecoaches, and raiding farmhouses. In Fall 1851, the Murietas committed seven murders in twelve days near Marysville, Calif. In November they were reported in the vicinity of Mount Shasta, where they stole horses and murdered miners.

In Spring 1852, the Indian chief Sapatorra captured Murieta and several of his men as they attempted to steal some horses. Sapatorra contacted the Los Angeles authorities that he had rounded up some Mexican horse thieves, but he did not know he had the famous Murieta in custody. The authorities told the chief to let them go. After whipping the men and taking their clothes, he did so. Meanwhile, the uproar the bandit leader had created had various law enforcement officers boasting that they would bring in Murieta for the reward money being offered. In July 1852, Major-General Joshua H. Bean organized a posse to wipe out the entire gang, but was stabbed to death one night.

Murieta skillfully avoided capture for the next year, but on May 17, 1853, Governor John Bigler signed a bill that authorized Captain Harry Love of the California Rangers to organize a body of twenty men to hunt down the outlaw and kill him. Love and his men were to be paid $150 per month, spread over a three-month period. Love and his posse cornered Murieta and seventy of his bandits in June 1853 near Arroyo Cantoova. The bandit leader, alerted to the presence of peace officers, abruptly broke camp and ordered his brigands to scatter in every direction. Love located the Murieta faction at the crack of dawn on June 25. The posse made a rush at the camp, catching Murieta as he was washing down his horse. He mounted his steed in a vain attempt to break away, but Love's posse shot Murieta's horse from under him and then shot Murieta himself. Gasping for his last breath, Murieta staggered a few more feet, collapsing in the dust, and said, "Don't shoot any more boys, the work is done." With that he died. The desperado, Three-fingered Jack Garcia, engaged the posse in a running gun battle for the next five miles before the lawmen killed their quarry. They cut off his left hand, the one with only three fingers, and brought it back as proof that the outlaw had not escaped them.

Captain Love, meanwhile, had ordered that Murieta's head be cut off and returned to the authorities for identification. Justice of the Peace A.C. Bain received the sworn affidavit of Father Dominic Blaine on Aug. 11, 1853, that this was indeed Murieta. Captain Love was awarded the sum of $6,000 by the grateful California legislature. The head of the bandit king was placed in a jar and taken down to King's Saloon on Sansome Street in San Francisco, where it was placed on display as a novelty by ghoulish promoters who collected a dollar from each person who wanted to see it. A superstition was attached to the head that all who came in possession of it were doomed to bad luck. Bartender King went bankrupt, and Deputy Sheriff Harrison, who next owned it, committed suicide. The third owner, a gunsmith named Natchez who bought the item at a public auction, was killed when his weapon accidentally went off.

Captain Love drove the remaining outlaws across the border back into Mexico, thus ending the scourge of lawlessness that plagued the California gold fields. Not everyone was satisfied, however, that Love had gotten the right man. Rumors circulated throughout the 1870s that Murieta had escaped to Sonora, where he eventually died. The body was thought by some to have been buried in the Jesuit cemetery in the village of Cucurpe.

Murphy, Jim, 1861-79, U.S., outlaw. Jim Murphy, the son of a Denton County, Texas, rancher, was close enough to Sam Bass and his gang that the Murphy family occasionally harbored the gang. In May 1878, Jim Murphy, his father, and his brother were arrested and charged with being accessories after the fact in Bass' robbing of the U.S. mails. Murphy won his release by offering to deliver Bass to the authorities.

Murphy helped Bass plan a robbery of a bank in Round Rock, Texas. As the gang was riding toward Round Rock,

Murphy slipped away and wired the gang's plans to the authorities, who ambushed the gang and seriously wounded Bass. He was found the next day, and died one day later, on July 21, 1878. Bass refused to identify the men riding with him.

Murphy, stigmatized for his betrayal of Bass and criticized in all quarters, died less than a year later, in June 1879, after swallowing poisonous eye lotion. The slow, painful death suggested that Murphy's death was not a suicide.

Murrel, John A. (Murrell, AKA: **The Great Western Land Pirate**), b.1794, U.S., outlaw. John A. Murrel was lionized in fictional tales that described him as The Great Western Land Pirate. He was no Robin Hood, however, but a vicious cutthroat and robber. He had the distinction of being the first bandit to terrorize and rob travelors along the Natchez Trace, the only trail through the wilderness from the Ohio Valley to Natchez, Miss.

Murrel befriended a young traveler named Virgil Stewart in 1834. Traveling along the Trace under another name, Murrel amused himself by telling Stewart about a bandit older brother of his, describing countless robberies and murders committed by the older brother. By the campfire one night, Murrel leaned his scarred and frightening face close to Stewart and said: "I might as well be out with it. I'm the older brother I've been telling you about."

Murrel told Stewart that he and his bandits had been stealing slaves and reselling them. "I have carried off more than a thousand slaves," Murrel told Stewart proudly, adding that he kept the fiercest, most powerful slaves for himself to add to the ranks of his slave army. Murrel believed Stewart was his friend and would join him in his dark enterprises. He detailed his plans to attack Natchez and New Orleans with thousands of armed slaves. The bandit hated the landed gentry of New Orleans and the southern aristocracy that somehow in the past had injured him

Outlaw John Murrel, right, with a henchman, carrying a murder victim to the swamp.

and his family. Murrel not only vowed to have his revenge, but meant to control the entire states of Louisiana and Mississippi.

To preserve his own life, Stewart not only placated Murrel but pretended to join his revolt. On the way to Murrel's camp deep in the wilderness of the Trace, Stewart learned the real reason for Murrel's hatred of the southern land owners. Years earlier, he had been caught horse-stealing and had been whipped and branded. He was a preacher at the time, and the humiliation of the public whipping caused him "to abandon the work of the Lord." Murrel blamed the very land owners he preyed upon as having caused him to turn outlaw and bandit. "My blacks will cut all their throats!" he vowed. "We will swim in rivers of blood!"

At Murrel's camp, Stewart witnessed scores of blacks marching about, heavily armed, preparing for the invasion of Natchez and New Orleans. Stewart took his opportunity to escape the camp in the middle of the night. Upon reaching Nashville, he told his horror story of John A. Murrel and the impending slave revolt. Stewart then led a small, heavily armed posse to the outlaw's camp, where they captured Murrel and his men. Murrel was returned to Nashville, where he stood trial for slave stealing and banditry. He was convicted and sent to prison for ten years, released in 1842, and once more disappeared into the Natchez Trace.

Musgrave, George, prom. 1900s, U.S., outlaw. George Musgrave was erroneously given credit for many of the crimes committed in the New Mexico Territory following the death of "Black Jack" Ketchum. Nevertheless, Marshal Creighton Foraker alerted neighboring states to watch out for Musgrave, who had settled with his family in Colorado. "Musgrave is an outlaw and desperado of the worst kind," Foraker warned Marshal George H. Green of Dalhart, Texas, "and I have been hunting him for the past nine years." A man fitting Musgrave's description was captured and held in custody in Texas, but this suspect proved not to be Foraker's nemesis. Musgrave, however, was eventually tried for murder in Albuquerque in 1907, but the alleged terrible outlaw was acquitted. See: **Foraker, Creighton.**

Musgrove, Lee H., d.1868, U.S., outlaw. Lee H. Musgrove, a Mississippian, ran a gang of road agents and livestock thieves noted for their barbarity. Musgrove settled in the 1850s in Napa, Calif., where he developed a reputation as a tough gunfighter. He was forced to flee California in 1863 after he killed a man who disparaged the Confederacy. In Nevada, where Musgrove journeyed to next, he killed two more men. His next stop was in the Idaho Territory, where he operated as an Indian trader and dealer in stolen goods. When he killed another man there, he was forced to move again, this time to the Wyoming Territory, where he organized a gang of thieves and rustlers who ranged from Texas to Kansas. The gang was credited with at least twelve murders.

Colorado lawman Dave Cook came after the Musgrove Gang and whittled their numbers down one by one, killing or arresting them. Cook finally caught Musgrove in the Wyoming Territory. Musgrove was jailed in Denver, Colo., and Cook cleverly anticipated and headed off an attempt by his sidekick, Ed Franklin, to break him out of jail. On Nov. 23, 1868, a crowd stormed the jail where Musgrove was being held and lynched him.

Mysterious Dave, See: **Mather, Dave H.**

Mysterious Kid, See: **Lewis, Elmer.**

N

Neagle, David, c.1847-1926, and **Field, Stephen J.,** 1816-99, U.S., lawmen-mur. David S. Terry resigned as chief justice of the California Supreme Court in order to kill U.S. Senator David C. Broderick in a duel. The charges brought against Terry were dismissed, but he was ostracized. Only slowly did he regain a place in public life.

As an attorney, Terry met Sarah Hill, who was suing U.S. senator William Sharon, a Nevada millionaire, to force him to honor a written marriage contract between them. When Senator Sharon died, Terry took charge of Hill's fight for the estate, and the two were soon married. In September 1888, Justice Stephen Field ruled against Sarah Terry, and a courtroom scene ended with both Terrys in jail. David Terry swore revenge. David Neagle, a former city marshal of Tombstone, Ariz., was appointed bodyguard to Justice Field. Though born in Boston Neagle grew up in the San Francisco Bay area, where he earned a reputation for

The argumentative Judge David S. Terry who was killed by David Neagle in 1889.

being a handy man with a gun while roaming through the mining camps of the Pacific Slope. At various times, he was a gambler, politician, saloon keeper, and lawman. During the height of the Earp-Clanton feud in 1880, Neagle served as deputy sheriff of Tombstone. He remained unbiased in his dealings with both the Earps and Clantons, and succeeded in furthering his career with election to the city marshal's post in January 1882. However, he failed to win the shrievalty, and then moved on to other western boom towns. Then in 1888, Neagle, having re-established himself in San Francisco, became embroiled in the Terry-Field altercation.

The following August, the Terrys were among the passengers on a train from Los Angeles to San Francisco who had breakfast in the station dining room in Lathrop. There they spotted Justice Field. As Mrs. Terry rushed back to the train, her husband approached Field and slapped his face. Neagle drew his revolver and warned Terry, who nevertheless attacked the judge again. Neagle fatally shot Terry in the chest just as Mrs. Terry returned with a gun of her own. Neagle was arrested for murder, and at the insistence of Mrs. Terry, Justice Field was charged with complicity. The case against Field was quickly dismissed. After a month, the U.S. Circuit Court also

dismissed all charges against David Neagle, who returned to San Francisco where he lived quietly. Mrs. Terry was later committed to a mental institution at Stockton, Calif.

Nevill, Charles L., prom. 1870s-80s, U.S., lawman. A member of the Texas Rangers, Charles Nevill located the outlaw Sam Bass near Round Rock, Texas, in 1878. Bass was severely wounded when Nevill found him, and afterward took him to jail where Bass died. In 1880, Captain Nevill was sent into Jeff Davis County, Texas, to chase down the Jesse Evans gang and the troublesome Potter boys. Nevill was well qualified for these tasks, after helping to suppress the Horrell-Higgins Feud in Lampasas County in the late 1870s. Nevill was well respected and liked by his subordinates, and was a meticulous note keeper who assiduously recorded his movements in Texas while pursuing outlaws. He served as sheriff of Presidio County from 1885-88, before settling down on his ranch south of Alpine. See: **Evans, Jesse; Horrell-Higgins Feud.**

Newcomb, George (AKA: **Bitter Creek; Slaughter's Kid**), d.1895, U.S., outlaw. George Newcomb left his home in Fort Scott, Kan., while still a youth. In Texas, Newcomb worked for cattleman John Slaughter and became known as "Slaughter's Kid." In 1883, Newcomb moved on to Oklahoma, working as a cowboy in the Cherokee Strip ranching country. While in Oklahoma, he earned the nickname Bitter Creek by frequently belting out the lyrics, "I'm a wild wolf from Bitter Creek/ And it's my night to howl."

Newcomb left ranching to become a member of both the Dalton and Doolin gangs, both of which

Outlaw George Newcomb, dead, 1895.

robbed a number of banks and trains. In July, 1892, Newcomb and other members of the Dalton gang rode into the town of Adair, Okla., just before an evening train was to arrive. They robbed the depot and then attacked the train, escaping unharmed after exchanging gunfire with some lawmen on the train. In September 1893, Newcomb was nearly killed in Ingalls, Okla., where he and the Doolin gang had gone for a rest. While they were in the saloon, several lawmen arrived and began surrounding the building. When Newcomb sensed something wrong, he took a look outside, and got on his horse. He was identified, fired on, and injured in the exchange, but escaped.

By May 1895, Newcomb had a $5,000 reward on his head. When he and fugitive Charley Pierce stopped at the Dunn ranch so Newcomb could see teenage Rose Dunn, the reward proved too great a temptation for the Dunn brothers. As Newcomb and Pierce dismounted, the brothers opened fire on them, hitting them both. The following day, the Dunns loaded both bodies into a wagon to take them in for the reward. Newcomb groaned and asked for a glass of water. The surprised Dunns shot him again, this time killing him. See: **Doolin, William**.

Newman, Bud, prom. 1890s, U.S., outlaw. Bud Newman was a member of the Taylor gang of Texas, which specialized in train robbery. Newman and others robbed a train at Coleman Junction, Texas, on June 9, 1898, and he was later captured at the Taylor camp at Sonora, Texas. Newman was jailed and later escaped. He was killed by lawmen.

Newton General Massacre, 1871, U.S., mur. The bloody shootout in Newton, Kan., in 1871, in which five men were killed and several others wounded, was the result of a feud between cowboy Hugh Anderson and a burly railroad foreman, Mike McCluskie. The railroad boss had killed gambler William Bailey, a close friend of Anderson's, and the cowboy had vowed revenge. At about 1 a.m. on Aug. 20, 1871, Anderson returned to Newton from a trail drive and sought out McCluskie, finding him at Perry Tuttle's Dance Hall, where the the deadly railroader was playing faro. Anderson wasted no time; he immediately marched up to the table where McCluskie sat and pulled his pistol, pointing it at McCluskie's head and shouting: "You are a cowardly s.o.b.! I will blow the top of your head off!" With that he fired a shot, the bullet hitting McCluskie's neck.

The railroad man, however, was a massive brute, and the wound only slowed him down a bit. He half rose in his chair, gushing blood from his neck, and pulled his own pistol, aiming it at Anderson. But when McCluskie squeezed the trigger, the gun misfired while Anderson got off another shot that struck McCluskie in the leg. McCluskie toppled to the floor and his gun finally went off, the bullet ploughing into the floorboard beneath him. Anderson fired one more shot, which entered McCluskie's

back. McCluskie was not without friends in the saloon. These cowboys and friends of Anderson's began to exchange fire in a wild gun battle. Jim Riley and Patrick Lee, McCluskie's friends, fired on Anderson, hitting him twice in the leg. Henry Kearnes and Billy Garrett, Anderson's companions, opened up on Lee and Riley, these men advancing against each other with guns blazing. Lee fell, shot in the stomach and dying. Bullets from his gun and that of Riley's smashed into Kearnes and Garrett, striking both men in the chests and killing them.

Several men tried to stop the murderous battle and received painful wounds for their efforts: Jim Martin, from Texas, stepped forward, motioning for the men to stop and was struck by a bullet. He clutched his neck where an artery had been severed and then stumbled through the saloon's swinging doors to fall dead into the dusty street. Jim Wilkinson, who had not taken part in the shooting and who had been standing near the bar, was singled out by Jim Riley. Riley sent a bullet toward the unarmed cowboy, blowing off the tip of his nose. When the gun smoke began to clear, five men were dead or dying and five others were wounded. Anderson's friends carried him from the saloon and put him on a horse, speeding him out of Newton. He would die in another gun battle two years later in Medicine Lodge, Kan. McCluskie was dead, as were Jim Martin, Patrick Lee, Henry Kearnes, and Billy Garrett. This gun battle, only equalled in ferocity and number of deaths at a single time by the Earp-Clanton battle in Tombstone in 1881, was the worst gunfight in the Old West, one that took place within less than three minutes and in which about forty to fifty shots were fired. No lawmen made an appearance to stop the fight. By the time the local sheriff was informed of the battle, all those involved were either dead or had left town. See: **Anderson, Hugh**.

Nix, Evett, prom. 1880s-90s, U.S., lawman. Evett Nix served as marshal of the Oklahoma Territory, during the time the Bill Doolin Gang roamed the prairies. It was Nix who in 1885 first appointed as deputy U.S. Marshal the famous western lawman Heck Thomas. Thomas of course, went on to capture members of the Doolin Gang, Sam Bass, and the Dalton brothers.

In his campaign to drive the Doolins out of the territory, Nix also recruited the services of some of the best known lawmen the Old West had ever seen, including Frank Canton, an active participant in the Johnson County War; Chris Madsen, a swaggering soldier-of-fortune who had fought with Garibaldi in Italy and the French Foreign Legion, and Bill Tilghman who became the fourth Nix appointee. Tilghman, a feared gunman in his own right, had served as marshal of Dodge City before coming to the Oklahoma Territory. Thomas, Madsen, and Tilghman formed the core of Marshal Nix' "Oklahoma Guardsmen." Each man was assigned to a different quadrant of Doolin's territory.

In December 1895, Tilghman captured Doolin in a health spa at Eureka Springs, where he was soaking his rheumatic bones. Doolin was reading a newspaper in the bathhouse when Tilghman stormed in. He did not recognize the lawman and did not have time to react before Tilghman pointed a six-shooter at his face. Tilghman cabled the happy news to Nix that day. "I have him. Will be home tomorrow." A throng of 5,000 spectators lined the street of Guthrie to catch sight of Doolin. The "King of the Oklahoma Outlaws," was given a large feast that night at the swankiest hotel in town. Six months later, in July 1896, Doolin escaped from the Guthrie jail. He was tracked by Heck Thomas to a farmhouse in Lawson and was killed while trying to avoid arrest. See: **Doolin, William M.; Thomas, Henry Andrew; Tilghman, William Matthew, Jr.; Canton Frank M.; Johnson County War.**

O

Oden, Lon, prom. late 1800s, U.S., lawman. Serving as a Texas Ranger along the Mexican border in the late 1800s Lon Oden was involved in several gun fights while in the company of ranger John Hughes. In 1889 in Shafter, Texas, Oden and Hughes were watching the entrance to an abandoned silver mine shaft when three ore thieves and Ernest St. Leon, an undercover man, appeared. All three outlaws were killed in the ensuing fight.

In 1893 Oden was traveling on assignment with Hughes and ranger Jim Putnam. The three lawmen arrested Desidario Duran at the Mexican settlement in the border town of San Antonio Colony, Texas. When the rangers spotted three more wanted men on their way out of town, Putnam guarded Duran while Oden and Hughes chased the other fugitives. Fugitive Florencio Carrasco was killed by the rangers who returned to San Antonio just in time to rescue Putnam from a threatening mob.

O'Folliard, Thomas, 1858-80, U.S., gunman-outlaw. Tom O'Folliard was one of the Old West's most legendary gunmen, despite being killed at age twenty-two. A horse thief and cattle rustler, O'Folliard was the son of Irish immigrant parents who died in a smallpox epidemic in Monclova, Mex. The boy was raised by relatives in Uvalde, Texas. In 1878, O'Folliard began his foray into crime by stealing horses for Emil Fritz, one of the gunmen involved in the Lincoln County War. As a result, O'Folliard made the acquaintance of Billy the Kid, who was aligned with the Alexander McSween faction.

In the climactic battle of the "war" on July 15-19, 1878, O'Folliard and the rest of the McSween men were holed up inside an adobe fort on the outskirts of Lincoln, N.M. The buildings were besieged by Sheriff George Peppin and his lawmen for almost three days. The two factions exchanged shots with only one injury reported: Charlie Crawford, who was struck by a bullet from Fernando Herrera, one of McSween's men. The siege ended on the third day when a column of thirty-five soldiers marched into Lincoln with two howitzers and a Gatling gun. Though the army professed neutrality in the long and bitter struggle, the commanding officer nevertheless, sympathized with the anti-McSween group led by Lawrence Murphy.

The adobe building was set on fire, which led to the forcible evacuation of the women and a number of McSween regulars who no longer wanted to fight. O'Folliard was one of a dozen men left inside the smoldering abode. As the dense smoke choked off the oxygen, O'Folliard decided to blast his way to freedom. He ran out the back door with Harvey Morris, who was felled by a bullet from one of the soldier's guns. When O'Folliard stopped to help him, a bullet tore through his shoulder. Badly wounded, but still able to move, O'Folliard made his way to the river embankment where soon after, he was able to rejoin Billy the Kid.

For the next two years, O'Folliard and the Kid were active as livestock thieves and were observed together as far south as Texas. With a price on their heads, and Pat Garrett relentlessly pursuing them through the Southwest, O'Folliard, the Kid, and four other outlaw brigands managed to stay ahead of the law until Dec. 19, 1880, when they rode into Fort Sumner, N.M., where Garrett and Lon Chambers had laid a trap for them inside the town. Tom Pickett and O'Folliard were riding side by side down the dusty street when Garrett appeared from out of the shadow and ordered them to halt. O'Folliard tried to reach for his gun, but a bullet tore through his chest just below the heart. Billy the Kid and the rest of the gang escaped the ambush unhurt and headed out of town. Mortally wounded, O'Folliard feebly attempted to follow close behind, but it was too much trouble. "Don't shoot Garrett. I'm killed," O'Folliard said. He asked Garrett to spare him further pain, and to put an end to his misery. But the sheriff would have none of it. In his last few minutes, O'Folliard asked if someone might inform his grandmother in Texas of his tragic, violent death. Finally he uttered his last words, "Oh my God, is it possible I must die?" He was buried in the Fort Sumner cemetery where Charlie Bowdre and Billy the Kid would one day be interred. See: **Billy the Kid**.

O.K. Corral, 1881, U.S., gunfight. In 1881, the long-smoldering feud between the Earp Brothers and the Clanton-McLowery Gang of rustlers and outlaws boiled over into one of the most explosive confrontations in western history—the gunfight at the O.K. Corral in Tombstone, Ariz. The Clanton-McLowery Gang, led by Ike Clanton, had been rustling cattle and several of its members were involved in a recent stagecoach robbery, which they tried to blame on John H. "Doc" Holliday, a friend of Wyatt Earp. The Earp Brothers, lawmen in the area, began to pressure the Clantons, and the Clantons retaliated by challenging the Earps to meet them at the O.K. Corral on Oct. 26, 1881.

At about 1 p.m., a town drunk approached Wyatt, Morgan, and Virgil Earp and Doc Holliday and said: "There are some men who want to see you fellas down at the O.K. Corral."

"Who are these men?" Wyatt Earp asked.

"The McLowery brothers, the Clantons, and Billy Claiborne."

Turning to his brothers, Wyatt simply said: "Let's go." The Earps and Holliday then walked solemnly down the street, four abreast, turned a corner onto Fremont Street and, in the middle of the block, approached the small OK Corral, which was wedged between two adobe buildings. Sheriff John Behan, a thoroughly corrupt sheriff who was in league with the outlaw faction, tried to stop the Earps from confronting the Clanton-McLowery Gang, but Wyatt Earp ordered him to step aside and he did. Inside the Corral stood Ike and Billy Clanton, Frank and Tom McLowery, and Billy Claiborne, who worked at the Clanton ranch outside of Tombstone.

Virgil Earp, town marshal, ordered the Clantons and McLowerys to throw up their hands, telling them they were under arrest. At that moment Frank McLowery and Billy Clanton reached for their pistols. Virgil Earp shouted: "Hold on! I don't mean that! I have come to disarm you."

A few more words were exchanged and then Billy Clanton drew his pistol as did Wyatt Earp. As the guns of the lawmen and outlaws roared, Ike Clanton fled, deserting his brother and friends. In the deafening fusillade, more than fifty bullets were fired within a few minutes. Morgan and Virgil Earp and Doc Holliday were wounded. Tom and Frank McLowery were killed, as was Billy Clanton. Billy Claiborne, wounded, fled, following the direction Ike Clanton had earlier taken. Only Wyatt Earp, who had cooly fired his six-gun with deadly accuracy, remained unharmed when the smoke cleared.

Behan later arrested the Earps for murder, but they were acquitted since Virgil Earp was performing his duties as a lawman by attempting to disarm the outlaws, who were carrying weapons in violation of a town ordinance. The gunfight at the O.K. Corral did not end the bloody feud. Morgan Earp was later shot and killed from ambush by Clanton gunmen. Wyatt Earp and others tracked down the four men who committed the murder, executing each one. Wyatt and Virgil Earp, who had been permanently crippled from his wound at the O.K. Corral gunfight, then went to the family homestead in California. See: **Clanton-McLowery Gang; Earp, Wyatt Berry Stapp; Holliday, John Henry.**

Old Bill, See: **Miner, William.**

Olguin, Clato, and **Olguin, Jesus Maria,** and

Olguin, Antonio, prom. 1893, U.S., outlaws. The border between Mexico and the U.S. remained in dispute for many years. When Texas was ceded to the U.S. in 1845, ending a ten-year civil war, the international boundary was established at the bed of the Rio Grande River. In 1854 the natural bends of the river voided this agreement when its channel southward shifted, leaving a portion of Mexican territory on the north side of the river and a slip of land known as Pirate Island (six miles long and six miles wide) between the old and new bed.

The physical configuration of Pirate Island made it a natural habitat for rustlers, bandits, and criminal fugitives, plus it was beyond the jurisdiction of both the Mexican and U.S. governments. Some 300 Mexicans lived on Pirate Island, including the murderous Olguin family who owned the *Tres Jacales* (Three Huts) ranch. Clato Olguin, family patriarch, was a retired border outlaw who was spending his last days in quiet retirement. His sons, however, were still active in their criminal pursuits. Jesus Maria, for example, had been charged with cattle theft and resisting arrest. When Deputy Sheriff R.E. Bryant failed to bring in the younger Olguin on an arrest warrant, the Texas Rangers were brought into the case.

On June 29, 1893, Captain Frank Jones, accompanied by Corporal Karl Kirchner, privates F.F. Tucker, E.D. Aten, J.W. Saunders, and Deputy R.E. Bryant departed from Ysleta with writs demanding the arrest of Jesus Maria Olguin and his son Severio. When the party arrived at the ranch, they found Clato, several women, and a small boy. Jesus had decamped to the home of his brother, Antonio. The Rangers pursued the fugitives three miles up the river into a kind of no man's land, where it was impossible to distinguish Mexican territory from Texas. There they found two Mexicans—one of them Jesus Maria Olguin—on horseback. They turned and fled at the sight of the Texas Rangers and raced toward an encampment of four adobe huts.

The lawmen proceeded cautiously from hut to hut, when suddenly the Olguins opened fire. Captain Jones returned their fire, but a second furious volley riddled his chest with lead. The other Rangers rushed to his side, which afforded the Olguins the perfect opportunity to escape. The Mexican authorities rounded up the Olguins and lodged them in a jail at Juarez—beyond the pale of U.S. justice. It is doubtful they were ever seriously prosecuted for the crime. See: **Jones, Frank.**

Olinger, John Wallace, prom. 1870s, U.S., lawman. John Olinger was the brother of peace officer Bob Olinger, who was killed by Billy the Kid during a jail break. During the Lincoln County War, he was deputized by Sheriff George Peppin to do battle against Alexander McSween's band of "Regulators." His first notable gunfight occurred near Lincoln, N.M., on Apr. 30, 1878, when his posse caught up with Frank McNab, Ab Sanders, and Frank Coe, eight miles outside of town. A fast and furious gunfight ensued, and when the smoke cleared, McNab lay dead, Sanders was badly wounded, and Coe, who was out of ammunition, quietly surrendered.

Olinger hung up his holster shortly after becoming embroiled in a domestic dispute near Seven Rivers, N.M. On Aug. 16, 1878, William H. Johnson, Olinger's partner in a cattle ranching business, got into a quarrel with his father-in-law Henry Beckwith. The argument escalated into violence when Beckwith shot Johnson in the neck and chest with a double barreled shotgun. Olinger retaliated by opening fire on Beckwith. He wounded him in the cheek and nose, but Beckwith survived the attack. John Olinger was arrested and taken to Fort Stanton, but was later released. Afterward he retired to pursue more peaceful endeavors.

Olinger, Robert A., c.1841-81, U.S., lawman. As a boy Olinger moved with his family from Ohio to Oklahoma. In 1876 he was named marshal of Seven Rivers in Lincoln County, N.M. However, he was suspected of consorting with an outlaw band and was dismissed from his post. Two years later he fought in the Lincoln County War on the side of the Santa Fe Gang against John Chisum and Alexander McSween.

Although Olinger was twice employed as a lawman, he seemed better suited to fighting range wars than upholding the peace. This was evidenced by several incidents. In 1878 he shot and killed a Mexican named Pas Chavez in Seven Rivers. Olinger extended his hand in friendship to Chavez. But as the Mexican took it, Olinger, without warning jerked Chavez off balance and fired a fatal shot into his stomach. The following year he ambushed John Hill outside Seven Rivers. In January 1881, Olinger was appointed deputy U.S. Marshal. The office apparently held no special significance for him, because he was later arrested in Las Vegas for carrying illegal firearms.

Olinger met up with Billy the Kid in Lincoln, N.M., when the notorious gunfighter was safely incarcerated behind bars and was waiting to die on the gallows. As the day of execution approached, Bob Olinger delighted in taunting the Kid by crossing off the days on a calendar leading up to his fateful appointment with the hangman on May 13, 1881. Occasionally Olinger would stick a shotgun in the Kid's face, reminding him that death awaited those who

defied the law. All the while Billy the Kid waited for the right opportunity to make his escape and settle accounts with the swaggering Bob Olinger. On Apr. 28, 1881, Olinger escorted five prisoners to the courthouse and then proceeded down the street to the Wortley Hotel for supper. J.W. Bell was left to guard the Kid, who somehow managed to obtain a gun inside the jail. Hearing two shots ring out from the courthouse, Olinger ran into the street where he heard the news that Bell was dying and Billy the Kid had escaped. From a second-floor window overlooking the street, Billy the Kid called Olinger. "Hello Bob," he taunted. Godfrey Gauss, who was attending to Bell, ran for cover, but a blast from the Kid's shotgun caught Olinger in the head and neck. The Kid threw his weapon into the street shouting: "You won't follow me any more with that gun!" See: **Billy the Kid; Lincoln County War; Olinger, John Wallace; Salazar, Hijino.**

Olive, Isom Prentice, (AKA: **Print**), 1840-86, U.S., gunman. A native of Mississippi, Isom Prentice Olive moved to Texas at an early age with his parents. At the outbreak of the Civil War, "Print" Olive, as he was known to his friends, was among the first to enlist in the Confederate forces. He served with distinction in Hood's Texas Division and with him saw action at such major battles as Gettysburg.

When the war ended, Olive returned to Texas and set about raising a large herd of cattle. He moved northward with his cattle, sold some of them, and kept the rest as the basis for the even larger herds he intended to raise in the huge expanse of Nebraska. Olive claimed a huge chunk of land in that state, a spread that ran for hundreds of miles along the Platte River. Not a proponent of the "live and let live" philosophy, Olive hired a virtual army of cowboys to run his cattle and, equally as important, to protect his land.

Olive was the main power of Custer County, where his ranch was located. His near total control of the area made the intrusion of two homesteading farmers, Ami Ketchum and Luther Mitchell, appear all the more courageous. The two large families established side-by-side farms on property to which Olive apparently felt he had claim. In November 1878, after sending the homesteaders repeated warnings to "get out or get killed," Olive sent his brother, Robert, to Mitchell's farm, along with a large number of his armed cowhands. The farmers were prepared for a confrontation and returned the cowboys' fire. Robert Olive was killed in the ensuing gun battle and the rest of Print Olive's men were driven away.

Olive was infuriated by the outcome of the skirmish and

used his clout with county officials to have Ketchum and Mitchell arrested and turned over to him. Olive took the farmers to a deserted area near Clear Creek. He ordered his men to tie the two with ropes and then shot Mitchell in the back, reputedly saying, "That's the way you gave it to my brother." Olive then had both men hanged from a tree. In a final gesture of fury, he ordered a large fire built under the suspended bodies, and when the members of a vigilante committee arrived, they found corpses charred beyond recognition.

The brutality of the murders created such public outrage against Olive that, despite his sizable political influence, the governor was forced to order his arrest and trial for murder. Olive and one of his top lieutenants, Fred Fisher, were found Guilty and sentenced to life imprisonment at the Nebraska State Penitentiary. Olive's cowboy army was utterly incensed at the verdict and sentence and threatened to try to prevent Olive's incarceration. To forestall an attempted raid on the courthouse where Olive was being held, President Rutherford B. Hayes ordered federal troops into the territory.

The extreme precautions helped to see Olive safely into prison, but after two years of expensive legal work, Olive and Fisher were released on the grounds that because their trial was not held in Custer County where the murders had been committed, it had not been properly conducted. Although freed from prison, Olive discovered that his years away had cost him dearly. Rustlers had raided and greatly diminished his herds, and settlers were encroaching on his vast empire. His reputation as the murderer of homesteaders spread amongst the new settlers and hatred for him abounded. In 1882, Olive took what remained of his herd and moved into Kansas. However, he found the same difficulty with farmers there. Olive attempted to establish himself in Dodge City, but a highly organized farmers' group called The Grange thwarted his efforts.

Olive finally gave up the cattle business, sold his remaining herd, and moved to Trail City, Colo., where he purchased a saloon. The great cattle baron came to a sudden and less than heroic end in 1886. A cowboy, Joe Sparrow, annoyed because Olive owed him ten dollars, walked into Olive's saloon and without warning shot him in the head, killing him instantly.

O'Neill, William Owen (AKA: **Buckey**), 1860-98, U.S., lawman. According to a contemporary report, William "Buckey" O'Neill was "the most many-sided man Arizona ever produced." Indeed, William O'Neill wore many hats in his lifetime. He was at various times a gambler, lawyer, soldier, politician, and sheriff, and one of Teddy Roosevelt's Rough Riders.

O'Neill was raised in Washington, D.C., but he made his way west in 1879 where he landed a job in Arizona as a newspaperman for the Phoenix *Herald*. In between working for the paper and attending to family matters, O'Neill served as deputy for Marshal Henry Garfias. In 1888, after working in Prescott and Tombstone as an itinerant newsman, O'Neill was elected sheriff of Yavapai County. He quickly earned a reputation for himself as an uncompromising foe of crime by conducting an exhaustive three-week, 600-mile search for four men who robbed a railroad safe at Diablo Canyon, east of Flagstaff, Ariz. He caught up with the bandits at Wah Weep Canyon in southern Utah and returned them to the Yuma Territorial Prison. Following an unsuccessful congressional bid in 1894 and again in 1896, O'Neill was elected mayor of Prescott on Jan. 1, 1898. A month later the battleship *Maine* blew up in Havana Harbor, and within days the U.S. was at war with Spain. O'Neill organized the Arizona volunteers into a crack fighting unit which became Troop A of the fabled Rough Riders outfit. O'Neill did not live long enough to bask in their glory; in July of 1898, he was shot in the head during a skirmish with the Spanish at San Juan Hill.

Oriental Saloon, prom. 1870s-80s, U.S., gambling hall. Tombstone, in the Arizona Territory was notorious as the meanest mining town in the western frontier, and Tombstone's Oriental Saloon was similarly renowned. As many as 200 men may have been shot to death there in pointless, even idiotic arguments that originated in the Oriental. On one occasion, John Ringo invited Louis Hancock to have a drink with him. When Hancock agreed and asked for a beer, Ringo said, "No man drinks beer with me. I don't like beer." Ringo finally shot Hancock who allegedly was buried with a bottle of beer.

The original Oriental was started by Jim Vizina in a canvas tent with two wagon loads of whiskey. It later moved to an actual building that was lavishly decorated by the new owner, Mike Joyce. Joyce later sold out to Lou Rickabaugh, who gave a quarter interest to Wyatt Earp for protection purposes. Gunmen Bat Masterson and Luke Short ran the gambling tables, with Earp and his friend Doc Holliday often present. Earp and Doc Holliday left town following the gunfight at O.K. Corral. Tombstone's silver mine died out, and the Oriental folded with it. See: **Earp, Wyatt Berry Stapp; Short, Luke.**

O'Rourke, John (AKA: Michael O'Rourke; Johnny

Behind the Deuce), 1862-82, U.S., gunman-gambler. Johnny Behind The Deuce, or John O'Rourke, started his brief but colorful career as a gambler and a gunman working as a hotel porter as he learned his trades of shooting and cards. In early 1878 the 16-year-old turned up in Tucson, Ariz., and by 1880 he was famous as an expert card player. Suspicions surfaced that O'Rourke was also a thief who would steal from stuporous drunks, but few were willing to accuse the young card sharp, fearful of his shooting expertise. In January 1881, a miner named Henry Schneider called O'Rourke a thief when his pack was missing from his Charleston shack. O'Rourke put a bullet between his accuser's eyes and was taken off to Tombstone by Marshal George McKelvey before the miners could lynch the hot-headed young man. In Tombstone, a mob gathered clamoring for the gunslinger's blood but Wyatt Earp held them off with a shotgun long enough for O'Rourke to be moved to a Tucson jail, from which he soon escaped.

The most popular theory regarding O'Rourke's end—he was just twenty-one at the time—was that as a fugitive he encountered Johnny Ringo, an infamous character who was Earp's enemy, in July 1882. Supposedly figuring he was paying his rescuer, Earp, back for saving him from the lynch mob, O'Rourke shot and killed Ringo as he slept beneath a tree in Turkey Creek Canyon. Later, Pony Deal, one of Ringo's friends, played cards with John O'Rourke in Sulphur Springs Valley, and accused him of being a card cheat and a murderer, and shot him dead in the ensuing gunfight.

Outlaw, Bass, d.1894, U.S., lawman-gunman. Born into a good family in Georgia, Bass Outlaw was a slight man with a good education, refined manners, and a serious drinking problem. After allegedly murdering a man in Georgia in 1855, Outlaw enlisted in the Texas Rangers, winning promotion to sergeant but, when discovered drunk on duty in Alpine, he was dismissed. Later obtaining an appointment as U.S. deputy marshall Outlaw was continually reprimanded for drinking.

Bass Outlaw, train robber.

In 1889, in Sierra del Carman, Coahuila, Mex., Outlaw, John Hughes, and Walter Durbin had been guarding bullion shipments from a silver mine for several weeks. One night, between trips, a drunken Outlaw fought with a Mexican worker shooting and killing him when the man pulled a knife. The three Texans left quickly for the Rio Grande, after Hughes and Durbin had subdued Outlaw. On Dec. 25, 1889 a midnight ambush was sprung near Vance, Texas, by Outlaw, Hughes, fellow Ranger Ira Aten and Deputy Sheriff Will Terry on the fugitive Odle brothers as they attempted to sneak back into Texas from Mexico for Christmas. Will and Alvin Odle were killed.

In El Paso, Texas, to be a court witness on Apr. 5, 1894, Outlaw got drunk and fired a shot into Tillie Howard's brothel. Challenged by Constable John Selman and Texas Ranger Joe McKidrict, Outlaw threatened them as well, then fired point blank at McKidrict's head. He then shot at Selman, missing but almost blinding the constable with the gun powder blast. Selman shot Outlaw in the chest and, as the wounded man staggered back, Outlaw fired twice more, wounding Selman, before stumbling away. Surrendering to Ranger Frank McMahon, Outlaw was led into a nearby saloon where he collapsed, dying four hours later.

Owens, Perry, 1852-1919, U.S., lawman. Born and raised in Tennessee, Commodore Perry Owens, named after naval hero Commodore Oliver Perry, spent some time in Indiana before following the cattle trails west in his late teens. With his long blond hair, hand-tooled chaps, sombrero, and a long barreled Colt .45 with a double row of ammunition on his gun belt, Perry was a gaudy cowboy. By the time he rode into Apache County in the Arizona Territory in 1881, his skill as a gunman was renowned. In 1886, hired by a railroad contractor to protect a herd of horses, Owens was rushed by a band of Indians who attempted to start a stampede, but he forced them off by fatally wounding two of them. The reputation he gained from

Commodore Perry Owens, western lawman.

this incident and his honesty earned him an appointment as sheriff. The dangerous Apache country was full of rowdy and often lawless cattle ranchers who liked to tear up saloons and Navaho Indians who stole horses. Owens kept both elements under some control.

Owens' most famous gun battle occurred on Sept. 4, 1887, when he rode into Holbrook looking for fugitive Andy Blevans, who was wanted for his stealing horses. Owens found Blevans on his porch and informed him that he was under arrest. Blevans ran inside, slammed the door, and fired one shot before Owens' lethal blast knocked him across the room. Leaping from the porch just as Andy's brother John Blevans charged around the house to shoot at him, Owens felled his assailant with a single shot, spinning around in time to shoot the Blevans' brother-in-law, Moses Roberts, through the head. Almost simultaneously, Sam Houston Blevans, the youngest brother, left the house and was killed by Owens before he could fire. Only John Blevans survived Owens' bullets.

Although this gunfight further enhanced Owen's standing as a lawman, public opinion gradually turned against him as the era of the gunfighter passed and his skill with a gun became more feared than respected. Owens quit his post in 1896, finishing his days doing a variety of jobs and drinking heavily. Owens died in 1919.

P

Packer, Alferd G. (Alfred, AKA: **John Schwartze**), 1847-1907, U.S., mur. Alferd G. Packer was born in rural Colorado and received minor education as a child. He grew up crude and rough-hewn, with no thought of humanity and very little inclination toward civilized behavior. As a prospector, Packer lived in the hills, surviving on the meat of animals, and at one point, survived on the meat of men. In the early 1870s, a prospector struck it rich in the wildness of the San Juan Mountains outside of Salt Lake City, Utah. A horde of silver-seeking novices flooded Salt Lake City, all bent on digging their fortunes out of the mountains.

Alferd Packer, 1873.

Few of them knew how to construct a mine, let alone locate veins of silver once the mining had begun. Hardly any of these eastern "greenhorns" even knew which part of the mountain range to prospect. Nineteen of these flabby-armed, clean-shaven tenderfeet set off toward the San Juan Mountains with a single guide, Alferd Packer, in Fall 1873.

This proved to be one of the worst and coldest winters in Colorado. Game went to ground, and other than what the prospectors carried on their backs, there was nothing to eat. Packer, who had claimed to be a hunter, found no game, and when the food ran out, the prospecting party grew desperate. Packer promised his clients that he would lead them back to civilization, but he had no idea where he was or where he should take his party. He was lucky enough to stumble into the camp of a friendly Indian tribe led by Chief Ouray. The chief fed the party and kept them warm for days in his lodgings, but he warned the prospectors that if they did not return to Salt Lake City, all of them would perish in the desolate white wilderness. After a council meeting, ten men in the party elected to return to civilization.

Alferd Packer was not one of them. A loud-mouth and braggart, Packer laughed at the men quitting the expedition, saying that they were giving up a fortune that was not far away, that silver in gleaming chunks could be found along the Gunnison River. He was adamant in not leading the ten men back to Salt Lake City. They must push on to fortune, he cried out. He made no mention that he was broke and that the grubstake the prospectors had given him was all he possessed. He had nothing back in Salt Lake City but a bevy of angry creditors looking for him.

Chief Ouray argued with Packer, but the kindly Indian finally gave in and agreed to supply the guide and the ten men still determined to plunge forward into the icy wilderness. Ouray cautioned the party to stay close to the Gunnison River, telling them that if they went into the mountains, the only thing they would find would be frozen death. Packer pooh-poohed these dire statements saying that, if need be, the party could always take refuge in the Los Pinos Indian Agency, located near the river. Actually, Alferd G. Packer had no idea where the agency could be found. The party marched out into a blinding snowstorm and within a few weeks provisions had run out. The group fell to arguing, and four men said they would strike out for the Indian agency. Packer refused to guide them, saying that they were fools, that silver was waiting for them just over the next range of mountains.

The four men left, and after days of stumbling about in the high snow drifts and through severe storms, two of the men finally staggered into the agency. Packer led the other five men—Miller, Noon, Humphreys, Swan, and Bell—into the frozen regions where they found a deserted trapper's cabin. Here the party cooked, ate its last meal, and then went to sleep. They realized they were about to die of starvation and cold. When the party was asleep, Packer stood up and reached for his rifle. Quickly, he went from one sleeping form to the other, firing a single shot into each man's head.

Miller, hearing the shots, according to later evidence, jumped up and tried to defend himself, but Packer was on him in an instant, smashing the butt of his rifle down so hard on Miller's head that he split his victim's skull and broke the stock of his weapon. He rifled the pockets of the dead prospectors and collected several thousand dollars. Packer apparently intended to carry out the crime first, but now he was faced with death by starvation. He contemplated his problem for hours, or so he later claimed, and then he decided that his victims would serve to keep him alive.

He fell upon the dead men with a large hunting knife, slicing away the flesh about the breast and stripping the flesh from the rib cages. He took these gory pieces of human remains to a snowbank and froze them. The next day, he packed the flesh in his shoulder packs and departed. For two weeks, Packer struggled against the deep snow, eating the human remains to keep up his strength. He reached the Los Pinos Agency in February 1874 and still had some strips of "human beef jerky," as it was later described.

The cannibal, once he spotted the buildings of the agency, grew nervous about carrying about the remains of his victims. He later stated: "When I espied the agency from the top of the hill, I threw away the strips of flesh I had left, and I confess that I did so reluctantly, as I had grown fond of human flesh, especially that portion around the breast." Once inside a warm cabin at the agency, Packer sat down among startled residents, who gaped at his mottled flesh, his popped eyes, his bloated face. His clothes hung on him in rags and his limbs were blue from the intense cold. Warm food was brought to him, but Packer could not swallow it. He drank only liquor and remained drunk for some time.

Alferd Packer, 1883.

General Adams, the commander at the agency, knew Packer had led an expedition into the mountains to look for silver. He asked the so-called guide where his party was. Packer gave him evasive answers, saying that the men wandered off and froze to death. When Packer began spending lavishly, buying expensive items at the agency, getting drunk, and tipping extravagantly, the general grew suspicious and arrested Packer. On Apr. 4, 1874, two of Chief Ouray's Indians found the strips of human flesh Packer had discarded near the agency. Packer was charged with murdering the very men he had been hired to protect, but the intrepid guide claimed innocence. He told General Adams that he only participated in the cannibalism begun by others to stay alive. Packer told a fantastic story of how he came upon four of the men after they had killed Swan, the oldest in their ranks, and were carving his body for food. They also split Swan's money, which was how Packer came to have his pockets full of cash, or so he claimed.

The four then attacked each other, killing and eating the flesh of the victims until, Packer insisted, he and Bell were the only survivors. When Bell attacked him, he defended himself and was forced to kill Bell. He was then forced to use Bell's corpse for food. This was the tale told by Alferd Packer. General Adams ordered Packer to take lawman H. Lauter and a small party to the cabin where the murders and cannibalism had taken place. Packer quickly agreed, but after the party groped about in the wildness for several weeks, it was evident to Lauter that Packer had no intention of taking him to the murder cabin. When Packer tried to lose the small party in a woods, Lauter arrested him and sent him back to the agency. Lauter and others went on, and two weeks later, discovered the cabin and the mutilated corpses. When Lauter found that each man had been shot in the head, he realized Packer's tale was a complete fabrication and that the guide was a mass murderer.

When he returned to the agency with his discoveries, however, Lauter found that Packer had been allowed freedom within the agency and had simply walked away, escaping. For almost ten years, authorities searched for the missing Packer who seemed to have utterly vanished. Then, on Mar. 12, 1883, one of the men who had been part of the original prospecting group spotted a man on a Salt Lake City street and walked up to him. "You're Alferd Packer," the man gasped.

"I am not," Packer said angrily. "I am John Schwartze. Who is Alferd Packer?"

As Packer began to walk away, the man called a policeman standing nearby and Packer was arrested and taken to Lake City, Colo., where, on Apr. 3, 1883, he was placed on trial for cannibalism and murder. Packer sat in the witness chair and cried out that he was innocent, that he had killed only in self-defense and that to stay alive he had eaten the human flesh of the man who had tried to murder him. He asked jury members that, if in his position, would they not do the same? The jury did not agree, and Packer was found Guilty and sentenced to be executed.

Packer appealed while lawyers unearthed a loophole in the law. The newly created Colorado constitution had no provision for the fate of convicted murderers. After many legal delays, Packer was granted a new trial in 1885. His lawyers got the charge reduced to manslaughter. He was again found Guilty, but he received a forty-year sentence instead of death. (As the Packer legend has been passed down over the years, a tale has been told of Judge Melville Gerry, admonishing Packer at his sentencing: "They was sivvin Demmycrats in Hinsdale County, and ye et five of 'em, God damn ye!")

A model inmate in the state prison, Packer was released in 1901. He moved to a ranch near Denver, Colo., where he worked as a cowboy. He died in the bunkhouse on Apr. 24, 1907, after having consumed a large amount of chicken, eating mostly the white meat from the breast.

Padgett, George W., d.1881, U.S., outlaw. A dispute over a head of cattle on its way to the Kansas slaughter houses ended in murder on July 26, 1881. George Padgett, a notorious cattle thief, murdered W.H. Stephens on the North Fork of the Canadian River after quarreling over the cattle. Padgett was apprehended and hanged for murder at Fort Smith (Ark.) on Sept. 9, 1881.

Parish, Frank, d.1864, U.S., outlaw. The Montana Vigilance Committee planned to hang five proven criminals in January 1864 and also voted to hang Frank Parish as a preventive measure. Despite a lack of evidence against Parish, the Vigilance Committee reasoned that because he had a bad reputation, associated with the wrong people, and was an "outsider," he was a viable candidate for lynching. Parish used his final moments to confess to a number of crimes, including the theft of livestock and a $2,500 stagecoach robbery a year earlier.

Parker, Isaac C. (AKA: **Hanging Judge**), 1838-96, U.S., lawman Isaac Parker, the famous "hanging judge," served as the Republican congressman from Missouri, and was named to the federal bench in 1875 by President Ulysses S. Grant. A native of Maryland, Parker resettled in Ohio early on in his life. He was admitted to the Ohio bar in 1859, when he was twenty-one. Lured by the promise of adventure, Parker headed west to St. Joseph, Mo., where there was a critical need for lawyers. Legal experience counted for very little in those days, but there was plenty of opportunity for a man with ambition and determination.

In 1864 Parker was elected state's attorney for the Twelfth Judicial Circuit of Missouri. Four years later he was elected judge of the Twelfth Judicial Circuit for a six-year term. He only served four years, because in 1870 the politically ambitious jurist gave up his seat to seek a term in Congress, representing the Sixth Missouri District. A turncoat Democrat who took advantage of Abraham Lincoln's popularity in the North, Parker ran as a Republican and was easily elected. Parker became familiar with Indian issues through his work for the Congressional Committee on Territories. In 1872 he sponsored a measure to organize the territorial government for the Indian country in the Western District of Arkansas. Parker drew favorable attention to himself, which convinced President Grant to appoint him chief justice for the territory of Utah upon completion of his term in March 1875. However, Utah was a considerable distance from Missouri, and since the area was scheduled for statehood anyway, the chances were good that the territorial offices were going to be abolished. Instead, Parker prevailed upon Grant to name him to the recently vacated judgeship at Fort Smith (Ark.), which the president was only too happy to do. The appointment was named, and Parker, at age thirty-six, became the youngest judge on the federal bench in an untamed, lawless land. On May 2, 1875, the newly appointed judge arrived at the fort with his wife and two children.

Parker's record for imposing the death sentence and the conviction ratio in his court were unequaled by any other jurist. During Parker's first eight weeks on the bench, of eighteen people tried for murder, fifteen were convicted; six of those were sentenced to death; eight received long prison terms; and one was shot to death while trying to escape.

Parker's jurisdiction was the Western District of Arkansas, which included the crime-ridden Indian Territory. In Parker's twenty-one years on the bench, 13,490 cases had been docketed. Out of this grand total, 9,454 persons were convicted by a trial jury or had voluntarily entered pleas of guilty. Parker sentenced 160 people to the gallows.

Judge Isaac C. Parker.

Seventy-nine of those sentenced were hanged, two were killed while trying to escape, forty-six were commuted to prison terms by the president, two died in jail while awaiting execution, and two others were pardoned. In response to allegations of unfairness, Parker's defenders pointed out that sixty-five deputy marshals had been killed in the line of duty in that twenty-one year period. Accused of leading juries, Parker said, "I tell you a jury should be led! If they are guided they will render justice." Parker always insisted on the death sentence in cases of murder. He routinely cried while passing sentence, sobbing again as he watched the hangings from the window of his chambers. In defense of what many considered high-handed tactics, the judge took considerable credit for eradicating open lawlessness in the Indian territories.

During Parker's tenure, multiple hangings attended by large crowds of spectators were commonplace. These spectacles brought Parker national publicity, and his court became known as the Court of the Damned. Legal authorities finally began to call for moderation of his conduct. When, after 1889, the Supreme Court allowed appeals from Parker's Indian Territory Court for the first time, thirty of forty-six condemned people were found to have had unfair trials. Sixteen of those who had been condemned to death were acquitted and the others received jail terms.

In response, Parker criticized "the laxity of the Courts" and the Supreme Court's concentration on "the flimsiest technicalities." Even the prisoners in Parker's courtroom began to challenge him. Henry Starr interrupted Parker's death sentence pronouncements saying, "If I am a monster, you are a fiend, for I have put only one man to death, while almost as many men have been slaughtered by your jawbone as Samson slew with the jawbone of that other historic ass."

Parker did sentence Starr to death, but the case was later reversed by the Supreme Court. Although in 1895 Congress removed the Indian Territory from Parker's jurisdiction, the judge died on Nov. 17, 1896, before the actual transfer took place. During Parker's long period of illness, Judge John E. Carland of the District of South Dakota presided over his court. Many welcomed the news of Parker's death, including the inmates of the Fort Smith jail who passed the word from cell to cell. "The devil's shore got de ole cuss dis time!" one prisoner rejoiced. Others praised him as the greatest judge in the history of the west. See: **Maledon, George.**

Parker, Robert Leroy, See: **Cassidy, Butch.**

Pattee, James Monroe (AKA: **Lottery King**), prom. 1870s, U.S., gambler. When it came to fleecing the public through crooked lotteries, New Hampshire-born James Monroe Pattee had few peers. After deciding that the quiet academic life of a writing teacher was too sedate for him, Pattee headed west to seek his fortune in land speculation. By 1868, he had amassed a small fortune in a California mining venture which encouraged him to organize the "Cosmopolitan Benevolent Association of California Grand Fair," ostensibly created to defray the debts of the Nevada City school district. Pattee eventually moved east to Omaha, Neb., where he held a series of "Great Legal Drawings" between 1871-73. It was a legitimate enterprise by all accounts, with most of the proceeds given to hospitals and libraries. In 1873, Nebraska outlawed the lotteries, which for Pattee was probably just as well, since he was suspected of issuing duplicate and triplicate tickets during one of these games.

Things were different in neighboring Wyoming, where the price of doing business was a $100 payoff to the county sheriff, who signed a three month license authorizing Pattee to do business in the territory. In the spring of 1875, Pattee was in Laramie where he ordered 40,000 handbills from a local newspaper publisher promoting his newest lottery scheme. The take was enormous, with Pattee depositing $4,000 to $5,000 a day in the local bank. It was estimated that the "Lottery King" sold more than $7 million in ticket sales during the first year alone. Much of the revenue came from out-of-town advertisements placed in the New York *Herald*. Pattee shrewdly realized that it was a good policy to keep his victims a safe distance away. Meanwhile, he set himself up as a pillar of Wyoming society by contributing to charities and to local churches.

Each month, Pattee offered 70,755 prizes, totaling $200,000-$275,000. A single grand prize was $50,000. The smallest payout was fifty cents, but to lure the victim into his web, he would notify them that it would cost more than the value of the prize itself to mail their winnings, and so he was offering them instead a share of stock in the "Bullion Gold and Silver Mining Company" worth $10. It was a first-rate pyramid scheme, as Pattee encouraged them to sell five new shares in return for a free share. The newspapers got wind of the fraud and launched several campaigns aimed at driving the Lottery King from their midst, but Pattee simply picked up his stakes when things began to get hot and headed for Cheyenne, where he started the "Cheyenne State Lottery," supposedly managed by Marshal S. Pike, president of the state bank. Editor Orange Judd of the *American Agriculturalist* lamented: "Poor Wyoming, were not the grasshoppers enough?" When the reformers threatened Pattee's livelihood, he quietly left Wyoming and crossed the Canadian border, as always, remaining one step ahead of the law. A Kansas editor recalled that the con man was proud of his own villainy. "He said his conscience did not trouble him, that people wanted to be humbugged, and it was his business to do it."

Paul, Robert H., prom. 1890-93, U.S., lawman. The election of a new president in 1888 also meant another turnover in the federal marshal's service. After Benjamin Harrison's presidential victory, Robert H. Paul, also a Republican, was named Arizona marshal on Mar. 4, 1890. Born in Massachusetts, Paul made his way west to California with the rest of the forty-niners in the Gold Rush. He served for a time as the sheriff of Calaveras County, Ariz., before signing on with the Wells Fargo Co., in 1872. During the marshalcy of Crawley P. Dake, Paul earned a reputation for himself as a resolute foe of the highwaymen who were running rampant in the Arizona Territory. In one famous case in early 1881, Paul made use of the steam locomotives to make an arrest in Yuma. The shotgun-wielding lawman arrived in town to occupy a commercial establishment caught in bankruptcy proceedings. A year later he became a political foe of the Earp faction, and in 1888 he made the newspapers again after gunning down several bandits in Chihuahua, Mex.

Arizonians greeted his appointment with enthusiasm, for no single lawman had earned the respect of his peers as an incorruptible force against evil as had "Bob" Paul. Crime was on everyone's mind those days, as many of the law-abiding residents of the territory who supported statehood feared that the lawless conditions would delay the inevitable entry into the union. The Arizona *Daily Citizen* noted that

Paul was "known throughout the Southwest as a fearless man who has frequently taken his life into his own hands in pursuit of criminals."

Paul disappointed his supporters by his failure to pursue action against thirteen outlaw brigands who ambushed and robbed army paymaster Joseph Wham near Fort Thomas on May 11, 1889. The bandits made off with $29,000 in one of the most celebrated robberies to occur in the territory in many years. Deputy William Breakenridge, a former county official in Tombstone, and a close friend of Sheriff John Behan, became convinced that the robbers had fled

Marshal of Arizona from 1890-93, Robert H. Paul.

to the nearby Mormon settlement of Pima. As a result of an informer's tip, Breakenridge arrested several Mormons for the crime. The elders of the church were convinced that these baseless arrests were another example of anti-Mormon persecution. Marshal William Kidder Meade, who occupied the office before Paul, was labeled the instigator of the trumped up case against the Wham defendants. The suspects in the grueling month-long trial were acquitted, which hastened Meade's demise.

Paul adopted a cautious wait and see posture regarding the Wham case. Anxious not to offend the Mormon community, the new marshal did little more than offer a $500 reward for the arrest of the suspects. While Paul vacillated, officials from Graham County arrested Mark E. Cunningham and Lyman and Warren Follett in May 1890, charging the men with robbery and cattle theft. The Folletts were eventually sentenced to a two-year prison term.

Government examiners who audited Robert Paul's office in April 1892, reported that the marshal abused the powers of his office by selecting unqualified veniremen or prospective jurors. According to the report, juries in Paul's jurisdiction were composed of "loafers, bar-room bums, and the 'ragged reubens' of the community, especially about Tucson where the marshal resides." Unlike neighboring New Mexico, Paul was able to get away with this practice because the territory did not have U.S. commissioners to regulate the jury process. The examiners also found instances of financial impropriety. He "is not a successful businessman," complained the auditor, but he "manages to successfully manipulate the business of office...to make his maximum fees." The inadequacies of the fee system lingered until the term of Creighton Foraker, when marshals were finally paid a steady salary.

Before Paul could make an accounting of himself, a political change necessitated his removal. When Democrat Grover Cleveland recaptured the White House in 1892, he selected a political ally, Louis C. Hughes, to serve as governor of the Arizona Territory. Hughes in turn, supported the re-appointment of William Kidder Meade to the marshalcy. Meade was appointed on May 8, 1893, and Bob Paul, who, more than anyone seemed to fit the popular image of the gun-slinging western lawman, was out. See: **Meade, William Kidder.**

Peacock, Lewis, d.1871, U.S., gunman. Lewis Peacock, a powerful land owner near the town of Pilot Grove, Texas, led a gang of post-Civil War fighters in a feud against a faction headed by Bob Lee. Because Peacock was involved in the Reconstruction Union League, a group which helped former slaves, the dispute had racial overtones.

The first major skirmish of the four-year feud began in April 1868. Following several bushwhackings and killings Peacock and Lee and their followers finally engaged at Pilot Grove where Peacock was wounded, but no one was killed. On June 15, 1868, Peacock and his band were staying at a farm in Hunt County, Texas, when Lee's gang ambushed them. The Peacock faction suffered three fatalities.

In December 1868, Peacock was leading Union soldiers and a few of his own men on a hunt for Lee when they were again ambushed. One soldier died in the fighting. The final foray occurred on June 13, 1871, at Pilot Grove. Although Lee had been killed in late 1869, the revenge murders continued. Two of Lee's friends, Dick Johnson and Joe Parker, saw Peacock, who was hiding in Pilot Grove. After keeping watch all night, Johnson and Parker shot and mortally wounded Peacock as he came out to get firewood.

Phelps, Edward, prom. 1866-71, U.S., lawman-fraud. Edward Phelps replaced Milton Duffield, who occupied the marshalcy of Arizona from 1863-66. Phelps was a Californian who was the surgeon-in-chief at Fort Whipple, Ariz., up to the time of his appointment in June 1866. Commenting on the selection of Phelps, the Prescott *Arizona Miner* noted that President Andrew Johnson "reposes special trust and confidence in the integrity, ability, and diligence of Edward Phelps, and has by and with the advice of and consent of the Senate, appointed him marshal."

Phelps did little to live up to the accolades bestowed upon him by the local media. In 1869, unhappy jurors complained that the marshal had not paid them. A year later Phelps was criticized for conducting the census three months late. More serious were the charges of financial impropriety leveled against Phelps in August 1870. U.S. District Attorney Converse W.C. Rowell filed a complaint against Phelps charging him with misappropriating public monies and squandering a $10,000 advance he received in 1867. In a strongly worded memo to Phelps advising him of the nature of the complaint, the clerk noted that: "you have entirely failed thus far to render due account of the expenditures of $10,000 advanced you in March 1867, an instance of official neglect which this office regards with strong displeasure." Phelps defended his actions on the grounds that he did not have the proper authority to advance funds to census deputies, and that he could not pay outstanding bills until they were first examined by the treasury department.

Dissatisfied with his earnings, and restless in his job, Phelps announced in January 1871, his intentions to embark on a cruise to Sonora, Mex. On Jan. 28, the U.S. Consul in Guaymas received word that the vacationing Phelps had left for Mazatlan on an English man-of-war. A month later it was clear to all that the marshal was not coming back, and very well may have absconded with $12,000 in federal money. The accusation was not fully confirmed when in April, Mexican bandits murdered Phelps for the money in his possession. President Ulysses S. Grant, no doubt embarrassed by the state of affairs in the Southwest, waited three months before naming Isaac Q. Dickason the new marshal. See: **Dickason, Isaac.**

Pickett, Tom, 1858-1934, U.S., lawman-gunman. Raised in Decatur, Texas, Tom Pickett was caught stealing cattle at the age of seventeen. His father, a former officer for the Confederacy and a member of the Texas legislature, mortgaged the family home to pay the heavy fine. Pickett served for a short time as a Texas Ranger, followed a cattle drive to Kansas, and became a gambler. Following rustler Dave Rudabaugh to New Mexico, Pickett was a peace officer in Las Vegas and in White Oaks before hiring on as a cowhand with Charlie Bowdre in the Fort Sumner area. He was soon rustling cattle with Rudabaugh, Bowdre, Billy the Kid, Billy Wilson, and Tom O'Folliard.

When O'Folliard was killed by Pat Garrett's posse in Fort Sumner, Pickett and his cohorts fled and hid out in a one-room house made of rock. On Dec. 23, 1880, Bowdre went out at dawn to feed his horse and was riddled with bullets by Pat Garrett's posse, which had sneaked up on the house during the night. Fatally wounded, Bowdre stumbled back inside and was pushed back out by Billy the Kid, who instructed him to "kill some of the s.o.b.s before you die." The siege began. Garrett shot one of the fugitives' horses dead and drove the others away to prevent the rustlers' escape. The posse then left in shifts and went to a nearby ranch to eat. At about 4 p.m., a wagon arrived with provisions, and Garrett and his men started cooking a meal. The hungry rustlers surrendered, filing out and allowing themselves to be disarmed. Released on a $300 bail, Pickett stayed in Las Vegas for a while before drifting into northern Arizona where he hooked up with the Hash Knife gang and was part of the Graham-Tewksbury feud. Wounded in the leg during a foray, Pickett returned to punching cattle and married in 1888, wandering again after his wife and baby both died in childbirth.

The rest of Pickett's days were spent gambling, bar tending, prospecting for gold, working as a cowhand, and serving as a deputy U.S. marshall when Woodrow Wilson was president. After he was forced to have his leg amputated, Pickett returned to northern Arizona where he died in Pinetop at the age of seventy-six. He was buried in Winslow, Ariz. See: **Billy the Kid; Rudabaugh, David.**

Pierce, Abel Head (AKA: **Shanghai Pierce**), prom. 1870s-80s, U.S., gunman. Abel Pierce was a vain and proud cowboy who erected a $10,000 monument so that he would not be forgotten in death. Known in the cow towns as "Shanghai Pierce," Abel earned a fortune in the booming cattle breeding business— and then squandered it on liquor in hundreds of saloons west of the Pecos. His unruly behavior was not appreciated, especially by Wyatt Earp, who had more than one run-in with this man. The forty-foot bronze monument, which Pierce built at a cost of $10,000 stands on his ranch at Tres Palacios Creek in Bay City, Texas.

Western gunman Abel Head "Shanghai" Pierce.

Pierce, Charles, d.1895, U.S., outlaw. After an unsuccessful career as a horse racer in Pawnee, Okla., Charles Pierce became a member of the infamous Dalton Gang in the 1890s, until they were destroyed in a gun battle at Coffeyville, Kan. After that, he rode with William Doolin's gang. One of the Dalton Gang's triumphs was the July 15, 1892, train robbery. The gang sneaked into the little town of Adair, Okla., about fifteen minutes before the arrival of the 9:42 p.m. train. Capturing the depot at gunpoint, they robbed the station, then went to chosen spots to wait for the train. When it arrived, they appropriated the cab, firing at the passengers to keep them on board, and drove a wagon up to the express car door. A gun battle with guards resulted in injuries but no deaths as the bandits fled with their haul.

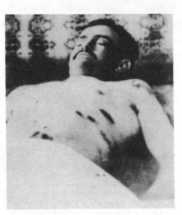

Outlaw Charley Pierce in death.

Pierce's final battle was an ambush on May 2, 1895. After Doolin's gang split up, Pierce and George "Bitter Creek" Newcomb teamed up and rode to the Dunn Ranch on the Cimarron River to visit Newcomb's lover, the famous "Rose of the Cimarron, and to collect $900 owed Newcomb by Rose's brothers. Approaching the house the fugitives were ambushed, shot out of their saddles by the brothers who wanted to collect the large bounty on their heads. Both bodies were thrown into a wagon to be taken to Guthrie, but when Newcomb, who had lived through the night, sat up and begged for water, he was given another bullet. See: **Doolin, William M.**

Plummer, Henry, 1837-64, U.S., lawman-gunman. Henry Plummer was the prototype of the deceitful sheriff who is shown in the end to be a villain. Plummer was believed to have killed as many as fifteen men, and his gang of outlaws was alleged to have murdered 102 victims.

Plummer traveled west from his native New England when he was fifteen, and became marshal of Nevada City, Calif., in 1856 at the age of nineteen. He killed the angry husband of a woman he was having an affair with, and was sentenced to ten years but was pardoned. He also allegedly robbed a Wells Fargo office in Washoe, killing another man, and again escaped prison, this time by bribing a jailer before he could be tried. Moving on to Oregon Plummer killed a sheriff, drifted to Washington to pursue several more romantic adventures, and participated in the murder of a man in Orofino, Idaho. Working in a gambling casino in Lewistown, Idaho, in 1862, Plummer rounded up a gang of thieves and brigands and ordered the assassination of a member of a vigilante committee.

In Bannack, Mont., in the fall of 1862, Plummer promoted himself as a vigilante from Lewiston and was soon elected sheriff. His gang, known as the Innocents, stepped up its activities, and the sheriff erected a scaffold to punish the villains. But the few who hanged on it were not members of the Innocents, many of whom worked for Plummer as deputies. The organization grew so large that secret handshakes and code words were instituted so one Innocent could recognize another. The ambitious sheriff soon extended his operations to Virginia City, where he forced the lawman to abscond. Plummer gunned down former cohort Jack Cleveland, who was trying to blackmail him into sharing the gang's profits. He was taken home by a local butcher, Hank Crawford, who kept Cleveland alive for several more hours, and he told the story of Plummer's deceit and corruption with his last gasps. Crawford began to relate the tale, and Plummer soon drove him from the area, but the damage had been done as Virginia City and Bannack residents formed their own vigilance committee, excluding the sheriff. From late 1863, the Vigilantes of Montana hanged dozens of suspected criminals, including a number of Innocents. Plummer made no attempt to leave town, believing he was not in danger. One theory maintains that Plummer made a deal with the vigilantes and was double-crossed.

Outlaw leader Henry Plummer, hanged in 1864.

On Jan. 10, 1864, a sobbing Plummer and two of his comrades were taken to the gallows that he himself had built. Begging for mercy, the former lawman pleaded that his tongue be cut out and all of his limbs hacked off, after which he could be left in a cabin in the hills. But no one took his suggestions, and he was hanged.

Pointer, Johnny, d.1894, U.S., outlaw. Johnny Pointer of Eureka Springs, Ark., had been a problem to his parents since he was twelve years old. That year he set fire to a neighbor boy. Then Pointer stabbed another local boy, for which his father bailed him out again. This pattern of juvenile delinquency continued until manhood when he began pilfering horses. Johnny Pointer was arrested in Decatur, Texas, and jailed for this serious offense in 1891. Like always, he counted on his father to put up the bail money. The elder Pointer obliged, and the son walked free. On his way back to Arkansas, Johnny met up with Ed Vandever and William Bolding, who were also heading that way. They had completed their business in Texas, and were in possession of a sizeable bankroll. On the night of Dec. 25, 1891, the three men set up camp near a farm belonging to W.G. Baird at Wilburton, in the Choctaw Nation. The next morning the mangled remains of Bolding and Vandever were found in an adjacent creek. The team of horses, the provisions, and the men's money had disappeared with Pointer. At McAlester, Pointer was arrested after trying to sell the equipment.

Appearing before Judge Isaac Parker at Fort Smith (Ark.), Pointer was cool as ice and not moved by the grief his parents exhibited. When the sentence of death was passed, Pointer asked the judge if it might not be too much trouble if he could name the hour of his execution. Parker allowed the request and Pointer decided upon 3:30 p.m., on Sept. 24, 1894, as the time for his execution. As the minutes counted down, Pointer suddenly lost his nerve. He was granted a fifteen minute delay for him to properly compose himself. On the scaffold the once defiant young Pointer turned white with fear. He was dropped into eternity a moment later.

Poker Alice, See: Ivers, Alice.

Ponce, Noratto, d.1865, U.S., outlaw. The leader of a group of bandits from 1860-65, Noratto Ponce gunned down a man at Governor's Saloon in the town of Hayward, Calif., on Oct. 3 1865. The killing occurred following a heated argument during a poker game. Ponce shot the man and rode away unmolested. Sheriff Harry Morse and a deputy caught up with Ponce a few days later. The lawmen and outlaw exchanged gunfire and though Ponce was severely wounded and his horse was shot out from under him, the bandit escaped. In November Morse heard that Ponce was at the home of Jose Rojos in Contra Costa County, recovering from his wounds. When Morse arrived at the house, he saw Ponce steal into the surrounding brush. Both men opened fire simultaneously, and Morse shot and killed Ponce.

Powell, Sylvester, d.1877, U.S., gunman. A usually quiet man Sylvester Powell became crazed when drunk. A driver for the Southwestern Stage Company, Powell was alleged to have killed two men while drunk in Wichita, Kan., where he lived. On New Year's Day, Powell and Albert Singleton were getting drunk in the afternoon when they came across a horse owned by E.R. Dennison and tried to take it. Dennison came forward and made a comment which caused Powell to stun him with a fierce blow from a neck yoke he was carrying. Although Powell ordered Dennison not to turn him in, soon Marshall Mike Meagher was pushing Powell toward the city jail.

That night, stage company official W.A. Brown got Powell released. After threatening to kill Meagher, Powell went looking for a pistol. He then found the marshall in an outhouse behind Jim Hope's saloon. Sneaking up to the building, Powell fired two bullets through the planks. One hit Meagher in the calf and the other tore through his coat. The marshal leaped toward Powell and a third bullet grazed his hand. Powell took off down an alley, firing back at Meagher as he ran. Limping, Meagher caught up with Powell in front of Charles Hill's drugstore and shot Powell in the chest, killing him instantly.

Powers, Bill, See: Evans, Christopher.

Pratt, John, prom. 1866-76, U.S., lawman. Massachusetts native John Pratt succeeded Abraham Cutler as marshal of the New Mexico Territory on Mar. 3, 1866. Pratt was a former military officer who had seen action with the Second Kansas Cavalry in 1862. Pratt was a Unionist whose sympathies were with the Republican Party, which coincided nicely with the then current state of affairs in New Mexico politics. The Santa Fe Ring, a Republican "machine" headed by District Attorney Stephen B. Elkins and Thomas B. Catron was coming into power, and would soon control the patronage and economic resources of the entire territory. It was therefore necessary to have a fellow Republican in the marshal's office.

Pratt established headquarters in Albuquerque, and as one of his first official acts, he assisted Elkins in prosecuting Abraham Cutler for embezzlement. (It was Pratt who released Cutler on bond, whereby the former marshal fled to the East Coast but later returned to face trial and was acquitted.)

During the Reconstruction period, Pratt and a force of special deputies uncovered evidence of a slavery ring in New Mexico operating in violation of federal laws. On Sept. 26,

1868, Pratt informed Elkins that he had delivered 150 offenders who had violated the Peonage laws in New Mexico to Special Commissioner William Griffith who oversaw the enforcement of this law.

Marshal Pratt greatly expanded the powers of his office during his ten years of service. He provided better care for prisoners assigned to his jurisdiction and closely involved the county sheriffs, many of whom were invited to serve as special deputies. Pratt's warm dealings with members of the Santa Fe Ring brought conflict of interest charges down on his head. But the marshal did little to assuage his critics and seemed more concerned about placating Elkins, who owned the First National Bank of Santa Fe—Pratt sat on the board of directors of this institution—than in prosecuting the perpetrators of the Colfax County War which broke out in the fall of 1875. Pratt, and the other local authorities, failed to identify the gang who killed Parson T.J. Tolby near Cimarron. Tolby had threatened to expose some shady dealings involving the Maxwell Land Grant Company, a real estate consortium owned by William R. Morley and which Elkins had a financial stake in. Tolby was going to point the finger at Judge Joseph Palen, who had moved against the settlers living on land owned by the company. Tolby's friends organized a vigilante band, and arrested several members of the ring in Cimarron. Two of the accused killers were lynched by the mob.

Pratt distanced himself from the Colfax County War until August 1875, when he refused to execute a warrant for the arrest of Mrs. William R. Morley for removing an envelope in the mails at Cimarron. Interestingly, the warrant was issued by Thomas Catron who was an enemy of Morley. It was no doubt prepared in order to harass the Morley family, and may in fact have been recalled by Catron at the last minute. According to one source, Pratt was slow to move against Mrs. Morley because the gunfighter Clay Allison vowed serious reprisals. "Bring that woman to trial and not a man will come out of the courtroom alive," he warned. Pratt's refusal to carry out the law reflected the growing factionalism in New Mexico politics, and the power the marshal was now able to wield. Pratt lasted until May 1876, when Elkins decided that he wanted Ohioan John E. Sherman, Jr. to assume the marshalcy. For his many long years of service, Elkins used his influence with President Ulysses S. Grant to reward Pratt with the position of secretary of the New Mexico Territory. The incumbent secretary, William G. Ritch, was summarily dismissed. His job performance was never a consideration. Elkins would later boast that President Grant "would not do it unless by my consent." See: **Colfax County War; Cutler, Abraham.**

Q

Quantrill, William Clarke, 1837-65, U.S., outlaw. The name of William Clarke Quantrill has gone down in history as one associated with wholesale destruction and mass murder, even among those who supported his cause as a Confederate guerrilla during the Civil War. The early life of Quantrill suggests anything but the bloody butcher he was to become. Born in Canal Dover, Ohio, Quantrill was well educated, coming from a respectable middle-class family. He taught Bible school and lived a quiet life until the age of twenty when he rode west seeking adventure, reaching Utah in 1857. Here, down on his luck, Quantrill turned to stealing horses. By the time he moved east in 1859, his nature was that of a brigand and an outlaw.

The West had hardened him, changed him into an unscrupulous and vicious bandit. In Kansas he posed as a jayhawker, raiding pro-slavery farms and ranches with other bandits. Quantrill claimed he was freeing slaves, but this was only a ruse. He looted the livestock of these ranches and took along what slaves were present, later reselling the stolen herds of cattle and horses, as well as the slaves. The anti-slavery movement in the U.S. at the time was only a matter of booty to Quantrill. Quantrill had obtained a job as a schoolteacher and used the position to cover his true activities, that of a thief and killer.

In December 1860, Quantrill persuaded five gullible young Quakers to join him in raiding pro-slavery farms. The first of these to be raided was the farm of Morgan Walker in Jackson County. Quantrill told the Quakers that the aim of the raid was to free Walker's slaves and none of the whites on the Walker farm should be spared if they resisted the liberation of the blacks. Quantrill had by then arranged to sell all of Walker's slaves as soon as he captured them. But hours before the raid took place, Quantrill inexplicably warned the pro-slavery men at Walker's farm. Quantrill then rode into an ambush that he himself had arranged, and three of the Quakers were shot dead.

The slave owners gathered around the mounted Quantrill, weapons raised. Before they could fire, a strange look came into the bandit's eyes. Solemnly, he leaned forward in his saddle. Torchlight flickered across his dark features as he told the leery slave owners that he was a pro-slavery man from Maryland and that he and his brother had been attacked in California by Quakers. His brother had been killed, he said, and he had been wounded, left for dead. With this lie on his lips, Quantrill added: "I have spent my days trailing my brother's murderers, and the three dead men you see before you were part of that band."

This outlandish fabrication was wholly accepted by the pro-slavery men. When the Civil War began months later Quantrill had no trouble in recruiting a large number of them to his guerrilla banner under which he claimed to be fighting for the Confederacy. He was joined by hard-riding gunmen who were as ruthless as he, such men as William "Bloody Bill" Anderson, George Todd, Fletcher Taylor, Arch Clements, the Younger Brothers, and Frank and Jesse James. (Jesse James was too young to join the guerrilla force led by Quantrill at the onset of the Civil War but joined the band in 1864.)

Todd, William H. Gregg, and William Haller became his lieutenants and, along with Anderson, would later lead their own bands of guerrillas, their ranks swollen with outlaws, murderers, thieves—the flotsam of the war. The first raid Quantrill made in the sullied name of the Confederacy was against Olathe, Kan. He and his men looted the town of its gold and goods, then burned it to the ground. The dozens of unarmed men left alive after the raid were lined up and shot to death at Quantrill's orders.

Although he never officially enlisted in the Confederate army, Quantrill did travel to Richmond, Va., in 1864, obtaining a commission as a captain from President Jefferson Davis. This was but a sanction sought by Quantrill to cover the many crimes he had already committed, including the slaughterhouse destructions of a whole town, Lawrence, Kan., which Quantrill raided with 450 men in 1863. Lawrence had long been pro-Union, a bastion of anti-slavery. This peaceful farming community was also the home of James H. Lane, U.S. senator from Kansas and the leader of the Jayhawkers, pro-Union forces that also operated as guerrillas.

Quantrill, before the raid, ordered his men to be utterly ruthless, to slay every adult male in Lawrence, to create such havoc and destruction that Lane himself would be blamed for bringing this wrath down upon his own constituents. Lane would, Quantrill insisted, be in such disgrace as a result of the Lawrence raid, that he would be recalled from Washington. "His own people will execute him," Quantrill prophesized. "They will burn him at the stake for what we are about to do."

En route to Lawrence, Quantrill and his men took local residents prisoner and ordered them at gunpoint to lead them around Union lines. As these captive guides performed their duties, they were summarily shot by Quantrill's guerrillas. Camping outside of Lawrence, Quantrill learned that the local garrison of Union troops had marched off to face other Confederate forces. On the morning of Aug. 21, 1863, Quantrill and his men swarmed into the undefended town. James Lane was in Lawrence at the time and when he heard the rebel yell, he leaped from his bed in his nightshirt and ran into a cornfield where he hid throughout the raid.

Weeks earlier, the wives, mothers, and sisters of many of Quantrill's men who had been living in Kansas City had been placed in a three-story hotel, confined to the upper floors, at the orders of Union general Thomas C. Ewing. The old structure collapsed, the third and second floors folding inward some days later, and many of these women, along with their children, were crushed to death. Among them were Matilda Anderson and Christie McCorkle Kerr, sisters of Bloody Bill Anderson and John McCorkle, two of Quantrill's riders who, because of the Kansas City disaster, had turned into bloodthirsty monsters. Quantrill's riders had whipped themselves into a frenzy days before the raid by talking about these grievances, both real and imagined. By the time the guerrillas appeared in Lawrence, they were wholly disposed to show no mercy.

After looting the banks and stores of gold, cash, and supplies, Quantrill ordered the entire city put to the torch. As Lawrence burned, scores of men and boys were rounded up and their hands were tied behind their backs. The wives, mothers, and sisters of these men were lined up and forced to watch as Quantrill's bands of hooting, drunken murderers shot their loved ones to death one by one or in groups. When the hysterical women tried to interfere, they were knocked down, tied up, or threatened with guns. Anderson, McCorkle, and such bloody killers as Arch Clements delighted in making target practice out of their victims. They ordered some to run for their lives then shot them in the back, laughing uproariously at the hideous murders.

Senator S.M. Thorpe and Dr. J.F. Griswald (or Griswold), both pro-Union, were dragged from their homes and surrounded by dozens of Quantrill's jeering killers and shot to death. Even after these men were dead, scores of the guerillas used their bodies for target practice. Judge A. Carpenter and his wife were chased through their house and back yard by guerrillas. As Mrs. Carpenter clung to her husband, pleading for his life, a Quantrill man leaned forward and shot the judge in the head. Quantrill, impassively viewing the slaughter, then ordered the victims' bullet-ridden bodies tossed into the burning buildings to hide the massacre.

A blacksmith who had tried to resist the invaders was tied to another man and both men were shot with one bullet by Anderson and then dragged into a burning building. The flames burned away the ropes binding these men. Both were still alive as they tried to crawl out of the flaming building but were again shot and tossed back into the inferno. Dozens of men continued firing at them as they staggered about screaming through the flames until they roasted to death. Quantrill's killers had slaughtered 185 men and boys and had left twenty-four others wounded before their cruel leader ordered a retreat after learning that Union troops were riding toward Lawrence. The town

was by then a smoldering black ruin, with 154 homes and businesses burned to gutted stubble. In four hours, between 5 and 9 a.m., Quantrill had wiped out an entire community. He and his men rode off, burdened by loot, most of them drunk.

Try as they might, Union troops failed to capture the mass killer Quantrill, who later rode to Texas with some of his men and attacked helpless wagon trains, killing dozens more. Toward the end of the war, Quantrill's odious reputation had spread across the frontier. Regular Confederate officers and soldiers were offended by his deeds and he was shunned by southern troops. Moving back to Missouri, Quantrill made a few skirmishes against Union outposts, but his band of guerrillas was fast dwindling. Those who were not killed in his ranks, deserted his banner, realizing he was a branded outlaw and that the Confederate cause was lost. Following the war there would be retribution for the innumerable crimes committed by Quantrill.

The guerrilla leader, with only twenty men, next moved into Kentucky. Here he planned to surrender to Union forces, to pass himself and his worst killers off as regular Confederate troops. He thought to obtain a pardon, as was the case with all regular captured Confederate troops. He knew that to surrender in either Missouri or Kansas where he and his men had committed their murderous acts would mean certain execution. On May 10, 1865, weeks after Confederate general Robert E. Lee had surrendered in the east, Quantrill and what was left of his band took refuge in a barn outside of Smiley, Ky.

As a rainstorm swept the area, Union captain Edward Terrell, an old foe of Quantrill's, learned of the guerrillas' presence and led a large force of Union troops against the barn. As Terrell's men appeared, Quantrill shouted: "It's every man for himself!" Several guerrillas shot their way to freedom. Quantrill and Clark Hockinsmith rode out of the barn but Quantrill's horse was killed. The guerrilla leader fell to the ground and then tried to climb aboard Hockinsmith's horse, helped by Richard Glasscock.

A volley from the Union troops blasted Hockinsmith, Glasscock, and Quantrill who fell to the ground, their horses collapsing next to them. Quantrill had been hit in the hand. He stood up and began to run toward some woods but another bullet struck him in the neck, then another in the spine. He fell, paralyzed, to the earth. He was carried to a farmhouse by Union troops; here the guerrilla leader told Captain Terrell he was dying. He was taken to the military hospital in Louisville and died gasping for breath and begging for his life on June 5, 1865. He was buried in a hidden grave and, in December 1877, his remains were removed to Dover Canal (now Dover), Ohio, to rest in the family plot. What was left of Quantrill's force

William Clarke Quantrill

Quantrill in uniform.

Arch Clements, executioner.

Captain George Todd

Frank James, guerrilla.

Lawrence, Kan., a few weeks before Quantrill's guerrilla raiders attacked the thriving pro-Union town.

Jesse James, guerrilla.

Lawrence, Kan., in utter ruins after Quantrill's murderous raid in 1863 when his men torched the city.

surrendered on July 26, 1865. See: **Anderson, William; James, Jesse; Younger Brothers, The.**

R

Raidler, William (AKA: **Little Bill**), prom. 1895, U.S., outlaw. An educated man from Pennsylvania Dutch stock Bill Raidler drifted into Texas and became part of the infamous Bill Doolin gang. Raidler had met Doolin in Oklahoma when they were both cowboys. A cowboy, convict, and robber of trains and banks, Raidler was involved in many gunfights, the most well-known of which took place in 1895. In Spring 1895, the Doolin gang was jumped by a posse near Dover, Okla. A forty-minute fray ensued in which nearly two hundred shots were exchanged. After Tulsa Jack Blake was killed, Raidler and three cohorts grabbed two horses and double mounting, galloped away to safety.

On May 20, 1895, the Doolin gang was robbing a bank at Southwest City, Mo., when irate citizens began to fire at them. As the bandits tried to flee, store owners Oscar and Joe Seaborn stepped out of their shop. Raidler rode past and fired at Oscar, but the bullet passed through Oscar's body and into Joe, killing him instantly. Near Elgin, Kan., on Sept. 6, Raidler was hiding out at Sam Moore's ranch when he was jumped at dusk by Bill Tilghman and two other law enforcement officers. Raidler fired back but was hit in the wrist by a rifle slug. Dropping his gun and running, Raidler was brought down by the bullets of Deputy W.C. Smith. Wounded in the neck, both sides, and in the back,

Outlaw Bill Raidler.

Raidler somehow survived. His final battle was near Bartlesville, Okla., in October 1895. Hiding in a cave, Raidler was discovered by Heck Thomas and two Osage scouts. When Raidler saw the men approaching, he ambushed them. Thomas fired back with a .45-90 Winchester and a bullet ripped into Raidler's hand. Dropping his rifle and racing into the bush, Raidler chopped off two of his damaged fingers and managed to hide in a tree to avoid capture. One week later he was wounded and apprehended by Tilghman and two other officers. Tried and convicted, Raidler served time and was later released on parole from an Ohio prison with the help of Tilghman. Raidler later married but never regained his health and lived out the rest of his years disabled. See: **Doolin, William.**

Rattlesnake Dick, See: **Barter, Richard.**

Raynor, William P., d.1885, U.S., outlaw. Gunfighter William Raynor, known as "the best-dressed bad man in Texas," died in El Paso, Texas, on Apr. 14, 1885. Contemporary newspaper reports indicate that Raynor was playing faro in the Gem Saloon and objected to a move the dealer, a young man by the name of Bob Cahill, made with his hands. Raynor left the table and began drinking heavily with a friend, Charlie "Buck" Linn. After a time, Raynor started looking for a fight. Wyatt Earp happened to be standing at the bar and Raynor approached him and tried to goad him into a gunfight. Earp, however, indicated that he was unarmed and Raynor moved on to his next target, "Cowboy" Bob Rennick, who was sitting at the faro table with Cahill. Raynor insulted Rennick, specifically about his white cowboy hat. Rennick, also, indicated that he was unarmed.

As Raynor walked to a back room, Rennick reconsidered and borrowed a gun from Cahill. Raynor saw the transaction and came running into the room with his guns drawn. He fired five or six shots, all of them missing Rennick. Rennick fired twice, hitting Raynor once in the shoulder and once in the stomach. The injured man staggered out into the street and managed to board a horse-drawn streetcar. As Raynor was being taken to a doctor, Linn, who had been drinking in another saloon, raced into the Gem thinking that Cahill had shot his friend. Both men fired and Cahill put a bullet through Linn's heart, killing him instantly. Raynor died an hour later after asking that his mother be told that he "died game." Cahill was arrested for murder but released on a $10 bond after a coroner's inquest. He never went to trial.

Reavis, James Addison (AKA: **The Baron of Arizona; Caballero de los Colorados**), d.1908, U.S., fraud-forg. A land swindle of monumental proportions withstood the close scrutiny of some of the finest legal minds of the American Southwest for nearly a decade before Spanish scholar and linguist Mallet Prevost took a closer look. Only then did he discover that James Addison Reavis, the notorious "Red Baron of Arizona," was not the real estate mogul he pretended to be. The vast acreage he had acquired over the years was the result of an elaborate forgery which took shape in the early 1870s.

James Reavis served in the Confederate army during the

Civil War. During this period he discovered his talents as a "penman." Armed with a forged pass, he found he could easily fool the camp sentries and slip away from his regiment. His ability to duplicate the signatures of his commanding officers kept him away from the front lines for the duration of the Civil War. When the South was defeated and Reavis' military career came to an end, the forger returned to private life in St. Louis, where he found

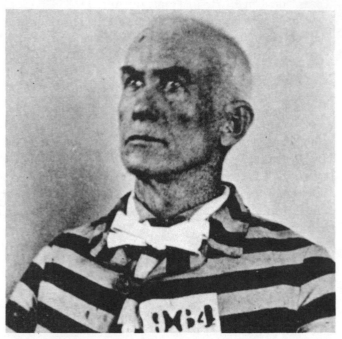

James Addison Reavis, the "Red Baron of Arizona," in prison garb.

work as a streetcar conductor. This was not to his liking, however, and in time he decided to open a real estate business that pandered to a somewhat shady clientele. One of his customers promised a sizable commission if Reavis could come up with a quitclaim on a large parcel of land. The forger put his talents to good use by producing an authentic-looking document that was accepted by the courts without question. Encouraged by the ease with which he had deceived the authorities, Reavis went on to help other St. Louis residents forge property titles. But when the police became aware of certain improprieties, Reavis closed shop and headed west.

By the time he reached Santa Fe, N.M., he had squandered the bulk of his small, illegal fortune. But he managed to find a job in the records division of a governmental agency, which handled the claims of Spanish and Mexican residents whose lands were ceded to the U.S. at the close of the Mexican War. The U.S. was bound by the terms of the 1848 Treaty of Guadelupe Hidalgo to restore the rightful land to the owners and to honor all legitimate claims. While toiling over reams of documents—much of it printed in Spanish—Reavis stumbled upon an idea that on the surface seemed so simple one could only wonder why

no one had thought of it sooner.

He decided to forge Mexican and Spanish land documents—some of which had been prepared by religious monks hundreds of years earlier—and then lay claim to existing properties under the name of Miguel de Peralta, a fictional character Reavis invented to lend legitimacy to the fraud. Reavis carefully went over the quality of the parchment paper, the type of ink the ancient scribes used, and even went so far as to whittle an identical quill. He attached an identity to the imaginary nobleman Miguel de Peralta. According to Reavis' own account the Spanish don was a lineal descendant of King Ferdinand, who had been awarded a princely title, military honors, and fabulous wealth. He went on to say that he was related to the family. His half-brother was Juan de Peralta, an itinerant gambler who had arrived in Arizona in 1851 to purchase a large tract of land.

Reavis spent years putting it all together. He created generations of Peraltas, awarding Miguel's descendants with ten million acres of prime land in Arizona which had once been the province of Spain. By 1870 the real estate huckster had traveled through Guadalajara, Lisbon, Madrid, Seville, and Mexico City placing his forged deeds, mortgages, and family wills in all the important libraries, monasteries, and archives—exactly where the lawyers were most likely to look.

At last everything was in place and Reavis was ready to spring his little surprise on the people of Arizona. He appeared in Prescott some time in the late 1870s with an accomplice named Dr. George Willing. Reavis claimed that the doctor had purchased rights to a portion of the Peralta lands in Arizona for $1,000. But then he was poisoned to death (by Reavis, allegedly) and the grant reverted back to the con man for $30,000. The forged documents proved it, of course. In 1881 Reavis went before the surveyor general of the U.S. with certified copies of the falsified papers. Notices soon appeared in the towns of Silver King, Pinal, Florence, Globe, Casa Grande, and Tempe advising the residents who owned homes on Reavis property that they were obligated to pay taxes. Not even the Southern Pacific Railroad or the Silver King Mine, which had business interests in this area, were exempt. A battery of lawyers, many of them employed by the railroad and mining concerns, did as Reavis anticipated. They searched through state Torrens records and the ancient parchment land grants only to discover to their dismay that Reavis' claim of ownership was valid.

The Southern Pacific was obliged to pay $50,000 as a first down payment for a right-of-way through Arizona and New Mexico. The Silver King Mine contributed $25,000, and thousands of ranchers, homesteaders, and business people were forced to follow suit. Reavis collected his taxes and rental fees with impunity. Overnight he had become one of the wealthiest land entrepreneurs in Arizona. But in the back of his mind he feared that he may have gone too far. To fool any government people who might be snooping around, he plucked a young Mexican woman off the street, sent her to a finishing school, and then married her. Reavis told his business associates that the woman, Maria Sanchez, was a direct descendant of the Peralta royal line. They had twin boys, who were educated by private tutors and attended to by a battery of servants. The family lived ostentatiously in opulent mansions in New York, Washington, St. Louis, and Mexico. Reavis even took his family to Spain where they received all the courtesies of the royal house, including an audience before King Alfonso.

In March 1890 the charade ended unceremoniously when the Spanish historian and expert linguist Mallet Prevost took a second look at some of the parchment documents. Through chemical analysis he determined that while the first few pages of each file were genuine, the succeeding sheets of paper were produced in a much later period. Mallet further noticed important differences in the script. The writing of the genuine Spanish monks was done in iron ink. Reavis' forgeries were written in common dogwood ink. Important birth register pages had been noticeably altered. It was not like the ancient scribes to change a record after the fact.

With these facts in hand, James Reavis was brought before the Land Grant Court in Santa Fe, where his frauds were exposed. He was charged with criminal fraud and sentenced to serve six years in the Phoenix Penitentiary beginning in April 1890. He emerged in 1899 a broken, dissolute man without family or friends. Reavis' wife had divorced him years earlier and had taken the children to Denver. The remaining years of his life were spent on the streets of Santa Fe, where Reavis hustled for spare change. He died in 1908.

Red Buck, See: **Waightman, George.**

Red Light Saloon, 1880-82, U.S., pros. Known as the "worst whorehouse in Kansas," the notorious Red Light Saloon in Caldwell existed for two years of "violent, obscene and godless" action. Two town marshals died on the premises and a third was murdered as he left the saloon after a night of debauchery. Arriving in Caldwell in 1880, Mag and George Woods, who had run a brothel in Delano, Kan., opened up the two-story dance hall, saloon, and bordello on Chisholm Street. The first floor was the ballroom, saloon, and the Woods' living quarters, with the second floor reserved for the prostitutes' rooms. Several attempts were made to close the raucous Red Light. Women who worked there were notorious for luring patrons from outside, knocking them out, and robbing them. After a cowboy was murdered at the bar a prostitute who had been upstairs with him earlier pulled off his bandanna and dipped it in his blood. Angry earlier because he had underpaid her, she was satisfied that "now I have a souvenir from the cheapskate."

In August 1881, cowboy Charlie Davis visited the Red Light. When he got into a fight that night with one of the prostitutes, George Woods intervened and Davis shot him through the chest. Davis was never caught, despite Mag Woods' offer of a $500 reward. Woods apparently had a restraining influence in the operation; after his death the Red Light became still more rowdy and boisterous. On June 22, 1882, two cowboys killed Marshal George Brown inside the saloon when he came after them. The routine headline of the Caldwell *Standard,* "The Red Light Must Go," was supported by the passage of a new ordinance which allowed the local courts to run unwanted elements out of town. The new marshal was given authority to clean up the saloons, notably the Red Light. Realizing that her business days were numbered, Mag Woods sold all her liquor and fixtures in August 1882, boarded up the brothel and left for the train station. Jeering citizens followed her but were stopped short in their celebration when a rush of flame and smoke brought them back to the Red Light, which Woods had set on fire. Although the saloon was completely destroyed, the surrounding buildings incurred only minor damage.

Red Sash Gang, prom. 1887-92, U.S. outlaws. The Red Sash Gang, so called because of the article of clothing they wore for identification, took part in some of the bloodiest fighting in the Johnson County range war between cattlemen and homesteaders in Wyoming. In addition to being the most feared band of rustlers in the Powder River area, it also preyed on the homesteaders and was responsible for the deaths of many of them. Among its most heinous acts of violence were the murders of Nathan Champion and Nick Rae on Apr. 8, 1892. Champion and Rae barricaded themselves in a ranch house on the Champion Ranch when Major Frank Wolcott, then leader of the Red Sash Gang, led a large raiding party on the ranch. One of the party, a gunslinger known only as the Texas Kid, murdered Rae. Members of the party who shot Champion to death were never identified.

The persistent violence of the range war took another

kind of toll as well; even Frank Canton, another leader of the Red Sash Gang and a hardened veteran of gunfighting, could not take it. Between fits of insomnia, he had fearsome nightmares, screaming in his sleep for his confederates to get their guns and horses.

Ultimately, the U.S. Army arbitrated the dispute. With the end of the Johnson County War, the Red Sash Gang faded away.

Reed, Charlie, d.1883, U.S., gunman. A rustler and cowboy Charlie Reed was a drifter. He became involved in a rustling ring headed by John Selman and John Larn in the mid-1870s in the Fort Griffin, Texas, area. On Jan. 17, 1877, Reed and another rustler, Billy Bland, rode into town drunk, firing their guns. They went to the Beehive Saloon and Dance Hall where they continued shooting. When Deputy Sheriff W.R. Cruger and County Attorney William Jeffries arrived to arrest the drunken cowboys, Bland fired and wounded Cruger. An open battle raged with several men wounded or killed. Bland was fatally shot; Jeffries, although hit in the chest, survived. A cavalry officer was killed and a young lawyer, Dan Barron, was shot in the chest. Reed fled on foot, leaving Texas the next day. In 1883, in an Ogallala, Neb., saloon, Reed, drunk again, got into a fight with a man named Dumas whom he shot and killed. An angry mob gathered and Reed was hanged.

Reed, Jim, 1845-74, U.S., outlaw. One of the many paramours of bandit queen Belle Starr, Jim Reed was an outlaw who occasionally worked as a lawman in the common tradition of the Old West. Originally from Vernon County, Mo., Reed rode with Tom Starr's band of assassins. While he was living with 13-year-old Myra Belle Shirley, Reed murdered a man named Shannon and fled from Missouri to California with Belle and their young daughter. Another child, Ed Reed, who would grow up to allegedly murder his mother, was born in California, where Reed supported the family by highway robbery. After he was identified in a stagecoach heist, Reed went back east with his brood. With two other outlaws, Reed tortured an elderly Creek Indian until he told them where he had hidden a $30,000 cache of gold.

With his share of the loot, Reed took Belle to Texas, where she began to play the part of the Bandit Queen. Starr opened a stable which was kept well stocked by Reed's frequent forays into Oklahoma Indian Territory with Tom Starr and his gang of horse thieves. In August 1874, Reed was shot and killed by Deputy Sheriff John T. Morris of Lamar County, Texas, a former partner in stagecoach robberies and stock thefts who presumably collected the $4,000 bounty out on Reed's head. After burying Reed, Starr left her children with relatives and began to build her own legend. See: **Reed, Edwin; Starr, Belle.**

Reed, Nathaniel (AKA: **Texas Jack**), 1862-1950, U.S., outlaw. A clever outlaw who parlayed his mostly successful career as a train robber into a still more lucrative career in show business, Nathaniel Reed was a long-haired young man from Arkansas who decided when he was twenty-three to give up punching cattle in the Oklahoma Territory and become a train robber instead. Adopting the name Texas Jack, Reed joined with several others for his first holdup, robbing a train in Colorado and netting the considerable sum of about $6,000. Organizing and leading several bank and stage robberies in Texas, the Arizona Territory, California, and Colorado, Reed had a profitable decade. His luck ran out when he attempted a robbery in the Oklahoma Territory. With accomplices Buzz Luckey, Tom Smith, Tom Root, and several others, Reed thought they were looting $60,000 from the express car; they were instead confronted by an ambush party lead by Deputy U.S. Marshal Bud Ledbetter. Badly wounded in the ensuing gunfight, Reed went home to Arkansas. Luckey and Root fought it out with pursuers and murdered lawman Newton LaForce. When they were captured, Root turned informer. A murder charge was brought against Luckey, and Reed was captured.

Judge Isaac Parker sentenced Luckey to death, and Reed's stiff sentence was postponed while Luckey's appeal was heard by the U.S. Supreme Court. Luckey's murder conviction was overturned, and Reed got a lighter sentence than Luckey because he was not present when LaForce was slain. After serving two years, Reed was released on parole. Texas Jack decided to switch careers and went on the road with a show pragmatically titled *Texas Jack, Train Robber.* It proved to be more lucrative than his career as a thief, and the former convict created an encore number with his autobiography, *The Life of Texas Jack,* which sold 70,000 copies. Reed died at the age of 88 in Oklahoma City.

Regulator War, 1841-44, U.S., outlaw feud. In 1840, a vigilante movement committee in Shelby County caused a polarization that turned east Texas into a war zone. Like most of the West in those days, Shelby County was overrun with murderers, counterfeiters, thieves, and corrupt county officials making law and order an impossibility. The Regulators vigilante group was under the leadership of Charles Jackson, a steamboat operator of dubious character who apparently created the organization more for personal profit and control than for controlling local undesirables. When Jackson was murdered, the position went to Watt Moorman, who made Jackson look good by comparison. The Regulators soon were reduced to the level of the outlaw forces they had been organized to drive out.

In 1841, a counter movement appeared on the scene. Unfortunately the Moderators, as they were known, attracted the same criminal elements that the Regulators had; though theoretically fighting against criminals, the groups in fact spent most of their time killing and wounding each other. All of Shelby County was soon involved in the fray, often pitting neighbor against neighbor and one relative against another. Within a three-year span, the Moderators were able to weed out the outlaws from their ranks and, by 1844, were ready to take on the Regulators in a full out battle. A bloodbath was prevented by the intervention of Sam Houston, president of the Republic of Texas, who sent in the militia; the onset of the Mexican War further dissipated the conflict in Shelby. The vigilante war resulted in eighteen official deaths, with hundreds more severely wounded or maimed for life. Feuds among the Regulators and Moderators continued for decades, the animosity between the two groups maintained into the twentieth century.

Reno Brothers, d.1868, U.S., outlaws. The political, economic, and social unrest of the post-Civil War era produced several prominent outlaw gangs, including the Youngers, the James Brothers, and the Reno Brothers. The Reno family settled near the present city of Seymour, Ind., in 1816 and had considerable success in farming. Beginning in the fall of 1865, four of the six Reno children—Frank Reno, born on July 27, 1837; John Reno, born on July 23, 1839; Simeon Reno, born on Aug. 2, 1843; and William Reno,

Frank Reno, leader of the Reno Brothers, first to rob a train in America, in 1866.

born on May 15, 1848—formed a gang that terrorized the Seymour area for the next four years.

In Spring 1866, the gang robbed the Clinton County, Ind., Treasury. Frank Reno was arrested for the robbery but was soon acquitted. On Oct. 6, 1866, the Renos committed what

is believed to be the first formal U.S. train robbery, a crime that has been incorrectly attributed to the better-known James gang. John and Simeon Reno and another gang member, Franklin Sparks, boarded an Ohio & Mississippi train as it pulled out of the Seymour depot. After knocking a guard unconscious, they pushed out two safes from the moving car at a spot three miles from town where the rest of the gang waited for them. They managed to break open one safe containing $15,000 but failed to crack the second one holding $30,000 worth of cash and gold. The Adams Express Company, which had been assigned to guard the train, called in the Pinkerton Agency. Before long Pinkerton's agents had infiltrated the town of Seymour and gained the Renos' confidence. In Spring 1867, the Renos struck again. This time their target was the Daviess County Treasury in Gallatin, Mo., which they robbed of $22,065. The Pinkertons, believing that a direct confrontation with the gang in Seymour would endanger innocent lives, devised a plan for kidnapping the gang's leader, John Reno. They arranged to have a special train pass through the Seymour station while one of their operatives enticed Reno out on the platform as the train pulled into the station. Six Pinkerton agents descended from the train and snatched Reno, carrying him back onto the moving train before anyone in the crowd realized what was happening. The Reno gang, when informed of the kidnapping, pursued the train but never caught it. John Reno was given a quick trial, convicted, and sent under armed guard to the state penitentiary.

Meanwhile, Frank Reno took over leadership of the gang and led his men over the state, robbing county treasury offices, post offices, and trains. In February 1868, the gang robbed the Harrison County Treasury office at Magnolia, Iowa, of $14,000. The Pinkertons traced the gang to Council Bluffs, Ia. After posting a round-the-clock watch on a saloon run by a former counterfeiter, they discovered that Michael Rogers, an upstanding resident, was a frequent visitor to the saloon. When it also was learned that Rogers had an old police record, the Pinkertons followed him. Four days later, Frank Reno was observed entering Rogers' home by the back door. The detectives staged a raid on the home and arrested Rogers, Frank Reno, and two prominent counterfeiters, William Perkins and Miles Ogle. They were sent to the jail in Council Bluffs from which they escaped on Apr. 1, leaving a message scrawled on the wall saying "April Fool."

On May 2, 1868, the Renos staged their most daring and profitable robbery. A gang of at least two dozen men robbed an Ohio and Mississippi Valley train stopped at Marshfield, Ind., thirteen miles south of Seymour. They forced open the train's two safes and got away with a record $96,000 in cash and valuables. The Pinkertons set off once again on their trail. Three members of the gang, Franklin Sparks, John J. Moore, and Henry Jerrell, were captured five days after the robbery but a vigilante group overwhelmed six Pinkerton agents guarding them just outside of Seymour and hanged the three men. On July 22, William and Simeon Reno were arrested in Indiana and on Aug. 4 taken under heavy guard to the New Albany jail. The Pinkertons followed the rest of the gang to Windsor, Canada where they finally arrested Frank Reno, Charlie Anderson, and Michael Rogers. Rogers was released for lack of concrete evidence and immediately fled the area.

The Pinkerton agents applied for extradition of the remaining three men to the U.S. The process was slow and complicated and twice while William Pinkerton waited for its completion, criminals sympathetic to the Renos tried to kill him. After seemingly interminable wrangling over the terms of extradition, the Canadian government released the prisoners to the Pinkerton detectives who, on Oct. 7, took them via steamboat to Cleveland. From there they traveled overland to the New Albany jail where they joined their fellow gang members. On the evening of Dec. 12, 1868, a group of vigilantes broke into the New Albany jail and one by one lynched all of the members of the Reno gang.

Reynolds Gang, prom. 1860s, U.S., outlaws. Because of the story that it had hidden a great treasure somewhere in the Colorado Territory, the Reynolds Gang won a place in that state's folklore. Their infamous execution also stands as a black page in Colorado history. Brothers Jim and John Reynolds came to Colorado Territory around Bayou Salado, or South Park, around 1863. Because they had money and no visible work or other means of support there were increasing suspicions that they were highwaymen. Although there was no evidence against them the fact that they were from Texas was sufficient provocation for them to be put in an internment compound for Confederate sympathizers in Denver. The Reynolds soon escaped and returned to Texas where they began to work as Confederate irregulars, stealing gold for the southern cause.

The twenty-member gang got $40,000 in gold on their first strike on the Santa Fe Trail. When Jim Reynolds said something about the booty belonging to Jeff Davis and the Confederacy, about twelve men pulled out of the deal, taking their share with them. The Reynolds brothers then allegedly buried the rest, though there were other reports which claimed that it was divided up among the other remaining gang members. Several more robberies were managed by the gang, including a $10,000 gold dust heist from a stagecoach. In Spring 1864 the gang suffered severe losses; one member was slain and only Jake Stowe and John

Reynolds escaped. Jim Reynolds and four accomplices were tried in Denver; all were given life sentences. The death sentence was ruled out because none of them had ever killed anyone. Kept in jail until mid-summer, they were turned over to the charge of Colonel John M. Chivington of the 3rd Colorado Cavalry in August. Chivington secretly tried the men, who were sentenced to be hanged as Confederate conspirators. Fearful that it was exceeding its authority, the military tribunal made the announcement that the prisoners would be taken to Fort Leavenworth, Kan., where their case would be reviewed.

Captain Cree left with the five prisoners on Aug. 19 and returned a few days later to report that they had been killed while trying to escape. Famous scout Dick Wooten found the corpses of the Reynolds Gang members lashed to trees and riddled with bullet holes near Russelville, a ghost town. Cree claimed he had been given orders to shoot the prisoners at the first chance. This explanation was rejected because it reflected badly on Chivington, an upstanding officer and a Methodist minister. When Chivington cruelly massacred the Cheyenne Indians at Sand Creek three months later, public revulsion over the Reynolds murders swept through Colorado. In 1871 John Reynolds returned to the Colorado Territory, supposedly to retrieve the loot hidden in the Handcart Gulch and Spanish Peaks. Committing several holdups he was eventually mortally wounded, allegedly telling the secret of where the booty was hidden to a penny-ante outlaw named Brown, who died a drunken vagrant in Wyoming Territory, presumably never having found the loot. A century after the Reynolds Gang exploits, fortune hunters continued to tear up the region in search of the treasure.

Richardson, Levi, 1851-1879, U.S., gunman. Levi Richardson's awkwardness and slowness did not extend to his prowess with a gun, but a falling out with an old friend led to his demise. He came from Wisconsin to Dodge City and frequented the Long Branch Saloon, where he gambled, drank, and ignored the law set down by Wyatt Earp against carrying sidearms in town. One of his card-playing cronies was a young gambler called "Cock-Eyed" Frank Loving, whom he had known for years by the time they both fell in love with the same dance-hall girl in 1879.

Although Richardson had killed several men and Loving had never been in a gunfight, neither was ready to back down in this dispute. They quarrelled on the street one day in early March. Richardson hit the unarmed Loving in the face. Loving walked away, but vowed to a friend that he would shoot Richardson next time he saw him.

A month passed before the showdown occurred. Both

men wore their guns to the Long Branch Saloon on the night of Apr. 5. They sat down the bar from one another where they could study each other in the mirror, until Richardson broke the silence by muttering under his breath. This annoyed Loving, who turned to Richardson and demanded, "If you have anything to say to me, say it to my face."

The two moved toward one another until there was barely an arm's length between them, although they did position themselves on either side of a stove. They both drew their guns at once, and ducked. For several seconds they jumped around with the stove between them to try to dodge if the other fired a shot. Although an eyewitness stated that their pistols almost touched, Richardson missed when he finally did shoot, then panicked and started to fan the gun. After he got off his fifth ineffectual shot, Loving threw him to the floor, then fired several shots of his own into Richardson's chest.

Loving was tried for murder, but acquitted. Despite his violation of the gun-carrying statute, his vow to kill Richardson, and the fact that he was kneeling on top of him when he shot him, Loving was ruled to have acted in self-defense.

Riggs, Barney, d.1900, U.S., gunman. West Texas gunman Barney Riggs was frequently involved in gun fights. He killed his employer in Arizona in a fight over a woman, for which he was sentenced to life imprisonment at the Yuma Territorial Prison. While he was there, in October 1887, seven Mexican convicts with knives jumped Superintendent Thomas Gates and demanded to be released. Assistant superintendent Johnny Behan secured the gate. A general fray erupted as the convicts scrambled to get guns. As guards clubbed and fired at prisoners, three convicts, Lopez, Vasquez, and Bustamente, were gunned down by Officer B.F. Hartlee. By then a convict named Puebla had embedded a knife in Gates' neck. As Vasquez, who was still alive, pushed the superintendent in front of him as a shield, Gates shouted to Riggs to grab the fallen Lopez' gun and help him. Riggs grabbed the pistol and shot Puebla in the chest. Officer Hartlee aimed at Riggs, then suddenly realized that he was helping Gates, and fired instead at Puebla, hitting him in the back just as Riggs fired into Puebla's leg. A convict named Sprague helped Riggs carry the wounded Gates to safety. Riggs won a pardon and returned to Texas.

Near Toyah, Texas, Riggs began ranching and married the sister of Sheriff Bud Frazer, then becoming involved in the Frazer versus Killin' Jim Miller feud. In 1897, Fort Stockton, Texas, outlaws John Denson, Bill Earhart, and Miller decided to go after Riggs. As the three set out for Pecos, where Riggs was living, drinking and carousing along the way, lawman Dee Harkey sent Riggs a telegram to warn him. He carefully avoided them all day, but the next morning Riggs was substitute bartending for a friend at R.S. Johnson's saloon. He was alone behind the bar when Earhart and Denson burst in. Earhart shot and grazed Riggs, who pulled a gun and killed Earhart with a shot between the eyes. Riggs' pistol cartridges slid loose in the process; as he fumbled with his weapon, Denson grabbed him, but then fled. As Denson went through the door Riggs raced after him, and brought him down in the street with a bullet in the back of his head. Riggs surrendered himself to Harkey, who quickly released him.

In 1900, Riggs was living in Fort Stockton, Texas, when a family dispute angered his step-grandson enough to shoot and kill Riggs. See: **Miller, James B.**

Riley (Reily), Jim, b.1853, U.S., gunman. Jim Riley earned a small place in western folklore by participating in the famous Newton's General Massacre in Newton, Kan., on Aug. 20, 1871. Until this time, not much was known about this brawling, but sickly young man who became a follower of Mike McCluskie.

Ten days after McCluskie killed gambler Bill "William Bailey" Wilson, Hugh Anderson rounded up a group of Texas cowboys to avenge his death. They found McCluskie on Aug. 20, 1871, enjoying a game of faro in Perry Tuttle's dance hall and saloon in Newton's red-light district. Around 1 a.m., Anderson burst into the saloon and pointed a gun at McCluskie. He then shot McCluskie in the neck, arm, and back. In the wild shooting melee that followed, a Texan named Jim Martin was struck in the neck after trying to serve as peacemaker. Riley, who had been minding his own business up to this time, calmly locked the doors of Tuttle's and drew out his gun. He shot Anderson twice in the leg and shot two other Texans, Billy Garrett and Henry Kearnes; both of whom later died of chest wounds. See: **Newton General Massacre; McCluskie, Mike.**

Riley, Thomas, d.1868, U.S., outlaw. Tough guy Thomas Riley encountered Sheriff Tim Smith outside Carson City, Nev., in June 1868. The two men quarreled briefly, but when Smith tried to exert his legal authority on the irascible Riley, he was shot and killed. A few days later Riley turned up in Dayton, Nev., where he was recognized by Asa Kenyon, who organized a posse to give chase.

Riley then mounted a horse and attempted to ride out

of town, but he was closely pursued by the posse, who opened fire. The skirmish ended when Riley realized he was running low on ammunition. After wounding posse member H.A. Comins, Riley turned the gun on himself to avoid being taken back to jail.

Ringo, John (**John Ringgold**), d.1882, U.S., gunman. Rumors surrounded John Ringo in his lifetime, and legend follows him today, but few of the facts about him are certain. It is known that he was better educated than most western gunfighters, having attended William and Jewell College in Liberty, Mo., and being known for his ability to quote Shakespeare. He was arrested in 1877 along with John Wesley Hardin, Mannen Clements, and Bill Taylor. Upon his release, he drifted west, settling in Tombstone, Ariz., a town his legend helped put on the map.

In Tombstone, he continued to associate with criminals, including the Clantons and the McLowerys. He played both sides of the law himself, serving briefly as a sheriff's deputy and rustling cattle outside of town. He drank hard, and it was this that led to most of the verifiable shooting incidents in his short life. In December 1879, Ringo was drinking in the Crystal Palace Saloon when a man made a remark to a woman passing by outside. Offended by the comment, Ringo pistol-whipped the man, then shot him in the throat.

Ringo was killed in Turkey Creek Canyon outside of Tombstone in July 1882. At first it was believed Ringo committed suicide, but he was also scalped. Suspicion fell on Buckskin Frank Leslie, his drinking companion of Ringo's last two weeks, but Pony Deal, who knew Ringo as well as anyone, believed the killer was a fellow gambler called Johnny O'Rourke. Whether he was right or wrong, Deal killed O'Rourke over Ringo's death. Wyatt Earp also later claimed to have killed Ringo in retaliation for the murder of his brother Morgan.

It isn't hard to trace where most of the legends about Ringo originated. It was easy enough for people to assume he had been born in Missouri, because he had gone to school there, and that he was born around the early fifties, because he appeared to be about thirty when he was killed. People assumed he took part in the Texas range wars, as his first arrest took place in Austin around that time. He was an enemy of the Earp family, so he may have been one of the four men who bushwhacked Virgil Earp as he left the Oriental Saloon three nights after Christmas 1881. Otherwise, there is little evidence to support his reputation as one of the most lethal outlaws of the Old West. See: **Earp Brothers; Hardin, John Wesley.**

Robber's Roost, prom. 1880s-90s, U.S., hideout. Robber's Roost, along with Hole-in-the-Wall and Brown's Hole, was one of the safest hideouts used by western outlaws. It was tucked away in southeastern Utah's Wayne County, high on the San Rafael Swell plateau summit. The arid countryside offered springs of water for invaders to utilize. On the east was the Green River; the only other routes into the hideaway were from Dandy Crossing and Hanksville. Lookouts in the Roost could see anyone trying to enter from a long distance away, so that approaching posses were not safe. Desperados who hid out at the Robber's Roost included Butch Cassidy, the Sundance Kid, Bob Lee, O.C. Hanks, Harry Tracy, Black Jack Ketchum, Elza Lay, the Missouri Logans, and Dave Lant.

Roberts, Andrew L. (AKA: **Buckshot**), d.1878, U.S., outlaw. A man with a questionable past, Andrew Roberts was thought to be an army deserter, ex-convict, and ardent foe of the Texas Rangers—to which he once belonged. As for Roberts' nickname, Buckshot, there were three possibilities as to how he acquired it. He was fond of using a shotgun, he was always leaving a town followed closely by a load of buckshot, or he was wounded by buckshot and never had the lead removed. He joined the Lincoln County posse which murdered rancher John Tunstall in 1878.

A short time later Sheriff William Brady, who led the raid on Tunstall's ranch, was himself killed by the so-called "Regulators." Roberts realized that he was next on the list to die, so he decided to confront his pursuers at Blazer's Mill, N.M. He armed himself with a pair of six-guns and a Winchester rifle and rode to where these Regulators— George and Frank Coe, Billy the Kid, Henry Brown, Dick Brewer, Charlie Bowdre, and John Middleton—were preparing to take their evening meal. After spotting Roberts, Frank Coe tried to persuade his one-time friend to surrender peaceably. Roberts knew that the Regulators had killed Billy Morton and Frank Baker, two other members of the posse who helped kill Tunstall, after they had laid down their arms. He decided instead to take his chances.

Dick Brewer said he was going to arrest Roberts. Followed by Bowdre, Brown, and George Coe, Brewer confronted Roberts who was still discussing matters with Frank Coe. Charlie Bowdre leveled his gun at Roberts and ordered him to surrender. Roberts refused and, as he grabbed his Winchester, Bowdre fired. A bullet tore through his mid-section and out his back, but he managed to stagger inside Blazer's outhouse where he found a .50-caliber buffalo gun. Brewer and his men encircled the outhouse and again ordered Roberts to surrender, but the wounded gunman issued a steady stream of curses.

Roberts aimed at Brewer and, using the powerful buffalo gun, blew off the top of the Regulator's head. The earlier wounds Roberts had sustained however, ebbed away at his strength. "I'm killed," he told Dr. Emil Blazer, a retired dentist who owned the mill. "No one can help me. It's all over." Blazer conveyed this information to the posse, which left the area to find help for their wounded comrades, Coe and Middleton. When they returned they found Roberts lying dead. He was buried next to Brewer behind the mill.

Roberts, Daniel Webster, 1841-1935, U.S., lawman. A native of Mississippi, Daniel Roberts joined the Company D unit of the Texas Rangers under the direction of Rufe Perry in 1874. Four years later he was promoted to captain and stationed in Sabinal. Roberts was one of the legendary frontiersmen who had a hand in breaking up some of the most dangerous criminal gangs to threaten the peace of the state, including the Mason County Mob, which was dispersed in 1875. In 1880, Roberts and his men were in West Texas where they arrested the Potter gang, and members of the Jesse Evans bunch. When peace had been restored, Roberts sent dispatches to Austin demanding that his men be given fair credit for their part in the roundup. His men revered him, and called him "one of God's noblemen." In 1882, Daniel Roberts resigned his commission because of his wife's deteriorating health, and in 1914 he published a memoir of his adventures with the Texas Rangers.

Roberts, Jim, 1859-1934, U.S., lawman-gunman. A gunfighter for the Tewksbury clan in the Arizona Pleasant Valley War, Jim Roberts was a suspect in the shooting murder of one of the older members of the Graham family and was known to have taken part in several shooting skirmishes.

In a Pleasant Valley, Ariz., gunfight on Aug. 10, 1887, Roberts and five other gunfighters fought their enemies from inside a ranch cabin. Seven cowboys led by Tom Tucker besieged the cabin, from the cover of which the Tewksbury men killed two and wounded three of Tucker's cowhands. John Paine was pinned under his horse. Roberts shot off his right ear and Jim Tewksbury killed him as he tried to run away. John Tewksbury and Bill Jacobs were murdered at dawn on Sept. 2, 1887. Again, Roberts held out along with several other Tewksbury men in another cabin siege. At the end of the day they were able to make their escape but could not help abandoning the two bodies. Another Pleasant Valley skirmish took place on Sept. 16,

1887. The Tewksbury men were ambushed at Cherry Creek and had to shoot back from the blankets they slept in. Jim Roberts and Jim Tewksbury drove off their assailants when they shot Joe Underwood in both legs and fatally wounded Harry Middleton.

When the feud was over, Roberts was cleared of charges and turned lawman for the rest of his life. He spent his later years in Clarkdale, Ariz., where he worked as a special officer for the U.S. Verde Copper Company. In 1928, two thieves robbed the Clarkdale Bank and were racing away in their getaway car when Roberts saw them. Although he was near seventy, he killed one of the bandits with his single-action Colt. The car crashed, and Roberts single-handedly captured the other robber, who surrendered to him quietly. After all his gunfights, Roberts died of a heart attack in 1934.

Roberts, Judd, d.1887, U.S., outlaw. Judd Roberts led four others in 1885, robbing and murdering a Fredericksburg, Texas, rancher named Brautigen. Rangers captured Roberts and a cohort and both were transferred to the supposedly "escape proof" jail in San Antonio. Lynching fever was high in Fredericksburg at the time. When a third Roberts gang member was captured soon after, the local prison "immediately and mysteriously" burned to the ground with the outlaw inside.

Four months after their capture Roberts and his confederate escaped and Roberts began stealing horses in the Panhandle. Regularly visiting friends and relatives in Williamson County, Roberts was soon trailed by Texas Ranger Ira Aten. In April 1887 Roberts, who knew Aten was after him, found out that the Ranger had become friendly with rancher George Wells. Looking for revenge Roberts rode to Wells' ranch and met Aten who ordered him to surrender. Both men fired simultaneously and the wounded Roberts fled, escaping to the Panhandle. Two months later Roberts returned to Williamson County again and had a run-in with rancher John Hughes. Trying to sneak up on Hughes at his Liberty Hill spread in Burnet County, the outlaw stepped onto Hughes' porch at dawn and was confronted by Aten, who had spent the night there waiting for Roberts. Roberts was again wounded in the gunfire, again in his shooting hand, and once more escaped to the Panhandle.

By July 1887, Roberts had established himself at a ranch in the Panhandle and was courting the owner's daughter. One day, at about 200 yards from the ranch house, Roberts was jumped by Hughes and Aten, who had trailed him for weeks. In the face of drawn guns Roberts tipped his gun toward his adversaries and began firing through his holster's open end. Aten's jacket was ripped with a bullet, but Roberts took six shots from chest to groin. While dying, he confessed to Brautigen's murder and was then carried by wagon to his would-be bride's arms, where he died.

Robertson, Ben F. (AKA: **Ben Wheeler; Ben F. Burton**), 1854-84, U.S., lawman-outlaw. The son of a respected Texas family, with a brother who became general land agent for the state, Ben F. Robertson, fled the state in 1878. Following a dispute Robertson severely wounded his opponent and left, abandoning his wife and four children and going to Cheyenne where he worked as a cowboy for a few years. He eventually went to Indianola, Neb.

In Nebraska Robertson, using the name Ben F. Burton, married Alice Wheeler in November 1881. After living with Wheeler at her parents' house for a year, Robertson deserted his second wife and went to Caldwell, Kan., where he was appointed deputy by Marshal Henry Brown in December 1882 and lived under the alias of Ben Wheeler. When his second wife tracked him down to Caldwell he convinced her to go back to Indianola by promising to send money to her and their child. On Apr. 11, 1883, Robertson was one of five lawmen who surrounded the camp of stock thief Ross and his family near Hunnewell, Kan. When dawn came, the posse ordered Ross to surrender. Instead the robber and his two sons opened fire. Thirty minutes later one of Ross' sons was dead and the other wounded, and Ross gave up. On Nov. 21, Robertson accompanied Cash Hollister, who was going to arrest Chet Van Meter in Caldwell. When Robertson ordered Van Meter to put up his hands the fugitive responded by firing. Hollister and Robertson shot Van Meter dead.

On Apr. 30, 1884, Henry Brown and Robertson traveled to Medicine Lodge, allegedly in search of a killer but actually intending to rob the Medicine Valley Bank in what would come to be known as one of the West's most notorious robberies. Accompanied by John Wesley and William Smith, the two men rode into Medicine Lodge in a driving rain. When Robertson, Brown and Wesley entered the bank in the morning they found President E.W. Payne and cashier George Geppert inside. Payne reached for a gun and was fatally wounded by Brown, while Robertson turned in panic to Geppert. Although Geppert raised his hands above his head, Robertson shot him twice and Geppert stumbled into the vault, locked the door, and died. Riding out of town with the posse after them, the three outlaws were soon chased into a box canyon and surrendered after a two hour siege.

Locked in a log building the three robbers were descended on by a mob at about 9 p.m. As Brown tried to run away he was shot down and killed. Robertson ran in the opposite direction, but a bullet set his vest on fire, making him an easy target; he was gunned down by three bullets—one in his right arm, and two shooting off two fingers of his left hand—before he had run 100 yards. Robertson was taken with Smith and Wesley to a tree and ropes were draped over it. Although he begged for mercy, swearing he would tell "many things that would interest the community at large," he was hanged along with his cohorts. See: **Brown, Henry Newton.**

Rogers, Bob, 1873-95, U.S., outlaw. Easily impressed by the lurid tales of the Dalton Gang, 19-year-old Bob Rogers decided in 1892, to follow in their footsteps. That year he stole a dozen horses from the Cherokee Nation and transported them into Arkansas where they were sold. Rogers was arrested by Deputy Marshal Heck Bruner and brought before Judge Isaac Parker, who decided to release him on probation because of his age. "This is your first offense lad," Parker said. "If you continue in this path of life, death may be the penalty." Rogers paid scant attention to the warning.

On Nov. 3, 1892, Rogers got into a drunken altercation with Deputy Constable Jess W. Elliott, a Cherokee who had arrived in Catoosa (Okla.) to serve papers on another criminal offender. Rogers, a man with a quick, violent temper, knocked Elliott to the floor and nearly beat him to death. Bystanders separated the pair and hustled Rogers out of the pool hall before he killed the man. Elliott was revived and put back on his horse. However, Rogers was still lurking in the shadows and as Elliott attempted to ride out of town, he was dragged off of the horse and stabbed three times in the neck. The unfortunate constable died within twenty minutes. The townspeople built a fire and watched over the body while someone went to get Deputy Marshal John Taylor. A witness to the tragedy described what Rogers did next. He "rode through the fire, ran them off, kicked and stamped the lifeless body of his victim, put on and wore his hat for a while, looked through the papers in his pocket and left."

Rogers evaded capture for the next several months. He organized a gang of desperados on the frontier and returned to the Indian Territory to rob the Missouri-Kansas-Texas Railroad at Kelso, Mo., the Mound Valley Bank in Labette County, Kan., and the Kansas and Arkansas Valley train. The slippery Rogers evaded the lawmen at every turn. On Jan. 8, 1894, he was seemingly cornered at the home of his brother-in-law Henry Daniels. Deputy Marshal W.C. Smith found Rogers sitting before the fire. Daniels was instructed to go upstairs and bring down gang member Bob

Stiteler for the ride back to jail. But as the men were about to leave the house, Rogers whirled around and knocked the lawman to the floor. Stiteler was quickly recaptured, but Rogers continued to remain at large. Two weeks later Heck Bruner's posse killed two other gang members and arrested Dynamite Jack near Big Creek. Again, Bob Rogers succeeded in avoiding the trap. His end finally came on Mar. 13, 1895, when Deputy Marshal Jim Mayes located the fugitive at his

Outlaw Bob Rogers.

father's house in Horseshoe Mound (Okla.) The dwelling was surrounded by peace officers who trained a gun on every window and door, should Rogers decide to make another run for it.

Rogers' father answered the door, and when he was advised about the hopelessness of his son's situation, he pointed to the upstairs bedroom.

"Come down, Bob, and surrender," Mayes called out.

"Come up and get me!" came the reply.

Deputies W.C. McDaniel, C.E. Smith, and Phil Williams cautiously proceeded up the darkened stairwell when a volley of fire erupted from the bedroom. McDaniel was killed instantly, and Williams was severely wounded in the arm. The officers reformed outside the home and braced for what appeared to be a siege. Shots were exchanged, but Rogers remained defiant. "I'll give up after I'm killed!" he shouted. More than three hundred bullets pierced the building, but Rogers did not sustain so much as a scratch. Many minutes passed. Finally Rogers offered to come out if he could be allowed to keep his weapon. Mayes instructed Rogers to "keep the muzzle down."

Rogers appeared outside the door with McDaniel's abandoned Winchester. "Do you have a warrant for me?" the felon demanded.

"We don't need one," Mayes answered.

With that, Bob Rogers raised the muzzle of his gun. Before he could fire a dozen guns took aim and fired, fatally shooting the youth.

Ross, Kit, 1861-86, U.S., outlaw. A Cherokee half-breed named Kit Ross, incurred the wrath of his neighbor Jonathan Davis one night in 1883, when, in a drunken stupor, he rode his horse into his neighbor's home. Davis, whose wife was ill at the time, forcibly ejected Ross and admonished him not to return. The two men seemed to have reconciled their differences and agreed to live peaceably. However, Ross continued to harbor bitterness toward Davis. His attitude festered for a long time, until the two men ran into each other on Dec. 20, 1885, at a store in Choteau (Okla.). Ross was obviously drunk again.

"Kit, I believe we will have some snow," Davis said, good naturedly. "Yes, I believe we will," Ross replied. With that, he whipped out his pistol and discharged two shots into Davis' back. The half-breed was arrested and convicted of murder at Fort Smith (Ark.). Before he was hanged on Aug. 6, 1886, he told the jury: "Well, they done it to me."

Rowdy Joe, See: Lowe, Joseph.

Rudabaugh, David, 1840-86, U.S., outlaw. After coming to notoriety in the late 1870s as the head of a gang of thieves and rustlers in Texas, David Rudabaugh shifted his activities to Kansas by 1878. Leading four men in a train holdup at Kinsley on Jan. 27, Rudabaugh was caught, with Edgar West, in camp a few days later by Bat Masterson and his posse. When Rudabaugh went for his gun John Joshua Webb stopped him and forced him to surrender. Two of his accomplices were arrested later but Rudabaugh bargained for release by informing against his cohorts.

Promising to go straight and "earn his living on the square" Rudabaugh drifted to New Mexico and soon was thieving again. In 1879 he reunited with some of his cronies from Kansas and they terrorized the city for six months, committing train and stagecoach robberies as the "Dodge City Gang," which was supported by City Marshall John Joshua Webb, Rudabaugh's former enemy. When Webb was arrested on murder charges in 1880, the gang broke up. Trying to release Webb from jail Rudabaugh managed only to murder peace officer Deputy Sheriff Lino Valdez. Rudabaugh fled to Fort Sumner and joined forces with Billy the Kid's gang. After several shooting and rustling forays and the stubborn pursuit of Pat Garrett, Rudabaugh surrendered along with the Kid in December 1880.

On Nov. 30-31, 1880, Billy the Kid, Billy Wilson and Rudabaugh rode into White Oaks, N.M., and ran into Deputy Sheriff James Redman. When they shot at him he hid behind Will Hudgen's saloon but several local citizens ran into the street and chased the fugitives out of town. Hiding at Jim Greathouse's ranch they were accosted by a posse at dawn but managed to escape by trading their hostage, Greathouse, for Deputy Sheriff James Carlyle. At midnight Carlyle tried to escape through a window but was killed by gunfire which may have come from either the outlaws or the posse. After discovering their murdered colleague, the angry posse burned down the ranch house but Rudabaugh and his companions had already escaped.

Trailed by the resolute Pat Garrett, Billy the Kid, Wilson, Rudabaugh, Tom O'Folliard, Charlie Bowdre, and Tom Pickett rode wearily into Fort Sumner, N.M., on Dec. 19, 1880, and were confronted by Garrett's posse which had been hiding in an old post hospital building. In the shooting match Rudabaugh's horse was killed and he rode out of town behind Wilson. O'Folliard was fatally wounded and surrendered, dying within an hour. Rudabaugh and the other outlaws holed up in an abandoned cabin near Stinking Springs.

The determined Garrett and his posse tracked the outlaws down to Stinking Springs and surrounded the hideout. Bowdre stepped outside at dawn and was killed. When the remaining four tried to retrieve their horses Garrett killed one and shot the reins of the others away. After an all-day hold out, Rudabaugh waved the white flag and the bandits surrendered. After being convicted of murder and sentenced to death, Rudabaugh was held in a Las Vegas prison where Webb was serving time. Webb, Rudabaugh, Thomas Duffy, and H.S. Wilson tried unsuccessfully to shoot their way out on Sept. 19, 1881, Duffy was mortally wounded. Two months later, Webb and Rudabaugh escaped by digging their way out through the walls; they fled to Mexico where Webb disappeared. On Feb. 18, 1886 Rudabaugh was involved in a cantina card game in Parral, Mex., which broke up over accusations of cheating. Rudabaugh and a Mexican man faced off and Rudabaugh shot him through the head. When another player drew and fired Rudabaugh shot him through the heart. Unable to find his horse, Rudabaugh returned to the cantina, which was now in total darkness. On entering, Rudabaugh was jumped and decapitated. See: **Billy the Kid.**

Rumley, Charles S., prom. 1853, U.S., lawman. Charles S. Rumley succeeded John G. Jones as the territorial marshal of New Mexico on Apr. 5, 1853. His appointment was engineered by Hugh N. Smith, a politically connected member of the Masonic Order and a champion of the anti-home rule movement. Smith ran a thriving commercial business in Santa Fe and was able to convince President Franklin Pierce to name Rumley to the key post after some considerable arm bending.

During his short tenure of office (Rumley served only five months and was replaced by Charles Blumner on Dec. 10, 1853), Charles Rumley contributed very little. Shortly

before he stepped down, he organized a posse to track down several Mexicans who were responsible for the murder of an Apache tribal chief in the village of Dona Ana. Rumley asked Mexican officers to arrest the suspects, but they refused. As the area in which the crime occurred was not officially incorporated into the U.S. until the Gadsden Purchase was completed later that year, military officials from Fort Fillmore were reluctant to deploy their forces into disputed land to look for the Mexicans. Rumley quietly disbanded the posse and returned to Santa Fe. See: **Blumner, Charles.**

Russell, Baldy, See: **Mitchell, William.**

Russell, Richard Robertson (AKA: **Dick**), 1858-1922, U.S., lawman. At the age of thirteen, Richard Russell arrived in Menard County, Texas, where he worked as a cowboy. With the money he earned, Russell purchased 100 head of cattle. Russell enlisted in the Texas Rangers in 1880 and was stationed in Kimble County. From 1886-96, Russell was sheriff of Menard, but continued to send part of his paycheck to friends and business associates who purchased cattle for his growing ranch. When his law enforcement days were over, Russell devoted his energies to the Cattle Raiser's Association, where he served as an officer for many years. Russell became a successful rancher and then moved to San

Richard Russell

Antonion in 1905. He became president of the State Bank and lived in San Antonio until his death on June 28, 1922.

Russian Bill, See: **King, Sandy.**

Rynning, Thomas H., 1866-1941, U.S., lawman. Orphaned at twelve, Tom Rynning drifted west when he was a teenager to work as a cowboy and a teamster in Texas. In 1885, he joined the Eighth U.S. Cavalry and was transferred from Texas to Arizona where he took part in the final campaign against Geronimo. In 1891 he left the service to work as a performer in Buffalo Bill Cody's Wild West Show. He later rode during the Spanish-American War with Teddy Roosevelt's Rough Riders. After marrying and settling in Arizona Territory, Rynning was appointed captain of the Rangers there in 1902, a post he held for five years until he was appointed superintendent of the Yuma Territorial Prison.

In 1902, in Douglas, another Arizona Ranger named Webb investigated a gunshot in the Douglas' Cowboy Saloon and was threatened at gunpoint by the owner whom Webb killed with two shots. Rynning and two other rangers went into the saloon. One of the rangers was wounded, but Rynning ended the conflict by shooting the gambler who had wounded his man. In 1904, Rynning and ranger Dave Allison trailed the one-armed murderer of a schoolteacher to his hideout in the Chiricahua Mountains, burst inside, and wounded him in the leg and hip. In Summer 1906 in northern Mexico, a group of miners revolted against the U.S. engineers in the Cananea Mountains. Rynning was made a colonel and placed in command of 300 volunteers from the U.S. who had been accepted by the Mexican army. In a subsequent battle, Rynning was attacked by three Mexican snipers, all of whom he wounded and drove away. Rynning died at the age of seventy-five in 1941.

S

Said, John (AKA: **Rattlesnake Jack**), d.1882, U.S., gunman. John Said had single-handedly turned the quiet little town of Weiser City, Idaho, into his own private playground. Most often he could be found inside the Gem Saloon, carousing until dawn. On the evening of Nov. 21, 1882, the freewheeling cowboy ordered the bartender, John Smith, to serve drinks all around. "Rattlesnake Jack," as he was called, told Smith to put it on his bill, which the bartender could not do, given Said's poor credit history. Said produced a six-shooter and pointed it in Smith's face. When several other men rushed to the bartender's defense, Said backed away from the fight and retreated into the street, where Deputy Sheriff George Porter tried to arrest him. Said whipped out his pistol and fired at the deputy, but Porter was faster on the draw; he discharged a bullet into Said's hip. Thinking the matter was over, Porter retired to the saloon, only to find that Said was still itching for a fight. Said re-entered the saloon and shot Porter in the leg. Porter returned fire from his shotgun hitting Said in the chest, but only one barrel of the gun worked. When Said managed to pin the officer to the wall, Hans Matson, a bystander, shot and killed Said.

St. Leon, Ernest (AKA: **Diamond Dick**), d.1891, U.S., lawman. The son of a refugee from France, Ernest St. Leon was raised in San Antonio, Texas. He studied law but later joined the U.S. Cavalry, participated in a number of Indian campaigns, and eventually was promoted to sergeant. He was alleged to have shot and killed three Indians who had slain one of his men. St. Leon left the army in the 1880s and joined the Texas Rangers' Company D, where he gained the nickname "Diamond Dick" because he enjoyed decorating himself with large diamonds.

A drinking problem got St. Leon kicked out of the Rangers, but Corporal John Hughes sent him on an undercover mission which he managed so well that he was soon reinstated and given other clandestine assignments. In 1889, in Shafter, Texas, St. Leon, pretending to be an ore thief, went with three criminals and a mule train to an abandoned mine shaft. Rangers Lon Oden and John Hughes were waiting in the darkness and called to the criminals to surrender. A fight erupted, with St. Leon opening up on the thieves at close range. All three criminals were slain and buried on the mountainside. In 1891, St. Leon and a deputized citizen arrested three cowboys, but St. Leon decided to release them. All five man went to a bar to drink together. There a fight erupted and St. Leon and the deputy were shot. The deputy died immediately, St. Leon the next day.

Salazar, Hijino, 1863-1936, U.S., gunman. At the age of fifteen, Hijino Salazar signed on with the Alexander McSween faction, which was then engaged in a bloody range war in Lincoln County, N.M., against Lawrence Murphy, a politically connected businessman who controlled a large general store known as the "House," which sold beef to the government. Salazar participated in only one gunfight of note. This occurred on July 15-19, 1878, when the Murphy faction laid siege to the McSween store in Lincoln. Salazar was trapped inside the building when the opposing forces set the adobe hut on fire. The young Mexican waited until the cover of darkness before he attempted an escape. After releasing the bolt, he slipped out the back, but a hail of bullets tore into his back, chest, and side.

Though seriously wounded, Salazar realized his only chance for survival was to feign death. As Murphy's men walked among the fallen McSween men, gunman Andy Boyle said it might be a good idea to pump one more shot into what appeared to be the lifeless frame of Salazar. His companion, a man named Pierce, commented that they should not waste the bullet. When they had gone, Salazar crawled toward the Rio Bonito River where he refreshed himself in the water. He then made his way to his brother's home where he received medical attention. After recovering his health, Salazar joined Governor Lew Wallace's "Lincoln County Rifleman" brigade, which helped restore law and order to the countryside. Salazar had one last confrontation with the criminal world before hanging up his gun and living a quiet life. In April 1881, Salazar supplied Billy the Kid, with a file and other necessary tools which enabled him to shoot his way out of the Lincoln County jail. See: **Billy the Kid**.

Sample, Omer W. (AKA: **Red, George Lincoln**), 1860-84, U.S., outlaw. Omer Sample was born in Missouri, but confined much of his criminal activity to the Arizona Territory, where he rode with the John Heath outlaw gang. On Dec. 7, 1883, Sample and his cohorts robbed a store in Clifton, and brutally murdered several men and a woman. Sample, Tex Howard, and Dan Kelly fled into the mountains during the middle of a blinding snowstorm and were thus able to escape the posse sent out to track them down. On Dec. 17, he was captured near Black Jack Canyon, forty miles south of Tombstone. With a bullet deeply lodged in his back, Sample was returned to Tombstone with other members of the gang who had been previously arrested and taken into custody.

The jury handed down a Guilty verdict in the Clifton shooting on Feb. 20, 1884, and sentenced Sample to death on the gallows. He protested the decision, arguing that he and Heath were miles away at the time of the robbery. A vigilante mob took matters in hand and strung up Heath from a pole. Sample was hanged on Mar. 8, 1884, with four other men. See: **Heath, John**.

Sand Creek Massacre, 1864, U.S., mur. John Chivington was the minister and soldier who commanded the slaughter of as many as 450 Indian men, women, and children in the Sand Creek Massacre of Nov. 29, 1864, in the Cheyenne Territory in Colorado. Known as the "Fighting Parson," Chivington preached the gospel in Illinois, Ohio, Missouri, Kansas, and Nebraska before settling in Denver, Colo., in 1860 to preside over the First Methodist Episcopal Church. Chivington spread the good word throughout the mining camps, and opened the first permanent Methodist Sunday school in Denver. When the Civil War broke out, Governor William Gilpin awarded Chivington an active commission. He became a hero to the Union sympathizers in New Mexico by driving the Confederate army out of the territory as a result of a lethal surprise attack he launched at La Glorieta Pass, east of Santa Fe.

Chivington did not return to the pulpit but continued his military career in active pursuit of hostile Indians who rode the Colorado plains. On the morning of Nov. 29, 1864, Colonel Chivington led the Third Colorado Volunteers against a docile tribe of Cheyenne encamped at Sand Creek. The Indians believed they were under the protection of the U.S. Army, but Chivington saw matters differently. He ordered his men to take no prisoners. The soldiers carried out the mandate with ruthless abandon, raping and slaughtering the Indians—mainly women and children. Returning to Denver, the troopers displayed the grisly souvenirs collected at the scene before a cheering throng of spectators. They held aloft Indian scalps and the genitalia of the victims.

Following the mass murder, an investigation was carried out by the Committee on the Conduct of the War, the military, and a joint congressional committee in March 1865. Chivington was publicly censured for his actions, and an attempt was made to court-martial him, but since he had resigned his commission in January 1865, there was little the government could do in the way of punishment. According to most sources, Chivington allegedly was never

able to work again, tainted by the stigma of the massacre. In reality he moved to Denver, Colo., and got a job as an under-sheriff, a post he held for several years until his death in 1894. Chivington was said to have performed honorably and won the respect of those who worked with him, despite his notorious past. See: **Reynolds Gang**.

Sanders, Osee, 1847-76, U.S., outlaw. Thomas S. Carlyle and his Cherokee wife were sitting on the veranda in their Tahlequah (Okla.) home in the Indian Territory on the night of Aug. 6, 1875, when Osee Sanders, twenty-nine, and an unnamed confederate rode up to their gate on horseback. Carlyle knew Sanders and welcomed him to his home. He sent his son to open the gate for the two men, when suddenly Sanders brandished a pistol. The Indian woman turned and fled into the tall grass with her son as the shots rang out. When she returned, she found her husband lying in a pool of blood. His money was gone, $1,200 in cash, and Cherokee Court warrants had been removed from the house. Sanders was arrested the next day, but the second man escaped and was never found. Brought before Judge Isaac Parker, the accused man refused to identify his associate. Sanders was convicted and hanged at Fort Smith (Ark.) on Sept. 8, 1876.

San Francisco Vigilance Committee, prom. 1851-56, U.S., law enfor. agency. The state of lawlessness brought on by the discovery of gold in California became a growing concern among the peaceful citizens of San Francisco. In 1851 the population of the city was estimated to be 30,000, with a relative amount of saloons and gambling halls. Yet only twelve policemen were assigned to safeguard the lives and property of the San Francisco citizens. Alarmed that the criminal element was poised to take over the city, William T. Coleman and eleven other civic leaders organized the Vigilance Committee in June 1851. They wrote a controversial five-point constitution that essentially allowed members to take the law into their own hands when the situation demanded.

The committee took its first action June 10, 1851, when burglar John Jenkins attempted to cross the Bay towing a stolen safe. Jenkins was arrested and housed in the headquarters of the Vigilance Committee on Battery Street. The committee passed the death sentence and gave warning to all by ringing the bell on the Monumental Engine Company firehouse. The execution of Jenkins had an immediate effect. The criminal classes paused, and for a short time the city was quiet.

California governor John McDougall issued a written protest, but privately, he applauded their efforts. Nevertheless, the committee temporarily disbanded operations on Sept. 16, only to quietly reorganize some months later. The shooting of James King, editor of the San Francisco *Bulletin*, on May 14, 1856, instigated a renewal of vigilantism in the city. Armed with artillery, the vigilantes forced the sheriff to hand over the two murderers, Charles Cora and James Casey, who were promptly taken to the scaffold and hanged. By August, support for the Vigilance Committee waned. Gradually the movement evolved to one of political activism through more legitimate channels. They renamed the committee the People's Party, and remained a force in local politics for many years. See: **Coleman, William Tell**.

Scarborough, George W., d.1900, U.S., lawman.

The son of a Baptist preacher, George W. Scarborough became a Texas cowboy, a lawman, and a range detective. He served as Jones County sheriff and as a U.S. deputy marshall in the El Paso area in the 1890s, dealing with gunmen John Selman, Wes Hardin, and Jeff Milton. Scarborough played his part in a plan to lure fugitive cattle rustler Martin Morose back across the Texas-Mexico border,

Western lawman George Scarborough.

when he met Morose on a bridge over the Rio Grande late on the night of June 21, 1895. As Scarborough and Morose crossed over the bridge into Texas, Deputy Marshall Jeff Milton and Texas Ranger Frank McMahon opened fire and killed Morose.

John Selman, Scarborough's fellow lawmen and also his friend, accused Scarborough of stealing money from Morose's corpse. At 4 a.m. on Easter Sunday, Apr. 2, 1896, Scarborough came into El Paso's Wigwam Saloon where Selman sat drinking himself into a stupor. They went into the alley to quarrel and Scarborough drew his gun and fired, hitting Selman and then shooting into the prostrate form of the old gunman three more times. As he lay dying, Selman gasped out to a gathering crowd, "you know I am not afraid of any man; but I never drew my gun." Scarborough was found Not Guilty of murdering his one-time friend.

In July 1898 he assisted Jeff Milton in a search of eastern Arizona for outlaw Bronco Bill Walters. Finding him near Solomonville the officers shot it out with Walters and his companions Red Pipkin and Bill Johnson. Walters, who lived only to be sent to jail, was shot out of his saddle, Pipkin fled to safety on foot after his horse was killed, and Johnson was mortally wounded.

Scarborough later resigned from his post as deputy and became a detective for the Grant County Cattleman's Association. On Apr. 5, 1900, he was working near San Simon, Ariz., assisted by rancher Walter Birchfield as they traced some rustlers associated with Butch Cassidy's notorious Wild Bunch. The two detectives chased the outlaws into a canyon where a bullet from bandit Harvey Logan's gun tore through Scarborough's leg and killed his mount. Abandoning the hunt, Birchfield rode to San Simon to get a wagon. That night he transported Scarborough to the railroad and sent him to Deming, N.M., where his leg was amputated. Scarborough died the next day. See: **Selman, John**.

Scurlock, Josiah G. (AKA: Doc), d.1882, U.S., gunman.

In 1868, in his home state of Tennessee, Josiah G. Scurlock got into a fight with his brother-in-law over a calf. When his brother-in-law tried to push the animal away, Scurlock threatened, "Don't you dare drive that cow beyond my gate. I'll kill you if you do." His brother-in-law persisted and Scurlock emptied both barrels of a shotgun into his body. Fleeing to South America he worked his way back through Mexico toward the U.S., hiring on as a cowhand on John Chisum's sprawling ranch. In 1876, Scurlock was involved in the killing of his friend Mark Harkins, later ruled an accidental death.

After marrying a native of New Mexico, Scurlock secured a small spread of his own but left it to hire on as one of the McSween "Regulators" during the Lincoln County War. On Mar. 9, 1878, in Steel Springs, N.M., Scurlock and several other Regulators followed Dick Brewer in a hunt for murder suspects Billy Morton and Frank Baker, whom they captured. An argument about the fugitives on the trip back to Lincoln ended with the

Western gunman Josiah Scurlock.

posse killing Baker and Morton, with Regulator William McCloskey slain in the gunfire. Scurlock also was present at the Blazer's Mill gunfight in which Dick Brewer and Buckshot Roberts were killed, and he also participated in the Regulator raid on a Pecos County cow camp near Black River in Lincoln County. Scurlock, Charlie Bowdre, George Coe, Henry Brown, and three Anglos—one may have been Billy the Kid—along with eleven Mexicans attacked an Indian camp, driving off the herders and taking all the horses, killing two Indians, and wounding two others.

Tiring of cattle rustling and living as a fugitive, Scurlock rejoined his family, working on Pete Maxwell's ranch in Fort Sumner. By 1882 he was at John Chisum's ranch at Seven Rivers, N.M., and there he began cursing and threatening Fred Roth with a gun. Roth, who was carrying a baby, went inside his house, put down the baby and picked up a rifle, then went back outside and told Scurlock he was ready. Both men fired and Scurlock was hit with two or three slugs. Collapsing, he told Roth, "That's enough. You've got me, Fred. Don't shoot any more." Roth tried to fire again but was stopped by bystander Elias Bly. Scurlock died minutes later. See: **Lincoln County War; Regulator War.**

Selman, John, 1839-96, U.S., lawman-gunman. Son of an English schoolteacher, John Selman was raised in Arkansas and moved with his family to Grayson, Texas, in 1858 at age nineteen. During the Civil War he joined the Confederate cavalry and was stationed in Oklahoma, but in 1863 deserted and went to Fort Davis, Texas, with his family. Enlisting in the state militia in 1864, Selman worked for frontier defense and soon was elected lieutenant by his neighbors.

John Selman, schoolteacher turned western lawman.

Marrying Edna de Graffenreid a year later, they moved to Colfax County, N.M., in 1869, but returned to Texas, near Fort Griffin, after a year. In the 1870s Selman was involved in several conflicts with Indians, allegedly killing several. He was also believed to have murdered a local man named Haulph.

Selman became a close friend and business partner of John Larn, a gunfighter and rustler who became sheriff of Shackleford County. Selman also became acquainted with western figures Bat Masterson, Doc Holliday, "Killin'" Jim Miller, Jesse Evans, Wyatt Earp, and Pat Garrett. Though he owned a saloon and other property, Selman rustled cattle with Larn. In 1876, he was helping arrest a suspect named Hampton who was unarmed and half deaf. Neither Larn nor Selman were aware of his condition, and after Hampton apparently ignored Larn's command to stop, Selman emptied his gun into him. Larn and Selman subsequently returned to rustling. Texas Rangers were pressured to put an end to their exploits, which resulted in bushwhackings from both sides.

When Larn was arrested and murdered by a mob in early 1878, Selman fled the country. While he was gone his wife, pregnant with their fifth child, died. Selman drifted back into Lincoln County with his brother, Tom Selman, later that summer and formed "Selman's Scouts," a gang of outlaws who rustled cattle and robbed stores until pressure from the U.S. Army caused them to disband. Before their break-up, in May 1878 Selman was ambushed by a local farmer enraged at his rustling, and Selman killed the man with his buffalo gun. In September, Selman murdered a gunman named Hart as they competed for leadership of a Lincoln County gang. Selman shot Hart without warning as they waited together in a cabin for a meal. The next month Selman murdered a trouble-making "Selman Scout" in a fight over a poker hand when they were camped out on the Pecos River.

In the next several years Selman drifted around the West, rustling, robbing, and occasionally working in Mexico, Texas, and New Mexico. He married again, lost his second wife, and moved to El Paso in 1888 after being cleared of rustling charges in Texas. After leading several cattle drives he was elected to the post of city constable in 1892. In 1893 he married a 16-year-old girl. In 1894 he murdered deputy U.S. Marshal Bass Outlaw who, while drunk, murdered Texas Ranger Joe McKidrict in a brothel. Selman was shot and wounded in the fight and used a cane for the rest of his life.

The next year he killed the famous gunfighter John Wesley Hardin who allegedly had taken money from the body of outlaw Martin Morose, with whose wife he was having an affair, and then reneged on his promise to split the take with Selman. He killed Hardin by shooting him in the back. The murder trial resulted in a hung jury with a retrial scheduled, but Selman was killed before the case again came to court. A heavy drinker by that time, Selman was in a near stupor on April 5, 1896, when fellow lawman George W. Scarborough met him in an El Paso saloon. They stepped into an alley to discuss their fight over the money Selman believed Scarborough had gotten from Morose's corpse. Scarborough fired four shots into Selman who never drew his gun. He died the next day. See: **Hardin, John Wesley; Scarborough, George W.**

Shadley, Lafe, d.1893, U.S., lawman. An Oklahoman law officer, Lafe Shadley, gained fame for his clashes with outlaws during the 1890s. In 1892, in Osage County, Shadley crossed the trail of bank robber and rustler Dan "Dynamite Dick" Clifton. When Shadley tried to take Clifton, a gunfight left Clifton wounded in the neck, but he escaped.

Lawmen around the Ingalls, Okla., area were informed that outlaw Bill Doolin and six of his Oklahombres gang members were tearing up the town. Two wagons of officers headed toward Ingalls. Coming in from the south at around 10 a.m. was Shadley, along with W.C. Roberts, Jim Masterson, Henry Keller, George Cox, Hi Thompson, and H.A. Janson. Their wagon circled Ingalls and stopped by a grove of trees near the residence of Dr. Pickering. At the same time a wagon driven by Dick Speed, accompanied by John W. Hixon, J.S. Burke, Tom Houston, Red Lucas and Ike Steel, rode in from the north. Men from the posse infiltrated the town and shooting began when Speed fired on Bitter Creek Newcomb. Arkansas Tom Jones, who was firing from a hotel window, fatally shot Speed and the injured Newcomb rode out of town. Doolin and four of the Oklahombres began shooting from inside a saloon and the gunfire became so intense that a local boy, Del Simmons, and a stray horse were both slain.

When Doolin and his gunmen raced to a nearby livery stable Shadley hid behind the dead horse and fired on the front door of the stable. Then Bill Dalton, Tulsa Jack Blake, and Red Buck Waightman came tearing through the door on horseback as Doolin and Dan Clifton rode out the back door. Jones' sniping fire wounded Houston and one of Hixon's bullets clipped Dalton's horse in the jaw. Dalton spurred the wounded animal on but Shadley dropped the horse with a bullet to its leg. Dalton grabbed some wire cutters and began ripping at a fence which blocked his way out of town. Shadley hid behind a storm cellar, crawled under a fence, and then was spotted by Dalton who pumped three bullets into his body. Dalton finished cutting up the fence, jumped up behind Doolin, and sprinted out of Ingalls. Jones surrendered after another hour of gun fire and the battle was over. Shadley and Houston were taken to Stillwater, along with Speed's corpse, and their relatives and friends were called in. Both lawmen died the next morning. See: **Doolin, William.**

Shepherd, Oliver, d.1868, U.S., outlaw. During the Civil War Oliver Shepherd battled and robbed with the Missouri guerrillas before joining the James-Younger Gang of outlaws which included Jesse James and Cole, John, James, and Robert Younger. On Feb. 13, 1866, Shepherd and eleven other gang members committed the first daylight bank robbery in the U.S. in Liberty, Mo. Shooting broke out as the robbers were riding out of town with the stolen $57,000. George Wymore, a college student, was caught in the fire and killed.

On Mar. 21, 1868, eight members of the James-Younger Gang, including Shepherd, rode into Russelville, Ky., and robbed the Southern Bank of Kentucky of $14,000. Bank president Nimrod Long was wounded in the head and the gang fled, shooting as they left. An intensive manhunt followed and George Shepherd, Oliver's cousin, was arrested. The gang dispersed with Oliver returning to Missouri trailed by a Kentucky posse. In Jackson County, Mo., he was confronted by another posse and ordered to surrender. Shepherd instead drew his gun and attempted to shoot his way to safety. He was killed, with twenty bullets tearing into his body.

Sherman, James D. (AKA: **Jim Talbot**), d.1896, U.S., gunman. James D. Sherman, also known as "Jim Talbot," assisted in trailing a cattle herd from Texas to Caldwell, Kan., in 1881. In Caldwell, Sherman rented a house for his wife and two children. Known as a desperado, he spent several weeks drinking with friends and carousing around town. On Dec. 17, 1881, he and six of his friends, Bob Bigtree, Dick Eddleman, Tom Love, Bub Munson, George Speers, and Jim Martin went on a Friday night drinking binge, became abrasive and threatened to kill a local newspaper editor and Mike Meagher, a former marshal. The next morning Meagher protested to Marshal John Wilson, who soon arrested Love for shooting off his gun. Sherman and his gang jumped Wilson and released Love. When Wilson asked Meagher for help the gang again threatened to murder Meagher.

At 1 p.m. Wilson arrested Martin and fined him for carrying a gun. Deputy Marshal Will Fossett walked down the street with him so Martin could get funds to pay the fine. Sherman, Eddleman, Munson, and Love grabbed Martin and Sherman fired two shots at Wilson, then began running with Meagher and Wilson chasing him. When he reached the Opera House Sherman turned and fired his Winchester, killing Meagher with a bullet through the chest. An angry mob went after the cowboys. Speers was fatally shot and most of the gang's horses were wounded as the men rode out of town. Pursued several miles into Indian Territory by the irate citizens, the gang hid in a dugout. After they wounded W.E. Campbell their pursuers retreated.

In 1894 Sherman was arrested at his ranch in California, probably for murdering a man in Mendocino County. In 1895 his trial for the murder of Meagher ended in a hung jury and he was acquitted at a second trial. In August 1896

Sherman returned to his Ukiah, Calif., ranch. A concealed assassin—possibly John Meagher avenging his brother's death, but more probably Sherman's wife's lover—fired a shotgun when Sherman was fifty feet from his gate, severing his spinal cord and killing him instantly.

Sherman, John E., Jr., 1846-1912, U.S., lawman. When John Pratt stepped down after serving ten years as New Mexico's marshal, Republican party boss Stephen B. Elkins named John E. Sherman, Jr., his replacement, with the blessing of President Ulysses S. Grant. Sherman was a member of an old and highly respected Ohio family. He was the nephew of both Senator John Sherman and General William Tecumseh Sherman, who sliced through Georgia during the climactic days of the Civil War. John Sherman's political connections extended all the way to the White House. His business partner was Frederick Grant, son of the president.

Marshal Sherman assumed his duties on May 24, 1876. He was greeted unenthusiastically by the residents of the territory who sensed that his appointment was little more than another example of political cronyism. Sherman took over at a time when the Colfax County War was in full swing and lawlessness pervaded the territory. Highway robbers and cattle rustlers threatened the southern counties, and stagecoaches were routinely held up outside Albuquerque. In January 1876, cattle baron John Chisum became one of the victims of the holdup men when his stagecoach was waylaid in Cook's Canyon, east of Silver City. Fortunately for Chisum, he managed to conceal most of his money from the thieves who made off with only $100. Chisum was an outspoken critic, who complained about the increase in cattle rustling in the territory. Not even the U.S. Cavalry was able to track down the rustlers who raided Blazer's Mill in February 1876. The unhappy cattle barons took matters into their own hands the following July when they seized suspected horse thief Jose Segura from the local jail and hanged him.

Sherman seemed powerless to do anything about the lawlessness. He only succeeded in inflaming the strained relations between the press and the marshal's office when he reappointed Robert Widenmann, the impetuous young deputy marshal who created a storm of controversy by notifying the authorities in Washington that the murder of businessman John H. Tunstall was engineered by the Santa Fe Ring, of which Sheriff William Brady was a member. (Brady had arrested Widenmann on charges of fomenting a riot during the time he tried to bring accused murderer Jesse Evans to justice.) Sherman demonstrated surprising political independence by reappointing Widenmann. But he realized that the charges against his deputy were politically inspired by the Lawrence Murphy-James Dolan clique, who were influential in neighboring Lincoln County. (Widenmann was a Democrat, the Murphy-Dolan faction was aligned with the Republican Santa Fe Ring.) The rival press castigated Sherman, but a few of the journals found his stance to be an enviable one. The *News and Press* congratulated Sherman for exhibiting "remarkably good taste and good judgment."

Marshal Sherman not only had to contend with range wars in Colfax and Lincoln counties, but outlaw Billy the Kid and his renegade gang were at large and causing trouble in the territory. In November 1880, Deputy Marshal Pat Garrett and his posse were sent out to capture Billy the Kid after Sherman secured federal murder warrants for several survivors of the Lincoln County War. Garrett was accompanied by Robert A. Olinger, a man with a suspicious past who had aligned himself with the Murphy-Dolan faction in the Lincoln County War. Sherman deputized Olinger, which was a costly decision in hindsight.

Garrett ambushed Billy the Kid's gang in Fort Sumner on Dec. 19, 1880. One member of the gang, Tom O'Folliard, was killed. As Garrett closed in on his quarry, he suddenly realized that the commissions of his posse were scheduled to expire on New Year's Day, 1881. It so happened that Marshal Sherman was occupied with personal matters in Washington, D.C., and was indisposed to correct this technicality of the law. This oversight directed further criticism at Sherman but it was a moot point when Billy the Kid was captured on Dec. 23.

Sherman returned from Washington to bask in the favorable limelight of the media. He turned the spectacle of Billy the Kid's incarceration in the Santa Fe jail into a carnival sideshow by marching an army of bug-eyed tourists past the cell. On Mar. 4, 1881, the Kid complained to the governor about the way he was being treated. "He lets every stranger...see me through curiosity...but will not let a single one of my friends in." Billy the Kid was sentenced to hang in Lincoln. Deputy marshals Olinger and James W. Bell were assigned by Sherman to guard the prisoner, but the Kid was too smart for them. On Apr. 28, 1881, the Kid wrestled a gun away from Bell and killed him before making his escape. Olinger, who was drinking at a nearby saloon, was gunned down in the streets by the vengeful Kid who recalled the taunting manner of the deputy. On May 5, the *New Mexican* reported that Billy the Kid had targeted Marshal Sherman for death, but before this threat could be carried out, Pat Garrett killed him at Fort Sumner.

John Sherman concluded his term of office on Mar. 2, 1882, under a cloud of scandal and public censure. Back in Washington Secretary of the Treasury John Sherman—his uncle—was implicated in a scandal which caused him to lose considerable patronage. Without his clout in Washington, the nephew was forced out of office by his political opponents. During his six years as New Mexico marshal, Sherman was accused of many things, including public drunkenness, failure to pay jurors, and an inability to track down liquor runners who were selling whiskey to the Indians. In his favor, Sherman had exhibited uncharacteristic political independence from the Santa Fe Ring, something his predecessor was never able to do, and had introduced a degree of professionalism to the office. See: **Billy the Kid**; **Colfax County War**; **Lincoln County War**; **Olinger, Robert**; **Pratt, John**; **Widenmann, Robert A.**

Shirley, Myra Belle, See: **Starr, Belle.**

Shonsey, Mike, prom. 1890s-1900s, U.S., gunman. Moving to Wyoming's cattle country from Ohio, Mike Shonsey started out as a cowboy but soon became ranch foreman. During the infamous Johnson County War he joined forces with the powerful cattlemen and hired on as a gunman with the Wyoming Cattle Growers' Association. On Apr. 9, 1892, Shonsey rode into the camp of the Regulators association stating that he had found fourteen rustlers at the KC Ranch. The Regulators spread out before dawn to catch them, with Shonsey and five men posting themselves in a gulch behind a ranch cabin. When the Regulators closed in they only found Nate Champion and Nick Ray along with unemployed ranch hands Ben Jones and Bill Walker. Jones and Walker came out of the cabin at dawn and were captured. But when Ray appeared, shooting erupted and he was wounded. Champion covered the dying Ray and helped him back inside. In mid-afternoon Jack Flagg, a small-time rancher, came by and was shot at but escaped. Flagg left his wagon behind and the Regulators set it on fire and pushed it against the cabin. Champion came out firing a six-gun and a Winchester and ran barefoot toward the gulch. When Shonsey and his five companions opened fire, Champion fell with twenty-eight bullet holes in his body. The Regulators pinned a note to the dead man's shirt which read, "Cattle thieves, beware."

In May 1893 at a cattle camp twenty miles northeast of Lusk, Wyo., Shonsey found Dudley Champion, twin brother of the slain Nate. After a short talk with him Shonsey pulled a gun, shot Champion, and ran from the camp. Champion, whose gun was jammed with dirt, died without firing a shot. Shonsey went to Lusk, where he was released after pleading self-defense to a murder charge, then headed to Cheyenne to catch a southbound train. He eventually returned to Wyoming where he died of old age. He was one of the last survivors of the Johnson County War.

Shores, Cyrus Wells, (AKA: **Doc**), 1844-1934, U.S., gunman. Cyrus Wells Shores received both his name and his nickname from the doctor who delivered him. Leaving his hometown near Detroit, Mich., for Montana Territory at the age of twenty-two, Wells worked as a bullwhacker driving ox teams then as a hunter and trapper. He purchased a wagon and hauled ties for the Union Pacific Railroad, brought freight to mining camps, and transported government supplies from Fort Hays to Camp Supply, Okla., for several years. Selling the wagon in 1871, he purchased a herd of cattle which he drove up the Chisholm Trail. Over the next seven years he lived in Kansas selling and buying cattle.

Shores married in 1877 and moved with his wife to Gunnison, Colo., and set up a freight company to supply the many local gold camps. In October 1880, he was in his cabin holding his infant son when Jack Smith and Tom Lewis began shooting in the town's streets. Shores picked up a Winchester and ran outdoors to chase the ruffians. After exchanging gunfire he was shot at by a pursuing posse of fifteen men, but apparently was unharmed. The posse captured Smith and Lewis. In 1884 Shores was elected Gunnison County sheriff, a post he held for eight years. He later served as a deputy U.S. marshal and a Denver and Rio Grande railroad detective. When about 250 Italian and Austrian coal miners went on strike in December 1891 in Crested Butte, Colo., Sheriff Shores gathered two dozen deputies and traveled to the community to end the conflict. The posse's midnight arrival was met by 150 irate miners who fired on the men. Dashing behind the railroad track bed, the posse returned fire. Shores told his men to aim low and as a result thirty-six miners were wounded, and only one was seriously hurt. No posse members were shot and the strike soon ended.

In 1915, Shores was appointed Salt Lake City chief of police. During his career Shores associated with Wild Bill Hickok, Jim Clark, and Tom Horn. Perhaps the most notorious fugitive he captured was the American cannibal Alferd Packer. Shores retired in Gunnison and died there at the age of eighty-nine.

Short, Luke, 1854-93, U.S., gunman. Though a small man, Luke Short was a mean, ruthless, and deceitful gunfighter who earned the nickname of "Undertaker's Friend." For example, a man he once quarrelled with protested when Short put his hand under his coat. Short said, "I'm not trying to pull a gun. I haven't got a gun in there, see!" as he pulled out a gun and murdered the man. Short was part of the Dodge City Gang led by Wyatt Earp and Bat Masterson which controlled a large piece of the vice action in the Plains region.

Short grew up in Texas and became a cowboy at sixteen. At age twenty-two, in 1876, he started a new career as a

Luke Short, western gambler and gunman.

bootlegger, selling whiskey to the Sioux Indians, which was a federal offense. At least six men died from Short's bullets as he defended his franchise. The U.S. Army finally put him out of business and Short soon turned scout for the U.S. Army, then advanced to gambling in Leadville, Colo. His surefire system was simple. He collected when he won, welshed when he lost, and killed men who owed him money and would not pay. By 1879 Short was in Dodge City, Kan., where he became friends with Earp, following him later to the Arizona Territory and becoming a dealer at the infamous Oriental Saloon where Short continued to garner a reputation as a gunfighter. One day a man named Charley Storms, while playing cards at the Oriental, called Short a cheat and got the drop on him. Masterson broke it up and got Storms to leave, but later that afternoon Storms returned, walked over to Short, and began to trace the outline of Short's mustache with his .45. Short whipped out his Colt and killed Storms with three bullets before the other man fired a shot.

Returning to Dodge City in 1881 Short bought the Long Branch Saloon which he turned into a wildly successful combination bar, casino, and brothel. When a reform movement gripped the town the local government decided to ban women employees in saloons. Since this statute would obviously put a damper on Short's business he fought against it with his gun but he and his backers were soon driven out of town. Short lodged a complaint in Topeka, Kansas' state capital. When the governor did nothing Short started sending telegrams to all his friends. Earp, Doc Holliday, Masterson, Charlie Bassett, Shotgun Collins, Neal Brown, and many more notorious gunmen poured into town, calling themselves the Dodge City Peace Commission. The reformers gave in quickly, inviting Short to reopen his saloon and run it the way he wanted.

Short later sold the Long Branch and moved on to Fort Worth, Texas, where he opened and ran the White Elephant Saloon and several other gambling saloons and brothels. When gambling was outlawed he became the most success-

Gunman Luke Short (top row center), surrounded by members of the "Dodge City Peace Commissioners."

ful underground gambling house owner in town. When, in 1887, Longhair Jim Courtright, who had been a Fort Worth city marshal and then headed his own detective agency, came in to shake down saloons for protection payoffs, Short was unimpressed by Courtright's reputation as a top gunslinger. He shot off Courtright's thumb as the ex-marshal tripped back the hammer of his gun, then killed him with three shots as Courtright reached for a second gun. In 1890 saloon owner Charles Wright tried to muscle Short out of business. When Wright came after him Short shot his challenger. Short died in 1893 of natural causes at the age of thirty-nine. See: **Oriental Saloon**.

Siddons, Belle (AKA: **Madame Vestal; Lurline Monte Verde**), d.1881, U.S., gambler. The history of the Old West is marked by dozens of colorful anecdotes concerning famous female outlaws and gamblers; Poker Alice and Calamity Jane are but a few. Belle Siddons etched her name into Western folklore in the years following the Civil War. She was a highly educated Missouri woman, who served as a Confederate spy during the war. She later married a U.S. Army surgeon, who was stationed in Texas. After her husband's death in 1869, Belle supported herself through gambling. For a period of twelve years, Belle Siddons wandered the West, operating her own casinos in Denver, Colo., Wichita, Kan., and Deadwood, S.D.

While working in Deadwood, she made the acquaintance

of Archie McLaughlin, a notorious stagecoach robber who was well known throughout South Dakota. Siddons became McLaughlin's lover, but the romance was short-lived. When McLaughlin told her of an upcoming heist, she accidentally made the secret known. On Nov. 3, 1878, McLaughlin was captured outside of Fort Laramie. He was dragged from the stagecoach in which he was riding and lynched by vigilantes in the wilderness. A highly romanticized contemporary drawing of the hanging depicts Siddons in evening clothes, draped over the prostate body of her dead lover. Whether she was witness to the deed or not, is not known. However, in her grief she became addicted to drugs and was found unconscious one night in a San Francisco opium den. She died a few hours later. See: **McLaughlin, Archie.**

Silva, Vincente, 1845-95, U.S., outlaw. Las Vegas, N.M., in the 1890s, was home to a vicious gang of Latin Americans called Silva's White Caps, or Forty Bandits. The gang's leader, Vincente Silva, was born in Bernalillo County and arrived in Las Vegas in 1875. His gang, which committed all varieties of crime, often met in Silva's Imperial Saloon on Moreno Street. The gang held the area in a virtual stranglehold until October 1892, when they decided to hang fellow gang member Pat Maes for an infraction. The gang gradually disintegrated after this and Silva was eventually murdered by former members. He was buried at Campo de los Cadillos on May 19, 1895.

Sippy, Benjamin, prom. 1881, U.S., lawman. Benjamin Sippy served as city marshal of Tombstone, Ariz., until January 1881 when he was temporarily replaced by Virgil Earp. However, Earp managed to hold on to the post only for a couple of months before losing the election to Sippy. The marshal is given credit for saving the life of a roughneck named John O'Rourke, who had murdered a man in Charleston. Sippy, Virgil Earp, and John Behan, transported the prisoner back to Tombstone where a lynch mob threatened to string him up from the rafters. However, it has been rumored that Wyatt Earp intervened and saved O'Rourke from a "red necktie party." When Sippy resigned his post, he was again replaced by Virgil Earp.

Siringo, Charles Angelo, 1855-1928, U.S., lawman. Considered by many, including outlaw Butch Cassidy, as the finest of the Pinkerton detectives, Charles Angelo Siringo was born in Texas and worked as a cowhand from the time he was thirteen. At twenty-two he went out to join the search for 17-year-old killer Billy the Kid but was forced to give up after he lost all his money gambling. Siringo later worked as a grocer in Kansas for two years. On a visit to Chicago, he went to a blind phrenologist, who "read" the shape of his skull and told him he should be a detective. Siringo joined the Pinkerton Detective Agency and began a twenty-year career, building an enviable record of getting his man.

Trailing fugitives through deserts and blizzards, Siringo lived with moonshiners and disguised himself as a wanted criminal to convince Efie Landusky, a member of the Hole-in-the-Wall Gang, to tell him where infamous outlaw Harvey Logan hid out. The detective later barely escaped being killed when he infiltrated a union which was at the center of the Couer d'Alene labor riots of the 1890s. After twenty years with the agency Siringo retired to write about his adventures. One of his pamphlets was called *Two Evil Isms: Pinkertonism and Anarchism*. He published several books but died a poor man in Los Angeles in 1928, solitary to the end.

Pinkerton detective Charles Siringo.

Skinner, Cyrus, d.1864, U.S., outlaw. A California and Idaho saloon owner, Cyrus Skinner was brought to Montana by Sheriff Henry Plummer in the early 1860s to operate a Bannack, Mont., bar. Plummer's gang of outlaws, the Innocents, met at the clapboard saloon run by Skinner. The bar also served as a place to get information about wagon and stagecoach shipments of gold from the mines; keeping a sharp ear Skinner would listen as his customers got drunk and talked too much, later passing the details on to Plummer.

Skinner himself rarely participated in the robberies but one time, when he learned on extremely short notice of a lucrative shipment, he went with Innocent member Bob Zachery to hold up the stagecoach. They murdered the driver and netted a hefty $250,000 in gold. A ruthless opportunist, Skinner was around when an Innocent murdered a friendly Bannack Indian—Skinner grabbed the dead man's scalp and hung it above his bar for atmosphere.

After Henry Plummer was hanged by vigilantes on Jan. 10, 1864, his bartender stayed in the area, apparently believing he could brazen it out. The lynchings continued. and it became obvious that some of the condemned men would implicate the barkeeper. Nevertheless, Skinner stayed. On Jan. 25, 1864, the vigilantes took Skinner from his porch. Despite his protests that all they had on him were a "heap of suspicions" and no proof, they led him to the gallows that same day. Skinner broke away and ran, pleading with the vigilantes to shoot him instead of subjecting him to the sometimes slow process of hanging. His pleas fell on deaf ears and his captors returned him to the gallows.

Slade, Joseph Alfred (AKA: **Jack**), 1824-64, U.S., outlaw. Gunfighter Jack Slade was known to the famous author and humorist Mark Twain as a kind-hearted individual despite a reputation that suggested otherwise. After encountering Slade in a saloon in 1861, Twain reported that the gunman was "so friendly and so gentle-spoken that I warmed to him in spite of his awful history."

Western gunfighter Joseph Slade.

The "awful history" Twain referred to began in 1824 when the future gunfighter was born in the little town of Carlyle, Ill. While still in his youth, Slade headed west to the raw cowtowns of the Southwest. He served in the U.S. Army during the Mexican War and later was hired by the Central Overland California and Pike's Peak Express Company to serve as a line superintendent. His success was closely tied to the safety of stagecoach drivers who covered long stretches of roadway in the Colorado Territory. In 1858, the year that Slade went to work for the Express Company, word came down that a French Canadian named Jules Bene was stealing horses and using the company offices at Julesburg, Colo., to hide fugitive members of his gang.

Julesburg was as rough and unsavory a place as there ever was. The population never went over 2,000 but with the dawn of each day it was a foregone conclusion that someone would be shot in the streets. Slade arrived in town intent on bringing Bene to justice. Hearing of this, the Frenchman fired five shots into his pursuer. "Bury him," Bene ordered his henchmen. Slade, having miraculously

survived the shooting, was about to be lynched when Ben Ficklin, superintendent of the Central Overland Company, suddenly appeared. He persuaded Bene to cut Slade down with the promise that he would leave the state immediately. On his own now, Slade spent some time recovering from his wounds. He returned to work with the Overland company, awaiting the chance to get revenge on Bene. Finally Slade received word that Bene and his associates were holed up near Slade's ranch in Cold Springs, waiting for him to appear.

The hunter quickly became the prey when Jack Slade seized Bene at gunpoint in front of the ranch and strapped him to a post. Slade amused himself by using Bene for target practice. He fired several shots into his legs and arms until he grew tired of it. "To hell with it," he said, stuck the barrel of the pistol into Bene's mouth, and pulled the trigger. For good measure he cut off both of Bene's ears, keeping one of them for a watch fob. The nature of the crime shocked even the most hardened gunfighter. Slade was someone to be reckoned with.

Slade and his wife Virginia pushed on to Virginia City, Mont., in 1861 after he was charged with assaulting a Fort Halleck resident. The couple tried farming but Slade's obsessive drinking habits got him into trouble with the law. He instigated numerous fights, free-for-alls, and mini riots, which compelled a local vigilante mob to order him from their city for good. Slade complied but for some reason known only to himself he decided to stop by the local watering hole for a last drink on Mar. 10, 1864. He guzzled down a shot and defied the locals to draw on him. The vigilantes rushed into the bar, grabbed him by the arms, and dragged him out to the hanging tree. Then, for the first time in his life, the gunman showed genuine fear. "My God!" he wailed. "Must I die like this? Oh, my poor wife!" Slade was hanged just before his wife arrived to plead for his life. Afterward the body was placed in the street where it was claimed by Virginia.

Mrs. Slade dressed the body down in raw alcohol and prepared to return the corpse to Illinois for burial. She got only as far as Salt Lake City before decomposition set in. Slade was buried in the Mormon Cemetery on July 20, 1864.

Slaughter, John Horton (AKA: **Texas John; Don Juan**), 1841-1922, U.S., lawman. Born in Louisiana, John Horton Slaughter moved with his family at the age of three months to a land grant in Texas. His family settled near Lockhart and began raising cattle. When the Civil War began, Slaughter fought Indians as a "Minute Man of the Texas Rangers." Slaughter continued battling Indians throughout the 1870s, and eventually settled in the middle of Apache country.

At the close of the war, Slaughter began a ranch of his own in Atascosa and Frio counties. Slaughter married, started a family, and for the next few years acted as trail boss on a number of cattle drives and developed his ranch. Although he was successful, he decided to move to Arizona in 1878. In 1884, Slaughter purchased the 65,000-acre San Bernardino Grant, which extended from Arizona down into Mexico. His operation was large and sophisticated, employing at least twenty cowhands and some thirty families who harvested the crops.

Slaughter was not afraid to use his guns to settle a dispute. He was involved in a number of gun fights over the years, and always emerged unscathed. In 1886, he was elected sheriff of Cochise County with the particular project of checking lawlessness in Tombstone and Galeyville. Slaughter was successful here, too, and was reelected in 1888. The clean-up task was largely accomplished by 1890, and Slaughter retired from law enforcement to tend to his cattle ranch in Arizona and slaughterhouse in Los Angeles.

Cochise County, Ariz., sheriff John Slaughter.

Following a brief absence in 1906 to serve in the territorial assembly, Slaughter concentrated on his business and eventually bought a meat market in Charleston and two butcher shops in Bisbee. The wealth he accumulated also turned Slaughter into something of a banker, handling mortgages for many of his neighbors. Slaughter died peacefully at the age of eighty.

Slaughter Kid, See: **Lewis, Elmer.**

Slaughter's Kid, See: **Newcomb, George.**

Smith, Bill, d.1902, U.S., outlaw. At the turn of the century, Bill Smith led a gang of train robbers and rustlers in Arizona and Utah. In 1901 the Arizona Rangers were created to bring order to the lawless land. In October of that year, Smith and his cohorts robbed a Union Pacific train in Utah, afterwards stealing a herd of horses to take back to their Arizona hideout at the forks of the Black River. Spotted by three rangers and six cowboys, they were tracked by these men who decided that one of the rangers should go for help while the others kept watch on the outlaws' cabin.

Smith and his brother were outside the cabin at dusk when Rangers Carlos Tefio and Bill Maxwell came after them. Bill Smith ran back into the cabin but his brother pretended to surrender, dragging his rifle on the ground, then abruptly raising it and firing into Tefio's stomach. Mortally wounded, Tefio fired his Winchester and hit two of Smith's gang members. Bill Smith then opened fire on Maxwell, shooting him through the hat before murdering him with a bullet in the eye. The outlaws then fled from their hideout. Later that same year, Smith went into Douglas, Ariz., for the nightlife and was approached by Ranger Dayton Graham and policeman Tom Vaughan in front of a store. When the officers asked Smith what he was doing, he pulled a six-gun and fired, seriously wounding both lawmen, then escaped. Graham recovered and tracked Smith through gambling dens. He finally caught up with him in 1902 at a monte table in a Southern Arizona town. Smith tried to go for his gun but Graham murdered him, firing two bullets into his stomach and one into his head. Found sewn into the lining of Smith's coat were steel hacksaw blades.

Smith, Jack, d.1890, U.S., gunman. An outlaw who served time in the Colorado penitentiary in 1880, Jack Smith, not long after his release, pistol-whipped a former lawman named Barrett in White Pine, and afterward escaped to Cripple Creek. In late October 1880 near Gunnison, Colo., Tom Lewis and Smith left the White Pine mining camp and began to drink excessively. Meeting lawmen escorting a counterfeiter on the road, Smith and Lewis arbitrarily decided to release the prisoner and hold the officers at gunpoint, after which they rode into town and started shooting randomly in the streets. A passerby was wounded and the two outlaws rode out of town with twenty men chasing them. During a running fight they escaped but were captured the next day in Lake City.

In 1890 in Cripple Creek, Colo., Smith led protestors against authorities in the Bull Hill War, during which there were riots, murders, and the destruction of mines. When one of Smith's men was arrested, Smith marched to the town jail and started shooting at the locks on cells. The city marshal moved in on the gunman and began firing, mortally wounding Smith.

Smith, Richard, d.1889, U.S., outlaw. Thomas Pringle was gunned down as he strolled through the woods outside Wheelock, in the Choctaw Nation on Mar. 28, 1888. The killer was Richard Smith, who attempted to hide his trail by wading through a shallow lake. However, he had left several distinguishing footprints in the soft marshy ground near where Pringle had fallen. A comparison was made between the heels of Smith's boots and the tracks left behind in the mud. Even though the killer had pulled the tacks out of the soles of the boots, the corresponding holes were still visible. It was all the evidence needed for a conviction. Smith was hanged at Fort Smith (Ark.) on Jan. 25, 1889.

Smith, Thomas (AKA: **Bear River Smith**), 1830-70, U.S., lawman. A western lawman who became famous for keeping order by using his fists instead of a gun, Thomas Smith was, according to

New York city policeman-turned-western-lawman, Thomas "Bear River" Smith.

most of his biographers, a policeman in New York City for about six years in the late 1850s or early 1860s and allegedly learned how to fight with his hands on a tough Bowery beat. Smith may have then either fought in the New York Draft Riots of 1863 or moved west before the Civil War. By 1865 he was working for several different freight companies in the Wyoming, Utah, and Colorado territories until 1868, when he became a construction worker at the "end of the track" of the Union Pacific Railroad, in Bear River, Wyoming Territory. Friction between the often rowdy railroad workers and the townspeople resulted in the forming of a vigilance committee. After three railroad workers were captured by the vigilantes who seemed about to hang them, Smith initiated a counterattack, set fire to the jail, and captured most of the vigilantes in a store. Peace was being negotiated when Smith shot a man named Nuckles who may have fired on him first. A battle broke out that left fourteen men dead. Smith was seriously wounded by the time the Fort Brodges U.S. Cavalry arrived. Never tried for his misdeeds, Smith was nicknamed "Bear River" after the fight, and given the post of marshal by the appreciative Union Pacific authorities.

By the time Smith became marshal at Kit Carson in Colorado Territory in 1869, he had stopped using a gun, instead settling fights with his fists. The Abilene, Kan., mayor appointed Smith marshal of that unruly town and Smith's first act was to decree it illegal to carry a gun within city limits. In a few months Abilene had been transformed from a rowdy town to a peaceful place.

But then, as a favor to another sheriff, Smith left Abilene to capture a man named Andrew McConnell on charges of murder. It was an act that doomed him. For, after he found McConnell with his partner, Moses Miles, Smith was cut down with rifle fire as soon as he was in range of the outlaws. As he lay dying, Miles and McConnell almost decapitated him with an ax. Abilene reverted to its turbulent ways until Wild Bill Hickock restored order in 1871. Stories of Smith's exploits have appeared in dime novels and adventure stories, with titles such as *Bear River Smith: Two-Fisted Marshal of Abilene.*

Smith, Tom, d.1893, U.S., lawman. Born in Texas, Tom Smith became a law enforcement officer in Texas and Oklahoma. He also served as a deputy U.S. marshal in the 1870s. A decade later Smith worked for the powerful Wyoming Stock Growers' Association, an organization which sought to drive out homesteaders seeking to settle the grazing lands of the western plains.

Smith faithfully served the interests of the wealthy cattle barons. At Powder River on Nov. 1, 1891, the association ordered Smith and detectives Joe Elliott, Fred Coates, and Frank Canton to rid the territory of accused rustler Nate Champion. In the early morning, Smith and his men congregated outside a cabin owned by Ross Gilbertson on the Powder River. As the men approached the building one of their guns accidentally discharged, touching off a panic. They rushed the cabin with guns blazing. Champion attempted to defend himself but was cut down by Smith's bullets. The governor and two U.S. senators intervened on behalf of the Stock Growers' Association and helped Smith gain back his freedom.

In Spring 1892, Smith was sent into Texas to hire gunfighters for the Johnson County War which raged in Wyoming. Smith found twenty-six men willing to work for $5 dollars a day and they were promised an additional $50 for every homesteader they shot down. These so-called "Regulators" were given a list of seventy men targeted for murder. However, the plan collapsed and most of the gunfighters were driven out of town or arrested. Smith was taken into custody and held until Summer 1893. Following his release, he returned to Gainesville, Texas, but was shot down by a man in a quarrel on board a train.

Sontag Brothers, prom. 1880s-90s, U.S., outlaws. George and John Sontag were born in Minnesota in the 1860s. The boys were three years apart in age, living with

Brothers in crime George and John Sontag.

their mother and her second husband in Mankato. George, the younger of the two, went to work as a train brakeman and then later as a grocery clerk in Nebraska. He embezzled money from his employer and was sentenced to the state prison. After serving about a year, George escaped with another convict. He later returned to jail on his own volition to complete the original sentence, which ended in 1887.

Meanwhile, John Sontag had moved to Los Angeles in 1878 where he went to work on the Southern Pacific Railroad as a brakeman. He was badly injured in an industrial accident and continued to harbor deep resentment against his employers during his convalescence. Short of cash, Sontag found employment with a Visalia, Calif., farmer named Chris Evans, who also had an intense dislike for the railroad. Together these men decided to avenge themselves.

On Jan. 21, 1889, they boarded a train at Goshen, Calif., and robbed the express car clerk of $600. A month and a day later they repeated the same crime at Pixley, only this time the take was $5,000. Having escaped detection John Sontag returned to Mankato in May 1891. He confessed to his brother George all he had done. John Sontag returned to California a month later to sample the pickings. Reunited with Evans, they attempted to rob the Southern Pacific but were driven off by Detective Len Harris. Having failed, John headed back to Minnesota where he enlisted George to the cause. After carefully considering the matter

the Sontag brothers decided that the most likely plum would be train No. 3 out of Chicago, which stopped at Western Union Junction, Wis., on the evening of Nov. 5, 1891. The robbery went off like clockwork, and the brothers rejoined their relatives in Racine, $9,800 richer.

After this the Sontags traveled west to rendezvous with Evans. The three held up a passenger train at Collis Station, in Fresno, Calif., on Aug. 1, 1892, making off with three sacks of money. Later, George Sontag boarded the same train in the suburbs of Fresno where he joined in the conversation with the excited passengers who recounted the robbery minute by minute. His actions aroused the suspicion of the local authorities. Detective Smith and Deputy Sheriff Witty ordered George Sontag to appear at headquarters and answer a few questions. How was it, they wanted to know, that Sontag happened to be on the same train right after the robbery? Meanwhile, Smith and several deputies went back to Evans' home to question him at length. The daughter told the men that her father was not home, whereby they pushed aside a portiere and found John Sontag. He leveled a shotgun at the officers who attempted to flee. Evans drew his own weapon and fired upon Witty who fell to the floor dead.

John Sontag and his friend Chris Evans were now fugitives. Meanwhile, George was quietly arrested and placed on trial for the Fresno train robbery on Oct. 25, 1892. On Nov. 3, after a Guilty verdict had been returned, he was sentenced to life imprisonment at Folsom. His brother and Chris Evans were given help by the villagers northeast of Visalia, frustrating efforts to arrest the pair.

Posse that captured the wounded Chris Evans.

But Evans, who along with Sontag had been wounded in an earlier gunfight, was trapped in a straw shack outside Visalia. Barely able to walk, he was taken into custody. John Sontag was captured soon after.

Meanwhile, George Sontag plotted his escape from Folsom Prison. He ingratiated himself with a fellow convict named William Fredericks who had been imprisoned for holding up the Mariposa stage. On June 27, 1893, the two, armed with smuggled weapons, seized the lieutenant of the guards. Using the man as a shield, Sontag, Williams, and four other hardcases marched through the gates under the watchful gaze of the tower guards who trained a Gatling gun on them. As they approached the brink of a deep gulch the lieutenant managed to extricate himself from his captors. At the precise moment he leaped over the cliff the Gatling gun opened fire. George Sontag was badly wounded in the affray, but miraculously survived. On July 3, 1893, his brother John succumbed to his own gunshot wounds and died in the Fresno jail. It was a hard blow for his brother. Chris Evans went on trial for murder on Nov. 28, 1893. George Sontag volunteered to give evidence against his former associate after explaining that Mrs. Evans had mistreated his mother when she had come to California to nurse John. Based on his testimony, the jury returned a Guilty verdict against Evans who was sentenced to life imprisonment. Evans made a bid for freedom on Dec. 28, 1893. He seized a knife and held it to the throat of jailer Ben Scott, who opened the door and let him out. The desperado, having recovered sufficiently from his wounds, made his way back to the ranch in Visalia. He remained there until Feb. 19, 1894, when a posse surrounded the house and took him prisoner. Evans surrendered and was returned to the state prison to serve out a life sentence. George Sontag was pardoned on Mar. 21, 1908. He went to work at Tim McGrath's gambling resort on Pacific Street in San Francisco before settling down to write his memoirs.

Soto, Juan (AKA: **The Human Wildcat**), d.1871, U.S., outlaw. The notoriety that earned Juan Soto a place in the history of the U.S. West came at the end of his life. Soto was of mixed Indian and Mexican heritage and became notorious in California as a thief and murderer. Soto and two other men robbed a store in Sunol, Calif., on Jan. 10, 1871, killing a clerk and shooting a number of rounds into the living quarters of the store owners, apparently for no purpose at all.

Soto and his men were then tracked by Sheriff Harry Morse and a deputy. The lawmen followed the outlaws into the Sausalito Valley about fifty miles outside the town of Gilroy. Morse and the deputy found Soto and a dozen of his followers inside a makeshift hideout. Soto drew his gun on the sheriff when the lawman told him he was under arrest. After a short and uneventful skirmish, Morse broke free and pursued Soto outside. Arriving outside ahead of

the lawman, Soto had attempted to mount a horse. But the animal spooked and ran away leaving the hapless gunfighter behind with nowhere to hide. Soto ran for some 150 yards before Morse was able to draw a bead on the outlaw. Even at this significant distance the sheriff's aim was true, as he nailed the bandit with a single shot. As Soto, now wounded, ran back toward the sheriff, Morse fired a second shot. This time, the bullet found its mark, striking the "Human Wildcat" in the head. Soto died almost instantly.

The "Human Wildcat" Juan Soto.

Spaniard, Jack (Jack Sevier), 1861-89, U.S., gunman. Orphaned at an early age, Jack Sevier took the name of Spaniard while living on Spaniard Creek between Muskogee and Webbers Falls, Okla. Jack Spaniard was described by the local press as "a man of desperate and reckless character, who held human life at a very low estimate." This opinion seemed true after Spaniard, a half-blood Cherokee, murdered Deputy Marshal William Erwin. At Fort Smith (Ark.) the jury weighed the evidence (much of it circumstantial) and returned a Guilty verdict after only one hour of deliberation. Spaniard was hanged on Aug. 30, 1889.

Spradley, A. John (AKA: **A.J.**), 1853-1940, U.S., lawman. Born into a Simpson County, Miss., farming family, A. John Spradley was the oldest of nine children and lived with his family until 1871, when he was eighteen. One day a local boy, Jack Hayes, with whom Spradley had previously fought, and his brother, Bill Hayes, confronted Spradley and his brother, Bill Spradley. When the Hayes brothers pulled derringers and began to fire, John Spradley brought out an old cap and ball pistol and shot them both. The Hayes' died that night and Spradley fled to Texas, where he worked at his uncle's Nacogdoches farm and then at a mill. He was appointed deputy sheriff of Nacogdoches County in 1880 and became sheriff one year later, a post he held for thirty years. He then served four years as deputy U.S. marshal. Spradley often wore a steel shirt under his clothes for protection.

In the summer of 1884, Spradley arrested Bill Rogers and was taking him to jail when Whig Rogers, Bill's drunken brother, tried to stop him. Spradley released Bill, warning Whig to settle down. Bill Rogers then pulled out a gun, fired twice at the deputy, and one of the bullets tore through Spradley's back. Though he was not expected to live, a silk handkerchief pulled through the wound apparently healed it. Three years later Spradley was confronted by a young man with a gun who had a grudge against him, and Spradley narrowly missed being killed when the youth fired at him. The assailant escaped but was soon arrested and sent to jail. On July 16, 1893, in Longsport, La., Spradley was waylaid by saloon keeper Joel Goodwin, who had nursed a two-year grudge against Spradley for arresting him for murdering an employee. Informed that Goodwin was after him, Spradley armed himself with a shotgun as well as his usual revolver. Goodwin waited at the depot and began firing his Winchester at Spradley as the train pulled in. Spradley fired his shotgun, instantly killing Goodwin. Goodwin's distraught wife then shot at Spradley, but the train pulled out before anyone else was injured.

During his years as a deputy, Spradley owned part interest in a Nacogdoches saloon, but sold out after one of his nearly fatal gunfights and afterward became an ardent prohibitionist. When he retired from his job as a lawman, Spradley became a farmer and was involved in politics until he died in 1940.

Sprole, Lincoln, d.1886, U.S., outlaw. Lincoln Sprole lived on a farm belonging to Sam Paul, in Paul's Valley, Chickasaw Nation. Sprole, a disagreeable sort, quarreled with Ben Clark and his 18-year-old son over the watering of some livestock at a well. On May 30, 1885, Clark and his son went into the town of White Bead Hill to purchase some provisions. As they were returning to the ranch, the father and son were ambushed by Sprole, who had concealed himself in a thicket alongside the road. Clark tumbled from the buckboard mortally wounded, just as the frightened horses bolted. The teenage boy tried futilely to regain control of the rig, but Sprole's next volley shattered his leg.

The youth writhed in pain as Sprole slowly advanced on him; the muzzle of the gun pointing ominously at his head. Ignoring his pleas for mercy, Lincoln Sprole shot the unarmed youth in the breast and collar bone. Clark died in six hours. His son died eleven days later. Sprole left the country, but was tracked down by Deputy Marshal John Williams and returned to Fort Smith (Ark.) to stand trial. The murderer was convicted and hanged on July 23, 1886. The *Elevator* of Aug. 9, 1886, expressed the sentiments of the community when it observed that: "It is only to be regretted that he has not two necks to break instead of one."

Standard, Jess, 1854-1935, U.S., gunman. Working as a cowboy for Pink Higgins in Texas during the 1870s, Jess Standard participated in the violent and bloody Horrell-Higgins feud in Lampasas County.

Western gunman Jess Standard.

On Mar. 26, 1877, several members of the Higgins gang ambushed brothers Sam and Mart Horrell as they rode to court in Lampasas. When Sam was thrown from his horse, Mart charged his assailants, firing. The Higgins men fled. On June 14, 1877, the feud ignited in the Lampasas streets when Frank Mitchell was slain and Bill Wren was wounded, but none of the Horrell men were hit. In July 1877, in Lampasas County, Standard and thirteen others followed Higgins to the headquarters of Horrell, pinning them inside the bunk and ranch houses and wounding two of their men. After a two-day siege, ammunition ran low and the Higgins faction left the ranch.

Standard eventually moved his family to Tuscola, Texas, where he farmed and worked as a carpenter.

Standefer, Wiley W., prom. 1876-78, U.S., lawman. Wiley Standefer succeeded the ineffectual Francis Goodwin as Arizona marshal on Aug. 15, 1876. Before embarking on a career in law enforcement, Standefer owned a ranch in California. He was a Georgian by birth who secured his appointment to the marshalcy through his warm dealings with his predecessor Goodwin, who no doubt intervened on his behalf with Governor Anson Safford.

Standefer had a respectable record during his brief two-year term. He spent much of his time attempting to track down the highwaymen who had been running roughshod across the territory for many months. In April-May of 1877, Standefer and his Indian guide Al Sieber encountered a gang of outlaws near Ehrenberg. They wounded one of the gunmen and took a second man to jail. The prisoner turned out to be an undercover postal agent. Marshal Standefer also had the distinction of overseeing the execution of convicted murderer James Malone on Mar. 15, 1878. It was the first time in Arizona history that a hanging had been carried out under federal court order.

Standefer's good record was marred by an ugly incident that occurred on Aug. 12, 1878, when one of the Arizona Territory's best loved residents, Jack Swilling, died in his jail cell from disease and dehydration. Swilling and his companion Andrew Kirby were arrested in May 1878 and charged with the Apr. 19 robbery of a stagecoach near Wickenburg. The local courts decided to drop the charges in favor of the federal courts who assumed the case and the attending court costs. The prisoners were placed in the custody of Deputy Marshal Joseph W. Evans, who escorted the two men from Prescott to Yuma. Swilling's friends were outraged that he should be treated in such a disgraceful manner. Swilling was bound over for trial and incarcerated in the Yuma jail; an unsanitary hellhole parched by the dry desert heat. Swilling, who suffered serious health problems, which were aggravated by the conditions in the jail, died in his cell. In the eyes of the local residents he was a martyr whose untimely death was caused by government bureaucrats. Andrew Kirby was ordered released shortly thereafter. On this note of discord, Standefer stepped down as marshal and was replaced by Crawley P. Dake on June 12, 1878. See: **Dake, Crawley P.**

Starr, Belle (**Myra Belle Shirley**), 1848-89, U.S., outlaw. Born in Carthage, Mo., the notorious Belle Starr moved with her family at the age of sixteen to Scyene, Texas, just outside of Dallas. In the 1860s, Starr became involved with bank robber Cole Younger, Jesse James' partner. The couple spent several months together in a small cabin on the Oklahoma Strip while Younger was hiding out from the law after robbing several banks. After Younger rejoined the James gang, Starr gave birth to a daughter, Pearl, who was thought to be Younger's child. Starr's next romance was with another bank robber, Jim Reed. Along with Reed and two other criminals in 1869, Starr robbed a California prospector suspected of having hit a rich vein. The four tortured the prospector until he told them where his gold was hidden, and they got away with $30,000.

After Reed was shot in a gun fight in 1874, Starr and an Indian outlaw named Blue Duck organized a horse-and-cattle-rustling ring. Starr then married a Cherokee Indian named Sam Starr and continued stealing livestock. Belle and Sam Starr were arrested in 1883 and sentenced to six months in jail. After their release, they returned to rustling and were arrested again in 1886. Although they appeared before "hanging" Judge Isaac Parker at Fort Smith, they were released for lack of evidence.

Sam Starr was shot and killed in a barroom brawl in December 1886. Starr's last lover was a Creek Indian named Jim July. On Feb. 3, 1889, after riding part of the

The infamous Belle Starr.

way to Fort Smith with July, Starr turned back to her home in Younger's Bend. A gunman apparently lying in wait shot her off her horse. She was found by a passing traveler who took her home to her daughter. When she died, Pearl had her tombstone engraved with the following inscription:

"Shed not for her the bitter tear,
Nor give the heart to vain regret,
'Tis but the casket that lies here,
The gem that fills it sparkles yet."

Starr, Henry (AKA: **The Bearcat**), 1873-1921, U.S., rob. As a teenager on the Oklahoma Strip, Henry Starr, alleged nephew of notorious robber and livestock rustler Belle Starr, received initiation as a livestock rustler. In the late 1890s, Starr, who was part Cherokee Indian, organized a gang that specialized in robbing small banks in the Oklahoma, Texas, and Arkansas areas.

Bank robber Henry Starr.

Starr shot and killed Floyd Wilson, a deputy of Judge Isaac Parker, in 1903. Although convicted and sentenced to death, he managed to appeal his case successfully and was released. Parker persisted, and Starr was retried for the same crime, convicted again, but was saved a second time by a pardon from President Teddy Roosevelt. Only a month later, Starr, Kid Wilson, and three other men robbed a bank in Bentonville, Ark., of $11,000. Starr and Wilson were captured in Colorado Springs, Colo., in July 1903. After serving a five-year term in prison, Starr was released and immediately returned to robbing banks. In 1914, Starr earned himself a "first" in the history of crime by using an automobile to escape from the scenes of his crimes. Starr's innovation stood him in good stead for the next six years until the police also began using cars. While escaping from a successful bank robbery in Harrison, Ark., in 1921, Starr's car broke down, and he was overtaken by a motor-driven posse. He was shot and killed in the ensuing gun battle.

A Winchester automatic rifle owned by outlaw Henry Starr.

Starr, Tom, 1813-90, U.S., outlaw. An extremely violent character, even for the Wild West, Tom Starr, a full-blooded Cherokee Indian, fathered a vicious clan of eight sons and two daughters who, along with their children, nephews, and cousins, made up the notorious Starr clan gang.

Born in Tennessee, Starr was brought to the Oklahoma territory by his parents. By the time he was twenty, Starr was six feet seven inches tall and accomplished with a bowie knife. After killing David Buffington, a rival tribesman, Starr went unpunished. In 1843, with no apparent motivation, he burned an entire family to death. Leading groups of half-breeds, whites, and Indians on horse-rustling raids, Starr became hated and feared. His enemies attacked his homestead in 1845, killing his father and his brother, Buck Starr, twelve. Starr postponed his horse stealing long enough to get revenge and was alleged to have slain all thirty-two raiders, torturing them slowly before they died.

After the mass murders, Starr returned to thievery and rustling. Jim Reed was a member of the Starr gang. His young lover would come to be known as Belle Starr when she later married "Uncle" Tom's son, Sam. Before his retirement in the 1880s, Starr's territory, now part of Adair County, Okla., was known as the most dangerous in the region. Starr, who was alleged to have murdered more than 100 men, also traveled into Texas on his crime sprees. After his death in 1890, clan members apparently decided to rewrite history, telling journalists that Uncle Tom Starr was a charming man "full of fun and eager to josh folks."

Stephens, John, d.1887, U.S., outlaw. John Stephens left the Delaware reservation the night of May 28, 1886, to do away with his enemies who had testified against him in a larceny case. He headed for the home of Mrs. Annie Kerr, who was sleeping in her bedroom. Stephens chopped the woman into a bloody pulp and did the same with her 16-year-old son who slept on a pallet near the front door. When the deed was done, Stephens rode to the home of Dr. Pyle, who had also testified against him. Using the ax again, he struck the doctor and his wife in the head and beat their child. Pyle lingered for six days before succumbing to his wounds. Brought before Judge Isaac Parker, Dr. Pyle's wife exhibited the wounds inflicted in the back of her head by Stephens. Fourteen pieces of bone had to be removed from her skull. Consequently, Stephens was found Guilty, and was hanged on Jan. 14, 1887.

Stewart, Dr. Henri, 1844-79, U.S., gunman. Henri Stewart was a respected physician who had studied at Harvard and Yale before accepting a position as ship's doctor on a vessel that traversed the coast of California, South America, and Cuba. In 1877 he inexplicably abandoned his wife and four children, who were living in Ohio, to seek new adventures in the western Indian territories. Stewart joined legendary outlaw Sam Bass and his gang of train robbers which terrorized Texas for a brief, but bloody four-year period in the late 1870s. During an attempted holdup of a Missouri-Kansas-Texas train near Caddo (Okla.) in the Choctaw Indian Territory in May 1879, Stewart shot and killed J.B. Jones. He was captured in Missouri, and was brought to Fort Smith (Ark.) where he was hanged on Aug. 29, 1879. See: **Bass, Samuel**.

Stiles, William Larkin (AKA: **William Larkin**), d.1908, U.S., outlaw-gunman-lawman. Gunman William Stiles, who allegedly killed his father when he was twelve, became notorious around the turn of the century in the Southwest. After assisting lawman Jeff Milton, Stiles was hired by Willcox, Ariz., marshal Burt Alvord. Together they formed a gang of train robbers which included George and Louis Owens, Jack Dunlap, Bravo Juan Yoas, and Bob Brown. On Apr. 8, 1900, Stiles, recently released from jail,

William Stiles

visited Alvord and other gang members at the Cochise County courthouse. While being guided from the cell by jailer George Bravin, Stiles pulled a gun and demanded Bravin's keys. Stiles shot Bravin and released the prisoners.

In January 1908, in Nevada, Stiles, then deputy sheriff, shot a man to death while arresting him. The victim's 12-year-old son then shot and killed Stiles.

Stilwell, Frank C., c.1857-1882, U.S., gunman. Frank

C. Stilwell, younger brother of noted lawyer and army scout, S.E. "Comanche Jack" Stilwell, was born circa 1857 in the border area between Kansas and Missouri. He arrived in Arizona in 1878 and went to work as a miner and teamster in Mohave County. After his initial stint of legitimate employment, Stilwell signed on with N.H. Clanton and his gang of cattle rustlers in Tombstone.

Stilwell apparently kept his rustling activities a secret since he was also appointed deputy sheriff of Cochise County (of which Tombstone was the county seat). Even during his tenure as a law enforcement officer, Stilwell involved himself in a stage-robbing partnership with Pete Spence. Stilwell's criminal activities came to light when he and Spence robbed the Tombstone-Bisbee stage of $3,000 and were arrested. The pair went to trial and were acquitted. However, Wyatt Earp, making a reputation for himself as a tough law enforcement officer, brought them back for a second trial. Again they were acquitted. Stilwell was considered a prime suspect in the wounding of Virgil Earp on Dec. 28, 1881, and of Morgan Earp's murder on Mar. 18, 1882. Two days after Morgan Earp's murder, Wyatt Earp and several of his men encountered Stilwell and Ike Clanton, who was believed to be behind the murders of the two Earp brothers. Clanton and Stilwell split up. Stilwell's bullet-riddled body was discovered later.

Stinson, Joe, 1838-1902, U.S., gunman. After migrating to the California gold fields in the 1850s, Joe Stinson joined the California Column during the Civil War and marched with them into New Mexico. After the war ended, Stinson stayed in New Mexico where he was a miner. Although not overly successful, he gathered together enough money to open a saloon in Elizabethtown, N.M. In October 1871, Stinson shot and killed a belligerent drunk, Wall Henderson, who threatened to burn down Stinson's saloon. After killing Henderson, Stinson moved his business to Santa Fe, where he was involved in several other shootings, none of them fatal. On June 24, 1886, after drinking all night with Reddy McCann, the pair argued and Stinson threw McCann out. When McCann returned to resume the argument, Stinson pulled a gun and fired point-blank into his face. Surprisingly McCann survived, although missing the base of his nose. By 1890, Stinson was enfeebled by alcoholism. He lived on a $10-a-month veteran's pension. In 1895, he was admitted to the National Home for Disabled Soldiers near Los Angeles where he died in 1902.

Stockton, Port 1854-81, U.S., lawman-gunman. Port

Stockton and his brother, Ike, both showed an early inclination toward wildness. When 17-year-old Port was charged with attempted murder, Ike helped him escape. Port then drifted for a few years, spent some time in Dodge City, and finally settled in Lincoln County, N.M., where Ike had opened a saloon. In 1876, after marrying, Port moved to Trinidad, Colo., with Ike. In October 1876, in Cimarron, N.M., after shooting and killing an unarmed man, Juan Gonzales, in Lambert's Saloon, Port was arrested. Once again, Ike helped him escape and the pair returned to Trinidad where Port, two months later, shot and killed another unarmed man. Ike came to the rescue and saved Port from the posse that had arrested him.

The Stocktons moved to Animas City, Colo., where Port was appointed city marshal. However, enraged citizens ran him out of town after he shot at a barber who had nicked him with a razor. After a brief stint as marshal in Rico, Colo., a job he lost when his reputation caught up with him, Port and his family moved to a shack near Farmington, N.M. In Farmington, Port joined suspected rustlers Harge Eskridge and James Garret. On Jan. 10, 1881, ten days after the three shot up a New Year's Eve party, Alf Graves, a rancher who had fought with Port, rode past Stockton's home with Frank Coe and several other friends. Stockton grabbed a Winchester and demanded that Graves come back and settle the argument. They spoke briefly, and Graves pulled out a gun, and killed Stockton. After Port's death an outbreak of rustling in the area caused Governor Lew Wallace to issue a reward for Ike Stockton's arrest. In September 1881, in Durango, Colo., Ike was shot in the leg. His leg was amputated and he died shortly thereafter.

Storms, Charles, d.1881, U.S., gunman. As a professional gunfighter, Charles Storms was envious of the reputation of gunslingers such as Bat Masterson and Wild Bill Hickok. When Jack McCall walked into Carl Mann's Saloon in Deadwood, S.D., on Aug. 2, 1876, and shot Hickok in the back of the head, Storms, sitting nearby, grabbed one of Hickok's pistols for a souvenir.

However, Storms' career as a gunfighter never blossomed. He lived through several gunfights in Deadwood, but his career ended in Tombstone, Ariz., on Feb. 21, 1881. After drinking whiskey, Storms argued with Luke Short, a professional gambler, and eventually slapped him. Bat Masterson interceded and separated the two men before any shots were fired. An hour later Storms reappeared and grabbed Short as though he intended to pull him into the street. As Storms was attempting to draw his pistol, Short quickly drew his and shot Storms in the chest killing him instantly. Short was found Not Guilty on grounds of self

defense and released.

Stoudenmire, Dallas, 1843-82, U.S., lawman. Dallas Stoudenmire's career as the marshal of El Paso, Texas, was short but distinguished. Beginning with the day of his appointment, Apr. 11, 1881, his presence had a calming influence on a violent town, as he repeatedly showed himself

El Paso marshal Dallas Stoudenmire.

able to outdraw and outshoot anyone looking for trouble. He was the typical western lawman, even carrying his two six-guns in his belt because he found holsters too cumbersome in a gunfight. During his year in office, however, a feud developed between Stoudenmire and the wealthy Manning brothers. Stoudenmire and his deputy, Doc Cummings, believed that the Mannings had hired gunmen to assassinate them, beginning with shots fired at Stoudenmire in the dark just six days after he took office. The attempts continued on Stoudenmire's and Cummings' lives for a year, until Stoudenmire left town briefly to marry Isabella Sherrington. During Stoudenmire's absence, the Mannings killed Cummings in the Coliseum Saloon (the Mannings owned the Coliseum, along with part interests in most of the other saloons in town, and one of the biggest cattle ranches in Texas). A hearing determined that the Mannings acted in self defense.

Stoudenmire began drinking heavily. Although he had signed a truce with George, Frank, and James Manning, he repeatedly threatened to kill them when he was drunk. By Autumn 1882, he was asked to resign from the marshal's office by the El Paso Vigilance Committee.

Stoudenmire was drunk on the night of Sept. 18. He sought out George "Doc" Manning at his saloon to pick a fight with him. An employee of Manning's, Walter Jones, tried unsuccessfully to intercede. Doc Manning drew first, but his shot was stopped by pocketful of letters Stoudenmire was carrying in his shirt. After Stoudenmire wounded Manning in the arm, he caught Stoudenmire in a bear hug to prevent him from firing again. Their wrestling carried them out the front door just as James Manning arrived. James killed Stoudenmire with a shot to the head, but George picked up one of Stoudenmire's guns and vented his rage by pistol-whipping the corpse.

At their trial for Stoudenmire's murder, James and George Manning were again ruled to have killed in self-defense.

Strawhim, Samuel (Strawan), 1845-69, U.S., gunman. Known in Hays City, Kan., as a vicious killer and gunfighter, Samuel Strawhim ignored vigilantes that ordered him to leave town, and pistol-whipped one of their leaders, Alonzo B. Webster. However, when "Wild Bill" Hickok became sheriff in August 1869, Strawhim left town. On Sept. 27, he returned with eighteen cowboys. The gang took over John Bitter's Leavenworth Beer Saloon where Strawhim declared he was going to "kill someone tonight just for luck." Strawhim, who threatened to break every glass in the saloon, was challenged and shot dead by Hickok. Some reports say Hickok turned his back on Strawhim, saw the gunman drawing on him in a mirror, turned, and fired first. Others claim Hickok simply drew faster. See: **Hickok, James Butler.**

Stuart's Stranglers, prom. 1884, U.S., vigil. Gran-

ville Stuart was a prominent Montana stockman, who, frustrated by the ranchers and homesteaders who were stealing his cattle, decided to go after the those responsible. Stuart claimed he had the proof of their crimes: "Near our home ranch we discovered one rancher whose cows invariably had twin calves and frequently triplets, while the range cows in that vicinity were nearly all barren, and would persist in hanging around this man's corral, envying his cows, their numerous children, and bawling and lamenting their own childless fate. This state of affairs continued until we were obliged to call around that way and threaten to hang the man if his cows had any more twins."

In 1884 at a Miles City, Mont., meeting, while serving as the secretary of the Montana Stock Grower's Association, Stuart heard the complaints of 429 other cattlemen who demanded an immediate end to the rustling. "The Montana cattlemen were as peaceable and law abiding a body of men as could be found anywhere," Stuart later recalled. "But they had $35 million worth of property scattered over 75,000 square miles of practically uninhabited country and it had to be protected from thieves. The only way to do it was to make the penalty for stealing so severe that it would lose its attraction." The Miles City delegation demanded that a vigilante army of hired gunmen be raised, but Stuart told them that he thought such an extreme action would be foolhardy and would lead to unnecessary loss of life. Instead, he argued, why not handle this matter quietly with their own band of men.

Stuart organized a group called the Stranglers, and in the next few months they lived up to their name by lynching every suspected horse thief and cattle rustler they found hiding in the territory. There seemed to be no limit to their savagery. Once they came upon a half-breed boy they accused of rustling. With little in the way of hard evidence, the Stranglers forced the lad to entertain them with his fiddle during a drunken, debauched party that lasted all night. At dawn, the boy was hanged.

The Stranglers made good on their promise to implement frontier vigilantism, but the rustling continued. In desperation, the Montana stockman finally decided to import hired gunmen. A secret plan was carried out, but few people outside the stockmen themselves ever learned the real truth about the roundup of cattle thieves. Newspaperman Owen Wister, who went on to write the classic novel of the Old West, *The Virginian*, claimed to have been told the true story during a visit to Montana in the early 1890s. Wister described what followed: "It happened like a visit from the Destroying Angel. The ringleaders among the cattle thieves suddenly died, as it were, in one night. There may have been twenty, there may have been fifty, who met their deaths in this way. I am not certain of the number, but I know that the stroke was the result of long and elaborate preparation, that when it fell it was a single stroke and a clean one, and those physically concerned with the killings were never known in Montana. Their names did not come to light; they were brought into the state for this purpose and they left it shut invisible in a freight car on the Northern Pacific Railway." In truth, Wister never visited Montana. He heard the story while traveling through Wyoming which was caught in the midst of a range war of its own: the Johnson County War. See: **Johnson County War.**

Sundance Kid, The (**Harry Longabaugh**), c.1863-1908, U.S., outlaw. Born and raised in Mont Clare, Pa., Harry Longabaugh moved to Wyoming in his youth, becoming a horse thief while still in his teens. He was apprehended, and from August 1887 until February 1889, he served a sentence in the Sundance jail, and henceforth was known as The Sundance Kid. Returning to a life of crime, Longabaugh robbed banks and trains, and rustled cattle, and became a frequent user of the craggy Robber's Roost in the western Rocky Mountain Hole-in-the-Wall area. In 1892, Longabaugh was captured with Harry Bass, Bert

The Sundance Kid.

Charter, and Bill Madden following a failed train robbery near Malta, Mont., but he escaped, and a short time later he met Butch Cassidy for the first time. Years later their paths crossed again while they both worked at a Wyoming ranch. Soon thereafter, Cassidy formed the Wild Bunch gang.

The Wild Bunch robbed a bank in Belle Fourche, S.D., in 1897, but Longabaugh and three others were arrested. Escaping from a jail in Deadwood, S.D., Longabaugh participated in crime for the next five years, living a lavish life that included frequent vacations in New Orleans and Denver. He also began to consort with Etta Place, a former schoolteacher. Longabaugh escaped a posse led by Sheriff Joe Hazen on June 5, 1899, after robbing a train at Wilcox Siding, Wyo., with "Flat Nose" George Curry and Harvey Logan. Logan killed Hazen during the shootout.

Accompanied by Etta Place, Longabaugh fled to Argentina in 1902, where he met Cassidy and became his partner in a cattle ranch. The trio migrated to Bolivia, where, in 1905, Longabaugh was caught in a bedroom with the wife of a neighboring rancher, and forced to shoot the irate husband in the shoulder. In 1907, Longabaugh and Place returned to the U.S. for a vacation. After visiting New York, the pair journeyed to Denver, where Place was hospitalized for appendicitis. While waiting for her release, Longabaugh met up with a few old friends, and after becoming quite drunk, wounded a bartender during a gunfight.

Upon returning to Bolivia, Longabaugh and Cassidy went to work for a mining company, supplementing their income with occasional bank robberies. In 1908, the pair robbed a mule train near San Vicente, Bol. Two days later they were recognized in the plaza at San Vicente and surrounded by police and a cavalry troop. Despite overwhelming odds, Longabaugh shot the cavalry commander, seized his ammunition belt, and retreated with Cassidy into the safety of a nearby restaurant. After dark, while still hopelessly surrounded, Longabaugh attempted to sneak across the plaza to reach a cache of arms. He was cut down by a barrage of bullets, but Cassidy dragged him to safety. With Longabaugh seriously wounded, Cassidy ended his friend's life with a gunshot to the head before Cassidy himself was killed. Some later claimed Cassidy survived and did not die until 1937. See: **Cassidy, Butch; Wild Bunch, The.**

Sutton-Taylor Feud, 1840s-70s, U.S. The Sutton-Taylor feud began in the late 1840s in South Carolina where the Sutton and Taylor families were neighbors. After the Civil War, William E. Sutton, and his family moved to Clinton, Texas. Coincidentally, so did the Taylor family. A truce existed between the two families until Mar. 25, 1868, when William Sutton, then deputy sheriff of Bastrop, Texas, shot and killed Charley Taylor on suspicion of stock theft. Later that year, on Dec. 24, when Sutton shot and killed Buck Taylor in a saloon in Clinton, the feud began with renewed vigor. Each family recruited gangs of about 200 members. On Sutton's side were lawman Jack Helm, cattleman Shanghai Pierce, and Indian fighter Old Joe Tumlinson. Fighting with the Taylors were the hostile Clements brothers and an East Texas cousin, John Wesley Hardin.

On Aug. 26, 1870, an ambush at the home of Henry Kelly, related to the Taylors by marriage, resulted in the shooting deaths of Kelly and his brother, William Kelly. Jack Helm, a Texas State Police captain, who had come with Doc White and John Meador to arrest Henry Kelly, was fired for his part in the killings. James "Jim" Taylor, son of murdered Pitkin Taylor, first tracked Bill Sutton down on Apr. 1, 1873, in Cuero, Texas. In Cuero, Taylor and his friends badly wounded Sutton. Then on Mar. 11, 1874, when Sutton, along with his young wife and child, had just boarded a steamboat in Indianola, Texas, bound for New Orleans, Jim and William "Bill" Taylor appeared and shot and killed Sutton and Sutton's friend, Gabe Slaughter. Although the Taylors escaped, they were ambushed and killed the following year by Sutton supporters. The feud, virtually over, claimed about forty lives. See: **Taylor, Jim**.

T

Tall Texan, The, See: **Kilpatrick, Benjamin.**

Taylor, Jack Hays, d.1869, U.S., gunman-outlaw. A feud between the Suttons and Taylors in Texas broke out in 1867 and became the bloodiest in the state's history. Many of the Sutton faction were lawmen while the Taylors were an anti-Reconstruction southern Texas family. Jack Hays Taylor, the son of Texas ranger Creed Taylor, was an expert shot with a pistol and cold-blooded as well. In November 1867, he and his brother, Phillip "Doboy" Taylor, were in Mason, Texas, when soldiers from Fort Mason harassed them. One soldier knocked Hays' hat to the ground, and Hays calmly drew his pistol then shot him. More soldiers poured in and demanded that the murderer be handed over to them. A gunfight ensued, during which the Taylor brothers shot and killed an army sergeant and fled town. With the excuse of hunting the fugitives, the Suttons stepped up the feud. On Aug. 23, 1869, a posse of Sutton Regulators led by Jack Helm ambushed the Taylor residence and fired on Creed. Phillip, though wounded, escaped. Hays Taylor rode into the midst of the posse firing his gun and wounded five Regulators. The Regulators then opened fire and killed Jack Hays Taylor.

Taylor, Jim, 1852-75, U.S., gunman. Jim Taylor became the Taylor leader during a feud between the Suttons and Taylors. Jim's father, Pitkin Taylor, was ambushed by the Suttons in 1872. He died six months after the ambush and Jim, with his brother Bill Taylor, swore revenge on the Sutton faction leader, Bill Sutton. In the following months, the Taylors killed three Sutton men. The Sutton-Taylor feud began in the 1840s and ended with the death of Jim Taylor in 1875.

On Apr. 1, 1873, a band of Taylor men led by Jim opened fire on Bill Sutton in a pool room. Sutton, though critically wounded, recovered. In June, Jim and several friends gunned down Sutton man Jim Cox and a companion. The following month, Jim and a relative, John Wesley "Wes" Hardin, the West's most feared gunman, were in Albuquerque, Texas, when they spied Jack Helm, a Sutton leader, in the company of six friends. Hardin aimed his shotgun at Helm and shot him through the chest while Taylor pumped several bullets into his head. Then on Mar. 11, 1874, Hardin informed Jim that Bill Sutton and his family were sailing from Indianola on a steamer. Jim and Bill Taylor rushed to the ship and spotted the Sutton family

gathered on the deck. A gunfight followed and Jim killed Sutton while Bill shot Gabe Slaughter in the head. The Suttons retaliated by lynching Scrape Taylor, Jim White, and Kute Tuggle on June 20. In turn, the Taylors assassinated the new Sutton leader, Rube Brown, who was also the Cuero town marshal.

On Dec. 27, 1875, Jim Taylor and a few friends rode into Clinton, Texas. They had left their horses with Martin King when a Sutton posse charged into town and began firing. King released the animals and Taylor and two friends found themselves cut off. Dashing through King's house, the three were stopped by Sutton man Kit Hunter who shot Jim in the arm. The Sutton posse surrounded the Taylor men, opened fire, and killed them. With the death of the Taylor faction's young and aggressive leader, the feud quickly ended.

Taylor, Phillip (AKA: **Doboy**), d.1871, U.S., gunman-outlaw. The son of Texas Ranger Creed Taylor and the younger brother of Jack Hays Taylor, Phillip "Doboy" Taylor became another of the casualties of the Sutton-Taylor feud, the bloodiest in Texas history. Following a gunfight in Mason, Texas, in which Hays and Doboy killed two soldiers, the two were declared "wanted" by Reconstruction authorities. Becoming fugitives, the brothers were aggressively pursued by the Suttons, many of whom were law enforcement officials. A posse of Sutton Regulators ambushed the Taylor home on Aug. 23, 1869, killing Hays and wounding Doboy in the arm. Doboy next was attacked by Sutton Regulators on Sept. 7 in William Connor's house near Pennington, Texas, in the company of two friends named Kelleson and Cook. Kelleson was killed, but Doboy and Cook escaped. In November 1871, Sim Holstein and Doboy quarreled about a job Doboy wanted. Doboy drew his pistol, fired, and missed. Holstein grabbed the gun and shot him three times. Doboy Taylor died six hours later. See: **Taylor, Jack Hays; Sutton-Taylor Feud; Taylor, Pitkin.**

Taylor, Pitkin, d.1873, U.S., gunman. A member of the gun-slinging Taylor family, whose legendary feud with the Suttons of Clinton, Texas, dated back to the 1840s when both factions still resided in South Carolina, Pitkin Taylor was one of the later victims of the feud. Pitkin was a brother of Creed Taylor, a family patriarch who outlived his two sons Phillip and Jack Hays Taylor. Late one night in October 1872, Pitkin heard what he thought to be the sound of a cowbell ringing in his pasture. He loaded his shotgun and went out to see what was causing the commotion. In the pitch darkness, a team of gunmen opened fire on him before he could get a shot off. Pitkin Taylor lingered until March 1873, when he succumbed to his wounds. At the funeral, Jim and Bill Taylor vowed to avenge Pitkin's death, and eventually, they did. See: **Sutton-Taylor Feud; Taylor, Phillip; Taylor, William.**

Taylor, William prom. 1872-75, U.S., gunman. William "Bill" Taylor, the brother of Jim Taylor and the son of Pitkin Taylor, involved himself in the famous Sutton-Taylor feud after he and Jim swore to avenge their father's killing by Sutton Regulators. The brothers got their revenge on Mar. 11, 1874, in the presence of Sutton's wife and child, when Jim killed Bill Sutton and Bill shot Gabe Slaughter in the head. The Taylors escaped but Bill later was arrested and jailed in Indianola. On Sept. 15, 1875, in the midst of a fierce tropical storm that battered the coast of Texas, Bill escaped from jail but helped rescue several people from the flooding waters. Later imprisoned in 1877, he shared the Austin jail with his relative John Hardin. The following year, Bill Taylor was arrested again and charged with horse theft, forgery, and assault, but was not imprisoned. He left Texas after 1881 and moved to Indian Territory, where, according to family members, he became a lawman and, ironically, was killed by a criminal. See: **Hardin, John Wesley; Sutton-Taylor Feud.**

Tewksbury, Edwin, d.1904, U.S., gunman-lawman. John D. Tewksbury and his Indian wife had three sons, Edwin, James, and John, Jr. In 1880 the family moved to Pleasant Valley, Ariz., and began raising sheep. A feud broke out in 1887, when the Tewksburys opposed the Hash Knife cowboys and the Grahams, a ranching family. The Grahams and the cowboys, who believed sheep ruined the grazing land for cattle, ambushed the Tewksbury clan twice. In the first ambush, the Tewksburys were at a hideout when Edwin Tewksbury, posted as a lookout, spied a cowboy crawling toward the camp. He called to his brother, Jim, who shot and killed the cowboy, allowing the Tewksburys to escape. Then, on Sept. 2, the Grahams ambushed and killed John Tewksbury and Bill Jacobs. The surviving Tewksburys, trapped in a cabin, fended off a day-long assault before escaping. The feud ended shortly thereafter. Nearly five years later, John Graham, the leader of the Graham faction, was ambushed and fatally wounded while driving a load of grain into Tempe, Ariz. Before he died, he named Edwin Tewksbury and John Rhodes as his murderers. The two were arrested and spent two and a half years in jail before they were acquitted in 1896. Edwin Tewksbury served as constable of Globe, Ariz., and deputy of Gila County until his death in 1904. See: **Tewksbury, Jim.**

Tewksbury, Jim, d.1888, U.S., gunman. Jim Tewksbury was a violent member of the Tewksbury family, who began raising sheep in Pleasant Valley, Ariz., angering the Hash Knife cowboys and the Grahams, a ranching family. Graham offered a $500 reward for the death of one of the sheepherders and $1,000 for the clan leader John Tewksbury, Sr. Outnumbered, the Tewksburys were forced to move their herds from camp to camp. Jim, alerted by his brother, Edwin, killed one of the Hash Knife cowboys when they attempted to ambush the sheepherders. The other cowboys were afraid to move, and their injured companion bled to death. On Aug. 10, 1887, eight cowboys led by Tom Tucker rode to Jim's cabin, hoping to fight. A shootout ensued in which Jim and his friends killed Hampton Blevins and John Paine, and wounded Tucker, Bob Gillespie, and Bob Carrington. Two weeks after John, Sr., and Bill Jacobs were killed in ambush, the Tewksburys were attacked at dawn by several cowboys. Jim Tewksbury and Jim Roberts, firing from their blankets, killed Harry Middleton and wounded Joe Underwood before driving off the others. Jim Tewksbury died in his cabin in 1888 of consumption. See: **Tewksbury, Edwin.**

Texas Billy, See: **Thompson, William.**

Texas Jack, See: **Reed, Nathaniel.**

Texas Property Wars, 1840s, U.S., feud. A feud in rural Texas in the early 1840s, became so violent that the intercession of Texas president Sam Houston was required. Two factions of Shelby County, the Regulators and the Moderators, became embroiled over issues ranging from cattle stealing to law and order to property rights. Poor record keeping by earlier Mexican authorities and fraud perpetrated by crooked land speculators caused one of the bloodiest wars in Texas history. Houston recognized that

Shelby County was in a state of anarchy and commanded all citizens to lay down their arms and return to their homes. An uneasy peace existed until the Mexican War, when both sides vented their frustrations on a common enemy.

Texas Rangers, 1826- , U.S., lawmen. The Texas Rangers were formed in 1826 at the urging of Governor Steven Austin, who wanted twenty to thirty Rangers in the field at all times. The Rangers, an independent law enforcement agency, became the most controversial, as well as the most fabled, lawmen in the U.S. According to legend, they always got their man, yet they had a penchant for pursuing outlaws and fugitives across state and country borders, frequently into Mexico. The pre-Civil War rangers of the Wild West were as much villains as heroes, however. Heroes such as Ben McCulloch, Big Foot Wallace, Frank Jones, John Coffee Hays, and Leander McNelly are remembered with such rangers-turned-villains as Bass Outlaw, Ben Thompson, and Scott Cooley. For a short period, they were disbanded, then re-established in 1873 and they captured several notorious outlaws including King Fisher, Sam Bass, and John Hardin. The twentieth-century rangers came under sharp criticism for anti-black, anti-Chicano, and anti-labor views. A state legislative committee found that they consistently ignored civil rights, killed criminals without provocation, and frequently murdered their prisoners. In one incident during WWI, nine Rangers shot and killed fifteen Mexicans in cold blood. The nine were dismissed, but no criminal charges were ever brought against them.

When Ma Ferguson was elected governor, she fired the entire Ranger force because they openly supported her opponent. The only Ranger she did not fire was Frank Hamer, the Ranger on special assignment who was one of the lawmen, who killed Clyde Barrow and Bonnie Parker in 1934. Ferguson appointed her own people as replacements. The Ferguson Rangers, as the group came to be called, was one of the most corrupt law enforcement agencies ever formed, made up of thieving murderers. Ferguson's successor disbanded the agency and reformed it under the Department of Public Safety. The Texas AFL-CIO, in 1967, called for their disbandment, claiming they were used as tax-paid strikebreakers. The State Supreme Court ruled against the Rangers, claiming they used excessive force in breaking up a United Farm Workers strike. In the 1970s, a candidate for governor ran a very strong, albeit unsuccessful, campaign calling for the abolition of the Rangers. Their status at present is unresolved.

Thomas, Henry Andrew (AKA: **Heck**), 1850-1912, U.S., lawman. One of the Wild West's most effective lawmen, Henry Andrew Thomas, apprehended many notorious outlaws including members of the Doolin gang, the Dalton gang, and the Sam Bass gang. A native of Athens, Ga., Thomas was a courier in the Civil War when he was twelve. He joined the Atlanta police force after the war and gained fame as a fearless fighter after being wounded in one of the city's race riots. He and his wife moved to Texas in 1875 where he worked as a guard for the Texas Express Company. He was promoted to detective in 1876 after preventing a train robbery by hiding the money in an unlit stove. As detective, he led posses that captured several members of the Sam Bass gang. Thomas turned to bounty hunting in 1885, capturing two murderers,

Lawman Heck Thomas.

brothers Jim and Pink Lee. Pursuing the brothers another time, Thomas gave them the chance to surrender as was his custom. The brothers declined and fired on Thomas, who killed them in the shootout.

Thomas was appointed deputy U.S. marshal later that year and moved to Fort Smith, Ark. Under the jurisdiction of "Hanging Judge" Isaac Parker, Thomas pursued outlaws and fugitives in the Indian Territory. During his tenure, fifteen Indian Territory officers were killed while Thomas, often singlehandedly, brought in numerous outlaws. On his first excursion, for example, he apprehended eight murderers, a bootlegger, a horse thief, and seven other outlaws. Another time, while riding alone, he brought in four murderers. His wife divorced him by 1888, and by 1891, he and Chris Madsen, another deputy U.S. marshal, were trailing the Dalton and Doolin gangs. The Daltons, desperate to avoid the two lawmen, attempted to simultaneously rob two banks in Coffeyville, Kan., to get enough money to go to South America. Most of the gang was slaughtered during the attempt, Thomas and Madsen arriving shortly after the gunfire ceased.

Thomas and Madsen, joined by William Tilghman, tracked the Doolin gang, and Thomas captured and killed several members. In 1893, the three lawmen, later known as the "Three Guardsmen," were assigned to tame Perry, a town in Oklahoma Territory, and within three years, they arrested more than 300 wanted men. In 1896, Thomas collected the reward for killing William Doolin. According to one story, he led a posse to Doolin's cabin at night and engaged the outlaw in a shootout. Another story told of how Thomas found Doolin dead of consumption, blasted the corpse twice with his shotgun, took the body in, and gave the $5,000 reward money to Doolin's widow. The lawman moved to Lawton, in the Oklahoma Territory, in 1902, and served for seven years as the town's chief of police. He retired in 1909 after a heart attack and died on Aug. 15, 1912. See: **Dalton Brothers; Doolin, William M.; Tilghman, William Matthew, Jr.**

Thompson, Ben, 1842-84, U.S., gunman. Born in Knottingly, Yorkshire, England on Nov. 11, 1842, western gambler and gunfighter Ben Thompson immigrated to Austin, Texas, with his family in 1849. He had his first gunfight in 1858, when he shot another teenager in the back with a load of buckshot as the other boy turned and fled. After finishing his schooling, Thompson went to work as a printer. In 1860, he moved to New Orleans, where he worked in the related field of book binding. While pursuing

Ben Thompson, the deadly western gunman.

these conventional occupations, Thompson got into more fights, showing the tendency toward violence that would later dominate his life.

When the Civil War began, Thompson joined the Confederate Army and served in Texas, New Mexico, and Louisiana. Various accounts indicate that Thompson split his attention during those years between soldiering and other activities such as gambling and smuggling whiskey. He was wounded and mustered out of the army in 1863 and married soon after. He got into a shootout in Austin in 1865, was arrested and jailed, and bribed the two men guarding him to let him escape. He went to Mexico with the two former jailers and served with distinction as a mercenary soldier in the employ of Emperor Maximilian.

For the next fifteen years, Thompson divided his time between Texas and Kansas and was involved in several shootings. He saved the life of a judge in Austin in 1867, but the following year he shot his brother-in-law in the side (he claimed he just meant to scare him) for beating up Thompson's wife. Thompson turned himself in but got into an argument with a magistrate, whose life he threatened and who sentenced him to four years as a result. Thompson served two years of the sentence. In 1869, in a saloon in Ogallalie, Kan., he shot the gun out of the hand of a man who was causing trouble by pointing it at the other men at the bar as a joke. He said afterward, "I just wanted to slow him down a bit before he got himself into real trouble." Thompson later owned and operated the Bull's Head Saloon in Abilene, Kan., with an old friend, Phil Coe, but sold out and moved to Ellsworth, Kan., in 1873. There he got into the most famous gunfight of his career when his brother, Billy Thompson, shot and killed the popular sheriff C.B. Whitney. He told Billy to get out of town, saying, "You've shot Whitney, our best friend." After Billy left, Thompson stayed to face the angry crowd alone. Ben finally surrendered to Sheriff Wyatt Earp who ordered Thompson to throw down his gun or be killed. Whitney exonerated Billy on his deathbed, acknowledging that the shooting was accidental; when Billy was tried in 1877, he was acquitted.

In 1881, Thompson was elected marshal of Austin, Texas. He was a highly effective lawman but gave the job up the following year after killing Jack Harris, the owner of the Vaudeville Variety Theater in San Antonio. On Mar. 11, 1884, fourteen months after he was acquitted of Harris' murder, Thompson and his friend, John "King" Fisher, were watching a show at the Vaudeville Theater in San Antonio when Jack Harris' two partners, Joe Foster and William Simms, started a gunfight in which Thompson was killed and Foster and Fisher were mortally wounded. See: **Earp, Wyatt Berry Stapp; Fisher, John King.**

Thompson, Thomas, d.1884, U.S., outlaw. Whiskey smuggler Thomas Thompson was executed at Fort Smith (Ark.) on July 11, 1884, for murdering James O'Holeran.

He killed his partner O'Holeran, on Sept. 20, 1883, in the Chickasaw Nation and then dumped the body into a well.

Thompson, William (AKA: **Texas Billy**), c.1845-88, U.S., gunman. The younger brother of the notorious western gunman Ben Thompson, William "Billy" Thompson continually needed his brother's protection. A less accurate gunman than Ben, he was more cold-blooded. When he was very young, his parents emigrated from Yorkshire, England, to Austin, Texas. The brothers enlisted in the Texas Mounted Rifles during the Civil War. Billy killed a fellow soldier and, with his brother's help, deserted and escaped to the Indian Territory, where he turned to gambling. After the war, he followed his brother to Ellsworth, Kan. One night in August 1873, Billy got drunk and in a rage shot and killed Sheriff C.B. Whitney. Ben helped his brother get out of town to sleep off his drunkenness. Billy then returned

Gunfighter Billy Thompson.

to Ellsworth for a few days before fleeing to Buena Vista, Colo., where the outlaws made him mayor of the town. Three years later, he was captured by Texas Rangers and extradited to Kansas, where he was eventually acquitted of murder. Allegedly, his brother used threats and bribes to clear Billy.

Billy returned briefly to Austin before following his brother to Dodge City, Kan. He then wandered into Nebraska, found employment, and supposedly shot off Texan Jim Thompson's finger. The rancher shot Billy in the back, and Bat Masterson helped him escape from Ogallala. Drifting down to Texas, by coincidence he was in San Antonio and reportedly saw his brother and King Fisher gunned down by three killers in 1884. Unarmed, Billy did not take revenge, but merely cried over the body of his protector. He wandered around the streets of San Antonio for a few days and then left town. After that, little is known of the younger Thompson brother. After reportedly hiding out in El Paso for a few months after committing murder in Corpus Christi, Texas, rumors persist that Billy Thompson was killed in Laredo, Texas, in 1888. See: **Masterson, Bat; Thompson, Ben.**

Thornton, John, d.1892, U.S., outlaw. John Thornton was a profligate, drunken sadist, who had taken indecent liberties with his daughter. When the unfortunate girl finally attempted to put her life in order and married her sweetheart, the besotted father raced to where the young couple was staying and shot her with a pistol. He was arrested and convicted after a short trial. Thornton, a man of considerable girth, was hanged at Fort Smith (Ark.) on June 28, 1892. It was a gruesome sight for the spectators who came to witness the hanging. The rope nearly severed Thornton's head from the torso; only the tendons in his neck saved him from decapitation.

Three-Fingered Jack. See: **Gallagher, Jack; Garcia, Manuel; McDowell, Jack.**

Tidball, Zan L., prom. 1882, U.S., lawman. Recommended to the Arizona marshalcy by Senator Edward Platt of New York, Zan L. Tidball, a former Department of Justice examiner seemed to be the right man for a tough job when he took office July 18, 1882. Eastern politicians spoke of his credentials in glowing terms. William E. Chandler, a senator from New Hampshire, described Tidball as a "most capable and deserving" individual. Arizona leaders were not impressed, nor were they pleased that an outsider should be selected to replace Marshal Crawley P. Dake. "Why he was appointed is more than we can say," complained the Arizona *Miner*.

Marshal Zan L. Tidball.

Tidball made a powerful enemy in Joseph C. Tiffany, a San Carlos Indian agent who was charged with perjury, embezzlement, and conspiracy against the agency he served. Tidball was assigned to investigate Tiffany's illegal dealings with the Tucson freight firm of Lord & Williams. Tiffany had drawn a deputy marshal from Fort Thomas into the scheme and had allowed several suspected Indian murderers to escape. The accused embezzler had fled to New York, where he was arrested by the local police on Oct. 26, 1882. Tiffany was returned to New Mexico to stand trial, but given the absence of Marshal Tidball and District Attorney James A. Zabriskie, who were in Washington at work on the Star Route fraud cases—involving government mail fraud in Arizona—the trial was suspended. Tiffany eventually succeeded in winning a decision of *nolle prosequis* on Dec. 3, 1883. A year later the Congressional Committee on Expenditures brought in the redoubtable Tiffany to testify about the conduct of Tidball. Seizing the opportunity to retaliate, the former Indian agent accused the marshal of bribing a defense witness in the embezzlement case, George Smerdon, and causing Smerdon to flee to Mexico where he died of yellow fever. Tiffany accused the marshal of other misdeeds, but nothing came of the charges and the case was quietly dropped.

Tidball encountered other problems. He was indirectly responsible for the escape of the renegade Apache chieftain Geronimo. In the summer of 1883, Marshal Tidball was presented with a warrant for the capture of the famed warrior, who at the time was in Mexico. Geronimo indicated his intention to surrender to the army which wanted him on cattle rustling charges. The Apache leader, with a head of cattle, was met at the border by Lieutenant Britton Davis, who then set up camp near a ranch in Sulphur Springs Valley. Tidball, who held in his hand a warrant for Geronimo's arrest on the charge of murder, demanded that Davis hand over the warrior. In the throes of a dilemma —Davis knew Geronimo would not go with Tidball—the young lieutenant tricked the marshal by allowing Geronimo to drive his herd of cattle a few miles north of the encampment. In the meantime, Davis drank himself into a stupor and passed out, allowing Geronimo to flee.

Tilghman, William Matthew, Jr., 1854-1924, U.S., lawman. A lawman who held several positions in Dodge City, Kan., Lincoln County, Oklahoma Territory, and Oklahoma City, Okla., Bill Tilghman was credited with bringing in several outlaws, including Bill Raidler, Kid Donnor, John Braya, and Bill Doolin. At the age of twenty-three, Tilghman was a deputy under Dodge City sheriff Charlie Bassett. Tilghman was appointed city marshal of Dodge City in 1884, serving two years, and he helped to establish and enforce the no-guns-in-Dodge rule. In 1892, Tilghman accepted an appointment as deputy U.S. marshal and brought in several Kansas outlaws alive. In 1893, Tilghman, Chris Madsen, and Henry "Heck" Thomas brought law to the town of Perry, where the three became known as the "Three Guardsmen." Tilghman also tangled with Jennie "Little Britches" Stevens and "Cattle" Annie Mc-Dougal. The Three Guardsmen tracked the Doolin gang,

capturing several members.

Tilghman earned a reputation for never killing unnecessarily. In one instance, on Sept. 6, 1895, he shot and severely wounded Doolin gang member Bill Raider, but nursed him back to health so he could travel. Tilghman also captured Bill Doolin in Eureka Springs, Ark., and locked him up in the wooden jailhouse in Guthrie, Oklahoma Territory. Doolin escaped, and was later apprehended by Henry Thomas. Tilghman served as sheriff of Lincoln County, Oklahoma Territory, in 1900, and eleven years later as chief of po-

Lawman Bill Tilghman.

lice of Oklahoma City, retiring three years later at the age of sixty. He was persuaded to come out of retirement in 1924 and clean up Cromwell, Okla. There, a shady and very drunk prohibition officer, Wiley Lynn, shot and killed the 70-year-old Tilghman as he led Lynn to jail. See: **Doolin, William M.; Thomas, Henry Andrew.**

Tobler, George, d.1890, U.S., outlaw. George Tobler and Irvin Richmond were competing for the attentions of the same woman at a dance held at Cache Bottom, in the Choctaw Nation on the evening of Apr. 30, 1889. As the evening wore on, Tobler became increasingly distressed over his prospects with this woman. He stood sullenly by as Richmond waltzed across the floor with the woman. In a jealous rage, Tobler produced a pistol and shot Richmond dead. He was arrested immediately, remanded to Fort Smith (Ark.) and hanged on Jan. 30, 1890.

Towerly, William, 1870-87, U.S., outlaw. A horse thief in Indian Territory, William Towerly killed two lawmen. On Nov. 29, 1887, Towerly camped on the Arkansas River with Dave Smith, another horse thief, Lee Dixon, and Dixon's wife. Lawmen Frank Dalton and James Cole approached the camp on horseback, carrying warrants for Smith's arrest. Smith shot Dalton in the chest, and as the Dixons joined the firing at Cole, Towerly ran up to Dalton and shot him through the mouth and then through the head. Cole killed Smith and the Dixons, and Towerly fled to his family's home near Atoka in Indian Territory. In December, lawmen Ed Stokley and Bill Moody learned of his whereabouts and set up an ambush. One morning as Towerly emerged from his house, Stokley shouted, "Hands up!" Towerly went for his gun and both officers fired at the same time, hitting him in the shoulder and leg. Towerly dropped his gun and collapsed to the ground. As Stokley approached, Towerly grabbed his gun and shot the lawman in the groin and heart. While the outlaw was trying to reload, Towerly's sister and mother jumped Moody and dragged him into the house. Moody finally shook them free, walked outside, and killed Towerly.

Tracy, Harry, 1877-1902, U.S., outlaw. By the end of his criminal career, Harry Tracy had earned himself a reputation as one of the U.S.' most violent outlaws. He demonstrated no criminal tendencies until the age of fifteen,

Outlaw Harry Tracy.   **David Merrill.**

when he met another 15-year-old Vancouver, Wash., resident, David Merrill. Although Merrill was the instigator of their joint criminal activities, Tracy soon exceeded him.

Tracy's and Merrill's first prison sentence—twenty days for stealing geese—did not discourage them. After practicing shooting pistols at a local barracks until they became expert shots, the two started off on a run of petty offenses that ended with Tracy's arrest for house-breaking in Provo, Utah, for which he was sentenced on July 10, 1897 to a year in prison. On Oct. 8, Tracy and three other prisoners working on a labor gang outside the prison walls escaped. Tracy traveled to Colorado, where he joined the "Robbers Roost" gang, whose members included Merrill, Dave Lant, Pat Johnson, and John Bennett. When the gang murdered a young man named William Strang, a posse set out after them, catching up with them on Mar. 1, 1898, outside Craig, Colo. During a gun battle, a deputy sheriff was killed. Although the gang escaped, they were tracked down again on Mar. 4 by another posse that captured Lant, Tracy, Johnson and Bennett. Johnson, accused of the Strang murder, was extradited to Wyoming, where he was tried and acquitted due to a lack of a evidence. Bennett was lynched by a mob, and Tracy and Lant escaped from jail but were

recaptured the next day. They escaped again and this time Tracy rejoined Merrill.

Tracy and Merrill returned to Portland, Ore., where they set about terrorizing the citizenry with a series of robberies

Harry Tracy's body on display.

and holdups. Merrill was arrested on Feb. 6, 1899, and Tracy was arrested the following day. Both men were found Guilty of robbery and were sentenced to the Salem prison on Mar. 22, Tracy for twenty years and Merrill for fifteen. On June 9, 1902, after having a rifle smuggled in to them, Tracy and Merrill broke out of prison. The two men eluded authorities, mostly by breaking into private citizens' homes, and forcing them to provide food, weapons, and supplies, and taking hostages to assure that their demands were met. On June 28, Merrill and Tracy had a falling out. Tracy said later that their argument proved Merrill had turned informer. One report had it that the two men stepped off in a back-to-back duel but Tracy shot Merrill in the back. Another account stated that Tracy merely killed Merrill as he slept.

Tracy remained at large until Aug. 6, 1902, when a posse surprised him on a ranch near Creston, Wash. Tracy managed to dash into an adjoining wheat field. The posse fired volleys of shots into the field but heard Tracy fire only one shot in return. The following morning, Sheriff Gardner of Lincoln County and his posse searched the field, where they found Tracy dead, a suicide. One of his legs had been shattered by two of the rifle balls fired by the posse. He had attempted to stop the flow of blood with a bandage, but when it became obvious he could not escape, Tracy apparently decided to make good on his promise that he would never be caught alive, and shot himself in the head. His body was returned to Salem prison for identification and was displayed to the inmates as an object lesson in the rewards of a life of crime. The men who finally stopped Harry Tracy received a reward of $4,100.

Tualisto, d.1883, U.S., outlaw. On July 6, 1881, Tualisto, a member of the Creek Indian tribe, robbed and murdered Emanuel Cochran, who was passing through the Choctaw Nation. A deputy marshal named Beck quietly began assembling evidence against Tualisto, and was preparing to issue an arrest warrant when Tualisto was convicted within the tribal court on an unrelated charge of larceny. The court adjudged him Guilty and ordered that he be strapped to the whipping post and flogged. After enduring the punishment, Tualisto was released to Deputy Beck who led him away. The Indian renegade was convicted of murder and hanged at Fort Smith (Ark.) on June 29, 1883. Before he was dropped to eternity, he announced to the spectators that the four buttons sewn into his hat were taken from the four white men he had killed.

Tucker, Tom, prom. 1880s-1908, U.S., gunman-lawman. A cowboy who occasionally hired himself out to feuding factions, Tom Tucker rode with the Hash Knife Gang in Arizona and with Oliver Lee in New Mexico. On Aug. 10, 1887, while riding with the Hash Knife Gang, who were feuding with the Tewksburys, Tucker led seven cowboys to the cabin of Jim Tewksbury. A shootout ensued, during which John Paine and Hampton Blevins were killed, and Bob Gillespie and Bob Carrington were wounded. Tucker was shot and seriously wounded. He crawled to Bob Sigsby's cabin, where he slowly recovered. Tucker later rode with Lee while he was feuding with the Good family. Tucker killed several Chinese during a shootout at Silver City, N.M., in 1889, and was later tried and acquitted on the grounds of self-defense. In 1908, Tucker became an undersheriff in Santa Fe, N.M., and helped Dee Harkey corner the outlaw band led by Jim Nite. Tucker died in Texas. See: **Tewksbury, Jim.**

Tulsa Jack, See: **Blake, Jack.**

Turner, Ben, d.1873, U.S., gunman. Cowboy Ben Turner worked for the Horrell brothers during the Horrell-Higgins feud in Lampasas, Texas. On Mar. 19, 1873, state police officers came to Lampasas to arrest Clint Barkley, a member of the Horrell faction. Turner, with Barkley, and Mart, Tom, and Sam Horrell, killed three officers as they entered Jerry Scott's saloon. Turner later helped Mart Horrell and Scott break out of jail in Georgetown, Texas. In December 1873, Ben Horrell was killed by Mexicans in Lincoln County, N.M. In revenge, his brothers began indiscriminately killing local Mexicans. A group of angry Mexicans shot and killed Turner in a gunfight.

Tyler, Jesse, d.1900, U.S., lawman. Utah lawman Jesse Tyler brought in stolen cattle and rustlers, and frequently pursued Butch Cassidy's Wild Bunch. He was bested by a group of rustlers in February 1899 in the San Rafael Valley, and another time was sued by the wife of a horse thief for retrieving stolen horses from her corral. On May 16, 1900, Tyler led a posse after cattle rustlers near Thompson, Utah. Thinking they were riding up to an Indian camp, Tyler and deputy Sam Jenkins dismounted, left their horses, and approached unarmed. The camp turned out to be that of the band of rustlers led by Harvey Logan. The lawmen turned to run and Logan opened fire, shooting both men in the back. The rest of the posse fled, abandoning the bodies of Tyler and Jenkins for two days. See: **Logan, Harvey.**

Tyng, George, prom. 1870-74, U.S., lawman. George Tyng, the successor to the Arizona marshalcy of the disgraced Isaac Dickason, was believed to be descended from an old and respected Massachusetts family that founded the settlement of Tyngsborough. In July 1872, he was hired by the army to provide beef to the remote military installations

Marshall George Tyng (seated below, left) with two companions in 1874.

in Arizona and was later appointed to complete the unexpired term of the Yuma County sheriff. Tyng resigned his post a year later to accept a position with the firm of William B. Hooper and Company of Ehrenberg (Ariz.). In

January 1874 while still working in the private sector, Tyng was recruited to serve the Arizona marshalcy. Commenting on Tyng's chances for returning a degree of professionalism to the job, the Prescott *Arizona Miner* noted: "We learn from a friend in Washington that Arizona marshals have until now stood in bad repute."

Tyng failed to justify the newspaper's confidence. He found the office to be in disarray and could not find existing records left behind by his predecessors whom he accused of "maladministration." However, the new marshal acted in a reticent, unsure manner himself, concerning the unpaid claims filed against Dickason's office. He did little to address current or past problems and then took a sixty-day leave of absence for health reasons. Tyng's resignation took effect on Dec. 15, 1874; he was succeeded by Francis H. Goodwin. See: **Dickason, Isaac; Goodwin, Francis H.**

U

Updyke, David, d.1866, U.S., lawman-outlaw. A notoriously crooked lawman who consorted with known felons, David Updyke was elected sheriff of Ada County, Idaho, in 1865. He was closely watched by the Payette Vigilance Committee, who waited until the opportune moment to punish him for suspected wrongdoing. On Sept. 28, 1865, committee members arrested Updyke on a charge of defrauding the revenue and failing to arrest a hardcase outlaw named West Jenkins. Freed on bond, Updyke learned of the fate that befell outlaw John Clark, who was lynched by the Vigilance Committee. Fearing for his life, the former lawman slipped out of town and fled to Boise. On Apr. 14, 1866, Updyke and a companion were found hanging by their necks in a barn at Sirup Creek. A note pinned to the dead sheriff's chest accused him of being "an aider of murderers and horse thieves." The next day an anonymous note appeared in Boise that further explained the committee's actions. "Dave Updyke: Accessory after the fact to the Port Neuf stage robbery, accessory and accomplice to the robbery of the stage near Boise City in 1864, chief conspirator in burning property on the overland stage line, guilty of aiding and assisting escape of West Jenkins, and the murderer and others while sheriff, and threatening lives and property of an already outraged and long suffering community."

V

Vasquez, Tiburcio, c.1838-75, U.S., outlaw. A criminal by the time he was in his teens, Tiburcio Vasquez quickly went on to bigger things. Vasquez, half Indian, was born and raised in California. He was barely eighteen years old when he engaged in his first gunfight. In about 1856, Vasquez abducted the daughter of a wealthy Mexican rancher who lived in the Livermore Valley. The rancher followed them and demanded the return of his daughter. When Vasquez refused the rancher pulled out a gun and fired a shot into the young desperado's arm, shattering the bone. With that Vasquez rode away alone. In about 1855, Vasquez stabbed to death a Monterey man, but evaded the authorities and was never charged.

Vasquez specialized in horse stealing and cattle rustling and was arrested and sent to prison for five years at San Quentin in 1857. After an escape in 1859 and subsequent recapture on theft charges, Vasquez was freed from jail on Aug. 13, 1863. Following his third conviction, this time for armed robbery, Vasquez was returned to jail. He was released on June 4, 1870, only to begin a new career robbing the stagecoach lines.

Vasquez and his band gained a reputation up and down the California coast as notorious outlaws. In Summer 1872 the bandits held up a stage near Arroyo Cantua in the northern part of the state. While en route to their hideout they were confronted by a posse led by Alameda County sheriff Harry Morse, the constable of Santa Cruz, and the San Benito County sheriff. In the gunfight that followed, Vasquez was shot in the chest. Bandit Francisco Barcenas was killed, and a third man, Garcia Rodriguez was badly injured.

Bandit Tiburcio Vásquez.

Rodriguez was tracked down by the posse two days later and died not long afterward, but Vasquez escaped to the mountains where he nursed himself back to health.

The Mexican bandit resumed his outlawry on Aug. 26, 1873, when he and six accomplices looted the town of Tres Pinos, Calif., murdering sheepherder William Redford, an old man known as Davidson, and teamster James Riley. While this was going on, Jose Chavez hit a small boy over the head with a club, rendering him unconscious. This cold-blooded act of violence was typical of the outlaw gang. The Tres Pinos shootout sufficiently aroused the ire of the community. Posses were quickly formed, and an $8,000 reward was offered by the state for the capture of the fearsome Vasquez.

Tiburcio Vasquez and his gang robbed a Kingston hotel and some stagecoaches before they were finally overtaken by one of the posses on their home ground in Alison Canyon, Los Angeles County in December 1874. The bandit was hiding out in an adobe shack owned by "Greek" George Allen when the posse broke through the doors. George Beers injured Vasquez, who attempted to make a break for freedom through the back window. Beers took aim and brought down Vasquez with a volley of buckshot. The bandit survived his wounds and was taken back to stand trial for the murders of the three Tres Pinos men. Vasquez was convicted, and sentenced to death. On Mar. 19, 1875, he was hanged at San Jose, Calif.

W

Wade, "Kid", 1862-84, U.S., outlaw. Kid Wade was a horse thief and all around bad man, who rode with Doc Middleton's outlaw gang, terrorizing northern Nebraska and the Dakotas. After Middleton was apprehended, Wade took over leadership of the gang. Shortly thereafter, Wade was arrested on a charge of horse theft and was sentenced to Anamosa State Prison for one year. In 1883, he was released from custody, and promptly returned to his old haunts in the Niobrara River country. In no time there were reports of widespread horse thievery involving the Kid and his henchmen. Law enforcement officers pursued the Kid into Iowa where he was finally captured at Le Mars and taken to Yankton, S.D. He escaped and was tracked by a posse. Wade was captured and taken back to Basset, Custer County, Neb., where the angry townsmen took matters into their own hands. On the night of Feb. 8, 1884, Wade was dragged from the house where he was being held and lynched.

Waightman (Weightman), George (AKA: **Red Buck**), d.1895, U.S., outlaw. George Waightman was a member of the egregious Bill Doolin gang of bank robbers, active in the Southwest during the 1880s and 1890s. Born in the Lone Star State of Texas, Waightman was a horse thief, bank robber, and cold-blooded killer who would shoot a man down at the slightest provocation. In 1889 he was arrested by Heck Thomas in Oklahoma for horse stealing, a serious offense in those days, and was sentenced to spend three years in jail. After completing his sentence, Waightman joined up with Bill Doolin.

Oklahoma bandit George "Red Buck" Waightman, dead, 1895.

There was a streak of meanness in Waightman that even Doolin—who was never shy with a gun himself—found appalling. After robbing a train outside Dover, Okla., on Apr. 3, 1895, the Doolin mob found themselves encircled by a local posse. Tulsa Jack Blake was killed in the ensuing gunfight, and Waightman's horse was shot out from under him. He jumped on Bitter Creek Newcomb's mount and made a getaway with the remnants of the gang.

Doolin and his men passed a farm where several horses were grazing in the pasture. Waightman jumped off his horse and scaled the farmer's fence. Just as he was about to ride off with one of the unattended horses, the owner suddenly burst out of the house and demanded that Waightman leave at once. Without a word Red Buck turned and fired on the hapless preacher. Later that day, Doolin discussed the matter with Bill Dalton, his second in command. It was agreed that Waightman should be drummed out of the gang. They broke camp, leaving Red Buck behind. Without the gang's protection, the peace officers soon caught up with the murderer. In Arapaho, Okla., on Oct. 2, 1895, a posse of lawmen surrounded Waightman's hideout and demanded he surrender. Waightman tried to shoot his way to freedom, but was cut down instantly. See: **Doolin, William M.**

Wait, Frederick T. (**Waite**, AKA: **Dash Wait**), 1853-95, U.S., gunman. Frederick Wait, a cowboy and a quarter Cherokee Indian, married an Indian woman and moved to Lincoln County, N.M., where he found a job as a Regulator under John Tunstall, an English rancher. When the Lincoln County War broke out, Wait rode with Billy the Kid. On Apr. 1, 1878, Wait, "the Kid," Henry Brown, John Middleton, and Jim French ambushed Sheriff William Brady and four other lawmen on the streets of Lincoln. The five rose from concealment behind an adobe wall and opened fire, killing Brady and another lawmen. Wait and the Kid ran toward the two bodies to seize their rifles and received grazing wounds from Deputy Billy Matthews, who had run for cover when the shooting began. The ambushers then rode out of Lincoln.

Along with three other Regulators, Wait encountered Buckshot Roberts at Blazer's Mill on Apr. 4. In the ensuing gunfight, Dick Brewer, the Regulator's leader, was killed. The others rode off, leaving Roberts fatally wounded.

Wait followed Billy the Kid into the Texas Panhandle when the outlaw prudently decided to leave New Mexico. There, a posse captured him, but he escaped. When Tom O'Folliard and Billy the Kid returned to New Mexico, Wait moved back to the Cherokee Nation in Indian Territory and became a tax collector. He died at the age of forty-two in 1895. See: **Billy the Kid.**

Walker, Joe, 1850-98, U.S., outlaw. Joe Walker never

knew his father, a Texas rancher who died when Walker was an infant. After her husband's death, Walker's mother turned their ranch property over to the management of her brother, Dr. Whitmore, who merged his herds with theirs. Whitmore subsequently moved to a ranch in northern Arizona and later was killed in a skirmish with Indians. His widow, along with her two sons, George and Tobe, sold the Arizona ranch and moved to Carbon County, Utah, eventually becoming a prominent ranching and banking family. After the death of his mother, Walker traveled to Utah to make a property settlement with the Whitmores, who denied their relationship to him as well as his claim to a portion of their property. The cowboy took jobs in ranches and at a sawmill, awaiting a chance for revenge.

Walker hounded the Whitmores for some time. In 1895, he became a wanted man for shooting up the town of Price, Utah, where he caused considerable property damage. Then he joined a band of outlaws at Robbers Roost. Stealing horses and rustling cattle, he frequently took Whitmore stock. In 1896 a posse intercepted him, and after a running gunfight and a fifteen-mile chase, the rustler escaped to Robbers Roost. In 1897 Walker quarrelled with fellow rustler C.L. Maxwell after stealing some Whitmore horses, and Maxwell informed sheriffs C.W. Allred and Azariah Tuttle of Walker's whereabouts which allowed them to catch Walker by surprise. Walker scaled a canyon wall, then wounded Tuttle as Allred raced for help. The outlaw and the wounded lawman held each other at bay for several hours until nightfall when Walker brought Tuttle a bucket of water and then escaped.

Walker threw in with the Wild Bunch and Butch Cassidy a few months later, and on Apr. 21, aided the gang in the Castle Gate payroll robbery by cutting the telegraph wires. The robbery netted $8,000. Walker returned to raiding Whitmore cattle. In May 1898, he and another cowboy, Johnny Herring, were again rustling Whitmore cattle. They were camped near Thompson, Utah, when a nine-man posse caught up with them one night. The posse thought Herring was Butch Cassidy and at dawn, just as Walker stirred awake, the posse opened fire and slaughtered the two men in their bedrolls. See: **Cassidy, Butch.**

Walker, William, d.1889, U.S., outlaw. William Walker and his father, David Walker, were leaders of a wild outlaw band that terrorized Christian County, Mo., in the late 1890s. They reportedly had as many as 400 members in their gang at one time and were known as the Bald Knobbers. Those who dared to testify against Walker and his clan were summarily executed by gang members. In 1888, five witnesses came forward to describe a robbery and

several murders committed by Walker and his Knobbers, but these men were lynched by Walker and his men before they could testify in court.

Missouri bandit and killer William Walker, hanged in 1889.

All five witnesses were mutilated, a large gash made on the forehead of each as a symbol of the informant. William and David Walker, along with John Matthews, one of their men, were convicted of killing Charles Green and Charles Edins. All three were sentenced to be hanged at Ozark, Mo., on May 10, 1889.

The three men were taken to a scaffold and, before a large crowd, were forced at gunpoint to jump off a crude gallows. The ropes around their necks were too long, and William Walker's rope ripped his neck, causing blood to spurt. He was dragged back to the top of the scaffold and forced to wait until his father and Matthews, their knees on the ground, had slowly strangled to death. As William Walker screamed in agony, causing the crowd to look away, another rope was affixed around his neck and the bandit was once again hanged. Walker was pushed off the scaffold and dangled for fifteen minutes before he, too, strangled to death.

Wallace, William Alexander Anderson (AKA: **Bigfoot**), 1817-99, U.S., lawman-gunman. In 1836, a brother and a cousin of "Bigfoot" Wallace were murdered by Mexicans in the Goliad Massacre. The tall Virginian then relocated to La Grange County, Texas, and continued his travels to Travis County in 1840, finally settling in San Antonio in 1842. During these long months on the road Wallace extracted his revenge against the Mexican population of the Southwest until he was at last satisfied that he had

Lawman and gunman William Alexander Anderson Wallace.

evened the score. From there he joined the Texas Rangers

and later fought in the Mexican War. In 1858, Wallace was named a captain in the Texas Rangers, fighting both Indians and outlaws with equal ferocity. He was considered to be somewhat of an expert when it came to tracking wanted fugitives and escaped slaves in West Texas. For a number of years, Wallace rode shotgun on the San Antonio-El Paso stagecoach lines, which often resulted in shootouts with would-be robbers. When his gun fighting days were over, Wallace bought a ranch in Frio County, where he died on Jan. 7, 1899.

Walters, William E. (AKA: **Bill Anderson; Billy Brown; Bronco Billy**), b.1869, U.S., outlaw. William E. Walters, born at Fort Sill, Indian Territory, worked as a cowboy and later as a section hand for the Santa Fe Railroad. Walters turned gunman and bandit in Arizona during the late 1890s, at one point joining the Black Jack Ketchum gang. He was credited with shooting several men and committing a number of robberies with his own gang after leaving Ketchum. Walters and others attempted to rob a train at Grants Station, N.M., but lawmen drove them off

Outlaw William E. Walters.

with heavy gunfire. Walters was tracked down by a posse led by Jeff Milton, who shot Walters in a duel. Walters was convicted of train robbery and sent to prison for life. He was released in 1917 and moved to Hachita, N.M., where he worked as a wrangler for the Diamond A Cattle Company. Walters was killed when he fell from a windmill tower he was repairing.

Warner, Matt, See: Christianson, Willard Erastus.

Watson, Jack, d.1890, U.S., gunman-lawman. Shot in the instep while fighting in the Confederate army, Jack Watson suffered a pronounced limp throughout the remainder of his life following the Civil War. He worked as a cowboy for years, enlisted for a brief time with the Texas Rangers, and frequently was hired by Texas ranchers to track down rustlers. On one occasion in 1880 some cattlemen hired him to capture a horse thief. Watson followed the outlaw for nearly a week before overtaking him one morning as he was cooking breakfast over an open fire. Watson killed the rustler and ate the dead man's breakfast.

Four years later, on Feb. 7, 1884, the local marshal of Montrose, Colo., arrested Watson for drunkenness and a judge fined him all the money he possessed, $85. Watson was furious. When he mounted his horse he began searching for the marshal and judge. When he found them, he opened fire, hitting and wounding the lawman in the arm and the judge in the side. Then he exchanged fire with some citizens and rode out of town. A price of $600 was placed on his head. Watson was later arrested by Sheriff C.W. Shores of Gunnison County, a one-time fellow cowboy of the fugitive, for knifing a man at Crystal mining camp. After Watson won acquittal of the charge, Shore offered him a position as deputy sheriff. Watson accepted and served faithfully as a lawman until his assassination in 1890. Watson had been working undercover in Price, Utah, and had made many local enemies. These men hired a gunman named Ward to kill Watson. One evening as Watson stumbled drunk out of a saloon in Price, Ward shot him from behind a hay wagon. He then was killed with Ward's second volley as he crawled back into the saloon to retrieve his gun.

Webb, John Joshua (AKA: **Samuel King**), 1847-82, U.S., lawman-gunman. Serving most of his adult life as a lawman, John Joshua Webb was also a hunter, teamster, surveyor, hired gun, and member of the notorious Dodge City Gang in Las Vegas, N.M. Born on Feb. 13, 1847, in Iowa, Webb traveled west in 1871, becoming a buffalo hunter and then a surveyor in Colorado. He drifted from Deadwood to Cheyenne, Wyo., to Dodge City, Kan. He found work as a lawman in Dodge City in the late 1870s, and later became a deputy sheriff of Ford County. When the Santa Fe and the Denver & Rio Grande railroad disputed over the right-of-way through the Grand Canyon of the Arkansas River, Webb accepted employment as a gunman to smooth the struggle. He also became close friends with Dave Rudabaugh, a train robber he arrested in 1878.

In 1880, Webb accepted the position of city marshal of Las Vegas, N.M. While marshal, he joined the Dodge City Gang led by Justice of the Peace Hyman Neill, known as "Hoodoo Brown." On Mar. 2, 1880, Webb shot and killed Michael Kelliher after a fight. Regardless of his status as a marshal, Webb was convicted of murder and sentenced to hang. Rudabaugh attempted to break Webb out of jail on Apr. 30 but was unsuccessful. Webb's sentence was appealed and commuted to life in prison. When Rudabaugh was put in prison with Webb, the pair along with two other prisoners, attempted to escape on Sept. 19, 1881. One of their party, Thomas Duffy, was killed. Then on Dec. 3, along with five other convicts, Webb and Rudabaugh escaped after digging their way out of their cell with a knife and a pickax. They raced to Texas and then to Mexico, where Rudabaugh was later killed. John Webb returned to Kansas, took the name "Samuel King," and worked in Kansas and Nebraska as a teamster. He died of smallpox in 1882 in Arkansas.

Weightman, George, See: **Waightman, George.**

West, Frank, d.1886, U.S., lawman. Deputy Marshal Frank West tangled with the murderous Sam Starr on two occasions. Starr, a full-blood Cherokee Indian, married the famous female outlaw Belle Starr, and together they caused trouble among the citizens living in the Indian territories. A week before the Christmas holiday in 1886, Belle Starr and Sam were invited to a dance given at the home of Mrs. Lucy Surratt near Whitefield on the Canadian River. Sam Starr was in an ugly mood and was already intoxicated by the time he arrived at the party, where he spotted lawman Frank West. "You are the son of a bitch who shot me and killed my horse that day in the cornfield!" West denied having ever laid eyes on Starr, but he could not be placated. Starr drew out his pistol and shot West through the neck. Before he fell, the lawman managed to unholster his own weapon and fire. The bullet landed in Starr's chest, and within two minutes, both men lay dead. See: **Starr, Belle.**

Bandit queen Belle Starr whose husband Sam Starr was shot and killed by lawman Frank West in 1886.

West, Richard (AKA: **Little Dick**), d.1898, U.S., outlaw. After William Doolin was killed in 1896, the last surviving member of his gang, Richard "Little Dick" West, tried to form another gang, recruiting novices. West named his outfit the Al Jennings gang, after the leader of the group he had fallen in with, but Jennings, his brothers, and their friends, the O'Malley brothers, looked to West to guide them in robbing trains.

Outlaw "Little Dick" West, shown dead, 1898.

Their first attempted train robbery occurred near Oklahoma City on Aug. 16, 1897, at Edmond. While they looked at the door of an express car they had just stopped, a conductor asked them what they were doing. The outlaws panicked and ran for their horses. West had no choice but to follow.

West set up another train robbery near Muskogee, Okla., but his gang failed him again. They refused to attempt a bank job because they saw armed guards inside. They waylaid a Rock Island train in Indian Territory under the control of the Chickasaw Nation, but used all the dynamite they had by mistake in their first attempt to blow the train's safe. The car containing the safe was blown apart, but the safe was unharmed, so they robbed the passengers, from whom they collected $300 in cash, some whiskey, and a stalk of bananas. During the holdup, Al Jennings' mask fell from his face. Someone who recognized him alerted lawman William Matthew Tilghman.

West took his share of the robbery and headed on alone. Tilghman hunted him down in a stable near Guthrie, Okla. On Apr. 7, 1898, West was currying his horse when Tilghman ordered him to surrender. West fired on Tilghman and tried to get away on foot, but the lawman killed him with one shot.

Jennings and his gang were later caught. Jennings was given a long sentence, of which he served less than five years. See: **Doolin, William; Tilghman, William Matthew, Jr.**

Wheeler, Grant, d.1895, U.S., outlaw. Grant Wheeler was a train and bank robber who raided through California, Arizona, and New Mexico during the mid-1890s. Wheeler, along with Joe George, another western desperado, stopped a Southern Pacific train near Cochise, Ariz., on Jan. 3, 1895. They forced their way into the express car at gunpoint and set a charge of dynamite next to the express car safe. The bandits used too much dynamite and the resulting explosion sent a shipment of Mexican silver dollars sky high. Wheeler and Grant spent several hours collecting the coins, gathering about $1,000 before they gave up the exhausting work. For years thereafter, tourists and prospectors collected the silver dollars in an area of several blocks. Wheeler and George fled to California where George attempted a lone holdup and was shot to death.

Outlaw Grant Wheeler.

Some weeks later, Wheeler appeared in a saloon in Deming, N.M., where he got into an argument over a bar girl. He was wounded in the resulting gunfight. Recovering from his wound, Wheeler learned that he was being tracked by several posses for his robbery of the Southern Pacific train. Former sheriff of Tombstone, Ariz., and railroad detective William Breakenridge trailed Wheeler to Mancos, Colo. There, on Apr. 25, 1895, Breakenridge and Wheeler shot it out and Wheeler was wounded. The embattled outlaw, however, refused to surrender, continuing to exchange shots with Breakenridge while dodging behind rocks. Wheeler soon exhausted all of his ammunition, except for his last bullet, with which he shot himself in the head, committing suicide.

Wheeler, Harry, d.1925, U.S., lawman. The son of an army officer, Harry Wheeler served as an army scout, Arizona Ranger, sheriff, and army captain. Under the command of Nelson A. Miles, Wheeler was a scout in the Spanish-American War and during the military campaign against Indian chief Geronimo. Wheeler joined the Arizona Rangers in 1902, and killed a robber named Bostwick while the man had a group of saloon patrons lined up against the wall. When Wheeler burst into the bar, he and Bostwick exchanged fire. Wheeler shot Bostwick in the chest, killing him.

Wheeler was appointed captain of the Rangers two years later, replacing Thomas Rynning. In February 1907, in Benson, Ariz., the Ranger captain fatally wounded J.A. Tracy, a man who was threatening a couple boarding a train. Apparently Tracy was infatuated with the man's female companion. Following a gun battle during which Wheeler was shot twice and Tracy four times, both men shook hands and wished each other a quick recovery. Tracy died shortly afterwards on the train before reaching Tucson.

Lawman Harry Wheeler.

In 1909, the Arizona Rangers disbanded and Wheeler was later elected sheriff of Cochise County. He led the group responsible for the 1917 "Bisbee Deportation" in which 1,200 striking laborers were forcibly removed from the town. After serving as captain in the army during WWI, Wheeler was defeated in a re-election bid for the position of sheriff of Cochise County.

Whitley, William, d.1888, U.S., outlaw. Gunman William Whitley was a member of Brack Cornett's outlaw band, which pulled off many successful train robberies in Texas, including the one at McNeil in 1888. In September of that same year, Marshal John Rankin received word that Whitley and his cohorts were planning another hold up. With Deputy Duval West and a compliment of Texas Rangers, Rankin sequestered himself in the express car of the train that Whitley planned to rob. When the train steamed out of Harwood, Texas, on Sept. 22, 1888, the lawmen were on board. About three miles east of town, eight to ten men appeared on the tracks. The gunfire from the express car drove the would-be robbers off, and in the subsequent shootout with the gang in Floresville on Sept. 25, Whitley was shot and killed. See: **Cornett, Brack.**

Whitney, Chauncey Belden (AKA: **Cap**), 1842-73, U.S., lawman. One of the first settlers of Ellsworth, Kan., in 1867, Chauncey Whitney was the town's first sheriff. He built the Ellsworth Jail, and in 1868, fought in the Battle of Beecher Island, in which several armed "scouts" killed attacking Indians who were armed with only spears and arrows. He later served as city marshal, deputy sheriff, and county sheriff. On Aug. 15, 1873, when he was thirty-one, Whitney was killed when Billy Thompson, brother of Ben Thompson, accidentally shot the lawman in the shoulder and breast. The bullet fragments pierced a lung before becoming embedded in his spine. Whitney lingered in great agony for three days before he died. See: **Thompson, Ben.**

Widenmann, Robert A., d.1930, U.S., lawman. On Feb. 18, 1878, Alexander A. McSween's partner John Tunstall was gunned down while allegedly resisting arrest by deputy sheriffs Jesse Evans, Frank Baker, and Tom Hill. It was the latest round of violence in the Lincoln County War, pitting Lawrence J. Murphy, owner of a large general store known as The House, against McSween, Tunstall, and John Chisum, who objected to the monopolistic practices of the cattle raisers who hid behind the veil of the corrupt Republican Santa Fe Ring.

Murphy's partner, James J. Dolan, obtained the necessary legal papers to arrest Tunstall and several of his associates. But when Tunstall refused, he was shot down by Evans, a known cattle rustler. Marshal John Sherman ordered the arrest of Evans and his outlaw band who had escaped from the Lincoln County Jail in 1877. He assigned the task of bringing in these men to a young deputy who had come from the east, Robert A. Widenmann. After receiving a tip that Evans was hiding at Murphy's ranch, Widenmann dispatched his men to the location only to find the gunman had fled.

Deputy Widenmann finally caught up with his prey on Feb. 13, 1878, but Evans threatened to shoot him if he had the temerity to try to bring him to justice. Widenmann, supported by U.S. troops, surrounded the Dolan store, which he believed to be guarded by Evans' men. Marshal Sherman appealed to Washington for permission to engage the troops against the Evans band, but was disappointed by the reply. "It does not appear why the arrest of four men cannot be made without troops." The request was denied.

Unable to locate Evans inside the Dolan mercantile store, Widenmann recklessly went after Sheriff William Brady's deputies, who were occupying Tunstall's store. He ordered the soldiers of the posse to "shoot it out" on the streets of Lincoln, but realizing the absurdity of such an order, the army lieutenant in charge refused. Incensed by the high-handed actions of Widenmann, Brady and his deputies arrested the young easterner and bound him over for trial.

Widenmann pressured the authorities in Washington and the British ambassador to investigate what he believed to be an organized conspiracy to murder Tunstall. (Tunstall was a British citizen.) The perpetrators were none other than the Santa Fe Ring of which Sheriff Brady was a member. The letter had a devastating and immediate effect. Governor Samuel B. Axtell had the letter published in the *New Mexican*, and when Marshal Sherman finally saw it, he promptly revoked Widenmann's commission as a deputy. The move was supported by Axtell, who had sided with the Dolan faction all along. For days the controversy simmered in the press. The *New Mexican* sided with the Santa Fe Ring and denounced Widenmann as a traitor to the territory by going to a foreign government for aid. The rival Cimarron *News and Press* scolded Sheriff Brady and members of the clique for failing to uphold the laws.

Realizing that this was nothing more than a political war of words between the Republican ring and Widenmann's Democratic supporters, Sherman reappointed Widenmann on Mar. 30, 1878. The Cimarron *News and Press* greeted the announcement with jubilation. The Murphy-Dolan faction retaliated by filing robbery and murder charges against the deputy and several of the McSween men. Widenmann and Billy the Kid were arrested by Deputy Sheriff George W. Peppin on Apr. 1, 1878, for the recent murders of Brady and Sheriff George Hindman. Widenmann was soon released, however, only to be rearrested on two more occasions for abusing his authority and resisting an officer of the law. The harassment of Widenmann by the Dolan faction continued unabated. The deputy was accused of provoking the Lincoln County War in the pages of the *New Mexican*. "That scrub (Widenmann) was to a great degree responsible for the disturbed conditions...in Lincoln County." The editor went on to say that Widenmann had offered perjured testimony to the jurors in his court appearances. "We are neither surprised nor disappointed as we have long since...pronounced him an unmitigated liar and scoundrel."

In May 1878, erroneous reports filtered out of Lincoln County that Widenmann had been killed by the Dolan faction. In actuality, he was very much alive and later traveled to England, where he tried to interest John H. Tunstall's father in a shady business deal. Widenmann eventually returned to the U.S. but elected to retire to Ann Arbor, Mich., where he worked quietly in his father's hardware store. Widenmann died in 1930, and up until his death, he believed that Thomas Catron, an influential member of the Santa Fe ring, had spies keep him under constant surveillance. See: **Catron, Thomas Benton; Lincoln County War; Sherman, John E., Jr.**

Wild Bill Hickok, See: **Hickok, James Butler.**

Wild Bunch, prom. 1880s-90s, U.S., outlaws. In the late 1880s and through the 1890s, when the West was being tamed in dozens of frontier towns, the last bastion of the outlaw was Hole-in-the-Wall, a seemingly impenetrable fortress of towering cliffs, deep gorges and mountainous retreats. This was the hideout of the last of the great outlaw bands, The Wild Bunch. The shelter was located where the state lines of Utah, Colorado, and Wyoming now meet and only those who belonged to the infamous band knew the treacherous path to the high mountain hideout. Another less celebrated hideout for Wild Bunch members was Robber's Roost in Southeastern Utah.

The hundreds of members of the Wild Bunch were part of a loose federation of mostly cowboys who had turned outlaw following the disastrous blizzards of 1888. After the blizzards drastically reduced the great herds of cattle in the West and caused the collapse of thousands of small ranches, many owners and their hands turned to other means to survive. Many turned to crime, rustling cattle, robbing banks and trains, drifting to Hole-in-the-Wall when the great posses led by Joe LeFors, William Breakenridge, and others hunted them across the plains.

Living in huts and small cabins built on a small plateau, Wild Bunch members worked together or continued their lone banditry, occasionally joining larger bands of outlaws from the Wild Bunch community. The most notorious Wild Bunch members were the McCarty Brothers, George "Flat Nose" Curry, Butch Cassidy, the Sundance Kid, Ben "The Tall Texan" Kilpatrick, Harvey Logan, William Carver, Ellsworth Lay, O.C. Hanks, and Harry Tracy, but scores more, who occasionally rode with the infamous members, continued to inhabit Hole-in-the-Wall in the early 1900s. Beyond the super star bandits, the most notable of the many outlaws who rode in and out of Hole-in-the-Wall for twenty years and were classified as members of the Wild Bunch were:

Dave Atkins, a ranch hand who turned to train robbery and murder while in his mid-twenties. He was fast on the draw, but backed down twice from pulling his gun on Harry Longbaugh (or Longabaugh), who was called The Sundance Kid. On one occasion Atkins made fun of the Kid because of his preference for Ralston's cereal food. Sundance finished his bowl of cereal, stood up, and gave a speech about its "healthy properties." He then invited Atkins, while resting his hands on his two holstered six-guns, to have a bowl. Atkins reluctantly sat down, ate some of the cereal, and then quickly agreed with the Kid that it was the best tasting food he had ever eaten.

Jack Bennett, a freightman who brought the Wild Bunch supplies to Hole-in-the-Wall and occasionally rode with some of its members in various holdups. In March 1898, a posse caught Bennett and lynched him from the crossbars of a Wyoming ranch.

The famous Wild Bunch photo of Butch Cassidy and friends.

William Cruzan, robber.

O.C. Hanks, robber.

Elza Lay, robber.

Ben Kilpatrick, robber.

Above, Dave Lant, outlaw.
Right, Tom O'Day, thief.

James Lowe, thief.

Bob Lee, train robber.

Will Roberts, rustler.

Jesse Linsley, horse thief.

Dave Atkins, train robber.

Frank Elliott, robber.

Sam "Laughing Sam" Carey, who received his ironic name because he never smiled and displayed a mean streak that was often lethal. Carey, one of the first to use Hole-in-the-Wall as a hideout, began robbing trains and banks in the late 1880s with the Taylor Brothers, Bud Denslow, and H. Wilcox. Carey operated throughout Wyoming, Montana, and South Dakota. Carey's gang was shot to pieces by citizens in Spearfish, S.D., and he alone survived, riding back to Hole-in-the-Wall where another Wild Bunch member pried three bullets from his body. Carey rested for a week, then rode out to rob another bank.

Joseph Chancellor, born in Texas, made his reputation as a gunfighter in Oklahoma. He was caught rustling cattle and was sent to the penitentiary in Santa Fe. He was released on Jan. 28, 1897. The 37-year-old Chancellor drifted into Hole-in-the-Wall as late as 1904. He was so addicted to cigarettes that his fingers were completely stained yellow and he got up several times each night to smoke a dozen or so cigarettes before going back to sleep.

William Cruzan, who was thirty-three in 1901 when he arrived at Hole-in-the-Wall after serving several years in prison for rustling and robbery. He preferred to commit robberies alone and was shot to death in 1905 while trying to rob a train single-handedly.

Frank "Peg-Leg" Elliot was twenty-one when he reached Hole-in-the-Wall, where he met Robert Eldredge, another cowboy turned horse and cattle thief. These two rode out to rob a train in October 1891, and were trapped by a posse and shot to death.

Swede Johnson, a pathological murderer, rode into Hole-in-the-Wall in 1898 and befriended Harry Tracy and Dave Lant who were as trigger-happy as Johnson. Willie Strang, a witless 17-year-old, dumped a pitcher of water on Johnson and Johnson went crazy, emptying his six-gun into Strang. For this murder Johnson was tracked down and sent to the Wyoming State Prison for life.

Bob Lee, cousin of Harvey and Lonnie Logan, was one of the first outlaws to ride into Hole-in-the-Wall. He later brought the Logans, and Harvey Logan became one of the most feared members of the Wild Bunch and its worst six-gun killer. Lee participated in several robberies and was later sent to prison.

Jesse Linsley, horse thief, ex-convict, rode into Hole-in-the-Wall about 1899. He committed some minor robberies, but he did not have the stomach for the kind of train robberies committed by Butch Cassidy and others, especially since they used dynamite to blow open locked express cars. Linsley vanished in 1901.

James Lowe, a 32-year-old train robber when he arrived in Hole-in-the-Wall in 1903, led many raids against trains and banks and was killed by lawmen in 1910.

Tom O'Day, a hardcase cowboy from Wyoming, joined the Wild Bunch in 1899 and participated in several bank robberies. Occasionally he rode with Butch Cassidy, but usually he operated as a lone bandit, which pleased other Wild Bunch members since O'Day seldom bathed and reportedly "smelled like a skunk" most of the time. O'Day attempted to rob the bank in Casper, Wyo., was arrested, and sent to prison to serve a long term.

Will Roberts, cowboy turned gunman and outlaw, used the alias "Dixon." He robbed many banks and trains before he was captured and sent to prison. He was one of the last important members of the Wild Bunch, which ceased to exist after 1910.

Willard Erastus Christianson (Matt Warner), one of the original inhabitants of Hole-in-the-Wall, participated in several holdups but retired early from outlawry. However, he maintained a sort of general store and hotel in Hole-in-the-Wall, selling supplies to the outlaws and offering them necessities. He later wrote a fine account of the Wild Bunch that stands as a classic in the western field.

Little remains of the old Hole-in-the-Wall hideout used by the Wild Bunch except the skeletal remains of a few shacks. Little is left to prove that the worst criminals in the U.S. ever inhabited this barren mountainous area. When they were present, however, no lawman or posse dared to enter Hole-in-the-Wall. Peace officers of the day estimated that as many as 100 to 200 outlaws were hidden in its rocky recesses at one time, an army of ruthless killers no sheriff thought to capture at one time. See: **Bullion, Laura; Briant, Elijah S.; Carver, William; Cassidy, Butch; Christianson, William Erastus; Curry, George; Hanks, Orlando Camillo; Ketchum, Thomas E.; Kilpatrick, Benjamin; Lay, William Ellsworth; Logan, Harvey; McCarty Brothers; Sundance Kid, The; Tracy, Harry.**

Williamson, Robert M. (AKA: Three Legged Willie), prom. 1850s, U.S., lawman.

Robert Williamson walked with a peg attached to one knee; the result of a childhood disability that withered his leg—hence the nickname Three Legged Willie. He was sent to Shelbyville to set up a district court in an area unaccustomed to the intrusions of the federal government. The residents of Shelby County, Texas, referred to District Judge Robert Williamson's brand of western justice as "Willie's Law," and with good reason.

The judge opened the session in a crude, improvised courtroom in the back of a general store. One of the local toughs looked at Williamson with benign amusement. He hurled a bowie knife at the bench and exclaimed: "This sir, is the law in Shelby County." The judge was not taken aback by the threat. Williamson pulled out his pistol and plunked it down on the desk. "This is the constitution that overrules your law!" he exclaimed.

Wilson, Aaron, 1855-76, U.S., outlaw. Fifty-six-year-old James Harris closed up his dry goods store in Beatty, Kan., in 1875. He packed his worldly possessions in a wagon and embarked on a perilous journey through Indian territory with his 12-year-old son. The man and the boy were making their way to Texas when they set up camp for the night at Wichita Agency, a remote outpost near Fort Sill (Okla.) on Oct. 12, 1875. Aaron Wilson, twenty, introduced himself to Harris and asked if he might share with them their evening meal.

The trusting Harris invited Wilson to spend the night in their camp. Wilson thanked them and settled down for the night. A few minutes after midnight, the boy was awakened by the anguished cries of his father who Wilson had attacked with an ax. The youngster pleaded with Wilson to spare his life, but the gunman had no intentions of granting the request. The boy attempted to flee, but was cut down by a load of buckshot from Wilson's rifle.

When the bloody deed was over, Wilson scalped his victims before he made off with their horses and a new suit of clothes. The murderer proudly displayed the scalps of his victims to the local Indians, thinking that they might grant him special favors. The Indian chief reported the matter to officials at Fort Sill, who tracked down Wilson and arrested him. The remorseless murderer appeared before Judge Isaac Parker who commented: "You have been tried and found guilty of that most revolting and terrible of crimes known to the land as murder. You have been aided and advised by experienced counsel, who have done all that could be done by any one under the most conclusive and convincing set of facts which made up the damning evidence of your guilt...I beg of you not to waste a moment of time, but to at once devote yourself to the preparation of your soul to meet its God." With that, Wilson was sentenced and taken away to await his execution on Apr. 21, 1876.

Wilson, George (James C. Casharego), 1870-96, U.S., outlaw. On July 30, 1896, George Wilson was the last man to be executed on the Fort Smith (Ark.) gallows. Wilson was a thief, swindler, and master forger who had been convicted of murdering Zachariah W. Thatch at their campfire near Keokuk Falls in the Creek Indian Territory on May 15, 1895. Wilson dumped the body in a stream and made off with the dead man's possessions. He was cap-

tured a few days later. At first he told the marshals that he was a nephew of Thatch, a claim which was later proved false. Finally Wilson broke down and admitted that his real name was James Casharego, and he was from Conway, Ark.

Wilson denied killing Thatch, but deputy marshals who closely examined the camp-site unearthed traces of blood extracted from a fissure in the ground. Judge Isaac Parker, who had sent many men to the gallows since taking his place on the bench in 1875, passed sentence. "Even nature revolted against your crime," he told the condemned man. "The earth opened up and drank up the blood, held it in a fast embrace until the time it should appear against you; the water too, threw up its dead and bore upon its placid bosom the foul evidence of your crime." An appeal was filed to the Su-

James C. Casharego, better known as outlaw George Wilson.

preme Court, but the conviction was upheld. Wilson was resentenced and summarily executed. The George Wilson hanging closed out a long and colorful chapter in the history of the Old West.

Wilson, John B. (AKA: **Juan Bautista**), prom. 1870s, U.S., lawman. John Wilson served as the justice of the peace at Lincoln, N.M., during the time of the Lincoln County War. He was a veteran of the Mexican War, having served with the First Regiment of Illinois Volunteer Infantry. He settled in the New Mexico Territory in 1849 and presided over the inquest into the 1878 murder of John Tunstall. The jury consisted of Frank Coe, Ben Ellis, George Barber, and John Newcomb, all McSween partisans. See: **Lincoln County War.**

Wilson, Sinker, d.1876, U.S., outlaw. In 1867 Sinker Wilson murdered Datus Cowan in the Cherokee Nation. Wilson was arrested, tried, and convicted of this crime in 1867, but escaped from the federal court at Van Buren, Ark., and remained at large until he was recaptured by U.S. marshals. On June 24, 1876, he was resentenced by Judge

Isaac Parker. The defendant was hanged three months later on Sept. 8, 1876.

Wilson, Vernon Coke, 1855-92, U.S., lawman. Born in Abingdon, Va., Vernon Wilson was a nephew of Texas governor Richard Coke. In 1876, at the age of twenty-one, Wilson joined the Texas Rangers Company A, Frontier Battalion, which was commanded by Neal Coldwell. In 1878, Wilson participated in one of the most legendary rides in the history of the Old West—from Austin to San Saba County—where he warned the Rangers that outlaw Sam Bass was holed up in Round Rock.

Wilson made rapid advances in his chosen career. In 1885, he served as chief of the Mounted Inspectors in Arizona and in New Mexico, where he was a candidate for sheriff. In 1892, the Southern Pacific Railroad employed him as a special detective investigating train robbery cases. While serving in this

Vernon Coke Wilson, shot and killed while attempting to arrest members of the Evans-Sontag robbery gang.

capacity, he was sent to California to investigate the Evans-Sontag Case. Considered to be one of the most feared gunslingers on the right side of the law, Wilson claimed to have put twenty-seven men in their graves. However, while in pursuit of the Evans-Sontag gang, he was shot down outside a mountain cabin near Sampsons Flat, Fresno County, Calif., on Sept. 13, 1892. It is believed that Chris Evans fired the fatal shot. See: **Sontag Brothers**.

Wilson, William, d. 1875, U.S., gunman. On Aug. 2, 1875, Lincoln County, N.M., resident William Wilson ambushed his former employee Bob Casey from behind an adobe wall. Wilson was tried for murder on Oct. 18, 1875 at the U.S. District Court and was sentenced to die on the scaffold. By order of the governor, the execution was postponed until Dec. 6. He was actually hanged four days later in the Lincoln County jail yard, but the job was badly botched. The morticians discovered shortly after placing Wilson's body in the wooden coffin, that the dead man was still alive. He had miraculously survived the ten-minute ordeal. The jailers tried a second time, and after twenty

minutes, Wilson was pronounced dead. He was the first man to be legally hanged in Lincoln County.

Wolcott, Frank, prom. 1892, U.S., gunman. A retired U.S. army major, Frank Wolcott was selected to lead the vigilante raid against the Johnson County, Wyo., rustlers who had threatened the livelihood of the powerful Wyoming Stock Growers Association in April 1892. Wolcott and his heavily armed "militia" men found themselves surrounded by U.S. Army troops and Johnson County gunmen led by Sheriff Red Angus at the TA Ranch near Buffalo. The Johnson County War ended with a whimper in the court-rooms of Cheyenne. Afterward, Wolcott served for a few years as justice of the peace in Glenrock. See: **Johnson County War**.

Woodruff, Len, prom. 1880s, U.S., outlaw. Len Woodruff worked as an LX cowboy in Oldham County, Texas, before opening a bar in Tascosa. On Mar. 21, 1886, he engaged a group of LS cowboys in a pitched gun battle that left Ed King, Frank Valley, and Fred Chilton dead. Woodruff had taken refuge in the back room of an adobe cafe and had fired on Valley and Chilton when they attempted to charge the building. King was shot down moments earlier. Woodruff left town, but was eventually tracked down, returned to stand trial for murder, and acquitted. He was last seen in 1889, during the height of the Oklahoma land rush.

Worthington, Nick, 1846-78, U.S., outlaw. Horse thief and three-time convicted felon Nick Worthington "died with his boots on," according to published reports in the Santa Fe *New Mexican* in June 1878. His tragic demise occurred outside Lambert's Hotel in Cimarron, when a group of men from Colorado happened to recognize him as the leader of an outlaw band wanted by the government for stealing sixty mules from Fort Elliot, Texas. One of the Colorado men ordered him to raise his hands and surrender, but Worthington ran off into the street, where a rifle shot fired by Texan W.N. Peet, whose orders were to capture Worthington, caught him in the middle of the back, and he fell to the ground dead. It was later discovered that Worthington owned a hog farm near Jacksboro, Texas, and had murdered two black soldiers there.

Wren, William R., prom. 1877, U.S., gunman-lawman. William Wren was a cattle rancher in Lampasas County, Texas. He became Pink Higgins' chief lieutenant in a feud with the Horrell brothers. On Mar. 26, 1877, Wren, Higgins, and several others ambushed Mart and Sam Horrell. They shot Sam from his horse, and though they wounded Mart, he charged the ambushers and single-handedly dispersed them. Wren was wounded in a battle with seven Horrell men in Lampasas on June 14. Frank Mitchell, Higgins' brother-in-law, was killed, and Wren was wounded. The following month, Higgins and fifteen men besieged the Horrell ranch. The assault lasted two days, during which two of Horrell's men were wounded. Higgins had to withdraw when his ammunition ran low. Wren was severely wounded in a street fight later that year, and signed a truce at the insistence of Texas Ranger major John B. Jones. Wren later became a county sheriff.

Wyatt, Nathaniel Ellsworth (AKA: **Zip; Wild Charlie; Dick Yaeger**), 1863-95, U.S., outlaw. Nathaniel Wyatt was the son of an Indiana farmer. He turned to outlawry after his brother, Nim "Six Shooter Jack" Wyatt, was killed in Texline, Texas. Nathaniel robbed various U.S.

Outlaw Zip Wyatt, photographed only a few hours before he died of wounds.

postal stations, retail stores, and trains in the Southwest before retreating to Indiana, where he was arrested and returned to Oklahoma by Chris Madsen. However, he escaped from the jail in Guthrie and returned to the Indian Territory, where some his most famous gunfights occurred.

In the little village of Todd, on Mar. 29, 1894, Wyatt and two henchman held up a Blaine County store owned and operated by E.H. Townsend. When the proprietor put up some resistance, the robbers shot him dead in the presence of his wife and children. The next month in Dewey County, Okla., Wyatt murdered County Treasurer Fred Hoffman.

After the successful robbery of a Santa Fe train in Whorton, Okla., on May 9, 1894, that left the station master dead, Wyatt and his gang went across the border into Kansas. Wyatt and his gang were cornered in Pryor's Grove by Sheriff Andrew Balfour, who produced an arrest warrant. Wyatt wheeled and fired on the sheriff, instantly killing him.

Wyatt, a trigger-happy gunman, was pursued throughout the Old West for several years before a posse finally caught up with him outside Skeleton Creek, Okla., on Aug. 3, 1895. Wyatt had drifted off to sleep in a cornfield when Ad Poak and Tom Smith crept up on him with their rifles drawn. Without giving him a chance to respond, they opened fire. "Don't shoot any more. I'm bad hit," Wyatt said. He was taken to Enid, Okla., where he died Sept. 7.

Y

Yager, Erastus (AKA: **Red**), d.1864, U.S., outlaw. A nineteenth-century outlaw informant, Erastus Yager revealed the identities of several members of the Innocents outlaw gang, bringing about the gang's destruction. In December 1863, a vigilante committee captured Yager while he was carrying messages to gang agents who held up wagons and stages carrying large sums of money. Yager claimed he worked for Sheriff Henry Plummer, the leader of the Innocents, and told the vigilantes that Sheriff Plummer directed the activity of the Innocents while telling the public he was trying to rid the area of them. Yager also revealed how the organization was structured, how orders were handed down, and the password "innocent." He further revealed the names of twenty-six key members of the gang. The vigilance committee, while appreciating Yager's information, hanged him in Stinkingwater Valley on Jan. 4, 1864.

Younger Brothers, prom. 1860s-70s, U.S., outlaws. The three Younger brothers, Thomas "Cole" Coleman, Robert, and James, grew up in Kansas in the 1850s when the state was torn between the pro-slavery factions and the abolitionists of the North who sought to keep slavery out of the territories. The Youngers were growing up in Lee's Summit, Mo., when their father was killed, presumably by Northerners. When the Civil War came, Cole Younger joined William Quantrill's band of Confederate marauders who rode through border states creating havoc against the Union. In 1863 Cole met 16-year-old Myra Belle Shirley while he was stationed in Texas. Their courtship produced an illegitimate child, according to Shirley, who achieved notoriety as the legendary outlaw Belle Starr.

Jim Younger, who was only eleven when the war started, followed his older brother into the ranks of the Quantrill raiders in the vain hope of avenging his father's death. They rode together for the duration of the conflict, until Quantrill was mortally wounded at Smiley, Kan. Jim was captured and jailed at a military prison in Alton, Ill., where he was held until the waning months of 1865. About a year later, Cole Younger and Frank James, who was also a former member of Quantrill's Raiders, decided to form an outlaw band.

Cole Younger, his taste for adventure whetted by the Civil War, joined the Frank and Jesse James holdup gang in 1866. They robbed a bank in Liberty, Mo., and then fled to Texas and Louisiana to spend their loot. At an opportune time, Cole returned to Missouri where he inveigled his brothers to join him. Jim left the farm to ride with the newly formed James-Younger Gang.

Bob was too young to have fought in the Civil War, but he joined his older brothers in 1868 and 1872 respectively. Jesse James was the acknowledged leader of this Western outlaw gang, but he never got along well with Cole. The Younger Brothers and the James boys committed a string of bank robberies and train holdups throughout Missouri and the surrounding states in the late 1860s, continuing through the next decade. As was their custom when the law was in pursuit, the Younger-James gang retreated to Texas and laid low until things settled down in Missouri.

The highly publicized exploits of this renegade band led to stepped-up pressure for their arrest. By 1874 the Pinkerton National Detective Agency entered the affray, sending several of their best agents to Missouri to capture Jesse James and the Youngers. In March 1874, Jim Younger and his cousin John went into hiding at a friend's house in Monegaw Springs, Mo. Having discovered their location, agents Louis J. Lull and John Boyle disguised themselves as cattle buyers to garner some useful information. The Youngers were in hiding at Theodorick Snuffer's home in Monegaw Springs when the Pinkerton men appeared at the door asking for directions. When they had gone, the Youngers loaded up their weapons and rode off in pursuit. They caught up with them on the Chalk Level Road, and demanded that the "cattle buyers" identify themselves. Jim Younger collected their rifles while John stood guard. A moment later, agent Lull produced a hidden pistol and shot John Younger through the throat. Before he fell to the ground, he fired several shotgun blasts which killed Lull. Deputy Sheriff Ed Daniels, who accompanied the two Pinkertons, was gunned down in a similar fashion. John Younger, who had killed a man for the first time when he was only fifteen, died of his wounds a short time later.

The three remaining Youngers rode with the James Brothers and three other men into Northfield, Minn., on Sept. 7, 1876, to rob the First National Bank. The ill-timed holdup went awry from the beginning when three bank employees, F.J. Wilcox, A.E. Bunker, and Joseph Lee Heywood, refused to cooperate. Bunker turned and fled out the door, but Wells wounded him with a bullet outside. Jesse James and Bob Younger shot cashier Heywood to death, then ran outside to rejoin the gang. Pandemonium broke loose, when the incensed residents of Northfield learned what had transpired. A storekeeper, A.E. Manning, exchanged shots with Bob Younger. Bill Chadwell and Clell Miller, who had rerouted the gang from Mankato to Northfield because they feared the vigilantes there, were shot off their horses. A medical student, Henry Wheeler,

Cole Younger

Bob Younger

Jim Younger

John Younger

The disastrous raid of the James-Younger gang in Northfield, Minn., 1876, saw the capture of the Younger Brothers.

Cole Younger, 1890.

Bob Younger, 1890.

Jim Younger, 1890.

Cole Younger in old age.

took aim on Miller, and leveled him. Bill Chadwell was also killed. Bob Younger, who was severely wounded in the hand, was snatched up by his brother, Cole, who galloped out of town. Jesse and Frank James fled from the area, not really caring about the plight of the Youngers who sought refuge in a thicket near Medalia, Minn.

Cole, Jim, and Charlie Pitts did as much as they could for brother Bob, who was weakened by the loss of blood. On Sept. 21, a posse caught up with the Youngers and demanded their immediate surrender. They replied by firing on the lawmen, which commenced one last bloody shoot-out. Pitts was killed. Cole was shot seven times, and James was hit five times. Bob emerged from behind the embankment with his hands raised. "They're all down except me," he said. A final shot clipped Bob in the cheek before the lawmen took the prisoners back to jail.

The three brothers entered a plea of guilty to robbery and murder. All three were sentenced to life in the Still-water penitentiary. Bob Younger was a model prisoner. He studied medicine and cooperated with the guards in every way. However, his health was frail. He contracted tuberculosis and died on Sept. 16, 1889. Cole and Jim were paroled in 1901, but were required under the terms of the Deming Act to live in Minnesota. The brothers went into business selling tombstone monuments, and later, insurance. Jim fell in love with a newspaper writer, Alice Miller, but was not permitted to marry under the strict parole terms handed down by the state. Despondent, he killed himself on Oct. 19, 1902. Cole Younger received an official pardon in 1903. He eventually reunited with Frank James in a touring Wild West show. Before he died on Feb. 21, 1916, Cole went on the lecture circuit preaching the evils of crime. See: **James, Jesse Woodson**.

Yountis, Oliver (AKA: **Crescent Sam**), d.1892, U.S., outlaw. Kentucky-born Oliver Yountis rode with the Doolin-Dalton gang in Oklahoma in the early 1890s. Yountis is credited with murdering a man in Spearville, Kan., during the commission of a bank robbery in November 1892. Ford County Sheriff Chalk Beeson followed the gang into Oklahoma. They surrounded Yountis at his home, and when he appeared on the porch, Marshals Heck Thomas, and Chris Madsen cut him down during a furious exchange of shots. The lawmen recovered $4,500 of the stolen loot.

WESTERN LAWMEN

The task of enforcing the laws of the U.S. in the untamed nineteenth-century Western frontier was often left to the marshals and sheriffs of the respective areas. The word "marshal" was originally a corruption of the German "marah" and "calc," which together mean "horsekeeper," but the status for those who held the title of marshal gradually improved until by the Middle Ages the rank of marshal was for the commander of great armies.

In the U.S., the office of marshal, adopted from the earlier British model, was attached to each federal district court. The marshal was authorized to carry out all "lawful precepts," as determined by the federal bench. The president appointed the marshal with the consent of the Senate. They were originally compensated from an inadequate fee system, which was revised over time so that the marshal could charge a municipality a fee equal to that of a state office. The federal marshals who were sworn to uphold the law on the frontier faced many obstacles, notably Congress' failure to assess stiff penalties to those who resisted arrest. By the 1850s, federal marshals policed a vast stretch of territory, assisted by county sheriffs, city marshals, and precinct constables. They had "acquired the primary duty of enforcement within the territories" and were "the sole police power in pioneer communities."

The Texas Rangers were organized in 1826 to protect American settlers from Indian attacks. During the Texas war for independence this paramilitary force served as a border patrol. Though they refused to wear any kind of uniform, or even salute their superior officers, the Rangers were a highly disciplined outfit noted for their marksmanship. They adopted the Colt six-shooter as their preferred weapon, and in time the gun became synonymous with the settlement of the West. With the taming of the the West, the Rangers became less important. By 1935 they were absorbed into the state highway patrol, but they will always figure prominently in the legends and folklore of the Old West. The following compilation is presented as supplemental information, designed as ready reference of prominent western figures and also includes those who, for the most part, receive little or no mention in the main text of this volume.

A

Abeyta, Agapito, a lawman of Mora County, in the New Mexico Territory, implicated in the murder of John Doherty.

Adams, Charles, a detective for the postal service who led posses throughout the New Mexico Territory, capturing several bandits during the Lincoln County War.

Adams, J.H., a New Mexico deputy marshal who was killed with Marshal Cornelius Finley in 1878.

Alarid, Eugenio, a lawman and outlaw, was a policeman in Las Vegas, N.M., in the 1890s and a member of Silva's White Caps.

Alexander, E.M., a captain of the Texas State Police from 1870 to 1873.

Allee, Alfred Y., appointed deputy sheriff of Karnes County, Texas, in 1882, made deputy sheriff of Frio County, Texas. He shot and killed robber Brack Cornett in 1888.

Allen, Abe, a lawman, was a deputy U.S. marshal for the Indian Nations working out of Judge Isaac Parker's court in the 1880s and 1890s.

Allison, Charles, a lawman and outlaw, was appointed deputy sheriff of Conjos County, Colo., but soon organized a band of outlaws.

Allison, Dave, a lawman, was the sheriff of Pecos

City, Texas, in the 1890s.

Alston, Fielding, a lawman, served as a lieutenant in the Texas Rangers in 1847.

Alvord, Burton (Burt), a lawman and outlaw, was deputy sheriff in Cochise County, Ariz., under Sheriff John Slaughter in 1886. He became town constable of Fairbank in the early 1890s, then town constable of Wilcox where he killed Bill King. Alvord later led a band of train robbers.

Anderson, Bernard, a deputy marshal in the New Mexico Territory.

Anderson, J.E., a New Mexico deputy marshal, who had previously served as assistant secretary of the territory.

Anderson, William H., appointed U.S. deputy marshal in Dallas after the Civil War, tracked Bill Collins into Canada where they shot and killed each other in a gunfight.

Andrew, Robert, a detective and lawman, was a deputy sheriff in Oklahoma. He arrested Ragged Bill and discovered the Doolin gang hideout.

Andrews, Captain M., a lawman, commanded the Texas Rangers in 1837.

Archibald, Albert W., was appointed marshal of New Mexico on Sept. 13, 1861, but decided against accepting the position and moved to Colorado.

Armstrong, Charles, a lawman, served as a Texas Ranger and fought Mexicans on the border during WWI.

Armstrong, John Barclay, enlisted with the Travis Rifles in 1871 and joined the Texas Rangers in 1875. He helped capture John King Fisher in 1874 and tracked and captured John Wesley Hardin in 1877. Retired as a captain in 1882 and died May 1, 1913.

Arrington, George W., joined the Texas Rangers in 1875, and brought in sixteen alleged murderers and twenty other felons from the Panhandle in July 1878. He was appointed captain of Company C, and later served as sheriff of Wheeler County for eight years. He died at his ranch on Mar. 31, 1923.

Ascarate, Guadalupe, a sheriff in the New Mexico Territory who was eventually replaced by Pat Garrett.

Aten, Edwin, joined the Texas Rangers after his brother Ira Aten and was assigned to Company D.

Aten, Ira, joined the Texas Rangers in 1883, and became captain of Company D. He was elected sheriff of Castro County in 1893. He tracked and shot down outlaw Judd Robberts and two cattle rustlers, Alvin Odle and Will Odle.

B

Baca, Elfego, was a prominent lawman in New Mexico for several years as well as an attorney and prosecutor. He was involved in a shoot-out at Tom Slaughter's ranch.

Bailey, Marvin E., a lawman, was a Texas Ranger in 1907.

Baird, P.C., a lawman, served as sergeant of Company D, Texas Rangers for several years and in 1888 was elected sheriff of Mason County. He served for ten years and died on Mar. 9, 1928.

Baker, A.R., a lawman, served as a Texas Ranger under Captain Frank Johnson in 1906.

Baker, Frank, an outlaw and lawman, served as a deputy sheriff in the Lincoln County War and rode in the posse that killed John Tunstall. He was killed by Billy the Kid on Mar. 10, 1878.

Baker, J.H., a lawman, served in Company C of the Texas Rangers around 1907.

Ballard, Charles, deputy marshal, serving at Roswell, New Mexico.

Barela, Mariano, the sheriff of Mesilla, New Mexico, who later became a deputy U.S. marshal.

Barker, Dudley S., a lawman, served in Company B as a Texas Ranger in 1896 and helped break up a gang terrorizing the town of San Saba in 1897.

Barler, W.L., a lawman, served as a Texas Ranger and as the sheriff and tax collector of Terrell County.

Barringer, J.C., a lawman, served as a Texas Ranger in 1886 under Captain G.H. Schmidt.

Bartley, C.C., a lawman, was the sheriff of Val Verde County, Texas, in 1909.

Barton, Charles, a lawman, served in Company D of the Texas Rangers in 1887.

Bassett, Charles E., a lawman who served as sheriff of Ford County, Kan., in 1873, and was made marshal of Dodge City after Ed Masterson was killed. He appointed Wyatt Earp special deputy.

Bauman, Wes, a lawman, worked as a deputy U.S. marshal for the Indian Nations and worked out of Judge Isaac Parker's courtroom in the 1880s and 1890s.

Baylor, George Wythe, a West Texas Confederate soldier-turned-lawman, served with the Texas Rangers from 1879 to 1885, attaining the rank of major. He was a legislator and judge before he died on Mar. 27, 1916.

Bean, Roy, the "law West of the Pecos," served as a California Ranger before his election as justice of the peace of Pecos County in 1882. Bean died on Mar. 16, 1903.

Bean, Samuel G., a sheriff and deputy marshal in the New Mexico Territory.

Beckner, Frederick (Burckner), a lawman, who was appointed sheriff of Dona Ana County, N.M.,

on Mar. 28, 1863.

Beckwith, John H., a lawman and brother of Robert, was a deputy sheriff under Sheriff William Brady during the Lincoln County War of New Mexico, and was killed by a rustler.

Beckwith, Robert W., a lawman and brother of John, was a deputy sheriff under Sheriff William Brady during the Lincoln County War of New Mexico, and was killed during the battle at the McSween house.

Behan, John, an Arizona lawman, was a deputy under Sheriff Shibbell in Tombstone and was elected sheriff of Cochise County. He killed Dick Tolby and was in Tombstone during the O.K. Corral gunfight. He died in Tucson in 1917.

Bell, Bob, a lawman, served in Company D of the Texas Rangers in 1887.

Bell, Hamilton, the sheriff of Ford County, Kan., for thirty years following lawman Bat Masterson, he arrested more alleged outlaws, with a warrant, than any other lawman in the West. He lived past the age of ninety.

Bell, J. W. (AKA: **Lone Bell**), a lawman, was a Texas Ranger in the mid-1870s, and a deputy sheriff under Pat Garrett during the Lincoln County War. He was killed by Billy the Kid while he was guarding the outlaw in the Lincoln courthouse on Apr. 28, 1881.

Berstein, Morris, a deputy sheriff in the New Mexico Territory.

Best, Phil, a lawman, was a Texas Ranger, Company B in 1889 under Captain Sam McMurry.

Bingham, George, a lawman, was a Texas Ranger killed by Jesse Evans.

Birchfield, Steve, a lawman, served as deputy sheriff of Cochise County, Ariz., under Sheriff C.S. Fly. He rode with the posse that battled the Black

Jack Ketchum Gang at Mud Springs.

Blackburn, Leslie, a deputy sheriff at Tombstone, Arizona.

Blackwell, C.J., a lawman, served as a Texas Ranger in 1919.

Blumner, Charles, was appointed Marshal of the New Mexico Territory on Dec. 10, 1853.

Bobbitt, A.A. (AKA: **Gus**), a lawman and gunman, was a deputy U.S. marshal in Oklahoma but returned to ranching. He entered into feud with cattlemen in Pontotoc County, was arrested, and lynched in February 1909.

Boles, Thomas, a lawman, was a U.S. marshal for the western district of Arkansas. He was appointed by President Chester Arthur in 1882.

Boston, Riley, a lawman, served in Company D of the Texas Rangers in 1887.

Bowers, Edward G., a lawman who served as sheriff of Yavapai County, New Mexico.

Bracken, J.W., a lawman, was a Texas Ranger, Company B in 1889 under Captain Sam McMurry.

Brady, William, a lawman and outlaw, was appointed sheriff of Lincoln County in 1878. He deputized Murphy's employees, formed a posse, and killed John Tunstall. He was ambushed and killed by Billy the Kid and other Tunstall Regulators shortly thereafter.

Breakenridge, William M. (**Billy, Billie**), a lawman, served as deputy under Sheriff John Behan of Tombstone, Ariz., in the early 1880s. He later worked as a detective for the SP Railroad, and died on Jan. 31, 1931.

Brent, James R., a buffalo hunter and lawman, served as chief deputy to John Poe when Poe succeeded Pat Garrett as sheriff of Lincoln County. Brent was deputy in the mid-1880s.

Brewer, Richard M., a gunman and lawman, worked for John Tunstall as leader of the Regulators in the Lincoln County War. As deputy sheriff, he captured the Jesse Evans gang. Brewer was killed at Blazer's Mill by Buckshot Roberts on Apr. 4, 1878.

Briant, Elijah S. (**Lige**), a lawman, was the druggist and sheriff of Sonora, Sutton County, Texas. In a gun battle, he killed Will Carver and George Kilpatrick on Apr. 2, 1901. He served as a county judge and died on Dec. 22, 1932.

Bridges, Jack L., a lawman, served in Hays City, Kan., as a deputy U.S. marshal in 1869, and was later assigned to Wichita where he killed horse thief J.E. Ledford. He became marshal of Dodge City, Kan., in the early 1870s.

Britton, Ed, a lawman, was a Texas Ranger, Company B in 1889 under Captain Sam McMurry.

Brooks, J.A., a lawman, served as a sergeant in the Texas Rangers in 1919.

Brooks, James Abijah, a lawman, joined the Texas Rangers in 1882 and served with Company F and A. He was made a captain in May 1889, resigned in 1906, and died on Jan. 15, 1944.

Brooks, William (AKA: **Buffalo Billy**), a lawman and gunman, was the first town marshal of Newton, Kan., in the early 1870s, and participated in the Newton War. He was the assistant town marshal of Dodge City in 1872 where he killed or wounded fifteen men.

Brown, A.W., a lawman, was a Texas Ranger in Company B in 1909.

Brown, Angus (AKA: **Arapaho; Red**), a lawman, was the sheriff of Buffalo, Wyo., in 1892. He was killed by two young cowboys.

Brown, George S., a lawman, served as city marshal of Caldwell, Kan., and was killed on June 22, 1882, by Jim Bean.

Brown, Henry Newton (Hendry), an outlaw and lawman, was a Regulator in the Lincoln County War and then deputy sheriff of Tascosa. In Caldwell, Kan., he was assistant town marshal and then marshal on Dec. 2, 1882. With Ben Wheeler and others, he robbed the bank at Medicine Lodge on Apr. 30, 1884, and was killed by a mob.

Brown, Neal (AKA: Skinny), a lawman in Dodge City, Kan., in the late 1870s, was a deputy under Bill Tilghman in Oklahoma. Brown was with Tilghman when he chased the Doolin gang.

Bruner, Heck, a lawman, was a deputy U.S. marshal for the Indian Nations working out of Judge Isaac Parker's court in the 1880s and 1890s.

Brunner, Neal, a lawman, was a deputy U.S. marshal in Indian Territory in the late 1890s, working out of Judge Parker's federal court at Fort Smith.

Bryant, Ed, a lawman, served as a Texas Ranger in 1896.

Burke, A.F., a deputy sheriff in Tombstone, Ariz., in the 1880s.

Burke, J.S. (Steve), a lawman, served under E.D. Nix as a deputy U.S. marshal in the Fourth District, Texas. He helped capture Cattle Annie and Little Britches. Burke later became an evangelist.

Burroughs, W.H., a lawman, was a deputy sheriff in Nacogdoches County, Texas, under Sheriff Milton Mast. Burroughs aided in the capture of Wild Bill Longely.

Bursum, Holm O., a lawman, who in the 1890s, served as sheriff of Sorocco County, in the New Mexico Territory.

Burts, Matthew (Matt), an outlaw and lawman, robbed a train with a gang led by Burt Alvord and served briefly as a deputy town constable in Pearce, Ariz., in 1899. He was imprisoned for robbery, and killed by a ranching neighbor in November 1925.

Burwell, W.M., a lawman, served as a Texas Ranger in 1896.

Buttner, A.F., a deputy marshal in the New Mexico Territory.

C

Cameron, John, a lawman, served in Company E as a Texas Ranger in 1892.

Campbell, J.E, a lawman, was a sergeant in the Arizona Rangers in 1903.

Canton, Frank M., a lawman and gunman, was elected deputy sheriff of Jacksboro, sheriff of Johnson County, Wyo., in 1882, and served as a deputy U.S. marshal in Oklahoma under Marshal Nix. Canton captured Teton Jackson in 1887 while sheriff of Buffalo and was later appointed adjutant general of four states by the governors.

Carlyle, James, a lawman, was a deputy sheriff in Las Vegas, N.M., and was killed by Billy the Kid on Dec. 1, 1880.

Carnes, H.A., a lawman, served in Company C of the Texas Rangers around 1907.

Carr, "Bat", a gambler and businessman, was made city marshal of Caldwell, Kan., and appointed Willis Metcalf and Henry Newton Brown as his deputies.

Carr, T. Jeff, a lawman, was made the first sheriff of Laramie County, Wyoming Territory, in 1869. He made Wild Bill Hickok check his guns in Cheyenne and in 1876 arrested Jack McCall, the man who shot Hickok.

Carson, Joe, a lawman, was the constable of Las Vegas, N.M., wounded James Lowe in a shoot-out, and was killed by outlaw John Dorsey on Jan. 22, 1880 (or 1884).

Carson, Thomas, a lawman, he served in Company

D and E of the Texas Rangers and fought the Chris Evans Gang in 1880.

Carson, Tom, a lawman and nephew of Kit Carson, was a deputy city marshal of Abilene, Kan., under Wild Bill Hickok. He was killed at Dodge City, Kan.

Caruthers, L.B., a lawman, served with the Texas Rangers during the Higgins-Horrell feud and fought the Evans gang in 1880.

Castle, Kit, a lawman, was elected sheriff of Unitah County, Wyo., killed two horse thieves, and, while serving as mayor, pistol-whipped five men into returning to their cell.

Charlton, John B. (Jack), a soldier in the Indian Territory, who chased several outlaws, including Red McLaughlin.

Chavez, Francisco (Frank), a lawman, who served as sheriff of Santa Fe, N.M.

Chew, Bob, a lawman, served as a Texas Ranger in 1896.

Christianson, Willard Erastus (AKA: **Matt Warner; Ras Lewis**), an outlaw and brother-in-law of outlaw Tom McCarty, robbed trains and banks with Butch Cassidy, Elza Lay, and McCarty from 1878, served a prison sentence, became a lawman, and died Dec. 21, 1938.

Clark, Ben, a lawman at Clifton, Ariz., who killed Black Jack Christian in April 1897.

Clark, G.H., a lawman, served as a Texas Ranger in 1886 under Captain G.H. Schmidt.

Clements, Emanuel, Jr. (Mannie), a lawman, served under Sheriff Dave Allison as deputy sheriff at Pecos City, Texas, from 1894. He later worked for Jim Miller during the Miller-Frazer feud and served as constable of El Paso.

Clements, W.T. (AKA: **Slick**), a lawman, served

as a Texas Ranger in Company D in the 1870s.

Clever, Charles P., a lawman born in Prussia, who in the 1850s, served as marshal in the New Mexico Territory.

Coalson, Doug, a lawman, served as a Texas Ranger in Company D in the 1870s.

Coe, Chas, a lawman and outlaw, killed two men in Grayson County, Texas, in 1884 and was indicted for murder.

Colbert, Paden, a lawman, served out of Fort Smith, Ark., as a deputy U.S. marshal for the Indian Territory in the 1880s and 1890s. He led the posse that killed Ned Christie.

Colcord, Charles F., a lawman, served as a deputy U.S. marshal for the Indian Territory in the 1880s and 1890s. A friend of Bill Tilghman, he was elected city marshal of Oklahoma City in August 1890.

Coldwell, Captain **Neal**, a soldier and lawman, was made captain of Company F of the Texas Rangers under Major John B. Jones in June 1874, captain of Company A in 1876, and resigned in 1883 to become a rancher.

Coleman, Dan, a lawman, served as a Texas Ranger in 1894 as a private in Company E.

Coleman, E.E., a lawman, served as a Texas Ranger in 1894 as a private in Company F.

Collier, W.W., a lawman, was made a Texas Ranger at the age of eighteen.

Collins, John, a New Mexico lawman, who was a deputy marshal in Santa Fe.

Conklin, Charles, a deputy marshal in Las Vegas, N.M., whose pursuit of twelve train robbers in 1879 led to their arrests.

Conley, Ed, a lawman, served as a Texas Ranger in 1896.

Connell, Ed, a lawman, served as a Texas Ranger in 1894 as a private in Company B.

Connelly, Charles T., a lawman, was city marshal of Coffeyville, Kan., when the Dalton Gang attempted to rob the town's two banks. Connelly was the fifth person the Daltons killed during the robberies.

Cook, Thalis T., a lawman, served as a Texas Ranger for several years in the 1880s and 1890s and killed many outlaws including Fine Gilliland and the Friar brothers.

Cooke, C.G., a lawman, served as a Texas Ranger in 1894 as a private in Company F.

Cooley, Corydon E., a deputy marshal in Springerville, N.M., who rid his jurisdiction of desperadoes in 1877.

Cooley, Scott, a lawman and gunman, killed deputy sheriff John Wohrle during the Mason County War in Texas in 1875 to avenge Wohrle's killing Tim Williamson. He formed a gang that continued to terrorize Mason County until he mysteriously fell dead in 1876.

Cooper, Harry, a deputy marshal in New Mexico, who was accused of stealing courtroom evidence in 1899.

Copeland, Charles, a lawman, Copeland was a deputy U.S. marshal for the Indian Nations working out of Judge Isaac Parker's court in the 1880s and 1890s.

Costley, Solon, a lawman, served as a Texas Ranger in the early 1890s.

Cottle, A.R., a lawman, was appointed chief deputy U.S. marshal of the northern district of Oklahoma on July 1, 1903, and served several decades.

Cotton, Mitchell, a lawman, served on the Texas State Police and killed D.C. Applewhite on Sept. 30, 1871.

Courtright, Timothy Isaiah (AKA: **Long-Haired Jim**), a lawman and outlaw, was elected city marshal of Fort Worth, Texas, in 1876, and named Bill Woody deputy. As deputy U.S. marshal in 1883 under Marshal Johnson, Courtright became a fugitive after his posse killed two ranchers. He was later acquitted.

Craighead, Charlie, a lawman, was a deputy sheriff of Val Verde County, Texas, in 1909.

Crawford, Ed, a lawman, served on the Ellsworth, Kan., police force in the early 1870s. Crawford was discharged for killing suspected murderer Cad Pierce, and was himself later killed by Pierce's brother.

Culver, Martin S., a member of Major Tobin's Rangers, who fought numerous battles along the Rio Grande.

Cummings, Samuel M. (AKA: **Doc**), a lawman, was the deputy marshal of El Paso, Texas, in 1881 under Dallas Stoudenmire and was killed by Jim Manning on Feb. 14, 1882.

Cunningham, William P., a lawman in the New Mexico Territory during the 1890s.

Cury, W.S., a lawman, was the sheriff of Pima County, Ariz., from 1873 to 1877.

Cutler, Abraham, was brought from Kansas to serve as marshal of the New Mexico Territory, beginning Aug. 16, 1862.

D

Dake, Albert, a lawman during the 1880s, in the New Mexico Territory.

Dake, Crawley P., became marshal of the New Mexico Territory in 1878.

Dallam, Richard, a miner and merchant, who became marshal of the New Mexico Territory in 1846.

Dalton, Bob, a lawman turned outlaw, formed the Dalton Gang in 1891 with his brothers and robbed banks throughout Kansas. He and most of the gang were killed attempting to simultaneously rob two banks at Coffeyville on Oct. 5, 1892.

Dalton, Frank, a deputy U.S. marshal, stationed at Fort Smith, in the Indian Territories. Brother of Bob, Emmett, and Gratton Dalton.

Dalton, Gratton, a deputy U.S. marshal, who became an outlaw member of the Dalton gang.

Daniels, Ben Jamin F., a lawman, served in Arizona as a deputy sheriff and later joined Theodore Roosevelt's Rough Riders. In 1901 Roosevelt appointed Daniels U.S. marshal of Arizona and New Mexico territories.

Davidson, James, a corrupt lawman, commanded the Texas state police as adjutant general from 1870 to 1873.

Davis, E.K., a lawman, served as deputy sheriff of Custer County, Mont., in 1880, and was part of a group of famous Montana manhunters.

Davis, Levi, a lawman, was a Texas Ranger in 1907.

Delling, M.G. (AKA: **Blaze**), a lawman, served as a Texas Ranger in Company B from September 1900 to December 1906.

Delony, Lewis S., a lawman and deputy, became a Texas Ranger in 1877. Served as deputy sheriff in Clinton.

Dibrell, John L., a lawman, served as a Texas Ranger in Company C for five years and as a deputy U.S. marshal for thirteen years.

Dickason, Isaac Q., a lawman, was appointed marshal of the New Mexico Territory on Apr. 15, 1871.

Doherty, John, a lawman, served as sheriff of Mora County, N.M., and was later murdered.

Dolan, Patrick, a lawman, joined the Texas Rangers in 1874, was made a lieutenant in 1876, and in January 1878, was appointed captain of Company F by Major Jones.

Donahue, Cornelius (AKA: **Lame Johnny**), a lawman and an outlaw, moved to Texas to become a cowboy, but a physical impairment led him to horse thievery; left Texas and became deputy sheriff of Deadwood; was arrested as a horse thief, and returned to Deadwood, but on his return trip a masked man abducted him. Was found hung from a tree in 1878.

Donley, Ed, a lawman, served as a Texas Ranger in 1896.

Donnelly, Dr., a lawman, served as a Texas Ranger in the 1890s and in 1897 helped break up a gang terrorizing San Saba.

D'Orgenay, Francis J.L., was the first western marshal, appointed to jurisdiction of the Orleans Territory in 1804.

Dow, E.A., a lawman in Lincoln County, N.M., during the 1870s.

Dow, Leslie, a lawman and gunman, killed Zack Light in a gunfight in the late 1880s, became sheriff of Eddy County, Texas, on Nov. 27, 1896, and was killed in April 1896 by the former sheriff, Dave Kemp.

Dow, Luke, a lawman, served as a Texas Ranger in Company E from 1890 to 1892 and was later sheriff of Maverick County.

Downing, William, a lawman, was deputy sheriff of Willcox, Ariz., under Burt Alvord in the late 1890s, and allowed the outlaw Alvord and his gang to escape.

Duffield, Milton B., a lawman from West Virginia,

who was appointed marshal of Arizona on Mar. 10, 1863.

Dunavan, C.T., a chief deputy marshal who investigated the robbery of an Army paymaster in Graham County, N.M. on May 11, 1889.

Dunman, William Hickman, a lawman, joined the Texas Rangers in 1874. He died in 1905.

Dunn, Amasa G., was a deputy marshal during the 1860s, in the New Mexico Territory.

Durbin, Walter, a lawman, served as a corporal in Company D of the Texas Rangers in 1886 and 1887.

Durham, George P., a lawman, was one of McNelly's Rangers from 1875 to 1878, and then became foreman on the King ranch.

Durst, S.O. (AKA: **Sod**), a lawman, joined Company F of the Texas Rangers in 1918 and served two years. He joined Company A in 1921 and quit in 1922. He was elected sheriff of Kimble County and later served as special ranger for the Gulf Oil Corporation.

E

Earp, Morgan, a lawman and gunman, was city marshal of Butte, Mont., when he killed Billy Brooks. He was appointed sheriff of Pima County, Ariz., in 1879, and a policeman in Tombstone in 1880. He was shot and killed while playing billiards on Mar. 18, 1882.

Earp, Virgil, a lawman and gunman, was appointed city marshal of Tombstone, Ariz., in 1880, lost an election, and later was appointed marshal again. Virgil died in 1905.

Earp, Wyatt Berry Stapp, a lawman and gunman, was appointed marshal of Ellsworth, Kan., in 1873, marshal of Wichita in 1874, and marshal of Dodge

City in 1876. He was appointed deputy city marshal in 1880 by Virgil. Wyatt died on Jan. 13, 1929.

Edwards, W.R., a lawman, was a deputy sheriff of Val Verde County, Texas, in 1909.

Ervin, Christopher Columbus, a lawman, was a court officer in the Choctaw Nation in the 1870s.

Evans, Joseph, a deputy marshal in the New Mexico Territory.

Evans, Rut, a lawman, served in Company E as a Texas Ranger in 1892.

Evetts, J.H., a lawman, was a Texas Ranger in 1896.

Ezekiels, Alexander, a lawman and expert manhunter during the 1890s, in the New Mexico Territory.

F

Faber, Charles, deputy sheriff and town constable of Las Animas, Colo., in the 1870s. Shot and killed by Clay Allison in 1876 at a town dance when he attempted to remove Clay's and John Anderson's guns.

Fain, William, a Kansas lawman, who in 1858, organized his own "army" of possemen, until federal authorities ordered them to disband.

Fall, Philip, a rustler turned lawman, who in the 1890s served as a deputy marshal in Las Cruces, N.M.

Farr, Edward, a lawman, was elected sheriff of Walsenburg, Colo., in 1897. He was killed by Will Carver when Farr's posse encountered the Ketchum-Carver gang in 1899.

Farr, Jeff B., a lawman and brother of Edward, Farr served as sheriff of Huerfano County, Colo., for several years.

Ferguson, Andy, a lawman, was a Texas Ranger in 1896.

Finley, Cornelius, a New Mexico lawman, who was murdered by outlaws on Sept. 2, 1878.

Fisler, John King (AKA: **King Fisher**), a lawman and a gunman, served as sheriff in Uvalde County. Killed in shootout with Ben Thompson in 1884.

Flapp, George W., a lawman, was the first marshal of Caldwell, Kan., in 1880. He was disliked and shot dead in the back in 1885.

Flint, Ed, a lawman, was a Texas Ranger in 1896.

Foraker, Charles, a rancher who became a deputy marshal in New Mexico Territory in February 1903.

Foraker, Creighton M., a rancher with his brother Charles, he was appointed U.S. Marshal of New Mexico Territory on July 22, 1897.

Forbes, Harry, served as chief deputy of Roswell, New Mexico.

Forbes, William R., a deputy marshal in the New Mexico Territory.

Ford, John Salman (AKA: **Rip**), a lawman and legislator, was made captain of the Texas Rangers in 1849, killed Chief Buffalo Hump, and fought many bandits, including Cortina. He died on Nov. 3, 1897.

Fornoff, Fred, a lawman, was the captain of the New Mexico Mounted Police during the state's territorial days.

Forsyth, J.P., a lawman, was sheriff of Panola County, Texas, for eighteen years and never carried a pistol.

Frazer, George A. (AKA: **Bud**), a lawman, joined the Texas Rangers and later served as deputy sheriff of Fort Stockton, Texas. He was elected sheriff of Pecos City in 1890 and 1892, and was killed in a saloon on Sept. 14, 1896, by rival marshal James Miller.

Fulgam, James, a lawman, was a Texas Ranger in 1896.

Fullerton, C.B., a lawman, served as a Texas Ranger in 1894 as a private in Company B.

Fusselman, Charles H., a lawman, served in Company D of the Texas Rangers in 1887.

G

Gabriel, Peter, a lawman, was sheriff of Pima County, Ariz., in 1883 and 1885. He pursued the Red Jack Gang and shot and killed ex-deputy Joe Phy in a duel on May 3, 1888.

Gardner, Raymond Hatfield (AKA: **Arizona Bill**), a lawman, was born in 1846 and became a deputy U.S. marshal and later an Arizona Ranger. He buffaloed Doc Holliday in 1881.

Garrett, Buck, a lawman and nephew of Pat Garrett, fought in the Johnson County War in 1892, was deputy U.S. marshal in the Chickasaw Nation, and sheriff of Ardmore. He led the posse that killed outlaw Bill Dalton.

Garrett, Patrick Floyd, a lawman, was made sheriff of Lincoln County in November 1880 and killed Tom O'Folliard, Charles Bowdre, and later Billy the Kid in July 1881. He became a Texas Ranger, resigned in 1885, and was killed on Feb. 28, 1908.

Gildea, Augustus M. (**Gus**), a lawman and cowboy, was a part-time Texas Ranger in Company D and F, and was a deputy sheriff from 1881 to 1889. He died on Aug. 10, 1935.

Gillett, James Buchanan, a lawman, joined Captain Roberts' Texas Rangers in 1875, killed outlaw

Dick Dublin, served as sheriff of El Paso, and as sheriff of Brewster County in the 1890s. In 1937, he was the first person appointed a lifetime captain of the Rangers.

Gilliland, Jim, appointed a deputy marshal of the New Mexico Territory in 1893, he was suspected of cattle rustling a year later.

Gilson, Bill, a lawman, served as a peace officer in northern Texas in 1874.

Glasgow, Mr., a lawman, was a deputy sheriff of Georgetown, N.M., and killed outlaw Boyd Dempster on Dec. 26, 1881.

Goodlet, Bill, a lawman turned gunman, was a member of the Dodge City Gang in Las Vegas, N.M.

Goodnight, Charles, a lawman and gunman, was a Texas Ranger in 1857 and drove cattle after the Civil War. He fought outlaws and Indians for many years in Texas, New Mexico, and California. Goodnight outlived most of his Old West comrades dying in Tucson, Ariz., on Dec. 12, 1929, at the age of ninety-three.

Goodwin, Francis H., a lawman who served as U.S. Marshal of the New Mexico Territory between February, 1875, and July, 1876.

Gosling, Harold L., a lawman, was appointed U.S. marshal of the Western District of Texas in 1884 and was killed by two stage robbers in his custody en route to a prison on a train.

Graham, Dayton, a lawman who became a sergeant in the Arizona Rangers; killed Bill Smith in a shootout.

Graham, Samuel, a lawman, joined Company A of the Texas Rangers in July 1878, was discharged in 1880, and later reenlisted. He led the posse that captured Albert Gross.

Green, George, a lawman, was a New Mexico marshal in 1907.

Gregory, Walter, a lawman, serving as a marshal in the Arizona Territory in 1905.

Griego, Francisco (AKA: **Pancho**), a lawman and gunman, was city marshal of Santa Fe, N.M., and was killed by Clay Allison in 1875.

Griffith, William M., a lawman who served as marshal of the Arizona Territory between June 15, 1897, and June 6, 1901.

Grimes, A.C., a lawman, served as a lieutenant of the Texas Rangers in 1886 under Captain G.H. Schmidt.

Guyse, Buck, a lawman and outlaw, deserted from the Texas Rangers and fled to New Mexico Territory and was arrested by Pat Garrett.

H

Hall, Edward L., a lawman who was appointed marshal of the New Mexico Territory on May 16, 1893.

Hall, Frank W., a deputy marshal in the New Mexico Territory during the 1890s.

Hall, Jesse Lee, a lawman, served as city marshal of Sherman, Texas, joined the Texas Rangers in 1876.

Hall, Jesse Leigh (AKA: **Lee; Red; Colorado Grande**), a lawman, became deputy sheriff of Grayson County, Texas, in 1876 and later joined the Texas Rangers. He was in the Pat Garrett posse that killed Charles Bowdre and captured Billy the Kid.

Hall, T.L., a lawman, as deputy sheriff led a posse that killed outlaw train robber Mitch Lee.

Hamer, Frank, a lawman, joined the Texas Rangers in 1906, served as city marshal of Navasota, two years later, rejoined the Rangers in 1915, and was made captain of Company C. Hamer tracked down fugitives Clyde Barrow and Bonnie Parker and organized the ambush that killed them in May 1934.

Hanson, William, a lawman, served as a captain of the Texas Rangers in 1919.

Harkey, D.R. (Dee), a lawman, served as deputy sheriff in San Saba County, Texas, under his brother Joe and at the age of seventeen, arrested Jim Miller. He held several other positions as a peace officer in Texas and New Mexico.

Harrell, Jack, a lawman, served as a Texas Ranger in the 1890s and in 1897 helped break up a gang terrorizing San Saba.

Harris, James, a gunman and former lawman, was killed while dueling Bob Majors at Santa Cruz, Calif., in the 1880s.

Harrison, Richard, served as a special deputy beginning in September 1886, at La Marcia, in the Arizona Territory.

Harwell, Jack, a lawman, served as a Texas Ranger in 1896.

Hawkins, Jack, a lawman, served in Company D of the Texas Rangers and was a member of the famous Montana manhunters.

Hayden, Carl, a lawman in the Arizona Territory, who in 1910 became one of the first officers to use an automobile.

Hays, John Coffee (Jack), a lawman, became a captain in the Texas Rangers in 1840 and fought several battles with Indians. He was elected the first sheriff of San Francisco in April 1850, and died on Apr. 25, 1883.

Head, Lafayette, served as a deputy marshal in the New Mexico Territory, beginning in 1858.

Helrs, C.F., a lawman, served as a Texas Ranger in 1896.

Helm, Jack, a lawman and outlaw, was appointed a special officer by the state police in 1869 and fought in the Sutton-Taylor feud. He led the posse that killed Hays Taylor on Aug. 23, 1869, and was killed by Wes Hardin and Jim Taylor in July 1873.

Hereford, Frank H., a lawman, who served as a deputy marshal in the New Mexico Territory.

Herredia, Clato, a lawman, scouted for the Texas Rangers in 1880 during the Jesse Evans gang round-up.

Hess, John, a lawman, served as a Texas Ranger in 1896.

Hickey, Mike, a lawman, who in 1885 served as vice-president of the Anti-Chinese Labor Association in Arizona.

Hickman, Tom, a lawman, served as a Texas Ranger in the 1880s and 1890s for more than twelve years in Company B and later as captain of Company C.

Hickok, James Butler (AKA: **Wild Bill**), a gunman and lawman, served as a constable in the 1860s and as town marshal of Abilene, Kan., in 1872. He was credited with killing thirty to eighty-five men including Sam Strawhorn, Bill Mulvey, Bill Thompson, and David McCandles. On Aug. 2, 1876, Jack McCall shot and killed Hickok in Deadwood, S.D.

Higgins, Fred, a lawman, served as a deputy sheriff of Globe, Ariz., in 1895 and led the attack on the Black Jack Christian hideout in which Christian was killed. He fought the Black Jacks in 1896 under Sheriff C.S. Fly.

Hildreth, William (Billy), a lawman, was made a deputy when John Slaughter was elected sheriff of Tombstone, Ariz. He fought the Black Jacks as a deputy of Sheriff C.S. Fly and was a friend of Burt Alvord.

Hill, John, a lawman, who during 1860s served as a deputy marshal at Albuquerque, N.M.

Hill, Tom, a lawman, serving as a New Mexico deputy marshal, who was a member of the posse that killed John Tunstall on Feb. 18, 1878.

Hindman, George, a lawman and gunman, was a deputy sheriff in Lincoln County under Sheriff William Brady and rode in the posse that killed John Tunstall. He was killed by Billy the Kid and John Middleton on Apr. 1, 1878.

Holliday, John Henry (AKA: **Doc**), was deputized by Virgil Earp to abet the efforts against the Clanton gang, which culminated with a gunfight at the O.K. Corral on Oct. 26, 1881. He died in a sanatarium in 1887.

Hollister, Cassius M. (AKA: **Cash**), lawman and deputy U.S. marshal. Shot in 1884 while attempting to arrest an adulterer.

Holmes, W.A. (AKA: **Hunky Dory**), a lawman, served as a deputy sheriff under Sheriff Glen Reynolds of Gila County, Ariz. He was murdered by the Apache Kid and his men, while transporting the outlaw to Tuma Prison.

Hopkins, Arthur A., a lawman, who served as a deputy marshal in the Arizona Territory.

Hopkins, Gilbert W., a lawman and mining engineer who became a deputy marshal in the New Mexico Territory in 1864.

Horn, Tom, worked as Pinkerton detective, during which time he was charged with and convicted of murdering a Wyoming boy. Horn was hanged on Nov. 20, 1903, in Cheyenne, though many still believed he was innocent.

Horton, George, a lawman, was a Texas Ranger in 1896 as a private in Company D.

Houston, Tom, a lawman, served as Oklahoma law officer during early 1890s. Killed in shoot-out with Doolin gang.

Hudson, R.M. (AKA: **Duke**), a lawman, served in Company C of the Texas Rangers in 1907.

Hughes, John Reynolds, a lawman, joined the Texas Rangers, Company D, in 1887 and was made captain in 1893. He arrested and killed numerous outlaws and committed suicide in 1946, at the age of eighty-nine.

Hume, James B., a Wells Fargo detective, investigated more than 350 stagecoach and train robberies.

Hunnicut, J.R., a lawman, served as a Texas Ranger in 1919.

Hunnicutt, M.P., a lawman, served as a captain of the Texas State Police from 1870 to 1873.

Hunt, Frank J., a lawman, served as a deputy sheriff of Caldwell, Kan., under Sheriff George Flatt in the late 1870s. In a gunfight with four outlaws, he and the four outlaws were killed.

I

Irvan, Tom, a lawman, served as sheriff of Custer County, Mont., and was one of the famous Montana manhunters.

J

Jefferson, Dunk, a lawman, served as a Texas Ranger in 1877 under Pat Dolan and was one of his most efficient men.

Jennings, Napoleon Augustus, lawman. Became a Texas Ranger in 1876 and was with Jesse Lee Hall when the Rangers ended the Sutton-Taylor feud.

Johnson, Charles, a lawman, served in Company E as a Texas Ranger in 1892.

Johnson, Jack (AKA: **Turkey Creek**), lawman and

gunman. Former Dakota goldminer, he moved to Arizona after killing his partners. Was deputy marshal to Wyatt Earp and part of posse that killed Frank Stillwell.

Johnson, John (AKA: **Liver Eating**), a lawman and friend of Buffalo Bill Cody, was constable of Coulson, Mont., in the 1870s and was deputy sheriff of Coulson in 1880.

Johnson, Tom, a lawman, served in Company B of the Texas Ranger in 1896 and was a deputy U.S. marshal for the Indian Nations working out of Judge Isaac Parker's court in the 1880s and 1890s.

Johnson, William H., a lawman and gunman. Confederate captain in Civil War. Made deputy to Sheriff William Brady during the Lincoln County War.

Jones, Frank, a lawman, served in Company A, Company F in 1874, and Company D in 1878 of the Texas Rangers. He served as captain in 1887 and was killed by outlaws on June 30, 1893.

Jones, Fred, a lawman, was a deputy sheriff of Val Verde County, Texas, in 1909.

Jones, Gus (AKA: **Buster**), a lawman, was a Texas Ranger stationed in Alice, Texas, in 1906.

Jones, John B., a lawman, joined the Texas Rangers before the Civil War and was commissioned as the commander of the Frontier Battalion of the Rangers during the Texas reconstruction. In 1877, Jones ended the Horrell-Higgins feud, and died on June 19, 1881.

Jones, John G., a lawman, who on Mar. 12, 1851, became the first U.S. marshal under civilian rule, of the New Mexico Territory.

Jones, Nat B. (AKA: **Kiowa**), a lawman, joined the Texas Rangers under Captain Bill McDonald. He died around 1928.

Jones, Walter, a lawman, served in Company D of the Texas Rangers in 1887.

K

Karnes, Quill, a lawman, was a Texas Ranger stationed in Alice, Texas, in 1906.

Kaseman, George A., a lawman who served as a deputy marshal in the New Mexico Territory.

Kemp, Dave, an outlaw, killed a man in Texas, moved to New Mexico, killed Sheriff Les Dow. Later served as a lawman in Eddy County, N.M.

Kennon, Louis, a lawman, who in the 1880s served as a deputy marshal at Silver City, New Mexico.

Kimball, George, a lawman, who served as sheriff and deputy marshal of Lincoln County, N.M., beginning in 1879.

King, Frank, a lawman, was a deputy sheriff of Phoenix, Ariz., and a guard at Yuma prison in 1889. He fought the Black Jack Christian gang in 1896 at Nogales.

King, Jim, a lawman, served in Company D of the Texas Rangers in 1887.

King, Lou, a lawman, served as deputy sheriff of Custer County, Mont., in 1880, and was part of a group of famous Montana manhunters.

Kirchner, Karl, a lawman, served as a sergeant in Company D of the Texas Rangers in 1894.

Kosterlitsky, Emilio, a Mexico lawman, was the leader of the Rurales near the end of the nineteenth century.

Krummeck, Charles, a lawman, was a deputy sheriff of Santa Cruz, N.M., where he shot and killed a man in December 1880.

Kuhley, Charles, a lawman, he served as a Texas

Ranger in 1886 under Captain G.H. Schmidt.

L

Lambert, Charles Frederick (AKA: Kid Lambert), a lawman, arrested three killers at sixteen and was made a deputy sheriff. He was appointed to the New Mexico Mounted Police and pursued the Hole-in-the-Wall Gang and Black Jack Ketchum's gang. He was made a U.S. special officer, and after WWII, became a deputy sheriff.

Landrum, James David, a lawman, served as a Texas Ranger, as a deputy sheriff of Haskell County in 1901, and then as deputy sheriff of Abilene. He served on the Waco police force from 1912 to 1917 and later on the Dallas police force and died in 1942.

Lane, Van, a lawman, served as a Texas Ranger in the 1890s and in 1897 helped break up a gang terrorizing San Saba.

Langford, N.P., a lawman, was known as a "law and order officer" in Montana at the time of Sheriff Plummer's Innocents gang.

Larkin, Sam, a lawman, served in Company C of the Texas Rangers around 1907.

Larn, John M., an outlaw turned lawman, killed a rancher in Colorado and a sheriff in New Mexico. He rustled cattle while sheriff of Shackleford County, Texas, in the late 1870s.

Latham, James V., a lawman, enlisted in the Texas Rangers, Company D in 1880, 1884, and 1893 and fought the Evans gang. He served as a deputy sheriff of El Paso County for two years and as a deputy in New Mexico. He died on Nov. 17, 1936.

Latta, Oscar, a lawman, served as a Texas Ranger in the 1890s, and was a deputy sheriff of Kimble County, Texas, in February 1897. He was later elected sheriff and helped defeat the Crane-Knight gang. He rejoined the Texas Rangers in 1939.

Laughlin, J.T. (Tom), a lawman, was a Texas Ranger in 1907.

Leatherwood, Robert N., a lawman, was sheriff of Pima County, Ariz., in 1883 and captured a train-robbing gang.

Ledbetter, James F. (AKA: Bud), a lawman, was a deputy U.S. marshal in the 1880s and then town marshal of Vinita, Okla., in 1893. As a deputy U.S. marshal under E.D. Nix, he captured the Al Jennings gang. He was police chief of Muskogee, Okla., and then county sheriff.

Lee, Oliver, a lawman who became a deputy marshal in the New Mexico Territory in 1894.

Lefors, Joseph, a detective in Wyoming who fought battles with the Hole-in-the-Wall Gang, he was later appointed a deputy U.S. marshal.

Lewis, Lon, a lawman, served briefly as a Texas Ranger in 1889 before his appointment as deputy U.S. marshal of Oklahoma and the Indian Territory. Lewis was named the first sheriff of Tulsa County, Okla.

Lewis, W.W., a lawman, served in Company D, Texas Rangers under Captain Dan W. Roberts. He became a merchant and died in 1934.

Long, John (AKA: Rivers), a lawman, was deputized for a raid upon the McSween house on July 19, 1878, during the Lincoln County War.

Long, Steve (AKA: Big Steve), a lawman and outlaw, ran the "Bucket of Blood" saloon in Laramie City, Wyo., and appointed himself assistant marshal. Long and his two partners were lynched on Oct. 28, 1868.

Loomis, A.W., a lawman, served as a deputy marshal in the New Mexico Territory.

Loomis, H.W., a lawman, was a chief deputy U.S. marshal in New Mexico Territory and killed train robber Cole Estes on Oct. 2, 1896.

Love, Harry, a lawman, served as a Texas Ranger in the 1850s, and allegedly brought in the head of Murieta, the Mexican outlaw.

Love, H.M., a lawman, who serving as a deputy marshal in New Mexico, was wounded while in pursuit of Samuel Ketchum on July 16, 1899.

Lowe, Joseph (AKA: **Red Joe; Rowdy Joe; Monte Joe**), a lawman, a gambler and one-time lawman, served as a Texas Ranger at Camp San Saba in 1866.

Lozier, Doctor, a lawman, served as a Texas Ranger in 1896.

M

McCall, Thomas P., a lawman, was the first sheriff of Medina County, Texas, in 1858, and was later a deputy sheriff in Bexar County. McCall became sheriff and served for a decade.

McCauley, William, a lawman, served as a Texas Ranger in the 1890s and in 1897 helped break up a gang terrorizing San Saba.

McClure, Robert, a lawman, served as a Texas Ranger in the 1890s and in 1897 helped break up a gang terrorizing San Saba.

McCord, Myron, a lawman, who was appointed marshal of the Arizona Territory on June 6, 1901.

McCuiston, O.W., a lawman, who while sheriff of Raton, Ariz., in 1894, became embroiled in a railway strike.

McDonald, William Jesse (AKA: **Captain Bill**), a lawman, was a deputy sheriff at Wood County and then sheriff of Wichita County. He served as a special Texas Ranger and was appointed captain in 1893. Appointed a deputy U.S. marshal of northern Texas and southern Kansas and he was made captain of Company B, Texas Rangers before becoming a U.S. marshal.

McIntire, James (**Jim McIntyre**), a Texas gunman and lawman from 1860, was at different times a Texas Ranger, city marshal of Las Vegas, deputy sheriff, cowboy, hunter, gambler, and outlaw with a $1,000 reward on his head for the deaths of two men in American Valley, N.M.

McIntosh, T.W., a lawman, who served as a deputy marshal at Prescott, Ariz.

McKidrict, Joe, a lawman, was a Texas Ranger. McKirdict also shot and fatally wounded deputy U.S. marshal, Bass Outlaw.

McKinney, Thomas L. (AKA: **Tip**), a lawman, was a deputy sheriff under famous lawman Pat Garrett, and was present when Garrett killed Billy the Kid. McKinney killed Bob Edwards on May 8, 1881, in a shoot-out with the gunman.

McMahon, Francis Marion, a lawman, joined Company D of the Texas Rangers under J.R. Hughes in September 1893 and arrested Bass Outlaw on Apr. 4, 1894. He was a deputy U.S. marshal under Dick Ware, and died on Mar. 6, 1940.

McMillan, Private, a lawman, served as a Texas Ranger in 1919.

McMurry, Sam A., a lawman, served for several years in the 1880-90s as captain of Company B, Texas Rangers.

McNeel, J.S., Jr., a lawman, served in Company E as a Texas Ranger in 1892.

McNeel, P.J., a lawman, served in Company E as a Texas Ranger in 1892.

McNelly, Leander H., a lawman, was commissioned as captain of the state police on July 1, 1870, and commanded the "Special Ranger Force" in 1874 which patrolled the Mexico border. He died on Sept. 4, 1877.

McNew, William, a lawman, served as deputy marshal of Dona Ana County, New Mexico.

Maddox, Allen R., a lawman, served in Company B of the Texas Ranger in 1896.

Madsen, Chris, a lawman, served as chief deputy U.S. marshal under Marshal William Grimes in the Territories in 1889, and then under E.D. Nix in the 1890s, John Shelby from 1897 to 1898, Marshal Hamner till 1902, and marshals Paden Colbert and Abernathy. In 1910 he was appointed marshal, and died in 1947.

Mahorn, Tom, a lawman, was a Texas Ranger, Company B, in 1889 under Captain Sam McMurry.

Maledon, George, a lawman, was a policeman at Fort Smith, Ark., and a deputy sheriff in Sebastian County. He later served as the hangman of the federal court at Fort Smith.

Marsden, Crosby, a lawman, was a Texas Ranger in 1907.

Martinez, Romulo, a lawman, was sheriff of Santa Fe County, N.M., between 1881 and 1884.

Mason, Barney, a gunman and lawman, killed John Farris in self-defense at Fort Sumner, N.M., in 1880. He was a deputy to Sheriff Garrett.

Mast, Milton, the sheriff of Nacogdoches County, Texas, who captured Wild Bill Longley on June 26, 1877.

Masterson, Edward J. (AKA: **Little Ed**), a lawman and brother of Bat Masterson, was the Dodge City, Kan., town marshal and was killed by cowboys on Apr. 9, 1878.

Masterson, James P., a lawman and brother of Bat Masterson, was a law officer in Dodge City, Kan., in 1885, deputy sheriff of Colfax County, and then a deputy U.S. marshal in Indian Territory, serving under E.D. Nix. He fought the Doolin gang and was part of the posse that forced Arkansas Tom to surrender.

Masterson, Robert (AKA: **Smiling Bob**), a lawman and brother of Bat Masterson, was marshal of Trinidad, Colo., in 1882 and reportedly killed twenty-one men.

Masterson, William Barclay (AKA: **Bat**), a famous lawman, was deputy town marshal of Dodge City, Kan., was elected Ford County sheriff in the 1870s, and was later city marshal of Dodge City, Kan., when he helped capture outlaw Dave Rudabaugh. Appointed deputy U.S. marshal of the New York district in 1905, he resigned in 1907 and died on Oct. 25, 1921.

Mather, Dave H. (AKA: **Mysterious Dave**), an outlaw and lawman, was one of the Dodge City gang in Las Vegas, N.M. On Jan. 26, 1880, as assistant marshal of Las Vegas, he killed Joe Costillo.

Matthews, Frank, a lawman, served as a Texas Ranger in 1919.

Matthews, Jacob B., a gunman and lawman, served in the Tennessee Cavalry in the Civil War, and was a deputy sheriff under Sheriff Brady during the Lincoln County War. He died in 1904.

Meade, William Kidder, a lawman, was appointed U.S. marshal for the Arizona Territory on July 8, 1885.

Middleton, C.P., a lawman, was a Texas Ranger in Company B in 1909.

Miles, Hod, an outlaw turned deputy sheriff, who in January 1888, killed Jake Gibson, purported to be his fifth victim.

Millard, George, a lawman, served as a Texas Ranger in 1919.

Miller, James B. (**Jim**), an outlaw and lawman, was a deputy sheriff in Pecos, Texas, in the 1890s, was appointed town constable, and later served as a Texas Ranger. He killed Sheriff Bud Frazer and was suspected of forty other killings including Pat Garrett and A.A. Bobbitt. A mob lynched him on Apr. 19, 1909, at Ada, Okla.

Miller, John, a lawman, a deputy marshal of Tucson, Ariz., during the 1870s.

Milton, Jeff Davis, a lawman, served as police chief of El Paso, Texas, and became a deputy U.S. marshal at Fairbanks, Ariz. He captured outlaw William E. Walters (AKA: **Bronco Bill**) and killed John Patterson (AKA: **Three-Fingered Jack**).

Montgomery, David, a lawman, serving in 1878 as chief deputy marshal of Lincoln County, N.M.

Moore, George, a lawman, Texas Ranger.

Moore, Jeff B., a lawman, mercenary, and cowboy, fought Indians in Argentina before he served several terms as sheriff of Crockett County, Texas.

Moore, John, a lawman, served as a Texas Ranger in 1896.

Morgan, Joe, a gunman and lawman, fought deputy sheriff Ben Williams in Las Cruces, N.M., on Sept. 15, 1895, with Albert Fall. He was later a deputy sheriff and Oliver Lee supporter.

Morris, W.T. (AKA: **Brack**), a lawman, served in Company D as a Texas Ranger in 1882 and was sheriff of Karnes County, Texas, when he was killed on June 13, 1901.

Morrison, Alexander L., Jr., a lawman, Morrison served as chief deputy to his father in Santa Fe County, N.M.

Morrison, Alexander L., Sr., a lawman, was appointed marshal of Santa Fe, N.M., on Mar. 2, 1882.

Mossman, Burton C., a lawman, was the first captain of the Arizona Rangers.

Mowbray, George W., a lawman, was a posseman under Heck Thomas, Bill Tilghman, and Chris Madsen in the early 1890s and was appointed deputy U.S. marshal by E.D. Nix. He fought the Cook gang, the Doolin gang, the Buck gang, and the Cherokee Bill gang.

Murchison, Ivan, a lawman, served as a Texas Ranger under Captain Frank Johnson in 1906.

N

Natus, Joe, a lawman, served as a private in Company F of the Texas Rangers in 1894.

Neagle, David, a lawman and one of the fastest gunfighters, killed Judge David Terry while serving as a deputy U.S. marshal in California. He was sheriff of Tombstone, Ariz., in the late 1870s.

Neal, Doc, a lawman, served as a Texas Ranger in 1896.

Neal, Edgar T., a lawman, served as a Texas Ranger in Company B in the 1890s and was elected sheriff of San Saba County for several terms.

Neeley, A.A., a lawman, served as a Texas Ranger in 1894 as a private in Company B.

Neil, Edgar, a lawman, served as a Texas Ranger in 1896.

Neis, Tony, a lawman, who in 1881 was assigned to escort Billy the Kid to trial at Mesilla, N.M.

Nevill, Charles L., a lawman, served as a Texas Ranger, and was lieutenant of Company E in 1879, and later captain. Arrested a wounded Sam Bass in 1878, broke up the Jesse Evans gang, and captured the Potter gang. Served as sheriff of Presidio County from 1885 to 1888.

Newell, J. Benson, a lawman and nephew of Creighton Foraker, was appointed a U.S. marshal in New Mexico Territory in 1907.

Newhall, James T., a lawman, serving during the 1870s, as a deputy marshal in the New Mexico Territory.

Newman, Jim, a lawman and outlaw, he consorted

with John Hardin in the 1860s. He later lived in Texas and New Mexico Territory.

Newton, J.O., a lawman, was the adjutant general of the Texas Rangers in 1907.

Nichols, Frank P., a lawman, was deputy sheriff of Springer, N.M., and shot and killed outlaw John Scott on May 17, 1883.

Nix, Evett Dumas, a lawman, was the U.S. Marshal of Oklahoma and the Indian Nations in the 1890s. He employed more than 100 deputies who arrested and jailed several thousand suspected criminals.

O

O'Grady, John, a lawman, served as a Texas Ranger in the early 1890s.

Olinger, Robert A., an outlaw, crooked U.S. marshal, and deputy sheriff of Lincoln County, N.M., was indicted for his participation in the Lincoln County War, and was killed by Billy the Kid on Apr. 28, 1881.

O'Neill, John H. "Jack", a lawman at Fort Thomas, N.M., during the late 1880s.

Osborn, William S., a lawman, Osborn served as a deputy marshal at Prescott, Ariz., north of Phoenix, during the 1870s.

Outlaw, Bass L., a lawman, joined Company E of the Texas Rangers in 1855 and changed to Company D in 1887, resigned in 1894 after shooting up the town of Alpine, and was appointed deputy U.S. marshal. Outlaw was killed by Ranger John Selman on Apr. 5, 1894.

Owens, Will, a lawman, served as a Texas Ranger in 1886 under Captain G.H. Schmidt.

P

Palmer, Edward, a lawman, served in Company D of the Texas Rangers in 1894.

Parker, F.D., a lawman, served as deputy marshal at Prescott, Ariz., who in 1876, apprehended an Army clerk attempting to steal a payroll.

Paul, John V., a lawman, serving as an Arizona marshal, who in 1890 was accused of deporting Chinese laborers.

Paul, Robert H., a lawman, was sheriff and constable of Calaveras County, Calif., from 1854 to 1861. He became a deputy U.S. marshal in Tucson, Ariz., and arrested Pony Deal in 1881. As sheriff of Pima County he battled Red Jack and Charles Hensley.

Pauli, Louis, a lawman, served as a Texas Ranger in 1892.

Payne, Ransom, a lawman, served as a deputy U.S. marshal in the 1890s in Indian Territory and pursued the Dalton gang.

Peak, Junius (June), a lawman, served as a deputy sheriff of Dallas, Texas, after the Civil War and became one of the special Rangers recruited to break up the Bass gang, which they did in 1878. He resigned on Mar. 15, 1880, and died in Dallas in 1934.

Penwell, E.S., a lawman, Penwell served as a deputy marshal in the Arizona Territory during the 1870s.

Peppin, George, a lawman and gunman, was the sheriff of Lincoln County, Ariz., during the Lincoln County War.

Perry, Cicero R. (AKA: Rufe), a lawman and Indian fighter, joined the Texas Rangers under Jack Hays in 1844 and became commander of Company D in 1874. He resigned several years later and died on Oct. 7, 1898.

Perry, Ollie, a lawman, served as a Texas Ranger in the 1890s, and in 1897 helped break up a gang terrorizing San Saba.

Phelps, E.M., a lawman, served as a colonel in Company C of the Texas Rangers in 1907.

Phelps, Edward, a lawman, served as U.S. Marshal of the Arizona Territory from 1863-66.

Phillipowski, Lyon, a lawman and Dolan factionist, was a deputy sheriff of Lincoln County, N.M., and killed William Burns, a clerk at Murphy store, in a duel.

Phillips, Charles A., a lawman, served as a deputy marshal in the Arizona Territory during the 1860s.

Phy, Josephus, a lawman, served as deputy sheriff of Pinal County, Ariz., under Pete Gabriel and was discharged in 1885. Phy ran for sheriff and Gabriel killed him in a gunfight.

Pickard, E.B., a lawman, served as a marshal in the New Mexico Territory during the 1890s.

Pickett, Sam, a lawman, served as a Texas Ranger in 1886 under Captain G.H. Schmidt.

Pickett, Tom, an outlaw and lawman, stole cattle and was captured with outlaw Billy the Kid in New Mexico on Dec. 23, 1880. Pickett later served as a Ranger and died peacefully on May 14, 1934, in Arizona.

Pinkerton, Allen, the founder of the famous detective agency, who was hired privately to track down criminals, including the James gang.

Platt, Rudd, a lawman, was a Texas Ranger, Company B, in 1889 under Captain Sam McMurry.

Platt, Sam, a lawman, was a Texas Ranger, Company B, in 1889 under Captain Sam McMurry.

Platt, Tom, a lawman, was a Texas Ranger, Company B, in 1889 under Captain Sam McMurry.

Plummer, Henry, an outlaw leader and lawman, organized in Idaho in early 1860 the worst gang of cutthroats in the West. Plummer and over thirty members of the gang were lynched by vigilantes in 1864. He was about to become U.S. marshal of the Territory.

Poe, John W., a gunman and lawman, was town marshal and deputy U.S. marshal of Fort Griffin, Kan., became a deputy sheriff, and helped Sheriff Pat Garrett track Billy the Kid. He was elected sheriff of Lincoln County, N.M., in 1882 and died in July 1925.

Porterie, J.A., a lawman, served as a marshal in New Mexico Territory, and in 1907 was accused but exonerated of killing an Hispanic.

Potter, Dell, a lawman, served as deputy marshal at Dona Ana County, N.M., during the 1890s.

Pratt, John, a lawman, served as U.S. marshal of the New Mexico Territory between March 1866 and May 1876.

Premont, Charles, a lawman, served in Company E as a Texas Ranger in 1892.

Price, Sterling, a lawman, was a Texas Ranger, Company B, in 1889 serving under Captain Sam McMurry.

Pridgen, Bolivar Jackson, a senator from 24th District from Price Creek Settlement, DeWitt County, Texas.

Putts, Henry, a lawman, served as a Texas Ranger in 1886 under Captain G.H. Schmidt.

Q

Queen, Lee, a lawman, served as a Texas Ranger in 1896.

R

Rader, Bud, a lawman, served in Company E as a Texas Ranger in 1892.

Rankin, John, a lawman, was a marshal in Texas and helped kill outlaw William Whitley.

Redus, Roscoe, a lawman, served as a sergeant in Company B of the Texas Rangers in 1909.

Reid, F.J., a lawman, was a deputy sheriff of Val Verde County, Texas, in 1909 under Sheriff C.C. Bartley.

Reynolds, N.O. (AKA: **Nage**), a lawman, commanded Company E of the Texas Rangers in 1878. He helped break up the Horrell-Higgins feud and warned Rangers of an attack at Round Rock by Sam Bass.

Rigdon, Terrell, a lawman, served in Company E as a Texas Ranger in 1892.

Roberts, Andrew L. (AKA: **Bill Williams; Buckshot; William Albert Roberts; Bill Roberts**), a Texas Ranger, outlaw, and member of King Fisher's gang in New Mexico, Buckshot Roberts was killed in the gun battle at Blazer's Mill in 1878 after having killed Dick Brewer.

Roberts, Daniel Webster, a lawman, joined the Texas Rangers and served under Rufe Perry in 1874. He was made captain in 1878 and broke up outlaw gangs such as the Mason County Mob, the Potter boys, and the Jesse Evans gang. He resigned in 1882.

Roberts, Ross, a lawman, was a deputy sheriff of Val Verde County, Texas, in 1909 under Sheriff C.C. Bartley.

Robinson, D.S., a lawman, served in Company E as a Texas Ranger in 1892.

Robinson, Jim R., a lawman, served as a Texas Ranger in 1886 under Captain G.H. Schmidt.

Rogers, C.L. (AKA: **Kid**), a lawman, served as a Texas Ranger in 1896.

Rogers, Ernest, a lawman, served in Company D of the Texas Rangers in 1887.

Rogers, Ike, a lawman, was a deputy under U.S. Marshal Crum, and captured Cherokee Bill on Jan. 29, 1895. He was killed at Fort Gibson in 1897.

Rogers, J.H., a lawman for fifty years, joined the Texas Rangers in 1882 and was appointed U.S. marshal, but returned to the Rangers and served as a captain in Company C in 1907.

Rogers, L.T., a lawman, served as a colonel in Company C of the Texas Rangers in 1907.

Romero, Bernardo, a lawman, the nephew of Trinidad Romero, served as a deputy marshal in the New Mexico Territory.

Romero, Cleofes, a lawman and sheriff of San Miguel County, N.M., during the 1890s.

Romero, Miguel A., a lawman, served as deputy marshal at Las Vegas, N.M.

Romero, Secundino, a lawman, served as U.S. Marshal of New Mexico beginning in 1912.

Romero, Trinidad, a lawman, served as U.S. Marshal of the New Mexico Territory beginning Nov. 7, 1889.

Rosenthal, William, a lawman, served as a deputy in the New Mexico Territory during the 1870s.

Ross, T.M., a lawman, served as a private in Company F of the Texas Rangers in 1894 and as captain of Company B of the Texas Rangers in 1909.

Roundtree, Oscar J., a lawman, served as a Texas Ranger under Captain Frank Johnson in 1906.

Rucker, E.C., a lawman, Rucker was deputy sheriff of Tularosa, N.M., and sided with John Good in the

Tularosa feud.

Rudabaugh, David, an outlaw and briefly city marshal of Las Vegas, N.M., rode with the Roark Gang, Doc Holliday, and Billy the Kid. He was shot and beheaded by vigilantes in Mexico.

Rudd, W.L. (AKA: Colorado Chico; Little Red), a lawman, served under Lee Hall in McNelly's Rangers in the 1870s and was elected sheriff of Karnes County in the 1880s. He died at age ninety-four in 1938.

Rumley, Charles S., a lawman, served as U.S. marshal of the New Mexico Territory beginning Apr. 5, 1853.

Rusk, Dave, a lawman, was a deputy U.S. marshal for the Indian Nations working out of Judge Isaac Parker's court in the 1880s and 1890s.

Russell, Richard Robertson (Dick), a lawman, joined the Texas Rangers in 1880, served as sheriff of Menard, Texas, from 1886 to 1896, and died on June 28, 1922.

Russell, Stillwell, a lawman, served in the New Mexico Territory during the 1870s.

Rynning, Thomas H., a lawman, commanded the Arizona Rangers in the 1890s and 1900s.

S

Sallis, W.F., a lawman, served in Company B of the Texas Rangers in 1909.

Saunders, J.W., a lawman, served in Company D of the Texas Rangers in 1894.

Scarborough, George W., a lawman, was elected sheriff of Jones County, Texas, in 1885, served for several terms. He killed John Selman in 1895 while a deputy U.S. marshal of El Paso. He was killed by the Will Carver gang on Apr. 5, 1900.

Schmidt, Frank, a lawman, served in Company D of the Texas Rangers in 1887 under Captain Frank Jones.

Schmidt, G.H., a lawman, was the captain of a company of Texas Rangers in 1886.

Schmidt, Will, a lawman, served in Company D of the Texas Rangers in 1894.

Scotten, Ed H., a lawman, served under Jim Gillett as assistant city marshal of El Paso in 1882, and died on Sept. 2, 1884.

Seale, James, a lawman, served in Company B of the Texas Rangers in 1909.

Selman, John, a Texas lawman and outlaw, allegedly rustled with John Larn around Fort Griffin, Texas. He befriended Billy the Kid during the Lincoln County War, and killed Wes Hardin in August 1895. George Scarborough killed him on Apr. 6, 1896.

Selman, John, Jr., a lawman, deputized as an Arizona marshal in 1899.

Sena, George, a lawman, was removed as a sheriff of Lincoln County, N.M., in 1896, for failure to enforce the law.

Sena, Jose D., a lawman, served as a deputy marshal of Santa Fe County, N.M., during the 1860s.

Sena y Baca, Jesus Maria, a lawman, became a deputy marshal in the New Mexico Territory in 1858.

Shaffenburg, M.A., a lawman, served as a marshal in the Colorado Territory during the 1860s.

Sharp, Mike, a lawman, was a deputy sheriff of Val Verde County, Texas, in 1909 under Sheriff C.C. Bartley.

Sheridan, J.J., a lawman, served as a deputy marshal in the New Mexico Territory, during the 1890s.

Shibbell, Charles, a lawman, served as sheriff of Pima County, Ariz., from 1877 to 1879 and appointed Wyatt Earp as deputy to replace Virgil Earp. Deputy Sheriff John Behan replaced Shibell as sheriff.

Sieber, Albert, a lawman and Indian scout, commanded a scout and police force as a deputy U.S. marshal, employing at different times the Apache Kid, Frank Leslie, and Tom Horn. He died in 1907.

Sieker, Edward A., a lawman and one of the Sieker brothers, served as a Texas Ranger in Company D under Dan Roberts and led the attack against the Jesse Evans gang in 1880.

Sieker, Frank, a lawman and one of the Sieker brothers, joined the Texas Rangers and served on Company B. He was shot and killed in a battle with Mexican horse thieves in May 1885.

Sieker, Lamartine P. (AKA: **Lamb**), a lawman and one of the Sieker brothers, joined Company D of the Texas Rangers and in 1884 was made quartermaster general. He served as a Ranger for nineteen years and died in 1914.

Sieker, Tom, a lawman and one of the Sieker brothers, served on the Texas Rangers and lived in Dallas.

Simms, Pink, a lawman and cowboy, served as a lawman in Texas and hunted individual outlaws of the Wild Bunch with Charles Siringo.

Sippy, Benjamin, a lawman, served as city marshal of Tombstone, Ariz., until January 1881, and was replaced by Virgil Earp who lost the following election to Sippy.

Siringo, Charles, a gunman, was a cowboy detective who pursued outlaws and rustlers throughout the West. He joined the Pinkerton Agency in the 1890s and worked for them for twenty-two years.

Sitters, Joe, a lawman, served in Company D of the Texas Rangers in 1894.

Slaughter, John Horton, a lawman, was sheriff of Cochise County, Ariz., during the 1880s.

Smith, Colonel, a lawman, was the colonel of the Texas Rangers of Headquarters Company of Austin, Texas, in 1919.

Smith, J.H., a lawman, served as a deputy marshal in the New Mexico Territory, and was shot to death while in pursuit of the outlaw Samuel Ketchum.

Smith, Simeon H., a lawman, served as a deputy marshal in the New Mexico Territory during the 1850s.

Smith, Thomas J. (AKA: **Bear River**), a lawman, served as a police officer in Bear River, Wyo., during the "Bear River troubles." He was appointed the first marshal of Abilene, Kan., in 1870. Known as the "No gun marshal," he was shot and killed on Nov. 2, 1870.

Smith, William, a lawman, was a deputy U.S. marshal for the Indian Nations working out of Judge Isaac Parker's court in Fort Smith, Ark., in the 1880s and 1890s.

Snearly, W.J., a lawman, served as a Texas Ranger in 1877 under Pat Dolan and was one of his most efficient men.

Sowell, A.J., a lawman, served as a Texas Ranger in 1870-71, and later wrote and published several Texas history books. He died in 1922.

Spradley, A. John, a lawman, served as deputy sheriff of Nacogdoches County, Texas, in 1880 under Sheriff Dick Orton and was elected sheriff in 1881. He served for several years, solved many murder cases such as the Truitt murder, and tracked outlaws.

Standefer, Wiley W., a lawman, served as U.S. Marshal of the Arizona Territory from Aug. 15, 1876, until June 12, 1878.

Stephens, R.M., a lawman, served as a sheriff in the New Mexico Territory during the 1850s.

Stiles, William Larkin (Billie), an outlaw, rode with Burt Alvord as a lawman and outlaw in Arizona in the 1890s and 1900s, and was killed in 1908.

Stilwell, Frank C., a gunman and lawman, was a deputy sheriff under Sheriff Behan in Tombstone, Ariz., and was shot and killed in 1881 during the grand jury investigation of Morgan Earp's shooting death.

Stilwell, Simpson (AKA: **Commanche Jack; John**), a gunman and lawman, scouted for the Army in Texas, served as a deputy U.S. marshal in the Indian Nations, and brought in several outlaws.

Stockton, Port (**William Porter**, AKA: **Porter Stogden**), an outlaw, lawman, and brother of Ike, shot and killed Juan Gonzales in October 1876 in Cimarron, N.M., and was killed on Jan. 10, 1881, by Alfred Graves.

Stoudenmire, Dallas, a lawman and gunman, joined Company A of the Texas Rangers in 1874, was city marshal of El Paso in 1881, and killed several men before his death in the early 1880s.

Sullivan, W. John L., a lawman, served as a sergeant in Company B of the Texas Rangers in 1889 and 1896.

Sunday, Jesse, a lawman, served as sheriff of the Sabine district, Cherokee Nation in the late 1880s.

T

Taylor, Creed, a lawman, joined the Texas Rangers under Captain Hays, fought in many battles, and died Dec. 27, 1906, at age eighty-six.

Terrell, Arthur, a lawman, was a Texas Ranger, Company B, in 1889 under Captain Sam McMurry.

Therringer, T.M., a lawman, Therringer served as a deputy marshal in the Arizona Territory during the 1870s.

Thomas, Henry Andrew (**Heck**), a lawman and one of the "Three Guardsmen," served in the Indian Nations as a deputy U.S. marshal in 1877, and as a special Texas Ranger in 1883. He helped break up the Dalton, Doolin, and Casey gangs, and captured the Lee gang. He died on Aug. 15, 1912.

Thompson, Ben (AKA: **Shotgun Ben**), a gunman and lawman in Texas, served as city marshal of Austin, Texas. He killed thirty-two men, and was killed in ambush with King Fisher in March 1884. Bat Masterson called him the West's greatest gunfighter.

Throckmorton, Sergeant, a lawman, served as a sergeant in the Texas Rangers in 1896.

Tidball, Zan L., a lawman, was appointed U.S. Marshal of the Arizona Territory on July 18, 1882.

Tilghman, William Matthew, Jr., a lawman, served as marshal of Dodge City, Kan., as sheriff of Ford County, and was the first city marshal of Perry, Okla. He became a deputy U.S. marshal under E.D. Nix and brought in outlaws Bill Doolin and Henry Starr. Tilgham was killed by prohibition officer Wiley Lynn on Nov. 1, 1924.

Tolbit, John, a lawman, was a deputy U.S. marshal for the Indian Nations working out of Judge Isaac Parker's court in the 1880s and 1890s.

Townsend, Everett E., a lawman, served in Company E as a Texas Ranger in 1892.

Townsley, Bob, a lawman, served in Company E as a Texas Ranger in 1892.

Townsley, Forest, a lawman, served in Company E as a Texas Ranger in 1892.

Trentham, Charles, a lawman, was a Texas Ranger who killed a man in Marfa, Texas, and escaped to New Mexico with a friend.

Tucker, George, a lawman, served in Company D of the Texas Rangers in 1894 and 1896.

Tucker, Tom, a lawman and gunfighter, served as deputy marshal in Las Cruces, N.M., during the 1850s.

Turnbo, L.S. (Kirk), a lawman, Turnbo served under Colonel Baylor as a Texas Ranger and made first lieutenant in his outfit before he was named to fill the post of sheriff for Reeves County, Texas, on Aug. 20, 1885.

Turner, George, a lawman and Arizona deputy marshal, was shot to death by Indians in September 1881.

Turner, Marion, a gunman and lawman, was a part-time assistant sheriff under Sheriff Peppin of Lincoln County, N.M., who led an army of men against Billy the Kid and his Regulators who were in hiding.

Tyner, Andrew, a lawman, served as sheriff of Yuma County, Ariz., during the 1870s.

Tyng, George, a lawman, served as sheriff of Yuma County, Ariz., during the 1860s.

U

Updyke, David, a lawman, was elected sheriff of Ada County, Idaho, in 1865. He was lynched on Apr. 14, 1866, for allegedly aiding horse thieves and murderers.

Utting, Charles, a lawman, served as a deputy marshal in the Arizona Territory.

V

Valdez, Antonio Jose (AKA: **El Mico; El Patas de Rana**), an outlaw and lawman, was one of Silva's White Caps of Las Vegas, N.M., shot and killed Vicente Silva from behind, and later became city marshal of Wagon Mound, N.M.

Vandenburg, B.C. (Bob), a lawman and U.S. cavalryman, served as deputy sheriff of Ford County in 1872 and as marshal of Dodge City, Kan., from 1881 to 1883.

W

Wakefield, Lyman, a lawman, served as the sheriff of Cochise County, Ariz., in the 1890s. He shot and killed outlaw Pedro Chavez.

Wallace, William Alexander Anderson (AKA: **Bigfoot**), a lawman, fought Mexicans for several years before joining the Texas Rangers under Captain Hays. He was made captain in 1858 and fought outlaws along the border. Bigfoot Wallace died on Jan. 7, 1899.

Ware, R.C. (Dick), a lawman, served as a Texas Ranger in 1878 and shot Sam Bass at Round Rock. He served as sheriff of Mitchell County, Texas, 1880-81, 1887-88, as U.S. marshal of West Texas in 1884, and was killed by constable John Selman at El Paso.

Webb, John Joshua (AKA: **Samuel King**), an outlaw, member of the Dodge City gang in Las Vegas, N.M., and city marshal of Las Vegas, murdered Michael Kelliher on Mar. 2, 1880, was condemned to hang, but escaped from jail with David Rudabaugh in 1881, and died of smallpox the following year.

Welch, John, a lawman, was Judge Roy Bean's deputy in 1893.

Welles, Justus P., a lawman, served as a deputy marshal in the Arizona Territory.

Wernett, John, a lawman, was a deputy sheriff of Val Verde County, Texas, in 1909 under Sheriff C.C. Bartley.

West, Duval, a lawman, was a Texas deputy U.S. marshal in 1886 to 1888, and helped kill outlaw William Whitley. He was later a federal judge.

Weston, Parker, a lawman, served as a Texas Ranger under Captain Frank Johnson in 1906.

Wheeler, Ben, a lawman and outlaw, was a companion of Billy the Kid during the Lincoln County War, robbed the Medicine Lodge, Kan., bank with Marshal Henry Brown and others on Apr. 30, 1884, and was lynched.

Wheeler, Harry, a lawman, served as an Arizona Ranger and then as sheriff of Cochise County, Ariz., for several years.

White, Coley, a lawman, served as the deputy sheriff of Travis County, Texas, in 1907.

White, Dudley, a lawman, served as a Texas Ranger in 1907.

White, Fred, a lawman, the marshal of Tombstone, Ariz., who was killed by "Curley Bill" Brocius in October 1880.

White, Golf, a lawman, served in Company C of the Texas Rangers in 1907.

White, G.S., a lawman, served as a deputy U.S. marshal out of Fort Smith, Ark., in the 1890s.

White, Jack, a lawman, was once sheriff of Cochise County, Ariz.

White, J.C. (AKA: **Doc**), a lawman, served as Texas Ranger in 1907.

White, Scott, a lawman and politician, served as sheriff of Cochise County, Ariz., from 1892 to 1901.

White, Tom B., a lawman, served as a Texas Ranger under Captain Frank Johnson in 1906.

White, Will, a lawman, served as the sheriff of Wilson County, Texas, in 1907.

Whitney, Chauncey Belden., a lawman, was the first city marshal of Ellsworth, Kan., in 1871, and became sheriff of the county in 1872. He was killed on Aug. 18, 1873, by Billy Thompson, who claimed his gun fired by accident.

Widenmann, Robert A., a lawman, served as a deputy marshal in the New Mexico Territory during the 1870s.

Wiley, John M., a lawman, served as a deputy marshal in the New Mexico Territory.

Williams, Ben, a lawman, was the deputy sheriff of Las Cruces, N.M., and fought Joe Morgan and Albert Fall in a shoot-out on Sept. 15, 1895.

Wilson, Vernon Coke, a lawman, joined Company A, Texas Rangers in 1876 under Neal Coldwell and alerted the Rangers that Sam Bass was at Round Rock in 1878. He was chief of the Mounted Inspectors of Arizona and New Mexico Territories in 1885. As a deputy U.S. marshal assigned to track Chris Evans and John Sontag, he was killed by Evans on Sept. 13, 1892.

Wilson, William (AKA: **Buffalo Billy**), an outlaw and lawman, was arrested with Billy the Kid, served time in prison, received a pardon in 1896, and became sheriff of Terrell County, N.M. He was killed in 1911.

Worley (or Wohrle), John, a lawman and outlaw, was deputy sheriff in Mason County, Texas, and involved in the Hoodoo War in 1875. He was shot, stabbed, and scalped by Scott Cooley to avenge Wohrle's part in the death of Tim Williamson.

Wright, Milam, a lawman, was a deputy sheriff of Val Verde County, Texas, in 1909 under Sheriff C.C. Bartley.

Wright, Will, a lawman, served as a captain in the Texas Rangers during WWI.

WESTERN OUTLAWS AND GUNMEN

The homesteaders and fortune seekers who moved west into previously ungoverned Indian lands during the mid-nineteenth century faced enormous perils, including the many colorful gunfighters and desperados who etched their names into history in the fifty years before the western frontier officially "closed" in 1900. The exploits of these men have been greatly exaggerated in the popular culture of the late twentieth century. There really was a Billy the Kid, for example, though it is doubtful that he killed twenty-one men, one for every year of his life; according to his friend George Coe, this figure never exceeded nine. Similarly, Ben Thompson of Texas was said to have gunned down thirty men single-handedly, and John Wesley Hardin forty.

Lawlessness in the Old West was not confined to the main streets of wide-open towns like Abilene or Dodge City. The worst incidents of gun play often occurred in the era's range wars and personal feuds that sprang up in New Mexico, Arizona, and Texas. The Mason County War in particular was characterized by a violent clash between German homesteaders and native Texans. Their differences harkened back to the Civil War, when the Germans espoused the cause of the Union, and the natives took the side of the Confederacy. Erupting between them in 1875, a shooting war resulted in many casualties on both sides before the Texas Rangers restored order.

The era of the gunfighter was over by the turn of the century. Improvements in transportation, the encroachments of civilization, and a more efficient deployment of law enforcement personnel put an end to this colorful but violent chapter in U.S. history.

The following compilation is presented as supplemental information, designed as ready reference of prominent western figures and also includes those who, for the most part, receive little or no mention in the main text of this volume.

A

Adamson, Carl, rode with Jim Miller, helped kill Pat Garrett in New Mexico on Feb. 28, 1908.

Adkins, Dave, an outlaw, was a member Black Jack Ketchum's gang.

Aguelari, Epeminto, an outlaw, killed Jose A. Samora at Wallace, N.M., on Apr. 20, 1884.

Aguilar, Ceberiano, an outlaw, fought and died in the Harrold War of Lincoln County, N.M., in 1874.

Aguilar, Donaciano, an outlaw, was sentenced to life imprisonment in New Mexico on Nov. 24, 1909.

Aguilar, Reymundo, an outlaw, fought and died in the Harrold War of Lincoln County, N.M., 1874.

Aguillan, Felix, a member of the Castillo gang.

Aguirre, Jermin, a gunman, was shot on Aug. 8, 1875, near San Augustin Ranch, N.M.

Ake, Jeff was a Texas Reconstruction gunman.

Ake, William, a gunman and brother of Jeff Ake, fought in the Mason County feud in the 1870s.

"Alamosa Bill", an outlaw, was killed at El Paso, Texas, in April 1888.

Alarid, Eugenio, a lawman and outlaw, was a member of the Las Vegas, N.M., police force and a member of Vincente Silva's White Caps.

Alarid, Nasario, an outlaw, was sentenced to ninety-nine years in prison in New Mexico on Sept. 17, 1906.

Alexander, John, an outlaw, stole horses in Texas

and was shot and killed by a mob on May 25, 1874, in Belton.

Alford, George, an outlaw, was imprisoned five years for killing a sheriff in 1880 at Fort Worth, Texas.

Allen, Bill, a Texas outlaw and robber, occasionally rode with the Jesse Evans gang.

Allen, Billy (AKA: **The Kid**), a gunman in Deadwood, S.D., and New Mexico, killed several men.

Allen, "Bladder", an outlaw in Lincoln County, was jailed for stabbing a man in White Oaks, N.M.

Allen, Chas, an outlaw, robbed and killed a group of people in Virginia City for which he was hanged.

Allen, Frank, a gunman, was shot and killed in El Paso, Texas, in March 1881.

Allen, James, an outlaw, killed James Moorehead in Las Vegas, N.M., for ordering eggs on Mar. 2, 1880, and was killed by a posse after escaping from prison.

Allen, John, a outlaw member of the Dodge City gang, operating around Las Vegas, New Mexico.

Allen, Joseph, a gunman, was hanged on Apr. 19, 1909, at Ada, Okla., for his participation in a feud.

Allen, Malachi, an outlaw, killed two men in the Chickasaw Nation and was hanged at Fort Smith on Apr. 19, 1889.

Allison, Charles, a former deputy sheriff turned outlaw, robbed stages between Colorado and New Mexico. He was captured in 1881 by sheriff Matt Kyle, then by Frank Hyatt, and released in 1890.

Allison, Robert A. (AKA: **Clay**), a quick-draw gunman who killed at least fifteen men, moved between Colorado, New Mexico, and Texas as a cowhand. He led several lynch mobs and died on July 1, 1887, when a wagon wheel crushed his head.

Almer, Jack (**Jack Averill**, AKA: **Red Jack**), an outlaw and leader of the infamous Red Jack gang, was killed on Oct. 4, 1883, by a posse near Wilcox, Ariz.

Alsup, Wade, an outlaw, was lynched by fifteen masked men in Blue, Texas, on June 27, 1877.

Altman, Perry, a New Mexico gunman and the half-brother of Oliver Lee.

Alvarid, Juan, an outlaw, who was lynched in Socorro, N.M., on Aug. 16, 1882, for raping an 8-year-old girl.

Alverson, Leonard, a cowboy and gunman, was accused, with two others, of a Dec. 9, 1897, robbery at Steins Pass, N.M. They were imprisoned, but in 1899, Sam Ketchum confessed to the crime and the three men were freed.

Alvord, Burton, a deputy sheriff turned outlaw, led a gang that robbed trains in Arizona. Captured in Mexico by Arizona Rangers, he served two years in prison and died around 1910.

Amador, Martin, an outlaw, hanged for murder in Deming, N.M., on Jan. 13, 1908.

Amos, Fred was an outlaw and highwayman in California in the late 1860s.

Anderson, Ham, a gunman and cousin of John Hardin, used his guns in Dodge City, Kan., and Texas before he was killed in 1874.

Anderson, Jim, an outlaw with Bill Anderson's guerilla band. Anderson was killed in Texas in the 1860s.

Anderson, Reese, a gunman and cowboy who led a vigilante sweep of the Lower Judith Basin in Montana, 1884, captured and hanged twenty-three horse thieves.

Anderson, Scott, L., the trusted guard for the Northwestern Stage and Transportation Company, which transported gold in the Dakotas, killed Boston Joe when the stage robber attempted to take over $100,000 in gold.

Anderson, Tom, a gunman, was the brother of Black Jack Christian.

Anderson, William, a resident of Delano, the vice district of Wichita, Kan., was a drunken gunman who in 1873 was blinded in a shoot-out. Anderson died begging coins outside saloons.

Andrews, Hank, an outlaw, was lynched by vigilantes in February 1884, near Tularosa, N.M.

Anthony, Ernest, an outlaw horse thief, was jailed in Springer, N.M., in March 1885.

Apache Kid (Zenogalache, AKA: The Crazy One), an outlaw Apache Indian, along with a band of warriors, raided ranches and wagon trains throughout New Mexico and Arizona territories; reportedly died of consumption around 1910 after retiring to Mexico.

Apodaca, Maximo, an outlaw and convicted murderer of the Nesmith family in White Sands, N.M., committed suicide in prison on Nov. 4, 1885.

Applegate, Bill, an outlaw, led a gang of rustlers in New Mexico Territory in the 1870s. He was nearly captured by Seven Rivers.

Aragon, Serefin, a New Mexico Territory outlaw and cattle rustler.

Arajo, Justin, an outlaw in California, was lynched for shooting a man to death on July 12, 1877.

Arango, Doroter (AKA: Francisco "Pancho" Villa), an outlaw, cattle rustler, and Mexican revolutionist, successfully raided the U.S. border several times. He was killed on July 20, 1923, at Parral, Mex.

Archer Brothers, outlaws, robbed travelers, trains, and stages throughout Orange and Marion Counties of Indiana. Tom, Mort, and John Archer were lynched by vigilantes in March 1886 and Sam Archer was hanged July 10, 1886.

Arguello, A., an outlaw, murdered Asher Jones at Clayton, N.M., in 1881.

"Arizona Jack", a gunman and teamster, was lynched at Wagon Bed Springs, Kansas Territory, for shooting to death another teamster.

"Arkansas Bill", a gunman of Dodge City, Kan., in the late 1870s, claimed to kill twenty-two men.

Armstrong, Jack, an outlaw of Las Vegas, N.M., killed a bartender over the price of a drink.

Arquello, David, an outlaw, was hanged in Raton, N.M., on May 25, 1906.

Arrington, Willis, a Texas outlaw, was charged in 1881 with rustling cattle.

Ashby, George, an outlaw, stole horses in Montana and Texas, and killed a sheriff near Powder River and Little Missouri, Mont.

Asque, Joe (Joe Askew), an outlaw, rustled cattle near Hillsboro, N.M., around 1877 and cut himself down from a hangman's noose.

Atkins, David, an outlaw and member of the Black Jack Ketchum gang, robbed trains throughout New Mexico, West Texas, and Arizona.

Augustine, Robert, a cowboy and gunman, was arrested in 1863 for hurrahing San Antonio, Texas. Augustine was lynched by a mob after the court acquitted him.

Averill, James, and **Watson, Ella**, outlaws, rustled cattle. Their deaths in July 1889 at the hands of rival ranchers began the bloody Johnson County War.

Avila, Genovevo (AKA: El Cochumeno), a Mexican native who was a member of Vincente Silva's White Caps or Forty Thieves.

Ayers, Thomas G. a gunman, was killed by the Dalton gang in the Coffeyville, Kan., bank robberies on Nov. 5, 1892, while attempting to shoot a rifle.

B

Baca, Abran, an outlaw, murdered A.M. Conklin of Socorro, N.M., with others on Christmas Eve 1880. He was acquitted in 1881.

Baca, Antonio, an outlaw, murdered A.M. Conklin with others in 1880. He was killed attempting to escape jail on Dec. 29, 1880.

Baca, Celso, a murderer who beat Jose de la Cruz Sandoval to death in 1884 at Santa Rosa, N.M.

Baca, Cruz, an outlaw, murdered W.H. Allen of Hillsboro, N.M., in February 1887.

Baca, Jose, an outlaw and multiple offender, was sent to prison on Nov. 19, 1906, for the fifth time.

Baca, Manuel, an outlaw and member of Silva's White Caps in the 1890s, was the "judge" who ordered the execution of disloyal gang members.

Baca, Onofre, an outlaw, murdered A.M. Conklin with others in 1880 and was lynched on Mar. 31, 1881.

Baca, Patricio, an outlaw and the most notorious horse thief in northern New Mexico Territory, was killed in Chimayo in December 1875.

Bader, Pete was a gunman in the Mason County "Hoodoo War" of Texas. His brother, Charles Bader, was killed by John Ringo.

"Bad Nell", a Texas outlaw and cowboy. She operated around Fort Griffin in the 1870s.

Bailey, John, an outlaw and rustler, was shot and killed by Ranger P.C. Baird in Edward County, Texas, on July 29, 1884.

Baker, Chas, a gunman in the Lincoln County War and brother of Frank Baker, was captured by Ranger Jim Gillett in Texas and imprisoned for twenty-five years.

Baker, Cullen Montgomery, an outlaw and veteran guerilla soldier, fought reconstructionist soldiers and terrorized Texas for four years after the war. He was killed on Jan. 6, 1869, having killed twenty-six men in his fifteen years as a soldier.

Baker, Frank, an outlaw and member of the Jesse Evans gang, helped kill John Tunstall during the Lincoln County War. Billy the Kid killed Baker in March 1878 in retaliation.

Baldwin, Thurman (AKA: **Skeeter**), an outlaw and member of the Cook gang in Indian Territory, was captured after a bank robbery.

Ballard, Charles, a gunman, rode with the posse that captured Black Jack Ketchum in September 1896.

Ballew, Steve, a gunman, in 1870, shot and killed Jim Golden in Collin County, Texas, and was executed.

Bangs, "Cherokee", an outlaw and cattle rustler in Utah, led a gang in the 1890s which included Matt Warner.

Barbee, Claude, an outlaw, shot and killed deputy sheriff Hamilton on Gene Rhodes' ranch.

Barbour, John, an outlaw, was a member of the Brack Cornett gang of Texas in the 1880s. He was killed in the Indian Nations.

Barela, Manuel, a New Mexico gunman who killed a man in Las Vegas, only to be hanged by vigilantes in 1879.

Barela, Santos, an outlaw, was hanged on May 20, 1881, in Mesilla, N.M.

Barela, Ysabel, a gunman, was shot and killed by

John Kinney in Mesilla, N.M., on Nov. 2, 1877.

Barkley, Clinton, an outlaw wanted for murder, was a Horrell gunman in the Horrell-Higgins feud.

Barnes, Johnny was an Arizona and New Mexico outlaw.

Barnes, Seaborn (Sebe, AKA: **Nubbin's Colt**), an outlaw, joined the Sam Bass gang in 1878, was indicted for assault, and killed with Bass at Round Rock, Texas, in 1878.

Barnett, Wesley, an outlaw in the Indian Nations in the 1880s, was killed by police in 1889. He terrorized the Creek Indian capital.

Barrera, Calisto, an outlaw, murdered John D. Bohn on Aug. 16, 1882, near Sapello, N.M.

Barter, Richard (AKA: **Rattlesnake Dick; Dick Woods**), a California outlaw, stole horses and robbed mining camps. He was killed in July 1859 while his gang robbed a mule train.

Barton, Jerry, a gunman, ran a saloon in Charleston, Ariz., killed his partner, and was jailed for killing a Mexican in 1881.

Barton, "Kid", an outlaw, led a stage-robbing gang that operated at Raton Pass. He killed several people and was hanged in the late 1860s.

Basham, Tucker, an outlaw, was a member of Jesse James' gang.

Bass, Samuel (Sam), an outlaw who robbed stages in the Dakotas, organized a gang in Texas and robbed trains. He and another gang member were killed by Texas Rangers at Round Rock, Texas, in July 1878.

Basset, Harry, a gunman, was shot on Nov. 20, 1879, in Otero, N.M.

Baugh, Captain **Andrew T.**, a Texas outlaw and cattle rustler, was lynched in 1885 when caught with a herd of stolen cattle.

Baxter, Dan, a gunman, was shot and killed in August 1884 by Frank Thurmond in Deming, N.M.

Beach, Charles, a gunman, shot and killed a man who stabbed him in the Prescott, Ariz., courtroom on Dec. 3, 1883.

Beard, Edward T., a gunman in California, Oregon, and Arizona, ran a bar in Wichita, Kan., and died on Nov. 11, 1873, from wounds received from a shoot-out with rival saloon owner and gunman Rowdy Joe Lowe.

Beard, John, a gunman in the Mason County, Texas, "Hoodoo War," participated in the Horrell-Higgins feud.

Beard, Mose, brother of John, was a gunman in the Mason County, Texas, "Hoodoo War."

Beck, Frank, an outlaw, helped murder Joe Hickson on Oct. 28, 1884, at Good Hope, N.M.

Beck, H.O. (AKA: **Ole; Edward Welch**), an outlaw, was a cell mate of Ben Kilpatrick of the Wild Bunch and wanted to join the gang. He was shot and killed Mar. 13, 1912, during a train robbery in which Kilpatrick was also killed.

Beck, William Ellison (AKA: **Cyclone Bill**), an outlaw, who became a suspect in the robbery of an Army paymaster on May 11, 1889.

Beckwith, Henry, a gunman in the Lincoln County War, shotgunned his son-in-law on Aug. 16, 1878.

Beckwith, John H., a gunman and son of Henry, participated in the Lincoln County War.

Beckwith, Robert W., gunman in the Lincoln County War, was a member of the posse that killed John Tunstall. He was killed in the McSween fight July 19, 1878.

Bell, "Choctaw", an outlaw, was a member of the

Langford gang of Texas in the early 1880s. He was shot by a posse in 1881.

Bell, C.S., a gunman, lawman, and former Union spy, claimed he killed over thirty men.

Bell, Tom, a California outlaw, robbed stagecoaches with a gang he led, and was lynched by a sheriff in 1856.

Belmont, Courtney, a gunman, rode with Matt Zimmerman in the 1880s in Nebraska.

Belmont, Dick, a gunman, rode with Matt Zimmerman but went to Kansas after Matt was killed. Belmont was shot dead in Stockton.

Benavides, Santos, an outlaw, murderer and horse thief, was lynched in Albuquerque, N.M., Dec. 29, 1880.

Bennett, George, a outlaw and member of the Bill Dalton gang, was killed in 1893 at Longview, Texas, during a bank robbery.

Bentley, Charley, an outlaw, escaped from jail at White Oaks, N.M., in March 1881.

Berry, James, an outlaw and member of the Sam Bass gang, was caught by lawmen after the train robbery at Big Spring.

Bewley, Jim, a gunman, was killed in Oregon attempting to break the smallpox quarantine.

Bickerstaff, Benjamin F., an outlaw and guerilla soldier, looted Federal supplies and fought soldiers throughout Texas. He was shot and killed by citizens of Alvarado in April 1869.

Bideno, Juan, an outlaw, killed the trail boss during a cattle drive from Texas to Kansas. A posse which included John Hardin pursued Bideno, and Hardin killed him in Bluff Creek, Kan.

"Big Sandy" was an outlaw in California in the 1850s.

Bill, Charles, an outlaw, was run out of the New Mexico Territory on Feb. 6, 1906.

Billee, John, an outlaw, murdered W.P. Williams with the help of Thomas Willis. Billee and Willis were captured by deputies Will Ayers, James Wilkerson, and Perry DuVall, and hanged on Jan. 16, 1890.

Billy the Kid (William H. Bonney; William Antrim), a notorious outlaw, one of the "Regulators" in the Lincoln County War, 1870s-1880s. He ambushed Sheriff Brady, and was slain on July 14, 1881, at Fort Sumner by Pat Garrett in the home of Pete Maxwell.

Bishop, Miles was an outlaw in New Mexico, in the mid-1860s.

Bishop, Pete, a gunman and saloon owner, killed two men in December 1871.

Bivins, Bill, a Wyoming outlaw, was jailed for train robbery near Atlantic City in 1877.

Bivins, Lige, an outlaw, was a member of a gang of raiders in Bell, Texas, during the Civil War.

Black, Blackie, a gunman and teamster, killed several men in Texas in the early 1850s.

Black, Isaac, an outlaw and member of the Doolin gang, was killed by a posse near Enid, Okla., on Aug. 1, 1895.

Black, Jim, a train robber in the New Mexico Territory.

Black, John, a train robber in the New Mexico Territory.

Black, Pope, an outlaw, was shot and killed in the Florida Mountains, N.M., while resisting arrest, December 1882.

Black, Robert (AKA: Arkansaw), an outlaw, eluded lynching by challenging the vigilantes to a fight.

Blackburn, Duncan (AKA: **Tom**), an outlaw, robbed stages in 1877 in Deadwood, Dakota Territory. He disappeared after Boone May killed four bandits.

Blackwell, James, an outlaw, shot and killed W.B. Foster in Raton, N.M., on Aug. 8, 1882.

Blain, Joe, an outlaw, shot and killed Joe Pitman in Luna Valley, N.M., on Feb. 18, 1888.

Blake, John, (AKA: **Tulsa Jack**), an outlaw and member of the Doolin-Dalton gang, was killed by lawmen following the Rock Island train robbery near Dover, Okla., in 1895.

Blevins, John, a gunman, fought in the Pleasant Valley, Ariz., War and against the Tewksburys in their feud with the Grahams.

Blevins, M. (AKA: **F.C. Marklin**), an outlaw, escaped from the Texas penitentiary in 1884, at the age of twenty.

Blind Joe, a gunman, was killed on the Mescalero Apache Reservation in January 1908.

Blue Duck, a gunman, friend of Belle Starr, and half-breed Indian, allegedly killed a farmer in 1886 and was sentenced to die. He was later pardoned.

Blun, Kenry, an outlaw, shot George C. Quaries on Sept. 20, 1884, at Fairview, N.M.

Bobbitt, Angus A. (**Gus**), a gunman and former lawman, led a faction in the Pontotoc County War against cattlemen Jesse West and Joseph Allen. He was killed in ambush in February 1909.

Bogan, Dan, an outlaw, was wanted in Wyoming and indicted for murder in Texas in 1881.

Boggs, Thomas O., a gunman and a mountain man around Taos, N.M., in 1844, was a friend and associate of Kit Carson.

Boles, Charles E. (AKA: **Black Bart**), an outlaw, successfully robbed twenty-seven stages in California in the early 1880s. He was captured in 1883 and sent to San Quentin prison. He was released on Jan. 23, 1888, and disappeared.

Bolt, William James, an outlaw, was hanged in Lincoln on June 18, 1886.

Boot, Joseph, an outlaw, was captured and imprisoned in 1899 after attempting his first stage robbery with Pearl Hart.

Borne, Dutch Henry, an outlaw, and the leader of a group of horse and mule thieves in the 1870s throughout Texas, Kansas, and the Indian Nations.

Bothwell, Albert J., a gunman and head of the cattle barons of Sweetwater, Wyo., who ordered the lynching of Jim Averill and Ella Watson, precipitating the Johnson County War. Bothwell was driven out of the county by other ranchers and disappeared.

Boucher, William, an outlaw and cowboy of Tombstone, Ariz., was suspected of stage robbery and killed on Mar. 25, 1888, by Sheriff Billy Breakenridge's posse.

Bowdre, Charles, an outlaw and right hand to Billy the Kid in the Lincoln County War, was killed on Dec. 20, 1880, awaiting trial for the murder of Buckshot Roberts.

Bowers, George, gunman, was killed in the Lincoln County War on July 19, 1878.

Boyce, Mart, a gunman and faro dealer in Caldwell, Kan. In 1883, he was killed by Marshal H. Brown.

Boyce, Reuben H. (AKA: **Rube**), an outlaw in Kimble County, Texas, led a gang of rustlers. He was arrested for murder on Jan. 24, 1878, and died on May 23, 1927, in Texas.

Boyd, Thomas M., Jr., an outlaw, shot and killed John Foundation in Lake Valley, N.M., on Aug. 15, 1884.

Boyle, Andrew was a gunman in the Lincoln County War.

Boyle, Robert H. (AKA: **Hornsburg**), an outlaw, shot Pat Slavin in Magdalena, N.M., on May 28, 1881.

Boyle, "Sport", a gunman, was a member of the Dodge City gang in Las Vegas, N.M.

Brady, Jack, an outlaw in 1892, Brady stole $50,000 from a Wells-Fargo coach and was killed by a detective.

Brady, William, the outlaw sheriff of Lincoln County during the war in 1878, formed the posse of deputies and known outlaws that killed John Tunstall. He was ambushed and shot by Billy the Kid and others shortly after.

Brann, William Cowper, a newspaperman, engaged Captain T.E. Davis in a gunfight on Apr. 1, 1898, in which both men were killed.

Brazil (or Brazel), Wayne, a gunman, confessed to the Feb. 28, 1908, shooting of Pat Garrett. He was acquitted following a trial.

Brazzelton, William, an outlaw, robbed stagecoaches in Arizona, while wearing various disguises. He was killed in August 1878.

Brent, Henry, an outlaw, was run out of Bannack, Mont., by vigilantes and killed during a fight with Indians.

Brewer, Richard M., a gunman formerly of the Murphy-Dolan faction in the Lincoln County War, was named leader of the Regulators in 1878 and led a posse after Tunstall's murderers. Brewer was killed in the Blazer's Mill battle.

Brinster, Joseph, an outlaw, was hanged in Isleta, Texas, on July 5, 1883.

Broadwell, Richard (Dick, AKA: **Texas Jack**), an outlaw and member of the Dalton gang, robbed

banks and trains throughout Kansas and Oklahoma, and was killed during the Coffeyville, Kan., raid on Oct. 5, 1892.

Brocius, William (AKA: **Curley Bill; Graham**), an outlaw leader in Tombstone, Ariz., shot and killed the Haslett brothers with Johnny Ringo in June 1881 at Hachita, N.M. He was reportedly shotgunned by Wyatt Earp.

Brock, Leonard Calvert, an outlaw, was a member of the Rube Burrow gang that robbed trains in Texas and Alabama. He was captured and died on Nov. 10, 1890, after jumping from the fourth floor of the jail after confessing to train robbery.

Broderick, David C., a gunman and politician in California, was killed by Judge David S. Terry in a duel in the 1850s.

"Bronco Charlie", an outlaw, was lynched near Miles City, Mont., in the late 1880s.

Brooks, William L. (AKA: **Buffalo Billy**), a lawman and gunman, participated in the Newton War in Kansas during which fourteen men were killed. He was killed in 1874 by Morgan Earp.

Brophy, Hank, an outlaw, rustled cattle in New Mexico.

Brown, Billy, a gunman, killed his best friend on Aug. 19, 1880, near Fort Sill, was arrested in Texas, and hanged in Fort Smith.

Brown, Bob, an outlaw, attempted to rob a train at Fairbanks, Ariz., with a gang. He was captured and served a prison term in Yuma, Ariz.

Brown, Henry Newton, an outlaw and member of Billy the Kid's gang who went to Arizona, became the city marshal of Caldwell, Kan. He led a gang that robbed a bank in Medicine Lodge on Apr. 30, 1884. He was captured and hanged.

Brown, Robert C., an outlaw, attempted to rob a train with his gang at Fairbanks, Ariz., on Feb. 20,

1900. He was captured, imprisoned in Yuma, and disappeared after his release.

Brown, Sam (AKA: **Long-Haired Sam**), a gunman in the Nevada mining camps, killed fifteen men and was shot and killed on July 7, 1861.

Brown, W.E., an outlaw, was shot and killed by Sheriff Turnbo on Sept. 6, 1887, in Pecos, Texas.

Browning, William (AKA: **Browney**), an outlaw and train robber in Illinois in the 1900s, was killed in Texas while robbing a bank.

Brunton, "Tex", an outlaw, fled from Texas, California, and Oklahoma.

Bryant, Charles (AKA; **Black Face Charlie; Black Eyed Charlie**), an outlaw and member of the Doolin-Dalton gang, was killed in a duel with a lawman named Short in Hennessey, Okla., in 1891.

Buck Gang, the infamous outlaw Indian gang of Okmulgee, Cherokee Nation, raped, murdered, and robbed for thirteen days. They were captured and hanged on July 1, 1896. Led by Rufus Buck, the gang was Sam Sampson, Maomi July, Lewis Davis, and Lucky Davis.

Buckley, James (AKA: **Coal Oil Jimmy**), an outlaw stage robber and murderer, was killed in January 1871.

Bull, John C., a gunman, killed a farmer in Montana in 1867. He was tried, acquitted in 1882, and died in 1928.

Bullion, Laura, the girlfriend of several outlaws including Bill Carver and Ben Kilpatrick; helped Kilpatrick rob a train and was imprisoned in 1901 for currency forgery.

Bunch, Eugene, an outlaw, robbed an express car in Texas and was killed on Aug. 21, 1892, near Franklin.

Burbridge, William, an outlaw, shot and killed William Heine on Apr. 12, 1881, in San Marcial, N.M.

Burleson, Pete, an outlaw, shot and killed Tom Driscoll in Springer, N.M., on Jan. 16, 1884. Driscoll died sixteen days later.

Burrows, James Buchanan, an outlaw and brother of Rube, robbed trains with his brother in 1886-87 and was captured in 1888. He died in the Montgomery, Ala., jail of natural causes.

Burrow, Reuben Houston (AKA: **Rube; Charles Davis**), a famed outlaw leader and train robber whose gang operated in Texas, Arkansas, Missouri, and Alabama. He was killed on Oct. 7, 1890, in Linden, Ala.

Burt, Sam, an outlaw, was lynched by the Committee of 601 on Dec. 17, 1875, in Montana Territory.

Burts, Matthew (Matt), a lawman and part-time Arizona outlaw, rode with Burt Alvord, Billie Stiles, and the Owens brothers. He ranched in California, and was murdered in 1925 during a dispute over water rights.

Buster, John, an outlaw and member of the silver gang, killed William Holland in Seven Rivers in December 1884.

C

Caballero, Guadalupe (AKA: **The Owl**), an outlaw and the chief spy and rustler for Vicente Silva's White Caps in Las Vegas, N.M. Caballero was sentenced to ten years as an accessory to Pat Maes' hanging.

Cameron, Andrew, an outlaw, shot and killed Donaciano Tafoya on Apr. 25, 1881, in New Mexico.

Campbell, William, an outlaw, rode with Jesse Evans, killed Thomas King on Dec. 6, 1896, and was acquitted of murder.

Campbell, William, a Texas gunman and cowboy, was killed in a gun battle with Babe and Andy Moye on the streets of Ogalalla, Neb., after insulting Babe.

Campbell, William (AKA: **The Kid**), an outlaw, was a member of the Ashly gang of Montana in 1884. He was killed by lawmen.

Canton, Frank M., a gunman and lawman, was a rancher, cowboy, sheriff, and adjunct general of four states. Lived in Oklahoma, Wyoming, Alaska, and Montana.

Capehart, Tom, an outlaw, was a member of the Black Jack Ketchum gang.

Carbajal, Antonio, a gunman, fatally wounded Bernardino Chavez on Dec. 8, 1897, at Mesilla, N.M.

Cardenas, Manuel, a gunman, was suspected of murder in November 1875 at Cimarron, N.M.

Cardis, Louis, an outlaw, led the Mexican faction in the El Paso Salt War and was killed by Judge Howard in 1877.

Carl, Peter, an outlaw, shot and killed Harry Huber in a saloon in Rincon, N.M., on Aug. 31, 1884.

Carlile, William L., an outlaw and the last of the Old West train robbers, was captured and imprisoned in the 1900s.

Carlisle, John, a Texas outlaw, was hanged in 1893 for conspiracy to commit murder.

Carmondy, Patric, an outlaw, was jailed with Mexican conspirators Jagola and Gonzales, for killing William Wiggins. The three escaped from jail in Socorro, N.M., in October 1888.

Carrhert, George, a gunman, was killed in Bannack, Mont., during a duel in 1863.

Carrolla, Jose M. (AKA: **Portuguese Jo**), an outlaw and member of the Wild Bill Martin Gang, was shot and killed by John Perry on June 19, 1877.

Carson, Christopher (AKA: **Kit**), the legendary scout, mountain man, and Indian fighter, ranged throughout the West and lived on the Santa Fe Trail near Cimarron, N.M.

Carson, Joe, a gunman and city marshal of Las Vegas, N.M., was a member of the Dodge City gang in Las Vegas and was killed in a saloon gunfight.

Carter, "Tex", a gunfighter for Jim Lacy, Opium Bob, and Dutch Charley Bates, escaped a lynch mob on Mar. 22, 1881, at Rawlins, Wyo., and later became a sheriff in Nebraska.

Carver, William, an outlaw and a Texas cowboy, rode with the Black Jacks, the Wild Bunch, and the High Five gang. While robbing with the Kilpatrick brothers, he was killed by a posse led by Sheriff Lige Briant in 1901 outside of Sonora, Texas.

Casey, Joe, an outlaw, was jailed by Sheriff Bob Paul in 1882 in Tucson, Ariz., escaped several times, and was hanged.

Casey, John P., an outlaw horse thief, was apprehended in the Black Hills of New Mexico in June 1889.

Casharago, James, an outlaw and prison escapee, was hanged in Fort Smith on July 30, 1896, for the murder of Zack Thatch.

Cassidy, Butch (George Leroy Parker), an outlaw, led the Wild Bunch, which robbed trains and banks in Utah, Nevada, Wyoming, Colorado, New Mexico, and other states. He and Harry Longbaugh, the Sundance Kid, were allegedly killed in Bolivia or Argentina in 1908.

Castillo, Candido, an outlaw with rewards for him totaling $2,400, was shot and killed by a posse near Espanola, N.M., in 1884.

Castillo, Manuel, was Candido's younger brother.

Catfish Kid, an outlaw, reportedly killed deputy Sheriff L.S. Pierce in a gunfight and others, and was imprisoned for murder. He was present when three LS cowboys were killed in March 1886 at Tascosa, Texas.

Catron, Jim (AKA: **The Pagnas Stage Robber**), an outlaw, was shot and killed by a guard in the 1880s at Fort Garland, Colo.

Chaco, Icnacio, an outlaw, was a member of the Castillo gang.

Chacon, Augustin (AKA: **Paludo; Peledo; the Hairy One**), an outlaw, led a gang who murdered and robbed in Arizona and escaped jail and execution twice before he was captured by the deputy sheriff of Cochise County, Burt Alvord. He was hanged on Nov. 21, 1901.

Chadwell, William (AKA: **Bill Stiles**), an outlaw and member of the James-Younger gang, was killed on Sept. 7, 1876, during the First National Bank of Northfield, Minn., robbery.

Chamberlain, Samuel E. (AKA: **Peloncillo Jack**), a gunman and soldier of fortune in the 1840s, later became a general in the Civil War, and died in Worcester, Mass, in 1908.

Champion, Nathan D., an outlaw and rustler, was killed with Nick Ray by cattleman in their cabin in Kaycee, Wy.

Chaves, Juan, a New Mexico outlaw and horse thief, was captured by the 9th Cavalry in February 1876.

Chaves, Paz, an outlaw, stole horses around Boquilla, N.M.

Chavez, Antonio, an outlaw, was shot and killed during a holdup outside San Simon, N.M., on May 21, 1880.

Chavez, Carlos, an outlaw, was hanged for slaying Yum Kee in Silver City, N.M., in 1884.

Chavez, Fernando, an outlaw, was lynched in Las Lunas, N.M., on Oct. 6, 1881.

Chavez, Josefito, an outlaw and horse thief, was a gunman in the Lincoln County War.

Chavez, Pedro, an outlaw and member of Augustin Chacon's gang in the 1890s, was arrested for robbery, escaped prison at Tuscon, Ariz., and was killed in a gun battle with Sheriff Wakefield.

Chavez y Baca, Jose was a gunman in the Lincoln County War.

Chavez y Chavez, Jose, an outlaw and member of Vicente Silva's White Caps, was the last surviving member of the gang. He was sentenced to life imprisonment.

Chenowith, Otto, a Wyoming outlaw and horse thief, Chenowith was placed in a sanatarium in the East.

"Cherokee Bob" was a gunman in the 1860s in mining camps of Idaho an Montana.

Cherry (AKA: **The Kid**), an outlaw, was a member of Ike Stockton's gang. Dyson Eskridge shot him in the back.

Chilton, Fred, a cowboy and gunman, was one of three cowboys killed by Len Woodward on Mar. 21, 1886, at Tascosa, Texas.

Choalt, Frank, an outlaw, escaped from a prison train on Apr. 16, 1906.

Christian, William (AKA: **Black Jack**), an outlaw who committed several robberies throughout Oklahoma, Arizona, and New Mexico; Christian was ambushed and killed at his hideout near Clifton, Ariz.

Christianson, Willard Erastus (AKA: **Matt Warner; Ras Lewis**), an outlaw and brother-in-law of outlaw Tom McCarty, robbed trains and banks with Butch Cassidy, Elza Lay, and McCarty from 1878, served a prison sentence, became a lawman, and died Dec. 21, 1938.

Christie, Ned, an outlaw Cherokee Indian, killed Marshal Dan Maples and others, stole horses, and was killed by a large posse on Nov. 2, 1892, in the Cherokee Nation.

Claiborne, William F. (AKA: **Billy the Kid**), a gunman and cowhand, moved to Cochise County, Ariz., when John Slaughter bought the old McLowery ranch. He survived the O.K. Corral gunfight and was killed by Buckskin Frank Leslie in Tombstone in November.

Clancy, John, an outlaw, allegedly robbed a stage in September 1879 near Tecolote, N.M., and was tried and acquitted.

Clanton, Finneas, although not as active an outlaw as his brothers, he did serve a prison sentence for cattle stealing.

Clanton, Isaac (Ike), a gunman who was a member of the Clanton family in Cochise County, Ariz. He was unarmed when the Earps and Doc Holliday advanced on them at the O.K. Corral. His brother William "Billy" Clanton, who carried a gun, was killed.

Clanton, N.H. (AKA: **Old Man**), the head of the Clanton clan in Cochise County, N.M., was accused by the Earps of rustling, ambushing smugglers, and harboring rustlers. He was never prosecuted or arrested for these alleged crimes.

Clanton, Robert, a gunmen who killed Jerome and Dick Maddox and Lew Coates in a gunfight in Portland, Mo., in 1863. Clanton escaped to Texas, but was apprehended twenty-five years later for murder.

Clanton, William (Billy), a gunman, took a horse Wyatt Earp claimed belonged to him, and thus precipitated the gunfight at the O.K. Corral in which Billy, sixteen, was killed along with Frank and Tom McLowery.

Clark, Benjamin, a gunman and Indian scout, fought and killed renegade and hostile Indians most of his life. He served with Bat Masterson and scouted for General Nelson Miles in the Indian Wars, 1874.

Clark, Jap, was a New Mexico gunman, who lasted into the 20th century, until his imprisonment in 1908.

Clark, Thomas (AKA: **Pennsylvania Butch**), an outlaw, was a member of the gang that held up a train outside Marcus, Ill. He was arrested and sent to the prison at Joliet.

Clements, Emanuel, Jr. (AKA: **Mannie**), a lawman, gunman, and son of Emanuel Sr. of Gonzales County, Texas, participated in the Miller-Frazer feud in Pecos, Texas, in 1891 and was killed in El Paso while a lawman on Dec. 29, 1908.

Clements, Emanuel, Sr. (AKA: **Mannen**), an outlaw, cousin, and cohort of John Hardin, killed two men in July 1871 in Indian Territory, jailed in Kansas by Bill Hickok, and released on request of Hardin. He was killed at Ballinger, Texas, on Mar. 29, 1887.

Clements, James, a gunman, brother of Emanuel Sr., and cousin of John Hardin, drove cattle with Hardin and helped him kill six Mexican herders near Newton, Kan., in 1871.

Clements, John Gibson (AKA: **Gip**), a gunman and youngest of the Clements brothers, helped cousin Wes Hardin disarm several deputies of Bill Hickok in 1871, and send them back to Abilene, Kan., pantless. Clements died in Runnels County, Texas.

Clements, Joseph, a cowboy, gunman, and one of the Clements brothers, trailed John Hardin's herd in 1874 to Comanche County.

Cleveland, George, a black outlaw, was a member of Kit Joy's gang and was killed by the gang after escaping from jail at Silver City, N.M., on March 1884.

Clifton, Daniel (AKA: **Dynamite Dick**), outlaw and member of the Doolin-Dalton gang, participated in several train and bank robberies and escaped from the Guthrie, Okla., jail, freeing thirteen prisoners including Bill Doolin.

Clum, John P., a gunman and Apache Indian agent in Arizona, sided with the Earps against the "cowboys" in Tombstone.

Clyde, Charles, an outlaw, was arrested for stealing mules in April 1884.

Coal Oil Jimmie, a rustler and stage robber, who was also involved in the Cimarron War.

Cockerill, Tilton, an outlaw and former army officer, led the group that robbed a train at Verdi, Neb., on Nov. 4, 1870.

Cockrane, Thomas, a gunman in the Lincoln County War, was a member of the posse that killed John Tunstall.

Coe, Chas, a lawman and outlaw, killed two men in Grayson County, Texas, in 1884, and was indicted for murder.

Coe, Frank, a gunman in the Lincoln County War, was charged with the murder of Buckshot Roberts with Billy the Kid and others.

Coe, George Washington, a gunman in the Lincoln County War, was charged with the murder of Buckshot Roberts, received amnesty, and died in Roswell in 1942.

Coe, Phillip Haddox, called the greatest gunfighter of Texas, was killed by Bill Hickok in 1871 at Abilene, Kan.

Collins, George, an outlaw train robber and partner of Bill Rudolph, killed a Pinkerton detective and was hanged on Mar. 26, 1904.

Collins, Henry, a gunman and cousin of Joel, allegedly helped Sam Bass rob a train in 1878 at Mesquite, Texas.

Collins Joel, an outlaw, joined Sam Bass in a train robbery near Big Springs, Neb., and was killed by soldiers near Hays City, Kan.

Collins, William, an outlaw, joined Sam Bass after his brother, Joel, was killed and participated in a train robbery. He was arrested, escaped, and fled to Canada where he and U.S. Marshal Bill Anderson shot and killed each other.

Colville, James, an outlaw and rustler, was apprehended in March 1883 by the militia of A.J. Fountain.

Connor, Al, an outlaw, was one of five brothers chased by Texas Rangers for many months in the 1880s.

Connor, Bill, an outlaw, was one of five brothers chased by Texas Rangers for many months in the 1880s.

Connor, Fred, an outlaw, was one of five brothers chased by Texas Rangers for many months in the 1880s.

Connor, John, an outlaw, was one of five brothers chased by Texas Rangers for many months in the 1880s.

Connor, Willis, an outlaw, was one of five brothers chased by Texas Rangers for many months in the 1880s.

Cook, Jim, an outlaw and brother of William Cook, was wounded while resisting arrest in the Cherokee Nation.

Cook, William Tuttle (Bill), leader of the outlaw Cook gang, committed several bold robberies throughout the Indian Territory. He was arrested Jan. 11, 1895, and sentenced to forty-five years imprisonment in the federal prison at Albany, N.Y.

Cooley, Scott, a lawman and gunman, killed deputy

sheriff John Worley during the Mason County War in Texas, in 1875, to avenge the death of Tim Williamson. He formed a gang that continued to seek vengeance for Williamson's death until Major John B. Jones and his Texas Rangers ended the violence.

Cooper, Ira, a gunman, helped end the Lee-Good feud in Tularosa, N.M.

Cooper, Jim, a gunman and rancher, participated in the Lee-Good feud in Tularosa, N.M.

Cooper, Tom (AKA: **Tom Kelly**), an outlaw, rustled cattle in Hillsboro, N.M., in 1877.

Copeland, James, an outlaw, led the most successful outlaw gang which robbed, killed, and rustled cattle throughout the South and Texas. He was captured and executed at Augusta, Miss., on Oct. 30, 1857.

Corman, Burt, an outlaw, shot and killed Matt Craig on Dec. 27, 1886, in Fairview, N.M.

Corna, Silveria, an outlaw, murdered Tavian Pacheco on July 15, 1882, in Sabinal, N.M.

Cornett, Brack, an outlaw and member of the Bill Whitley gang, robbed banks and trains throughout Texas. Whitley was killed on Sept. 25, 1888, and Cornett was tracked and killed by Sheriff Alfred Allee.

Cortez, Gregorio, a Texas rustler and outlaw, killed Karnes County sheriff Morris, then killed Gonzales County sheriff Robert Glover, was jailed for eight years, and pardoned.

Cortina, Juan, (**Juan Nepomucena Cortinas**, AKA: **Cheno**), a Mexican bandit chieftain, led raids against towns north of the Rio Grande River during the 1850s. He captured the U.S. Army garrison at Brownsville, Texas. After Texas Rangers killed several of Cortina's leaders, the Mexican bandit retired and died in 1892.

Costillo, Can, a New Mexico outlaw, was wanted for murder.

Coughlin, Pat, an outlaw cattle rustler and friend of Billy the Kid, was apprehended by John W. Poe but released after the only witness was gunned down.

Coulter, Ed, an outlaw, was lynched by vigilantes in New Mexico in October 1881.

Courtright, Timothy Isaiah (AKA: **Long-Haired Jim**), a notorious gunman, participated in the May 1883 American Valley murders. He was killed in an accidental shooting in February 1887.

Craft, James H., an outlaw and partner of Charles G. Walrath, murdered William Shook by Ojo Caliente, N.M., and was lynched on June 30, 1879, with Walrath.

Crane, Jim, an outlaw in Arizona and New Mexico, who died in a shoot-out in 1881.

Cravens, Ben, a lone Oklahoma outlaw, rustled cattle and escaped jail several times. He was captured in July 1894 and given a long prison term but escaped by killing a guard. He was recaptured in November 1896, but escaped again.

Crawford, Foster, an outlaw who rode with Elmer "The Slaughter Kid" Lewis, robbed and murdered in Texas. The pair were captured by Texas Rangers, jailed, and lynched on Feb. 27, 1896.

Crawford, "Salecooler" was a gunman in the Lincoln County War, and died at Fort Stanton in 1878.

Crockett, David, a gunman said to be related to Davy Crockett, escaped from the Texas prison in 1872. He and an accomplice allegedly killed three black soldiers in cold blood. The two were shot dead while attempting to escape arrest.

Crompton, Zacariah, an outlaw and horse thief, on Dec. 20, 1873, with several others, killed Isidoro Patron, Isidoro Padilla, Dario Balazar, and Jose Candelaria in Lincoln County.

Crosthwaite, Charles H., a gunman and news-paperman, was hanged for killing George W. Johnson in January 1889.

Crowe, Patrick, an outlaw, robbed a train in 1894 and stole diamonds in Denver. He was captured in Cincinnati and sentenced to three years in prison.

Cruz, Florentino, an outlaw in Arizona and New Mexico, was killed by Wyatt Earp in 1882.

Cullin, Ed (AKA: **Shoot 'em Up Dick**), an outlaw, was a member of Black Jack Ketchum's gang and was killed during a train robbery in December 1897.

Cummins, James Robert (AKA: **James Johnson; Old Jim**), an outlaw and member of the James gang, he was present during several robberies, and eventually settled in Missouri where the law forgot about him. He published a book about his life in 1903.

Curry, George L. (AKA: **Flat Nose; Tom Dilly**), an outlaw, rustler, and member of the infamous Wild Bunch, taught the skills of robbery to Harvey Logan, whom he raised. He was shot and killed after a bank robbery in 1900, by the sheriff of Vernal, Utah.

Curry, John, an outlaw, was killed along with Dick Rodgers on Mar. 13, 1885, attempting to help a prisoner escape from the Springer jail.

Cush, Old John, an outlaw and member of the Black Jack Ketchum gang, was captured by Jeff Milton and sent to prison.

D

Dalton, Christopher (AKA: **Kit; Charles Bell; Thomas Mabry**), an outlaw and second cousin of the Dalton brothers, robbed and looted along the North-South border during the Civil War and claimed he rode with the James gang and the Bass gang. He died in 1920.

Dalton, Emmett (AKA: **Charley McLaughlin**), an outlaw and member of the Dalton gang, survived the raid on Coffeyville but was apprehended while attempting to rescue his brother Bob. He served over fourteen years in prison, moved to Hollywood, Calif., and wrote *When the Daltons Rode.*

Dalton, Grattan, a Kansas deputy marshal and outlaw, who robbed trains and was killed during the Coffeyville bank robbery attempt on Oct. 5, 1892.

Dalton, J. Frank (AKA: **Happy Jack**), an outlaw, was wanted in Limestone County, Texas, in 1886 for horse theft. He later claimed he was Jesse James.

Dalton, Robert, a lawman-turned-outlaw, formed the Dalton gang in 1891, with his brothers. The Daltons robbed banks throughout Kansas. He and most of the gang were killed attempting to simultaneously rob two banks at Coffeyville on Oct. 5, 1892.

Dalton, William (Bill), an outlaw and a member of the California legislature, joined Bill Doolin's gang after the death of his brothers, and became a leader of the Doolin-Dalton gang. Lawmen killed him September 1895.

Daly, James, an outlaw and member of Three-Fingered Jack McDowell's gang, ran a gambling house and saloon in Aurora and killed at least two men in cold blood. When vigilantes captured Daly and three other gang members, he took poison but they lynched him anyway.

Damewood, Boston, a California outlaw and highwayman, was lynched by a mob of 200 in Los Angeles.

Daniels, Bill, led a gang of outlaws who robbed the Tucumcari, N.M., bank and shot a boy who was holding his hands in the air.

Daugherty, Roy (AKA: **Arkansas Tom Jones**), an outlaw and member of the Doolin-Dalton gang, was captured at Ingalls, Okla., and served seventeen years in prison. He returned to crime and was killed by law officers on Aug. 16, 1924.

Davenport, Jim, a Texas outlaw and cowboy, was accused of killing Elk Hereford, fought with Texas Rangers, and was killed by Ranger Wright in Cotulla, Texas, in 1899.

Davis, George, an outlaw and member of the Jesse Evans gang, was a gunman in the Lincoln County War.

Davis, Hog, a gunman who killed Peter Hildreth and was in return shot to death in 1872.

Davis, Jack, an outlaw, was a friend of Bill Longley and robbed trains with Sam Bass and Joel Collins.

Davis, "Lucky", a half-black Creek Indian and member of the infamous Buck gang, was hanged on July 1, 1896.

Day, Alfred, a gunman in the Taylor faction in the Sutton-Taylor feud and a friend of John Hardin, he allegedly shot Bill Sutton in the back in 1876. He wrote a book on his life in the 1930s.

Dayson, Curtis, an outlaw, was a member of the Cook gang in Indian Territory. He was captured after a bank robbery.

Deal, Pony (Charles Ray), a Dodge City gunman, claimed to kill Johnny O'Rourke in 1882, after O'Rourke had killed Deal's friend, Johnny Ringo.

Dedrick, Sam, a gunman and rancher, Dedrick lived in White Oaks, N.M., and was a friend of Billy the Kid.

Delaney, William E. (AKA: Bill Johnson; Morman Bill), an outlaw suspected of murder in Pennsylvania, was a member of a gang in Arizona. He was captured by Deputy Ben Daniels and hanged in Tombstone in March 1884.

Deloach, Tom, shot and killed Joe Holland in September 1885 outside of El Paso, Texas.

Demmons, Dan, an outlaw, led a gang in Texas and New Mexico in the 1870s. He was captured in 1880.

Dempster, Boyd, an outlaw, was shot and killed in Georgetown, N.M., on Dec. 26, 1881, by Deputy Sheriff Glasgow.

de Rana, Patas (AKA: **El Coyote**), an outlaw and member of Silva's White Caps, shot and killed Vicente Silva by orders of the gang on May 19, 1895. The gang's breakup came after one of them was ordered hanged by the gang court.

Devine, James (AKA: **Jones; James Johnson; Curran**), an outlaw, was lynched in Raton, N.M., on Apr. 16, 1881.

Dial, J.I., a gunman, allegedly killed a freighter on Mar. 14, 1872, in Mexico. He was killed near El Paso.

Dilion, Jerry, an outlaw, killed Captain Paul Dowlin on May 5, 1877, by Fort Stanton, N.M.

Dodds, John, a gunman, was a companion of Dick Rogers of Raton, N.M.

Dolan, James J., a gunman and businessman, led the Murphy-Dolan faction in the Lincoln County War and was suspected of riding with the posse that killed John Tunstall. He was charged with the murder of H.J. Chapman on Feb. 18, 1879.

Doolin, William M. (Bill, AKA: Will Barry), an outlaw, led a gang that robbed trains and banks in Oklahoma, New Mexico, Missouri, and Kansas. He either died of tuberculosis or was shot and killed by lawman Heck Thomas in August 1896.

Doran, Major A.S., a gunman and soldier, killed about ten men and was shot dead in Hot Springs, Ark., in 1888.

Dorsey, John, an outlaw, was lynched for killing Constable Joe Carson in Las Vegas, N.M., on Jan. 22, 1880 (or 1884).

Dow, Leslie (Les), a gunman and lawman, shot and killed Zack Light during an argument while bartender at Seven Rivers, N.M., in the late 1880s. He later became sheriff of Eddy County and was killed by former sheriff Dave Kemp at Carlsbad.

Dowd, Daniel, an outlaw companion of Bill Delaney, was hanged in March 1884, in Tombstone and buried on Boot Hill.

Downing, William, an outlaw and member of the Alvord-Stiles gang, was deputy sheriff of Willcox, Ariz., who allowed the gang to escape after a train robbery. Killed over thirty men and was shot dead by Sheriff Billy Speed in August 1900 at Willcox.

Dublin, Dell, an outlaw, was captured in Coryell, Texas, for murder.

Dublin, Dick, an outlaw and brother of Dell, was captured in Coryell, Texas, for murder.

Duboise, E. Leon, an outlaw, was imprisoned in February 1886.

Dudley, Nathan Augustus Monroe, a gunman and lieutenant colonel stationed at Fort Stanton, N.M., sided with the Murphy-Dolan faction during the Lincoln County War and besieged the McSween house. Tried and acquitted for his actions.

Duffy, Thomas, an outlaw, was jailed for killing Thomas Bishop in Liberty, N.M., on Sept. 19, 1880, and was shot and killed while attempting to escape the Las Vegas jail.

Dugi, Giovanni (AKA: **Dagi; Duque**), an outlaw, was lynched on June 4, 1879, in Las Vegas, N.M.

Duke, Frank, an outlaw and cattle rustler, was imprisoned in the Socorro, N.M., jail in 1884.

Duncan, Dick, an outlaw and nephew of the Ketchums, hanged for murder in 1891 at Eagle Pass, Texas.

Dunlap, John (AKA: **Three-Fingered Jack**), an outlaw, train robber, and member of Black Jack Christian's gang, was shot by a guard in 1881, left for dead by the gang, and taken to Tombstone where he informed on the others.

Dunn, Rose (AKA: **Rose of Cimarron**), an outlaw, lover of George Newcomb, and friend of the Dalton-Doolin gang, helped Newcomb escape from a gunbattle outside Ingalis, Indian Territory, and served time in a U.S. reformatory.

Dupont, John, an outlaw, shot and killed Bartole Garcia on Jan. 14, 1883, in La Joya, N.M.

Dwindle, Charlie, a gunman, was arrested for the murder of John Byers, near Springer, N.M., in March 1883.

E

Earhart, Bill, a gunman, fought with Oliver Lee in the feud in Tularosa, N.M. He was killed in Pecos, Texas, Fall 1896.

Edwards, Joseph M. (AKA: **Bob**), an outlaw, was killed by Sheriff Thomas L. McKinney in Rattlesnake Springs, N.M., on May 8, 1881.

Elliott, Frank (AKA: **Peg-Leg**), an outlaw and part-time member of the Dalton gang, was arrested and charged with robbery on Oct. 27, 1891.

Elliott, James, a gunman, shot and killed James Fay on February 1884, in Lake Valley, N.M.

Ellis, Charles, a Texas outlaw, was charged with train robbery and murder in 1898.

Ellis, William, a gunman, shot and killed J.S. McAlpin on Apr. 18, 1886, in La Luz, N.M.

Elmoreau (AKA: **Frenchy**), an outlaw and member of Ike Stockton's gang, was lynched in October 1881 in Socorro, N.M.

"El Pollo", horse thief, was captured near Socorro and shot by a lynch mob on Feb. 8, 1869.

Elvard, Juan, an outlaw, he was lynched in August 1882 in Socorro, N.M.

Enbree, Jack, a gunman, shot and wounded Laramie, Wy., rancher E.M. Dixon and was imprisoned for two years. He was killed on Jan. 23, 1889, when he returned to threaten Dixon.

Escobar, Rafael, an outlaw, was lynched by a vigilance committee at Jackson, Calif., in the 1850s.

Eskridge, Dyson, an outlaw and murderer, was a member of Ike Stockton's gang.

Eskridge, Harge, an outlaw rustler and brother of Dyson, was a member of Ike Stockton's gang.

Espinosa, Julian, the oldest of the outlaw "Bloody Espinosas," robbed and killed in the 1850s-60s with his brother in New Mexico and Colorado. Mountain man Tom Tobin killed Juan and his nephew in 1863.

Espinosa, Vivian, the younger of the outlaw "Bloody Espinosas," was killed by posseman Joe Lamb near Cripple Creek, Colo., in 1863.

Espinoso, Selzo, an outlaw, was lynched on Oct. 6, 1881, in Las Lunas, N.M.

Espolin, Jose, a gunman, was accused of murdering Mescalero merchant A.H. Howe in 1886.

Estabo, Tranquellano, a gunman, shot up Phoenix, Ariz., in 1895 and was arrested by Sheriff Cicero Stewart and Dee Harkey.

Estes, Cole, a gunman who was shot to death robbing a train on Oct. 2, 1896.

Evan, Tom, an outlaw, robbed a bank with three others in Limestone, Indian Territory, on Jan. 23, 1888, and was killed.

Evans, Christopher (AKA: Bill Powers), an outlaw, led a train robbing gang after the railroad took his land. Caught by a posse in 1893, he was charged with murder and sent to prison for life. Paroled in 1911, he died in 1917.

Evans, Dan, an outlaw, who killed a cowboy in the Creek Nation and was hanged at Fort Smith in 1875.

Evans, Jesse, outlaw leader of the Evans gang, fought on the Murphy-Dolan side in the Lincoln County War of New Mexico. He was sent to prison for rustling but escaped in 1882 and was never heard from again.

F

Falkner, Frederick, an outlaw, was hanged Aug. 19, 1892.

Fall, Albert, a gunman, lawyer, congressman, and rancher in New Mexico, fought Ben Williams on Sept. 15, 1895, on the streets of Las Cruces, N.M.

Fall, Philip, the brother of Albert, a cattle rustler and outlaw, who later became a deputy marshal.

Fallon, Charles, a cowboy and gunman, with companion Long-Haired Owens, fought one of the fiercest gun battles known in the West on July 4, 1884, at Lewistown, Mont., against the Stuart cowboy-vigilantes. Fallon was killed, shot nine times.

Farley, Hutch, an Indian scout, killed the Indian that killed his father at the battle at Beecher's Island, Colo., in November 1868.

Farrington, Hilary, an outlaw and train robber; served under Quantrill in 1870 and was captured in Vinita, Indian Territory.

Farrington, Levi, an outlaw and train robber; brother of Hilary, served under Quantrill in 1870 and was captured in Vinita, Indian Territory.

Farris, William, an outlaw, was a member of the

Cook gang in the Indian Territory. He was captured after a bank robbery.

Felshaw, Jake, an outlaw, who participated in a train robbery near Bowie, N.M. on Jan. 6, 1894.

Ferris, Henry, a Colorado gunman and lawyer, was killed in Sterling in 1873.

Fields, Tom, an outlaw, robbed a train near Samuels, Texas, in 1891, was captured by Rangers, and received a life sentence.

Finch, William, an outlaw, stole two horses and two guns in Fort Sill, Texas, in 1882 and was hanged in Fort Smith in 1883 after killing two soldiers.

Finley, Jim, an outlaw, stole cattle around Socorro, N.M., and was killed by Joel Fowler.

Finnessy, Tom was a gunman and friend of Martin McRose.

Fisher, Bill, a Texas outlaw, was wanted in 1886 for killing J.S. Vaughn. He was arrested and tried.

Fisher, Dick, an outlaw, was wanted in Texas and found dead near Cimarron, N.M., in 1871.

Fisher, John K. (King), a gunman and suspected outlaw gang leader, became deputy sheriff of Uvalde, and was killed by a concealed assassin in March 1884.

Fitzpatrick, Mike, an outlaw, shot Judge Halliday in the 1870s and was killed by Marshal Jack Johnson.

Flint, John, an outlaw, killed several men in the year following the Civil War in Doaksville, Indian Territory, and was convicted of murder and hanged by federal authorities.

Floyd, Henry, an outlaw and member of Bill Henderson's gang in 1876. Arrested in Dodge City and lynched by a mob in June at Albany, Texas.

Floyd, W.S. (AKA: **William Wardell; Taylor;**

Simmons), an outlaw, was killed in May 1884 near Flora Vista, N.M.

Flynt, John, an outlaw and member of the Wallington gang. Robbed a train in 1891 in Val Verde County, Texas, and killed himself during a battle.

Follett, Lyman, an outlaw who was involved in the robbery of an Army paymaster on May 11, 1889.

Follett, Warren, the brother of Lyman, who was involved in the robbery of an Army paymaster on May 11, 1889.

Folsom, Tandy, an outlaw, killed a man on the Indian Territory border in February 1881 and was hanged at Fort Smith.

Fooy, Sam, an outlaw, was hanged on Sept. 3, 1875, in Fort Smith for killing a school teacher.

Ford, Charles, an outlaw, member of the James gang, and brother of Robert Ford, committed suicide in his home on May 6, 1884.

Ford, Robert, a gunman, shot Jesse James in the back of the head on Apr. 3, 1882, and was pardoned by Governor T.T. Crittenden. Killed in June 1892.

Foster, Joseph, a gunman and gambler, was shot and killed by King Fisher in San Antonio, Texas, in 1884 when Fisher and Ben Thompson were shot by unknown gunmen.

Fountain, Albert Jennings., a gunman, soldier, editor, and lawyer, killed B.F. Williams on Dec. 7, 1870, in El Paso, Texas, and defended Billy the Kid in his first trial in Mesilla, N.M. He disappeared in the White Sands on Jan. 31, 1896.

Fowler, Joel, a gunman, gambler, and rancher, killed over twenty men, and was lynched on Jan. 21, 1884, in Socorro, N.M.

Freeman, Frank, a New Mexico gunman and a factor in the Lincoln County War, was killed in Cimarron in late 1876.

French, Jim, an outlaw, member of the Cook gang, and gunman in the Lincoln County War, ambushed Brady and Hindman on Apr. 1, 1878, with Billy the Kid. He was killed by lawmen.

Frescan, Cesario, an outlaw, shot and killed Nicanor Garcia near La Mesilla, N.M., on Dec. 10, 1886.

Frink, D.B., a gunman and member of the Truckee, Calif., Committee of 601, was accidentally killed in November 1874.

G

Gagen, Richard F., an outlaw, was one of the conspirators in the June 17, 1877, murder of Captain R.N. Calhoun.

Gallagher, Bill (Barney), an outlaw, was killed in 1876 by John Slaughter in South Springs, N.M.

Gallagher, J.G., a gunman, shot and killed Alberto Martinez in January 1883 in the Steeple Rock district of New Mexico.

Gallagher, Jack (AKA: Three-Fingered Jack), an outlaw and member of the Plummer gang was hanged by vigilantes on Jan. 13, 1864, in the Montana Territory.

Gallegos, Jose Trujillo, a gunman, killed Miguel Montano in March 1885 at Pederval, N.M.

Gallegos, Leandro, an outlaw, was a member of Vicente Silva's White Caps in Las Vegas, N.M.

Gallegos, Nestor, an outlaw, was a member of Vicente Silva's White Caps in Las Vegas, N.M.

Gallegos, Pantaeleon, a gunman in the Lincoln County War, rode in the posse that killed John Tunstall on Feb. 18, 1878.

Galvin, John, a gunman in the Lincoln County War, was indicted in 1879 for his participation.

Garfias, Pete, an outlaw, allegedly robbed a train in 1883 and was killed in a battle.

Garrett, Joe, an outlaw, was a member of Ike Stockton's gang.

Garza, Catarino, a gunman and self-styled rebel, organized a gang of over 300 men, crossed the border into Mexico, fought against Diaz, and was defeated. Arrested for violating International Law, he was killed in Cuba during a revolution.

George, Joe, an outlaw, allegedly robbed an SP train near Wilcox with Grant Wheeler.

German, Joe, a gunman, was killed by Frank Leslie in Eureka, N.M., on June 22, 1881.

Gibbons, James, a gunman, was charged with murder in 1891 at Clayton, N.M.

Gibbs, Bill (AKA: The Panther of the Boston Mountains), an outlaw, killed five men and was shot and killed by a lawman.

Gibson, Con, a gunman in the Miller-Frazer feud of Reeves County, Texas, was killed in the 1890s in Phoenix, N.M.

Gibson, Volney, a gunman, shot and killed Kyle Terry in 1889 at the courthouse in Galveston, Texas, for killing L.E. Gibson.

Gilbreth, Bud (AKA: Cook), an outlaw, was a companion of Ike Stockton.

Gilliand, Jim, an accused rustler, joined the Oliver Lee faction in the Lee-Good feud in Tularosa, N.M.

Gilliland, Fine, a cowboy, shot and killed Henry Harrison Powe on a roundup. He was shot and killed by lawmen, including Thalis Cook, Jim Gillett, and Ranger Jim Putman.

Gilson, Chris, a gunman, participated in the Newton, Kan., gunfight in 1867 which left fourteen gunmen dead.

Gladden, George, a gunman in the "Hoodoo War" in Mason County, Texas, was arrested on charges that included a jail break, received a 99-year sentence, was pardoned.

Glanton, John Joel, a gunman, was outlawed by Sam Houston when he fought on both sides in the Regulator-Moderator War in East Texas. He was arrested, escaped, and led a gang of scalp hunters. He was later killed by Indians in 1850 at Yuma, Colo.

Golden, John, a gambler and gunman, was lynched by a mob in 1876 outside Fort Griffin, Texas.

Goldensen, an outlaw, was hanged in September 1888 for the murder of Mami Kelley.

Goldsby, Crawford (AKA: **Cherokee Bill**), an outlaw and killer, he was also a member of the Cook gang. He was hanged for murder on Mar. 17, 1896.

Gomez, Juan, an outlaw, escaped from prison and was recaptured on Feb. 16, 1907.

Gonzales, Marcus, an outlaw, was jailed in La Veta, Colo., and lynched by a mob in July 1877.

Gonzolez, Gabriel, a gunman, killed Adolf Harmon in Springer, N.M., in Aug. 1, 1907, and started a feud.

Gonzolez, Juan, an outlaw, stole horses and was killed in Albuquerque, N.M., in October 1876.

Gonzolez y Blea, Manuel (AKA: **El Mellado**), an outlaw, was a member of Vicente Silva's White Caps of Las Vegas.

Gonzolez y Blea, Martin (AKA: **El Moro**), an outlaw, was a member of Vicente Silva's White Caps of Las Vegas.

Good, John H., gunman and rancher, along with others, shot and killed Charles Dawson on Dec. 8, 1885, in La Luz, N.M.; was involved in the feud with Oliver Lee.

Good, Walter, a gunman and son of John Good, started the Good-Lee feud by ambushing George McDonald on June 13, 1888. He was found dead in the White Sands of New Mexico.

Goodlet, Bill, a lawman turned gunman, Goodlet was a member of the Dodge City gang in Las Vegas, N.M.

Goodman, William, an outlaw, escaped from the Las Vegas jail along with Rudabaugh and Webb, on Dec. 3, 1881.

Goodnight, Charles, a lawman, was a Texas Ranger in 1857 and drove cattle after the Civil War. He fought outlaws and Indians for many years in Texas, New Mexico, and California, and died in Tucson, Ariz., on Dec. 12, 1929, at the age of ninety-three.

Gordon, Lon, an outlaw and member of the Bill Cook gang in Oklahoma, was killed near Sapulpa, Okla., after the Chandler bank robbery.

Gordon, Mike, a gunman, was shot in Las Vegas, N.M., on July 19, 1879.

Gordon, Tom, an outlaw, was lynched in Socorro on Mar. 10, 1881.

Grady, Tom, an outlaw, rustled cattle and murdered John Carney on Dec. 14, 1885, in Lake Valley, N.M.

Graham, Albert (Abbs; AKA: **Charles Graves; Ace Carr**), an outlaw and member of the Jesse Evans gang, robbed throughout New Mexico and West Texas. He was arrested, but either died or left the country, as he never appeared in court.

Graham, Charles (AKA: **Bud Davis**), an outlaw and member of the Jesse Evans gang and brother of Abbs, was captured and accused of killing a man while shooting up Jonesboro.

Graham, Dollay (AKA: **George Davis; George Graves**), an outlaw and one of the Graham brothers who rode with Jesse Evans in Lincoln County, N.M. He was killed when the gang was captured in West Texas.

Graham, John D., a gunman in the feud with the Tewksburys in Pleasant Valley, Ariz., was killed in Holbrook in September 1887.

Graham, Thomas H., a gunman in the feud with the Tewksburys and brother of John, was ambushed and killed at Tempe, Ariz., in August 1892.

Grant, Joe, a gunman and bounty hunter, attempted to bring in Billy the Kid. The Kid shot him, and he died on Jan. 10, 1880.

Graves, Mit, a gunman, allegedly killed two members of the Truitt family in connection with a feud in Hood County, Texas, in 1874.

Graves, "Whiskey Bill", an outlaw and member of the Plummer gang, was lynched by vigilantes at Bitter Root in January 1864.

Greathouse, James (AKA: **Whiskey Jim**), a former deputy sheriff labelled an outlaw by ranger Patrick Garrett, ran a way station on the White Oaks-Las Vegas, N.M., road. Shot to death southeast of Socorro.

Green, Thomas, a gunman in the Lincoln County War, rode with the posse that killed John Tunstall on Feb. 18, 1878.

Green, Tom, an outlaw, was indicted for murder in 1877 at Parker County, Texas.

Grey, Dick was an outlaw in Arizona and New Mexico.

Griego, Francisco (AKA: **Pancho**), an outlaw and former city marshal of Santa Fe, N.M., was killed by Clay Allison on Nov. 1, 1875, at Cimarron, N.M.

Griffin, George a Texas and New Mexico gunman, was given to shooting up a town while drunk.

Griffith, Ben, a guerilla outlaw under Cullen Baker in the Texas reconstruction war, was killed by three citizens of Glarkville in 1868.

Gross, Albert (AKA: **John Gunter**), an outlaw and member of the Evans gang, was captured by rangers near Shafter, Texas, on July 3, 1880. He escaped jail but was recaptured by Ranger Sam Graham.

Guyse, Buck, a lawman and outlaw, deserted the Texas Rangers and fled to New Mexico where he was arrested by Pat Garrett.

H

Halderman, Bill, an outlaw, was hanged with his brother Tom in Tombstone, Ariz., on Nov. 16, 1900, for killing a man.

Halderman, Tom, an outlaw, was hanged with his brother Bill in Tombstone, Ariz., on Nov. 16, 1900, for killing a man.

Hale, John, a gunman and foreman of the Manning ranch near El Paso, Texas. Killed Gus Krempkau in 1881 and was killed by Marshal Stoudenmire.

"Halfbreek Jack", an outlaw, was lynched near Yellowstone by the Montana Stranglers in 1884 for rustling cattle.

Hall, Bill, an outlaw, was the first prisoner of Yuma Prison in 1875.

Hall, Charles (AKA: **Tex**), rustled cattle near Hillsboro, N.M., in 1877.

Hanks, Orlando Camillo (AKA: **Charley Jones; Deaf Charley**), an outlaw and the last and toughest of Butch Cassidy's Wild Bunch, robbed trains in Montana and New Mexico from the 1880s. He was killed in 1902 by Sheriff Pink Taylor after killing a lawman.

Hannah, James (AKA: **Socorro Jim**), a gunman, was shot on Mar. 17, 1883, in Middle Camp, N.M.

Hardin, Bill, a gunman and first cousin to John Hardin, was lynched by a mob after killing a man near Engle, N.M., in the 1880s.

Hardin, John Wesley (Wes), Texas's most deadly gunman, killed over thirty people. Hardin fought for the Taylors in the Sutton-Taylor feud. Captured by Ranger John Armstrong in 1877, he was released in 1894 after eighteen years in prison. He was killed by Constable John Selman in El Paso, Texas, in July 1895.

Hardin, Joseph, the brother of Wes. Although not active as a criminal, he was lynched in June 1874, after he brandished a shotgun in his brother's defense.

Hardin, Mart, an outlaw, was charged with conspiracy in the murder of Bud Frazer committed in 1893 by Jim Miller.

Harlin, J.J (AKA: **Off Wheeler**), an outlaw, was named on a Las Vegas, N.M., poster reading: "Notice! To Thieves, Thugs, Fakirs and Bunko-Steerers...you have until ten p.m. to leave town, or be invited to Attend a Grand Neck-Tie Party."

Harmon, Adolf, an outlaw, was shot and killed by Gabriel Gonzolez, ten years after Harmon killed Deputy Sheriff Esteban Trujillo on Jan. 22, 1897.

Harmon, Albert, a gunman, shot and killed Tomas Salazar in January 1908 at Springer, N.M.

Harmon, Augustin, a gunman, was sentenced to twenty-five years in prison for killing Ricardo Lovato of Springer, N.M.

Harper, Chas, an outlaw and member of the Plummer gang, was hanged at Florence, Idaho, in 1891.

Harrington, Frank E., the conductor of the Fort Worth Express train, shot and critically wounded Tom Ketchum on Aug. 16, 1899. Harrington was wounded in the forearm and Ketchum was captured the following day and later executed at Clayton, N.M.

Harris, James, a gunman and former lawman, was killed while dueling Bob Majors at Santa Cruz, Calif., in the 1880s.

Harrold, Benjamin, a gunman and one of five Harrold brothers of Lampasas County, Texas, was killed while resisting arrest on Dec. 20, 1873, leading to an earlier Lincoln County War.

Harrold, Martin was one of the five Harrold brothers.

Harrold, Merritt was one of the five Harrold brothers.

Harrold, Samuel was one of the five Harrold brothers.

Harrold, Thomas, one of the five Harrold brothers, moved back to Texas with his three brothers due to escalating violence.

Hart, Pearl (Pearl Taylor), an outlaw and mother of two children, a miner, committed the "comic opera" stage holdup between Globe and Riverside with Joe Boot. Hart was arrested, sent to prison, and released after having served five years of her sentence.

Hartnett, Splay Foot, an outlaw, was lynched by the Montana Stranglers in 1884.

Haslett, Bill, gunman and rancher, with his brother Ike, ambushed and killed two men on June 12, 1881, who were attempting to take over his ranch. Bill and Ike were killed in Eureka on June 22.

Haslett, Ike, a gunman, was the brother of Bill Haslett.

Hasley, Sam, an outlaw, killed several men and joined the war against the Texas reconstructionists in Bell County.

Hassells, Samuel (Bob Hayes), an outlaw and member of the Black Jack Ketchum gang, was killed in a battle with lawmen.

Hawkins, Henry, who led a band of outlaws named the "Mesa Hawks," robbing trains in the New Mexico Territory in 1897.

Hawks, George, a gunman, shot and killed John M. Berry on Jan. 18, 1887, in Flagstaff, Ariz.

Hawley, C.B., an outlaw, confessed to stage robbery in 1882 near Globe, Ariz., and was lynched.

Hays, Bob, an outlaw and member of Black Jack Christian's gang, was killed on Aug. 6, 1896, after an aborted bank robbery at Nogales, Ariz.

Head, Harry (AKA: Harry the Kid), a Tombstone outlaw, was accused by Wyatt Earp of robbing the Benson stage when Bud Philpot was killed. He was killed by the Haslett brothers and Billy Leonard in 1881.

Heath (or Heith), John, an alleged outlaw, was charged with robbery and murder at Tombstone, Ariz. A mob lynched him after he was convicted of second-degree murder and robbery on Feb. 21, 1884.

Hedgepeth, Marion C., an outlaw in Missouri, Montana, Colorado, and Wyoming, was a rustler, horse thief, and bank robber. He was killed in 1910 in Chicago, Ill., while attempting a robbery.

Hedges, William (AKA: Pawnee Bill), an outlaw, was listed in the Las Vegas, N.M., poster warning all "Thieves, Thugs, Fakirs and Bunko-Steerers" to leave town before 10 p.m. or be invited to "a Grand Neck-Tie Party."

Hefferman, Art, an outlaw, who shot a man at Virginia City in March 1871 and was lynched by vigilantes.

Heffridge, Bill, an outlaw and member of the Sam Bass gang in 1877, was killed in Kansas during a gun battle.

Heffron, Augustus (Gus), an outlaw and friend of Dave Crockett, was captured in the gun battle with lawmen at Cimarron, N.M., in October 1876, where Crockett was killed. He escaped and was not heard from again.

Helm, Boone, an outlaw, murderer, and robber, was a member of several gangs, including the "Destroying Angels" and the Plummer gang. He was hanged in Virginia City by vigilantes on Jan. 13, 1864.

Helm, Charles, a gunman and cowboy buried in Tombstone's Boot Hill, was shot and killed by Billie McCauley in 1882 after arguing about whether to drive cattle fast or slow.

Helm, Jack, a lawman and outlaw, fought for the Suttons in the Sutton-Taylor feud and terrorized DeWitt and surrounding counties. His posse killed Hays Taylor on Aug. 23, 1869. John Hardin and Jim Taylor killed him in July 1873.

Henderson, Bill, an outlaw, robbed stages, trains, and stole horses in Texas and New Mexico in the 1880s and was lynched in Texas.

Henderson, Wall, an outlaw, was shot and killed on Nov. 14, 1871, by John W. Stinson in Elizabethtown, N.M.

Hernandez, Mariano, an outlaw, allegedly killed a man and was lynched at San Jose, Calif., in 1850.

Herndon, Al, an outlaw and member of the Sam Bass gang, was captured in 1878.

Herrera, Nestor, an outlaw, was one of Vicente Silva's White Caps in Las Vegas, N.M.

Herring, Bob, a Texas outlaw and member of Joe Baker's gang, stole horses from 1885-1894 and was imprisoned for thirty-five years following a gunfight at Dallas in 1899.

Hetherington, Joe, an Englishman outlaw, was lynched by vigilantes in San Francisco, Calif., on July 29, 1856.

Hicks, Milt was an outlaw in Arizona and New Mexico.

Hilderman, George (AKA: **The Great American Pie-Eater**), an outlaw, was a member of the Plummer gang.

Hill, Frank, an outlaw and rustler who was killed by a posse in New Mexico in March, 1880.

Hill, George W., a gunman, shot and killed Pooler and Juan Romero in March 1884 in the Vermejo Valley, N.M., and was captured in 1879 by Sheriff Pete Burleson.

Hill, Joe, a gunman, was friends with Jim Hughes, John Ringo, and Curly Bill. He died when a horse fell on him.

Hill, Tom (AKA: **Tom Chelson**), an outlaw and member of the Jesse Evans gang, rode with the posse that killed John Tunstall on Feb. 18, 1878.

Hindman, George, a lawman and gunman who rode in the posse that killed John Tunstall, was ambushed and killed by Billy the Kid and two others on Apr. 1, 1878.

Hinton, John,, an outlaw in the New Mexico Territory in 1896.

Hite, Clarence, an outlaw and relative of Wood Hite, allegedly helped the James gang rob a train at Winston, Mo., in the 1870s.

Hite, Robert Woodson (AKA: **Wood**), an outlaw and cousin of Jesse James, robbed trains with the James gang and was killed in 1881 by Dick Liddell.

Hoges, Henry, a gunman, was arrested for the March 1883 murder of John Byers.

Holden, "Judge", a gunman, fought in the Mexican War and was a member of the scalp-hunting Glanton gang.

Holliday, John Henry (AKA: **Doc; Tom McKey; John Powers**), the gunman and companion of Wyatt Earp, followed the Earps from Dodge City to Tombstone, and joined O.K. Corral gunfight. Holliday died in 1887 at a sanitarium in Glenwood Springs, Colo.

Holloway, Russ, an outlaw, killed a man in 1879 in Earth County, Texas, and fled. He returned in 1927 and surrendered himself but was released as no indictment was standing.

Holzhay, Reimund (AKA: **Black Bart**), a German immigrant and outlaw, was captured in 1889 while robbing a train single handedly. He received a life sentence.

Horan, John (AKA: **Pete**), was a gunman and miner, and was hanged by Sheriff Henry Plummer for murder in 1863.

Horn, Tom, the famous lawman, gunman, and scout, initially worked in the frontier as a gunman for hire. He was hanged at Cheyenne, Wyo., on Nov. 20, 1903, for murdering a 14-year-old boy from ambush.

Horrell, Sam, a New Mexico rancher and outlaw.

House, Eddie, an outlaw, was charged with the murder of a Lincoln County sheepherder but was acquitted in 1881.

House, Thomas Jefferson (AKA: **Tom Henry**), an outlaw and horse thief, killed Joe Carson, constable of Las Vegas, N.M., on Jan. 22, 1880 (or 1884). He was lynched on Feb. 7.

Houston, Temple L., a gunman, state senator, and son of Texas governor Sam Houston, killed Ed Jennings in Woodward, Okla. Houston was acquitted of murder, and died in Woodward, Aug. 15, 1905.

Hovey, Walter (AKA: **Fatly Ryan**), an outlaw, was a member of the Black Jack Ketchum gang.

Howard, Charles, an outlaw and member of the later Robert McKemie gang, was captured in 1878 along with McKemie.

Howard, James (Tex, AKA: **Tex Willis; Jack Howard**), an outlaw, was the scout for a Bisbee, Ariz., robbery in 1883 during which several people were killed. Howard was arrested and hanged in 1884.

Howard, Joe, an alleged outlaw and horse thief, was lynched in 1873 at Franklin, Mo.

Howard, Joe, a gunman in Lincoln County, N.M., in 1877, killed Chihuahua, a Cherokee Indian.

Howell, Bennett, a gunman and cowboy, was killed with two others by Billy the Kid on June 5, 1881, in John Chisum's camp.

Howland, Big Dan, an outlaw, Howland murdered J.W. Lacy, a relative of Ike Stockton in May 1881 at the insistence of the vigilantes in Farmington, N.M.

Hoyt, George R., a gunman and cowboy, was shot by Wyatt Earp while "hurrahing" Dodge City. His arm was amputated and he died.

Hubert, Joe (AKA: **Joe Roberts**), an outlaw, rustled cattle in 1877 near Hillsboro, N.M., and was convicted of mail robbery.

Hudgens, John, a gunman, shot and killed Louis Montjeau in January 1885 at White Oaks.

Hudson, Hugh, a Peacock gunman in the late 1860s Lee-Peacock feud, was shot and killed after he was accused of killing a man.

Hughes, Jim, an Arizona and New Mexico outlaw, died on Nov. 2, 1899.

Hughes, Wilson (AKA: **Texas Jack**), an outlaw, was a member of the Ike Stockton gang.

"Human Tiger, The", an outlaw and rustler, was killed while attempting to escape from A.J. Fountain's militia in 1877.

"Humpy Jack", an alleged outlaw, was shot and killed in his cabin in 1884 by the vigilante Montana Stranglers.

Hunt, Richard (AKA: **Zwing Hunt**), an outlaw, robbed the Tombstone Mining and Milling Co. with Billy "the Kid" Grounds and killed M.C. Peel. Deputy Billy Breakenridge killed Grounds and wounded Hunt. Escaped while jailed at Tombstone.

Hunter, Bill (AKA: **Tex**), an outlaw, was a member of Ike Stockton's gang.

Hunter, Bill, an outlaw and member of the Plummer gang in the 1860s, was the last of the gang, lynched by vigilantes.

Hurley, John, a gunman in the Lincoln County War, rode with the posse that killed John Tunstall on Feb. 18, 1878.

I

Irwin, Nat (AKA: **Tex**), an outlaw, rustled cattle in New Mexico and was captured by A.J. Fountain's militia in March 1883.

Isom, Ben, an outlaw, shot a man at Howe Station, Texas, in 1885 and was killed by the sheriff.

Ivers, Alice (AKA: **Poker Alice**), a woman gambler well-known from Tombstone to Deadwood, carried a pistol in her vest and wounded a man who attempted to stab her husband. She witnessed the killing of Bill Hickok.

Ives, George, an outlaw and a member of the Plummer gang of Montana Territory, was hanged on Jan. 3, 1864, at Alder Gulch.

J

Jackson, Frank (Blockey), one of the toughest outlaws of Texas, joined Sam Bass in 1877. After Texas Rangers killed Bass and Sebe Barnes on July 19, 1878, Jackson moved to Arizona.

Jackson, James, a gunman, killed James Williams on May 12, 1884, in Lake Valley, N.M.

Jackson, Tom, an outlaw who was involved in a train robbery at Bowie, New Mexico, on Jan. 6, 1894.

Jacobs, Ben, a gunman, killed John Findlay on Nov. 5, 1882, in White Oaks, N.M.

James, Frank (Alexander Franklin AKA: Buck; Frank Vaughn), an outlaw and brother of Jesse James, rode with the James-Younger gang on most of their robberies. He surrendered to Governor T.T. Crittenden after Jesse was killed. He was acquitted of murder and robbery, lived peacefully in Kearny, and died on Feb. 19, 1915.

James, Jesse Woodson, the famous outlaw and leader of the James-Younger gang, robbed banks and trains for sixteen years. Born on Sept. 4, 1847, he was shot in the back of the head by Robert Ford in his home in St. Joseph, Mo., on Apr. 3, 1881.

Jamieson, George, an outlaw, stole horses around Folsom, N.M., in the early 1900s.

Janes, John, an outlaw, was hanged in Lincoln, N.M., on June 18, 1886.

Jenkins, James Gilbert, an outlaw, stole horses and robbed and killed strangers, companions, law officers, and Indians throughout the U.S. between 1846 and 1864. He was hanged in Napa County, Calif., in 1864.

Jenkins, Tom, a gunman from Dawson, N.M., shot a prostitute for shooting his brother on Aug. 15, 1907.

Jennings, Aphonso J. (Al), an outlaw, led the Jen-

nings gang, beginning his fourteen week criminal career after Temple Houston killed his brother Ed. Captured by Marshal Bud Ledbetter, Al served five years in prison and became a lawyer after his release.

Jennings, Frank, an outlaw and brother of Al, was a member of the train robbing gang. He was captured with Al and imprisoned.

Johnson, "Arkansas", an outlaw and member of the Sam Bass gang, was killed at Salt Creek, Texas, by Rangers on June 12, 1878.

Johnson, Bill, a gunman who rode with Bronco Bill Walters, was killed by Jeff Milton and George Scarborough.

Johnson, Chas, an outlaw and member of the Backus gang, was lynched by the "Hoodoos" on June 12, 1878, in Mason County, Texas.

Johnson, Dan, an outlaw and accomplice of Jim Nite, Johnson was apprehended by deputy U.S. Marshal Dee Harkey near Sacramento Sinks, N.M., in 1908.

Johnson, DeWitt C., an outlaw, was hanged in Lincoln, N.M, on Nov. 19, 1886.

Johnson, Jack (AKA: Turkey Creek), a gunman, joined the Earps in Tombstone in 1882 and was indicted for murder. He left town and was later killed.

Johnson, Otter, an outlaw, shot and killed Norman Buck in Deming, N.M., and received a three-year prison sentence.

Johnson, Peter (AKA: Toppy), an outlaw, rustled cattle in New Mexico and served a prison sentence in Santa Fe.

Johnson, Richard (Dick), a Lee gunman in the Lee-Peacock feud in Grayson County, Texas, in the late 1860s, may have been Peacock's murderer on July 1, 1871.

Johnson, Samuel (AKA: **Rattlesnake Sam**), an outlaw in Canoncito, N.M., was killed by a bartender on Dec. 3, 1879.

Johnson, "Swede", an outlaw, rode with Butch Cassidy in the Powder River bunch, killed a cowboy in 1899, and was killed by lawmen.

Johnson, Tobe, an outlaw, rustled cattle around Hillsboro, N.M., in 1877.

Johnson, William H., a gunman in the Lincoln County War, was indicted in 1879 for his participation.

Jones, "Acorn Head", an outlaw, stole horses and was lynched by vigilantes in Sumner County, Kan., on July 27, 1874.

Jones, "Chubby", an outlaw and member of Dutch Henry's gang, was lynched with eight others at Sweet Water Creek, Texas.

Jones, John, a gunman in the Lincoln County War, was charged, along with Marion Turner with the July 19, 1879, murder of Alexander A. McSween.

Jones, John, an outlaw, was killed with his brother Jim after robbing a train near Hugo, Colo.

Jones, John, an outlaw who stabbed George Wagstaff to death in Blossburg, N.M., in 1897.

Jones, "Ranger", a Texas gunman, was shot from his horse and killed in ambush near Buffalo, Wyo., during the Cattleman's War.

Jones, Tom was a gunman in the Lincoln County War of New Mexico.

Jones, William (AKA: **Canada Bill**), a gunman, was allegedly one of the hidden snipers that shot and killed Ben Thompson and John Fisher in San Antonio, Texas, in 1884.

Jordan, Francisco, an outlaw, was lynched on Nov. 25, 1881, in Cuchilla Negra, N.M.

Joseph, Martin (AKA: **Bully Josey**), a gunman, was hanged at Fort Smith in 1882 for killing a woman.

Joy, Christopher (AKA: **Kit**), an noted outlaw, robbed trains with his gang before his capture in March 1884. He escaped jail once and was sent to prison.

July, Naomi, an outlaw Creek Indian and member of the Buck gang, was hanged on July 1, 1896.

K

Kay, Jim, an outlaw, rustled cattle near Socorro, N.M., and was killed by Joel Fowler.

Kearney, Frank, an outlaw, escaped from the Las Vegas, N.M., jail on Dec. 3, 1881, with outlaws Dave Rudabaugh and John Webb.

Keaton, Pierce, a Texas cowboy and outlaw, attempted to hold up a train on June 9, 1898, at Coleman Junction, and was captured in Sutton County. He was imprisoned, paroled in 1916, and died in 1931.

Kellam, William (AKA: **Cherokee Bill**) was a gunman for Oliver Lee in the Lee-Good feud in Tularosa, N.M.

Kelly, Bill, an outlaw, broke out of jail, killed a deputy, and was charged with murder in 1885 at Brazos County, Texas.

Kelly, Dan (AKA: **Yorky**), an outlaw, raided Bisbee, Ariz., with a gang in December 1883. Several people were killed, and Yorky was tried, convicted of murder, and hanged on Mar. 8, 1884.

Kelly, Edward O. (AKA: **Red**), on June 8, 1892, shot and killed Bob Ford, the murderer of Jesse James, in Ford's saloon in South Creede, Colo. He was released from prison after eight years and was killed in Oklahoma City by a lawman in 1904.

Kelly, Jack, an outlaw, escaped from the Las Vegas, N.M., jail on Dec. 3, 1881, with outlaws Dave Rudabaugh and John Webb.

Kemp, David, an outlaw, shot and killed a man in Texas, moved to New Mexico, killed Sheriff Les Dow. He had previously served as a lawman in Eddy County, N.M.

Kennedy, Charles, a mountain man and outlaw according to his wife, killed his baby daughter and robbed and killed many travelers near Eagle Nest, N.M. He was lynched on Oct. 7, 1870.

Kenny, Robert, a gunman, shot and killed Julius Lancleve in March 1878 at Palomas, N.M.

Ketchum, Samuel, an outlaw, joined the Black Jacks in the mid-1890s and led the gang in his brother's absence in 1899. He was captured and died on July 24, 1899.

Ketchum, Thomas E. (AKA: **Black Jack**), an outlaw and the youngest of the Ketchum brothers, led a gang which robbed trains in New Mexico, West Texas, and Arizona. He was hanged on Apr. 25, 1901.

Kettle Jack, an outlaw, led a gang in the Big Horn Mountains, Wyo. His gang was lynched by 150 vigilantes in 1889, but he got away.

Kilmartin, Jack, a gunman and civilian Indian scout, pursued rustlers and outlaws around Fort Sill, Okla., and was shot and killed while spying on rustlers.

Kilpatrick, Benjamin (AKA: **The Tall Texan; Benjamin Arnold**), an outlaw and member of the Wild Bunch, robbed trains and banks in Nevada, Missouri, Montana, and Texas. He was killed on Mar. 13, 1912 while robbing the SP train stopped at Sanderson Draw, Texas.

King, "Cowboy Bill", a gunman and ranch foreman in Sonorra, N.M., was killed by Burt Alvord in the 1890s.

King, Ed, a gunman and cowboy at the LS ranch in Oldham county, Texas, was killed in a shoot-out with Len Woodruff, an LX cowboy.

King, Luther, an outlaw, was accused by the Earps of robbing the Benson stage and killing the driver, Bud Philpot.

King, Sandy, an outlaw and member of Curly Bill's gang in Arizona and New Mexico, was hanged by the Shakespeare, N.M., vigilance committee on Jan. 1, 1881, for stealing a horse and being "a damned nuisance."

Kingsbury, Jack, an outlaw, killed a cowboy at Calabasas, Ariz., in 1882, and fled to Mexico where he was killed by lawmen.

Kinney, John, a gunman for hire and a cattle rustler, fought in the El Paso Salt War in 1877 and for Dolan in the Lincoln County War. He served five years in prison for rustling, and died in Arizona in 1919.

Kirby, Andrew, an outlaw who was implicated in the stagecoach robbery at Wickenburg, Ariz., on Apr. 19, 1878.

Kirk, George, an outlaw, was lynched on July 13, 1881, at Virginia City, Nev.

Kitt, George, a gunman in the Lincoln County War, rode with the posse that killed John Tunstall on Feb. 18, 1878.

Kloehr, John Joseph, a gunman and resident of Coffeyville, Kan., Kloehr was credited with having shot and killed Bob Dalton, Bill Broadwell, Grat Dalton, and Texas Jack, and having wounded Emmet Dalton during the Dalton gang's attempted raid on two Coffeyville banks. Kloehr died of natural causes in 1927.

Knight, Jim, an outlaw, robbed the Longview, Texas, bank with his brother Jourdan on Feb. 6, 1897. He was captured by a posse and received a life sentence.

Knight, Jourdan, an outlaw, robbed the Longview, Texas, bank with his brother Jim on Feb. 6, 1897, and was killed in Bear Creek, Texas, by a law officer.

Kosterlitsky, Colonel **Emilo**, a former U.S. army soldier and the commander of the Mexican Rurales in Sonora, Mex., hated bandits and lynched several while in command in the 1900s.

Kresling, Charles, a gunman in the Lincoln County War, was indicted for his participation.

Kuhns, Marvin (AKA: **J.W. Wilson**), an outlaw, was jailed on Dec. 12, 1890, in Fort Wayne, Ind., with five gunshot wounds.

L

Lacy, Robert, a gunman and gambler, he killed a man and was the alleged leader of a group of gunmen. Lacy was lynched by a mob in Rawlins, Wyo., in 1877.

Lamb, Thomas N., an outlaw who was involved in the robbery of an Army paymaster in Graham County, N.M. on May, 11, 1889.

"Lame Johnny", an outlaw, allegedly robbed a stage in 1878 and was hanged in Deadwood, S.D., in 1879.

Lane, George (AKA: **Clubfoot**), an outlaw and deputy under outlaw sheriff Henry Plummer of Virginia City, Montana Territory. He was hanged on Jan. 13, 1864, with Boone Helm.

Lang, Bill was an outlaw in Arizona and New Mexico.

Langston, Sell, a gunman, along with John B. Schlaepfer killed two men and wounded another during a shoot-out in March 1884.

Langworthy, Charles, a gunman, shot John Jackson on June 15, 1885.

Lara, Ruperto, an outlaw, participated in the killing of George Nesmith's family on Aug. 17, 1882, in White Sands, N.M.

L'archeveque, Sostenes, an outlaw and immigrant from France, L'archeveque operated in the 1870s around West Texas and was killed in Texas.

Largo, Jesus, an outlaw and horse thief, was lynched in August 1877 outside Lincoln, N.M.

Largo, Juan, an outlaw, led a gang of horse thieves around the Boquilla, N.M., and was lynched in August 1877.

Larn, John M., an outlaw turned lawman, killed a rancher in Colorado and a sheriff in New Mexico. He rustled cattle while sheriff of Shackleford County, Texas, in the late 1870s. He was killed on June 23, 1878, by vigilantes.

Latterner, Charles, a New Mexico criminal wanted for forgery in 1893.

Lawless, Bill, a cowboy and outlaw, killed a man in McLennon County, Texas, in 1870 and was killed near Cameron.

Lay, William Ellsworth (AKA: **Elza; Elzy; William McGinnis**), an outlaw and member of the Wild Bunch, robbed a train with the Black Jack Ketchum gang. He was captured and served seven years in prison. The last of the Wild Bunch, he died many years after his release.

Layton, G.I., an outlaw, alleged robber, and killer, was lynched by a vigilance committee on June 17, 1852, at Sonora, Calif.

Layton, Juan, a gunman, killed Alejandro Maes on Oct. 23, 1881, in Canoncito, N.M.

Lea, Smith, a gunman, killed Catarino Romero in June 1885 at Lincoln, N.M.

Lee, B.B., an outlaw, was killed by Joe Farr in 1868 at Hempstead, Texas.

Lee, Bob, a gunman, was a companion of Dick Rogers in Raton, N.M., and attempted to break a friend out of jail in Springer.

Lee, Clem, an outlaw and leader of a gang that robbed the Reno stage, was arrested in Virginia City, Mont.

Lee, James, an outlaw, led a gang in the 1880s that stole horses around Cooke County, Texas. He and his brother Pink were killed on Dec. 7, 1885, by a posse led by Heck Thomas and Jim Taylor.

Lee, Mitch, an outlaw and member of the Kit Joy gang, was killed by Deputy Sheriff T.L. Hall on Mar. 13, 1884.

Lee, Oliver Milton, one of the best gunmen, was the primary agitator in the Lee-Good feud in Tularosa. He had A.J. Fountain killed, and was an enemy of Pat Garrett.

Lee, Pink, an outlaw and brother of James Lee, stole horses and was killed with his brother on Dec. 7, 1885.

Lee, Robert E., an outlaw and cousin of Harvey Logan, was a member of the Curry gang and the Wild Bunch. He robbed a train in Wyoming on June 2, 1899, and was arrested, imprisoned, and released in February 1907.

Lee, Robert E., an outlaw, was involved in reconstruction troubles in North Texas after the Civil War. After several confrontations with the federal authorities and soldiers, he was killed in ambush in Hopkins County on June 26, 1869.

Leland, William (AKA: **Butch**), an outlaw and rustler in New Mexico, was killed by A.J. Fountain's militia in March 1888.

Lemons, Dan, a rustler and outlaw who was arrested in March 1880, at Lincoln County, New Mexico.

Lenta, Antonio, an outlaw aligned with the Clay-tons, and served time for killing Hop Lee in 1891.

Leonard, Bill, an outlaw and stage robber in Arizona, was killed by the Haslett brothers in June 1881.

Leroy, Billy, an outlaw, robbed stages and was lynched in 1881.

LeRoy, Kitty, a gunfighter and gambler, was one of the West's best women gamblers. In 1876 she ran a saloon in Deadwood. Her many lovers included Sam Bass and Bill Hickok. Her fourth husband grew jealous and killed her in 1878.

Leslie, Nashville Franklin (AKA: **Buckskin Frank**), a deadly gunman in Arizona, killed ten to thirteen men including Mike Killeen and Billy Claiborne in 1881, and claimed he killed John Ringo. He served eight years in Yuma prison for murder in 1889.

Levy, Jim, a gunman and a gambler, mortally wounded C.H. Harrison in 1877 at Deadwood, S.D.

Lewis, Bill, an outlaw, stole horses in Parker County, Texas, in 1881, and was imprisoned for life for robbing the U.S. Mail.

Lewis, Elmer (AKA: **Slaughter Kid; Mysterious Kid**), an outlaw, robbed the bank at Wichita Falls, Texas, with Foster Crawford. He was arrested by Marshal W.D. McDonald and hanged by a mob.

Lewis, Jim (AKA: **Arizona Bill**), an outlaw, attempted to "run the town" of Crested Butte, Colo., and was killed by Marshal Hatch on Sept. 30, 1881.

Leyba, Marino, an outlaw, led a gang of horse thieves and robbers who killed Colonel Charles Potter and was killed in Golden, Colo.

Liddell, James Andrew (AKA: **Dick**), an outlaw who robbed with Kit Dalton and the James gang, turned himself in to Sheriff Timberlake after Jesse James was killed, served several years in prison, and died a natural death in 1893.

Light, Zachary, a gunman and one of the best shots in Mason County, Texas, Zachary Light wounded "Judge" Adams, and was shot and killed by Les Dow in Seven Rivers, N.M., while attempting to rob him.

Lockhart, Del, a New Mexico outlaw, was lynched in October 1881.

Logan, Harvey (AKA: **Kid Curry**), a cowboy and rustler, participated in many Wild Bunch train robberies, later joined the Black Jacks, and allegedly killed nine men. He killed himself after a train robbery near Parachute, Colo.

Logan, Lonie, an outlaw and member of the Wild Bunch gang and brother of Harvey Logan, Lonie Logan was killed by a posse in February 1900 in Missouri.

Logwood, William, a gunman, shot and killed Juan Chavez y Pino on July 11, 1882, in the Nogal Mountains.

Long, John, an outlaw, was wanted for killing Marshal George Wellman in 1892 in Johnson County, Wyo.

Long, John (AKA: **Rivers**) was a gunman in the Lincoln County War. He died in Arizona.

Long, Steve (AKA: **Big Steve**), a lawman and outlaw, ran the Bucket of Blood saloon in Laramie City, Wyo., and was appointed deputy marshal. Long and his two partners were lynched on Oct. 28, 1868.

Longley, William Preston (AKA: **Wild Bill; Rattling Bill; Tom Jones; Jim Patterson; Jim Webb; Bill Black; Bill Henry; Bill Jackson**), a gunfighter, Longley allegedly killed just ten fewer men than Wes Hardin. Not an outlaw, he was hanged Oct. 11, 1878.

Love, Harry, a lawman and former Texas Ranger, Harry Love was allegedly a Mexican outlaw in the 1850s.

Loving, Frank (AKA: **Cock-Eyed Frank**), a Dodge City gambler, killed Levi Richardson, and was gunned down by another gambler in 1882 in Trinidad, Colo.

Lowe, James (AKA: **James West**), an outlaw and horse thief, was lynched in Las Vegas, N.M., on Feb. 7, 1886.

Lowe, Joseph (AKA: **Red Joe; Rowdy Joe; Monte Joe**), gunman and gambler, Lowe consorted with Sam Bass and Joel Collins and was reputedly violent and a good gunfighter. He was killed on Feb. 11, 1899, by E.A. Kimmel, an ex-police officer, while unarmed.

Lucas, Elmer (AKA: **Chicken**), an outlaw and part-time member of the Bill Cook gang, was captured in Indian Territory, after a bank robbery. He received a fifteen-year sentence in Detroit's federal prison.

Lucero, Aban, a gunman, shot and killed a man in Galisteo, N.M., on Feb. 9, 1891.

Lucero, Cecilio, an outlaw in Silva's White Caps, killed two cousins, Benizno Martinez and Juan Gallegos, and was lynched.

Lucero, Francisco, an outlaw, was jailed in 1891 in Clayton, N.M.

Lucero, Quinia, an outlaw, shot and killed Jose A. Samora on Apr. 20, 1884, in Wallace, N.M.

Lucero, Sostenes, an outlaw in Silva's White Caps, with Juan Romero, shot and killed gang member Antonio Rael.

Lucero, Tomas, an outlaw in Silva's White Caps of Las Vegas, N.M., died in the 1940s.

Lujan, Martiniano, a gunman, shot and killed Martias Mirival on Feb. 21, 1890, near Lincoln, N.M.

Luna, Melchior, a gunman, shot Manuel Sanchez on Feb. 20, 1883, in Belen, N.M.

Luttrell, Charles, an outlaw, killed a witness in 1880 to Sam Sparks's murder in Lee County, Texas, and fled to Denison. Captured in 1893, he was hanged after attempting escape several times.

Lyons, Hayes, an outlaw and deputy under outlaw Sheriff Henry Plummer in Silver City, Montana Territory, was lynched on Jan. 14, 1864.

M

McCall, Jim, an outlaw, rustled cattle near Springer, N.M., in the 1880s.

McCall, John (Jack, AKA: **Broken Nose Jack; Bill Sutherland**), a gunman, shot and killed Bill Hickok on Aug. 2, 1876. He was hanged for murder on Mar. 1, 1877.

McCanles, David C., a gunman, was killed by Bill Hickok on July 12, 1861, at Red Rock Ranch in Nebraska.

McCarty, Bill, an outlaw, brother of Tom McCarthy, and brother-in-law of Matt Warner, joined Butch Cassidy and the Wild Bunch, and was killed during the Delta, Colo., bank robbery.

McCarty, Henry (AKA: **Billy the Kid**), an outlaw and member of the Aelbee gang in South Dakota, was frequently confused with New Mexico's Billy the Kid.

McCarty, Tom, an outlaw, brother of Bill McCarty, and brother-in-law of Matt Warner, joined Butch Cassidy and the Wild Bunch and was killed during a gunfight in Montana.

McCauley, Hamp, an outlaw, was lynched by vigilantes in Napa, Calif., after he was tried for murder in 1851.

McCloskey, Andy, a gunman and buffalo hunter, dueled with another man at Camp Supply, Texas, in 1872. Both men were killed.

McCloskey, Sam, a gunman, was injured in the Lincoln County War.

McCoy, "One-Legged Jim", an outlaw, killed Sheriff Charles McKinney in La Salle County, Texas, and was hanged in San Antonio in 1887.

McCullough, Green, an outlaw, was lynched in San Antonio, Texas.

McDaniels, J., an outlaw and member of the Pitts-Yeager gang, was killed in 1884 in Texas.

McDaniels, Jim, a gunman in the Lincoln County War, participated in the McSween gunfight on July 19, 1879.

McDaniels, William (AKA: **Bud**), an outlaw and former guerilla soldier, rode with the James gang.

McDonald, J., a gunman, shot and killed his friend Robert Taylor on Jan. 13, 1890, in Clayton, N.M.

McDonald, Walter, a gunman, shot Thomas Richards in 1884 in Coeur de'Alene, N.M.

McDougal (or McDoulet), Annie, (AKA: **Cattle Annie**) an outlaw, at eighteen, associated with the Doolin gang and was suspected of stealing livestock and selling whiskey. Steve Burke captured her and Bill Tilghman caught her partner Little Britches and they were sent to reform school.

McDowell, Jack (AKA: **Three-Fingered Jack**), an outlaw, led a gang of outlaws and was lynched in Aurora, Nev., in February 1864.

McGrand, Ed, a gunman, received a life sentence in 1876 for killing a man in Nebraska.

McGuire, Edward, an outlaw, sheltered horse thieves on his New Mexico ranch and was caught.

McIntire, James, a Texas gunman and lawman from 1860, was Ranger, city marshal of Las Vegas, deputy sheriff, cowboy, hunter, gambler, and outlaw with a $1,000 reward on his head for the deaths of two men near Silver City, N.M.

McIntyre, Chas, a gunman, was jailed in 1874 at Belmont, Neb., for drawing his pistol, and was later lynched.

McKeague, Neal, a gunman and gambler, was killed at Church's Ferry, Dakota Territory in 1890 by a barkeeper.

McKemie, Robert (AKA: **Little Reddie from Texas**), an outlaw and member of the Sam Bass gang of the Dakotas in the 1870s.

McKinney, Thomas L., a New Mexico gunman who was also a lawman, accompanied Pat Garrett to the shoot-out with Billy the Kid on July 14, 1881.

McLaughlin, M. (AKA: **Red**), an outlaw and robber, escaped jail in Springer, N.M., on July 4, 1884.

McLowery, Frank, a gunman, was one of the three cowboys killed by the Earps in the O.K. Corral shoot-out on Oct. 26, 1881.

McLowery, Thomas, a gunman and the brother of Frank, was killed in the O.K. Corral shoot-out by the Earps.

McMains, Oscar P., a New Mexico reverend who was active in the disorder surrounding the Maxwell Land Grant.

McManus, Irving, an outlaw, rode with the Black Jack Ketchum gang in the 1890s.

McMasters, Sherman, an outlaw, rode with Wyatt Earp from 1879 to 1881, stole a horse, and was killed in the Texas Panhandle.

McNab, Frank, a gunman in the Lincoln County War, was killed in Bonito, N.M., in 1878.

McNew, Bill, a gunman and accused rustler, fought with Oliver Lee in the Lee-Good feud in Tularosa, N.M.

McRose, Martin, an outlaw, rustled cattle and was killed by El Paso city marshal Jeff Milton.

McWilliams, Sam (AKA: **the Verdigris Kid**), an outlaw and member of the Cook gang in the Indian Territory, was killed by lawmen in 1895.

Mace, Cal, an outlaw and Gunnison, Colo., gambler, was wanted for killing two men in Texas, and was killed by Jim McClease at Gunnison in the 1890s.

Mace, John, a gunman in the Lincoln County War, was indicted in 1878 for his participation. He was killed by a posse in 1880.

Maes, Juanito, an outlaw, stole horses around Boquilla, N.M.

Maes, Patricio, an outlaw and member of the White Caps, was hanged by the gang on Oct. 23, 1892, as a suspected traitor.

Maes, Zenon, an outlaw, was a member of Silva's White Caps.

Maestas, German (Herman), an outlaw and member of Silva's White Caps, was hanged on May 25, 1894, in Las Vegas for killing his common-law wife and her lover.

Mahoney, John, an outlaw, Mahoney was one of the gang that killed Jock Harriman on Dec. 10, 1883, in Wallace, N.M.

Majors, Robert, a gunman, shot and killed ex-Texas Ranger James Harris in a shoot-out at Santa Cruz, Calif., in the early 1880s.

Maldonado, Manuel, an outlaw, was a member of Silva's White Caps.

Mallory, L.P., a youthful troublemaker who was wanted for forgery in 1886.

Malone, James, an outlaw, executed for murder on Mar. 15, 1878, in the Arizona Territory.

Mamby, Henry, a gunman, shot and killed D.B. Griffin on May 11, 1884, in Vermijo, N.M.

Mancy, Mitchell E. (AKA: **Mitch; Mike Manning**), a gunman, shot and killed Juan Patron in Puerto de Luna, N.M., on Apr. 12, 1884.

Mankiller, Smoker, an outlaw Cherokee Indian, was hanged for killing a man at Fort Smith, Indian Territory, on Sept. 3, 1875.

Manning, A.E., a merchant in Northfield, Minn., and gunman, shot Cole Younger and Bill Chadwell on Sept. 7, 1876, while the James-Younger gang robbed the bank.

Manning, James, a gunman, was one of the brothers in an El Paso feud with Marshal Dallas Stoudenmire. In 1882, James shot Stoudenmire in the head and was acquitted of murder.

Mansker, Jim, a gunman, was killed at Miles City, Mont., in 1894 during a gunfight.

Mares, Hilario, an outlaw, was a member of Silva's White Caps.

Marlowe Brothers, outlaw brothers, Boone, Alf, Epp, Charley, and George Marlow were horse thieves who killed a lawman in 1889. During the battle that ensued two of the brothers were killed. Boone was poisoned by bounty hunters, and George and Charley fled to California.

Marshall, Charles, a gunman in the Lincoln County War, rode with the posse that killed John Tunstall on Feb. 18, 1878.

Martin, Charles, a gunman in the Lincoln County War, was indicted in 1878 for his participation.

Martin, Robert, an outlaw, who in 1879, led a gang in the Arizona Territory.

Martin, William (AKA: **Hurricane Bill**), a gunman, was jailed for playing cards, matching Holliday, and assault. He fled to Castroville, Texas, after he was forced to marry a prostitute.

Martin, William (AKA: **Wild Bill; Jones**), an outlaw in Lincoln County, was killed by John Perry in June 1887.

Martinez, Atanacio, a gunman, claimed he shot and killed Morris J. Bernstein in Lincoln County, a shooting credited to Billy the Kid.

Mason, Barney, a gunman, lawman, and Sheriff Garrett's deputy, killed John Farris in self-defense at Fort Sumner, N.M., in 1880.

Massagee, George, an outlaw, convicted of robbing a post office in the New Mexico Territory.

Masterson, Edward J., older brother of Bat Masterson, who served as town marshal in Dodge City, Kan., and was killed by two cowboys on Apr. 9, 1878.

Masterson, James P., a gunman and lawman, brother of Bat Masterson; took part in the arrest of the Doolin gang in 1893.

Masterson, Robert (AKA: **Smiling Bob**), another brother of Bat, Robert was marshal in Trinidad, Colo., in 1882. He reportedly killed twenty-one men.

Masterson, William Barclay (AKA: **Bat**), served as sheriff of Ford County, Kan., as city marshal in Dodge, and deputy U.S. marshal for the New York District. Bat killed one of the men who murdered his brother and helped apprehend Dave Rudabaugh and his gang. He died while working as a newspaper sports writer in 1921.

Mather, David H. (AKA: **Mysterious Dave**), an outlaw, was one of the Dodge City gang in Las Vegas, N.M.

Mathias, Oscar, a gunman, shot John Coddington on Sept. 30, 1882, at Three Rivers, N.M.

Matthews, Jacob B., a gunman, served in the Tennessee Cavalry in the Civil War, and was a gunman employed as deputy sheriff by L.G. Murphy during the Lincoln County War. He died in 1904.

Maxwell, Peter Menard, a cowboy and gunman, was a friend of Billy the Kid in Lincoln County. Pat Garrett shot and killed the Kid in Maxwell's bedroom in July 1881. He died on June 21, 1898.

May, D. Boone, a gunman and stage guard in Deadwood, S.D., and Cheyenne, Wyo., killed several stage robbers in the 1870s.

Meade, William, a gunman, shot J.E. "Dobe" Johnson on Feb. 24, 1884, in Hillsboro, N.M.

Means, Colonel Thomas, a gunman, was lynched on Jan. 1, 1867, for attempting to murder his father-in-law in Taos, N.M.

Medlock, John, an outlaw, was hanged on May 25, 1906, in Raton.

Medran, Florentino, an outlaw, was a member of Silva's White Caps.

Meeks, Henry Wilbur (Bob), an outlaw and member of the Wild Bunch, was imprisoned in the 1900s, and died in an insane asylum on Nov. 22, 1912, in the State Hospital in Evanston, Wyo.

Menczer, Augustus (Gus), a gunman and Texas saloon owner, killed several men after a shoot-out with his business partner in Raton, N.M., in 1882. A mob lynched him on June 28, 1882.

Meras, Nica, an outlaw, stole horses in Lincoln County and was shot in 1877.

Merideth, Charles, an outlaw, killed "Red" Dent Kyes in Clayton, N.M, in March 1890.

Merrill, David, an Oregon outlaw, Merrill rode with Harry Tracy who killed him in 1899, after a prison escape.

Mes, Cruz, an outlaw and horse thief, was killed with Roman and Pancho on a road near White Sands, N.M., in 1876.

Mes, Felipe, a gunman in the Lincoln County War, rode with the posse that killed John Tunstall on Feb. 18, 1878.

Mes, Pancho, an outlaw horse thief, was killed with Roman and Cruz on a road near White Sands, N.M., in 1876.

Mes, Roman, an outlaw horse thief, was killed with Pancho and Cruz on a road near White Sands, N.M., in 1876.

Metcalfe, "Wild Bill", an outlaw, fled Loma Parda, N.M., in November 1877 after killing a man. He was jailed and lynched by a mob.

Middleton, Chas, an outlaw, wanted by the sheriff of Bastrop County, Texas, in 1886.

Middleton, John, an outlaw and cousin of Jim Reed, rode with Quantrill and killed Sheriff J.H. Black in Texas, and was shot and killed southwest of Fort Smith.

Middleton, John, an outlaw and gunman who along with Billy the Kid became a part of the posse of Regulators in Lincoln County and ambushed Sheriff William Brady and George Hindman on Apr. 1, 1878.

Middleton, Thomas (AKA: Doc), led an outlaw gang of horse thieves in Nebraska, 1870s-1890s. He died in 1913.

Miera, Pantaleon, an outlaw, stole horses and killed men in New Mexico. He was lynched in Albuquerque, N.M., on Dec. 29, 1880.

Miller, Clelland, an outlaw in the James-Younger gang, was active in the 1870s, before his death during the robbery of the First National Bank at Northfield, Minn., in September 1876.

Miller, Eli (AKA: Slick), a New Mexico outlaw, was captured by A.J. Fountain.

Miller, James B., a gunman, professional killer, and occasional lawman in Pecos, Texas, in the 1890s, killed Sheriff Bud Frazer and was suspected of forty other killings including Pat Garrett and A.A. Bobbitt. A mob lynched him in 1909 at Ada, Okla.

Miller, Jesse (AKA: **Jesse Williams; Jeff Davis**), an outlaw, was a member of the Cole Estes gang of train robbers in New Mexico.

Miller, Captain John, a gunman, killed thirty-two men in his life before he was killed in 1888 by John Ables, a tenant on his farm in Jonesboro, Indian Territory, who claimed Miller attacked him.

Miller, S.C., a gunman, shot John Saun in November 1885 in San Marcial, N.M.

Miller, "Wild Bill", an outlaw, was killed by lawmen in Corwell County, Texas, on Jan. 13, 1869.

Mills, Alexander H., a gunman and murderer, rode with the posse that killed John Tunstall on Feb. 18, 1878.

Miner, William, an outlaw, robbed stages for forty years and died in a Georgia prison in 1913.

Mitchell, William (AKA: **John W. King**), an outlaw, killed men in the Hood County, Texas, feud and received a life sentence in 1912 in Texas. He escaped from jail at the age of seventy.

Montoya, Jose F., an outlaw, was a member of Silva's White Caps.

Montoya, Narciso, an outlaw, killed Luis Gallegos and was lynched in Taos, N.M., on June 10, 1881.

Montoya, Ramon, a gunman in the Lincoln County War, rode with the posse that killed John Tunstall on Feb. 18, 1878.

Moon, Jim, an outlaw, led a gang that stole mules from Texas and New Mexico army posts in 1870.

Moore, Lester, a gunman, was buried on Boothill in Tombstone, Ariz. His tombstone reads "Here lies Lester Moore, Four Slugs from a .44, No Les, No More."

Moore, Thomas, a gunman in the Lincoln County War, rode with the posse that killed John Tunstall on Feb. 18, 1878.

Moore, William, an outlaw, horse thief, and murderer, rode with John Casey in New Mexico and later fled to Alaska.

Morgan, Frank, an outlaw, who held up the San Marcial, N.M., stage on May 15, 1881, and was killed.

Morgan, Joe, a gunman and lawman, fought Deputy Sheriff Ben Williams in Las Cruces, N.M., on Sept. 15, 1895, with Albert Fall. He was later a deputy sheriff and Oliver Lee supporter.

Morrell, Ed, an outlaw and author of a book, aided the escape of Chris Evans from a California jail in 1893.

Morris, Harvey, a gunman in the Lincoln County War, was killed during the McSween gunfight on July 19, 1878.

Morris, W.C., a gunman, Morris dueled with "Editor Shannan" and killed him at Visalia, Calif., in 1860.

Morrissey, Peter, a New Mexico outlaw, was killed in June 1877 by a posse.

Morton, William, a gunman in the Lincoln County War, rode with the posse that killed John Tunstall in February. He was killed by Billy the Kid in March 1878.

Mosely, "Scar Face", an outlaw, was killed by the Montana Stranglers close to Glendive, Mont., in 1884.

Mosier, Henry, a gunman who participated in the killing of Jock Harriman in Wallace, N.M. on Dec.

10, 1883.

Moyer, Ace, a gunman and founder of Laramie, Wyo., was hanged with his brother Con in 1868.

Moyer, Con, a gunman and founder of Laramie, Wyo., was hanged with his brother Ace in 1868.

Munson, Henry, an outlaw and member of the Bill Cook gang of Oklahoma, was killed on Aug. 2, 1894, during a battle at Sapulpa, Okla.

Murieta, Joaquin, the half-mythical "King of the California Outlaws," reportedly killed Texas Ranger Harry Love before he was killed in 1853 by a posse.

Murietta, Procopio, an outlaw and nephew of Joaquin Murieta, once terrorized Santa Cruz, Calif., and rode with Timbucio Vasquez in the late 1860s.

Murillo, Zeke, an outlaw, led a gang of rustlers headquartered in Shakespeare, N.M.

Murphy, John, an outlaw, sentenced for train robbery at Las Vegas, N.M. in 1905.

Murphy, Lawrence G., an immigrant from Ireland who became a judge, shopkeeper, and post trader in Lincoln County, died on Oct. 20, 1878, during the height of the Lincoln County War, which he reportedly started.

Musgrave, George, an outlaw, was a member of the Black Jack Ketchum gang in the 1890s in New Mexico.

Musgrove, Lee H., an outlaw, led a gang in the 1860s after the Civil War in Colorado.

Muskgrove, M., an outlaw, was a member of Black Jack Christian's gang.

N

Nangway, Charles, an outlaw, murdered a rancher on June 3, 1885, near Lake Valley, N.M.

Nash, Joe, a gunman in the Lincoln County War, was indicted for his participation in 1878.

Neel, John S., a gunman, shot J.N. New on June 19, 1883, on the Penasco.

Neill, Hyman G. (AKA: **Hoodoo Brown**), an outlaw and justice of the peace, was one of the Dodge City gang, and was run out of Las Vegas, N.M.

Nelson, Bob, an outlaw, was a member of Wild Bill Martin's gang in Lincoln, N.M.

Nelson, Mart, a gunman, killed seven people in Bonito, N.M., on May 4 1885.

Newcomb, George (AKA: **Bitter Creek; Slaughter's Kid**), an outlaw and member of the Dalton and Doolin gangs of Oklahoma in 1890s, was killed near Pawnee, Okla.

Newman, Bud, an outlaw with the Taylor gang of West Texas, was captured in 1898, and killed in an escape attempt.

Newman, Jim, a lawman and outlaw, consorted with Wes Hardin in the 1860s. He later lived in Texas and New Mexico.

Nicholson, William (AKA: **Flap Jack Bill**), an outlaw, Nicholson was lynched by a mob on Oct. 1, 1881, in Sanders, N.M.

Nite, Jim, an outlaw and member of the Dalton gang, was apprehended by Deputy U.S. Marshal Dee Harkey near Sacramento Sinks, N.M., in 1908.

Nolan, Francisco, an outlaw, was a member of the Castillo gang.

Noranjo, Aristotle, an outlaw, was lynched on Oct. 6, 1881, in Las Lunas, N.M.

Norfleet, J. Frank, a gunman and rancher in Gonzales County, Texas, tracked, captured, and sent to prison a gang that conned him out of more than $100,000.

O

O'Day, Tom, an outlaw, robbed banks in the Black Hills in the 1890s and was imprisoned in 1903 for horse theft.

O'Dell, Bill, a gunman, was killed with his brother Tom by lawmen in Texas in December 1880.

O'Dell, Tom, a gunman, was killed with his brother Bill by lawmen in Texas in December 1880.

Odle, Alvin, an outlaw, escaped from the Burnet, Texas, jail with his brother William in 1889, fled to Mexico, and was later killed by Rangers Outlaw and Hughes in Edwards County, Texas.

Odle, William, an outlaw, escaped from the Burnet, Texas, jail with his brother Al in 1889, fled to Mexico, and was later killed by Rangers Outlaw and Hughes in Edwards County, Texas.

O'Folliard, Thomas, an outlaw, friend of Billy the Kid, and cohort in the Lincoln County War, was killed in ambush by Pat Garrett's posse on Dec. 19, 1880. O'Folliard is buried alongside Billy the Kid.

O'Laughlin, Jimmy, an outlaw, broke out of jail on June 1885.

Olinger, John Wallace, a gunman in the Lincoln County War and brother of Robert, was indicted for his participation.

Olinger, Robert A., an outlaw, crooked U.S. marshal, and deputy sheriff of Lincoln County, was indicted for his participation in the Lincoln County War, and he was killed by Billy the Kid on Apr. 28, 1881.

Omohundro, John B. (AKA: **Texas Jack**), a scout and gunman, tracked horse thieves and led massacres of Indian tribes in the 1850s-60s, in Texas, Kansas, Arizona, and New Mexico. He died in 1888.

O'Neill, Thomas, a gunman, killed Walter Byers in Dawson, N.M.

Orr, John (AKA: **Donaldson**), an outlaw and member of Wild Bill Martin's gang, was killed by a gang led by John Perry in June 1877.

Owens, George, an outlaw and member of the Alvord-Stiles gang of Arizona, was imprisoned for a train robbery committed in 1899.

Owens, Louis (**Lewis**), an outlaw and brother of George, robbed trains with a gang, and was captured and imprisoned in 1900.

P

Padilla, Pablo, an outlaw, stole horses and cattle around Valencia County, N.M., and was lynched in January 1872.

Paine, John, a Texas gunfighter, fought for the Grahams in the Tonto Basin, Ariz., war in the 1880s.

Paine, Manfred, an outlaw and son of a suspected killer, shot and killed his father in Washington, as well as the lawman who arrested him.

Palmeter, Page, a gunman, shot and killed Harry Walters on Oct. 27, 1883. in Raton, N.M.

Parker, George Leroy, See: **Cassidy, Butch**

Parrott, George (AKA: **Big Nose George**), an outlaw, led a gang in a train robbery in 1878 but was thwarted. Captured in 1880, he was lynched after receiving a death sentence from the court.

Pate, James, an outlaw, was arrested on Nov. 17, 1906, for murder.

Patterson, Ferd, an outlaw, was killed either in a barber's chair or in a hotel lobby in Idaho or Walla Walla, Wash., in the 1860s.

Patterson, Frank was an outlaw in Arizona and New Mexico.

Paxton, Louis, a gunman in the Lincoln County War, was indicted in 1879 for his participation.

Peacock, Lewis, a western outlaw and gunman.

Pearl, William S., a gunman, killed a soldier in Fort Stanton, N.M., and was lynched on Jan. 23, 1883, by other soldiers.

Pell, Henry (AKA: **Henry Thompson; Long Henry**), a gunman who lived in Missouri, Texas, and Montana, killed seven men before he was gunned down in 1902.

Peppin, George, a lawman who aligned himself with outlaws during a feud in Lincoln County, N.M. on July 19, 1879.

Perkins, Louis, an outlaw, was captured with Charlie Allison in Albuqerque, N.M., in June 1881.

Perry, Samuel R., a gunman in the Lincoln County War, Samuel Perry was indicted in 1879 for his participation.

Petal, Gabriel, an outlaw, was a member of Silva's White Caps.

Phillipowski, Lyon, a lawman who was involved in a shoot-out with a store clerk in Lincoln County, N.M. on Oct. 21, 1874.

Pickett, Tom, an outlaw and lawman, stole cattle and was captured with Billy the Kid in New Mexico on Dec. 23, 1880. He later served as a U.S. marshal and died on May 14, 1934, in Arizona.

Pierce, Charles, an outlaw, joined the Dalton gang and later the Doolin gang, in Oklahoma in the 1890s. He was killed on May 2, 1895, near Pawnee, along with George Newcomb.

Pino y Pino, Pablo, a gunman in the Lincoln County War, was indicted in 1879 for his participation.

Pipkin, Red, an outlaw, rode with Bronco Bill Walters.

Pitman, Joe, a gunman, shot and killed Dick Blain on Feb. 18, 1888, in Luna Valley, N.M.

Pitts, Charles, an outlaw and member of the Younger gang, Charles Pitts was killed after the failed robbery of the Northfield, Minn., bank on Sept. 7, 1876.

Plummer, Henry, an outlaw leader and lawman, organized the Innocents, one of the worst gang of cutthroats in the West, in the early 1860s. Plummer was lynched by vigilantes in 1864.

Poe, John W., a gunman and deputy to Pat Garrett, was with Garrett when he killed Billy the Kid on July 14, 1881.

Polanco, Librado, an outlaw, was the secretary of Silva's White Caps, and received a life sentence for robbery.

Porter, Frank, an outlaw, was killed eighty miles west of Albuquerque, N.M., in April 1888, by a posse.

Potter, Andrew Jackson, an outlaw turned Methodist preacher, scouted and fought hostiles in New Mexico and Texas from 1847, and died in October 1895.

"Powder Bill", an outlaw, was hired to kill A.J. Fountain but did not attempt the murder.

Powell, Buck, a gunman in the Lincoln County War, was indicted for his participation.

Power, William (**Bill**, AKA: **Joe; Tim Evans**), an outlaw and member of the Dalton gang, was killed by John Kloehr in the Coffeyville, Kan., bank robbery, in 1892.

Powers, Doc, a New Mexico gunman, who killed a man in Council Springs, on June 27, 1888.

Price, Elmer, an outlaw, was sent to prison. He was refused pardon twice: first on Feb. 6, 1909, and then on Apr. 27, 1912.

Putman, Ed (AKA: **Ed Sibley**), an outlaw killed by Texas Rangers on Dec. 1, 1906, at Del Rio, Texas, during a shoot-out. Putman was wanted for killing two men over a sheep deal.

Q

Quantrill, William Clark, an outlaw, commanded a group of guerrilla fighters in the Civil War that raided the towns of Centralia and Lawrence in the 1860s. The Dalton, James, and Younger brothers rode with him, and he was killed in Kentucky on June 5, 1865.

Queen, Richard, an outlaw, was jailed in Socorro, N.M., on Aug. 17, 1906.

Queen, Vic, an outlaw, rode with Martin McRose in New Mexico.

Quinlan, Tom (AKA: **Tex**), an outlaw, escaped from the Las Vegas jail with Webb and Rudabaugh on Dec. 3, 1881.

R

Radigan, Thomas, an outlaw, rode with Ike Stockton's gang.

Rael, Antonio, an outlaw, was a member of Silva's White Caps, and was killed by gang members Juan Romero and Sostenas Lucero.

Raidler, William (AKA: **Little Bill**), an outlaw, joined the Dalton-Doolin gang in Oklahoma in 1892, and was captured in 1895. After his release from prison, Raidler quit crime.

Randall, William, an outlaw and horse thief, shot and killed Constable Joe Carson on Jan. 22, 1880 (or 1884), and was himself killed in Las Vegas.

Rande, Frank (AKA: **Charles Van Zandt**), an outlaw in Iowa, Illinois, and Indiana in the 1870s, was shot and killed by guards while in prison in March 1884.

Rascon, Eugenio, a gunman, shot and killed Demas Garcia in New Mexico on Nov. 18, 1883.

Raynolds, Joseph, stole a horse from Captain Jack Crawford, was captured, convicted, and served eighteen months in prison.

Real, Acasio, an outlaw, was a member of Silva's White Caps.

Real, Procopio, an outlaw, was a member of Silva's White Caps.

Realis, Pablo, an ax murderer who killed his wife and sister-in-law on July 19, 1848, in Santa Fe, N.M., was the first murderer reported in the first English newspaper in New Mexico Territory.

Redding, Robert, a New Mexico gunman, shot and killed a Central City, Colo., man in October 1888.

Redfield, Len, a suspected outlaw in Arizona, was lynched in 1877 for allegedly robbing a stagecoach.

Reed, Ed, the son of Belle Starr and Jim Reed, he was a suspected stagecoach and train robber.

Reed, Jim, an outlaw and paramour of Belle Starr, was wanted in Central Texas for robbery. He was killed in 1874.

Reese, James, a gunman in the Lincoln County War. He fought in the gun battle July 19, 1879, between the McSween and Murphy factions.

Remine, Richard, an outlaw, was hanged at Silver City, N.M., in March 1881.

Reynolds, Laris, an outlaw, rode with Ike Stockton's gang.

Richardson, Robert, a gunman, Richardson shot and killed Louis Lesser on Nov. 12, 1881, in Teseque, N.M.

Riggs, Barney, an outlaw in Texas in the 1880s, he was killed at Fort Stockton in 1900.

Riley, John Henry, a gunman and immigrant from Ireland, was a leader of the Murphy-Dolan faction in the Lincoln County War in New Mexico. He died in 1916.

Ringo, John (John Ringgold), a gunman prominent in Texas, Arizona, and New Mexico, killed several men before his body was found outside Tombstone in July 1882.

Rivera, Petronilio, a gunman, killed a man on Oct. 23, 1884, in Tularosa, N.M.

Roach, John was a gunman and gambler in Kingston, N.M.

Roberts, Andrew L. (AKA: Buckshot), a Texas Ranger, outlaw, and member of King Fisher's gang in New Mexico, killed Dick Brewer and was killed in the gun battle at Blazer's Mill, N.M., in 1878.

Robertson, Ben F. (AKA: Ben Wheeler), a lawman and outlaw, was a companion of Billy the Kid during the Lincoln County War, robbed the Medicine Lodge, Kan., bank with Marshal Henry Brown and others on Apr. 30, 1884, and was lynched.

Robertson, William, a gunman, was shooting at an enemy when police killed him in April 1880.

Rodriguez, Jesus, a gunman and horse thief, participated in the Lincoln County War.

Rogers, Annie, girlfriend of outlaw Kid Curry, was charged with Curry as an accomplice, imprisoned in the Tennessee Penitentiary, and released on June 19, 1902.

Rogers, Bob, an Indian Territory outlaw from 1893, murdered a lawman and was later killed by a posse in Horseshoe Mound (Okla.) on Mar. 13, 1895.

Rogers, David, an outlaw, arrested in 1889 for complicity in the robbery of an Army paymaster in the New Mexico Territory.

Rogers, Dick, an outlaw, attempted to break a friend from jail on Mar. 13, 1885, and was killed.

Romero, Cristobel, an outlaw, was lynched in 1884 near Los Lunas.

Romero, Damon, an outlaw and murderer, was hanged in Springer, N.M., on Feb. 2, 1883.

Romero, Juan, an outlaw and member of Silva's White Caps, killed gang member Antonio Rale with Sostenas Lucero. He died in Raton in 1931.

Romero, Ricardo (AKA: El Romo), an outlaw, was Silva's first lieutenant in the White Caps.

Romero, Torevio, a gunman, Romero killed Francisco Martinez on Mar. 25, 1886, in Rio Quemado, N.M.

Romero, Vincent, a gunman in the Lincoln County War, was killed in the McSween gunfight on July 15, 1878.

Roth, Fred, a gunman, shot and killed James Spurlock in Spring 1885 on John Chisum's Ranch.

Rucker, E.C., a New Mexico lawman, but also aligned with the outlaw, John Good.

Rudabaugh, David, an outlaw and briefly city marshal of Las Vegas, N.M., rode with the Roark gang, Doc Holliday, and Billy the Kid. He was shot and beheaded by vigilantes in Mexico.

Rudolph, Bill (AKA: **The Missouri Kid**), an outlaw and murderer, robbed banks in Missouri with George Collins the 1900s, and was captured in 1904. He was imprisoned and hanged on May 8.

Ruff, Rufus (AKA: **Windy**), an outlaw, was lynched in Mora County, N.M., for killing Charles Norton.

Rush, Matt, an outlaw and suspected rustler, was killed by Tom Horn on July 9, 1900, near Brown's Hole, Wyo.

Russell, T.N., a gunman and citizen of Coffeyville, Kan., killed Dick Broadwell when the Dalton gang attempted to robbed two banks on Oct. 5, 1892.

Ryan, "Fatty", an outlaw, was an early hold-up artist in Arizona.

Ryan, P., a gunman, shot and killed Charles Walker on June 23, 1881, in San Marcial, N.M.

Rynerson, William L., a gunman and legislator, killed Territorial Chief Justice John P. Slough in Santa Fe, N.M., and was acquitted. Later, he was a Dolan gunman in the Lincoln County War.

S

Sage, Lee, an outlaw, rustled cattle and was born in Robber's Roost country.

Sagolia, Manuel, a gunman in the Lincoln County War, rode with the posse that killed John Tunstall on Feb. 18, 1878.

Said, John (AKA: **Rattlesnake Jack**), an Idaho outlaw, was shot and killed by the sheriff and posse in Weiser City in November 1882.

Sais, Carlos, an outlaw, was sentenced to be hanged for murder on Dec. 17, 1906.

Salas, Justo, a New Mexico gunman who was involved in a 1900 shoot-out at a dance hall.

Salazar, Hijino was a gunman in the Lincoln County War.

Sample, Omer W., an outlaw and member of the Heath gang, was hanged in Tombstone for robbery on March 8, 1884.

Sampson, Sam, an outlaw and member of the Buck gang in the Indian Territory, was hanged on July 1, 1896.

Sanders, George, an outlaw, was a member of the Cook gang in the Indian Territory. He was killed by lawmen.

Sandobal, Juan, an outlaw, was lynched on Dec. 15, 1871, in Las Lunas, N.M.

Sandoval, Anastacio, a gunman, shot and killed Cypriano Montoya on Mar. 20, 1884, in Anton Chico, N.M.

Sandoval, Remigio (AKA: **El Gavilan**), an outlaw, and member of Silva's White Caps in New Mexico.

Sanez, Doroteo, an outlaw, was a lieutenant in John Kinney's gang of professional gunmen. He was killed in July 1877 by A.J. Fountain's militia.

Santleben, August, a gunman, ran a stage line from 1867 between Texas and Mexico and killed several Mexican outlaw and hostile Indians. He died on Sept. 19, 1911.

Saunders, William, a gunman, shot Sid Moore in June 1885 in White Oaks, N.M.

Schroeder, S., an outlaw, was jailed in Las Vegas, N.M., and escaped on Dec. 3, 1881, with David Rudabaugh and John Webb.

Scorgins, John (**Bill**), a gunman in the Lincoln

County War, was indicted for the murder of Buckshot Roberts.

Scott, E., a wanted outlaw with a reward for his arrest, killed several men on Dec. 20, 1873, in Lincoln County, N.M.

Scott, John, an outlaw, shot and killed by Springer, N.M., Deputy Sheriff Frank P. Nichols on May 17, 1883.

Scurlock, Josiah, G. (AKA: **Doc**), a gunman and friend of Billy the Kid, left when he was indicted for the murder of Buckshot Roberts, but later returned to New Mexico. In 1882, during an argument, Fred Roth shot and killed him.

Seaman, Carey, a gunman and resident of Coffeyville, Kan., wounded Dick Broadwell and shot Emmett Dalton when the Dalton gang attempted to rob two Coffeyville banks on Nov. 5, 1892.

See, James, a Texas outlaw, murderer, and rustler in the 1860s, died in California in 1887.

Segura, Jose, an outlaw and leader of a gang of horse thieves, was lynched by vigilantes on July 10, 1876, near Fort Stanton.

Selman, John, a Texas lawman and gunman, allegedly rustled with John Larn around Fort Griffin, Texas. He befriended Billy the Kid during the Lincoln County War, and killed John Hardin in August 1895. George Scarborough killed him on Apr. 6, 1896.

Sharp, Milton A., a California outlaw, robbed the Bodie stage four times in June and September 1880.

Shears, John, a gunman, killed W.W. Pruner on June 2, 1888.

Sheedy, Ben, an outlaw, was shot while attempting to escape arrest in Lincoln, N.M., in September 1887.

Sheehan, Larry, an outlaw, led a group of train robbers in 1887, in the New Mexico Territory.

Sheet Iron Jack, a California outlaw known as a "Robinhood," was lynched by vigilantes from Idaho and Montana.

Short, Luke, a gunfighter who killed two men, was one of the Dodge City gang that followed Wyatt Earp to Tombstone, Ariz. He died in December 1893.

Sias, Carlos, an outlaw and murderer, was hanged in January 1907 in Socorro, N.M.

Silva, Vincente, an outlaw, leader of Silva's Forty Bandits (also known as Silva's White Caps), a gang of robbers and murderers in Las Vegas, N.M. Silva was killed by members of the gang in 1895.

Simms, W.H. (AKA: **Billy**), a saloon keeper in San Antonio, who in 1884, was suspected of killing King Fisher and Ben Thompson.

Siringo, Charles Angelo, a gunman and cowboy detective, chased outlaws and rustlers throughout Texas, New Mexico, and the Montanas in the 1890s. He died in California in 1928.

Sisneros, Dionicio (AKA: **Candelas**), an outlaw, was a member of Silva's White Caps. He was sentenced to life imprisonment.

Slade, Joseph Alfred (AKA: **Jack**), a gunman in Montana, Idaho, and Colorado territories, was hanged by vigilantes in 1864.

Slaughter, John Horton (AKA: **Texas John**), a gunman, lawman, and rancher in South Arizona who was involved in many gunfights over the years; in 1886 was elected sheriff of Cochise County. He died on Feb. 15, 1922.

Smith, William (**Bill, Billie**), a Kansas cowboy-turned-outlaw, robbed the Medicine Lodge bank with a gang led by Marshal Henry Brown and killed two men on Apr. 30, 1884. He was lynched while awaiting trial.

Smith, James, a gunman, on Feb. 18, 1894, shot C.F. Hilton.

Smith, Joe, an Texas outlaw, was arrested for murder in New Mexico by Texas Rangers.

Smith, Sam (AKA: **Fred Wyat**), was a gunman in the Lincoln County War.

Smith, Six Shooter, a New Mexico gunmen who enjoyed wounding people without killing them.

Snider, William (AKA: **Bill Caveness**), an outlaw who was arrested at Springerville, Ariz. in November, 1877.

Snow, Bud was an outlaw in Arizona and New Mexico.

Snow, Charles (AKA: **Johnson**), a gunman, was killed in New Mexico on Aug. 12, 1881.

Snyder, Jess, an outlaw, was a member of the Cook gang in the Indian Territory. He was captured after a bank robbery.

Sontag, George C. (AKA: **George Bohm**), an outlaw in the 1880s and 1890s, robbed several trains in California with Chris Evans and was released from prison in 1908.

Sontag, John, an outlaw and brother of George, robbed trains in Illinois and California in the 1890s with Chris Evans. He was wounded in a shoot-out with police officers and died in a Fresno, Calif., jail in 1893.

Spawn, George (AKA: **Buffalo Bill**), a New Mexico outlaw and cattle rustler.

Spence, Pete, a gunman and friend of the Clantons in Tombstone, Ariz., in the early 1880s, who reportedly killed Morgan Earp.

Spencer, Charles, an outlaw, horse thief, and murderer, was jailed in Silver City, N.M., and escaped in March 1884 with the Kit Joy gang.

Sperry, Sam was a gunman in the Lincoln County War.

Starr, Belle, outlaw, romantically involved with bank robbers Cole Younger and Jim Reed, later married outlaw Sam Starr, with whom she served a jail sentence. She was killed in February 1889.

Starr, Henry (AKA: **The Bearcat**), an outlaw nephew of Belle Starr who robbed banks from the 1890s, was killed in Harrison, Ark., in 1921 while attempting to rob a bank.

Stevens, Jennie (AKA: **Little Britches**) an outlaw connected with the Doolin gang, Little Britches rustled cattle and horses in the Osage Nation with Cattle Annie McDougal. She was arrested in 1894 and sent to the Federal Reformatory in Framingham, Mass.

Stevens, Stephens, a gunman in the Lincoln County War, was charged with the murder of Buckshot Roberts.

Stiles, William Larkin, an outlaw, rode with Burt Alvord as a lawman and outlaw in Arizona in the 1890s and 1900s, and was killed in 1908.

Stilwell, Frank C., a gunman, lawman, and cowboy in Texas and Tombstone, Ariz., was shot down in 1882 during the grand jury investigation of the killing of Morgan Earp.

Stilwell, Simpson (AKA: **Commanche Jack**), a gunman and lawman, scouted for the Army in Texas, and brought in several outlaws.

Stinson, Joe, a gunman, shot Wall Henderson in October 1871.

Stockton, Isaac (AKA: **Ike**), an outlaw and leader of a gang of robbers in northern New Mexico, Stockton was shot and wounded by lawmen, captured, and died after having his leg amputated on Sept. 27, 1881.

Stockton, Thomas, a rancher who owned a popular

overnight stage stop near Trinidad, Colo., killed several rustlers in the 1870s and was allegedly tried for murder.

Stockton, Port, an outlaw, lawman, and brother of Ike, shot and killed Juan Gonzales in October 1876 in Cimarron, N.M., and was killed on Jan. 10, 1881, by Alfred Graves.

Storms, Charles, a gunman, gambler, and friend of Bat Masterson in Kansas and Arizona, was killed by Luke Short in 1881.

Stoudenmire, Dallas, a lawman and gunman in New Mexico and Texas, Stoudenmire shot and killed several men before his death in 1882.

Sullivan, James, a gunman who, in April 1884, killed John Houston, at Black Hawk, New Mexico.

Sundance Kid, The (Harry Longabaugh or Longbaugh), an outlaw and horse wrangler from Colorado who worked in Sundance, Wyo. He rode with the "Wild Bunch of Robbers' Roost." The Sundance Kid and Butch Cassidy fled to South America where he was reportedly killed by government soldiers in either Bolivia or Argentina in 1908.

Swilling, Hank was an outlaw in Arizona and New Mexico.

T

Taggart, Frank, an outlaw and member of the train robbing Kit Joy gang, Taggart was killed on Mar. 13, 1884, by a posse led by Deputy Sheriff T.L. Hall.

Tattenbaum, William (AKA: Russian Bill), a gunman in Tombstone, Ariz., was lynched on Jan. 1, 1881, for horse theft.

Taylor, Jack Hays, a gunman and brother of Phillip Taylor, killed a cavalry soldier and became

a fugitive in the Sutton-Taylor feud of South Texas. A Sutton posse ambushed and killed him near the Taylor home on Aug. 23, 1869.

Taylor, Jack J., an outlaw, led a gang of train robbers and killers in Arizona and New Mexico. He received a life sentence for train robbery in 1888.

Taylor, Jim, a gunman and son of Pitkin Taylor, led the Taylor faction in the Taylor-Sutton feud in 1873 in South Texas. He gunned down several men and was killed in December 1875.

Taylor, Phillip (AKA: Doboy), a gunman and brother of Jack Hays Taylor, participated in the Sutton-Taylor feud, and was gunned down in November 1871 near Kerrville, Texas.

Taylor, Pitkin, a gunman, led the Taylors in the Taylor-Sutton feud which began in 1867. He was gunned down outside his home by the Suttons in October 1872 and died in March 1873.

Taylor, Steve, an outlaw, stole money at Custer County, Mont., in 1884, and was arrested in New Mexico.

Taylor, William, the son of Pitkin Taylor, participated in the Taylor-Sutton feud and killed men with his brother Jim. He rode with their relative, Wes Hardin, and was imprisoned in 1877.

Telfrin, Count Feador (AKA: Russian Bill), an outlaw and son of a Russian countess, was hanged in November 1881 at Shakespeare for rustling cattle.

Telles, Jose, an outlaw, was executed on Apr. 3, 1903, in Santa Fe, N.M.

Telles, Octoviano, a New Mexico outlaw who eluded authorities until his arrest on Aug. 13, 1907.

Terry, Kyle, a gunman, killed Henry Williams in February 1886 at Houston, Texas, shotgunned Ned Gibson on Jan. 21, 1888, at Wharton. Volney Gibson shot and killed Terry on Jan. 21, 1890, in Galveston.

Tewksbury, Edwin, a gunman in the Graham-Tewksbury feud in Globe County, Ariz., helped kill John Graham and was arrested. He became constable of Globe County and later deputy sheriff of Gila County.

Tewksbury, Jim, a gunman in the feud and brother of Edwin Tewksbury, killed several members of the Graham faction, and died of consumption in 1888.

"Texas Jack", an outlaw, was shot and killed in February 1881 in Rincon, N.M.

Thomas, Charles was an outlaw and cattle rustler in New Mexico.

Thompson, Ben, a gunman and lawman in Texas, killed thirty-two men, and was ambushed with King Fisher in March 1884. Bat Masterson called him the West's greatest gunfighter.

Thompson, John (AKA: **Kid**), an outlaw, twice robbed a train near Los Angeles, Calif., in December 1893 and February 1895 with a man named Johnson. He was imprisoned in Summer 1895.

Thompson, William (AKA: **Texas Billy**), a gunman and brother of Ben, engaged in several gunbattles with lawmen and ranchers in Kansas, Texas, and Nebraska. He was killed in Laredo, Texas.

Thurmond, Frank, a gunman, shot and killed Dan Baxter in August 1881 in Deming, N.M.

Tobin, Thomas, a famous frontiersman, gunman, and mountain man, was shot by Kit Carson's son, and died in 1902.

Todd, Captain **George W.**, an outlaw, fought along side Cole Younger in Bill Anderson's guerilla army and was killed after the war.

Towerly, William, an outlaw horse thief, who in less than a month killed two law officers and was himself shot dead by U.S. Marshal Bill Moody in December 1887.

Tracy, Harry, an outlaw who rode with the Hole-in-the-Wall Gang and Dave Merrill in Washington, killed Merrill during a prison escape and committed suicide in 1902.

Trentham, Charles, an outlaw and Texas Ranger, killed a man in Marfa, fled to New Mexico, and then to the Indian Territory.

Trujillo, Antonio Maria, an outlaw in New Mexico, was hanged for high treason on Feb. 18, 1883.

Trujillo, Julian, an outlaw, was one of Silva's White Caps.

Tucker, Jim, an outlaw and murderer, poisoned W.F. Fletcher and was shot and killed on May 20, 1882, in Pinos Altos, N.M., by Deputy Sheriff Henry Barton.

Tucker, Tom, a gunman in the Graham-Tewksbury feud in Arizona, joined Oliver Lee in his feud in Tularosa, N.M.

Turner, Ben, a gunman employed by the Horrell brothers in the Horrell-Higgins feud in the 1870s, was gunned down by angry citizens in December 1873.

Turner, Marion, a gunman in the Lincoln County War and deputy sheriff in Lincoln, was indicted with John Jones on July 19, 1878, for the murder of Alexander McSween.

U

Ulibarri, Francisco, an outlaw and Comanche Indian, Francisco Ulibarri was a member of Silva's White Caps.

Updyke, Dave, corrupt lawman turned stagecoach robber in and around the Idaho Territory. Hanged by vigilantes in April 1866.

Urieta, Leandro, an outlaw, was shot in Mesilla,

N.M., on Nov. 2, 1877, by Sheriff Mariano Barela.

Utter, Charles (AKA: **Sentimental Charley; Colorado Charley**), a gunman, friend, and cohort of Bill Hickok, made Hickok's tombstone and dealt cards at Socorro, N.M., and El Paso, Texas.

V

Valdez, Antonio Jose (AKA: **El Patas de Rana**), an outlaw and member of Silva's White Caps, shot Vicente Silva in the back and was jailed. He was later appointed Marshal of Wagon Mound.

Valley, Frank, a gunman and cowboy on the LS ranch in Tascosa, Texas, was killed by Len Woodruff in 1886.

Varela, Marcos, an outlaw and member of Silva's White Caps and a nephew of Vicente Silva.

Vasquez, Tiburcio, a notorious California outlaw and murderer, was captured and hanged in San Jose, Calif., in 1875.

Vega, Cruz, an outlaw, was lynched by a mob in Cimarron, N.M., on Oct. 30, 1875, for allegedly murdering Reverend T.J. Tolby.

Vialpando, J.M. was an outlaw member of Silva's White Caps.

Vialpando, Juan de Dios, an outlaw and member of Silva's White Caps, killed two men and was hanged on Nov. 19, 1895, in Santa Fe.

W

Wade, "Kid", an outlaw and horse thief in northern Nebraska and the Dakotas, rode with Doc Middleton, and later formed his own gang. The Kid was lynched in February 1884 at Bassett, Neb.

Waightman, George (**Weightman**, AKA: **Red Buck**), an outlaw and member of the Doolin gang, was captured and imprisoned by Heck Thomas in 1889. Waightman was killed in a gunfight with lawmen near Arapaho, Okla., on Oct. 2, 1895.

Wait, Frederick T. (AKA: **Dash Wait**), a gunman and a quarter-blood Cherokee Indian, was employed by John Tunstall in the Lincoln County War, riding with outlaw Billy the Kid as a "Regulator." Wait died in 1895 at the age of forty-two in Indian Territory.

Wakefield, E.H., a gunman in the Lincoln County War, rode with the posse that killed John Tunstall on Feb. 18, 1878.

Walker, Joe, an outlaw, rustled cattle with the Robbers Roost outlaws in Utah, and robbed banks with Butch Cassidy and the Wild Bunch before a posse shot him to death in May 1898 at Thompson.

Walker, Thomas J., a gunman, shot and killed Albert Kjellstrom in January 1885 in Socorro, N.M.

Walker, William, a gunman and mercenary commander, attempted to conquer the western section of Mexico, led a private army to Nicaragua in 1855, became president of Nicaragua in 1857, and was captured and executed in Trujillo, Honduras, on Sept. 12, 1860.

Walker, William, an outlaw and alleged leader of the "Bald Knobbers," a gang of over 400 members, was hanged in May 1889 at Ozark, Mo.

Wall, William, an outlaw, was a member of the Wild Bunch. He was imprisoned and then released on Jan. 11, 1900, with Matt Warner.

Wallace, Dan (AKA: **Texas Dan**), an outlaw, robbed and killed a rancher near San Antonio, Texas, and was captured in the late 1880s.

Wallace, William Alexander Anderson (AKA: **Bigfoot**), a gunman and Texas Ranger, fought Mexicans throughout the mid- and early 1800s to avenge the deaths of his brother and cousin. He rode shotgun on a Texas stage line, and died near Austin on Jan. 7, 1899.

Walrath, Charles G., an outlaw, shot and killed William Shook; hanged.

Walters, William E. (AKA: **Bill Anderson; Billy Brown; Bronco Bill**), an outlaw, rode with the Black Jack Ketchum gang in the late 1890s. Released from prison in 1917, he died a few years later.

Warderman, Bill, an outlaw, was a member of the Black Jack Ketchum gang.

Warner, M. (AKA: **Doc**), an outlaw, murdered Thomas Colligan on Feb. 20, 1883, near Rio Quemado, N.M.

Warner, Matt (**Willard Erastus Christianson,** AKA: **Morman Kid**), an outlaw, bank robber, and friend to Butch Cassidy and the Wild Bunch; after serving time for murder he became a justice of the peace and a deputy sheriff. He died in 1938 at age seventy-four.

Warren, James, a gunman, shot W.F. Markham on Sept. 2, 1886.

Washington, George, an outlaw, was lynched in June 1882 in Lincoln, N.M.

Waters, Buck was a gunman in the Lincoln County War.

Watson, Sam, a gunman and saloon keeper in Folsom, N.M., shot and killed a gambler named Fred Brown.

Watts, Henry, an outlaw and horse thief, was captured in June 1881 with Charlie Allison in Albuquerque, N.M.

Watts, John, an outlaw and rustler who was killed by the militia in New Mexico in March 1883.

Webb, Gilbert, an outlaw, arrested for complicity

in the robbery of an Army paymaster at Fort Thomas, Arizona, on May 11, 1889.

Webb, John Joshua (AKA: **Samuel King**), an outlaw, member of the Dodge City gang in Las Vegas, N.M., and city marshal of Las Vegas, murdered Michael Kelliher on Mar. 2, 1880, was condemned to hang, but escaped from jail with David Rudabaugh in 1881 and died of small pox the following year.

Webb, Wilfred, an outlaw, arrested for complicity in the robbery of an Army paymaster at Fort Thomas, on May 11, 1889.

Wells, Charles Knox Polk, an admitted outlaw and murderer, robbed banks and trains, and allegedly killed over thirty men including an uncle and a jailer. He was convicted of murder in May 1882 and received a life sentence.

Welsh, Tom, an outlaw, killed Joe Hickson in Good Hope, N.M., on Oct. 28, 1884.

Wesley, John (AKA: **Harry Hill**), a cowboy and outlaw, attempted to rob the Medicine Lodge Bank on Apr. 30, 1884, with Marshal Henry Brown and two others. Brown was killed attempting to escape a lynch mob.

West, Richard (AKA: **Little Dick**), an outlaw and member of the Doolin gang, was the last of the gang to die. He joined the Jennings gang and was killed in 1898 by lawman William Matthew Tilghman.

Whealington, Tom (AKA: **Red River Tom**), an outlaw, was shot and killed with Dick Rogers while attempting to break a friend out of jail in Springer, N.M., on Mar. 13, 1885.

Wheeler, Grant, an outlaw, robbed trains in the 1890s and was trailed by railroad detective William Breakenridge. He killed himself on Apr. 25, 1895, at Mancos, Colo., after he was wounded and cornered by lawmen.

Wheeler, James, an outlaw, shot and killed Adolph

Davidson in Chance City, N.M., in April 1886.

White, Ham, a murderer and stage robber on the road between San Antonio and Austin, Texas.

Whitley, William, an outlaw and member of Brack Cornett's gang, was killed on Sept. 25, 1888, at Floresville, Texas.

Wiggin, W., an outlaw, was lynched in San Marcial, N.M., in Sept. 1882.

Williams, Ben, a lawman who was involved in a shoot-out with fellow lawmen, Albert Fall and Joe Morgan, at Las Cruces, N.M., on Sept. 15, 1895.

Williams, Charles, an outlaw, was lynched near Harshaw, N.M., in November 1883.

Williams, Jess, an outlaw, was a member of the Black Jack Christian's gang.

Willis, Thomas, an outlaw, murdered W.P. Williams with the help of John Billee. Billee and Willis were captured by deputies Will Ayers, James Wilkerson, and Perry DuVall, and hanged on Jan. 16, 1890.

Wilson, Jim, an outlaw, shot and killed Dane Williams in Central City, N.M., on Mar. 20, 1886.

Wilson, William (AKA: **Buffalo Bill**), an outlaw and lawman, was arrested with Billy the Kid, served time in prison, received a pardon in 1896, and became sheriff of Terrell County, N.M. Wilson was killed in 1911.

Wilson, William, an outlaw, shot and killed Robert Casey in Lincoln, N.M., and was hanged twice on Dec. 10, 1875.

Wolcott, Frank, a gunman and mercenary commander, led an army of gunfighters and soldiers to quell the Johnson County War in April 1892. The U.S. army ended the war and the mercenaries were arrested and later acquitted.

Wolz, Charles, a gunman in Lincoln County, N.M.,

was part of the posse that shot and killed John Tunstall on Feb. 18, 1878.

Woodruff, Len, a cowboy and gunman, instigated a gunfight between LX and LS cowboys on Mar. 21, 1886, in Oldham County, Texas.

Worley, John, a lawman and outlaw, was deputy sheriff in Mason County and involved in the Hoodoo War in 1875. He was shot, stabbed, killed, and scalped by Scott Cooley to avenge Worley's part in the death of Tim Williamson.

Worthington, Nick, a New Mexico and Colorado outlaw, stole horses and killed several men before he was shot and killed by civilians in Cimarron, N.M., in June 1878.

Wyatt, Nathaniel Ellsworth (AKA: **Zip, Dick Yeager; Wild Charlie**), Oklahoma outlaw, stole livestock and robbed post offices before he was wounded, captured, and imprisoned in Enid, where he died from his wounds on Sept. 7, 1895.

Y

Yager, Erastus (AKA: **Red**), an outlaw and messenger for Sheriff Henry Plummer's gang, the Innocents, who later revealed the identities of Plummer and his gang. He was lynched in January 1864.

Young, Cole (AKA: **Cole Estes**), an outlaw and a member of the Black Jack Ketchum gang of Arizona and New Mexico, was killed by Marshal Loomis during a bank robbery in Nogales on Oct. 2, 1896.

Young, William, an outlaw, was hanged in March 1881 in Silver City, N.M.

Younger, James (Jim), an outlaw and member of the Younger gang, robbed banks and trains with his brothers Cole and Bob, and outlaws Jesse and Frank James. He was captured and imprisoned after the failed Northfield, Minn., bank raid on Sept. 21, 1876, and released on July 14, 1901. He killed himself in

October 1902.

Younger, John, an outlaw, and member of the Younger gang, was killed by Pinkerton detective Louis Lull in St. Clair County, Mo., in March 1874.

Younger, Robert (Bob), an outlaw, a member of the Younger gang, and youngest of the Younger brothers, was severely wounded in the 1876 Northfield raid. He was captured in Stillwater, Minn., and died of his wounds on Sept. 16, 1889.

Younger, Thomas Coleman (Cole), an outlaw, Younger brother, and leader of the Younger gang, was wounded and captured following the Northfield bank raid, and pardoned in July 1901. He died on Feb. 21, 1916.

Yountis, Oliver (AKA: Crescent Sam), an outlaw and member of the Doolin-Dalton gang, was killed by lawmen at his home near Orlando, Okla., by Chris Madsen after the gang's first bank robbery in 1892.

Z

Zamora, Francisco, a gunman for McSween in the Lincoln County War, was killed during the McSween gunbattle on July 19, 1878.

THE WILD WEST
IN PHOTOS & ILLUSTRATIONS

Abilene, Kan.:

In the days of Wild Bill Hickok, Abilene saw shootings almost daily, such as the wild gunfight (right) in a local bar when one gunmen refused the drink of another, or drunken cowboys flavoring their fun by riding atop pool tables (below).

Amarillo, Texas:

The fate that befell mashers on the Texas & Pacific line near Amarillo, according to the *Police Gazette*.

Austin, Texas:

A teeming street in Austin in the 1870s; at the left of the restaurant is Ben Thompson's saloon.

Bannack, Mont.:

Three bandits who robbed the Adams Express car in a passenger train near Bannack were rounded up by vigilantes and promptly hanged, a fate that became all too familiar in the lawless West when citizens, angered over vacilating courts, meted out their own brand of swift and self-satisfying justice.

Bear River, Wyo.:

Down this hardscrabble main street, the fearless lawman "Bear River Tom" Smith earned his reputation as a peacemaker who would not back down from any gunslinger.

Billings, Mont.:

On Saturday night, the cowboys and scarlet ladies of every saloon in Billings performed impossible dances atop bars, tables and, in the instance shown below, upon a baby grand piano, much to the consternation of the piano player.

Billy the Kid:

The legendary gunfighter and killer became a mythical figure in the West during his own time. He is shown below at Stinking Springs where Pat Garrett and a strong posse captured the Kid and his men, and at right (top) shooting deputy Bob Olinger when escaping jail in Lincoln, N.M., and at right (bottom) being killed by Garrett in a dark bedroom at the Maxwell Ranch.

Black Bart:

California bandit Black Bart, shown at left robbing a stage, robbed alone and wore socks over his boots so he could not be tracked; his real name was Charles E. Boles, shown bottom left, a gentleman outlaw who enjoyed writing bits of doggeral (bottom right) which he left in empty strongboxes to vex pursuing possemen.

ARREST. STAGE ROBBER.

☞ These Circulars are for the use of Officers and Discreet Persons only. ☜

About one o'clock P. M. on the 3d of August, 1877, the down stage between Fort Ross and Russian River, was stopped by a man in disguise, who took from Wells, Fargo & Co.'s express box about $300 in coin and a check for $205 32, on Granger's Bank, San Francisco, in favor of Fisk Bros. On one of the way-bills left with the box, the robber wrote as follows :

I've labored long and hard for bread—
For honor and for riches—
But on my corns too long you've trod,
You fine haired sons of bitches.
BLACK BART, the Poet.

Driver, give my respects to our friend, the other driver; but I really had a notion to hang my old disguise hat on his weather eye.

Respectfully
B. B

It is believed that he went into the Town of Guernieville about daylight next morning.

———

About three o'clock P. M , July 25th, 1878, the down stage from Quincy, Plumas Co., to Oroville, Butte Co., was stopped by one masked man, and from Wells, Fargo & Co.'s box taken $379 coin, one diamond ring said to be worth $200, and one silver watch valued at $25. In the box, when found next day, was the following [Fac simile.]

here I lay me down to sleep
to wait the coming morrow
perhaps success perhaps defeat
And everlasting sorrow
I've labored long and hard for bread
for honor and for riches
But on my corns too long you've trod
You fine haired sons of bitches
let come what will I'll try it on
My condition can't be worse
and if there's money in that Box
Tis munny in my purse

Black Bart
the Po8

About eight o'clock A. M. of July 30th, 1878, the down stage from La Porte to Oroville was robbed by one man, who took from express box a package of gold specimens valued at $50, silver watch No. 716,996, P. S. Bartlett, maker.

It is certain the first two of these crimes were done by the same man, and there are good reasons to believe that he did the three.

There is a liberal reward offered by the State, and Wells, Fargo & Co. for the arrest and conviction of such offenders. For particulars, see Wells, Fargo & Co.'s "Standing Reward" Posters of July 1st, 1876.

It will be seen from the above that this fellow is a character that would be remembered as a scribbler and something of a wit or wag, and would be likely to leave specimens of his handwriting on hotel registers and other public places.

If arrested, telegraph the undersigned at Sacramento. Any information thankfully received.

J. B. HUME, Special Officer Wells, Fargo & Co.

Bodie, Calif.:

One of the worst hell-holes of the Old West, Bodie boasted impromptu gunfights or death threats at any hour, such as when a pool player took someone else's turn (shown at left top), or a mountain man insisting at gunpoint he receive a drink in payment for a human ear he had recently sliced from an opponent (see left, bottom left), or a street gunfight which erupted because a man stepped on a cowboy's toe (see left, bottom right). Bodie's females were equally fierce; at left a school teacher horsewhips a local physician for gossiping about her, and bottom, the notorious female cardsharp, Madame Moustache, is shown fighting off two thieves after her night's winnings; she killed one and wounded the other.

Broken Bow, Neb.:

Left, a Burlington train near Broken Bow being robbed by bandits so un-chivalrous as to take the wallets and valuables of passengers, including female travelers.

Brown's Hole, Wyo.:

Ison Dart, left, one of the few black gun-slingers of the Old West, was killed near Brown's Hole by the feared stock detective and bounty hunter Tom Horn.

Butte, Mont.:

Below, armed police in Butte are shown emptying a bordello on notorious Galena Street and being threatened by incensed brothel customers deprived of their female companions.

Calamity Jane:

The most publicized woman of the Old West, Calamity Jane, shown left in buckskins as a cavalry scout, was little more than a camp follower of gunmen, a one-time bordello tart and, in later years, a hopeless alcoholic. Posters of her, such as that at top right, did much to promote a fame she never earned, especially her non-existent love affair with James Butler "Wild Bill" Hickok; she is shown in old age at Hickok's grave in Tombstone where, upon her deathbed insistence, she was finally buried, lying through eternity next to a man who hardly knew her in life.

California Gold Camps:

Law and lawmen did not exist in the wild California gold camps, which caused gold hunters to protect their wives and homes with guns, such as the miner at left, shooting a would-be rapist attacking his wife.

Cherry Creek, Colo.:

Vigilantes attacking a man *suspected* of bank robbery in Cherry Creek, a town where no one took any chances.

Cheyenne, Wyo.:

Cheyenne, shown top left in the mid-1870s, was a gambler's paradise, but woe to the cardsharp who cheated. At left bottom, a lady card player accuses a dealer of using marked cards, and below, noted card cheat George Devol, seated left, is confronted by Wild Bill Hickok and his deadly six-gun after Devol dealt from the bottom.

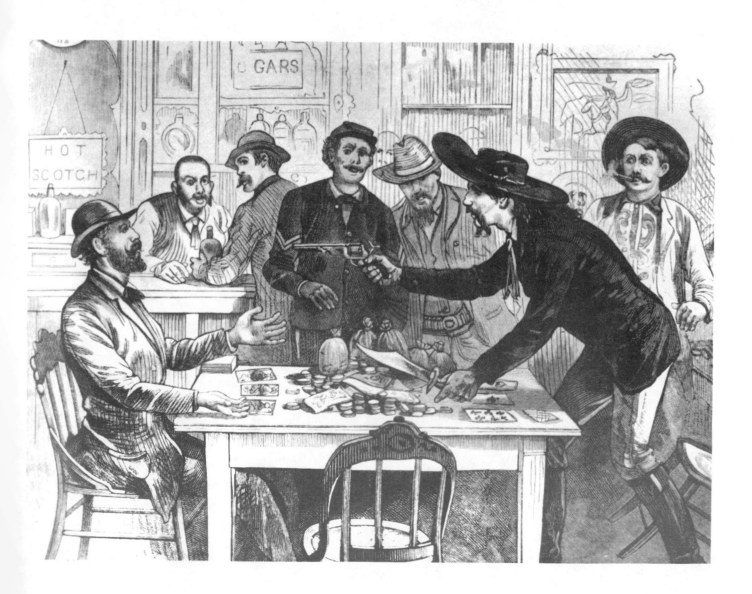

Chinese Riots:

With the great Chinese migration to the West Coast following the Civil War rose intense racist hatreds which burst forth in riots against these hapless Orientals; at left thugs attack Chinese coolies in Denver's Chinatown, beating them and cutting off their pigtails. At right, Chinese immigrants are attacked in downtown Denver by angry crowds fearing loss of jobs. In San Francisco, below, a coolie is murdered and mutilated by white workers.

Circleville, Utah:

The peaceful homestead at right is the birthplace of one of the West's most celebrated bandits, Butch Cassidy, born Robert Leroy Parker, who led the Wild Bunch on numerous train robberies.

Coffeyville, Kan.:

The Dalton Brothers played in Coffeyville as small boys; they returned to their home town as fierce bandits in 1892 to rob two banks, but those citizens who once had repaired the boys' shoes and sold them candy shot them to pieces. At left is the only survivor of the disastrous raid, Emmett Dalton; on opposite page, top, is one of the shot-up banks the Daltons invaded, and, bottom, the dead bodies of (clockwise from bottom) Bob Dalton, Bill Powers, Dick Broadwell, and Grat Dalton.

Colfax County, N.M.:

In the after-dinner duel between the homicidal gunman, Clay Allison (left), and Chunk Colbert, who reportedly invited Allison to dinner, Colbert chatted amiably through the meal and then drew on his guest, his gun barely clearing the tabletop before quick-draw Allison shot him dead.

Colorado City, Colo.:

Paris-born Eleanor Dumont, a celebrated cardsmith also known as Minnie the Gambler, tolerated no quick deals. She is shown, bottom left, taking a horsewhip to a dealer whom she caught slipping a cold deck to her sweetheart and fellow gambler, Charlie Utter (shown hand up, mildly protesting the attack).

Copperas Cove, Texas:

An artist of the *Police News* captures the agonizing death of horse thief Thomas Polk at the hands of citizens of Copperas Cove, a town that has long since vanished from the Texas map.

Cripple Creek, Colo.:

A hotel clerk in Cripple Creek insists that a group of vaga-
bounds and loafers pay for their rooms before departing;
note the man at left immediately depositing his pocket watch
in payment. Men were shot for less in Cripple Creek, one
hapless cowboy being riddled with bullets after refusing to
pay for a shot of whiskey.

Davenport, Wash.:

August 6, 1902: Harry Tracy, last of the Wild Bunch riders, had escaped from prison and was trapped on a ranch, top, by possemen, shooting it out to the last bullet which he saved for himself; his body is shown above, still clutching his six-gun, and was later placed on display, below.

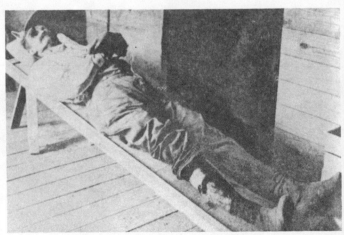

Deadwood, S.D.:

Below, outside of Deadwood, the town where Wild Bill Hickok was shot in the back while playing cards, a lone bandit is shown forcing a passenger of a stagecoach to play poker for his wallet while other passengers, with sacks tied over their heads, wait their turns to be fleeced.

Deer Lodge, Mont.:

A cowboy evangelist, angered over a snoring parishioner, fires a bullet above the head of the dozing man in Deer Lodge, where there was little rest for the weary and wicked.

Delta, Colo.:

Two outlaws, recently slain in an abortive hold-up, are shown in death; posing dead bandits and gunmen before the ancient cameras of the West was not only popular but profitable; this photo was sold for a dozen years at $1 a copy, a hefty price in those days for such a gruesome souvenir.

Deming, Ariz.:

Bandits terrifying members of a railroad crew in Deming; the crewmember at right is being ordered to throw a switch which will send the oncoming express onto a siding where it will become easy prey to the outlaws. So many trains were robbed between 1865 and 1900 that railroads could not hire enough detectives to track down the robbers.

Denver, Colo.:

Below, lady gambler Madame Vestel encounters vigilantes who have slain bandits that were once her customers at the poker table. While one of Madame's girls weeps over a fallen lover, the lady gambler pleads vainly for the life of the outlaw being lynched at right. Opposite page, top, Denver females riding the stage from Denver to Idaho Springs fight off a masked bandit; at bottom, outlaw Frank Williams (seated) is arrested while lounging in Denver's rail station.

Dodge City, Kan.:

One of the wildest towns of the Wild West, Dodge City was lawless and lusty, its citizens shunning reform and refinement. Opposite page, top, a group of masked rowdies, one even disguised as an Indian, hold a temperance leader at gunpoint while they busily burn his books and pamphlets; at bottom, a view of roughshod Front Street, scene of many a shootout. Below, the most celebrated Dodge City courtesan, Dora Hand, captivates her drunken admirers while she toasts the "Queen of the Cowtowns." She was later killed accidentally by Spike Kennedy, a cowboy who loved her.

Dodge City, Kan.:

At left, Dodge City mayor James H. "Dog" Kelley, and, bottom, one of the greatest group of lawmen ever gathered in the Old West: seated (left to right), Charles E. Bassett, Wyatt Earp, M. C. Clark, Neil Brown; standing (left to right) W. H. Harris, Luke Short, Bat Masterson. Opposite page, top, the celebrated Long Branch saloon, the scene of the infamous shoot-out between Levi Richardson and Cock-Eyed Frank Loving; below, Chalk Beeson, owner of the Long Branch, a man who loved peace but found only violence and gun smoke.

Ellsworth, Kan.:

Ellsworth was a town packed with drunken cowboys who delighted in terrorizing local residents such as the merchant below, forced to dance inside a circle of bullets until the arrival of Wyatt Earp and other intrepid lawmen who stripped the gunmen of their weapons and locked them up or shot them down.

El Paso, Texas:

El Paso was a tough bordertown where gunfights were common and lawmen did not live long enough to retire. Two of the town's most celebrated peace-makers, El Paso chief of police Jeff Milton and U.S. Deputy Marshal George Scarborough, shown top right, were the exceptions. At right is the first floor bar of the famous Gem Saloon. The upstairs gambling den was robbed by the famous outlaw, John Wesley Hardin. Below, right, an artist's sketch shows how Hardin (the man beneath the lamp) was shot in the back by John Selman while the notorious gunman was shooting dice in the Acme Saloon.

Eureka, Calif.:

The most shocking shootout in Eureka's history occurred when the top gambler in town, Gus Botto (shown lying on the floor), was gunned down by rival cardsharp Jesse Bigelow (in the vest), shown fending off Botto's many friends, explaining that he had been forced to shoot Botto when the gambler demanded his free tickets to the opera house.

Feather River, Calif.:

The gold camps on Feather River were wild places where villains and outlaws ran rampant. At right a heroic pioneer woman shoots a would-be rapist. Below, left, vigilantes storm the local saloon to drag out three bandits (shown below, right), dangling a short time later from a river bridge.

Fort Benton, Mont.:

The cowboy who insisted upon riding his horse to his room in the Grand Union Hotel exchanged gunfire with the manager and others, and lost; the horseman was killed before reaching the top of the stairs and fourteen .44 slugs were later dug out of his body.

Fort Scott, Kan.:

Captain Sam Walker, shown holding pistol, center right, arrests a gang of border ruffians in 1858 during a racially troubled era.

Fort Sill, Okla.:

Geronimo, the once fierce Apache warrior chief, is shown menacing the camera, gun in hand; the old chief was by then little more than a side show for the few tourists visiting the reservation. Geronimo sold this photo of himself for 10 cents a copy to curious easterners.

Fort Smith, Ark.:

Above, sitting in ominous shadows with many of his homemade ropes on display and clippings of his executions adorning the wall of his office, is George Maledon, the official hangman for Judge Isaac Parker at Fort Smith. He executed more than eighty outlaws and had no regrets. Upon his retirement, Maledon toured small town America, detailing to open-mouthed citizens how he had gladly "sent damned sinners to hell."

Fort Worth, Texas:

A haven for outlaws and bandits in the late 1890s, Fort Worth's most notorious madam was Fannie Porter, shown right, whose luxurious brothel was home to the infamous Wild Bunch. Below, the most notorious members of the Wild Bunch pose for a Fort Worth photographer: seated (left to right), Harry Longbaugh (The Sundance Kid), Ben Kilpatrick (The Tall Texan), and Robert Leroy Parker (Butch Cassidy); standing, William Carver and the deadly Harvey Logan, also known as Kid Curry.

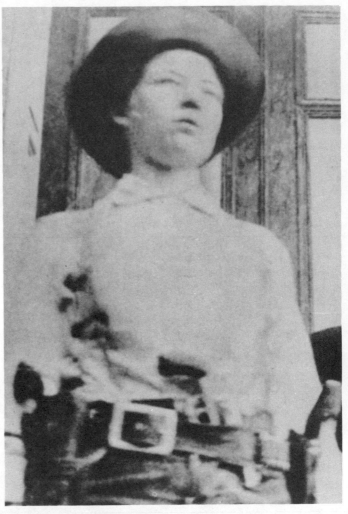

Hanksville, Utah:

The above photo was taken of a 17-year-old cowhand working for the Gibbons Ranch in 1883; he was Robert Leroy Parker who would go on to become the notorious bandit, Butch Cassidy.

Pearl Hart:

Female bandit Pearl Hart, above, was the last person to rob a stagecoach in the Old West; left, Hart holding rifle on passengers, and partner Joe Boot loot the Globe stage in 1899.

Hays City, Kan.:

Two U.S. cavalrymen lay dead outside of a Hays City dancehall, c.1880, killed in a drunken brawl only hours earlier. The town was one of the deadliest in Kansas, where even tough sheriffs like Wyatt Earp and Bat Masterson had trouble keeping order.

Helena, Mont.:

Opposite page, top: standing at left, cigar in mouth, in this Helena saloon is outlaw Lonny Logan, brother of Harvey Logan, the infamous Kid Curry; opposite page, bottom, Helena in 1869. Below, a Helena woman and her friends attack the local barber for spreading gossip about the woman's virtue, a painful custom in Helena where loose lips brought out the horsewhips.

Holbrook, Ariz.:

At left is one of the toughest lawmen in the West, Sheriff Commodore Perry Owens, who in 1887 single-handedly faced a lethal family of horse thieves, killing three and wounding the fourth. Owens came out unscathed.

Hole-in-the-Wall:

Next page, top, the trail leading into the remote outlaw haven known as Hole-in-the-Wall where members of the Wild Bunch hid from the law. Below, in this remote area, shielded by canyon walls, Butch Cassidy, the Sundance Kid, Bill Carver, Kid Curry, Ben Kilpatrick and others planned their daring robberies. The bandits would ride from this hideout to commit their bank and train robberies and then scurry back through narrow rocky passageways to elude posses that never seemed to find the way into Hole-in-the-Wall. The hideout is located where the Wyoming, Utah, and Colorado state lines join together.

Indian Territory (Okla.-Ark.):

On the left is the legendary peacemaker, Bill Tilghman (pronounced Tyman), shown in his youth with another lawman. Tilghman was responsible for tracking down scores of outlaws, including members of the notorious Bill Doolin gang. He never used his weapons unless necessary, and was known to those he pursued as a fair and honest man. Opposite page, top, celebrated lawyer and gunman, Temple Houston (third from left), bareheaded, rests with possemen during the pursuit of an outlaw gang in the Indian Territory; below, vigilantes hold three horse thieves (at left) while a posse member climbs a telegraph pole to tie the ropes that will take the lives of the outlaws.

Indian Territory:

From the 1880s to the turn of the century the Indian Territory was a haven for the worst outlaws of the Old West, including such bandits as Dan Clifton (left), better known as Dynamite Dick, staunch member of the Doolin Gang. Below, two other members of the Doolin bunch, Charley Pierce and George "Bitter Creek" Newcomb, lying dead, July 1895, shot by bounty hunters. At bottom is the venerable lawman, Bill Tilghman, posing in old age with his trusty Winchester.

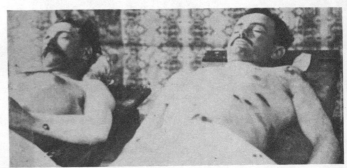

Jesse James:

The most celebrated bandit in western history, Jesse James, is shown at right, circa 1879, bearded, famous, and lethal. His reputation was so great that bank tellers and train guards quaked at the sound of his name. He reveled in his notoriety and even wrote his own press release about a robbery he had committed, handing it to the engineer of a train before riding away with his men. James was no cavalier, however, but a murderous thief, as shown below where Jesse (center) shoots a helpless cashier during a bank robbery. He had already shot and killed the bank president, shown dead on the floor.

Jesse James:

Left, James is shown pointing his pistol squarely at the head of a terrified express car guard while his men round up the train crew during one of his many train robberies; below, Jesse (left) takes a train passenger's wallet and watch. Opposite page, top, the James gang is shown robbing a stagecoach, and, bottom, telling campfire tales at their Missouri hideout.

Jesse James:

The disastrous raid on Northfield, Minn., in 1876 is shown above; the citizens shot the James gang to pieces; left, Jesse being killed by Bob and Charlie Ford; below, Jesse in death. Opposite page, top left, Jesse's coffin being taken to its gravesite; top right, members of the James' family hear gang members vow revenge for Jesse's assassination; and below, Jesse's personal effects being auctioned; at bottom, both columns, the typical dime novel publications that exploited the James legend.

457

THE MAN ON THE BLACK HORSE:
OR,
The James Boys' First Ride in Missouri.
By D. W. STEVENS.

Johnson County War:

The Johnson County War in Wyoming raged from 1889 to 1892 and took hundreds of lives, mostly those in the farming and small ranching communities, deaths brought about by gunmen hired by the cattle barons to maintain control of the plains. Small rancher and gunman Nate Champion is shown below, left; he stood up to the cattle kings and was shot to death.

Kid Curry:

The deadliest gunman of the West in the 1890s was Harvey Logan, known as Kid Curry. He is shown at left with mistress Laura Bullion. At bottom left, Curry's hands reach through the bars of his cell to loop a rope around an unsuspecting guard in one of his many escapes. Below right, Curry is shown disguised as a tramp, a photo taken only hours after his capture; at bottom right, Curry is shown in two death poses; he killed himself when the posse closed in on him.

Laramie, Wyo.:

The saloons in Laramie were places of danger and havoc; at left, a wild fight ensues when a visitor refuses to buy a round of drinks for the local barflys; below, masked terrorists lynch and rape hapless Chinese workers in Laramie during the anti-Chinese riots.

Lawrence, Kan.:

The massacre at Lawrence, Kan., on Aug. 21, 1863, tainted the cause of the Confederacy during the Civil War in that it was conducted by Confederate guerrillas under the command of the ruthless killer and outlaw, William Clarke Quantrill. His raiders slaughtered 185 defenseless men and boys, and wounded scores more before looting and torching the town. Quantrill and his men fled at the sound of approaching Union troops and many, including the infamous leader, were later tracked down and killed. It was while riding with Quantrill that Frank and Jesse James learned the methods of gunmanship and murder.

Leadville (Dakota Territory):

Leadville thronged with gunmen and thieves during the 1870s; below, left, stagecoach bandits outside Leadville are shown robbing passengers; bottom left, a typical shootout between lawmen and bandits; right, Wild Bill Raymond, a Leadville gunman, poses with a .44-caliber pistol in hand; his other holstered pistol indicates that he was a cross-draw pistoleer.

Lewiston, Mont.:

Below, diminutive Billy Calder, a gunman convicted of a double murder, is about to be hanged on a crudely constructed gallows; he stands on planks, beneath which is a deep hole. The planking will be yanked away by the rope attached to it, and Calder will plummet downward into a hole that will serve as his grave. Such were the utilitarian ways of the West.

Lincoln, Neb.:

Below, armed cowboys hiding their faces beneath crude masks were photographed outside of Lincoln cutting a farmer's barbed wire at the orders of their cattle baron boss. Wire penned in the range and led to bloody range wars for thirty years across the plains states.

Lincoln County, N.M.:

In a *Police Gazette* sketch, Billy the Kid is shown killing a saloon owner; the man had the nerve to pull a gun after drinking with the Kid. Although no record exists of such a killing, the portrait is in keeping with the Kid's ruthless character; the boy gunman thrilled to the smell of his own gunsmoke and murdered with alarming regularity, claiming twenty-one lives before his death at age twenty-one.

Marshall, Texas:

A drunken gunman objecting to the presence of an eastern troupe of actors is shown fatally shooting actor Benjamin C. Porter to death while Maurice Barrymore, father of John, Ethel, and Lionel, tries to fend off the attack which occurred in the depot restaurant of the Texas and Pacific Railroad.

Miles City, Kan.:

Hatred for foreigners was deep-rooted in the West; here cowboys attack visiting British travelers simply because the "cut of their clothes" was strange and their accents odd.

Missoula, Mont.:

Cowboys terrorize Chinese coolies who worked for the railroad by chasing them through Missoula's streets; they would tie up the hapless Chinese and then cut their pigtails, strip them and often shoot off their toes and fingers to prevent them from taking jobs from white laborers. Opposite page, top, a Missoula minister is ordered out of town, and, bottom, passengers in a snow sled are robbed of their valuables by masked bandits.

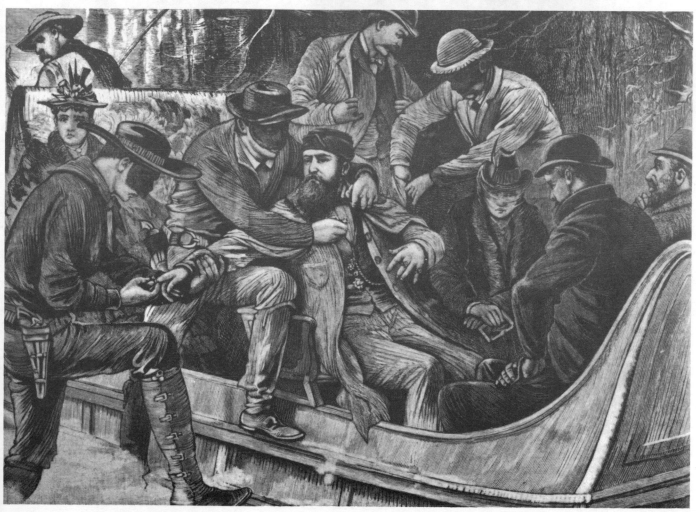

Mountain Meadow Massacre (Utah):

Sketches on the page opposite show the horrific Mountain Meadow Massacre of September 1857 and the slaying of 140 immigrants of a pioneer wagon train. The bloody massacre was led by renegade Mormon bishop John D. Lee, who at first told the immigrants that if they surrendered to him and his men, giving up their gold and property, they would be spared. When the immigrants surrendered, Lee ordered them all killed. It took twenty years before Lee was identified as the instigator of the massacre. After two trials, he was convicted and condemned to death. Lee is shown, top right, writing his memoirs while awaiting execution; middle right, in his coffin; and, bottom, being shot by a firing squad hidden behind a tent wall on March 23, 1877, at Salt Lake City, Utah. The executioners insisted upon anonymity, believing the Mormons would take vengeance on them if their identities were known.

Joaquin Murieta

Known as the "Robin Hood of the El Dorado," Mexican bandit Joaquin Murieta was a mysterious legend in his own time, a daring, dashing bandit—some said murderous and ruthless—who raided throughout the San Joaquin and Sacramento Valleys of California until enormous posses tracked him and his band down, decapitating the bandit and displaying his severed head; at left a posse battles Murieta's men near Marysville; below, Murieta in a heroic pose before Sonoran immigrants after subduing a cruel landowner.

New Albany, Ind.:

The Reno Brothers robbed the first train in American history at Marshfield, Ind., on May 12, 1868, but the gang was rounded up and jailed in the small prison at left in New Albany; below, on the night of Dec. 12, 1868, vigilantes broke into the jail and removed the Renos and hanged them one by one, firing bullets into each bandit as they jerked at rope's end.

Panamint, Calif.:

Few towns in the Gold Rush days equalled Panamint in wild revelry and lethal shootouts; below, a gunman named Jones is shot to death in the Dexter tent saloon while in the act of trying to sell his six-gun to a money-lender; unarmed, he was vulnerable to those who would kill him for his boots and hat.

Pecos, Texas:

Above, a Pecos saloon with gambling table in full operation; the man in the white hat seated next to the waiter in the apron is Jim "The Killer" Miller, one of the most feared assassins in the West, a ruthless killer-for-hire who reportedly shot and killed famed lawman Pat Garrett from ambush. Miller was later hanged with a group of Oklahoma cattlemen who conspired to kill a cattle baron to obtain his land.

Pinto, Ariz.:

A cowboy brought into court on a charge of disorderly conduct, responds angrily to the verdict, threatening both the rural judge and the cavalry officer who arrested him.

Henry Plummer:

A dramatic artist's sketch shows a small army of masked Montana vigilantes returning home after peforming their gruesome chore, leaving the notorious sheriff-turned-outlaw Henry Plummer dangling from a tree limb; Plummer, in reality, was hanged on a gallows that he himself helped to build, on Jan. 10, 1864.

Prescott, Ariz.:

No place in unsettled Arizona was safe in the 1880s, not even a court of law; here a man accused of murder is about to stab to death the chief witness against him following his damning testimony. Such conduct was not the exception but the norm.

Redlodge, Idaho:

Left, the *Police News* offered this sketch to illustrate how domestic quarrels were solved in rural Idaho; miner John Gump and his wife argued violently and settled the matter outside their tent in a duel to the death. The outcome was not stated.

Robber's Roost:

High on the San Rafael Swell plateau in Wayne County, Utah, was Robber's Roost, shown below, which served as a hideout for much-wanted outlaws such as the McCarty brothers, Butch Cassidy, and other members of the notorious Wild Bunch.

St. Louis, Mo.:

Any editor who wrote the truth about the wheeler-dealer land and cattle barons of the West risked his life; at right an editor who has exposed the crooked operations of a land magnate reaches for a gun to defend himself against the attack of the real estate baron while, below, a crowd gathers outside at the sound of gunshots.

San Antonio, Texas:

Left, the roaring cowtown of San Antonio in 1876, showing the pride of the town, Hord's Hotel, a four-story resort where the sheets where changed once a week; below, the Variety Theater where gunfighters Ben Thompson and John King Fisher were shot to death while watching a comedy on the second floor in 1884.

San Francisco, Calif.:

Rival newspapermen in San Francisco settled their grievances as did the gunslingers of the cowtowns; below, James Casey shoots James King, editor of the *Bulletin*, over a recent editorial. This sensational shooting caused Casey to be jailed; he was later dragged from his cell by members of the San Francisco Vigilance Committee and lynched.

San Francisco, Calif.:

In the turbulent 1850s, San Francisco residents resorted to the gun rather than reason; opposite page, top, a defiant broker is threatened with death after the value of Comstock shares declined; opposite, bottom, a typical scene of mayhem in a brothel. Right, top, the violent Sydney Ducks gang (former prisoners from the penal colony in Sydney, Australia) battling gold seekers in a tent city outside of town; right, center, fires set by the Sydney Ducks along San Francisco's waterfront; bottom, right, vigilantes erecting makeshift gallows to combat the wild crime wave.

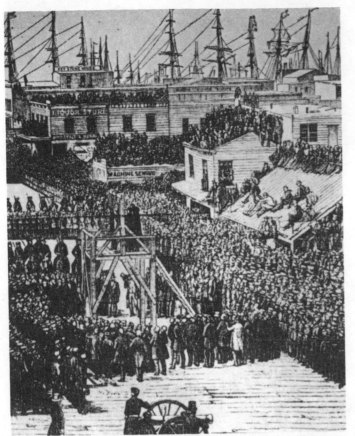

San Francisco, Calif.:

The sprawling, teeming town became so lawless in the mid-1850s that the only force that could overcome the gangs, thugs, and crooks was the Vigilance Committee, which took matters into its own hands and began to round up bandits and killers, summarily hanging them after quick trials (and sometimes with no trials at all); at left, thousands gather to see outlaws Hetherington and Brace go to the gallows on July 29, 1856; below, fires rage through the Barbary Coast, set by a gang called the Hounds so that its members could freely loot the burning buildings quickly evacuated by terrified residents; opposite page, top, armed vigilantes are shown erecting a gallows upon which to hang San Francisco's killers; opposite page, bottom, another view of the execution of Hetherington and Brace.

Belle Starr:

The most notorious female of the Old West was Belle Starr, who, like Calamity Jane, promoted her own image as a daring lady bandit, although she confined her thieving to stray horses and occasional cattle rustling; she is best remembered as a consort of outlaws, having had torrid affairs with such notorious men as Cole Younger of the James-Younger band and other fearsome gunmen including Sam Starr, Jim July, and Blue Duck. She

is shown below in an outlaw hideout in Sarcoxie, Mo., her dinner interrupted by raiders who fatally shot her brother, Ed Shirley, a renegade. It was this incident that allegedly set Belle on the outlaw trail. Opposite page, top left, Belle in her early twenties, bottom left, a reward poster for Sam and Belle Starr; top right, Belle posing as a lady bandit in her later years; and bottom, right, Belle being shot and killed from ambush by an unknown killer.

REWARD
☞ **$10,000** ☜
IN GOLD COIN
*Will be paid by the U. S. Government
for the apprehension*
DEAD OR ALIVE
of
SAM and BELLE STARR

*Wanted for Robbery, Murder, Treason
and other acts against the peace
and dignity of the U. S.*

THOMAS CRAIL
Major, 8th Missouri Cavalry, Commanding

Stroud, Okla.:

The last important outlaw in Oklahoma, Henry Starr, left, was the first bandit to use a car in a bank robbery; above, the People's Bank in Stroud, robbed by Starr and his men on March 27, 1915; Starr would survive many shootouts, only to be killed in 1921 while robbing another bank.

Tipton, Wyo.:

The Wild Bunch, led by Butch Cassidy, stopped a Union Pacific flyer near Tipton on Aug. 29, 1900, and blew off the locked door of the express car, below, wrecking the entire car; at left is the posse riding a fast train before pursuing the Wild Bunch on horseback for this robbery.

Tombstone, Ariz.:

The wildest town of the Wild West in the late 1870s
was Tombstone where gunfights, murder, and robbery
were daily occurences. Until the arrival of the Earp
brothers, Tombstone's law was hit-and-miss, with
the outlaw and bandit reigning supreme. Below, left,
a group of drunken cowboys insist a bartender buy
a round for a skeleton found on the desert; below,
right, Tombstone cowboys abusing Chinese coolies;
bottom, left, Lampasas Jake, the Cowboy Evangelist,
threatens a saloon congregation with bullets while
ordering them to their knees to pray; bottom, right,
bandits terrorizing a visiting eastern dude.

Tombstone, Ariz.:

Opposite page, top, the "fashionable" Cosmopolitan Hotel, where Doc Holliday lived with Big Nose Kate Fisher; opposite page, bottom, angry patrons displeased with the show, threaten the manager of Tombstone's Birdcage Theater; this page, top, the celebrated gunfight between the Earp and Clanton-McLowery factions at the O.K. Corral; and, bottom, visiting Englishmen are abused by Tombstone cowboys who deride the visitors' attire.

Topeka, Kan.:

Topeka was the scene of many a gun battle, but the most bizarre incident occurred in the Kansas House of Representatives where Boston Corbett, the reported killer of John Wilkes Booth, Lincoln's assassin, ran amuck. Corbett (shown below as a special officer in the assembly) threatened to kill several state congressmen for stalling legislation; he finally surrendered his weapon without shooting anyone and was sent to a lunatic asylum.

Tucson, Ariz.:

Bandits in the 1870s and 1880s plagued the trains of
the Southern Pacific, particularly near Tuscon; below,
a bandit gang has stopped a flyer, forcing the brakeman, kneeling, to light a stick of dynamite to threaten
the express car guard into opening the door to the
car.

Virginia City, Nev.:

Gamblers in Virginia City took their losses seriously; left, a heavy loser ends his life after exhausting his funds at faro; below, bold bandits ride into the Old Montana Club to rob the roulette table; opposite page, top, a train is robbed outside of Virginia City but retribution is swift; the bandits meet their fate in a quick lynching by vigilantes, shown below.

Cattle Kate Watson:

The legendary Cattle Kate rustled Wyoming cattle with her lover Jim Averill until cattle barons ordered their executions; in the montage below, Cattle Kate and Averill are dragged from their ranch house and taken to a remote spot and hanged; opposite page, top left, Cattle Kate in a sketch about a year before her death; top right, a graphic illustration of the lynching of Kate and Averill; bottom, the cottonwood tree from which the rustlers were hanged.

Wichita, Kan.:

Wichita was a wild cowboy town for twenty years, one
that even Wyatt Earp found difficult to tame; below,
on a typical Saturday night, a gang of gunmen ride
past a Wichita saloon, firing at other gunslingers who
have stepped outside to "have some fun."

Women of the West:

Calamity Jane (Martha Jane Canary), below, a marvelous fraud, dressed in buckskin and told one and all she had been a scout for General Custer and that Wild Bill Hickok had secretly married her before his untimely death in Leadville; Calamity insisted upon being buried next to Hickok, a wish that was granted.

Laura Bullion, above, was a consort of outlaws, a mistress to many members of the Wild Bunch—first with Harvey Logan, called Kid Curry, then with Ben Kilpatrick, called The Tall Texan; she was arrested with Kilpatrick and sent to prison. Upon her release she disappeared.

Etta Place, at right, a one-time schoolteacher, became enamored with the Sundance Kid, becoming his mistress; after accompanying the Kid and Butch Cassidy to South America, she deserted the outlaws when she knew their end was near, going to New York and oblivion.

Lotta Crabtree, above, was the top entertainer at Tombstone's Bird Cage Theater; many a battle was waged over her affections, which she showered upon countless admirers during the days of Wyatt Earp.

Callie Lewis, above, the teenage second wife of John Wesley Hardin, the deadliest gunfighter of the Old West, a man who claimed to have killed forty men; she left Hardin shortly after the wedding.

Rose of Cimarron, above, reportedly the teenage sweetheart of bandit George "Bitter Creek" Newcomb; her real name was Rose Dunn and the girl posing here may have been a nameless vagrant passed off as Rose by lawman Bill Tilghman, who wanted to protect the real Miss Dunn.

Squirrel Tooth Alice, right, was one of Dodge City's more attractive fallen angels, whose company was widely sought; she poses here with a live squirrel in her lap, hence her odd sobriquet.

Fannie Porter, above, the most infamous madam in Texas, whose Fort Worth bordello was the private resort for members of Butch Cassidy's Wild Bunch; it was in Porter's brothel that the Sundance Kid reportedly met the love of his life, Etta Place.

Cattle Kate Watson, right, dressed in feminine finery, mounted on a horse near one of the pens housing the cattle rustled by her lover, Jim Averill, whose business caused them both to be lynched.

Belle Starr, left, in a typical pose designed to promote her lady bandit image—gun in hand, another on hip; she was a poor shot and an inept bandit, but the outlaws of the Indian Territory found her irresistable.

BIBLIOGRAPHY

NOTE: Tens of thousands of sources have been consulted by the author in researching the *Encyclopedia of Western Lawmen & Outlaws* over the last twenty-five years. What follows are basic book references which the reader may find helpful in further reading and research. Space does not permit citing the tens of thousands of periodical, newspaper, pamphlet, court document, and transcript sources also consulted by the author.

A

Abbott, E.C., and Smith, Helena Huntington. *We Pointed Them North: Recollections of a Cow Puncher.* New York: Farrar & Rinehart, 1939.

Abbott, Lawrence F. *Impressions of Theodore Roosevelt.* New York: Doubleday, 1920.

Abbott, Newton Carl. *Montana in the Making.* Billings, Mont.: Gazette Printing Co., 1931.

Abel, Annie Heloise (ed.). *The Official Correspondence of James S. Calhoun, While Indian Agent at Santa Fe and Superintendent of Indian Affairs in New Mexico, 1849-1852.* Washington, D.C.: U.S. Government Printing Office, 1915.

Abernathy, John R. *"Catch-'Em-Alive Jack": The Life and Adventures of an American Pioneer.* New York: Association Press, 1936.

_____. *In Camp with Roosevelt; or, the Life of John R. (Jack) Abernathy.* Oklahoma City, Okla.: Times-Journal, 1933.

Adams, Ramon F. (ed.). *The Best of the American Cowboy.* Norman: University of Oklahoma Press, 1957.

_____. *A Fitting Death for Billy the Kid.* Norman: University of Oklahoma Press, 1960.

_____. *From the Pecos to the Powder.* Norman: University of Oklahoma Press, 1965.

_____. *The Old-Time Cowhand.* New York: Macmillan, 1961.

Adams, Ward R. *History of Arizona.* Phoenix, Ariz.: Record, 1930.

Adler, Alfred. *Billy the Kid: A Case Study in Epic Origins.* Berkeley: University of California Press, 1951.

Agee, George W. *Rube Burrows, King of Outlaws, and His Band of Train Robbers.* Chicago: Hennebery, 1890.

Aiken, Albert W. *Rocky Mountain Rob, the California Outlaw; or the Vigilantes of Humburg Bar.* New York: Beadle & Adams, 1871.

Aikman, Duncan. *Calamity Jane and the Lady Wildcats.* New York: Henry Holt, 1927.

_____. (ed.) *The Taming of the Frontier.* New York: Prospect Press, 1925.

Akeny, Nesmith. *The West as I Knew It.* Lewiston, Idaho: R.G. Bailey Printing, 1938.

Albach, James R. *The Annals of the West.* Pittsburgh, Pa.: W.S. Haven, 1857.

Alldredge, Eugene Perry. *Cowboys and Coyotes.* Nashville, Tenn.: Marshall & Bruce, 1945.

Allen, Allyn. *The Real Book About the Texas Rangers.* Garden City, N.Y.: Garden City Books, 1952.

Allen, Dr. William A. *Adventures with Indians and Game; or Twenty Years in the Rocky Mountains.* Chicago:

A.W. Bowen, 1903.

Alley, John. *City Beginnings in Oklahoma Territory.* Norman: University of Oklahoma Press, 1939.

Aloutte. *Quantrell: The Terror of the West.* New York: M.J. Ivers, 1881.

Alvarez, N. *The James Boys in Missouri.* Clyde, Ohio: Ames, 1907.

American Guide Series (compiled by WPA writers).

_____. *Arizona; A State Guide.* New York: Hastings House, 1940.

_____. *Arkansas; A Guide to the State.* New York: Hastings House, 1941.

_____. *California; A Guide to the Golden State.* New York: Hastings House, 1939.

_____. *Cincinnati; A Guide to the Queen City and Its Neighbors.* Cincinnati, Ohio: Weiesen-Hart Press, 1943.

_____. *Colorado; A Guide to the Highest State.* New York: Hastings House, 1941.

_____. *Idaho; A Guide in Word and Picture.* New York: Oxford University Press, 1937.

_____. *Iowa; A Guide to the Hawkeye State.* New York: Viking Press, 1938.

_____. *Kansas; A Guide to the Sunflower State.* New York: Viking Press, 1939.

_____. *Kentucky; A Guide to the Bluegrass State.* New York: Harcourt, Brace, 1939.

_____. *Louisana; A Guide to the State.* New York: Hastings House, 1945.

_____. *Minnesota; A State Guide.* New York: Viking Press, 1938.

_____. *Mississipppi; A Guide to the Magnolia State.* New York: Hastings House, 1938.

_____. *Missouri; A Guide to the "Show Me" State.* New York: Duell, Sloan & Pearce, 1941.

_____. *Montana; A State Guide.* New York: Viking Press, 1939.

_____. *Nebraska; A Guide to the Cornhusker State.* New York: Viking Press, 1939.

_____. *New Mexico; A Guide to the Colorful State.* New York: Hasting House, 1940.

_____. *New Orleans City Guide.* Boston: Houghton Mifflin, 1938.

_____. *Oklahoma; A Guide to the Sooner State.* Norman: University of Oklahoma Press, 1941.

_____. *The Oregon Trail.* New York: Hastings House, 1939.

_____. *Provo; Pioneer Mormon City.* Portland, Ore.: Binfords & Mort, 1942.

_____. *A South Dakota Guide.* Pierre, S.D.: Pierre, 1938.

_____. *Tennessee; A Guide to the State.* New York: Hastings House, 1939.

_____. *Texas; A Guide to the Lone Star State.* New York: Hastings House, 1940.

_____. *Tulsa; A Guide to the Oil Capital.* Tulsa, Okla.: Mid-West Printing, 1938.

_____. *West Virginia; A Guide to the Mountain State.* New York: Oxford University Press, 1941.

_____. *Wyoming; A Guide to Its History, Highways, and People.* New York: Oxford University Press, 1941.

American Heritage. *American Heritage Picture History of the Civil War.* New York: American Heritage, 1960.

Anderson, Frank W. *Bill Miner: Train Robber.* Calgary,

Alberta, Can.: Frontiers, 1963.

Anderson, Galuska. *A Border City During the Civil War.* Boston: Little, Brown, 1908.

Anderson, George B. (ed.). *History of New Mexico: Its Resources and People.* Los Angeles: Pacific States, 1907.

Andreas, A.T., and Cutler, W.G. *History of the State of Kansas.* Chicago: n.p., 1883.

———. *History of the State of Nebraska.* Chicago: Western Historical, 1882.

Andrews, C.C. (ed.). *Minnesota in the Indian and Civil Wars.* 2 vols. St. Paul: State of Minnesota, 1890-93.

Angel, Myron (ed.). *History of Nevada.* Oakland, Calif.: Thompson & West, 1881.

———. *History of Placer County.* Oakland, Calif.: Thompson & West, 1882.

———. *History of San Luis Obispo County, California.* Oakland, Calif.: Thompson & West, 1883.

Ankeny, Nesmith. *The West as I Knew It.* Lewiston, Idaho: R.G. Bailey, 1953.

Annals of San Francisco. New York: Western Press, 1855.

Anthony, Irving. *Paddle Wheels and Pistols.* Philadelphia: Macrae Smith, 1929.

Applegate, Frank G. *The Apache Kid: "Folk-Say: A Regional Miscellany."* Norman: University of Oklahoma Press, 1931.

———. *Native Tales of New Mexico.* Philadelphia: J.B. Lippincott, 1932.

Appleman, Roy E. *Charlie Siringo, Cowboy Detective.* Washington, D.C.: Potomac Corral, the Westerners, 1968.

Appler, Augustus C. *The Guerrillas of the West; or The Life, Character and Daring Exploits of the Younger Brothers.* St. Louis: Eureka, 1876.

———. *The Younger Brothers.* New York: Frederick Fell, 1955.

Archambeau, Ernest R. (ed.). *Old Tascosa, 1885-1888.* Canyon, Texas: Panhandle Plains Historical Society, 1966.

Argall, Phyllis. *The Truth About Jesse James.* Sullivan, Mo.: Lester B. Dill & Rudy Turilli, 1953.

Arizona, The Grand Canyon State. New York: Hastings House, 1940.

Arnold, Oren, and Hale, John P. *Hot Irons: Heraldry of the Range.* New York: Macmillan, 1940.

———. *Thunder in the Southwest: Echoes from the Wild Frontier.* Norman: University of Oklahoma, 1937.

———. *Wild Life in the Southwest.* Dallas: Banks Upshaw, 1935.

Arrington, A.W. *Desperadoes of the Southwest.* New York: W.H. Graham, 1847.

———. *The Rangers and Regulators of the Tanaha.* New York: R.M. Dewitt, 1856.

Arthur, George Clinton. *Bushwhacker.* Rolla, Mo.: Rolla Printing, 1938.

Ashbaugh, Don. *Nevada's Turbulent Yesterday.* Los Angeles: Westernlore Press, 1963.

Ashton, Wendall J. *The Voice of the West: Biography of a Pioneer Newspaper.* New York: Duell, Sloan, & Pearce, 1950.

Ashurst, Henry Fountain. *The Diary of Henry Fountain Ashurst.* Tucson: University of Arizona, n.d.

Athearn, Robert G. *High Country Empire.* New York: McGraw-Hill, 1953.

———. *Rebel of the Rockies.* New Haven, Conn.: Yale University, 1962.

Atherton, Gertrude. *California, an Intimate History.* New York: Harper & Brothers, 1914.

———. *My San Francisco.* Indianapolis, Ind.: Bobbs-Merrill, 1946.

Atherton, Lewis. *The Cattle Kings.* Bloomington: Indiana University Press, 1961.

Atkinson, S.W. *Adventures of Oklahoma Bill.* n.p., 1906.

Atkinson, T.W. *Oriental and Western Siberia.* New York: Harpers, 1858.

Authentic History of Sam Bass and His Gang. Denton, Texas: Monitor Job Office, 1878.

Axford, Joseph Mack. *Around Western Campfires.* New York: Pageant Press, 1964.

B

Baber, Daisy F., as told by Bill Walker. *Injun Summer.* Caldwell, Ohio: Caxton Press, 1952.

———. *The Longest Rope: The Truth About the Johnson County Cattle War.* Caldwell, Idaho: Caxton Printers, 1940.

Baca, Carlos Cabeza de. *Vicente Silva, New Mexico's Vice King of the Nineties.* n.p., 1938.

Baca, Fabiola Cabeza de. *We Fed Them Cactus.* Albuquerque: University of New Mexico Press, 1954.

Bailey, Harry H. *When New Mexico Was Young.* Las Cruces, N.M.: Las Cruces Citizen, 1948.

Bailey, Robert G. *River of No Return. (The Great Salmon River of Idaho).* Lewiston, Idaho: Bailey-Blake, 1935.

Baird, Josie. *Tom Bond, Bronc-Buster, and Trail Driver.* Sweetwater, Texas: Watson-Focht, 1960.

Bakarich, Sarah Grace. *Empty Saddles: A New Version of the Earp-Clanton Fight.* n.p., 1946.

———. *Gunsmoke.* n.p., 1947.

———, and Bennett, Kathelen M. *There's Treasure in Our Hills.* n.p., 1947.

Baker, Joseph E. (ed.). *Past and Present of Alameda County, California.* Chicago: S.J. Clarke, 1914.

Baker, Pearl. *The Wild Bunch at Robbers Roost.* New York: Abelard-Schuman, 1971.

Baldwin, Gordon. *The Warrior Apaches.* Tucson, Ariz.: Dale S. King, 1966.

Ball, Eve. *Ma'am Jones of the Pecos.* Tucson: University of Arizona Press, 1968.

———. *Ruidoso, The Last Frontier.* San Antonio, Texas: Naylor, 1963.

Ball, Larry D. *The United States Marshals of New Mexico and Arizona Territories, 1846-1912.* Albuquerque: University of New Mexico Press, 1978.

Ballenger, T.H. *Around Tahlequah Council Fires.* Muskogee, Okla.: Motter Bookbinding, 1935.

Ballert, Marion. *Billy the Kid: A Date with Destiny.* Seattle, Wash.: Superior, 1970.

———. *Complete & Authentic Life of Jesse James.* New York: Frederick Fell, 1953.

———. *Younger Brothers.* San Antonio, Texas: Naylor, 1961.

Bancroft, Hubert Howe. *California Inter Pocula.* San Francisco: The History Company, 1888.

———. *History of Arizona and New Mexico.* San Francisco: Bancroft, 1889.

———. *History of California.* 7 vols. San Francisco: San Francisco History, 1884-1890.

———. *History of Nevada, Colorado, and Wyoming, 1540-1888.* San Francisco: The History Company, 1889.

———. *History of the North Mexican States and Texas.* San Francisco: History, 1889.

———. *History of the Pacific States.* 39 vols. San Francisco: Bancroft-Whitney, 1883-92.

——. *History of Washington, Idaho and Montana.* San Francisco: History, 1887.

——. *Outlaws.* San Francisco: Historical, 1887.

Bankson, Russell A. *The Klondike Nugget.* Caldwell, Idaho: Caxton Printers, 1935.

Bannorris, Amanda. *The Female Land Pirate.* Cincinnati, Ohio: E.E. Barclay, 1848.

Bard, Floyd. *Horse Wrangler: Sixty Years in the Saddle in Wyoming and Montana.* Norman: University of Oklahoma Press, 1960.

Barker, Eugene C. *The Life of Stephen F. Austin.* Nashville, Tenn.: Cokesbury Press, 1925.

Barker, Frances. *From the Green Mountains to the Prairies.* Great Barrington, Mass.: Berkshire Courier Press, 1955.

Barnard, Evan G. *A Rider of the Cherokee Strip.* Boston: Houghton Mifflin, 1936.

Barnes, William Croft. *Apaches & Longhorns.* Los Angeles: Ward Ritchie Press, 1941.

Barney, Libeus. *Letter's of the Pike's Peak Gold Rush.* San Jose, Calif.: Talisman Press, 1959.

Barnum, G.H. *Rube Burrow, The Famous Outlaw, Murderer, and Train Robber.* Chicago: Published by Author, 1890.

Barsness, Larry. *Gold Camp.* New York: Hastings House, 1962.

Bartholomew, Ed. *A Biographical Album of Western Gunfighters.* Houston: Frontier Press of Texas, 1958.

——. *Black Jack Ketchum: Last of the Hold-Up Kings.* Houston: Frontier Press of Texas, 1955.

——. *Cullen Baker: Premier Texas Gunfighter.* Houston: Frontier Press of Texas, 1954.

——. *Henry Plummer: Montana Outlaw Boss.* Ruidoso, N.M.: Frontier Books, 1960.

——. *Jesse Evans: A Texas Hideburner.* Houston: Frontier Press of Texas, 1955.

——. *Kill or Be Killed: A Record of Violence in the Early Southwest.* Houston: The Frontier Press of Texas, 1953.

——. *Some Western Gunfighters.* Toyahvale, Texas: Frontier Book, n.d.

——. *Western Hardcases.* Ruidoso, N.M.: Frontier Book, 1960.

——. *Wild Bill Longley: A Texas Hard-Case.* Houston: Frontier Press of Texas, 1953.

——. *Wyatt Earp, 1879-1882: The Man and the Myth.* Toyahvale, Texas: Frontier Book, 1964.

——. *Wyatt Earp, 1848-1880: The Untold Story.* Toyahvale, Texas: Frontier Books, 1963.

Barton, D.S., and McCorkle, John (ed.) *Three Years with Quantrell.* Armstrong, Mo.: Armstrong Herald Printing, 1914.

Baskin, R.N. *Reminiscences of Early Utah.* Salt Lake City, Utah: Tribune-Reporter, 1914.

Bassett, Samuel Clay. *Buffalo County, Nebraska, and Its People.* Chicago: S.J. Clarke, 1916.

Beals, Frank Lee. *Buffalo Bill.* Chicago: Wheeler, 1943.

Bearss, Edwin C., and Gibson, A.M. *Fort Smith, Little Gibraltar on the Arkansas.* Norman: University of Oklahoma Press, 1969.

Bechdolt, Frederick Ritchie. *Tales of the Oldtimers.* New York: Century, 1924.

——. *When the West Was Young.* New York: Century, 1924.

Beck, Warren A. *New Mexico: A History of Four Centuries.* Norman: University of Oklahoma Press, 1962.

Beckett, V.B. *Baca's Battle.* Houston, Texas: Stagecoach Press, n.d.

Beebe, Lucius, and Clegg, Charles. *The American West.* New York: E.P. Dutton, 1955.

——. *Hear the Train Blow.* New York: E.P. Dutton, 1952.

——. *Shoot if You Must.* New York: D. Appleton Century, 1943.

——. *U.S. West: The Saga of Wells Fargo.* New York: E.P. Dutton, 1949.

Beers, George A. *Vasquez; or the Hunted Bandits of San Joaquin.* New York: Robert M. DeWitt, 1875.

Beidler, X. *Vigilante.* Norman: University of Oklahoma Press, 1965.

Bell, Horace. *On the Old West Coast.* New York: William Morrow, 1930.

——. *Reminiscences of a Ranger.* Los Angeles: Yarnell, Caystile, & Mathes, 1881.

Belle, Frances P. *Life and Adventures of the Celebrated Bandit Joaquin Murieta.* Chicago: Reagan, 1925.

Bennett, Edwin Lewis. *Boom Town Boy in Old Creede Colorado.* Chicago: Sage Books, 1966.

Bennett, Estelline. *Old Deadwood Days.* New York: J.H. Sears, 1928.

Benson, Henry C. *Life Among the Choctaw Indians and Sketches of the Southwest.* Cincinnati, Ohio: L. Swormstedt & A.

Benton, Jesse James. *Cow by the Tail.* Boston: Houghton Mifflin, 1943.

Berry, Gerald L. *The Whoop-Up Trail.* Edmonton, Alberta, Can.: Applies Art Productions, 1953.

Betenson, Lula. *Butch Cassidy, My Brother.* Provo, Utah: Brigham Young University Press, 1975.

Billington, Ray A. *America's Frontier Heritage.* New York: Holt, Rinehart & Winston, 1966.

——. *The Far Western Frontier 1830-1860.* New York: Harper & Brothers, 1956.

Billy the Kid: Las Vegas Newspaper Account of His Career, 1880-81. Waco, Texas: W.M. Morrison, 1958.

Birney, Herman Hoffman. *Vigilantes.* Philadelphia: Penn, 1929.

Bishop, William. *Old Mexico and Her Lost Provinces.* New York: Harper, 1883.

Black, A.P. *End of the Long Horn Trail.* Selfridge, N.D.: Selfridge Journal, 1936.

Blacker, Erwin R. (ed.). *The Old West in Fact.* New York: Ivan Obolensky, 1962.

Blackmar, Frank W. *Charles Robinson. The First Free-State Governor of Kansas.* Topeka, Kan.: Crane, 1900.

Blanchard, Leola Howard. *The Conquest of Southwest Kansas.* Wichita, Kan.: Wichita Eagle Press, 1931.

Blanchard, Rufus. *Discovery and Conquests of the Northwest with History of Chicago.* Chicago: Cushing, Thomas, 1881.

Bland, T.A. *Life of Albert B. Meacham.* Washington D.C.: T.A. & M.C. Bland, 1883.

Blankenship, Russell. *And There Were Men.* New York: Alfred A. Knopf, 1942.

Bliss, Frank E. *The Life of Hon. William F. Cody Known as Buffalo Bill, the Famous Hunter, Scout and Guide.* Hartford, Conn.: Published by Author, 1879.

Block, Eugene B. *Great Stagecoach Robbers of the West.* New York: Doubleday, 1962.

——. *Great Train Robberies of the West.* New York: Coward-McCann, 1959.

Bloss, Roy S. *Pony Express-the Great Gamble.* Berkeley, Calif.: Howell-North, 1939.

Bloyd, Levi. *Jefferson County History.* Fairbury, Neb.: Holloway, n.d.

Blythe, T. Roger (ed.). *A Pictorial Souvenir and Historical Sketch of Tombstone, Arizona.* Tombstone, Ariz.: Tombstone Epitaph, 1946.

Boddam-Whetham, John. *Western Wanderings.* R. Bentley and Son, 1874.

Boggs, Mae Helene Bacon. *My Playhouse was a Concord Coach.* Oakland, Calif.: Howell-North Press, 1942.

Boller, Henry A. *Among the Indians.* Philadelphia: T. Ellwood Zell, 1868.

Bonney, Edward. *Banditti of the Prairies.* Chicago: Homewood, 1890.

Booker, Anton S. *Wildcats in Petticoats.* Girard, Kan.: Haldeman-Julius, 1945.

Botkin, Benjamin A. (ed.) *A Treasury of Mississippi River Folklore.* New York: Crown, 1955.

———, and Harlow, Alvin F. *A Treasury of Railroad Folklore.* New York: Crown, 1953.

———. *A Treasury of Southern Folklore.* New York: American Legacy Press, 1984.

———. *A Treasury of Western Folklore.* New York: Crown, 1951.

Bowman, Lynn. *Los Angeles, Epic of a City.* Berkeley, Calif.: Howell-North Books, 1974.

Boyd, William Harland, and Rodgers, Glendon J. (eds.). *San Joaquin Vignettes.* Bakersfield, Calif.: Kern County Historical Society, 1955.

Boyer, Glenn G. (ed.) *I Married Wyatt Earp: The Recollections of Josephine Sarah Marcus Earp.* Tucson: University of Arizona Press, 1976.

———. *An Illustrated Life of Doc Holliday.* Glenwood Springs, Colo.: Reminder, 1966.

———. *Suppressed Murder of Wyatt Earp.* San Antonio: Naylor, 1967.

Boynton, Percy Holmes. *The Rediscovery of the Frontier.* Chicago: University of Chicago Press, 1931.

Brackett, L.P. *Our Western Empire.* Philadelphia: Bradley, Garretson, 1881.

Bradley, Glenn Danford. *The Story of the Santa Fe.* Boston: R. G. Badger, 1920.

Bradley, R.T. *Lives of Frank and Jesse James.* St. Louis: J.W. Marsh, 1882.

———. *The Outlaws of the Border.* St. Louis: J.W. Marsh, 1880.

Brady, Jasper Ewing. *Tales of the Telegraph.* New York: Doubleday & McClure, 1899.

Branch, Edward Douglas. *The Cowboy and His Interpreters.* New York: D. Appleton, 1926.

———. *The Hunting of the Buffalo.* New York: D. Appleton, 1929.

———. *The Sentimental Years.* New York: Appleton Century, 1934.

———. *Westward: The Romance of the American Frontier.* New York: D. Appleton, 1930.

Brandt, Fred. *Fascinating San Francisco.* San Francisco: Published by Author, 1924.

Brashear, Minnie M. *Mark Twain, Son of Missouri.* Chapel Hill: University of North Carolina Press, 1934.

Bratt, John. *Trails of Yesterday.* Lincoln, Neb.: University Publishing, 1921.

Brayer, Garnet M. and Herbert O. *American Cattle Trails.* Bayside, N.Y.: Western Range Cattle Industry Studies, 1952.

Brayer, Herbert O. *Range Murder.* Evanston, Ill.: Branding Iron Press, 1955.

———. *William Blackmore: the Spanish-Mexican Land Grants of New Mexico and Colorado 1863-1878.* Denver: Bradford-Robinson, 1949.

Breakenridge, William M. *Helldorado: Bringing the Law to the Mesquite.* Boston: Houghton Mifflin, 1928.

Breihan, Carl W. *Badmen of Frontier Days.* New York: Robert M. McBride Co., 1957.

———. *The Complete and Authentic Life of Jesse James.* New York: Frederick Fell, 1953.

———. *The Day Jesse James Was Killed.* New York: Frederick Fell, 1961.

———. *Escapades of Frank & Jesse James.* New York: Frederick Fell, 1974.

———. *Great Gunfighters of the West.* San Antonio, Texas: Naylor, 1962.

———. *Great Lawmen of the West.* New York: Signet, 1978.

———. *The Killer Legions of Quantrill.* Seattle, Wash.: Hangman Press, 1971.

———. *The Man Who Shot Jessie James.* New York: A.S. Barnes, 1979.

———. *The Outlaw Brothers: The True Story of Missouri's Younger Brothers.* San Antonio, Texas: Naylor, 1961.

———. *Outlaws of the Old West.* New York: Bonanza Books, 1967.

———. *Quantrill and His Civil War Guerrillas.* Denver: Sage Books, 1959.

———. *Younger Brothers.* San Antonio: Naylor, 1961.

Brent, Rafer (ed.). *Great Western Heroes.* New York: Bartholomew House, 1957.

Brent, William. *The Complete and Factual Life of Billy the Kid.* New York: Frederick Fell, 1964.

———, and Brent, Milarde. *The Hell Hole.* Yuma, Ariz.: Southwest Printers, 1962.

Briggs, C.W. *The Reign of Terror in Kansas.* Boston: n.p., 1856.

Briggs, Harold Edward. *Frontiers of the Northwest.* New York: Appleton-Century, 1940.

Briggs, L. Vernon. *Arizona and New Mexico, 1882.* Boston: Privately Printed, 1932.

Brininstool, Earl Alonzo. *Fighting Red Cloud's Warriors.* Columbus, Ohio: Hunter-Trader-Trapper, 1926.

Bristow, Joseph Quayle. *Tales of Old Fort Gibson.* New York: Exposition Press, 1961.

Broaddus, J. Morgan. *The Legal Heritage of El Paso.* El Paso: Texas Western Press, 1963.

Bronson, Edgar Beecher. *The Red-Blooded Heroes of the Frontier.* New York: A.C. McClurg, 1910.

Brooks, Juanita. *The Moutain Meadows Massacre.* Stanford, Calif.: Stanford Universtiy Press, 1962.

Brophy, Frank Cullen. *Arizona Sketch Book: Fifty Historical Sketches.* Phoenix, Ariz.: Ampco Press, 1952.

Brosnan, Cornelius James. *History of the State of Idaho.* New York: Charles Scribner's Sons, 1918.

Brothers, Mary Hudson. *Billy the Kid.* Farmington, N.M.: Hustler Press, 1949.

———. *A Pecos Pioneer.* Albuquerque: University of New Mexico Press, 1943.

Brown, Dee. *The Gentle Tamers: Women of the Old West.* New York: G.P. Putnam's Sons, 1958.

———, and Schmitt, Martin F. *Trail Driving Days.* New York: Charles Scribner's Sons, 1952.

Brown, James Cabell. *Calabaza.* San Francisco: Valleau & Peterson, 1892.

Brown, Jesse, and Willard, A.M. *The Black Hills Trails.* Rapid City, S.D.: Rapid City Journal, 1924.

Brown, John. *Twenty-Five Years a Parson in the Wild West.* Fall River, Mass.: n.p., 1896.

Brown, John Henry. *Reminiscences and Incidents of the Early Life of San Francisco.* San Francisco: Mission Journal, 1929.

Brown, John P. *Old Frontiers.* Kingsport, Tenn.: Southern, 1938.

Brown, Mark H., and Felton, W.R. *Before Barbed Wire.* New York: Henry Holt, 1956.

———. *The Frontier Years.* New York: Henry Holt, 1955.

———. *The Plainsmen of the Yellowstone.* New York: G.P.

Putnam's Sons, 1961.

Brown, Robert L. *Ghost Towns of the Colorado Rockies.* Caldwell, Idaho: Caxton Printers, 1968.

Brown, Robert R. (ed.). *History of Kings County.* Handford, Calif.: A.H. Canoston, 1940.

Brown, Will C. *Sam Bass and Company.* New York: New American Library, 1960.

Brown, William Adams. *Morris Ketchum Jesup: A Character Sketch.* New York: Charles Scribner's Sons, 1910.

Brown, William G. *Life of Oliver Ellsworth.* New York: Macmillan, 1905.

Browne, J. Ross. *Adventures in Apache Country: A Tour Through Arizona and Sonora, 1864.* Tucson: University of Arizona Press, 1974.

Bruce, Robert. *The Fighting Norths and Pawnee Scouts.* New York: Privately Printed, 1932.

Bruffey, George A. *Eighty-One Years in the West.* Butte, Mont.: Butte Miner, 1925.

Bryan, Jerry. *An Illinois Gold Hunter in the Black Hills.* Springfield, Ill.: State Historical Society, 1960.

Bryant, Will. *Great American Guns and Frontier Fighters.* New York: Grossett & Dunlap, 1961.

Buckbee, Edna Bryan. *Pioneer Days of Angel's Camp.* Angel's Camp: Calaveras Californian, 1932.

_____. *The Saga of Old Tuolumne.* New York: Press of the Pioneers, 1935.

Buel, James William. *The Border Bandits.* Chicago: Donohue, Henneberry, 1893.

_____. *The Border Outlaws.* St. Louis: Historical, 1881.

_____. *Heroes of the Plains.* St. Louis: Historical, 1881.

_____. *The James Boys.* Chicago: M.A. Donohue, n.d.

_____. *Jesse and Frank James and Their Comrades in Crime, the Younger Brothers, the Notorious Border Outlaws.* Baltimore: I. & M. Ottenheimer, 1902.

_____. *Life and Marvelous Adventures of Wild Bill, the Scout.* Chicago: Belford, Clarke, 1880.

_____. *The True Story of Wild Bill Hickok.* New York: Atomic Books, 1946.

Buffum, George Tower. *On Two Frontiers.* Boston: Lothrop, Lee & Shepard, 1918.

_____. *Smith of Bear City.* New York: Grafton Press, 1906.

Buley, R.C. *The Old Northwest: Pioneer Period, 1815-1840.* 2 vols. Indianapolis: Indiana Historical Society, 1950.

Burch, John P. *Charles W. Quantrell: A True History of Guerrilla Warfare on the Missouri and Kansas Border During the Civil War of 1861-1865 as Told by Capt. Harrison Trow.* Vegas, Texas: Privately Printed, 1923.

Burchell, Robert A. *The San Francisco Irish, 1848-1880.* Berkeley: University of California Press, 1980.

Burdick, Usher Lloyd. *Jim Johnson, Pioneer.* Williston, N.D.: Privately Printed, 1941.

_____. *Life and Exploits of John Goodall.* Watford City, N.D.: McKenzie County Farmer, 1931.

_____. *Tales from Buffalo Land.* Baltimore: Wirth Brothers, 1939.

Burgess, Opie Rundle. *Bisbee Not So Long Ago.* San Antonio, Texas: Naylor, 1967.

Burke, John M. *"Buffalo Bill" From Prairie to Palace.* Chicago: Rand McNally, 1893.

Burke, Martha Jane. *Life and Adventures of Calamity Jane By Herself.* Livingston, Mont.: Post Print, 1936.

Burlingame, Merrill G., and Toole, K. Ross. *A History of Montana.* New York: Lewis Historical, 1957.

_____. *The Montana Frontier.* Helena: Montana State, 1942.

Burnham, Frederick Russell. *Scouting on Two Continents.* Garden City, N.Y.: Doubleday, Page, 1926.

_____. *Taking Chances.* Los Angeles: Haynes, 1944.

Burns, Robert Homer, Gillespie, Andrew Springs, and Richardson, Willing Gay. *Wyoming's Pioneer Ranches.* Laramie, Wyo.: Top-of-the-World Press, 1955.

Burns, Walter Noble. *The Robin Hood of El Dorado.* New York: Coward-McCann, 1932.

_____. *The Saga of Billy the Kid.* New York: Grosset & Dunlap, 1926.

_____. *Tombstone, An Iliad of the Southwest.* Garden City, N.Y.: Doubleday, Page, 1927.

Burroughs, Burt E. *Tales of an Old "Border Town."* Fowler, Ind.: Benton Review, 1925.

Burroughs, John Rolfe. *Where the Old West Stayed Young.* New York: William Morrow, 1962.

Burrows, William E. *Vigilante!* New York: Harcourt Brace Jovanovich, 1976.

Burt, Maxwell Struthers. *The Diary of A Dude Wrangler.* New York: Charles Scribner's Sons, 1924.

_____. *Powder River: Let 'Er Buck.* New York: Farrar & Rinehart, 1938.

Burton, Jeff. *Black Jack Christian, Outlaw.* Santa Fe, N.M.: Press of the Territorian, 1967.

_____. *Dynamite and Six-Shooter.* Santa Fe, N.M.: Palomino Press, 1970.

Bush, Ira Jefferson. *Gringo Doctor.* Caldwell, Idaho: Caxton Press, 1939.

Buss, Henry. *Wanderings in the West, During the Year 1870.* London: Thomas Danks, 1870.

Butterfield, Roger. *The American Past.* New York: Simon & Schuster, 1947.

Byington, Lewis F., and Lewis, Oscar (eds.). *The History of San Francisco.* San Francisco: S.J. Clarke, 1931.

C

Cady, John Henry. *Arizona's Yesterday.* Los Angeles: Privately Published, 1916.

Cain (or Calin), Ella M. *The Story of Bodie.* Sonora, Calif.: Mother Lode Press, 1956.

Calkins, Ernest E. *They Broke the Prairie.* New York: Charles Scribner's Sons, 1937.

Callaway, Lewis L. *Montana's Righteous Hangmen.* Norman: University of Oklahoma Press, 1982.

Callison, John J. *Bill Jones of Paradise Valley, Oklahoma.* Chicago: M.A. Donohue, 1914.

Callon, Milton W. *Las Vegas, New Mexico, the Town That Wouldn't Gamble.* Las Vegas, N.M.: Las Vegas Daily Optic, 1962.

Campos, Ruben M. *El folklore literario de Mexico.* Mexico: Talleres Graficos de la Nacion, 1929.

Canfield, Chauncey L. *Diary of a Forty-Niner.* New York: M. Shephard, 1906.

Canton, Frank M. *The Autobiography of Frank M. Canton.* Norman: University of Oklahoma Press, 1954.

_____. *Frontier Trails.* Boston: Houghton Mifflin, 1930.

Cantonwine, Alexander. *Star Forty-Six, Oklahoma.* Oklahoma City: Pythian Times, 1911.

Carey, Henry L. (ed.). *The Thrilling Story of Famous Boot Hill and Modern Dodge City.* Dodge City, Kan.: Herbert Etrick, 1937.

Carlisle, William L. *Bill Carlisle, Lone Bandit: An Autobiography.* Pasadena, Calif.: Trail's End, 1946.

Caroll, John Alexander (ed.). *Pioneering in Arizona.* Tucson: Arizona Pioneers Historical Society, 1964.

Carr, Harry. *The West Is Still Wild.* Boston: Houghton Mifflin, 1932.

Carr, John. *Pioneer Days in California.* Eureka, Calif.:

Times, 1891.

Carson, John. *Doc Middleton, the Unwickedest Outlaw.* Santa Fe, N.M.: Press of the Territorian, 1966.

————. *The Union Pacific: Hell on Wheels.* Santa Fe, N.M.: Press of the Territorian, 1968.

Carter, W.N. *Harry Tracy, The Desperate Outlaw.* Chicago: Laird & Lee, 1902.

Caruthers, William. *Loafing Along the Death Valley Trails.* Ontorio, Calif.: Death Valley, 1951.

Carver, Charles. *Brann and the Iconoclast.* Austin: University of Texas Press, 1957.

Casady, Klina E. *Once Every Five Years: A History of Cheyenne, Oklahoma, 1892-1972.* Oklahoma City: Metro Press, 1974.

Case, Nelson. *History of Labette County, Kansas, From the First Settlement to the Close of 1892.* Topeka, Kan.: Crane, 1893.

Case, Theodore (ed.). *History of Kansas City, Missouri.* Syracuse, N.Y.: Mason, 1880.

Casey, Robert J. *The Black Hills and Their Incredible Characters.* Indianapolis, Ind.: Bobbs-Merrill, 1949.

————. *Pioneer Railroad.* New York: McGraw-Hill, 1948.

————. *The Texas Border and Some Borderliners.* New York: Bobbs-Merrill, 1950.

Castel, Albert. *A Frontier State at War: Kansas, 1861-1865.* Ithaca, N.Y.: Cornell University Press, 1958.

————. *William Clarke Quantrill: His Life and Times.* New York: Frederick Fell, 1962.

Castleman, Harvey N. *The Bald Knobbers.* Girard, Kan.: Haldeman-Julius, 1944.

————. *Sam Bass, The Train Robber.* Girard, Kan.: Haldeman-Julius, 1944.

————. *The Texas Rangers.* Girard, Kan.: Haldeman-Julius, 1944.

Cattermole, E.G. *Famous Frontiersmen, Pioneers and Scouts.* Chicago: Coburn & Newman, 1883.

Caughey, John Walton. *California.* New York: Prentice Hall, 1953.

————. *History of the Pacific Coast.* Los Angeles: Published by Author, 1933.

Chalfant, Willie Arthur. *Gold, Guns & Ghost Towns.* Stanford, Calif.: Stanford University Press, 1947.

————. *Outposts of Civilization.* Boston: Christopher, 1928.

————. *The Story of Inyo.* Chicago: W.B. Conkey, 1922.

Chamberlain, Newell D. *The Call of Gold: True Tales on the Gold Road to Yosemite.* Mariposa, Calif.: Gazette Press, 1936.

Chambers, Henry E. *Mississippi Valley Beginnings.* New York: G.P. Putnam's Sons, 1922.

Channing, Edward. *History of the United States.* 6 vols. New York: Macmillan, 1905-25.

Chapel, Charles Edward. *Guns of the Old West.* New York: Coward-McCann, 1961.

————. *Levi's Gallery of Long Guns and Western Riflemen.* San Francisco: Levi Strauss, n.d.

————. *Levi's Gallery of Western Guns and Gunfighters.* San Francisco: Levi Strauss, n.d.

Chapman, Arthur. *The Pony Express.* New York: G.P. Putnam's Sons, 1932.

Chapman, Berlin Basil. *The Founding of Stillwater.* Oklahoma City: Times-Journal, 1948.

Charles, Mrs. Tom. *More Tales of Tularosa.* Alamogordo, N.M.: Bennett Printing, 1961.

————. *Tales of the Tularosa.* Alamogordo, N.M.: n.p., 1963.

Chatterton, Fenimore C. *Yesterday's Wyoming.* Aurora, Colo.: Powder River, 1957.

Cheek, W. Raymond. *The Story of an American Pioneer*

Family. New York: Exposition Press, 1960.

Chicago and Northwestern Railway Company. *Yesterday and Today.* Chicago: Rand, McNally, 1905.

Chicago Tribune. *A Century of Tribune Editorials, 1847-1947.* Chicago: Chicago Tribune, 1947.

Chilton, Charles. *The Book of the West.* Indianapolis, Ind.: Bobbs-Merrill, 1962.

Chisholm, Joe. *Brewery Gulch.* San Antonio, Texas: Naylor, 1949.

————, and Cohn, Alfred. *Take the Witness.* New York: Frederick A. Stokes, 1934.

Chittenden, Hiram Martin. *The American Fur Trade of the Far West.* 2 vols. Stanford, Calif.: Academic Reprints, 1954.

————. *History of Early Steamboat Navigation on the Missouri River.* New York: Francis P. Harper, 1903.

Chrisman, Harry E. *Fifty Years on the Owl Hoot Trail.* Chicago: Sage Books, 1969.

————. *The Ladder of Rivers: The Story of I.P. (Print) Olive.* Denver: Sage Books, 1962.

————. *Lost Trails of the Cimarron.* Denver: Sage Books, 1961.

Christie, Octavius F. *Dickens and His Age.* London: Heath, Cranton, 1939.

Churchill, Allen. *A Pictorial History of American Crime 1849-1929.* New York: Holt, Rinehart & Winston, 1964.

City Council of Women's Clubs. *Pioneer Stories.* Meade County, Kan.: n.p., 1950.

Clairmonte, Glenn. *Calamity Jane Was Her Name.* Denver: Sage Books, 1959.

Clampitt, John Wesley. *Echoes From the Rocky Mountains.* Chicago: Clarke, 1888.

Clark, Charles M. *A Trip to Pike's Peak.* San Jose, Calif.: Talisman Press, 1958.

Clark, Ira G. *Then Came the Railroads.* Norman: University of Oklahoma Press, 1958.

Clark, O.S. *Clay Allison of the Washita.* Attica, Ind.: G.M. Williams, 1920.

Clarke, Mary Whatley. *The Palo Pinto Story.* Fort Worth, Texas: Manney, 1956.

Claussen, W. Edmunds. *Cimarron-"Last of the Frontier."* Boyertown, Pa.: n.p., 1948.

Clay, John. *My Life on the Range.* Norman: University of Oklahoma Press, 1962.

————. *The Tragedy of Squaw Mountain.* Chicago: Traders Print, n.d.

Clay-Clopton, Virginia. *A Belle of the Fifties.* New York: Da Capo Press, 1969.

Cleaveland, Agnes Morley. *Satan's Paradise, from Lucien Maxwell to Fred Lambert.* Boston: Houghton Mifflin, 1952.

Cleaveland, Norman, and Fitzpatrick, George. *The Morleys.* Albuquerque, N.M.: Calvin Horn, 1971.

Cleland, Robert Glass. *California Pageant, the Story of Four Centuries.* New York: Alfred A. Knopf, 1946.

————. *The Cattle on a Thousand Hills: Southern California, 1850-1870.* San Marino, Calif.: Huntington Library, 1941.

————. *From Wilderness to Empire.* New York: Alfred A. Knopf, 1949.

————. *History of California: The American Period.* New York: Macmillan, 1922.

————. *The Irvine Ranch of Orange County, 1810-1950.* San Marino, Calif.: Huntington Library, 1952.

————, and Putnam, Frank B. *Isaias W. Hellman and the Farmers and Merchants Bank.* San Marino, Calif.: Huntington Library, 1965.

Clemens, Samuel Langhorne (Mark Twain, Pseud.). *Life*

on the Mississippi. Boston: James R. Osgood, 1883.
———. Roughing It. Chicago: F.G. Gilmer, 1872.
Clum, John P. It All Happened in Tombstone. Flagstaff, Ariz.: Northland Press, 1965.
Clum, Woodworth. Apache Agent. Boston: Houghton Mifflin, 1936.
Coan, Charles Florus. A History of New Mexico. Chicago: American Historical Society, 1925.
Coates, Robert M. The Outlaw Years: The History of the Land Pirates of the Natchez Trace. New York: Literary Guild of America, 1930.
Coblentz, Stanton Arthur. Villains and Vigilantes. New York: Thomas Yoseloff, 1957.
Coburn, Walt. Pioneer Cattleman in Montana: The Story of Circle C Ranch. Norman: University of Oklahoma Press, 1968.
———. Stirrup High. New York: Julian Messner, 1957.
Cody, Louisa Frederici. Memories of Buffalo Bill. New York: D. Appleton, 1919.
Cody, William Frederick. An Autobiography of Buffalo Bill. New York: Cosmopolitan Book, 1920.
———. Buffalo Bill's Own Story of His Life and Deeds. Chicago: John R. Stanton, 1917.
———. Life and Adventures of "Buffalo Bill." Chicago: John R. Stanton, 1917.
———. The Life of the Hon. William F. Cody, Known as Buffalo Bill. Hartford, Conn.: F.E. Bliss, 1879.
———. Story of Wild West and Camp-Fire Chats. Richmond, Va.: B.F. Johnson, 1888.
———. True Tales of the Plains (William F. Cody), Frontiersman and Late Chief of Scouts, U.S. Army. New York: Empire Books, 1908.
Coe, Charles H. Juggling a Rope. Pendleton, Ore.: Hamley, 1927.
Coe, George Washington. Frontier Fighter: The Autobiography of George W. Coe. Boston: Houghton Mifflin, 1934.
Coe, Urling C. Frontier Doctor. New York: Macmillan, 1939.
Coe, Wilber. Ranch on the Ruidoso: The Story of a Pioneer Family in New Mexico, 1871-1968. New York: Alfred A. Knopf, 1968.
Cole, Philip G. Montana in Miniature. Kalispell, Mont.: O'Neill Printers, 1966.
Coleman, John Winston, Jr. Stage Coach Days in the Bluegrass. Louisville, Ky.: Standard Press, 1935.
Coleman, Max M. From Mustanger to Lawyer. San Antonio, Texas: Carleton Printing, 1952.
Collier, William Ross-Westrate, and Victor, Edwin. Dave Cook of the Rockies. New York: Rufus Rockwell Wilson, 1936.
Collins, Dabney Otis. Great Western Rides. Denver: Sage Books, 1961.
———. The Hanging of Bad Jack Slade. Denver: Golden Ball Press, 1963.
Collins, Dennis. The Indians' Last Fight; or The Dull Knife Raid. Girard, Kan.: Appeal of Reason, 1915.
Collins, Hubert E. Warpath and Cattle Trail. New York: William Morrow, 1928.
Collins, Lewis. History of Kentucky. Covington, Ky.: Collins, 1874.
Collinson, Frank. Life in the Saddle. Norman: University of Oklahoma Press, 1963.
Combs, Joseph F. Gunsmoke in the Redlands. San Antonio, Texas: Naylor, 1968.
Complete Official History of Rube Burrows and His Celebrated Gang. Birmingham, Ala.: Lyman & Stone, n.d.
Conard, Howard L. (ed.). Encyclopedia of the History of Missouri, a Compendium of History and Biography for Ready Reference. 6 vols. New York: Haldeman, Conard, 1901.
———. Uncle Dick Wootton: The Pioneer Frontiersman of the Rocky Mountains. Chicago: R.R. Donnelley & Sons, 1957.
Conger, Roger N. Texas Rangers: Sesquicentennial Anniversary, 1823-1973. Fort Worth, Texas: Heritage Publications, 1973.
Conkling, Roscoe P., and Conkling, Margaret B. The Butterfield Overland Mail, 1857-1869. Glendale, Calif.: Arthur H. Clark, 1947.
Conn, William. Cow-Boys and Colonels. London: Griffith, Farran, Okeden & Welsh, 1887.
Connable, Alfred, and Silberfarb, Edward. Tigers of Tammany Hall: Nine Men Who Ran New York. New York: Holt, Rinehart & Winston, 1967.
Connell, Robert, Sr. Arkansas. New York: Paebar, 1947.
Connelley, William Elsey. Quantrill and the Border Wars. Cedar Rapids, Iowa: Torch Press, 1909.
———. Wild Bill and His Era. New York: Press of the Pioneers, 1933.
Conner, Daniel Ellis. Joseph Reddeford Walker and the Arizona Adventure. Norman: University of Oklahoma Press, 1956
Cook, David J. Hands Up; or Twenty Years of Detective Life in the Mountains and on the Plains. Denver: W.F. Robinson Printing, 1897.
Cook, James Henry. Fifty Years on the Old Frontier, as Cowboy, Hunter, Guide, Scout and Ranchman. New Haven, Conn.: Yale University Press, 1923.
———. Longhorn Cowboy. New York: G.P. Putnam's Sons, 1942.
Cook, Jim (Lane). Lane on the Llano, Being the Story of Jim (Lane) Cook. Boston: Little, Brown, 1936.
Cook, John R. The Border and the Buffalo. Topeka, Kan.: Crane, 1907.
Cookridge, E.H. The Baron of Arizona. New York: John Day, 1967.
Coolidge, Dane. Arizona Cowboys. New York: E.P. Dutton, 1938.
———. Fighting Men of the West. New York: E.P. Dutton, 1932.
———. Gringo Gold: A Story of Joaquin Murieta, the Bandit. New York: E.P. Dutton & Co., 1939.
Cooper, Frank C. Stirring Lives of Buffalo Bill, Colonel Wm. F. Cody, Last of the Great Scouts, and Pawnee Bill, Major Gordon W. Lillie, White Chief of the Pawnees. New York: Parsons, 1912.
Cordley, Rev. Richard D. History of Lawrence, Kansas. Lawrence, Kan.: E.F. Caldwell, 1895.
Corle, Edwin. Billy the Kid. New York: Duell, Sloane, & Pearce, 1953.
———. Desert Country. New York: Duell, Sloan & Pearce, 1941.
———. The Gila River of the Southwest. New York: Rinehart, 1951.
———. The Royal Highway (El Camino Real). New York: Bobbs-Merrill, 1949.
Corner, William (ed.). San Antonio de Bexar: A Guide and History. San Antonio, Texas: Bainbridge & Corner, Christmas, 1890.
Cossley-Batt, Jill Lillie Emma. The Last of the California Rangers. New York: Funk & Wagnalls, 1928.
Countant, C.G. The History of Wyoming. Laramie, Wyo.: Chaplin, Spafford & Mathison, 1899.
Coursey, O.W. Beautiful Black Hills: A Comprehensive Treatise on the Black Hills of South Dakota. Mitchell, S.D.: Educator Supply, 1926.
———. Wild Bill (James Butler Hickok). Mitchell, S.D.:

Educator Supply, 1924.

Cowan, Robert Ellsworth. *Range Rider*. Garden City, N.Y.: Doubleday, Doran, 1930.

———, and Boutwell Dunlap. *Bibliography of the Chinese Question in the United States*. San Francisco: A.M. Robertson, 1909.

Cox, Robert V. *Deadly Pursuit*. New York: Cameron House, 1977.

Cox, William R. *Luke Short and His Era*. Garden City, N.Y.: Doubleday, 1961.

Crabb, Richard E. *Empire on the Platte*. New York: World, 1967.

Crandall, Allen. *The Man from Kinsman*. Sterling, Colo.: Published by Author, 1933.

Crane, Walter R. *Gold and Silver*. New York: John Wiley & Sons, 1908.

Crawford, Lewis Ferandus. *Rekindling Camp Fires: The Exploits of Ben Arnold (Connor)*. Bismarck, N.D.: Capital Books, 1926.

Crawford, Samuel J. *Kansas in the Sixties*. Chicago: A.C. McClurg, 1911.

Crawford, Thomas Edgar. *The West of the Texas Kid, 1881-1910*. Norman: University of Oklahoma Press, 1962.

Creer, Leland. *Utah and the Nation*. Seattle: University of Washington Press, 1929.

Crichton, Kyle S. *Law and Order, Ltd.: The Rousing Life of Elfego Baca of New Mexico*. Glorieta, N.M.: Rio Grande Press, 1928.

Crites, Arthur S. *Pioneer Days in Kern County*. Los Angeles: Ward Ritchie Press, 1951.

Crockett, George Louis. *Two Centuries in East Texas*. Dallas: Southwest Press, 1932.

Croft-Cook, Rupert, and Meadmore, W.S. *Buffalo Bill, the Legend, the Man of Action, the Showman*. London: Sidwick & Jackson, 1952.

Crouch, Carrie J. *A History of Young County, Texas*. Austin: Texas State Historical Association, 1956.

Croy, Homer. *Corn Country*. New York: Duell, Sloan & Pearce, 1947.

———. *He Hanged Them High*. New York: Duell, Sloan & Pearce, 1952.

———. *Jesse James Was My Neighbor*. New York: Duell, Sloan & Pearce, 1949.

———. *Last of the Great Outlaws: The Story of Cole Younger*. New York: Duell, Sloan & Pearce, 1956.

———. *Trigger Marshall: The Story of Chris Madden*. New York: Duell, Sloan & Pearce, 1958.

Crumbine, Samuel J. *Frontier Doctor*. Philadelphia: Dorrance, 1948.

Culley, John Henry. *Cattle, Horses & Men of the Western Range*. Los Angeles: Ward Ritchie Press, 1940.

Cummins, Jim. *Jim Cummins' Book*. Denver: Reed, 1903.

Cunningham, Eugene. *Famous in the West*. El Paso, Texas: Hicks-Haywood, 1926.

———. *Triggernometry: A Gallery of Gunfighters*. New York: Press of the Pioneers, 1934.

Cunningham, James Charles. *The Truth About Murietta: Anecdotes and Facts Related by Those Who Knew Him and Disbelieve His Capture*. Los Angeles: Wetzel, 1938.

Curry, Mrs. Bell. *Parsons, Labette County, Kansas*. Parson, Kan.: Bell Bookcraft Shop, n.d.

Curry, J.C. *The Indian Police*. London: Faber & Faber, 1935.

Curtis, Albert. *Fabulous San Antonio*. San Antonio, Texas: Naylor, 1955.

Cushman, Dan. *The Great North Trail*. New York: McGraw-Hill, 1966.

Custer, George Armstrong. *My Life on the Plains*. New York: Sheldon, 1874.

D

Dacus, Joseph A. *Life and Adventures of Frank and Jesse James, the Noted Western Outlaws*. St. Louis: N.D. Thompson, 1880.

———. *Illustrated Lives and Adventures of Frank and Jesse James and the Younger Brothers, The Noted Western Outlaws*. St. Louis: N.D. Thompson, 1882.

Daggett, Stuart. *Chapters on the History of the Southern Pacific*. New York: Ronald Press, 1922.

Daggett, Thomas F. *Billy LeRoy, the Colorado Bandit; or the King of American Highwaymen*. New York: Richard K. Fox, Police Gazette, 1881.

———. *The Outlaw Brothers, Frank and Jesse James*. New York: Richard K. Fox, Police Gazette, 1881.

Dale, Edward Everett. *Cow Country*. Norman: University of Oklahoma Press, 1965.

———, and Lytton, Gaston. *Cherokee Cavaliers*. Norman: University of Oklahoma Press, 1939.

———, and Wardell, Morris L. *History of Oklahoma*. New York: Prentice-Hall, 1948.

———. *The History of the Ranch Cattle Industry in Oklahoma*. Washington, D.C.: American Historical Association, 1920.

———. *The Range Cattle Industry*. Norman: University of Oklahoma Press, 1960.

Dale, Henry. *Adventures and Exploits of the Younger Brothers, Missouri's Most Daring Outlaws, and Companions of the James Boys*. New York: Street & Smith, 1890.

Dalton, Emmett. *Beyond the Law*. New York: J.S. Ogilvie, 1918.

———. *The Dalton Brothers and Their Astounding Career of Crime*. New York: Frederick Fell, 1954.

———, and Jungmeyer, Jack. *When the Daltons Rode*. Garden City, N.Y.: Doubleday, Doran, 1931.

Dalton, Kit. *Under the Black Flag*. Memphis, Tenn.: Lockhart, 1914.

Dana, J.G. *Sutter of California*. New York: Halcyon House, 1938.

Dana, Rocky, and Harrington, Marie. *The Blonde Ranchero*. Los Angeles: Dawson's Book Shop, 1960.

Dane, G. Ezra. *Ghost Town*. New York: Tudor, 1941.

Daniels, Jonathan. *The Devil's Backbone*. New York: McGraw-Hill, 1962.

———. *Frontier on the Potomac*. New York: Macmillan, 1946.

Darrah, William Culp. *Powell of the Colorado*. Princeton, N.J.: Princeton University Press, 1962.

David, Robert B. *Malcolm Campbell, Sheriff*. Casper, Wyo.: Wyomingana, 1932.

Davidson, Levette J. and Blake, Forrester (eds.). *Rocky Mountain Tales*. Norman, Okla.: University of Oklahoma Press, 1947.

Davis, Carlyle C. *Olden Times in Colorado*. Los Angeles: Phillips, 1916.

Davis, Clyde. *The Arkansas*. New York: Farrar & Rinehart, 1940.

Davis, Jean. *Shallow Diggin's*. Caldwell, Idaho: Caxton Printers, 1963.

Davis, Mary Lee. *Sourdough Gold*. Boston: W.A. Wilde, 1933.

Davis, Reuben. *Recollections of Mississippi and the Mis-*

sissippians. Boston: Houghton Mifflin, 1889.

Davis, W.W.H. *El Gringo: Or New Mexico and Her People.* Santa Fe, N.M.: Rydal Press, 1938.

Day, B.F. *Gene Rhodes, Cowboy.* New York: Julian Messner, 1954.

Day, Jack Hays. *The Sutton-Taylor Feud.* San Antonio, Texas: Sid Murray & Sons, 1937.

Dean, Henry Clay. *Crimes of the Civil War.* Baltimore: William T. Smithson, 1868.

Dearment, Robert K. *Bat Masterson: The Man and the Legend.* Norman: University of Oklahoma Press, 1979.

Debo, Angie. *The Cowman's Southwest.* Glendale, Calif.: Arthur H. Clark, 1953.

_____. *A History of the Indians of the United States.* Norman: University of Oklahoma Press, 1970.

_____. *The Rise and Fall of the Choctaw Republic.* Norman: University of Oklahoma Pres, 1934.

_____. *And Still the Waters Run.* Princeton, N.J.: Princeton University Press, 1940.

_____. *Tulsa: From Creek Town to Oil Capital.* Norman: University of Oklahoma Press, 1943.

Dee, D. *Lowdown on Calamity Jane.* Rapid City, S.D.: Rapid City Guide, 1932.

Delay, Peter J. *History of Yuba and Sutter Counties.* Los Angeles: Historic Record, 1924.

Delony, Lewis S. *40 Years a Peace Officer.* Abilene, Texas.: Published by Author, 1937.

Denison, Merrill. *Klondike Mike.* New York: Morrow & Co., 1943.

Denton, B.E. *A Two-Gun Cyclone.* Dallas: B.E. Denton, 1927.

de Quille, Dan. *The Big Bonanza.* New York: Thomas Y. Crowell, 1947.

Dc Vcny, William. *The Establishment of Law and Order on Western Plains.* Portland, Ore.: Optimist Print, 1915.

DeVoto, Bernard. *Across the Wide Missouri.* Boston: Houghton Mifflin, 1947.

Dewees, W.B. *Letters from Texas.* Louisville, Ky.: New Albany Tribune Plant, 1852.

Dick, Everett. *The Sod-House Frontier, 1854-1890.* New York: D. Appleton-Century, 1937.

_____. *Vanguards of the Frontier.* New York: D. Appleton-Century, 1941.

Dicker, Laverne Mau. *The Chinese in San Francisco.* New York: Dover, 1979.

Dickson, Arthur Jerome (ed.). *Covered Wagon Days.* Cleveland: Arthur H. Clark, 1929.

Dillon, Richard. *California Trail Herd.* Los Gatos, Calif.: Talisman Press, 1961.

Dimsdale, Thomas J. *The Vigilantes of Montana.* Helena, Mont.: State Publishing, 1915.

Dixon, Clive K. *The Life of "Billy" Dixon.* Dallas: P.L. Turner, 1914.

Dobie, Charles Caldwell. *San Francisco's Chinatown.* New York: D. Appleton-Century, 1936.

_____. *San Francisco: A Pageant.* New York: D. Appleton Century, 1939.

Dobie, James Frank. *Coronado's Children.* Garden City, N.Y.: Garden City, 1930.

_____. *The Flavor of Texas.* Dallas: Dealey and Lowe, 1936.

_____. *Guide to Life and Literature of the Southwest.* Dallas: Southern Methodist University Press, 1952.

_____. *The Longhorns.* Boston: Little, Brown, 1941.

_____. *The Mustangs.* New York: Bantam Books, 1954.

_____. *A Vaquero of the Brush Country.* Dallas: Southwest Press, 1929.

Dodge, I.F. *Our Arizona.* New York: Scribner's, 1929.

Dodge, Richard Irving. *Our Wild Indians.* Hartford, Conn.: A.D. Worthington, 1883.

_____. *The Plains of the Great West.* New York: G.P. Putnam's Sons, 1877.

Dolan, J.R. *The Yankee Peddlers of Early America.* New York: Clarkson N. Potter, 1964.

Donaldson, Thomas. *Idaho of Yesterday.* Caldwell, Idaho: The Caxton Printers, 1941.

Dorsett, Lyle W. *The Queen City.* Boulder, Colo.: Pruet Publishers, 1977.

Dorsey, Florence. *Master of the Mississippi.* Boston: Houghton Mifflin, 1941.

Dorsey, George A. *Traditions of the Arikara.* Washington, D.C.: Carnegie Institution, 1904.

Dosch, Henry Ernst. *Vigilante Days at Virginia City.* Portland, Ore.: Fred Lockley, 1924.

Douglas, Clarence Brown. *History of Tulsa, Oklahoma.* Chicago: S.J. Clarke, 1921.

_____. *Territory Tales.* El Reno, Okla.: El Reno American, 1951.

Douglas, Claude Leroy. *Cattle Kings of Texas.* Dallas: Cecil Baugh, 1939.

_____. *Famous Texas Feuds.* Dallas: Turner, 1936.

_____. *The Gentlemen in White Hats.* Dallas: South-West Press, 1934.

Douglas, Ford. *The Cattle Rustlers of Wyoming.* New York: J.S. Ogilvie, 1916.

Drago, Harry Sinclair. *Great American Cattle Trails.* New York: Dodd, Mead, 1965.

_____. *The Great Range Wars.* New York: Dodd, Mead, 1970.

_____. *Lost Bonanzas.* New York: Dodd, Mead, 1966.

_____. *Notorious Ladies of the Frontier.* New York: Dodd, Mead, 1969.

_____. *Outlaws on Horseback.* New York: Dodd, Mead, 1964.

_____. *Red River Valley.* New York: Clarkson N. Potter, 1962.

_____. *Road Agents and Train Robbers.* New York: Dodd, Mead, 1973.

_____. *Roads to Empire.* New York: Dodd, Mead, 1968.

_____. *The Steamboaters.* New York: Dodd, Mead, 1967.

_____. *Wild, Woolly & Wicked.* New York: Clarkson N. Potter, 1960.

Drake, Samuel G. *Biography and History of the Indians of North America.* Philadelphia: Charles de Silver, 1860.

Drannan, Capt. William F. *Thirty-One Years on the Plains and in the Mountains.* Chicago: Rhodes & McClure, 1899.

Draper, William R. *A Cub Reporter in the Old Indian Territory.* Girard, Kan.: E. Haldeman-Julius, 1946.

_____. *Exciting Adventures Along the Indian Frontier.* Girard, Kan.: E. Haldeman-Julius, 1946.

_____, and Mabel. *Old Grubstake Days in Joplin.* Girard, Kan.: E. Haldeman-Julius, 1946.

Dresser, Albert. *California's Pioneer Mountaineer of Rabbit Gulch.* San Francisco: Published by Author, 1930.

Driggs, Benjamin Woodbury. *History of Teton Valley, Idaho.* Caldwell, Idaho: Caxton Printers, 1926.

Driggs, Howard Roscoe. *Westward America.* New York: G.P. Putnam's Sons, 1942.

Driscoll, R.E. *Seventy Years of Banking in the Black Hills.* Rapid City, S.D.: Gate City Guide, 1948.

Driver, Harold E. *Indians of North America.* Chicago: Chicago University Press, 1961.

Drucker, Philip. *Indians of the Northwest Coast.* Garden City, N.Y.: The Natural History Press, 1963.

Drury, Aubrey. *California, An Intimate Guide.* New York: Harper & Brothers, 1935.

_____. *John A. Hooper and California's Robust Youth.* San Francisco: Arthur W. Hooper, 1952.

Drury, Wells. *An Editor on the Comstock Lode.* San Francisco: Elder, 1913.

Drzazga, John. *Wheels of Fortune.* Springfield, Ill.: Charles C. Thomas, 1963.

Duffus, Robert L. *The Santa Fe Trail.* New York: Tudor Publishing, 1930.

_____. *The Tower of Jewels: Memories of San Francisco.* New York: W. W. Norton, 1960.

Duncan, L. Wallace (ed.). *History of Montgomery County, Kansas, by Its Own People.* Iola, Kan.: Iola Register, 1903.

Dunlap, Carol. *California People.* Salt Lake City, Utah: Peregrene Smith Books, 1982.

Dunlop, Richard. *Doctors of the American Frontier.* Garden City, N.Y.: Doubleday, 1965.

Dunn, Allan. *Carefree San Francisco.* San Francisco: Elder, 1913.

Dunn, J.B. *Perilous Trails of Texas.* Dallas: Southwest Press, 1952.

Dunn, John P. *Massacres of the Mountains.* New York: Harper and Brothers, 1886.

Dunning, Harold Marion. *The Life of Rocky Mountain Jim (James Nugent).* Boulder, Colo.: Johnson, 1967.

Dunraven, Earl of (Windham, Thomas Wyndham-Quin). *Hunting in the Yellowstone.* New York: Macmillan, 1925.

_____. *Past Times and Pastimes.* London: Hodder & Stoughton, 1922.

Durham, Philip, and Jones, Everett L. *The Negro Cowboys.* New York: Dodd, Mead, 1965.

Dutton, Bertha P. (ed.). *Indians of the Southwest.* Santa Fe, N.M.: Southwestern Association of Indian Affairs, 1963.

Duval, John C. *The Adventures of Big Foot Wallace, the Texas Ranger and Hunter.* Macon, Ga.: J.W. Burke, 1871.

_____. *Early Times in Texas.* Austin, Texas: H.P.N. Gammel, 1892.

Dykes, Jefferson C. *Billy the Kid: The Bibliography of a Legend.* Albuquerque: University of New Mexico Press, 1952.

Dykstra, Robert R. *The Cattle Towns.* New York: Alfred A. Knopf, 1968.

E

Earle, Alice Moore. *Stage Coach and Tavern Days.* London: Macmillan, 1927.

Earle, J.P. *History of Clay County and Northwest Texas.* Henrietta, Texas: n.p., 1900.

Eaton, Frank. *Pistol Pete, Veteran of the Old West.* Boston: Little, Brown, 1952.

Eaton, Jeanette. *Bucky O'Neill of Arizona.* New York: William Morrow, 1949.

Edgar, William Crowell. *Judson Moss Bemis, Pioneer.* Minneapolis Minn.: The Bellman Company, 1926.

Edwards, J.B. *Early Days in Abilene.* Abilene, Texas: C.W. Wheeler, 1896.

Edwards, John Newman. *Noted Guerrillas, or the Warfare of the Border.* St. Louis: Bryan, Brand, 1877.

_____. *Shelby and His Men.* Cincinnati, Ohio: Miami Printing, 1867.

_____. *Shelby's Expedition to Mexico.* Kansas City: Kansas City Times, 1872.

Egan, Ferol. *Fremont, Explorer for a Restless Nation.* Garden City, N.Y.: Doubleday, 1977.

Eggan, Fred. *Social Organization of the Western Pueblos.* Chicago: University of Chicago Press, 1950.

Eikemeyer, Carl. *Over the Great Navajo Trail.* New York: J.J. Little, 1900.

Eisele, Wilbert E. *The Real "Wild Bill" Hickok.* Denver: William H. Andre, 1931.

Ellet, Charles. *The Mississippi and Ohio Rivers.* Philadelphia: J.B. Lippincott, Grambo, 1853.

Ellett, Elizabeth Fries Lummis. *Summer Rambles in the West.* New York: J.C. Riker, 1853.

Elliott, David Stewart. *Last Raid of the Daltons.* Coffeyville, Kan.: Coffeyville Journal, 1892.

Ellis, Amanda M. *Bonanza Towns: Leadville and Cripple Creek.* Colorado Springs, Colo.: Dentan Printing, 1954.

_____. *Pioneers.* Colorado Springs, Colo.: Dentan Printing, 1955.

Elman, Robert. *Fired in Anger: The Personal Handguns of American Heroes and Villains.* Garden City, N.Y.: Doubleday, 1968.

_____. *Badmen of the West.* Secaucus, N.J.: Ridge Press, 1974.

Emmett, Chris. *Fort Union and the Winning of the Southwest.* Norman: University of Oklahoma Press, 1965.

_____. *Shanghai Pierce, a Fair Likeness.* Norman: University of Oklahoma Press, 1953.

Emrich, Duncan. *It's An Old Wild West Custom.* New York: Vanguard Press, 1949.

Erskine, Gladys. *Broncho Charlie: A Saga of the Saddle.* New York: Thomas Y. Crowell, 1934.

Erwin, Allen A. *The Southwest of John H. Slaughter, 1841-1922.* Glendale, Calif.: Arthur H. Clark, 1965.

Evans, Max. *Long John Dunn of Taos.* Los Angeles: Westernlore Press, 1959.

Ewers, John C. *The Blackfeet: Raiders on the Northwestern Plains.* Norman: University of Oklahoma Press, 1958.

_____., et al. *Views of a Vanishing Frontier.* Omaha, Neb.: Center for Western Studies, Joslyn Art Museum, 1984.

F

Fable, Edmund Jr. *Billy the Kid, the New Mexican Outlaw.* Denver: Denver, 1881.

Fallwell, Gene. *The Texas Rangers.* Texarkana, Texas: Connell Printing, 1959.

Fanning, Pete. *Great Crimes of the West.* San Francisco: Ed Barry, 1929.

Farber, James. *Texans with Guns.* San Antonio, Texas: Naylor, 1950.

_____. *Those Texans.* San Antonio, Texas: Naylor, 1945.

Farish, T.E. *The Gold Hunters of California.* Chicago: M.A. Donohue, 1904.

_____. *History of Arizona.* San Francisco: Filmer Brothers Electrotype, 1915-18.

Farmer, Elihu J. *The Resources of the Rocky Mountains.* Cleveland: Leader Printing, 1883.

Farrow, Marion Humphreys. *Troublesome Times in Texas.* San Antonio, Texas: Glegg, 1957.

Fast, Howard Melvin. *The Last Frontier.* New York: Duell, Sloan & Pearce, 1942.

Faulk, Odie B. *Dodge City.* New York: Oxford University

Press, 1977.

_____. *The Geronimo Campaign.* New York: Oxford University Press, 1969.

_____. *Tombstone: Myth and Reality.* New York: Oxford University Press, 1972.

Faulkner, Virginia. *Roundup: A Nebraska Reader.* Lincoln: University of Nebraska Press, 1957.

Featherston, Edward Baxter. *A Pioneer Speaks.* Dallas: Cecil Baugh, 1940.

Feder, Sid. *Longhorns and Short Tales of Victoria and the Gulf Coast.* Victoria, Texas: Victoria Advocate, 1958.

Ferguson, Charles D. *The Experiences of a Forty-Niner During Thirty-Four Years' Residence in California and Australia.* Cleveland, Ohio: Williams, 1888.

Ferguson, Fergus. *From Glasgow to Missouri and Back.* Glasgow, Scot.: T.D. Morison, 1878.

Ferguson, William. *America by River and Rail.* London: J. Nisbet, 1856.

Fergusson, Erna. *Erna Fergusson's Albuquerque.* Albuquerque, N.M.: Armitage Editions, 1947.

_____. *Murder & Mystery in New Mexico.* Albuquerque, N.M.: Armitage Editions, 1948.

_____. *Our Southwest.* New York: Alfred A. Knopf, 1940.

Fergusson, Harvey. *Rio Grande.* New York: Alfred A. Knopf, 1933.

Fewtrell, Malcolm. *The Train Robbers.* London: Arthur Barker, 1964.

Fielder, Mildred (ed.). *Lawrence Country for the Dakota Territory Centennial.* Lead: Seaton Printing, 1960.

_____. *Wild Bill and Deadwood.* Seattle, Wash.: Superior, 1965.

Fieldhouse, D.K. *The Colonial Empires.* New York: Delacorte Press, 1965.

Fierman, Floyd D., and West, John. *Billy the Kid, the Cowboy Outlaw.* Philadelphia: Maurice Jacobs Press, 1965.

Finger, Charles Joseph. *Adventures Under Sapphire Skies.* New York: William Morrow, 1931.

_____. *The Distant Prize.* New York: Appleton-Century, 1935.

_____. *Foot-Loose in the West.* New York: William Morrow, 1932.

_____. *Frontier Ballards.* Garden City, N.Y.: Doubleday, Page, 1927.

Finley, James B. *Autobiography of Reverend James B. Finley or Pioneer Life in the West.* Cincinnati, Ohio: Cranston

Fisher, O.C. *It Occurred In Kimble.* Houston, Texas: Anson Jones Press, 1937.

_____, with Dykes, J.C. *King Fisher: His Life and Times.* Norman: University of Oklahoma Press, 1966.

_____. *The Texas Heritage of the Fishers and the Clarks.* Salado, Texas: Anson Jones Press, 1963.

Fisher, Vardis, and Holmes, Opal Laurel. *Gold Rushes and Mining Camps of the Early American West.* Caldwell, Idaho: Caxton Printers, 1968.

Flagg, Oscar H. *A Review of the Cattle Business in Johnson County, Wyoming, Since 1882.* Cheyenne, Wyo.: Vic Press, 1967.

Flanagan, Mike. *Out West.* New York: Harry N. Abrams, 1987.

Fletcher, Baylis John. *Up the Trail in '79.* Norman: University of Oklahoma Press, 1968.

Fletcher, Ernest M. *The Wayward Horseman.* Denver: Sage Books, 1958.

Flexner, James T. *Steamboats Come True: American Inventors in Action.* New York: Viking Press, 1944.

Flint, Timothy. *A Condensed Geography and History of the Western States, or The Mississippi Valley.* 2 vols. Cincinnati, Ohio: E.H. Flint, 1828.

_____. *Recollections of the Last Ten Years.* Boston: Cummings, Hilliard, 1826.

Florin, Lambert. *Boot Hill: Historic Graves of the Old West.* Seattle, Wash.: Superior, 1966.

_____. *Ghost Town Album.* Seattle, Wash.: Superior, 1962.

Fogarty, Kate Hammond. *The Story of Montana.* New York: A.S. Barnes, 1916.

Folmsbee, Stanley J., et al. *History of Tennessee.* New York: Lewis Historical, 1960.

Folwell, William Watts. *A History of Minnesota.* St. Paul: Minnesota Historical Society, 1921-30.

Foote, Stella Adelyne. *Letters from Buffalo Bill.* Billings, Mont.: Foote, 1954.

Forbes, Gerald. *Guthrie: Oklahoma's First Capital.* Norman: Univesity of Oklahoma Press, 1938.

Ford, John Salmon. *Rip Ford's Texas.* Austin: University of Texas Press, 1963.

Foreman, Grant. *Advancing the Frontier.* Norman: University of Oklahoma Press, 1933.

_____. *The Five Civilized Tribes.* Norman: University of Oklahoma Press, 1934.

_____. *Fort Gibson.* Norman: University of Oklahoma Press, 1936.

_____. *A History of Oklahoma.* Norman: University of Oklahoma Press, 1942.

_____. *Indian Removal.* Norman: University of Oklahoma Press, 1932.

_____. *Muskogee: The Biography of an Oklahoma Town.* Norman: University of Oklahoma Press, 1943.

_____ (ed.). *A Pathfinder in the Southwest, The Itinerary of Lt. A.W. Whipple.* Norman: University of Oklahoma Press, 1940.

_____. *Pioneer Days in the Early Southwest.* Cleveland: Arthur H. Clark, 1926.

Forrest, Earle R. *Arizona's Dark and Bloody Ground.* Caldwell, Idaho: Caxton Printers, 1953.

_____, and Hill, Edwin B. *Lone War Trail of Apache Kid.* Pasadena, Calif.: Trail's End, 1947.

_____. *Missions and Pueblos of the Old Southwest.* Cleveland: Arthur H. Clark, 1929.

Forsee, Peter A. *Five Years of Crime in California.* Ukiah City, Calif.: Forsee, 1867.

Fortier, Alcee. *A History of Louisiana.* New York: Manz & Joyand, 1904.

Fortson, John. *Pott County and What Has Come of It.* Shawnee, Okla.: Pottawatomie County Historical Society, 1936.

Fossett, Frank. *Colorado: A Historical, Descriptive and Statistical Work.* Denver: Daily Tribune Steam Printing House, 1876.

_____. *Colorado: Its Gold and Silver Mines.* New York: C.G. Crawford, 1879.

Foster-Harris. *The Look of the Old West.* New York: Viking Press, 1955.

Foy, Eddie, and Harlow, Alvin F. *Clowning Through Life.* New York: E.P. Dutton, 1928.

Frackelton, Will. *Sagebrush Dentist.* Chicago: A.C. McClurg, 1941.

Francis, Francis, Jr. *Saddle and Moccasin.* London: Chapman & Hall, 1887.

Franke, Paul. *They Plowed Up Hell in Old Cochise.* Douglas, Ariz.: Douglas Climate Club, 1950.

Franks, J.M. *Seventy Years in Texas.* Gatesville, Tex., 1924.

Frantz, Joe B., and Choate, Julian Ernest, Jr. *The American Cowboy: The Myth and the Reality.* Norman: University of Oklahoma Press, 1955.

Fraser, Mrs. Hugh and Hugh C. *Seven Years on the Pacific Slope*. New York: Dodd, Mead, 1914.

Frazer, Robert W. *Forts of the West*. Norman: University of Oklahoma Press, 1965.

Frederick, James Vincent. *Ben Holladay, the Stagecoach King*. Glendale, Calif.: Arthur H. Clark, 1940.

Freeman, G.D. *Midnight and Noonday, or Dark Deeds Unraveled*. Caldwell, Kan.: G.D. Freeman, 1890.

Freeman, James W. (ed.). *Prose and poetry of the live stock industry of the United States*. Denver: Franklin Hudson, 1905.

Freeman, Lewis Ransome. *Down the Yellowstone*. New York: Dodd, Mead, 1922.

French, Chauncey Del. *Railroadman*. New York: Macmillan, 1938.

French, George (ed.). *Indianola Scrap Book*. Victoria, Texas: Victoria Advocate, 1936.

French, Joseph Lewis. (ed.). *The Pioneer West*. Boston: Little, Brown, 1923.

French, Wild James. *Wild Jim, the Texas Cowboy and Saddle King*. Antioch, Ill.: W.J. French, 1890.

French, William John. *Some Recollections of a Western Ranchman: New Mexico, 1883-1899*. London: Methuen, 1927.

Fridge, Ike. *History of the Chisum war*. Electra, Texas: J.D. Smith, 1927.

Frink, Maurice. *Cow Country Cavalcade*. Denver: Old West, 1954.

———, Jackson, W. Turrentine, and Spring, Agnes W. *When Grass Was King*. Boulder: University of Colorado Press, 1956.

Frison, Paul. *First White Woman in the Big Horn Basin*. Worland, Wyo.: Worland Press, 1962.

———. *Grass Was Gold*. Worland, Wyo.: Worland Press, 1966.

Fuess, Claude M. *Carl Schurz, Reformer, 1829-1906*. New York: Dodd, Mead, 1932.

Fugate, F.L. *The Spanish Heritage of the Southwest*. El Paso, Texas: Western Press, 1952.

Fugina, Captain Frank J. *Lore and Lure of the Upper Mississippi River*. Winona, Minn.: Privately Printed, 1945.

Fulcher, Walter. *The Way I Heard It: Tales of the Big Bend*. Austin: University of Texas Press, 1959.

Fulkerson, H.S. *Early Days in Mississippi*. Vicksburg, Miss.: Vicksburg Printing, 1885.

———. *Random Recollections of Early Days in Mississippi*. Vicksburg, Miss.: Vicksburg, 1885.

Fuller, George W. *A History of the Pacific Northwest*. New York: Alfred A. Knopf, 1931.

———. *The Inland Empire of the Pacific Northwest*. Denver: H.G. Linderman, 1928.

Fuller, Henry C. *Adventures of Bill Longley*. Nacogdoches, Texas: Baker Printing, n.d.

———. *A Texas Sheriff*. Nacogdoches, Texas: Baker Printing, 1931.

Fulton, Maurice Garland. *History of the Lincoln County War*. Tucson: University of Arizona Press, 1968.

———, and Horgan, Paul. *New Mexico's Own Chronicle*. Dallas: Banks Upshaw, 1937.

———. *Roswell in Its Early Years*. Roswell, N.M.: Hall-Poorbaugh Press, 1963.

Fultz, Hollis B. *Famous Northwest Manhunts and Murder Mysteries*. Elma, Wash.: Elma Chronicle, 1955.

Furlong, Thomas. *Fifty Years A Detective*. St. Louis: C.E. Barnett, 1912.

Fyfe, H. Hamilton. *The Real Mexico*. London: William Heinemann, 1914.

G

Gage, Jack R. *The Johnson County War Is a Pack of Lies*. Cheyenne, Wyo.: Flintlock, 1967.

———. *Tensleep and No Rest*. Casper, Wyo.: Prairie, 1958.

Gann, Walter. *Tread of the Longhorns*. San Antonio, Texas: Naylor, 1949.

Gantt, Paul H. *The Case of Alfred Packer, the Man Eater*. Denver: University of Denver, 1952.

Ganzhorn, Jack. *I've Killed Men*. London: Robert Hale, 1940.

Gard, Wayne. *The Chisholm Trail*. Norman: University of Oklahoma Press, 1954.

———. *Fabulous Quarter Horse: Steel Dust*. New York: Duell, Sloan & Pearce, 1958.

———. *Frontier Justice*. Norman: University of Oklahoma Press, 1949.

———. *The Great Buffalo Hunt*. New York: Alfred A. Knopf, 1959.

———. *Rawhide Texas*. Norman: University of Oklahoma Press, 1965.

———. *Sam Bass*. New York: Houghton Mifflin, 1936.

Gardiner, Charles Fox. *Doctor at Timberline*. Caldwell, Idaho: Caxton Printers, 1939.

Gardner, Raymond Hatfield. *The Old Wild West*. San Antonio, Texas: Naylor, 1944.

Garland, Hamlin. *The Captain of the Gray-Horse Troop*. New York: Harper & Brothers, 1902.

———. *A Daughter of the Middle Border*. New York: Macmillan, 1921.

———. *Roadside Meetings*. New York: Macmillan, 1930.

Garrett, Patrick Floyd, and Upson, Ash. *The Authentic Life of Billy the Kid*. New York: Macmillan, 1927.

Garretson, Martin S. *The American Bison*. New York: New York Zoological Society, 1938.

Garst, Doris Shannon. *The Story of Wyoming and Its Constitution and Government*. Douglas, Wyo.: Douglas Enterprise, 1938.

———. *When the West Was Young*. Douglas, Wyo.: Douglas Enterprise, 1942.

———, and Garst, Warren. *Wild Bill Hickok*. New York: Julian Messner, 1952.

Garwood, Darrel. *Crossroads of America: The Story of Kansas City*. New York: W.W. Norton, 1948.

Gates, Paul Wallace. *Illinois Central Railroad and Its Colonization Work*. Cambridge, Mass.: Harvard University Press, 1934.

Gay, Felix M. *History of Nowata County*. Stillwater, Okla.: Redlands Press, 1957.

George, Andrew L. *The Texas Convict: Thrilling and Terrible Experiences of a Texas Boy*. Austin, Texas: Ben C. Jones, 1893.

George, Todd Menzies. *Just Memories, and Twelve Years with Cole Younger*. Kansas City: Quality Hill Printing, 1959.

Gibbons, Rev. James Joseph. *In the San Juan, Colorado: Sketches*. Chicago: Press of Calumet Book & Engraving, 1898.

Gibbs, Josiah F. *The Mountain Meadow Massacre*. Salt Lake City, Utah: Salt Lake Tribune, 1910.

Gibson, Arrell M. *The Life and Death of Colonel Albert Jennings Fountain*. Norman: University of Oklahoma Press, 1965.

Gibson, Rev. Otis. *The Chinese in America*. Cincinnati, Ohio: Hitchcock & Walden, 1877.

Gilfillan, Archer B. *A Goat's Eye View of the Black Hills*. Rapid City, S.D.: Dean & Dean, 1953.

Gillett, James Buchanan. *Six Years With the Texas Rangers*,

1875 to 1881. Lincoln: University of Nebraska Press, 1976.

Gillis, O.J. *To Hell and Back Again, Its Discovery, Description, and Experiences; or, Life in the Penitentiary of Texas and Kansas.* Little Rock, Ark.: Democrat Printing, 1906.

Gilmore, Harry. *Four Years in the Saddle.* New York: Harper and Brothers, 1866.

Ginty, Elizabeth Beall. *Missouri Legend.* New York: Random House, 1938.

Gipson, Fred. *Fabulous Empire: Colonel Zack Miller's Story.* Boston: Houghton Mifflin, 1946.

Gish, Anthony. *American Bandits.* Girard, Kan.: Haldeman-Julius, 1938.

Gittinger, Roy. *The Formation of the State of Oklahoma.* Norman: University of Oklahoma Press, 1939.

Glasscock, Carl Burgess. *Bandits of the Southwest Pacific.* New York: Frederick A. Stokes, 1929.

_____. *Big Bonanza: The Story of the Comstock Trade.* Indianapolis, Ind.: Bobbs-Merrill, 1931.

_____. *Gold in Them Hills: The Story of the West's Last Wild Mining Days.* Indianapolis, Ind.: Bobbs-Merrill, 1932.

_____. *A Golden Highway: Scenes of History's Greatest Gold Rush Yesterday and Today.* Indianapolis, Ind.: Bobbs-Merrill, 1934.

_____. *Lucky Baldwin.* Indianapolis, Ind.: Bobbs-Merrill, 1933.

_____. *Then Came Oil.* New York: Bobbs-Merrill, 1938.

_____. *The War of the Copper Kings: Builders of Butte and Wolves of Wall Street.* Indianapolis, Ind.: Bobbs-Merrill, 1935.

Glazier, Willard. *Down the Great River.* Philadelphia: Hubbard Brothers, 1883

_____. *Ocean to Ocean on Horseback.* Philadelphia: Hubbard, 1896.

Goetzmann, William H. *Army Exploration in the American West, 1803-1863.* New Haven, Conn.: Yale University Press, 1959.

_____. *Exploration and Empire: The Explorer and the Scientist in the Winning of the American West.* New York: Alfred A. Knopf, 1966.

_____. *Exploring the American West, 1803-1879.* Washington: Division of Publications, National Park Service, U.S. Department of the Interior, 1966.

Goodsmith, Elliott S. *The Story of a Forty-Niner.* Chicago: n.p., 1930.

Goodwin, Cardinal. *The Trans-Mississippi West.* New York: D. Appleton, 1927.

Goodykoontz, Colin B. *Home Missions on the American Frontier.* Caldwell, Idaho: Caxton, 1939.

Goplen, Arnold O. *The Career of the Marquis de Mores in the Badlands of North Dakota.* Bismarck: State Historical Society of North Dakota, 1946.

Gordon, Mike. *I Arrest Pearl Starr, and Other Stories of Adventure as a Policeman in Fort Smith, Arkansas, for 40 Years.* Fort Smith, Ark.: Press-Atgus, 1958.

Gordon, S. *Recollections of Old Milestown.* Miles City, Mont.: Independent Printing, 1918.

Gordon, Welche. *Jesse James and His Band of Notorious Outlaws.* Chicago: Laird & Lee, 1891.

Gorman, Harry M. *My Memoires of the Comstock.* New York: Sutton-House, 1939.

Gosnell, H. Allen. *Guns on the Western Waters.* Baton Rouge, La.: Louisiana State University Press, 1949.

Goss, Helen Rocca. *The Life and Death of a Quicksilver Mine.* Los Angeles: Historical Society of Southern California.

Gould, E.W. *Fifty Years on the Mississippi.* St. Louis, Mo.: Nixon-Jones, 1889.

Goulder, W.A. *Reminiscences of a Pioneer.* Boise, Idaho: Timothy Regan, 1909.

Graham, Jean. *Tales of the Ozark River Country.* Clinton, Mo.: Press of Martin Printing, 1929.

Grant, Bruce. *The Cowboy Encyclopedia.* New York: Rand McNally, 1951.

Grant, Jack. *Trail Dust and Gun Smoke: Factual Stories of a Cowboy's Life.* New York: Vantage Press, 1965.

Grant, Joseph D. *Redwoods and Reminiscences.* San Fransisco: Save the Redwoods League & the Menninger Foundation, 1973.

Graves, Richard S. *Oklahoma Outlaws.* Fort Davis, Texas: Frontier Books, 1968.

Gray, Arthur Amos. *Men Who Built the West.* Caldwell, Idaho: Caxton Printers, 1945.

Gray, Frank S. *Pioneering in Southwest Texas.* Austin, Texas: Steck, 1949.

Green, J.H. *Gambling Unmasked! or The Personal Experience of J. H. Green, the Reformed Gambler.* Philadelphia: Privately Published, 1847.

_____. *The Secret Band of Brothers; or The American Outlaws.* Philadelphia: Privately Published, 1847.

Greene, Capt. Jonathan H. *A Desperado in Arizona, 1858-1860.* Santa Fe, N.M.: Stagecoach, 1964.

Greer, James K. *Grand Prairie.* Dallas, Texas: Tardy, 1935.

Greer, James Kimmins. *Bois d'arc to Barb'd Wire; Ken Carey: Southwestern Frontier Born.* Dallas, Texas: Dealey & Lowe, 1936.

_____. (ed.). *Buck Barry: A Texas Ranger and Frontiersman.* Dallas, Texas: Southwest Press, 1932.

_____. *Colonel Jack Hays: Texas Frontier Leader and California Builder.* New York: E.P. Dutton, 1952.

Greever, William S. *The Bonanza West: The Story of the Western Mining Rushes, 1848-1900.* Norman: University of Oklahoma Press, 1963.

Gregg, Andrew K. *New Mexico in the Nineteenth Century: A Pictorial History.* Albuquerque: University of New Mexico Press, 1968.

Gregg, Andy. *Drums of Yesterday: The Forts of New Mexico.* Santa Fe, N.M.: Press of the Territorian, 1968.

Gregg, Jacob Ray. *Pioneer Days in Malheur County.* Los Angeles: Lorrin L. Morrison, 1950.

Gregg, Josiah. *The Commerce of the Prairies.* Lincoln: University of Nebraska, 1967.

Gregg, Kate L. (ed.). *The Road to Santa Fe.* Albuquerque: University of New Mexico Press, 1952.

Gregory, Lester. *True Wild West Stories.* London: Andrew Dakers, n.d.

Grinnell, George B. *The Cheyennes: Their History and Ways of Life.* 2 vols. New York: Cooper Square, 1962.

_____. *The Fighting Cheyennes.* New York: Charles Scribner's Sons, 1915.

Grisham, Noel. *Tame the Reckless Wind: The Life and Legends of Sam Bass.* Austin, Texas: San Felipe Press, 1968.

Griswold, Don and Jean. *The Carbonate Camp Called Leadville.* Denver: University of Denver Press, 1951.

Grover, David H. *Diamondfield Jack: A Study in Frontier Justice.* Reno: University of Nevada Press, 1968.

Guernsey, Charles Arthur. *Wyoming Cowboy Days.* New York: G.P. Putnam's Sons, 1936.

Guild, Josephus Conn. *Old Times in Tennessee.* Nashville, Tenn.: Eastman & Howell, 1878.

Guinn, J.M. *A History of California, and an Extended History of Its Southern Coast Counties.* Los Angeles:

Historic Record, 1907.

———. *Historical and Biographical Record of Southern California*. Chicago: Chapman, 1902.

———. *History of the State of California and Biographical Record of Sacramento Valley, California*. Chicago: Chapman, 1906.

———. *History of the State of California and Biographical Record of San Joaquin County*. Los Angeles: Historic Record, 1909.

Guyer, James S. *Pioneer Life in West Texas*. Brownwood, Texas: n.p., 1938.

H

Hafen, Leroy R. (ed.). *Colorado Gold Rush: Contemporary Letters and Reports, 1858-1859*. Glendale, Calif.: Arthur H. Clark, 1941.

———, and Young, Francis Marion. *Fort Laramie and the Pageant of the West*. Glendale, Calif.: Arthur H. Clark, 1938.

——— and Ann. *Handcrafts for Zion*. Glendale, Calif.: Arthur H. Clark, 1860.

———, and Rister, Carl Coke. *Western America*. New York: Prentice-Hall, 1941.

Hagan, William T. *American Indians*. Chicago: University of Chicago Press, 1961.

———. *Indian Police and Judges: Experiences in Acculturation and Control*. New Haven, Conn.: Yale University Press, 1966.

Hagedorn, Hermann. *Roosevelt in the Badlands*. Boston: Houghton Mifflin, 1921.

Hailey, John. *The History of Idaho*. Boise, Idaho: Syms-York, 1910.

Hale, Horace. *Education in Colorado 1861-1885*. Denver: News, Printing, 1885.

Haley, J. Evetts. *Charles Goodnight: Cowman and Plainsman*. Boston: Houghton Mifflin, 1936.

———, and Holden, William Curry. *The Flamboyant Judge: James D. Hamlin*. Canyon, Texas: Palo Duro Press, 1972.

———. *George W. Littlefield, Texan*. Norman: University of Oklahoma Press, 1943.

———. *Jeff Milton: A Good Man with a Gun*. Norman: University of Oklahoma Press, 1948.

———. *Jim East: Trailhand and Cowboy*. Canyon, Texas: n.p., 1931.

———. *A Texan Looks at Lyndon: A Study in Illegitimate Power*. Canyon, Texas: Palo Duro Press, 1964.

———. *The XIT Ranch of Texas and the Early Days of the Llano Estacado*. Chicago: Lakeside Press, 1929.

Hall, Angelo. *Forty-One Thieves: A Tale of California*. Boston: Cornhill, 1919.

Hall, Frank. *History of the State of Colorado*. Chicago: Blakeley Printing, 1889.

Hall, Frank O., and Whitten, Lindsey H. *Jesse James Rides Again*. Lawton, Okla.: LaHoma, 1948.

Hall, J.M. *The Beginnings of Tulsa*. Tulsa, Okla.: n.p., 1933.

Hall, James. *The Harpe's Head: A Legend of Kentucky*. Philadelphia: Key & Biddle, 1833.

———. *Sketches of History: Life and Manners in the West*. Philadelphia: H. Hall, 1835.

———. *Statistics of the West, At the Close of the Year 1836*. Cincinnati, Ohio: J.A. James, 1836.

———. *The West: Its Commerce and Navigation*. Cincinnati:

H.W. Derby, 1848.

Hall, Trowbridge. *California Trails: Intimate Guide to the Old Mission*. New York: Macmillan, 1920.

Hall-Quest, Olga W. *Wyatt Earp, Marshal of the Old West*. New York: Farrar, Straus & Cudahay, 1956.

Halsell, H.H. *The Old Cimarron*. Lubbock, Texas: Published by Author, 1944.

———. *Cowboys and Cattleland*. Nashville, Tenn.: Parthenon Press, 1937.

Hambleton, Chakley J. *A Gold Hunter's Experience*. Chicago: Published by Author, 1898.

Hamer, Philip M. *Tennessee: A History*. New York: American Historical Society, 1933.

Hamilton, James McClellan. *From Wilderness to Statehood: A History of Montana, 1805-1900*. Portland, Ore.: Binsford & Mort, 1957.

Hamilton, Jonathan Newman. *A Storeboat on the Ohio River*. Cincinnati, Ohio: Published by Author, n.d.

Hamilton, Patrick. *Resources of Arizona*. San Francisco: Bancroft, 1884.

Hamilton, William Baskerville. *Anglo-American Law on the Frontier*. Durham, N.C.: Duke University Press, 1953.

Hamilton, Winifred Oldham. *Wagon Days on Red River*. Raton, N.M.: Daily Range, 1947.

Hamlin, Lloyd and Rose. *Hamlin's Tombstone Picture Gallery*. Glendale, Calif.: Western Americana Press of Glendale, 1960.

Hamlin, William Lee. *The True Story of Billy the Kid*. Caldwell, Idaho: Caxton Printers, 1959.

Hammond, Dorothy M., and Hendricks, George. *The Dodge City Story*. Indianapolis, Ind.: Bobbs-Merrill, 1964.

Hamner, Laura V. *Light n'Hitch*. Dallas: American Guild Press, 1958.

———. *The No-Gun Man of Texas*. Amarillo, Texas: Published by Author, 1935.

———. *Short Grass and Longhorns*. Norman: University of Oklahoma Press, 1942.

Hanchett, Lafayette. *The Old Sheriff*. New York: Margent Press, 1937.

Hanes, Colonel Bailey C. *Bill Doolin Outlaw O.T.* Norman: University of Oklahoma Press, 1968.

Haney, Lewis. *A Congressional History of Railways in the United States*. Madison: University of Wisconsin Press, 1910.

Hanged by the Neck Until You Be Dead. Brooklyn, N.Y.: W.C. Wilton, 1877.

Hansen, Gladys C., and Heintz, William F. *The Chinese in California*. Portland, Ore.: Richard Abel, 1970.

———. *San Francisco Almanac*. San Rafael, Calif.: Presidio Press, 1980.

Hansen, Harvey J., and Miller, Jeanne Thurlow. *Wild Oat in Eden: Sonoma County in the 19th Century*. Santa Rosa, Calif.: n.p., 1962.

Hanson, Joseph Mills. *The Conquest of the Missouri*. New York: Murray Hill, 1946.

Hardin, John Wesley. *The Life of John Wesley Hardin*. Norman: University of Oklahoma Press, 1961.

Hardy, Allison. *Wild Bill Hickok, King of Gun-Fighters*. Girard, Kan.: Haldeman-Julius, 1943.

Hardy, Mary Duffus. *Through Cities and Prairie Lands*. New York: R. Worthington, 1881.

Hare, F.A. *The Last of the Bushrangers: The Capture of the Kelly Gang*. Chicago: Weeks, 1892.

Harkey, Dee. *Mean as Hell*. Albuquerque: University of New Mexico Press, 1948.

Harlow, Victor Emmanuel. *The Most Picturesque Personality in Oklahoma, Al Jennings*. Oklahoma City, Okla.: Harlow, 1912.

Harman, Samuel W. *Belle Starr, the Female Desperado.* Houston: Frontier Press of Texas, 1954.

———. *Cherokee Bill, the Oklahoma Outlaw.* Houston: Frontier Press of Texas, 1954.

———. *Hell on the Border.* Fort Smith, Ark.: Phoenix, 1898.

Harolds Club. *Pioneer Nevada.* Reno, Nev.: Harolds Club, 1951.

Harper, Minnie Timms, and Dewey, George. *Old Ranches.* Dallas: Dealey & Lowe, 1936.

Harriman, Alice. *Pacific History Stories.* San Francisco: Whitaker & Ray, 1903.

Harrington, Fred Harvey. *Hanging Judge.* Caldwell, Idaho: Caxton Printers, 1951.

Harris, Frank. *My Reminiscences As a Cowboy.* New York: Charles Boni, 1930.

Harris, Phil. *This Is Three Forks Country.* Muskogee, Okla.: Hoffman Printing, 1965.

Harris, Sallie B. *Hide Town in the Texas Panhandle: 100 Years in Wheeler County and Panhandle of Texas.* Hereford, Texas: Pioneer Books, 1968.

Harrison, Fred. *Hell Holes and Hangings.* New York: Ballentine Books, 1968.

———. *The West's Territorial Prisons, 1861-1912.* New York: Ballantine Books, 1973.

Hart, Adolphus M. *History of the Valley of the Mississippi.* New York: Newman & Ivison, 1853.

Hart, Albert Bushnell (ed.). *American History Told by Contemporaries.* New York: Macmillan, 1910.

Hart, Herbert M. *Old Forts of the Southwest.* Seattle, Wash.: Superior, 1964.

Hart, William Surrey. *My Life East and West.* Boston: Houghton Mifflin, 1929.

Harvey, Clara Toombs. *Not So Wild the Old West.* Denver: Golden Bell Press, 1961.

Haskell, Henry C., and Fowler, Richard B. *City of the Future: A Narrative History of Kansas City, 1850-1950.* Kansas City: Frank Glenn, 1950.

Hattich, William. *Pioneer Magic.* New York: Vantage Press, 1964.

Havighurst, Walter. *Annie Oakley of the Wild West.* New York: Macmillan, 1954.

———. *Voices on the River, The Story of the Mississippi Waterways.* New York: Macmillan, 1964.

Havins, T.R. *Something About Brown (A History of Brown County, Texas).* Brownwood, Texas: Banner Printing, 1958.

Hawes, Harry B. *Frank and Jesse James in Review for the Missouri Society.* Washington D.C.: n.p., 1939.

Hawkeye, Harry. *The Dalton Brothers and Their Gang: Fearsome Bandits of Oklahoma and the Southwest.* Philadelphia: Kerner & Getts, 1908.

———. *Rube Burrows, the Outlaw.* Baltimore: I.& M. Ottenheimer, 1908.

———. *Tracy, the Outlaw, King of Bandits.* Baltimore: I.& M. Ottenheimer, 1908.

Hawley, James H. (ed.). *History of Idaho, the Gem of the Mountains.* Chicago: S.J. Clarke, 1920.

Haydon, Arthur Lincoln. *The Riders of the Plains.* Chicago: A.C. McClurg, 1910.

Hayes, Augustus Allen, Jr. *New Colorado and the Santa Fe Trail.* New York: Harper & Brothers, 1880.

Hayes, Jess G. *Apache Vengeance.* Albuquerque: University of New Mexico Press, 1954.

———. *Boots and Bullets: The Life and Times of John W. Wentworth.* Tucson: University of Arizona Press, 1968.

———. *Sheriff Thompson's Day-Turbulence in the Arizona Territory.* Tucson: University of Arizona Press, 1968.

Hazen, R.W. *History of the Pawnee Indians.* Fremont, Neb.: Fremont *Tribune*, 1893.

Hearn, Walter. *Killing of Apache Kid.* n.p, n.d.

Hebert, Frank. *40 Years Prospecting and Mining in the Black Hills of South Dakota.* Rapid City, S.D.: Rapid City *Daily Journal*, 1921.

Hedges, J.B. *Henry Villard and the Railways of the Northwest.* New Haven, Conn.: Yale University Press, 1930.

Hedgpeth, Nelie McGraw. *My Early Days in San Francisco.* San Francisco: Victorian Alliance, 1974.

Heermans, Forbes. *Thirteen Stories of the Far West.* Syracuse, N.Y.: C.W. Bardeen, 1887.

Heizer, Robert F., and Almquist, Alan F. *The Other Californians: Prejudice and Discrimination Under Spain, Mexico, and the United States to 1920.* Berkeley: University of California Press, 1971.

Helper, Hinton. *The Land of Gold.* Baltimore: H. Taylor, 1855.

Hemphill, Vivia. *Down the Mother Lode.* Sacramento, Calif.: Purnell's, 1922.

Henderson, Jeff S. (ed.). *100 Years in Montague County, Texas.* Saint Jo, Texas: Ipta Printers, 1958.

Henderson, Richard B. *Maury Maverick: A Political Biography.* Austin: University of Texas Press, 1970.

Hendricks, George David. *The Bad Man of the West.* San Antonio, Texas: Naylor, 1941.

Hendrix, John M. *If I Can Do It on Horseback: A Cow-Country Sketchbook.* Austin: University of Texas Press, 1964.

Hendron, J.W. *The Story of Billy the Kid.* Santa Fe, N.M.: Rydal Press, 1948.

Hening, H.B. (ed.). *George Curry, 1861-1947: An Autobiography.* Albuquerque: University of New Mexico Press, 1958.

Hennessy, W.B. *Tracy, the Bandit; or, the Romantic Life and Crimes of a Twentieth Century Desperado.* Chicago: M.A. Donohue, 1902.

Henry, Stuart Oliver. *Conquering Our Great American Plains.* New York: E.P. Dutton, 1930.

Hepburn, A. *Complete Guide to the Southwest.* New York: Doubleday, 1963.

Hereford, Robert A. *Old Man River.* Caldwell, Idaho: Caxton, 1943.

Herman, Robert D. *Gambling.* New York: Harper & Row, 1967.

Hertzog, Peter. *A Dictionary of New Mexico Desperadoes.* Santa Fe, N.M.: Press of the Territorian, 1965.

———. *Legal Hangings.* Sante Fe, N.M.: Press of the Territorian, 1966.

———. *Little Known Facts About Billy the Kid.* Santa Fe, N.M.: Press of the Territorian, 1963.

———. *Old Town Albuquerque.* Santa Fe, N.M.: Press of the Territorian, 1962.

Hicks, Edwin P. *Belle Starr and Her Pearl.* Little Rock, Ark.: Pioneer Press, 1963.

Higginson, Thomas Wentworth. *Travellers and Outlaws: Episodes in American History.* New York: C.T. Dillingham, 1888.

Hill, Alice Polk. *Tales of the Colorado Pioneers.* Denver: Pierson & Gardner, 1884.

Hill, Forest G. *Roads, Rails and Waterways.* Norman: University of Oklahoma Press, 1957.

Hill, J.L. *End of the Cattle Trail.* Long Beach, Calif.: George W. Moyle, 1920.

Hill, James M. *Mining Districts of the Western United States.* Washington, D.C.: U.S. Government Printing Office, 1912.

Hill, John Alexander. *Stories of the Railroad.* New York: Doubleday & McClure, 1899.

Hill, W.A. *Historic Ways...* Hays, Kan.: News, 1938.
———. *Rome, the Predecessor of Hays.* Hays, Kan.: n.p, n.d.

Hine, Robert V. *The American West: An Interpretive History.* Boston: Little, Brown, 1973.

Hinton, Arthur Cherry, and Godsell, Philip H. *The Yukon.* New York: Macrae Smith, 1955.

Hinton, Richard J. *Hand-Book of Arizona.* San Francisco: Upham, 1878.

History of Placer County. Oakland, Calif.: Thompson & West, 1882.

History of the Arkansas Valley, Colorado. Chicago: O.L. Baskin, 1881.

Hitchcock, Frank. *A True Account of the Capture of Frank Rande, "The Noted Outlaw."* Peoria, Ill.: J.W. Franks & Sons, 1897.

Hitchcock, Mary E. *Two Women in the Klondike: The Story of a Journey to the Gold-Fields of Alaska.* New York: G.P. Putnam's Sons, 1899.

Hittell, John S. *The Commerce and Industries of the Pacific Coast.* San Francisco: A.L. Bancroft, 1882.
———. *A History of the City of San Francisco.* San Francisco: A.L. Bancroft, 1878.

Hittell, Theodore H. *History of California.* San Francisco: N.J. Stone, 1898.

Hobbs, James. *Wild Life in the Far West: Personal Adventures of a Border Mountain Man.* Hartford, Conn.: Wiley, Waterman & Eaton, 1872.

Hobbs, Richard Gear. *Glamorland: The Ozarks.* Manhattan, Kan.: n.p., 1944.

Hodge, Frederick Webb (ed.). *Handbook of American Indians North of Mexico.* Washington D.C.: U.S. Government Printing Office, 1907.

Hoebel, E. Adamson. *The Cheyennes.* New York: Henry Holt, 1960.

Hoffman, Charles Fenno. *A Winter in the West.* Chicago: Fergus, 1882.

Hogan, Ray. *The Life and Death of Clay Allison.* New York: New American Library, 1961.
———. *The Life and Death of Johnny Ringo.* New York: New American Library, 1963.

Hogan, William Ransom. *The Texas Republic.* Norman: University of Oklahoma Press, 1946.

Hogg, Thomas E. *Authentic History of Sam Bass and His Gang.* Denton, Texas: Monitor Job Office, 1878.

Holbrook, Stewart H. *Dreamers of the American Dream.* Garden City, N.Y.: Doubleday, 1957.
———. *Far Corner: A Personal View of the Northwest.* New York: Macmillan, 1952.
———. *Holy Old Mackinaw: A Natural History of the American Lumberjack.* New York: Macmillan, 1938.
———. *Let Them Live.* New York: Macmillan, 1938.
———. *Little Annie Oakley and Other Rugged People.* New York: Macmillan, 1948.
———. *The Rocky Mountain Revolution.* New York: Henry Holt, 1956.
———. *The Story of American Railroads.* New York: Crown, 1947.
———. *Wild Bill Tames the West.* New York: Random House, 1952.

Holcombe, R.I. (ed.). *History of Marion County, Missouri.* St. Louis: E.F. Parkins, 1884.

Holden, W.C. *Alkali Trails.* Dallas: The Southwest Press, 1930.

Holland, Gustavus Adolphus. *History of Parker County and the Double Log Cabin.* Weatherford, Texas: Herald, 1937.
———. *The Man and His Monument: The Man Was J.R. Couts, His Monument the Citizens National Bank.* Weatherford, Texas: Herald, 1924.

Hollon, W. Eugene. *Frontier Violence: Another Look.* New York: Oxford University Press, 1974.
———. *The Southwest Old and New.* New York: Alfred A. Knopf, 1961.

Holloway, Carroll C. *Texas Gun Lore.* San Antonio, Texas: Naylor, 1951.

Homsher, Lola M. (ed.). *South Pass, 1868: James Chisholm's Journal of the Wyoming Gold Rush.* Lincoln: University of Nebraska Press, 1960.

Hooker, William Francis. *The Prairie Schooner.* Chicago: Saul Brothers, 1918.

Hoole, W. Stanley. *The James Boys Rode South.* Tuscaloosa, Ala.: Published by Author, 1955.

Hopper, W.L. *Famous Texas Landmarks.* Dallas: Arrow Press, 1966.

Hopping, Richard C. *A Sheriff-Ranger in Chuckwagon Days.* New York: Pageant Press, 1952.

Horan, James D. *Across the Cimmaron.* New York: Crown, 1956.
———. *The Authentic Wild West—The Gunfighters.* New York: Crown, 1976.
———. *The Authentic Wild West—The Lawmen.* New York: Crown, 1980.
———. *The Authentic Wild West—The Outlaws.* New York: Crown, 1977.
———. *Desperate Men: Revelations from the Sealed Pinkerton Files.* New York: G.P. Putnam's Sons, 1949.
———. *Desperate Women.* New York: G.P. Putnam's Sons, 1952.
———. *The Great American West.* New York: Crown, 1959.
———. *The Life of Tom Horn.* New York: Crown, 1978.
———, and Sann, Paul. *Pictorial History of the Wild West.* New York: Crown, 1954.
———. *The Pinkertons, The Detective Dynasty That Made History.* New York: Crown, 1967.
———, and Swiggett, Howard. *The Pinkerton Story.* New York: G.P. Putnam's Sons, 1951.
———. *The Trial of Frank James Brown.* New York: Crown, 1978.
———. *The Wild Bunch.* New York: New American Library, 1958.

Horn, Calvin. *New Mexico's Troubled Years: The Story of the Early Territorial Governors.* Albuquerque, N.M.: Horn & Wallace, 1963.

Horn, Tom. *Life of Tom Horn: A Vindication.* Denver: Louthan, 1904.

Horton, Thomas F. *History of Jack County.* Jacksboro, Texas: Gazette, 1932.

Hough, Emerson. *The Story of the Cowboy.* New York: D. Appleton, 1897.
———. *The Story of the Outlaw.* New York: Outing, 1907.

House, Boyce. *City of Flaming Adventure.* San Antonio, Texas: Naylor, 1949.
———. *Cowtown Colonist.* San Antonio, Texas: Naylor, 1946.
———. *Oil Field Fury.* San Antonio, Texas: Naylor, 1954.
———. *Texas Treasure Chest.* San Antonio, Texas: Naylor, 1956.

House, Edward Mandell. *Riding For Texas.* New York: Reynal & Hitchcock, 1936.

Howard, Helen Addison. *Northwest Trail Blazers.* Caldwell, Idaho: Caxton Printers, 1963.

Howard, Joseph Kinsey. *Montana, High, Wide and Handsome.* New Haven, Conn.: Yale University Press, 1943.

Howard, Robert West, (ed.). *This Is the West.* New York: Rand McNally, 1957.

Howard, Sarah Elizabeth. *Pen Pictures of the Plains.* Denver: Reed, 1902.

Howbert, Irving. *Memories of a Lifetime in the Pike's Peak Region.* New York: G.P. Putnam's Sons, 1925.

Howe, Charles Willis. *Timberleg of the Diamond Trail.* San Antonio, Texas: Naylor, 1949.

Howe, Elvon L. (ed.). *Rocky Mountain Empire.* Garden City, N.Y.: Doubleday, 1950.

Hoyt, Henry Franklin. *Frontier Doctor.* Boston: Houghton Mifflin, 1929.

Hubbard, Freeman H. *Railroad Avenue.* New York: McGraw-Hill, 1945.

Hubbard, Harry D. *Building the Heart of an Empire.* Boston: Meador, 1937.

Hubbs, Barney. *Robert Clay Allison: Gentleman Gunfighter, 1840-1887.* Pecos, Texas: n.p., 1966.

Huckabay, Ida Lasater. *Ninety-four Years in Jack County, 1854-1948.* Austin, Texas: Steck, 1949.

Hudson, Wilson M. *Andy Adams, His Life and Writings.* Dallas: Southern Methodist University Press, 1964.

_____, and Maxwell, Allen (eds.). *The Sunny Slopes of Long Ago.* Dallas: Southern Methodist University Press, 1966.

Hueston, Ethel. *Calamity Jane of Deadwood Gulch.* Indianapolis, Ind.: Bobbs-Merrill, 1937.

Hughes, Dan de Lara. *South From Tombstone.* New York: Methuen, 1938.

Hughes, John R. *The Killing of Bass Outlaw.* Austin, Texas: Brick Row Books, 1963.

Hughes, Marion. *Oklahoma Charley.* St. Louis: John P. Wagner, 1910.

Hughes, Richard B. *Pioneer Years in the Black Hills.* Glendale, Calif.: Arthur H. Clark, 1957.

Hughes, W.J. *Rebellious Ranger: Rip Ford and the Old Southwest.* Norman: University of Oklahoma Press, 1964.

Hulbert, Archer Butler. *The Historic Highways of America.* Cleveland: A.H. Clark, 1905.

_____. *Waterways of Westward Expansion.* Cleveland: A.H. Clark, 1903.

Hull, Clifton E. *Shortline Railroads of Arkansas.* Norman: University of Oklahoma Press, 1969.

Hullah, John. *The Train Robber's Career: A Life of Sam Bass.* Chicago: Belford, Clarke, 1881.

Hultz, Fred S. *Range Beef Production in the Seventeen Western States.* New York: John Wiley & Sons, 1930.

Humphrey, Seth King. *Following the Prairie Frontier.* Minneapolis: University of Minnesota Press, 1931.

Humphreys, J.R. *The Lost Towns and Roads of America.* Garden City, N.Y.: Doubleday, 1961.

Hungerford, Edward. *Wells Fargo: Advancing the American Frontier.* New York: Random House, 1949.

Hunt, Frazier. *Cap Mossman, Last of the Great Cowmen.* New York: Hastings House, 1951.

_____. *The Long Trail From Texas: The Story of Ad Spaugh, Cattleman.* New York: Doubleday, Doran, 1940.

_____. *The Tragic Days of Billy the Kid.* Caldwell, Idaho: Caxton Printers, 1959.

Hunt, Inez, and Draper, Wanetta W. *To Colorado's Restless Ghosts.* Denver: Sage Books, 1960.

Hunt, Lenoir. *Bluebonnets and Blood.* Houston: Texas Books, 1938.

Hunt, R.D. *California and the Californians.* San Francisco: Lewis, 1926.

Hunt, Rockwell D. *California Ghost Towns Live Again.* Stockton, Calif.: College of the Pacific, 1948.

_____. *California's Stately Hall of Fame.* Stockton, Calif.: College of the Pacific, 1950.

_____, and Van De Grift Sanchez, Nellie. *A Short History of California.* New York: Thomas Y. Crowell, 1929.

Hunter, John Marvin, and Rose, Noah H. *Album of Gunfighters.* Bandera, Texas: n.p., 1951.

_____. *Peregrinations of a Pioneer Printer: An Autobiography.* Grand Prairie, Texas: Frontier Times, 1954.

_____. *The Story of Lottie Deno, Her Life and Times.* Bandera, Texas: Four Hunters, 1959.

_____ (ed.). *The Trail Drivers of Texas.* Nashville, Tenn.: Cokesbury Press, 1925.

Hunter, Lillie Mae. *The Moving Finger.* Borger, Texas: Plains Printing, 1956.

Hunter, Louis C. and B.J. *Steamboats on the Western Rivers.* Cambridge, Mass.: Harvard University Press, 1949.

Huntington, George. *Robber and Hero: The Story of the Raid on the First National Bank, Minnesota.* Northfield, Minn.: Christian Way, 1895.

Huntington, William. *Bill Huntington's Both Feet in the Stirrups.* Billings, Mont.: Western Livestock Reporter Press, 1959.

_____. *Bill Huntington's Good Men and Salty Cusses.* Billings, Mont.: Western Livestock Reporter Press, 1952.

Hunton, John. *John Hunton's Diary.* Lingle, Wyo.: Flannery, 1956.

Hurd, C.W. *Boggsville: Cradle of the Colorado Cattle Industry.* Boggsville, Colo.: Bent County *Democrat*, 1957.

Hutchens, John K. *One Man's Montana: An Informal Portrait of a State.* Philadelphia: J.B. Lippincott, 1964.

Hutchinson, W.H. *Another Notebook of the Old West.* Chico, Calif.: Hurst & Yount, 1954.

_____. *Another Verdict for Oliver Lee.* Clarendon, Texas: Clarendon Press, 1965.

_____. *A Bar Cross Man: The Life & Personal Writings of Eugene Manlove Rhodes.* Norman: University of Oklahoma Press, 1956.

_____. *A Notebook of the Old West.* Chico, Calif.: Hurst, 1947.

_____. *The Rhodes Reader: Stories of Virgins, Villains, and Varmints.* Norman: University of Oklahoma Press, 1957.

_____, and Mullin, R.N. *Whiskey Jim and a Kid Named Billy.* Clarendon, Texas: Clarendon Press, 1967.

Hutto, Nelson A. *The Dallas Story, from Buckskins to Top Hat.* Dallas: William S. Henson, 1953.

Hyde, Albert E. *Billy the Kid and the Old Regime in the Southwest.* Ruidoso, N.M.: Frontier Books, 1961.

Hyde, George E. *Pawnee Indians.* Denver: University of Denver Press, 1951.

Illustrations of Contra Costa County. Oakland, Calif.: Smith & Elliott, 1878.

I

Ingersoll, Ernest. *Knocking Around the Rockies.* New York: Harper, 1883.

Ingham, George Thomas. *Digging Gold Among the Rockies.* Philadelphia: Hubbard Brothers, 1888.

Ingraham, Prentiss. *Wild Bill, the Pistol Dead Shot.* New York: Beadle & Adams, 1882.

Inman, Henry. *The Great Salt Lake Trail.* New York: Macmillan, 1898.

_____. *The Old Santa Fe Trail.* New York: Macmillan, 1897.

Irenholm, U.C. *The Shoshonis: Sentinels of the Rockies.* Norman: University of Oklahoma Press, 1964.

Irwin, Inez Haynes. *Angels and Amazons: A Hundred Years of American Women.* Garden City, N.Y.: Doubleday, Doran, 1934.

Isely, Bliss, and Richards, W.M. *Four Centuries in Kansas.* Wichita, Kan.: McCormick-Mathers, 1936.

Issler, Anne Roller. *Stevenson at Silverado.* Caldwell, Idaho: Caxton Printers, 1939.

J

Jackson, Donald, and Spence, Mary Lee (eds.). *The Expeditions of John Charles Fremont.* Urbana: University of Illinois Press, 1970.

——— (ed.). *Letters of the Lewis and Clark Expedition.* Urbana: University of Illinois Press, 1962.

Jackson, Joseph Henry. *Anybody's Gold: The Story of California's Mining Towns.* New York: Appleton-Century, 1941.

———. *Bad Company.* New York: Harcourt, Brace, 1949.

———. *The Creation of Joaquin Murieta.* n.p., 1948.

———. *Tintypes in Gold: Four Studies in Robbery.* New York: Macmillan, 1939.

Jackson, Mary E. *Bank and Train Robbers.* Chicago: Henneberry, 1881.

———. *The Life of Nellie C. Bailey.* Topeka, Kan.: R.E. Martin, 1885.

Jackson, Orich. *The White Conquest of Arizona.* Los Angeles: West Coast Magazine, 1908.

Jackson, Ralph Semmes. *Home on Double Bayou: Memories of an East Texas Ranch.* Austin: University of Texas Press, 1961.

Jackson, W. Turrentine. *Treasure Hill.* Tucson: University of Arizona Press, 1963.

Jahns, Pat. *The Frontier World of Doc Holliday.* New York: Hastings House, 1957.

James, Daniel. *Mexico and the Americas.* New York: Frederick A. Praeger, 1963.

James, Edgar. *James Boys: Deeds and Daring.* Baltimore: I. & M. Ottenheimer, 1912.

———. *The Lives and Adventures, Daring Hold-ups, Train and Bank Robberies of the World's Most Desperate Bandits and Highwaymen—The Notorious James Brothers.* Baltimore: I. & M. Ottenheimer, 1913.

James, Edwin. *Account of an Expedition from Pittsburgh to the Rocky Mountains.* Philadelphia: H.C. Carey & I. Lea, 1822.

James, Frank. *Frank James and His Brother Jesse.* Baltimore: I. & M. Ottenheimer, 1915.

James, Jesse Edward, Jr. *Jesse James, My Father.* Independence, Mo.: Sentinel, 1899.

James, Jesse Lee. *Jesse James and the Lost Cause.* New York: Pageant Press, 1961.

James, Marquis. *The Cherokee Strip: A Tale of an Oklahoma Boyhood.* New York: Viking Press, 1945.

———. *They Had Their Hour.* Indianapolis, Ind.: Bobbs-Merrill, 1934.

James, Thomas. *Three Years Among the Indians and Mexicans.* Philadelphia: J.B. Lippincott, 1962.

James, Vinton Lee. *Frontier and Pioneer Recollections of Early Days in San Antonio and West Texas.* San Antonio, Texas: Published by Author, 1938.

James, William F., and McMurray, George H. *History of San Jose, California.* San Jose, Calif.: Cawston, 1933.

Jameson, Henry B. *Heroes by the Dozen.* Abilene, Kan.: Shadinger-Wilson, 1961.

———. *Miracle of the Chisholm Trail.* Abilene, Kan.: Tri-State Chisholm Trail Centennial Commission, 1967.

Jannewein, J. Leonard. *Calamity Jane of the Western Trails.* Huron, S.D.: Dakota Books, 1953.

Jaramillo, Cleofas M. *Shadows of the Past.* Santa Fe, N.M.: Seton Village Press, 1941.

Jeffrey, John Mason. *Adobe and Iron.* La Jolla, Calif.: Prospect Avenue Press, 1969.

Jelinek, George. *Ellsworth, Kansas, 1867-1947.* Salina, Kan.: Consolidated, 1947.

———. *90 Years of Ellsworth and Ellsworth County History.* Ellsworth, Kan.: Messenger Press, 1957.

Jenkins, A.O. *Olive's Last Roundup.* Loup City, Nebr.: Sherman County Times, n.d.

Jenkins, John H., and Frost, Gordon. *I'm Frank Hamer: The Life of a Texas Peace Officer.* New York: The Pemberton Press, 1968.

———. *Neither the Fanatics nor the Faint-Hearted.* Austin, Texas: The Pemberton Press, 1963.

Jenkinson, Michael. *Ghost Towns of New Mexico.* Albuquerque: University of New Mexico Press, 1967.

Jennewein, J. Leonard. *Calamity Jane of the Western Trails.* Huron, S.D.: Dakota Books, 1953.

———, and Boorman, Jane (eds.). *Dakota Panorama.* Sioux Falls, S.D.: Midwest-Beach Printing, 1961.

Jennings, Alphonso J. *Beating Back.* New York: D. Appleton, 1914.

———. *Number 30664, by Number 31539.* Hollywood, Calif.: Pioneer Press, 1941.

———. *Through the Shadows with O. Henry.* New York: H.K. Fly, 1921.

Jennings, Napoleon A. *A Texas Ranger.* New York: Charles Scribner's Sons, 1899.

Jensen, Ann (ed.). *Texas Ranger's Diary and Scrapbook.* Dallas: Kaleidograph Press, 1936.

Jerrett, Herman Daniel. *California's El Dorado, Yesterday and Today.* Sacramento, Calif.: Press of Jo Anderson, 1915.

Jocknick, Sidney. *Early Days on the Western Slope of Colorado.* Denver: Carson-Harper, 1913.

Johannsen, Albert. *The House of Beadle and Adams and Its Nickel and Dime Novels.* Norman: University of Oklahoma Press, 1950.

John of Joinville. *The Life of St. Louis.* trans. Rene Hague. New York: Sheed & Ward, 1955.

Johnson, Dorothy. *Famous Lawmen of the Old West.* New York: Dodd, Mead, 1963.

———. *Some Went West.* New York: Dodd, Mead, 1965.

Johnson, G.C. *Wagon Yard.* Dallas: William T. Tardy, 1938.

Johnson, W.A. *History of Anderson County, Kansas.* Garnett, Kan.: Kauffman & Iler, 1877.

Johnson, W.F. *History of Cooper County, Missouri.* Cleveland: Historical, 1919.

Johnston, Charles Haven Ladd. *Famous Scouts, Including Trappers, Pioneers, and Soldiers of the Frontier.* Boston: L.C. Page, 1910.

Johnston, Harry V. *The Last Roundup.* Minneapolis, Minn.: H.V. Johnston, 1950.

———. *My Home on the Range: Frontier Life in the Bad Lands.* St. Paul, Minn.: Webb, 1942.

Jones, Haloway R. *John Muir and the Sierra Club.* San Francisco: Sierra Club, 1965.

Jones, Horace. *The Story of Rice County.* Wichita, Kan.: Wichita *Eagle*, 1928.

Jones, Lloyd. *Life and Adventures of Harry Tracy.* Chicago: Jewett & Lindrooth, 1902.

Jones, Mat Ennis. *Fiddlefooted.* Denver: Sage Books,

519

1966.

Jones, W.F. *The Experiences of a Deputy U.S. Marshal of the Indian Territory.* Tulsa, Okla.: n.p., 1937.

Jordin, John F. *Memories.* Gallatin: North Missourian Press, 1904.

Judson, Katherine Berry. *Montana: The Land of Shining Mountains.* Chicago: A.C. McClurg, 1909.

K

Kane, Larry. *100 Years Ago with the Law and the Outlaw.* n.p., n.d.

Karolevitz, Robert F. *Newspapering in the Old West.* Seattle, Wash.: Superior, 1965.

Karsner, David. *Silver Dollar: The Story of the Tabors.* New York: Covici, Friede, 1932.

Keating, Bern. *The Flamboyant Mr. Colt.* New York: Doubleday, 1978.

_____. *Texas Rangers.* New York: Promontory Press, 1975.

Keatinge, Charles Wilbur. *Gold Miners of Hard Luck; or, Three-Fingered Jack.* Cleveland: Arthur Westbrook, 1927.

Keeler, Bronson C. *Leadville and Its Silver Mines.* Chicago: E.L. Ayer, 1879.

Keeler, Charles. *San Francisco and Thereabout.* San Francisco: A.M. Robertson, 1912.

_____. *San Francisco Through Earthquake and Fire.* San Francisco: P. Elder, 1906.

Keeler, Ralph. *Vagabond Adventures.* Boston: Fields, Osgood, 1870.

Keith, Agnes Newton. *Three Came Home.* Boston: Little, Brown, 1947.

Keith, Billy. *Days of Anguish, Days of Hope.* New York: Doubleday, 1972.

Keith, Elmer. *Shotguns by Keith.* New York: Stackpole, 1967.

_____. *Sixguns by Keith.* Harrisburg, Pa.: Stackpole, 1955.

Keithley, Ralph. *Bucky O'Neill: He Stayed with 'Em While He Lasted.* Caldwell, Idaho: Caxton Printers, 1949.

Keleher, William A. *The Fabulous Frontier: Twelve New Mexico Items.* Santa Fe, N.M.: Rydal Press, 1945.

_____. *Maxwell Land Grant, a New Mexico Item.* Santa Fe, N.M.: Rydal Press, 1942.

_____. *Violence in Lincoln County, 1869-81.* Albuquerque, N.M.: University of New Mexico Press, 1957.

Keller, Morton. (ed.). *Theodore Roosevelt: A Profile.* New York: Hill & Wang, 1967.

Kelley, Thomas P. *The Black Donnellys.* New York: Signet Books, 1955.

_____. *Jesse James.* New York: Export, 1950.

Kelly, Charles, and Hoffman, Birney. *Holy Murder: The Story of Porter Rockwell.* New York: Minton, Balch, 1934.

_____. *The Outlaw Trail.* New York: Devin-Adair, 1959.

Kelly, Erick P. *On the Staked Plain, El Llano Estacado.* New York: Macmillan, 1940.

Kelly, Robin A. *The Sky Was Their Roof.* London: Andrew Melrose, 1955.

Kelly, Thomas P. *Jesse James, His Life and Death.* New York: Export, 1950.

Kelsey, D.M. *History of Our Wild West and Stories of Pioneer Life.* Chicago: Thompson & Thomas, 1901.

Kemp, Ben W., and Dykes, J.C. *Cow Dust and Saddle Leather.* Norman: University of Oklahoma Press, 1968.

Kendall, George Wilkins. *Narrative of the Texas Santa Fe Expedition.* New York: Harper & Brothers, 1856.

Kendall, John S. *History of New Orleans.* New York: Lewis, 1922.

Kennedy, Captain. *Jesse James' Mysterious Warning: or, the Raid That Almost Failed.* Baltimore: I. & M. Ottenheimer, 1915.

_____. *Jesse James' Thrilling Raid: or the Daylight Robbery of the Harkness Bank.* Baltimore: I. & M. Ottenheimer, 1913.

_____. *Jesse James' Wild Leap: or, the Hold-Up of the Through Express.* Baltimore: I. & M. Ottenheimer, 1915.

Kennedy, Michael S. (ed.). *Cowboys and Cattleman.* New York: Hastings House, 1964.

Kenner, Charles L. *A History of New Mexican-Plains Indian Relations.* n.p., n.d.

Kent, Lewis. *Leadville in Your Pocket.* Denver: Daily Times Steam Printing House, 1880.

Kent, William. *Reminiscences of Outdoor Life.* San Francisco: A.M. Robertson, 1929.

Kerby, R.L. *The Confederate Invasion of New Mexico and Arizona.* Los Angeles: Westernlore, 1958.

Key, Della Tyler. *In the Cattle County: History of Potter County, 1887-1966.* Quanah-Witchita Falls, Texas: Nortex Offset, 1972.

King, Dick. *Ghost Towns of Texas.* San Antonio, Texas: Naylor, 1953.

King, Ernest L. *Main Line: Fifty Years of Railroading with the Southern Pacific.* Garden City, N.Y.: Doubleday, 1948.

King, Frank M. *Mavericks: The Salty Comments of an Old-Time Cowpuncher.* Pasadena, Calif.: Trail's End, 1947.

_____. *Pioneer Western Empire Builders.* Pasadena, Calif.: Trail's End, 1946.

_____. *Wranglin' the Past: Being Reminiscences of Frank M. King.* Pasadena, Calif.: Trail's End, 1946.

King, Grace. *New Orleans: The Place and the People.* New York: Macmillan, 1937.

King, Leonard. *From Cattle Rustler to Pulpit.* San Antonio, Texas: Naylor, 1943.

Kinnaird, Lawrence. *History of the Greater San Francisco Bay Region.* New York: Lewis Historical, 1966.

Kinyon, Edmund. *The Northern Mines.* Nevada City, Calif.: Union, 1949.

Kirsch, Robert, and Murphy, William S. *West of the West.* New York: E.P. Dutton, 1967.

Kittrel, Norman G. *Governors Who Have Been and Other Public Men of Texas.* Houston, Texas: Dealy-Adey-Elgin, 1921.

Klasner, Lily. *My Girlhood Among Outlaws.* Tucson: University of Arizona Press, 1972.

Klette, Ernest. *The Crimson Trail of Joaquin Murieta.* Los Angeles: Wetzel, 1928.

Kluckhohn, Clyde, and Leighton, Dorthea. *The Navaho.* Garden City, N.Y.: Doubleday, 1962.

Knapp, A.E. (ed.). *Pioneers of the San Juan Country.* Durango, Colo.: Durango Printing, 1952.

Kneedler, H.S. *Through Storyland to Sunset Seas.* Chicago: Knight, Leonard, 1895.

Knight, Edward. *Wild Bill Hickok.* Franklin, N.H.: Hillside Press, 1959.

Knight, Oliver. *Fort Worth: Outpost on the Trinity.* Norman: University of Oklahoma Press, 1953.

Knowles, Horace (ed.). *Gentlemen, Scholars and Scoundrels.* New York: Harper & Brothers, 1959.

Koenigsberg, Moses. *King News—An Autobiography.* New York: Frederick A. Stokes, 1941.

Koller, Larry (ed.). *The American Gun.* New York: Madison Books, 1961.

———. *The Fireside Book of Guns.* New York: Simon & Schuster, 1959.

Koop, W.E. *Billy the Kid.* Kansas City: Kansas City Posse of Westerners, 1965.

Krakel, Dean F. *The Saga of Tom Horn: The Story of a Cattlemen's War.* Laramie, Wyo.: Powder River, 1954.

Kroll, Harry Harrison. *Rogue's Company: A Novel of John Murrell.* Indianapolis, Ind.: Bobbs-Merrill, 1943.

Kupper, Winifred. *The Golden Hoof: The Story of the Sheep of the Southwest.* New York: Alfred A. Knopf, 1945.

Kuykendall, Ivan Lee. *Ghost Riders of the Mogollon.* San Antonio, Texas: Naylor, 1954.

Kuykendall, William Littlebury. *Frontier Days: A True Narrative of Striking Events on the Western Frontier.* Published by Author, 1917.

Kyner, James H. *End of the Tracks.* Caldwell, Idaho: Caxton Printers, 1937.

L

Lackey, B. Roberts. *Stories of the Texas Rangers.* San Antonio, Texas: Naylor, 1955.

La Croix, Arda. *Billy the Kid.* New York: J.S. Ogilvie, 1907.

Ladd, Robert E. *Eight Ropes to Eternity.* Tombstone, Ariz.: Tombstone Epitaph, 1965.

La Farge, Oliver. *A Pictorial History of the American Indian.* New York: Crown, 1956.

———. *Santa Fe: The Autobiography of a Southwestern Town.* Norman: University of Oklahoma Press, 1959.

La Follette, Robert Hoath. *Eight Notches, "Lawlessness and Disorder, Unlimited".* Albuquerque, N.M.: Valiant Printing, 1950.

La Font, Don. *Rugged Life in the Rockies.* Casper, Wyo.: Prairie, 1951.

Laine, Tanner. *Campfire Stories.* Lubbock, Texas: Ranch House, 1965.

Lake, Carolyn (ed.). *Under Cover for Wells Fargo.* Boston: Houghton Mifflin, 1969.

Lake, Stuart N. *He Carried a Six-Shooter: The Biography of Wyatt Earp.* New York: Peter Nevill, 1952.

———. *Wyatt Earp, Frontier Marshal.* Boston: Houghton Mifflin, 1931.

Lamar, Howard Roberts. *Dakota Territory, 1861-1889: A Study of Frontier Politics.* New Haven, Conn.: Yale University Press, 1956.

———. *The Far Southwest, 1846-1912: A Territorial History.* New Haven, Conn.: Yale University Press, 1966.

——— (ed.). *A Reader's Encyclopedia of the American West.* New York: Thomas Y. Crowell, 1977.

Lamb, Arthur H. *Tragedies of the Osage Hills.* Pawhuska, Okla.: Osage Printery, 1935.

Lane, Allen Stanley. *Emperor Norton, the Mad Monarch of America.* Caldwell, Idaho: Caxton Printers, 1939.

Lang, Lincoln A. *Ranching With Roosevelt.* Philadelphia: J.B. Lippincott, 1926.

Langford, Nathaniel Pitt. *Vigilante Days and Ways.* Chicago: A.L. Burt, 1890.

Langtry, Lillie. *The Days I Knew.* New York: George H. Doran, 1925.

Lardner, W.B., and Brock, M.J. *History of Placer and Nevada Counties, California.* Los Angeles: Historic Record, 1924.

Larson, T.A. *History of Wyoming.* Lincoln: University of Nebraska Press, 1965.

Lathrop, Amy. *Tales of Western Kansas.* Kansas City: La Rue Printing, 1948.

Laughlin, Clarence John, and Cohn, David L. *New Orleans and Its Living Past.* Boston: Houghton Mifflin, 1941.

Laughlin, Ruth. *Caballeros.* New York: D. Appleton, 1931.

Laune, Seigniora Russell. *Sand in Your Eyes.* Philadelphia: J.B. Lippincott, 1956.

Laut, Agnes C. *Pilgrims of the Santa Fe.* New York: Frederick A. Stokes, 1931.

———. *The Romance of the Rails.* New York: Robert M. McBride, 1928.

Lavender, David. *The American Heritage History of the Great West.* New York: American Heritage, 1965.

———. *The Big Divide.* Garden City, N.Y.: Doubleday, 1948.

———. *Land of Giants, The Drive to the Pacific Northwest.* New York: Doubleday, 1958.

———. *Nothing Seemed Impossible.* Palo Alto, Calif.: American West, 1975.

———. *The Rockies.* New York: Harper & Row, 1968.

Lavine, Sigmund. *Allan Pinkerton, America's First Private Eye.* New York: Dodd, Mead, 1963.

Lawson, W.B. *The Indian Outlaw, or Hank Starr: the Log Cabin Bandit.* Orville, Ohio: Frank T. Fries, n.d.

———. *Jesse James at Long Branch; or, Playing for a Million.* New York: Street & Smith, 1898.

Layne, J. Gregg. *Annals of Los Angeles, From the Arrival of the First White Man to the Civil War, 1769-1861.* San Francisco: California Historical Society, 1935.

Layres, Augustus. *Both Sides of the Chinese Question.* San Francisco: A.F. Woodbridge, 1877.

———. *The Other Side of the Chinese Question.* San Francisco: n.p., 1876.

Leach, A.J. *A History of Antelope County, Nebraska.* Chicago: Lakeside Press, 1909.

Leakey, John. *The West that was from Texas to Montana.* Dallas: Southern Methodist University Press, 1958.

Leckenby, Charles H. *The Tread of the Pioneers...Some Highlights in the Dramatic and Colorful History of Northwestern Colorado.* Steamboat Springs, Colo.: Pilot Press, 1945.

Leckie, William H. *The Buffalo Soldiers.* Norman: Oklahoma University Press, 1967.

Lee, John Doyle. *The Lee Trial! An Expose of the Mountain Meadow Massacre.* Salt Lake City, Utah: Tribune Printing, 1875.

———. *The Mormon Menace, Being the Confession of John D. Lee, Danite.* New York: Home Protection, 1905.

Lee, Mabel Barbee. *Cripple Creek Days.* New York: Doubleday, 1958.

Lee, Rose Hum. *The Chinese in the United States of America.* Hong Kong: Hong Kong University Press, 1960.

Lee, Samuel D. *San Francisco's Chinatown.* San Francisco: Central District Coordinating Council, 1940.

Lee, Susan E. *These Also Served: Brief Histories of Pioneers.* Las Lunas, N.M.: Published by Author, 1960.

Leedy, Carl H. *Golden Days in the Black Hills, by "The Old Timer."* n.p., n.d.

Leeson, Michael A. *History of Montana.* Chicago: Warner, Beers, 1885.

LeFors, Joe. *Wyoming Peace Officer.* Laramie, Wyo.: Laramie Printing, 1953.

Leftwich, Bill. *Tracks Along the Pecos.* Pecos, Texas: Pecos Press, 1957.

Lemley, Vernon. *The Old West, 1849-1929*. Osborne, Kan.: n.p., 1929.

Lemon, John J. *The Northfield Tragedy; or, the Robber's Raid*. St. Paul, Minn.: Published by Author, 1876.

Leonard, Elizabeth Jane, and Goodman, Julia Cody. *Buffalo Bill: King of the Old West*. New York: Library, 1955.

Leonard, John C., et al. *History of Davies and Gentry Counties, Missouri*. Topeka, Kan.: Historical, 1922.

Lesson, Michael A. *History of Montana, 1739-1885*. Chicago: Warner, Beer, 1885.

Lesure, Thomas B. *Adventures in Arizona*. San Antonio, Texas: Naylor, 1956.

Levy, Jo Ann L. *Behind the Western Skyline*. Los Angeles: Coldwell Banker, 1981.

Lewis, Alfred Henry. *The Sunset Trail*. New York: A.S. Barnes, 1905.

Lewis, Flannery. *Suns Go Down*. New York: Macmillan, 1937.

Lewis, John Woodruff. *The True Life of Billy the Kid*. New York: Frank Tousey, 1881.

Lewis, Lloyd. *It Takes All Kinds*. New York: Harcourt, Brace, 1947.

_____, and Smith, Henry Justin. *Oscar Wilde Discovers America*. New York: Harcourt, Brace, 1936.

Lewis, Meriwether, and Clark, William. *The Journals of Lewis and Clark*. Boston: Houghton Mifflin, 1953.

_____. *The Letters of the Lewis and Clark Expedition*. Urbana: University of Illinois Press, 1962.

Lewis, Oscar. *High Sierra Country*. New York: Duell, Sloan & Pearce, 1955.

_____. *Silver Kings*. New York: Alfred A. Knopf, 1947.

_____. *This Was San Francisco*. New York: David McKay, 1962.

Lewis, Tracy Hammond. *Along the Rio Grande*. New York: Lewis, 1916.

Lewis, Willie Newberry. *Between Sun and Sod*. Clarendon, Texas: Clarendon Press, 1938.

Liggett, William Sr. *My Seventy-Five Years Along the Mexican Border*. New York: Exposition Press, 1964.

Lillie, Gordon William. *Life Story of Pawnee Bill*. Topeka, Kan., n.p., 1916.

Lindquist, Allan Sigvard. *Jess Sweeten, Texas Lawman*. San Antonio, Texas: Naylor, 1961.

Lindsay, Charles. *Big Horn Basin*. Lincoln: University of Nebraska Press, 1932.

Linford, Velma. *Wyoming, Frontier State*. Denver: Old West, 1947.

Lingle, Robert T., and Linford, Dee. *The Pecos River Commission of New Mexico and Texas*. Santa Fe, N.M.: Rydal Press, 1961.

Lloyd, Everett. *Law West of the Pecos: The Story of Roy Bean*. San Antonio, Texas: Naylor, 1936.

Lloyd, John. *The Invaders: A Story of the "Hole-in-the-Wall" Country*. New York: R.F. Fenno, 1910.

Lloyd-Owen, Frances. *Gold Nugget Charlie: A Narrative Compiled From the Notes of Charles E. Masson*. London: George C. Harrap, 1939.

Lockley, Fred. *Oregon Folks*. New York: Knickerbocker Press, 1927.

Lockwood, Francis Cummins. *Arizona Characters*. Los Angeles: Times-Mirror, 1928.

_____. *Pioneer Days in Arizona*. New York: Macmillan, 1932.

Logan, Herschel C. *Buckskin and Satin*. Harrisburg, Pa.: Stackpole, 1954.

Logue, Roscoe. *Tumbleweeds and Barb Wire Fences*. Amarillo, Texas: Russell Stationery, 1935.

_____. *Under Texas and Border Skies*. Amarillo, Texas: Russell Stationery, 1935.

Long, Haniel. *Pinon Country*. New York: Duell, Sloan & Pearce, 1941.

Long, Katherine W., and Siciliano, Samuel A. *Yuma From Hell-Hole to Haven*. Yuma, Ariz.: Yuma County Chamber of Commerce, 1950.

Look, Al. *Unforgettable Characters of Western Colorado*. Boulder, Colo.: Pruett Press, 1966.

Looney, Ralph. *Haunted Highways: The Ghost Towns of New Mexico*. New York: Hastings House, 1968.

Lorant, Stefan. *The Life and Times of Theodore Roosevelt*. New York: Doubleday, 1959.

Lord, John. *Frontier Dust*. Hartford, Conn.: E.V. Mitchell, 1926.

Lotchin, Roger W. *San Francisco - 1846-1856*. New York: Oxford University Press, 1974.

Lounsberry, Clement A. *History of North Dakota*. Chicago: S.J. Clarke, 1917.

Love, Nat. *The Life and Adventures of Nat Love, Better Known in the Cattle Country as "Deadwood Dick," by Himself*. Los Angeles: Wayside Press, 1907.

Love, Robertus. *The Rise and Fall of Jesse James*. New York: G. P. Putnam's Sons, 1926.

Lovell, Emily Kalled. *A Personalized History of Otero County, New Mexico*. Alamorgordo, N.M.: Star, 1963.

Low, Frederick F. *Some Reflections of an Early California Governor*. Sacramento, Calif.: Sacramento Book Collectors Club, 1959.

Lowie, Robert H. *The Crow Indians*. New York: Farrar & Rinehart, 1935.

_____. *Indians of the Plains*. New York: McGraw-Hill, 1954.

Lowther, Charles C. *Dodge City, Kansas*. Philadelphia: Dorrance, 1940.

Lucia, Ellis. *Klondike Kate: The Life and Legend of Kitty Rockwell, the Queen of the Yukon*. New York: Hastings House, 1962.

_____. *The Saga of Ben Holladay, Giant of the Old West*. New York: Hastings House, 1959.

_____. *Tough Men, Tough Country*. Englewood Cliffs, N.J.: Prentice-Hall, 1963.

Ludlow, Fitzhugh. *The Heart of the Continent*. New York: Hurd and Houghton, 1870.

Ludlum, Stuart D. (ed.). *Great Shooting Stories*. Garden City, N.Y.: Doubleday, 1947.

Lyman, Albert R. *Indians and Outlaws: Settling of the San Juan Frontier*. Salt Lake City, Utah: Bookcraft, 1962.

Lyman, George Dunlap. *John Marsh, Pioneer: The Life Story of a Trail-Blazer on Six Frontiers*. New York: Charles Scribner's Sons, 1930.

_____. *Ralston's Ring*. New York: Charles Scribner's Sons, 1937.

_____. *The Saga of the Comstock Lode*. New York: Charles Scribner's Sons, 1934.

Lyon, Peter. *The Wild, Wild West*. New York: Funk & Wagnalls, 1969.

Lyons, B.J. *Thrills and Spills of a Cowboy Rancher*. New York: Vantage Press, 1959.

M

McAfee, Ward. *California's Railroad Era*. San Marino, Calif.: Golden West Books, 1973.

McCallum, Henry D., and Frances T. *The Wire That Fenced the West*. Norman: University of Oklahoma Press, 1965.

McCarty, John L. *Adobe Walls Bride.* San Antonio, Texas: Naylor, 1955.

_____. *The Enchanted West.* Dallas: Doctor Pepper, 1944.

_____. *Maverick Town: The Story of Old Tascosa.* Norman: University of Oklahoma Press, 1946.

_____ (ed.). *Some Experiences of Boss Neff in the Texas and Oklahoma Panhandle.* Amarillo, Texas: Globe News, 1941.

McCarty, Lea Franklin. *The Gunfighters.* Berkeley, Calif.: Mike Roberts, 1959.

McCauley, James Emmitt. *A Stove-Up Cowboy's Story.* Dallas: University of Texas Press, 1943.

McClintock, John S. *Pioneer Days in the Black Hills.* Deadwood, S.D.: Published by Author, 1939.

McClure, Alexander Kelly. *Three Thousand Miles Through the Rocky Mountains.* Philadelphia: J.B. Lippincott, 1869.

McConnell, H.H. *Five Years a Cavalryman; or, Sketches of Regular Army Life on the Texas Frontier.* Jacksboro, Texas: J.N. Rogers, 1889.

McConnell, J.L. *Western Characters.* New York: Redfield, 1853.

McConnell, William John. *Early History of Idaho.* Caldwell, Idaho: Caxton Printers, 1913.

_____. *Frontier Law: A Story of Vigilante Days.* New York: World Book, 1924.

McCool, Grace. *So Said the Coroner: How They Died in Old Cochise.* Tombstone, Ariz.: Tombstone Epitaph, 1968.

McCorkle, John. *Three Years with Quantrill: A True Story.* Armstrong, Mo.: Armstrong Herald, 1914.

McCormick, Robert R. *The American Empire.* Chicago: Chicago Tribune, 1952.

McCoy, Joseph G. *Historic Sketches of the Cattle Trade.* Kansas City: Ramsey Millet & Hudson, 1874.

McCready, Albert L. *Railroads in the Days of Steam.* New York: American Heritage, 1960.

MacCreary, Henry. *A Story of Durant, "Queen of Three Valleys."* Durant, Okla.: Democrat Printing, 1946.

McDearmon, Ray. *Without the Shedding of Blood: The Story of Dr. U.D. Uzell, and of Pioneer Life at Old Kimball.* San Antonio, Texas: Naylor, 1953.

McDermott, John Francis (ed.). *Frenchmen and French Ways in the Mississippi Valley.* Chicago: University of Illinois Press, 1969.

_____. *The Lost Panoramas of the Mississippi.* Chicago: University of Chicago Press, 1958.

MacDonald, A.B. (ed.). *Hands Up! True Stories of the Six-Gun Fighters of the Old Wild West.* New York: Bobbs-Merrill, 1927.

McGee, John H. *Rice and Salt.* San Antonio, Texas: Naylor, 1962.

McGeeney, P.S. *Down at Stein's Pass: A Romance of New Mexico.* Boston: Angel Guardian Press, 1909.

McGiffin, Lee. *Ten Tall Texans.* New York: Lothrop, Lee & Shepard, 1956.

McGinnis, Edith B. *The Promised Land.* Boerne, Texas: Topperwein, 1947.

McGinty, Billy, and Eyler, Glenn, Jr. *The Old West.* Stillwater, Okla.: Redlands Press, 1958.

McGloin, John Bernard. *San Francisco: The Story of a City.* San Rafael, Calif.: Presidio Press, 1978.

Macguire, H.N. *The Black Hills of Dakota: A Miniature History of Their Settlement, Resources, Production and Prospects.* Chicago: Jacob S. Gantz, 1879.

_____. *The Coming Empire: A Complete and Reliable Treatise on the Black Hills, Yellowstone and Big Horn Regions.* Sioux City, Iowa: Watkins & Snead, 1878.

McIntire, James. *Early Days in Texas: A Trip to Hell and Heaven.* Kansas City: McIntire, 1902.

McIntire, Josephine. *Boot Hill.* Boston: Chapman & Grimes, 1945.

McKee, Irving. *"Ben-Hur" Wallace.* Berkeley: University of California Press, 1947.

McKelvie, Martha. *The Fenceless Range.* Philadelphia: Dorrance, 1960.

McKennon, C.H. *Iron Men: A Saga of the Deputy United States Marshals Who Rode the Indian Territory.* Garden City, N.Y.: Doubleday, 1967.

McKeown, Martha Ferguson. *The Trail Led North: Mont Hawthorne's Story.* New York: Macmillan, 1948.

McKittrick, Myrtle M. *Vallejo, Son of California.* Portland, Ore.: Binfords & Mort, 1944.

MacLane, John F. *A Sagebrush Lawyer.* New York: Pandick Press, 1953.

McLeod, Alexander. *Pigtails and Gold Dust.* Caldwell, Idaho: Caxton Printers, 1947.

Macleod, William Christie. *The American Indian Frontier.* New York: Alfred A. Knopf, 1928.

McMaster, S.W. *Sixty Years on the Upper Mississippi.* Rock Island: n.p., 1893.

MacMinn, George R. *The Theatre of the Golden Era in California.* Caldwell, Idaho: Caxton Printers, 1941.

McMullen, Jerry. *Paddle Wheel Days in California.* Palo Alto, Calif.: Stanford University Press, 1944.

McMurray, Floyd L. *Westbound.* New York: Charles Scribner's Sons, 1943.

McNeal, Thomas Allen. *When Kansas Was Young.* New York: Macmillan, 1922.

McNeil, Cora. *Mizzoura.* Minneapolis, Minn.: Mizzoura, 1898.

McNitt, Frank. *The Indian Traders.* Norman: University of Oklahoma Press, 1962.

Macomb, John N. *Exploring Expedition from Santa Fe, New Mexico, to the Junction of the Grand and Green Rivers of the Great Colorado of the West.* Washington, D.C.: U.S. Government Printing Office, 1876.

McPherren, Ida. *Empire Builders.* Sheridan, Wyo.: Star, 1942.

_____. *Imprints on Pioneer Trails.* Boston: Christopher, 1950.

_____. *Trail's End.* Casper, Wyo.: Prairie, 1938.

McReynolds, Robert. *Thirty Years on the Frontier.* Colorado Springs, Colo.: El Paso Publishing, 1906.

McRill, Albert. *And Satan Came Also.* Oklahoma City, Okla.: Britton, 1955.

McWilliams, Carey. *North from Mexico.* New York: Greenwood Press, 1948.

_____. *Southern California Country: The Cults of California.* New York: Duell, Sloan & Pearce, 1946.

Madison, Virginia. *The Big Bend Country of Texas.* Albuquerque: University of New Mexico Press, 1955.

_____, and Stillwell, Hallie. *How Come It's Called That?* Albuquerque: University of New Mexico Press, 1958.

Majors, Alexander. *Seventy Years on the Frontier.* Chicago: Rand McNally, 1893.

Maltby, W.J. *Captain Jeff, or Frontier Life in Texas with the Texas Rangers.* Colorado, Texas: Whipkey, 1906.

Mangam, William Daniel. *The Clarks: An American Phenomenon.* New York: Silver Bow Press, 1941.

_____. *The Clarks of Montana.* New York: Silver Bow Press, 1939.

Mangan, Frank J. *Bordertown.* El Paso, Texas: Carl Hertzog, 1964.

Manly, William Lewis. *Death Valley in 1840.* Santa Barbara, Calif.: Wallace Hebberd, 1929.

Mann, Etta Donnan. *Four Years in the Governor's Mansion in Virginia, 1910-1914.* Richmond, Va.: Diet Press,

1937.

Marshall, James. *Elbridge A. Stuart, Founder of Carnation Company.* Los Angeles: Carnation, 1949.

———. *Santa Fe, The Railroad That Built an Empire.* New York: Random House, 1945.

Marshall, Jim. *Swinging Doors.* Seattle, Wash.: Frank McCaffrey, 1949.

Marshall, Otto Miller. *The Wham Paymaster Robbery.* Pima, Ariz.: Pima Chamber of Commerce, 1967.

Marshall, T.M. *A History of the Western Boundary of the Louisiana Purchase, 1819-1841.* Berkeley: University of California Press, 1924.

Marshall, Theodora Britton, and Evans, Gladys Crail. *They Found It In Natchez.* New Orleans, La.: Pelican, 1939.

Marshall, Thomas M. *Early Records of Gilpin County, Colorado, 1859-1861.* Boulder: University of Colorado Press, 1920.

Martin, Charles L. *A Sketch of Sam Bass, The Bandit.* Norman: University of Oklahoma Press, 1956.

Martin, Douglas D. *An Arizona Chronology: The Territorial Years, 1846-1912.* Tucson: University of Arizona Press, 1963.

———. *The Earps of Tombstone.* Tombstone, Ariz.: Tombstone Epitaph, 1959.

———. *Silver, Sex and Six Guns: Tombstone Sage of the Life of Buckskin Frank Leslie.* Tombstone, Ariz.: Tombstone Epitaph, 1962.

———. *Tombstone's Epitaph.* Albuquerque: University of New Mexico Press, 1951.

Martin, Edward Winslow. *History of the Grange Movement; or, the Farmer's War Against Monopolies. . . etc.* Chicago: National, 1874.

Martin, George Washington. *The First Two Years in Kansas.* Topeka, Kan.: State Printing Office, 1907.

Martin, Jack. *Border Boss: Captain John R. Hughes.* San Antonio, Texas: Naylor, 1942.

Martin, V. Covert. *Stockton Album Through the Years.* Stockton, Calif.: Simard Printing, 1959.

Masterson, Vincent Victor. *The Katy Railroad and the Last Frontier.* Norman: University of Oklahoma Press, 1952.

Masterson, William Barclay ("Bat"). *Famous Gunfighters of the Frontier.* Houston: Frontier Press of Texas, 1957.

———. *The Tenderfoot's Turn.* Utica, N.Y.: Savage Arms, 1909.

Matlock, J. Eugene. *Gone Beyond the Law.* Dallas: Mathis, Van Nort, 1940.

Matthews, Sallie Reynolds. *Interwoven: A Pioneer Chronicle.* El Paso, Texas: Carl Hertzog, 1958.

Mattison, Ray H. *Roosevelt and the Stockmen's Association.* Bismarck: State Historical Society of North Dakota, 1950.

Mayer, Frank H., and Roth, Charles B. *The Buffalo Harvest.* Denver: Sage Books, 1958.

Mayer, Robert. (ed.). *San Francisco.* Dobbs Ferry, N.Y.: Oceana Publications, 1974.

———. *Los Angeles, a Chronological and Documentary History.* Dobbs Ferry, N.Y.: Oceana, 1978.

Mayfield, Eugene O. *The Backbone of Nebraska.* Omaha, Neb.: Burkley Printing, 1916.

Maynard, Louis. *Oklahoma Panhandle: A History and Stories of No Man's Land.* Privately Printed, 1956.

Mayo, Morrow. *Los Angeles.* New York: Alfred A. Knopf, 1933.

Mazzanovich, Anton. *Trailing Geronimo.* Los Angeles: Gem, 1926.

Mazzula, Fred and Jo. *Al Packer, a Colorado Cannibal.* Denver: Published by Authors, 1968.

———. *Brass Checks and Red Lights.* Denver: Published by Authors, 1966.

———. *Outlaw Album.* Denver: A.B. Hirschfeld Press, 1966.

Meecham, A.B. *Wigwam and War-Path; or, the Royal Chief in Chains.* Boston: John P. Dale, 1875.

Memorial and Genealogical Record of Texas. Chicago: Goodspeed Brothers, 1894.

Mencken, August. *By the Neck.* New York: Hastings House, 1942.

Menefee, Eugene L., and Dodge, Fred A. *History of Tulare and Kings Counties California.* Los Angeles: Historic Record, 1913.

Mercer, Asa Shinn. *The Banditti of the Plains.* Cheyenne, Wyo.: Published by Author, 1894.

Metz, Leon Claire. *Dallas Stoudenmire: El Paso Marshall.* New York: Pemberton Press, 1969.

———. *John Selman: Texas Gunfighter.* New York: Hastings House, 1966.

———. *Pat Garrett: The Story of a Western Lawman.* Norman: University of Oklahoma Press, 1974.

Michelson, Charles. *The Ghost Talks.* New York: G.P. Putnam's Sons, 1944.

———. *Mankillers at Close Range.* Houston: Frontier Press of Texas, 1958.

Middagh, John. *Frontier Newspaper: The El Paso Times.* El Paso, Texas: Western College Press, 1958.

Millard, Bailey. *History of the San Francisco Bay Region.* Chicago: American Historical Society, 1924.

Miller, Benjamin S. *Ranch Life in Southern Kansas and the Indian Territory.* New York: Fless & Ridge Printing, 1896.

Miller, Floyd. *Bill Tilghman: Marshal of the Last Frontier.* New York: Doubleday, 1968.

Miller, George, Jr. *Missouri's Memorable Decade.* Columbia, Mo.: E.W. Stephens, 1898.

———. *Trial of Frank James for Murder.* Columbus, Mo.: E.W. Stephens, 1898.

Miller, Joaquin. *An Ilustrated History of the State of Montana.* Chicago: Lewis, 1894.

Miller, Joseph. *Arizona, A State Guide.* New York: Hastings House, 1956.

———. *Arizona, The Last Frontier.* New York: Hastings House, 1956.

———. *The Arizona Rangers.* New York: Hastings House, 1972.

———. *The Arizona Story.* New York: Hastings House, 1952.

Miller, Nina Hull. *Shutters West.* Denver: Sage Books, 1962.

Miller, Nyle H., and Snell, Joseph W. *Great Gunfighters of the Kansas Cowtowns, 1867-1886.* Lincoln: University of Nebraska Press, 1963.

———, Langsdorf, Edgar, and Richmond, Robert W. *Kansas, a Pictorial History.* Topeka: Kansas State Historical Society, 1961.

———. *Kansas Frontier Police Officers Before TV.* Topeka: Kansas State Historical Society, 1958.

———. et al. *Kansas in Newspapers.* Topeka: Kansas State Historical Society, 1963.

———. *Some Widely Publicized Western Police Officers.* Lincoln, Neb.: n.p., 1958.

———, and Snell, Joseph W. *Why the West Was Wild.* Topeka: Kansas State Historical Society, 1963.

Miller, Ronald Dean. *Shady Ladies of the West.* Los Angeles: Westernlore Press, 1964.

Miller, Thomas Lloyd. *The Public Lands of Texas, 1519-1970.* Norman: University of Oklahoma Press, 1972.

Miller, W. Henry. *Pioneering North Texas.* San Antonio, Texas: Naylor, 1953.

Miller, William Alexander. *Early Days in the Wild West.* n.p., 1943.

Mills, Edward Laird. *Plains, Peaks and Pioneers.* Portland, Ore.: Binfords & Mort, 1947.

Mills, Lester W. *A Sagebrush Saga.* Springfield, Utah: Art City, 1956.

Mills, William W. *Forty Years at El Paso, 1858-1898.* El Paso, Texas: Carl Hertzog, 1962.

Milner, Joe E., and Forrest, Earle R. *California Joe, Noted Scout and Indian Fighter.* Caldwell, Idaho: Caxton Printers, 1935.

Miner, Frederick Roland. *Outdoor Southland of California.* Los Angeles: Times-Mirror Press, 1923.

Minor, Charles L.C. *The Real Lincoln, from the Testimony of his Contemporaries.* Gastonia, N.C.: Atkins-Rankin, 1928.

Mitchell, John D. *Lost Mines of the Southwest.* Phoenix, Ariz.: Journal, 1933.

Mitchell, Lige. *Daring Exploits of Jesse James and His Band of Border Train and Bank Robbers.* Baltimore: I. & M. Ottenheimer, 1912.

Mix, Olive Stokes, and Heath, Eric. *The Fabulous Tom Mix.* Englewood Cliffs, N.J.: Prentice-Hall, 1957.

Mix, Tom. *The West of Yesterday.* Los Angeles: Times-Mirror Press, 1923.

Moaks, Sim. *The Last of the Mill Creek and Early Life in Northern California.* Chico, Calif.: n.p., 1923.

Mokler, Alfred James. *History of Natrona County, Wyoming.* Chicago: Lakeside Press, 1923.

Monaghan, Jay (ed.). *Civil War on the Western Border 1854-1865.* Boston: Little, Brown, 1955.

———. *The Great Rascal.* New York: Bonanza Books, 1951.

———. *Last of the Bad Men.* New York: Bobbs-Merrill, 1946.

———. *The Legend of Tom Horn, Last of the Bad Men.* New York: Bobbs-Merrill, 1946.

———. *The Overland Trail.* New York: Bobbs-Merrill, 1947.

Monroe, Arthur Worley. *San Juan Silver.* Grand Junction, Colo.: Grand Junction Sentinel, 1940.

Montague, Joseph. *Wild Bill, a Western Story.* New York: Chelsea House, 1926.

Montgomery, Cora. *Eagle Pass.* New York: G.P. Putnam's Sons, 1852.

Moody, Ralph. *Stagecoach West.* New York: Thomas Y. Crowell, 1967.

———. *Wells Fargo.* Boston: Houghton Mifflin, 1961.

Moore, John M. *The West.* Wichita Falls, Texas: Wichita Printing, 1935.

Mootz, Herman Edwin. *The Blazing Frontier.* Dallas: Tardy, 1936.

———. *"Pawnee Bill." A Romance of Oklahoma.* Los Angeles: Excelsior, 1928.

Morgan, Dale L. *The Humboldt, Highroad of the West.* New York: Farrar & Rinehart, 1943.

Morgan, Edward E.P. *God's Loaded Dice; Alaska, 1897-1930.* Caldwell, Idaho: Caxton Printers, 1948.

Morgan, Jonnie R. *The History of Wichita Falls.* Oklahoma City, Okla.: Economy, 1931.

Morgan, Leon. *Shooting Sheriffs of the Wild West.* Racine, Wis.: Whitman, 1936.

Morgan, Thomas B. *Spurs on the Boot.* New York: Longmans, 1941.

Morgan, Wallace M. *History Kern County, California.* Los Angeles: Historic Record, 1914.

Morison, Elting E. et al. (eds.). *Letters of Theodore Roosevelt.* Cambridge, Mass.: Harvard University Press, 1951.

Morleigh. *Life in the West....* London: Saunders & Otley, 1842.

Morris, Eastin. *The Tennessee Gazetteer.* Nashville, Tenn.: W. Hassell Hunt, 1834.

Morris, Henry Curtis. *Desert Gold and Total Prospecting.* Washington D.C.: Published by Author, 1955.

Morris, Leopold. *Pictorial History of Victoria and Victoria County "Where the History of Texas Began."* San Antonio, Texas: Clements, 1953.

Morris, Lerona Rosamond (ed.). *Oklahoma-Yesterday, Today, Tomorrow.* Guthrie, Okla.: Co-Operative, 1930.

Morris, Lucile. *Bald Knobbers.* Caldwell, Idaho: Caxton Printers, 1939.

Morris, Maurice. *Rambles in the Rocky Mountains.* London: Smith, Elder, 1864.

Morrison, William Brown. *Military Posts and Camps in Oklahoma.* Oklahoma City: Harlow, 1936.

Morse, Frank P. *Cavalcade of Rails.* New York: E.P. Dutton, 1940.

Moss, William Paul. *Rough and Tumble: The Autobiography of a West Texas Judge.* New York: Vantage Press, 1954.

Mott, Mrs. D.W. (ed.). *Legends and Lore of Long Ago (Ventura County, California).* Los Angeles: Wetsel, 1929.

Mowry, Sylvester. *Arizona and Sonora.* New York: Harper & Brothers, 1864.

Mullane, William H. (ed.). *This Is Silver City, 1882-1891.* 4 vols. Silver City, N.M.: Silver City Enterprise, 1963-1967.

Mullin, Robert N. *The Boyhood of Billy the Kid.* El Paso, Texas: Texas Western Press, 1967.

———. *A Chronology of the Lincoln County War.* Santa Fe, N.M.: Press of the Territorian, 1966.

——— (ed.). *Maurice Garland Fulton's History of the Lincoln County War.* Tucson: University of Arizona Press, 1968.

Mumey, Nolie. *Calamity Jane, 1852-1903: A History of Her Life and Adventure in the West.* Denver: Range Press, 1950.

———. *Creede, Colorado.* Denver: Artcraft Press, 1949.

———. *Hoofs to Wings: The Pony Express.* Boulder, Colo.: Johnson, 1960.

———. *Poker Alice.* Denver: Artcraft Press, 1951.

Munsell, M.E. *Flying Sparks.* Kansas City: Tierman-Dart, 1914.

Murbarger, Nell. *Ghosts of the Adobe Walls.* Los Angeles: Westernlore Press, 1964.

———. *Sovereigns of the Sage.* Palm Desert, Calif.: Desert Magazine Press, 1958.

Murdock, John C. *Under the Covenant: The Story of the Mormons.* New York: Vantage Press, 1966.

Murphy, Celeste G. *The People of the Pueblo; or, the Story of Sonoma.* Sonoma, Calif.: Published by Author, 1935.

Murphy, Thomas F. *The Hearts of the West.* Boston: Christopher, 1928.

Murrell, John A. *Life and Adventures of John A. Murrell.* Philadelphia: T.B. Peterson & Brothers, 1845.

Musick, John R. *Mysterious Mr. Howard.* New York: G.W. Dillingham, 1896.

———. *Stories of Missouri.* New York: American Book, 1897.

Myers, John Myers. *The Death of the Bravos.* Boston: Little, Brown, 1962.

———. *Doc Holliday.* Boston: Little, Brown, 1955.

———. *The Last Chance: Tombstone's Early Years.* New York: E.P. Dutton, 1950.

———. *San Francisco's Reign of Terror.* New York: Doubleday 1966.

Myers, S.D. (ed.). *Pioneer Surveyor, Frontier Lawyer: The Personal Narrative of O.W. Williams, 1877-1902.* El Paso, Texas: Texas Western College Press, 1966.

Mylar, Isaac L. *Early Days at the Mission San Juan Bautista.* Watsonville, Calif.: Evening Pajaronian, 1929.

The Mysteries and Miseries of San Francisco. New York: Dick & Fitzgerald 1853.

N

Nadeau, Reni. *Los Angeles, from Mission to Modern City.* New York: Longmans, Green 1960.

Nahm, Milton C. *Las Vegas and Uncle Joe.* Norman: University of Oklahoma Press, 1964.

Nash, Jay Robert. *Almanac of World Crime.* New York: Doubleday, 1981.

———. *Bloodletters and Badmen, A Narrative Encyclopedia of American Criminals From the Pilgrims to the Present.* New York: M. Evans, 1973.

———. *Look for the Woman.* New York: M. Evans, 1981.

Neal, Dorothy Jensen. *Captive Mountain Waters: A Story of Pipe Line and People.* El Paso, Texas: Western Press, 1961.

Ned, Nebraska. *Buffalo Bill and His Daring Adventures in the Romantic Wild West.* Baltimore: I. & M. Ottenheimer, 1913.

Neff, Boss S. *Some Experiences in the Texas and Oklahoma Panhandle.* Amarillo, Texas: The Globe News, 1941.

Neider, Charles (ed.) *The Great West.* New York: Coward-McCann, 1958.

Nelson, Bruce. *Land of the Dakotahs.* Minneapolis: University of Minnesota Press, 1946.

Nelson, Oliver M., and Debo, A. *The Cowman's Southwest.* Glendale, Calif.: Arthur H. Clark, 1953.

Nesbit, Charles Francis. *An American Family, the Nesbits of St. Clair.* Washington D.C.: n.p., 1932.

Neville, A.W. *The History of Lamar County (Texas).* Paris, Texas: Texas, 1937.

———. *The Red River Valley, Then and Now.* Paris, Texas: Texas, 1948.

Neville, Amelia Ransome. *The Fantastic City: Memoirs of the Social and Romantic Life of Old San Francisco.* Boston: Houghton Mifflin, 1932.

Newmark, Harris. *Sixty Years in Southern California.* New York: Knickerbocker Press, 1916.

Newmark, Marco R. *Jottings in Southern California History.* Los Angeles: Ward Ritchie Press, 1955.

Newsom, J.A. *The Life and Practice of the Wild and Modern Indian.* Oklahoma City, Okla.: Harlow, 1923.

Newton, Harry J. *Yellow Gold of Cripple Creek.* Denver: Nelson, 1928.

Nicholl, Edith M. *Observations of a Ranch Woman in New Mexico.* New York: Macmillan, 1898.

Nichols, Alice. *Bleeding Kansas.* New York: Oxford University Press, 1954.

Nicholson, Irene. *The X in Mexico: Growth Within Tradition.* London: Faber and Faber, 1965.

Nix, Evett Dumas. *Oklahombres.* St. Louis: Eden, 1929.

Nolan, Frederick W. *The Life & Death of John Henry Tunstall.* Albuquerque: University of New Mexico Press, 1965.

———. *The Sound of Their Music.* New York: Walter, 1978.

Nolen, Oren Warder. *Galloping Down the Texas Trail.* Odem, Texas: Privately Printed, 1947.

Nordyke, Lewis T. *The Angels Sing.* Clarendon, Texas: Clarendon Press, 1964.

———. *Cattle Empire: The Fabulous Story of the 3,000,000 Acre XIT.* New York: William Morrow, 1949.

———. *The Great Roundup.* New York: William Morrow, 1955.

———. *John Wesley Hardin, Texas Gunman.* New York: William Morrow, 1957.

———. *The Truth About Texas.* New York: Thomas Y. Crowell, 1957.

North, Escott. *The Saga of the Cowboy.* London: Jarrolds, 1942.

Noyes, Alva Josiah. *In the Land of the Chinook.* Helena, Mont.: State, 1917.

———. *The Story of Ajax: Life in the Big Hole Basin.* Helena, Mont.: State, 1914.

Nunis, Doyce B., Jr. (ed.). *The Golden Frontier: The Recollections of Herman Francis Reinhart, 1851-1869.*

Nunn, W.C. *Texas Under the Carpetbaggers.* Austin: University of Texas Press, 1962.

Nunnelley, Lela S. *Boothill Grave Yard.* Tombstone, Ariz.: Tombstone Epitaph, 1952.

Nuttall, Thomas. *A Journal of Travels into the Arkansas Territory During the Year 1819.* Norman: University of Oklahoma Press, 1980.

Nye, Nelson C. *Pistols for Hire: A Tale of the Lincoln County War and the West's Most Desperate Outlaw William (Billy the Kid) Bonney.* New York: Macmillan, 1941.

O

Oates, Stephen B. *Confederate Cavalry West of the River.* Austin: University of Texas Press, 1961.

O'Brien, Robert. *California Called Them: A Saga of Golden Days and Roaring Camps.* New York: McGraw-Hill, 1951.

———. *This Is San Francisco.* New York: Whittlesey House, 1948.

O'Byrne, John. *"Pike's Peak or Bust," and Historical Sketches of the Wild West.* Colorado Springs, Colo.: n.p., 1922.

O'Connor, Richard. *Bat Masterson.* New York: Doubleday, 1957.

———. *Pat Garrett.* New York: Ace Books, 1960.

———. *Wild Bill Hickok.* New York: Doubleday, 1959.

O'Dell, Scott. *Country of the Sun: Southern California, an Informal History and Guide.* New York: Thomas Y. Crowell, 1957.

Oden, Bill. *Early Days on the Texas-New Mexico Plains.* Canyon, Texas: Palo Duro Press, 1965.

Odens, Peter. *Outlaws, Heroes and Jokers of the Old Southwest.* Yuma, Ariz.: Southwest Printers, 1964.

O'Flaherty, Daniel. *General Jo Shelby.* Chapel Hill: University of North Carolina Press, 1954.

Ogg, Frederick Austin. *The Opening of the Mississippi.* New York: Macmillan, 1904.

Ogle, Ralph Hedrick. *Federal Control of the Western Apaches.* Albuquerque: University of New Mexico Press, 1970.

Oglesby, Carl. *The Yankee and Cowboy War.* Mission, Kan.: Sheed, Andrews & McMeel, 1976.

Oklahoma: A Guide to the Sooner State. Norman, Okla.: U.S. W.P.A., 1945.

Older, Cora. *Love Stories of Old California.* New York: Coward-McCann, 1940.

———. *San Francisco: Magic City.* New York: Longmans, Green, 1961.

Older, Fremont and Cora. *George Hearst: California Pioneer.* Los Angeles: Westernlore, 1966.

Olmsted, Frederick Law. *A Journey Through Texas.* New York: Dix & Edwards, 1857.

Olson, Edmund T. *Utah, a Romance in Pioneer Years.* Salt Lake City, Utah: Published by Author, 1931.

Olson, James C. *History of Nebraska.* Lincoln: University of Nebraska Press, 1955.

Olsson, Jan Olof. *Welcome to Tombstone.* trans. Maurice Michael. London: Elek Books, 1956.

O'Meara, James. *The Vigilance Committee of 1856.* San Francisco: Nash, 1932.

O'Neal, Bill. *Encyclopedia of Western Gunfighters.* Norman: University of Oklahoma Press, 1979.

O'Neal, James Bradas. *They Die But Once.* New York: Knight, 1935.

Opler, Morris E. *An Apache Life-Way.* Chicago: University of Chicago Press, 1941.

O'Reilly, Harrington. *Fifty Years on the Trail: A True Story of Western Life.* London: Chatto & Windus, Piccadilly, 1889.

Osgood, Ernest Staples. *The Day of the Cattleman.* Minneapolis: University of Minnesota Press, 1929.

Otero, Pear Miquel Antonio. *My Life on the Frontier, 1864-1882.* 2 vols. New York: The Press of the Pioneers, 1935.

———. *My Nine Years as Governor of the Territory of New Mexico, 1897-1906.* Albuquerque: University of New Mexico Press, 1940.

———. *The Real Billy The Kid.* New York: Rufus Rockwell Wilson, 1936.

Otis, Elwell S. *The Indian Question.* New York: Sheldon, 1878.

Outerbridge, Henry. *Captain Jack: His Story as Told to Henry Outerbridge.* New York: Century, 1928.

Outlawry and Justice in Old Arizona. Tucson, Ariz.: L.A. Printers, 1965.

Overholser, Joel F. *A Souvenir History of Fort Benton, Montana.* Fort Benton, Mont.: The River Press, n.d.

Ovitt, Mabel. *Golden Treasure.* Dillon, Mont.: Privately Printed, 1952.

Owens, Meroe J. *A Brief History of Sherman County, Nebraska.* Norfolk, Neb.: Norfolk News, 1952.

P

Pace, Dick. *Golden Gulch: The Story of Montana's Fabulous Alder Gulch.* Butte, Mont.: n.p., 1962.

Paddock, Capt. B.B. *A Twentieth Century History and Biographical Record of North and West Texas.* Chicago: Lewis, 1906.

Paden, Irene D., and Schlichtmann, Margaret E. *The Big Oak Flat Road: An Account of Freighting From Stockton to Yosemite Valley.* San Francisco: n.p., 1955.

Page, Elizabeth. *Wagons West.* New York: Farrar & Rinehart, 1930.

Page, Henry Markham. *Pasadena; Its Early Years.* Los Angeles: Lorrin L. Morrison, 1964.

Paine, Albert Bigelow. *Captain Bill McDonald, Texas Ranger.* New York: J.J. Little & Ives, 1909.

———. *Mark Twain's Notebook.* New York: Harper & Brothers, 1935.

Paine, Bayard H. *Pioneers, Indians and Buffaloes.* Curtis, Neb.: Curtis Enterprise, 1935.

Paine, Lauran. *Texas Ben Thompson.* Los Angeles: Westernlore Press, 1966.

———. *Tom Horn, Man of the West.* Barre, Mass.: Barre, 1963.

Paine, Swift. *Eilley Orrum, Queen of the Comstock.* New York: Bobbs-Merrill, 1929.

Pannell, Walter. *Civil War on the Range.* Los Angeles: Welcome News, 1943.

Paredes, Americo. *With a Pistol in his Hand: A Border Ballad and Its Hero.* Austin: University of Texas Press, 1958.

Pares, Richard. *Yankees and Creoles.* Cambridge, Mass.: Harvard University Press, 1956.

Park, Robert. *History of Oklahoma State Penitentiary at McAlester, Okla.* McAlester, Okla.: McAlester Printing, 1914.

Parke, Adelia. *Memoirs of an Old Timer.* Weiser, Idaho: Signal-American, 1955.

Parker, Amos Andrew. *Trip to the West and Texas.* Concord, N.H.: White & Fisher, 1835.

Parker, James. *The Old Army Memories, 1872-1918.* Philadelphia: Dorrance, 1929.

Parker, Watson. *Gold in the Black Hills.* Norman: University of Oklahoma Press, 1966.

Parkes, Henry Bamford. *A History of Mexico.* London: Eyre & Spottiswoods, 1962.

Parkhill, Forbes. *The Law Goes West.* Denver: Sage Books, 1956.

———. *The Wildest of the West.* New York: Henry Holt, 1951.

Parkman, Francis. *The Oregon Trail.* New York: Modern Library, 1949.

Parmer, Charles B. *For Gold and Glory.* New York: Carrick & Evans, 1939.

Parrish, Joe. *Coffins, Cactus and Cowboys: The Exciting Story of El Paso, 1536 to Present.* El Paso, Texas: Superior, 1964.

Parrish, Randall. *The Great Plains: The Romance of Western American Exploration, Warfare and Settlement, 1527-1870.* Chicago: A.C. McClurg, 1907.

Parrish, William E. *David Rice Atchison of Missouri: Border Politician.* Columbia: University of Missouri Press, 1961.

———. *Turbulent Partnership: Missouri and the Union, 1861-1865.* Columbia: University of Missouri Press, 1963.

Parson, Mabel. *A Courier of New Mexico.* n.p., n.d.

Parsons, Chuck. *The Capture of John Wesley Hardin.* College Station, Texas: Young West, n.d.

Parsons, George Frederick. *Life and Adventures of James W. Marshall.* Sacramento, Calif.: J.W. Marshall & W. Burke, 1870.

Parsons, George W. *The Private Journal of George Whitwell Parsons.* Phoenix: Arizona Statewide Archival and Records Project, 1939.

Parsons, John E. *The Peacemaker and Its Rivals.* New York: William Morrow, 1950.

Patterson, C.L. *Sensational Texas Manhunt.* San Antonio, Texas: Sid Murray & Son, 1939.

Patton, Fred J. *History of Fort Smith, Arkansas.* Ft. Smith, Ark.: Chamber of Commerce, n.d.

Paul, Rodman W. *California Gold: The Beginning of Mining in the Far West.* Cambridge, Mass.: Harvard University Press, 1947.

———. *Mining Frontiers of the Far West 1848-1880.* New York: Holt, Rinehart & Winston, 1963.

Paxson, Frederick L. *History of the American Frontier, 1763-1793*. Boston: Houghton Mifflin, 1924.

———. *The Last American Frontier*. New York: Macmillan, 1910.

Paxton, W.M. *Annals of Platte County*. Kansas City, Mo.: Hudson Kimberley, 1897.

Payne, Albert Bigelow. *Captain Bill McDonald, Texas Ranger*. New York: Little & Ives, 1909.

Payne, Doris Palmer. *Captain Jack, Modoc Renegade*. Portland, Ore.: Binford & Mort, 1938.

Payne, Ransom. *The Dalton Brothers and Their Astounding Career of Crime*. Chicago: Laird & Lee, 1892.

Peak, Howard W. *A Ranger of Commerce; or, 52 Years on the Road*. San Antonio, Texas: Naylor, 1929.

Peake, Ora Brooks. *The Colorado Range Cattle Industry*. Glendale, Calif.: Arthur H. Clark, 1937.

Pearson, Jim Berry. *The Maxwell Land Grant*. Norman: University of Oklahoma Press, 1961.

Peattie, Roderick (ed.). *The Black Hills*. New York: Vanguard Press, 1952.

———. *The Inverted Mountain; Canyons of the West*. New York: Vanguard Press, 1948.

Peavey, John R. *From the Thorny Hills of Duval to the Sleepy Rio Grande*. Brownsville, Texas: Springman-King, 1963.

Peavy, Charles D. *Charles A. Siringo, a Texas Picaro*. Austin, Texas: Steck-Vaughn, 1967.

Peck, Anne Merriman. *Southwest Roundup*. New York: Dodd, Mead, 1950.

Pelzer, Louis. *The Cattlemen's Frontier*. Glendale, Calif.: Arthur H. Clark, 1936.

Pence, Mary Lou, and Homsher, Lola M. *The Ghost Towns of Wyoming*. New York: Hastings House, 1956.

Penfield, Thomas. *Dig Here!* San Antonio, Texas: Naylor, 1962.

———. *Western Sheriffs and Marshals*. New York: Grossett & Dunlap, 1955.

Penrose, Charles Bingham. *The Johnson County War*. Laramie: University of Wyoming, 1939.

———. *The Rustler Business*. Douglas, Wyo.: Douglas Budget, 1959.

Penrose, Matt R. *Pots O' Golds*. Reno, Nev.: A. Carlisle, 1935.

Perkins, Jacob R. *Trails, Rails and War: The Life of General Grenville M. Dodge*. Indianapolis, Ind.: Bobbs-Merrill, 1929.

Perrigo, Lynn I. *Our Spanish Southwest: Its Peoples and Cultures*. New York: Holt, Rinehart, Winston, 1971.

Perry, George Sessions. *Texas, a World in Itself*. New York: McGraw-Hill Book, 1942.

Peterson, P.D. *Through the Black Hills and Bad Lands of South Dakota*. Pierre, S.D.: Fred Orlander, 1929.

Peyton, Green. *San Antonio, City in the Sun*. New York: McGraw-Hill Book, 1946.

Peyton, John Lewis. *Over the Alleghenies and Across the Prairies*. London: Simkin, Marshall, 1869.

Phares, Ross. *Bible in Pocket, Gun in Hand*. Garden City, N.Y.: Doubleday, 1964.

———. *Reverend Devil, A Biography of John A. Murrell*. New Orleans, La.: Pelican, 1941.

———. *Texas Tradition*. New York: Henry Holt, 1954.

Phelan, James. *History of Tennessee*. Boston: Houghton Mifflin, 1888.

Phelps, Alonzo. *Contemporary Biography of California's Representative Men*. 2 vols. San Francisco: A.L. Bancroft, 1881-1882.

Phillips, Michael James. *History of Santa Barbara County, California*. Chicago: S.J. Clarke, 1927.

Phillips, Paul Chrisler. *The Fur Trade*. 2 vols. Norman: University of Oklahoma Press, 1961.

Phillips, William. *The Conquest of Kansas, by Missouri and Her Allies*. Boston: Phillips, Sampson, 1856.

Pickett, Calder M. *Ed Howe: Country Town Philosopher*. Lawrence: Unviersity Press of Kansas, 1968.

Pierce, Frank Cushman. *A Brief History of the Lower Rio Grande Valley*. Menasha, Wis.: George Banta, 1917.

Pierce, N.H., and Brown, Nugent E. *The Free State of Menard: A History of the County*. Menard, Texas: Menard News Press, 1946.

Pinkerton, A. Frank. *Jim Cummins: Or, the Great Adams Express Robbery*. Chicago: Laird & Lee, 1887.

Pinkerton, Allan. *Mississippi Outlaws and the Detectives*. New York: G.W. Carleton 1881.

Pinkerton, William A. *Train Robbers*. Jamestown, Va.: International Chiefs of Police Association, 1907.

Piper, Edwin Ford. *Barbed Wire and Wayfarers*. New York: Macmillan, 1924.

Pitts, Dr. J.R.S. *Life and Bloody Career of the Executed Criminal James Copeland*. Jackson, Miss.: Pilot, 1874.

Pleasants, William James. *Twice Across the Plains, 1849, 1856*. San Francisco: W.M. Brunt Co., 1906.

Plenn, Jaime H., and LaRoche, C.J. *The Fastest Gun in Texas*. New York: American Library, 1956.

———. *Saddle in the Sky: The Lone Star State*. Indianapolis, Ind.: Bobbs-Merrill, 1940.

———. *Texas Hellion: The True Story of Ben Thompson*. New York: American Library, 1955.

Pocock, Roger S. *Following the Frontier*. New York: McClure, Phillips, 1903.

Poe, John William. *The Death of Billy the Kid*. Boston: Houghton Mifflin, 1933.

Poe, Sophie A. *Buckboard Days*. Caldwell, Idaho: Caxton Printers, 1936.

Pointer, Larry. *In Search of Butch Cassidy*. Norman: University of Oklahoma, 1977.

Police Gazette, Editor of. *The Pictorial Life and Adventures of John A. Murrel*. Philadelphia: T.B. Peterson & Brothers, 1848.

Polk, Stella Gipson. *Mason and Mason County: A History*. Austin, Texas: Pemberton Press, 1966.

Pope, John. *A Tour Through the Southern and Western Territories of the United States of America*. New York: C.L. Woodward, 1888.

Porter, A. Toomer. *Lead On!* New York: G.P. Putnam's Sons, 1898.

Potter, Colonel Jack. *Cattle Trails of the Old West*. Clayton, N.M.: Laura R. Krehbiel, 1939.

———. *Lead Steer and Other Tales*. Clayton, N.M.: Leader Press, 1939.

Powell, Addison M. *Trailing and Camping in Alaska*. New York: A. Wessells, 1909.

Powell, John Wesley. *Exploration of the Colorado River of the West and Its Tributaries*. Washington, D.C.: U.S. Government Printing Office, 1875.

Powell, Philip Wayne. *Soldiers, Indians, and Silver*. Berkeley: University of California Press, 1952.

Powers, Alfred. *Redwood Country: The Lava Region and the Redwoods*. New York: Duell, Sloan & Pearce, 1949.

Powers, Laura Bride. *Old Monterey, California's Adobe Capital*. San Francisco: San Carlos Press, 1934.

Prassel, Frank Richard. *The Western Peace Officer. A Legacy of Law and Order*. Norman: University of Oklahoma Press, 1972.

Prather, H. Bryant. *Come Listen to My Tale*. Tahlequah, Okla.: Pan Press, 1964.

———. *Texas Pioneer Days*. Dallas: Egan, 1965.

Preece, Harold. *The Dalton Gang, End of An Outlaw Era*.

New York: Hastings House, 1963.

———. *Living Pioneers: The Epic of the West by Those Who Lived It.* New York: World, 1952.

———. *Lone Star Man: Ira Aten.* New York: Hastings House, 1963.

Prentis, Noble L. *Southwestern Letters.* Topeka: Kansas Publishing House, 1882.

Preston, Paul. *Wild Bill, the Indian Slayer.* New York: Robert M. DeWitt, n.d.

Prettyman, W.S. *Indian Territory.* Norman: University of Oklahoma Press, 1957.

Price, Con. *Memories of Old Montana.* Hollywood, Calif.: Highland Press, 1945.

Price, G.G. *Death Comes to Billy the Kid.* Greenburg, Kan.: Signal, 1940.

Price, Sir Rose Lambart. *A Summer in the Rockies.* London: Sampson Low, Marston, 1898.

Price, S. Goodale. *Black Hills, the Land of Legend.* Los Angeles: De Vorrs, 1935.

———. *Ghosts of Golconda: A Guide Book to Historical Characters and Locations in the Black Hills of South Dakota.* Deadwood, S.D.: Western, 1952.

———. *Saga of the Hills.* Hollywood, Calif.: Cosmo, 1940.

Pride, W.F. *The History of Fort Riley.* n.p, 1926.

Priestley, Herbert Ingram. *The Coming of the White Man, 1492-1848.* New York: Macmillan, 1929.

Priet, Guillermo. *San Francisco in the Seventies: The City as Viewed by a Mexican Political Exile.* trans. Edwin S. Marby. San Francisco: John Henry Nash, 1938.

Prince, L. Bradford. *A Concise History of New Mexico.* Cedar Rapids, Iowa: Torch Press, 1912.

———. *Historical Sketches of New Mexico.* New York: Leggat Brothers, 1883.

———. *The Student's History of New Mexico.* Denver: Publishers Press, 1913.

Puckett, James L., and Ellen. *History of Oklahoma and Indian Territory and Homeseekers Guide.* Vinita, Okla.: Chieftan, 1906.

Q

Quaife, Milo Milton. *Checagou: From Indian Wigwam to Modern City, 1673-1835.* Chicago: University of Chicago Press, 1933.

———. *Chicago and the Old Northwest, 1673-1835: A Study of the Evolution of the Northwestern Frontier, Together with a History of Fort Dearborn.* Chicago: University of Chicago Press, 1913.

———. *Chicago's Highways Old and New: From Indian Trails to Motor Road.* Chicago: D.F. Keller, 1923.

Quick, Herbert. *One Man's Life: An Autobiography.* Indianapolis, Ind.: Bobbs-Merrill, 1925.

Quiett, Glenn Chesney. *Pay Dirt, A Panorama of American Gold Rushes.* New York: D. Appleton-Century, 1936.

———. *They Built the West.* New York: D. Appleton Century, 1934.

Quigg, Lemuel Ely. *"Gentleman" George Ives, a Montana Desperado.* Houston: Frontier Press of Texas, 1958.

Quinn, John Philip. *Fools of Fortune, or Gambling and Gamblers.* Chicago: W.B. Conkey, 1890.

———. *Gambling and Gambling Devices.* Canton, Ohio: J.P. Quinn, 1912.

Quinn, Vernon. *War-Paint and Powder-Horn.* New York: Frederick A. Stokes, 1929.

R

Raine, William McLeod, and Barnes, Will C. *Cattle.* New York: Doubleday, Doran, 1930.

———. *Famous Sheriffs and Western Outlaws.* Garden City, N.Y.: Doubleday, Doran, 1929.

———. *45-Caliber Law: The Way of Life of the Frontier Peace Officer.* Evanston, Ill.: Row, Peterson, 1941.

———. *Guns of the Frontier: The Story of How Law Came to the West.* Boston: Houghton Mifflin, 1940.

Rainey, George. *The Cherokee Strip.* Guthrie, Okla.: Cooperative, 1933.

———. *No Man's Land.* Guthrie, Okla.: Cooperative, 1937.

Ralph, Julian E. *Our Great West: A Study of the Present Conditions and Future Possibilites of the New Commonwealths and Capitals of the United States.* New York: Harper & Brothers, 1893.

Rambo, Ralph. *Trailing the California Bandit Tiburcio Vasquez, 1835-1875.* San Jose, Calif.: Rosicrucian Press, 1968.

Ramsdell, Charles. *San Antonio, a Historical and Pictorial Guide.* Austin: University of Texas Press, 1959.

Ramsdell, Charles W. *Reconstruction in Texas.* New York: Columbia University Press, 1910.

Rankin, M. Wilson. *Reminiscences of Fronter Days, Including an Authentic Account of the Thornburg and Meeker Massacre.* Denver: Smith-Brooks, 1938.

Raper, A.F. *The Tragedy of Lynching.* Chapel Hill: University of North Carolina Press, 1933.

Rascoe, Burton. *Belle Starr, The Bandit Queen.* New York: Random House, 1941.

Rascoe, Jesse Ed. *Some Western Treasures.* Cisco, Texas: Frontier Books, 1964.

Rath, Ida Ellen. *Early Ford County.* North Newton, Kan.: Mennonite Press, 1964.

———. *The Rath Trail.* Wichita, Kan.: McCormick-Armstrong, 1961.

Rathjen, Frederick W. *The Texas Panhandle Frontier.* Austin: University of Texas Press, 1973.

Ray, Bright. *Legends of the Red River Valley.* San Antonio, Texas: Naylor, 1941.

Ray, Clarence E. *The Alabama Wolf: Rube Burrow and His Desperate Gang of Highwaymen.* Chicago: Regan, 1910.

———. *The Border Outlaws, Frank & Jesse James.* Chicago: Regan, n.d.

———. *Buffalo Bill, the Scout.* Chicago: Regan, n.d.

———. *The Dalton Brothers.* Chicago: Regan, n.d.

———. *Famous American Scouts.* Chicago: Regan, n.d.

———. *Harry Tracy, Bandit, Highwayman and Outlaw of the Twentieth Century.* Chicago: Regan, n.d.

———. *The James Boys.* Chicago: Regan, n.d.

———. *The James Boys and Bob Ford.* Chicago: Regan, 1893.

———. *Jesse James' Daring Raid.* Chicago: Regan, n.d.

———. *Jesse James and His Gang of Train Robbers.* Chicago: Regan, n.d.

———. *Life of Bob and Cole Younger with Quantrell.* Chicago: Regan, 1916.

———. *The Oklahoma Bandits: The Daltons and Their Desperate Gang.* Chicago: Regan, n.d.

———. *Rube Burrow, King of Outlaws and Train Robbers.* Chicago: Regan, n.d.

———. *The Younger Brothers.* Chicago: Regan, n.d.

Ray, G.B. *Murder at the Corners.* San Antonio, Texas: Naylor, 1957.

Ray, Grace Ernestine. *Wily Women of the West.* San Antonio, Texas: Naylor, 1972.

Ray, Sam Hill. *Border Tales: Stories of Texas-New Mexico.* El Paso, Texas: Commercial, 1964.

Ray, Worth S. *Down in the Cross Timbers.* Austin, Texas: Published by Author, 1947.

Rayburn, Otto Ernest. *The Eureka Springs Story.* Eureka Springs, Ark.: Times-Echo Press, 1954.

_____. *Ozark Country.* New York: Duell, Sloan & Pearce, 1941.

Rayfield, Alma C. *The West That's Gone.* New York: Carleton Press, 1962.

Raymar, Robert George. *Montana, the Land and the People.* Chicago: Lewis, 1930.

Raymond, Dora Neill. *Captain Lee Hall of Texas.* Norman: University of Oklahoma Press, 1940.

Raynor, Ted. *Old Timers Talk in Southwestern New Mexico.* El Paso: Texas Western Press, 1960.

Rea, Ralph. *Boone County and Its People.* Van Buren, Ark.: Press-Argus, 1955.

Redford, Robert. *The Outlaw Trail.* New York: Grosset & Dunlap, 1979.

Redmond, Dennis M. *"Four Sixes to Beat."* El Paso, Texas: n.p, 1965.

Redmond, Frank. *The Younger Brothers.* St. Louis: Dramatic, 1901.

Reese, John Walter and Lillian Estelle. *Flaming Feuds of Colorado County.* Salado, Texas: Anson-Jones Press, 1962.

Reichard, Gladys A. *Navaho Religion.* New York: Bollingen Foundation, 1950.

Reid, Col. J.M. *Sketches and Anecdotes of the Old Settlers and New Comers.* Keokuk, Iowa: R.R. Ogden, 1876.

Reid, Samuel C., Jr. *The Scouting Expeditions of McCulloch's Texas Rangers.* Philadelphia: G.B. Zieber, 1848.

Reinhardt, Richard. *Out West on the Overland Train.* Palo Alto, Calif.: American West, 1967.

Reinhart, Herman Francis. *The Golden Frontier: The Recollections of Herman Francis Reinhart, 1851-1869.* Austin: University of Texas, 1962.

Rennert, Vincent Paul. *The Cowboy.* New York: Crowell-Collier Press, 1966.

_____. *Western Outlaws.* New York: Crowell-Collier Press, 1968.

Reno, John. *Life and Career of John Reno.* Indianapolis, Ind.: Indianapolis Journal, 1879.

Rensch, Hero Eugene and Ethel Grace. *Historic Spots in California: The Southern Counties.* Stanford, Calif.: Stanford University Press, 1932.

_____. *Historic Spots in California: Valley and Sierra Counties.* Stanford, Calif.: Stanford University Press, 1933.

Reps, John W. *Cities of the American West: A History of Frontier Urban Planning.* Princeton, N.J.: Princeton University Press, 1979.

Revoil, Benedict. *The Hunter and Trapper in North America.* trans. W.H. Davenport Adams, New York: Thomas Nelson & Sons, 1874.

Reynolds, John N. *The Twin Hells: A Thrilling Narrative of Life in the Kansas and Missouri Penitentiaries.* Chicago: Bee, 1890.

Reynolds, M.G. *Spanish and Mexican Land Laws.* St. Louis: Buxton, 1895.

Rhoades, William. *Recollections of Dakota Territory.* Fort Pierre, S.D.: n.p., 1931.

Rhodes, James Ford. *History of the United States from the Compromise of 1850.* New York: Macmillan, 1900.

Rhodes, James Ford. *History of the United States from the Compromise of 1850 to the McKinley-Bryan Campaign of 1898.* 8 vols. New York: Macmillan, 1920.

Rich, Everett (ed.). *The Heritage of Kansas.* Lawrence: University of Kansas Press, 1961.

Richards, Stanley. *Black Bart.* Wolfeboro, N.H.: Christopher Davies, 1966.

Richardson, Albert D. *Beyond the Mississippi.* Hartford, Conn.: American, 1867.

Richardson, Gladwell. *Two Guns, Arizona.* Santa Fe, N.M.: Press of the Territorian, 1968.

Richardson, R.N. *Texas, the Lone Star State.* New York: Prentice-Hall, 1943.

Richardson, Rupert Norval. *Adventuring With a Purpose: Life Story of Arthur Lee Wasson.* San Antonio, Texas: Naylor, 1951.

_____. *The Comanche Barrier to South Plains Settlement.* Glendale, Calif.: Arthur H. Clark, 1933.

_____, and Rister, Carl Coke. *The Greater Southwest.* Glendale, Calif.: Arthur H. Clark, 1934.

Rickard, T.A. *A History of American Mining.* New York: McGraw, 1932.

_____. *Through the Yukon and Alaska.* San Francisco: Mining & Scientific Press, 1909.

Rickards, Colin. *"Buckskin Frank" Leslie: Gunman of Tombstone.* El Paso, Texas: Western College Press, 1964.

_____. *Charles Littlepage Ballard, Southwesterner.* El Paso: Texas Western Press, 1966.

_____. *The Gunfight at Blazer's Mill.* El Paso: Texas Western Press, 1974.

_____. *Mysterious Dave Mathers.* Santa Fe, N.M.: Press of the Territorian, 1968.

Ricketts, William Pendleton. *50 Years in the Saddle.* Sheridan, Wyo.: Star, 1942.

Riddle, Jeff C. *The Indian History of the Modoc War, and the Cause That Led to It.* n.p, 1914.

Ridge, John Rollin (Yellow Bird). *The Life and Adventure of Joaquin Murieta, the Celebrated California Bandit.* Norman: University of Oklahoma Press, 1969.

Ridings, Sam P. *The Chisholm Trail.* Guthrie, Okla.: Cooperative, 1936.

Riegel, Robert E. *America Moves West.* New York: Henry Holt, 1930.

_____. *The Story of the Western Railroads.* New York: Macmillan, 1926.

Rieseberg, Felix Jr. *Golden Gate: The Story of San Francisco Harbor.* New York: S. Paul, 1940.

Rifkin, Shepard. *King Fisher's Road.* Greenwich, Conn.: Fawcet, 1963.

Ringgold, Jennie Parks. *Frontier Days in the Southwest: Pioneer Days in Old Arizona.* San Antonio, Texas: Naylor, 1952.

Rister, Carl Coke. *Fort Griffin on the Texas Frontier.* Norman: University of Oklahoma Press, 1956.

_____. *Land Hunger.* Norman: University of Oklahoma Press, 1942.

_____. *No Man's Land.* Norman: University of Oklahoma Press, 1948.

_____. *The Southern Plainsmen.* Norman: University of Oklahoma Press, 1938.

_____. *The Southwestern Frontier: 1865-1881.* Cleveland: Arthur H. Clark, 1928.

Rittenhouse, Jack D. *Cabezon: A New Mexico Ghost Town.* Santa Fe, N.M.: Stagecoach Press, 1963.

_____. *The Man Who Owned Too Much: Together with an 1895 Newspaper Account of the Life of Lucien Maxwell.* Houston, Texas: Stagecoach Press, 1958.

_____. *Outlaw Days at Cabezon.* Santa Fe, N.M.: Stagecoach Press, 1964.

Roberts, Bruce. *Springs from Parched Ground.* Uvalde, Texas: Hornby Press, 1950.

Roberts, Daniel Webster. *Rangers and Sovereignty*. San Antonio, Texas: Wood Printing and Engraving, 1914.

Roberts, Lou Conwary. *A Woman's Reminiscences of Six Years im Camp with Texas Rangers*. Austin, Texas: Press of von Boechmann-Jones, 1928.

Robertson, Frank C., and Harris, Beth Kay. *Soapy Smith, King of the Frontier Con Men*. New York: Hastings House, 1961.

Robertson, Pauline Durrett, and R.L. *Panhandle Pilgrimage: Illustrated Tales Tracing History in the Texas Panhandle*. Canyon, Texas: Staked Plains Press, 1976.

Robertson, Ruth T. *Famous Bandits; Brief Accounts of the Lives of Jesse James, Cole Younger, Billy the Kid and Others...* Washington D.C.: Washington Bureau, 1928.

Robinson, Charles. *The Kansas Conflict*. New York: Harper & Brothers, 1882.

Robinson, Duncan W. *Judge Robert McAlpin Williamson, Texas' Three-Legged Willie*. Austin: Texas State Historical Association, 1948.

Robinson, Sara T.L. *Kansas: Its Interior and Exterior Life*. Boston: Crosby, Nichols, 1856.

Robinson, W.W. *Panorama, a Picture History of Southern California*. Los Angeles: Title Insurance and Trust, 1953.

Robinson, William Henry. *The Story of Arizona*. Phoenix, Ariz.: Berryhill, 1919.

Rock, Marion Tuttle. *Illustrated History of Oklahoma*. Topeka, Kan.: C.B. Hamilton & Son, 1890.

Rockfellow, John Alexander. *The Log of an Arizona Trailblazer*. Tucson, Ariz.: Acme Printing, 1933.

Rockwell, Wilson (ed). *Memoirs of a Lawman: Autobiography of Cyrus Wells Shores*. Denver: Sage Books, 1962.

———. *New Frontier: Saga of the North Fork*. Denver: World Press, 1938.

———. *Sunset Slope: True Epics of Western Colorado*. Denver: Big Mountain Press, 1955.

———. *Utes: A Forgotten People*. Denver: Sage Books, 1956.

Rodney, William. *Joe Boyle: King of the Klondike*. Toronto, Ontario, Can.: McGraw-Hill Ryerson, 1974.

Roe, Edward Thomas. *The James Boys*. Chicago: A.E. Weeks, 1893.

Roe, Frank G. *The Indian and the Horse*. Norman: University of Oklahoma Press, 1955.

———. *The North American Buffalo*. Toronto, Ontario, Can.: University of Toronto Press, 1951.

Roenigk, Adolph. *Pioneer History of Kansas*. Lincoln, Kan.: Publish by Author, 1933.

Roff, Joe T. *A Brief History of Early Days in North Texas and the Indian Territory*. Allen, Okla.: Pontotoc County Democrat, 1930.

Rogers, Fred B. *Soldiers of the Overland: Being Some Account of the Services of General Patrick Edward Conner & His Volunteers in the Old West*. San Francisco: Grabhorn Press, 1938.

Rogers, John William. *The Lusty Texans of Dallas*. New York: E. P. Dutton, 1951.

Rogers, Justus H. *Colusa Country*. Orland, Calif.: Published by Author, 1891.

Rojas, Arnold R. *California Vaquero*. Fresno, Calif.: Academy Library Guild, 1953.

Rolle, Andrew F. *California, A History*. Arlington Heights, Ill.: Harlan Davidson, 1978.

——— (ed.). *The Road to Virginia City: The Diary of James Knox Polk Miller*. Norman: University of Oklahoma Press, 1960.

Rollins, Philip Ashton. *The Cowboy*. New York: Charles Scribner's Sons, 1922.

Rollinson, John K. *Hoofprints of a Cowboy and U.S. Ranger; Pony Trails in Wyoming*. Caldwell, Idaho: Caxton Printers, 1941.

———. *Wyoming Cattle Trails*. Caldwell, Idaho: Caxton Printers, 1948.

Rolt-Wheeler, Francis William. *The Book of Cowboys*. Boston: Lothrop, Lee & Shepard, 1921.

Root, Frank A., and Connelley, William Elsey. *The Overland Stage to California*. Topeka, Kan.: Published by Authors, 1901.

Rosa, Joseph G. *Alias Jack McCall: A Pardon or Death?*. Kansas City: Kansas City Posse of Westerners, 1967.

———. *The Gunfighter, Man or Myth?* Norman: University of Oklahoma Press, 1969.

———. *They Called Him Wild Bill*. Norman: University of Oklahoma Press, 1964.

———. *The West of Wild Bill Hickok*. Norman: University of Oklahoma Press, 1982.

Rosa, Joseph, and May, Robin. *Gun Law*. Chicago: Contemporary Books, 1977.

Rose, Victor M. *The Life and Services of Gen. Ben McCulloch*. Philadelphia: Pictorial Bureau of the Press, 1888.

———. *The Texas Vendetta, or the Sutton-Taylor Feud*. New York: J.J. Little, 1880.

Rosen, Rev. Peter. *Pa-ha-sa-pah; or the Black Hills of South Dakota*. St. Louis: Nixon-Jones, 1895.

Ross, Marvin C. *The West of Alfred Jacob Miller*. Norman: University of Oklahoma Press, 1951.

Ross, Nancy Wilson. *Westward the Women*. New York: Alfred A. Knopf, 1944.

Rothert, Otto A. *The Outlaws of Cave-in-Rock*. Cleveland: Arthur H. Clark, 1924.

Rouse, M.C. *A History of Cowboy Flat-Campbell-Pleasant Valley*. Guthrie, Okla.: Privately Printed, 1960.

Rowan, Richard Wilmer. *A Family of Outlaws*. Fort Wayne, Ind.: n.p., 1955.

———. *The Pinkertons, A Detective Dynasty*. Boston: Little, Brown, 1931.

Rowland, Dunbar. *History of Mississippi*. Chicago: S.J. Clarke, 1925.

Royce, Josiah. *California From the Conquest in 1846 to the Second Vigilance Committee in San Francisco*. New York: Houghton Mifflin, 1886.

Royce, Sarah. *A Frontier Lady's Recollections of the Gold Rush and Early California*. New Haven, Conn.: Yale University Press, 1932.

Rush, N. Orwin. *Mercer's Banditti of the Plains*. Tallahassee: Florida State University Library, 1961.

Russell, Carl Parcher. *One Hundred Years in Yosemite*. Palo Alto, Calif.: Stanford University Press, 1931.

Russell, C.W. (ed.). *Memoirs of Colonel John S. Mosby*. Boston: Little, Brown, 1917.

Russell, Don. *The Lives and Legends of Buffalo Bill*. Norman: University of Oklahoma Press, 1960.

Ruth, Kent. *Great Day in the West: Forts, Posts, and Rendezvous Beyond the Mississippi*. Norman: University of Oklahoma Press, 1963.

———. *Oklahoma, A Guide to the Sooner State*. Norman: University of Oklahoma Press, 1957.

Rutledge, Col. Dick. *A Few Stirring Events in the Life of Col. Dick Rutledge, Only Living Indian Scout of the Early Frontier Days of the West*. Denver: n.p., 1930.

Ryan, Ed. *Me and the Black Hills*. Custer, S.D.: Published by Author, 1951.

Ryan, J.C. *A Skeptic Dude in Arizona*. San Antonio, Texas: Naylor, 1952.

Rye, Edgar. *The Quirt and the Spur*. Chicago: W.B. Conkey, 1909.

S

Sabin, Edwin LeGrand. *Wild Men of the Wild West.* New York: Thomas Y. Crowell, 1929.

Sage, Lee. *The Last Rustler: The Autobiography of Lee Sage.* Boston: Little, Brown, 1930.

Sahula-Dyckes, Ignatz. *Alias Linson; or, the Ghost of Billy the Kid.* New York: Pageant Press, 1963.

Salisbury, Albert and Jane. *Here Rolled the Covered Wagons.* Seattle, Wash.: Superior, 1948.

Samuel, Ray, Huber, Leonard, and Ogden, Warren C. *Tales of the Mississippi.* New York: Hastings House, 1955.

Samuels, Charles. *The Magnificent Rube: The Life and Gaudy Times of Tex Rickard.* New York: McGraw-Hill, 1957.

Sanders, Helen Fitzgerald. *A History of Montana.* 3 vols. Chicago: Lewis, 1913.

_____, and Bertsche, William H., Jr. (eds.). *X. Beidler: Vigilante.* Norman: University of Oklahoma Press, 1957.

Sandmeyer, Elmer C. *The Anti-Chinese Movement in California.* Urbana: University of Illinois Press, 1939.

Sandoz, Mari. *The Buffalo Hunters.* New York: Hastings House, 1954.

_____. *The Cattlemen.* New York: Hastings House, 1958.

_____. *Love Song of the Plains.* New York: Harper & Brothers, 1961.

Sands, Frank. *A Pastoral Prince.* Santa Barbara, Calif.: n.p., 1893.

Santee, Ross. *Apache Land.* New York: Charles Scribner's Sons, 1947.

_____. *Lost Pony Tracks.* New York: Charles Scribner's Sons, 1953.

Santerre, George H. *Dallas' First Hundred Years, 1856-1956.* Dallas: Book Craft, 1856.

Saunders, Arthur C. *The History of Bannock County, Idaho.* Pocatello, Idaho: Tribune, 1915.

Saunders, Charles Francis. *The Southern Sierras of California.* Boston: Houghton Mifflin, 1923.

Savage, James Woodruff, et al. *History of the City of Omaha, Nebraska.* New York: Munsell, 1894.

Savage, Pat. *One Last Frontier: A Story of Indians, Early Settlers and Old Ranches of Northern Arizona.* New York: Exposition Press, 1964.

Sawyer, Eugene Taylor. *The Life and Career of Tiburcio Vasquez.* San Francisco: Bacon, 1875.

Saxon, Lyle. *Fabulous New Orleans.* New York: D. Appleton-Century, 1928.

_____. *Father Mississippi.* New York: Century, 1927.

Scanland, John Milton. *Life of Pat F. Garrett and the Taming of the Border Outlaw.* El Paso, Texas: Carleton F. Hodge, 1952.

Schaefer, Jack. *Heroes Without Glory: Some Good Men of the Old West.* Boston: Houghton Mifflin, 1965.

Schatz, August Herman. *Opening a Cow Country: A History of the Pioneer's Struggle in Conquering the Prairie South of the Black Hills.* Ann Arbor, Mich.: Edwards Brothers, 1939.

Schell, Herbert Samuel. *South Dakota, Its Beginnings and Growth.* New York: American Book, 1942.

Scherer, James A.B. *The First Forty-Niner.* New York: Minton Balch, 1925.

_____. *"The Lion of the Vigilantes": William T. Coleman and the Life of Old San Francisco.* Indianapolis, Ind.: Bobbs-Merrill, 1939.

Schmedding, Joseph. *Cowboy and Indian Trader.* Caldwell, Idaho: Caxton Printers, 1951.

Schmidt, Heinie. *Ashes of My Campfire.* Dodge City, Kan.: Journal, 1952.

Schmitt, Jo Ann. *Fighting Editors: The Story of Editors Who Faced Six-Shooters with Pen and Won.* San Antonio, Texas: Naylor, 1958.

Schmitt, Martin F. (ed.). *General George Crook: His Autobiography.* Norman: University of Oklahoma Press, 1946.

_____, and Brown, Dee. *The Settler's West.* New York: Charles Scribner's Sons, 1955.

Schoenberger, Dale T. *The Gunfighters.* Caldwell, Idaho: Caxton Printers, 1971.

Schofer, Jerry P. *Urban and Rural Finnish Communities in California: 1860-1960.* San Francisco: R & E Research Associates, 1975.

Schomackers, Günter. *The Wild West.* London: Macdonald & Jane's, 1977.

Schoolcraft, Henry Rowe. *Narrative of an Expedition through the Upper Mississippi to Itasca Lake.* New York: Harper & Brothers, 1834.

_____. *Travels in the Central Portions of the Mississippi Valley.* New York: Collins & Hannay, 1825.

Schoolfield, F.E. *Captain Alex F. Boss, Western Rivers Pilot from 1824-1850.* Cincinnati, Ohio: Public Library of Cincinnati, n.d.

Schrantz, Ward L. *Jasper County, Missouri, in the Civil War.* Carthage, Mo.: Carthage Press, 1923.

Schultz, Vernon B. *Southwestern Town: The Story of Willcox, Arizona.* Tucson: University of Arizona Press, 1964.

Schurz, Carl. *The Autobiography of Carl Schurz.* New York: Charles Scribner's Sons, 1961.

Scobee, Barry. *Fort Davis, Texas, 1583-1960.* El Paso, Texas: Published by Author, 1960.

_____. *Old Fort Davis.* San Antonio, Texas: Naylor, 1947.

_____. *The Steer Branded Murder.* Houston: Frontier Press of Texas, 1952.

Scott, George Ryley. *Such Outlaws as Jesse James.* London: Gerald S. Swann, 1943.

Scott, George W. *The Black Hills Story.* Fort Collins, Colo.: Published by Author, 1953.

Scott, Kenneth D. *Belle Starr in Velvet.* Tahlequah, Okla.: Pan Press, 1963.

Scott, Mel G. *The San Francisco Bay Area: A Metropolis in Perspective.* Berkeley: University of California Press, 1959.

Secrest, William B. *Joaquin.* Fresno, Calif.: Saga-West, 1967.

_____. *Juanita.* Fresno, Calif.: Saga-West, 1967.

Seeley, Charles Livingstone. *Pioneer Days in the Arkansas Valley in Southern Colorado.* Denver: Published by Author, 1932.

Segale, Sister Blandina. *At the End of the Santa Fe Trail.* Columbia, Ohio: Columbia Press, 1932.

Sell, Henry Blackman, and Weybright, Victor. *Buffalo Bill and the Wild West.* New York: Oxford University Press, 1955.

Senn, Edward L. *"Wild Bill" Hickok, "Prince of Pistoleers."* Deadwood, S.D.: n.p., 1939.

Settle, Raymond W., and Lund, Mary. *Empire on Wheels.* Palo Alto, Calif.: Stanford University Press, 1949.

Settle, William A., Jr. *Jesse James Was His Name.* Columbia: University of Missouri Press, 1966.

Severin, Timothy. *Explorers of the Mississippi.* New York: Alfred A. Knopf, 1968.

Seymour, Flora Warren. *Indian Agents of the Old Frontier.* New York: D. Appleton-Century, 1941.

_____. *The Story of the Red Man.* Longmans, Green, 1929.

Shackleford, William Yancey. *Belle Starr, The Bandit Queen.* Girard, Kan.: Haldemann-Julius, 1943.

_____. *Buffalo Bill Cody, Scout and Showman.* Girard, Kan.: Haldemann-Julius, 1944.

_____. *Gunfighters of the Old West.* Girard, Kan.: Halde-mann-Julius, 1943.

Shackleton, B. Close. *Handbook of Frontier Days of Southeast Kansas.* Privately Printed, 1961.

Shaner, Dolph. *The Story of Joplin.* New York: Stratford House, 1948.

Sharp, Paul F. *Whoop-Up Country: The Canadian-American West, 1865-1885.* Minneapolis: University of Minnesota Press, 1955.

Sheldon, Addison Erwin. *Nebraska Old and New: History, Stories, Folklore.* Lincoln: University of Nebraska, 1937.

Shell, Leslie Doyle, and Hazel M. *Forgotten Men of Cripple Creek.* Denver: Big Mountain Press, 1959.

Sheller, Roscoe. *Bandit to Lawman.* Yakima, Wash.: Franklin Press, 1966.

_____. *Ben Snipes: Northwest Cattle King.* Portland, Ore.: Binsford & Mort, 1957.

Sheridan, Sol N. *History of Ventura County, California.* Chicago: S.J. Clarke, 1926.

Sherman, James E., and Barbara H. *Ghost Towns of Arizona.* Norman: University of Oklahoma Press, 1969.

Shields, Robert William. *Seymour, Indiana and the Famous Story of the Reno Gang.* Indianapolis, Ind.: H. Lieber, 1939.

Shinkle, James D. *Fifty Years of Roswell History, 1867-1917.* Roswell, N.M.: Hall-Poorbaugh Press, 1964.

_____. *Reminiscences of Roswell Pioneers.* Roswell, N.M.: Hall-Poorbaugh Press, 1966.

Shinn, Charles Howard. *Graphic Description of Pacific Coast Outlaws.* Los Angeles: Westernlore Press, 1958.

_____. *Mining Camps: A Study in American Frontier Government.* New York: Alfred A. Knopf, 1948.

Shipman, Mrs. O.L. *Letters, Past and Present...* n.p., n.d.

_____. *Taming the Big Bend: A History of the Extreme Western Portion of Texas from Fort Clark to El Paso.* Marfa, Texas: n.p., 1926.

Shippey, Lee. *It's an Old California Custom.* New York: Vanguard Press, 1948.

Shirk, George H. *Oklahoma Place-Names.* Norman: University of Oklahoma Press, 1965.

Shirley, Glenn. *Belle Starr and Her Times.* Norman: University of Oklahoma Press, 1982.

_____. (ed.). *Buckskin Joe; Being the Unique and Vivid Memoirs of Edward Jonathan Hoyt.* Lincoln: University of Nebraska Press, 1966.

_____. *Buckskin and Spurs: A Gallery of Frontier Rogues and Heroes.* New York: Hastings House, 1958.

_____. *Heck Thomas, Frontier Marshal.* Philadelphia: Chilton, 1962.

_____. *Henry Starr, Last of the Real Bad Men.* New York: David McKay, 1965.

_____. *Law West of Fort Smith.* New York: Henry Holt, 1957.

_____. *Outlaw Queen: The Fantastic True Story of Belle Starr.* Derby, Conn.: Monarch Books, 1960.

_____. *Pawnee Bill: A Biography of Major Gordon W. Lillie.* Albuquerque: University of New Mexico Press, 1958.

_____. *Shotgun for Hire: The Story of "Deacon" Jim Miller, Killer of Pat Garrett.* Norman: University of Oklahoma Press, 1970.

_____. *Six-Gun and Silver Star.* Albuquerque: University of New Mexico Press, 1955.

_____. *Temple Houston.* Norman: University of Oklahoma Press, 1980.

_____. *Toughest of Them All.* Albuquerque: University of New Mexico Press, 1953.

_____. *West of Hell's Fringe: Crime, Criminals, and the Federal Peace Officer in Oklahoma Territory, 1889-1907.* Norman: University of Oklahoma Press, 1978.

Shoemaker, Floyd (ed.). *Missouri, Day by Day.* 2 vols. Jefferson City, Mo.: Mid-State Printing, 1942.

_____. *Missouri and Missourians: Land of Contrasts and People of Achievements.* 5 vols. Chicago: Lewis, 1943.

Shumard, George. *The Ballad and History of Billy the Kid.* Clovis, N.M.: Tab, 1966.

Simpson, C.H. *Life in the Far West; or, a Detective's Thrilling Adventures Among the Indians and Outlaws of Montana.* Chicago: Rhodes & McClure, 1893.

Simpson, S.R. *Llano Estacado; or, the Plains of West Texas.* San Antonio, Texas: Naylor, 1957.

Sims, Judge Orland L. *Gun-Toters I Have Known.* Austin, Texas: Encino Press, 1967.

Sinise, Jerry. *Pink Higgins: The Reluctant Gunfighter.* Quanah, Texas: Nortex Press, 1974.

Siringo, Charles A. *A Cowboy Detective, an Autobiography.* Chicago: W.B. Conkey, 1912.

_____. *The History of Billy the Kid.* Santa Fe, N.M.: Published by Author, 1920.

_____. *A Lone Star Cowboy.* Sante Fe, N.M.: Published by Author, 1919.

_____. *Riata and Spurs: The Story of a Lifetime Spent in the Saddle as a Cowboy and Ranger.* Boston: Houghton Mifflin, 1927.

_____. *A Texas Cowboy, or Fifteen Years on the Hurricane Deck of A Spanish Pony.* Chicago: M. Umbdenstock, 1885.

_____. *Two Evil Isms, Pinkertonism and Anarchism.* Chicago: Published by Author, 1915.

Skelton, Charles L. *Riding the Pony Express West.* New York: Macmillan, 1937.

Sloan, Richard E. (ed.). *History of Arizona.* Phoenix, Ariz.: Record, 1930.

_____. *Memoires of an Arizona Judge.* Stanford, Calif.: Stanford University Press, 1932.

Small, Floyd B. *Autobiography of a Pioneer.* Seattle, Wash.: Published by Author, 1916.

Small, Joe Austell (ed.). *The Best of True West.* New York: Julian Messner, 1964.

Small, Kathleen Edwards, and Smith, J. Larry. *History of Tulare County, California.* Chicago: S.J. Clarke, 1926.

Smith, C. Alphonso. *O. Henry Biography.* Garden City, N.Y.: Doubleday, Page, 1916.

Smith, Cornelius C., Jr. *William Sanders Oury: History Maker of the Southwest.* Tucson: University of Arizona Press, 1968.

Smith, Duane A. *Rocky Mountain Mining Camps.* Bloomington: Indiana University Press, 1967.

Smith, Frank Meriweather (ed.). *San Francisco Vigilance Committee of '56.* San Francisco: Barry, Baird, 1883.

Smith, Gene, and Smith, Jayne Barry. *The National Police Gazette.* New York: Simon & Schuster, 1972.

Smith, Grant H. *The History of the Comstock Lode 1850-1920.* Reno: University of Nevada Bulletin, 1943.

Smith, Helena Huntington. *The War on Powder River.* New York: McGraw-Hill, 1966.

Smith, Jedediah S. *The Southwestern Expedition of Jedediah S. Smith: His Personal Account of the Journey to California, 1826-1827.* Glendale, Calif.: Arthur H. Clark, 1977.

Smith, Tevis Clyde, Jr. *From the Memories of Men.* Brownwood, Texas: Published by Author, 1954.

_____. *Frontier's Generation.* Brownwood, Texas: Published by Author, 1931.

Smith, Waddell F. (ed.). *The Story of the Pony Express.*

San Francisco: Hesperian House, 1960.

Smith, Wallace. *Garden of the Sun.* Los Angeles: Lymanhouse, 1939.

_____. *Prodigal Sons: The Adventures of Christopher Evans and John Sontag.* Boston: Christopher, 1951.

Smith, Wallace. *Oregon Sketches.* New York: G.P. Putnam's Sons, 1925.

Snell, Joseph W. *Painted Ladies of the Cowtown Frontier.* Kansas City: Kansas City Posse of Westerners, 1965.

Sollis, Roberta Beed. *Calamity Jane: A Study in Historical Criticism.* Helena, Mont.: Western Press, 1958.

Sonney, Louis S. *The American Outlaw.* n.p, n.d.

Sonnichsen, Charles Leland. *Alias Billy the Kid.* Albuquerque: University of New Mexico Press, 1955.

_____. *Billy King's Tombstone: The Private Life of an Arizona Boom Town.* Caldwell, Idaho: Caxton Printers, 1942.

_____. *Cowboys and Cattle Kings.* Norman: University of Oklahoma Press, 1950.

_____. *The Grave of John Wesley Hardin.* College Station: Texas A & M University Press, 1979.

_____. *I'll Die Before I'll Run.* New York: Harper & Brothers, 1951.

_____. *Outlaw: Bill Mitchell Alias Baldy Russell.* Denver: Sage Books, 1965.

_____. *Pass of the North.* El Paso: Texas Western Press, 1968.

_____. *The Story of Roy Bean, Law West of the Pecos.* New York: Macmillan, 1943.

_____. *Ten Texas Feuds.* Albuquerque: University of New Mexico Press, 1951.

_____. *Tularosa.* New York: Devin-Adair, 1960.

Sorenson, Alfred R. *Early History of Omaha; or, Walks and Talks Among the Old Settlers.* Omaha, Neb.: Daily Bee, 1876.

_____. *Hands Up! or The History of a Crime.* Omaha, Neb.: Barkalow Brothers, 1877.

_____. *The Story of Omaha from the Pioneer Days to the Present Time.* Omaha, Neb.: National, 1923.

Soule, Frank, and Gilran, John H, and Nisbet, James. *The Annals of San Francisco.* New York: D. Appleton, 1855.

South, Colon. *Out West; or, From London to Salt Lake City and Back.* London: Wyman & Sons, 1884.

Sparks, William. *The Apache Kid, a Bear Fighter and Other True Stories of the Old West.* Los Angeles: Skelton, 1926.

Speer, Marion A. *Western Trails.* Huntington Beach, Calif.: Huntington Beach News, 1931.

Speer, William. *China and California.* San Francisco: Marvin & Hitchcock, 1853.

_____. *A Humble Plea in Behalf of the Immigrants from the Empire of China.* San Francisco: Office of the Oriental, 1856.

_____. *The Oldest and the Newest Empire: China and the United States.* Hartford, Conn.: S.S. Scranton, 1870.

Speer, William S., and Brown, John Henry (eds.). *The Encyclopedia of the New West.* Marshall, Texas: United States Biographical, 1881.

Spencer, Mrs. George E. *Calamity Jane: A Story of the Black Hills.* New York: Cassell, 1887.

Spindler, Will Henry. *Rim of the Sandhills: A True Picture of the Old Holt County Horse Thief-Vigilante Days.* Mitchell, S.D.: Educator Supply, 1941.

_____. *Yesterday's Trails.* Gordon, Neb.: Gordon Journal, 1961.

Sprague, Marshall. *Massacre, the Tragedy at White River.* Boston: Little, Brown, 1957.

_____. *Money Mountain: The Story of Cripple Creek Gold.* Boston: Little, Brown, 1953.

Sprague, William F. *Women and the West: A Short Social History.* Boston: Christopher, 1940.

Spring, Agnes Wright. *The Cheyenne and Black Hills Stage and Express Routes.* Glendale, Calif.: Arthur H. Clark, 1949.

_____. *Colorado Charley, Wild Bill's Pard.* Boulder, Colo.: Pruett Press, 1968.

_____. (ed.). *Pioneer Years in the Black Hills.* Glendale, Calif.: Arthur H. Clark, 1957.

_____. *Seventy Years: A Panoramic History of the Wyoming Stock Growers' Association.* Cheyenne, Wyo.: Privately Printed, 1942.

_____. *William Chapin Deming, of Wyoming, Pioneer Publisher, and State and Federal Official.* Glendale, Calif.: Arthur H. Clark, 1944.

Spurr, Josiah Edward. *Through the Yukon Gold Diggings.* Boston: Eastern, 1900.

Stambaugh, J. Lee and Lillian J. *A History of Collin County, Texas.* Austin: Texas State Historical Association, 1958.

Stanley, Edwin J. *Life of Rev. L.B. Stateler; or, Sixty-Five Years on the Frontier.* Nashville, Tenn.: M.E. Church South, 1907.

Stanley, F. (pseud. for Father Stanley Crocchiola). *The Alma (New Mexico) Story.* n.p., n.d.

_____. *The Antonchico (New Mexico) Story.* n.p, n.d.

_____. *Clay Allison.* Denver: World Press, 1956.

_____. *The Clayton (New Mexico) Story.* n.p, n.d.

_____. *Dave Rudabaugh: Border Ruffian.* Denver: World Press, 1961.

_____. *Desperadoes of New Mexico.* Denver: World Press, 1953.

_____. *The Duke City: The Story of Albuquerque, New Mexico, 1706-1956.* Pampa, Texas: Pampa Print, 1963.

_____. *The Elizabethtown (New Mexico) Story.* n.p., 1961.

_____. *The Folsom (New Mexico) Story.* Pantex, Texas: Published by Author, 1962.

_____. *Fort Bascom Comanche-Kiowa Barrier.* Pampa, Texas: Pampa Print, 1961.

_____. *Fort Stanton.* Pampa, Texas: Pampa Print, 1964.

_____. *Fort Union (New Mexico).* n.p, 1953.

_____. *The Grant That Maxwell Bought.* Denver: World Press, 1952.

_____. *The Kingston (New Mexico) Story.* Pantex, Texas: Published by Author, 1961.

_____. *The La Belle (New Mexico) Story.* Pantex, Texas: n.p., 1962.

_____. *The Lake Valley (New Mexico) Story.* Pep, Texas: n.p, 1964.

_____. *The Lamy (New Mexico) Story.* Pep, Texas: n.p., 1966.

_____. *The Las Vegas Story.* Denver: World Press, 1951.

_____. *The Lincoln (New Mexico) Story.* Pep, Texas: n.p., 1964.

_____. *Longhair Jim Courtright: Two Gun Marshal of Fort Worth.* Denver: World Press, 1957.

_____. *The Mogollon (New Mexico) Story.* Pep, Texas: n.p., 1968.

_____. *No More Tears for Black Jack Ketchum.* Denver: World Press, 1958.

_____. *One Half Mile from Heaven; or, the Cimarron Story.* Denver: World Press, 1949.

_____. *The Otero (New Mexico) Story.* Pantex, Texas: n.p., 1962.

_____. *The Private War of Ike Stockton.* Denver: World Press, 1959.

_____. *Raton Chronicle.* Denver: World Press, 1948.

_____. *Rodeo Town.* Denver: World Press, 1953.

_____. *The Seven Rivers (New Mexico) Story.* Pep, Texas: n.p., 1963.

_____. *The Shakespeare (New Mexico) Story.* Pantex, Texas: Published by Author, 1961.

_____. *Socorro: The Oasis.* Denver: World Press, 1950.

_____. *The Springer (New Mexico) Story.* Pantex, Texas: Published by Author, 1962.

_____. *Story of the Texas Panhandle Railroads.* Borger, Texas: Hess, 1976.

_____. *The White Oaks (New Mexico) Story.* n.p., 1961.

Stansbery, Lon R. *The Passing of the 3D Ranch.* Tulsa, Okla.: George W. Henry, 1930.

Stanton, G. Smith. *When the Wildwood Was in Flower.* New York: J.S. Ogilvie, 1910.

Stanton, Irving W. *Sixty Years in Colorado.* Denver: n.p., 1922.

Starkey, Marion L. *The Cherokee Nation.* New York: Alfred A. Knopf, 1946.

Starkie, Walter. *The Waveless Plain.* London: John Murray, 1938.

Steckmesser, Kent Ladd. *The Western Hero in History and Legend.* Norman: University of Oklahoma Press, 1965.

Steele, Robert V.P. *Between Two Empires: The Life Story of California's First Senator.* Boston: Houghton Mifflin, 1969.

Steele, S.B. *Forty Years in Canada.* New York: Dodd, Mead, 1915.

Steen, Ralph W. (ed.). *The Texas News: A Miscellany of Texas History in Newspaper Style.* Austin, Texas: Steck, 1955.

Steffen, Jerome O. *The American West.* Norman: University of Oklahoma Press, 1979.

Stellman, Louis J. *Mother Lode: The Story of California's Gold Rush.* San Francisco: Harr Wagner, 1934.

Stephenson, Nathaniel Wright. *Texas and the Mexican War.* New Haven, Conn.: Yale University Press, 1921.

Sterling, Hank. *Famous Western Outlaw-Sheriff Battles.* New York: Rainbow Books, 1954.

Sterling, William Warren. *Trails and Trials of a Texas Ranger.* n.p., 1959.

Stevens, Brevet-Major Isaac I. *Campaigns of the Rio Grande and of Mexico.* New York: D. Appleton, 1851.

Stevenson, Robert Louis. *Across the Plains.* New York: Charles Scribner's Sons, 1892.

Stevenson-McDermott, Myra E. *Lariat Letters.* Liberal, Kan.: n.p., 1907.

Steward, A.J.D. (ed.). *The History of the Bench and Bar of Missouri.* St. Louis: Legal, 1898.

Stewart, Dora Ann. *Government and Development of Oklahoma Territory.* Oklahoma City: Harlow, 1933.

Stewart, Edgar I. *Custer's Luck.* Norman: University of Oklahoma Press, 1955.

Stewart, Robert. *Sam Steele.* Garden City, N.Y.: Doubleday, 1979.

Stoll, William T. *Silver Strike: The True Story of Silver Mining in the Coeur d'Alenes.* Boston: Little, Brown, 1932.

Stone, Arthur L. *Following Old Trails.* Missoula, Mont.: Morton John Elrod, 1913.

Stone, Will Hale. *Twenty-Four Years a Cowboy and Ranchman in Southern Texas and Old Mexico.* Published by Author, 1905.

Stong, Phil. *Gold in Them Hills.* Garden City, N.Y.: Doubleday, 1957.

Stout, Ernest. *The Younger Brothers.* Chicago: Dramatic, 1902.

_____. *The Younger Brothers' Last Raid.* Chicago: Dramatic, 1902.

_____. *The Youngers' Last Stand.* Chicago: Dramatic, 1902.

_____. *The Youngers Out West.* Chicago: Dramatic, 1902.

Stout, F.E. *Rube Burrows; or, Life, Exploits and Death of the Bold Train Robber.* Aberdeen, Miss.: n.p., 1890.

Stout, Tom (ed.). *Montana, Its Story and Biography.* Chicago: American Historical Society, 1921.

Stover, Elizabeth Matchett (ed.). *Son-of-a-Gun Stew; a Sampling of the Southwest.* Dallas: University of Dallas Press, 1945.

Strahorn, Carrie Adell. *Fifteen Thousand Miles by Stage.* New York: G.P. Putnam's Sons, 1911.

Strahorn, Robert E. *To the Rockies and Beyond.* Omaha: New West, 1879.

_____. *Wyoming, Black Hills and Big Horn Region.* Cheyenne, Wyo.: Western Press, 1877.

Strate, David K. *Sentinel to the Cimarron.* Dodge City, Kansas: Cultural Heritage and Arts Center, 1970.

Straus, Ralph. *Coaches and Carriages.* London: M. Secher, 1912.

Strauss, Levi. *Levi's Round-Up of Western Sheriffs.* San Francisco: Levi Strauss, n.d.

Streeter, Floyd Benjamin. *Ben Thompson, Man With A Gun.* New York: Frederick Fell, 1957.

_____. *The Kaw: The Heart of a Nation.* New York: Farrar & Rinehart, 1941.

_____. *Prairie Trails and Cow Towns.* Boston: Chapman & Grimes, 1936.

Strong, Capt. Henry W. *My Frontier Days & Indian Fights on the Plains of Texas.* Dallas: n.p, 1926.

Stuart, Granville. *Forty Years on the Frontier.* 2 vols. Cleveland: Arthur H. Clark, 1925.

Sullivan, Dulcie. *The LS Brand: The Story of a Texas Panhandle Ranch.* Austin: University of Texas Press, 1968.

Sullivan, Frank S. *A History of Meade County, Kansas.* Topeka, Kan.: Crane, 1916.

Sullivan, W. John L. *Twelve Years in the Saddle for Law and Order on the Frontiers of Texas.* Austin, Texas: Von Boeckman-Jones, 1909.

Sumner, Charles. *The Crime Against Kansas.* Washington, D.C.: Buell & Blanchard, 1856.

Sutherland, William Alexander. *Out Where the West Begins.* Las Cruces, N.M.: Southwest, 1942.

Sutley, Zachary Taylor. *The Last Frontier.* New York: Macmillan, 1933.

Sutton, Fred Ellsworth. *Hands Up! Stories of the Six Gun Fighters of the Old West.* Indianapolis, Ind.: Bobbs-Merrill, 1926.

Sutton, Robert C., Jr. *The Sutton-Taylor Feud.* Quanah, Texas: Nortex Press, 1974.

Swallow, Alan (ed.). *The Wild Bunch.* Denver: Sage Books, 1966.

Swan, Oliver G. *Covered Wagon Days.* New York: Grosset & Dunlap, 1928.

_____. (ed.). *Frontier Days.* Philadelphia: Macrae-Smith, 1928.

Swanton, John R. *The Indians of the Southeastern United States.* New York: Greenwood Press, 1969.

Sweet, Willis. *Carbonate Camps, Leadville and Ten-Mile of Colorado.* Kansas City: Ramsey, Millett & Hudson, 1879.

Sweetman, Luke D. *Back Trailing on Open Range.* Caldwell, Idaho: Caxton Printers, 1951.

Swessinger, Earl A. *Texas Trail to Dodge City.* San Antonio, Texas: Naylor, 1950.

Switzler, William F. *Switzler's Illustrated History of Missouri, from 1541 to 1877.* St. Louis: C.R. Barns, 1879.

T

Tallent, Annie D. *The Black Hills: or, The Last Hunting Ground of the Dakotahs.* St. Louis: Nixon-Jones Printing, 1899.

Targ, William. *The Great American West.* New York: World, 1946.

Taylor, Drew Kirksey. *Taylor's Thrilling Tales of Texas.* San Antonio, Tex.: Guaranty Bond Printing, 1926.

Taylor, Morris F. *Trinidad, Colorado Territory.* Trinidad, Colo.: Trinidad State Junior College, 1966

Taylor, Ralph C. *Colorado, South of the Border.* Denver: Sage Books, 1963.

Taylor, Thomas Ulvan. *Bill Longley and His Wild Career.* Bandera, Texas: Frontier Times, 1925.

_____. *The Chisholm Trail and Other Routes.* San Antonio, Texas: Naylor, 1936.

Taylor, William. *California Life Illustrated.* New York: n.p., 1860.

_____. *Seven Years' Street Preaching in San Francisco, California.* New York: Published By Author, 1856.

Terhune, Albert Payson. *Famous Hussies of History.* New York: World, 1943.

Tevis, James. *Arizona in the 50s.* Albuquerque: University of New Mexico Press, 1954.

Thane, Eric. *High Border Country.* New York: Duell, Sloan & Pearce, 1942.

Thoburn, Joseph B., and Wright, Muriel H. *Oklahoma: A History of the State and Its People.* 4 vols. New York: Lewis Historical, 1929.

_____. *A Standard History of Oklahoma.* 5 vols. Chicago: American Historical Society, 1916.

Thomas, D.K. *Wild Life in the Rocky Mountains; or, the Lost Million Dollar Gold Mine.* C.E. Thomas, 1917.

Thompson, Albert W. *The Story of Early Clayton, New Mexico.* Clayton, N.M.: Clayton News, 1933.

_____. *They Were Open Range Days; Annals of a Western Frontier.* Denver: World Press, 1946.

Thompson, George G. *Bat Masterson, The Dodge City Years.* Topeka: Kansas State Printing Plant, 1943.

Thompson, Goldianne. *History of Clayton and Union County, New Mexico.* Denver, Colo.: Monitor, 1962.

Thompson, Henry C. *Sam Hildebrand Rides Again.* Bonne Terre, Mo.: Steinbeck, 1950.

Thompson, Mary, et al. *Clayton: The Friendly Town of Union County, New Mexico.* Denver: Monitor, 1962.

Thorndike, Thaddeus. *Lives and Exploits of the Daring Frank and Jesse James.* Baltimore: I. & M. Ottenheimer, 1909.

Thorp, Nathan Howard. *Story of the Southwestern Cowboy, Pardner of the Wind.* Caldwell, Idaho: Caxton Printers, 1945.

Thorp, Raymond W., and Bunker, Robert. *Crow Killer.* New York: Signet, 1958.

_____. *Spirit Gun of the West; the Story of Doc W.F. Carver.* Glendale, Calif.: Arthur H. Clark, 1957.

Thrapp, Dan L. *Al Sieber: Chief of Scouts.* Norman: University of Oklahoma Press, 1964.

Tibbles, Thomas Henry. *Buckskin and Blanket Days: Memories of a Friend of the Indians.* Garden City, N.Y.: Doubleday, 1957.

Tice, J.H. *Over the Plains and on the Mountains.* St. Louis: Industrial Age Printing, 1872.

Tilden, Freeman. *Following the Frontier With F. Jay Haynes.* New York: Alfred A. Knopf, 1964.

Tilghman, Zoe A. *Marshal of the Last Frontier.* Glendale, Calif.: Arthur H. Clark, 1949.

_____. *Outlaw Days.* Oklahoma City: Harlow, 1926.

_____. *Spotlight: Bat Masterson and Wyatt Earp as U.S.*

Deputy Marshals. San Antonio, Texas: Naylor, 1960.

Tillotson, F.H. *How To Be A Detective.* Kansas City: Hailman Printing, 1909.

Timmons, William. *Twilight on the Range: Recollections of a Latterday Cowboy.* Austin: University of Texas Press, 1962.

Tinkham, George H. *California Men and Events: Time 1769-1890.* Stockton, Calif.: Record, 1915.

_____. *History of San Joaquin, California.* Los Angeles: Historic Record, 1923.

_____. *A History of Stockton from Its Organization Up to the Present Time.* San Francisco: W.H. Hinton, 1880.

Tolbert, Frank X. *An Informal History of Texas: From Cabeza de Vaca to Temple Houston.* New York: Harper & Brothers, 1961.

Tombstone Map and Guide. Tombstone, Ariz.: Devere, 1969.

Tomlinson, William P. *Kansas in Eighteen Fifty-Eight.* New York: H. Dayton, 1859.

Toole, K. Ross. *Montana: An Uncommon Land.* Norman: University of Oklahoma Press, 1959.

Torchiana, Henry Albert William van Coenen. *California Gringos.* San Francisco: Paul Elder, 1930.

_____. *Story of the Mission Santa Cruz.* San Francisco: Paul Elder, 1933.

Toulouse, Joseph H. and James R. *Pioneer Posts of Texas.* San Antonio, Texas: Naylor, 1936.

Towle, Virginia Rowe. *Vigilante Woman.* South Brunswick, N.Y.: A.S. Barnes, 1966.

Townshend, R.B. *The Tenderfoot in New Mexico.* London: John Lane, 1923.

Train, Arthur. *On the Trail of the Bad Men.* New York: Charles Scribner's Sons, 1925.

Travers, James W. *California: Romance of Clipper Ships and Gold Rush Days.* Los Angeles: Wetzel, 1949.

Trenholm, Virginia Cole. *Footprints on the Frontier: Saga of the La Ramie Region of Wyoming.* Douglas, Wyo.: Douglas Enterprise, 1945.

_____, and Carley, Maurine. *Wyoming Pageant.* Casper, Wyo.: Prairie, 1946.

Trinka, Zena Irma. *Out Where the West Begins, Being the Early and Romantic History of North Dakota.* St. Paul, Minn.: Pioneer, 1920.

Triplett, Col. Frank. *Conquering the Wilderness.* New York: N.D. Thompson, 1883.

_____. *History, Romance and Philosophy of Great American Crimes and Criminals.* Hartford, Conn.: Park, 1885.

_____. *The Life, Times, and Treacherous Death of Jesse James.* St. Louis: J.H. Chambers, 1882.

Truman, Benjamin Cummings. *Life, Adventures and Capture of Tiburcio Vasquez.* Los Angeles: Los Angeles Star, 1874.

Turner, F.J. *The Frontier in American History.* New York: Henry Henry Holt, 1920.

_____. *The United States, 1830-1850.* New York: Holt, 1935.

Turner, Fitzhugh. *Dirty Little Coward of Fauquier County.* Warrentonn, Va.: n.p., 1953.

Turner, John Peter. *The North-West Mounted Police, 1873-1893.* 2 vols. Ottawa, Ontario, Can.: Edmund Cloutier, 1950.

Turner, Mary Honeyman Ten Eyck. *Avery Turner, Pioneer Railroad and Empire Builder of the Great Southwest.* Amarillo, Texas: Southwestern, 1933.

_____. *These High Plains.* Amarillo, Texas: Russell Stationery, 1941.

Tuttle, Charles R. *History of Kansas.* Madison, Wis.: Interstate, 1876.

Twain, Mark [Samuel Clemens]. *Roughing It.* Hartford,

Conn.: American, 1872.

Twitchell, Ralph E. *Historical Sketch of Governor William Carr Lane*. Santa Fe: New Mexico Historical Society, 1917.

———. *The History of Military Occupation of the Territory of New Mexico*. Chicago: Rio del Grande Press, 1963.

———. *The Leading Facts of New Mexican History*. Cedar Rapids, Iowa: Torch Press, 1911-1917.

Tyler, George W. *The History of Bell County*. San Antonio, Texas: Naylor, 1936.

U

Udall, David King, and Pearl Udall Nelson. *Arizona Pioneer Mormon*. Tucson: Arizona Silhouettes, 1959.

Underhill, Ruth Murray. *The Navajos*. Norman: University of Oklahoma Press, 1958.

———. *Red Man's America*. Chicago: University of Chicago Press, 1953.

Upton, Charles Elmer. *Pioneers of El Dorado*. Placerville, Calif: Published by Author, 1906.

Urquhart, Lena M. *Roll Call: The Violent and Lawless*. Denver: Golden Bell Press, 1967.

V

Vandor, Paul E. *History of Fresno County, California*. Los Angeles: Historic Record, 1919.

Van Nada, M.L. (ed.). *The Book of Missourians*. Chicago: T.J. Steele, 1906.

Van Tramp, John C. *Plain and Rocky Mountain Adventure*. Columbus, Ohio: Gilmore & Segner, 1866.

———. *Prairie and Rocky Mountain Adventures*. Columbus, Ohio: Segner & Condit, 1867.

Vaughan, Joe. *The Only True History of Frank James, Written by Himself*. Pine Bluff, Ark.: Sarah E. Snow, 1926.

Vaughn, Robert. *Then and Now or Thirty-Six Years in the Rockies*. Minneapolis, Minn.: Tribune, 1900.

Verckler, Stewart P. *Cowtown-Abilene: The Story of Abilene, Kansas, 1867-1875*. New York: Carlton Press, 1961.

Vernon, Joseph S., and Booth, Capt. Henry. *Along the Old Trail: A History of the Old and a Story of the New Santa Fe Trail*. Cimarron, Kan.: Tucker-Vernon, 1910.

———. *Dodge City and Ford County, Kansas*. Larned, Kan.: Tucker-Vernon, 1911.

Vestal, Stanley (pseud. of Walter S. Campbell). *Dodge City, Queen of Cow Towns*. New York: Harper & Brothers, 1951.

———. *Jim Bridger, Mountain Man*. New York: William Morrow, 1946.

———. *Joe Meek, The Merry Moutain Man*. Caldwell, Idaho: Caxton Printers, 1952.

———. *The Missouri*. New York: Farrar & Rinehart, 1945.

———. *The Old Santa Fe Trail*. Boston: Houghton Mifflin, 1939.

———. *Queen of Cowtowns, Dodge City*. New York: Harper & Brothers, 1952.

———. *Short Grass Country*. New York: Duell, Sloan & Pearce, 1941.

———. *Sitting Bull*. New York: Houghton Mifflin, 1932.

———. *Wagons West: Story of the Old Trail to Santa Fe*. New York: American Pioneer Trails Association, 1946.

———. *Warpath and the Council Fire*. New York: Random House, 1948.

Vickers, C.L. (ed.). *History of the Arkansas Valley, Colorado*. Chicago: O.L. Baskin, 1881.

Violette, Eugene Morrow. *A History of Missouri*. New York: D.C. Heath, 1918.

Visscher, William Lightfoot. *Buffalo Bill's Own Story of His Life and Deeds*. n.p., 1917.

Voorhees, Luke. *Personal Recollections of Pioneer Life on the Mountains and Plains of the Great West*. Cheyenne, Wyo.: Privately Printed, 1920.

W

Wagoner, Jay J. *Arizona Territory, 1863-1912*. Tucson: University of Arizona Press, 1970.

———. *History of the Cattle Industry*. Tucson: University of Arizona, 1952.

Walden, Arthur Treadwell. *A Dog-Puncher on the Yukon*. Boston: Houghton Mifflin, 1928.

Waldo, Edna La Moore. *Dakota, an Informal Study of Territorial Days Gleaned from Contemporary Newspapers*. Bismarck, N.D.: Capital, 1932.

Walker, Henry J. *Jesse James "the Outlaw," Jesse Woodson James alias J. Frank Dalton 1848-1951*. Des Moines, Iowa: Wallace Homestead, 1961.

Walker, Stanley. *Home to Texas*. New York: Harper & Brothers, 1956.

Walker, Tacetta B. *Stories of Early Days in Wyoming*. Casper, Wyo.: Prairie, 1936.

Walker, Tom. *Fort Apache*. New York: Avon, 1977.

Wallace, Betty. *Gunnison County*. Denver: Sage Books, 1960.

———. *History With the Hide Off*. Denver: Sage Books, 1965.

Wallace, Ernest, and Hoebel, E.A. *The Comanches*. Norman: University of Oklahoma Press, 1952.

Wallace, Lew. *Lew Wallace: An Autobiography*. New York: Harper & Brothers, 1906.

Wallack, L.R. *American Pistol and Revolver*. New York: Winchester Press, 1979.

Waller, Brown. *Last of the Great Western Train Robbers*. South Brunswick, N.Y.: A.S. Barnes, 1968.

Wallis, George A. *Cattle Kings of the Staked Plains*. Dallas: American Guide Press, 1957.

Walls, Jim and Phil. *Chinatown, San Francisco*. Stanford, Calif.: Howell-North, 1960.

Walsh, Richard John. *The Making of Buffalo Bill*. Indianapolis, Ind.: Bobbs-Merrill, 1928.

Walter, George W. *The Loomis Gang*. Prospect, N.Y.: Prospect Books, 1953.

Walter, William W. *The Great Understander: True Life Story of the Last of the Wells Fargo Shotgun Express Messengers*. Aurora, Ill.: Published by Author, 1931.

Walters, Lorenzo D. *Tombstones's Yesterday*. Tucson, Ariz.: Acme Printing, 1928.

Walton, Augustus. *A History of Detection, Conviction, Life and Designs of John A. Murrel, The Great Western Land Pirate*. Athens, Tenn.: George White, 1835.

Walton, William M. *The James Boys of Old Missouri*. Cleveland: Arthur Westbrook, 1907.

———. *Life and Adventures of Ben Thompson, the Famous Texan*. Houston, Texas: Frontier Press, 1954.

Waltrip, Lela, and Rufus. *Cowboys and Cattlemen*. New

York: David McKay, 1967.

Ward, Don (ed.). *Bits of Silver: Vignettes of the Old West.* New York: Hastings House, 1961.

Ward, Joseph O. *My Grandpa Went West.* Caldwell, Idaho: Caxton Printers, 1956.

Ward, Margaret. *Cimarron Saga.* n.p., 1940.

Ward, William. *The Dalton Gang, the Bandits of the Far West.* Cleveland: Arthur Westbrook, n.d.

———. *Harry Tracy, the Death Dealing Oregon Outlaw.* Cleveland: Arthur Westbrook, 1908.

———. *The James Boys of Old Missouri.* Cleveland: Arthur Westbrook, 1907.

———. *Jesse James' Blackest Crime.* Cleveland: Arthur Westbrook, 1909.

———. *Jesse James' Dash for Fortune.* Cleveland: Arthur Westbrook, n.d.

———. *Jesse James' Midnight Attack.* Cleveland: Arthur Westbrook, 1910.

———. *Jesse James' Mid-Winter Lark.* Cleveland: Arthur Westbrook, n.d.

———. *Jesse James' Race for Life.* Cleveland: Arthur Westbrook, n.d.

———. *The Younger Brothers, the Border Outlaws.* Cleveland: Arthur Westbrook, 1908.

Warden, Ernest A. *Infamous Kansas Killers.* Wichita, Kan.: McGuin, 1944.

———. *Thrilling Tales of Kansas.* Wichita, Kan.: Wichita Eagle Press, 1932.

Ware, Captain Eugene F. *The Indian War of 1864.* New York: St. Martin's Press, 1960.

Warman, Cy. *Frontier Stories.* New York: Charles Scribner's Sons, 1898.

———. *The Story of the Railroad.* New York: D. Appleton, 1898.

Warner, Matt. *The Last of the Bandit Riders.* Caldwell, Idaho: Caxton Printers, 1940.

Warner, Opie L. *A Pardoned Life: Life of George Sontag.* San Bernardino, Calif.: Index Print, 1909.

Watanabe Ryusaku. *Bandits on Horseback.* Tokyo: Chuo Koron-sha, 1964.

Waters, Frank. *The Colorado.* New York: Rinehart, 1946.

———. *Midas of the Rockies.* Newbury Park, Calif: Sage, Swallow, 1972.

———. *The Story of Mrs. Virgil Earp: The Earp Brothers of Tombstone.* New York: Clarkson N. Potter, 1960.

Waters, L.L. *Steel Trails to Santa Fe.* Lawrence: University of Kansas Press, 1951.

Waters, William. *A Gallery of Western Badmen.* Covington, Ky. Americana, 1954.

Watrous, Ansel. *History of Larimer County, Colorado.* Fort Collins, Colo.: Courier, 1911.

Watson, Frederick. *A Century of Gunmen; a Study in Lawlessness.* London: Ivor Nicholson & Watson, 1931.

Way, Thomas E. *Frontier Arizona.* New York: Carlton Press, 1950.

———. *Sgt. Fred Platten's Ten Years on the Trail of Redskins.* Williams, Ariz.: Williams News Press, 1963.

Way, W.J. (Jack). *The Tombstone Story.* Tucson, Ariz.: Livingston Press, 1965.

Weadock, Jack. *Dust of the Desert: Plain Tales of the Desert and the Border.* New York: D. Applton-Century, 1936.

Weaver, John. *El Pueblo Grande.* Los Angeles: Ward Ritchie Press, 1973.

Webb, Walter Prescott. *The Great Frontier.* Boston: Houghton Mifflin, 1952.

———. *The Great Plains.* Boston: Ginn, 1931.

——— (ed.). *The Handbook of Texas.* 2 vols. Austin: Texas State Historical Society, 1952.

———. *The Story of the Texas Rangers.* New York: Grosset & Dunlap, 1957.

———. *The Texas Rangers, A Century of Frontier Defense.* Boston: Houghton Mifflin, 1935.

Webb, W.E. *Buffalo Land; an Authentic Account of the Discoveries, Adventures, and Mishaps of a Scientific and Sporting Party in the Wild West.* Chicago: E. Hannaford, 1872.

Weber, David. *The Lost Trappers.* Albuquerque: University of New Mexico Press, 1970.

———. *The Taos Trappers.* Norman: University of Oklahoma Press, 1968.

Weinstein, Alfred A. *Barbed Wire Surgeon.* New York: Macmillan, 1948.

Wellman, Paul I. *The Blazing Southwest.* London: W. Foulshar, 1961.

———. *Death on Horseback.* New York: J.B. Lippincott, 1934.

———. *A Dynasty of Western Outlaws.* Garden City, N.Y.: Doubleday, 1961.

———. *Glory, God and Gold.* Garden City, N.Y.: Doubleday, 1954.

———. *The Indian Wars of the West.* Garden City, N.J.: Doubleday, 1947.

———. *Spawn of Evil.* Garden City, N.Y.: Doubleday, 1964.

———. *The Trampling Herd.* New York: Carrick & Evans, 1939.

Wells, Evelyn, and Peterson, Harry Austin. *The '49ers.* Garden City, N.Y.: Doubleday, 1949.

———. *Fremont Older.* New York: D. Appleton-Century, 1936.

Wendland, Michael F. *The Arizona Project.* Kansas City: Sheed, Andrews & McMeel, 1977.

West, John O. *Billy the Kid, Hired Gun or Hero.* Dallas: Southern Methodist University Press, 1966.

West, Ray B., Jr. (ed.). *Rocky Mountain Cities.* New York: W.W. Norton, 1949.

Westermeier, Clifford P. *Trailing the Cowboy.* Caldwell, Idaho: Caxton Printers, 1955.

Western Kansas Cattle Growers Assoc. *Brand Book.* n.p., 1882, 1883, 1884, 1885.

Westerners, The. *Brand Book.* Los Angeles: Los Angeles Corral, 1947.

———. *The Smoke Signal.* 13 vols. Tucson, Ariz.: Tucson Corral, n.d.

Westphall, Victor. *Thomas Benton Catron and His Era.* Tucson: University of Arizona Press, 1973.

Wetmore, Helen Cody. *Last of the Great Scouts: The Life Story of Col. William F. Cody.* Duluth, Minn.: Duluth Press, 1899.

Wharton, Clarence Ray. *L'Archeveque.* Houston, Texas: Anson Jones Press, 1941.

———. *History of Fort Bend County.* San Antonio, Texas: Naylor, 1939.

Wharton, J.E. *History of the City of Denver.* Denver: Byers & Dailey, 1866.

Wheeler, Col. Homer Webster. *Buffalo Days; Forty Years in the Old West.* Indianapolis, Ind.: Bobbs-Merrill, 1925.

———. *The Frontier Trail; or, from Cowboy to Colonel.* Los Angeles: Times-Mirror Press, 1923.

Whisenand, Emma Boge. *This Is Nebraska.* Kansas City: Burton, 1942.

White, Dale. *Bat Masterson.* New York: Julian Messner, 1960.

White, Michael C. *California All the Way Back to 1828.* Los Angeles: Glen Dawson, 1956.

White, Owen Payne. *The Autobiography of a Durable Sinner.* New York: G.P. Putnam's Sons, 1942.

_____. *Lead and Likker.* New York: Minton, Balch, 1932.

_____. *My Texas 'Tis of Thee.* New York: G.P. Putnam's Sons, 1936.

_____. *Out of the Desert: The Historical Romance of El Paso.* El Paso, Texas: McMath, 1923.

_____. *Texas, an Informal Biography.* New York: G.P. Putnam's Sons, 1945.

_____. *Them Was the Days; From El Paso to Prohibition.* New York: Minton, Balch, 1925.

_____. *Trigger Fingers.* New York: G.P. Putnam's Sons, 1926.

White, S.E. *Arizona Nights.* New York: McClure, 1907.

Whiting, F.B. *Grit, Grief and Gold: A True Narrative of an Alaskan Pathfinder.* Seattle, Wash.: Peacock, 1933.

Whittemore, Margaret. *One-Way Ticket to Kansas: The Autobiography of Frank M. Stahl.* Lawrence: University of Kansas Press, 1959.

Whymper, Frederick. *Travel and Adventure in the Territory of Alaska.* London: John Murray, 1868.

Wickersham, James. *Old Yukon: Tales, Trails and Trials.* Washington D.C.: Washington Law Book, 1938.

Wilbarger, Josiah W. *Indian Depredations in Texas.* Austin, Texas: Hutchings Printing House, 1889.

Wilder, Daniel W. *The Annals of Kansas.* Topeka, Kans.: George W. Martin, 1875.

Wilhelm, Stephen R. *Cavalcade of Hooves and Horns.* San Antonio, Texas: Naylor, 1958.

_____. *Texas, Yesterday and Tomorrow.* Houston, Texas: Gulf, 1947.

Williams, Albert N. *The Black Hills, Mid-Continent Resort.* Dallas: Southern Methodist University Press, 1952.

Williams, Amelia W., and Barker, Eugene C. (eds.). *The Writings of Sam Houston.* Austin: University of Texas Press, 1938-1943.

Williams, Brad, and Pepper, Choral. *Lost Legends of the West.* New York: Holt, Rinehart & Winston, 1970.

_____. and _____. *The Mysterious West.* New York: World, 1967.

Williams, Charlean Moss. *Washington, Hemstead County, Arkansas.* Houston, Texas: Anson-Jones Press, 1951.

Williams, Harry. *Texas Trails; Legends of the Great Southwest.* San Antonio, Texas: Naylor, 1932.

Williams, Henry Llewellyn. *"Buffalo Bill."* London: George Routledge & Sons, 1887.

Williams, J.S. *Old Times in West Tennessee.* Memphis, Tenn.: W.G. Cheeney, 1873.

Williams, Judge Oscar Waldo. *A City of Refuge.* n.p., n.d.

_____. *The Old New Mexico, 1879-1880.* n.p., n.d.

_____. *Pioneer Surveyor, Frontier Lawyer: The Personal Narrative of O.W. Williams, 1877-1902.* El Paso: Texas Western College Press, 1966.

Williams, R.H. *With the Border Ruffians.* New York: E.P. Dutton, 1907.

Williams, Walter, and Shoemaker, Floyd Calvin. *Missouri, Mother of the West.* Chicago: American Historical Society, 1930.

Williamson, Thames. *Far North Country.* New York: Duell, Sloan & Pearce, 1944.

Williard, James F., and Goodykoontz, Collin B. (eds.). *The Trans-Mississippi West.* Boulder: University of Colorado Press, 1930.

Willison, George Finlay. *Here They Dug the Gold.* New York: Brentano's, 1931.

_____. *Saints and Strangers.* New York: Reynal & Hitchcock, 1945.

Wilson, Don W. *Governor Charles Robinson of Kansas.* Wichita: University of Kansas Press, 1975.

Wilson, Edward. *An Unwritten History: A Record from the Exciting Days of Early Arizona.* Phoenix, Ariz.: McNeill, 1915.

Wilson, Neill Compton (ed.). *Deep Roots: The History of Blake, Moffitt, and Towne, Pioneers in Paper Since 1855.* San Francisco: Privately Printed, 1955.

_____. *400 California Street: A Century Plus Five.* San Francisco: Bank of California, 1969.

_____. *Silver Stampede.* New York: Macmillan, 1936.

_____. *Silver Stampede, the Career of Death Valley's Hell-Camp.* New York: Macmillan, 1937.

_____, and Taylor, Frank J. *Southern Pacific: The Roaring Story of a Fighting Railroad.* New York: McGraw-Hill Book, 1952.

_____. *Treasure Express: Epic Days of the Wells Fargo.* New York: Macmillan, 1936.

Wilson, R.L. *The Colt Heritage.* New York: Simon & Schuster, 1979.

Wilson, Rufus Rockwell, and Sears, Ethel M. *History of Grant County, Kansas.* Wichita, Kan.: Wichita Press, 1950.

_____. *Out of the West.* New York: Press of the Pioneers, 1933.

Wilstach, Frank J. *The Plainsman Wild Bill Hickok.* Garden City, N.Y.: Sun Dial Press, 1937.

_____. *Wild Bill Hickok, the Prince of Pistoleers.* New York: Doubleday, Page, 1926.

Winch, Frank. *Thrilling Lives of Buffalo Bill.* New York: S.L. Parsons, 1911.

Winchell, Lilbourne Alsip. *History of Fresno County, and the San Joaquin Valley.* Fresno, Calif.: A.H. Cawston, 1933.

Winget, Dan. *Anecdotes of Buffalo Bill.* Chicago: Historical, 1927.

Winn, Mary Day. *The Macadam Trail: Ten Thousand Miles by Motor Coach.* New York: Alfred A. Knopf, 1931.

Winsor, Justin. *The Westward Movement.* Boston: Houghton Mifflin, 1899.

Winther, Oscar Osburn. *The Great Northwest: A History.* New York: Alfred A. Knopf, 1947.

_____. *The Old Oregon Country: A History of Frontier Trade, Transportation, and Travel.* Palo Alto, Calif.: Stanford University Press, 1950.

_____. *The Transportation Frontier; Trans-Mississippi West, 1865-1890.* New York: Rinehart & Winston, 1964.

_____. *Via Western Express & Stagecoach.* Palo Alto, Calif.: Stanford University Press, 1945.

Wisehart, David. *The Fur Trade of the American West, 1807-1840.* Lincoln: University of Nebraska Press, 1979.

Wisehart, M.K. *Sam Houston: American Giant.* Washington D.C.: Robert B. Luce, 1962.

Wissler, Clark. *The American Indian.* New York: Oxford University Press, 1938.

Wister, Fanny Kemble (ed.). *Owen Wister Out West: His Journals and Letters.* Chicago: University of Chicago Press, 1958.

Witcher, W.C. *The Reign of Terror in Oklahoma.* Fort Worth, Texas: Published by Author, 1923.

With the Pinkertons. New York: McFadden, 1940.

Wolfe, W.C. (ed.). *Men of California.* San Francisco: Western Press Reporter, 1925.

Wolle, Muriel Sibell. *The Bonanza Trail, Ghost Towns and Mining Camps of the West.* Bloomington: Indiana University Press, 1953.

_____. *Montana Pay Dirt: A Guide to the Mining Camps of the Treasure State.* Denver: Sage Books, 1963.

_____. *Stampede to Timberline, the Ghost Towns and Mining Camps of Colorado.* Denver: Artcraft Press, 1949.

Wood, Raymund F. *California's Agua Fria: The Early History of Mariposa County.* Fresno, Calif.: Academy Library Guild, 1954.

Wood, Richard Coke. *Calaveras, the Land of Skulls.* Sonora, Calif.: Mother Lode Press, 1955.

———. *Murphys, Queen of the Sierra: A History of Murphys, Calaveras County, California.* Angel's Camp, Calif.: Calaveras Californian, n.d.

Woods, Betty. *Ghost Towns and How to Get to Them.* Santa Fe, N.M.: Press of the Territorian, 1964.

Woods, Henry F., and Morgan, Edward E.P. *God's Loaded Dice: Alaska, 1897-1930.* Caldwell, Idaho: Caxton Printers, 1948.

Woods, S.D. *Lights and Shadows of Life on the Pacific Coast.* New York: Funk & Wagnalls, 1910.

Woodson, William H. *History of Clay County, Missouri.* Topeka, Kan.: Historical, 1920.

Wooldridge, Maj. J.W. *History of Sacramento Valley, California.* Chicago: Pioneer Historical, 1931.

Wooten, Dudley G. (ed.). *A Comprehensive History of Texas.* Dallas: William G. Scarff, 1898.

Wooten, Mattie Lloyd (ed.). *Women Tell the Story of the Southwest.* San Antonio, Texas: Naylor, 1940.

Wormser, Richard. *The Yellowlegs, The Story of the United States Cavalry.* Garden City, N.Y.: Doubleday, 1966.

Wortham, Louis J. *A History of Texas: From Wilderness to Commonwealth.* 5 vols. Fort Worth, Texas: Wortham-Molyneaux, 1924.

Wright, George F. *History of Sacramento County.* Oakland, Calif.: Thompson & West, 1880.

Wright, Muriel H. *The Story of Oklahoma.* Oklahoma City: Webb, 1930.

Wright, Robert M. *Dodge City, The Cowboy Capital and the Great Southwest.* Wichita, Kan.: Wichita Eagle Press, 1913.

———. *Dodge City, the Cowboy Capital.* Wichita, Kan.: Wichita Eagle Press, 1917.

Wright, William. *History of the Big Bonanza.* San Francisco: A.L. Bancroft, 1876.

Wyllys, Rufus Kay. *Arizona, the History of a Frontier State.* Phoenix, Ariz.: Hobson & Herr, 1950.

Wyman, Walker D. *Nothing But Prairie and Sky: Life on the Dakota Range in the Early Days.* Norman: University of Oklahoma Press, 1954.

Wynn, Marcia Rittenhouse. *Desert Bonanza: Story of Early Randeburg, Mojave Desert Mining Camp.* Culver City, Calif.: M.W. Samelson, 1949.

Y

Yoakum, Henderson K. *History of Texas.* New York: Redfield, 1856.

Yost, Nellie Snyder. *The Call of the Range: The Story of the Nebraska Stock Growers' Association.* Denver: Sage Books, 1966.

———. *Medicine Lodge.* Chicago: Sage Books, 1970.

Young, Betty Lou. *Pacific Palisades, Where the Mountains Meet the Sea.* Los Angeles: Pacific Palisades Historical Society Press, 1983.

Young, Charles E. *Dangers on the Trail in 1865.* Geneva, N.Y.: W.Y. Humphrey, 1912.

Young, Frederick R. *Dodge City.* Dodge City, Kan.: Boot Hill Museum, 1972.

Young, Harry (Sam). *Hard Knocks, A Life Story of the Vanishing West.* Portland, Ore.: Wells & Company, 1915.

Young, John P. *San Francisco: A History of the Pacific Coast Metropolis.* San Francisco: S.J. Clarke, 1912.

Young, Otis E., Jr. (ed.). *The First Military Escort on the Santa Fe Trail.* Glendale, Calif.: Arthur H. Clarke, 1952.

Young, S. Glenn. *Life and Exploits of S. Glenn Young, World-Famous Law Enforcement Officer.* Herrin, Ill.: Mrs. S. Glenn Young, 1924.

Young, Dr. S.O. *True Stories of Old Houston and Houstonians.* Houston, Texas: Oscar Springer, 1913.

Younger, Coleman. *The Story of Cole Younger by Himself.* Chicago: Press of the Henneberry, 1903.

Younger, Scout. *True Facts of the Lives of America's Most Notorious Outlaws.* n.p., n.d.

Younghusband, Francis E. *The Heart of a Continent.* London: John Murray, 1896.

Z

Zink, Wilbur A. *The Roscoe Gun Battle: Younger Brothers vs. Pinkerton Detectives.* Appleton City, Mo.: Democrat, 1967.

Zornow, William Frank. *Kansas: A History of the Jayhawk State.* Norman: University of Oklahoma Press, 1957.

INDEX

Note: In this comprehensive index, the reader and researcher will find that, in addition to all proper names from text, place names include police organizations, detective agencies, railroads, banks, ranches, saloons, hotels, and other institutions which are shown with their locations, as well as events (Newton General Massacre, Gunfight at the O.K. Coral). Alternate names for the more celebrated entries are shown in cross-reference citations. Military persons of the Civil War are designated as representing the Confederacy (C.S.A.) or the Union (U.S.A.), and persons in the U.S. cavalry operating in the West following the war (U.S.A.).

Abernathy, Marshal, 340
Abeyta, Agaptio, 324
Ables, John, 386
Acme Saloon (El Paso, Texas), 149
Adams, Charles, 324
Adams, General, 251
Adams, Jake, 126
Adams, J.H., 324
Adams, Judge, 381
Adams, Spencer, 103
Adams Express Company, 69, 182, 267
Adamson, Carl, 136, 137, 233, 350
Adkins, Dave, 350
Adkins, George, 38
Aelee Gang, 382
Aguelari, Epeminto, 350
Aguilar, Ceberiano, 350
Aguilar, Donaciano, 350
Aguilar, Reymundo, 350
Aguillan, Felix, 350
Aguirre, Jermin, 350
Ake, Jeff, 350
Ake, William, 350
Alamosa Bill, 350
Alamo Saloon, 158
Alarid, Eugenio, 324, 350
Alarid, Nasario, 350
Alcatraz Federal Penitentiary, 66
Alexander, E.M., 324
Alexander, John, 350
Alexander, Robert, 222
Alexander, William, 1
Alexander Mitchell Bank (Lexington, Mo.), 174
Alfonso, King, 265
Alford, George, 351
Alhambra Saloon (Tombstone, Ariz.), 77, 116
Alhambra Club (Dodge City, Kan.), 198
Allee, Sheriff **Alfred Y.**, 5, 86, 324, 363
Allen, Abe, 324
Allen, Bill (Leadville, Colo.), 164, 165
Allen, Bill (Texas), 351
Allen, Billy, 351
Allen, Bladder, 351
Allen, Charles (Big Time Charlie), 1-2
Allen Chas, 351
Allen, Frank, 351
Allen, George, 308
Allen, J.A., 182, 232

Allen, Jack, 217
Allen, James, 351
Allen, John, 351
Allen, Joseph, 2, 233, 351, 356
Allen, Malachi, 2, 351
Allen, W.H., 353
Allison, Charlie, 324, 351, 389, 398
Allison, Clay, Jr., 4
Allison, Dave (prom. 1904), 275
Allison, Dave (prom. 1890s), 324, 329
Allison, John, 2, 3
Allison, Mary, 2
Allison, Monroe, 2
Allison, Patsy, 4
Allison, Robert A. (Clay), 2-5, 81, 83, 142, 258, 332, 334, 351, 371
Allred, Sheriff C.W., 310
Almer, Jack (Red Jack), 5, 351
Alston, Fielding, 325
Alsup, Wade, 351
Altman, Perry, 351
Alvarid, Juan, 351
Alverson, Leonard, 351
Alvord, Burton, 5-6, 11, 61, 107, 109, 221, 293, 325, 328, 331, 335, 347, 351, 358, 360, 378, 394
Alvord-Stiles Gang, 366, 388
Amador, Martin, 351
American Horse, 6
Ames, Rep. Oakes (Mass.), 89
Ames, W.A., 182
American Agriculturalist, 253
American Mining Co. (Lake Valley, N.M.), 87
American Valley Murders, 363
Amos, Fred, 351
Anamosa State Prison, 309
Anderson, Bernard, 325
Anderson, Charles, 11
Anderson, Charlie, 268
Anderson, David L. (Billy Wilson, Buffalo Billy), 6-7, 42, 134, 135, 255, 273, 274
Anderson, Ham, 148, 351
Anderson, Hugh, 7, 37, 145, 220, 242, 269
Anderson, James, 228
Anderson, J.E., 325
Anderson, Jim, 351
Anderson, John, 332
Anderson, Matilda, 260
Anderson, Reese, 8, 351
Anderson, Scott L., 8, 351
Anderson, Tom, 352
Anderson, William (Bloody Bill), 8-9, 173, 259, 260, 396, 351
Anderson, William (prom. 1870s), 9-10, 32, 217, 352
Anderson, U.S. Marshal William H., 10, 83, 325, 362
Anderson, Wilson, 216
Andrew, Robert, 10, 325
Andrews, Hank, 352
Andrews, Capt. M., 325
Angel Island State Prison (Calif.), 35
Angus, Sheriff Red, 193, 319
Annapolis Naval Academy, 141
Ansara, Pete, 142
Anthony, Ernest, 352
Anti-Chinese Labor Association, 335

Antrim, Catherine Bonney (McCarty), 38, **39**
Antrim, Henry, See: **Billy the Kid**
Antrim, Joseph, 38
Antrim, William Henry Harrison, 38, **39**
Apache Government Scouts, 10
Apache Kid (Zenogalache, The Crazy One), 10-11, 49, 336, 346, 352
Apodaca, Maximo, 352
Applegate, Bill, 352
Applewhite, D.C., 330
Aragon, Serefin, 352
Arajo, Justin, 352
Arango, Doroter, 352
Arbor Restaurant (Virginia City, Mont.), 132
Archer, John, 11, 352
Archer, Morton, 11, 352
Archer, Samuel, 11, 352
Archer, Thomas, 11, 352
Archer Brothers, 11, 352
Archibald, Albert W., 79, 325
Arcine, James, 11
Arguello, A., 352
Arizona Bandit, The, 153
Arizona Citizen, The, 51
Arizona *Daily Citizen*, 253
Arizona Jack, 352
Arizona Miner, 108, 302
Arizona Mirror, 104, 254, 306
Arizona Rangers, 6, 11, 71, 141, 221, 236, 286, 313, 328
Arizona State Prison (Yuma, Ariz.), 6, 11
Arkansas Bill, 352
Arkansas Tom Jones, See: **Daugherty, Roy**
Armijo, Gov. Manuel (N.M.), 36-37, 82
Armstrong, Charles, 325
Armstrong, Jack, 352
Armstrong, John Barclay (McNelly's Bulldog, Texas Rangers), 12-**13**, 148, 191, 325, 371
Arquello, David, 352
Arrington, George W. (Texas Rangers), 13-14, 325
Arrington, Willis, 352
Arthur, Pres. Chester A., 12, 93, 327
Ascarate, Guadalupe, 325
Ashby, George, 352
Askew, Daniel H., 232
Asque (or Askew), Joe, 352
Atchison, Topeka & Santa Fe Railroad, 220
Atchley Ranch (Table Mountain, N.M.), 10
Aten, E.D., 245
Aten, Edwin (Texas Rangers), 14, 15, 325
Aten, Franklin (Texas Rangers), 15
Aten, Ira (Texas Rangers), **14**-15, 168, 189, 248, 271, 272, 325
Atkins, Dave, 315, **316**
Atkins, David, 352
Atlanta Federal Penitentiary (Ga.), 201
Atlantic and Pacific Railroad, 219
Augustine, Robert, 352
Austin, Harris, 15
Austin, Gov. Steven, 300
Averill, James (Jim), 15-(**16, 17**)-18, 65, 71, 193, 352, 356
Averill, Thomas (Buffalo Vernon), 18
Avila, Genovevo, 352
Axtell, Gov. Samuel B. (N.M.), 41, 83, 315
Ayers, Thomas G., 98, 100, 353
Ayers, Will, 37, 355, 399

Babb, T.C., 98

Baca, Abran, 353
Baca, Antonio, 353
Baca, Celso, 353
Baca, Cruz, 353
Baca, Elfego, 19-20, 325
Baca, Jose, 353
Baca, Manuel, 353
Baca, Onofre, 353
Baca, Patricio, 353
Backus, Elijah, 226
Backus, Pete, 226
Backus Gang, 376
Bader, Charles, 353
Bader, Pete, 138, 226, 353
Bad Man's Territory, 170
Bad Nell, 353
Bailey, John (John Mason), 20, 353
Bailey, Marvin E., 325
Bailey, William, See: Wilson, Bill
Bain, A.C., 238
Baird, P.C. (Texas Rangers), 20, 325, 353
Baird, W.G., 257
Baker, A.R., 325
Baker, Chas, 353
Baker, Cullen Montgomery, 20-23, 353, 371
Baker, Mrs. Cullen (Martha Foster), 21
Baker, Mrs. Cullen (Jane Petty), 20, 21
Baker, Frank, 38, 40, 52, 123, 131, 161, 211, 223, 224, 231, 270, 278, 314, 325, 353
Baker, J.H., 325
Baker, Joc, 373
Baker, John, 140
Balazar, Dario, 363
Bald Knobbers Gang, 310, 397
Baldwin, Lucius M., 98, 100
Baldwin, Thurman (Skeeter), **23**, 84, 85, 353
Balfour, Sheriff Andrew, 320
Ball, Charles, 98
Ballard, Charles (lawman), 325
Ballard, Charles (gunman), 353
Ballew, Steve, 353
Bancroft, Hubert Howe, 79
Bangs, Cherokee, 353
Bank Exchange Saloon (Raton, N.M.), 231
Banks, Sheriff William, 45, 48
Bank Saloon (Cuero, Texas), 101
Barbee, Claude, 353
Barber, Acting Gov. Amos (Wyo.), 193
Barber, George, 318
Barber, John, 210
Barbour, John, 353
Barcenas, Francisco, 308
Bardsley, Sheriff, 27
Barela, Manuel, 353
Barela, Mariano, 326, 397
Barela, Santos, 353
Barela, Ysabel, 353
Barker, Dudley S., 326
Barkley, Clinton, 23-24, 167, 305, 354
Barler, Dudley S., 326
Barler, W.L., 326
Barnell, John, 25
Barnes, Johnny, 354
Barnes, Seaborn (Nubbins Colt, Sebe), 24-25, 27, 28, 29, 172, 354, 376
Barnes, William E., 231
Barnett, Wesley, 25, 354
Barnum, P.T., 130

Barrera, Calisto, 354
Barrickman, Alex, 148
Barringer, J.C., 326
Barron, Dan, 266
Barrow, Clyde, 300, 335
Barstow, S.T., 35
Barter, Richard (Rattlesnake Dick), 25, 354
Bartley, C.C., 326, 344, 348, 349
Barton, Charles, 326
Barton, Dep. Sheriff Henry, 396
Barton, Sheriff James R., 126
Barton, Jerry, 354
Barton, Kid, 354
Bascom, Lt. George N. (U.S.A.), 25
Bascom Affair, 25-26
Basham, Tucker, 184, 354
Bass, Harry, 296
Bass, Samuel (Sam), 14, 24-25, **26-(27, 28)**-29, 107,
    143, 172, 209, 217, 222, 238, 239, 241, 242, 292,
    300, 319, 344, 348, 349, 354, 362, 365, 373, 376,
    381, 383
Bassett, Charles E. (Charlie), 29-30, 113, 198, 228,
    283, 303, 326
Bassett, Harry, 354
Bass Gang, 342, 354, 355, 364, 373, 376
Baugh, Andrew T., 30, 354
Bauman, Wes, 326
Baxter, Dan, 354, 396
Baylock, Celia (Mattie), 120
Baylor, Col., 348
Baylor, George Wythe, 326
Beach, Charles, 354
Beach, Rex, 65
Bean, Anna, 30
Bean, Francis, 30
Bean, Jim, 327
Bean, Maj.-Gen. Joshua H., 30, 238
Bean, Judge **Roy**, 30-(31)-32, 326
Bean, Mrs. Roy (Virginia Chavez), 31
Bean, Samuel G., 326
Bean, Sam (brother of Roy Bean), 30
Beard, Edward T. (E.T., Red), 10, 32, 217, 354
Beard, Mose, 354
Beard Brothers, 138
Beard's Dance Hall (Wichita, Kan.), 32
Bear River Smith: Two-Fisted Marshal of Abilene,
    287
Bear River Tom, See: **Smith, Thomas J.**
Beaubien, Carlos, 32-33, 82
Beaubien, Narcisco, 32
Beck, Frank, 354
Beck, H.O. (Ole), 33, **201**, 202, 354
Beck, William Ellison, 354
Beckner, Frederick, 326
Beckwith, Henry, 33, 192, 246, 354
Beckwith, Jennings, 33
Beckwith, John H., 33, 326, 354
Beckwith, Robert W., 33, 41, 326, 354
Beckwourth (or Beckwith) **James**, 33-34
Beebe's Hardware Store (Ellsworth, Kan.), 112
Beehive Saloon and Dance Hall, 266
Beers, George, 308
Beeson, Ben, 68
Beeson, Sheriff Chalk, 323
Behan, Sheriff **John** (Cochise County), 34, 51, 76,
    88, 114, **115**, 116, 118, 119, 164, 245, 254, 269,
    284, 326, 327, 346, 347
Beidler, John X., 34-35
Bell, Bob, 326

Bell, Choctaw, 354
Bell, C.S., 155, 355
Bell, Hamilton B., 35, 325
Bell, James W. (Texas Rangers), 35, 44, 246, 281,
    326
Bell, Tom (Dr. Thomas J. Hodges), 35-36, 142, 355
Bella Union Saloon (San Francisco, Calif.), 108
Bell Gang, 36
Belmont, Courtney, 355
Belmont, Dick, 355
Belt, Judge, 36
Benavides, Santos, 355
Bene, Jules, 285
Benjamin, Bert, 47, 48
Bennett, George, 355
Bennett, Jack, 315
Bennett, John, 304
Bent, Gov. Charles (N.M.), 32, 36-37, 93
Bent, St. Vrain and Company, 36
Bentley, Charley, 355
Bernstein, Morris, 326
Bernstein, Morris J., 384
Berry, James, 26, 355
Berry, John M., 373
Best, Phil, 326
Bewley, Jim, 355
Bickerstaff, Benjamin F., 37, 355
Bickford, George, 162
Bideno, Juan, 7, 37, 145, 355
Big Bowl, Chief, 33
Bigler, Gov. John (Calif.), 238
Big Sandy, 355
Bigtree, Bob, 280
Bill, Charles, 355
Billee, John, 37-38, 355, 399
Billy the Kid (William H. Bonney, Henry Antrim,
    Kid Antrim, William Antrim, Henry Mc-
    Carty, Patrick Henry McCarty), 6, 7, 33, 38-
    (39)-45, 52, 54, 71, 81, 105, 123, 131, **134**,
    135, 136, 161, 210, 211, 212, 215, 222, 223,
    231, 233, 244, 245, 246, 255, 270, 273, 274,
    276, 279, 281, 284, 309, 315, 326, 327, 328,
    333, 334, 336, 339, 341, 342, 343, 345, 348,
    349, 350, 353, 355, 356, 357, 362, 363, 365,
    367, 368, 371, 374, 375, 383, 384, 385, 387,
    388, 389, 392, 393, 397, 399
Bingham, George, 326
Bingham, John (Texas Ranger), 89, 123
Birchfield, Steve, 326
Birchfield, Walter, 278
Bisbee, Ariz. (Massacre), 45, 101, 102, 154
Bisbee (Ariz.) Deportation, 314
Bishop, Miles, 355
Bishop, Pete, 355
Bishop, Thomas, 366
Bitter Creek, See: **Newcomb, George**
Bivins, Bill, 222, 355
Bivins, Lige, 355
Bixler, Ease, 168
Blachey, A.T., 220
Black, Blackie, 355
Black, Isaac (Ike), 45, 355
Black, Sheriff J.H., 385
Black, Jim, 355
Black, John, 355
Black, Pope, 355
Black, Robert, 355
Black Bart (Charles E. Boles, Charles E. Bolton),
    45-(46)-47, 236, 356

Blackburn, Duncan, 47, 222, 356
Blackburn, Leslie, 327
Blackburn, Judge W.A., 202
Black Face Charlie, See: Bryant, Charles
Black Jack Christian, See: Christian, Will
Black Jack Christian's Gang, 366, 373, 387, 399
Black Jack Ketchum's Gang, 335, 337, 338, 350, 352, 359, 364, 373, 375, 378, 379, 381, 383, 387, 398, 400
Black Jacks, See: Black Jack Ketchum's Gang
Black Jim, 66
Blackwell, C.J., 327
Blackwell, James, 356
Blackwell, Okla., 47-48
Blain, Dick, 389
Blain, Joe, 356
Blaine, Father Dominic, 238
Blake, John (Tulsa Jack), 48, 106, 107, 263, 280, 309, 356
Bland, Billy, 266
Blaylock Celia, 111
Blazer, Dr. Emil, 52, 271
Blevins, Andy (Andy Cooper), 48-49, 141, 249
Blevins, Charles, 49
Blevins, Hampton, 49, 299, 305
Blevins, John, 49, 249, 356
Blevins, M., 356
Blevins, Sam Houston, 49, 249
Blevins Family, 48-49
Blind Joe, 356
Bloody Espinosas, 367
Blue Duck, 49, 291, 356
Blumner, Charles, 49, 78, 79, 274, 327
Blun, Kenry, 356
Bly, Elias, 279
Bobbitt, Angus A., 2, 233, 327, 340, 356, 386
Bogan, Dan, 356
Boggs, Sheriff J., 25
Boggs, Thomas O., 356
Bogles, Gus, 49-50
Bogus Charley, 66
Bojorques, Narcisco, 50
Bolding, William, 257
Boles, Charles E., See: Black Bart
Boles, Thomas, 327
Bolt, William James, 356
Bolton, Charles E., See: Black Bart
Bolton, Martha, 128, 161
Bonner, Thomas D., 34
Bonney, Kathleen (or Catherine), 38
Bonney, William H., See: Billy the Kid
Bonney, William, 38
Boot, Joseph (Joe), 152, 356, 372
Booth, Gov. Newton, 124
Boot Hill (Tombstone, Ariz.), 373
Border Boss, See: Hughes, John Reynolds
Border, Peter, 85
Borne, Henry, See: Dutch Henry
Boston Joe, 8, 222, 352
Boston, Riley, 327
Boswell, N.K., 69, 216
Bothwell, Albert J., 16, 17 , 356
Boucher, Billy, See: Grounds, Billy
Bowdre, Charles (Charlie), 7, 40, 41, 42, 45, 52, 134, 135, 136, 244, 255, 270, 274, 279, 333, 334, 356
Bowen, John (Chick), 231
Bowers, Edward G., 327
Bowers, George, 356
Bowles, Tom, 81

Bowman, Mason T., 3
Bowman, Dep. Wess, 75
Boyce, Mart, 356
Boyce, Newt, 55
Boyce, Reuben H., 50, 356
Boyd, Thomas M., Jr., 356
Boyet, Johnny, 121
Boyle, Andrew (Andy), 212, 276, 357
Boyle, John, 321
Boyle, Robert H., 357
Boyle, Sport, 357
Brack Cornett Gang, 353, 399
Bracken, J.W., 327
Bradley, Jim, 144
Brady, Jack, 357
Brady, Sheriff William, 38, 41, 44, 54, 81, 123, 131, 161, 193, 211, 212, 215, 231, 270, 281, 309, 314, 315, 326, 327, 336, 337, 340, 355, 357, 369, 385
Brann, William Cowper, 50, 357
Brannan, Sam, 82
Brassfield, George, 204
Bravin, George, 293
Bray, Neil, 60
Braya, John, 303
Brazil (or Brazel), Wayne, 136, 137
Brazzleton, William, 50-51, 357
Breakenridge, William Milton, 51-52, 53, 116, 254, 313, 315, 327, 356, 375, 399
Brennan, Molly, 227
Brent, Henry, 357
Brent, James R., 327
Brewer, Richard M. (Dick), 39, 40-41, 52, 54, 80, 161, 211, 212, 224, 270, 271, 278, 309, 327, 344, 357, 391
Brewster, C.L., 98
Briant, Elijah S. (Lige), 52, 66, 327, 359
Bridges, Dep. U.S. Marshal Jack L., 52-53, 327
Brighton, J.V., 76
Brink, Doc, 155, 156
Brinster, Joseph, 357
Briscoe, Joseph, 133, 134
Bristol, Judge Warren, 44
Bristow, Benjamin H., 104
Britton, Ed, 327
Broadwell, Richard (Dick), 96, 98, 99, 100, 357, 378, 392, 393
Brocius, William (Curly Bill, William B. Graham), 51, 53, 76, 93, 114, 120, 203, 349, 357, 374, 378
Brock, Leonard Calvert, 53, 59, 60, 357
Brock, W.L., 59
Broderick, Sen. David C., 241, 357
Brodie, Gov. A.W. (Ariz.), 153
Bronco Charlie, 357
Brooks, Billy, 332
Brooks, Rep. James (New York), 89
Brooks, James Abijah (Texas Rangers), 53-54, 327
Brooks, William L. (Buffalo Billy), 54, 327, 357
Brophy, Hank, 357
Brown, Angus (Arapaho Red), 54, 327
Brown, Billy, 357, See also: Brown, William, 56
Brown, Bob, 109, 293, 357
Brown, Charlie, 225
Brown, Charles, 100
Brown, Dep. Charlie, 112
Brown, David J. (Cooke), 121
Brown, Fred, 398
Brown, George, 139

Brown, Marshal George S., 265, 327
Brown, Marshal Henry, 272
Brown, Henry Newton (Hendry), 40, 52, 54-55, 161, 270, 279, 309, 328, 349, 357, 394, 398, 399
Brown, Hoodoo, See: Neill, Hyman
Brown, H.S., 149
Brown, Jim, 223
Brown, Joe, 78
Brown, Maud, 139
Brown, Neal, 198, 283, 328
Brown, Robert C., 357
Brown, Rube, 298
Brown, Sam (Long-Haired Sam), 55, 358
Brown, W.A., 257
Brown, W.E., 358
Brown, William, 56, See also: Brown, Billy, 357
Browning, William, 358
Brown's Hole, 270
Bruner, Dep. Marshal Heck, 272, 273, 328
Brunner, Neal, 328
Bruton, Tex, 358
Bryant, Charles (Black Face Charlie), 56, 96, 358
Bryant, Ed, 328
Bryant, Dep. Sheriff R.E., 245
Buchanan, Frank, 16, 17, 18
Buchanan, Pres. James, 79
Buck, Norman, 376
Buck, Rufus, 56-58, 358
Bucket of Blood Saloon, The (Laramie, Wyo.) 216, 338, 381
Buck Gang, 56-58, 170, 358, 377, 392
Buckley, James, 358
Buckley, Jim, 221
Buckskin Frank, See: Leslie, Nashville Franklin
Buffalo Bill, See: Cody, William Frederick
Buffalo Bill's Wild West Show, 80, 81, 275
Buffalo Billy, See: Anderson, David L.; Brooks, William L.
Buffalo Hump, Chief, 333
Buffington, David, 292
Bull, John C., 358
Bull Hill War, 286
Bullion, Laura (Della Rose), 58, 69, 70, 201, 358
Bull's Head Saloon and Gambling House (Abilene, Kan.), 81, 146, 301
Bunch, Eugene, 58-59, 60, 358
Bunker, A.E., 183, 321
Buntline, Ned (Edward Zane Carroll Judson), 59, 80
Burbridge, Bill, 231, 358
Burke, A.F., 328
Burke, Frank, 122
Burke, J.S. (Steve), 280, 328
Burke, U.S. Marshal Steve, 57
Burke, Steve, 360
Burleson, Pete, 358, 374
Burnett, Joseph, 197
Burnett, William, 225
Burns, Richard, 176
Burns, William, 343
Burrell, Berry B., 233
Burroughs, W.H., 328
Burrow, James Buchanan (Jim), 59-60, 358
Burrow (or Burrows), Reuben Houston (Rube), 59-61, 357, 358
Burrow Brothers Gang, 53, 58
Bursum, Holm O., 328

Burt, Sam, 358
Burton, Isaac, 61
Burts, Matthew, 61-62, 328, 358
Burwell, W.M., 328
Bushnell, John, 182
Bussey, W.H., 79
Buster, John, 358
Butler, Ben, 182
Butler, Dick, 236
Buttner, A.F., 328
Byers, John, 366, 374
Byers, Walter, 388

Caballero, Guadalupe (The Owl), 63, 358
Cabinet Saloon (Woodward, Okla.), 190
Cadete, Chief, 63
Cahill, Bob, 263
Cahill, Frank P., 38
Cain, Neil, 88
Calabaza, Ariz., 63
Calamity Jane (Martha Jane Canary or Cannary), 47, 63, 158
Caldwell Standard, 265
Cale, Jim, 131
Calhoun, R.N., 369
California House (Marysville, Calif.), 35, 36
California Rangers, 30, 133, 238
Callicott, Bill (Texas Ranger), 206
Calverly, Bob, 67
Calvert, Mary, See: Lay, Mary Calvert
Cameron, Andrew, 358
Cameron, John, 328
Campbell, Billy, 217
Campbell, J.E., 328
Campbell, George, 196
Campbell, W.E., 280
Campbell, William (Lincoln County War), 42
Campbell, William (outlaw), 358
Campbell, William (Ashley gang), 359
Campbell, William (Texas gunman), 359
Campbell and Hatch's Billiard Parlor (Tombstone, Ariz.), 90, 120
Camp Grant Massacre, 63-64, 104
Canada Bill, 126
Canadian Pacific Railroad, 235
Canary (or Cannary), Martha Jane, See: Calamity Jane
Canby, Gen. Edward R.S., 65
Candelaria, Jose, 363
Canton, Frank M. (Joe Horner), 16, 17, 18, 64-65, 71, 72, 109, 193, 242, 266, 287, 328, 359
Capehart, Tom, 359
Captain Jack (Keintpos), 65
Carbajal, Antonio, 359
Cardenas, Manuel, 3, 83, 359
Cardis, Louis, 359
Carey, Sen. Joseph M. (Wyo.), 193
Carey, Sam (Laughing Sam), 317
Carillo, Gov. Jose Antonio (Calif.), 33-34
Carl, Peter, 359
Carland, Judge John E., 253
Carlisle, John, 359
Carlyle, Dep. Sheriff James (Jim), 6, 7, 42, 328
Carlyle, Thomas S., 277
Carmondy, Patric, 359

Carnes, H.A., 328
Carney, John, 370
Carney, Thomas, 66
Carpenter, Judge A., 260
Carpenter, Charles T., 98
Carr, Bat, 328
Carr, Bob (English Bob), 35, 36
Carr, Dep. Marshal, 15
Carr, T. Jeff, 328
Carrasco, Florencio, 168, 244
Carrhert, George, 359
Carrington, Bob, 299, 305
Carroll, Billy, 103
Carroll, Marshal John, 94
Carrolla, Jose M., 359
Carson, Joe, 105, 328, 359, 365, 374, 390
Carson, Kit (Christopher), 66, 329, 356, 359
Carson, Kit, III, 122, 396
Carson, Thomas (prom. 1871), **66**
Carson, Thomas (prom. 1880), 123, 328
Carter, C., 61
Carter, Tex, 359
Carter, William, 36
Caruthers, L.B., 329
Carver, William (News), 52, 58, **66**, 67, 162, 199,
     200, 208, 315, 327, 332, 345, 358, 359
Casey, James, 278
Casey, Joe, 359
Casey, John, 359, 386
Casey, Robert (prom. 1875), 161
Casey, Robert (d.1875), 319, 399
Casey Gang, 347
Casharago, James, 359
Casper (Wyo.) *Mail*, 18
Cassidy, Butch (Robert LeRoy Parker), 52, 66, **67-
     (68)**-70, 74, 143, 162, 198, 200, 201, 206, 207,
     208, 209, 213, 214, 215, 219, 270, 278, 284, 296,
     305, 310, 315, **316**, 317, 329, 359, 361, 371, 377,
     381, 382, 389, 397, 398
Cassidy, Mike, 67
Castillo, Candido, 359
Castillo, Manuel, 359
Castillo Gang, 350, 388
Castle, Kit, 329
Castleton, Kate, 121
Caswell, Alex, 223
Catfish Kid, 360
Catron, Jim, 360
Catron, Thomas Benton, 70, 82, 83, 257, 258, 315
Cattle Annie, See: McDougal, Annie
Cattle Kate, See: Ella Watson
Cattleman's War (Wyo.), 377
Cattle Raiser's Association, 274
Cave-In-the-Rock (Ohio), 150
Central Overland California and Pike's Peak Ex-
     press Company, 285
Chaco, Icnacio, 360
Chacon, Augustin (The Hairy One), 11, 70-71, 236,
     360
Chadwell, Bill (Bill Stiles), 178, 182, 183, 321, 323,
     360, 384
Chaffee, Jerome B., 82
Chalmers, Lee, 93
Chamberlain, Samuel E., 360
Chambers, Gus, 57
Chambers, Lon, 7, 71, 134, 244
Champion, Dudley, 71, 72, 282
Champion, Nathan D., 64, 65, 71, 193, 213, 215, 265,
     282, 287, 360

Chancellor, Joseph, 317
Chandler, Sen. William E. (N.H.), 302
Chandler, Sen. Zachariah (Mich.), 92, 93
Chapman, Houston (H.J.), 42, 365
Chapman, John, 67
Charles, Mrs. Tom, 11
Charles Hill's Drugstore (Wichita, Kan.), 257
Charter, Bert, 296
Charlton, John B. (Jack), 329
Chaves, Juan, 360
Chaves, Paz, 360
Chavez, Antonio, 360
Chavez, Bernardino, 359
Chavez, Carlos, 360
Chavez, Fernando, 360
Chavez, Jose, 308
Chavez, Josefito, 360
Chavez, Pas, 246
Chavez, Pedro, 348, 360
Chavez, Virginia, See: Bean, Mrs. Roy
Chavez y Baca, Jose, 360
Chavez y Chavez, Jose, 360
Chavez y Pino, Juan, 381
Chenowith, Otto, 360
Cherokee Bill, See: **Goldsby, Crawford**
Cherokee Bill Gang, 341
Cherokee Bob, 360
Cherokee Strip, The, See: Indian Territory
Cherry (The Kid), 360
Chew, Bob, 329
Cheyenne (Wyo.) *Weekly Mail*, 17
Cheyenne (Wyo.) *Mail Leader*, 16
Chicago *Herald*, 72
Chicago, Rock Island, and Pacific Express Railroad,
     180, 184
Chihuahua, 375
Childers, John, Jr., 72-73
Childers, John, Sr., 72
Childers, Mrs. John, Sr. (Katy Vann), 72
Chilton, Fred, 319, 360
Chinese Riots, 73
Chisholm Trail, 282
Chisum, John, 38, 40, 41, 70, 80, 81, 123, 192, 210,
     211, 212, 223, 246, 278, 279, 281, 314, 375,
     392
Chivington, Col. John M. (U.S.A.), 34, 51, 268, 277
Choalt, Frank, 360
Choate, Boone, 86
Choate, Crockett, 155
Choate, John, 155
Chouteau, Auguste, 32
Christian, Bob, 73
Christian, William (Black Jack), 73, 107, 109, 127,
     153, 160, 202, 329, 335, 352, 360
Christianson, Teenie, 219
Christianson (or Christiansen) **Willard Erastus**,
     (Matt Warner, Mormon Kid), 67, 68, 74,
     219, 317, 329, 353, 360, 382, 398
Christianson, Mrs. Willard Erastus (Rose Morgan),
     74
Christie, Ned, 74-75, 170, 329
Cimarron, 189
Cimarron *News and Press*, 3, 83, 315
Cimarron War, 362
Cincinnati *Enquirer*, 104
City Hotel (Ingalls, Okla.), 106
City National Bank (Wichita Falls, Texas), 89, 210
Claiborne, William (Billy the Kid), 75, 76, 114, 116,

118, 119, 209, 245, 361, 380
Clancy, John, 361
Clanton, Finneas (Finn), 75, 77, 114, 120
Clanton, Joseph Isaac (Ike), 75, 88, 114, **115**, 116, 118, 119, 120, 153, 164, 244, 245, 293, 361
Clanton, Newman H. (Old Man Clanton), 75, 76, 77, 92, 114, **115**, 120, 209, 293, 361
Clanton, Peter, 114
Clanton, Robert, 361
Clanton, William (Billy), 75, 76, 114, **115**, 118, 119, 245, 361
Clanton Brothers, 116, 118, 154, 245, 270, 326
Clanton Family, 361
Clanton House Hotel (Fort Thomas, Ariz.), 75
Clanton-McLowery Gang, 5, 34, 53, 75, 76, 88, 113, 114, 120, 121, 138, 148, 164, 244
Clark, Ben, 290
Clark, Ben (lawman), 329
Clark, Benjamin, 361
Clark, Edmond, 226
Clark, Edward A., 11
Clark, Atty. Gen. George, 205
Clark, G.H., 329
Clark, Jap, 361
Clark, Jim Cummings, 77, 282
Clark, John, 307
Clark, Richard Brinsley Sheridan, 77
Clar, Thomas, 361
Clarke, Judge Gaylord Judd, 130
Clay County Savings Bank (Liberty Mo.), 174
Clayton, William H.H., 78
Clements, Arch, 259, 260, **261**
Clements, Joe, 233, 296
Clements, Emmanuel, Jr., (Mannie), **78**, 329, 361
Clements, Emmanuel, Sr., (Mannen), **78**, 145, 147, 148, 233, 270, 296, 361
Clements, James, 361
Clements, John Gibson, 361
Clements, Joseph, 361
Clements, Manning, 138
Clements, W.T., 329
Clements Brothers, 361
Clements Family, 147
Cleveland, George, 361
Cleveland, Pres. Grover, 10, 78, 219, 254
Cleveland, Jack, 256
Clever, Charles P., 78-79, 329
Clifton, Daniel (Dynamite Dick), 48, **79**, 106, 280, 362
Clifton House (Colfax County, N.M.), 3, 81
Clover, Sam, 72
Clum, Mayor John, **115**, 116
Clum, John P., 362
Clyde, Charles, 362
C.M. Condon Bank (Coffeyville, Kan.), **95**, 98
Coal Oil Jimmie, 362
Coalson, Doug, 329
Coates, Fred, 64, 71, 287
Coates, Lew, 361
Coble, John, 166, 167
Cochise, Chief, 25, 26, 79
Cochran, Dr., 29
Cochran, Emanuel, 305
Cockerill, Tilton, 362
Cock-Eyed Frank, See: Loving, Frank
Cockrane, Thomas, 362
Coddington, John, 385
Cody, William Frederick (Buffalo Bill), 59, 80, 155, 158, **159**, 192, 212, 224, 337

Coe, Chas, 329, 362
Coe, Frank, 33, 80-81, 192, 215, 224, 232, 246, 270, 294, 318, 362
Coe, George Washington, 52, 80, 81, 270, 279, 350, 362
Coe, James, 303
Coe, Philip Haddox, 81, 158, 301, 362
Coffelt, Matt, 208
Cohron, John, 145
Cohron, William C. (Billy), 37, 145
Coke, Richard, 319
Colbert, Chunk, 3, 81-82
Colbert, Paden, 329, 340
Colbert, Zachary, 2
Colcord, Charles F., 329
Cold Branch Ranch (Cooke County, Texas), 207
Coldwell, Capt. Neal (Texas Rangers), 319, 329, 349
Cole, James, 82
Cole Estes Gang, 386
Coleman, Dan, 329
Coleman, E.E., 329
Coleman, Jim, 165
Coleman, Lewis, 2, 3
Coleman, William Tell, 82, 277
Colfax County War (N.M.), 82-83, 258, 281
Colfax, Schuyler, 89
Coliseum Saloon (El Paso, Texas), 295
Coliseum Variety Theater, 225
College, William Jewell, 174
Collier, W.W., 329
Colligan, Thomas, 398
Collins, Ben, 83
Collins, Bill, 10,
Collins, George, 362, 392
Collins, Henry, 362
Collins, Joel (Joe), 10, 26, **27**, 83, 217, 362, 365, 381
Collins, John, 329
Collins, Sam, 139
Collins, William, 83, 325, 362
Colombo Saloon (Telluride, Colo.), 77
Colorado & Southern Railroad, 199
Colquitt, Gov. Oscar Branch (Texas), 87
Columbian Exposition (World's Fair, Chicago, 1893-94)
Columbus Federal Prison (Ohio), 191
Colville, James, 362
Comanche, 61
Comins, H.A., 270
Comique Theater, 113
Commanche Tony, 180
Committee of 601, 369
Compton, W.W., 112
Concordia Tin Min (Boliv.), 70
Coney Island Saloon (El Paso, Texas), 78
Congressional Committee on Expenditures, 303
Conklin, A.M., 353
Conklin, Charles, 329
Conley, Ed, 329
Connell, Ed, 330
Connelly, Charles T., 83-84, 100, 330
Connor, Al, 362
Connor, Bill, 362
Connor, Fred, 362
Connor, John, 362
Connor, Ned, 35, 36
Connor, William, 298
Connor, Willis, 362
Cook, C.G., 330
Cook, David J., 84, 240

Cook, J.H., 19, 20
Cook, James, 138, 139, 362
Cook, Thalis T. (Texas Ranger), **84**, 138, 330, 369
Cook, William Tuttle (Bill), 23, **84-85**, 138, 139, 362, 370
Cook Brothers, 139
Cook Gang, 23, 140, 170, 341, 353, 365, 367, 369, 370, 381, 383, 387, 392, 394
Cooley, Corydon E., 330
Cooley, Scott (Texas Ranger), **85**, 138, 194, **226**, 300, 330, 349, 362, 399
Coop, John, 232, 233
Cooper, Charles, 3
Cooper, Clay, 110
Cooper, Harry, 330
Cooper, Ira, 363
Cooper, Jim, 110, 363
Cooper, Tom, 363
Copeland, Charles (Charley), 75, 330
Copeland, James, **85**, 363
Cora, Charles, 278
Corman, Burt, 363
Corna, Silveria, 363
Cornett, Brack, 1, 85-86, 314, 324, 363, 399
Cortez, Gregorio, 86-87, 363
Cortina, Juan (Juan Nepomuceno Cortinas), **87**, 127, 128, 224, 333, 363
Cosmopolitan Hotel (Tombstone, Ariz.), 209
Costillo, Can, 363
Costillo, Joe, 340
Costley, Solon, 330
Cottle, A.R., 330
Cotton, Mitchell, 330
Cougar, Charles, 145
Coughlin, Pat, 363
Coulter, Ed, 363
Courtright, Jim, 222, 283
Courtright, Timothy Isaiah (Long-Haired Jim), 87-88, 330, 363
Cowan, Datus, 318
Cowboy Saloon (Douglas, Ariz.), 275
Cox, George, 280
Cox, Jim, 298
Cox, Capt. S.P., 9, 177
Coy, Jacob, 125, 126
Craft, James. H.
Craig, Matt, 363
Craighead, Charlie, 330
Crane, Jim, 88, 92, 116, 153, 154, 209, 363
Crane-Knight Gang, 338
Cravens, Ben, 48, **88**, 363
Crawford, Charlie, 244
Crawford, Ed, 88-89, 112, 140, 330
Crawford, Foster, **89**, 210, 224, 363, 380
Crawford, Hank, 256
Crawford, Capt. Jack, 390
Crawford, Salecooler, 363
Credit Mobiler, 89
Cree, Capt., 268
Creek Light Horse Police Force (Okla.), 140
Crittenden, Gov. Thomas T. (Mo.), 129, 184, 186, 368, 376
Crockett, David, 363, 373
Crockett, Davy, 363
Crompton, Zacariah, 363
Cross, Bob, 165
Crosthwaite, Charles H., 364
Crow, Jack, 204
Crow Killer, See: **Johnson, John**

Crowe, Patrick, 364
Croy, Homer, 94
Crozier and Nutter Store (Cushing, Okla.), 190
Cruger, Sheriff William R., 205, 266
Crumpton, Bood, 89-90
Cruz, Florentino (Indian Charley), 76, 90, 119, 120, 164, 191, 223, 364
Cruzan, William, 317
Crystal Palace (Dennison, Texas), 217, 270
Cubine, George, 83, 100
Cullin, Ed, 364
Culver, Martin S., 330
Cummings, Samuel M. (Doc), 90, 330
Cummins, James Robert (Jim), 8, 178, 180, 184, **187**, 364
Cummings, Doc, 225, 226, 294
Cunningham, Mark E., 254
Cunningham, William P., 330
Curly Bill, See: **Brocius, William**
Curry, George (Big Nose, Flat Nose), 68, 69, **90**, 162, 200, 213, 296, 315, 364
Curry, John, 364
Curry, Kid, See: **Logan, Harvey**
Curry, W.S., 330
Curtin, Gen. Samuel R., 156
Cush, Old John, 364
Cutler, Abraham, 90-91, 107, 257, 330
Cutler, Carrie F., 90
Custer, Gen. George Armstrong, 80, 156

Dake, Albert, 330
Dake, Crawley P., **92**-93, 253, 291, 302, 330
Dallam, Richard, 93, 330
Dalton, Adeleine, 94, 96, 98
Dalton, Charles, 96
Dalton, Christopher, 364
Dalton, Emmett, 94, **95**, 96, 97, 98, 100-01, 364, 378, 393
Dalton, Mrs. Emmett (Julia Johnson), 97, 100
Dalton, Dep. Marshal Frank, 82, 94, **95**, 331
Dalton, Gratton (Grat), 84, 94, **95**, 97, 98, **99**, 100, 122, 331, 364, 378
Dalton, Henry, 96
Dalton, J. Frank, 93-**94**, 188, 191, 303, 364
Dalton, Kit, 380
Dalton, Lewis, 94, 96
Dalton, Littleton, 96
Dalton, Robert (Bob), 94, **95**, 96, 97, 98, **99**, 100, 106, 331, 364, 378
Dalton, William Marion (Bill), 48, 79, 94, **95**, 96, 106, 309, 364
Dalton, M.L., 2
Dalton Brothers, 56, 83, 94-(**95**, **99**)-101, 150, 170, 188, 242
Dalton Gang, 224, 241, 256, 272, 300, 330, 331, 342, 347, 353, 355, 357, 364, 366, 387, 388, 390, 392, 393
Daly, James, 101, 221, 364
Damewood, Boston, 364
Daniels, Benjamin F., **101**, 102, 221, 331, 365
Daniels, Bill, 364
Daniels, E.B., 181
Daniels, Ed, 321
Daniels, Henry, 272
D'Argentcourt, Louisa, 77
Dart, Isom, 166

Daugherty, Roy (Arkansas Tom Jones), 48, **101**, 106, 168, 280, 340, 364
Davenport, Jim, 365
Davidson, Adolph, 399
Davidson, Adjutant Gen. James, 137, 331
Davies County Savings Bank (Gallatin, Mo.), 177, 267
Davis, Lt. Britton, 303
Davis, Gov. E.J. (Texas), 155
Davis, E.K., 331
Davis, George, 365
Davis, Henry, See: **Brock, Leonard Calvert**
Davis, Hog, 365
Davis, Jack, 26, 27, 28, 365
Davis, Jefferson, 259, 268
Davis, Jonathan, 273
Davis, Levi, 331
Davis, Lewis, 56-**58**, 358
Davis, Lucky, 56-**58**, 358, 365
Davis, Martha, 57
Davis, T.E., 50, 357
Dawson, Charles, 140, 370
Day, Alfred, 101, 365
Day, Dep. P., 214
Dayson, Curtis, 84, 85, 365
Deady, Matthew Paul, 102
Deal, Pony, 114, 248, 270, 342, 365
Dean, Henry Clay, 178
Dean, John, 126
Dedrick, Sam, 365
Deer Lodge Penitentiary, 143
Deger, Larry, 102
Deggs, Leroy, 12
de Graffenreid, Edna, 279
de la Cruz Sandoval, Jose, 353
Delaney, William E., 365, 366
Delaney, William E. (Mormon Bill), 101, 102, 154
Delano, Columbus, 82
de la Torre, Miguel, 168
Delling, M.G., 331
Deloach, Tom, 365
Delony, Lewis S., 103, 331
DeMerritt, Josephine (Jo), 32, 217
Demmons, Dan, 365
Dempsey, Jack, 89
Dempster, Boyd, 334, 365
Dennison, E.R., 257
Denslow, Bud, 317
Denson, John, 269
Denver and Rio Grande Railroad, 67, 311
Denver (Col.) Mint, 27
Department of Public Safety, 300
de Rana, Patas (El Coyote), 103, 365
Destroying Angels Gang, 373
Devere, Leona, 204
Devine, James, 365
Devol, George, 103-04
Dial, J.I., 365
Diamond A Cattle Company (N.M.), 311
Diamond A Ranch (N.M.), 153
Diamond Dick, See: St. Leon, Ernest
Diaz, Porfirio, 1, 87
Dibrell, John L., 331
Dickason, Isaac Q., 104, 254, 305, 331
Diehl, Bill, 10, 11
Diggs, James, 104
Dilion, Jerry, 365
Dillinger, John, 188
Dillingham, Dep. Bill, 218

Dixon, Billy, 110
Dixon, Bob, 192, 208
Dixon, Bud (Bill), 147, 148
Dixon, Charles, 192, 208
Dixon, E.M., 367
Dixon, Lee, 82, 303
Dixon, Simpson, 144, 192, 208
Dixon, Tom, 148
Dixon Brothers, 192
Dobson, Bill, 36
Dodds, John, 365
Dodge, Capt. F.S. (U.S.A.), 21
Dodge City Gang, 105, 131, 273, 311, 334, 340, 348, 357, 370, 385, 398
Dodge City Peace Commission, 283
Dodge City Peace Commissioners, **283**
Dodge City *Times*, 66, 102, 113
Dodge House (Dodge City, Kan.), 113
Doherty, John, 324, 331
Dolan, James J., 38, 42, 52, 80, **105**, **210**, 211, 229, 314, 365, 378
Dolan, Lt. Patrick (Texas Rangers), 202, 331, 336, 346
Dolan Gang, 212, 314
Donahue, Cornelius (Lame Johnny), 105, 331
Donahue, Florencio, 3
Donley, Ed, 331
Donnelly, Dr., 331
Donnor, Kid, 303
Donovan, William, 125
Doolin, William M. (Bill), 48, 79, 96, 98, 101, **106-07**, 109, 263, 280, 300, 301, 303, 309, 313, 333, 347, 362, 364, 365
Doolin Gang, 10, 45, 168, 170, 189, 190, 227, 241, 242, 256, 263, 300, 303, 309, 325, 328, 336, 340, 341, 347, 355, 360, 381, 384, 387, 389, 390, 397
Doolin-Dalton Gang, 323, 356, 358, 362, 364, 392, 400
Doran, Major, 365
D'Orgenay, Francis J.L., 331
Dorsey, Frank, 89, 210
Dorsey, John, 328, 365
Dow, E.A., 331
Dow, Leslie (Les), 107, 198, 331, 337, 366, 378, 381
Dow, Luke, 331
Dowd, Daniel, 366
Dowli, Paul, 365
Downing, William, **107**, 331, 366
Driscoll, Tom, 358
Dublin, Dell, 366
Dublin, Dick, 137, 334, 366
Duboise, E. Leon, 366
Dudley, Lt. Col. Nathan Augustus Monroe (U.S.A.), 41, 366
Duffield, Milton B., 107-**08**, 140, 254, 331
Duffy, Thomas, 274, 312, 366
Dugi, Giovanni, 366
Duke, Benton, 165
Duke, Frank, 366
Dumont, Eleanore (Madame Moustache), 108-09
Dunagan, James H., 105
Dunavan, C.T., 332
Duncan, Dick, 366
Duncan, Jack, 207
Duncan, James, 148
Dunlap, Jack (Three-Fingered Jack), **109**, 293, 366
Dunman, William Hickman, 332
Dunn, Amasa G., 332

Dunn, Bee, 109
Dunn, Bill, 65, 109, 242, 256
Dunn, Dep. Bill, 107
Dunn, Calvin, 109
Dunn, Dal, 109
Dunn, George, 109
Dunn, Sheriff John, 213
Dunn, Rose (Rose of the Cimarron), 242, 392
Dupont, John, 366
Duran, Desidario, 168, 244
Duran, Rosa, 153
Durant, Thomas C., 89
Durbin, Walter, 248, 332
Durham, George P., 332
Durst, S.O., 332
Dutch John, 35
Dutch Henry (Henry Borne), 109, 229, 377
DuVall, Perry, 37, 355, 399
Dwindle, Charlie, 366
Dynamite Dick, See: **Clifton, Daniel**
Dynamite Jack, 273

Eagan, Sheriff W.F. (Dad), 24, 26, 28
Earhart, Bill, 110, 269, 366
Earp, Adelia, 110
Earp, Allie, 121
Earp, James, 110, **111**, 114, 119, 121
Earp, Josie, 120
Earp, Martha, 110
Earp, Morgan, 76, 90, 93, 110, **111**, 112, 113, 114,
    116, 118, 119, 120, 121, 154, 163, 164, 191, 223,
    245, 293, 332, 347, 357
Earp, Newton, 110, 121
Earp, Nicholas, 110
Earp, Virgil, 53, 75, 76, 92, 93, 110, **111**, 113, 114,
    116, 118, 119, 120, 121, 163, 223, 245, 270, 284,
    293, 332, 336, 346
Earp, Virginia, 110
Earp, Warren, 119, 120, 121, 191, 223
Earp, Wyatt Berry Stapp, 4, 30, 34, 51, 53, 59, 75,
    76, 84, 88, 90, 92, 110-(**111**, **115**, **117**)-21, 119,
    121, 148, 153, 154, 163, 191, 198, 217, 228, 229,
    244, 245, 247, 248, 255, 268, 279, 283, 284, 293,
    301, 326, 332, 337, 346, 357, 361, 364, 373, 374,
    375, 383, 393
Earp Brothers, 75, 76, 93, 120, 138, 164, 228, 244,
    270, 374
Earp-Clanton Feud, 241, 242
Earp-Holliday Clan, 5
East, Jim, 133
Eddleman, Dick, 280
Edins, Charles, 310
Edwards, Joseph M. (Bob), 223, 339, 366
Edwards, W.R., 332
Eldredge, Robert, 317
Eldrich, O.M., 167
Elevator, 121, 290
Elkins, Dist. Atty. Stephen B., 70, 82, 257, 258, 281
Elliott, Frank (Peg-Leg), **316**, 317, 366
Elliott, James, 366
Elliott, Dep. Constable Jess W., 272
Elliott, Joe, 64, 71, 72, 287
Elliott, Joe (Little Joe), 121
Elliott, Thomas, 15
Elliott, William (Colorado Bill), 121
Ellis, Ben, 318

Ellis, Charles, 366
Ellis, William, 366
Ellison, Samuel, 79
Elmoreau, 366
El Paso Salt War, 359, 378
El Paso Vigilance Committee, 295
El Paso (Texas) *Times*, 149
El Pollo, 367
Elvard, Juan, 367
Enbree, Jack, 367
Ervin, Christopher Columbus, 332
Erwin, Dep. Marshal William, 289
Escobar, Rafael, 121, 367
Eskiminzin, Chief, 64
Eskridge, Dyson, 360, 367
Eskridge, Harge, 294, 367
Espinosa, Felipe, 122
Espinosa, Julian, 122, 367
Espinosa, Victorio, 122
Espinosa, Vivian, 367
Espinosa Brothers, 122
Espinoso, Selzo, 367
Espolin, Jose, 367
Estabo, Tranquellano, 122, 150, 367
Estes, Cole, 338, 367, 386, 399
Evans, Christopher (Chris, Bill Powers), **122**-23,
    288, 319, 329, 349, 367, 386, 394
Evans, Dan, 367
Evans, Jesse, 38, 40, 52, 123, 141, 211, 241, 271, 279,
    281, 314, 326, 327, 358, 367
Evans, Dep. Marshal Joseph W., 92, 291, 332
Evans, Rut, 332
Evans, Tom, 122
Evans-Sontag Case, 319
Evetts, J.H., 332
Ewing, Gen. Thomas C., 260
Ezekiels, Alexander, 231, 332

Faber, Dep. Sheriff Charles, 4, 332
Fain, William, 332
Falkner, Frederick, 367
Fall, Albert B., 130, 150, 341, 349, 367, 386, 399
Fall, Phillip, 332, 367
Fallon, Charles, 367
Fannin, Dep. Marshal H.D., 204
Fanny Butler, 61
Farley, Hutch, 367
Farmers and Merchants Bank (Delta, Colo.), 220
Farr, Sheriff Edward (Colo.), 69, 199, 332
Farr, Jeff B., 322
Farr, Joe, 379
Farrington, Hilary, 367
Farrington, Levi, 367
Farris, John, 384
Farris, William, 23, 84, 85, 367
Fay, James, 366
Feigel, Henry, 11
Feliz, Reyes, 238
Feliz, Rosita, 236
Fellows, Dick, 124
Felshaw, Jake, 368
Ferber, Edna, 189
Ferguson, Andy, 333
Ferguson, Ma, 300
Ferguson & Biggs California Laundry (San Francisco, Calif.), 47

Ferguson Rangers, 300
Fernandez, Juan, 35, 36
Ferris, Henry, 368
Fetterman, Capt. William J., 6
Fetterman Massacre, 6
Ficklin, Ben, 285
Field, Stephen J., 241, 341
Fields, Tom, 368
Finch, William, 124, 368
Findlay, John, 376
Finley, Marshal Cornelius, 324, 333
Finley, Jim, 368
Finnessey, Tom, 149, 368
First Methodist Episcopal Church, 277
First National Bank (Northfield, Minn.), **179**, 232, 360, 386, 400
First National Bank of Coffeyville (Kan.), 97, 98, 183
First National Bank of Denver (Col.), 67
First National Bank of Santa Fe (N.M.), 258
First National Bank of Winnemuca, Nev., 201
Fisher, A.S., 23
Fisher, Bill, 368
Fisher, Dick, 368
Fisher, Fred, 247
Fisher, John King (King Fisher), 124-**(25)**-26, 300, 301, 325, 333, 339, 344, 347, 368, 377, 391, 396
Fisher, Kate (Katherine Elder; Big Nose), **111**, 116, 163-64
Fitch, Ed (Texas Ranger), 196
Fitzpatrick, Mike, 368
Fitzsimmons, Bob, 120
Flagg, Jack, 64, 72, 282
Flatt, George W., 125, 169, 333, 336
Flint, Ed, 333
Flint, John (prom. 1891), 194
Flint, John (prom. 1860s-70s), 368
Flores, Ceferino, 86
Flores, Gen. Juan, 126, **205**, **206**
Floyd, Charles Arthur (Pretty Boy), 188
Floyd, Henry, 368
Floyd, W.S., 368
Fly, Sheriff C.S., 119, 326, 335
Flying H Ranch (N.M.), 105
Flynn, Jim, 118
Flynt, John, 368
Follett, Lyman, 254, 368
Follett, Warren, 254, 368
Folsom, Tandy, 368
Folsom State Prison (Calif.), 122, 289
Fontes, Andres, 126
Foote, Jack, 184
Fooy, Sam, 368
Foraker, Charles, 126, 333
Foraker, Creighton M., **126-27**, 239, 254, 333, 341
Forbes, Harry, 333
Forbes, William R., 333
Ford, Charles, 128, **129**, 184, **185**, 186, 188, 368
Ford, John S. (Rip), **127-28**, 333
Ford, Robert (Bob), 93, **128-30**, 161, 162, 184, **185**, 186, 188, 189, 197, 368, 376, 377, 381
Ford Brothers, 27, 188
Ford's Tent Saloon, **129**
Foreign Miners Act, 238
Foretone Hotel (South Creede, Colo.), 197
Fornoff, Fred, 333
Forrest, Gen. Nathan Bedford, 80
Forsyth, J.P., 333
Fort Worth and Denver Railroad, 59, 60
Forty Bandits, 284

Forty Thieves Gang, See: Silva's White Caps
Forty Years a Gambler on the Mississippi, 103
Fossett, U.S. Marshal William D., 45, 280
Foster, Amanda, 138, 139
Foster, Bell, 21, 22
Foster, Joe, 125, 126, 301
Foster, M.E., 50, 368
Foster, Martha, See: Baker, Mrs. Cullen
Foster, W.B., 356
Fountain, Albert, 130
Fountain, Albert Jennings, 130, 136, 208, 362, 368, 375, 380, 386, 390
Fountain, Henry, 130, 136
Fountain Ranch (Calif.), 124
Fowler, Joel, 131, 368, 377
Foy, Eddie, 113
Franc, Otto, 68
Franklin, Annie, 10, 32, 217
Franklin, Ed, 240
Franks, G.W., 69, 198, 199
Frazer, George A. (Bud), **131**, 233, 269, 333, 340, 372, 386
Fredericks, William, 289
Free Rovers, The, 30
Fremont, John C., 93
French, A.H., 130
French, Jim, 40, 84, 85, 131, 161, 170, 309, 369
Frescan, Cesario, 369
Friar, Art, 168,
Friar, Jubel, 168
Friar Brothers, 330
Frink, D.B., 369
Fritz, Emil, 244
Fulgam, James, 333
Fullerton, C.B., 333
Fulsom, Edward, 131
Funny, Squirrel, 170
Fusselman, Charles H., 333

Gabriel, Peter, 132, 333, 343
Gagen, Richard F., 369
Gallagher, Bill, 369
Gallagher, Jack (Three-Fingered Jack), 110, 132, 155, 369
Gallagher, J.G., 369
Gallegos, Jose Trujillo, 369
Gallegos, Juan, 381
Gallegos, Leandro, 369
Gallegos, Luis, 386
Gallegos, Nestor, 369
Gallegos, Pantaeleon, 369
Galveston (Texas) *Tribune*, 50
Galvin, John, 369
Garcia, Bartole, 366
Garcia, Manuel (Three-Fingered Jack), 132-33, 238
Garcia, Nicanor, 369
Gardner, J.E., **27**
Gardner, Raymond Hatfield, 333
Gardner, Sheriff, 197, 304
Garfias, Marshal Henry, 247
Garfias, Pete, 369
Garfield, Pres. James, 73, 89
Garner, John Nance (Cactus Jack), 136
Garner's Saloon (Mason, Texas), 20
Garret, James, 294
Garrett, Billy, 269

Garrett, Buck, 333
Garrett, Joe, 369
Garrett, Marshal John, 56
Garrett, Patrick Floyd (Pat), 7, 42, **43**, 44, 45, 71, 133-(35, 36)-37, 208, 212, 222, 223, 233, 242, 244, 255, 273, 274, 279, 281, 326, 327, 333, 334, 339, 340, 343, 350, 355, 357, 371, 380, 383, 385, 386, 388, 389
Garza, Catarino, 369
Gates, Superintendent Thomas, 269
Gathings, James, 137
Gathings, Col. J.J., 137
Gauss, Godfrey, 246
Gay, Det. Daniel (Sacramento, Calif. PD), 36
Gem Saloon (El Paso, Texas), 263, 276
Gentry, Doc, 126
George, Joe, 313, 369
Geppert, George, 55, 272
German, Joe, 369
Geronimo, 10, 165, 275, 302, 313
Gerren, Sheriff, 26
Gerry, Judge Melville, 251
Gibbons, James, 369
Gibbs, Bill, 369
Gibson, Con, 233, 369
Gibson, Jake, 340
Gibson, L.E., 369
Gibson, Ned, 395
Gibson, Volney, 369, 395-96
Gilbertson, Ross, 71, 72, 287
Gilbreth, Bud, 369
Gildea, Augustus M., 333
Gill, Bobby, 102
Gillespie, Bob, 299, 305
Gillespie, John C., 51
Gillett, James Buchanan, 137, 138, 333, 345, 353, 369
Gilliland, Fine, 84, 137-38, 330, 369
Gilliland, James, 130, 136, 208, 334, 369
Gilmore, Robert, 66
Gilpin, Gov. William, 277
Gilson, Bill, 334
Gilson, Chris, 369
Gladden, George, 138, 370
Glanton, John Joel, 370
Glanton Gang, 374
Glasgow, Dep. Sheriff, 365
Glasgow, Mr., 334
Glass, Maggie, 139
Glasscock, Richard, 260
Glispen, Sheriff, 183
Globe Restaurant (El Paso, Texas), 196
Glover, Sheriff Robert M., 86, 363
Goff, Dr. W.L., 97
Golden, Jim, 353
Golden, John, 370
Golden Glow Ranch (Lincoln County, N.M.), 81
Goldensen, 370
Goldsby, Crawford (Cherokee Bill), 84, 85, **138-**(39)-40, 170, 344, 370
Gonzales, Juan, 294, 350
Gonzales, Juan, 347, 370, 395
Gonzales, Marcus, 370
Gonzales, Pedro, 238
Gonzalez, Sheriff Dario, 14
Gonzalez, Jesus, 86
Gonzolez, Gabriel, 370, 372
Gonzolez y Blea, Manuel, 370
Gonzolez y Blea, Martin, 370

Good, John, 140, 208, 344
Good, John H., 370, 392
Good, Walter, 140, 208, 370
Goodall, Henry, 172
Goodbread, Joseph, 172
Good-Lee Feud, See: Lee-Good Feud
Goodlet, Bill, 370
Goodman, Sgt. Thomas M., 9
Goodman, William, 370
Goodnight, Charles, 2, 334, 370
Goodnight-Loving Trail, 2
Goodwin, Francis H., 140, 290, 306, 334
Goodwin, Joel, 290
Gordon, James, 155-56
Gordon, Lon, 84, 140, 370
Gordon, Mike, 163, 370
Gordon, Tom, 370
Gosling, Harold L, 141, 334
Gosper, Gov. John J. (Ariz.), 92
Gould, J.C., 104
Governor's Saloon, 257
Grace, Mike, 10
Grady, Tom, 370
Graham, Albert (Charles Graves, Ace Carr), 141, 370
Graham, Carson, 167
Graham, Charles, 141, 370
Graham, Dayton, 141, 286, 334
Graham, Dollay, 141, 371
Graham, John D., 141, 371, 396
Graham, Samuel, 334, 371
Graham, Thomas H., 141, 371
Graham, William, See: Brocius, Curly Bill
Graham Brothers, 141, 356
Graham-Tewksbury Feud (Ariz., Pleasant Valley War), 48, 141, 255, 356, 371, 396
Grand Central Hotel (Socorro, N.M.), 131
Grange, The, 247
Grannon, Riley, 141
Grant, Frederick, 281
Grant, Joe, 42, 371
Grant, Pres. Ulysses Simpson, 64, 65, 78, 160, 252, 254, 258, 281
Grant County Cattleman's Association, 278
Granville Stuart Ranch (Mont.), 8
Graves, Alf, 294
Graves, Alfred, 347, 395
Graves, Mit, 235, 371
Graves, Whiskey Bill, 371
Greathouse, James (Jim), 6, 273, 371
Gregg, William H., 259
Gregory, Walter, 334
Green, Charles, 310
Green, Edward W., 174
Green, George, 334
Green, Marshal George H., 239
Green, Thomas, 371,
Green, Tom, 371
Green Front Saloon (San Antonio, Texas), 151
Greenwood, Caleb, 33
Greer, John, 36
Grey, Dick, 371
Grey, Fanny, 217
Griego, Francisco (Pancho), 3, 83, 141-42, 334, 371
Griffin, B.G., 176
Griffin, Frank, 176
Griffin, George, 371
Griffith, Ben, 371

Griffith, Comm. William, 258
Griffith, William M., 334
Grimes, A.C., 334
Grimes, Dep. Sheriff Ellis (Hoke), 24, 28, 172
Grimes, Marshal William, 340
Gristy, Bill (Bill White), 35, 36
Griswald (or Griswold), Dr. J.F., 260
Gross, Albert, 334, 371
Gross, John, 123
Grounds, Billy (Billy Boucher), 51, 356
Grounds, Robert (Bob), 106
Guadalupe Canyon (N.M.) Massacre, 76
Gustavson, Nicholas, 183
Guy, Marshal James, 207
Guyse, Buck, 334, 371
Gylam, Jack, 167

Hackett, George W., 46
Hainer, Al, 67
Hairy One, The, See: **Chacon, Augustin**
Halderman, Bill, 371
Halderman, Tom, 371
Hale, John, 196, 371
Halfbreed Jack, 371
Hall, Bill, 371
Hall, Charles, 371
Hall, Edward L., 126, 334
Hall, Frank W., 334
Hall, Jesse Lee (Red), 29, 125, **143**, 191, 334, 336
Hall, Jesse Leigh, 334
Hall, Lee, 345
Hall, T.L., 334, 380, 395
Hall, W.H., 71
Haller, William, 259
Hamer, Frank, 300, 334
Hamilton, Sheriff, 353
Hamner, Marshal, 340
Hampton, Silas, 143
Hancock, Louis, 247
Hancock, Winfield, 73
Hand, Dora (Fannie Keenan), 30, 113, 114, 198, 228
Hanging Judge, The, See: **Parker,** Judge **Isaac**
Hanks, Orlando Camillo (Deaf Charley, O.C.), 69,
    143, 162, 200, 201, 270, 315, **316**, 371
Hannah, James, 372
Hannehan, Jim, 125,
Hannehan, Tom, 125
Hanrahan, Jim, 110
Hansford, Judge John, 172
Hanson, William, 335
Happy Jack, See: Morco, John
Hardin, Bill, 372
Hardin, Jane Bowen, 146, 149
Hardin, John Wesley, 7, 12, 37, 78, 143-(**44, 46, 49**)-
    50, 155, 156, 216, 233, 270, 278, 279, 296, 298,
    299, 300, 325, 335, 342, 345, 350, 351, 355, 361,
    365, 372, 373, 381, 387, 393, 395
Hardin, Joseph (Joe), 148, 372
Hardin, Mart, 372
Hardin, Judge William B., 144
Harding's Trading Post (Medicine Lodge, Kan.), 7
Hargraves, Dick, 150
Harkey, Sheriff **Dee** (Phoenix, Ariz.), 122, 150, 198,
    269, 305, 335, 367, 376, 388
Harkey, Sheriff Joe, 150
Harkins, Mark, 278

Harlin, J.J., 372
Harmon, Adolf, 370, 372
Harmon, Albert, 372
Harmon, Augustin, 372
Harmon Arnett Ranch, 190
Harpe, Wiley (Little), 150
Harpe, William Micajah (Big), 150
Harper, Chas, 372
Harrell, Jack, 335
Harriman, Jock, 383, 387
Harrington, Frank, 199, 372
Harris, Jack, 125, 126, **151**, 301
Harris, James (d.1875), 318
Harris, James (prom. 1880s), 335, 372, 384
Harris, Det. Len, 288
Harris, O.D., 178
Harris House Hotel (Wichita, Kan.), 53
Harrison, Pres. Benjamin, 253
Harrison, C.H., 380
Harrison, Dep. Sheriff, 238
Harrison, Richard, 335
Harrison, Det. Robert (Sacramento, Calif. PD), 36
Harrison, Rollie (Hard Luck), 216
Harrison County Treasury (Magnolia, Iowa), 267
Harrold, Benjamin, 372
Harrold, Martin, 372
Harrold, Merritt, 372
Harrold, Samuel, 372
Harrold, Thomas, 372
Harrold Brothers, 372
Harrold War, 350
Harry, Capt. Edmund (Creek Lighthorse Police,
    Indian Territory), 57
Hart, Ernest, 151
Hart, Frederick, 151
Hart, Pearl, 151-53, 356, 372
Hartlee, B.F., 269
Hartnett, Splay Foot, 372
Harvey, James, 85
Harwell, Jack, 335
Hasbrouck, L.B., 54
Hash Knife Gang, 299, 305
Hash Knife Ranch (N.M.), 236, 255
Haslett, Bill, 88, 154, 372
Haslett, Ike, 88, 154, 372
Haslett Brothers, 53, 88, 373, 380
Hasley, Sam, 373
Hassan, Henry, 57
Hassan, Rosetta, 57
Hassells, Samuel, 153, 373
Haswell, Charles, C., 96
Hatch, Bob, 120
Hatch, Marshal, 380
Hatch's Saloon, 119
Hawkins, Henry, 373
Hawkins, Jack, 335
Hawks, George, 373
Hawley, C.B., 373
Hayden, Carl, 335
Hayes, Bill, 289
Hayes, Jack, 289
Hayes, John Coffee, 335
Hayes, Pres. Rutherford B., 41, 247
Hays, Bob, 73, 153, 160, 373
Hays, Bill, 205
Hays, John Coffey (Jack), **153**, 300, 342, 347, 348
Haywood, Dep. Marshal Nat, 227
Hazen, Sheriff Joseph, 69, 214, 296
Head, Harry (Harry the Kid), 88, 116, 153-54, 209,

373
Head, Lafayette, 195, 335
Heath (or Heith) **John**, 102, **154**, 276, 277, 373
Heath Gang, 392
Hedgepeth, Marion C., 373
Hedges, William, 373
Hefferman, Art, 373
Heffridge, Bill, 26, 27, 373
Heffron, Augustus, 373
Heine, William, 358
Heintzelman, Maj. S.P., 127
Heirs, C.F., 335
Heith, John, See: **Heath, John**
Helldorado, 52
Helm, Boone, 132, 154-55, 373, 379
Helm, Charles, 373
Helm, Jack, 147, 155, 296, 298, 335, 373
Henderson, Bill, 368, 373
Henderson, Wall, 293, 373, 395
Henry, O. (William Sydney Porter), 50, 143, 191
Henry Plummer Gang, 132
Hensley, Charles, 342
Hereford, Elk, 365
Hereford, Frank H., 335
Herndon, Albert, 24
Hernandez, Mariano, 373
Herndon, Al, 373
Herne, Jim, 19
Herredia, Clato, 335
Herrera, Fernando, 244
Herrera, Nestor, 373
Herring, Bob, 373
Herring, Johnny, 68, 310
Herron, Sheriff Jim, 191
Hess, John, 335
Hetherington, Joe, 374
Hewey, Vergil, 215
Heywood, Joseph Lee, 183, 321
Hickey (or Hicks), James, 75
Hickey, Mike, 335
Hickman, Tom, 335
Hickok, James Butler (Wild Bill), 4, 59, 63, 76, 81, 84, 110, 145, 146, 155-(**57, 59**)-60, 171, 209, 217, 282, 287, 294, 295, 328, 329, 335, 361, 362, 382, 397
Hickok, Lorenzo, 155, 156
Hickok, Polly Butler, 155
Hickok, William Alonzo, 155
Hickory, Sam, 160
Hicks, Dep. Marshal Dick, 213
Hicks, Milt, 374
Hickson, Joe, 354, 398
Higgins, Fred R., 153, 160, 335
Higgins, John Pinckney Calhoun (Pink), 24, **160-61**, 167, 290, 320
High Five Gang, 73, 359
Hildebrand, Sam, 180
Hilderman, George, 374
Hildreth, Peter, 365
Hildreth, William, 335
Hill, Frank, 374
Hill, George W., 374
Hill, Joe, 374
Hill, John (prom. 1860s), 335
Hill, John (d.1879), 246
Hill, Sarah, 241
Hill, Tom, 52, 123, 161, 211, 314, 336, 374
Hilton, John, 71
Hindman, Dep. **George W.**, 41, 131, 211, 212, 215,

231, 315, 336, 369, 374, 385
Hinton, John, 374
High, George, 150,
Hite, Clarence, 184, 374
Hite, George, 177
Hite, Robert Woodson (Wood), 128, 129, 161-62, 181, 184, 374
Hixon, John W., 280
Hockinsmith, Clark, 260
Hodges, Dr. Thomas J., See: **Bell, Tom**
Hoerster, Daniel, 138, 226
Hoffman, Fred, 320
Hogan, Ed, 152
Hoges, Henry, 374
Hogue, Ed, 88
Holden, Judge, 374
Holder, Lewis, 162
Holdout Jackson, 162
Holdson, James, 226
Hole-in-the-Wall (Colo.), 63, 66, 68, 69, 72, 162, 165, 198, 208, 213, 215, 270, 296, 315, 317
Hole-in-the-Wall Gang, 143, 284, 338, 396
Holland, Joe, 365
Holland, William, 358
Holliday, John Henry (Doc), 34, 76, 90, 92, 93, **111**, 113, 114, 116, 118, 120, 121, **162-65**, 191, 223, 228, 244, 245, 247, 279, 283, 336, 345, 361, 374, 392
Hollingsworth, C.L., 98
Hollister, Cassius M. (Cash), 165, 272, 336
Holloway, Russ, 374
Holmes, W.A. (Bill), 11, 336
Holstein, Sim, 298
Holzhay, Reimund, 374
Homestead Mine, 223
Hood, Elizabeth, 35
Hoodoo Brown, See: Neill, Hyman G.
Hoodoo War, See: **Mason County War**
Hoover, Mayor George M. (Dodge City, Kan.), 113
Hoover, Tuck, 165
Hopkins, Arthur A., 336
Hopkins, Gilbert W., 336
Hop Lee, 380
Hope, Mayor Jim (Wichita, Kan.), 112
Hope's Saloon (Wichita, Kan.), 231, 257
Horan, John, 374
Horn, Tom, 10, 165-(**66**)-**67**, 209, 231, 282, 336, 346, 374, 392
Horner, Joe, See: **Canton, Frank**
Horrell, Ben, 167, 305
Horrell, John, 167
Horrell, Martin, 23, 24, 161, 167, 290, 305, 320
Horrell, Merritt, 23, 161, 167
Horrell, Sam, 23, 24, 161, 167, 290, 305, 320, 374
Horrell, Tom, 23, 24, 167, 305
Horrell Brothers, 23, 161, 194, 305, 320
Horrell Clan, 161
Horrell-Higgins Feud (Texas), 23-24, 167-68, 194, 241, 290, 305, 329, 337, 344, 396
Horseman, William, 126
Horton, George, 336
House, Thomas Jefferson, 374
House of Murphy, The (Lincoln County, N.M.), 210, 211, 212, 223
Houston, John, 395
Houston, Sam, 168, 189, 219, 266, 299, 370, 374
Houston, Dep. Sequoyah, 139
Houston, Temple L., **168**, 189, 190, 374, 376
Houston, Tom, 168, 280, 336

Houston (Texas) *Post*, 50
Houston & Texas Central Railroad, 27
Hovey, Walter, 375
Howard, Charles, 375
Howard, James, 375
Howard, Joe (d.1873), 375
Howard, Joe (prom. 1877), 375
Howard, Judge, 359
Howard, Gen. O.O. (U.S.A.), 25
Howard, Tex, 197, 276
Howard, Tillie, 248
Howe, A.H., 367
Howell, Bennet, 375
Howland, Big Dan, 375
Hoyt, George R., 113, 375
Hoyt, Gov. John P. (Mich.), 92
Huber, Harry, 359
Hubert, Joe, 375
Hudgen, Will, 273
Hudgens, John, 375
Hudson, Charlie, 155
Hudson, Hugh, 375
Hudson, R.M., 336
Huerta, Gen. Victoriano, 1, 87
Hughes, Chester, 60
Hughes, Jim, 374, 375
Hughes, John Reynolds (Border Boss), 14-15, **168**,
    244, 248, 271, 276, 336, 339, 388
Hughes, Louis C., 254
Hughes, Wilson, 375
Hughes and Wasson Bank (Richmond, Mo.), 176
Human Tiger, The, 375
Human Wildcat, The, See: **Soto, Juan**
Hume, James B., 47, 336
Humphreys, Bill, 161
Humpy Jack, 375
Hunnicut, J.R., 336
Hunnicut, M.P., 336
Hunt, J. Frank, 126, 165, 168-69, 336
Hunt, James, 54
Hunt, Richard (Zwing), 51, 375
Hunter, Bill, 375
Hunter, Bill (prom. 1860s), 375
Hunter, Kit, 298
Hunter, Marvin, 201
Huntsville (Texas) Penitentiary, 87
Hurley, Johnny, 211, 375
H-X Bar Ranch (Indian Territory), 106
Hyatt, Frank, 351

Iconoclast, The, 50
Illinois Central Railroad, 60
Immigration Service, 234
Imperial Saloon, 284
Imperial Valley Irrigation System, 207
Indian Territory (Cherokee Strip) (Okla.), 25, 56-
    58, 63, 83, 84, 88, 94, 104, 106, 143, 145, **170**,
    190, 191, 207, 231, 252, 253, 266, 272, 277, 280,
    302, 309, 313, 320, 328, 329, 331, 361, 383
Indian Wars, 361
Innocents Gang, The, (Henry Plummer Gang), 218,
    256, 285, 321, 338, 369, 371, 372, 373, 374, 375,
    399
International Bank (Nogales, Ariz.), 73, 153
Iron Mountain Railroad, 180
Irvan, Tom, 336

Irwin, Nat, 375
Isbel, L.P., 74
Isham's Hardware Store (Coffeyville, Kan.), 100
Ishtanubbee, Gibson, 170
Isom, Ben, 375
Ivers, Alice (Poker Alice), 170-**71**, 375
Ives, George, 375

Jackson, Charles W., 172, 267
Jackson, Frank (Blockey), 24, 27, 28, 29, 107, 172,
    376
Jackson, James, 376
Jackson, Joe, See: **Brock, Leonard Calvert**
Jackson, John (prom. 1885), 379
Jackson, John H. (prom. 1882), 93
Jackson, Teton, 328
Jackson, Tom, 376
Jacobs, Ben, 376
Jacobs, Bill, 48, 271, 299
James, Annie Ralston, 181
James, Calvin, 172
James, Frank (Alexander Franklin James), 97, 129,
    130, 133, 173, 174, **175**, 176, 177, 178, **179**,
    180, 181, 184, 186, **187**, 188, 189, 232, 259,
    261, 280, 321, 323, 376, 400
James, Jesse, Jr., 181, **185**, **187**
James, Jesse Woodson (Dingus), 8, 27, 60, 93-94,
    97, **129**, 161, 172-(**75**, **79**, **85**)-89, 191, 197,
    232, 259, **261**, 291, 321, 323, 364, 376, 377,
    380, 400
James, Mary, 181, **185**
James, Robert (prom. 1850), 173
James, Robert (b.1878), 181
James, Rev. William, 181
James, Mrs. Zerelda Mimms (Zerelda Mimms),
    129, 174, 181, **185**
James Brothers, 96
James Gang, 343, 364, 374, 380, 381, 382
James-Younger Gang, 176, 177, 180, 181, 280, 360,
    376, 386
Jamison, George, 376
Janes, John, 376
Janson, H.A., 280
Jaramillo, Heraldo, 105
Jaybird-Woodpecker War (Texas), 15, 189
Jefferson, Dunk, 336
Jeffries, William, 266
Jenkins, James Gilbert, 189, 376
Jenkins, John, 277
Jenkins, Dep. Sam F., 214, 305
Jenkins, Tom, 376
Jenkins, West, 307
Jennings, Alphonso J. (Al), 89, **93**, 189-(**90**)-91, 207,
    313, 338, 376
Jennings, Edward, 189, 190, 374
Jennings, Frank, 189, 190, 191, 376
Jennings, Judge J.D.F., 189, 190
Jennings, John, 189, 190
Jennings, Napoleon Augustus, 191, 336
Jennings Brothers, 190
Jennison's Jayhawkers, 26
Jerrell, Henry, 268
Jerry Scott's Saloon (Lampasas, Texas), 305
Jesse Evans Gang, 329, 335, 338, 341, 344, 351, 365,
    370, 371, 374

Jim Hope's Saloon, See: Hope's Saloon
Jinglebob Ranch (N.M., owned by John Chisum), 38, 40
John Bitters' Beer Saloon (Hays City, Kan.), 156
Johnny Behind the Deuce, See: **O'Rourke, John**
Johnson, Andrew, 254
Johnson, Arkansas Tom, 24, 27, 28, 376
Johnson, Bill (d.1881), 90
Johnson, Bill (d.1898), 278, 376
Johnson, Charles, 336
Johnson, Chas., 376
Johnson, Dan, 150, 376, 388
Johnson, Dewitt C., 376
Johnson, George W., 364
Johnson, Capt. Frank (Texas Rangers), 341, 344, 349
Johnson, Jack (Turkey Creek), 90, 119, 120, 191-92, 223, 336, 376
Johnson, Marshal Jack, 368
Johnson, J.E. (Dobe), 385
Johnson, Jim, 210,
Johnson, John (Liver-Eating), **192**, 337
Johnson, Julia, See: Dalton, Mrs. Emmett
Johnson, Lee, 197
Johnson, Otter, 376
Johnson, Pat, 304
Johnson, Peter, 376
Johnson, Richard (Dick), **192**, 208, 254, 376
Johnson, Robe, 377
Johnson, R.S., 269
Johnson, Samuel, 377
Johnson, Dep. Marshal Sid, 97
Johnson, Swede, 317, 377
Johnson, Tom, 337
Johnson, William H., 33, 192, 246, 337, 377
Johnson County War (Wyo.), 15-18, 64, 71, 166, 193, 213, 215, 242, 265, 266, 282, 287, 296, 319, 333, 352, 356, 399
Jones, Acorn Head, 377
Jones, Arkansas Tom, See: Daugherty, Roy
Jones, Asher, 352
Jones, Ben, 72, 282
Jones, Dep. Bill (Red Bill), 126
Jones, Chubby, 377
Jones, Factor, 236
Jones, Capt. Frank (Texas Rangers), 15, **194**, 245, 300, 337, 345
Jones, Fred, 337
Jones, Gus, 337
Jones, J.B., 293
Jones, Jefferson, 194
Jones, Jim, 195
Jones, John (d.1879), 33, 41, 194, 212, 377, 396
Jones, John (d.1900), **195**
Jones, Maj. John B. (Texas Rangers), 28, 29, 167, **194**, 202, 320, 329, 331, 337, 363
Jones, John G., 194-95, 274, 337
Jones, Nat B., 337
Jones, Payne, 176
Jones, Ranger, 377
Jones, Stanton T., 235
Jones, Tom, 377
Jones, Walter, 295
Jones, Walter (Texas Ranger), 337
Jones, William (Canada Bill), 103, 377
Jones, W.R., 68, 214
Jones Brothers, 195
Jordan, Francisco, 377
Jordan, Kirk, 54

Joseph, Martin, 377
Joy, Christopher (Kit), 361, 377
Joyce, Mike, 164, 247
Jurata, Padre, 238
Juarez, Benito, 87, 130
Judah, Theodore, 90
Judd, Orange, 253
Judson, Edward Zane Carroll, See: **Buntline, Ned**
July, Jim, 291
July, Naomi, 56-**58**, 358, 377

Kalijah, Seaborn, 196
Kansas and Arkansas Valley Railroad, 272
Kansas City & Missouri Railroad, 84
Kansas City *Journal*, 186, 221
Kansas Pacific Railroad, 27
Karnes, Sheriff John (Comanche, Texas), 147
Karnes, Quill, 337
Kaseman, George A., 337
Kay, Jim, 377
K.C. Ranch (Wyo.), 64, 72, 282
Kearnes, Henry, 242, 269
Kearney, Frank, 377
Kearney, Kent, 136
Kearny, Gen. Stephen Watts (U.S.A.), 32, 37, 93
Keating, Lawrence, 139
Keating's Saloon, Battle of, 196
Keaton, Pierce, 197, 377
Keintpos, See: **Captain Jack,** 65
Kellam, William, 377
Keller, Henry, 280
Kelley, Mami, 370
Kelley, Mayor James H. (Dog) (Dodge City, Kan.), 102, 113, 114, 198, 228
Kelley, William D., 89
Kelliher, Michael, 311, 348, 398
Kells, Commander, 205
Kelly, Bill, 377
Kelly, Daniel (Yorky), 102, 154, 197, 276, 377
Kelly, Edward O. (Red), 130, **197**, 377
Kelly, Henry, 155, 296
Kelly, Jack, 378
Kelly, Constable W.C., 126
Kelly, William (prom. 1873), 155, 296
Kelly, William (d.1887), 196
Kemp, Albert, 172
Kemp, David (Dave), 107, 197-98, 331, 337, 366, 378
Kennedy, Charles, 2-3, 378
Kennedy, James W. (Spike), 30, 113, 114, 198, 228
Kennon, Louis, 337
Kenny, Robert, 378
Kenyon, Asa, 269
Kerr, Mrs. Annie, 292
Kerr, Christie McCorkle, 260
Ketchum, Ami, 246, 247
Ketchum, Samuel (Sam), 58, 198, 199, 339, 351, 378
Ketchum, Thomas E. (Black Jack), 58, 69, 127, **198-(99)**-200, 207, 239, 311, 326-27, 346, 353, 366, 372, 378
Ketchum Brothers, 378
Ketchum-Carver Gang, 332
Ketchum Gang, 66
Kettle, Jack, 200, 378
Kid Curry, See: **Logan, Harvey**

Kid Lewis, See: Lewis, Elmer
Kile, John, 156
Killeen, May, See: Leslie, Killeen May
Killeen, Mike, 380
Killin' Jim, See: **Miller, Jim**
Kilmartin, Jack, 378
Kilpatrick, Benjamin (Ben, The Tall Texan), 33, 52, 58, 66, 67, 68, 69, 70, 162, **200-(201)-202**, 208, 213, 315, **316**, 354, 358, 378
Kilpatrick, George, 52, 200, 327
Kimball, George, 337
Kimble County, Texas, 202
Kimmel, E.A., 217, 381
Kimmel, Glendolene, 167
King, Billy (Cowboy Bill), 5-6, 325, 378
King, David, 90
King, Ed, 319, 378
King, Frank, 73, 153, 202-03, 337
King, James, 82
King, Jim, 337
King, Lou, 337
King, Luther, 88, 116, 154, 209, 378
King, Martin, 298
King, Sandy, 203, 378
King, Thomas, 358
King, Capt. William (Sacramento, Calif. PD), 36
King Ranch (Texas), 53, 224
Kingsbury, Jack, 378
King's Saloon (San Francisco, Calif.), 238
Kinnear & Co. Stagecoach, 116
Kinney, J.J., 97, 210
Kinney, John, 378, 392, 393
Kirby, Andrew, 291, 378
Kirchner, Karl, 245, 337
Kirk, George, 378
Kirkham, Capt. (U.S.A.), 22
Kirksey, Bill, 207
Kirkwood, Samuel J., 92
Kiser, W.H., 126
Kit Joy Gang, 380, 395
Kitt, George, 378
Kjellstrom, Albert, 397
Kloehr, John Joseph, 100, 378, 390
Knight, Jim, 378, 379
Knight, Jourdon, 378, 379
Knott, A.W., 98
Koppel's Store (Round Rock, Texas), 24, 28
Kosterlitsky, Emilio, 337, 379
Krempkau, Gus, 196, 371
Kresling, Charles, 379
Krummeck, Charles, 337
Kuhley, Charles, 337
Kuhns, Marvin, 203, 379
Kuhns, Walter, 203
Ku Klux Klan, 160
Kuykendall, Mark, 196
Kuykendall, Judge W.L., 158, 196
Kyes, Red Dent, 385
Kyle, Sheriff Matt, 351

Labreu, Jason, 204
Lackey, John, 145
Lacy, Isaac, 2
Lacy, Robert, 204, 379
Lady Gay Saloon and Dance Hall (Dodge City, Kan.), 102, 227, 228

LaFlore, Chief Charley, 97
LaForce, Newton, 266
Laird, Marshal Elmer, 203
Lambert, Charles Frederick, 338
Lamb, James, 204-05
Lamb, Joe, 367
Lamb, Thomas N., 379
Lambert, Henry, 3, 199
Lambert's Hotel (Cimarron, N.M.), 319
Lambert's Saloon (Cimarron, N.M.), 3, 294
Lame Johnny, 379
Lancleve, Julius, 378
Landrum, James David, 338
Landusky, Efie, 284
Landusky, Pike, 213
Lane, George (Clubfoot), 132, 155, 379
Lane, Sen. James H. (Kan.), 90, 259
Lane, Jim, 155
Lane, Gov. William Carr (N.M.), 79
Lane, Van, 338
Lang, Bill, 379
Langford, N.P., 338
Langford Gang, 355
Langston, Sell, 379
Langtry, Lily, 31, 32
Langworthy, Charles, 379
Lanihan, Priv. Jerry, 156
Lanihan, Dep. Peter, 156
Lant, Dave, 270, 304, **316**, 317
Lantier, Ike, 161
Lara, Ruperto, 379
L'archeveque, Sostenes, 379
Large, Georgia, 233
Largo, Jesus, 379
Largo, Juan, 379
Larkin, Sam, 338
Larn, John M., 205, 206, 279, 338, 345, 379, 393
Las Cuevas, Mex., War, 205-06
Latche, James, 181
Latham, James V., 206, 338
Latta, Oscar, 338
Latterner, Charles, 379
Laughlin, J.T., 338
Lauter, H., 251
Lawless, Bill, 379
Lawson, George, 79, 162
Lay, Mary Calvert, 207
Lay, William Ellsworth (Elza, Elzy), 68, 69, 162, 198, 199, 200, 206-07, 270, 315, **316**, 329, 361, 379
Layton, G.I., 379
Layton, Juan, 379
Lea, Smith, 379
Leach, William, 207
Leatherwood, Sheriff Robert N., 73, 338
Leavenworth Beer Saloon, 295
Leavenworth (Kan.) Federal Penitentiary, 2, 191
Ledbetter, Marshal **James F.** (Bud), 190-91, **207,** 266, 338, 376
Ledford, J.E., 53, 327
Lee, B.B., 379
Lee, Bob, 380
Lee, Clem, 380
Lee, Cyrus, 98
Lee, James, 207-08, 300, 380
Lee, Mitch, 334, 380
Lee, Oliver Milton, 130, 136, 208, 305, 338, 351, 366, 369, 377, 380, 383, 386, 396
Lee, Patrick, 242

Lee, Pink, 207, 208, 300, 380, 380
Lee, Robert (Bob), **208**, 212, 213, 215, 270, **316**, 317, 380
Lee, Robert E. (Bob), 192, **208**, 254, 380
Lee, Gen. Robert E., 128, 260
Lee, Tom, 207
Lee Gang, 208, 347
Lee-Good Feud, 363, 369, 377, 380, 383
Lee-Peacock Feud, 192, 208, 375
Lefors, Joseph, 69, 166, 167, 208-09, 315, 338
Leiva, Mariano, 134
Leland, William, 380
Lenta, Antonio, 380
Leonard, Bill, 88, 116, 153, 154, 209, 373, 380
LeRoy, Bill, 234
Leroy, Billy, 380
LeRoy, Kitty, 209, 380
Leshhart, Charles, 32
Leslie, May Killeen, 209
Leslie, Nashville Franklin (Buckskin Frank), 75, 76, 116, **209**-10, 270, 346, 361, 369, 380
Lesser, Louis, 391
Levy, Jim, 380
Lewis, Alexander, 210
Lewis, Bill, 380
Lewis, Callie, 149
Lewis, Elmer (Kid Lewis, Mysterious Kid, Slaughter Kid), **89, 210**, 224, 363, 380
Lewis, Jake, 138
Lewis, Jim, 380
Lewis, Lon, 338
Lewis, Tom, 282, 286
Lewis, W.W., 338
Leyba, Marino, 380
Liberty Hill Ranch, 271
Liddell, James Andrew (Dick), 128, 129, 130, 161, 184, 186, 374, 380, 381
Life of Texas Jack, The, 266
Light, Zackary, 331, 366, 381
Lincoln, Pres. Abraham, 90, 107, 108, 144, 252
Lincoln County War (N.M.), 33, 38, 41, 44, 51, 52, 54, 80, 81, 123, 131, 134, 161, 192, 194, 210-12, 215, 223, 229, 231, 244, 246, 246, 276, 278, 281, 309, 315, 318, 326, 327, 328, 338, 342, 345, 353, 354, 355, 356, 357, 362, 363, 365, 365, 366, 367, 368, 369, 371, 375, 377, 378, 379, 381, 382, 383, 384, 385, 386, 387, 388, 389, 390, 391, 392, 393, 394, 397, 398, 399, 400
Lindsey, Seldon T., 212
Line Ferry (Sulphur River, Ark.), 21
Linn, Charlie (Buck), 263
Linsley, Jesse, **316**, 317
Little, Tom, 176
Little Bill, See: Raidler, William
Little Britches, See: Stevens, Jennie
Little Dick, See: West, Richard
Little Reddie from Texas, See: McKemie, Robert
Liver-Eating Johnson, See: Johnson, John
Lloyd, Abner N., 143
Lobato, Paula, 32
Lockhart, De., 381
Logan, Harvey (Kid Curry), 66, 67, 68, 69, 90, 162, 200, 201, 208, 212-(13)-15, 278, 284, 296, 305, 315, 317, 364, 380, 381, 391
Logan, John A., 89
Logan, Johnny, 212, 215
Logan, Lonie (or Lonnie), 68, 208, 212, 213, 215, 317, 381
Logan Brothers, 270

Logwood, William, 381
Long, John (prom. 1878-81), 131, 215-16, 338, 381
Long, John (prom. 1892), 381
Long, Nimrod, 176, 280
Long, Steve (Big Steve), **216**, 338, 381
Longabaugh (or Longbaugh), Harry, See: Sundance Kid
Long Branch Saloon (Dodge City, Kan.), 217, 268, 269, 283
Longfellow House (Clifton, Ariz.), 71
Long-Haired Jim, See: **Courtright, Timothy Isaiah**
Long-Haired Owens, 367
Long-Haired Sam, See: **Brown, Sam**
Longley, Bill, 365
Longley, William Preston, (Wild Bill, Bill) **216**, 328, 340, 381
Longwill, Robert, 83
Loomis, A.W., 338
Loomis, H.W., 338, 400
Lord & Williams, 302
Los Pinos Indian Agency, 250
Louis Segerman's Restaurant (Caldwell, Kan.), 126
Louisville and Nashville Railroad, 60, 61
Lovato, Ricardo, 372
Love, Cy, 2
Love, Capt. Harry (Calif. Rangers), 133, 238, 339, 381, 387
Love, H.M., 339
Love, Sheriff Thomas D., 85
Love, Tom, 280
Love, Tony, 172
Love, Dep. W.H., 69, 199
Loving, Frank (Cock-Eyed Frank), 30, 217, 268, 269, 381
Loving, Oliver, 2
Lowe, James (d.1910), **316**, 317
Lowe, James (James West) (d.1880s), 328, 381
Lowe, Joseph (Rowdy Joe), 10, 32, **217**, 339, 381
Lowe, Kathryn (Rowdy Kate), 217
Lozier, Dr., 339
Lund, Dep. Sheriff Alfred, 47, 48
Lucas, Elmer (Chicken), 84, 85, 381
Lucas, Red, 280
Lucero, Aban, 381
Lucero, Cecilio, 381
Lucero, Cesario, 5
Lucero, Francisco, 381
Lucero, Quinia, 381
Lucero, Sostenes, 381, 390
Lucero, Tomas, 381
Lujan, Martiniano, 381
Luckey, Buzz, 266
Lull, Louis J., 181, 321, 400
Luna, Melchior, 381
Luttrell, Charles, 382
Lynn, Wiley, 303, 347
Lyon, Montague (Monte Jack), 35, 36
Lyon House (Springfield, Mo.), 156
Lyons, Haze (Hays), 132, 155, 218, 382

Mabry, W.S., 133
McAlester, Dep. Marshal, 2
McAlpin, J.S., 366
McCaffry, U.S. Dist. Attorney James E., 104
McCall, Jack (Bill Sutherland), 63, 158, 160, 171,

294, 328, 335
McCall, Jim, 382
McCall, John (Broken Nose Jack), 219, 382
McCall, Thomas P., 219, 339
McCanles, David C., 155, 157, 335, 382
McCanles, Monroe, 155
McCann, Reddy, 293
McCarty, Bill, 67, 68, 74, 219, 220, 382
McCarty, Catherine, 38
McCarty, Fred, 68, 220
McCarty, George, 74
McCarty, Henry, 382
McCarty, Joseph, 38
McCarty, Patrick, 38
McCarty, Patrick (d.1887), 219
McCarty, Patrick Henry, See: Billy the Kid
McCarty, Tom, 67, 74, 219, 220, 329, 360, 382
McCarty Brothers, 315
McCauley, Hamp, 382
McCauley, W.J. (Texas Rangers), 23, 339
McCaulley, Billie, 373
McClain, Judge John, 176
McClease, Jim, 383
McClelland, Andrew, 15
McClelland, Hugh, 15
McCloskey, Andy, 382
McCloskey, Sam, 382
McCloskey, William, 40, 223, 224, 278
McCloud, Jim, 167
McClure, Bob (Texas Rangers), 23, 339
McCluskie, Arthur, 7, 8, 220
McCluskie, Mike, 7, 220, 242, 269
McConnell, Andrew, 220, 287
McCool, Len, 65
McCord, Myron, 221, 339
McCorkle, John, 260
McCory, Arthur, 180
McCoy, One-Legged Jim, 382
McCuiston, O.W., 339
McCulloch, Ben, 300
McCullough, Green, 382
McCullough, John, 4
McDaniel, Jim, 38
McDaniel, W.C., 273
McDaniels, J., 382
McDaniels, Jim, 382
McDaniels, William, 382
McDonald, Bill, 337
McDonald, George, 140, 208, 370
McDonald, Dep. J.H., 221
McDonald, Walter, 382
McDonald, Marshal W.D. (Bill), 210, 380
McDonald, Capt. W.J. (Texas Rangers), 89, 339
McDougal, Annie (Cattle Annie), 303, 328, 360, 381
McDougall, Gov. John, 278
McDowell, Jack (Three-Fingered Jack), 100, 221-22, 364, 382
McDowell, William, 177
Mace, John, 383
McEhanie, Bill, 96
McGee, Orpheus, 222
McGrand, Ed, 382
McGrath, Price, 222
McGrath, Tim, 289
McGregg, Buck, 48
McGuire, Edward, 382
McIntire, James, 222, 339, 382
McIntosh, T.W., 339
McIntyre, Chas, 383

McKeague, Neal, 383
McKemie (or McKimie), Robert, (Little Reddie from Texas), 222, 375, 383
McKenna, Aleck, 98
McKenzie, Kenneth, 33
McKidrict, Joe (Texas Ranger), 248, 279, 339
McKinley, William, 221
McKinney, Charles, 382
McKinney, Thomas L. (Tip), 135, 339, 366, 383
McLaughlin, Archie, 223, 284
McLaughlin, M., 383
McLaughlin, Red, 329
McLowery, Frank, 75, 76, 114, 115, 118, 119, 164, 245, 361, 383
McLowery, Tom, 75, 76, 114, 115, 118, 119, 164, 245, 361, 383
McLowery (or McLaury) Brothers, 53, 118, 245
McLowery Ranch, 361
McMahon, Francis Marion (Frank), 149, 223, 248, 278, 339
McMains, Rev. Oscar P., 83, 383
McManus, Irving, 383
McMasters, Jim, 133
McMasters, Sherman, 90, 119, 120, 191, 223, 383
McMillan, Frank, 184
McMillan, John, 35
McMurry, Capt. Sam, 326, 327, 339, 340, 343, 347
McNab, Frank, 33, 40, 52, 80, 192, 215, 223-24, 246, 383
McNack, Wallace, 25
McNeel, J.S., Jr., 339
McNeel, P.J., 339
McNelly, Capt. Leander H. (Texas Rangers), 12, 205, 224, 300, 339, 345
McNelly's Bulldog, See: Armstrong, John Barclay
McNew, William, 130, 339, 383
McRose, Martin, 149, 383, 390
McRose, Mrs. Martin, 149
McSween, Alexander, 33, 38, 39, 40, 41, 42, 70, 81, 105, 131, 194, 211, 212, 215, 216, 223, 244, 246, 276, 278, 314, 315, 326, 377, 396
McSween, Susan, 39
McSween-Tunstall Faction, 52, 54, 80, 212, 318
McVay, Ellis, 225
McVeagh, U.S. Attorney Gen. Wayne, 92
McWilliams, Sam (Verdigris Kid), 84, 85, 383
Madden, Bill, 296
Maddox, Allen R., 340
Maddox, Dick, 361
Madsen, Dep. U.S. Marshal Christian (Chris), 48, 106, 168, 224, 242, 243, 300, 303, 320, 323, 340, 341, 400
Maes, Alejandro, 379
Maes, Juanito, 383
Maes, Patricio (Pat), 284, 358, 383
Maes, Pete, 63
Maes, Zenon, 383
Maestas, German, 383
Maguire, Andy, 176
Mahoney, John, 383
Mahoney, Thomas, 219
Mahorn, Tom, 340
Maine, 247
Majors, Robert (Bob), 335, 372, 383
Majors & Waddell Express Co., See: Russell, Majors & Waddell
Maldonado, Manuel, 383
Maledon, George, 225, 340
Mallory, L.P., 383

Malone, James, 291, 383
Mamby, Henry, 384
Man, John, 66
Mancy, Mitchell E., 384
Mankiller, Smoker, 384
Manley, Abler, 225
Manley, Amos, 225
Mann, Carl, 158, 294
Mann, Hiram, 104
Mann, Jim, 12, 148
Manning, A.B., 183
Manning, A.E., 321, 384
Manning, Frank, 225, 295
Manning, George, 295
Manning, Gyp, 112
Manning, James, 90, 112, 225-26, 295, 330, 384
Manning, Joe, 112
Manning, John, 225
Manning Brothers, 90, 112, 196, 294
Mann's Saloon (Deadwood, S.D.), 171
Mansfield, Billy, See: McLaughlin, Archie
Mansker, Jim, 384
Maples, Dan, 361
Maples, Sam, 75
Mares, Hilario, 384
Markham, W.F., 398
Marlowe, Alf, 226, 384
Marlowe, Boone, 226, 384
Marlowe, Charley, 226, 384
Marlowe, Epp, 226, 384
Marlowe, George, 226, 384
Marlowe Brothers, 384
Marsden, Crosby, 340
Marshall, Charles, 384
Martin, Charles, 384
Martin, Jack, 110
Martin, Jim (d.1871), 242, 269
Martin, Jim (prom. 1881), 280
Martin, R.A.C., 178
Martin, Robert, 384
Martin, William, 384
Martin, William (d.1887), 384
Martinez, Alberto, 369
Martinez, Atanacio, 384
Martinez, Benizno, 381
Martinez, Francisco, 391
Martinez, Juan, 167
Martinez, Romulo, 340
Mason, Barney, 135, 340, 384
Mason County Mob, 271, 344
Mason County (Texas) War (Hoodoo War), 85,
     138, 194, 349, 350, 353, 354, 363, 399
Massagee, George, 384
Massey, Robert, 226
Massie, William Rodney, 158
Massingill, William, 131
Mast, Sheriff Milton, 328, 340
Masterson, Bat, See: **Masterson, William Barclay**
Masterson, Catherine, 226, 227
Masterson, Edward J. (Ed), 30, 102, 226-27, 228,
     340, 384
Masterson, Dep. James P., 101, 113, **227**, 280, 340,
     384
Masterson, Robert, 340, 384
Masterson, Thomas, 226, 227
Masterson, William Barclay (Bat), 30, 102, 109, 113,
     114, 116, **117**, 118, 168, 198, 226, 227-(**28**)-29,
     247, 273, 279, 283, 294, 302, 326, 340, 347, 361,
     384, 395, 396

Matador Saloon (Lampasas, Texas), 23, 167
Mather, Cotton, 105
Mather (or Mathers), **David H.** (Mysterious Dave),
     105, **229**, 340, 384
Mathes, Frances, 207
Mathias, Oscar, 384
Matthews, Frank, 340
Matthews, Dep. **Jacob B.** (Billy, J.B.), 41, 211, 215,
     229-30, 231, 309, 340, 384
Matthews, John, 310
Matthews, William, 42
Matson, Hans, 276
Maverick Act (Wyo.), 16
May, D. Boone, 47, 356, 385
May, Col. George, 158
Mayes, Dep. Marshal Jim, 273
Mayfield, John, 12
Maximillian, Emperor, 13, 301
Maxwell, Bill, 286
Maxwell, C.L., 310
Maxwell, Deluvina, 44, 45
Maxwell, Gunplay, 67
Maxwell, Lucien Bonaparte, 82
Maxwell, Peter Menard, 135, 136, 279, 355, 385
Maxwell Land Grant Company, 258
Maxwell Land Grant Frauds, 70, 82, 83, 383
Maxwell Ranch (N.M.), 44, 45
Meacham, Albert B., 65
Meade, William, 385,
Meade, Marshal William Kidder, 254, 340
Meador, John, 296
Mcagher, John, 231, 281
Meagher, Marshal **Michael**, 112, 231, 257, 280
Means, Col. Thomas, 385
Medicine Valley Bank (Medicine Lodge, Kan.), 55,
     398, 399
Medlock, John, 385
Medran, Florentino, 385
Meeks, Henry Wilbur (Bob), 68, 385
Meldrum, Bob, 231
Melton, Ernest, 85, 139
Menczer, Augustus, 231, 385
Meras, Nica, 385
Merideth, Charles, 385
Merrill, David, **304**, 385, 396
Mershon, Dep. Marshal, 204
Mes, Cruz, 385
Mes, Felipe, 385
Mes, Pancho, 385
Mes, Roman, 385
Mesa Hawks, 373
Mescalero Apache Reservation, 356
Messila Guard (N.M.), 79
Messler, Dep. James, 73
Metcalf, Wild Bill, 385
Metcalf, Willis, 328
Mexican Rurales, 379
Mexican Sam, 77
Mexican War, 30, 35, 300, 310, 318
Mickey Free, See: Tellez, Felix
Middleton, Chas, 385
Middleton, C.P., 340
Middleton, Eugene, 11
Middleton, Harry, 271, 299
Middleton, Joe, 232
Middleton, John (N.M.), 40, 52, 161, 211, 231-32,
     270, 336, 385
Middleton, John (Ark.), 385,
Middleton, Thomas (Doc), **232**, 309, 385, 397

Miera, Pantaleon, 385
Miles, Hod, 340
Miles, Moses, 221, 287
Miles, Gen. Nelson A., 192, 227, 313, 361
Millard, George, 340
Miller, Alice, 323
Miller, Clelland (Clell), 178, **179**, 180, 181, 182, 183, 232, 321, 323, 385
Miller, Ed, 178, 180, 185
Miller, Eli, 385
Miller, Mayor James (Ellsworth, Kan.), 112
Miller, James B. (Killer Miller, Killin' Jim, Jim the Killer, Deacon), 1, 78, 83, 131, 136, 137, **232-(33)**-34, 269, 279, 219, 333, 335, 340, 350, 372, 386
Miller, Jesse, 386
Miller, Joe, 54
Miller, John, 341
Miller, Judge, 158
Miller, S.C., 386
Miller, Wild Bill, 386
Miller-Frazer Feud, 329, 361, 369
Mills, Alexander, H., 386
Mills, James, 234
Milton, Dave, 74
Milton, Jeff Davis, 109, 149, **234**, 278, 293, 311, 341, 376, 383
Mimms, John, 174,
Mimms, Zerelda, See: James, Mrs. Zerelda Mimms
Miner, William (Old Bill), 234, 386
Minster, Henry W., 235
Mint Gambling Saloon (Deadwood, N.D.), 209
Miranda, Guadelupe, 82
Mirival, Martias, 382
Missouri-Kansas & Texas Railroad, 97, 210, 272, 293
Missouri Pacific Railroad, 182
Mitchell, Frank, 161, 167, 290, 320
Mitchell, Luther, 246, 247
Mitchell, William (Baldy Russell), 235, 386
Mobile and Ohio Railroad, 53
Moderators, The, 299
Modoc War, 65
Montana Livestock Association, 209, 295
Montana Stranglers, 371, 372, 375, 387
Montana Vigilance Committee, 252
Monte Jack, See: Lyon, Montague
Montgomery, David, 341
Montjeau, Louis, 375
Montoya, Cypriano, 392
Montoya, Jose F., 386
Montoya, Narciso, 386
Montoya, Ramon, 386
Monumental Engine Company (San Francisco, Calif.), 277
Moody, Bill, 303, 396
Moon, Jim, 386
Moore, Bob, 180
Moore, Eugenia, **95**, 97
Moore, George, 341
Moore, Jeff B., 341
Moore, John, 341
Moore, John J., 268
Moore, Lester, 386
Moore, Dep. Sheriff Morris, 24, 28, 172
Moore, Sam, 263
Moore, Sid, 393
Moore, Susanna, 156
Moore, Thomas, 386

Moore, William, 235, 386
Moorehead, James, 351
Moorman, Watt, 267
Morco, John (Happy Jack), 110, 235
Morgan, Frank, 386
Morgan, J.B., 147
Morgan, J.D., 49
Morgan, Joe, 341, 349, 386, 399
Morgan, Rose, See: Christianson, Mrs. Willard Erastus
Morgan, Sam, 90
Morley, William R., 83, 258
Morman Bill, See: **Delaney, William E.**
Morman Kid (Matt Warner), See: **Christianson, Willard Erastus**
Morose, Martin, 278, 279
Morrel, Ed, 122, 386
Morris, Charles, 81
Morris, Harvey, 194, 244, 386
Morris, Dep. Sheriff John T., 266
Morris, W.C., 386
Morris, Sheriff W.T. (Brack), 86, 341
Morrison, Alexander L., Sr., 341
Morrissey, Peter, 386
Morse, Sheriff **Harry N.** (Henry Nicholson Morse), 47, 50, 235-36, 257, 289, 308
Morton, William (Billy, Buck), 38, 40, 52, 131, 211, 223, 224, 231, 270, 278, 386
Mosby's Raiders (C.S.A.), 13
Mosely, Scar Face, 386
Mosier, Henry, 386
Moss, George, 236
Mossman, Capt. **Burton C.** (Arizona Rangers), 12, 71, 221, **236**, 341
Mountaineer House (Auburn, Calif.), 35
Mountain Meadows Massacre, 154
Mount Valley Bank (Labette County, Kan.), 272
Mowbray, George W., 341
Mowry, Sylvester, 90
Moye, Andy, 359,
Moye, Babe, 359
Moyer, Ace, 216, 387
Moyer, Con, 216, 387
Moyer Brothers, **216**
Mulverson, Sheriff William, 49
Mulvey (Melvin or Mulrey), Bill, 156, 335
Munson, Bub, 280
Munson, Henry, 84, 140, 387
Murchison, Ivan, 341
Murieta, Joaquin, 35, 132, 133, 236-(37)-38, 339, 387
Murietta, Procopio, 387
Murietta, Tex, 194
Murillo, Zeke, 387
Murphy, Henderson, 28
Murphy, James W. (Jim), 24, 27, 28, 29, 172, 238-39
Murphy, John, 387
Murphy, Lawrence G., 38, 40, 52, 70, 105, **210**, 211, 229, 244, 276, 314, 385, 387
Murphy-Dolan Faction (Lincoln County, N.M., War), 33, 38, 40, 41, 44, 54, 70, 80, 194, 212, 281, 315, 357, 365, 366, 367, 391
Murrel, John A. (The Great Western Land Pirate), **239**
Musgrave, George (Muskgrove), 239, 387
Musgrove, Lee H., 84, 239-40, 387
Muskgrove, M., 387
Musgrove-Franklin Gang, 84

Mysterious Dave, See: **Mather, David**
Mysterious Kid, See: **Lewis, Elmer**

Norton, George, 176
Norton, Marshal J.W., 112

Nangway, Charles, 387
Naranjo, Francisquito, 19
Nash, Joe, 212, 387
Natchez Trace, 239
National Home for Disabled Soldiers (Los Angeles, Calif.), 293
Natus, Joe, 341
Navarro, Angel, 128
Neagle, David, 241, 341
Neal, Doc, 341
Neal, Edgar T., 341
Nebraska State Prison, 232, 247
Neel, John S., 387
Neeley, A.A., 341
Neil, Edgar, 341
Neill, Hyman G. (Hoodoo Brown), 105, 311, 387
Neis, Tony, 341
Nelson, Bob, 387
Nelson, Mart, 387
Nesmith, George, 379
Nesmith Family, 352
Nevill, Charles L., 50, 241, 341
Newcomb, George (Bitter Creek, Slaughter's Kid), 96, 106, 109, **241**-42, 256, 280, 309, 387, 389, 392
Newcomb, Ed (Indian), 67
Newcomb, John, 318
Newell, J. Benson, 341
Newhall, James T., 341
Newman, Bud, 197, 242, 387
Newman, Jim, 341, 387
New Mexico Bar Association, 70
New Mexico Sanitary Association, 107
New Mexico State Prison (Santa Fe, N.M.), 7, 69
New Mexico Territorial Prison, 207
New Orleans and Northwestern Railroad, 58
News and Press, 281
Newton, J.O., 342
Newton General Massacre, 7, 66, 242, 269
Newton War, 357
New York Draft Riots, 287
New York *Herald*, 253
New York *Sun*, 89
New York *Telegraph*, 229
New York *Tribune*, 108
Nichols, Frank P., 342, 393
Nicholson, Sol, 137
Nicholson, William, 387
Nickell, Kels P., 166
Nickell, Willie, 166, 167
Nite, Jim, 150, 305, 387
Nix, Marshal Evett D., 207, 242-43, 328, 338, 340, 341, 342, 347
Nixon, Tom, 26, 27, 229
Nolan, Francisco, 387
Noranjo, Aristotle, 387
Norberg's Store (McDermott, Indian Territory), 57
Norfleet, J. Frank, 387
Northern Pacific Railroad, 143
Northwestern Stage and Transportation Company, 8, 351
Norton, Brocky Jock, 66
Norton, Charles, 392
Norton, Col. Charles, 66

Oakley, Annie, 80
O'Brien, Patrick, 189
Occidental Saloon (Caldwell, Kan.), 126
Ocobock Brothers Bank (Corydon, Iowa), 178
O'Connor, Barney, 55
O'Day, Tom (Peep), 67, 68, 213, 214, **316**, 317, 388
O'Dell, Albert, 204-05
O'Dell, Bill, 388
O'Dell, Tom, 388
Oden, Lon, 168, 244, 276
Odle, Alvin, 15, 168, 248, 388
Odle, William, 15, 168, 248, 388
Odle Brothers, 248
Odeneal, T.B., 65
O'Folliard, Thomas, 7, **39**, 41, 42, 45, 71, 134, 136, 194, 244, 255, 274, 281, 309, 333, 388
Ogg, Billy, 110
Ogle, Miles, 267
O'Grady, John, 342
Ohio & Mississippi Railroad, 267
O'Holeran, James, 301, 302
O.K. Corral (Tombstone, Ariz.), 5, 34, 75, 113, **115**, 120, 121, 209, 244-45, 247, 326, 336, 361, 374, 383
Oklahoma National Guard, 65
O.K. Stable, 132
O'Laughlin, Jimmy, 388
Old Bill, See: **Miner, William**
Old Cottage Bar Ranch (N.M.), 7
Olguin, Antonio, 245
Olguin, Clato, 245
Olguin, Jesus Maria, 15, 194, 245
Olguin, Severio, 194, 245
Olinger, John Wallace, 192, 245, 388
Olinger, Dep. Robert A. (Bob), 35, **43**, 44, 194, 245, 246, 281, 342, 388
Olive, Isom Prentice, 246-47
Olive, Robert, 246
Olympic Dance Hall (Las Animas, Colo.), 4
O'Malley, Morris, 190, 191
O'Malley, Pat, 190, 191
O'Malley Brothers, 313
Omohundro, John B. (Texas Jack), **159**, 388
O'Neill, John H. (Jack), 342
O'Neill, Thomas, 388
O'Neill, William Owen (Buckey), 247
Opera House (Caldwell, Kan.), 280
Orcutt's Store (McDermott, Indian Territory), 57
Oriental Saloon (Tombstone, Ariz.), 75, 114, 116, 119, 121, 164, 247, 270, 283
O'Rourke, John (Johnny Behind the Deuce), 247, 270, 284
Orr, John, 388
Orr, Thomas, 21, 22, 23
Ortega, Juan, 79
Orton, Sheriff Dick, 346
Osborn, William S., 342
Otero, Celestino, 20
Otero, Miguel A., 79
Ouray, Chief, 250
Outlaw U.S. Marshal Bass, 15, 223, **248**, 279, 300, 339, 342, 388
Outlaws of Missouri, 129

Overland Hotel (Denver, Colo.), 84
Owens, Commodore Perry, 248-49
Owens, George, 109, 293, 388
Owens, Louis (Lewis), 109, 293, 388
Owens, Sheriff Perry, 48-49
Owens, Will, 342
Owens Brothers, 358
Ozona (Texas) *Kicker*, 201

Pacheco, Tavian, 363
Packer, Alferd G., 250-51, 282
Paddleford, Walter, 122
Padgett, George W., 251
Padilla, Isidoro, 363
Padilla, Pablo, 388
Paine, John, 271, 299, 305, 388
Paine, Manfred, 388
Palen, Judge Joseph, 82, 258
Palmer, Edward, 342
Palmeter, Page, 388
Parchmeal, William, 11
Parish, Frank, 132, 252
Parker, Bonnie, 300, 335
Parker, F.D., 342
Parker, George Leroy, See: **Cassidy, Butch**
Parker, Judge Isaac C. (The Hanging Judge), 1, 11,
    49, 57, 65, 78, 84, 85, 94, 96, 104, 121, 139, 143,
    160, 162, 170, 207, 210, 219, 222, 225, **252**-53,
    257, 266, 272, 277, 292, 300, 318-19, 324, 326,
    328, 330, 337, 345, 346, 347
Parker, Joe, 192, 254
Parker, Robert Leroy, See: **Cassidy, Butch**
Parramore, Green, 145
Parrott, George, 388
Pate, James, 388
Patron, Isidoro, 363
Patron, Juan, 383
Pattee, James Monroe, 253
Patterson, Ferd, 389
Patterson, Frank (Kan.), 114
Patterson, Frank (Ariz., N.M.), 389
Patterson, Sen. James W. (N.H.), 89
Patterson, John, 341
Paul, John V., 342
Paul, Sheriff **Robert H.** (Bob), 5, 88, 116, 153, 164,
    209, 253-**54,** 342, 359
Pauli, Louis, 342
Pawnee Indian Agency, 90
Paxton, Louis, 389
Payette Vigilance Committee, 307
Payne, E.W., 55, 272
Payne, Ransom, 342
Peacock, A.J., 228
Peacock, Lewis, 192, 208, 254, 389
Peak, Capt. Junius (June) (Texas Rangers), 24, 27,
    28, 342
Pearl, William S., 389
Peel, M.C., 375
Peeler, Oscar, 233
Peet, W.N., 319
Pegleg Gang, 50
Pell, Henry, 389
Pendencia Ranch (Eagle Pass, Texas), 125
Pennsylvania Fiscal Agency, 89
Penwell, E.S., 342
Peppin, Sheriff George (Dad), 41, 215, 244, 246, 315,

342, 348, 389
Perez, Mariana, 130
Perkins, Louis, 389
Perkins, William, 267
Perkins Store (Holbrook, Ariz.), 49
Perry, Sheriff C.C., 85
Perry, Cicero, R., 342
Perry, Commodore Olive, 248
Perry, John, 359, 384
Perry, Ollie, 343
Perry, Rufe, 271, 344
Perry, Samuel, 389
Perry Tuttle's Dance Hall, 220, 269
Peshaur, George, 112
Pesqueira, Gov., 92
Petal, Gabriel, 389
Peters, Shadrach, 2
Petty, Hubbard, 21
Petty, Jane, See: Baker, Mrs. Cullen
Phelps, Edward, 104, 254-55, 343
Phelps, E.M., 343
Phelps-Dodge Copper Mining Co. (Bisbee, Ariz.),
    45
Philips, U.S. Marshal John, 25, 196
Phillipowski, Lyon, 343, 389
Phillips, Charles, A., 343
Phillips, Samuel F., 92
Philpot, Budd, 88, 116, 153, 164, 209, 373, 378
Phoenix *Herald*, 247
Phoenix Penitentiary, 265
Phy, Josephus (Joe), 132, 333, 343
Pickard, E.B., 343
Pickering, Dr., 280,
Pickett, Sam, 343
Pickett, Tom, 7, 42, 71, 134, 135, 244, 255, 274, 343,
    389
Pico, Andres, 126
Pierce, Abel Head (Shanghai Pierce), 112, 147, **255,**
    296
Pierce, Cad, 88, 140, 330
Pierce, Pres. Franklin, 274
Pierce, Charley, 96, 106, 109, 242, **256,** 389
Pierce, Milo, 194
Pike, Marshal S., 253
Pilgrim's Progress, 180
Pine Ridge Indian Reservation (Dakota Territory),
    105
Pinkerton, Allan, 181, 343
Pinkerton, William, 60, 61, 268
Pinkerton Detective Agency, 59, 60, 61, 69, 148, 165,
    166, 173, 177, 181, 182, 184, 215, 231, 232,
    235, 267, 268, 284, 321, 346
Pino y Pino, Pablo, 389
Pipes, Sam, 24
Pipkin, Red, 278, 389
Pitman, Joe, 356, 389
Pitts, Charlie (Samuel Wells), 178, 182, 183, 389
Pitts, James, 141, **179**
Place, Etta, 214, 296
Platt, Sen. Edward (N.Y.), 302
Platt, Rudd, 343
Platt, Sam, 343
Platt, Tom, 343
Pleasant Valley War, See: **Graham-Tewksbury Feud**
Plummer, Sheriff **Henry,** 154, 218, **256,** 284, 285,
    321, 338, 343, 374, 379, 382, 389, 399
Plummer Gang, See: Innocents, The
Poak, Ad, 320
Poe, Frank, 135

Poe, John W., 327, 343, 363, 389
Pointer, Johnny, 256-57
Poker Alice, See: Ivers, Alice
Polanco, Librado, 389
Pollard, Edward, 204
Pollard, Mrs. Edward, 204
Pomeroy, Sen. Samuel, 107, 108,
Ponce, Noratto, 235, 257
Pontotoc County War, 356
Pony Express, 80
Porter, Fannie, 70, 214
Porter, Frank, 389
Porter, Dep. Sheriff George, 276
Porterie, J.A., 343
Porters, John, 25
Potter, Andrew Jackson, 389
Potter, Charles, 380
Potter, Dell, 343
Potter Gang, 271, 341, 344
Powder Bill, 389
Powe, Henry Harrison, 137, 138, 369
Powell, Buck, 389
Powell, George, 76
Powell, Sylvester, 231, 257
Power, William, 389
Powers, Bill, 98, 99, 100
Powers, Doc, 390
Pratt, Marshal John, 83, 257-258, 281, 343
Preece, William, 90
Premont, Charles, 343
Prevost, Mallet, 263, 265
Price, Elmer, 390
Price, Robert, 36
Price, Sterling, 343
Price, Gen. Sterling (C.S.A.), 9, 80, 93
Pridgen, Bolivar Jackson, 343
Pringle, Thomas, 287
Pritchett, Lt. W.T. (Texas Rangers), 137
Proctor, Dep. Sheriff Richard, 167
Pruiett, Moman, 2
Pruitt, Port, 83
Pruner, W.W., 393
Putnam, Ed, 390
Putnam, Jim (Texas Ranger), 84, 138, 244, 369
Putney, Walt, 68, 213, 214
Putts, Henry, 343
Pyle, Dr., 292

Quantrill, William Clarke, 8, 77, 93, 94, 173, 259-(61)-62, 321, 367, 385, 390
Quaries, George C., 356
Queen, Kelp, See: Lewis, Alexander
Queen, Lee, 343
Queen, Richard, 390
Queen, Vic, 149, 389
Quinette, 124
Quinlan, 390

Radcliff, George, 96
Rader, Bud, 344
Radigan, Thomas, 390
Rae, Nick, 265
Rael, Antonio, 382, 390

Rafferty, John, 180
Ragged Bill, 325
Raidler, William (Little Bill), 106, 263, 303, 390
Ralls, J.G., 1
Ranchero, 128
Randall, William, 390
Rande, Frank, 390
Randlett, Capt., 206
Rankin, Marshal John, 314, 344
Ransom and Murray Saloon (Ingalls, Okla.), 106
Rascon, Eugenio, 390
Rash, Matt, 166
Rattlesnake Dick, See: Barter, Richard
Ray, Nick, 64, 72, 193, 282, 360
Raynolds, Joseph, 390
Raynor, William P., 263
R.C. Ranch (Ariz.), 77
Read, James, 78
Reagan, Sheriff Richard, 146
Real, Acasio, 390
Real, Procopio, 390
Realis, Pablo, 390
Reavis, James Addison (The Baron of Arizona), 263-(64)-65
Reconstruction Union League, 208, 254
Red Buck, See: Waightman, George
Redding, Robert, 390
Redfield, Len, 390
Redford, William, 308
Red Front Saloon (Newton, Kan.), 220
Red Jack, 342
Red Jack Gang, 5, 333, 351
Red Light Saloon and Dance Hall (Caldwell Kan.), 169, 265
Redman, Dep. Sheriff James, 6, 273
Red Sash Gang, 213, 215, 265-66
Redus, Roscoe, 344
Reed, Charlie, 266
Reed, Ed, 266, 390
Reed, Jim, 170, 180, 266, 291, 292, 385, 390, 394
Reed, Atty. J. Warren, 1, 139, 160, 210
Reed, Nathaniel (Texas Jack), 266, 378
Reese, James, 390
Regulators, The, 299, 327, 328, 357
Regulator War, 266-67, 370
Reid, F.J., 344
Reilly, Ben, 14
Remine, Richard, 391
Rennick, Bob (Cowboy), 263
Reno, Frank, 267, 268
Reno, John, 267
Reno, Maj. Marcus, 122
Reno, Simeon, 267, 268
Reno, William, 267, 268
Reno Brothers, 11, 27, 180, 267-68
Reynolds, Sheriff Glenn, 10, 11
Reynolds, Jim, 268
Reynolds, John, 268
Reynolds, Laris, 391
Reynolds, Lt. N.O., 137, 344
Reynolds, Starke, 137
Reynolds Gang, 268
Rhodes, Eugene Manlove, 107
Rhodes, Gene, 353
Rhodes, John, 141, 299
Rhodius, Charley, 208
Rich, Charlie, 158
Richards, Richard, 139
Richards, Thomas, 382

Richardson, Levi, 30, 217, 268-69, 381
Richardson, Robert, 391
Richmond, Irvin, 303
Rickabaugh, Lou, 247
Rickard, Tex, 89
Rigdon, Terrell, 344
Riggs, Barney, 269, 391
Riley, Bob, 194
Riley, James, 308
Riley, James H., 80, 210, 211
Riley, Jim (or Reily), 242, 269
Riley, John Henry, 391
Riley, Thomas, 269
Rinehart, Sheriff Frank, 190
Ringo, John (John Ringgold), 75, 76, 78, 93, 114,
    120, 138, 148, 226, 247, 248, 270, 353, 357, 373,
    380, 391
Ritch, William G., 258
Rio Bravo, 205
Rivera, Petronillo, 391
Roach, John, 391
Roark Gang, 345
Robber's Roost, 67, 68, 74, 270, 296, 304, 310, 315,
    381, 392
Roberts, Andrew L. (Buckshot), 40-41, 44, 52, 54,
    80, 81, 211, 212, 270-71, 278, 309, 327, 344, 356,
    362, 385, 391, 393, 394
Roberts, Daniel Webster (Texas Rangers), 50, 271,
    338, 344
Roberts, Jim, 271, 299
Roberts, Judd, 14, 168, 271-72
Roberts, Moses, 49, 249
Roberts, Ross, 344
Roberts, William (Indian Billy), 68, **316**, 317
Roberts, W.C., 280
Robertson, Ben F. (Wheeler, Ben), **55**, 165, 272, 328,
    349, 399
Robertson, J.B.A., 224
Robertson, William, 391
Robey, Henry, 172
Robidoux, Antoine, 32
Robin, Tom, 234
Robinson, D.S., 344
Robinson, Dep. Frank, 127
Robinson, Jim R., 344
Robinson, Lt., 206
Robinson's Circus, 103
Robledo, Martin, 86
Robson, Dep. Frank, 73
Rocking Chair Ranch (Texas), 13
Rock Island Railroad, 190, 313
Rodgers, Jim, 37, 145
Rodriguez, Jesus, 391
Roerig, Peter, 88, 116, 153
Roff, Andy, 207
Roff, James, 207
Rogers, Annie, 391
Rogers, Bill, 290
Rogers, Bob, 272-**73**, 391
Rogers, C.L., 344
Rogers (Rodgers), Dick, 364, 365, 380, 391, 398
Rogers, Ernest, 344
Rogers, Isaac (Ike), 139, 344
Rogers, J.H., 344
Rogers, L.T., 344
Rogers, Michael, 267, 268
Rogers, Whig, 290
Rojos, Jose, 257
Rollieri, Jimmy, 46

Romero, Bernardo, 344
Romero, Catarino, 379
Romero, Cleofes, 344
Romero, Cristobel, 391
Romero, Damon, 391
Romero, Juan (d.1884), 374
Romero, Juan (d.1931), 382, 390, 391
Romero, Miguel A., 344
Romero, Pooler, 374
Romero, Ricardo, 391
Romero, Secundino, 127, 344
Romero, Torevio, 391
Romero, Trinidad, 344, 344
Romero, Vincent, 194, 391
Ronan, Charles, 66, 228
Roosevelt, Pres. Franklin D., 136
Roosevelt, Pres. Theodore, 34, 101, 136, 152, 166,
    221, 224, 229, 247, 292, 331
Root, Tom, 266
Rosche, Louis, 108, 109
Rosenthal, William, 344
Rose of the Cimarron, See: Dunn, Rose
Ross, Dep. Sheriff, 19, 20
Ross, Kit, 273
Ross, T.M., 344
Ross Gang, 55
Roth, Fred, 279, 391, 393
Rough Riders, 34, 152, 221, 224, 247, 275, 331
Roundtree, Oscar J., 344
Rowden Store (Cass County, Texas), 22
Rowdy Joe, See: **Lowe, Joseph**
Rowell, Dist, Atty. Converse W.C., 104, 254
Royal Canadian Mounted Police, 235
Rucker, E.C., 344, 391
Rudabaugh, David (Dave), 6, 7, 42, 105, 134, 135,
    255, 273-74, 311, 312, 340, 345, 348, 370, 377,
    378, 385, 390, 391, 392, 398
Rudd, W.L., 345
Rudolph, Bill, 362, 392
Ruff, Rufus, 392
Rumley, Charles S., 195, 274, 345
Runnels, Gov. Hardin R. (Texas), 127, 128
Rush, Matt, 392
Rusk, Dave, 74, 345
Rusk Prison (Huntsville, Texas), 149
Russell, Baldy, See: **Mitchell, William**
Russell, Majors & Waddell Express Co., 80, 155
Russell, Richard Robertson (Dick), **274**, 345
Russell, Stillwell, 345
Russell, T.N., 392
Russian Bill, 203
Rutherford, Marshal S. Morton, 57, 207
Ryan, Bill, 184
Ryan, Fatty, 392
Ryan, P., 392
Ryland, Ike P., 133
Rynerson, William L., 392
Rynning, Thomas H., 274, 313, 345

Sacramento *Union*, 130
Safford, Gov. Anson Peacely-Killen, 140, 290
Sage, Lee, 392
Sagolia, Manuel, 392
Said, John (Rattlesnake Jack), 276, 392
St. James Hotel (Cimarron, N.M.), 3
St. Joseph *Gazette*, 186

St. Leon, Ernest (Diamond Dick), 168, 244, 276
St. Louis, Arkansas and Texas Railroad, 60
St. Louis *Dispatch*, 181
St. Vrain, Ceran, 36
Sais, Carlos, 392
Saiz (or Sanez), Doroeto, 130, 392, 393
Salas, Justo, 392
Salazar, Hijino, 194, 276, 392
Salazar, Thomas, 372
Salcido, Pablo, 71
Salem Prison (Ore.), 304
Sallis, W.F., 345
Saloon Number 10 (Deadwood, N.D.), 158, 171
Samora, Jose A., 350, 382
Sample, Omer W. (Red), 197, 276, 392
Sampson, Sam, 56-**58**, 358, 392
Samuels, Archie Peyton, 173, 181
Samuels, Dr. Reuben, 173
Samuels, Zerelda James, 174, **175**, 181, 186
San Carlos Indian Agency (N.M.), 10
Sanchez, Manuel, 382
Sanchez, Maria, 265
Sand Creek Massacre, 34, 51, 268, 277
Sandel, M.H., 78
Sanders, Ab, 33, 80, 192, 215, 224, 246
Sanders, George, 84, 392
Sanders, Osee, 277
Sandobal, Anastacio, 392
Sandoval, Remigio, 392
Sanez (or Saiz), Doroteo, 130, 392
San Francisco *Bulletin*, 278
San Francisco *Chronicle*, 124
San Francisco County, 153
San Francisco Vigilance Committee, 277-78
San Quentin Prison (Calif.), 47, 124, 126, 235, 308
Santa Cruz *Daily Echo*, 124
Santa Fe *New Mexican*, 91, 281, 315
Santa Fe Prison, 199
Santa Fe Railroad, 56, 97, 105, 190, 199, 311, 320
Santa Fe (N.M.) Ring, 70, 82, 211, 212, 246, 257, 258, 281, 314
Santa Fe Trail, 268
Santa Fe *Weekly Gazette*, 79
Santleben, August, 392
Sarber, Marshal John, 73
Saunders, J.W., 245, 345
Saunders, William, 392
Sayles, Det. Bill (Pinkerton), 215
Scales, Clinton, 139
Scanlan, John, 11
Scarborough, U.S. Marshal **George W.**, 149, 214, **278**, 279, 345, 376, 393
Scherer, James A.B., 82
Schieffelin, Edward, 114
Schlaepfer, John B., 379
Schmidt, Frank, 345
Schmidt, Capt. G.H., 326, 329, 334, 338, 342, 343, 344, 345
Schmidt, Will, 345
Schnabel, Henry, 86
Schneider, Henry, 248
Schonchin John, 66
Schroeder, S., 392
Schufeldt and Son Store (Lenapah, Okla.), 85
Scorgins, John, 392
Scott, A.D., 60-61
Scott, Ben, 289
Scott, E., 393
Scott, Jerry, 23

Scott, John, 393
Scotten, Ed H., 345
Scurlock (or Skurlock), **Josiah G.** (Doc), 40, 52, **278**-79, 393
Seaborn, Joe C., 48, 79, 263
Seaborn, Oscar, 263
Seale, James, 345
Seaman, Carey, 100, 393
See, James, 393
Seely, Isham, 170
Segovia, Manuel, 211
Segura, Jose, 281, 393
Seligman, Sigmund, 79
Selman, John, 149, 345
Selman, John, Sr., 149, 150, 205, 223, 233, 248, 266, 278, **279**, 342, 345, 348, 372, 393
Selman, Tom, 279
Sena, George, 345
Sena, Jose, 345
Senate Saloon (Ballinger, Texas), 78
Sena y Baca, Jesus Maria, 79, 345
Seven Rivers Gang, 215
Seven Springs Ranch (N.M.), 223
Seward, Sec. of State William, 108
Sexton Bank (Riverton, Iowa), 184
Shadley, Lafe, 168, 279-80
Shaffenburg, M.A., 345
Shaffer, George (Sombrero Jack), 38
Sharkey, Tom, 120
Sharon, Sen. William (Nev.), 241
Sharp, Mike, 345
Sharp, Milton A., 393
Shaw, Bob, 227
Shaw, Mayor John B., 176
Shea, John, 220
Shea, Patrick, 196
Shears, John, 393
Sheedy, Ben, 393
Sheehan, Larry, 393
Sheeks, David, 26
Sheet Iron Jack, 393
Sheets, John W., 177
Shelby, John, 340
Shelley, Bill, 65
Shelley, John, 65
Shepherd, George, 280
Shepherd, Oliver, 280
Shepherd, W.H., 98
Sheridan, J.J., 345
Sheridan, Gen. Philip H., 80
Sherman, James D., 231, 280-81
Sherman, Marshal **John E., Jr.**, 105, 258, 281-82, 314, 315
Sherman, Sen. John, 281
Sherman, Gen. William Tecumseh, 281
Sherrington, Isabella, 295
Shibbell, Sheriff Charles (Pima County, Ariz.), 34, 114, 326, 346
Shine, John, 45
Shinn, Lloyd, 102
Shirley, John, 182
Shirley, Myra Belle, See: **Starr, Belle**
Shonsey, Mike, 72, 282
Shook, William, 363, 398
Shores, Cyrus Wells (Doc), 282, 311
Short, Marshal Ed, 56, 96
Short, Luke, 53, 247, 282-**83**, 294, 393, 395
Shotgun Collins, 283
Shufeldt & Son General Store (Lenapah, Okla.), 139

Shull, Sarah, 155
Sias, Carlos, 393
Siddons, Belle (Madame Vestal), 223, 283-84
Sieber, Al, 10, 165, 290, 346
Sieker, Edward A., 346
Sieker, Frank, 346
Sieker, Capt. Lamartine P. (Texas Rangers), 14, 346
Sieker, Tom, 346
Siever, William, 25
Sigsby, Bob, 305
Silva, Henry, 224
Silva, Vicente, 63, 103, 284, 348, 365, 369, 393
Silva's White Caps, 103, 324, 348, 350, 352, 353, 358,
    365, 369, 370, 373, 381, 382, 383, 384, 385, 389,
    390, 391, 393, 394, 396, 397
Silver City *Enterprise*, 126
Silver King Mine, 264
Silver Tip, See: Wall, Billy
Simmons, Del, 106, 280
Simmons, Jesse, 20
Simmons, John, 20
Simpson, Ray, 220
Simms, Pink, 346
Simms, W.H. (Billy), 125, 126, 301, 393
Singer, Sheriff Fred, 228
Singleton, Albert, 257
Sippy, Benjamin, 284, 346
Siringo, Charles Angelo, 69, 215, **284**, 346, 346, 393
Sisneros, Dionicio, 393
Sitters, Joe, 346
Sitting Bear, Chief, 6
Six-Shooter Jimmy, 5
Skinner, Cyrus, 25, 284-85
Skinner, George, 25
Slade, Joseph A. (Jack), 80, **285**, 393
Slade, Virginia, 285
Slaughter, Gabe, 297, 298
Slaughter, Sheriff, John Horton (Texas John), 5, 75,
    222, 241, 285-**86**, 325, 335, 346, 361, 393
Slaughter, John (prom. 1876), 369
Slaughter, Tom, 19
Slaughter Kid, See: **Lewis, Elmer**
Slaughter's Kid, See: **Newcomb, George**
Slavin, Pat, 357
Slough, Justice John P., 392
Smerdon, George, 303
Smith, Bean-Belly, 203
Smith, Bill (Six-Shooter) (prom. 1897), 90
Smith, Bill, (d.1902), 141, 286, 334
Smith, C.E., 273
Smith, Charley, 54
Smith, Col., 346
Smith, Dave, 82, 303
Smith, Det., 288
Smith, Frank, 105
Smith, Henry, 196
Smith, Hugh N., 274
Smith, Jack (d.1878), 223
Smith, Jack (prom. 1880), 282, 286
Smith, James, 394
Smith, J.H., 346
Smith, Jim, 35
Smith, Joe, 394
Smith, John, 276
Smith, Marcus Aurelius, 51
Smith, Pegleg, 33
Smith, Richard, 287
Smith, Sam, 40, 394
Smith, Sandy, See: **Moss, George**

Smith, Simeon H., 346
Smith, Six Shooter, 394
Smith, Stuttering, 162
Smith, Sheriff Tim, 269
Smith, Marshal Thomas J. (Bear River Smith), 221,
    287, 346
Smith, Tom (d.1893), 64, 71, 287-88
Smith, Tom (d.1899), 69, 199
Smith, Tom (prom. 1895), 266, 320
Smith, Dep. Marshal W.C., 139, 263, 272, 346
Smith, Dep. Marshal W.D., 213
Smith, William (Billie) (prom. 1883), **55**, 272,
    393
Smith, William (prom. 1876), 112, **117**
Snake River Cattlemen's Association, 231
Snearly, W.J., 346
Snider, William, 394
Snow, Bud, 394
Snow, Charles, 394
Snow, Red, 101
Snuffer, Theodorick, 321
Snyder, Jess, 23, 84, 394
Sohn, Alf, 106
Sombrero Jack, See: Shaffer, George
Sontag, George, 122, **288**, 289, 394
Sontag, John, 122, **288**, 289, 349, 394
Sontag Brothers, 288-89, 319
Soto, Juan (The Human Wildcat), 236, **289**
Southern Bank of Kentucky (Russellville, Ky.), 176,
    280
Southern Pacific Railroad, 31, 33, 52, 85, 124, 201,
    223, 231, 234, 264, 288, 313, 319, 327
Southern Railroad, 235
Sowell, A.J., 346
Spaniard, Jack (Jack Sevier), 289
Spanish-American War, 34, 143, 275, 313
Sparks, Franklin, 267, 268
Sparks, Sam, 382
Sparrow, Joe, 247
Spawn, George, 394
Speed, Dep. Billy, 107, 366
Speed, Dick, 106, 168, 280
Speers, George, 280
Spence, Det. Lowell (Pinkerton), 215
Spence, Pete, 76, 90, 114, **115**, 116, 119, 120, 293,
    394
Spencer, Al, 170
Spencer, Charles, 394
Sperry, Sam, 394
Spicer, Wells, 119
Spites, Off., 146
Spotswood, Thomas, 24, 27
Spotted Horse, 55
Spradley, A. John, 289, 346
Spradley, Bill, 289
Sprole, Lincoln, 290
Spurlock, James, 392
Stacy, Elias, 183, 232
Standard, Jess, 290
Standefer, Wiley W., 92, 290-91, 346
Standifer, Bill, 161
Stanley, Emma, 32
Star Route Fraud Cases, 303
Starr, Belle (Myra Belle Shirley), **49**, 151, 170, 182,
    232, 266, **291**, 292, **312**, 321, 356, 391, 394
Starr, Buck, 292
Starr, Henry (The Bearcat), 170, 252, 291-**92**, 347,
    394
Starr, Jim, 394

Starr, Pearl, 291
Starr, Sam, 232, 291, 292, 312, 394
Starr, Tom, 266, 292
State Hospital (Evanston, Wyo.), 385
Staunton, Dick, 74
Staunton, Ike, 74
Steadman, David C., 1
Steel, Ike, 280
Steele, Gen. William, 206
Stein, Ed, 207, 208
Stephens, John, 292
Stephens, R.M., 346
Stephens, W.H., 251
Sterling, John, 110
Stevens, Ben, 83, 91
Stevens, Jennie (Little Britches), 303, 360, 381
Stevens, Stephen, 394
Stevenson, Robert Louis, 82
Stewart, Sheriff Cicero, 122, 150, 367
Stewart, Dr. Henri, 292-93
Stewart, Lew, 53
Stewart, Virgil, 239
Stiles, William Larkin, (Billy), 6, 61, 109, 221, **293**, 347, 358, 394
Stilwell, Frank C., 76, 90, 114, 116, 119, 120, 164, 191, 223, 293, 337, 347, 394
Stilwell, Simpson E. (Comanche Jack), 293, 347, 394
Stinson, Joe, 293, 394
Stinson, John W., 373
Stiteler, Bob, 272-73
Stockton, Ike (Isaac), 294, 347, 360, 366, 367, 369, 375, 390, 391, 394
Stockton, Port (William Porter), 293-94, 347, 395
Stockton, Thomas, 394
Stockton Ranch (Tombstone, Ariz.), 51
Stokley, Ed, 303, 304
Stoneman, Gen. George, 63
Storms, Charles (Charley), 283, 294, 395
Stoudenmire, Dallas, 90, 165, 196, 225, **294**-95, 330, 347, 371, 384, 395
Stowe, Jake, 268
Strang, William, 304, 317
Strawhim, Samuel, 156, **157**, 219, 295, 335
Stuart, Granville, 295
Stuart's Stranglers, 295
Sublett, Phil, 146
Sullivan, James, 395
Sullivan, Matthew, 54
Sullivan, W.J.L. (Texas Rangers), 23, 347
Sundance Kid, The (Harry Longabaugh or Long-baugh), 66, 67, 68, 69, 70, 90, 162, 200-01, 207, 208, 209, 213, 214, 215, 270, **296**, 315, 381, 389
Sunday, Jesse, 347
Surratt, Mrs. Lucy, 312
Sutton, Mike, 102
Sutton, William, 101, 147, 224, 296, 298, 365
Sutton Clan, 78
Sutton-Taylor Feud, 101, 143, 147, 155, 191, 224, 296-97, 298, 299, 335, 336, 365, 372, 395
Swan Land and Cattle Company, 166
Sweet, A.M., 217
Swilling, Hank, 119, 395
Swilling, Jack, 92, 290

Tabor, Sen. Horace, 77
Taff, George, 236

Tafoya, Donaciano, 358
Taft, Pres. William Howard, 127
Taggart, Frank, 395
Talbot, Jim, See: **Sherman, James D.**
Tall Texan, The, See: **Kilpatrick, Benjamin**
TA Ranch (Buffalo, Wyo.), 319
Tarver, Benjamin C., 210
Tate, Ralph, 56
Tattenbaum, William, 395
Taylor, Bill, 197
Taylor, Buck, 147, 297
Taylor, Charley, 296
Taylor, Creed, 147, 224, 298, 347
Taylor, Fletcher, 259
Taylor, Jack Hays (Hays Taylor), 155, 298, 335, 373, 395
Taylor, Jack J., 395
Taylor, Jeff, 197
Taylor, James (Jim) (1852-75), 101, 147, 155, 297, 299, 335, 373, 395
Taylor, Jim, 208, 380
Taylor, Dep. Marshal John, 272
Taylor, Josiah, 147
Taylor, Phillip (Doboy), 155, 298, 395
Taylor, Pink, 78, 143, 371
Taylor, Pitkin, 147, 296, 298-99, 395
Taylor, Robert H., 128
Taylor, Rufus, 147
Taylor, Scrape, 298
Taylor, Steve, 395
Taylor, William (Bill), 78, 147, 148, 270, 297, 298, 299, 395
Taylor Brothers, 317
Taylor Clan, 147
Taylor Gang, 387
Teapot Dome Scandal, 150
Teel, Maj. T.T., 125
Tefio, Carlos, 286
Telfrin, Count Feador, 395
Telles, Jose, 395
Telles, Octoviano, 395
Tellez, Felix (Mickey Free), 25, 79
Tennessee Cavalry, 340
Terrell, Arthur, 347
Terrell, Capt. Edward, 260
Terrell, Zeke, 161
Territorial Police (Indian Territory), 97
Terry, Judge David S., 241, 341, 357
Terry, Kyle, 369, 395
Terry, Sen. T.W. (Mich.), 92
Terry, Sheriff Will, 15
Tewksbury, Edwin, 141, 299, 396
Tewksbury, James (Jim), 141, 271, 299, 305, 396
Tewksbury, Mrs. John, 48
Tewksbury, John D., 48, 141, 271, 299
Tewksbury, John, Jr., 141, 299
Tewksbury Clan, 271, 305, 356, 371
Texas and Pacific Railroad, 27, 59, 60
Texas Billy, See: **Thompson, William**
Texas Central Railroad, 24
Texas Express Company, 300
Texas Kid, 265
Texas Jack (1862-1950), See: **Reed, Nathaniel**
Texas Jack (d. 1881), 396
Texas Jack, Train Robber, 266
Texas Mounted Rifles, 302
Texas Property Wars, 299
Texas Rangers, 1, 11, 12-13, 14, 15, 24, 27, 28, 29, 50, 53, 54, 87, 89, 103, 127, 128, 131, 136,

137, 143, 148, 153, 161, 191, 194, 202, 205, 206, 209, 222, 223, 226, 234, 244, 245, 248, 255, 270, 271, 274, 275, 276, 279, 300, 302, 310, 311, 314, 325, 326, 390
Texas State Police, 130, 167
Thatch, Zachariah W., 318, 359
Therringer, T.M., 347
Thomas, Charles, 396
Thomas, Eleasar, 65
Thomas, Henry Andrew (Heck), 74, 107, 168, 208, 224, 242, 243, 263, **300-01**, 303, 323, 341, 347, 365, 380, 397
Thomas, J.L., 174, 176
Thomason, Dep. Sheriff John, 177-78
Thompson, Ben, 81, 110, 112, **117**, **125**, 126, 146, 151, 158, 228, 300, **301**, 302, 314, 333, 347, 349, 350, 368, 377, 393, 396
Thompson, Bill, 335
Thompson, Dan, 25
Thompson, John, 396
Thompson, Hi, 280
Thompson, Texan Jim, 302
Thompson, Thomas, 301
Thompson, William (Billy, Texas Billy), 110, 112, 117, 228, 301, **302**, 314, 396
Thornhill, Jim, 213
Thornton, John, 302
Thornton, Nep, 59
Thornton, Oliver, 214
Thorpe, Sen. S.M., 260
Three-Fingered Jack, See: **Dunlap, Jack; Gallagher, Jack; Garcia, Manuel; McDowell, Jack**
Throckmorton, Sgt., 347
Thurmond, Frank, 354, 396
T.I.C. Commercial Agency (Fort Worth, Texas), 88
Tidball, Zan L., **302-03**, 347
Tiffany, Joseph C., 302, 303
Tilghman, Marshal William Matthew, Jr. (Bill), 53, 101, 107, 113, 198, 224, 228, 229, 242, 243, 263, 300, **303**, 313, 328, 329, 341, 347, 360, 398
Timberlake, Sheriff, 380
Tipple, Anson, 158
Tobin, Tom, 122, 396
Tobin, Capt. W.G. (Texas Rangers), 127, 128, 330
Tobler, George, 303
Todd, Capt. George W., 259, **261**, 396
Toga-de-chuz, Chief, 10
Tolbert, Paden, 74
Tolbit, John, 347
Tolby, Dick, 34, 326
Tolby, Rev. T.J., 83, 258, 397
Topeka *Daily Commonwealth*, 77
Towerly, William, 82, **303-04**, 396
Townsend, Everett E., 347
Townsend, E.H., 320
Townsend, Marshal Joe, 78
Townsley, Forest, 347
Tracy, Harry, 162, 270, **304**, 315, 317, 385, 396
Tracy, J.A., 313, 314
Travis Rifles, 12
Tremaine, Harry, 126
Trentham, Charles, 347, 396
Tres Jacales (Three Huts) Ranch, 245
Trimmel, Dep. John, 86
Trittle, Gov. Frederick A., 93
Trousdale, David A., 33, **201**, 202
Truitt, James, 235
Truitt Family, 235, 346, 371
Trujillo, Antonio Maria, 93, 396

Trujillo, Dep. Sheriff Esteban, 372
Trujillo, Julian, 396
Tubbs, Frank, 171
Tucker, F.F., 245
Tucker, George, 347
Tucker, Jim, 396
Tucker, Tom, 271, 299, 348, 396
Tucson *Citizen*, 64, 104
Tucson *Daily Arizona Journal*, 92
Tucson Committee of Public Safety, 64
Tuggle, Kute, 298
Tulsa Jack, See: **Blake, John**
Tumilson, Joe, 147, 296
Tunstall, John H., 33, 38, **39**, 40, 52, 81, 105, 123, 133, 161, 210, 211, **212**, 223, 231, 270, 281, 309, 314, 315, 318, 325, 327, 336, 353, 354, 357, 362, 365, 369, 371, 374, 375, 378, 384, 385, 386, 387, 392, 397, 399
Turilli, Rudy, 94
Turnbo, L.S., 348
Turner, Ben, 305, 396
Turner, George, 348
Turner, Marion, 41, 348, 377, 396
Turner Hall Opera House (San Antonio, Texas), 125
Tutt, Davis, 156, **157**
Tuttle, Sheriff Azariah, 310
Tuttle, Perry, 7
Tuttle's Dance Hall (Newton, Kan.), 7
Twain, Mark, 285
Two Evil Isms: Pinkertonism and Anarchism, 284
Tyler, Sheriff Jesse, 90, 214, 305
Tyner, Andrew, 348
Tyng, George, 104, **305-06**, 348

Ulivarri, Francisco, 396
Underwood, Henry, 24, 26, 27
Underwood, Joe, 271, 299
Union Pacific Railroad, 26, 68, 73, 89, 193, 195, 200, 207, 208, 214, 282, 286, 287
United Express Company, 182
United Farm Workers, 300
Updegraff, Al, 227, 228
Updyke, David, 307, 348, 396
Upson, M.A., 40
Urieta, Leandro, 396
U.S. Supreme Court, 139, 160, 193, 210, 253, 266
U.S. Verde Copper Company, 271
Utah State Prison, 74
Utter, Charles, 397
Utting, Charles, 348

Vaden, John, 101
Valdez, Antonio Jose, 103, 348, 397
Valdez, Dep. Sheriff Lino, 273
Valencia, Joaquin, 238
Valentine, Ed, 7
Valley, Frank, 319, 397
Vandenburg, B.C., 348
Van Devanter, Willis, 193
Vandever, Ed, 257
Van Meter, Chet, 165, 272
Vann, Katy, See: Childers, Mrs. John, Sr.

Vann, Sherman, 139
van Sickles, Henry, 55
Varela, Marcos, 397
Vasquez, Tiburcio, 308, 397
Vaudeville Variety Theater (San Antonio, Texas), 125, 301
Vaughn, Sheriff Tom (Douglas, Ariz.), 141, 286
Vega, Cruz, 3, 83, 142, 397
Vega, Luis, 3
Vennoy, Marshal, 72, 73
Verdigris Kid, See: McWilliams, Sam
Vermillion, Texas Jack, 119, 120
Vialpando, J.M., 397
Vialpando, Juan de Dios, 397
Victoria, Queen, 80
Vigilance Committee, See: **San Francisco Vigilance Committee**
Villa, Francisco (Pancho), 1, 87
Vincente Silva's Forty Thieves, See: Silva's White Caps
Virginia Hotel (Virginia City, Mont.), 132
Virginian, The, 295
Vivian, C.B., 133
Vizina, Jim, 247

Waddill, H.B. (Texas Ranger), 202
Wade, Kid, 309, 397
Wadkins, John, 207
Wages, Gale H., 85
Wages Family, 85
Wagner, Jack, 227, 228
Wagstaff, George, 377
Waightman (or **Weightman**), **George** (Red Buck), 106, 280, **309**, 397
Wait, Frederick T. (Dash Wait), 161, 309, 397
Wakefield, E.H., 397
Wakefield, Lyman, 348
Waldrip, Will, See: **Brock, Leonard Calvert**
Walker, A.M., 227
Walker, Bill, 72, 282
Walker, Charles, 392
Walker, David, 310
Walker, George, 310
Walker, Joe, 68, 309-10, 397
Walker, Morgan, 259
Walker, Thomas J., 397
Walker, Tobe, 310
Walker, William (d.1860), 397
Walker, William (d.1889), **310**, 397
Wall, Jim, 47, 222
Wall, William (Silver Tip), 67, 397
Wallace, Ben, 178
Wallace, Dan, 397
Wallace, Jim, 51
Wallace, Judge, 118
Wallace, Gov. Lew (N.M.), 41, 42, **43**, 81, 276, 294
Wallace, William Alexander Anderson (Big Foot), 300, 310-11, 348, 397
Walrath, Charles G., 363, 398
Walrus Saloon (Denver, Colo.), 217
Walter, Harry, 389
Walters, Emma, 229
Walters, Joseph, 217
Walters, William E. (Bill, Bronco Billy), 278, **311**, 341, 376, 389, 398
Ward, Johnny, 25

Warderman, Bill, 398
Ware, R.C. (Dick) (Texas Rangers), 24, 29, 339, 348
Warner, Dave, 167
Warner, M., 398
Warner, Matt (Morman Kid), See: **Christianson, Willard Erastus**
Warren, Sen. Francis E. (Wyo.), 193
Warren, James, 398
Washington, George, 398
Washington, John, 208
Watchman, 61
Waters, Buck, 398
Waterson, Nellie, 130, 197
Watson, Ella (Cattle Kate), 15-(**16, 17**)-18, 65, 71, 193, 352, 356
Watson, Jack, 311
Watson, Peg-Leg, 165
Watson, Sam, 398
Watson, Thomas, 18
Watts, Henry, 398
Watts, John, 398
Wayt, Fred, 40
Webb, Dep. Sheriff Charles (Comanche County, Texas), 147
Webb, Gilver, 398
Webb, John Joshua, 163, 273, 274, 311-13, 348, 370, 377, 378, 390, 393, 398
Webb, Wilfred, 231, 398
Webster, Mayor A.B., 228
Webster, Alonzo B., 295
Wedding, Reyburn, 72
Weightman, George (Red Buck), See: **Waightman, George**
Welch, John, 348
Welles, Justus P., 348
Wellman, Marshal George, 381
Wellman, Horace, 155, 156
Wells, Charles Knox Polk, 398
Wells, George, 271
Wells Fargo Co., 5, 25, 33, 35, 45, 46, 47, 88, 124, 153, 154, 164, 223, 234, 253, 256, 336, 357
Welsh, Tom, 398
Welty, Bert, 88
Wernett, John, 348
Wesley, John (d.1885), **55**, 272, 398
Wesley, John, 144
West, Dep. Duval, 314, 348
West, Edgar, 273
West, Frank, 312
West, James, 398
West, Jesse, 2, 233, 356
West, Richard (Dick, Little Dick), 106, 190, **313**, 398
Western Exchange Hotel (Sacramento, Calif.), 35, 36
Westfall (or Westphal), William, 184
Weston, Parker, 349
Wham, Maj. Joseph (U.S.A.), 51, 231, 254
Wham case, 51-52
Whealington, Tom, 398
Wheeler, Alice, 272
Wheeler, Ben, See: Ben Robertson
Wheeler, Grant, 313, 369, 398
Wheeler, Sheriff **Harry**, 45, 313-14, 349
Wheeler, Henry, 182, 183, 232, 321
Wheeler, James, 398
When the Daltons Rode, 364
Whicher, John W., 181
White, Charley, 163

White, Coley, 349
White, Doc, 296
White, Dudley, 349
White, Marshal Fred, 53, 114, 349
White, Golf, 349
White, G.S., 349
White, Ham, 399
White, Jack, 349
White, James, 176
White, J.C., 349
White, Jim, 298
White, Scott, 349
White, Tom B., 349
White, Will, 349
White Elephant Saloon (Fort Worth, Texas), 88, 283
Whitley, William (Bill), 85, 86, 314, 344, 348, 363, 399
Whitman, Lt. Royal Emerson (U.S.A.), 63, 64
Whitmore, Dr., 310
Whitney, Sheriff **Chauncey Belden,** 88, 112, 235, 301, 302, 349
Widenmann, Dep. U.S. Marshal **Robert A.,** 211, 281, 314-15, 349
Wiggin, W., 399
Wiggins, Luther, 226
Wiggins, William, 359
Wigwam Saloon (El Paso, Texas), 278
Wilcox, H., 317
Wild Bill Hickok, See: **Hickok, James Butler**
Wild Bill Martin Gang, 359, 388
Wild Bunch, The, 33, 52, 58, 66, 67, 68, 69, 70, 90, 162, 198, 199, 200, 201, 206, 207, 208, 209, 213, 214, 215, 278, 296, 305, 310, 315, 346, 354, 359, 371, 378, 379, 380, 381, 382, 385, 389, 397
Wiley Bear, 25
Wiley, John M., 349
Wilkerson, James, 37, 355
Wilkinson, Dep. Marshal James, 104
Wilkinson, Jim, 242
Wilkinson, Noah, 231
William, W.P., 37
William and Jewell College (Liberty, Mo.), 270
William B. Hooper and Company (Ehrenberg, Ariz.), 305
Williams, Ben, 341, 349, 367, 386, 399
Williams, B.F., 130, 368
Williams, Charles, 399
Williams, Dane, 399
Williams, Henry, 395
Williams, James, 376
Williams, Jess, 73, 153, 399
Williams, Dep. Marshal John, 290
Williams, Mike, 81, 158
Williams, Mollie, 210
Williams, Old Bill, 33
Williams, Phil, 273
Williams, Sid, 79
Williams, Capt. Thomas (Texas Rangers), 23
Williams, W.P., 355, 399
Williamson, James A., 83
Williamson, Robert M. (Three Legged Willie), 317
Williamson, Tim, 85, 226, 330, 349, 363, 399
Willing, Dr. George, 264
Willis, Thomas, 37-38, 355, 399
Wilson, Aaron, 318
Wilson, Bill (William Bailey), 7, 220, 242, 269
Wilson, Billy, See: **Anderson, David L.**
Wilson, Floyd, 292
Wilson, George (James C. Casharego), **318**

Wilson, Henry, 194
Wilson, H.S., 274
Wilson, Jim, 399
Wilson, Dep. Marshal John, 126, 280
Wilson, John B. (Juan Bautista), 318
Wilson, Dep. U.S. Marshal Joseph, 160
Wilson, Kid, 292
Wilson, Sinker, 318
Wilson, Vernon Coke, 319, 349
Wilson, William (d.1875), 319, 399
Wilson, William (d.1911), 349, 399
Wilson, Pres. Woodrow, 255
Windham, John, 234
Winters, Jim, 213, 214
Wister, Owen, 295
Witty, Sheriff, 288
Wolcott, Maj. **Frank,** 64, 193, 265, 319, 399
Wolf, Arch, 75
Wolz, Charles, 399
Wood, George, 126
Woodruff, Len, 319, 397, 399
Woods, George, 265
Woods, James, 155, 156
Woods, Mag, 265
Woodward, Len, 360
Woody, Bill, 330
Wooten, Dick, 268
World's Columbian Exposition (World's Fair, Chicago, 1893-94), 77, 80, 151
Worley (or Wohrle), Dep. Sheriff John, 85, 226, 330, 349, 363, 399
Worthington, Nick, 319, 399
Wortley Hotel (Lincoln, N.M.), 246
Wren, William R. (Bill), 24, 167, 290, 320
Wright, Charles, 283
Wright, Milam, 349
Wright, Will, 349
Wyatt, Nathaniel Ellsworth (Zip, Dick Yeager), 45, 320, 399
Wyatt, Nim (Six Shooter Jack), 320
Wymore, George (Jolly), 174, 280
Wyoming Stock Growers' Association, 16, 64, 166, 193, 282, 287, 319
Wyoming State Prison, 317

XIT Ranch (Texas), 13, 15

Yager, Erastus (Red), 321, 399
Yantis, Ole, 106, 168
Yeager, Charles, 141
Yeager, Dick, See: **Wyatt, Nathaniel Ellsworth**
Yellow Hand, Chief, 80, 224
Yoas, Bravo Juan, 109, 293
Yonker, Bronco Sue, 140
Young, Cole, 338, 367, 386, 399
Young, George, 150
Young, Tom, 21
Young, William, 399
Younblood, Dr. B., 97
Younger, Bruce, 394
Younger, James (Jim), 174, 176, 178, **179**, 180, 181, 182, 183, 188, 280, 321, **322**, 323, 399
Younger, John, 181, 280, 321, **322**, 400

Younger, Robert (Bob), 174, 176, 178, **179**, 182, 183, 188, 280, 321, **322**, 323, 400
Younger, Thomas Coleman (Cole), 173, 174, 176, 178, **179**, 180, 182, 183, 188, 232, 280, 291, 321, **322**, 323, 384, 396, 400
Younger Brothers, 94, 96, 97, 174, 259, 321-22, 390, 400
Younger Gang, 389, 400
Yountis, Oliver (Crescent Sam), 323, 400
Yuma State Prison, 92, 202, 336, 337
Yuma Territorial Prison, 152, 247, 269, 275
Yum Kee, 360

Zabriskie, Dist. Atty. James A., 303
Zachery, Bob, 284
Zamora, Francisco, 194, 400
Zapata, Emiliano, 87
Zimmerman, Matt, 355